2002 Edition

The BOOK of

BASEBALL RECORDS

MAJOR LEAGUE BASEBALL RECORDS

WORLD SERIES RECORDS

CHAMPIONSHIP SERIES RECORDS

ALL-STAR GAME RECORDS

HALL OF FAME RECORDS

SEYMOUR SIWOFF, Editor and Publisher

500 Fifth Avenue, New York, NY 10110

© Copyright 2002 by Seymour Siwoff

A STATEMENT FROM THE PUBLISHER

THE BOOK OF BASEBALL RECORDS is the most accurate baseball record book ever published. It is produced by the acknowledged authority for sports history, information and statistics.

THE BOOK OF BASEBALL RECORDS contains four major sections

- REGULAR-SEASON RECORDS
- WORLD SERIES RECORDS
- CHAMPIONSHIP SERIES RECORDS
- ALL-STAR GAME RECORDS

Each section lists records in the following order:
- LIFETIME • SEASON • GAME • INNING

If a single-game record was set in a game that extended into extra innings, the record for a nine-inning game is also listed.

The index, and various tables showing annual leaders in major categories, are located at the back of the book.

YEARS: Hyphenated items are inclusive and consecutive.

CLUB & LEAGUE RECORDS: Generally disregard the following seasons:
1918 - abbreviated due to World War I
1972, 1981, 1994 & 1995 - shortened seasons
1994 - League Championship Series not played
1904 & 1994 - World Series not played

International Standard Book Number: 0-917050-04-5

Library of Congress Control Number: 2001127147

COMMISSIONERS

Kenesaw M. Landis	1920-1944
Albert B. Chandler	1945-1951
Ford C. Frick	1951-1965
William D. Eckert	1965-1968
Bowie K. Kuhn	1969-1984
Peter V. Ueberroth	1984-1989
A. Bartlett Giamatti	1989
Francis T. Vincent	1989-1992
Allan H. Selig	1998-

AMERICAN LEAGUE PRESIDENTS

B. Bancroft Johnson	1901-1927
Ernest S. Barnard	1927-1931
William Harridge	1931-1959
Joseph E. Cronin	1959-1973
Leland S. MacPhail, Jr.	1974-1983
Robert W. Brown	1984-1994
Gene A. Budig	1994-1999

NATIONAL LEAGUE PRESIDENTS

Morgan G. Bulkeley	1876
William A. Hulbert	1877-1882
Arthur H. Soden	1882
Abraham G. Mills	1883-1884
Nicholas E. Young	1885-1902
Harry C. Pulliam	1903-1909
John A. Heydler	1909
Thomas J. Lynch	1910-1913
John K. Tener	1913-1918
John A. Heydler	1918-1934
Ford C. Frick	1934-1951
Warren C. Giles	1951-1969
Charles S. Feeney	1970-1986
A. Bartlett Giamatti	1987-1989
William D. White	1989-1994
Leonard S. Coleman, Jr.	1994-1999

ABBREVIATIONS

LEAGUES

ML	Major leagues
AL	American League
NL	National League
AA	American Association
UA	Union Association
PL	Players League

CLUBS

Alt	Altoona
Ana	Anaheim
Ari	Arizona
Atl	Atlanta
Balt	Baltimore
Bos	Boston
Brk	Brooklyn
Buff	Buffalo
Cal	California
Chi	Chicago
Cin	Cincinnati
Clev	Cleveland
Col	Colorado
Colu	Columbus
Det	Detroit
Fla	Florida
Hart	Hartford
Ind	Indianapolis
KC	Kansas City
LA	Los Angeles
Lou	Louisville
Mil	Milwaukee
Minn	Minnesota
Mtl	Montreal
NY	New York
Oak	Oakland
Phil	Philadelphia
Pitt	Pittsburgh
Prov	Providence
Rich	Richmond
Roch	Rochester
StL	St. Louis
StP	St. Paul
SD	San Diego
SF	San Francisco
Sea	Seattle
Syr	Syracuse
TB	Tampa Bay
Tex	Texas
Tol	Toledo
Tor	Toronto
Wash	Washington
Wil	Wilmington
Wor	Worcester

GENERAL

g	games
dh	doubleheader
1g	first game
2g	second game
inn	inning
n	night game

BATTING

ab	at-bats
r	runs
h	hits
tb	total bases
1b	singles
2b	doubles
3b	triples
hr	home runs
rbi	runs batted in
sh	sacrifice hits
sf	sacrifice flies
bb	walks
hp	hit by pitch
so	strikeouts
sb	stolen bases
cs	caught stealing

lob	left on base
ba	batting average
slg	slugging percentage
pct	percentage
avg	average
DH	designated hitter

FIELDING

tc	total chances
ca	chances accepted, errorless
po	putouts
a	assists
e	errors
dp	double plays
tp	triple plays
pb	passed balls

PITCHING

lhp	left-handed pitcher
rhp	right-handed pitcher
gs	games started
cg	complete games
gf	games finished
sv	saves
sho	shutouts
era	earned run average
ip	innings pitched
er	earned runs
bfp	batters faced
hb	hit batters
wp	wild pitches
bk	balks

NATIONAL LEAGUE CLUB HISTORY

NUMBER	CLUB	YEARS
#1	Chicago	1876-
#2	Boston	1876-1952 to Milwaukee #32
#3	New York (Mutual Club)	1876
#4	Philadelphia (Athletic Club)	1876
#5	Hartford	1876-1877
#6	St. Louis	1876-1877
#7	Cincinnati	1876-1880
#8	Louisville	1876-1877
#9	Indianapolis	1878
#10	Milwaukee	1878
#11	Providence	1878-1885
#12	Buffalo	1879-1885
#13	Cleveland	1879-1884
#14	Syracuse	1879
#15	Troy	1879-1882
#16	Worcester	1880-1882
#17	Detroit	1881-1888
#18	New York	1883-1957 to San Francisco #33
#19	Philadelphia	1883-
#20	St. Louis	1885-1886
#21	Washington	1886-1889
#22	Kansas City	1886
#23	Pittsburgh	1887-
#24	Indianapolis	1887-1889
#25	Cleveland	1889-1899
#26	Brooklyn	1890-1957 to Los Angeles #34
#27	Cincinnati	1890-
#28	St. Louis	1892-
#29	Baltimore	1892-1899
#30	Louisville	1892-1899
#31	Washington	1892-1899
#32	Milwaukee	1953-1965 to Atlanta #37
#33	San Francisco	1958-
#34	Los Angeles	1958-
#35	Houston	1962-
#36	New York	1962-
#37	Atlanta	1966-
#38	Montreal	1969-
#39	San Diego	1969-
#40	Colorado	1993-
#41	Florida	1993-
#42	Arizona	1998-
#43	Milwaukee	1998-

AMERICAN LEAGUE CLUB HISTORY

NUMBER	CLUB	YEARS
#1	Chicago	1901-
#2	Milwaukee	1901 to St. Louis #9
#3	Cleveland	1901-
#4	Detroit	1901-
#5	Washington	1901-1960 to Minnesota #13
#6	Boston	1901-
#7	Baltimore	1901-1902 to New York #10
#8	Philadelphia	1901-1954 to Kansas City #12
#9	St. Louis	1902-1953 to Baltimore #11
#10	New York	1903-
#11	Baltimore	1954-
#12	Kansas City	1955-1967 to Oakland #16
#13	Minnesota	1961-
#14	Washington	1961-1971 to Texas #20
#15	Anaheim	1961-
#16	Oakland	1968-
#17	Kansas City	1969-
#18	Seattle	1969 to Milwaukee #19
#19	Milwaukee	1970-1997 to National League #43
#20	Texas	1972-
#21	Seattle	1977-
#22	Toronto	1977-
#23	Tampa Bay	1998-

INDIVIDUAL BATTING RECORDS

SERVICE (See INDIVIDUAL PITCHING RECORDS for pitchers' service)

Most Seasons, Lifetime
26   Deacon McGuire, AA:Tol. 1884; Clev. 88; Roch. 90; Wash. 91
                  NL:Det. 85,88; Phil. 86-88; Wash. 92-99; Brk. 1899-1901
                  AL:Det. 02-03,12; NY 04-07; Bos. 07-08; Clev. 08,10

Most Seasons, Consecutive, Lifetime
25   Bobby Wallace, NL:Clev. 1894-98; StL. 1899-1901,17-18; AL:StL. 1902-16
                  Eddie Collins, AL:Phil. 1906-14,27-30; Chi. 15-26

Most Seasons, League
25   Eddie Collins, AL:Phil. 1906-14,27-30; Chi. 15-26
24   Pete Rose, NL:Cin. 1963-78,84-86; Phil. 79-83; Mtl. 84

Most Seasons, Consecutive, League
25   Eddie Collins, AL:Phil. 1906-14,27-30; Chi. 15-26
24   Pete Rose, NL:Cin. 1963-78,84-86; Phil. 79-83; Mtl. 84

Most Leagues, Lifetime
4   By many players. Last:
                  Lave Cross, AA 1887-89,91; Lou. 1887-88; Phil. 1889,91; PL 1890; Phil. 1890;
                  NL 1892-1900; Phil. 1892-97; StL. 1898-1900; Clev. 1899; Brk. 1900;
                  AL 1901-07; Phil. 1901-05; Wash. 1906-07

Most Clubs, Lifetime
12   Deacon McGuire, AA:Tol. 1884; Clev. 88; Roch. 90; Wash. 91; NL:Det. 85,88; Phil. 86-88;
                  Wash. 92-99; Brk. 1899-1901; AL:Det. 02-03; NY 04-07; Bos. 07-08; Clev. 08,10
                  Since 1900:
10   Tommy Davis, NL:LA 1959-66; NY 67; Hou. 69-70; Chi. 70,72AL:Chi. 68; Sea. 69;
                  Oak. 70-71; Balt. 72-75; Cal. 76; KC 76

Most Clubs, League
9   Dan Brouthers, NL:Troy 1879-80; Buff. 81-85; Det. 86-88; Bos. 89; Brk. 92-93;Balt. 94-95;
                  Lou. 95; Phil. 96; NY 1904
                  Since 1900:
8   Juan Beniquez, AL:Bos. 1971-72,74-75; Tex. 76-78; NY 79; Sea. 80;
                  Cal. 81-85; Balt. 86; KC 87; Tor. 87-88
                  Chris Jones, NL:Cin 1991; Hou. 92; Col. 93-94; NY 95-96; SD 97; Ari. 98; SF 98, Mil. 2000

Most Clubs, Season
4   By many players; Last:
                  Dave Martinez, AL:TB-Tex.-Tor; NL:Chi. 2000

Most Clubs, League, Season
4   Tom Dowse, NL:Lou-Cin.-Phil.-Wash. 1892
                  Frank Huelsman, AL:Chi.Det.-StL.-Wash. 1904
                  Paul Lehner, AL:Phil.-Chi.-StL.-Clev. 1951
                  Ted Gray, AL:Chi.-Clev.-NY-Balt. 1955

Most Clubs, One Day
2   Max Flack, NL:Chi.-StL. May 30, 1922
                  Cliff Heathcote, NL:StL.-Chi. May 30, 1922
                  (Flack & Heathcote traded for each other between games of doubleheader)
                  Joel Youngblood, NL:NY-Mtl. Aug. 4, 1982

One Club, Most Seasons
23   Brooks Robinson, AL:Balt. 1955-77
                  Carl Yastrzemski, AL:Bos. 1961-83
22   Cap Anson, NL:Chi. 1876-97
                  Mel Ott, NL:NY 1926-47
                  Stan Musial, NL:StL. 1941-63 (1945 Military Service)

One Club, Most Seasons, Consecutive
23	Brooks Robinson, AL:Balt. 1955-77
	Carl Yastrzemski, AL:Bos. 1961-83
22	Cap Anson, NL:Chi. 1876-97
	Mel Ott, NL:NY 1926-47
	Stan Musial, NL:StL. 1941-63 (1945 Military Service)

POSITIONS

Most Positions, Lifetime
9	By many players

Most Positions, League
9	By many players

Most Positions, Season, Since 1900
9	Sam Mertes, AL:Chi. 1902
	Jack Rothrock, AL:Bos. 1928
	Bert Campaneris, AL:KC 1965
	Cesar Tovar, AL:Minn. 1968
	Shane Halter, AL:Det. 2000
	Scott Sheldon, AL:Tex. 2000
	Jimmy Walsh, NL:Phil. 1911
	Gene Paulette, NL:StL. 1918
	Jose Oquendo, NL:StL. 1988

Most Positions, Game
9	Bert Campaneris, AL:KC Sept. 8, 1965 (13 inn)
	Cesar Tovar, AL:Minn. Sept. 22, 1968
	Scott Sheldon, AL:Tex. Sept. 6, 2000
	Shane Halter, AL:Det. Oct. 1, 2000

Most Games, One Day, One Position
3	Clyde Barnhart, NL:Pitt. Oct. 2, 1920 (3B)
	Pat Duncan, NL:Cin. Oct. 2, 1920 (LF)

BATTING AVERAGE

Most Seasons Leading Major Leagues
11	Ty Cobb, AL:Det. 1907,09-15,17-19

Most Seasons, Consecutive, Leading Major Leagues
7	Ty Cobb, AL:Det. 1909-15

Most Seasons Leading League
12	Ty Cobb, AL:Det. 1907-15,17-19
8	Honus Wagner, NL:Pitt. 1900,03-04,06-09,11
	Tony Gwynn, NL:SD 1984, 87-89, 94-97

Most Seasons, Consecutive, Leading League
9	Ty Cobb, AL:Det. 1907-15
6	Rogers Hornsby, NL:StL. 1920-25

Highest Batting Average, Lifetime, Since 1900 (Minimum: 5000 at-bats)
.367	Ty Cobb, AL:Det. 1905-26; Phil. 27-28
.359	Rogers Hornsby, NL:StL. 1915-26,33; NY 27; Bos. 28; Chi. 29-32

Highest Batting Average, Season
.442	Tip O'Neill, AA:StL. 1887
.438	Hugh Duffy, NL:Bos. 1894
	Since 1900:
.424	Rogers Hornsby, NL:StL. 1924
.422	Napoleon Lajoie, AL:Phil. 1901

Most Seasons, .400 or higher Batting Average (Minimum: 400 at-bats)
3	Jesse Burkett, NL:Clev. 1895-96; StL. 99
	Rogers Hornsby, NL:StL. 1922,24-25
	Ty Cobb, AL:Det. 1911-12,22

Most Seasons, Consecutive, .400 or higher Batting Average (Minimum: 400 at-bats)
2	Jesse Burkett, NL:Clev. 1895-96
	Rogers Hornsby, NL:StL. 1924-25
	Ty Cobb, AL:Det. 1911-12

Most Seasons, .300 or higher Batting Average (Minimum: 400 at-bats)
19	Ty Cobb, AL:Det. 1907-13,15-25; Phil. 27
17	Stan Musial, NL:StL. 1942-44, 46-58, 62

Most Seasons, Consecutive, .300 or higher Batting Average (Minimum: 400 at-bats)
16   Honus Wagner, NL:Lou. 1898-99; Pitt. 1900-13
          Tony Gwynn, NL:SD 1984-99
12   Lou Gehrig, AL:NY 1926-37

Lowest Batting Average, Lifetime (Minimum: 5000 at-bats)
.218   George McBride, AL:Mil. 1901, Wash. 08-20, NL:Pitt. 1905; StL. 05-06

Lowest Batting Average, League (Minimum: 5000 at-bats)
.224   Ed Brinkman, AL:Wash. 1961-70; Det. 71-74; Tex.-NY 75
.232   Mickey Doolan, NL:Phil. 1905-13; Chi.-NY 16; Brk. 18

Lowest Batting Average, Season (Minimum: 400 at-bats)
.166   Jim Canavan, NL:Chi, 1892 (439 at-bats)
          Since 1900:
.179   Rob Deer, AL:Det. 1991 (448 at-bats)
.184   Bill Hallman, NL:Phil. 1901 (445 at-bats)

SLUGGING PERCENTAGE

Most Seasons Leading Major Leagues
12   Babe Ruth, AL:Bos. 1918-19; NY 20-21,23-24,26-31

Most Seasons, Consecutive, Leading Major Leagues
6   Babe Ruth, AL:NY 1926-31

Most Seasons Leading League
13   Babe Ruth, AL:Bos. 1918-19; NY 20-24,26-31
9   Rogers Hornsby, NL:StL. 1917,20-25; Bos. 28; Chi. 29

Most Seasons, Consecutive, Leading League
7   Babe Ruth, AL:Bos. 1918-19; NY 20-24
6   Rogers Hornsby, NL:StL. 1920-25

Highest Slugging Percentage, Lifetime (Minimum: 5000 at-bats)
.690   Babe Ruth, AL:Bos. 1914-19; NY 20-34 NL:Bos. 35

Highest Slugging Percentage, League (Minimum: 5000 at-bats)
.692   Babe Ruth, AL:Bos. 1914-19; NY 20-34
.585   Barry Bonds, NL:Pitt. 1986-92; SF 93-2001

Highest Slugging Percentage, Season
.863   Barry Bonds, NL:SF 2001
.847   Babe Ruth, AL:NY 1920

Most Seasons, .700 or higher Slugging Percentage (Minimum: 400 at-bats)
9   Babe Ruth, AL:NY 1920-21,23-24,26-28,30-31
2   Rogers Hornsby, NL:StL. 1922,25
         Larry Walker, NL:Col. 1997,99

Most Seasons, Consecutive, .700 or higher Slugging Percentage (Minimum: 400 at-bats)
3   Babe Ruth, AL:NY 1926-28

Most Seasons, .600 or higher Slugging Percentage (Minimum: 400 at-bats)
13   Babe Ruth, AL:Bos. 1919; NY 20-24,26-32
7   Rogers Hornsby, NL:StL. 1921-25; Bos. 28; Chi. 29

Most Seasons, Consecutive, .600 or higher Slugging Percentage (Minimum: 400 at-bats)
7   Babe Ruth, AL:NY 1926-32
5   Rogers Hornsby, NL:StL. 1921-25

Lowest Slugging Percentage, Lifetime (Minimum: 5000 at-bats)
.264   George McBride, AL:Mil. 1901; Wash. 08-20 NL:Pitt.-StL. 05; StL. 06

Lowest Slugging Percentage, League (Minimum: 5000 at-bats)
.280   Mark Belanger, AL:Balt. 1965-81
.307   Mickey Doolan, NL:Phil. 1905-11; Chi.-NY 16; Brk. 18

Lowest Slugging Percentage, Season (Minimum: 400 at-bats)
.197   Jim Lillie, NL:KC 1886
         Since 1900:
.206   Pete Childs, NL:Phil. 1902
.225   Charlie Moran, AL:Wash.-StL. 1904

PLATE APPEARANCES

Most Plate Appearances, Lifetime
15,890   Pete Rose, NL:Cin. 1963-78,84-86; Phil. 79-83; Mtl. 84

Most Plate Appearances, League
15,890   Pete Rose, NL:Cin. 1963-78,84-86; Phil. 79-83; Mtl. 84
13,992   Carl Yastrzemski, AL:Bos. 1961-83

Most Plate Appearances, Season
773   Len Dykstra, NL:Phil. 1993
758   Wade Boggs, AL:Bos. 1985

Most Plate Appearances, Game
8 By many players; Last:
   Darryl Hamilton, AL:Mil. Aug. 28, 1992
   Mike Cameron, NL:Cin. May 19, 1999
   Extra-Inning Game:
12 Felix Millan, NL:NY Sept. 11, 1974 (25 inn)
   John Milner, NL:NY Sept. 11, 1974 (25 inn)
11 Rudy Law, AL:Chi. May 8 , 1984 (25 inn)
   Carlton Fisk, AL:Chi. May 8, 1984 (25 inn)
   Harold Baines, AL:Chi. May 8, 1984 (25 inn)

Most Plate Appearances, Inning
3 Larry Murphy, AA:Wash. June 17, 1891
   Marty Callaghan, NL:Chi. Aug. 25, 1922 (4th)
   Billy Cox, NL:Brk. May 21, 1952 (1st)
   Pee Wee Reese, NL:Brk. May 21, 1952 (1st)
   Duke Snider, NL:Brk. May 21, 1952 (1st)
   Gil Hodges, NL:Brk. Aug. 8, 1954 (8th)
   Dusty Baker, NL:Atl. Sept. 20, 1972 (2nd)
   Luis Quinones, NL:Cin Aug. 3, 1989 (1st)
   Mariano Duncan, NL:Cin. Aug. 3, 1989 (1st)
   Stan Javier, NL:SF July 15, 1997 (7th)
   Ted Williams, AL:Bos. July 4, 1948 (7th)
   Sammy White AL:Bos. June 18, 1953 (7th)
   Gene Stephens, AL:Bos. June 18, 1953 (7th)
   Tom Umphlett, AL:Bos. June 18, 1953 (7th)
   Johnny Lipton, AL:Bos. June 18, 1953 (7th)
   George Kell, AL:Bos. June 18, 1953 (7th)
   Darryl Hamilton, AL:Tex. Apr. 19, 1996 (8th)

REACHING BASE SAFELY

Most Times Reaching Base Safely, Lifetime
5929 Pete Rose, NL:Cin. 1963-78, 84-86; Phil. 79-83; Mtl. 84

Most Times Reaching Base Safely, League
5929 Pete Rose, NL:Cin. 1963-78, 84-86; Phil. 79-83; Mtl. 84
5468 Ty Cobb, AL:Det. 1905-26; Phil. 27-28

Most Times Reaching Base Safely, Season
   Since 1900:
379 Babe Ruth, AL:NY 1923
342 Barry Bonds, NL:SF 2001

Most Times Reaching Base Safely, Game
8 Piggy Ward, NL:Cin. June 18, 1893
   Since 1900:
7 Ben Chapman, AL:NY May 24, 1936
   Cliff Heathcote, NL:Chi. Aug. 25, 1922
   Cookie Lavagetto, NL:Brk. Sept. 23(1g), 1939
   Mel Ott, NL:NY Apr. 30, 1944
   Rennie Stennett, NL:Pitt. Sept. 16, 1975
   Sean Casey, NL:Cin. May 19, 1999
   Extra-Inning Game:
9 Max Carey, NL:Pitt. July 7, 1922 (18 inn)
   Johnny Burnett, AL:Clev. July 10, 1932 (18 inn)

Most Times Reaching Base Safely, Inning
3 Ned Williamson, NL:Chi. Sept. 6, 1883 (7th)
   Tommy Burns, NL:Chi. Sept. 6, 1883 (7th)
   Fred Pfeffer, NL:.Chi. Sept. 6, 1883 (7th)
   Herman Long, NL:Bos. June 18, 1894 (1g; 1st)
   Bobby Lowe, NL:Bos. June 18, 1894 (1g;1st)
   Hugh Duffy, NL:Bos. June 18, 1894 (1g;1st)
   Pee Wee Reese, NL:Brk. May 21, 1952 (1st)
   Sammy White, AL:Bos. June 18, 1953 (7th)
   Gene Stephens, AL:Bos. June 18, 1953 (7th)
   Tom Umphlett, AL:Bos. June 18, 1953 (7th)

GAMES

Most Seasons Leading Major Leagues
8 Cal Ripken, AL:Balt. 1983-84, 87, 91-93,96-97

Most Seasons, Consecutive, Leading Major Leagues
3	Steve Garvey, NL:LA 1980-82
	Cal Ripken, AL:Balt. 1991-93

Most Seasons Leading League
9	Cal Ripken, AL:Balt. 1983-84,87,89,91-93, 96-97
6	Ernie Banks, NL:Chi. 1954-55,57-60
	Steve Garvey, NL:LA 1977-78,80-82; SD 85

Most Seasons, Consecutive, Leading League
4	Del Pratt, AL:StL. 1913-16
	Brooks Robinson, AL:Balt. 1961-64
	Ernie Banks, NL:Chi. 1957-60
	Dale Murphy, NL:Atl. 1982-85

Most Games, Lifetime
3562	Pete Rose, NL:Cin. 1963-78,84-86 Phil. 79-83; Mtl. 84

Most Games, League
3562	Pete Rose, NL:Cin. 1963-78,84-86 Phil. 79-83; Mtl. 84
3308	Carl Yastrzemski, AL:Bos. 1961-83

Most Games, Consecutive, Lifetime
2632	Cal Ripken, AL:Balt., May 30, 1982–Sept. 19, 1998

Most Games, Consecutive, League
2632	Cal Ripken, AL:Balt., May 30, 1982–Sept. 19, 1998
1207	Steve Garvey, NL:LA-SD Sept. 2, 1975-July 29(1g), 1983

Most Games, One Club
3308	Carl Yastrzemski, AL:Bos. 1961-83
3076	Hank Aaron, NL:Mil./Atl., 1954-74

Most Games, Season
165	Maury Wills, NL:LA 1962
164	Cesar Tovar, AL:Minn. 1967

Most Seasons, 150 or more Games
17	Pete Rose, NL:Cin. 1963,65-66,69-78; Phil. 79-80,82-83
15	Cal Ripken, AL:Balt. 1982-93, 96-98

Most Seasons, Consecutive, 150 or more Games
13	Willie Mays, NL:NY 1954-56; SF 58-66
12	Cal Ripken, AL:Balt. 1982-93

Most Seasons, 100 or more Games, Lifetime
23	Pete Rose, NL:Cin. 1963-78,84-85; Phil. 79-83; Mtl. 84

Most Seasons, 100 or more Games, League
23	Pete Rose, NL:Cin. 1963-78,84-85; Phil. 79-83; Mtl. 84
22	Carl Yastrzemski, AL:Bos. 1961-80, 82-83

Most Seasons, Consecutive. 100 or more Games
23	Pete Rose, NL:Cin. 1963-78,84-85; Phil. 79-83; Mtl. 84
20	Carl Yastrzemski AL:Bos. 1961-80

Most Games, One Day, Since 1900
3	Clyde Barnhart, NL:Pitt. Oct. 2, 1920
	Pat Duncan, NL:Cin. Oct. 2, 1920
	Fred Nicholson, NL:Pitt. Oct. 2, 1920
	Morrie Rath, NL:Cin. Oct. 2, 1920
	Jim Tierney, NL:Pitt. Oct. 2, 1920

AT-BATS

Most Seasons Leading Major Leagues
6	Doc Cramer, AL:Phil. 1933-34; Bos. 38,40; Wash. 41; Det. 42

Most Seasons, Consecutive, Leading Major Leagues
3	Doc Cramer, AL:Bos. 1940-Wash. 41-Det. 42
	Dave Cash, NL:Phil. 1974-76

Most Seasons Leading League
7	Doc Cramer, AL:Phil. 1933-35; Bos. 38,40; Wash. 41; Det. 42
4	Abner Dalrymple, NL:Chi. 1880,82,84-85
	Pete Rose, NL:Cin. 1965,72-73,77

Most Seasons, Consecutive, Leading League
3	Sparky Adams, NL:Chi. 1925-27
	Dave Cash, NL:Phil. 1974-76
	Doc Cramer, AL:Phil. 1933-35; Bos. 40-Wash. 41-Det. 42
	Bobby Richardson, AL:NY 1962-64

Most At-Bats, Lifetime
14,053	Pete Rose, NL:Cin. 1963-78,84-86; Phil. 79-83; Mtl. 84
11,988	Carl Yastrzemski, AL:Bos. 1961-83

Most At-Bats, Season
705	Willie Wilson, AL:KC 1980
701	Juan Samuel, NL:Phil. 1984

Most Seasons, 600 or more At-Bats
17	Pete Rose, NL:Cin. 1963,65-66,68-78; Phil 79-80,82
13	Cal Ripken, AL:Balt. 1983-87, 89-93, 96-98

Most Seasons, Consecutive, 600 or more At-Bats
13	Pete Rose, NL:Cin. 1968-78; Phil. 79-80
12	Nellie Fox, AL:Chi. 1951-62

Most At-Bats, Game
8	By many NL players prior to 1900
7	By many players since 1900

Extra-Inning Game:
11	Carson Bigbee, NL:Pitt. Aug. 22, 1917 (22 inn)
	Charlie Pick, NL:Bos. May 1, 1920 (26 inn)
	Tony Boeckel, NL:Bos. May 1, 1920 (26 inn)
	Ralph Garr, NL:Atl. May 4, 1973 (20 inn)
	Dave Schneck, NL:NY Sept. 11, 1974 (25 inn)
	Dave Cash, NL:Mtl. May 21, 1977 (21 inn)
	Johnny Burnett, AL:Clev. July 10, 1932 (18 inn)
	Edward Morgan, AL:Clev. July 10, 1932 (18 inn)
	Irv Hall, AL:Phil. July 21, 1945 (24 inn)
	Bobby Richardson, AL:NY June 24, 1962 (22 inn)
	Cecil Cooper, AL:Mil. May 8 1984 (25 inn)
	Rudy Law, AL:Chi. May 8, 1984 (25 inn)
	Carlton Fisk, AL:Chi. May 8, 1984 (25 inn)
	Julio Cruz, AL:Chi. May 8, 1984 (25 inn)

Most At-Bats, Doubleheader
13	Rabbit Maranville, NL:Pitt. Aug. 8, 1922
	Billy Herman, NL:Chi. Aug. 21, 1935
	Dave Philley, AL:Chi. May 30, 1950

Extra Innings:
14	Joe Christopher, NL:NY May 31, 1964 (32 inn)
	Jim Hickman, NL:NY May 31, 1964 (32 inn)
	Ed Kranepool, NL:NY May 31, 1964 (32 inn)
	Roy McMillan, NL:NY May 31, 1964 (32 inn)
	Frank Thomas, NL:NY May 31, 1964 (32 inn)
	Jesus Alou, NL:SF May 31, 1964 (32 inn)
	Rick Monday, AL:KC June 17, 1967 (28 inn)
	Ramon Webster, AL:KC June 17, 1967 (28 inn)

Most At-Bats, Inning
3	By many players; Last:
	Gene Stephens, AL:Bos June 18, 1953 (7th)
	Geoge Kell, AL:Bos. June 18, 1953 (7th)
	Luis Quinones, NL:Cin. Aug. 3, 1989 (1st)

RUNS

Most Seasons Leading Major Leagues
8	Babe Ruth, AL:Bos. 1919; NY 20-21,23-24,26-28

Most Seasons, Consecutive, Leading Major Leagues
3	Eddie Collins, AL:Phil. 1912-14
	Babe Ruth, AL:Bos. 1919; NY 20-21,26-28
	Ted Williams, AL:Bos. 1940-42
	Mickey Mantle, AL:NY 1956-58
	Pete Rose, NL:Cin. 1974-76

Most Seasons Leading League
8	Babe Ruth, AL:Bos. 1919; NY 20-21,23-24,26-28
5	George Burns, NL:NY 1914,16-17,19-20
	Rogers Hornsby, NL:StL. 1921-22,24; NY 27; Chi. 29
	Stan Musial, NL:StL. 1946,48,51-52,54

Most Seasons, Consecutive, Leading League
3	King Kelly, NL:Chi. 1884-86
	Chuck Klein, NL:Phil. 1930-32
	Duke Snider, NL:Brk. 1953-55
	Pete Rose, NL:Cin. 1974-76
	Ty Cobb, AL:Det. 1909-11
	Eddie Collins, AL:Phil. 1912-14
	Babe Ruth, AL:Bos. 1919-NY 20-21; 26-28
	Ted Williams, AL:Bos. 1940-42
	Mickey Mantle, AL:NY 1956-58

Most Runs Scored, Lifetime
2248   Rickey Henderson, AL:Oak.. 1974-84,89-95,98; NY 85-89; Tor. 93; Ana. 97; Sea. 2000; NL:SD 96-97, 2001; NY 99-2000

Most Runs Scored, League
2245   Ty Cobb, AL:Det. 1905-26; Phil. 27-28
2165   Pete Rose, NL:Cin. 1963-78,84-86; Phil. 79-83; Mtl. 84

Most Runs Scored, Season
196   Billy Hamilton, NL:Phil. 1894
Since 1900:
177   Babe Ruth, AL:NY 1921
158   Chuck Klein, NL:Phil. 1930

Most Seasons, 100 or more Runs Scored
15   Hank Aaron, NL:Mil./Atl. 1955-70
13   Lou Gehrig, AL:NY 1926-38

Most Seasons, Consecutive, 100 or more Runs Scored
13   Lou Gehrig, AL:NY 1926-38
        Hank Aaron, NL:Mil./Atl. 1955-67

Most Runs Scored, Game
7   Guy Hecker, AA:Lou. Aug. 15(2g), 1886
6   Jim Whitney, NL:Bos. June 9, 1883
        Cap Anson, NL:Chi. Aug. 24, 1886
        Mike Tiernan, NL:NY June 15, 1887
        King Kelly, NL:Bos. Aug. 27, 1887
        Ezra Sutton, NL:Bos. Aug. 27, 1887
        Jimmy Ryan, NL:Chi. July 25, 1894
        Bobby Lowe, NL:Bos. May 3, 1895
        Ginger Beaumont, NL:Pitt. July 22, 1899
        Mel Ott, NL:NY Aug. 4(2g), 1934; Apr. 30(1g), 1944
        Frank Torre, NL:Mil. Sept. 2(1g), 1957
        Edgardo Alfonzo, NL:NY Aug. 30, 1999
        Johnny Pesky, AL:Bos. May 8, 1946
        Spike Owen, AL:Bos. Aug. 21, 1986

Most Games, Consecutive, Runs Scored
24   Billy Hamilton, NL:Phil. July 6-Aug. 2, 1894 (35 runs)
Since 1900:
18   Red Rolfe, AL:NY Aug. 9-25, 1939 (30 runs)
        Kenny Lofton, AL:Clev. Aug. 15-Sept. 3, 2000 (26 runs)
17   Ted Kluszewski, NL:Cin. Aug. 27-Sept. 13, 1954 (24 runs)

Most Runs Scored, Inning
3   Tommy Burns, NL:Chi. Sept. 6, 1883 (7th)
        Ned Williamson, NL:Chi. Sept. 6, 1883 (7th)
Since 1900:
3   Sammy White, AL:Bos. June 18, 1953 (7th)
2   By many NL players

HITS

Most Seasons Leading Major Leagues
7   Ty Cobb, AL:Det. 1907,09,11-12,15,17,19
        Pete Rose, NL:Cin. 1965,68,70,72-73,76; Phil. 81

Most Seasons, Consecutive, Leading Major Leagues
2   Dan Brouthers, NL:Buff. 1882-83
        Jesse Burkett, NL:Clev. 1895-96
        Ty Cobb, AL:Det. 1911-12
        Kirby Puckett, AL:Minn. 1988-89
        Ginger Beaumont, NL:Pitt. 1902-03
        Chuck Klein, NL:Phil. 1932-33
        Stan Musial, NL:StL. 1948-49
        Pete Rose, NL:Cin. 1972-73
        Tony Gwynn, NL:SD 1994-95

Most Seasons Leading League
8   Ty Cobb, AL:Det. 1907-09,11-12,15,17,19
7   Pete Rose, NL:Cin. 1965,68,70,72-73,76; Phil. 81
        Tony Gwynn, NL:SD 1984,86-87,89,94-96,97

Most Seasons, Consecutive, Leading League
3   Ty Cobb, AL:Det. 1907-09
        Tony Oliva, AL:Minn. 1964-66
        Kirby Puckett, AL:Minn. 1987-89
        Ginger Beaumont, NL:Pitt. 1902-04
        Rogers Hornsby, NL:StL. 1920-22
        Frank McCormick, NL:Cin. 1938-40

Most Hits, League

4256	Pete Rose, NL:Cin. 1963-78,84-86; Phil. 79-83; Mtl. 84
4191	Ty Cobb, AL:Det. 1905-26; Phil. 27-28

Most Hits, Season

257	George Sisler, AL:StL. 1920
254	Lefty O'Doul, NL:Phil. 1929
	Bill Terry, NL:NY 1930

Most Seasons, 200 or more Hits

10	Pete Rose, NL:Cin. 1965-66,68-70,73,75-77; Phil. 79
9	Ty Cobb, AL:Det. 1907,09,11-12,15-17,22,24

Most Seasons, Consecutive, 200 or more Hits

8	Willie Keeler, NL:Balt. 1894-98, Brk. 99-1901
	Since 1900:
7	Wade Boggs, AL:Bos. 1983-89
5	Chuck Klein, NL:Phil. 1929-33

Most Hits, Consecutive, Season

12	Mike Higgins, AL:Bos. June 19-21, 1938 (2-bb)
	Walt Dropo, AL:Det. July 14-15, 1952
10	Ed Delahanty, NL:Phil. July 13-14, 1897 (1-bb)
	Jake Gettman, NL:Wash. Sept. 10-11, 1897
	Ed Konetchy, NL:Brk. June 28-July 1, 1919
	Kiki Cuyler, NL:Pitt. Sept. 18-21, 1925 (1-bb)
	Chick Hafey, NL:StL. July 6-9, 1929 (2-bb)
	Joe Medwick, NL:StL. July 19-21, 1936 (1-bb)
	Buddy Hassett, NL:Bos. June 9(2g)-14, 1940 (1-bb)
	Woody Williams, NL:Cin. Sept. 5-6, 1943 (1-bb)
	Bip Roberts, NL:Cin. Sept. 19-23, 1992

Most Hits, Game

7	Wilbert Robinson, NL:Balt. June 10(1g), 1892
	Rennie Stennett, NL:Pitt. Sept. 16, 1975
6	By many AL players; Last:
	Damion Easley, AL:Det. Aug. 8, 2001
	Extra-Inning Game:
9	Johnny Burnett, AL:Clev. July 10, 1932 (18 inn)

Most Hits, Consecutive, Game

7	Wilbert Robinson, NL:Balt. June 10(1g), 1892
	Rennie Stennett, NL:Pitt. Sept. 16, 1975
6	By many AL players
	Extra-Inning Game:
7	Cesar Gutierrez, AL:Det. June 21, 1970 (2g, 12 inn)

Most Hits, First Major League Game

5	Fred Clarke, NL:Lou. June 30, 1894 (1-3b)
	Since 1900:
4	Ray Jansen, AL:StL. Sept. 30, 1910
	Art Shires, AL:Chi. Aug. 20, 1928 (1-3b)
	Russ Van Atta, AL:NY Apr. 25, 1933
	Spook Jacobs, AL:Phil. Apr. 13, 1954
	Ted Cox, AL:Bos. Sept. 18, 1977 (1-2b)
	Kirby Puckett, AL:Minn. May 8, 1984
	Billy Bean, AL:Det. Apr. 25, 1987 (2-2b)
	Casey Stengel, NL:Brk. Sept. 17, 1912
	Ed Freed, NL:Phil. Sept 11, 1942
	Willie McCovey, NL:SF July 30, 1959 (2-3b)
	Mack Jones, NL:Mil. July 13, 1961 (1-2b)
	Delino DeShields, NL:Mtl. Apr. 9, 1990 (1-2b)
	Derrick Gibson, NL:Col. Sept. 8, 1998 (1-2b)
	Extra-Inning Game:
5	Cecil Travis, AL:Wash. May 16, 1933 (12 inn)

Most Games, 6 or more Hits, Lifetime

2	Cal McVey, NL:Chi. July 22-25, 1876 (cons)
	Ed Delahanty, PL:Clev. June 2, 1890; NL:Phil. June 16, 1894
	Jim Bottomley, NL:StL. Sept. 16, 1924, Aug. 5, 1931
	Jimmie Foxx, AL:Phil. May 30, 1930 (13 inn), July 10, 1932 (18 inn)
	Doc Cramer, AL:Phil. June 20, 1932, July 13(1g), 1935
	Kirby Puckett, AL:Minn. Aug. 30, 1987; May 23, 1991 (11 inn)

Most Games, 5 or more Hits, Lifetime

14	Ty Cobb, AL:Det. 1905-26; Phil. 27-28
10	Willie Keeler, NL:NY 1892-93, 1910; Brk. 93,99-1902; Balt. 94-98
	Pete Rose, NL:Cin. 1963-78,84-86; Phil. 79-83; Mtl. 84

Most Games, 5 or more Hits, Season
4   Willie Keeler, NL:Balt. July 17, Aug. 14, Sept. 3, 6, 1897
       Stan Musial, NL:StL. Apr. 30, May 19, June 22, Sept. 22, 1948
       Tony Gwynn, NL:SD Apr. 18, 30, July 27, Aug. 4, 1993
       Ty Cobb, AL:Det. May 7, July 7, 12, 17, 1922

Most Games, 1 or more Hits, Season
135   Rogers Hornsby, NL:StL. 1922 (154 g)
       Chuck Klein, NL:Phil. 1930 (156 g)
       Wade Boggs, AL:Bos. 1985 (161 g)
       Derek Jeter, AL:NY 1999 (158 g)
       Ichiro Suzuki, AL:Sea. 2001 (157 g)

Most Games, Consecutive, 1 or more Hits, Lifetime
56   Joe DiMaggio, AL:NY May 15-July 16, 1941
45   Willie Keeler, NL:Balt. Sept 26, 1896-June 18, 1897
       NL Since 1900:
44   Pete Rose, NL:Cin. June 14-July 31, 1978

Most Games, Consecutive, 1 or more Hits, Season
56   Joe DiMaggio, AL:NY May 15-July 16, 1941
44   Willie Keeler, NL:Balt. Apr. 22-June 18, 1897
       Pete Rose, NL:Cin. June 14-July 31, 1978

Most Games, Consecutive, 1 or more Hits, Start of Season
44   Willie Keeler, NL:Balt. Apr. 22-June 18, 1897
       Since 1900:
34   George Sisler, AL:StL. Apr. 14-May 19, 1925
25   Charlie Grimm, NL:Pitt. Apr. 17-May 16, 1923

Most Hits, 2 Consecutive Games
12   Cal McVey, NL:Chi. July 22-25, 1876
       Since 1900:
11   Johnny Burnett, AL:Clev. July 9-11, 1932
10   Roberto Clemente, NL:Pitt. Aug. 22-23, 1970
       Rennie Stennett, NL:Pitt. Sept. 16-17, 1975
       Mike Benjamin, NL:SF June 13-14, 1995

Most Hits, Doubleheader
9   Fred Carroll, AA:Pitt. July 5, 1886
       Wilbert Robinson, NL:Balt. June 10, 1892
       Joe Kelley, NL:Balt. Sept. 3, 1894 (cons)
       Fred Lindstrom, NL:NY June 25, 1928
       Bill Terry, NL:NY June 18, 1929
       Ray Morehart, AL:Chi. Aug. 31, 1926
       George Case, AL:Wash. July 4, 1940
       Lee Thomas, AL:LA Sept. 5, 1961

Most Hits, 3 Consecutive Games
14   Willie Keeler, NL:Balt. Sept. 3-6, 1897
       Mike Benjamin, NL:SF June 11-14, 1995
13   Joe Cronin, AL:Wash. June. 19-22, 1933
       Walt Dropo, AL:Det. July 14-15, 1952

Most Hits, Inning
3   Tommy Burns, NL:Chi. Sept. 6, 1883 (7th; hr, 2-2b)
       Fred Pfeffer, NL:Chi. Sept. 6, 1883 (7th; 2b, 2-1b)
       Ned Williamson, NL:Chi. Sept. 6, 1883 (7th; 2b, 2-1b)
       Gene Stephens, AL:Bos. June 18, 1953 (7th; 2b, 2-1b)
       NL Since 1900:
2   By many NL players

Fewest Hits, Season (Most at-bats)
0   Bob Buhl, NL:Mil.-Chi. 1962 (70 at-bats)
       Bill Wight, AL:Chi. 1950 (61 at-bats)

Fewest Hits, Game (Most at-bats)
0   Charlie Pick, NL:Bos. May 1, 1920 (11ab, 26 inn)
       George Kell, AL:Phil. July 21, 1945 (10ab, 24 inn)

EXTRA-BASE HITS

Most Seasons Leading Major Leagues
7   Stan Musial, NL:StL. 1943-44,46,48-50,53

Most Seasons, Consecutive, Leading Major Leagues
4   Babe Ruth, AL:Bos. 1918-19; NY 20-21

Most Seasons Leading League
7   Honus Wagner, NL:Pitt. 1900,02-04,07-09
       Stan Musial, NL:StL. 1943-44,46,48-50,53
       Babe Ruth, AL:Bos. 1918-19; NY 20-21,23-24,28

Most Seasons, Consecutive, Leading League
4	Babe Ruth, AL:Bos. 1918-19; NY 20-21
3	Dan Brouthers, NL:Buff. 1885; Det. 86-87
	Honus Wagner, NL:Phil. 1902-04,07-09
	Rogers Hornsby, NL:StL. 1920-22
	Joe Medwick, NL:StL. 1935-37
	Johnny Mize, NL:StL. 1938-40
	Stan Musial, NL:StL. 1948-50
	Duke Snider, NL:Brk. 1954-56

Most Extra-Base Hits, Lifetime
1477	Hank Aaron, NL:Mil./Atl. 1954-74; AL:Mil. 75-76

Most Extra-Base Hits, League
1429	Hank Aaron, NL:Mil./Atl. 1954-74
1350	Babe Ruth, AL:Bos. 1914-19; NY 20-34

Most Extra-Base Hits, Season
119	Babe Ruth, AL:NY 1921
107	Chuck Klein, NL:Phil. 1930
	Barry Bonds, NL:SF 2001

Most Games, 4 or more Extra-Base Hits, League
5	Lou Gehrig, AL:NY 1926,28,30,32,34
	Joe DiMaggio, AL:NY 1936-37,41,48,50
4	Willie Stargell, NL:Pitt. 1965,68,70,73

Most Games, 4 or more Extra-Base Hits, Season
2	Henry Larkin, AA:Phil. June 16, July 29, 1885
	George Burns, AL:Clev. June 19(1g), July 23, 1924
	Jimmie Foxx, AL:Phil. Apr. 24, July 2(2g), 1933
	Joe Medwick, NL:StL. May 12, Aug. 4, 1937
	Billy Williams, NL:Chi. Apr. 9, Sept. 5, 1969
	Paul O'Neill, NL:Cin. May 11, Sept. 13, 1991
	Rafael Palmeiro, AL:Tex. July 15, Sept. 6, 1993
	Albert Belle, AL:Balt. Aug. 29, Sept. 23, 1999
	Shannon Stewart, AL:Tor. June 9, July 18, 2000

Most Extra-Base Hits, Consecutive, Season
7	Elmer Smith, AL:Clev. Sept. 4-5, 1921 (4-hr, 3-2b)
	Earl Sheely, AL:Chi. May 20-21, 1926 (1-hr, 6-2b)
6	Larry Walker, NL:Col. May 21-22, 1996 (1-hr, 3-3b, 2-2b)

Most Extra-Base Hits, Game
5	George Strief, AA:Phil. June 25, 1885 (4-3b, 1-2b)
	George Gore, NL:Chi. July 9, 1885 (2-3b, 3-2b)
	Larry Twitchell, NL:Clev. Aug. 15, 1889 (1-hr, 3-3b, 1-2b)
	Joe Adcock, NL:Mil. July 31, 1954 (4-hr, 1-2b)
	Willie Stargell, NL:Pitt. Aug. 1, 1970 (2-hr, 3-2b)
	Steve Garvey, NL:LA Aug. 28, 1977 (2-hr, 3-2b)
	Lou Boudreau, AL:Clev. July 14(1g), 1946 (1-hr, 4-2b)

Most Extra-Base Hits, 2 Consecutive Games
7	Ed Delahanty, NL:Phil. July 13-14, 1896 (4-hr, 1-3b, 2-2b)
	Red Schoendienst, NL:StL. June 5-6, 1948 (1 hr, 6-2b)
	Joe Adcock, NL:Mil. July 30-31, 1954 (5-hr, 2-2b)
	Larry Walker, NL:Col. May 21-22, 1996 (2-hr, 3-3b, 2-2b)
	Earl Sheely, AL:Chi. May 20-21, 1926 (1-hr, 6-2b)

Most Extra-Base Hits, Inning
3	Tommy Burns, NL:Chi. Sept. 6, 1883 (7th: 1-hr, 2-2b)
	Since 1900:
2	By many players

TOTAL BASES

Most Seasons Leading Major Leagues
6	Babe Ruth, AL:Bos. 1919; NY 21,23-24,26,28
	Stan Musial, NL:StL. 1943,46,48-49,51-52

Most Seasons, Consecutive, Leading Major Leagues
2   Dan Brouthers, NL:Buff. 1882-83
      Jimmy Ryan, NL:Chi. 1888-89
      Babe Ruth, AL:NY 1923-24
      Jimmie Foxx, AL:Phil. 1932-33
      Stan Musial, NL:StL. 1948-49 & 51-52
      Duke Snider, NL:Brk. 1953-54
      Hank Aaron, NL:Mil. 1959-60
      Frank Howard, AL:Wash. 1968-69
      Jim Rice, AL:Bos. 1978-79
      Mike Schmidt, NL:Phil. 1980-81
      Don Mattingly, AL:NY 1985-86
      Sammy Sosa, NL:Chi. 1998-99

Most Seasons Leading League
8   Hank Aaron, NL:Mil. 1956-57,59-61,63; Atl. 67,69
6   Ty Cobb, AL:Det. 1907-09,11,15,17
      Babe Ruth, AL:Bos. 1919; NY 21,23-24,26,28
      Ted Williams, AL:Bos. 1939,42,46-47,49,51

Most Seasons, Consecutive, Leading League
4   Honus Wagner, NL:Pitt. 1906-09
      Chuck Klein, NL:Phil. 1930-33
3   Ty Cobb, AL:Det. 1907-09
      Jim Rice, AL:Bos. 1977-79

Most Total Bases, Lifetime
6856   Hank Aaron, NL:Mil./Atl. 1954-74; AL:Mil. 75-76

Most Total Bases, League
6591   Hank Aaron, NL:Mil./Atl. 1954-74
5863   Ty Cobb, AL:Det. 1905-26; Phil. 27-28

Most Total Bases, Season
457   Babe Ruth, AL:NY 1921
450   Rogers Hornsby,NL:StL. 1922

Most Seasons, 400 or more Total Bases
5   Lou Gehrig, AL:NY 1927,30-31,34,36
3   Chuck Klein, NL:Phil. 1929-30,32

Most Seasons, Consecutive, 400 or more Total Bases
2   Lou Gehrig, AL:NY 1930-31
      Jimmie Foxx, AL:Phil. 1932-33
      Chuck Klein, NL:Phil. 1929-30
      Todd Helton, NL:Col. 2000-01

Most Seasons, 300 or more Total Bases
15   Hank Aaron, NL:Mil. 1955-63; Atl. 69,71
13   Lou Gehrig, AL:NY 1926-38

Most Seasons, Consecutive, 300 or more Total Bases
13   Lou Gehrig, AL:NY 1926-38
      Willie Mays, NL:NY 1954-57; SF 58-66

Most Total Bases, Game
18   Joe Adcock, NL:Mil. July 31, 1954 (4-hr, 1-2b)
16   Ty Cobb, AL Det. May 5, 1925 (3-hr, 1-2b, 2-1b)
      Lou Gehrig, AL:NY June 3, 1932 (4-hr)
      Jimmie Foxx, AL:Phil. July 10, 1932 (18 inn; 3-hr,1-2b,2-1b)
      Pat Seerey, AL:Chi. July 18, 1948 (1g; 11 inn; 4-hr)
      Rocky Colavito, AL:Clev June 10, 1959 (4-hr)
      Fred Lynn, AL:Bos. June 18, 1975 (3-hr, 1-3b, 1-1b)

Most Total Bases, 2 Consecutive Games
25   Ty Cobb, AL:Det. May 5-6, 1925
      Joe Adcock, NL:Mil. July 30-31, 1954

Most Total Bases, Doubleheader
22   Nate Colbert, NL:SD Aug. 1, 1972
21   Jimmie Foxx, AL:Phil. July 2, 1933 (19 inn)
      Al Oliver, AL:Tex. Aug. 17, 1980

Most Total Bases, Inning
8   Tommy Burns, NL:Chi. Sept. 6, 1883 (7th)
      Also by many players (2 home runs, inning)

SINGLES

Most Seasons Leading Major Leagues
6   Ty Cobb, AL:Det. 1907,09,11-12,15,17
      Nellie Fox, AL:Chi. 1952,54-57,59

Most Seasons, Consecutive, Leading Major Leagues
  4   Nellie Fox, AL:Chi. 1954-57

Most Seasons Leading League
  8   Nellie Fox, AL:Chi. 1952,54-60
  7   Tony Gwynn, NL:SD 1984,86-87,89,94-95, 97

Most Seasons, Consecutive, Leading League
  7   Nellie Fox, AL:Chi. 1954-60
  4   Brett Butler, NL:SF 1990; LA 1991-93

Most Singles, Lifetime
  3215   Pete Rose, NL:Cin. 1963-78,84-86; Phil. 79-83; Mtl. 84
  3053   Ty Cobb, AL:Det. 1905-26; Phil. 27-28

Most Singles, Season
  201   Willie Keeler, NL:Balt. 1898
               Since 1900:
  198   Lloyd Waner, NL:Pitt. 1927
  192   Ichiro Suzuki, AL:Sea. 2001

Most Singles, Game
  6   Hick Carpenter, AA:Cin. Sept. 12, 1883
               George Pinckney, AA:Brk. June 25, 1885
               By many players since 1900; Last:
               Floyd Robinson, AL:Chi. July 22, 1962
               Willie Davis, LA May 24, 1973 (19 inn)
               Extra-Inning Game:
  7   Johnny Burnett, AL:Clev. July 10, 1932 (18 inn)

Most Singles, Inning
  2   By many players

DOUBLES

Most Seasons Leading Major Leagues
  7   Tris Speaker, AL:Bos. 1912,14; Clev. 18,20-23

Most Seasons, Consecutive, Leading Major Leagues
  4   Tris Speaker, AL:Clev. 1920-23

Most Seasons Leading League
  8   Honus Wagner, NL:Pitt. 1900-02,04,06-09
               Stan Musial, NL:StL. 1943-44,46,48-49,52-54
               Tris Speaker, AL:Bos. 1912,14; Clev. 16,18,20-23

Most Seasons, Consecutive, Leading League
  4   Honus Wagner, NL:Pitt. 1906-09
               Tris Speaker, AL:Clev. 1920-23

Most Doubles, Lifetime
  793   Tris Speaker,AL:Bos. 1907-15; Clev. 16-26; Wash. 27; Phil. 28
  746   Pete Rose, NL:Cin. 1963-78,84-86; Phil. 79-83; Mtl. 84

Most Doubles, Season
  67   Earl Webb, AL:Bos. 1931
  64   Joe Medwick, NL:StL. 1936

Most Seasons, 50 or more Doubles
  5   Tris Speaker, AL:Bos. 1912; Clev. 20-21,23,26
  3   Paul Waner, NL:Pitt. 1928,32,36
               Stan Musial, NL:StL. 1944,46,53

Most Doubles, Game
  4   By many players; Last:
               Johnny Damon, AL:KC July 18, 2000
               Shannon Stewart, AL:Tor. July 18, 2000
               Jeff Bagwell, NL:Hou. June 14, 1996

Most Doubles, Consecutive, Game
4   Frank Bonner, NL:Balt. Aug. 4, 1894
Joe Kelley, NL:Balt. Sept 3, 1894
Dick Bartell, NL:Phil. Apr. 25, 1933
Ernie Lombardi, NL:Cin. May 8(1g), 1935
Willie Jones, NL:Phil. Apr. 20, 1949
Billy Williams, NL:Chi Apr. 9, 1969
Billy Werber, AL:Bos. July 17(1g), 1935 & NL:Cin. May 13, 1940
Mike Kreevich, AL:Chi. Sept. 4, 1937
Johnny Lindell, AL:NY Aug. 17, 1944
Lou Boudreau, AL:Clev. July 14(1g), 1946
Vic Wertz, AL:Clev. Sept. 26, 1956
Bill Bruton, AL:Det. May 19, 1963
Dave Duncan, AL:Balt. June 30(2g), 1975
Sandy Alomar, Jr., AL:Clev. June 6, 1997
Albert Belle, AL:Balt. Aug. 29 & Sept. 23(2g), 1999

Most Doubles, 2 Consecutive Games
6   Cap Anson, NL:Chi. July 3-4, 1883
Sam Thompson, NL:Phil. June 29-July 1, 1895
Red Schoendienst, NL:StL. June 5-6, 1948
Joe Dugan, AL:Phil. Sept. 24-25, 1920
Earl Sheely, AL:Chi. May 20-21, 1926
Hank Majeski, AL:Phil. Aug. 27-27, 1948
Kirby Puckett, AL:Minn. May 13-14, 1989

Most Doubles, 3 Consecutive Games
8   Red Schoendienst, NL:StL. June 5-6(dh), 1948
7   Joe Dugan, AL:Phil. Sept. 23-25, 1920
Earl Sheely, AL:Chi. May 20-22, 1926

Most Doubles, Inning
2   By many players.

Fewest Doubles, Season (Minimum: 500 at-bats)
4   Roy Thomas, NL:Phil. 1900 (531 at-bats)
5   Donie Bush, AL:Det. 1916 (550 at-bats)

TRIPLES

Most Seasons Leading Major Leagues
5   Sam Crawford, NL:Cin. 1902
AL:Det. 03,10,13-14

Most Seasons, Consecutive, Leading Major Leagues
2   Dave Orr, AA:NY 1885-86
Sam Crawford, NL:Cin. 1902-AL:Det. 03 & Det. 13-14
Elmer Flick, AL:Clev. 1906-07
Earle Combs, AL:NY 1927-28
George Brett, AL:KC 1975-76
Lance Johnson, AL:Chi. 1993-94
Jose Offerman, AL:KC 1998-Bos. 99
Cristian Guzman, AL:Minn. 2000-01

Most Seasons Leading League
6   Sam Crawford, NL:Cin. 1902; AL:Det. 1903,10,13-15
5   Sam Crawford, AL:Det. 1903,10,13-15
Willie Wilson, AL:KC 1980,82,85,87-88
Stan Musial, NL:StL. 1943,46,48-49,51

Most Seasons, Consecutive, Leading League
4   Lance Johnson, AL:Chi. 1991-94
3   Garry Templeton, NL:StL. 1977-79

Most Triples, Lifetime
312   Sam Crawford, NL:Cin. 1899-1902; AL:Det. 03-17

Most Triples, League
297   Ty Cobb, AL:Det. 1905-26; Phil. 27-28
252   Honus Wagner, NL:Lou. 1897-99; Pitt. 1900-17

Most Triples, Season
36   Owen Wilson, NL:Pitt. 1912
26   Joe Jackson, AL:Clev. 1912
Sam Crawford, AL:Det. 1914

Most Seasons, 20 or more Triples, Lifetime
5   Sam Crawford, NL:Cin. 1902; AL:Det. 03,12-14

Most Seasons, 20 or more Triples, League
4	Sam Crawford, AL:Det. 1903,12-14
	Ty Cobb, AL:Det. 1908,11-12,17
3	Dan Brouthers, NL:Det. 1887; Brk. 92; Balt. 94
	Roger Connor, NL:NY 1886-87; NY-StL. 94
	Sam Thompson, NL:Det. 1887; Phil. 94-95
	NL Since 1900:
2	By many players

Most Seasons, Consecutive, 20 or more Triples
3	Sam Crawford, AL:Det. 1912-14
2	Roger Connor, NL:NY 1886-87
	George Davis, NL:NY 1893-94
	Sam Thompson, NL:Phil. 1894-95

Most Triples, Game
4	George Strief, AA:Phil. June 25, 1885
	Bill Joyce, NL:NY May 18, 1897
	Since 1900:
3	By many players; Last:
	Shawon Dunston, NL:Chi. July 28, 1990
	Herm Winningham, NL:Cin. Aug. 15, 1990 (12 inn)
	Lance Johnson, AL:Chi. Sept. 23, 1995

Most Triples, Consecutive, Game
3	By many players

Most Triples, Inning
2	Harry Wheeler, AA:Cin. June 28, 1882(11th)
	Harry Stovey, AA:Phil. Aug. 18, 1884 (8th)
	Joe Hornung, NL:Bos. May 6, 1882 (8th)
	Heinie Peitz, NL:StL. July 2, 1895 (1st)
	Frank Shugart, NL:Lou. July 30, 1895 (5th)
	Buck Freeman, NL:Bos. July 25, 1900 (1st)
	Bill Dahlen, NL:Brk. Aug. 30, 1900 (8th)
	Curt Walker, NL:Cin. July 22, 1926 (2nd)
	Al Zarilla, AL:StL. July 13, 1946 (4th)
	Gil Coan, AL:Wash. Apr. 21, 1951 (6th)

Fewest Triples, Season (most at-bats)
0	Cal Ripken, AL:Balt. 1989 (646 at-bats)
	Sammy Sosa, NL:Chi. 1998 (643 at-bats)

HOME RUNS

Most Seasons Leading Major Leagues
11	Babe Ruth, AL:Bos. 1918-19; NY 20-21,23-24,26-29,31

Most Seasons, Consecutive, Leading Major Leagues
6	Ralph Kiner, NL:Pitt. 1947-52

Most Seasons Leading League
12	Babe Ruth, AL:Bos. 1918-19; NY 20-21,23-24,26-31
8	Mike Schmidt, NL:Phil. 1974-76,80-81,83-84,86

Most Seasons, Consecutive, Leading League
7	Ralph Kiner, NL:Pitt. 1946-52
6	Babe Ruth, AL:NY 1926-31

Most Home Runs, Lifetime
755	Hank Aaron, NL:Mil./Atl. 1954-74; AL:Mil. 75-76

Most Home Runs, League
733	Hank Aaron, NL:Mil./Atl. 1954-74
708	Babe Ruth, AL:Bos. 1914-19; NY 20-34

Most Home Runs, Season
73	Barry Bonds, NL:SF 2001
61	Roger Maris, AL:NY 1961

Most Seasons, 50 or more Home Runs
4	Babe Ruth, AL:NY 1920-21,27-28
	Mark McGwire, AL:Oak. 1996; AL:Oak-NL:StL. 97; NL:StL. 98-99
	Sammy Sosa, NL:Chi. 1998-2001

Most Seasons, Consecutive, 50 or more Home Runs
4	Mark McGwire, AL:Oak. 1996; AL:Oak.-NL:StL. 97, NL:StL. 98-99
	Sammy Sosa, NL:Chi. 1998-2001
2	Babe Ruth, AL:NY 1920-21; 27-28
	Ken Griffey, Jr. AL:Sea. 1997-98

Most Seasons, 40 or more Home Runs
11	Babe Ruth, AL:NY 1920-21,23-24,26-32
8	Hank Aaron, NL:Mil. 1957,60,62-63; Atl. 66,69,71,73

Most Seasons, Consecutive, 40 or more Home Runs
7	Babe Ruth, AL:NY 1926-32
5	Ralph Kiner, NL:Pitt. 1947-51
	Duke Snider, NL:Brk. 1953-57

Most Seasons, 30 or more Home Runs
15	Hank Aaron, NL:Mil. 1957-63,65; Atl. 66-67,69-73
13	Babe Ruth, AL:NY 1920-24, 26-33

Most Seasons, Consecutive, 30 or more Home Runs
12	Jimmie Foxx, AL:Phil. 1929-35; Bos. 36-40
10	Barry Bonds, NL:Pitt. 1992; SF 93-2001

Most Seasons, 20 or more Home Runs
20	Hank Aaron, NL:Mil. 1955-65; Atl. 66-74
16	Babe Ruth, AL:Bos. 1919; NY 20-34
	Ted Williams, AL:Bos. 1939-42,46-51,54-58,60
	Reggie Jackson, AL:Oak. 1968-75; Balt. 76; NY 77-80; Cal. 82,84-85

Most Seasons, Consecutive, 20 or more Home Runs
20	Hank Aaron, NL:Mil. 1955-65; Atl. 66-74
16	Babe Ruth, AL:Bos. 1919; NY 20-34

Most Home Runs, Consecutive Seasons
135	Mark McGwire, NL:StL. 98 (70)-99 (65)
114	Babe Ruth, AL:NY 1927 (60)-28 (54)

Most Home Runs, Season, Home
39	Hank Greenberg, AL:Det. 1938
38	Mark McGwire, NL:StL. 1998

Most Home Runs, Season, Road
36	Barry Bonds, NL:SF 2001
32	Babe Ruth, AL:NY 1927

Most Home Runs, Season, vs. Opponent
14	Lou Gehrig, AL:NY vs Clev. 1936
13	Hank Sauer, NL:Chi. vs Pitt. 1954
	Joe Adcock, NL:Mil. vs Brk. 1956

Most Home Runs, Season, vs. Opponent, Home
10	Gus Zernial, AL:Chi.-Phil. vs StL. 1951
9	Stan Musial, NL:StL. vs NY 1954

Most Home Runs, Season, vs. Opponent, Road
10	Harry Heilmann, AL:Det. vs Phil. 1922
9	Joe Adcock, NL:Mil. vs Brk. 1954
	Willie Mays, NL:NY vs Brk. 1955

Most Home Runs, One Month
20	Sammy Sosa, NL:Chi. June 1998
18	Rudy York, AL:Det. Aug. 1937

Most Home Runs, Game
4	Bobby Lowe, NL:Bos. May 30, 1894 (cons)
	Ed Delahanty, NL:Phil. July 13, 1896
	Chuck Klein, NL:Phil. July 10, 1936 (10 inn)
	Gil Hodges, NL:Brk. Aug. 31, 1950
	Joe Adcock, NL:Mil. July 31, 1954
	Willie Mays, NL:SF Apr. 30, 1961
	Mike Schmidt, NL:Phil. Apr. 17, 1976 (cons; 10 inn)
	Bob Horner, NL:Atl. July 6, 1986
	Mark Whiten, NL:StL. Sept. 7(2g), 1993
	Lou Gehrig, AL:NY June 3, 1932 (cons)
	Pat Seerey, AL:Chi. July 18, 1948 (11 inn)
	Rocky Colavito, AL:Clev. June 10, 1959 (cons)

Most Home Runs, Leadoff Batter, First Inning, Lifetime
79	Rickey Henderson, AL:Oak., 1974-84,89-95,98; NY 85-89; Tor. 93; Ana. 97; Sea. 2000
	NL:SD 96-97, 2001; NY 99-2000

Most Home Runs, Leadoff Batter, First Inning, League
72	Rickey Henderson, AL:Oak. 1974-84,89-95,98; NY 85-89; Tor. 93; Ana. 97; Sea. 2000
30	Bobby Bonds, NL:SF 1968-74; StL. 80; Chi. 81

Most Home Runs, Leadoff Batter, First Inning, Season
12	Brady Anderson, AL:Balt. 1996
11	Bobby Bonds, NL:SF 1973

Most Games, 3 or more Home Runs, Lifetime
6 Johnny Mize, NL:StL-NY; AL:NY

Most Games, 3 or more Home Runs, League
5 Johnny Mize, NL:StL., NY
   Sammy Sosa, NL:Chi.
   Joe Carter, AL:Clev.; Tor.

Most Games, 3 or more Home Runs, Season
3 Sammy Sosa, NL:Chi. 2001
2 Ted Williams, AL:Bos. 1957
   Doug DeCinces, AL:Balt. 1982
   Joe Carter, AL:Clev. 1989
   Cecil Fielder, AL:Det. 1990
   Geronimo Berroa, AL:Oak. 1996
   Carlos Delgado AL:Tor. 2001

Most Games, 2 or more Home Runs, Lifetime
72 Babe Ruth, AL:Bos. 1914-19; NY 20-34; NL:Bos. 35

Most Games, 2 or more Home Runs, League
71 Babe Ruth, AL:Bos. 1914-19; NY 20-34
63 Willie Mays, NL:NY/SF 1951-52,54-71; NY 72-73

Most Games, 2 or more Home Runs, Season
11 Hank Greenberg, AL:Det. 1938
   Sammy Sosa, NL:Chi. 1998

Most Games, Switch-Hitting Home Runs, Lifetime
11 Eddie Murray, AL:Balt.1977, 79, 81-82, 85, 87; Clev. 94; NL:LA 90
   Chili Davis NL:SF 1983, 87; AL:Cal. 88-89, 93-94, 96; Minn. 92; KC 97

Most Games, Switch-Hitting Home Runs, League
10 Mickey Mantle, AL:NY 1955-59, 61-62, 64
   Ken Caminiti, NL:Hou 1994, 99; SD 95-96, 98

Most Games, Switch-Hitting Home Runs, Season
4 Ken Caminiti, NL:SD 1996
3 Tony Clark, AL:Det. 1998

Most Switch-Hitting Home Runs, Inning, Lifetime
1 Carlos Baerga, AL:Clev. Apr. 8, 1993 (7th)

Most Home Runs, Consecutive At-Bats (*consecutive plate appearances)
4 Bobby Lowe, NL:Bos. May 30, 1894
   Bill Nicholson, NL:Chi. July 22-23, 1944
   Ralph Kiner, NL:Pitt. Aug. 15-16, 1947
   Ralph Kiner, NL:Pitt. Sept. 11-13, 1949
   Stan Musial, NL:StL. July 7-8, 1962
   Art Shamsky, NL:Cin. Aug. 12-14, 1966
   Deron Johnson, NL:Phil. July 10-11, 1971*
   Mike Schmidt, NL:Phil. Apr. 17, 1976
   Mike Schmidt, NL:Phil. July 6-7, 1979
   Tuffy Rhodes, NL:Chi. Oct. 3, 1993-Apr. 4, 1994
   Benito Santiago, NL:Phil. Sept. 14-15, 1996
   Barry Bonds, NL:SF May 19-20, 2001
   Lou Gehrig, AL:NY June 3, 1932
   Jimmie Foxx, AL:Phil. June 7-8, 1933
   Hank Greenberg, AL:Det. Jul 26-27, 1938*
   Ted Williams, AL:Bos. Sept. 17-20-21-22, 1957
   Charlie Maxwell, AL:Det. May 3-3, 1959
   Rocky Colavito, AL:Clev. June 10, 1959
   Willie Kirkland, AL:Clev. July 9(2g)-13, 1961
   Johnny Blanchard, AL:NY July 21-22-26, 1961*
   Mickey Mantle, AL:NY July 4-6, 1962
   Bobby Murcer, AL:NY June 24-24, 1970
   Mike Epstein, AL:Oak. June 15-16, 1971*
   Don Baylor, AL:Balt. July 1-2, 1975
   Larry Herndon, AL:Det. May 16-18, 1982*
   Bo Jackson, AL:KC July 17-Aug. 26, 1990
   Jeff Manto, AL:Balt. June 8-10, 1995
   Bobby Higginson, AL:Det. June 30-July 1, 1997
   Manny Ramirez, AL:Clev. Sept. 15-16, 1998

Most Home Runs, Consecutive Innings, Game
3 George Kelly, NL:NY Sept. 17, 1923
   Larry Parrish, NL:Mtl. July 30, 1978
   Andres Galarraga, NL:Col. June 25, 1995
   Carl Reynolds, AL:Chi. July 2(2g), 1930

Most Games, Consecutive, 1 or more Home Runs

8   Dale Long, NL:Pitt. May 19-28, 1956
      Don Mattingly, AL:NY July 8-18, 1987
      Ken Griffey, Jr., AL:Sea. July 20-28, 1993

Most Home Runs, 2 Consecutive Games (HR in each game)

5   Cap Anson, NL:Chi. Aug. 5-6, 1884
      Ralph Kiner, NL:Pitt. Aug. 15-16, 1947
      Ralph Kiner, NL:Pitt. Sept. 11(2g)-12, 1947
      Don Mueller, NL:NY Sept. 1-2, 1951
      Stan Musial, NL:StL. May 2, 1954 (dh)
      Joe Adcock, NL:Mil. July 30-31, 1954
      Billy Williams, NL:Chi. Sept. 8-10. 1968
      Nate Colbert, NL:SD Aug. 1, 1972 (dh)
      Mike Schmidt, NL:Phil. Apr. 17-18, 1976
      Dave Kingman, NL:Chi. July 27-28, 1979
      Gary Carter, NL:NY Sept. 3-4, 1985
      Barry Larkin, NL:Cin. June 27-28, 1991
      Geoff Jenkins, NL:Mil. Apr. 28-29, 2001
      Barry Bonds, NL:SF May 19-20, 2001
      Ty Cobb, AL:Det. May 5-6, 1925
      Tony Lazzeri, AL:NY May 23-24, 1936
      Carl Yastrzemski, AL:Bos May 19-20, 1976
      Mark McGwire, AL:Oak. June 27-28, 1987
      Joe Carter, AL:Clev. July 18-19, 1989
      Mark McGwire, AL:Oak. June 10-11, 1995
      Albert Belle, AL:Clev. Sept 18-19, 1995
      Matt Williams, AL:Clev. Apr. 25-26, 1997
      Manny Ramirez, AL:Clev. Sept. 15-16, 1998
      Edgar Martinez, AL:Sea. May 17-18, 1999

Most Home Runs, Doubleheader

5   Stan Musial, NL:StL. May 2, 1954
      Nate Colbert, NL:SD Aug. 1, 1972
4   Earl Averill, AL:Clev. Sept. 17, 1930
      Jimmie Foxx, AL:Phil. July 2, 1933
      Jim Tabor, AL:Bos. July 4, 1939
      Gus Zernial, AL:Chi. Oct. 1, 1950
      Charlie Maxwell, AL:Det. May 3, 1959
      Roger Maris, AL:NY July 25, 1961
      Rocky Colavito, AL:Det. Aug. 27, 1961
      Harmon Killebrew, AL:Minn. Sept. 21, 1963
      Bobby Murcer, AL:NY June 24, 1970
      Graig Nettles, AL:NY Apr. 14, 1974
      Otto Velez, AL:Tor. May 4, 1980
      Al Oliver, AL:Tex. Aug. 17, 1980

Most Home Runs, 3 Consecutive Games (HR in each game)

6   Tony Lazzeri, AL:NY May 23-24, 1936
      Gus Zernial, AL:Phil. May 13-16, 1951
      Manny Ramirez, AL:Clev. Sept. 15-17, 1998
      Ralph Kiner, NL:Pitt. Aug. 14-16, 1947
      Ralph Kiner, NL:Pitt. Sept. 10-11(2g), 1947
      Ralph Kiner, NL:Pitt. Sept. 11(2g)-12, 1947
      Frank Thomas, NL:NY Aug. 1-3, 1962
      Lee May, NL:Cin. May 24-28, 1969
      Mike Schmidt, NL:Phil. Apr. 17-20, 1976
      Barry Bonds, NL:SF May 18-20, 2001
      Barry Bonds, NL:SF May 19-21, 2001

Most Home Runs, 4 Consecutive Games (HR in each game)

8   Ralph Kiner, NL:Pitt. Sept. 10-12, 1947
7   Tony Lazzeri, AL:NY May 21-24, 1936
      Gus Zernial, AL:Phil. May 13-17, 1951
      Frank Howard, AL:Wash. May 12-16, 1968
      Pitchers' batting:
4   Ken Brett, NL:Phil. June 9-23, 1973

Most Home Runs, 5 Consecutive Games (HR in each game)

8   Frank Howard, AL:Wash. May 12-17; 14-18, 1968
      Barry Bonds, NL:SF May 17-21, 2001
      Barry Bonds, NL:SF May 18-22, 2001

Most Home Runs, 6 Consecutive Games (HR in each game)

10   Frank Howard, AL:Wash. May 12-18, 1968
9   Barry Bonds, NL:SF May 17-22, 2001

Most Home Runs, 7 Consecutive Games (HR in each game)
9	Don Mattingly, AL:NY July 8-17, 1987
7	Dale Long, NL:Pitt. May 19-26, 1956

Most Home Runs, 8 Consecutive Games (HR in each game)
10	Don Mattingly, AL:NY July 8-18, 1987
8	Dale Long, NL:Pitt. May 19-28, 1956

Most Home Runs, First Major League Game
2	Charlie Reilly, AA:Colu. Oct. 9, 1889
	Bob Nieman, AL:StL. Sept. 14, 1951
	Bert Campaneris, AL:KC July 23, 1964
	Mark Quinn, AL:KC Sept. 14(2g), 1999
1	By many NL players

Most Home Runs, First Two Major League Games
3	Charlie Reilly, AA:Colu. Oct. 9-10, 1889
	Joe Cunningham, NL:StL. June 30-July 1(2g), 1954
2	Earl Averill, AL:Clev. Apr. 16-17, 1929
	Zeke Bonura, AL:Chi. Apr. 17-18, 1934
	Bob Nieman, AL:StL. Sept. 14, 1951
	Bert Campaneris, AL:KC July 23, 1964
	Joe Lefebvre, AL:NY May 22-23, 1980
	Dave Stapleton, AL:Bos. May 30-31, 1980
	Tim Laudner, AL:Minn. Aug. 28-29, 1981
	Alvin Davis, AL:Sea. Apr. 11-13, 1984
	Sam Horn, AL:Bos. July 25-26, 1987
	Manny Ramirez, AL:Clev. Sept. 2-3, 1993
	Gabe Alvarez, AL:Det. June 22-23, 1998
	Mark Quinn, AL:KC Sept. 14(2g), 1999

Most Home Runs, Inning
2	Lou Bierbauer, PL: Brk. July 12, 1890 (3rd)
	Ed Cartwright, AA:StL. Sept. 23, 1890 (3rd)
	Charley Jones, NL:Bos. June 10, 1880 (8th)
	Bobby Lowe, NL:Bos. May 30, 1894 (3rd)
	Jake Stenzel, NL:Pitt. June 6, 1894 (3rd)
	Hack Wilson, NL:NY July 1(2g), 1925 (3rd)
	Hank Leiber, NL:NY Aug. 24, 1935 (2nd)
	Sid Gordon, NL:NY July 31(2g), 1949 (2nd)
	Andy Seminick, NL:Phil. June 2, 1949 (8th)
	Willie McCovey, NL:SF Apr. 12, 1973 (4th)
	John Boccabella, NL:Mtl. July 6. 1973 (6th)
	Lee May, NL:Hou. Apr. 29, 1974 (6th)
	Willie McCovey, NL:SF June 27, 1977 (6th)
	Andre Dawson, NL:Mtl. July 30, 1978 (3rd)
	Ray Knight, NL:Cin. May 13, 1980 (5th)
	Von Hayes, NL:Phil. June 11, 1985 (1st)
	Andre Dawson, NL:Mtl. Sept. 24, 1985 (5th)
	Dale Murphy, NL:Atl. July 27, 1989 (6th)
	Jeff Bagwell, NL:Hou. June 24, 1994 (6th)
	Jeff King, NL:Pitt. Aug. 8, 1995 (2nd)
	Jeff King, NL:Pitt. Apr. 30, 1996 (4th)
	Sammy Sosa, NL:Chi. May 16, 1996 (7th)
	Mike Lansing, NL:Mtl. May 7, 1997 (6th)
	Gary Sheffield, NL:Fla. July 13, 1997 (4th)
	Fernando Tatis, NL:StL. Apr. 23, 1999 (3rd)
	Eric Karros, NL:LA Aug. 22, 2000 (6th)
	Ken Williams, AL:StL. Aug. 7, 1922 (6th)
	Bill Regan, AL:Bos. June 16, 1928 (4th)
	Joe DiMaggio, AL:NY June 24, 1936 (5th)
	Al Kaline, AL:Det. Apr. 17, 1955 (6th)
	Jim Lemon, AL:Wash. Sept. 5, 1959 (3rd)
	Joe Pepitone, AL:NY May 23, 1962 (8th)
	Rick Reichardt, AL:Cal. Apr. 30. 1966 (8th)
	Cliff Johnson, AL:NY June 30, 1977 (8th)
	Ellis Burks, AL:Bos. Aug. 27, 1990 (4th)
	Carlos Baerga, AL:Clev. Apr. 8, 1993 (7th)
	Joe Carter, AL:Tor. Oct. 3, 1993 (2nd)
	Dave Nilsson, AL:Mil. May 17, 1996 (6th)
	Mark McGwire, AL:Oak. Sept. 22, 1996 (5th)

Most At-Bats, No Home Runs, Season
672	Rabbit Maranville, NL:Pitt. 1922
658	Doc Cramer, AL:Bos. 1938

GRAND SLAM HOME RUNS

Most Grand Slam Home Runs, Lifetime
23   Lou Gehrig, AL:NY 1923-39
18   Willie McCovey, NL:SF 1959-73,77-80; SD 74-76

Most Grand Slam Home Runs, Season
6   Don Mattingly, AL:NY 1987
5   Ernie Banks, NL:Chi. 1955

Most Grand Slam Home Runs, One Month
3   Rudy York, AL:Det. May 16, 22, 30, 1938
      Jim Northrup, AL:Det. June 24 (2), 29, 1968
      Larry Parrish, AL:Tex. July 4, 7, 10, 1982
      Mike Blowers, AL:Sea. Aug. 3, 14, 18, 1995
      Shane Spencer, AL:NY Sept. 18, 24, 27, 1998
      Eric Davis, NL:Cin. May 1, 3, 30, 1987
      Mike Piazza, NL:LA Apr. 9, 10, 24, 1998
      Devon White NL:Mil. May 10, 15, 20, 2001

Most Grand Slam Home Runs, Game
2   Tony Lazzeri, AL:NY May 24, 1936 (2nd, 5th)
      Jim Tabor, AL:Bos. July 4(2g), 1939 (3rd, 6th)
      Rudy York, AL:Bos. July 27, 1946 (2nd, 5th)
      Jim Gentile, AL:Balt. May 9, 1961 (1st, 2nd)
      Jim Northrup, AL:Det. June 24, 1968 (5th, 6th)
      Frank Robinson, AL:Balt. June 26, 1970 (5th, 6th)
      Robin Ventura, AL:Chi. Sept. 4, 1995 (4th, 5th)
      Chris Hoiles, AL:Balt. Aug. 14, 1998 (3rd, 8th)
      Nomar Garciaparra, AL:Bos. May 10, 1999 (1st, 8th)
      Tony Cloninger, NL:Atl. July 3, 1966 (1st, 4th)
      Fernando Tatis, NL:StL. Apr. 23, 1999 (3rd inn, both)

Most Grand Slam Home Runs, First Major League Game
1   Bill Duggleby, NL:Phil. Apr. 21, 1898 (2nd; 1st at-bat)
      Bobby Bonds, NL:SF June 25, 1968 (6th)

Most Consecutive Games with a Grand Slam Home Run
2   Jimmy Bannon, NL:Bos. Aug. 6-7, 1894
      Jimmy Sheckard, NL:Brk. Sept. 23-24, 1901
      Phil Garner, NL:Pitt, Sept 14-15, 1978
      Fred McGriff, NL:SD Aug. 13-14, 1991
      Eric Davis, NL:Cin. May 4-5, 1996
      Mike Piazza, NL:LA Apr. 9-10, 1998
      Sammy Sosa, NL:Chi. July 27-28, 1998
      Robin Ventura, NL:NY May 20(1g)-20(2g), 1999
      Babe Ruth, AL:NY Sept. 27-29, 1927
      Babe Ruth, AL:NY Aug. 6-7, 1929
      Bill Dickey, AL:NY Aug. 3-4, 1937
      Jimmie Foxx, AL:Bos. May 20-21, 1940
      Jim Busby, AL:Clev. July 5-6, 1956
      Brooks Robinson, AL:Balt. May 6-9, 1962
      Willie Aikens. AL:Cal. June 13(2g)-14, 1979
      Greg Luzinski, AL:Chi. June 8-9, 1984
      Rob Deer, AL:Mil. Aug. 19-20, 1987
      Mike Blowers, AL:Sea. May 16-17, 1993
      Dan Gladden, AL:Det. Aug. 10-11, 1993
      Ken Griffey, Jr. AL:Sea. Apr. 29-30, 1999
      Albert Belle, AL:Balt. June 14-15, 2000

RUNS BATTED IN (Since 1920 - Prior seasons not compiled on official scores)

Most Seasons Leading Major Leagues
5   Babe Ruth, AL:NY 1920-21,23,26,28

Most Seasons, Consecutive, Leading Major Leagues
3   Cecil Fielder, AL:Det. 1990-92

Most Seasons Leading League
5   Babe Ruth, AL:NY 1920-21,23,26,28
      Lou Gehrig, AL:NY 1927-28,30-31,34
4   Rogers Hornsby, NL:StL. 1920-22,25
      Hank Aaron, NL:Mil. 1957,60,63; Atl. 66
      Mike Schmidt, NL:Phil. 1980-81,84,86

Most Seasons, Consecutive, Leading League
3	Rogers Hornsby, NL:StL. 1920-22
	Joe Medwick, NL:StL. 1936-38
	George Foster, NL:Cin. 1976-78
	Cecil Fielder, AL:Det. 1990-92

Most Runs Batted In, Lifetime
2297	Hank Aaron, NL:Mil./Atl. 1954-74; AL:Mil. 75-76

Most Runs Batted In, League
2202	Hank Aaron, NL:Mil./Atl. 1954-74
1995	Lou Gehrig, AL:NY 1923-39

Most Runs Batted In, Season
191	Hack Wilson, NL:Chi. 1930
184	Lou Gehrig, AL:NY 1931

Most Seasons, 150 or more Runs Batted In, League
7	Lou Gehrig, AL:NY 1927,30-32,34,36-37
2	Hack Wilson, NL:Chi. 1929-30
	Sammy Sosa, NL:Chi. 1998, 2001

Most Seasons, Consecutive, 150 or more Runs Batted In, League
3	Babe Ruth, AL:NY 1929-31
	Lou Gehrig, AL:NY 1930-32
2	Hack Wilson, NL:Chi. 1929-30

Most Seasons, 100 or more Runs Batted In, League
13	Lou Gehrig, AL:NY 1926-38
	Jimmie Foxx, AL:Phil. 1929-35; Bos. 36-41
11	Hank Aaron, NL:Mil. 1955,57,59-63; Atl. 66-67,70-71

Most Seasons, Consecutive, 100 or more Runs Batted In, League
13	Lou Gehrig, AL:NY 1926-38
	Jimmie Foxx, AL:Phil. 1929-35; Bos. 36-41
8	Mel Ott, NL:NY 1929-36
	Willie Mays, NL:SF 1959-66

Most Runs Batted In, Game
12	Jim Bottomley, NL:StL. Sept. 16, 1924
	Mark Whiten, NL:StL. Sept. 7(2g), 1993
11	Tony Lazzeri, AL:NY May 24, 1936

Most Runs Batted In, Game, All of Team's Runs
8	George Kelly, NL:NY June 14, 1924
	Bob Johnson, AL:Phil. June 12, 1938
	Extra-Inning Game:
9	Mike Greenwell, AL:Bos. Sept. 2, 1996 (10 inn)

Most Runs Batted In, 2 Consecutive Games
15	Tony Lazzeri, AL:NY May 23-24, 1936
13	Nate Colbert, NL:SD Aug. 1, 1972 (dh)
	Mark Whiten, NL:StL. Sept. 7, 1993 (dh)

Most Runs Batted In, Doubleheader
13	Nate Colbert, NL:SD Aug. 1, 1972
	Mark Whiten, NL:StL. Sept. 7, 1993
11	Earl Averill, AL:Clev. Sept. 17, 1930
	Jim Tabor, AL:Bos. July 4, 1939
	Boog Powell, AL:Balt. July 6, 1966 (20 inn)

Most Games, Consecutive, Runs Batted In
17	Ray Grimes, NL:Chi. June 27-July 23, 1922
13	Taft Wright, AL:Chi. May 4-20, 1941
	Mike Sweeney, AL:KC June 23-July 4, 1999

Most Runs Batted In, Inning
8	Fernando Tatis, NL:StL. Apr. 23, 1999 (3rd)
6	Bob Johnson, AL:Phil. Aug. 29, 1937 (1g;1st)
	Tom McBride, AL:Bos. Aug. 4, 1945 (2g;4th)
	Joe Astroth, AL:Phil. Sept. 23, 1950 (6th)
	Gil McDougald, AL:NY May 3, 1951 (9th)
	Sam Mele, AL:Chi. June 10, 1952 (4th)
	Jim Lemon, AL;Wash. Sept. 5, 1959 (3rd)
	Carlos Quintana, AL:Bos. July 30, 1991 (3rd)
	Matt Stairs, AL:Oak. July 5, 1996 (1st)
	Matt Williams, AL:Clev. Aug. 27, 1997 (4th)

SACRIFICE HITS

Most Season Leading Major Leagues
4   Phil Rizzuto, AL:NY 1949-52

Most Seasons, Consecutive, Leading Major Leagues
4   Phil Rizzuto, AL:NY 1949-52

Most Seasons Leading League
6   Mule Haas, AL:Phil. 1930-32; Chi. 33-34,36
4   Otto Knabe, NL:Phil. 1907-08,10,13

Most Seasons, Consecutive, Leading League
5   Mule Haas, AL:Phil. 1930-32; Chi. 33-34
2   By many NL players; Last:
           Ricky Gutierrez, NL:Chi. 2000-01

Most Sacrifice Hits, League
511   Eddie Collins, AL:Phil. 1906-14,27-30; Chi. 15-26
392   Jake Daubert, NL:Brk. 1910-18; Cin. 19-24

Most Sacrifice Hits, Season (including Sacrifice Flies)
67   Ray Chapman, AL:Clev. 1917
46   Jimmy Sheckard, NL:Chi. 1909

Most Sacrifice Hits, Season (not including Sacrifice Flies)
46   Bill Bradley, AL:Clev. 1907
43   Kid Gleason, NL:Phil. 1905

Most Sacrifice Hits, Game
4   Cy Seymour, NL:Cin. July 25, 1902
           Jake Daubert, NL:Brk. Aug. 15(2g), 1914
           Red Killefer, AL:Wash. Aug. 27(1g), 1910
           Jack Barry, AL:Bos. Aug. 21, 1916
           Ray Chapman, AL:Clev. Aug. 31, 1919
           Felix Fermin, AL:Clev. Aug. 22, 1989 (10 inn)

Most Sacrifice Hits, Inning
2   Al Benton, AL:Det. Aug. 6, 1941 (3rd)

Fewest Sacrifice Hits, Lifetime (Most at-bats)
0   Harmon Killebrew, AL:Wash./Minn. 1954-74; KC 75 (8147 at-bats)

Fewest Sacrifice Hits, League (Most at-bats; Minimum: 6000 at-bats)
0   Harmon Killebrew, AL:Wash./Minn. 1954-74; KC 75 (8147 at-bats)
1   Dave Parker, NL:Pitt. 1973-83; Cin. 84-87 (7316 at-bats)

Fewest Sacrifice Hits, Season (Most at-bats)
0   Juan Samuel, NL:Phil. 1984 (701 at-bats)
           Al Simmons, AL:Phil. 1932 (670 at-bats)

SACRIFICE FLIES (Since 1954)

Most Seasons Leading Major Leagues
3   Ron Santo, NL:Chi. 1963,67,69

Most Seasons, Consecutive, Leading Major Leagues
1   By many players

Most Seasons Leading League
4   Brooks Robinson, AL:Balt. 1962,64,67-68
3   Ron Santo, NL:Chi. 1963,67,69
           Johnny Bench, NL:Cin. 1970,72-73
           Dante Bichette, NL:Col. 1996,98-99

Most Seasons, Consecutive, Leading League
2   Gil Hodges, NL:Brk. 1954-55
           Johnny Bench, NL:Cin. 1972-73
           Mike Schmidt, NL:Phil. 1979-80
           Dante Bichette, NL:Col. 1998-99
           Jackie Jensen, AL:Bos. 1954-55
           Minnie Minoso, AL:Chi. 1960-61
           Dave Johnson, AL:Balt. 1966-67
           Brooks Robinson, AL:Balt. 1967-68

Most Sacrifice Flies, Lifetime
128   Eddie Murray, AL:Balt. 1977-88, 96; Clev. 94-96; Ana. 97; NL:LA 89-91, 97; NY 92-93

Most Sacrifice Flies, League
127   Cal Ripken, AL:Balt. 1981-2001
113   Hank Aaron, NL:Mil./Atl. 1954-74

Most Sacrifice Flies, Season
19	Gil Hodges, NL:Brk. 1954
17	Roy White, AL:NY 1971
	Bobby Bonilla, AL:Balt. 1996

Most Sacrifice Flies, Game
3	Harry Steinfeldt, NL:Chi. May 5, 1909
	Ernie Banks, NL:Chi. June 2, 1961
	Vince Coleman, NL:StL. May 1, 1986
	Candy Maldonado, NL:SF Aug. 29, 1987
	Bob Meusel, AL:NY Sept. 15, 1926
	Russ Nixon, AL:Bos. Aug. 31(2g), 1965
	Don Mattingly, AL:NY May 3, 1986
	George Bell, AL:Tor. Aug. 14, 1990
	Chad Kreuter, AL:Det. July 30, 1994
	Juan Gonzalez, AL:Tex. July 3, 1999

Most Sacrifice Flies, Inning
1	By many players

WALKS (Since 1913)

Most Seasons Leading Major Leagues
11	Babe Ruth, AL:NY 1920-21,23-24,26-28,30-33

Most Seasons, Consecutive, Leading Major Leagues
4	Babe Ruth, AL:NY 1930-33

Most Seasons Leading League
11	Babe Ruth, AL:NY 1920-21,23-24,26-28,30-33
7	Barry Bonds, NL:Pitt. 1992; SF 94-97, 2000-01

Most Seasons, Consecutive, Leading League
4	Babe Ruth, AL:NY 1930-33
	Ted Williams, AL:Bos. 1946-49
	Barry Bonds, NL:SF 1994-97

Most Walks, Lifetime
2141	Rickey Henderson, AL:Oak., 1974-84,89-95,98; NY 85-89; Tor. 93; Ana. 97; Sea. 2000
	NL:SD 96-97, 2001; NY 99-2000

Most Walks, League
2042	Babe Ruth, AL:Bos. 1914-19; NY 20-34
1799	Joe Morgan, NL:Hou. 1963-71, 80; Cin. 72-79; SF 81-82; Phil. 83

Most Walks, Season
177	Barry Bonds, NL:SF 2001
170	Babe Ruth, AL:NY 1923

Most Seasons, 100 or more Walks
13	Babe Ruth, AL:Bos. 1919; NY 20-21,23-24,26-28,30-34
10	Mel Ott, NL:NY 1929-30,32,36-42

Most Seasons, Consecutive, 100 or more Walks
8	Frank Thomas, AL:Chi. 1991-98
7	Mel Ott, NL:NY 1936-42

Most Walks, Game
6	Walter Wilmot, NL:Chi. Aug. 22, 1891 (cons)
	Jimmie Foxx, AL:Bos. June 16, 1938 (cons)
	Andre Thornton, AL:Clev. May 2, 1984 (16 inn)
	NL Since 1900:
5	By many NL players; Last:
	Brett Butler, NL:SF Apr. 12, 1990
	Extra-Inning Game:
6	Jeff Bagwell, NL:Hou. Aug. 20, 1999 (16 inn)

Most Games, 5 or more Walks, League
4	Mel Ott, NL:NY Oct. 5, 1929(2g); Sept. 1(1g), 1933; June 17, 1943; Apr. 30(1g), 1944
2	Max Bishop, AL:Phil. Apr. 29, 1929; May 21(1g), 1930

Most Games, Consecutive, 1 or more Walks, Season
22	Roy Cullenbine, AL:Det. July 2-22, 1947
16	Jack Clark, NL:StL. July 18-Aug. 10, 1987
	Chipper Jones, NL:Atl. Aug. 19-Sept. 5, 1999

Most Walks, Consecutive, Season
7	Billy Rogell, AL:Det. Aug. 17-19, 1938
	Jose Canseco, AL:Oak. Aug. 4-5 1992
	Mel Ott, NL:NY June 16-18, 1943
	Eddie Stanky, NL:NY Aug. 29-30, 1950

Most Walks, Inning

2	By many players

Fewest Walks, Season (Minimum: 500 at-bats)

6	Art Fletcher, NL:NY 1915 (562 at-bats)
9	John Leary, AL:StL. 1914 (533 at-bats)

INTENTIONAL WALKS (Since 1955)

Most Seasons Leading Major League

5	Barry Bonds, NL:Pitt. 1992; SF 93,96-98

Most Seasons, Consecutive, Leading Major Leagues

4	Frank Robinson, NL:Cin. 1961-64

Most Seasons Leading League

7	Barry Bonds, NL:Pitt. 1992; SF 93-98
6	Wade Boggs, AL:Bos. 1987-92

Most Seasons, Consecutive, Leading League

7	Barry Bonds, NL:Pitt. 1992; SF 93-98
6	Wade Boggs, AL:Bos. 1987-92

Most Intentional Walks, Lifetime

355	Barry Bonds, NL:Pitt. 1986-92; SF 93-2001
228	George Brett, AL:KC 1973-93

Most Intentional Walks, Season

45	Willie McCovey, NL:SF 1969
33	Ted Williams, AL:Bos. 1957
	John Olerud, AL:Tor. 1993

Most Seasons, 20 or more Intentional Walks

10	Barry Bonds, NL:Pitt. 1989,91-92; SF 93,95-98, 2000-01
3	Frank Thomas, AL:Chi. 1993,95-96
	Ken Griffey, Jr., AL:Sea. 1991, 93, 97

Most Seasons Consecutive, 20 or more Intentional Walks

4	Willie McCovey, NL:SF 1968-71
	Barry Bonds, NL:Pitt 1995-98
2	Harmon Killebrew, AL:Minn. 1969-70
	Frank Howard, AL:Wash. 1970-71
	Mo Vaughn, AL:Bos. 1993-94
	Frank Thomas,AL:Chi. 1995-96

Most Intentional Walks, Game

3	By many players
	Extra-Inning Game:
5	Andre Dawson, NL:Chi. May 22, 1990 (16 inn)
4	Roger Maris, AL:NY May 22, 1962 (12 inn)
	Manny Ramirez, AL:Bos. June 5, 2001 (18 inn)

Most Intentional Walks, Inning

1	By many players

HIT BY PITCH

Most Seasons Leading Major Leagues

9	Minnie Minoso, AL:Clev.-Chi. 1951; Chi. 53-54,56-57,60-61; Clev. 58-59

Most Seasons, Consecutive, Leading Major Leagues

6	Minnie Minoso, AL:Chi. 1956-57,60-61; Clev. 58-59
	Ron Hunt, NL:SF 1968-70; Mtl. 71-73

Most Seasons Leading League

10	Minnie Minoso, AL:Clev.-Chi. 1951; Chi. 52-54,56-57,60-61; Clev. 58-59
7	Ron Hunt, NL:SF 1968-70; Mtl. 71-73; Mtl.-StL. 74

Most Seasons, Consecutive, Leading League

7	Ron Hunt, NL:SF 1968-70; Mtl. 71-73; Mtl.-StL. 74
6	Minnie Minoso, AL:Chi. 1956-57,60-61; Clev. 58-59

Most Hit By Pitch, Lifetime

267	Don Baylor, AL:Balt. 1970-75; Oak. 76,88; Cal. 77-82; NY 83-85; Bos. 86-87; Minn. 87
243	Ron Hunt, NL:NY 1963-66; LA 67; SF 68-70; Mtl. 71-74; StL. 74

Most Hit By Pitch, Season

50	Ron Hunt, NL:Mtl. 1971
35	Don Baylor, AL:Bos. 1986

Most Hit By Pitch, Game
3   By many players; Last:
Damion Easley, AL:Det. May 31, 1999
Richard Hidalgo, NL:Hou. Apr. 19, 2000

Most Hit by Pitch, Doubleheader
4   Frank Chance, NL:Chi. May 30, 1904
3   By many players

Most Hit By Pitch, Inning
2   Willard Schmidt, NL:Cin. Apr. 26, 1959 (3rd)
Frank Thomas, NL:NY Apr. 29, 1962 (1g; 4th)
Andres Galarraga, NL:Col. July 12, 1996 (7th)
Brady Anderson, AL:Balt. May 23, 1999 (1st)

Most Plate Appearances, Season, No Hit By Pitch
739   Sandy Alomar, Sr. AL:Cal. 1971
727   Lou Brock, NL:StL. 1973

STRIKEOUTS (Since 1910)

Most Seasons Leading Major Leagues
4   Babe Ruth, AL:Bos. 1918; NY 23-24,27
Rob Deer, AL:Mil. 1987-88; Det. 91; Det.-Bos. 93

Most Seasons, Consecutive, Leading Major Leagues
3   Hack Wilson, NL:Chi. 1928-30
Mike Schmidt, NL:Phil. 1974-76

Most Seasons Leading League
7   Jimmie Foxx, AL:Phil. 1929-31, 33, 35; Bos. 36, 41
6   Vince DiMaggio, NL:Bos. 1937-38; Pitt, 42-44; Phil. 45

Most Seasons, Consecutive, Leading League
4   Hack Wilson, NL:Chi. 1927-30
Vince DiMaggio, NL:Pitt. 1942-44; Phil. 45
Juan Samuel, NL:Phil. 1984-87
Reggie Jackson, AL:Oak. 1968-71

Most Strikeouts, Lifetime
2597   Reggie Jackson, AL:Oak. 1968-75,87; Balt. 76; NY77-81; Cal. 82-86
1936   Willie Stargell, NL:Pitt. 1962-82

Most Strikeouts, Season
189   Bobby Bonds, NL:SF 1970
186   Rob Deer, AL:Mil. 1987

Most Seasons, 100 or more Strikeouts, Lifetime
18   Reggie Jackson, AL:Oak. 1968-75; Balt. 76; NY 77-80; Cal. 82-86

Most Seasons, Consecutive, 100 or more Strikeouts, Lifetime
13   Reggie Jackson, AL:Oak. 1968-75; Balt. 76; NY 77-80

Most Seasons, 100 or more Strikeouts, League
18   Reggie Jackson, AL:Oak. 1968-75; Balt. 76; NY 77-80; Cal. 82-86
13   Willie Stargell, NL:Pitt. 1965-76,79

Most Seasons. Consecutive, 100 or more Strikeouts, League
13   Reggie Jackson, AL:Oak. 1968-75; Balt. 76; NY 77-80
12   Willie Stargell, NL:Pitt. 65-76

Most Strikeouts, Consecutive At-Bats, Season
15   Mike Thurman, NL:Mtl. July 24-Sept. 10, 1998
13   Jim Hannan, AL:Wash. July 24-Aug. 13, 1968

Most Strikeouts, Consecutive Plate Appearances, Season
12   Sandy Koufax, NL:Brk. June 24-Sept. 24, 1955
11   Dean Chance, AL:Cal. July 24-Aug. 13, 1966
Non-Pitcher:
9   Adolfo Phillips, NL:Chi. June 8-11, 1966
Eric Davis, NL:Cin. Apr. 24-25, 1987
Steve Balboni, AL:KC Aug. 20-22, 1984
Reggie Jackson, AL:Oak. July 6-11, 1987
Bo Jackson, AL:KC Sept. 16-19, 1988

Most Strikeouts, Game
5	By many players; Last: Richie Sexson, NL:Mil. May 29, 2001 (cons) John Jaha, AL:Oak. Apr. 20, 2000 (cons) **Extra-Inning Game:**
6	Carl Weilman, AL:StL. July 25, 1913 (15 inn, cons) Rick Reichardt, AL:Cal. May 31, 1966 (17 inn) Billy Cowan, AL:Cal. July 9, 1971 (20 inn) Cecil Cooper, AL:Bos. June 14, 1974 (15 inn) Sam Horn, AL:Balt. July 17, 1991 (15 inn) Alex Gonzalez, AL:Tor. Sept. 9, 1998 (13 inn) Don Hoak, NL:Chi. May 2, 1956 (17 inn)

Most Strikeouts, Inning
2	By many players.

Fewest Strikeouts, Season (Minimum: 500 at-bats)
3	Joe Sewell, AL:NY 1932 (503 at-bats)
5	Charlie Hollocher, NL:Chi. 1922 (592 at-bats)

Most Games, Consecutive, No Strikeouts, Season (non-pitcher)
115	Joe Sewell, AL:Clev. May 17-Sept. 19, 1929
77	Lloyd Waner, NL:Pitt.-Bos.-Cin. Apr. 24-Sept. 16, 1941

GROUNDED INTO DOUBLE PLAYS (Since 1933 in NL; Since 1940 in AL)

Most Seasons Leading Major Leagues
4	Jim Rice, AL:Bos. 1982-85

Most Seasons, Consecutive, Leading Major Leagues
4	Jim Rice, AL:Bos. 1982-85

Most Seasons Leading League
4	Ernie Lombardi, NL:Cin. 1933-34, 38; NY 44 Jim Rice, AL:Bos. 1982-85

Most Seasons, Consecutive, Leading League
4	Jim Rice, AL:Bos. 1982-85
2	Ernie Lombardi, NL:Cin. 1933-34 Frank McCormick, NL:Cin. 1940-41 Joe Torre, NL:Mil. 1964-65 Willie Montanez, NL:Phil.-SF 1975; SF-Atl. 76 Ray Knight, NL:Cin. 1980-81

Most Grounded into Double Plays, Lifetime
350	Cal Ripken, AL:Balt. 1981-2001
305	Hank Aaron, NL:Mil./Atl. 1954-74

Most Grounded Into Double Plays, Season
36	Jim Rice, AL Bos. 1984
30	Ernie Lombardi, NL:Cin. 1938

Most Grounded Into Double Plays, Game
4	Goose Goslin, AL:Det. Apr. 28, 1934 (cons) Joe Torre, NL:NY July 21, 1975 (cons)

Most Grounded Into Double Plays, 2 Consecutive Games
5	Zeke Bonura, NL:NY July 8-9, 1939
4	By many players

Most At-Bats, No Grounded Into Double Plays, Season
646	Augie Galan. NL:Chi. 1935
570	Dick McAuliffe, AL:Det. 1968

STOLEN BASES (Prior to 1898 stolen bases credited on fielder's choice)

Most Seasons Leading Major Leagues
6	Lou Brock, NL:StL. 1966,68,71-74 Rickey Henderson, AL:Oak. 1980, 82-83, 98, NY 88, NY-Oak. 89

Most Seasons, Consecutive, Leading Major Leagues
5	George Case, AL:Wash. 1939-43

Most Seasons Leading League
12	Rickey Henderson, AL:Oak. 1980-84,90-91,98; NY 85-86,88; NY-Oak. 89
10	Max Carey, NL:Pitt. 1913,15-18,20,22-25

Most Seasons, Consecutive, Leading League
9	Luis Aparicio, AL:Chi. 1956-62; Balt. 63-64
6	Maury Wills, NL:LA 1960-65 Vince Coleman, NL:StL. 1985-90

Most Stolen Bases, Lifetime
1395   Rickey Henderson, AL:Oak. 1979-84,89-95,98; NY 85-88; Tor.93; Ana. 97; Sea. 2000;
        NL:SD 96-97, 2001; NY 99-2000

Most Stolen Bases, League
1262   Rickey Henderson, AL:Oak. 1979-84,89-95,98; NY 85-88; Tor. 93; Ana. 97; Sea. 2000
938   Lou Brock, NL:Chi. 1961-64; StL. 64-79

Most Stolen Bases, Season
156   Harry Stovey, AA:Phil. 1888
      Since 1900:
130   Rickey Henderson, AL:Oak. 1982
118   Lou Brock, NL:StL. 1974

Most Seasons, 100 or more Stolen Bases
3   Rickey Henderson, AL:Oak. 1980, 82-83
      Vince Coleman, NL:StL. 1985-87

Most Seasons, Consecutive, 100 or more Stolen Bases
3   Vince Coleman, NL:StL. 1985-87
2   Rickey Henderson, AL:Oak., 1982-83

Most Seasons, 50 or more Stolen Bases
13   Rickey Henderson, AL:Oak. 1980-84, 90-91,98; NY 85-86,88; NY-Oak. 89; Oak.-Tor. 93
12   Lou Brock, NL:StL. 1965-76

Most Seasons, Consecutive, 50 or more Stolen Bases
12   Lou Brock, NL:StL. 1965-76
7   Rickey Henderson, AL:Oak. 1980-84; NY 85-86

Most Stolen Bases, Consecutive, League
50   Vince Coleman, NL:StL. Sept. 18, 1988-July 26, 1989
40   Tim Raines, AL:Chi. July 23, 1993-Aug. 4, 1995

Most Stolen Bases, Consecutive, Season
44   Vince Coleman, NL:StL. Apr. 3-July 26, 1989
32   Willie Wilson, AL:KC July 23-Sept. 23, 1980

Most Stolen Bases, Game
7   George Gore, NL:Chi. June 25, 1881
      Billy Hamilton, NL:Phil. Aug. 31(2g), 1894
      Since 1900:
6   Eddie Collins, AL:Phil. Sept. 11, 22(1g), 1912
      Otis Nixon, NL:Atl. June 16, 1991
      Eric Young, NL:Col. June 30, 1996

Most Stolen Bases, Inning
3   By many players; Last:
      Chris Stynes, AL:KC May 12, 1996 (1st)
      Eric Young, NL:Col. June 30, 1996 (3rd)

Most Stolen Home, Lifetime
54   Ty Cobb, AL:Det. 1905-26; Phil. 27-28

Most Stolen Home, League
54   Ty Cobb, AL:Det. 1905-26; Phil. 27-28
33   Max Carey, NL:Pitt. 1910-26, Brk. 26-29

Most Stolen Home, Season
8   Ty Cobb, AL:Det. 1912
7   Pete Reiser, NL:Brk. 1946

Most Stolen Home, Game
2   Honus Wagner, NL:Pitt. June 20, 1901
      Ed Konetchy, NL:StL. Sept. 30, 1907
      Joe Tinker, NL:Chi. June 28, 1910
      Larry Doyle, NL:NY Sept. 18, 1911
      Sherry Magee, NL:Phil. July 20, 1912
      Doc Gautreau, NL:Bos. Sept. 3(1g), 1927
      Joe Jackson, AL:Clev. Aug. 11, 1912
      Guy Zinn, AL:NY Aug. 15, 1912
      Eddie Collins, AL:Phil. Sept. 6, 1913
      Ty Cobb, AL:Det. June 18, 1915
      Bill Barrett, AL:Chi. May 1, 1924
      Vic Power, AL:Clev. Aug. 14, 1958 (10 inn)

Most Stolen Home, Inning
1   By many players

Highest Percentage Successful, Lifetime (Minimum: 300 attempts)
.853   Tony Womack, NL:Pitt. 1993-98; Ari. 99-2001 (313-267)

Highest Percentage Successful, League (Minimum: 300 attempts)
.857   Tim Raines, NL:Mtl. 1979-89 (740-634)
.833   Willie Wilson, AL:KC 1976-90, Oak. 1991-92 (792-660)

Highest Percentage Successful, Season (Minimum: 35 attempts)
.962   Max Carey, NL:Pitt. 1922 (53-51)
.943   Amos Otis, AL:KC 1970 (35-33)

Most Stolen Bases, None Caught, Season
21   Kevin McReynolds, NL:NY 1988
20   Paul Molitor, AL:Tor. 1994

CAUGHT STEALING (Since 1920 in A.L.; Since 1951 in N.L.)

Most Seasons Leading Major Leagues
6   Maury Wills, NL:LA 1961-63,65-66; Mtl.-LA 69

Most Seasons, Consecutive, Leading Major Leagues
3   Maury Wills, NL:LA 1961-63

Most Seasons Leading League
7   Maury Wills, NL:LA 1961-63,65-66; Pitt. 68; Mtl,-LA. 69
        Lou Brock, NL:Chi,-StL. 1964; StL. 67,71,73-74,76-77
6   Minnie Minoso, AL:Chi. 1952-54,57,60; Clev. 58

Most Seasons, Consecutive, Leading League
4   Ben Chapman, AL:NY 1931-34
        Rickey Henderson, AL:Oak. 1980-83
3   Maury Wills, NL:LA 1961-63
        Omar Moreno, NL:Pitt. 1980-82

Most Caught Stealing, Lifetime
333   Rickey Henderson, AL:Oak. 1979-84,89-95,98; NY 85-89; Tor. 93; Ana. 97; Sea. 2000
                NL:SD 97, 2001; NY 99-2000

Most Caught Stealing, League
307   Lou Brock, NL:Chi. 1961-64;- StL. 64-79
291   Rickey Henderson, AL:Oak. 1979-84,89-95,98; NY 85-89; Tor. 93; Ana. 97; Sea. 2000

Most Caught Stealing, Season
42   Rickey Henderson, AL:Oak. 1982 (172 attempts)
33   Lou Brock, NL:StL. 1974 (151 attempts)
        Omar Moreno, NL:Pitt. 1980 (129 attempts)

Most Caught Stealing, Game
3   By many players
        Extra-Inning Game:
4   Robby Thompson, NL:SF June 27, 1986 (12 inn)

Most Caught Stealing, Inning
2   Don Baylor, AL:Balt. June 15, 1974 (9th)
        Roberto Kelly, AL:NY Apr. 17, 1990 (2nd)
        Jim Morrison, NL:Pitt. June 15, 1987 (8th)
        Paul Noce, NL:Chi. June 26, 1987 (3rd)
        Donnell Nixon, NL:SF July 6, 1988 (6th)
        Tony Fernandez, NL:SD June 26, 1992 (5th)
        Eric Young, NL:Col. May 1, 1993 (8th)
        Phil Plantier, NL:SD Sept. 25, 1993 (5th)
        Derek Bell, NL:Hou. June 19, 1995 (4th)
        Larry Walker, NL:Col. Apr. 30, 1998 (8th)

PINCH HITTING

Most Games, Season
95   Lenny Harris, NL:NY 2001
81   Elmer Valo, AL:NY-Wash. 1960

Most At-Bats, Lifetime
591   Greg Gross, NL:Hou. 1973-76,89; Chi. 77-78; Phil 79-88
414   Gates Brown, AL:Det. 1963-75

Most At-Bats, Season
83   Lenny Harris, NL:NY 2001
72   Dave Philley, AL:Balt. 1961

Most Hits, Lifetime
151   Lenny Harris, NL:Cin. 1988-89,94-98; LA 89-93; NY 98, 2000-01; Col. 99; Ari. 2000
107   Gates Brown, AL:Det. 1963-75

Most Hits, Season
28   John Vander Wal, NL:Col. 1995
24   Dave Philley, AL:Balt. 1961

Most Hits, Consecutive, League
9   Dave Philley, NL:Phil. Sept. 9, 1958-Apr. 16, 1959

Most Hits, Consecutive, Season
8   Dave Philley, NL:Phil, Sept. 9-28, 1958
       Rusty Staub, NL:NY June 11-26(1g), 1983
7   Bill Stein, AL:Tex. Apr. 14-May 25, 1981
       Randy Bush, AL:Minn. July 5-Aug. 19, 1991

Most Home Runs, Lifetime
20   Cliff Johnson, NL:Hou. 1972-77; Chi. 80;
               AL:NY 1977-79; Clev. 79-80; Oak. 81-82; Tor. 83-86

Most Home Runs, League
18   Jerry Lynch, NL:Pitt. 1954-56,63-66; Cin. 57-63
16   Gates Brown, AL:Det. 1963-75

Most Home Runs, Season
7   Dave Hansen, NL:LA 2000
       Craig Wilson, NL:Pitt. 2001
5   Joe Cronin, AL:Bos. 1943

Most Home Runs, Consecutive At-Bats
3   Lee Lacy, NL:LA May 2, 6, 17, 1978
       Del Unser, NL:Phil, June 30, July 5, 10, 1979
2   Ray Caldwell, AL:NY June 10-11, 1915
       Joe Cronin, AL:Bos. June 17-17, 1943
       Charlie Keller, AL:NY Sept. 12-14, 1948
       Del Wilber, AL:Bos. May 6-10, 1953
       Johnny Blanchard, AL:NY July 21-22, 1961
       Chuck Schilling, AL:Bos. Apr. 30-May 1, 1965
       Ray Barker, AL:NY June 20-22, 1965
       Curt Motton, AL:Balt. May 15-17, 1968
       Gates Brown, AL:Det. Aug. 9-11, 1968
       Gary Alexander, AL:Clev. July 5-6, 1980
       Daryl Sconiers, AL:Cal. Apr. 30-May 7, 1983
       Alex Sanchez, AL:Det. July 20-23, 1985
       Rupert Jones, AL:Cal. June 20-28, 1987
       Randy Bush, AL:Minn July 14-19, 1991
       Jack Howell, AL:Cal. May 15-17, 1996
       Jeromy Burnitz, AL:Mil. Aug. 2-3, 1997
       Willie Greene, AL:Tor. June 20-30, 1999
       Shawn Wooten, AL:Ana. Apr. 21-27, 2001
       Brian Buchanan, AL:Minn. May 4-16, 2001
       Tino Martinez, AL:NY June 25-July 6, 2001

Most Grand Slam Home Runs, Lifetime
3   Ron Northey, NL:StL. Sept. 3, 1947; May 30, 1948; Chi. Sept. 18, 1950
       Willie McCovey, NL:SF June 12, 1960; Sept. 10, 1965; SD May 30, 1975
       Rich Reese, AL:Minn. Aug. 3, 1969; June 7, 1970; July 9, 1972

Most Grand Slam Home Runs, Season
2   Dave Johnson, NL:Phil. Apr. 30, June 3, 1978
       Mike Ivie, NL:SF May 28, June 30, 1978
       Darryl Strawberry, AL:NY May 2, Aug. 4, 1998

Most Walks, Lifetime
91   Elmer Valo, AL:Phil./KC 1940-43,46-56; Clev. 59; NY 60; Wash./Minn. 60-61
               NL:Phil. 56,61; Brk./LA 57-58

Most Walks, Season
20   Matt Franco, NL:NY 1999
18   Elmer Valo, AL:Wash. 1960

Most Runs Batted In, Season
25   Joe Cronin, AL:Bos. 1943
       Jerry Lynch, NL:Cin. 1961
       Rusty Staub, NL:NY 1983

ROOKIE BATTING

(No official rookie rule prior to 1957. Qualifiers based on 130-or-fewer previous at-bats)

Highest Batting Average (Minimum: 350 at-bats)
.408   Joe Jackson, AL:Clev. 1911
.373   George Watkins, NL:StL. 1930

Highest Slugging Percentage (Minimum: 350 at-bats)
.651   Rudy York, AL:Det. 1937
.621   George Watkins, NL:StL. 1930

Most Games
162   Jake Wood, AL:Det. 1961
       Bobby Knoop, AL:LA 1964
       George Scott, AL:Bos. 1966
       Richie Allen NL:Phil. 1964
       Johnny Ray, NL:Pitt. 1982
       Jeff Conine, NL:Fla. 1993

Most At-Bats
701   Juan Samuel, NL:Phil. 1984
692   Ichiro Suzuki, AL:Sea. 2001

Most Runs
152   Mike Griffin, AA:Balt. 1887
135   Roy Thomas, NL:Phil. 1899
       Since 1900:
133   Lloyd Waner, NL:Pitt. 1927
132   Joe DiMaggio, AL:NY 1936

Most Hits
242   Ichiro Suzuki, AL:Sea. 2001
223   Lloyd Waner, NL:Pitt. 1927

Most Games, Consecutive, Hits
34   Benito Santiago, NL:SD Aug. 25-Oct. 2, 1987
30   Nomar Garciaparra, AL:Bos. July 26-Aug. 29, 1997

Most Extra-Base Hits
89   Hal Trosky, AL:Clev. 1934
88   Albert Pujols, NL:StL. 2001

Most Total Bases
374   Hal Trosky, AL:Clev. 1934
       Tony Oliva, AL:Minn. 1964
360   Albert Pujols, NL:StL. 2001

Most Singles
198   Lloyd Waner, NL:Pitt. 1927
192   Ichiro Suzuki, AL:Sea. 2001

Most Doubles
52   Johnny Frederick, NL:Brk. 1929
47   Fred Lynn, AL:Bos. 1975

Most Triples
27   Jimmy Williams, NL:Pitt. 1899
      Since 1900:
25   Tommy Long, NL:StL. 1915
19   Joe Cassidy, AL:Wash. 1904
      Frank Baker, AL:Phil. 1909
      Joe Jackson, AL:Clev. 1911

Most Home Runs
49   Mark McGwire, AL:Oak. 1987
38   Wally Berger, NL:Bos. 1930
      Frank Robinson, NL:Cin. 1956

Most Runs Batted In
145   Ted Williams, AL:Bos. 1939
130   Albert Pujols, NL:StL. 2001

Most Sacrifice Hits (Since 1931)
28   Joe Hoover, AL:Det. 1943
      Jackie Robinson, NL:Brk. 1947
      Ozzie Smith, NL:SD 1978

Most Sacrifice Flies (Since 1954)
13   Willie Montanez, NL:Phil. 1971
      Gary Gaetti, AL:Minn. 1982

Most Walks (Since 1913)
107   Ted Williams, AL:Bos. 1939
100   Jim Gilliam, NL:Brk. 1953

Most Intentional Walks (Since 1955)
16   Alvin Davis, AL:Sea. 1984
14   Willie Montanez, NL:Phil. 1971

Most Hit By Pitch
21   Bucky Harris, AL:Wash. 1920
        David Eckstein, AL:Ana. 2001
20   Frank Robinson, NL:Cin. 1956

Most Strikeouts (Since 1910)
185   Pete Incaviglia, AL:Tex. 1986
168   Juan Samuel, NL:Phil. 1984

Fewest Strikeouts (Minimum: 500 at-bats)
10   Tommy Holmes, NL:Bos. 1942 (558 at-bats)
17   Joe Sewell, AL:Clev. 1920 (572 at-bats)

Most Stolen Bases (Since 1898)
110   Vince Coleman, NL:StL. 1985
66   Kenny Lofton, AL:Clev. 1992

Most Caught Stealing (Since 1920)
28   George Grantham, NL:Chi. 1923
23   Miguel Dilone, AL:Oak. 1978

Most Grounded Into Double Plays
28   George Kell, AL:Phil. 1944
26   Sid Gordon, NL:NY 1943

Fewest Grounded Into Double Plays (Minimum: 500 at-bats)
1   Ellis Burks, AL:Bos. 1987 (558 at-bats)
2   Tommy Holmes, NL:Bos. 1942 (558 at-bats)

INDIVIDUAL FIELDING
(Career percentage leaders based on 1000-game minimum; pitchers' minimum: 300 total chances)

FIRST BASE

Most Seasons, Lifetime
22   Willie McCovey, NL:SF 1959-73,77-80; SD 74-76

Most Seasons, League
22   Willie McCovey, NL:SF 1959-73,77-80; SD 74-76
20   Joe Judge, AL:Wash. 1915-32; Bos. 33-34

PERCENTAGE

Most Seasons Leading League
7   Ed Konetchy, NL:StL. 1910-11,13; Pitt. 14; Bos. 17-18; Brk. 19
        Charlie Grimm, NL:Pitt. 1920,23-24; Chi. 28,30-31,33
        Don Mattingly, AL:NY 1984-87, 92-94

Most Seasons, Consecutive, Leading League
5   Ted Kluszewski, NL:Cin. 1951-55
4   Don Mattingly, AL:NY 1984-87

Highest Percentage, Lifetime
.9959   Steve Garvey, NL:LA 1975-82; SD 83-87
.9958   Don Mattingly, AL:NY 1982-95

Highest Percentage, Season
1.000   Steve Garvey, NL:SD 1984
.999   Stuffy McInnis, AL:Bos. 1921

Lowest Percentage, Season, Since 1900
.970   John Doyle, NL:NY 1900
.972   Pat Newnam, AL:StL. 1910

GAMES

Most Seasons Leading League
9   Steve Garvey, NL:LA 1975-81; SD 84-85
7   Lou Gehrig, AL:NY 1926-28,32,36-38

Most Games, Lifetime
2413   Eddie Murray, AL:Balt. 1977-88,96; Clev. 94-96; NL:LA 1989-91; NY 92-93

Most Games, League
2247   Jake Beckley, NL:Pitt. 1888-89,91-96; NY 96-97; Cin. 1897-1903; St,L. 04-07
2227   Mickey Vernon, AL:Wash. 1939-43,46-48,50-55; Clev. 49-50,58; Bos. 56-57

Most Games, Consecutive
885   Lou Gehrig, AL:NY June 2, 1925-Sept. 27, 1930
652   Frank McCormick, NL:Cin. Apr. 19, 1938-May 24, 1942

Most Games, Season
162   Norm Siebern, AL:KC 1962
             Bill Buckner, AL:Bos. 1985
             Carlos Delgado, AL:Tor. 2000
             Bill White, NL:StL. 1963
             Ernie Banks, NL:Chi. 1965
             Steve Garvey, NL:LA 1976, 79-80; SD 85
             Pete Rose, NL:Phil. 1980, 82
             Jeff Bagwell, NL:Hou. 1996
             Eric Karros, NL:LA 1997

CHANCES ACCEPTED

Most Seasons Leading League
6   Bill Terry, NL:NY 1927-30,32,34
4   Wally Pipp, AL:NY 1915,19-20,22

Most Chances Accepted, Lifetime
25,000   Jake Beckley, NL:Pitt. 1888-89,91-96; NY 96-97; Cin. 1897-1903; StL. 04-07; PL:Pitt. 1890

Most Chances Accepted, League
23,687   Jake Beckley, NL:Pitt. 1888-89, 91-96; NY 96-97; Cin. 1897-1903; StL. 04-07
21,198   Mickey Vernon, AL:Wash. 1939-43,46-48,50-55; Clev. 49-50,58; Bos. 56-57

Most Chances Accepted, Season
1986   Jiggs Donahue, AL:Chi. 1907
1862   George Kelly, NL:NY 1920

Most Chances Accepted, Game
22   By many players; Last:
             Ernie Banks, NL:Chi. May 9, 1963
             Alvin Davis, AL:Sea. May 28, 1988
             Extra-Inning Game:
43   Walter Holke, NL:Bos. May 1, 1920 (26 inn)
34   Rudy York, AL:Det. July 21, 1945 (24 inn)
             Mike Epstein, AL:Wash. June 12, 1967 (22 inn)
             Rod Carew, AL:Cal. Apr. 13, 1982 (20 inn)

Fewest Chances Accepted, Game
0   Guy Hecker, AA:Lou. Oct. 9, 1887
             Al McCauley, AA:Wash. Aug. 6, 1891
             Bud Clancy, AL:Chi. Apr. 27, 1930
             Norm Cash, AL:Det. June 27, 1963
             Gene Tenace, AL:Oak. Sept. 1, 1974
             Mark McGwire, AL:Oak. Sept. 12, 1995
             Scott Cooper, AL:KC May 31, 1997 (8 inn.)
             Ripper Collins, NL:Chi. June 29, 1937

PUTOUTS

Most Seasons Leading League
6   Jake Beckley, NL:Pitt. 1892,94-95; Cin. 1900,02; StL. 04
             Frank McCormick, NL:Cin. 1939-42,44-45
             Steve Garvey, NL:LA 1974-78; SD 85
4   Wally Pipp, AL:NY 1915,19-20,22

Most Putouts, Lifetime
23,696   Jake Beckley, NL:Pitt. 1888-89,91-96; NY 96-97; Cin. 1897-1903; StL. 04-07; PL:Pitt. 1890

Most Putouts, League
22,438	Jake Beckley, NL:Pitt. 1888-89,91-96; NY 96-97; Cin. 1897-1903; St,L. 04-07
19,754	Mickey Vernon, AL:Wash. 1939-43,46-48,50-55; Clev. 49-50, 58; Bos. 56-57

Most Putouts, Season
1846	Jiggs Donahue, AL:Chi. 1907
1759	George Kelly, NL:NY 1920

Most Putouts, Game
22	Tom Jones, AL:StL. May 11, 1906
	Hal Chase, AL:NY Sept. 21(1g), 1906
	Don Mattingly, AL:NY July 20, 1987
	Alvin Davis, AL:Sea. May 28, 1988
	Ernie Banks, NL:Chi. May 9, 1963
	Extra-Inning Game:
42	Walter Holke, NL:Bos. May 1, 1920 (26 inn)
32	Mike Epstein, AL:Wash. June 12, 1967 (22 inn)
	Rod Carew, AL:Cal. Apr. 13, 1982 (20 inn)

Fewest Putouts, Game
0	Guy Hecker, AA:Lou. Oct. 9, 1887 (8 inn)
	Al McCauley, AA:Wash. Aug. 6, 1891
	Solly Hofman, NL:Chi. June 24, 1910 (8 inn)
	Ripper Collins, NL:StL. Aug. 21, 1935; Chi. June 29, 1937
	Dolf Camilli, NL:Phil. July 30, 1937
	Earl Torgeson, NL:Bos. May 30(1g), 1947
	Gary Thomasson, NL:SF July 31, 1977 (8 inn)
	Len Matuszek, NL:Phil. June 1, 1984
	Franklin Stubbs, NL:Hou. July 25, 1990
	Bud Clancy, AL:Chi. Apr. 27, 1930
	Rudy York, AL:Det. June 18, 1943
	Norm Cash, AL:Det. June 27, 1963 (8 inn)
	Bill Skowron, AL:Chi. May 15, 1966 (8 inn)
	Frank Robinson, AL:Bait. July 1, 1971
	Gene Tenace, AL:Oak. Sept. 1, 1974
	Greg Brock, AL:Mil. June 28, 1987
	Mark McGwire, AL:Oak. Sept. 12, 1995
	Scott Cooper, AL:KC May 31, 1997 (8 inn)
	Rafael Palmeiro, AL:Balt. June 23, 1997
	John Olerud, AL:Sea. July 17, 2000

ASSISTS

Most Seasons Leading League
8	Fred Tenney, NL:Bos. 1899, 1901-07
6	George Sisler, AL:StL. 1919-20,22,24-25,27
	Vic Power, AL:KC 1955,57; Clev. 59-61; Minn. 62

Most Assists, Lifetime
1865	Eddie Murray, AL:Balt. 1977-88,96; Clev. 94-96; NL:LA 89-91; NY 92-93

Most Assists, League
1662	Keith Hernandez, NL:StL. 1974-83; NY 83-89
1444	Mickey Vernon, AL:Wash. 1939-43,46-48,50-55; Clev. 49-50,58; Bos. 56-57

Most Assists, Season
184	Bill Buckner, AL:Bos. 1985
180	Mark Grace, NL:Chi. 1990

Most Assists, Game
8	Bob Skinner, NL:Pitt. July 22, 1954 (14 inn)
	Bob Robertson, NL:Pitt. June 21, 1971
	Darrell Evans, NL:SF May 30, 1981 (14 inn)
7	George Stovall, AL:StL. Aug. 7, 1912
	Ferris Fain, AL:Phil. June 9, 1949 (12 inn)

Fewest Assists, Game (Most Innings)
0	Ed Konetchy, NL:Pitt. July 17, 1914 (21 inn)
	Fred Merkle, NL:NY July 17, 1914 (21 inn)

Most Assists, Inning
3	By many players; Last:
	Eric Karros, NL:LA Sept. 5, 1999
	Wil Cordero, AL:Chi. July 29, 1998

ERRORS

Most Seasons Leading League (most errors)
6	Mo Vaughn, AL:Bos. 1992-94, 96-97; Ana. 2000
5	Dick Stuart, NL:Pitt. 1958-62
	Willie McCovey, NL:SF 1967-68,70-71,77

Most Errors, League, Since 1900
285	Hal Chase, AL:NY 1905-13; Chi. 13-14
252	Fred Tenney, NL:Bos. 1900-07,11; NY 08-09
	Fred Merkle, NL:NY 1907-16; Brk. 16-17; Cin. 17-20

Most Errors, Season
62	Joe Quinn, UA:StL. 1884
58	Cap Anson, NL:Chi. 1884

Since 1900:
43	Jack Doyle, NL:NY 1900
41	Jerry Freeman, AL:Wash. 1908

Fewest Errors, Season
Minimum: 150 games
0	Steve Garvey, NL:SD 1984 (159 g)
1	Stuffy McInnis, AL:Bos. 1921 (152 g)

Minimum: 1500 total chances
1	Stuffy McInnis, AL:Bos. 1921 (1652 tc)
3	Steve Garvey, NL:LA 1976 (1653 tc)

Most Errors, Game
5	John Carbine, NL:Lou. Apr. 29, 1876
	George Zettlein, NL:Phil. June 22, 1876
	Everett Mills, NL:Hart. Oct. 7, 1876
	Dude Esterbrook, NL:Buff. July 27, 1880
	Roger Connor, NL:Troy May 27, 1882
	Lew Brown, AA:Lou. Sept. 10, 1883
	Jack Gorman, UA:KC June 28, 1884
	Joe Quinn, UA:StL. July 4(1g), 1884

Since 1900:
4	Jock Menefee, NL:Chi. Oct. 6, 1901
	Johnny Lush, NL:Phil. June 11 & Sept. 15(2g), 1904
	Fred Tenney, NL:Bos. July 12(1g), 1905
	Todd Zeile, NL:Phil. Aug. 7, 1996
	Hal Chase, AL:Chi. July 23, 1913
	George Sisler, AL:StL. Apr. 14, 1925
	Jimmy Wasdell, AL:Wash. May 3, 1939
	Glenn Davis, AL:Balt. Apr. 18, 1991

Most Errors, Inning
3	Dolf Camilli, NL:Phil. Aug. 2, 1935 (1st)
	Al Oliver, NL:Pitt. May 23, 1969 (4th)
	Jack Clark, NL:StL. May 25, 1987 (3rd)
	George Metkovich, AL:Bos, Apr. 17, 1945 (7th)
	Tom McCraw, AL:Chi. May 3, 1968 (3rd)
	Willie Upshaw, AL:Tor. July 1, 1986 (5th)

Most Errorless Games, Consecutive
193	Steve Garvey, NL:SD June 26, 1983-Apr. 14, 1985
178	Mike Hegan, AL:Mil. Sept. 24, 1970-Oak. May 20, 1973

Most Errorless Games, Consecutive, Season
159	Steve Garvey, NL:SD 1984 (entire season)
119	Stuffy McInnis, AL:Bos. May 31(1g)-Oct. 2, 1921

Most Errorless Chances Accepted, Consecutive
1700	Stuffy McInnis, AL:Bos.-Clev. May 31(1g), 1921 - June 2, 1922
1633	Steve Garvey, NL:SD June 26, 1983-Apr. 15, 1985

Most Errorless Chances Accepted, Consecutive, Season
1319	Steve Garvey, NL:SD 1984 (entire season)
1300	Stuffy McInnis, AL:Bos. May 31(1g)-Oct. 2, 1921

DOUBLE PLAYS

Most Seasons Leading League
6	Keith Hernandez, NL:StL. 1977,79-81; NY 83-84
4	Stuffy McInnis, AL:Phil. 1912,14; Bos. 19-20
	Wally Pipp, AL:NY 1915-17,20
	Vic Power, AL:KC 1955; Clev. 59-60; Minn. 62
	Cecil Cooper, AL:Mil. 1980-83

Most Double Plays, Lifetime
2044	Mickey Vernon, AL:Wash. 1939-43,46-48,50-55; Clev. 49-50,58; Bos. 56-57; NL:Mil. 1959

Most Double Plays, League
2041	Mickey Vernon, AL:Wash. 1939-43,46-48,50-55; Clev. 49-50,58
1708	Charlie Grimm, NL:StL. 1918; Pitt. 19-24; Chi. 25-36

Most Double Plays, Season
194	Ferris Fain, AL:Phil. 1949
182	Donn Clendenon, NL:Pitt. 1966

Most Double Plays, Unassisted, Season
8	Jim Bottomley, AL:StL. 1936
	Bill White, NL:StL. 1961

Most Double Plays, Game
7	Curt Blefary, NL:Hou. May 4, 1969
6	Jimmie Foxx, AL:Phil. Aug. 24, 1935 (15 inn)
	Ferris Fain, AL:Phil. Sept. 1(2g), 1947
	George Vico, AL:Det. May 19, 1948
	Eddie Robinson, AL:Clev. Aug. 5, 1948
	Lee Thomas, AL:LA Aug. 23, 1963
	Bob Oliver, AL:KC May 14, 1971; NY Apr. 29, 1975
	John Mayberry, AL:KC May 16, 1972
	Rod Carew, AL:Minn. Aug. 29(1g), 1977 (10 inn)
	Kent Hrbek, AL:Minn. July 18, 1990
	Mark McGwire, AL:Oak. May 17, 1995

Most Double Plays, Unassisted, Game
2	By many players; Last:
	Richie Sexson, NL:Mil. Oct. 7, 2001
	Jason Giambi, AL:Oak. Aug. 2, 2000

TRIPLE PLAYS

Unassisted Triple Play
1	George Burns, AL:Bos. (Clev.) Sept. 14, 1923 (2nd)
	Johnny Neun, AL:Det. (Clev.) May 31, 1927 (9th)

SECOND BASE

Most Seasons, Lifetime
22	Joe Morgan, NL:Hou. 1963-71,80; Cin. 72-79; SF 81-82; Phil. 83; AL:Oak. 1984

Most Seasons, League
21	Eddie Collins, AL:Phil. 1908-14,27-28; Chi. 15-26
	Joe Morgan, NL:Hou. 1963-71,80; Cin. 72-79; SF 81-82; Phil. 83

PERCENTAGE

Most Seasons Leading League
9	Eddie Collins, AL:Phil. 1909-10,14; Chi. 15-16,20-22,24
6	Red Schoendienst, NL:StL. 1946, 49, 53, 55; StL.-NY 56; Mil. 58

Most Seasons, Consecutive, Leading League
3	Claude Ritchey, NL:Pitt. 1905-07
	Bret Boone, NL:Cin. 1995-97
	Nap Lajoie, AL:Clev. 1906-08
	Eddie Collins, AL:Phil. 1914-Chi. 15-16; Chi. 20-22
	Charlie Gehringer, AL:Det. 1935-37

Highest Percentage, Lifetime
.9894	Ryne Sandberg, NL:Phil. 1981; Chi. 82-94,96-97
.9870	Roberto Alomar, AL:Tor. 1991-95; Balt. 96-98; Clev. 99-2001

Highest Percentage, Season
.9967   Bret Boone, NL:Cin. 1997
.9966   Bobby Grich, AL:Cal. 1985

Lowest Percentage, Season, Since 1900
.914   Frank Truesdale, AL:StL. 1910
.927   John Farrell, NL:StL. 1903

GAMES

Most Seasons Leading League
8   Nellie Fox, AL:Chi. 1952-59
7   Craig Biggio, NL:Hou. 1992-98, 2001

Most Games, Lifetime
2651   Eddie Collins, AL:Phil. 1908-14,27-28; Chi. 15-26

Most Games, League
2651   Eddie Collins, AL:Phil. 1908-14,27-28; Chi. 15-26
2427   Joe Morgan, NL:Hou. 1963-71,80; Cin, 72-79; SF 81-82; Phil. 83

Most Games, Consecutive
798   Nellie Fox, AL:Chi. Aug. 7, 1955-Sept. 3, 1960
443   Dave Cash, NL:Pitt.-Phil. Sept. 20, 1973-Aug. 5, 1976

Most Games, Season
163   Bill Mazeroski, NL:Pitt. 1967
162   Jake Wood, AL:Det. 1961
        Bobby Grich, AL:Balt. 1973

CHANCES ACCEPTED

Most Seasons Leading League
9   Nellie Fox, AL:Chi. 1952-60
8   Bill Mazeroski, NL:Pitt. 1958,60-64,66-67

Most Chances Accepted, Lifetime
14,156   Eddie Collins, AL:Phil. 1908-14,27-28; Chi. 15-26

Most Chances Accepted, League
14,156   Eddie Collins, AL:Phil. 1908-14,27-28; Chi. 15-26
12,279   Joe Morgan, NL:Hou. 1963-71,80; Cin. 72-79; SF 81-82; Phil. 83

Most Chances Accepted, Season
1037   Frankie Frisch, NL:StL. 1927
988   Nap Lajoie, AL:Clev. 1908

Most Chances Accepted, Game
18   Cupid Childs, AA:Syr. June 1, 1890
        Terry Harmon, NL:Phil. June 12, 1971
17   Jimmy Dykes, AL:Phil. Aug. 28, 1921
        Nellie Fox, AL:Chi. June 12, 1952
Extra-Inning Game:
21   Eddie Moore, NL:Bos. May 17, 1927 (22 inn)
20   Willie Randolph, AL:NY Aug. 25, 1976 (19 inn)

Fewest Chances Accepted, Game (Most Innings)
0   Steve Yerkes, AL:Bos. June 11, 1913 (15 inn)
    Ken Boswell, NL:NY Aug. 7, 1972 (13 inn)

PUTOUTS

Most Seasons Leading League
10   Nellie Fox, AL:Chi. 1952-61
7   Fred Pfeffer, NL:Chi. 1884-89,91
        Billy Herman, NL:Chi. 1933,35-36,38-40; Brk. 42

Most Putouts, Lifetime
6526   Eddie Collins, AL:Phil. 1908-14,27-28; Chi. 15-26

Most Putouts, League
6526   Eddie Collins, AL:Phil. 1908-14,27-28; Chi. 15-26
5541   Joe Morgan, NL:Hou. 1963-71,80; Cin. 72-79; SF 81-82; Phil. 83

Most Putouts, Season
484   Bobby Grich, AL:Balt. 1974
466   Billy Herman, NL:Chi. 1933

Most Putouts, Game
12	Lou Bierbauer, AA:Phil. June 22, 1888
	Billy Gardner, AL:Balt. May 21, 1957 (16 inn)
	Bobby Knoop, AL:Cal. Aug. 30, 1966
	Vern Fuller, AL:Clev. Apr. 11, 1969 (16 inn)
	Tomas Perez, AL:Tor. Aug. 20, 1996 (14 inn)
11	Sam Wise, NL:Wash. May 9, 1893
	Bid McPhee, NL:Cin. Apr. 21, 1894
	Nap Lajoie, NL:Phil. Apr. 25, 1899
	Billy Herman, NL:Chi. June 28(1g), 1933
	Gene Baker, NL:Chi. May 27, 1955
	Charlie Neal, NL:LA July 2, 1959
	Julian Javier, NL:StL. June 27, 1964
	Extra-Inning Game:
15	Jake Pitler, NL:Pitt. Aug. 22, 1917 (22 inn)

Fewest Putouts, Game (Most Innings)
0	Roberto Alomar, NL:SD Sept. 28, 1988 (16 inn)
	Steve Yerkes, AL:Bos. June 11, 1913 (15 inn)
	Denny Doyle, AL:Cal. June 14, 1974 (15 inn)
	Damion Easley, AL:Det. July 8, 2000 (15 inn)

ASSISTS

Most Seasons Leading League
9	Bill Mazeroski, NL:Pitt. 1958,60-64,66-68
7	Charlie Gehringer, AL:Det. 1927-28,33-36,38

Most Assists, Lifetime
7630	Eddie Collins, AL:Phil. 1908-14,27-28; Chi. 15-26

Most Assists, League
7630	Eddie Collins, AL:Phil. 1908-14,27-28; Chi. 15-26
6738	Joe Morgan, NL:Hou. 1963-71,80; Cin. 72-79; SF 81-82; Phil. 83

Most Assists, Season
641	Frankie Frisch, NL:StL. 1927
572	Oscar Melillo, AL:StL. 1930

Most Assists, Game
12	Monte Ward, NL:Brk. June 10(1g), 1892
	Jim Gilliam, NL:Brk. July 21, 1956
	Jack Perconte, NL:LA Sept. 19, 1981
	Ryne Sandberg, NL:Chi. June 12, 1983
	Glenn Hubbard, NL:Atl. Apr. 14, 1985
	Juan Samuel, NL:Phil. Apr. 20, 1985
	Don Money, AL:Mil. June 24, 1977
	Tony Phillips, AL:Oak. July 6, 1986
	Harold Reynolds, AL:Sea. Aug. 27, 1986
	Extra-Inning Game:
15	Lave Cross, NL:Phil. Aug. 5, 1897 (12 inn)
	Since 1900:
13	Morrie Rath, NL:Cin. Aug. 26, 1919 (15 inn)
	Bobby Avila, AL:Clev. July 1, 1952 (19 inn)
	Willie Randolph, AL:NY Aug. 25, 1976 (19 inn)

Fewest Assists, Game (Most Innings)
0	Gordon Slade, NL:Cin. July 1(1g), 1934 (18 inn)
	Delino DeShields, NL:LA Aug. 3, 1996 (18 inn)
	Jerry Browne, AL:Clev. Sept. 21, 1989 (17 inn)

Most Assists, Inning
3	By many players

ERRORS

Most Seasons Leading League (Most)
5	Fred Pfeffer, NL:Chi. 1884-88
	Since 1900:
4	Larry Doyle, NL:NY 1908, 10,17,19
	Tito Fuentes,NL:SF 1971-72; SD 76; AL:Det. 77
	Billy Herman, NL:Chi. 1932-33,37,39
	Glenn Beckert, NL:Chi. 1966-67,69-70
	Bill Wambsganss, AL:Clev. 1917,19-20; Bos. 24
	Joe Gordon, AL:NY 1938,41-43
	Harold Reynolds, AL:Sea. 1987-90

Most Errors, Lifetime
828   Fred Pfeffer, NL:Troy 1882; Chi. 83-89,91,96-97; Lou. 92-95; NY 96; PL:Chi. 1890

Most Errors, League
754   Fred Pfeffer, NL:Troy 1882; Chi. 83-89,91,96-97; Lou. 92-95; NY 96
        Since 1900:
443   Larry Doyle, NL:NY 1907-16,18-20; Chi. 16-17
435   Eddie Collins, AL:Phil. 1908-14,27-28; Chi. 15-26

Most Errors, Season
92   Yank Robinson, AA:StL. 1886
88   Pop Smith, NL:Cin. 1880
        Bob Ferguson, NL:Phil. 1883
        Since 1900:
61   Kid Gleason, AL:Det. 1901
        Hobe Ferris, AL:Bos. 1901
55   George Grantham, NL:Chi. 1923

Fewest Errors, Season
        Minimum: 800 total chances
5   Bobby Grich, AL:Balt. 1973 (945 tc) 162 g
        Jose Oquendo, NL:StL. 1989 (851 tc) 156 g
        Minimum: 150 games
3   Jose Oquendo, NL:StL. 1990 (150 g) 678 tc
5   Bobby Grich, AL:Balt. 1973 (162 g) 945 tc

Most Errors, Game
9   Andy Leonard, NL:Bos. June 14, 1876
        Since 1900:
5   Piano Legs Hickman, AL:Wash. Sept. 29, 1905
        Nap Lajoie, AL:Phil. Apr. 22, 1915
4   By many NL players; Last:
        Casey Wise, NL:Chi. May 3, 1957

Fewest Errors, Game (Most Innings)
0   Felix Millan, NL:NY Sept. 11, 1974 (25 inn)
        Ted Sizemore, NL:StL. Sept. 11, 1974 (25 inn)
        Julio Cruz, AL:Chi. May 8, 1984 (25 inn)

Most Errors, Inning
3   Bid McPhee, NL:Cin. Sept. 23(1g), 1894 (6th)
        Claude Ritchey, NL:Pitt. Sept. 22, 1900 (6th)
        Bama Rowell, NL:Bos. Sept. 25, 1941 (3rd)
        Eddie Stanky, NL:Chi. June 20(1g), 1943 (8th)
        George Hausmann, NL:NY Aug. 13(2g), 1944 (4th)
        Kermit Wahl, NL:Cin. Sept. 18(1g), 1945 (11th)
        Davey Lopes, NL:LA June 2, 1973 (1st)
        Ted Sizemore, NL:StL. Apr. 17, 1975 (6th)
        Del Pratt, AL:StL. Sept. 1(2g), 1914 (4th)
        Bill Wambsganss AL:Clev. May 15, 1923 (8th)
        Bobby Doerr, AL:Bos. May 11, 1949 (2nd)
        Tim Cullen, AL:Wash. Aug. 30, 1969 (8th)

Most Errorless Games, Consecutive
123   Ryne Sandberg, NL:Chi. June 21, 1989-May 17, 1990
113   Denny Hocking, AL:Minn. Sept. 16, 1993-Sept. 13, 1999

Most Errorless Games. Consecutive, Season
90   Ryne Sandberg, NL:Chi. June 21-Oct. 1, 1989
86   Rich Dauer, AL:Balt. Apr. 10-Sept. 29, 1978

Most Errorless Chances Accepted, Consecutive, League
584   Ryne Sandberg, NL:Chi. June 20, 1989-May 18, 1990
506   Damion Easley, AL:Det. Aug. 20, 1999-July 21, 2000

Most Errorless Chances Accepted, Consecutive, Season
479   Manny Trillo, NL:Phil. Apr. 7-July 31, 1982
425   Rich Dauer, AL:Balt. Apr. 10-Sept. 30, 1978

DOUBLE PLAYS

Most Seasons Leading League
8   Bill Mazeroski, NL:Pitt. 1960-67
5   Nap Lajoie, AL:Clev. 1903,06-09
        Eddie Collins, AL:Phil. 1909-10,12; Chi. 16,19
        Bucky Harris, AL:Wash. 1921-25
        Bobby Doerr, AL:Bos. 1938,40,43,46-47
        Nellie Fox, AL:Chi. 1954,56-58,60
        Harold Reynolds, AL:Sea. 1986-88, 91; Balt. 93

Most Double Plays, Lifetime
1706   Bill Mazeroski, NL:Pitt. 1956-72
1568   Nellie Fox, AL:Phil. 1947-49; Chi. 50-63

Most Double Plays, Season
161   Bill Mazeroski, NL:Pitt. 1966
150   Jerry Priddy, AL:Det. 1950

Most Double Plays, Game
6   Bobby Knoop, AL:Cal. May 1(1g), 1966
         Joe Gordon, AL:Clev. Aug. 31(1g), 1949 (14 inn)
         Felix Millan, NL:Atl. Aug. 5, 1971 (17 inn)
         Bill Doran, NL:Hou. May 8, 1988

Most Double Plays, Unassisted, Game
2   Davy Force, NL:Buff. Sept. 15, 1881
         Claude Ritchey, NL:Lou. July 9(1g), 1899
         Mike Edwards, AL:Oak. Aug. 10, 1978
         Luis Alicea, AL:Ana. Aug. 8, 1997

Unassisted Triple Play
1   Mickey Morandini, NL:Phil. (Pitt.) Sept. 20, 1992 (6th)
         Randy Velarde, AL:Oak. (NY) May 29, 2000 (6th)

THIRD BASE

Most Seasons, Lifetime
23   Brooks Robinson, AL:Balt. 1955-77

Most Seasons, League
23   Brooks Robinson, AL:Balt. 1955-77
18   Mike Schmidt, NL:Phil. 1972-89

PERCENTAGE

Most Seasons Leading League
11   Brooks Robinson, AL:Balt. 1960-64,66-69,72,75
6   Ken Reitz, NL:StL. 1973-74,77-78,80; Chi. 81

Most Seasons, Consecutive, Leading League
6   Willie Kamm, AL:Chi. 1924-29
4   Willie Jones, NL:Phil. 1953-56

Highest Percentage, Lifetime
.9713   Brooks Robinson, AL:Balt. 1955-77
.9696   Ken Reitz, NL:StL. 1972-75,77-80; SF 76; Chi. 81; Pitt. 82

Highest Percentage, Season
.9909   Steve Buechele, AL:Tex. 1991
.9832   Gary Gaetti, NL:StL-Chi. 1998

Lowest Percentage, Season, Since 1900
.836   Piano Legs Hickman, NL:NY 1900
.860   Hunter Hill, AL:Wash. 1904

GAMES

Most Seasons Leading League
8   Brooks Robinson, AL:Balt. 1960-64,66,68,70
7   Ron Santo, NL:Chi. 1961,63,65-69

Most Games Lifetime
2870   Brooks Robinson, AL:Balt. 1955-77

Most Games, League
2870   Brooks Robinson, AL:Balt. 1955-77
2212   Mike Schmidt, NL:Phil. 1972-89

Most Games, Consecutive
576   Eddie Yost, AL:Wash. July 3, 1951-May 11, 1955
364   Ron Santo, NL:Chi. Apr. 19, 1964-May 31, 1966

Most Games, Season
164   Ron Santo, NL:Chi. 1965
163   Brooks Robinson, AL:Balt. 1961,64

CHANCES ACCEPTED

Most Seasons Leading League
9	Ron Santo, NL:Chi. 1961-69
8	Frank Baker. AL:Phil. 1909-10,12-14; NY 17-19
	Brooks Robinson, AL:Balt. 1960,63-64,66-69,74

Most Chances Accepted, Lifetime
8902	Brooks Robinson, AL:Balt. 1955-77
6636	Mike Schmidt, NL:Phil. 1972-89

Most Chances Accepted, Season
603	Harlond Clift, AL:StL. 1937
601	Jimmy Collins, NL:Bos. 1899

Most Chances Accepted, Game
13	Willie Kuehne, NL:Pitt. May 24, 1889
	Jerry Denny, NL:NY May 29, 1890
	Bill Shindle, NL:Balt. Sept. 28, 1893
	Bill Joyce, NL:Wash. May 26, 1894
	Art Devlin, NL:NY May 23(1g), 1908
	Tony Cuccinello, NL:Brk. July 12(1g), 1934
	Roy Hughes, NL:Chi. Aug. 29(2g), 1944
	Wid Conroy, AL:Wash. Sept. 25, 1911
	Extra-Inning Game:
16	Jerry Denny, NL:Prov. Aug. 17, 1882 (18 inn)
	Since 1900:
14	Jimmy Collins, AL:Bos. June 21, 1902 (15 inn)
	Ben Dyer, AL:Det. July 16, 1919 (14 inn)
	Don Hoak, NL:Cin. May 4(2g), 1958 (14 inn)

Fewest Chances Accepted, Game (Most Innings)
0	Harry Steinfeldt, NL:Chi. Aug. 22, 1908 (15 inn)
	Heinie Groh, NL:Cin. Aug. 26(2g), 1919 (15 inn)
	Tony Boeckel, NL:Bos. June 16; Sept. 12(1g), 1921 (15 inn)
	Dean Palmer, AL:KC Sept. 24, 1997 (15 inn)

PUTOUTS

Most Seasons Leading League
8	Eddie Yost, AL:Wash. 1948,50-54,56; Det. 59
7	Pie Traynor, NL:Pitt. 1923,25-27,31,33-34
	Willie Jones, NL:Phil. 1949-50,52-56
	Ron Santo, NL:Chi. 1962-67,69
	Tim Wallach, NL:Mtl. 1982-85, 87-88; LA 94

Most Putouts, Lifetime
2697	Brooks Robinson, AL:Balt. 1955-77
2288	Pie Traynor, NL:Pitt. 1921-35,37

Most Putouts, Season
252	Jimmy Collins, NL:Bos. 1900
243	Willie Kamm, AL:Chi. 1928

Most Putouts, Game
10	Willie Kuehne, NL:Pitt. May 24, 1889
	Since 1900:
9	Pat Dillard, NL:StL. June 18, 1900
7	Bill Bradley, AL:Clev. Sept. 21(1g), 1901; May 13, 1909
	Harry Riconda, AL:Phil. July 5(2g), 1924
	Ossie Bluege, AL:Wash. June 18, 1927
	Ray Boone, AL:Det. Apr. 24, 1954

Fewest Putouts, Game (Most Innings)
0	Ryne Sandberg, NL:Chi. Aug. 17, 1982 (21 inn)
	Vern Stephens, AL:Bos. July 13, 1951 (19 inn)
	Don Wert, AL:Det. Aug. 23(2g), 1968 (19 inn)
	Jim Gantner, AL:Mil. May 1, 1991 (19 inn)

ASSISTS

Most Seasons Leading League
8	Brooks Robinson, AL:Balt. 1960,63-64,66-69,74
7	Ron Santo, NL:Chi. 1962-68
	Mike Schmidt, NL:Phil. 1974,76-77,80-83

Most Assists, Lifetime
6205	Brooks Robinson, AL:Balt. 1955-77
5045	Mike Schmidt, NL:Phil. 1972-89

Most Assists, Season
412	Graig Nettles, AL:Clev. 1971
404	Mike Schmidt, NL:Phil. 1974

Most Assists, Game
11	Deacon White, NL:Buff. May 16, 1884
	Jerry Denny, NL:NY May 29, 1890
	Damon Phillips, NL:Bos. Aug. 29, 1944
	Chris Sabo, NL:Cin. Apr. 7, 1988
	Kevin Young, NL:Pitt. June 25, 1995
	Frank Baker, AL:NY May 24, 1910 (19 inn)
	Ken McMullen, AL:Wash. Sept. 26(1g), 1966
	Mike Ferraro, AL:NY Sept. 14, 1968
	Doug DeCinces, AL:Cal. May 7, 1983 (12 inn)
	Extra-Inning Game:
12	Bobby Byrne, NL:Pitt. June 8(2g), 1910 (11 inn)

Fewest Assists, Game (Most Innings)
0	Sibby Sisti, NL:Bos July 5, 1940 (20 inn)
	Toby Harrah, AL:, Tex. Sept. 17, 1977 (17 inn)

Most Assists, Inning
3	By many players

ERRORS

Most Seasons Leading League (Most)
5	Pie Traynor, NL:Pitt. 1926,28,31-33
	Jim Tabor, AL:Bos. 1939-43

Most Errors, Lifetime
359	Jimmy Austin, AL:NY 1909-10; StL. 11-22,25-26,29

Most Errors, League, Since 1900
359	Jimmy Austin, AL:NY 1909-10; StL. 11-22,25-26,29
324	Pie Traynor, NL:Pitt. 1921-35,37

Most Errors, Season
91	Piano Legs Hickman, NL:NY 1900
64	Sammy Strang, AL:Chi. 1902

Fewest Errors, Season
	Minimum: 450 chances
5	Don Money, AL:Mil. 1974 (472 tc) 157 g
9	Robin Ventura, NL:NY 1999 (452 tc) 160 g
	Minimum: 150 games
5	Don Money, AL:Mil. 1974 (157 g) 472 tc
8	Ken Reitz, NL:StL. 1980 (150 g) 387 tc

Most Errors, Game
6	Jim Donnelly, UA:KC July 16, 1884
	Joe Moffett, AA:Tol. Aug. 2, 1884
	Joe Werrick, AA:Lou. July 28, 1888
	Billy Alvord, AA:Tol. May 22, 1890
	Joe Mulvey, NL:Phil. July 30, 1884
	Since 1900:
5	Dave Brain, NL:Bos. June 11, 1906
4	By many AL players; Last:
	Edgar Martinez, AL:Sea. May 6, 1990

Fewest Errors, Game (Most Innings)
0	Tony Boeckel, NL:Bos. May 1, 1920 (26 inn)
	Jimmy Johnston, NL:Brk. May 1, 1920 (26 inn)
	Vance Law, AL:Chi. May 8, 1984 (25 inn)

Most Errors, Inning
4   Lew Whistler, NL:NY June 19, 1891 (4th)
     Bob Brenly, NL:SF Sept. 14, 1986 (4th)
     Jimmy Burke, AL:Mil. May 27, 1901 (4th)

Most Errorless Games, Consecutive
99   John Wehner, NL:Pitt.-Fla.-Pitt. Aug. 2, 1992-Sept. 29, 2000
88   Don Money, AL:Mil. Sept. 28(2g), 1973-July 16, 1974

Most Errorless Games, Consecutive, Season
86   Don Money, AL:Mil. Apr. 5-July 16, 1974
85   Jeff Cirillo, NL:Col. June 20-Oct. 7, 2001

Most Errorless Chances Accepted, Consecutive
261 Don Money, AL:Mil. Sept. 28(1g), 1973-July 16, 1974

Most Errorless Chances Accepted, Consecutive, Season
257 Don Money, AL:Mil. Apr. 5-July 16, 1974
228 Jeff Cirillo, NL:Col. June 20-Oct. 7, 2001

DOUBLE PLAYS

Most Seasons Leading League
6   Heinie Groh, NL:Cin. 1915-16;18-20; NY 22
     Ron Santo, NL:Chi. 1961,64,66-68,71
     Mike Schmidt. NL:Phil. 1978-80,82-83,87
5   Ken Keltner, AL:Clev. 1939,41-42,44,47
     Frank Malzone, AL:Bos. 1957-61

Most Seasons, Consecutive, Leading League
5   Frank Malzone, AL:Bos. 1957-61
3   Ken Boyer, NL:StL. 1958-60
     Ron Santo, NL:Chi. 1966-68
     Mike Schmidt, NL:Phil. 1978-80
     Jeff Cirillo, NL:Mil. 1998-99; Col. 2000

Most Double Plays, Lifetime
618 Brooks Robinson, AL:Balt. 1955-77
450 Mike Schmidt, NL:Phil. 1972-89

Most Double Plays, Season
54   Graig Nettles, AL:Clev. 1971
45   Darrell Evans, NL:Atl. 1974
     Jeff Cirillo, NL:Mil. 1998

Most Double Plays, Game
4   Pie Traynor, NL:Pitt. July 9(1g), 1925
     Johnny Vergez, NL:Phil. Aug. 15, 1935
     Denny Walling, NL:Hou. May 8, 1988
     Edgardo Alfonzo, NL:NY May 14, 1997
     Shane Andrews, NL:Chi. Sept. 23, 2000
     Andy Carey, AL:NY July 31(2g), 1955
     Felix Torres, AL:LA Aug. 23, 1963
     Ken McMullen, AL:Wash. Aug. 13, 1965
     Jack Howell, AL:Cal. May 17, 1989
     Scott Brosius, AL:NY July 6, 2000

Most Double Plays, Unassisted, Season
4   Joe Dugan, AL:NY 1924
3   Harry Wolverton, NL:Phil. 1902
     Heinie Groh, NL:Cin. 1915

Most Double Plays, Unassisted, Game
1   By many players

SHORTSTOP

Most Seasons, Lifetime
20   Bobby Wallace, NL:StL. 1899-1901,17-18; AL:StL. 1903-16
                Bill Dahlen, NL:Chi. 1891-98; Brk. 1899-1903,11; NY 04-07; Bos. 08-09
                Luke Appling, AL:Chi. 1930-43,45-50

Most Seasons, League
20   Bill Dahlen, NL:Chi. 1891-98; Brk. 1899-1903,11; NY 04-07; Bos. 08-09
                Luke Appling, AL:Chi. 1930-43,45-50
                N.L. Since 1900:
19   Rabbit Maranville, NL:Bos. 1912-20,29-31; Pitt. 21-23; Chi. 25; Brk. 26; StL. 27-28
                Chris Speier NL:SF 1971-77,87-89; Mtl. 77-84; StL. 84; Chi. 85-86
                Dave Concepcion NL:Cin. 1970-88
                Ozzie Smith, NL:SD 1978-81, StL. 82-96

PERCENTAGE

Most Seasons Leading League
8   Everett Scott, AL:Bos. 1916-21; NY 22-23
               Lou Boudreau, AL:Clev. 1940-44,46-48
               Luis Aparicio, AL:Chi. 1959-62; Balt. 63-66
               Ozzie Smith, NL:SD 1981; StL. 82,84-87,91,94

Most Seasons, Consecutive, Leading League
8   Everett Scott, AL:Bos. 1916-21; NY 22-23
               Luis Aparicio, AL:Chi. 1959-62; Balt. 63-66
5   Hughie Jennings, NL:Balt. 1894-98
               NL Since 1900:
4   Eddie Miller, NL:Bos. 1940-42; Cin. 43
               Ozzie Smith, NL:StL. 1984-87

Highest Percentage, Lifetime
.9830   Omar Vizquel, AL:Sea. 1989-93; Clev. 94-2001
.9796   Larry Bowa, NL:Phil. 1970-81; Chi. 82-85; NY 85

Highest Percentage, Season
.9955   Cal Ripken, AL:Balt. 1990
.9938   Rey Ordonez, NL:NY 1999

Lowest Percentage, Season, Since 1900
.861   Bill Keister, AL:Balt. 1901
.891   Otto Kruger, NL:StL. 1902

GAMES

Most Seasons Leading League
12   Cal Ripken, AL:Balt. 1983-84,87-96
6   Mickey Doolan, NL:Phil. 1906,09-13
               Arky Vaughan, NL:Pitt. 1933-34,36,38-40
               Roy McMillan, NL:Cin. 1952-54,56-57; Mil. 61

Most Games, Lifetime
2581   Luis Aparicio, AL:Chi. 1956-62,68-70; Balt. 63-67; Bos. 71-73
2511   Ozzie Smith, NL:SD 1978-81; StL. 82-96

Most Games, Consecutive
2216   Cal Ripken, AL:Balt. July 1, 1982-July 14, 1996
584   Roy McMillan, NL:Cin, Sept. 16, 1951-Aug. 6, 1955

Most Games, Season
165   Maury Wills, NL:LA 1962
163   Tony Fernandez, AL:Tor. 1986

CHANCES ACCEPTED

Most Seasons Leading League
8   Ozzie Smith, NL:SD 1978,80-81; StL. 83,85,87-89
7   Luis Aparicio, AL:Chi. 1956-61,68

Most Chances Accepted, Lifetime
12,624   Ozzie Smith, NL:SD 1978-81; StL. 82-96
12,564   Luis Aparicio, AL:Chi. 1956-62,68-70; Balt. 63-67; Bos. 71-73

Most Chances Accepted, Season
984   Dave Bancroft, NL:NY 1922
969   Donie Bush, AL:Det. 1914

Most Chances Accepted, Game

19	Danny Richardson, NL:Wash. June 20(1g), 1892
	Eddie Joost, NL:Cin. May 7, 1941
17	Bobby Wallace, AL:StL. June 10, 1902
	Extra-Inning Game:
21	Eddie Miller, NL:Bos. June 27, 1939 (23 inn)
18	Fred Parent, AL:Bos. July 9, 1902 (17 inn)
	Chico Carrasquel, AL:Chi. July 13, 1951 (19 inn)
	Skeeter Webb, AL:Det. July 21, 1945 (24 inn)
	Pete Runnels, AL:Wash. June 3, 1952 (17 inn)
	Ron Hansen, AL:Chi. Aug. 29(1g), 1965 (14 inn)

Fewest Chances Accepted, Game (Most Innings)

0	Irv Ray, NL:Bos. Aug. 15, 1888 (12 inn)
	Eddie Feinberg, NL:Phil. May 19, 1939 (12 inn)
	Billy Jurges, NL:NY Sept. 22, 1942 (12 inn)
	John Gochnaur, AL:Clev. July 14, 1903 (12 inn)
	Billy Rogell, AL:Det. June 16, 1937 (12 inn)
	Manuel Lee, AL:Tex. Apr. 29, 1994 (12 inn)

PUTOUTS

Most Seasons Leading League

6	Rabbit Maranville, NL:Bos. 1914-17,19; Pitt. 23
	Cal Ripken, AL:Balt. 1984-85,88-89,91-92

Most Putouts, Lifetime

5133	Rabbit Maranville, NL:Bos. 1912-20,29-31; Pitt. 21-23; Chi. 25; Brk. 26; StL. 27-28
4548	Luis Aparicio, AL:Chi. 1956-62,68-70; Balt. 63-67; Bos. 71-73

Most Putouts, Season

425	Hughie Jennings, NL:Balt. 1895
	Donie Bush. AL:Det. 1914
	NL Since 1900:
407	Rabbit Maranville, NL:Bos. 1914

Most Putouts, Game

11	Shorty Fuller, NL:NY Aug. 20, 1895
	Hod Ford, NL:Cin. Sept. 18, 1929
	John Cassidy, AL:Wash. Aug. 30(1g), 1904
	Extra-Inning Game:
14	Monte Cross, NL:Phil. July 7, 1899 (11 inn)

Fewest Putouts, Game (Most Innings)

0	Jose Offerman, NL:LA July 7, 1993 (20 inn)
	Deivi Cruz, AL:Det. June 5, 2001 (18 inn)

Most Putouts, Inning

3	By many players

ASSISTS

Most Seasons Leading League

8	Ozzie Smith, NL:SD 1979-81; StL. 82,85,87-89
7	Luke Appling, AL:Chi. 1933,35,37,39,41,43,46
	Luis Aparicio, AL:Chi. 1956-61,68
	Cal Ripken, AL:Balt. 1983-84,86-87,89,91,93

Most Assists, Lifetime

8375	Ozzie Smith, NL:SD 1978-81; StL. 82-96
8016	Luis Aparicio, AL:Chi. 1956-62,68-70; Balt. 63-67; Bos. 71-73

Most Assists, Season

621	Ozzie Smith, NL:SD 1980
583	Cal Ripken, AL:Balt. 1984

Most Assists, Game

14	Herman Long, NL:Bos. May 6, 1892 (14 inn)
	Tommy Corcoran, NL:Cin. Aug. 7, 1903
	Bud Harrelson, NL:NY May 24, 1973 (19 inn)
13	Bobby Reeves, AL:Wash. Aug. 7, 1927
	Alex Gonzalez, AL:Tor. Apr. 26, 1996
	Extra-Inning Game:
15	Rick Burleson, AL:Cal. Apr. 13, 1982 (20 inn)

Fewest Assists, Game (Most Innings)
0	Jack Coffey, NL:Bos. July 26, 1909 (17 inn)
	Tony Batista, AL:Balt. Sept. 30, 2001 (15 inn)

Most Assists, Inning
4	Craig Grebeck, AL:Chi. May 2, 1995

ERRORS

Most Seasons Leading League (Most)
6	Dick Groat, NL:Pitt. 1955-56,59,61-62; StL. 64
	Rafael Ramirez, NL:Atl. 1981-85; Hou. 89
5	Luke Appling, AL:Chi. 1933,35,37,39,46

Most Errors, League, Since 1900
689	Donie Bush, AL:Det. 1908-21; Wash. 21-23
676	Honus Wagner, NL:Pitt. 1901-17

Most Errors, Season
115	Bill Schindle, PL:Phil. 1890
106	Joe Sullivan, NL:Wash, 1893
	Since 1900:
95	John Gochnaur, AL:Clev. 1903
81	Rudy Hulswitt, NL:Phil. 1903

Fewest Errors, Season
	Minimum: 700 tc
6	Tony Fernandez, AL:Tor. 1989 (741 tc) 140 g
9	Larry Bowa, NL:Phil. 1972 (715 tc) 150 g
	Minimum: 150 games
3	Cal Ripken, AL:Balt. 1990 (161 g) 680 tc
4	Rey Ordonez, NL:NY 1999 (154 g) 640 tc

Most Errors, Game
7	Jimmy Hallinan, NL:NY July 29, 1876
	Germany Smith, AA:Brk. June 17, 1885
	Since 1900:
5	Charlie Babb, NL:NY Aug. 24(1g), 1903
	Charlie Babb, NL:Brk. June 20, 1904
	Phil Lewis, NL:Brk. July 20, 1905
	Donie Bush, AL:Det. Aug. 25(1g), 1911
	Extra-Inning Game:
6	Bill O'Neill, AL:Bos. May 21, 1904 (13 inn)

Fewest Errors, Game (Most Innings)
0	Rabbit Maranville, NL:Bos. May 1, 1920 (26 inn)
	Robin Yount, AL:Mil. May 8, 1984 (25 inn)

Most Errors, Inning
4	Shorty Fuller, NL:Wash. Aug. 17, 1888 (2nd)
	Len Merullo, NL:Chi. Sept. 13(2g), 1942 (2nd)
	Ray Chapman, AL:Clev. June 20, 1914 (5th)

Most Errorless Games, Consecutive
101	Rey Ordonez, NL:NY June 14, 1999-Mar. 29, 2000
95	Cal Ripken, AL:Balt. Apr. 14-July 27, 1990
	Omar Vizquel, AL:Clev. Sept. 26, 1999-July 21, 2000

Most Errorless Games, Consecutive, Season
100	Rey Ordonez, NL:NY June 14-Oct. 4, 1999
95	Cal Ripken, AL:Balt. Apr. 14-July 27, 1990

Most Errorless Chances Accepted, Consecutive
428	Cal Ripken, AL:Balt. Apr. 14-July 28(1g), 1990
419	Rey Ordonez, NL:NY June 13, 1999-Mar. 29, 2000

Most Errorless Chances Accepted, Consecutive, Season
428	Cal Ripken, AL:Balt. Apr. 14-July 28(1g), 1990
412	Rey Ordonez, NL:NY June 13-Oct. 4, 1999

DOUBLE PLAYS

Most Seasons Leading League
8	Cal Ripken, AL:Balt. 1983-85,89,91-92,94-95
5	Mickey Doolan, NL:Phil. 1907,09-11,13
	Dick Groat, NL:Pitt. 1958-59,61-62; StL. 64
	Ozzie Smith, NL:SD 1980; StL. 84, 86-87,91

Most Double Plays, League
1590	Ozzie Smith, NL:SD 1978-81; StL 82-96
1565	Cal Ripken, AL:Balt. 1981-96

Most Double Plays, Season
147	Rick Burleson, AL:Bos. 1980
137	Bobby Wine, NL:Mtl. 1970

Most Double Plays, Game
5	By many players; Last:
	Alex Rodriguez, AL:Tex. May 22, 2001
	Jose Vizcaino, NL:LA May 28, 1998
	Extra-Inning Game:
6	Bert Campaneris, AL:Oak. Sept. 13(1g), 1970 (11 inn)
	Ozzie Smith, NL:SD Aug. 25, 1979 (19 inn)
	Rafael Ramirez, NL:Atl. June 27, 1982 (14 inn)

Most Double Plays, Unassisted, Game
2	Lee Tannehill, AL:Chi. Aug. 4(1g), 1911

TRIPLE PLAYS

Unassisted Triple Play
1	Neal Ball, AL:Clev. (Bos.) July 19, 1909 (2nd)
	Ron Hansen, AL:Wash. (Clev.) July 30, 1968 (1st)
	John Valentin, AL:Bos. (Sea.) July 8, 1994 (6th)
	Ernie Padgett, NL:Bos. (Phil.) Oct. 6, 1923 (4th)
	Glenn Wright, NL:Pitt. (StL.) May 7, 1925 (9th)
	Jimmy Cooney, NL:Chi. (Pitt.) May 30, 1927 (4th)

OUTFIELD

Most Seasons, Lifetime
24	Ty Cobb, AL:Det. 1905-26; Phil. 27-28

Most Seasons, League
24	Ty Cobb, AL:Det. 1905-26; Phil. 27-28
22	Willie Mays, NL:NY/SF 1951-52,54-72; NY 72-73

PERCENTAGE

Most Seasons Leading League
5	Amos Strunk, AL:Phil. 1912,14,17; Bos. 18; Phil.-Chi. 20
4	Joe Hornung, NL:Bos. 1881-83, 87
	NL Since 1900:
3	Stan Musial, NL:StL. 1949,54,61
	Tony Gonzalez, NL:Phil. 1962,64,67

Most Seasons, Consecutive, Leading League
3	Joe Hornung, NL:Bos. 1881-83
	Gene Woodling, AL:NY 1951-53
	NL Since 1900:
2	By many players

Highest Percentage, Lifetime
.9949	Darryl Hamilton, AL:Mil. 1988-95; Tex. 96; NL:SF 97-98; Col. 98-99; NY 99-2001

Highest Percentage, League
.9932	Terry Puhl, NL:Hou. 1977-90
.9909	Amos Otis, AL:KC 1970-83

Highest Percentage, Season (Most Chances)
1.000	Curt Flood, NL:StL. 1966 (396 tc)
	Darryl Hamilton, AL:Tex. 1996 (389 tc)

Lowest Percentage, Season
.843	John Manning, NL:Phil. 1884
	Since 1900:
.872	Bill O'Neill, AL:Wash. 1904
.900	Mike Donlin, NL:Cin. 1903

GAMES

Most Seasons Leading League
6   George Burns, NL:NY 1914,16,19-20; Cin. 22-23
     Billy Williams, NL:Chi. 1964-68,70
     Dale Murphy, NL:Atl. 1982-85,87-88
5   Rocky Colavito, AL:Clev. 1959,65; Det. 61-63

Most Games, Lifetime
2938   Ty Cobb, AL:Det. 1905-26; Phil. 27-28
2843   Willie Mays, NL:NY/SF 1951-52,54-72; NY 72-73

Most Games, Consecutive
897   Billy Williams, NL:Chi.Sept. 22, 1963-June 13, 1969
511   Clyde Milan, AL:Wash. Aug. 12, 1910-Oct. 3, 1913

Most Games, Season
164   Billy Williams, NL:Chi. 1965
163   Leon Wagner, AL:Clev. 1964

CHANCES ACCEPTED

Most Seasons Leading League
9   Max Carey, NL:Pitt. 1912-13,16-18,21-24
     Richie Ashburn, NL:Phil. 1949-54,56-58
8   Tris Speaker, AL:Bos. 1909-10,12-15; Clev. 18-19

Most Chances Accepted, Lifetime
7290   Willie Mays, NL:NY/SF 1951-52,54-72; NY 72-73
7244   Tris Speaker, AL:Bos. 1907-15; Clev. 16-26; Wash. 27; Phil. 28

Most Chances Accepted, Season
557   Taylor Douthit, NL:StL. 1928
524   Chet Lemon, AL:Chi. 1977

Most Chances Accepted, Game
13   Earl Clark, NL:Bos. May 10, 1929
     Rolando Roomes, NL:Cin. July 28, 1989 (17 inn)
12   by many AL players

Most Chances Accepted, Left Field, Game
11   Joseph Hornung, NL:Bos. Sept. 23, 1881
     Dick Harley, NL:StL. June 30, 1898
     Topsy Hartsel, NL:Chi. Sept. 10, 1901
     Phil Clark, NL:SD May 1, 1993
     Paul Lehner, AL:Phil. June 25(2g), 1950
     Willie Horton, AL:Det. July 18, 1969
     Extra-Inning Game:
12   Tom McBride, AL:Wash. July 2, 1948 (12 inn)
     Rickey Henderson, AL:NY Sept. 11, 1988 (18 inn)
     Darin Erstad, AL:Ana. July 24, 2000 (12 inn)

Most Chances Accepted, Center Field, Game
13   Earl Clark, NL:Bos. May 10, 1929
12   Harry Bay, AL:Clev. July 19, 1904 (12 inn)
     Happy Felsch, AL:Chi. June 23, 1919
     Johnny Mostil, AL:Chi. May 22, 1928
     Lyman Bostock, AL:Minn. May 25(2g), 1977
     Ruppert Jones, AL:Sea. May 16, 1978 (16 inn)
     Rick Manning, AL:Mil. July 11, 1983 (15 inn)
     Gary Pettis, AL:Cal. June 4, 1985 (15 inn)
     Oddibe McDowell, AL:Tex. July 20, 1985 (15 inn)
     Claudell Washington, AL:NY May 30, 1988 (14 inn)

Most Chances Accepted, Right Field, Game

12	Tony Armas, AL:Oak. June 12, 1982
10	Greasy Neale, NL:Cin. July 13, 1920
	Casey Stengel, NL:Phil. July 30, 1920
	Bill Nicholson, NL:Chi. Sept. 17, 1945
	Bake McBride, NL:Phil. Sept. 8, 1978
	Raul Mondesi, NL:LA Sept. 25, 1995
	Jeromy Burnitz, NL:Mil. Sept. 17, 2001
	Extra-Inning Game:
13	Rolando Roomes, NL:Cin. July 28, 1989 (17 inn)

Fewest Chances Accepted, Left Field, Game (Most Innings)

0	Dave Philley, AL:Det. Aug. 3, 1957 (17 inn)
	Joe Delahanty, NL:StL. July 19. 1908 (16 inn)
	Gary Redus, NL:Cin. June 21, 1983 (16 inn)
	Vince Coleman, NL:StL. May 11, 1988 (16 inn)

Fewest Chances Accepted, Center Field, Game (Most Innings)

0	Bill Bruton, AL:Det. June 24, 1962 (22 inn)
	Ernie Orsatti, NL:StL. July 2(1g), 1933 (18 inn)

Fewest Chances Accepted, Right Field, Game (Most Innings)

0	Cap Peterson, AL:Wash. June 12, 1967 (22 inn)
	Lance Richbourg, NL:Bos. May 14, 1927 (18 inn)
	Art Shamsky, NL. Cin. July 19, 1966 (18 inn)

Most Chances Accepted, Inning

3	By many players

PUTOUTS

Most Seasons Leading League

9	Max Carey, NL:Pitt. 1912-13,16-18,21-24
	Richie Ashburn, NL:Phil. 1949-54,56-58
7	Tris Speaker, AL:Bos. 1909-10,13-15; Clev. 18-19

Most Putouts, Lifetime

7095	Willie Mays, NL:NY/SF 1951-52,54-72; NY 72-73
6794	Tris Speaker, AL:Bos. 1907-15; Clev. 16-26; Wash. 27; Phil. 28

Most Putouts, Season

547	Taylor Douthit, NL:StL. 1928
512	Chet Lemon, AL:Chi. 1977

Most Putouts, Game

12	Earl Clark, NL:Bos. May 10, 1929
	Lyman Bostock, AL:Minn. May 25(2g), 1977
	Extra-Inning Game:
13	Rolando Roomes, NL:Cin. July 28, 1989 (17 inn)

Most Putouts, Left Field, Game

11	Dick Harley, NL:StL. June 30, 1898
	Topsy Hartsel, NL:Chi. Sept. 10, 1901
	Paul Lehner, AL:Phil. June 25(2g), 1950
	Willie Horton, AL:Det. July 18, 1969
	Extra-Inning Game:
12	Tom McBride, AL:Wash. July 2, 1948 (12 inn)
	Rickey Henderson, AL:NY Sept. 11, 1988 (18 inn)
	Darin Erstad, AL:Ana. July 24, 2000 (12 inn)

Most Putouts, Center Field, Game

12	Earl Clark, NL:Bos. May 10, 1929
	Carden Gillenwater, NL:Bos. Sept. 11, 1946 (17 inn)
	Lloyd Merriman, NL:Cin. Sept. 7, 1951 (18 inn)
	Garry Maddox, NL:Phil. June 10, 1984 (12 inn)
	Lyman Bostock, AL:Minn. May 25(2g), 1977
	Harry Bay, AL:Clev. July 19, 1904 (12 inn)
	Ruppert Jones, AL:Sea. May 16, 1978 (16 inn)
	Rick Manning, AL:Mil. July 11, 1983 (12 inn)
	Gary Pettis, AL:Cal. June 4, 1985 (15 inn)
	Oddibe McDowell, AL:Tex. July 20, 1985 (15 inn)

Most Putouts, Right Field, Game
11	Tony Armas, AL:Oak. June 12, 1982
10	Bill Nicholson, NL:Chi. Sept. 17, 1945
	Raul Mondesi, NL:LA Sept. 25, 1995

Extra-Inning Game:
13	Rolando Roomes, NL:Cin. July 28, 1989 (17 inn)

Most Putouts, Consecutive, Game
7	Ben Chapman, AL:Bos. June 25, 1937 (RF)
6	Edd Roush, NL:Cin. July 4(1g), 1919 (CF)
	Dave Martinez, NL:Mtl. Sept. 8, 1990 (CF)

ASSISTS

Most Seasons Leading League
7	Carl Yastrzemski, AL:Bos. 1962-64,66,69,71,77
5	Roberto Clemente, NL:Pitt. 1958,60-61,66-67

Most Assists, Lifetime
450	Tris Speaker, AL:Bos. 1907-15; Clev. 16-26; Wash. 27; Phil. 28
356	Jimmy Ryan, NL:Chi. 1885-89,1891-1900

NL Since 1900:
339	Max Carey, NL:Pitt. 1910-26; Brk. 26-29

Most Assists, Season, Since 1900
44	Chuck Klein, NL:Phil. 1930
35	Sam Mertes, AL:Chi. 1902
	Tris Speaker, AL:Bos. 1909,12

Most Assists, Game
4	Bill Crowley, NL:Buff. May 24 & Aug. 27, 1880
	Fred Clarke, NL:Pitt. Aug. 23, 1910
	Ducky Holmes, AL:Chi. Aug. 21, 1903
	Lee Magee, AL:NY June 28, 1916
	Happy Felsch, AL:Chi. Aug. 14, 1919
	Bob Meusel, AL:NY Sept. 5(2g), 1921
	Sam Langford, AL:Clev. May 1, 1928

Extra-Inning Game:
5	Dusty Miller, NL:Cin. May 30(2g), 1895 (11 inn)

Most Assists, Inning
2	By many players

ERRORS

Most Seasons Leading League (Most)
7	Lou Brock, NL:Chi.-StL. 1964; StL. 65-68,72-73
5	Burt Shotton, AL:StL. 1912,14-16; Wash. 18
	Reggie Jackson, AL:Oak. 1968,70,72,75; Balt 76

Most Errors, Lifetime, Since 1900
271	Ty Cobb, AL:Det. 1905-26; Phil. 27-28
235	Max Carey, NL:Pitt. 1910-26; Brk. 26-29

Most Errors, Season
52	Ed Beecher, PL:Buff. 1890
47	George Van Haltren, NL:Balt.-Pitt. 1892

Since 1900:
36	Cy Seymour, NL:Cin. 1903
31	Roy Johnson, AL:Det. 1929

Fewest Errors, Season

Most total chances
0	Curt Flood, NL:StL. 1966 (396 tc)
	Darryl Hamilton, AL:Tex. 1996 (389 tc)

Most games
0	Rocky Colavito, AL:Clev. 1965 (162 g)
	Brett Butler, NL:LA 1991 (161 g)
	Luis Gonzalez, NL:Ari. 2001 (161 g)

Most Errors, Game
5	Jack Manning, NL:Bos. May 1, 1876
	Pop Snyder, NL:Lou. July 29, 1876
	Jim O'Rourke, NL:Bos. June 21, 1877
	Charlie Bennett, NL:Mil. June 15, 1878
	Mike Dorgan, NL:NY May 24, 1884
	Mike Tiernan, NL:NY May 16, 1887
	Marty Sullivan, NL:Chi. May 18, 1887
	Jim Clinton, AA:Balt. May 3, 1884
	Fred Tenney, UA:Wash. May 29, 1884
	Since 1900:
4	Kip Selbach, AL:Balt. Aug. 19, 1902
	Fred Nicholson, NL:Bos. June 16, 1922

Fewest Errors, Game (Most Innings)
0	Walt Cruise, NL:Bos. May 1, 1920 (26 inn)
	Les Mann, NL:Bos. May 1, 1920 (26 inn)
	Ray Powell, NL:Bos. May 1, 1920 (26 inn)
	Bernie Nies, NL:Brk. May 1, 1920 (26 inn)
	Zack Wheat, NL:Brk, May 1, 1920 (26 inn)
	Harold Baines, AL:Chi. May 8, 1984 (25 inn)
	Rudy Law, AL:Chi. May 8, 1984 (25 inn)

Most Errors, Inning
3	Jim Donahue, AA:KC July 4(2g), 1889 (1st)
	George Gore, NL:Chi. Aug. 8, 1883 (1st)
	Larry Herndon, NL:SF Sept. 6, 1980 (4th)
	Kip Selbach, AL:Wash. June 23, 1904 (8th)
	Harry Bay, AL:Clev. June 29(2g), 1905 (9th)
	Harry Heilmann, AL:Det. May 22, 1914 (1st)
	Herschel Bennett, AL:StL. Apr. 24, 1925 (8th)
	Scott Lusader, AL:Det. Sept. 9, 1989 (1st)

Most Errorless Games, Consecutive, Lifetime
392	Darren Lewis, AL:Oak.-NL:SF Aug. 21, 1990-June 29, 1994

Most Errorless Games, Consecutive, League
369	Darren Lewis, NL:SF July 13, 1991-June 29, 1994
336	Rich Amaral, AL:Sea.-Balt. Apr. 30, 1995-June 14, 2000

Most Errorless Games, Consecutive, Season
162	Rocky Colavito, AL:Clev. 1965
161	Brett Butler, NL:LA 1991
	Luis Gonzalez, NL:Ari. 2001

Most Errorless Chances Accepted, Consecutive, Lifetime
938	Darren Lewis, AL:Oak. Aug. 21-Oct. 3, 1990; NL:SF July 13, 1991-June 29, 1994

Most Errorless Chances Accepted, Consecutive, League
905	Darren Lewis, NL:SF July 13, 1991-June 29, 1994
573	Ken Griffey, Jr. AL:Sea. Apr. 16, 1992-Aug. 8, 1993

Most Errorless Chances Accepted, Consecutive, Season
396	Curt Flood, NL:StL. 1966
393	Devon White, AL:Tor. 1991

DOUBLE PLAYS

Most Seasons Leading League
6	Tris Speaker, AL:Bos. 1909,12,14-15; Clev. 16,25
5	Max Carey, NL:Pitt. 1912,15-16,18,21

Most Double Plays, Lifetime
135	Tris Speaker, AL:Bos. 1907-15; Clev. 16-26; Wash. 27; Phil. 28
86	Max Carey, NL:Pitt. 1910-26; Brk. 26-29

Most Double Plays, Season
15	Happy Felsch, AL:Chi. 1919
	Jack Tobin, AL:StL. 1919
12	Mel Ott, NL:NY 1929

Most Double Plays, Game
3	Candy Nelson, AA:NY June 9, 1887
	Jack McCarthy, NL:Chi. Apr. 26, 1905
	Ira Flagstead, AL:Bos. Apr. 19(2g), 1926

Most Double Plays, Unassisted, Lifetime
6	Tris Speaker, AL:Bos. 1909,10,14; Clev. 18

Most Double Plays, Unassisted, League
6   Tris Speaker, AL:Bos. 1909,10,14 (2); Clev. 18 (2)
2   By many NL players

Most Double Plays, Unassisted, Season
2   Socks Seybold, AL:Phil. Aug. 15; Sept. 10(1g), 1907
    Tris Speaker, AL:Bos. Apr. 21; Aug. 8, 1914
    Tris Speaker, AL:Clev. Apr. 18,29, 1918
    Jose Cardenal, AL:Clev. June 8; July 16, 1968
    Adam Comorosky, NL:Pitt. May 31, June 13, 1931

Most Double Plays, Unassisted, Game.
1   By many players; Last:
    Orlando Merced, NL:Pitt. July 1, 1996
    Brian McRae, AL:KC Aug. 23, 1992

CATCHER

Most Seasons, Lifetime
25   Deacon McGuire, AA:Tol. 1884; Clev. 88; Roch. 90; Wash. 91
    NL:Det. 1885,88; Phil. 86-88; Wash, 92-99; Brk. 1899-1901
    AL:Det. 1902-03,12; NY 04-06; Bos. 07; Clev. 10

Most Seasons, League
24   Carlton Fisk, AL:Bos. 1969,71-80; Chi. 81-93
21   Bob O'Farrell, NL:Chi. 1915-25,34; StL. 25-28,33,35; NY 28-32; Cin. 34

PERCENTAGE

Most Seasons Leading League
6   Gabby Hartnett, NL:Chi. 1928,30,34-37
    Jim Sundberg, AL:Tex. 1976-79; Mil. 84; KC 86

Most Seasons, Consecutive, Leading League
4   Gabby Hartnett, NL:Chi. 1934-37
    Jim Sundberg, AL:Tex. 1976-79

Highest Percentage, Lifetime
.9934   Darrin Fletcher, NL:LA 1989-90; Phil. 90-91; Mtl. 92-97; AL:Tor. 1998-2001

Highest Percentage, League
.9932   Bill Freehan, AL:Det. 1961,63-76
.9916   Johnny Edwards, NL:Cin. 1961-67; StL. 68; Hou. 69-74

Highest Percentage, Season (Most Chances)
1.000   Charles Johnson, NL:Fla. 1997 (973 tc)
    Chris Hoiles, AL:Balt. 1997 (630 tc)

GAMES

Most Seasons Leading League
8   Yogi Berra, AL:NY 1950-57
6   Gary Carter, NL:Mtl. 1977-82

Most Games, Lifetime
2226   Carlton Fisk, AL:Bos. 1969,71-80; Chi. 81-93
2056   Gary Carter, NL:Mtl. 1974-84,92; NY 85-89; SF 90; LA 1991

Most Games, Consecutive
312   Frankie Hayes, AL:StL.-Phil.-Clev. Oct. 2, 1943-May 5, 1946
217   Ray Mueller, NL:Cin. July 31, 1943-Oct. 1, 1944

Most Seasons, 100 or more Games
15   Bob Boone, NL:Phil. 1973-74,76-80; AL:Cal. 82-88; KC 89
13   Bill Dickey, AL:NY 1929-41
    Johnny Bench, NL:Cin. 1968-80

Most Seasons, Consecutive, 100 or more Games
13   Bill Dickey, AL:NY 1929-41
    Johnny Bench, NL:Cin. 1968-80

Most Games, Season
160   Randy Hundley, NL:Chi. 1968
155   Frankie Hayes, AL:Phil. 1944
    Jim Sundberg, AL:Tex. 1975

Most Games, Consecutive, Season
155 Ray Mueller, NL:Cin. 1944
    Frankie Hayes, AL:Phil. 1944

CHANCES ACCEPTED

Most Seasons Leading League
8 Ray Schalk, AL:Chi. 1913-17,19-20,22
    Yogi Berra, AL:NY 1950-52,54-57,59
    Gary Carter, NL:Mtl. 1977-82; NY 85,88

Most Chances Accepted, Lifetime
12,988 Gary Carter, NL:Mtl. 1974-84,92; NY 85-89; SF 90; LA 91

Most Chances Accepted, League
12,988 Gary Carter, NL:Mtl. 1974-84,92; NY 85-89; SF 90; LA 91
12,417 Carlton Fisk, AL:Bos. 1969,71-80; Chi. 81-93

Most Chances Accepted, Season
1214 Johnny Edwards, NL:Hou. 1969
1123 Dan Wilson, AL:Sea. 1997

Most Chances Accepted, Game
23 George Bignell, UA:Mil. Oct. 3, 1884
22 Sandy Nava, NL:Prov. June 7, 1884
    Since 1900:
20 Jerry Grote, NL:NY Apr. 22, 1970
    Sandy Martinez, NL:Chi. May 6, 1998
    Ellie Rodriguez, AL:Cal. Aug. 12, 1974
    Rich Gedman, AL:Bos. Apr. 29, 1986
    Bill Haselman, AL:Bos. Sept. 18, 1996
    Dan Wilson, AL:Sea. Aug. 8, 1997
    Extra-Inning Game:
25 Mike Powers, AL:Phil. Sept. 1, 1906 (24 inn)
    Brad Ausmus, AL:Det. July 8, 2000 (15 inn)
24 Steve Yeager, NL:LA Aug. 8, 1972 (19 inn)

Most Chances Accepted, Inning
5 Joe Garagiola, NL:StL. June 17, 1949 (8th)
4 By many players

PUTOUTS

Most Seasons Leading League
9 Ray Schalk, AL:Chi. 1913-20,22
8 Gary Carter, NL:Mtl. 1977-82, NY 85,88

Most Putouts, Lifetime
11,785 Gary Carter, NL:Mtl. 1974-84,92; NY 85-89; SF 90; LA 91
11,369 Carlton Fisk, AL:Bos. 1969,71-80; Chi. 81-93

Most Putouts, Season
1051 Dan Wilson, AL:Sea. 1997
1045 Mike Piazza, NL:LA 1997

Most Putouts, Game
20 Jerry Grote, NL:NY Apr. 22, 1970
    Sandy Martinez, NL:Chi. May 6, 1998
    Rich Gedman, AL:Bos. Apr. 29, 1986
    Dan Wilson AL:Sea. Aug. 8, 1997
    Extra-Inning Game:
22 Bob Schmidt, NL:SF June 22(1g), 1958 (14 inn)
    Tom Haller, NL:SF May 31(2g), 1964 (23 inn)
    Steve Yeager, NL:LA Aug. 8, 1972 (19 inn)
    Brad Ausmus, AL:Det. July 8, 2000 (15 inn)
    Ben Davis, NL:SD June 19, 2001 (15 inn)

Fewest Putouts, Game (Most Innings)
0 Wally Schang, AL:Bos. Sept. 13, 1920 (14 inn)
    Gene Desautels, AL:Clev. Aug. 11(1g), 1942 (14 inn)
    Jimmie Wilson, NL:Phil. Aug. 31(1g), 1927 (13 inn)
    Hal Finney, NL:Pitt. Sept. 22, 1931 (13 inn)

ASSISTS

Most Seasons Leading League
6   Bob Boone, NL:Phil. 1973 AL:Cal. 82-84,86,88
          Gabby Hartnett, NL:Chi. 1925,27-28,30,34-35
          Del Crandall, NL:Mil. 1953-54,57-60
          Jim Sundberg, AL:Tex. 1975-78,80-81

Most Assists, Lifetime
1835   Deacon McGuire, AA:Tol. 1884; Clev. 88; Roch. 90; Wash. 91
          NL:Det. 85,88; Phil. 86-88; Wash. 92-99; Brk. 1899-1901
          AL:Det. 02-03,12; NY 04-06; Bos. 07; Clev. 08,10

Most Assists, League
1810   Ray Schalk, AL:Chi. 1912-28
1593   Red Dooin, NL:Phil. 1902-14; Cin. 15; NY 15-16

Most Assists, Season
214   Pat Moran, NL:Bos. 1903
212   Oscar Stanage, AL:Det. 1911

Most Assists, Game
9   Mike Hines, NL:Bos. May 1, 1883
          Since 1900:
8   Wally Schang, AL:Bos. May 12, 1920
7   Ed McFarland, NL:Phil. May 7, 1901
          Fred Jacklitsch, NL:Brk. Apr. 21. 1903
          Bill Bergen, NL:Brk. Aug. 23(2g), 1909
          Jimmy Archer, NL:Pitt. May 24, 1918
          Bert Adams, NL:Phil. Aug. 21, 1919
          Benito Santiago, NL:SD May 15, 1989 (11 inn)

Fewest Assists, Game (Most Innings)
0   Bob Swift, AL:Det. July 21, 1945 (24 inn)
          Jimmie Wilson, NL:StL. Aug. 28, 1930 (20 inn)

Most Assists, Inning
3   Jocko Milligan, AA:Phil. July 26, 1887 (3rd)
          Les Nunamaker, AL:NY Aug. 3, 1914 (2nd)
          Ray Schalk, AL:Chi. Sept. 30, 1921 (8th)
          Bill Dickey, AL:NY May 13, 1929 (6th)
          Jim Sundberg, AL:Tex. Sept. 3, 1976 (5th)
          Bruce Edwards, NL:Brk. Aug. 15, 1946 (4th)
          Jim Campbell, NL:Hou. June 16(2g), 1963 (3rd)

ERRORS

Most Seasons Leading League (Most)
7   Ivey Wingo, NL:StL. 1912-13; Cin. 16-18,20-21
6   Birdie Tebbetts, AL:Det. 1939-40,42; Det.-Bos. 47; Bos. 48-49

Most Errors, Lifetime, Since 1900
234   Ivey Wingo, NL:StL. 1911-14; Cin. 15-26,29

Most Errors, League, Since 1900
234   Ivey Wingo, NL:StL. 1911-14; Cin. 15-26,29
218   Wally Schang, AL:Phil. 1913-17,30; Bos. 18-20; NY 21-25; StL. 26-29; Det. 31

Most Errors, Season
94   Nat Hicks, NL:NY 1876
          Since 1900:
41   Oscar Stanage, AL:Det. 1911
40   Red Dooin, NL:Phil. 1909

Fewest Errors, Season
          Minimum: 600 total chances
0   Charles Johnson, NL:Fla. 1997 (973 tc; 123 g)
          Chris Hoiles, AL:Balt. 1997 (630 tc; 87 g)
          Minimum: 150 games
4   Randy Hundley, NL:Chi. 1967 (152 g; 928 tc)
          Jim Sundberg, AL:Tex. 1979 (150 g; 833 tc)

Most Errors, Game

7	Jack Rowe, NL:Buff. May 16, 1883
	Dickie Lowe, NL:Det. June 26, 1884
	Billy Taylor, AA:Balt. May 29(1g), 1886
	Since 1900:
4	Gabby Street, NL:Bos. June 7, 1905
	John Peters, AL:Clev. May 16, 1918
	Lena Styles, AL:Phil. July 29, 1921
	Bill Moore, AL:Bos. Sept. 26(2g), 1927

Fewest Errors, Game (Most Innings)

0	Mike Powers, AL:Phil. Sept. 1, 1906 (24 inn)
	Buddy Rosar, AL:Phil. July 21, 1945 (24 inn)
	Bob Swift, AL:Det. July 21, 1945 (24 inn)
	Jerry Grote, NL:NY Apr. 15, 1968 (24 inn)
	Hal King, NL:Hou. Apr. 15, 1968 (24 inn)

Most Errors, Inning

4	Doggie Miller, NL:StL. May 24, 1895 (2nd)
	Since 1900:
3	Jeff Sweeney, AL:NY July 10, 1912 (1st)
	John Peters, AL:Clev. May 16, 1918 (1st)
	Andy Seminick, NL:Cin. July 16, 1952 (1st)
	Jeff Reed, NL:Mtl. July 28, 1987 (7th)

Most Errorless Games, Consecutive

172	Charles Johnson, NL:Fla. June 24, 1996-Sept. 28, 1997
159	Rick Cerone, AL:NY-Bos. July 5, 1987-May 8, 1989

Most Errorless Games, Consecutive, Season

123	Charles Johnson, NL:Fla. Apr. 1, 1997-Sept. 28, 1997
117	Buddy Rosar, AL:Phil. Apr. 16-Sept. 29(1g), 1946

Most Errorless Chances Accepted, Consecutive

1294	Charles Johnson, NL:Fla. June 23, 1996-Sept. 28, 1997
950	Yogi Berra, AL:NY July 28(2g), 1957-May 10(2g), 1959

Most Errorless Chances Accepted, Consecutive, Season

973	Charles Johnson, NL:Fla. Apr. 1, 1997-Sept. 28, 1997
668	Joe Girardi, AL:NY May 7-Sept. 29, 1996

PASSED BALLS

Most Seasons Leading League (Most)

9	Ernie Lombardi, NL:Cin. 1932,35-41; NY 45
5	Mickey Cochrane, AL:Phil. 1925-26,29,31-32
	Rick Ferrell, AL:StL. 1931; Wash. 39-40,44-46

Most Passed Balls, Season

99	Pop Snyder, NL:Bos. 1881
	Mike Hines, NL:Bos. 1883
	Since 1900:
35	Geno Petralli, AL:Tex. 1987
29	Frank Bowerman, NL:NY 1900

Fewest Passed Balls, Season (most total chances)

0	Bill Dickey, AL:NY 1931 (751 tc)
	Al Todd, NL:Pitt. 1937 (712 tc)

Most Passed Balls. Game

12	Alex Gardner, AA:Wash. May 10, 1884
10	Pat Dealey, NL:Bos. May 3, 1886
	Since 1900:
6	Rube Vickers, NL:Cin. Oct. 4, 1902
	Jerry Goff, NL:Hou. May 12, 1996
	Geno Petralli, AL:Tex. Aug. 30, 1987

Fewest Passed Balls, Game (Most Innings)

0	Carlton Fisk, AL:Chi. May 8. 1984 (25 inn)
	Jerry Grote, NL:NY Apr. 15, 1968 (24 inn)
	Hal King, NL:Hou. Apr. 15, 1968 (24 inn)

Most Passed Balls, Inning

5	Dan Sullivan, AA:StL. Aug. 9, 1885 (3rd)
4	Ray Katt, NL:NY Sept. 10, 1954 (8th)
	Geno Petralli, AL:Tex. Aug. 22, 1987 (7th)

DOUBLE PLAYS

Most Seasons Leading League
6   Gabby Hartnett, NL:Chi. 1925,27,30-31,34-35
      Yogi Berra, AL:NY 1949-52,54,56

Most Double Plays, League
217   Ray Schalk, AL:Chi. 1912-28
163   Gabby Hartnett, NL:Chi. 1922-40; NY 41

Most Double Plays, Season
29   Frankie Hayes, AL:Phil.-Clev. 1945
23   Tom Haller, NL:LA 1968

Most Double Plays, Game
4   Chris Hoiles, AL:Balt. Apr. 9, 1998
3   Jack O'Neill, NL:Chi. Apr. 26, 1905
      Bob O'Farrell, NL:Chi. July 9(2g), 1919 (11 inn)
      Shanty Hogan, NL:NY Aug. 19, 1931
      Ebba St. Claire, NL:Bos. Aug. 9, 1951
      Ron Hodges, NL:NY Apr. 23, 1978 (12 inn)
      Eddie Taubensee, NL:Cin. Apr. 23, 1999
      Damian Miller, NL:Ari. May 25, 1999

BASE RUNNERS CAUGHT STEALING

Most Base Runners Caught Stealing, Game
8   Duke Farrell, NL:Wash. May 11, 1897
      Since 1900:
6   Bill Bergen, NL:Brk. Aug. 23(2g), 1909
      Wally Schang, AL:Phil. May 12, 1915

Most Base Runners Caught Stealing, Inning
3   Jocko Milligan, AA:Phil. July 26, 1887 (3rd)
      Les Nunamaker, AL:NY Aug. 3, 1914 (2nd)
2   By many NL players

PITCHER

Most Seasons, Lifetime
27   Nolan Ryan, NL:NY 1966,68-71; Hou. 80-88; AL:Cal. 1972-79; Tex. 89-93

Most Seasons, Consecutive, Lifetime
26   Nolan Ryan, NL:NY 1968-71; Hou. 80-88; AL:Cal. 1972-79; Tex. 89-93

Most Seasons, League
23   Early Wynn, AL:Wash. 1939,41-44,46-48; Clev. 49-57,63; Chi. 58-62
22   Steve Carlton, NL:StL. 1965-71; Phil. 72-86; SF 86

Most Seasons, Consecutive, League
22   Sam Jones, AL:Clev. 1914-15; Bos. 16-21; NY 22,26; StL. 27 Wash. 28-31; Chi. 32-35
      Steve Carlton, NL:StL. 1965-71; Phil. 72-86; SF 86

PERCENTAGE

Most Seasons Leading League
4   Claude Passeau, NL:Phil.-Chi. 1939; Chi. 42-43,45
      Larry Jackson, NL:StL. 1957; Chi. 64-65; Phil. 68
3   Walter Johnson, AL:Wash. 1913,17,22

Most Seasons, Consecutive, Leading League
2   By many players

Highest Percentage, Lifetime (Minimum: 300 total chances)
.9911   Brad Radke, AL:Minn. 1995-2001
.9902   Woody Fryman, NL:Pitt. 1966-77; Phil. 68-72; Mtl. 75-76, 78-83; Cin. 77; Chi. 78

Highest Percentage, Season, Most total chances:
1.000   Frank Owen, AL:Chi. 1904 (151 tc)
      Randy Jones, NL:SD 1976 (112 tc)

GAMES

Most Seasons Leading Major Leagues
5   Firpo Marberry, AL:Wash. 1924-26,28,32

Most Seasons Leading League
6   Joe McGinnity, NL:Brk. 1900; NY 1903-07
     Firpo Marberry, AL:Wash. 1924-26, 28-29, 32

Most Games, Lifetime
1131   Jesse Orosco, NL:NY 1979, 81-87; LA 88, 2001; StL. 2000;
       AL:Clev. 89-91, Mil. 92-94, Balt. 95-99

Most Games, League
1050   Kent Tekulve, NL:Pitt. 1974-85; Phil. 85-88; Cin. 89
869   Dennis Eckersley, AL:Clev. 1975-77; Bos. 78-84,98; Oak. 87-95

Most Games, Consecutive, Since 1900
13   Mike Marshall, NL:LA June 18-July 3(1g), 1974
      Dale Mohorcic, AL:Tex. Aug. 6-20, 1986

Most Games, Season
106   Mike Marshall, NL:LA 1974
90   Mike Marshall, AL:Minn. 1979

CHANCES ACCEPTED

Most Seasons Leading League
12   Greg Maddux, NL:Chi. 1989-92; Atl. 93-96,98-2001
8   Bob Lemon, AL:Clev. 1948-54,56

Most Chances Accepted, Lifetime, Since 1900
1761   Christy Mathewson, NL:NY 1900-16; Cin. 16
1606   Walter Johnson, AL:Wash. 1907-27

Most Chances Accepted, Season
262   Ed Walsh, AL:Chi. 1907
216   John Clarkson, NL:Bos. 1889
      NL Since 1900:
168   Christy Mathewson, NL:NY 1908

Most Chances Accepted, Game
13   Nick Altrock, AL:Chi. Aug. 6, 1904
      Ed Walsh, AL:Chi. Apr. 19, 1907
12   Rip Sewell, NL:Pitt. June 6(2g), 1941
      Extra-Inning Game:
15   Ed Walsh, AL:Chi. July 16, 1907 (13 inn)
13   Leon Cadore, NL:Brk. May 1, 1920 (26 inn)

Fewest Chances Accepted, Game (Most Innings)
0   Milt Watson, NL:Phil. July 17, 1918 (20 inn)
      Red Ruffing, AL:NY July 23(1g), 1932 (15 inn)

Most Chances Accepted, Inning
4   Phil Regan, NL:Chi. June 6, 1969 (6th)
      Fernando Valenzuela, NL:LA Apr. 20, 1983 (3rd)
      Hideo Nomo, NL:LA Sept. 17, 1996 (6th)
3   By many AL players

PUTOUTS

Most Seasons Leading League
7   Greg Maddux, NL:Chi. 1989-92; Atl. 93,96,98
5   Bob Lemon, AL:Clev. 1948-49,52-54

Most Putouts, Lifetime, Since 1900
422   Greg Maddux, NL:Chi. 1986-92, Atl. 93-2001
387   Jack Morris, AL:Det. 1977-90; Minn. 1991; Tor. 92-93; Clev. 94

Most Putouts, Season
52	Al Spalding, NL:Chi. 1876
	Since 1900:
49	Nick Altrock, AL:Chi. 1904
	Mike Boddicker, AL:Balt. 1984
41	Kevin Brown, NL:LA 1999

Most Putouts, Game
7	Greg Maddux, NL:Chi. Apr. 29, 1990
6	Bert Blyleven, AL:Clev. June 24, 1984
	Eric King, AL:Det. July 8, 1986
	Extra-Inning Game:
7	Dick Fowler, AL:Phil. June 9, 1949 (12 inn)

Fewest Putouts, Game (Most Innings)
0	Babe Adams, NL:Pitt. July 17, 1914 (21 inn)
	Rube Marquard, NL:NY July 17, 1914 (21 inn)
	Saul Rogovin, AL:Chi. July 12, 1951 (17 inn)

Most Putouts, Inning
3	By many players; Last:
	Mike Moore, AL:Det. July 2, 1994 (8th)
	Darren Dreifort, NL:LA Sept. 5, 1999 (4th)

ASSISTS

Most Seasons Leading League
8	Greg Maddux, NL:Chi. 1990; Atl. 92-93,95-96,98, 2000-01
6	Bob Lemon, AL:Clev. 1948-49,51-53,56

Most Assists, Lifetime, Since 1900
1489	Christy Mathewson, NL:NY 1900-16; Cin. 16

Most Assists, League, Since 1900
1489	Christy Mathewson, NL:NY 1900-16; Cin. 16
1337	Walter Johnson, AL:Wash. 1907-27

Most Assists, Season
227	Ed Walsh, AL:Chi. 1907
168	John Clarkson, NL:Bos. 1889
	NL Since 1900:
141	Christy Mathewson, NL:NY 1908

Most Assists, Game
11	Al Orth, AL:NY Aug. 12, 1906
	Ed Walsh, AL:Chi. Apr. 19 & Aug. 12, 1907
	George McConnell, AL:NY Sept. 2(2g), 1912
	Mellie Wolfgang, AL:Chi. Aug. 29, 1914
	Rip Sewell, NL:Pitt. June 6(2g), 1941
	Extra-Inning Game:
12	Ed Walsh, AL:Chi. July 16, 1907 (13 inn)
	Nick Altrock, AL:Chi. June 7, 1908 (10 inn)
	Leon Cadore, NL:Brk. May 1, 1920 (26 inn)

Fewest Assists, Game (Most Innings)
0	Milt Watson, NL:Phil. July 17, 1918 (20 inn)
	Red Ruffing, AL:NY July 23(1g), 1932 (15 inn)

Most Assists, Inning
3	By many players

ERRORS

Most Seasons Leading League (Most)
5	Hippo Vaughn, NL:Chi. 1914-15,17,19-20
	Warren Spahn, NL:Bos. 1949-50,52; Mil. 54,64
4	Allen Sothoron, AL:StL. 1917-20
	Dizzy Trout, AL:Det. 1943-45,48
	Dean Chance, AL:LA 1963; Minn. 67-68; Det. 71
	Nolan Ryan, AL:Cal. 1975-78

Most Errors, Lifetime, Since 1900
90	Joe McGinnity, NL:Brk. 1900; NY 1902-08; AL:Balt. 1901-02
	Nolan Ryan,NL:NY 1966,68-71; Hou. 80-88; AL:Cal. 1972-79; Tex. 89-93

Most Errors, League, Since 1900
79	Rube Waddell, AL:Phil. 1902-07; StL. 08-10
75	Joe McGinnity, NL:Brk. 1900; 1902-08

Most Errors, Season
28	Jim Whitney, NL:Bos. 1881

Since 1900:
17	Doc Newton, NL:Cin.-Brk. 1901
15	Jack Chesbro, AL:NY 1904
	Rube Waddell, AL:Phil. 1905
	Ed Walsh, AL:Chi. 1912

Fewest Errors, Season (Most Chances)
0	Randy Jones, NL:SD 1976 (112 tc)
	Walter Johnson, AL:Wash. 1913 (103 tc)

Most Errors, Game
5	Ed Doheny, NL:NY Aug. 15, 1899

Since 1900:
4	Doc Newton, NL:Cin. Sept. 13(1g), 1900
	Lave Winham, NL:Pitt. Sept. 21(1g), 1903
	Buster Ross, AL:Bos. May 17, 1925

Fewest Errors, Game (Most Innings)
0	Leon Cadore, NL:Brk. May 1, 1920 (26 inn)
	Joe Oeschger, NL:Bos. May 1, 1920 (26 inn)
	Jack Coombs, AL:Phil. Sept. 1, 1906 (24 inn)
	Joe Harris, AL:Bos. Sept. 1, 1906 (24 inn)

Most Errors, Inning
3	Cy Seymour, NL:NY May 21, 1898 (6th)
	Tommy John, AL:NY July 27, 1988 (4th)
	Mike Sirotka, AL:Chi. Apr. 9, 1999 (5th)

Most Errorless Games, Consecutive, Lifetime
549	Dan Plesac, NL:Chi.-Pitt.-Ari.; AL:Tor. July 30, 1993-Sept. 30, 2001

Most Errorless Games, Consecutive, League
546	Lee Smith, NL:Chi.-StL. July 5, 1982-Sept. 22, 1992
517	Jesse Orosco, AL:Clev.-Mil.-Balt. June 28, 1990-May 10, 1999

Most Errorless Games, Consecutive, Season
89	Steve Kline, NL:StL. 2001
88	Wilbur Wood, AL:Chi. 1968

Most Errorless Chances Accepted, Consecutive
273	Claude Passeau, NL:Chi. Sept. 21, 1941-May 20, 1946
231	Rick Langford, AL:Oak. Apr. 13, 1977-Oct. 2, 1980

DOUBLE PLAYS

Most Seasons Leading League
5	Warren Spahn, NL:Mil. 1953,56,60-61,63
	Greg Maddux, NL:Chi. 1987,90-91; Atl. 94,96
4	Willis Hudlin, AL:Clev. 1929-31,34

Most Double Plays, Lifetime
83	Phil Niekro, NL:Mil./Atl. 1964-83,87; AL:NY 1984-85; Clev. 86-87; Tor. 87

Most Double Plays, League
82	Warren Spahn, NL:Bos./Mil. 1942,46-64; NY 65; SF 65
78	Bob Lemon, AL:Clev. 1941-42,46-58

Most Double Plays, Season
15	Bob Lemon, AL:Clev. 1953
12	Art Nehf, NL:NY 1920
	Curt Davis, NL:Phil. 1934
	Randy Jones, NL:SD 1976

Most Double Plays, Game
4	Milt Gaston, AL:Chi. May 17, 1932
	Hal Newhouser, AL:Det. May 19, 1948
3	By many NL players; Last:
	Larry McWiliams, NL:Pitt. June 3, 1983

Most Double Plays, Unassisted, League
2	Tex Carleton, NL:Chi. 1935; Brk. 40
	Claude Passeau, NL:Phil. 1938; Chi. 45

Most Double Plays, Unassisted, Game
1	By many players

INDIVIDUAL PITCHING RECORDS

SERVICE

Most Seasons, Lifetime
27   Nolan Ryan, NL:NY 1966,68-71; Hou. 80-88; AL:Cal. 1972-79; Tex. 89-93

Most Seasons, Consecutive, Lifetime
26   Nolan Ryan, NL:NY 1968-71; Hou. 80-88; AL:Cal. 1972-79; Tex. 89-93

Most Seasons, League
23   Early Wynn, AL:Wash. 1939,41-44,46-48; Clev. 49-57,63; Chi. 58-62
22   Steve Carlton, NL:StL. 1965-71; Phil. 72-86; SF 86

Most Seasons, Consecutive, League
22   Sam Jones, AL:Clev. 1914-15; Bos. 16-21; NY 22-26; StL. 27; Wash. 28-31; Chi. 32-35
        Steve Carlton, NL:StL. 1965-71; Phil. 72-86; SF 86

Most Leagues, Lifetime
4   Jerry Bakely, AA:1883,88,91; UA:84; NL:89; PL:90
        Cannonball Crane, UA:1884; NL:86,88-89,91-93; PL:90; AA:91
        Gus Weyhing, AA:1887-89,91; PL:1890; NL:1892-1901; AL:1901
        Frank Foreman, UA:1884; AA:85,89,91; NL:90-93,95-96; AL:1901-02

Most Leagues, Season
3   By many players

CLUBS

Most Seasons, One Club
21   Walter Johnson, AL:Wash. 1907-27
        Ted Lyons, AL:Chi. 1923-42,46
        Phil Niekro, NL:Mil./Atl. 1964-83,87

Most Seasons, Consecutive, One Club
21   Walter Johnson, AL:Wash. 1907-27
20   Warren Spahn, NL:Bos.-Mil. 1942,46-64
        Phil Niekro, NL:Mil./Atl. 1964-83

Most Clubs, Lifetime
12   Mike Morgan, AL:Oak. 1978-79; NY 82; Tor. 83; Sea. 85-87; Balt. 88; Minn. 98; Tex. 99
        NL:LA 89-91; Chi. 92-95,98; StL. 95-96; Cin. 96-97; Ari. 2000-01

Most Clubs, League
7   Gus Weyhing, NL:Phil. 1892-95; Pitt. 95; Lou. 95-96; Wash. 98-99; StL. 1900; Brk. 1900; Cin. 01
        Mike Maddux, NL:Phil. 1986-89; LA 90; SD 91-92; NY 93-94; Pitt. 95; Mtl. 98; Hou. 2000
        Kent Bottenfield, NL:Mtl. 1992-93; Col.93-94; SF 94; Chi. 96-97; StL. 98-99; Phil. 2000; Hou. 01
        Ken Sanders, AL:KC/Oak. 1964,66,68,76; Bos. 66; Mil. 70-72; Minn. 73; Clev. 73-74;Cal. 74; KC 76
        Ken Brett, AL:Bos. 1967-71; Mil. 72; NY 76; Chi. 76-77; Cal. 77-78; Minn. 79; KC 80-81
        Ed Farmer, AL:Clev. 1971-73; Det. 73; Balt. 77; Mil. 78; Tex. 79; Chi. 79-81; Oak. 83
        Greg Cadaret, AL:Oak. 1987-89; NY 89-92; KC 93; Tor. 94; Det. 94; Ana. 97-98; Tex. 98
        Mike Morgan, AL:Oak. 1978-79; NY 82; Tor. 83; Sea. 85-87; Balt. 88; Minn. 98; Tex. 99

Most Clubs, Major Leagues, Season
4   Willis Hudlin, AL:Clev.-Wash.; NL:StL.-NY 1940
        Ted Gray, AL:Chi.-Clev.-NY-Balt. 1955
        Mike Kilkenny, AL:Det.-Oak.-Clev NL:SD 1972

Most Clubs, League, Season
4   Ted Gray, AL:Chi.-Clev.-NY-Balt. 1955
3   By many NL players

GAMES

Most Seasons Leading Major Leagues
5 Firpo Marberry, AL:Wash. 1924-26,28,32

Most Seasons, Consecutive, Leading Major Leagues
3 Bill Hutchinson, NL:Chi. 1890-92
Ace Adams, NL:NY 1942-44
Steve Kline, NL:Mtl. 1999-2000; StL. 01
Firpo Marberry, AL:Wash. 1924-26

Most Seasons Leading League
6 Joe McGinnity, NL:Brk. 1900; NY 03-07
Firpo Marberry, AL:Wash. 1924-26,28-29,32

Most Seasons, Consecutive, Leading League
5 Joe McGinnity, NL:NY 1903-07
3 Ed Walsh, AL:Chi. 1910-12
Firpo Marberry, AL:Wash. 1924-26
Wilbur Wood, AL:Chi. 1968-70

Most Games, Lifetime
1131 Jesse Orosco, NL:NY 1979, 81-87; LA 88, 2001; StL. 2000;
AL:Clev. 89-91, Mil. 92-94, Balt. 95-99

Most Games, League
1050 Kent Tekulve, NL:Pitt. 1974-85; Phil. 85-88; Cin. 89
869 Dennis Eckersley, AL:Clev. 1975-77; Bos. 78-84,98; Oak. 87-95

Most Games, Season
106 Mike Marshall, NL:LA 1974 (0 starts)
90 Mike Marshall, AL:Minn. 1979 (1 start)

Most Games, Consecutive
13 Mike Marshall, NL:LA June 18-July 3(1g), 1974
Dale Mohorcic, AL:Tex. Aug. 6-20, 1986

GAMES STARTED

Most Seasons Leading Major Leagues
6 Robin Roberts, NL:Phil. 1950-55

Most Seasons, Consecutive, Leading Major Leagues
6 Robin Roberts, NL:Phil. 1950-55

Most Seasons Leading League
6 Robin Roberts, NL:Phil. 1950-55
5 Bob Feller, AL:Clev. 1940-41,46-48
Early Wynn, AL:Wash. 1943; Clev. 51,54,57; Chi. 59

Most Seasons, Consecutive, Leading League
6 Robin Roberts, NL:Phil. 1950-55
4 Wilbur Wood, AL:Chi. 1972-75
Dave Stewart, AL:Oak. 1988-91

Most Games Started, Lifetime
818 Cy Young, NL:Clev. 1890-98; StL. 1899-1900; Bos. 11; AL:Bos. 1901-08; Clev. 09-11

Most Games Started, Consecutive, Lifetime
595 Nolan Ryan, AL:Cal.-Tex.; NL:Hou. July 30, 1974-Sept. 22, 1993

Most Games Started, League
677 Steve Carlton, NL:StL. 1965-71; Phil. 72-86; SF 86
666 Walter Johnson, AL:Wash. 1907-27

Most Games Started, Consecutive, League
534 Steve Carlton, NL:StL.-Phil.-SF May 15, 1971-Aug. 5, 1986
532 Roger Clemens, AL:Bos.-Tor.-NY July 26, 1984-Oct. 5, 2001

Most Games Started, Season
74 Will White, NL:Cin. 1879
Since 1900:
51 Jack Chesbro, AL:NY 1904
48 Joe McGinnity, NL:NY 1903
No relief appearances:
49 Wilbur Wood, AL:Chi. 1972
44 Phil Niekro, NL:Atl. 1979

Most Games Started, Incomplete, Season
37	Steve Bedrosian, NL:Atl. 1985 (37 starts)
36	Stan Bahnsen, AL:Chi. 1972 (41 starts)

Most Games Started, No Complete Games, Season
37	Steve Bedrosian, NL:Atl. 1985
35	Wilson Alvarez, AL:Chi. 1996
	Sterling Hitchcock, AL:Sea. 1996
	Rick Helling, AL:Tex. 2000

Most Games Started, Opening Day, Lifetime
16	Tom Seaver, NL:NY 1968-77,83; Cin. 78-79,81; AL:Chi. 1985-86

Most Games Started, Opening Day, League
14	Walter Johnson, AL:Wash. 1910, 12-21, -23-24, 26
	Jack Morris, AL:Det. 1980-90; Minn. 91; Tor. 92-93
	Tom Seaver, NL:NY 1968-77,83; Cin. 78-79, 81
	Steve Carlton, NL:Phil. 72-75; 77-86

Most Games Started, Consecutive, Opening Day, League
14	Jack Morris, AL:Det. 1980-90; Minn. 91; Tor. 92-93
12	Robin Roberts, NL:Phil. 1950-61
	Tom Seaver, NL:NY 1968-77; Cin. 78-79

COMPLETE GAMES

Most Seasons Leading Major Leagues
7	Warren Spahn, NL:Bos. 1951; Mil. 57-60,62-63

Most Seasons, Consecutive, Leading Major Leagues
5	Robin Roberts, NL:Phil. 1952-56

Most Seasons Leading League
9	Warren Spahn, NL:Bos. 1949,51; Mil. 57-63
6	Walter Johnson, AL:Wash. 1910-11,13-16

Most Seasons, Consecutive, Leading League
7	Warren Spahn, NL:Mil. 1957-63
4	Walter Johnson, AL:Wash. 1913-16

Most Complete Games, Lifetime
751	Cy Young, NL:Clev. 1890-98; StL. 1899-1900; Bos. 11; AL:Bos. 1901-08; Clev. 09-11

Most Complete Games, League
552	Pud Galvin, NL:Buff. 1879-85; Pitt. 87-89,91-92; StL. 92
	Since 1900:
531	Walter Johnson, AL:Wash. 1907-27
437	Grover Alexander, NL:Phil. 1911-17,30; Chi. 18-26; StL. 26-29

Most Complete Games, Season
74	Will White, NL:Cin. 1879 (74 starts)
	Since 1900:
48	Jack Chesbro, AL:NY 1904 (51 starts)
45	Vic Willis, NL:Bos. 1902 (46 starts)

Most Complete Games, Consecutive, Lifetime
198	Jack Lynch, NL:Buff. 1881. NY 83-87,90

Most Complete Games, Consecutive, League
197	Jack Lynch, AA:NY 1883-87,90
187	Jack Taylor, NL:Chi. 1901-03,06; StL. 04-06
54	Cy Young, AL:Bos. 1903-04
	Earl Moore, AL:Clev. 1902-04

Most Complete Games, Consecutive, Season, Since 1900
39	Jack Taylor, NL:StL. 1904 (two relief appearances during streak)
37	Bill Dinneen, AL:Bos. 1904
23	Jack Taylor, NL:StL. 1904

SHUTOUTS

Most Seasons Leading Major Leagues
6	Cy Young, NL:Clev. 1892, 95-96; StL. 1900; AL:Bos. 03-04
	Since 1900:
4	Christy Mathewson, NL:NY 1902,05,07-08
	Grover Alexander, NL:Phil. 1911,15-16; Chi. 19
	Walter Johnson, AL:Wash. 1913-14,18,24
	Roger Clemens, AL:Bos. 1987-88,90,92

Most Seasons, Consecutive, Leading Major Leagues
3	Tommy Bond, NL:Bos. 1877-79
	Amos Rusie, NL:NY 1893-95
	Since 1900:
2	Jack Chesbro, NL:Pitt. 1901-02
	Christy Mathewson, NL:NY 1907-08
	Grover Alexander, NL:Phil. 1915-16
	Whitlow Wyatt, NL:Brk. 1940-41
	Jim Bunning, NL:Phil. 1966-67
	Cy Young, AL:Bos. 1903-04
	Walter Johnson, AL:Wash. 1913-14
	Allie Reynolds, AL:NY 1951-52
	Camilo Pascual, AL:Minn. 1961-62
	Tommy John, AL:Chi. 1966-67
	Roger Clemens, AL:Bos. 1987-88

Most Seasons Leading League
7	Grover Alexander, NL:Phil. 1911,13,15-17; Chi. 19
	Walter Johnson, AL:Wash. 1911,13-15,18-19,24

Most Seasons, Consecutive, Leading League
3	Tommy Bond, NL:Bos. 1877-79
	Amos Rusie, NL:NY 1893-95
	Grover Alexander, NL:Phil. 1915-17
	Walter Johnson, AL:Wash. 1913-15
	Roger Clemens, AL:Bos. 1990-92

Most Shutouts, Lifetime
110	Walter Johnson, AL:Wash. 1907-27
90	Grover Alexander, NL:Phil. 1911-17,30; Chi. 18-26; StL. 26-29

Most Shutouts, Season
16	George Bradley, NL:StL. 1876
	Grover Alexander, NL:Phil. 1916
13	Jack Coombs, AL:Phil. 1910

Most Seasons, 10 or more Shutouts
2	Ed Walsh, AL:Chi. 1906,08
	Grover Alexander, NL:Phil. 1915-16

Most Shutouts, Consecutive, Season
6	Don Drysdale, NL:LA May 14-18-22-26-31, June 4, 1968
5	Doc White, AL:Chi. Sept. 12-16-19-25-30, 1904

Most Shutouts, Doubleheader
2	Ed Reulbach, NL:Chi. vs Brk. Sept. 26, 1908 (5-0, 3-0)

Most Shutouts, One Month
6	Doc White, AL:Chi. Sept. 1904
	Ed Walsh, AL:Chi. Aug. 1906 & Sept. 1908
5	George Bradley, NL:StL. May 1876
	Tommy Bond, NL:Hart. June 1876
	Pud Galvin, NL:Buff. Aug. 1884
	Ben Sanders, NL:Phil Sept. 1888
	Don Drysdale, NL:LA May 1968
	Bob Gibson, NL:StL. June 1968
	Orel Hershiser, NL:LA Sept. 1988

Most Shutouts vs. One Club, League
23	Walter Johnson, AL:Wash. vs Phil. 1907-27
20	Grover Alexander, NL:Phil.-Chi.-StL. vs Cin. 1911-30

Most Shutouts vs. One Club, Season
5	Tony Mullane, AA:Cin. vs NY 1887
	Lady Baldwin, NL:Det. vs Phil. 1886
	Grover Alexander, NL:Phil. vs Cin. 1916
	Larry Jaster, NL:StL. vs LA 1966 (cons)
	Tom Hughes, AL:Wash. vs Clev. 1905

Most Clubs Shutout, Season
8	Bob Gibson, NL:StL. 1968
	Nolan Ryan, AL:Cal. 1972

Most Shutouts, Opening Game, Season
7	Walter Johnson, AL:Wash. 1910,14-15,17,19,24,26
3	Rip Sewell, NL:Pitt. 1943,47,49
	Chris Short, NL:Phil. 1965,68,70
	Rick Mahler, NL:Atl. 1982,86-87

Most Innings, Shutout Game
18   Monte Ward, NL:Prov. Aug. 17, 1882
        Carl Hubbell, NL:NY July 2(1g), 1933
        Ed Summers, AL:Det. July 19, 1909 (tie)
        Walter Johnson, AL:Wash. May 15, 1918

Most Scoreless Innings, Consecutive, Game
21   Joe Oeschger, NL:Bos. May 1, 1920
20   Joe Harris, AL:Bos. Sept. 1, 1906

Most Hits Allowed, Shutout
14   Larry Cheney, NL:Chi. Sept. 14, 1913
        Milt Gaston, AL:Wash. July 10(2g), 1928

Most Walks Allowed, Shutout
11   Lefty Gomez, AL:NY Aug. 1, 1941
9   Vinegar Bend Mizell, NL:StL. Sept. 1(1g), 1958
        A.J. Burnett, NL:Fla. May 12, 2001
        Extra-Inning Game:
10   Jim Maloney, NL:Cin. Aug. 19(1g), 1965 (10 inn)
        J.R. Richard, NL:Hou. July 6, 1976 (10 inn)

Most Scoreless Innings, Consecutive. Season
59.0   Orel Hershiser, NL:LA Aug. 30-Sept. 28, 1988
55.2   Walter Johnson, AL:Wash. Apr. 10-May 14, 1913

Most Shutouts Lost, League
65   Walter Johnson, AL:Wash. 1907-27
53   Phil Niekro, NL:Mil. 1964-65, Atl. 66-83,87

Most Shutouts Lost, Season
14   Jim Devlin, NL:Lou. 1876
        Since 1900:
11   Bugs Raymond, NL:StL. 1908
10   Walter Johnson, AL:Wash. 1909

Most Shutouts Lost, vs. One Club, Season
5   Jim Devlin, NL:Lou. (Hart.) 1876
        Walter Johnson, AL:Wash. (Chi.) 1909
        NL Since 1900:
4   Irv Young, NL:Bos. (Pitt.) 1906
        Lefty Leifield, NL:Pitt. (Chi.) 1906,10
        Tom Zachary, NL:Brk. (Pitt.) 1935
        Bob Veale, NL:Pitt. (SF) 1968

Most Shutouts Lost, One Month
5   Cherokee Fisher, NL:Cin. May 1876
        Walter Johnson, AL:Wash. July 1909
        NL Since 1900:
4   Irv Young, NL:Bos. July 1907
        George McQuillan, NL:Phil. June 1908
        Pete Schneider, NL:Cin. Aug. 1915
        Jess Petty, NL:Brk. Aug. 1927
        Freddie Fitzsimmons, NL:NY Sept. 1934
        Max Butcher, NL:Phil. Sept. 1938
        Jim McAndrew, NL:NY Aug. 1968
        Ken Reynolds, NL:Phil. July 1972

GAMES FINISHED

Most Seasons Leading Major Leagues
4   Mike Marshall, NL:Mtl. 1972-73, LA 74; AL:Minn. 79
        Dan Quisenberry, AL:KC 1980,82-83,85

Most Seasons, Consecutive, Leading Major Leagues
3   Mike Marshall, NL:Mtl. 1972-73; LA 74

Most Seasons Leading League
5   Mike Marshall, NL:Mtl. 1971-73; LA 74; AL:Minn. 79
        Firpo Marberry, AL:Wash. 1924-26,28-29
4   Ace Adams, NL:NY 1942-45
        Roy Face, NL:Pitt. 1958,60-62
        Mike Marshall, NL:Mtl. 1971-73; LA 74
        Rod Beck, NL:SF 1993-94, 97; Chi. 98

Most Seasons, Consecutive, Leading League
4	Ace Adams, NL:NY 1942-45
	Mike Marshall, NL:Mtl. 1971-73; LA 74
3	Firpo Marberry, AL:Wash. 1924-26
	Joe Page, AL:NY 1947-49
	Roberto Hernandez, AL:Chi. 1994-96

Most Games Finished, Lifetime
802	Lee Smith, NL:Chi. 1980-87; StL. 90-93; Cin. 96; Mtl. 97
	AL:Bos. 1988-90; NY 93; Balt. 94; Cal. 95-96

Most Games Finished, League
741	John Franco, NL:Cin. 1984-89, NY 90-2001
599	Sparky Lyle, AL:Bos. 1969-71; NY 72-78; Tex. 79-80, Chi. 82

Most Games Finished, Season
84	Mike Marshall, AL:Minn. 1979
83	Mike Marshall, NL:LA 1974

SAVES (Since 1969)

Most Seasons Leading Major Leagues
3	Rollie Fingers, NL:SD 1977-78; AL:Mil. 81
	Bruce Sutter, NL:Chi. 1979; StL. 82,84

Most Seasons, Consecutive, Leading Major Leagues
2	Rollie Fingers, NL:SD 1977-78

Most Seasons Leading League
5	Bruce Sutter, NL:Chi. 1979-80; StL. 81-82,84
	Dan Quisenberry, AL:KC 1980,82-85

Most Seasons, Consecutive, Leading League
4	Bruce Sutter, NL:Chi. 1979-80; StL. 81-82
	Dan Quisenberry, AL:KC 1982-85

Most Saves, Lifetime
478	Lee Smith, NL:Chi. 1980-87; StL. 90-93; Cin. 96; Mtl. 97
	AL:Bos. 1988-90; NY 93; Balt. 94; Cal. 95-96

Most Saves, League
422	John Franco, NL:Cin. 1984-89; NY 90-2001
324	Dennis Eckersley, AL:Clev. 1975-77; Bos. 78-84,98; Oak. 87-95

Most Saves, Season
57	Bobby Thigpen, AL:Chi. 1990
53	Randy Myers, NL:Chi. 1993
	Trevor Hoffman, NL:SD 1998

Most Saves, Month
15	Lee Smith, NL:StL. June 1993
	John Wetteland, AL:NY June 1996

Most Saves, Consecutive Appearances, Season
24	John Wetteland, AL:NY May 31-July 14, 1996
17	Lee Smith, NL:StL. May 24-June 28, 1993

NO-HIT GAMES (Minimum: 9 innings pitched; additional listings on pages 347-352)

Most Perfect Games, Lifetime
1	Lee Richmond, NL:Wor. June 12, 1880 (vs Clev.)
	Monte Ward, NL:Prov. June 17, 1880 (vs Buff.)
	Jim Bunning, NL:Phil. June 21, 1964 (vs NY)
	Sandy Koufax, NL:LA Sept. 9, 1965 (vs Chi.)
	Tom Browning, NL:Cin. Sept. 16, 1988 (vs LA)
	Dennis Martinez, NL:Mtl. July 28, 1991 (vs LA)
	Cy Young, AL:Bos. May 5, 1904 (vs Phil.)
	Addie Joss, AL:Clev. Oct. 2, 1908 (vs Chi.)
	Charlie Robertson, AL:Chi. Apr. 30, 1922 (vs Det.)
	Catfish Hunter, AL:Oak. May 8, 1968 (vs Minn.)
	Len Barker, AL:Clev. May 15, 1981 (vs Tor.)
	Mike Witt, AL:Cal. Sept. 30, 1984 (vs Tex.)
	Kenny Rogers, AL:Tex. July 28, 1994 (vs Cal.)
	David Wells, AL:NY May 17, 1998 (vs Minn.)
	David Cone, AL:NY July 18, 1999 (vs. Mtl.)

Most No-Hit Games, Lifetime
7	Nolan Ryan, AL:Cal. 1973,74,75; Tex. 90,91; NL:Hou. 1981

Most No-Hit Games, League
6   Nolan Ryan, AL:Cal. 1973,74,75; Tex. 90,91
4   Sandy Koufax, NL:LA 1962,63,64,65

Most No-Hit Games, Season
2   Johnny Vander Meer, NL:Cin. June 11 (Bos.); June 15 (Brk.), 1938
    Allie Reynolds, AL:NY July 12 (Clev.); Sept. 28 (Bos.), 1951
    Virgil Trucks, AL:Det May 15 (Wash.); Aug. 25 (NY), 1952
    Nolan Ryan, AL:Cal. May 15 (KC); July 15 (Det.), 1973

Most No-Hit Games, Consecutive
2   Johnny Vander Meer, NL:Cin. June 11 (Bos.)-June 15 (Brk.), 1938

Most Innings, No-Hit Game
10   Sam Kimber, AA:Brk. (Tol.) Oct. 4, 1884 (0-0)
    Hooks Wiltse, NL:NY (Phil.) July 4, 1908 (1-0)
    Fred Toney, NL:Cin. (Chi.) May 2, 1917 (1-0)
    Jim Maloney, NL:Cin. (Chi.) Aug. 19, 1965 (1-0)

ONE-HIT GAMES

Most One-Hit Games, Lifetime
12   Bob Feller, AL:Clev. 1936-41,45-56
    Nolan Ryan, NL:NY 1966,68-71; Hou. 80-88; AL:Cal. 1972-79; Tex. 89-93

Most One-Hit Games, League
12   Bob Feller, AL:Clev.v. 1936-41,45-56
7   Hoss Radbourn, NL:Prov. 1881-85; Bos. 86-89; Cin. 91
    NL Since 1900:
6   Steve Carlton, NL:StL. 1965-71; Phil. 72-86; SF 86

Most One-Hit Games, Season
4   Hugh Daily, UA:Chi. 1884
    Grover Alexander, NL:Phil. 1915
3   Addie Joss, AL:Clev. 1907
    Dave Stieb, AL:Tor. 1988

Most One-Hit Games, Consecutive, Season
2   Hugh Daily, UA:Chi. July 7-10, 1884
    Toad Ramsey, AA:Lou. July 29-31, 1886
    Charlie Buffinton, NL:Phil. Aug. 6-9, 1887
    Rube Marquard, NL:NY Aug. 28-Sept. 1, 1911
    Lon Warneke, NL:Chi. Apr. 17-22, 1934
    Mort Cooper, NL:StL. May 31-June 4, 1943
    Whitey Ford, AL NY Sept. 2-7, 1955
    Sam McDowell, AL:Clev. Apr. 25-May 1, 1966
    Dave Stieb, AL:Tor. Sept. 24-30, 1988

Most Innings, One-Hit Game
12.2   Harvey Haddix, NL:Pitt. (Mil.) May 26, 1959
10.0   Doc White, AL:Chi. (Clev.) Sept. 6, 1903
    Bobo Newsom, AL:StL. (Bos.) Sept. 18, 1934
    Bert Blyleven, AL:Tex. (Oak.) June 21, 1976

EARNED RUN AVERAGE (Since 1912 in NL; Since 1913 in AL - Prior seasons not compiled on official scores)

Most Seasons Leading Major Leagues
4   Lefty Grove, AL:Phil. 1926,29-31
    Greg Maddux, NL:Atl. 1993-95,98

Most Seasons, Consecutive, Leading Major Leagues
3   Lefty Grove, AL:Phil. 1929-31
    Greg Maddux, NL:Atl. 1993-95

Most Seasons Leading League
9   Lefty Grove, AL:Phil. 1926,29-32; Bos. 35-36,38-39
5   Grover Alexander, NL:Phil. 1915-17; Chi. 19-20
    Sandy Koufax, NL:LA 1962-66

Most Seasons, Consecutive, Leading League
5   Sandy Koufax,NL:LA 1962-66
4   Lefty Grove, AL:Phil. 1929-32

Lowest Earned Run Average, Lifetime (Minimum: 2000 innings)
2.33   Hippo Vaughn, NL:Chi. 1913-21
2.37   Walter Johnson, AL:Wash. 1913-27 (Excluding 1907-12)

Lowest Earned Run Average, Season (Qualifiers)
1.00   Dutch Leonard, AL:Bos. 1914
1.12   Bob Gibson, NL:StL. 1968

WINNING PERCENTAGE

Most Seasons Leading Major Leagues
5   Lefty Grove, AL:Phil. 1929-31,33; Bos. 38

Most Seasons, Consecutive, Leading Major Leagues
3   Lefty Grove, AL:Phil. 1929-31

Most Seasons Leading League
5   Lefty Grove, AL:Phil. 1929-31,33; Bos. 38
3   Sam Leever, NL:Pitt. 1901,03,05
        Ed Reulbach, NL:Chi. 1906-08

Most Seasons, Consecutive, Leading League
3   Ed Reulbach, NL:Chi. 1906-08
        Lefty Grove, AL:Phil. 1929-31

Highest Winning Percentage, Lifetime (Minimum: 200 wins)
.690   Whitey Ford, AL:NY 1950,53-67 (236-106)
.665   Christy Mathewson, NL:NY 1900-16; Cin. 16 (373-188)

Lowest Winning Percentage, Lifetime (Minimum: 100 wins)
.380   Si Johnson, NL:Cin. 1928-36; StL. 36-38; Phil. 40-43,46; Bos. 46-47 (101-165)
.406   Sid Hudson, AL:Wash. 1940-42,46-52; Bos. 52-54 (104-152)

Highest Winning Percentage, Season (Minimum: 15 decisions)
.947   Roy Face, NL:Pitt. 1959 (18-1)
.938   Johnny Allen, AL:Clev. 1937 (15-1)

GAMES WON

Most Seasons Leading Major Leagues
4   Joe McGinnity, NL:Balt. 1899; Brk. 1900; NY 03,06
        Grover Alexander, NL:Phil. 1911,15-17
        Robin Roberts, NL:Phil. 1952-55
        Warren Spahn, NL:Mil. 1953,57-58,60
        Tom Glavine, NL:Atl. 1991,93,98, 2000
        Roger Clemens, AL:Bos. 1986-87, Tor. 97-98

Most Seasons, Consecutive, Leading Major Leagues
4   Robin Roberts, NL:Phil. 1952-55

Most Seasons Leading League
8   Warren Spahn, NL:Bos. 1949-50; Mil. 53,57-61
6   Walter Johnson, AL:Wash. 1913-16,18,24
        Bob Feller, AL:Clev. 1939-41,46-47,51

Most Seasons, Consecutive, Leading League
5   Warren Spahn, NL:Mil. 1957-61
4   Walter Johnson, AL:Wash. 1913-16

Most Games Won, Lifetime
511   Cy Young, NL:Clev. 1890-98; StL. 1899-1900; Bos. 11; AL:Bos. 1901-08; Clev. 09-11

Most Games Won, League
417   Walter Johnson, AL:Wash. 1907-27
373   Christy Mathewson, NL:NY 1900-16; Cin. 16
        Grover Alexander, NL:Phil. 1911-17,30; Chi. 18-26; StL. 26-29

Most Games Won, Season
60   Hoss Radbourn, NL:Prov. 1884
        Since 1900:
41   Jack Chesbro, AL:NY 1904
37   Christy Mathewson, NL:NY 1908

Most Games Won, No Losses, Season
12   Tom Zachary, AL:NY 1929
10   Howie Krist, NL:StL. 1941

Most Seasons, 30 or more Games Won, Lifetime
7   Kid Nichols, NL:Bos. 1891-94,96-98

Most Seasons, 30 or more Games Won, League
7   Kid Nichols, NL:Bos. 1891-94,96-98
       Since 1900:
4   Christy Mathewson, NL:NY 1903-05,08
2   Cy Young, AL:Bos. 1901-02
       Walter Johnson, AL:Wash. 1912-13

Most Seasons, Consecutive, 30 or more Games Won
6   Tim Keefe, AA:NY 1883-84; NL:NY 85-88
5   Amos Rusie, NL:NY 1980-94
       Since 1900:
3   Christy Mathewson, NL:NY 1903-05
       Grover Alexander, NL:Phil. 1915-17
2   Cy Young, AL:Bos. 1901-02
       Walter Johnson, AL:Wash. 1912-13

Most Seasons, 20 or more Games Won, Lifetime
16   Cy Young, NL:Clev. 1891-98; StL. 1899-1900; AL:Bos. 1901-04,07-08

Most Seasons, 20 or more Games Won, League
13   Christy Mathewson, NL:NY 1901,03-14
       Warren Spahn, NL:Bos. 1947,49-51; Mil. 53-54,56-61,63
12   Walter Johnson, AL:Wash. 1910-19,24-25

Most Seasons, Consecutive, 20 or more Games Won, Lifetime
14   Cy Young, NL:Clev. 1891-98; StL. 1899-1900; AL:Bos. 01-04

Most Seasons, Consecutive, 20 or more Games Won, League
12   Christy Mathewson, NL:NY 1903-14
10   Walter Johnson, AL:Wash. 1910-19

Most Games Won, Consecutive, Lifetime
24   Carl Hubbell, NL:NY July 17, 1936-May 27, 1937
20   Roger Clemens, AL:Tor. -NY June 3, 1998-June 1, 1999

Most Games Won, Consecutive, Season
19   Tim Keefe, NL:NY June 23-Aug. 10, 1888
       Rube Marquard, NL:NY Apr. 11-July 3(1g), 1912
16   Walter Johnson, AL:Wash. July 3(2g)-Aug. 23(1g), 1912
       Smokey Joe Wood, AL:Bos. July 8-Sept. 15(2g), 1912
       Lefty Grove, AL:Phil. June 8-Aug. 19, 1931
       Schoolboy Rowe, AL:Det. June 15-Aug. 25, 1934
       Roger Clemens, AL:NY May 26-Sept. 19, 2001

Most Games Won, Consecutive, Start of Season
19   Rube Marquard, NL:NY Apr. 11-July 3(1g), 1912
15   Johnny Allen, AL:Clev. Apr. 23-Sept. 30(1g), 1937
       Dave McNally, AL:Balt. Apr. 12-July 30, 1969

Most Games Won, Consecutive, End of Season
17   Pat Luby, NL:Chi. Aug. 6(2g)-Oct. 3, 1890
       Since 1900:
16   Carl Hubbell, NL:NY July 17-Sept. 23, 1936
15   General Crowder, AL:Wash. Aug. 2-Sept. 25, 1932
       Roger Clemens, AL:Tor. June 3-Sept. 21, 1998

Most Games Won, vs. One Club, League
70   Grover Alexander, NL:Phil.-Chi.-StL. (vs Cin.) 1911-30
66   Walter Johnson, AL:Wash. (vs Det.) 1907-27

Most Games Won, vs. One Club, Season
12   Hoss Radbourn, NL:Prov. (vs Clev.) 1884
       Since 1900:
9   Ed Reulbach, NL:Chi. (vs Brk.) 1908
       Frank Smith, AL:Chi. (vs Wash.) 1904
       Ed Walsh, AL:Chi. (vs NY & Bos.) 1908
       Walter Johnson, AL:Wash. (vs Chi) 1912

Most Games Won, Consecutive, vs. One Club, League
24   Christy Mathewson, NL:NY (vs StL.) June 16, 1904-Sept. 15, 1908
       Carl Mays, AL:Bos.-NY (vs Phil.) Aug. 30, 1918-July 24, 1923

GAMES LOST

Most Seasons Leading Major Leagues
3   Pedro Ramos, AL:Wash. 1958-59; Minn. 61

Most Seasons, Consecutive, Leading Major Leagues
2   Jim Devlin, NL:Lou. 1876-77
       Red Ruffing, AL:Bos. 1928-29
       Pedro Ramos,AL:Wash. 1958-59
       Roger Craig, NL:NY 1962-63

Most Seasons Leading League
4   Bobo Newsom, AL:StL. 1934; StL.-Wash. 35; Det. 41; Phil. 45
       Pedro Ramos, AL:Wash. 1958-60; Minn. 61
       Phil Niekro, NL:Atl. 1977-80

Most Seasons, Consecutive, Leading League
4   Pedro Ramos, AL:Wash. 1958-60; Minn. 61
       Phil Niekro, NL:Atl. 1977-80

Most Games Lost, Lifetime
315   Cy Young, NL:Clev. 1890-98; StL. 1899-1900; Bos. 11; AL:Bos. 1901-08; Clev. 09-11

Most Games Lost, League
279   Walter Johnson, AL:Wash. 1907-27
261   Pud Galvin, NL:Buff. 1879-85; Pitt. 87-89,91-92; StL. 92
       NL Since 1900:
251   Eppa Rixey, NL:Phil. 1912-17, 19-20, Cin 21-33

Most Games Lost, Season
48   John Coleman, NL:Phil. 1883
       Since 1900:
29   Vic Willis, NL:Bos. 1905
26   Jack Townsend, AL:Wash. 1904
       Bob Groom, AL:Wash. 1909

Most Games Lost, No Wins, Season
13   Terry Felton, AL:Minn. 1982
12   Russ Miller, NL:Phil. 1928

Most Games Lost, Consecutive, Lifetime
27   Anthony Young, NL:NY May 6, 1992-July 24, 1993
19   Jack Nabors, AL:Phil. Apr. 28-Sept. 28, 1916

Most Games Lost, Consecutive, Season
19   Jack Nabors, AL:Phil. Apr. 28-Sept. 28, 1916
18   Cliff Curtis, NL:Bos. June 13(1g)-Sept. 20(1g), 1910
       Roger Craig, NL:NY May 4-Aug. 4, 1963

Most Games Lost, Consecutive, Start of Season
14   Joe Harris, AL:Bos. May 10-July 25, 1906
       Matt Keough, AL:Oak. Apr. 15-Aug. 8, 1979
13   Anthony Young, NL:NY Apr. 9-July 24, 1993

Most Games Lost, Consecutive, End of Season
19   Jack Nabors, AL:Phil. Apr. 28-Sept 28, 1916
18   Cliff Curtis, NL:Bos. June 13(1g) Sept 28(1g), 1910

Most Games Lost, Consecutive, Start of Career
16   Terry Felton, AL:Minn. Apr. 18, 1980-Sept 12, 1982

Most Games Lost, vs. One Club, Season
7   By many pitchers. Last:
       Cal McLish, NL:Cin. (vs Pitt.) 1960
       Camilo Pascual, AL:Wash. (vs NY) 1956

Most Games Lost, Consecutive, vs. One Club, League
14   Fred Beebe, NL:StL. (vs NY) July 15, 1906-Sept. 22, 1909
       Eppa Rixey, NL:Phil.-Cin. (vs Bos.) Oct. 3, 1916-May 21, 1921
       George Smith, NL:Phil. (vs Brk.) Sept. 3, 1920-June 25, 1922
       Bob Rush, NL:Chi. (vs Phil.) June 14, 1951-June 17, 1955
       Herm Wehmeier, NL:Cin.-Phil. (vs StL.) July 3, 1949-May 9, 1956
       Joe Bush, AL:Phil. (vs Bos.) June 2, 1914-July 5, 1917
       Slim Harriss, AL:Phil. (vs NY) July 2, 1920-May 30, 1924
       Danny MacFayden, AL:Bos. (vs Wash) Aug. 7, 1929-June 2, 1932

INNINGS PITCHED

Most Seasons Leading Major Leagues
5   Robin Roberts, NL:Phil. 1951-55

Most Seasons, Consecutive, Leading Major Leagues
5   Robin Roberts, NL:Phil. 1951-55

Most Seasons Leading League
7   Grover Alexander, NL:Phil. 1911-12,14-17; Chi. 20
5   Walter Johnson, AL:Wash. 1910,13-16
           Bob Feller, AL:Clev. 1939-41,46-47

Most Seasons, Consecutive, Leading League
5   Robin Roberts, NL:Phil. 1951-55
           Greg Maddux, NL:Chi. 1991-92; Atl. 93-95
4   Walter Johnson, AL:Wash. 1913-16

Most Innings, Lifetime
7356   Cy Young, NL:Clev. 1890-98; StL. 1899-1900; Bos. 11; AL:Bos. 1901-08; Clev. 09-11

Most Innings, League
5924   Walter Johnson, AL:Wash. 1907-27
5246   Warren Spahn, NL:Bos./Mil. 1942,46-64; NY 65-SF 65

Most Innings, Season
683   Will White, NL:Cin. 1879
           Since 1900:
464   Ed Walsh, AL:Chi. 1908
434   Joe McGinnity, NL:NY 1903

Most Seasons, 300 or more Innings, Lifetime
16   Cy Young, NL:Clev. 1891-98; StL. 1899-1900; AL:Bos. 1901-05, 07

Most Seasons, Consecutive, 300 or more Innings, Lifetime
15   Cy Young, NL:Clev. 1891-98; StL. 1899-1900; AL:Bos. 1901-05

Most Seasons, 300 or more Innings, League
12   Kid Nichols, NL:Bos. 1890-99,1901,04
           Since 1900:
11   Christy Mathewson, NL:NY 1901,03-05,07-08,10-14
9   Walter Johnson, AL:Wash. 1910-18

Most Seasons, Consecutive, 300 or more Innings, League
10   Kid Nichols, NL:Bos. 1890-99
           Cy Young, NL:Clev. 1891-98; StL. 1899-1900
           Since 1900:
9   Walter Johnson, AL:Wash. 1910-18
7   Grover Alexander, NL:Phil. 1911-17

Most Seasons, 200 or more Innings, Lifetime
20   Don Sutton, NL:LA 1966-80, Hou. 82; AL:Mil. 1982-84, Oak. 85, Cal. 85-86

Most Seasons, Consecutive, 200 or more Innings, Lifetime
19   Cy Young, NL:Clev. 1891-98; StL. 1899-1900; AL:Bos. 1901-08, Clev.09

Most Seasons, 200 or more Innings, League
18   Walter Johnson, AL:Wash. 1908-19,21-26
17   Warren Spahn, NL:Bos. 1947-52; Mil. 53-63

Most Seasons, Consecutive, 200 or more Innings, League
17   Warren Spahn, NL:Bos. 1947-52; Mil. 53-63
13   Eddie Plank, AL:Phil. 1901-13
           Red Ruffing, AL:Bos. 1928-30; NY 30-40

Most Innings, Game
26   Leon Cadore, NL:Brk. May 1, 1920
           Joe Oeschger, NL:Bos. May 1, 1920
24   Jack Coombs, AL:Phil. Sept. 1, 1906
           Joe Harris, AL:Bos. Sept. 1, 1906

BATTERS FACED

Most Seasons Leading League
7	Steve Carlton, NL:Phil. 1972-74,80-83
5	Walter Johnson, AL:Wash. 1910,13-16

Most Seasons, Consecutive, Leading League
4	Walter Johnson, AL:Wash. 1913-16
	Bob Lemon, AL:Clev. 1950-53
	Grover Alexander, NL:Phil. 1914-17
	Robin Roberts, NL:Phil. 1952-55
	Steve Carlton, NL:Phil. 1980-83
	Greg Maddux, NL:Chi. 1991-92; Atl. 93-94

Most Batters Faced, Lifetime
30,418	Cy Young, NL:Clev. 1890-98; StL. 1899-1900; AL:Bos. 1901-08,11; Clev. 09-11

Most Batters Faced, League
23,433	Walter Johnson, AL:Wash. 1907-27
21,547	Warren Spahn, NL:Bos./Mil. 1942,46-64; NY 65; SF 65

Most Batters Faced, Season
1807	Joe McGinnity, NL:NY 1903
1755	Ed Walsh, AL:Chi. 1908

Most Batters Faced, Game
67	George Derby, NL:Buff. July 3, 1883
	Since 1900:
57	Roy Patterson, AL:Chi. May 5, 1901
53	Bill Phillips, NL:Cin. June 24(2g), 1901
	Extra-Inning Game:
96	Leon Cadore, NL:Brk. May 1, 1920 (26 inn)
86	Jack Coombs, AL:Phil. Sept. 1, 1906 (24 inn)
	Joe Harris, AL:Bos. Sept. 1, 1906 (24 inn)

Most Batters Faced, Inning
22	Tony Mullane, NL:Balt. June 18(1g), 1894 (1st)
	Since 1900:
16	Doc Adkins, AL:Bos. July 8, 1902 (6th)
	Lefty O'Doul, AL:Bos. July 7(1g), 1923 (6th)
	Howard Ehmke, AL:Bos. Sept. 28, 1923 (6th)
	Hal Kelleher, NL:Phil. May 5, 1938 (8th)

Most Batters Retired, Consecutive, Season
41	Jim Barr, NL:SF Aug. 23-29, 1972
38	David Wells, AL:NY May 12-23, 1998

Most Batters Retired, Consecutive, Extra-Inning Game:
36	Harvey Haddix, NL:Pitt. (vs Mil.) May 26, 1959
28	Walter Johnson, AL:Wash. (vs NY) May 11, 1919

AT-BATS

Most Seasons Leading League
6	Grover Alexander, NL:Phil. 1911,14-17; Chi. 20
	Steve Carlton, NL:Phil. 1972-73,80-83
4	Ed Walsh, AL:Chi. 1908,10-12
	Walter Johnson, AL:Wash. 1913-16
	Bob Lemon, AL:Clev. 1948,50,52-53

Most Seasons, Consecutive, Leading League
4	Walter Johnson, AL:Wash. 1913-16
	Grover Alexander, NL:Phil. 1914-17
	Robin Roberts, NL:Phil. 1952-55
	Steve Carlton, NL:Phil. 1980-83

Most At-Bats, Lifetime
29,209	Cy Young, NL:Clev. 1890-98; StL. 1899-1900; AL:Bos. 1901-08,11; Clev. 09-11

Most At-Bats, League
21,663	Walter Johnson, AL:Wash. 1907-27
19,778	Warren Spahn, NL:Bos./Mil. 1942,46-64; NY 65; SF 65

Most At-Bats, Season, Since 1900
1690	Ed Walsh, AL:Chi. 1908
1658	Joe McGinnity, NL:NY 1903

Most At-Bats, Game
66	George Derby, NL:Buff, July 3, 1883
	Since 1900:
53	Roy Patterson, AL:Chi. May 5, 1901
49	Doc Parker, NL:Cin. June 21, 1901
	Bill Phillips, NL:Cin. June 24(2g), 1901
	Extra-Inning Game:
86	Leon Cadore, NL:Brk. May 1, 1920 (26 inn)
82	Joe Harris, AL:Bos. Sept. 1, 1906 (24 inn)

Most At-Bats, Inning
14	Howard Ehmke, AL:Bos. Sept. 28, 1923 (6th)
	Hal Kelleher, NL:Phil. May 5, 1938 (8th)

RUNS (Since 1900)

Most Seasons Leading Major Leagues
3	Phil Niekro, NL:Atl. 1977-79

Most Seasons, Consecutive, Leading Major Leagues
3	Phil Niekro, NL:Atl. 1977-79

Most Seasons Leading League
3	Burleigh Grimes, NL:Brk. 1923-24; Pitt. 28
	Hugh Mulcahy, NL:Phil. 1938-40
	Robin Roberts, NL:Phil. 1955-57
	Phil Niekro, NL:Atl. 1977-79
	Rick Mahler, NL:Atl. 1986,88; Cin. 89
	George Mullin, AL:Det. 1905-07
	Wilbur Wood, AL:Chi. 1972-73, 75

Most Seasons, Consecutive, Leading League
3	George Mullin, AL:Det. 1905-07
	Hugh Mulcahy, NL:Phil. 1938-40
	Robin Roberts, NL:Phil. 1955-57
	Phil Niekro, NL:Atl. 1977-79

Most Runs, Lifetime
2337	Phil Niekro, NL:Mil./Atl. 1964-83,87; AL:NY 1984-85; Clev. 86-87; Tor. 87

Most Runs, League
2117	Red Ruffing, AL:Bos. 1924-30; NY 30-42,45-46; Chi. 47
2037	Burleigh Grimes, NL:Pitt. 1916-17,28-29,34; Brk. 18-26; NY 27;
	Bos. 30; StL. 30-31,34; Chi. 32-33

Most Runs, Season
544	John Coleman, NL:Phil. 1883
	Since 1900:
224	Bill Carrick, NL:NY 1900
219	Joe McGinnity, AL:Balt. 1901

Most Runs, Game
24	Al Travers, AL:Det. May 18, 1912
21	Doc Parker, NL:Cin. June 21, 1901

Most Runs, Inning
13	Lefty O'Doul, AL:Bos. July 7(1g), 1923 (6th)
12	Hal Kelleher, NL:Phil. May 5, 1938 (8th)

EARNED RUNS (Since 1912 in NL; Since 1913 in AL – Prior seasons not compiled on official scores)

Most Seasons Leading Major Leagues
3	Burleigh Grimes, NL:Brk. 1922,24-25
	Wilbur Wood, AL:Chi. 1972-73,75

Most Seasons, Consecutive, Leading Major Leagues
2	Elmer Myers, AL:Phil. 1916-17
	Bump Hadley, AL:Chi.-StL. 1932-33
	Wilbur Wood, AL:Chi. 1972-73
	Burleigh Grimes, NL:Brk. 1924-25
	Robin Roberts, NL:Phil. 1955-56
	Sammy Ellis, NL:Cin. 1965-66

Most Seasons Leading League
3   Bobo Newsom, AL:StL. 1938; Wash. 42; Phil. 45
           Wilbur Wood, AL:Chi. 1972-73,75
           Burleigh Grimes, NL:Brk. 1922,24-25
           Murry Dickson, NL:StL. 1948; Pitt. 51-52
           Robin Roberts, NL:Phil. 1955-57
           Jack Fisher, NL:NY 1964-65,67

Most Seasons, Consecutive, Leading League
3   Robin Roberts, NL:Phil. 1955-57
2   Elmer Myers, AL:Phil. 1916-17
           Red Ruffing, AL:Bos. 1928-29
           Bump Hadley, AL:Chi.-StL. 1932-33
           Wilbur Wood, AL:Chi. 1972-73

Most Earned Runs, Lifetime
2012   Phil Niekro, NL:Mil./Atl. 1964-83,87; AL:NY 1984-85; Clev. 86-87; Tor. 87

Most Earned Runs, League
1833   Red Ruffing, AL:Bos. 1924-30; NY 30-42,45-46; Chi. 47
1798   Warren Spahn, NL:Bos./Mil. 1942,46-64; NY 65; SF 65

Most Earned Runs, Season
186   Bobo Newsom, AL:StL. 1938
155   Guy Bush, NL:Chi. 1930

HITS

Most Seasons Leading Major Leagues
5   Robin Roberts, NL:Phil. 1952-56

Most Seasons, Consecutive, Leading Major Leagues
5   Robin Roberts, NL:Phil. 1952-56

Most Seasons Leading League
5   Robin Roberts, NL:Phil. 1952-56
4   Jim Kaat, AL:Minn. 1965-67; Chi. 75

Most Seasons, Consecutive Leading League
5   Robin Roberts, NL:Phil. 1952-56
3   Wes Ferrell, AL:Bos. 1935-36; Bos.-Wash. 37
           Jim Kaat, AL:Minn. 1965-67

Most Hits, Lifetime
7078   Cy Young, NL:Clev. 1890-98; StL. 1899-1900; AL:Bos. 1901-08,11; Clev. 09-11

Most Hits, League
5490   Pud Galvin, NL:Buff. 1879-85; Pitt. 87-89,91-92; StL. 92
           Since 1900:
4920   Walter Johnson, AL:Wash. 1907-27
4868   Grover Alexander, NL:Phil. 1911-17,30; Chi. 18-26; StL. 26-29

Most Hits, Season
809   John Coleman, NL:Phil. 1883
           Since 1900:
415   Bill Carrick, NL:NY 1900
401   Joe McGinnity, AL:Balt. 1901

Most Hits, Game
36   Jack Wadsworth, NL:Lou. Aug. 17, 1894
           Since 1900:
26   Doc Parker, NL:Cin. June 21, 1901
           Al Travers, AL:Det. May 18, 1912
           Hod Lisenbee, AL:Phil. Sept. 11, 1936
           Extra-Inning Game:
29   Ed Rommel, AL:Phil. July 10, 1932 (last 17 inn of 18 inn gm)

Most Hits, Inning
13   Stump Weidman, NL:Det. Sept. 6, 1883 (7th)
           Since 1900:
12   Doc Adkins, AL:Bos. July 8, 1902 (6th)
11   Reggie Grabowski, NL:Phil. Aug. 4(2g), 1934 (9th)

Most Hits, Consecutive, Game
10   Bill Reidy, AL:Mil. June 2, 1901
           Heinie Meine, NL:Pitt. June 23, 1930

Most Hits, Consecutive, Inning
10   Bill Reidy, AL:Mil. June 2, 1901 (9th)
           Heinie Meine, NL:Pitt. June 23, 1930 (6th)

Fewest Hits, 2 Consecutive Complete Games
0	Johnny Vander Meer, NL:Cin. June 11-15, 1938
1	Howard Ehmke, AL:Bos. Sept. 7-11, 1923

Fewest Hits, 3 Consecutive Complete Games
3	Johnny Vander Meer, NL:Cin. June 5-15, 1938
5	By many players

Most Hitless Innings, Consecutive, Season
24	Cy Young, AL:Bos. Apr. 25-May 11, 1904
21	Johnny Vander Meer, NL:Cin. June 11-19, 1938

Most Extra-Base Hits, Game
16	George Derby, NL:Buff. July 3, 1883
10	Dale Gear, AL:Wash. Aug. 10(2g), 1901

SINGLES

Most Singles, Game
28	Jack Wadsworth, NL:Lou. Aug. 17, 1894
23	Bock Baker, AL:Clev. Apr. 28, 1901

Most Singles, Inning
10	Reggie Grabowski, NL:Phil. Aug. 4(2g), 1934 (9th)
	Elden Auker, AL:Det. Sept. 29(2g), 1935 (2nd)

DOUBLES

Most Doubles, Game
14	George Derby, NL:Buff. July 3, 1883
8	Edward Lafitte, AL:Det. Oct. 8(1g), 1911

Most Doubles, Inning
6	Lefty Grove, AL:Bos. June 9, 1934 (8th)
	Dustin Hermanson, NL:Mtl. July 22, 1999 (2nd)

TRIPLES

Most Triples, Game
9	Mike Sullivan, NL Clev. Sept. 3(1g), 1894
6	Al Travers, AL:Det. May 18, 1912

Most Triples, Inning
4	Firpo Marberry, AL:Det. May 6, 1934 (4th)
3	By many NL players

HOME RUNS

Most Home Runs, Lifetime
505	Robin Roberts, NL:Phil. 1948-61; Hou. 65-66; Chi. 66; AL:Balt. 1962-65

Most Home Runs, League
434	Warren Spahn, NL:Bos./Mil. 1942,46-64; NY 65; SF 65
422	Frank Tanana, AL:Cal. 1973-80; Bos. 81; Tex. 82-85; Det. 85-92; NY 93

Most Home Runs, Season
50	Bert Blyleven, AL:Minn. 1986
48	Jose Lima, NL:Hou. 2000

Fewest Home Runs, Season (Most Innings), Since 1900
0	Walter Johnson, AL:Wash. 1916 (371 inn)
	Vic Willis, NL:Pitt. 1906 (322 inn)

Most Home Runs, vs. One Club, Season
15	Jim Perry, AL:Clev. (vs. NY) 1960
13	Warren Hacker, NL:Chi. (vs. Brk.) 1956
	Warren Spahn, NL:Mil. (vs. Chi.) 1958

Most Home Runs, Game
7	Charlie Sweeney, NL:StL. June 12, 1886
	Since 1900:
6	Larry Benton, NL:NY May 12, 1930
	Sloppy Thurston, NL:Brk. Aug. 13(1g), 1932
	Bill Kerksieck, NL:Phil. Aug. 13(1g), 1939
	Tommy Thomas, AL:StL. June 27, 1936
	George Caster, AL:Phil. Sept. 24(1g), 1940

Most Home Runs, Inning

4	Henry Lampe, NL:Bos. June 6, 1894 (3rd)
	Larry Benton, NL:NY May 12, 1930 (7th)
	Bill Kerksieck, NL:Phil. Aug. 13(1g), 1939 (4th)
	Charlie Bicknell, NL:Phil. June 6(1g), 1948 (6th)
	Ben Wade, NL:Brk. May 28, 1954 (8th)
	Mario Soto, NL:Cin. Apr. 29, 1986 (4th)
	John Smoltz, NL:Atl. June 19, 1994 (1st)
	Jose Lima, NL:Hou. Apr. 27, 2000 (1st)
	Andy Benes, NL:StL. July 23, 2000 (2nd)
	Phil Norton, NL:Chi. Aug. 8, 2000 (4th)
	Steve Trachsel, NL:NY May 17, 2001 (3rd)
	Alan Embree, NL:Atl. May 20, 2001 (7th)
	George Caster, AL:Phil. Sept. 24(1g), 1940 (6th)
	Cal McLish, AL:Clev. May 22, 1957 (6th)
	Paul Foytack, AL:LA July 31(2g), 1963 (6th)
	Catfish Hunter, AL:NY June 17, 1977 (1st)
	Mike Caldwell, AL:Mil. May 31, 1980 (4th)
	Scott Sanderson, AL:NY May 2, 1992 (5th)
	Brian Anderson, AL:Cal. Sept. 5, 1995 (2nd)
	Dave Telgheder, AL:Oak. Sept. 21, 1996 (3rd)
	Dave Burba, AL:Clev. June 29, 2001 (4th)
	Pat Mahomes, AL:Tex. Aug. 17, 2001 (6th)

Most Home Runs, Consecutive, Inning

4	Paul Foytack, AL:LA (Clev.) July 31(2g), 1963 (6th)
3	By many NL players; Last:
	Dave Mlicki, NL:Hou. Sept. 29, 2001 (1st)

GRAND SLAM HOME RUNS

Most Grand Slam Home Runs, Lifetime

10	Nolan Ryan, NL:NY 1970; Hou. 84,85,88; AL:Cal. 1972,73,77; Tex. 90,93

Most Grand Slam Home Runs, League

9	Ned Garver, AL:StL. 1949,50,51,52; Det. 54,55; KC 59
	Jerry Reuss, NL:StL. 1971; Hou. 72,73; Pitt. 74,76; LA 79,80

Most Grand Slam Home Runs, Season

4	Ray Narleski, AL:Det. 1959
	Mike Schooler, AL:Sea. 1992
	Tug McGraw, NL:Phil. 1979
	Chan Ho Park, NL:LA 1999
	Matt Clement, NL:SD 2000

Most Grand Slam Home Runs, Month

3	Archie Stimmel, NL:Cin. Sept. 22,23 (2), 1901
	Chan Ho Park, NL:LA Apr. 12,23 (2), 1999
2	By many AL players; Last:
	Blake Stein, AL:KC Apr. 4-21, 2001

Most Grand Slam Home Runs, Game

2	Bill Phillips, NL:Pitt. (Chi.) Aug. 16, 1890 (Tommy Burns, Malachi Kittredge)
	Charlie Petty, NL:Wash. (Bos.) May 28, 1894 (Bobby Lowe, Henry Staley)
	Archie Stimmel, NL:Cin. (Brk.) Sept. 23, 1901 (Joe Kelley, Jimmy Sheckard)
	Jock Menefee, NL:Chi. (Bos.) Aug. 12(2g), 1903 (Joe Stanley, Pat Moran)
	Jack Scott, NL:Bos. (Phil.) Apr. 28, 1921 (Ralph Miller, Lee Meadows)
	June Green, NL:Phil. (StL.) July 6(2g), 1929 (Jim Bottomley, Chick Hafey)
	Luke Hamlin, NL:Brk. (NY) July 4(2g), 1938 (Dick Bartell, Gus Mancuso)
	Chan Ho Park, NL:LA (StL.) Apr. 23, 1999 (Fernando Tatis 2)
	Tex Shirley, AL:StL. (Bos.) July 27, 1946 (Rudy York 2)
	Jack Morris, AL:Det. (Bos.) Aug. 7(1g), 1984 (Bill Buckner, Tony Armas)
	Eric Plunk, AL:Oak. (Cal.) July 31, 1986 (Brian Downing, Bob Boone)

Most Games, Consecutive, Grand Slam Home Runs
2 Archie Stimmel, NL:Cin. Sept. 22-23(2), 1901
  Bubba Church, NL:Phil. Sept. 24-27, 1950
  Johnny Rutherford, NL:Brk. Sept. 14-23, 1952
  Jerry Reuss, NL:Pitt. June 26-July 2, 1976
  Tug McGraw, NL:Phil. Aug. 5-11, 1979
  John Tudor, NL:StL. Sept. 16-21, 1985
  Doug Bair, NL:Phil. July 7-9, 1987
  Tommy Greene, NL:Phil. Aug. 22-27, 1995
  Tim Pugh, NL:Cin. Apr. 25-30, 1996
  Brad Penny, NL:Fla. May 9-14, 2000
  Scott Elarton, NL:Hou. June 27-July 3, 2001
  Bob Kline, AL:Phil. June 14-16, 1934
  Earl Caldwell, AL:Bos. Sept. 10-15, 1948
  Ted Gray, AL:Det. May 18-22, 1951
  Bill Wight, AL:Det. Apr. 26-May 5, 1953
  Marion Fricano, AL:Phil. July 16-19, 1953
  Chuck Stobbs, AL:Wash. May 2-6, 1957
  Jim Bunning, AL:Det. July 29-Aug. 2, 1958
  Tex Clevenger, AL:Wash. June 13-14, 1959
  Dave Hillman, AL:Bos. June 2-8, 1960
  Camilo Pascual, AL:Minn. May 2-7, 1961
  Paul Foytack, AL:LA July 7-14, 1963
  Phil Ortega, AL:Wash. June 22-26, 1966
  John Henry Johnson, AL:Tex. Aug. 4-8, 1979
  Dave LaPoint, AL:Det. May 29-June 3, 1986
  Jeff Russell, AL:Tex. July 27-Aug. 2, 1988
  Lance McCullers, AL:Det. June 17-20, 1990
  Bryce Florie, AL:Mil. June 27-July 1, 1997
  Greg McCarthy, AL:Sea. Aug. 12-18, 1998
  Pedro Borbon, Jr., AL:Tor. Apr. 15-16, 2000
  Denny Neagle, AL:NY Aug. 7-12, 2000
  Andy Larkin, AL:KC Sept. 5-10, 2000

Most Grand Slam Home Runs, Inning
2 Bill Phillips, NL:Pitt. (Chi.) Aug. 16, 1890 (5th)
  Chan Ho Park, NL:LA (StL.) Apr. 23, 1999 (3rd)

Most Grand Slam Home Runs, Consecutive Innings
2 Jock Menefee, NL:Chi. (Bos.) Aug. 12, 1903 (3rd-Joe Stanley, 4th-Pat Moran)
  Jack Morris, AL:Det. (Bos.) Aug. 7, 1984 (1st-Bill Buckner, 2nd-Tony Armas)
  Eric Plunk, AL:Oak. (Cal.) July 31, 1986 (3rd-Brian Downing, 4th-Bob Boone)

WALKS

Most Seasons Leading Major Leagues
7 Nolan Ryan, AL:Cal. 1972-74,76-78; NL:Hou. 82

Most Seasons, Consecutive, Leading Major Leagues
5 Amos Rusie, NL:NY 1890-94
  Since 1900:
3 Togie Pittinger, NL:Bos. 1902-04
  Tommy Byrne, AL:NY 1949-50; NY-StL. 51
  Nolan Ryan, AL:Cal. 1972-74; 76-78
  Randy Johnson, AL:Sea. 1990-92

Most Seasons Leading League
8 Nolan Ryan, AL:Cal. 1972-74,76-78; NL:Hou. 80,82
6 Nolan Ryan, AL:Cal. 1972-74; 76-78
5 Amos Rusie, NL:NY 1890-94
  NL Since 1900:
4 Jimmy Ring, NL:Phil. 1922-25
  Kirby Higbe, NL:Chi.-Phil. 1939; Phil. 40; Brk. 41; Brk.-Pitt. 47
  Sam Jones, NL:Chi. 1955-56; StL. 58; SF 59
  Bob Veale, NL:Pitt. 1964-65,67-68

Most Seasons, Consecutive, Leading League
5 Amos Rusie, NL:NY 1890-94
  Since 1900:
4 George Mullin, AL:Det. 1903-06
  Jimmy Ring, NL:Phil. 1922-25

Most Walks, Lifetime
2795 Nolan Ryan NL:NY 1966,68-71; Hou. 80-88; AL:Cal. 1972-79; Tex. 89-93

Most Walks, League
1775 Early Wynn, AL:Wash. 1939,41-44,46-48; Clev. 49-57,63; Chi. 58-62
1717 Steve Carlton, NL:StL. 1965-71; Phil. 72-86; SF 86

Most Walks, Season
276	Amos Rusie, NL:NY 1890	
	Since 1900:	
208	Bob Feller, AL:Clev. 1938	
185	Sam Jones, NL:Chi. 1955	

Most Intentional Walks, Season
23	Mike Garman, NL:StL. 1975
	Dale Murray, NL:Cin.-NY 1978
	Kent Tekulve, NL:Pitt. 1982
19	John Hiller, AL:Det. 1974

Most Walks, Game
16	Bill George, NL:NY May 30(1g), 1887
	George Van Haltren, NL:Chi. June 27, 1887
	Henry Gruber, PL:Clev. Apr. 19, 1890
	Bruno Haas, AL:Phil. June 23, 1915
	Tommy Byrne, AL:StL. Aug. 22, 1951 (13 inn)
	NL Since 1900:
14	Henry Mathewson, NL:NY Oct. 5, 1906

Most Walks, Inning
8	Dolly Gray, AL:Wash. Aug. 28(1g), 1909 (2nd)
7	Tony Mullane, NL:Balt. June 18(1g), 1894 (1st)
	Bob Ewing, NL:Cin. Apr. 19, 1902 (4th)

Most Walks, Consecutive, Inning
7	Dolly Gray, AL:Wash. Aug. 28(1g), 1909 (2nd)
6	Brickyard Kennedy, NL:Brk. Aug. 31, 1900 (2nd)

Fewest Walks, Game (Most Innings)
0	Babe Adams, NL:Pitt. July 17, 1914 (21 inn)
	Cy Young, AL:Bos. July 4(2g), 1905 (20 inn)

Most Innings, Consecutive, No Walks
84.1	Bill Fischer, AL:KC Aug. 3-Sept. 30, 1962
72.1	Greg Maddux, NL:Atl. June 20-Aug. 12, 2001

Most Innings, Consecutive, No Walks, Start Of Season
52.0	Grover Alexander, NL:Chi. Apr. 18-May 17, 1923 (52 inn)

HIT BATTERS

Most Seasons Leading Major Leagues
6	Howard Ehmke, AL:Det. 1920-22; Bos. 23,25; Phil. 27

Most Seasons, Consecutive, Leading Major Leagues
5	Tommy Byrne, AL:NY 1948-50; NY-StL. 51; StL. 52

Most Seasons Leading League
6	Howard Ehmke, AL:Det. 1920-22; Bos. 23,25; Phil. 27
5	Don Drysdale, NL:LA 1958-61,65

Most Seasons, Consecutive, Leading League
5	Tommy Byrne, AL:NY 1948-50; NY-StL. 51; StL. 52
4	Don Drysdale, NL:LA 1958-61

Most Hit Batters, Lifetime
206	Walter Johnson, AL:Wash. 1907-27
154	Don Drysdale, NL:Brk./LA 1956-69

Most Hit Batters, Season
41	Joe McGinnity, NL:Brk. 1900
31	Chick Fraser, AL:Phil. 1901

Most Hit Batters, Game
6	Ed Knouff, AA:Balt. Apr. 25, 1887
	John Grimes, NL:StL. July 31(1g), 1897
	Since 1900:
4	By many players; Last:
	Scott Schoeneweis; AL:Ana. June 7, 2001
	Pedro Astacio, NL:Col. Apr. 22, 2001

Most Hit Batters, Inning
3   Pat Luby, NL:Chi. Sept. 5, 1890 (6th)
            Pink Hawley, NL:StL. July 4(1g), 1894 (cons; 1st)
            Pink Hawley, NL:Pitt. May 9, 1896 (7th)
            Walter Thornton, NL:Chi. May 18, 1898 (cons; 4th)
            Deacon Phillippe, NL:Pitt. Sept. 25, 1905 (1st)
            Ray Boggs, NL:Bos. Sept. 17, 1928 (9th)
            Raul Sanchez, NL:Cin. May 15(1g), 1960 (8th)
            Dock Ellis, NL:Pitt. May 1, 1974 (cons; 1st)
            Mark Gardner, NL:Mtl. Aug. 15, 1992 (1st)
            Tom Candiotti, NL:LA Sept. 13, 1997 (1st)
            C.J. Nitkowski, NL:Hou. Aug. 3, 1998 (cons; 8th)
            Bert Gallia, AL:Wash. June 20(2g), 1913 (1st)
            Harry Harper, AL:NY Aug. 25, 1921 (8th)
            Tom Morgan, AL:NY June 30, 1954 (3rd)
            Wilbur Wood, AL:Chi. Sept. 10, 1977 (cons; 1st)
            Bud Black, AL:Clev. July 8(2g), 1988 (4th)
            Bert Blyleven, AL:Minn. Sept. 28, 1988 (2nd)
            Steve Sparks, AL:Ana. May 22, 1999 (cons; 3rd)

Fewest Hit Batters, Season (Most Innings)
0   General Crowder, AL:Wash. 1932 (327 inn)
            Sandy Koufax, NL:LA 1966 (323 inn)

Fewest Hit Batters, Game (Most Innings)
0   Leon Cadore, NL:Brk. May 1, 1920 (26 inn)
            Joe Oeschger, NL:Bos. May 1, 1920 (26 inn)
            Ted Lyons, AL:Chi. May 24, 1929 (21 inn)

STRIKEOUTS

Most Seasons Leading Major Leagues
8   Walter Johnson, AL:Wash. 1910,12-14,16,18-19,21

Most Seasons, Consecutive, Leading Major Leagues
5   Rube Waddell, AL:Phil. 1903-07

Most Seasons Leading League
12   Walter Johnson, AL:Wash. 1910,12-19,21,23-24
7   Dazzy Vance, NL:Brk. 1922-28

Most Seasons, Consecutive, Leading League
8   Walter Johnson, AL:Wash. 1912-19
7   Dazzy Vance, NL:Brk. 1922-28

Most Strikeouts, Lifetime
5714   Nolan Ryan, NL:NY 1966,68-71; Hou. 80-88; AL:Cal. 1972-79; Tex. 89-93

Most Strikeouts, League
4000   Steve Carlton, NL:StL. 1965-71; Phil. 72-86; SF 86
3717   Roger Clemens, AL:Bos. 1984-96; Tor. 97-98; NY 99-2001

Most Strikeouts, Season
505   Matt Kilroy, AA:Balt. 1886 (50-foot distance)
           Since 1900:
383   Nolan Ryan, AL:Cal. 1973
382   Sandy Koufax, NL:LA 1965

Most Seasons, 300 or more Strikeouts, League
6   Nolan Ryan, AL:Cal. 1972-74,76-77; Tex. 89
3   Amos Rusie, NL:NY 1890-92 (50-foot distance)
            Sandy Koufax, NL:LA 1963,65-66
            Randy Johnson, NL:Ari. 1999-2001

Most Seasons, Consecutive, 300 or more Strikeouts, Lifetime
4   Randy Johnson, AL:Sea.-NL:Hou. 1998; NL:Ari. 99-2001
3   Amos Rusie, NL:NY 1890-92 (50-foot distance)
            Randy Johnson, NL:Ari. 1999-2001
            Nolan Ryan, AL:Cal. 1972-74

Most Seasons, 200 or more Strikeouts, Lifetime
15   Nolan Ryan, AL:Cal. 1972-74,76-79; Tex. 89-91; NL:Hou. 80,82,85,87-88

Most Seasons, 200 or more Strikeouts, League
11   Roger Clemens, AL:Bos. 1986-92,96; Tor. 97-98; NY 2001
10   Tom Seaver, NL:NY 1968-76,78

Most Seasons, Consecutive, 200 or more Strikeouts, League
9   Tom Seaver, NL:NY 1968-76
7   Rube Waddell, AL:Phil. 1902-07; StL. 08
      Walter Johnson, AL:Wash. 1910-16
      Roger Clemens, AL:Bos. 1986-92

Most Strikeouts, Game
20   Roger Clemens, AL:Bos. Apr. 29, 1986
      Roger Clemens, AL:Bos. Sept. 18, 1996
      Kerry Wood, NL:Chi. May 6, 1998
      Randy Johnson, NL:Ari. May 8, 2001 (first 9 inn of 11-inn game)
      Extra-Inning Game:
21   Tom Cheney, AL:Wash. Sept. 12, 1962 (16 inn)

Most Strikeouts, Consecutive, Game
10   Tom Seaver, NL:NY Apr. 22, 1970
8   Nolan Ryan, AL:Cal. July 9, 1972; Aug. 7, 1973
      Ron Davis, AL:NY May 4, 1981
      Roger Clemens, AL:Bos. Apr. 29, 1986
      Blake Stein, AL:KC June 17, 2001

Most Strikeouts, Consecutive, Start of Game
9   Mickey Welch, NL:NY Aug. 28, 1884 (50-foot distance)
      Since 1900:
8   Jim Deshaies, NL:Hou. Sept. 23, 1986
7   Joe Cowley, AL:Chi. May 28, 1986

Most Games, 10 or more Strikeouts, Lifetime
215   Nolan Ryan, NL:NY 1966,68-71; Hou. 80-88; AL:Cal. 72-79; Tex. 89-93

Most Games, 10 or more Strikeouts, Season
23   Nolan Ryan, AL:Cal. 1973
      Randy Johnson, NL:Ari. 1999-2001

Most Strikeouts, 2 Consecutive Games
34   Dupee Shaw, UA:Bos. July 19 (18)-21 (16), 1884 (50-foot distance)
33   Kerry Wood, NL:Chi. May 6 (20)-11 (13), 1998
32   Luis Tiant, AL:Clev. June 29 (13)-July 3 (19), 1968
      Nolan Ryan, AL:Cal. Aug. 7 (13)-12 (19), 1974
      Randy Johnson, AL:Sea. Aug. 8 (19)-15 (13), 1997
      Pedro Martinez, AL:Bos. Sept. 4 (15)-10 (17), 1999
      Pedro Martinez, AL:Bos. May 6 (17)-12 (15), 2000

Most Strikeouts, 3 Consecutive Games
48   Dupee Shaw, UA:Bos. July 16 (14)-19 (18)-21 (16), 1884 (50-foot distance)
47   Nolan Ryan, AL:Cal. Aug. 12 (19)-16 (9)-20 (19), 1974
43   Dwight Gooden, NL:NY Sept. 7 (11)-12 (16)-17 (16), 1984
      Randy Johnson, NL:Ari. June 25 (14)-30 (17)-July 5 (12), 1999
      Randy Johnson, NL:Ari. Apr. 28 (12)-May 3 (11)-8 (20), 2001
      Randy Johnson, NL:Ari. May 3 (11)-May 8 (20)-13 (12), 2001

Most Strikeouts, Inning
4   Bobby Mathews, AA:Phil. Sept. 30, 1885 (7th)
    Cannonball Crane, NL:NY Oct. 4, 1888 (5th,cons)
    Hooks Wiltse, NL:NY May 15, 1906 (5th,cons)
    Jim Davis, NL:Chi. May 27(1g), 1956 (6th,cons)
    Joe Nuxhall, NL:Cin. Aug. 11(1g), 1959 (6th)
    Pete Richert, NL:LA Apr. 12, 1962 (3rd,cons)
    Don Drysdale, NL:LA Apr. 17, 1965 (2nd,cons)
    Bob Gibson, NL:StL. June 7, 1966 (4th)
    Bill Bonham, NL:Chi. July 31(1g), 1974 (2nd)
    Phil Niekro, NL:Atl. July 29, 1977 (6th)
    Mario Soto, NL:Cin. May 17, 1984 (3rd,cons)
    Mike Scott, NL:Hou. Sept. 3, 1986 (5th)
    Paul Assenmacher, NL:Atl. Aug. 22, 1989 (5th)
    Tim Birtsas, NL:Cin. June 4, 1990 (7th)
    Mark Wohlers, NL:Atl. June 17, 1995 (9th,cons)
    Bruce Ruffin, NL:Col. July 25, 1996 (9th)
    Derek Wallace, NL:NY Sept. 13, 1996 (9th)
    Kirt Ojala, NL:Fla Sept. 16, 1998 (4th,cons)
    Archie Corbin, NL:Fla. Apr. 28, 1999 (7th)
    Jerry Spradlin, NL:SF July 22, 1999 (7th)
    Steve Kline, NL:Mtl. Aug 17, 1999 (7th,cons)
    Frankie Rodriguez, NL:Cin. July 22, 2001 (7th)
    Walter Johnson, AL:Wash. Apr. 15, 1911 (5th)
    Guy Morton, AL:Clev. June 11, 1916 (6th,cons)
    Ryne Duren, AL:LA May 18, 1961 (7th)
    Lee Stange, AL:Clev. Sept. 2, 1964 (7th)
    Mike Cuellar, AL:Balt. May 29, 1970 (4th,cons)
    Mike Paxton, AL:Clev. July 21, 1978 (5th,cons)
    Bobby Witt, AL:Tex. Aug. 2, 1987 (2nd,cons)
    Charlie Hough, AL:Tex. July 4, 1988 (1st)
    Matt Young, AL:Sea. Sept. 9, 1990 (1st)
    Paul Shuey, AL:Clev. May 14, 1994 (9th)
    Kevin Appier, AL:KC Sept. 3, 1996 (4th)
    Wilson Alvarez, AL:Chi. July 21, 1997 (7th,cons)
    Blake Stein, AL:Oak. July 27, 1998 (4th)
    Chuck Finley, AL:Ana. May 12, 1999 (3rd)
    Tim Wakefield, AL:Bos. Aug 10, 1999 (9th)
    Chuck Finley, AL:Ana. Aug. 15, 1999 (1st,cons)
    Chuck Finley, AL:Clev. Apr. 16, 2000 (3rd)
    Erik Hiljus, AL:Oak. June 30, 2001 (7th)

SACRIFICE HITS

Most Seasons Leading League
3   Eppa Rixey, NL:Phil. 1920; Cin. 21,28
    Earl Whitehill, AL:Det. 1931; Wash. 34-35

Most Sacrifices, Season
    Including sacrifice flies:
54   Stan Coveleski, AL:Clev. 1921
    Ed Rommel, AL:Phil. 1923
49   Eppa Rixey, NL:Phil. 1920
    Jack Scott, NL:Phil. 1927
    Excluding sacrifice flies:
35   Ed Brandt, NL:Bos. 1933
28   Earl Whitehill, AL:Det. 1931

SACRIFICE FLIES (Since 1955)

Most Seasons Leading Major Leagues
3   Charlie Hough, AL:Tex. 1987; Chi. 91; NL:Fla. 94

Most Seasons, Consecutive, Leading Major Leagues
2   Jamie Navarro, AL:Mil. 1992-93

Most Seasons Leading League
4   Charlie Hough, AL:Tex. 1987, 90; Chi. 91; NL:Fla. 94
3   Rick Reuschel, NL:Chi. 1976,80; SF 88
    Charlie Hough, AL:Tex. 1987, 90; Chi. 91
    Jamie Navarro, AL:Mil. 1992-93; Chi. 97

Most Seasons, Consecutive, Leading League
2   Ferguson Jenkins. NL:Chi. 1973-AL:Tex. 74
        Jack Morris, AL:Det. 1980-81
        Charlie Hough, AL:Tex. 1990-Chi. 91
        Jaime Navarro, AL:Mil. 1992-93

Most Sacrifice Flies, Lifetime
146   Nolan Ryan, NL:NY 1966,68-71; Hou. 80-88; AL:Cal. 72-79; Tex. 89-93

Most Sacrifice Flies, League
118   Rick Reuschel, NL:Chi. 1972-81,83-84; Pitt. 85-87; SF 87-91
114   Jack Morris, AL:Det. 1977-90; Minn. 91; Tor. 92-93; Clev. 94

Most Sacrifice Flies, Season
17   Larry Gura, AL:KC 1983
        Jaime Navarro, AL:Mil. 1993
15   Randy Lerch, NL:Phil. 1979

WILD PITCHES

Most Seasons Leading Major Leagues
6   Larry Cheney, NL:Chi. 1912-14; Brk. 16-18

Most Seasons, Consecutive, Leading Major Leagues
3   Larry Cheney, NL:Chi. 1912-14; Brk. 16-18

Most Seasons Leading League
6   Nolan Ryan, AL:Cal. 1972,77-78; Tex. 89; NL:Hou. 81,86
        Larry Cheney, NL:Chi. 1912-14; Brk. 16-18
        Jack Morris, AL:Det. 1983-85,87; Minn. 91; Clev. 94

Most Seasons, Consecutive, Leading League
3   Larry Cheney, NL:Chi. 1912-14; Brk. 16-18
        John Smoltz, NL:Atl. 1990-92
        Jack Morris, AL:Det. 1983-85

Most Wild Pitches, Lifetime
277   Nolan Ryan, NL:NY 1966,68-71; Hou. 80-88; AL:Cal. 72-79; Tex. 89-93

Most Wild Pitches, League
206   Jack Morris, AL:Det. 1977-90; Minn. 91; Tor. 92-93; Clev. 94
200   Phil Niekro, NL:Mil./Atl. 1964-83,87

Most Wild Pitches, Season
64   Bill Stemmeyer, NL:Bos. 1886
        Since 1900:
30   Red Ames, NL:NY 1905
26   Juan Guzman, AL:Tor. 1993

Most Wild Pitches, Game
10   Johnny Ryan, NL:Lou. July 22, 1876
        Since 1900:
6   J.R. Richard, NL:Hou. Apr. 10, 1979
        Phil Niekro, NL:Atl. Aug. 4(2g), 1979
        Bill Gullickson, NL:Mtl. Apr. 10, 1982
5   Charlie Wheatley, AL:Det. Sept. 27, 1912
        Jack Morris, AL:Det. Aug. 3, 1987 (10 inn)

Most Wild Pitches, Inning
4   Walter Johnson, AL:Wash. Sept. 21, 1914 (4th)
        Phil Niekro, NL:Atl. Aug. 4(2g), 1979 (5th)

Fewest Wild Pitches, Season (Most Innings)
0   Joe McGinnity, NL:NY 1906 (340 inn)
        General Crowder, AL:Wash. 1932 (327 inn)

Fewest Wild Pitches, Game (Most Innings)
0   Leon Cadore, NL:Brk. May 1, 1920 (26 inn)
        Jack Coombs, AL:Phil. Sept. 1, 1906 (24 inn)
        Joe Harris, AL:Bos. Sept. 1, 1906 (24 inn)

BALKS

Most Balks, Season
16	Dave Stewart, AL:Oak. 1988
11	Steve Carlton, NL:Phil. 1979

Most Balks, Game
5	Bob Shaw, NL:Mil. May 4, 1963
4	Vic Raschi, AL:NY May 3, 1950
	Bobby Witt, AL:Tex. Apr. 12, 1988
	Rick Honeycutt, AL:Oak., Apr. 13, 1988
	Gene Walter, AL:Sea. July 18, 1988
	John Dopson, AL:Bos. June 13, 1989

Most Balks, Inning
3	Milt Shoffner, AL:Clev. May 12, 1930 (3rd)
	Don Heinkel, AL:Det. May 3, 1988 (6th)
	Jim Owens, NL:Cin. Apr. 24, 1963 (2nd)
	Bob Shaw, NL:Mil. May 4, 1963 (3rd)
	Jim Gott, NL:Pitt. Aug. 6, 1988 (8th)

RELIEF PITCHING

Highest Percentage, Games Won, Lifetime (Minimum: 50 wins)
.708	Hugh Casey, NL:Chi. 1935; Brk. 39-42,46-48; Pitt. 49; AL:NY 49 (51-21)

Highest Percentage, Games Won, League (Minimum: 50 wins)
.704	Hugh Casey, NL:Chi. 1935; Brk. 39-42,46-48; Pitt. 49 (50-21)
.680	Eddie Rommel, AL:Phil. 1920-32 (51-24)

Most Games, Lifetime
1127	Jesse Orosco, NL:NY 1979, 81-87; LA 88, 2001; StL. 2000; AL:Clev. 89-91; Mil. 92-94; Balt. 95-99

Most Games, League
1050	Kent Tekulve, NL:Pitt. 1974-85; Phil. 85-88; Cin. 89
807	Sparky Lyle, AL:Bos. 1967-71; NY 72-78; Tex. 79-80; Chi. 82

Most Games, Consecutive, Lifetime
1078	Jesse Orosco, NL:NY-LA-StL; AL:Clev.-Mil.-Balt. July 20, 1982-Oct.5, 2001

Most Games, Consecutive, League
1050	Kent Tekulve, NL:Pitt.-Phil.-Cin. May 20, 1974-July 16, 1989
807	Sparky Lyle, AL:Bos.-NY-Tex.-Chi. July 4, 1967-Sept. 27(2g) 1982

Most Games, Season
106	Mike Marshall, NL:LA 1974
89	Mike Marshall, AL:Minn. 1979
	Mark Eichhorn, AL:Tor. 1987

Most Games Won, Lifetime
124	Hoyt Wilhelm, NL:NY 1952-56; StL. 57; Atl. 69-71; Chi. 70; LA 71-72 AL:Clev. 57-58; Balt. 58-62; Chi. 63-68; Cal. 69

Most Games Won, Consecutive, Start of Career
19	Rube Waddell, AL:Phil.-StL. July 21, 1902-June 11, 1908
12	Butch Metzger, NL:SF-SD Sept. 21, 1974-Aug. 8, 1976

Most Games Won, League
96	Roy Face, NL:Pitt. 1953,55-68; Mtl. 69
87	Sparky Lyle, AL:Bos. 1967-71; NY 72-78; Tex. 79-80; Chi. 82

Most Games Won, Season
18	Roy Face, NL:Pitt. 1959 (1 lost)
17	John Hiller, AL:Det. 1974 (14 lost)
	Bill Campbell, AL:Minn. 1976 (5 lost)

Most Games Lost, Lifetime
108	Gene Garber, NL:Pitt. 1969-72; Phil. 74-78; Atl. 78-87; AL:KC 1973-74, 87-88

Most Games Lost, League
98	Gene Garber, NL:Pitt. 1969-72; Phil. 74-78; Atl. 78-87
67	Hoyt Wilhelm, AL:Clev. 1957-58; Balt. 58-62; Chi. 63-68; Cal. 69
	Sparky Lyle, AL:Bos. 1967-71; NY 72-78; Tex. 79-80; Chi. 82

Most Games Lost, Season
16	Gene Garber, NL:Atl. 1979 (6 won)
14	Darold Knowles, AL:Wash. 1970 (2 won)
	John Hiller, AL:Det. 1974 (17 won)
	Mike Marshall, AL:Minn. 1979 (10 won)

Most Innings, Lifetime

1870	Hoyt Wilhelm, NL:NY 1952-56; StL. 57; Atl. 69-71; Chi. 70; LA 71-72 AL:Clev. 57-58; Balt. 58-62; Chi. 63-68; Cal. 69

Most Innings, League

1436.2	Kent Tekulve, NL:Pitt. 1974-85; Phil. 85-88; Cin. 89
1265.0	Sparky Lyle, AL:Bos. 1967-71; NY 72-78; Tex. 79-80; Chi. 82

Most Innings, Season

208.0	Mike Marshall, NL:LA 1974
168.1	Bob Stanley, AL:Bos. 1982

Most Innings, Game

18.1	Zip Zabel, NL:Chi. June 17, 1915
17.0	Eddie Rommel, AL:Phil. July 10, 1932

Most Strikeouts, Consecutive, Game

8	Ron Davis, AL:NY May 4, 1981
7	Randy Johnson, NL:Ari. July 18, 2001

DOUBLEHEADERS (Complete Games)

Most Doubleheaders, Lifetime

5	Joe McGinnity, AL:Balt. 1901; NL:NY 1903

Most Doubleheaders, League

3	Joe McGinnity, NL:NY 1903
2 ·	Joe McGinnity, AL:Balt. 1901
	Ed Walsh, AL:Chi. 1905,08
	Mule Watson, AL:Phil. 1918

Most Doubleheaders, Season

3	Joe McGinnity, NL:NY 1903
2	Joe McGinnity, AL:Balt. 1901
	Mule Watson, AL:Phil. 1918

Most Doubleheaders Won, League

3	Joe McGinnity, NL:NY 1903
1	By many players

Most Doubleheaders Won, Season

3	Joe McGinnity, NL:NY 1903
1	By many players; Last:
	Dutch Levsen, AL:Clev. 1926

Fewest Runs, Doubleheader

0	Ed Reulbach, NL:Chi. Sept. 26, 1908
1	Ed Walsh, AL:Chi. Sept. 29, 1908
	Carl Mays, AL:Bos. Aug. 30, 1918

Fewest Hits, Doubleheader

3	Tim Keefe, AA:NY July 4, 1883
6	Fred Toney, NL:Cin. July 1, 1917
	Hi Bell, NL:StL. July 19, 1924
7	Frank Owen, AL:Chi. July 1, 1905
	Ed Walsh, AL:Chi. Sept. 29, 1908

Fewest Walks, Doubleheader

0	Guy Hecker, AA:Lou. July 4, 1884
1	Ed Walsh, AL:Chi. Sept. 29, 1908
	Grover Alexander, NL:Phil. Sept. 23, 1916 & Sept. 3, 1917

PITCHING – ROOKIE SEASON

(No official rookie rule prior to 1957. Qualifiers based on less than 45 innings pitched.)

Most Games
88	Sean Runyan, AL:Det. 1998
78	Tim Burke, NL:Mtl. 1985

Most Complete Games
66	Jim Devlin, NL:Lou. 1876
	Matt Kilroy, NL:Balt. 1886
	Since 1900:
41	Irv Young, NL:Bos. 1905
35	Roscoe Miller, AL:Det. 1901

Most Shutouts
16	George Bradley, NL:StL. 1876
	Since 1900:
8	Russ Ford, AL:NY 1910
	Reb Russell, AL:Chi. 1913
	Fernando Valenzuela, NL:LA 1981

Most Shutouts, Consecutive, Start of Career
2	Al Spalding, NL:Chi. Apr. 25-27, 1876
	Jim Hughes NL:Balt. Apr. 18-22, 1898
	Al Worthington, NL:NY July 6-11, 1953
	Karl Spooner, NL:Brk. Sept. 22-26, 1954
	Slow Joe Doyle, AL:NY Aug. 25-30, 1906
	Johnny Marcum, AL:Phil. Sept. 7-11, 1933
	Boo Ferriss, AL:Bos. Apr. 29-May 6, 1945
	Tom Phoebus, AL:Balt. Sept. 15-20, 1966

Most Saves, Season
37	Kazuhiro Sasaki, AL:Sea. 2000
36	Todd Worrell, NL:StL. 1986

Most Games Won
47	Al Spalding, NL:Chi. 1876 (13 lost)
	Since 1900:
28	Grover Alexander, NL:Phil. 1911 (13 lost)
26	Russ Ford, AL:NY 1910 (6 lost)

Most Games Won, Consecutive
17	Pat Luby, NL:Chi. Aug. 6-Oct. 3, 1890
	Since 1900:
12	Hooks Wiltse, NL:NY May 29-Sept. 15, 1904
	Atley Donald, AL:NY May 9-July 25, 1939

Most Games Lost
48	John Coleman, NL:Phil. 1883 (48 lost)
	Since 1900:
26	Bob Groom, AL:Wash. 1909 (26 lost)
25	Harry McIntire, NL:Brk. 1905 (25 lost)

Most Games Lost, Consecutive
16	Dory Dean, NL:Cin. July 11-Sept. 12, 1876
	Since 1900:
15	Bob Groom, AL:Wash. July 6-Sept. 25, 1909
14	Anthony Young, NL:NY May 6-Sept. 29, 1992

Most Innings
591	Lee Richmond, NL:Wor. 1880
	Since 1900:
378	Irv Young, NL:Bos. 1905
332	Roscoe Miller, AL:Det. 1901

Fewest Hits, First Game (9 or more innings)
0	Bumpus Jones, NL:Cin. Oct. 15, 1892
	Since 1900:
1	Addie Joss, AL:Clev. Apr. 26, 1902
	Mike Fornieles, AL:Wash. Sept. 2(2g), 1952
	Billy Rohr, AL:Bos. Apr. 14, 1967
	Juan Marichal, NL:SF July 19, 1960
	Jimmy Jones, NL:SD Sept. 21, 1986

Most Scoreless Innings, Consecutive, Start of Career
25	George McQuillan, NL:Phil. May 8, Sept. 22-29, 1907
22	Boo Ferris, AL:Bos. Apr. 29-May 13, 1945

Most Sacrifice Flies (Since 1954)
14	Rich DeLucia, AL:Sea. 1991
12	George O'Donnell, NL:Pitt. 1954

Most Intentional Walks (Since 1955)
20	Ron Willis, NL:StL. 1967
16	Ken Sanders, AL:Bos.-KC 1966

Most Strikeouts
276	Dwight Gooden, NL:NY 1984
245	Herb Score, AL:Clev. 1955

Most Strikeouts, First Game
15	Karl Spooner, NL:Brk. Sept. 22, 1954
	J.R. Richard, NL:Hou. Sept. 5(2g), 1971
12	Elmer Myers, AL:Phil. Oct. 6(2g), 1915
	Steve Woodard, AL:Mil. July 28(1g), 1997

Most Strikeouts, Consecutive, First Game
7	Sammy Stewart, AL:Balt. Sept. 1, 1978 (2-4 inn)
6	Karl Spooner, NL:Brk. Sept. 22, 1954 (7-8 inn)
	Pete Richert, NL:LA Apr. 12, 1962 (2-4 inn)

Most Wild Pitches, First Game
5	Jake Seymour, AA:Pitt. Sept. 23, 1882
	Mike Corcoran, NL:Chi. July 15, 1884
	George Winkelman, NL:Wash. Aug. 2, 1886

CLUB BATTING - SEASON

	AL:1901-1960 NL:1900-1961 8 clubs 154 games		AL:1961-1968 NL:1962-1968 10.clubs 162 games		AL:1969- NL:1969- 12-16 clubs 162 games	
Highest Batting Average						
AL:	.3156	Det. 1921	.2673	NY 1962	.2930	Clev. 1996
NL:	.3185	NY 1930	.2794	Pitt. 1966	.2940	Col. 2000
Lowest Batting Average						
AL:	.2117	Chi. 1910	.2141	NY 1968	.2291	Mil. 1971
NL:	.2131	Brk. 1908	.2188	NY 1963	.2245	SD 1969
Highest Slugging Percentage						
AL:	.4890	NY 1927	.4416	NY 1961	.4845	Sea. 1997
NL:	.4809	Chi. 1930	.4407	SF 1962	.4830	Col. 2001
Lowest Slugging Percentage						
AL:	.2614	Chi. 1910	.3110	Chi. 1968	.3175	Cal. 1976
NL:	.2742	Bos. 1909	.3005	Hou. 1963	.3265	StL. 1986
Most At-Bats						
AL:	5646	Clev. 1936	5705	NY 1964	5781	Bos. 1997
NL:	5667	Phil. 1930	5767	Cin. 1968	5734	StL. 1979
Fewest At-Bats						
AL:	4827	Chi. 1913	5275	Balt. 1968	5185	Mil. 1971
NL:	4725	Phil. 1907	5305	Hou 1964	5333	Cin. 1983
Most Runs						
AL:	1067	NY 1931	841	Det. 1961	1009	Clev. 1999
NL:	1004	StL. 1930	878	SF 1962	968	Col. 2000
Fewest Runs						
AL:	380	Wash. 1909	463	Chi. 1968	511	Cal. 1971
NL:	372	StL. 1908	464	Hou 1963	468	SD 1969
Most Hits						
AL:	1724	Det. 1921	1509	NY 1962	1684	Bos. 1997
NL:	1783	Phil. 1930	1586	Pitt. 1966	1664	Col. 2000
Fewest Hits						
AL:	1061	Chi. 1910	1137	NY 1968	1188	Mil. 1971
NL:	1044	Brk. 1908	1168	NY 1963	1203	SD 1969
Most Total Bases						
AL:	2703	NY 1936	2455	NY 1961	2741	Sea. 1996
NL:	2684	Chi 1930	2483	Cin. 1965	2748	Col. 2001
Fewest Total Bases						
AL:	1310	Chi. 1910	1681	Chi. 1968	1694	Cal. 1969
NL:	1358	Brk. 1908	1618	Hou. 1963	1756	StL. 1986
Most Extra-Base Hits						
AL:	580	NY 1936	494	Minn. 1964	607	Sea. 1996
NL:	566	StL. 1930	512	Cin. 1965	598	Col. 2001
Fewest Extra-Base Hits						
AL:	179	Chi. 1910	273	Chi 1968	268	Cal. 1969
NL:	182	Bos. 1909	271	Hou. 1963	282	Atl. 1976
Most Singles						
AL:	1298	Det. 1921	1075	Chi. 1961	1202	Tex. 1980
NL:	1297	Pitt. 1922	1239	Pitt. 1967	1168	StL. 1971
Fewest Singles						
AL:	837	Wash. 1959	811	Balt. 1968	870	Tor. 1997
NL:	846	Brk. 1908	865	NY 1965	867	Mil. 2000

	AL:1901-1960 NL:1900-1961 8 clubs 154 games		AL:1961-1968 NL:1962-1968 10.clubs 162 games		AL:1969- NL:1969- 12-16 clubs 162 games
Most Doubles					
AL:	358	Clev 1930	257	Clev 1961 Bos 1962 Minn 1965	373	Bos. 1997
NL:	373	StL. 1930	281	Cin 1968	339	Mtl. 1997
Fewest Doubles					
AL:	116	Chi. 1910	154	NY 1968	151	Cal. 1969
NL:	110	Brk. 1908	156	NY 1963	170	Atl. 1976
Most Triples					
AL:	112	Balt. 1901 Bos. 1903	59	KC 1965	79	KC 1979
NL:	129	Pitt. 1912	66	StL. 1963	70	Pitt. 1970
Fewest Triples					
AL:	19	Balt. 1958	17	NY 1967 Bos. 1968	11	Balt. 1998
NL:	19	Bos. 1942	23	NY 1967	14	LA 1986 NY 1999
Most Home Runs					
AL:	193	NY 1960	240	NY 1961	264	Sea. 1997
NL:	221	NY 1947 Cin. 1956	207	Atl. 1966	249	Hou. 2000
Fewest Home Runs					
AL:	3	Chi. 1908	69	KC 1967	55	Cal. 1975
NL:	5	Phil. 1902	62	Hou. 1963	49	Hou. 1979
Most Grand Slam Home Runs					
AL:	10	Det. 1938	8	Minn. 1961 Bos. 1964	14	Oak. 2000
NL:	9	Chi. 1929	8	Mil. 1962	12	Atl. 1997 StL. 2000
Most Home Runs, Pinch-Hitters					
AL:	7	NY 1953-54, 60 Clev.& Det. 1958	10	NY 1961	12	Clev. 1999
NL:	12	Cin. 1957	9	Chi. 1962 NY 1962, 66	14	Ari. 2001 SF 2001
Most Grand Slam Home Runs, Pinch-Hitters					
AL:	2	Phil. 1931; Det. 1952 NY 1953; Bos. 1960	2	Chi.& NY 1961	3	Balt. 1982
NL:	2	NY 1934; Phil. 1945	1	By many clubs	3	By many clubs
Most Runs Batted In (Since 1920)					
AL:	995	NY 1936	791	NY 1962	960	Clev. 1999
NL:	942	StL. 1930	807	SF 1962	909	Col. 1996
Fewest Runs Batted In (Since 1920)					
AL:	440	Phil. 1945	431	Chi. 1968	477	Cal. 1971
NL:	354	Phil. 1942	420	Hou. 1963	431	SD 1969
Most Sacrifice Hits					
AL:	207	Chi. 1906	109	Chi. 1966	142	Minn. 1979
NL:	231	Chi. 1906	120	LA 1964	133	SD 1975
Fewest Sacrifice Hits					
AL:	41	Bos. 1957	35	Bos. 1964	16	Det. 1998 NY 2000
NL:	32	NY 1957	46	NY 1963	29	SD 2001
Most Sacrifice Flies (Since 1954)					
AL:	59	Clev. 1954-55 Chi. 1960	59	Minn. 1965	77	Oak 1984
NL:	66	StL. 1954	53	LA 1963	75	Col. 2000

	AL:1901-1960 NL:1900-1961 8 clubs 154 games		AL:1961-1968 NL:1962-1968 10.clubs 162 games		AL:1969- NL:1969- 12-16 clubs 162 games
Fewest Sacrifice Flies (Since 1954)					
AL:	27	Balt. 1955	23	Cal. 1967	25	TB 2001
NL:	26	StL. 1959	26	NY 1964	19	SD 1971
Most Walks					
AL:	835	Bos. 1949	681	LA 1961	775	Sea. 2000
NL:	732	Brk. 1947	616	NY 1962	729	SF 1970
Fewest Walks					
AL:	356	Phil. 1920	397	Chi. 1968	383	Det. 1975
NL:	283	Phil. 1920	345	StL. 1966	388	Col. 1993
Most Intentional Walks (Since 1955)					
AL:	66	NY 1957	79	Minn. 1965	78	Minn. 1969
NL:	91	Brk. 1956	101	Phil. 1967	102	Pitt. 1979
Fewest Intentional Walks (Since 1955)					
AL:	20	Wash. 1959	10	KC 1961	19	Sea. 1987 Tor. 1996; Det. 1999
NL:	22	LA 1958	29	NY 1962	27	Pitt. 1997
Most Hit by Pitch					
AL:	75	Chi. 1956	61	Det. 1968	92	Tor. 1996
NL:	52	NY 1917	53	Phil. 1962	100	Hou. 1997
Fewest Hit by Pitch					
AL:	5	Phil. 1937	15	Wash. 1962	11	Clev. 1976
NL:	9	Phil. 1939	17	Pitt. 1962	9	SD 1989
Most Strikeouts					
AL:	893	Wash. 1960	1125	Wash. 1965	1268	Det. 1996
NL:	1054	Phil. 1960	1203	NY 1968	1399	Mil. 2001
Fewest Strikeouts					
AL:	326	Phil. 1927	612	Chi. 1961	589	Tex. 1980
NL:	308	Cin. 1921	782	Atl. 1968	649	StL. 1975
Most Stolen Bases					
AL:	291	Wash. 1913	153	Chi. 1966	341	Oak. 1976
NL:	347	NY 1911	198	LA 1962	314	StL. 1985
Fewest Stolen Bases					
AL:	13	Wash. 1957	18	Bos. 1964	25	Clev. 1970
NL:	17	StL. 1949	22	SF 1967	23	Pitt. 1973
Most Caught Stealing					
AL:	119	Chi. 1923	82	Chi. 1967	123	Oak. 1976
NL:	149	Chi. 1924	77	LA 1965	120	Pitt. 1977
Fewest Caught Stealing					
AL:	11	KC 1960	11	Clev. 1961	15	Oak. 2000
NL:	8	Mil. 1958	27	Mil. 1962	16	Chi. 1970
Most Grounded into Double Plays					
AL:	170	Phil. 1950	157	Bos. 1965	174	Bos. 1990
NL:	166	StL. 1958	149	SF 1965	154	Atl. 1985 Hou. 2000
Fewest Grounded into Double Plays					
AL:	93	StL. 1944 NY 1952	79	KC 1967	81	Det. 1985
NL:	75	StL. 1945	79	LA 1965	76	Hou. 1983
Most Left on Base					
AL:	1334	StL. 1941	1244	Chi. 1964	1312	Det. 1993
NL:	1278	Brk. 1947	1218	NY 1962	1328	Cin. 1976
Fewest Left on Base					
AL:	925	KC 1957	995	KC 1966	975	Cal. 1992
NL:	964	Chi. 1924	1019	SF 1966	978	Col. 1993

BATTING AVERAGE

Most Seasons Leading League
22 **NL:**StL. 1915, 20-21, 34, 38-39, 42-44,
   46, 49, 52, 54, 56-57, 63, 71, 75, 79-80,
   85, 92
21 **AL:**Bos. 1903, 38-39, 41-42,44, 46, 49-50,
   64, 67, 75, 79, 81, 84-85, 87-90, 97

Most Seasons, Consecutive, Leading League
7 **NL:**Col. 1995-2001
5 **AL:**Phil. 1910-14

Most Players, .300 or Higher, Season
(Minimum: 300 at-bats)
8 **NL:**StL. 1930
7 **AL:**Phil. 1927

SLUGGING PERCENTAGE

Most Seasons Leading League
30 **AL:**Balt./NY 1901,20-21, 23-24,26-28,30-
   31,36-39, 43-45, 47-48, 51, 53-58,
   60-62, 86
22 **NL:**NY/SF 1889,91, 1904-05,08,10-11,19,23-
   24,27-28,35,45,47-48 52,61-63,89,93

Most Seasons, Consecutive, Leading League
6 **AL:**NY 1953-58
5 **NL:**Col. 1995-99

PLATE APPEARANCES

Most Batters, Game
71 **NL:**Chi. (Lou.) June 29, 1897
   Since 1900:
66 **NL:**Phil. (Chi.) Aug. 25, 1922
65 **AL:**Mil. (Tor.) Aug. 28, 1992
   Extra-Inning Game
104 **AL:**Chi. (Mil.) May 8, 1984 (25 inn)
103 **NL:**NY(StL.) Sept. 11, 1974 (25 inn)

Most Batters, Both Clubs, Game
125 **NL:**Phil. (66) Chi. (59) Aug. 25, 1922
108 **AL:**Clev. (58) Phil. (50) Apr. 29, 1952
   Extra-Inning Game:
202 **NL:**NY (103) StL. (99) Sept. 11, 1974
   (25 inn)
198 **AL:**Chi. (104) Mil. (94) May 8, 1984
   (25 inn)

Most Batters, Inning
23 **NL:**Chi. (Det.) Sept. 6, 1883 (7th)
   Since 1900:
23 **AL:**Bos. (Det.) June 18, 1953 (7th)
21 **NL:**Brk. (Cin.) May 21, 1952 (1st)

Most Batters, 3 Appearances, Inning
5 **NL:**Chi. (Det.) Sept. 6, 1883 (7th)
  AL: Bos. (Det.) June 18, 1953 (7th)
  NL Since 1900:
3 **NL:**Brk. (Cin) May 21, 1952 (1st)

Most Batters on Base, Inning
20 **NL:**Bos. (Det.) June 18, 1953 (7th)
19 **NL:**Bos. (Balt.) June 18, 1894 (1g; 1st)
   Brk. (Cin.) May 21, 1952 (1st)

Most Batters, Consecutive, On Base, Inning
19 **NL:**Brk. (Cin.) May 21, 1952 (1st)
13 **AL:**KC (Chi.) Apr. 21, 1956 (2nd)

Most Batters, On Base 3 Times, Inning
3 **NL:**Chi. (Det.) Sept. 6, 1883 (7th)
  Bos. (Balt.) June 18, 1894 (1g; 1st)
  AL: Bos. (Det.) June 18, 1953 (7th)
  NL Since 1900:
1 **NL:**Brk. (Cin.) May 21, 1952 (1st)

AT-BATS

Most At-Bats, Game
66 **NL:**Chi. (Buff.) July 3, 1883
   Since 1900:
58 **NL:**NY (Phil.) Sept. 2, 1925
   NY (Phil.) July 11, 1931
57 **AL:**Mil. (Tor.) Aug. 28, 1992
   Extra-Inning Game
95 **AL:**Chi. (Mil.) May 8, 1984 (25 inn)
89 **NL:**NY (StL.) Sept. 11, 1974 (25 inn)

Most At-Bats, Both Clubs, Game
106 **NL:**Chi (64) Lou (42) July 22, 1876
   Since 1900:
99 **NL:**NY (56) Cin. (43) June 9, 1901
   NY (58) Phil. (41) July 11, 1931
96 **AL:**Clev. (51) Phil. (45) Apr. 29, 1952
   Extra-Inning Game:
175 **NL:**NY (89) StL. (86) Sept. 11, 1974 (25 inn)
   AL: Chi. (95) Mil. (80) May 8, 1984 (25 inn)

Fewest At-Bats, Game
9 innings:
22 **NL:**Atl. (Cin.) Apr. 11, 1980
23 **AL:**Chi. (StL) May 6, 1917
   Clev. (Chi.) May 9, 1961
   Det. (Balt.) May 6, 1968
8 innings:
19 **AL:**Balt. (KC) Sept. 12, 1964
21 **NL:**Pitt. (StL.) Sept. 8, 1908
   Atl. (Pitt.) Sept. 6, 1986

Fewest At-Bats, Both Clubs, Game
9 innings:
46 **AL:**Balt. (19) KC (27) Sept. 12, 1964
48 **NL:**Bos. (25) Phil. (23) Apr. 22, 1910
   Brk. (24) Cin. (24) July 22, 1911
   Cin. (26) Atl. (22) Apr. 11, 1980

Fewest At-Bats, Innings
3 fielding putouts
0 **AL:**Wash. (Det.) Aug. 22, 1915 (2nd)
1 **NL:**Many clubs

RUNS

Most Seasons Leading League
25 **AL:**NY 1921,26-28,30-33,36-39,42-43,45,
   47,53-54,56-58,60,62,85,98
21 **NL:**Chi. 1876,78,80-86,88,
   1906,11,13,18,29,31,35,37, 67,84,89
   NY/SF 1889, 1904-05,08,10,12 14,16-17,19-
   21,23-24,27, 47-48,58,61-62,70

Most Seasons, Consecutive, Leading League
7 **NL:**Chi. 1880-86
   Since 1900:
5 **NL:**Brk. 1949-53
4 **AL:**Det. 1907-10
   NY 1930-33, 36-39
   Bos. 1948-51

Most Games, Consecutive, Scoring Runs
308 **AL:**NY Aug. 3, 1931-Aug. 2, 1933
208 **NL:**Cin. Apr. 3, 2000-May 23, 2001

Most Runs, Game
36 **NL:**Chi. (Lou.) June 29, 1897
   Since 1900:
29 **AL:**Bos. (StL.) June 8, 1950
   Chi. (KC) Apr. 23, 1955
28 **NL:**StL. (Phil.) July 6, 1929

Most Runs, Both Clubs, Game
49 **NL:**Chi. (26) Phil. (23) Aug. 25, 1922
36 **AL:**Bos. (22) Phil. (14) June 29, 1950

Most Runs, 2 Consecutive Games
53 **NL:**Chi. July 22-25, 1876
   Since 1900:
49 **AL:**Bos. June 7-8, 1950
45 **NL:**Pitt. June 20-22, 1925

Most Runs, 3 Consecutive Games
71 **NL:**Chi. July 20-25, 1876
56 **AL:**Bos. June 7-9, 1950
   NL Since 1900:
54 **NL:**Pitt. June 19-22, 1925

Most Runs, 4 Consecutive Games
88 **NL:**Chi. July 20-27, 1876
65 **AL:**Bos. June 5-8, 1950
   Since 1900:
59 **NL:**Chi. June 1-5, 1930

Most Runs, Inning
18 **NL:**Chi. (Det.) Sept. 6, 1883 (7th)
   Since 1900:
17 **AL:**Bos. (Det.) June 18, 1953 (7th)
15 **NL:**Brk. (Cin.) May 21, 1952(1st)

Most Runs, Both Clubs, Inning
19 **AA:**Wash. (14) Balt. (5) June 17, 1891 (1st)
   AL: Clev. (13) Bos. (6) Apr. 10, 1977 (8th)
18 **NL:**Chi. (18) Det. (0) Sept. 6, 1883 (7th)
   Since 1900:
17 **NL:**Bos. (10) NY (7) June 20, 1912 (9th)

Most Runs, Extra Inning
12 **AL:**Tex. (Oak.) July 3, 1983 (15th)
10 **NL:**KC (Det.) July 21, 1886 (11th)
   Bos. (NY) June 17, 1887 (10th)
   Cin. (Brk.) May 15, 1919 (13th)

Most Runs, Both Clubs, Extra Inning
12 **AL:**Minn. (11) Oak. (1) June 21, 1969 (10th)
   Tex. (12) Oak. (0) July 3, 1983 (15th)
11 **NL:**NY (8) Pitt. (3) June 15, 1929 (14th)
   NY (6) Brk. (5) Apr. 24, 1955 (10th)
   NY (6) Chi. (5) June 30, 1979 (11th)
   Pitt. (6) Chi. (5) Apr. 21, 1991 (11th)

Most Runs, 1st Inning
16 **NL:**Bos. (Balt.) June 18, 1894
   Since 1900:
15 **NL:**Brk. (Cin.) May 21, 1952
14 **AL:**Clev. (Phil.) June 18(2g), 1950

Most Runs, 2nd Inning
13 **NL:**NY (Clev.) July 19, 1890
   Atl. (Hou.) Sept. 20, 1972
   SD (Pitt.) May 31, 1994
   AL:KC (Chi.) Apr. 21, 1956

Most Runs, 3rd Inning
14 **NL:**Clev. (Wash.) Aug. 7, 1889
   Since 1900:
13 **NL:**SF (StL.) May 7, 1966
12 **AL:**NY (Wash.) Sept. 11(1g), 1949

Most Runs, 4th Inning
15 **NL:**Hart. (NY) May 13, 1876
   Since 1900:
14 **NL:**Chi. (Phil.) Aug. 25, 1922
13 **AL:**Chi. (Wash.) Sept. 26(1g), 1943

Most Runs, 5th Inning
14 **AL:**NY (Wash.) July 6, 1920
13 **NL:**Chi. (Pitt.) Aug. 16, 1890
   NL Since 1900:
12 **NL:**NY (Bos.) Sept. 3, 1926
   Cin. (Atl.) Apr. 25, 1977
   Mtl. (Chi.) Sept. 24, 1985

Most Runs, 6th Inning
14 **PL:**Phil. (Buff.) June 26, 1890
13 **AL:**Clev. (Bos.) July 7(1g), 1923
   Det. (NY) June 17, 1925
   NL: Mtl. (SF) May 7, 1997

Most Runs, 7th Inning
18 **NL:**Chi. (Det.) Sept. 6, 1883
   Since 1900:
17 **AL:**Bos. (Det.) June 18, 1953
13 **NL:**SF (SD) July 15, 1997

Most Runs, 8th Inning
16 **AL:**Tex. (Balt.) Apr. 19, 1996
13 **NL:**Brk. (Cin.) Aug. 8, 1954

Most Runs, 9th Inning
14 **NL:**Balt. (Bos.) Apr. 24, 1894
   Since 1900:
13 **AL:**Cal. (Tex.) Sept. 14, 1978
   Det. (Tex.) Aug. 8, 2001
12 **NL:**SF (Cin.) Aug. 23, 1961

Most Runs, 10th Inning
11 **AL:**Minn. (Oak.) June 21, 1969
10 **NL:**Bos. (NY) June 17, 1887
   NL Since 1900:
9 **NL:**Cin. (Phil.) Aug. 24(1g), 1947
   SD (Phil.) May 28, 1995

Most Runs, 11th Inning
10 **NL:**KC (Det.) July 21, 1886
   Since 1900:
9 **NL:**SD (Col.) June 28(2g), 1994
8 **AL:**Phil. (Det.) May 1, 1951
   Tex. (Sea.) Sept. 23, 1991

Most Runs, 12th Inning
11 **AL:**NY (Det.) July 26(1g), 1928
9 **NL:**Chi. (Pitt.) July 23, 1923

Most Runs, 13th Inning
10 **NL:**Cin. (Brk.) May 15, 1919
9 **AL:**Clev. (Det.) Aug. 5(1g), 1933

Most Runs, 14th Inning
8 **NL:**NY (Pitt.) June 15, 1929
7 **AL:**Clev. (StL.) June 3, 1935
   Det. (Mil.) May 27, 1991

Most Runs, 15th Inning
12 **AL:**Tex. (Oak.) July 3, 1983
7 **NL:**StL. (Bos.) Sept. 28, 1928

Most Runs, 16th Inning
8 **AL:**Chi. (Wash.) May 20, 1920
5 **NL:**Cin. (NY) Aug. 20, 1973
   Hou. (Cin.) Apr. 8, 1988

Most Runs, 17th Inning
7 **NL:**NY (Pitt) July 16, 1920
6 **AL:**NY (Det.) July 20, 1941

Most Runs, 18th Inning
5 **NL:**Chi. (Bos.) May 14, 1927
4 **AL:**Minn. (Sea.) July 19, 1969

Most Runs, 19th Inning
5 **NL:**NY (Atl.) July 4, 1985
4 **AL:**Clev. (Det.) Apr. 27, 1984

Most Runs, 20th Inning
4 **NL:**Brk. (Bos.) July 5, 1940
3 **AL:**Bos. (Sea.) July 27, 1969
      Wash. (Clev.) Sept. 14(2g), 1971

Most Runs, 21st Inning
4 **AL:**Chi. (Clev.) May 26, 1973
3 **NL:**SD (Mtl.) May 21, 1977

Most Runs, 22nd Inning
2 **AL:**NY (Det.) June 24, 1962
1 **NL:**Brk. (Pitt.) Aug. 22, 1917
      Chi. (Bos.) May 17, 1927
      Hou. (LA) June 3, 1989
      LA (Mtl.) Aug. 23, 1989

Most Runs, 23rd Inning
2 **NL:**SF (NY) May 31(2g), 1964
0 **AL:**Bos. (Phil.) Sept. 1, 1906
      Phil. (Bos.) Sept. 1, 1906
      Det. (Phil.) July 21, 1945
      Phil. (Det.) July 21, 1945
      Chi. (Mil.) May 8, 1984
      Mil. (Chi.) May 8, 1984

Most Runs, 24th Inning
3 **AL:**Phil. (Bos.) Sept. 1, 1906
1 **NL:**Hou. (NY) Apr. 15, 1968

Most Runs, 25th Inning
1 **NL:**StL. (NY) Sept. 11, 1974
      AL: Chi. (Mil.) May 8, 1984

Most Runs 26th Inning
0 **NL:**Bos. (Brk.) May 1, 1920
      Brk. (Bos.) May 1, 1920
      AL: No games

Most Runs, Both Clubs, 1st Inning
19 **AA:**Wash. (14) Balt. (5) June 17, 1891
16 **NL:**Bos. (16) Balt. (0) June 18, 1894
      AL: Oak. (13) Cal. (3) July 5, 1996
      NL Since 1900:
15 **NL:**Brk. (15) Cin. (0) May 21, 1952

Most Runs, Both Clubs, 2nd Inning
14 **AL:**Phil. (10) Det. (4) Sept. 23, 1913
      NY (11) Det. (3) Aug. 28(2g), 1936
      Chi. (8) Clev. (6) Sept. 2, 2001
13 **NL:**NY (13) Clev. (0) July 19, 1890
      Chi. (10) Pitt. (3) Aug. 25, 1922
      Brk. (11) NY (2) Apr. 29, 1930
      Atl. (13) Hou. (0) Sept. 20, 1972
      SD (13) Pitt. (0) May 31, 1994

Most Runs, Both Clubs, 3rd Inning
14 **NL:**Clev. (14) Wash. (0) Aug7, 1889
      Since 1900:
13 **AL:**Clev. (8) StL. (5) July 6, 1917
      Phil. (7) Bos. (6) July 4(2g), 1939
      Bos. (8) Det. (5) July 2, 1995
      NL: Brk. (9) Cin. (4) Aug. 22, 1929
      SF (13) StL. (0) May 7, 1966
      StL. (7) Atl. (6) Aug. 21, 1973

Most Runs, Both Clubs, 4th Inning
15 **NL:**Hart. (15) NY (0) May 13, 1876
      Chi. (14) Phil. (1) Aug. 25, 1922
14 **AL:**Chi. (12) Phil. (2) June 10, 1952

Most Runs, Both Clubs, 5th Inning
16 **NL:**Brk. (11) NY (5) June 3, 1890
      AL:NY (10) Clev. (6) Aug. 3, 1986
      NL Since 1900:
15 **NL:**Brk. (10) Cin. (5) June 12, 1949
      Phil. (9) Pitt. (6) Apr. 16, 1953

Most Runs, Both Clubs, 6th Inning
15 **AL:**Phil. (10) NY (5) Sept. 5(1g), 1912
      Det. (10) Minn. (5) June 13, 1967
      NL:NY (10) Cin. (5) June 12, 1979

Most Runs, Both Clubs, 7th Inning
18 **NL:**Chi. (18) Det. (0) Sept. 6, 1883
      Since 1900:
17 **AL:**Bos. (17) Det. (0) June 18, 1953
13 **NL:**Chi. (12) Cin. (1) May 28, 1925
      StL. (7) NY (6) June 26, 1940
      Phil. (10) Chi. (3) July 22(2g), 1945
      SF (13) SD (0) July 15, 1997

Most Runs, Both Clubs, 8th Inning
19 **AL:**Clev. (13) Bos. (6), Apr. 10, 1977
14 **NL:**NY (11) Pitt. (3), May 25, 1954
      Brk. (13) Cin. (1), Aug. 8, 1954
      Atl. (9) SD (5) Apr. 27(1g), 1975
      Col. (8) LA (6) June 29, 1996

Most Runs, Both Clubs, 9th Inning
17 **NL:**Bos. (10) NY (7), June 20, 1912
15 **AL:**Tor. (11) Sea. (4), July 20, 1984

Most Runs. Both Clubs, 10th Inning
12 **AL:**Minn. (11) Oak. (1), June 21, 1969
11 **NL:**NY (6) Brk. (5), Apr. 24, 1955

Most Runs, Both Clubs, 11th Inning
11 **AL:**Sea. (6) Bos. (5), May 16, 1969
      NL:NY (6) Chi. (5), June 30, 1979
      Pitt. (6) Chi (5) Apr. 21, 1991

Most Runs, Both Clubs, 12th Inning
11 **AL:**NY (8) Det. (3), May 14, 1923
      NY (11) Det. (0), July 26(1g), 1928
9 **NL:**Chi. (9) Pitt. (0), July 23, 1923
      NY (8) Brk. (1), May 30(2g), 1940
      Hou. (8) Cin. (1), June 2, 1966
      SD (5) Hou. (4), July 5, 1969

Most Runs, Both Clubs, 13th Inning
10 **NL:**Cin. (10) Brk. (0), May 15, 1919
9 **AL:**Clev. (9) Det. (0),Aug. 5(1g), 1933

Most Runs, Both Clubs, 14th Inning
11 **NL:**NY (8) Pitt. (3), June 15, 1929
8 **AL:**Det. (7) Mil. (1), May 27, 1991

Most Runs, Both Clubs, 15th Inning
12 **AL:**Tex. (12) Oak. (0), July 3, 1983
7 **NL:**StL. (7) Bos. (0), Sept. 28, 1928
      SF (4) LA (3), May 2, 1995

Most Runs, Both Clubs, 16th Inning
8 **AL:**Chi. (8) Wash. (0), May 20, 1920
5 **NL:**Cin. (4) Brk. (1), July 29, 1914
      Cin. (5) NY (0), Aug. 22, 1973
      Hou. (5) Cin. (0), Apr. 8, 1988
      Ari. (3) LA (2), Apr. 13, 1999

Most Runs, Both Clubs, 17th Inning
7 **NL:**NY (7) Pitt. (0), July 16, 1920
6 **AL:**NY (3) Bos. (3), Sept. 5(1g), 1927
      NY (6) Det. (0), July 20, 1941

Most Runs, Both Clubs, 18th Inning
5 **NL:**Chi. (5) Bos. (0), May 14, 1927
4 **AL:**Minn. (4) Sea. (0), July 19, 1969

Most Runs, Both Clubs, 19th Inning
7 **NL:**NY (5) Atl. (2), July 4, 1985
5 **AL:**Chi. (3) Bos. (2), July 13, 1951

Most Runs, Both Clubs, 20th Inning
4 **AL:**Bos. (3) Sea. (1), July 27, 1969
Wash. (3) Clev (1), Sept. 14(2g), 1971
NL: Brk. (4) Bos. (0), July 5, 1940

Most Runs, Both Clubs, 21st Inning
6 **AL:**Mil. (3) Chi. (3), May 8, 1984
3 **NL:**SD (3) Mtl. (0), May 21, 1977

Most Runs, 2 Consecutive Innings
21 **NL:**Pitt. (Bos.) June 6, 1894 (3-4)
Since 1900:
19 **AL:**Bos. (Phil.) May 2, 1901 (2-3)
Bos. (Det.) June 18, 1953 (6-7)
Mil. (Cal.), July 8, 1990 (4-5)
18 **NL:**Mtl. (SF), May 7, 1997 (5-6)

Most Runs, None Out, Inning
13 **NL:**Chi. (Det.) Sept. 6, 1883 (7th)
Since 1900:
12 **NL:**Brk. (Phil.) May 24, 1953 (8th)
11 **AL:**Det. (NY) June 17, 1925 (6th)

Most Runs, Two Out, Inning
13 **AL:**Clev. (Bos.) July 7, 1923 (6th)
KC (Chi.) Apr. 21, 1956 (2nd)
12 **NL:**Brk. (Cin.) May 21, 1952 (1st)
Brk. (Cin.) Aug. 8, 1954 (8th)

Most Runs, 2 Out, 0 On Base, Inning
12 **NL:**Brk. (Cin.) Aug. 8, 1954 (8th)
10 **AL:**Chi. (Det.) Sept. 2, 1959 (5th)

Most Runs, None Out, 1st Inning
9 **NL:**Phil. (NY) Aug. 13, 1948
8 **AL:**Clev. (Balt.) July 6, 1954
NY (Balt.) Apr. 24, 1960
Mil. (Balt.) Apr. 8, 1978
NY (Balt.) Sept. 25, 1990
Clev. (KC) May 9, 1995

Most Innings, Consecutive, Scored Season
17 **AL:**Bos. Sept. 15-17, 1903 (3 g)
14 **NL:**Pitt. July 31-Aug. 2, 1894 (3 g)
NY July 18-20, 1949 (3 g)
Col. May 4-7, 1999 (3 g)

Scoring Each Inning, Game
9 **AA:** Colu. (Pitt.) June 14, 1883
KC (Brk.) May 20, 1889
NL: Clev. (Bos.) Aug. 15, 1889
Wash. (Bos.) June 22, 1894
Clev. (Phil.) July 12, 1894
Chi. (Lou.) June 29, 1897
NY (Phil.) June 1, 1923
StL. (Chi.) Sept. 13, 1964
Col. (Chi.) May 5, 1999
AL: none

Scoring Each Inning, Game
(Did not bat in 9th)
8 **NL:**By many clubs
AL: Bos. (Clev.) Sept. 16, 1903
Clev. (Bos.) July 7, 1923
NY (StL.) July 26, 1939
Chi. (Bos.) May 11, 1949
KC (Oak.) Sept. 14, 1998

Most Innings Scored, Both Clubs, Game
(Nine inning games only)
15 **NL:**Phil. (8) Det. (7) July 1, 1887
Wash. (9) Bos. (6) June 22, 1894
AA:KC (9) Brk. (6) May 20, 1889
PL:NY (8) Chi. (7) May 23, 1890
Since 1900:
14 **NL:**NY (9) Phil. (5) June 1, 1923
StL. (8) Phil. (6) July 5, 1923
Pitt. (8) Chi. (6) July 6, 1975
LA (8) Chi. (6) May 5, 1976
Col. (8) LA (6) June 30, 1996
Col. (8) SD (6) Sept. 24, 2001
AL: Balt. (8) Phil. (6) May 7, 1901
StL. (7) Det. (7) Apr. 23, 1927
Det. (7) Chi. (7) July 2, 1940
Chi. (7) Det. (7) May 28, 1995
ML: Sea. (7) SF (7), June 12, 1999

Most Runs Overcome to Win Game
12 **AL:**Det. (Chi.) June 18, 1911
Phil. (Clev.) June 15, 1925
Clev. (Sea.) Aug. 5, 2001 (11 inn)
11 **NL:**StL. (NY) June 15(1g), 1952
Phil. (Chi.) Apr. 17, 1976 (10 inn)
Hou. (StL.) July 18, 1994

Most Runs, Opening Game, Season
21 **AL:**Clev. (StL.) Apr. 14, 1925
19 **NL:**Phil. (Bos.) Apr. 19, 1900 (10 inn)

Most Runs, Both Clubs, Opening Game
36 **NL:**Phil. (19) Bos. (17) Apr. 19, 1900 (10 inn)
35 **AL:**Clev. (21) StL. (14) Apr. 14, 1925

Most Players, 100 or more Runs, Season
7 **NL:**Bos. 1894
Since 1900:
6 **AL:**NY 1931
NL: Brk. 1953

Most Players Scoring A Run, Game
15 **NL:**Atl. (Fla.) Oct. 3, 1999
14 **AL:**Oak. (Tex.) Sept. 30, 2000

Most Players, 2 or more Runs, Game
10 **NL:**Chi. (Lou.) June 29, 1897
Since 1900:
9 **NL:**StL. (Chi.) Apr. 16, 1912
Chi. (Phil.) Aug. 25, 1922
StL. (Phil.) July 6(2g), 1929
Chi. (Col.) Aug. 18, 1995
AL: Bos. (Phil.) May 2, 1901
Clev. (Bos.) July 7(1g), 1923
NY (Chi.) June 26, 1931
NY (Phil.) May 24, 1936
Bos. (Phil.) June 29, 1950
Cal. (Tor.) Aug. 25, 1979
Minn. (Det.) June 4, 1994

Most Players, 3 or more Runs, Game
9 **NL:**Chi. (Buff.) July 3, 1883
Since 1900:
7 **AL:**Bos. (StL.) June 8, 1950
6 **NL:**NY (Phil.) Sept. 2(2g), 1925

Most Players, 4 or more Runs, Game
6 **NL:**Chi. (Clev.) July 24, 1882
Chi. (Lou.) June 29, 1897
Since 1900:
4 **NL:**StL. (Phil.) July 6(2g), 1929
AL: Bos. (StL.) June 8, 1950

Most Players, 5 or more Runs, Game
3 **NL:**Chi. (Clev.) July 24, 1882
Bos. (Phil.) June 20, 1883
Bos. (Pitt.) Aug. 27, 1887
NY (Brk.) Apr. 30(1g), 1944
Chi. (Bos.) July 3, 1945
AL: Clev. (Balt.) Sept. 2, 1902
Chi. (KC) Apr. 23, 1955

Most Players, 6 or more Runs, Game
2 **NL:**Bos. (Pitt.) Aug. 27, 1887
1 **AL:**Bos. (Chi.) May 8, 1946
Bos. (Clev.) Aug. 21, 1986

Most Runs, Two Players, Game
12 **NL:**Bos. (Pitt.) Aug. 27, 1887
Since 1900:
11 **NL:**NY (Brk.) Apr. 30(1g), 1944
10 **AL:**Clev. (Balt.) Sept. 2, 1902
Chi. (KC) Apr. 23, 1955

Most Players, 2 or more Runs, Inning
7 **NL:**Chi. (Det.) Sept. 6, 1883 (7th)
Since 1900:
6 **NL:**Brk. (Cin.) May 21, 1952 (1st)
Cin. (Hou.) Aug. 3, 1989 (1st)
5 **AL:**NY (Wash.) July 6, 1920 (5th)
NY (Bos.) June 21, 1945 (5th)
Bos. (Phil.) July 4, 1948 (7th)
Clev. (Phil.) June 18, 1950 (1st)
Bos. (Det.) June 18, 1953 (7th)
Mil. (Cal.) July 8, 1990 (5th)
Ana. (Chi.) May 12, 1997 (7th)

HITS

Most Seasons Leading League
25 **NL:**StL. 1901, 20-21, 26, 34, 38-40, 42-47,
49, 54, 56-57, 63-64, 75, 79-80, 83, 92
21 **AL:**Bos. 1903, 39-42, 45-46, 49-50, 54, 67,
70, 75, 81, 84-85, 87-90, 97

Most Seasons, Consecutive, Leading League
7 **NL:**StL. Col. 1995-2001
4 **AL:**Bos. 1939-42, 1987-90

Most Players, 200 or more Hits, Season
4 **NL:**Phil. 1929
AL: Det. 1937

Most Players, 100 or more Hits, Season
9 **NL:**Phil. 1893, 99, 1922, 23
NY 1928
Pitt. 1921, 37, 72, 76
StL. 1979
Ari. 2001
AL: Balt. 1973
Bos. 1984, 91, 99
Cal. 1978, 82, 88
Chi. 1977
Clev. 1997;
Det. 1934, 80, 2001
KC 1974, 77, 80, 82, 89
Mil. 1978, 91, 92;
Minn. 1989, 91
NY 1975, 77, 93;
Phil./Oak. 1925, 75
Sea. 2001
Tex. 1976, 96, 99
Tor. 1983, 88, 92

Most Hits, Game
36 **NL:**Phil. (Lou.) Aug. 17, 1894
Since 1900:
31 **NL:**NY (Cin.) June 9, 1901
AL: Mil. (Tor.) Aug. 28, 1992
Extra-Inning Game:
33 **AL:**Clev. (Phil.) July 10, 1932 (18 inn)

Most Hits, Consecutive, Game
12 **NL:**StL. (Bos.) Sept. 17, 1920
Brk. (Pitt.) Aug. 23, 1930
10 **AL:**Bos. (Mil.) June 2, 1901
Det. (Balt.) Sept. 20, 1983
Tor. (Minn.) Sept. 4, 1992

Most Hits, Both Clubs, Game
51 **NL:**Phil. (26) Chi. (25) Aug. 25, 1922
45 **AL:**Phil. (27) Bos. (18) July 8, 1902
Det. (28) NY (17) Sept. 29, 1928
Extra-Inning Game:
58 **AL:**Clev. (33) Phil. (25) July 10, 1932 (18 inn)
52 **NL:**NY (28) Pitt. (24) June 15, 1929 (14 inn)

Most Hits, 2 Consecutive Games
55 **NL:**Phil. Aug. 16-17, 1894
Since 1900:
51 **AL:**Bos. June 7-8, 1950
49 **NL:**Pitt. Aug. 7-8, 1922

Fewest Hits, Game, 10 or more innings:
0 **NL:** See No-Hit Games
1 **AL:**Clev. (Chi.) Sept. 6, 1903 (10 inn)
Bos. (StL.) Sept. 18, 1934 (10 inn)
LA (NY) May 22, 1962 (12 inn)
Oak. (Tex.) June 21, 1976 (10 inn)

Fewest Hits, Both Clubs, Game
1 **NL:**Chi. (0) LA (1) Sept. 9, 1965
2 **AL:**Clev. (1) StL. (1) Apr. 23, 1952
Chi. (1) Balt. (1) June 21, 1956
Balt. (1) KC (1) Sept. 12, 1964
Det. (0) Balt. (2) Apr. 30, 1967

Fewest Hits, 2 Consecutive Games
2 **AA:**Balt. July 28-29, 1886
NL:NY June 17-18, 1884
Cin. July 5-6, 1900
Bos. Sept. 28-30, 1916
NY Sept. 10-11, 1965
LA Sept. 26-27, 1981
SF Sept. 24-25, 1986
AL:NY Sept. 25-26, 1907
StL. Sept. 25-27, 1910
Chi. Aug. 10-11, 1917
Mil. June 18-19, 1974
Clev. Apr. 12-12, 1992
Det. May 3-4, 1996

Fewest Hits, Doubleheader
2 **AL:**Clev. (Bos.) Apr. 12, 1992
3 **NL:**Brk. (StL.) Sept. 21, 1934
NY (Phil.) June 21, 1964

Most Hits, No Runs, Game
14 **NL:**NY (Chi.) Sept. 14, 1913
AL: Clev. (Wash.) July 10, 1928
Extra-Inning Game:
15 **NL:**Bos. (Pitt.) July 10, 1901 (12 inn)
Bos. (Pitt.) Aug. 1, 1918 (21 inn)
AL: Bos. (Wash.) July 3, 1913 (15 inn)

Most Players, 1 or more Hits, Game
15 **NL:**Atl. (Fla.) Oct. 3, 1999
   StL (NY) Sept. 28, 1979 (11 inn)
14 **AL:**Clev. (StL.) Aug. 12, 1948

Most Players, 1 or more Hits, Both Clubs, Game
24 **NL:**StL (15) NY (9) Sept. 29, 1979 (11 inn)
   SF (13) LA (11) Sept. 19, 1998
23 **AL:**Minn. (12) Clev. (11) July 13, 1996

Most Players, 2 or more Hits, Game
10 **AA:**Brk. (Phil.) June 25, 1885
   NL: Pitt. (Phil.) Aug. 7, 1922
   NY (Phil.) Sept. 2, 1925
9 **AL:**By many, Last:
   Minn. (Hou.) June 6, 1999

Most Players, 3 or more Hits, Game
8 **NL:**Chi. (Det.) Sept. 6, 1883
   Since 1900:
7 **NL:**Pitt. (Phil.) June 12, 1928
   NY (Atl.) July 4, 1985 (19 inn)
   Cin. (Hou.) Aug. 3, 1989
   Cin. (Col.) May 19, 1999
   AL:NY (Phil.) June 28, 1939
   Chi. (KC) Apr. 23, 1955
   Oak. (Tex.) July 1, 1979 (15 inn)

Most Players, 4 or more Hits, Game
7 **NL:**Chi. (Clev.) July 24, 1882
   Since 1900:
5 **NL:**SF (LA) May 13, 1958
4 **AL:**Det. (NY) Sept. 29, 1928
   Chi. (Phil.) Sept. 11, 1936
   Bos. (StL.) June 8, 1950
   Oak. (Tex.) July 1, 1979 (15 inn)
   Mil. (Tor.) Aug. 28, 1992

Most Players, 5 or more Hits, Game
4 **NL:**Phil. (Lou.) Aug. 17, 1894
   Since 1900:
3 **NL:**NY (Cin.) June 9, 1901
   NY (Phil.) June 1, 1923
   AL: Det. (Wash.) July 30, 1917
   Clev. (Phil.) July 10, 1932 (18 inn)
   Wash. (Clev.) May 16, 1933 (12 inn)
   Chi. (Phil.) Sept. 11, 1936

Most Players, 6 or more Hits, Game
2 **AA:**Cin. (Pitt.) Sept. 12, 1883
   NL: Balt. (StL.) Sept. 3, 1897
   Since 1900:
1 By many clubs

Most Hits, Inning
18 **NL:**Chi. (Det.) Sept. 6, 1883, (7th)
   Since 1900:
16 **NL:**Cin. (Hou.) Aug. 3, 1989 (1st)
14 **AL:**Bos. (Det.) June 18, 1953 (7th)

Most Hits, Consecutive, Inning
10 **AL:**Bos. (Mil.) June 2, 1901 (9th)
   Det. (Balt.) Sept. 20, 1983 (1st; incl. bb)
   Tor. (Minn.) Sept. 4, 1992 (2nd)
   NL: StL. (Bos.) Sept. 17, 1920 (4th)
   StL. (Phil.) June 12, 1922 (6th)
   Chi. (Bos.) Sept. 7, 1929 1g (4th)
   Brk. (Pitt.) June 23, 1930 (6th)
   Phil. (Mil.) Sept. 22, 1999 (8th; incl. sh
   & two hbp)

Most Hits, Consecutive, No Outs, 1st Inning
8 **NL:**Phil (Chi.) Aug. 5, 1975
   Pitt. (Atl.) Aug. 26, 1975
   AL: Oak. (Chi.) Sept. 27, 1981
   NY (Balt.) Sept. 25, 1990

Most Players, 2 or more Hits, Inning
7 **NL:**Cin. (Hou.) Aug. 3, 1989 (1st)
5 **AL:**Phil. (Bos.) July 8, 1902 (6th)
   NY (Phil.) Sept. 10, 1921 (9th)

EXTRA-BASE HITS

Most Seasons Leading League
27 **AL:**Bos. 1903,12-14,40-42,44,46,49-50, 54-
   57,65,67,69-72,75-79
21 **NL:**StL. 1920-23,26-28,30,34,36-40, 42-
   44,46,49,52,80

Most Seasons, Consecutive, Leading League
5 **NL:**Chi. 1882-86
   StL. 1936-40
   Col. 1995-99
   AL:NY 1958-62
   Bos. 1975-79

Most Extra-Base Hits, Game
17 **AL:**Bos. (StL.) June 8, 1950
16 **NL:**Chi. (Buff.) July 3, 1883
   NL Since 1900:
15 **NL:**Phil. (Chi.) June 23, 1986
   Cin. (Col.) May 19, 1999

Most Extra-Base Hits, Both Clubs, Game
24 **NL:**StL. (13) Chi. (11) July 12, 1931
   AL: Clev. (15) Minn. (9) July 13, 1996

Fewest Extra-Base Hits, Game (Most Innings)
0 **NL:**Brk. (Bos.) May 1, 1920 (26 inn)
   AL: Det. (NY) Aug. 23, 1968 (19 inn)

Fewest Extra-Base Hits, Both Clubs, Game
(Most Innings)
0 **AL:**Chi. (NY) Aug. 21, 1933 (18 inn)
   NL: Bos. (Chi.) Sept. 21, 1901 (17 inn)

Most Extra-Base Hits, Inning
8 **NL:**Chi. (Det.) Sept. 6, 1883 (7th)
   Since 1900:
7 **AL:**StL. (Wash.) Aug. 7, 1922 (6th)
   Bos. (Phil.) Sept. 24, 1940 (6th)
   NY (StL.) May 3, 1951 (9th)
   Sea. (Bos.) Sept. 3, 1982 (6th)
   NL: Bos. (StL.) Aug. 25, 1936 (1st)
   Phil. (Cin.) June 2, 1949 (8th)
   Phil. (Cin.) July 6, 1986 (3rd)

TOTAL BASES

Most Seasons, Leading League
28 **AL:**NY 1921,23-24,26-28,30-31,36-39,43-
   45,47,51,53-62,93
19 **NL:**Chi. 1876,78,80-82,84-85,88,90, 1906,
   16,30-31,37,58,61,83,88-89

Most Seasons, Consecutive, Leading League
10 **AL:**NY 1953-62
7 **NL:**Brk. 1949-55

Most Total Bases, Game
60 **AL:**Bos. (StL.) June 8, 1950
58 **NL:**Mtl. (Atl.) July 30, 1978

Most Total Bases, Both Clubs, Game
81 **NL:**Cin. (55) Col. (26) May 19, 1999
77 **AL:**NY (50) Phil. (27) June 3, 1932
Extra-Inning Game:
97 **NL:**Chi. (49) Phil. (48) May 17, 1979 (10 inn)
85 **AL:**Clev. (45) Phil. (40) July 10, 1932 (18 inn)

Fewest Total Bases, Game (Most Innings)
0 **AA:**Tol. (Brk.) Oct. 4, 1884 (10 inn)
NL: Phil. (NY) July 4, 1908 1g (10 inn)
Chi. (Cin.) May 2, 1917 (10 inn)
Chi. (Cin.) Aug. 19, 1965 (10 inn)
Hou. (Pitt.) July 12, 1997 (10 inn)
AL: By many (9 inn)

Fewest Total Bases, Both Clubs, Game
2 **NL:**Chi. (0) LA (2) Sept. 9, 1965
AL: Det. (0) Balt. (2) Apr. 30, 1967

Most Total Bases, 2 Consecutive Games
102 **AL:**Bos. June 7-8, 1950
89 **NL:**Pitt. June 20-22, 1925

Most Total Bases, Inning
29 **NL:**Chi. (Det.) Sept. 6, 1883 (7th)
Since 1900:
27 **NL:**SF (Cin.) Aug. 23, 1961 (9th)
25 **AL:**Bos. (Phil.) Sept. 24, 1940 (6th)

SINGLES

Most Seasons Leading League
27 **NL:**StL. 1900-01,20,23,39,41-43,45,49,54,
56-57,61-64,71,75,77,79,85,87-89,92,93
24 **AL:**Wash./Minn. 1918,24,26,29,32-33,35,
37-39,41-42,44-45,69,71,73-77,89,92,96

Most Seasons, Consecutive, Leading League
5 **AL:**Minn. 1973-77
4 **NL:**StL. 1961-64
Col. 1998-2001

Most Singles, Game
28 **NL:**Phil. (Lou.) Aug. 17, 1894
Bos. (Balt.) Apr. 20, 1896
Since 1900:
26 **AL:**Mil. (Tor.) Aug. 28, 1992
23 **NL:**NY (Chi.) Sept. 21, 1931
Hou. (Atl.) May 30, 1976

Most Singles, Both Clubs, Game
37 **NL:**Balt. (21) Wash. (16) Aug. 8, 1896
Since 1900:
36 **NL:**NY (22) Cin. (14) June 9, 1901
AL: Chi. (21) Bos. (15) Aug. 15, 1922

Most Singles, Inning
12 **NL:**Cin. (Hou.) Aug. 3, 1989 (1st)
11 **AL:**Bos. (Det.) June 18, 1953 (7th)

Most Singles, Consecutive, Inning
10 **NL:**StL. (Bos.) Sept. 17, 1920 (4th)
8 **AL:**Wash. (Clev.) May 7, 1951 (4th)
Oak. (Chi.) Sept. 27, 1981 (1st)
Balt. (Tex.) May 18, 1990 (1st)

DOUBLES

Most Seasons Leading League
36 **AL:**Bos. 1912, 14, 41-42, 44, 46, 48-50, 52,
54-59, 62-64, 67, 70-72, 74-75,79, 83,85-
86, 88-89, 91, 93, 95, 97-98
27 **NL:**StL. 1920-24, 28-31, 33-34,36-
39,42,44,46,49,52-54, 56, 63, 69, 79-80

Most Seasons, Consecutive, Leading League
8 **AL:**Clev. 1916-23
5 **NL:**StL. 1920-24

Most Doubles, Game
14 **NL:**Chi. (Buff.) July 3, 1883
Since 1900:
13 **NL:**Chi.) July 12, 1931
12 **AL:**Bos. (Det.) July 29, 1990
Clev. (Minn.) July 13, 1996

Most Doubles, Both Clubs, Game
23 **NL:**StL. (13) Chi. (10) July 12, 1931
18 **AL:**Clev. (12) Minn. (6) July 13, 1996

Most Doubles, Inning
7 **NL:**Bos. (StL.) Aug. 25, 1936 (1st)
6 **AL:**Wash. (Bos.) June 9, 1934 (8th)

Most Doubles, Consecutive, Inning
5 **AL:**Wash. (Bos.) June 9, 1934 (8th)
4 **NL:**By many

Most Players, 2 or more Doubles, Inning
3 **NL:**Bos. (StL.) Aug. 25, 1936 (1st)
2 **AL:**NY (Bos.) July 3, 1932 (6th)
Tor. (Balt.) June 26, 1978 (2nd)

TRIPLES

Most Seasons Leading League
45 **NL:**Pitt. 1893, 97, 99-1900, 1902-04,08-09,
11-12, 16, 21-25, 28-30, 32-37, 43-44,50,
55-56, 58, 61-62, 64, 66-67, 69-72,78, 89,
92, 97
22 **AL:**Wash./Minn. 1923-24, 26, 31-37, 39,
45-46, 48, 53-54, 56, 60, 68, 70, 81, 96

Most Seasons, Consecutive, Leading League
7 **AL:**Wash. 1931-37
6 **NL:**Pitt. 1932-37

Most Triples, Game
9 **NL:**Balt. (Clev.) Sept. 3, 1894
Since 1900:
8 **AL:**Pitt. (StL.) May 30, 1925
6 **AL:**Chi. (Mil.) Sept. 15, 1901
Phil. (Det.) May 18, 1912
Chi. (NY) Sept. 17, 1920
Det. (NY) June 17, 1922

Most Triples, Both Clubs, Game
11 **NL:**Balt. (9) Clev. (2) Sept. 3, 1894
Since 1900:
9 **NL:**Pitt. (6) Chi. (3) July 4, 1904
Pitt. (8) StL. (1) May 30, 1925
AL: Det. (6) NY (3) June 17, 1922

Fewest Triples, Game, (Most Innings)
0 **NL:**Brk. (Bos.) May 1, 1920 (26 inn)
  AL: Mil. (Chi.) May 8, 1984 (25 inn)
  Chi. (Mil.) May 8, 1984 (25 inn)

Fewest Triples, Both Clubs, Game, (Most Innings)
0 **NL:**StL. (NY) Sept. 11, 1974 (25 inn)
  AL: Mil. (Chi.) May 8, 1984 (25 inn)

Most Triples, Inning
5 **AL:**Chi. (Mil.) Sept. 15, 1901 (8th)
4 **NL:**Bos. (Troy) May 6, 1882 (8th)
  Balt. (StL.) July 27, 1892 (7th)
  StL. (Chi.) July 2, 1895 (1st)
  Chi. (StL.) Apr. 17, 1899 (4th)
  Brk. (Pitt.) Aug. 23, 1902 (3rd)
  Cin. (Bos.) July 22, 1926 (2nd)
  NY (Pitt.) July 17, 1936 (1st)

Most Triples, Consecutive, Inning
4 **AL:**Bos. (Det.) May 6, 1934 (4th)
3 **NL:**By many; Last:
  Mtl. (SD) May 6, 1981 (9th)

HOME RUNS

Most Seasons Leading League
34 **AL:**NY 1915-17, 19-21, 23-31, 33, 36-47,51, 55-56, 58, 60-61
29 **NL:**NY/SF 1904-05, 07, 09, 12, 17, 24-25, 27-28, 31, 33-35, 37-39, 42-43, 45-48, 54, 62-64, 72, 2001

Most Seasons, Consecutive, Leading League
12 **AL:**NY 1936-47
7 **NL:**Brk. 1949-55

Most Home Runs, At Home, Season
149 **NL:**Col. 1996
134 **AL:**Tor. 2000

Most Home Runs, Away, Season
138 **NL:**SF 2001
136 **AL:**Balt. 1996

Most Home Runs vs. One Club, Season
48 **AL:**NY (KC) 1956
44 **NL:**Cin. (Brk.) 1956

Most Home Runs, One Month
58 **AL:**Balt. May 1987
  Sea. May 1999
55 **NL:**NY July 1947
  StL. Apr. 2000

Most Home Runs, Game
10 **AL:**Tor. (Balt.) Sept. 14, 1987
9 **NL:**Cin. (Phil.) Sept. 4, 1999

Most Home Runs, Both Clubs, Game
12 **AL:**Det. (7) Chi. (5) May 28, 1995
11 **NL:**Chi. (7) NY (4) June 11, 1967
  Pitt. (6) Cin. (5) Aug. 12, 1966 (13 inn)
  Chi. (6) Cin. (5) July 28, 1977 (13 inn)
  Chi. (6) Phil. (5) May 17, 1979 (10 inn)

Fewest Home Runs, Both Clubs, Game (Most Innings)
0 **NL:**Bos. (Brk.) May 1, 1920 (26 inn)
  AL: Bos. (Phil.) Sept. 1, 1906 (24 inn)
  Det. (Phil.) July 21, 1945 (24 inn)

Most Home Runs, Opening Game
6 **NL:**NY (Mtl.) Apr. 4, 1988
5 **AL:**NY (Phil.) Apr. 12, 1932
  Bos. (Wash.) Apr. 12, 1965
  Mil. (Bos.) Apr. 10, 1980
  Clev. (Tex.) Apr. 27, 1995

Most Home Runs, Both Clubs, Opening Game
7 **AL:**NY, (5) Phil. (2) Apr. 12, 1932
  Bos. (5), Wash. (2) Apr. 12, 1965
  Mil. (5), Bos. (2) Apr. 10, 1980
  Mil. (4), Cal. (3) Apr. 2, 1996
  NL:NY (6), Mtl. (1) Apr. 4, 1988
  Atl. (4), Cin. (3) Apr. 5, 1988
  Atl. (5), SF (2) Apr. 1, 1996

Most Home Runs, Only Runs, Game
6 **AL:**Oak. (Minn.) Aug. 3, 1991
5 **NL:**NY (Chi.) June 16, 1930
  StL. (Brk.) Sept. 1, 1953
  Cin. (Mil.) Apr. 16, 1955
  Chi. (Pitt.) Apr. 21, 1964
  Pitt. (LA) May 7, 1973
  Col. (SF) May 9, 1994
  Atl. (Col.) Apr. 19, 1998 (1g)

Most Home Runs, Both Clubs, Only Runs, Game
5 **NL:**SF (3) Mil. (2) Aug. 30, 1962
  Mtl. (3) SD (2) May 16, 1986
  Col. (4) Mtl. (1) July 9, 1995
  ML:AL:Balt. (3) NL:Atl. (2) June 5, 1998
4 **AL:**Clev. (4) NY(0) Aug. 2, 1956
  NY (4) Balt. (0) May 13(1g), 1973
  Balt. (3) Det. (1) Apr. 24, 1977
  Tor. (4) Det. (0) May 23, 1983
  Det. (4) NY (0) June 14, 1985
  Det (3) Cal. (1) July 31, 1991
  Minn (3) KC (1) June 18, 1992
  KC (3) Chi. (1) Apr. 11, 1999

Most Games, Consecutive, Home Runs
25 **AL:**NY June 1-29, 1941 (40)
  Det. May 25-June 19, 1994 (46)
  NL: Atl. Apr. 18-May 13, 1998 (45)

Most Games, Consecutive, Home Runs, Start of Season
13 **NL:**Chi. Apr. 13-May 2, 1954 (28)
10 **AL:**NY Apr. 5-16, 1999 (16)

Most Home Runs, 2-Game Span, Season
14 **NL:**Cin. Sept. 4-5, 1999
13 **AL:**NY June 28 (dh), 1939

Most Home Runs, 3-Game Span, Season
16 **AL:**Bos. June 17-19, 1977
15 **NL:**LA June 29-July 1, 1996
  Cin. Sept 3-5 & 4-6, 1999

Most Home Runs, 4-Game Span, Season
18 **AL:**Bos. June 16-19, 1977
  Oak. June 25-29, 1996
  NL: Hou. Aug 13-16, 2000

Most Home Runs, 5-Game Span, Season
21 **AL:**Bos. June 14-19, 1977
  NL: Cin. Sept. 4-7, 1999

Most Home Runs, 6-Game Span, Season
24 **AL:**Bos. June 17-22, 1977
22 **NL:**NY July 6-11, 1954
  Cin. Sept. 3-7 & 4-8, 1999

Most Home Runs, 7-Game Span, Season
26 **AL:**Bos. June 16-22, 1977
24 **NL:**NY July 5-11, 1954
     Cin. Sept. 1-7, 1999

Most Home Runs, 8-Game Span, Season
29 **AL:**Bos. June 14-22, 1977
26 **NL:**NY July 5-11, 1954

Most Home Runs, 9-Game Span, Season
30 **AL:**Bos. June 14-23 & 16-24, 1977
29 **NL:**Cin. Sept. 4-11, 1999

Most Home Runs, 10-Game Span, Season
33 **AL:**Bos. June 14-24, 1977
30 **NL:**Cin. Sept. 3-11, 1999

Most Home Runs, 15-Game Span, Season
39 **NL:**Mil. June 8-24, 1961
38 **AL:**Minn. Apr. 28-May 14 & May 1-16, 1964
     Bos. June 8-24, 1977
     Balt. May 5-19, 7-22, & 8-23, 1987
     Oak. June 14-29 & 17-July 2, 1996
     Sea. May 11-28, 1999

Most Home Runs, 20-Game Span, Season
51 **AL:**Sea. Apr. 28-May 19, 1999
47 **NL:**StL. Apr. 6-25, 7-26 & 8-27, 2000

Most Home Runs, 25-Game Span, Season
59 **AL:**Oak. June 25-July 23, 1996
     Sea. Apr. 23-May 19, Apr. 28-May 25,
     & Apr. 29-May 26, 1999
56 **NL:**StL. Apr. 7-May 2, 2000

Most Games, Consecutive, 2 or more HRs
9 **AL:**Clev. May 13-21, 1962
     Balt. May 8-16, 1987
     Balt. Aug. 3-11, 1996
8 **NL:**Mil. July 19-26, 1956
     Chi. June 25-July 1, 1961
     Mil. Aug. 8-15, 1965

Most Home Runs, Inning
5 **NL:**NY (Cin.) June 6, 1939 (4th)
     Phil. (Cin.) June 2, 1949 (8th)
     SF (Cin.) Aug. 23, 1961 (9th)
     AL: Minn. (KC) June 9, 1966 (7th)

Most Home Runs, Consecutive, Inning
4 **NL:**Mil. (Cin.) June 8, 1961 (7th)
     AL: Clev. (LA) July 31, 1963 (6th)
     Minn. (KC) May 2, 1964 (11th)

Most Home Runs, Both Clubs, Inning
5 **AL:**StL. (3) Phil. (2) June 8, 1928 (9th)
     Det. (4) NY (1) June 23, 1950 (4th)
     Balt. (4) Bos. (1) May 17, 1967 (7th)
     Minn. (4) Oak. (1) May 16, 1983 (9th)
     Clev. (3) Tex. (2) June 29, 1984 (5th)
     Balt. (3) Bos. (2) Sept. 10, 1985 (8th)
     Clev. (3) Mil. (2) Apr. 25, 1997 (4th)
     Det. (3) Balt. (2) Apr. 7, 2000 (5th)
NL:NY (3) Bos. (2) July 6, 1951 (3rd)
     Cin. (3) Brk. (2) June 11, 1954 (7th)
     Phil. (3) Chi. (2) Apr. 17, 1964 (5th)
     Chi. (3) Atl. (2) July 3, 1967 (1st)
     Pitt. (3) Atl. (2) Aug. 1, 1970 (7th)
     Cin. (3) Chi. (2) July 28, 1977 (1st)
     SF (3) Atl. (2) May 25, 1979 (4th)
     Cin. (4) Atl. (1) June 19, 1994 (1st)
     SF (3) Pitt. (2) July 27, 1997 (2g, 9th)
     Col (3) StL. (2) July 31, 1999 (3rd)
     Atl. (4) SF (1) May 20, 2001 (7th)

Most Home Runs, None on Base, Game
7 **AL:**Bos. (Tor.) July 4, 1977
6 **NL:**NY (Phil.) Aug. 13, 1939
     NY (Cin.) June 24, 1950
     Atl. (Chi.) Aug. 3, 1967
     Chi. (SD) Aug. 19, 1970
     Atl. (Cin.) May 31, 1996

Most Home Runs, None on Base,
Both Clubs, Game
10 **AL:**Det. (5) Chi. (5) May 28, 1995
8 **NL:**Col. (4) Mtl. (4) Aug. 14, 1999

Most Home Runs, None on Base, Inning
4 **NL:**NY (Phil.) Aug. 13, 1939 (4th)
     Atl. (SF) May 20, 2001 (7th)
     AL: Clev. (LA) July 31, 1963 (6th)
     Minn. (KC) May 2, 1964 (11th)
     Minn. (KC) June 9, 1966 (7th)
     Bos. (NY) June 17, 1977 (1st)
     Bos. (Tor.) July 4, 1977 (8th)
     Bos. (Mil.) May 31, 1980 (4th)
     Minn. (NY) May 2, 1992 (5th)
     Balt. (Cal.) Sept 5, 1995 (2nd)
     Sea. (Oak.) Sept. 21, 1996 (3rd)

Most Home Runs, Two Out, Inning
5 **NL:**NY (Cin.) June 6, 1939 (4th)
4 **AL:**Bos. (Det.) July 18, 1998 (4th)

Most Players, 50 or more Home Runs, Season
2 **AL:**NY 1961
1 **NL:**By many clubs

Most Players, 40 or more Home Runs, Season
3 **NL:**Atl. 1973
     Col. 1996, 97
2 **AL:**NY 1927, 30-31, 61
     Det. 1961
     Bos. 1969
     Sea. 1996-99
     Tor. 1999-2000
     Tex 2001

Most Players, 30 or more Home Runs, Season
4 **NL:**LA 1977, 97
     Col. 1995-97, 99
     Atl. 1998
     AL: Ana. & Tor. 2000

Most Players, 20 or more Home Runs, Season
7 **AL:**Balt. 1996
     Tor. 2000
6 **NL:**Mil. 1965

Most Players, 3 or more HRs, Game, Season
4 **NL:**Brk. 1950
     Cin. 1956
     Mil. 2001
3 **AL:**Clev. 1987
     Sea. 1996

Most Players, Home Runs, Game
8 **NL:**Cin. (Phil.) Sept. 4, 1999
7 **AL:**Balt. (Bos.) May 17, 1967
     Oak. (Cal.) June 27, 1996
     Det. (Tor.) June 20, 2000

Most Players, Home Runs, Both Clubs, Game
9 **NL:**NY (5) Brk. (4) Sept. 2, 1939
   NY (6) Pitt. (3) July 11, 1954
   Chi (5) Pitt. (4) Apr. 21, 1964
   Cin. (6) Atl. (3) Apr. 21, 1970
   LA (5) Atl. (4) Apr. 24, 1977
   Cin. (5) Chi. (4) July 28, 1977 (13 inn)
   Chi. (6) Mil. (3) Sept. 12, 1998
   Chi. (5) Col. (4) June 22, 1999
   Cin. (8) Phil. (1) Sept. 4, 1999
   AL:NY (5) Det. (4) June 23, 1950
   Minn. (5) Bos. (4) May 25, 1965
   Balt. (7) Bos. (2) May 17, 1967
   Cal. (5) Clev. (4) Aug. 30, 1970
   Bos. (5) Mil. (4) May 22(1g), 1977
   Cal. (5) Oak. (4) Apr. 23, 1985
   Balt. (5) Cal (4) July 1, 1994
   Det. (5) Balt. (4) Apr. 7, 2000
   Det. (7) Tor. (2) June 20, 2000
9 **ML:**Col (5) Sea. (4) June 9, 1999

Most Players, 3 or more Home Runs, Game
2 **NL:**Mil. (Ari.) Sept. 25, 2001
1 **AL:**By many clubs

Most Players, 2 or more Home Runs, Game
3 **NL:**Pitt. (StL.) Aug. 16, 1947
   Chi. (StL.) Apr. 16, 1955 (14 inn)
   NY (Pitt.) July 8, 1956
   Cin. (Mil.) Aug. 18, 1956
   Phil. (NY) Sept. 8, 1998
   Col. (Mtl.) Aug. 14, 1999
   Hou. (Chi.) Sept. 9, 2000
   AL: Bos. (StL.) June 8, 1950
   NY (Bos.) May 30, 1961
   Tor. (Balt.) Sept. 14, 1987
   Tor. (Cal.) July 14, 1990
   Det. (Chi.) May 28, 1995
   Sea. (Mil.) July 31, 1996
   Ana. (TB) Apr. 21, 2000
   Minn. (Mil.) July 12, 2001

Most Players, 2 or more Home Runs, Both Clubs, Game
4 **NL:**Pitt. (3) StL. (1) Aug. 16, 1947
   Col. (3) Mtl (1) Aug. 14, 1999
   AL: Det. (3) Chi. (1) May 28, 1995

GRAND SLAM HOME RUNS

Most Grand Slam HRs, Game
2 By many Clubs; Last:
   AL: Sea. (Chi.) Aug. 8(1g), 2000
   NL:LA (Fla.) May 21, 2000

Most Grand Slam HRs, Both Clubs, Game
3 **AL:**Balt. (2) Tex. (1) Aug. 6, 1986
   NL: Chi. (2) Hou. (1) June 3, 1987

Most Grand Slam HRs, 2 Consecutive Games
3 **NL:**Brk. Sept. 23(2g)-24, 1901
   Pitt. June 20-22(2g), 1925
   LA May 20-21, 2000
   AL: Mil. Apr. 10-12(2g), 1980
   Chi. May 18-19, 1996
   Sea. Aug. 7-8(1g), 2000

Most Games Consecutive, Grand Slam HR
3 **AL:**Mil. Apr. 7- 9, 1978
   Det. Aug. 10-12, 1993
2 **NL:**By many clubs

Most Grand Slam HRs, Inning
2 **NL:**Chi. (Pitt.) Aug. 16, 1890
       (5th: Burns, Kittridge)
   Hou. (NY) July 30, 1969
       (9th: Menke, Wynn)
   StL. (LA) Apr. 23, 1999
       (3rd: Tatis 2)
   AL: Minn. (Clev.) July 18, 1962
       (1st: Allison, Killebrew)
   Mil (Bos.) Apr. 12, 1980
       (2nd: Cooper, Money)
   Balt. (Tex.) Aug. 6, 1986
       (4th: Sheets, Dwyer)

Most Grand Slam HRs, Both Clubs, Inning
2 **NL:**Chi. (NY) May 18, 1950 (6th)
   Atl. (Cin.) Sept. 12(1g), 1974 (2nd)
   Chi. (Pitt.) Sept. 9, 1992 (6th)
   AL: Bos. (Wash.) June 18, 1961 (9th)
   Clev. (Tex.) Apr. 14, 1980 (1st)
   ML: Ana. (Ari.) June 9, 1998 (3rd)

RUNS BATTED IN (Since 1920)

Most Runs Batted In, Game
29 **AL:**Bos. (StL.) June 8, 1950
26 **NL:**NY (Brk.) Apr. 30, 1944
    Chi. (Col.) Aug. 18, 1995

Most Runs Batted In, Both Clubs, Game
43 **NL:**Chi. (24) Phil. (19) Aug. 25, 1922
35 **AL:**Bos. (21) Phil. (14) June 29, 1950
    Extra-Inning Game:
45 **NL:**Phil. (23)·Chi. (22) May 17, 1979 (10 inn)

Fewest RBIs, Both Clubs, Game (Most Innings)
0 **NL:**NY (Hou.) Apr. 15, 1968 (24 inn)
   AL: Wash. (Det.) July 16, 1909 (18 inn)
   Wash. (Chi.) May 15, 1918 (18 inn)

Most Runs Batted In, 2 Consecutive Game
49 **AL:**Bos. June 7-8, 1950
39 **NL:**Pitt. June 20-22, 1925

Most Runs Batted In, Inning
17 **AL:**Bos. (Det.) June 18, 1953 (7th)
15 **NL:**Brk. (Cin.) May 21, 1952 (1st)

Most Players, 100 or more RBIs, Season
5 **AL:**NY 1936
4 **NL:**Pitt. 1925
   Chi. 1929;
   Phil. 1929
   Col. 1996-97, 99
   Ari. 1999

SACRIFICE HITS

Most Sacrifice Hits, Season (Includes sac-flies):
310 **AL:**Bos. 1917
270 **NL:**Chi. 1908

Most Sacrifice Hits, Game
8 **AL:**NY (Bos.) May 4, 1918
Chi. (Det.) July 11, 1927
StL. (Clev.) July 23, 1928
Tex. (Chi.) Aug. 1, 1977
NL: Cin. (Phil.) May 6, 1926

Most Sacrifice Hits, Both Clubs, Game
11 **AL:**Wash. (7) Bos. (4) Sept. 1, 1926
9 **NL:**NY (5) Chi. (4) Aug. 29, 1921
Cin. (8) Phil. (1) May 6, 1926
SF (6) SD (3) May 23, 1970 (15 inn)

Most Sacrifice Hits, Inning
3 **AL:**Clev. (StL.) July 10, 1949 (5th)
Det. (Balt.) July 12, 1970 (2nd)
Oak. (KC) June 26(1g), 1977 (5th)
Clev. (Chi.) June 8, 1980 (6th)
Sea. (Cal.) Apr. 29, 1984 (6th)
Cal. (Det.) June 5, 1977 (8th)
Minn. (Mil.) July 26, 1991 (8th)
NL: Chi. (Mil.) Aug. 1962 (6th)
Phil. (LA) Sept. 23, 1967 (7th)
LA (SF) May 23, 1972 (6th)
Hou. (SD) Apr. 29, 1975 (7th)
Hou. (Atl.) July 6, 1975 (9th)
Pitt. (StL.) Sept. 20, 1988 (8th)

SACRIFICE FLIES (Since 1954)

Most Seasons Leading League
10 **NL:**Pitt. 1962, 65, 70, 82, 87-92
7 **AL:**NY 1962,74-75,85,95-97

Most Seasons, Consecutive, Leading League
6 **NL:**Pitt. 1987-92
3 **AL:**Balt. 1967-69
Mil. 1990-92
NY 1995-97

Most Sacrifice Flies, Game
5 **AL:**Sea. (Oak.) Aug. 7, 1988
4 **NL:**NY (SF) July 26, 1967
NY (Phil.) Sept. 23, 1972
StL. (Cin.) Sept. 2, 1980
Cin. (Hou.) May 5, 1982
SF (NY) Aug. 29, 1987
Pitt. (Phil.) Sept. 9, 1988
SF (SD) Sept. 14, 1988
Atl. (SD) May 23, 1991 (12 inn)
Mtl. (Fla.) May 24, 1994
Hou. (Pitt.) May 9, 1995
Hou. (Phil.) Sept. 8, 1995
SD (Col.) July 3, 2001

Most Sacrifice Flies, Both Clubs, Game
5 By many; Last:
AL: Bos. (3) KC (2) Aug. 27, 2000
NL: Cin (3) Pitt. (2) Apr. 29, 2000

Most Sacrifice Flies, Inning
3 **AL:**Chi. (Clev.) July 1(1g), 1962 (5th)
NY (Det.) June 29, 2000 (4th)
NY (Ana.) Aug. 19, 2000 (3rd)
2 **NL:**By many clubs

WALKS

Most Seasons Leading League
24 **AL:**NY 1902-03,10,13-14,26-28,30-34, 36-
39,43,45,53,94-95,97-98
20 **NL:**Brk./LA 1892, 1903,33-34,38-39, 41-
43,45-47,52-57,59,61
NY/SF 1904-08,20-21,23,50-51,64,68-71,
81-82,96,98, 2000

Most Seasons, Consecutive, Leading League
7 **AL:**Clev. 1917-23
6 **NL:**Brk. 1952-57

Most Walks, Game
19 **AA:**Lou. (Clev.) Sept. 21, 1887
18 **AL:**Det. (Phil.) May 9, 1916
Clev. (Bos.) May 20, 1948
17 **NL:**Chi. (NY) May 30, 1887
Brk. (Phil.) Aug. 27, 1903
NY (Brk.) Apr. 30, 1944
Hou. (Fla.) Aug. 20, 1999 (16 inn)
Extra-Inning Game
20 **AL:**Bos. (Det.) Sept. 17, 1920 (12 inn)

Most Walks, Both Clubs, Game
30 **AL:**Det. (18) Phil. (12) May 9, 1916
Wash. (19) Clev. (11) Sept. 14, 1971
(20 inn)
26 **NL:**Hou. (13) SF (13) May 4(2g), 1975

Fewest Walks, Game (Most Innings)
0 **NL:**LA (Mtl.) Aug. 23, 1989 (22 inn)
AL: Phil. (Bos.) July 4, 1905 (20 inn)

Fewest Walks, Both Clubs, Game (Most Innings)
0 **AL:**Wash. (Det.) July 22, 1904 (13 inn)
Bos. (Phil.) Sept. 9, 1907 (13 inn)
NL: Chi. (LA) July 27, 1980 (12 inn)

Most Walks, Doubleheader
25 **NL:**NY (Brk.) Apr. 30, 1944
23 **AL:**Clev. (Phil.) June 18, 1950

Most Walks, Both Clubs, Doubleheader
42 **NL:**Hou. (21) SF (21) May 4, 1975
32 **AL:**Balt. (18) Chi. (14) May 28, 1954
Det. (20) KC (12) Aug. 1, 1962
Tex. (17) Chi. (15) May 24, 1995

Fewest Walks, Doubleheader (Most Innings)
0 **NL:**StL. (NY) July 2, 1933 (27 inn)
AL: Det. (Phil.) Aug. 28, 1908 (20 inn)

Fewest Walks, Both Clubs, Doubleheader
1 **NL:**Brk. (0) Cin. (1) Aug. 6, 1905
Pitt. (0) Cin. (1) Sept. 7, 1924
StL. (0) Brk. (1) Sept. 22, 1929
2 **AL:**Det. (0) Phil. (2) Aug. 28, 1908 (20 inn)
Chi (1) Phil. (1) July 12, 1912
Chi. (0) Clev. (2) Sept. 6, 1930

Most Walks, 2 Consecutive Games
29 **AL:**Det. May 9-10, 1916
25 **NL:**NY Apr. 30 (dh), 1944
Hou. Apr. 28-29, 2000

Most Walks, No Runs, Game
11 **AL:**StL. (NY) Aug. 1, 1941
Wash. (NY) May 21, 1970
10 **NL:**Chi. (Cin.) Aug. 19, 1965 (1g; 10 inn)
NY (Hou.) July 6, 1976 (10 inn)
Mtl. (NY) Apr. 24, 1982
SF (Ari.) May 29, 2001 (18 inn)
Ari. (SD) Sept. 2, 2001 (13 inn)

Most Walks, Inning
11 **AL:**NY (Wash.) Sept. 11, 1949 (3rd)
9 **NL:**Cin. (Chi.) Apr. 24, 1957 (5th)

Most Walks, Consecutive, Inning
7 **AL:**Chi. (Wash.) Aug. 28, 1909 (2nd)
NL: Atl. (Pitt.) May 25, 1983 (3rd)

INTENTIONAL WALKS (Since 1955)

Most Seasons, Leading League
9 **NL:**Pitt. 1960, 68, 69, 78-80, 89, 91-92
AL:NY 1955, 57-58, 61-62, 64, 78, 88, 99

Most Seasons, Consecutive, Leading League
3 **NL:**Pitt. 1978-80
Hou. 1994-96
AL: Chi. 1994-96

Most Intentional Walks, Game
6 **NL:**SF (StL.) July 19, 1975
5 **AL:**Cal. (NY) May 10, 1967
Wash. (Clev.) Sept. 2, 1970
NY (Cal.) Aug. 29, 1978
Oak. (Clev.) July 16, 1991
Extra-Inning Game
7 **NL:**NY (Chi.) May 2, 1956 (17 inn)
Hou. (Phil.) July 3, 1984 (16 inn)
Chi. (Cin.) May 22, 1990 (16 inn)
6 **AL:**KC (Tex.) June 6, 1991 (19 inn)

Most Intentional Walks, Both Clubs, Game
7 **NL:**NY (4) Pitt. (3) June 27, 1979
6 **AL:**Cal. (5) NY (1) May 10, 1967
Extra-Inning Game
11 **NL:**NY (7) Chi. (4) May 2, 1956 (17 inn)
7 **AL:**By many; Last:
NY (4) Balt. (3) May 1, 1996 (10 inn)

Most Intentional Walks, Inning
3 By many clubs

Most Intentional Walks, Both Clubs, Inning
4 By many clubs

HIT BY PITCH

Most Hit by Pitch, Game
6 **AA:**Brk. (Balt.) Apr. 25, 1887
NL: Lou. (StL.) July 31 (1g), 1897
AL:NY (Wash.) June 20, 1913
NL Since 1900:
5 **NL:**Atl. (Cin.) July 2, 1969
Hou. (LA) Apr. 19, 2000

Most Hit By Pitch, Both Clubs, Game
9 **NL:**Det. (5) Ind. (4) Apr. 30, 1887
Since 1900:
7 **AL:**Det. (4) Wash. (3) Aug. 24, 1914
Minn. (4) KC (3) Apr. 13, 1971
KC (5) Tex. (2) Sept. 3, 1989
Oak. (5) Ana. (2) June 7, 2001
6 **NL:**Brk. (4) NY (2) July 17, 1900
Mtl. (4) Fla. (2) July 29, 1994
Fla. (4) Phil. (2) May 16, 1995 (10 inn)
Pitt. (4) Fla. (2) May 22, 1999
Pitt. (4) Hou. (2) Sept. 16, 2000
(10 inn)

Most Hit By Pitch, Inning
4 **NL:**Bos. (Pitt.) Aug. 19(1g), 1893 (2nd)
Since 1900:
3 **NL:**NY (Pitt.) Sept. 25, 1905 (1st)
Chi. (Bos.) Sept. 17, 1928 (9th)
Phil. (Cin.) May 15(1g), 1960 (8th)
Atl. (Cin.) July 2, 1969 (2nd)
Cin. (Pitt.) May 1, 1974 (1st)
StL. (Mtl.) Aug. 15, 1992 (1st)
SD (Col.) June 28, 1994 (11th)
Hou. (LA) Sept. 13, 1997 (1st)
Fla. (Hou.) Aug. 3, 1998 (8th)
Atl. (SD) Aug. 16, 2000 (8th)
StL. (SD) Sept. 26, 2000 (8th)
AL:NY (Wash.) June 20(2g), 1913 (1st)
Clev. (NY) Aug. 25, 1921 (8th)
Bos. (NY) June 20, 1954 (3rd)
Balt. (Cal.) Aug. 9, 1968 (7th)
Cal. (Chi.) Sept. 10, 1977 (1st)
Cal. (Clev.) July 8, 1988 (4th)
Oak. (Minn.) Sept. 28, 1988 (2nd)
Oak. (Sea.) Sept. 22, 1996 (5th)
Tor. (Chi.) July 15(2g), 1998 (7th)
TB (Ana.) May 22, 1999 (3rd)

STRIKEOUTS

Most Strikeouts, Game
20 **AL:**Sea. (Bos.) Apr. 29, 1986
Det. (Bos.) Sept. 18, 1996
NL: Hou. (Chi.) May 6, 1998
Extra-Inning Game:
26 **AL:**Cal. (Oak.) July 9, 1971 (20 inn)
22 **NL:**NY (SF) May 31(2g), 1964 (23 inn)
Cin. (LA) Aug. 8, 1972 (19 inn)

Most Strikeouts, Both Clubs, Game
31 **AL:**Tex. (18) Sea. (13) July 13, 1997
30 **NL:**Hou. (20) Chi. (10) May 6, 1998
Extra-Inning Game:
43 **AL:**Cal. (26) Oak. (17) July 9, 1971 (20 inn)
40 **NL:**SF (20) SD (20) June 19, 2001 (15 inn)

Most Strikeouts, 2 Consecutive Games
36 **AL:**Sea. Apr. 29-30, 1986
32 **NL:**Col. June 14-15, 1998

Most Strikeouts, Doubleheader
26 **NL:**Phil. (NY) Sept. 9, 1970
    SD (NY) May 29, 1971
    SF (Hou.) Sept. 5, 1971
25 **AL:**LA (Clev.) July 31, 1963
    Including Extra-Inning Game:
31 **NL:**Pitt. (Phil.) Sept. 22, 1958 (23 inn)
    NY (Phil.) Oct. 2, 1965 (27 inn)
27 **AL:**Clev. (Bos.) Aug. 25, 1963 (24 inn)

Most Strikeouts, Both Clubs, Doubleheader
44 **AL:**Det. (24) Balt. (20) Sept. 8, 1980
41 **NL:**Phil. (26) NY (15) Sept. 9, 1970
    SD (26) NY (15) May 29, 1971
    Chi. (21) NY (20) Sept. 15, 1971
    Including Extra-Inning Game:
51 **NL:**NY (30) Phil. (21) Sept. 26, 1975 (24 inn)
48 **AL:**KC (24) Det. (24) June 17, 1967 (28 inn)

Most Strikeouts, Start of Game
9 **NL:**Clev. (NY) Aug. 28, 1884
    Since 1900:
8 **NL:**LA (Hou.) Sept. 23, 1986
7 **AL:**Tex. (Chi.) May 28, 1986

Most Strikeouts, Consecutive, Game
10 **NL:**SD (NY) Apr. 22, 1970
8 **AL:**Bos. (Cal.) July 9, 1972
    Mil. (Cal.) Aug. 7, 1973
    Cal. (NY) May 4, 1981
    Sea. (Bos.) Apr. 29, 1986
    Mil.-NL (KC) June 17, 2001
    (ties AL record for pitching team)

Fewest Strikeouts, Game (Most Innings)
0 **NL:**NY (Cin.) June 26, 1893 (17 inn)
    Cin. (NY) Aug. 27, 1920 (17 inn)
    AL: Clev. (NY) June 7, 1936 (16 inn)

Fewest Strikeouts, Both Clubs, Game (Most Innings)
0 **AL:**Chi. (StL.) July 7, 1931 (12 inn)
    NL: Bos. (NY) Apr. 19, 1928 (10 inn)

Fewest Strikeouts, Doubleheader (Most Innings)
0 **NL:**Pitt. (Phil.) July 12, 1924 (21 inn)
    AL: Bos. (StL.) July 28, 1917 (20 inn)

Fewest Strikeouts, Both Clubs, Doubleheader
1 **AL:**Bos. (0) Clev. (1) Aug. 28, 1926
2 **NL:**NY (0) Brk. (2) Aug. 13, 1932
    StL. (0) Pitt. (2) Sept. 6, 1948

Most Strikeouts, Inning
4 **AA:**Pitt. (Phil.) Sept. 30, 1885 (7th)
    NL: Chi. (NY) Oct. 4, 1888 (5th)
    Cin. (NY) May 15, 1906 (5th)
    StL. (Chi.) May 27(1g), 1956 (6th)
    Mil. (Cin.) Aug. 11(1g), 1959 (6th)
    Cin. (LA) Apr. 12, 1962 (3rd)
    Phil. (LA) Apr. 17, 1965 (2nd)
    Pitt. (StL.) June 7, 1966 (4th)
    Mtl. (Chi.) July 31(1g), 1974 (2nd)
    Pitt. (Atl.) July 29, 1977 (6th)
    Chi. (Cin.) May 17, 1984 (3rd,cons)
    Chi. (Hou.) Sept. 3, 1986 (5th)
    Cin. (Atl.) Aug. 22, 1989 (5th)
    SF (Cin.) June 4, 1990 (7th)
    Chi. (Atl.) June 7, 1995 (9th,cons)
    SD (Col.) Sept. 19, 1995 (6th)
    Atl. (NY) Sept. 13, 1996 (9th)
    Chi. (Col.) July 25, 1996 (9th)
    Mtl. (Fla.) Sept. 16, 1998 (4th)
    Fla. (Chi.) Apr. 28, 1999 (7th)
    SF (SD) July 22, 1999 (7th)
    SF (Mil.) Aug. 17, 1999 (7th,cons)
    Mil. (Mtl.) May 5, 2000 (9th)
    Fla. (Cin.) July 22, 2001 (7th)
    AL: Bos. (Wash.) Apr. 15, 1911 (5th)
    Phil. (Clev.) June 11, 1916 (6th)
    Chi (LA) May 18, 1961 (7th)
    Wash. (Clev.) Sept. 2, 1964 (7th)
    Cal. (Balt.) May 29, 1970 (4th)
    Sea. (Clev.) July 21, 1978 (5th)
    Balt. (Tex.) Aug. 2, 1987 (2nd,cons)
    NY (Tex.) July 4, 1988 (1st)
    Bos. (Det.) Aug. 13, 1988 (6th)
    Bos. (Sea.) Sept. 9, 1990 (1st)
    Cal. (Clev.) Apr. 11, 1994 (9th)
    Det. (Clev.) May 14, 1994 (8th)
    Tor. (KC) Sept. 3, 1996 (4th)
    Det. (Chi.) July 21, 1997 (7th)
    TB (Oak.) July 27, 1998 (4th)
    NY (Ana.) May 12, 1999 (3rd)
    KC (Bos.) Aug. 10, 1999 (9th)
    Det. (Ana.) Aug. 15, 1999 (1st,cons)
    Tex. (Clev.) Apr. 16, 2000 (3rd)
    Tex. (Oak.) June 30, 2001 (7th)

GROUNDED INTO DOUBLE PLAYS

Most Grounded Into Double Plays, Game
7 **NL:**SF (Hou.) May 4, 1969
6 **AL:**Wash. (Clev.) Aug. 5, 1948
Bos. (Cal.) May 1, 1966
Balt. (KC) May 6, 1972
Clev. (NY) Apr. 29, 1975
Tor. (Minn.) Aug. 29, 1977 (1g; 10)
Bos. (Det.) Apr. 13, 1984
Mil. (Chi.) May 8, 1984 (25)
Bos. (Chi.) Apr. 27, 1989 (16)
Bos. (Minn.) July 18, 1990
Det. (Tor.) Apr. 16, 1996

Most Grounded Into Double Plays, Both Clubs, Game
9 **AL:**Bos. (6) Cal. (3) May 1, 1966
Bos. (6) Minn. (3) July 18, 1990
8 **NL:**Bos. (5) Chi. (3) Sept. 18, 1928
Extra-Inning Game:
9 **NL:**LA (5) NY (4) May 24, 1973 (19 inn)

STOLEN BASES

Most Seasons Leading League
29 **AL:**Chi. 1901-04,17,19,23-24,28-29,39,41-43,46-47,49,51-61,66
25 **NL:**Brk./LA 1890-92, 1900,03,38,42,46-53,55,58-65,70

Most Seasons, Consecutive, Leading League
11 **AL:**Chi. 1951-61
8 **NL:**Brk. 1946-53
LA 1958-65

Most Stolen Bases, Game
19 **AA:**Phil. (Syr.) Apr. 22, 1890
17 **NL:**NY (Pitt.) May 23, 1890
Since 1900:
15 **AL:**NY (StL.) Sept. 28, 1911
11 **NL:**StL. (Pitt.) Aug. 13, 1916 (2g; 5 inn)

Most Stolen Bases, Both Clubs, Game
21 **AA:**Phil. (19) Syr. (2) Apr. 22, 1890
20 **NL:**NY (17) Pitt. (3) May 23, 1890
Since 1900:
15 **AL:**StL. (8) Det. (7) Oct. 1, 1916
14 **NL:**NY (9) Bos. (5) June 20, 1912

Most Triple Steals, Game
2 **AL:**Phil. (Clev.) July 25, 1930
1 **NL:**By many clubs

Fewest Stolen Bases, Game (Most Innings)
0 **NL:**Bos. (Brk.) May 1, 1920 (26 inn)
AL: Det. (Phil.) July 21, 1945 (24 inn)
Phil. (Det.) July 21, 1945 (24 inn)

Fewest Stolen Bases, Both Clubs, Game (Most Innings)
0 **AL:**Det. (Phil.) July 21, 1945 (24 inn)
NL:NY (SF) May 31(2g), 1964 (23 inn)

Most Stolen Bases, Inning
8 **AL:**Wash. (Clev.) July 19, 1915 (1st)
NL: Phil. (NY) July 7(1g), 1919 (9th)

Most Stealing Home, Season
16 **NL:**Chi. 1911
15 **AL:**Chi. 1906

Most Stealing Home, Game
3 **AL:**Chi. (StL.) July 2, 1909
NL: Chi (Bos.) Aug. 23, 1909
NY (Pitt.) Sept. 18, 1911

Most Stealing Home, Inning
2 By many; Last:
NL: StL. (Brk.) Sept. 19, 1925 (7th)
AL: Oak. (KC) May 28, 1980 (1st)

CAUGHT STEALING

Most Caught Stealing, Game
8 **AL:**Balt. (Wash.) May 11, 1897
Since 1900:
6 **NL:**StL. (Brk.) Aug. 23, 1909
AL: StL. (Phil.) May 12, 1915
Chi. (Phil.) June 18, 1915

Most Caught Stealing, Inning
3 **AA:**Cin. (Phil.) July 26, 1887 (3rd)
AL: Det. (NY) Aug. 3, 1914 (2nd)
2 **NL:**By many clubs

LEFT ON BASE

Most Left on Base, Game
20 **AL:**NY (Bos.) Sept. 21, 1956
18 **NL:**By many clubs; Last:
Atl. (LA) June 23, 1986
Extra-Inning Game:
27 **NL:**Atl. (Phil.) May 4, 1973 (20 inn)
25 **AL:**Wash. (Clev.) Sept. 14, 1971 (20 inn)
KC (Tex.) June 6, 1991 (18 inn)

Most Left on Base, Both Clubs, Game
30 **NL:**Brk. (16) Pitt. (14) June 30, 1893
NY (17) Phil. (13) July 18, 1943
Atl. (18) Phil. (12) Aug. 30(1g), 1982
AL:NY (15) Chi. (15) Aug. 27, 1935
LA (15) Wash. (15) July 21, 1961
Extra-Inning Game:
45 **NL:**NY (25) StL. (20) Sept. 11, 1974 (25 inn)
AL:KC (25) Tex. (20) June 6, 1991 (18 inn)

Most Left on Base, No Runs, Game
16 **NL:**StL. (Phil.) May 24, 1994
AL: Sea. (Tor.) May 7, 1998
Extra-Inning Game:
19 **NL:**Ari. (SD) Sept. 2, 2001 (13 inn)

Fewest Left on Base, Game (Most Innings)
0 **AL:**Phil. (NY) June 22, 1929 (2g; 14 inn)
1 **NL:**Mil. (Pitt.) May 26, 1959 (13 inn)
Cin. (StL.) Aug. 30, 1989 (13 inn)

Fewest Left on Base, Both Clubs, Game
1 **NL:**LA (0) Chi. (1) Sept. 9, 1965
2 **AL:**Many games

Fewest Left on Base, 2 Consecutive Games
1 **AL:**NY Sept. 21-22, 1982
Det. May 3-4, 1996
NL: Pitt. Aug. 3-4, 1999

Most Left on Base, Doubleheader
 30 **AL:**Phil. (StL.) June 22, 1949
 29 **NL:**StL. (Phil.) Sept. 15, 1928
      Phil. (Mil.) May 15, 1955
      Extra Innings
 33 **NL:**Fla. (Pitt.) Aug. 18, 1995 (22 inn)
      AL:NY (Det.) July 20, 1998 (26 inn)

Most Left on Base, Both Clubs, Doubleheader
 49 **NL:**Brk. (25) Pitt. (24) July 24, 1926
      AL:NY (27) Chi. (22) Aug. 27, 1935

Fewest Left on Base, Doubleheader
 3 **AL:**Wash. (NY) Aug. 6, 1963
      Balt. (NY) Sept. 14, 1982
      Chi. (Sea.) Sept. 27, 1982
      NL:SF (Hou.) Sept. 24, 1978
      NY (Mtl.) Sept. 21, 1982

Fewest Left on Base, Both Clubs, Doubleheader
 10 **NL:**StL. (6) Bos. (4) July 19, 1924
 13 **AL:**Chi. (9) Phil. (4) July 18, 1918

PINCH-HITTERS

Most Pinch-Hitters, Game
 9 **NL:**LA (StL.) Sept. 22, 1959
      Mtl. (Pitt.) Sept. 5(2g), 1975
      LA (StL.) Sept. 1, 1982 (13 inn)
      LA (NY) Sept. 8, 1985 (14 inn)
      SF (LA) Sept. 28, 1986 (16 inn)
      Atl. (Mtl.) Sept. 21, 1993
      StL. (Cin.) Sept. 25, 1997 (14 inn)
 8 **AL:**Balt. (Chi.) May 28, 1954
      Balt. (NY) Sept. 25, 1984
      Minn. (Sea.) Sept. 13, 1986
      Extra-Inning Game:
 10 **AL:**Oak. (Chi.) Sept. 19, 1972 (15 inn)

Most Pinch-Hitters, Both Clubs, Game
 13 **NL:**LA (7) SD (6) Sept. 25, 1986
      Atl. (9) Mtl. (4) Sept. 21, 1993
 10 **AL:**Balt. (6) NY (4) Apr. 26, 1959
      Extra-Inning Game:
 14 **NL:**NY (7) Chi. (7) May 2, 1956 (17 inn)
      LA (9) StL. (5) Sept. 1, 1982 (13 inn)
      LA (7) Atl. (7) Sept. 18, 1986 (12 inn)
      SF (9) LA (5) Sept. 28, 1986 (16 inn)
      AL: Oak. (10) Chi. (4) Sept. 19, 1972 (15 inn)

Most Pinch-Hitters, Doubleheader
 10 **AL:**NY (Bos.) Sept. 6, 1954
      Balt. (Wash.) Apr. 19, 1959
      NL: StL. (Chi.) May 11, 1958
      StL. (Pitt.) July 13, 1958
      SF (Ari.) Sept. 23, 2000
      Extra-Innings:
 15 **NL:**Mtl. (Pitt.) Sept. 5, 1975 (19 inn)

Most Pinch-Hitters, Both Clubs, Doubleheader
 15 **NL:**Mil. (8) SF (7) Aug. 30, 1964
      SF (10) Ari. (5) Sept. 23, 2000
 14 **AL:**NY (10) Bos. (4) Sept. 6. 1954
      Extra innings:
 19 **NL:**Mtl. (15) Pitt. (4) Sept. 5, 1975 (19 inn)
 17 **AL:**NY (9) Wash. (8) Aug. 14, 1960 (24 inn)

Most Pinch-Hitters, Inning
 6 **NL:**SF (Pitt.) May 5, 1958 (9th)
      SD (SF) Sept. 16, 1986 (9th)
      Atl. (Mtl.) Sept. 21, 1993 (7th)
      AL: Det. (NY) Sept. 5, 1971 (7th)

Most Pinch-Hitters, Both Clubs, Inning
 8 **AL:**Chi. (5) Balt. (3) May 18, 1957 (7th)
      NL: Phil. (5) StL. (3) Apr. 30, 1961 (8th)
      NY (5) SF (3) Sept. 16, 1966 (9th)

Most Pinch-Hits, Game
 6 **NL:**Brk. (Phil.) Sept. 9, 1926
 4 **AL:**Clev. (Chi.) Apr. 22, 1930
      Phil. (Det.) Sept. 18, 1940
      Det. (Chi.) Apr. 22, 1953
      KC (Det.) Sept. 1, 1958
      NY (Clev.) Aug. 26, 1960 (11 inn)
      Clev. (Bos.) Sept. 21, 1967
      Oak. (Det.) Aug. 30, 1970
      Chi. (Oak.) Sept. 7, 1970
      Tex. (KC) June 8, 1995 (10 inn)
      Bos. (NY) Sept. 8, 1995

Most Pinch-Hits, Inning
 4 **NL:**Chi. (Brk.) May 21(2g), 1927 (9th)
      Phil. (Pitt.) Sept. 12, 1974 (8th)
      AL: Phil. (Det.) Sept. 18, 1940 (9th)
      Tex. (KC) June 8, 1995 (8th)
      Bos. (NY) Sept. 8, 1995 (8th)

Most Pinch-Hit Home Runs, Game
 2 **NL:**Phil. (StL.) June 2, 1928
      StL. (Brk.) July 21, 1930
      StL. (Cin.) May 12, 1951
      Chi. (Phil.) June 9, 1954
      NY (StL.) June 20, 1954
      SF (Mil.) June 4, 1958
      Phil. (Pitt.) Aug. 13, 1958
      NY (Phil.) Aug. 15, 1962 (13 inn)
      LA (Chi.) Aug. 8, 1963 (10 inn)
      NY (Phil.) Sept. 17, 1963
      NY (SF) Aug. 4, 1966
      Mtl. (Atl.) July 13(1g), 1973
      Chi. (Pitt.) Sept. 10, 1974
      LA (StL.) July 23, 1975
      Chi. (Hou.) Aug. 23, 1975
      LA (Chi.) Aug. 27, 1982
      SF (SD) Sept. 28, 1987
      NY (SF) May 4, 1991 (12 inn)
      Col. (LA) May 6, 1995
      Cin. (Atl.) June 22, 1995
      Hou. (Chi.) Sept. 28, 1995 (11 inn)
      Atl. (StL.) July 22, 1996
      NY (StL.) May 11, 1997
      Chi. (StL.) July 13, 1997
      Chi. (Mil.) Sept. 12, 1998
      Atl. (Mil.) May 25, 1999
      SD (Col.) July 2, 1999
      Ari. (LA) Apr. 12, 2001
      SF (Mtl.) Aug. 23, 2001
      AL: Clev. (Phil.) May 26, 1937
      NY (KC) July 23, 1955
      Clev. (Minn.) Aug. 15, 1965, (11 inn)
      Balt. (Bos.) Aug. 26, 1966 (12 inn)
      Det. (Bos.) Aug. 11, 1968 (14 inn)
      Sea. (NY) Aug. 2, 1969
      Minn. (Det.) July 31, 1970
      Minn. (Cal.) July 28(2g), 1974
      Sea. (NY) Apr. 27, 1979
      Chi. (Oak.) July 6(2g), 1980
      Minn. (Oak.) May 16, 1983
      Balt. (Tex.) May 5, 1984
      Balt. (Clev.) Aug. 12, 1985
      Tor. (Det.) June 14, 1986
      Tex. (Bos.) Sept. 1, 1986
      Cal. (Chi.) June 28, 1987
      Bos. (Chi.) Sept. 19, 1997 (10 inn)

Most Pinch-Hit Home Runs, Both Clubs, Game
3 **NL:**Phil. (2) StL. (1) June 2, 1928
   StL. (2) Brk. (1) July 21, 1930
   Col. (2) LA (1) May 6, 1995
   SD (2) Col. (1) July 2, 1999
2 **AL:**Many games. Last:
   Clev. (1) Tex. (1) May 15, 2001

Most Pinch-Hit. Home Runs, 2 Cons. Games
3 **NL:**Mtl. July 13-13, 1973
   SF Sept. 27-28, 1987
   Chi. Sept. 11-12, 1998
   AL: By many clubs

Most Pinch-Hit Home Runs, Inning
2 **NL:**NY (StL.) June 20, 1954 (6th)
   SF (Mil.) June 4, 1958 (10th)
   LA (Chi.) Aug. 8, 1963 (5th)
   LA (StL.) July 23, 1975 (9th)
   NY (SF) May 4, 1991 (9th)
   Cin. (Atl.) June 22, 1995 (8th)
   NY (StL.) May 11, 1997 (9th)
   Atl. (Mil.) May 25, 1999 (9th)
   SD (Col.) July 2, 1999 (9th)
   SF (Mtl.) Aug. 23, 2001 (9th)
   AL:NY (KC) July 23, 1955 (9th)
   Balt. (Bos.) Aug. 26, 1966 (9th)
   Sea. (NY) Apr. 27, 1979 (8th)
   Minn. (Oak.) May 16, 1983 (9th)
   Balt. (Clev.) Aug. 12, 1985 (9th)
   Tex. (Bos.) Sept. 1, 1986 (9th)
   Bos. (Chi.) Sept. 19, 1997 (9th)

Most Grand Slam HRs, Game
1 By many

Most Grand Slam HRs, Both Clubs, Game
2 **NL:**Bos. (1) NY (1) May 26, 1929
1 **AL:**By many

Most Walks, Inning
3 **NL:**Pitt. (Phil.) June 3, 1911 (9th)
   Brk. (NY) Apr. 22, 1922 (7th)
   Bos. (Brk.) June 2, 1932 (9th)
   Chi. (Phil.) July 29, 1947 (7th)
   StL. (NY) May 6, 1994 (9th)
   NY (Col.) May 18, 1997 (8th)
   Phil. (Pitt.) July 18, 1997 (6th)
   AL: Balt. (Wash.) Apr. 22, 1955 (7th)
   Wash. (Bos.) May 14, 1961 (9th)
   Sea. (Bos.) June 3, 1995 (9th)
   Tex. (Ari.) July 15, 1999 (9th)

Most Strikeouts, Game
5 **AL:**Det. (NY) Sept. 8, 1979
   NL: Chi. (Cin.) May 22, 1990 (16 inn)
   Cin. (SF) Sept. 20, 2000

Most Strikeouts, Both Clubs, Game
5 **AL:**NY (4) Bos. (1) July 4, 1955
   Wash. (4) Clev. (1) May 1, 1957
   Det. (4) Clev. (1) Aug. 4, 1967
   Det. (5) NY (0) Sept. 8, 1979
   NL:LA (3) Cin. (2) Sept. 16. 1990
   NY (3) SF (2) Aug. 19, 1996
   Phil. (3) Cin. (2) Apr. 26, 1997
   Hou. (4) NY (1) Aug. 30, 1999
   Cin (5) SF (0) Sept. 20, 2000
   Extra-Inning Game:
7 **NL:**Chi. (5) Cin. (2) May 22, 1990 (16 inn)

Most Strikeouts, Inning
3 By many; Last:
   NL: Col. (Tex.) July 12, 2001 (9th)
   AL:KC (Det.) July 9, 1995 (7th)

PINCH-RUNNERS

Most Pinch-Runners, Game
4 By many clubs
   Extra-Inning Game:
5 **NL:**Chi. (Hou.) Sept. 2, 1986 (18 inn)

Most Pinch-Runners, Inning
4 **AL:**Chi. (Minn.) Sept. 16, 1967 (9th)
   Oak. (Chi.) Sept. 24, 1975 (8th)
   Tex. (Cal.) Sept. 10, 1987 (9th)
   Ana. (Tex.) Sept. 23, 2000 (7th)
   NL:SD (Cin.) Aug. 10, 1978 (7th)

Most Runs, Inning
3 **AL:**Chi. (Minn.) Sept. 16, 1967 (9th)
   Chi. (Oak.) May 19, 1968 (5th)
   Oak. (Cal.) May 7, 1975 (7th)
   Minn. (Balt.) June 6, 1991 (9th)
   Tex. (Balt.) Apr. 19, 1996 (8th)
2 **NL:**By many; Last:
   Hou. (Chi.) Sept. 22, 2001

CLUB FIELDING — SEASON

	AL:1901-1960 NL:1900-1961 8 clubs 154 games		AL:1961-1968 NL:1962-1968 10 clubs 162 games		AL:1969- NL:1969- 12-16 clubs 162 games	
Highest Fielding Average						
AL:	.983	Clev 1949	.985	Balt. 1964	.988	Clev. 2000
NL:	.983	Cin. 1958	.982	Phil. 1966	.989	NY 1999
Lowest Fielding Average						
AL:	.928	Det. 1901	.969	LA 1961	.970	Oak. 1977
NL:	.936	Phil. 1904	.967	NY 1963	.969	Chi. 1974
Most Total Chances						
AL:	6895	Chi. 1907	6557	Chi. 1967	6653	Cal. 1983
NL:	6682	NY 1920	6601	Pitt. 1968	6661	Chi. 1977
Fewest Total Chances						
AL:	5596	Clev. 1945	5930	Det. 1962	5869	NY 2000
NL:	5655	Phil. 1955	5964	Cin. 1966	5907	Phil. 2000
Most Chances Accepted						
AL:	6655	Chi. 1907	6419	Chi. 1967	6499	Cal. 1983
NL:	6472	NY 1920	6462	Pitt. 1968	6508	Chi. 1977
Fewest Chances Accepted						
AL:	5470	Clev. 1945	5774	Det. 1962	5760	NY 2000
NL:	5545	Phil. 1955	5842	Cin. 1966	5804	Chi. 2001
Most Putouts						
AL:	4396	Clev. 1910	4520	NY 1964	4493	Minn. 1969
NL:	4359	Phil. 1913	4471	Cin. 1968	4480	Pitt. 1979
Fewest Putouts						
AL:	3907	Clev. 1945	4245	KC 1961	4188	Det. 1975
NL:	3887	Phil. 1907	4280	Phil. 1962	4223	Atl. 1979
Most Assists						
AL:	2446	Chi. 1907	1975	NY 1968	2077	Cal. 1983
NL:	2293	StL. 1917	2068	Chi. 1964	2104	Chi. 1977
Fewest Assists						
AL:	1493	NY 1948	1443	Det. 1962	1487	NY 2000
NL:	1437	Phil. 1957	1534	Cin. 1966	1462	NY 1989
Most Errors						
AL:	425	Det. 1901	192	LA 1961	191	Tex. 1975
NL:	408	Brk. 1905	210	NY 1962-63	199	Chi. 1974
Fewest Errors						
AL:	103	Clev. 1949	95	Balt. 1964	72	Clev. 2000
NL:	100	Cin. 1958	113	Phil. 1966	68	NY 1999
Most Double Plays						
AL:	217	Phil. 1949	186	Cal. 1966	206	Bos. & Tor. 1980
NL:	198	LA 1958	215	Pitt. 1966	197	Atl. 1985
Fewest Double Plays						
AL:	74	Bos. 1913	114	Det. 1962	114	KC 1969
NL:	94	Pitt. 1935	100	Hou. 1963	106	LA 1975
Most Triple Plays						
AL:	3	Det. 1911 Bos. 1924	2	Wash. 1968	3	Bos. 1979 Oak. 1979
NL:	2	By many	3	Phil. 1964 Chi. 1965	2	Hou. 1971, 78, 91 NY 1982 Cin. 1995
Most Passed Balls						
AL:	49	Balt. 1959	45	Chi. 1965	73	Tex. 1987
NL:	42	Bos. 1905	42	Atl. 1967	38	Atl. 1976
Fewest Passed Balls						
AL:	0	NY 1931	5	Minn. 1966	2	Tex. 1999
NL:	2	Bos. 1943	4	Chi. 1967	2	NY 1980 SD 1992

AVERAGE

Most Seasons Leading League
20 **NL:** Bos./Mil./Atl. 1878-79,82,84,91,97,99-
    1900,02,15-16,24,32-33,54,61-63,69,98
19 **AL:** StL./Balt. 1902,63-64,66,69,74-78,80,
    82,84,89,91,94-95,98,99

Most Seasons, Consecutive, Leading League
6 **AL:** Bos. 1916-21
   NL: StL. 1984-89

TOTAL CHANCES

Most Seasons Leading League
25 **NL:** Chi. 1884-87,89,97,99-1900,02,16,32,
    42, 47-48,50,59-61,64-65,72,
    74,77-78,80
18 **AL:** Chi. 1905-09,25,33,36,41, 46-47,49,59,
    65-67,70,91

Most Seasons, Consecutive, Leading League
4 **NL:** Pro. 1878-81
   Chi. 1884-87
   Since 1900:
5 **AL:** Chi. 1905-09
3 **NL:** Cin. 1924-26
   NY 1927-29, 33-35
   Chi. 1959-61
   Pitt. 1966-68
   StL. 1982-84

CHANCES ACCEPTED

Most Seasons Leading League
24 **NL:** Chi. 1883-87,89,90,97, 1902,16,32,
    42,47-48,50,62-65,72,74,77-78,80
18 **AL:** Chi. 1905,07-09,21,25,33,36,41,46-47,
    53,59,65-67,70,87

Most Seasons, Consecutive, Leading League
5 **NL:** Chi. 1883-87
   Since 1900:
4 **NL:** Chi. 1962-65
3 **AL:** Chi. 1907-09, 65-67
   Clev. 1928-30
   Bos. 1956-58

Most Chances Accepted, Game
55 **NL:** Pitt. (NY) June 7, 1911
54 **AL:** StL. (Phil.) Aug. 16, 1919
    Extra-Inning game:
119 **NL:** Bos. (Brk.) May 1, 1920 (26 inn)
110 **AL:** Det. (Phil.) July 21, 1945 (24 inn)

Most Chances Accepted, Both Clubs, Game
98 **NL:** Brk. (50) NY (48) Apr. 21, 1903
    NY (52) Cin. (46) May 15, 1909
    AL: Clev. (49) StL. (49) May 7, 1909

PUTOUTS

Most Seasons Leading League
19 **NL:** Brk./LA 1892, 1910,16,19-20,39-41,46,
    48-49,51-52,59,62,64,73,82,93
16 **AL:** Chi. 1905,09,12,17,22-23,39-41,51,59,
    63, 65-67,93

Most Seasons, Consecutive, Leading League
4 **NL:** Chi. 1905-08
3 **AL:** Chi. 1939-41, 65-67

Most Putouts, Game (Most Innings)
78 **NL:** Bos. (Brk.) May 1, 1920 (26 inn)
    Brk. (Bos.) May 1, 1920 (26 inn)
75 **AL:** Chi. (Mil.) May 8, 1984 (25 inn)

Most Putouts, Both Clubs, Game (Most Innings)
156 **NL:** Bos. (78) Brk. (78) May 1, 1920 (26 inn)
148 **AL:** Chi. (75) Mil. (73) May 8, 1984 (25 inn)

Most Players, 1 or more Putouts, 9-Inning Game
14 By many clubs; Last:
    NL: Cin. (Phil.) May 4, 2000
    AL: Minn. (Sea.) Sept. 13, 1996

**Most Players, 1 or more Putouts, Both Clubs,
9-Inning Game**
25 In many games; Last:
    NL: SD (14) SF (11) Sept. 26, 1997
    AL: Minn. (14) Sea. (11) Sept. 13, 1996

ASSISTS

Most Seasons Leading League
25 **NL:** Chi. 1882,83,85,97,99, 1916,42,4750,59,
    61-62,63-65,72-73,77-78,80,83,92
19 **AL:** Chi. 1905-09,21,25,33,36,41,46-49,65-67,
    69-70,88

Most Seasons, Consecutive, Leading League
6 **NL:** NY 1933-38
5 **AL:** Chi. 1905-09

Most Assists, Game
28 **NL:** Pitt. (NY) June 7, 1911
27 **AL:** StL. (Phil.) Aug. 16, 1919
    Extra-Inning game:
42 **AL:** Minn. (Clev.) Aug. 31, 1993 (22 inn)
41 **NL:** Bos. (Brk.) May 1, 1920 (26 inn)

Fewest Assists, Game
0 **AL:** Clev. (NY) July 4(1g), 1945
   NY (Clev.) Sept. 11, 1995
   Balt. (Oak.) June 20, 2000
   NL: NY (Phil.) June 25, 1989
   Cin. (Col.) Aug. 20, 1997

Most Assists, Both Clubs, Game
44 **AL:** Clev. (22) StL. (22) May 27, 1909
43 **NL:** Brk. (24) NY (19) Apr. 21, 1903
    Extra inning game:
72 **NL:** Bos. (41) Brk. (31) May 1, 1920 (26 inn)
    AL: Det. (38) Phil. (34) July 21,
    1945 (24 inn)

Fewest Assists, Both Clubs, Game
5 **AL:** Balt. (3) Clev. (2) Aug. 31, 1955
   Bos. (4) NY (1) Aug. 9, 1992
   Det. (4) Oak. (1) June 12, 1991
6 **NL:** Chi. (5) Phil. (1) May 2, 1957
   Phil. (3) SF (3) May 13, 1959
   Atl. (3) Hou. (3) Sept. 19, 1989
   LA (3) SF (3) Sept. 27, 1989
   Atl. (3) Mtl. (3) May 28, 1990
   Mtl. (3) NY (3) Sept. 10, 1991
   Cin (5) Chi (1) Aug. 26, 1998

Most Assists, Infield
22 **AL:** Sea. (NY) May 28, 1988
21 **NL:** NY (Pitt.) July 13, 1919
    Phil. (Bos.) May 30(2g), 1931
    Brk. (Pitt.) Aug. 18(2g), 1935
    StL. (NY) June 27, 1993
    Phil. (Mtl.) Apr. 17, 1996

Fewest Assists, Infield, Game
0 By many clubs; Last:
   NL: LA (Fla.) May 10, 1998
   AL: Balt. (Sea.) June 25, 2000

Most Assists Infield, Both Clubs, Game
38 **NL:** Brk. (20) Cin. (18) June 10, 1917
35 **AL:** Det. (19) Clev. (16) Apr. 18, 1924
    Chi. (18) Bos. (17) Sept. 17(2g), 1945
    Det. (18) TB (17) Aug. 1, 1998

Fewest Assists, Infield, Both Clubs, Game
2 **AL:** Wash. (0) Phil. (2) May 5, 1910
NL: Phil. (0) Chi. (2) May 2, 1957

Most Assists, Outfield, Game
5 **NL:** Pitt. (Phil.) Aug. 23, 1910
AL: NY (Bos.) Sept. 5(2g), 1921
Clev. (StL.) May 1, 1928

Most Assists, Inning
10 **AL:** Clev. (Phil.) Aug. 17, 1921
Bos. (NY) May 10, 1952
8 **NL:** Bos. (Phil.) May 1, 1911
Cin. (StL.) June 3, 1992

Most Players, 1 or more Assists, 9-Inning Game
11 **AL:** Wash. (Phil.) Oct. 3, 1920
Bos. (Phil.) May 1, 1929
Wash. (Balt.) Apr. 29(1g), 1956
Chi. (KC) Sept. 22(2g), 1970
NL: Brk. (Phil.) Apr. 22, 1953
Mtl. (Fla.) May 12, 1993
Chi. (NY) Aug. 7, 1996

ERRORS – MOST

Most Seasons Leading League
18 **AL:** Phil./KC/Oak. 1915-16, 18-21,36-41,
64,77-79, 82, 84
NL: Phil. 1883, 1904, 14, 19, 21, 30-36,
38, 42-43,45, 48, 59

Most Seasons, Consecutive, Leading League
7 **NL:** Phil. 1930-36
6 **AL:** Phil. 1936-41
StL. 1948-53

Most Errors, Game
24 **NL:** Bos. (StL.) June 14, 1876
Since 1900:
12 **AL:** Det. (Chi.) May 1, 1901
Det. (Chi.) May 6, 1903
11 **NL:** StL. (Pitt.) Apr. 19, 1902
Bos. (StL.) June 11, 1906
StL. (Cin.) July 3(2g), 1909

Most Errors, Both Clubs, Game
40 **NL:** Bos. (24) StL. (16) June 14, 1876
Since 1900:
18 **AL:** Chi. (12) Det. (6) May 6, 1903
15 **NL:** StL. (11) Pitt. (4) Apr. 19, 1902
Bos. (10) Chi. (5) Oct. 3, 1904

Most Errors, Inning, Since 1900
7 **AL:** Clev. (Chi) Sept. 20, 1905 (8th)
6 **NL:** Pitt. (NY) Aug. 20, 1903 (1g; 1st)

ERRORS – FEWEST

Most Seasons Leading League
25 **NL:** Cin. 1896, 1919,27,30,40-41,43,
57-58,60, 64-65,67,71-73,75-77,80-81,
83,90,95,97
19 **AL:** StL./Balt. 1938,43,60,63-64,66,69,
75-78,80,82,89,91,94-95,98-99

Most Seasons, Consecutive, Leading League
6 **AL:** Phil. 1909-14
Bos. 1916-21
4 **NL:** Chi. 1905-08

Most Errorless Games, Season
104 **AL:** Balt. 1998
NL: NY 1999

Most Errorless Games, Consecutive, Season
16 **NL:** StL. July 30-Aug. 16, 1992
15 **AL:** Tex. Aug. 4-19, 1996

Fewest Errors, Game (Most Innings)
0 **NL:** Bos. (Pitt.) Aug. 1, 1918 (21 inn)
SF (Cin.) Sept. 1, 1967 (21 inn)
SD (Mtl.) May 21, 1977 (21 inn)
Also see next listing

Fewest Errors, Both Clubs, Game (Most Innings)
0 **AL:** Chi. (Wash.) June 12, 1967 (22 inn)
NL: Chi. (Phil.) July 17, 1918 (21 inn)

DOUBLE PLAYS

Most Seasons Leading League
19 **NL:** Pitt. 1904,06,11,25,38,49,55,59-
67,70,72,94
15 **AL:** NY 1941-42,46,52,54-58,61,65,
72,84,89

Most Seasons, Consecutive, Leading League
9 **NL:** Pitt. 1959-67
5 **AL:** NY 1954-58

Most Double Plays, Game
7 **AL:** NY (Phil.) Aug. 14, 1942
NL: Hou. (SF) May 4, 1969
Atl. (Cin.) June 27, 1982 (14 inn)
StL. (Pitt) June 16, 1994 (10 inn)

Most Double Plays, Both Clubs, Game
10 **AL:** Minn. (6) Bos. (4) July 18, 1990
9 **NL:** Chi. (5) Cin. (4) July 3, 1929
LA (5) Pitt. (4) Apr. 15, 1961
Extra-Inning Game:
10 **NL:** Bos. (5) Cin. (5) June 7, 1925 (12 inn)
Cin. (6) NY (4) May 1, 1955 (16 inn)

Most Double Plays, Unassisted, Game
2 By many

**Most Double Plays, Unassisted,
Both Clubs, Game**
2 By many

Most Double Plays, Doubleheader
9 **AL:** Phil. (Clev.) Sept. 14, 1931
Bos. (StL.) June 25, 1950
NL: StL. (Cin.) June 11, 1944
Including Extra-Inning Game:
10 **AL:** Wash. (Chi.) Aug. 18, 1943 (23 inn)

Most Double Plays, Both Clubs, Doubleheader
13 **NL:** NY (7) Phil. (6) Sept. 28, 1939
Pitt. (8) StL. (5) Sept. 6, 1948
12 **AL:** Phil. (9) Clev. (3) Sept. 14, 1931
Bos. (7) Chi. (5) Sept. 15, 1947
NY (7) KC (5) July 31, 1955
Cal. (8) Bos. (4) May 1, 1966
Cal. (7) Balt. (5) May 19, 1988 (19 inn)

Most Games, Consecutive, Double Plays
25 **AL:** Bos. May 7-June 4, 1951 (38)
Clev. Aug. 21-Sept. 12, 1953 (38)
23 **NL:** Brk. Aug. 7-27, 1952 (36)

Most Double Plays, 2 Consecutive Games
10 **NL:** NY Aug. 12-13(1g) 1932
AL: Det. May 18-19, 1948
Clev. May 3-5, 1970
KC May 5-6, 1972

Most Double Plays, 3 Consecutive Games
13 **NL:** SF Apr. 24-26, 1987
12 **AL:** Bos. June 25-27, 1950
NY Apr. 19-21, 1952
Chi. Sept 2-3, 1973

Most Double Plays, 4 Consecutive Games
15 **NL:**SF Apr. 24-27, 1987
14 **AL:**Chi. July 12-14, 1951
   NY Apr. 18-21, 1952

Most Double Plays, 5 Consecutive Games
16 **AL:**NY Apr. 19-23, 1952
   NL:SF Apr. 22-27, 1987

TRIPLE PLAYS

Most Seasons, Consecutive, Triple Plays
4 **NL:**Pitt. 1968-71
3 **AL:**Det. 1910-12
   StL. 1915-17
   NY 1916-18
   Wash. 1921-23
   Bos. 1922-24, 65-67
   Balt. 1977-79
   Minn. 1982-84

Most Triple Plays, Season
3 **AL:**Det. 1911
   Bos. 1924, 79
   Oak. 1979
   NL: Phil. 1964
   Chi. 1965

Most Triple Plays, Game
2 **AL:**Minn. (Bos.) July 17, 1990 (4th, 8th)
1 **NL:**By many

Most Triple Plays, Both Clubs, Game
2 AL:Minn. (2) Bos. (0) July 17, 1990

Most Games, Consecutive, Triple Plays
2 AL:Det. June 6-7, 1908
1 NL:By many clubs

PASSED BALLS

Most Seasons Leading League (Most)
Since 1903:
22 **NL:**Bos.-Mil./Atl 1904-05,07,24,26,
   28-30,42,65-67,69-72,74-79
Since 1912:
14 **AL:**Chi. 1934,43,47-48,63-67,69-73

**Most Seasons, Consecutive, Leading League
(Most)**
7 **AL:**Tex. 1984-90
6 **NL:**Atl. 1974-79

Most Seasons Leading League (Fewest)
Since 1912:
18 **AL:**NY 1914,29,31,36-37,42,44,51-52,55,
   58,62-63,67-68,74,88-89
Since 1903:
15 **NL:**Bos.-Mil./Atl. 1913,15-16,20,35,37-38,
   43,45,49,57-59,62,83

**Most Seasons, Consecutive, Leading League
(Fewest)**
5 **NL:**SF 1960-64
3 **AL:**Clev. 1939-41

Most Passed Balls, Game
12 **AA**:Wash. (NY) May 10, 1884
10 **NL:**Bos. (Wash.) May 3, 1886
   Since 1900:
6 **NL:**Cin. (Pitt.) Oct. 4, 1902
   Hou. (Mtl.) May 12, 1996
   AL: Tex. (Det.) Aug. 30, 1987

Fewest Passed Balls, Game (Most Innings)
0 **NL:**Bos. (Brk.) May 1, 1920 (26 inn)
   Brk. (Bos.) May 1, 1920 (26 inn)
   AL: Chi. (Mil.) May 8, 1984 (25 inn)

Most Passed Balls, Both Clubs, Game
14 **AA:**Wash. (12) NY (2) May 10, 1884
11 **NL:**Troy (7) Clev. (4) June 16, 1880
   Since 1900:
6 **NL:**Cin. (6) Pitt. (0) Oct. 4, 1902
   Hou. (6) Mtl. (0) May 12, 1996
   AL: Tex. (6) Det. (0) Aug. 30, 1987

**Fewest Passed Balls, Both Clubs, Game
(Most Innings)**
0 **NL:**Bos.-Brk. May 1, 1920 (26 inn)
   AL: Bos.-Phil. Sept. 1, 1906 (24 inn)
   Det.-Phil. July 21, 1945 (24 inn)

CLUB PITCHING – SEASON

	AL:1901-1960 NL:1900-1961 8 clubs 154 games		AL:1961-1968 NL:1962-1968 10 clubs 162 games		AL:1969- NL:1969- 12-16 clubs 162 games
Lowest Earned Run Average					
AL:	2.16	Chi. 1917	2.45 Chi. 1967	2.83	Balt. 1969
NL:	2.18	Phil. 1915	2.49 StL. 1968	2.91	NY 1988
Highest Earned Run Average					
AL:	6.24	StL. 1936	4.79 KC 1962	6.38	Det. 1996
NL:	6.70	Phil. 1930	5.04 NY 1962	6.01	Col. 1999
Most No-Hit Games					
AL:	2	Bos. 1904,16 Clev. 1908 StL. 1917 NY 1951 Det. 1952	2 Bos. 1962	2	Cal. 1973
NL:	2	Cin. 1938 Brk. 1956 Mil. 1960	1 By many	2	Chi. 1972
Most No-Hit Games Against					
AL:	2	Chi. 1917 Phil. 1923	2 Det. 1967	2	Det. 1973 Cal. 1977
NL:	2	Phil. 1960	2 Chi. 1965	2	Col. 1996 SD 2001
Most Complete Games					
AL:	148	Bos. 1904	62 Det. 1961	94	Oak. 1980
NL:	146	StL. 1904	77 SF 1968	75	Chi. 1971
Fewest Complete Games					
AL:	26	KC 1957	18 KC 1964-65	1	TB 2001
NL:	27	Chi. 1958	24 Cin. 1968	1	Col. 1995
Most Shutouts Participating					
AL:	47	Chi. 1910	44 Cal. 1964	38	Cal. 1972
NL:	46	StL. 1908	47 NY 1968	42	NY 1969
Fewest Shutouts Participating					
AL:	7	By many	12 Chi. 1961	4	Tex. 2001
NL:	6	Phil. 1930	10 NY 1962	5	Hou. 2000
Most Shutouts Won					
AL:	30	Chi. 1906 (+2 ties)	28 Cal. 1964	23	Mil. 1971 Oak. 1972
NL:	32	Chi. 1907, 09	30 StL. 1968	28	NY 1969
Most Shutouts Lost					
AL:	29	Wash. 1909	23 Chi. 1968	27	Tex. 1972
NL:	33	StL. 1908	30 NY 1963	23	SD 1969, 76
Fewest Shutouts Won					
AL:	1	Chi. 1924, Wash. 1956	3 Chi. 1961	1	Sea. 1977, Balt. 1996, Oak. 1997, Ana. & KC 2001
NL:	1	Bos. 1928	4 Chi. & NY 1962 Mil. 1965	0	Col. 1993
Fewest Shutouts Lost					
AL:	0	NY 1932 (156g)	3 Minn. 1965	1	Mil. 1979, 82, Tor. 1993 Bos. 1995, Clev. 1996 Tex. 2001
NL:	1	Brk. 1953 (155g)	6 By many	0	Cin. 2000
Most 1-0 Games Won					
AL:	11	Wash. 1914	10 Cal. 1964	8	Balt. 1974
NL:	10	Pitt. 1908	8 StL. 1968	9	NY 1969 Hou. 1976
Most 1-0 Games Lost					
AL:	9	NY 1914	9 Chi. 1968	7	Tex. 1976
NL:	10	Pitt. 1914 Chi. 1916	10 Phil. 1967	7	Chi. 1968 NY 1973 LA 1976
Most 1-Hit Games					
AL:	3	By many	5 Balt. 1964	3	By many clubs
NL:	4	Chi. 1906, 09 Phil. 1907, 11, 15	3 LA,Mil.,Pitt. 1965	4	Phil. 1979 Cin. 1999

	AL:1901-1960 NL:1900-1961 8 clubs 154 games		AL:1961-1968 NL:1962-1968 10 clubs 162 games		AL:1969- NL:1969- 12-16 clubs 162 games

Most 1-Hit Games Against

AL:	5	StL. 1910 Clev. 1915	4	Wash. 1965	3	Cal. 1986
NL:	3	By many	4	NY 1965	3	By many

Most Games Decided By One Run

AL:	60	Phil. 1945	74	Chi. 1968	70	KC 1993
NL:	69	Cin. 1946	68	LA 1968	75	Hou. 1971

Fewest Games Decided By One Run

AL:	27	Clev. 1948	39	Minn. 1963 Det. 1967	30	Det. 1993 Sea. 1998
NL:	28	Brk. 1949	40	Phil. 1962	28	Mtl. 2001

Most 1-Run Games Won

AL:	38	NY 1943	38	Chi. 1967	40	Balt. 1970, 74
NL:	41	Cin. 1940	37	Phil. 1968	42	SF 1978

Fewest 1-Run Games Won

AL:	9	Clev. 1948	13	Minn. 1963	10	Sea. 1998
NL:	7	Bos. 1935	17	NY 1964	13	Pitt. 1996

Most 1-Run Games Lost

AL:	38	Phil. 1945	44	Chi. 1968	35	Chi. 1969, Clev. 1978 Balt. 1991
NL:	41	Cin. 1916, 46	39	NY 1962	43	Hou. 1971

Fewest 1-Run Games Lost

AL:	11	Bos. 1950	17	KC 1961, NY 1963 Det. 1966	10	Bos. 1986 NY 1998
NL:	12	Pitt. 1908, Brk. 1949	14	Phil. 1962	14	StL. 1975 Mtl. 1987

Most Saves (Since 1969)

AL:	-	-	-	-	68	Chi. 1990
NL:	-	-	-	-	61	Mtl. 1993

Fewest Saves

AL:	-	-	-	-	11	Tor. 1979
NL:	-	-	-	-	13	Chi. 1971

Most Innings

AL:	1465	Clev. 1910	1507	NY 1964	1498	Minn. 1969
NL:	1453	Phil. 1913	1490	Cin. 1968	1493	Pitt. 1979

Fewest Innings

AL:	1302	Clev. 1945	1415	KC 1961, NY 1966	1396	Det. 1975
NL:	1296	Phil. 1907	1427	Phil. 1962	1408	Atl. 1979

Most Batters Faced

AL:	6382	StL. 1936	6428	KC 1964	6660	Oak. 1997
NL:	6549	Phil. 1930	6380	LA 1962	6574	Col. 1999

Fewest Batters Faced

AL:	5559	Clev. 1945	5864	Balt. 1968	5799	Balt. 1971
NL:	5684	Brk. 1956	5941	LA 1966	5877	NY 1988

Most At-Bats

AL:	5653	StL. 1936	5666	Clev. 1964	5770	Oak. 1997
NL:	5763	Phil. 1930	5601	Cin. 1968	5741	Chi. 1974

Fewest At-Bats

AL:	4933	Clev. 1945	5237	Balt. 1968	5268	Balt. & Mil. 1971
NL:	5062	Phil. 1947	5368	Phil. 1963	5297	StL. 1978

Most Runs

AL:	1064	StL. 1936	863	KC 1961	1103	Det. 1996
NL:	1199	Phil. 1930	948	NY 1962	1028	Col. 1999

Fewest Runs

AL:	408	Phil. 1909	491	Chi. 1967	517	Balt. 1969
NL:	379	Chi. 1906	472	StL. 1968	532	NY 1988

Most Earned Runs

AL:	935	StL. 1936	764	KC 1962	1015	Det. 1996
NL:	1024	Phil. 1930	801	NY 1962	955	Col. 1999

Fewest Earned Runs

AL:	343	Chi. 1917	406	Chi. 1967	463	Balt. 1969
NL:	332	Phil. 1915	409	StL. 1968	465	NY 1988

	AL:1901-1960 NL:1900-1961 8 clubs 154 games		AL:1961-1968 NL:1962-1968 10 clubs 162 games		AL:1969- NL:1969- 12-16 clubs 162 games	
Most Hits						
AL:	1776	StL. 1936	1519	KC 1961	1734	Oak. 1997
NL:	1993	Phil. 1930	1577	NY 1962	1697	Col. 1997
Fewest Hits						
AL:	1163	NY 1955	1087	Clev. 1968	1194	Balt. 1969
NL:	1174	Pitt. 1909	1223	LA 1965	1215	LA 1975
Most Home Runs						
AL:	187	KC 1956	220	KC 1964	241	Det. 1996
NL:	185	StL. 1955	192	NY 1962	239	Col. 2001
Fewest Home Runs (Since 1949)						
AL:	78	Wash. 1952	87	Chi. 1967	80	Balt. 1976
		Balt. 1954				Clev. 1976
NL:	87	StL. 1949	65	LA 1968	68	SF 1976
Most Grand Slam Home Runs						
AL:	9	Chi. 1934	8	Clev. 1963	14	Det. 1996
		StL. 1938, 50				
NL:	8	Phil. 1933	6	Chi.,LA,Phil. 1962	12	Mtl. 2000
		Pitt. 1950-51		Mil. 1965		
		Chi. 1961				
Most Sacrifice Hits						
AL:	110	KC 1960	106	Chi. 1961	92	KC 1970
						Tor. 1980
NL:	106	NY 1956	99	Hou. 1964	112	SD 1975
Fewest Sacrifice Hits						
AL:	45	NY 1958	51	Balt. 1968	26	Bos. 1998
NL:	45	Mil. 1958	53	Phil. 1966	46	Ari. 1999
Most Sacrifice Flies (Since 1954)						
AL:	63	Balt. & KC 1955	64	KC 1961	80	Oak. 1997
NL:	79	Pitt. 1954	58	Hou. 1963	78	Col. 1993
Fewest Sacrifice Flies (Since 1954)						
AL:	29	KC 1958	17	Det. 1968	27	Cal. 1969
NL:	24	Brk. 1955	17	SF 1963	27	Cin. 1971, NY 1985
						LA 1987, Atl 1998
Most Walks						
AL:	827	Phil. 1915	713	LA 1961	784	Det 1996
NL:	671	Brk. 1946	601	Chi. 1962	737	Col. 1999
Fewest Walks						
AL:	359	Det. 1909	392	Minn. 1966	378	Bos. 1977
NL:	295	NY 1921	344	SF 1968	383	StL. 1993
Most Intentional Walks (Since 1955)						
AL:	59	KC 1955	78	Oak. 1968	94	Sea. 1980
		Clev. 1957				
NL:	84	Pitt. 1959	101	LA 1967	116	SD 1974
Fewest Intentional Walks (Since 1955)						
AL:	18	Det. 1959	21	Bos. & KC 1961	12	Minn. 2000
NL:	33	Brk. 1957	19	Hou. 1962	9	LA 1974
Most Hit Batters						
AL:	81	Phil. 1911	66	Chi. 1968	93	Bos. 2001
NL:	68	Brk. 1903	61	Phil. 1966	80	Pitt. 2001
Fewest Hit Batters						
AL:	5	StL. 1945	12	Chi. 1961	10	Balt. 1983
NL:	10	StL. 1948	17	Chi. 1964	11	Pitt. 1984
Most Strikeouts						
AL:	896	Det. 1946	1189	Clev. 1967	1266	NY 2001
NL:	1122	LA 1960	1122	Cin. 1964	1344	Chi. 2001
Fewest Strikeouts						
AL:	356	Bos. 1930	666	Wash. 1961	575	Mil. 1980
NL:	357	NY 1921	717	NY 1964	652	SD 1976

		AL:1901-1960 NL:1900-1961 8 clubs 154 games		AL:1961-1968 NL:1962-1968 10 clubs 162 games		AL:1969- NL:1969- 12-16 clubs 162 games
Most Wild Pitches						
AL:	67	Phil. 1936	73	Minn. 1964 Bos. 1968	94	Tex. 1986
NL:	70	LA 1958	83	Cin. 1965 Atl. 1966	96	Cin. 2000
Fewest Wild Pitches						
AL:	10	StL. 1930 Clev. 1943	27	Clev. 1962 NY 1962, 68	15	Bos. 1977
NL:	9	Cin. 1944	30	StL. 1964, 68 Phil. 1968	23	SD 1979, 85 Atl. 2000
Most Balks						
AL:	14	NY 1950	12	Bos. 1965 Balt. 1968	76	Oak. 1988
NL:	14	Phil. 1950	20	NY 1963	41	Mtl. 1988
Most Pitchers, 20 or more Games Won						
AL:	4	Chi. 1920	2	NY 1963	4	Balt. 1971
NL:	3	Pitt. 1902, Chi. 1903 NY 1904-05,13,20 Cin. 1923	2	Cin. 1962, 65 LA 1965 SF 1966	2	LA 1969; Chi. 1969 StL. 1985, Atl & SF 1993 Hou. 1999, Ari. 2001
Most Pitchers, 20 or more Games Lost						
AL:	3	Wash. 1904 StL. 1905 Phil. 1916	1	Minn. 1961 KC 1963 NY 1966	2	Chi. 1973
NL:	4	Bos. 1905-06	2	NY 1962, 65	1	SD 1969, 72, 74 Phil. 1973, Chi. & Mtl. 1974 NY 1977, Atl. 1977, 79

EARNED RUN AVERAGE

Seasons Leading League
Lowest:
26 **AL:** NY 1919-21,23,27,32,34-39,42-43,
47,52-53,55,57-58,60,76,78,81,97-98
25 **NL:** Brk./LA 1899, 1916,20,27-28,30,41,
55,57,60,63-66,72-75,77-78,82-83
Highest:
33 **NL:** Phil. 1914,18-34,36-42,45-46,56,61,
81,88-89,92
18 **AL:** StL./Balt. 1927,30,33,35-39,46-49,
51,83,91
Phil./KC/Oak. 1915-17,19,40-41,43,50,
54-55,59,61-62,64,67,84,93,97

Seasons, Consecutive, Leading League
Lowest:
6 **AL:** NY 1934-39
5 **NL:** Atl. 1997-2001
Highest:
17 **NL:** Phil. 1918-34
5 **AL:** StL. 1935-39

COMPLETE GAMES

Seasons Leading League
Most:
30 **NL:** Bos./Mil./Atl. 1877,85,90-91,93,
1905-06,13-14,16-18,37-38,47-51,
55-61,63,91,94-95
17 **AL:** NY:1914-15,21-23,32,34,37-39,42-43,
63,75,83,98, 2001
Fewest:
20 **NL:** Cin. 1893,95-97, 1934,36,38,48,54-55,
60,66-68,71-72,75,78,87,91, 2001
18 **AL:** Phil./KC/Oak. 1902,13,25,38-39,
45-46,50,55-57,64-66,78,85,92,97

Seasons, Consecutive, Leading League
Most:
7 **NL:** Mil. 1955-61
LA 1984-90
4 **AL:** Clev. 1951-54
Fewest:
7 **NL:** StL. 1916-22
6 **AL:** NY 1903-08

Most Incomplete Games, Consecutive
152 **AL:** TB. Apr. 14-Oct. 7, 2001
139 **NL:** NY Sept. 5, 1998-Aug. 14, 1999

Most Incomplete Games, Consecutive, Season
152 **AL:** TB. Apr. 14-Oct. 7, 2001
127 **NL:** Mil. May 16-Oct. 3, 1999

SHUTOUTS

Seasons Leading League
Most:
22 **NL:** Brk./LA 1928,30,40,47,49,56-57,
63-66,70-72,75,77,80-82,84,89,91
21 **AL:** NY 1920,24,27,32,34,37-39,42,
50-53,58-60,80-81,83,93,96,98
Fewest:
21 **NL:** Phil. 1883,93, 1920-23,30-31,38-42,
45,56,60,68,74,76,84,92
AL: Phil./KC/Oak. 1915,17,19-22,35,40-43,
50,54-55,60,62,65,79,93,97-98

Seasons, Consecutive, Leading League
Most:
7 **NL:** Chi. 1904-10
5 **AL:** Det. 1943-47
Fewest:
5 **NL:** Phil. 1938-42
4 **AL:** Phil. 1919-22, 40-43

Won, Consecutive, Season
6 **NL:** Pitt. June 2-8, 1903
5 **AL:** Balt. Sept. 2-6, 1974
Balt. Sept. 26-Oct. 1, 1995

Lost, Consecutive, Season
4 **NL:** Bos. May 19-23, 1906
Cin. July 30-Aug. 3, 1908
Cin. July 31-Aug. 3, 1931
Hou. June 20-23, 1963
Hou. Sept. 9-11, 1966
Chi. June 16-20, 1968
Atl. May 8-12, 1985
Chi. Apr. 27-May 1, 1992
AL: Bos. Aug. 2-6, 1906 (includes tie game)
Phil. Sept. 23-25, 1906
StL. Aug. 25-30, 1913
Wash. Sept. 19-22, 1958
Wash. Sept. 1-5, 1964

Won, vs. Opponent Season
10 **NL:** Pitt. (Bos.) 1906
8 **AL:** Chi. (Bos.) 1906
Clev. (Wash.) 1956
Oak. (Clev.) 1968

1-0 Games Won, Consecutive, Season
3 **AL:** Chi. Apr. 25-27, 1909
NL: StL. Aug. 31-Sept. 1, 1917

1-0 Games Lost, Consecutive, Season
3 **NL:** Brk. Sept. 7-8, 1908
Pitt. Aug. 31-Sept. 1, 1917
Phil. May 11-13, 1960
AL: StL. Apr. 25-27, 1909
Wash. May 7-10, 1909

Runs Scored, Shutout Game
28 **NL:** Prov. (Phil.) Aug. 21, 1883
Since 1900:
22 **NL:** Pitt. (Chi.) Sept. 16, 1975
21 **AL:** Det. (Clev.) Sept. 15, 1901
NY (Phil.) Aug. 13(2g), 1939

Runs Scored, Doubleheader Shutouts
26 **AL:** Det. (StL.) Sept. 22, 1936, (12,14)
19 **NL:** NY (Cin.) July 31, 1949 (10,9)

Innings, Consecutive
56 **NL:** Pitt. June 1-9, 1903
54 **AL:** Balt. Sept. 1-7, 1974

Innings, Consecutive, No Runs Scored
48 **AL:** Phil. Sept. 22-26, 1906
NL: Chi. June 15-21, 1968

SAVES (Since 1969)

Seasons Leading League
Most:
10 **NL:** Cin. 1969-70,72,74-76,90,92,96-97
8 **AL:** NY 1978,80,85-87,96,99, 2001
Fewest:
6 **NL:** StL. 1970,72,78-80,83
LA 1982,86-87,90,92,94
AL: KC 1970, 90, 97, 99-2001

Seasons, Consecutive, Leading League
Most:
3 NL: Cin. 1974-76
AL: NY 1985-87
Bos. 1998-2000
Fewest:
4 AL: Cal. 1972-75
3 NL: StL. 1978-80
Atl. 1987-89

INNINGS

Seasons Leading League
Most:
20 NL: Brk./LA 1892, 1910,16,19-20,39,40-41,
46,48-49,51-52,59,62,64,73,76,82,93
17 AL: Chi. 1901,05,09,12,17,22-23,39-41,51,
59,63,65-67,93
Fewest:
29 NL: Phil. 1884,88,98, 1902-03,07,15,17,
20-21,24,26-29,33-34,36,38,40,45,
47,55,59,62,88-89,92,97
22 AL: Phil./KC/Oak. 1906,15-17,23,26,
34-35,37,39-41,46,50-51,54,57,61-62,
65,67,84

Seasons, Consecutive, Leading League
Most:
3 NL: Brk. 1939-41
StL. 1943-45
AL: Chi. 1939-41, 65-67
Fewest:
4 NL: Phil. 1926-29
3 AL: NY 1907-09
Phil. 1915-17, 39-41

One Day
32 NL: SF (NY) May 31, 1964 (dh)
29 AL: Bos. (Phil.) July 4, 1905 (dh)
Bos. (NY) Aug. 29, 1967 (dh)
Wash. (Clev.) Sept. 14, 1971 (dh)

RUNS

Seasons Leading League
Most:
32 NL: Phil. 1883-84, 1904,14,19-33,35-39,
41-42,45-46,56,58,89,92
22 AL: Phil./KC/Oak. 1915-17,19-22,33,
40-41,43,54-55,59,61-62,64,67,
82,84,93,97
Fewest:
26 NL: Bos./Mil./Atl. 1877-79,89-91,97-99,
1916,37,47-48,53,56,58,92-2001
24 AL: NY 1919-20,22,23,27,34-39,41-43,
46-47, 52-53,57,76-78,81,98

Seasons, Consecutive, Leading League
Most:
15 NL: Phil. 1919-33
6 AL: StL. 1946-51
Fewest:
10 NL: Atl. 1992-2001
6 AL: NY 1934-39
Chi. 1962-67

EARNED RUNS (Since 1912)

Seasons Leading League
Most:
33 NL: Phil. 1914,18-34,36-39,41-42,45-46,
56,61,79,81,88-89,92
18 AL: StL./Balt. 1925,27,30,32-33,35-40,
46-49,51,88,91
Fewest:
27 AL: NY 1919-21,23,27,32,34-39,41-43,
46-47,52-53,55,57-58,76,78,81,97-98
18 NL: Brk./LA 1920,27,30,55,57,63,65-66,
73-75,77-78,83,87,89,91,96

Seasons, Consecutive, Leading League
Most:
17 NL: Phil. 1918-34
6 AL: StL. 1935-40
Fewest:
6 AL: NY 1934-39
Balt. 1968-73
5 NL: Atl. 1997-2001

HITS

Seasons Leading League
Most:
29 NL: Phil. 1904,14,19,21-33,35-38,41,45-46,
56,58,60,68-69,89
17 AL: StL. 1913,17,31-33,36-41,46-51
Fewest:
27 AL: NY 1919-23,27,34-37,39,41-42,46-47,
49,52-53,55,57-58,63,76,78,81,96,98
24 NL: Brk./LA 1902,16,27-28,30,41,46-49,
56-57,60,62,64-66,72-75,80,85, 2000

Seasons, Consecutive, Leading League
Most:
13 NL: Phil. 1921-33
6 AL: StL. 1936-41, 46-51
Fewest:
8 NL: Chi. 1903-10
4 AL: NY 1934-37

HOME RUNS

Seasons Leading League
Most:
22 NL: Bos./Mil./Atl. 1878,93-94,96,98-1900,
02-03,05-08,10-11,45,64,70-72,77-78
19 AL: Phil./KC/Oak. 1920-23,32,36,38-42,
52,54-57,62,64,91
Fewest:
24 NL: Pitt. 1888,85-86,98, 1902-05,13,15-18,
20-21,35,40,46,58,60-61,65,69,75
23 AL: Clev. 1903-04,11,14,18,20-21,23,25,27,
32-34,36-37,39-40,45,51,53,76,78,94

Seasons, Consecutive, Leading League
Most:
8 AL: StL. 1924-31
5 NL: Phil. 1927-31
NY 1940-44
Fewest:
6 AL: Balt. 1956-61
5 NL: Cin. 1921-25
Mil. 1953-57

SACRIFICE FLIES (Since 1954)

Seasons Leading League
Most:
9 **AL:** Clev. 1969,71,74,82,84-87,91
NL: Phil. 1958,60,69,72,81,87,91-92,97
Fewest:
17 **NL:** LA 1955-56,60,65,73-74,76-78,82,84,
86-89,97, 2000
10 **AL:** Balt. 1962-63,67,71-72,78-80,89,95
Chi. 1956-57,63,66,75,81,83,87,93,96

Seasons,Consecutive,Leading League
Most:
4 **AL:** Clev. 1984-87
2 **NL:** Pitt. 1954-55
Cin. 1956-57,67-68
Hou. 1963-64
SF 1994-95
Fla. 1998-99
Fewest:
4 **NL:** LA 1986-89
3 **AL:** Balt. 1978-80

WALKS

Seasons Leading League
Most:
22 **AL:** Phil./KC/Oak. 1913,15-19,24,33-36,
42,55,62,64,66,79,82-83,93-94,97
18 **NL:** Chi. 1880,88,94, 1914,25-27,31,54-58,
60,62,80,87,92
Fewest:
25 **AL:** Chi. 1906-09,11,13,15-19,
25,30,39-41,51,55-57,63-65,82-83
20 **NL:** Pitt. 1887,89, 1900-02,06-07,09-10,
19-20,35-36,42,59-61,80,90-91

Seasons, Consecutive, Leading League
Most:
5 **AL:** Phil. 1915-19
NL: Chi. 1954-58
Fewest:
6 **NL:** Cin. 1922-27
5 **AL:** Chi. 1915-19

INTENTIONAL WALKS (Since 1955)

Seasons Leading League
Most:
14 **AL:** Det. 1956,74,85-86,88-96,98
8 **NL:** SD 1969,72,74,76-77,80,93-94
Fewest:
12 **NL:** Brk./LA 1955-57,69,71,73-78, 2000
11 **AL:** Wash./Minn. 1965-66,73-75,92-94,
96, 2000-01

Seasons, Consecutive, Leading League
Most:
9 **AL:** Det. 1988-96
3 **NL:** Pitt. 1957-59
Fewest:
6 **NL:** LA 1973-78
3 **AL:** NY 1956-58
KC 1969-71
Minn. 1973-75,92-94

STRIKEOUTS

Seasons Leading League
Most:
33 **NL:** Brk./LA 1920,22-29,36,40,45-46,
48-63,66,74,84,97
18 **AL:** NY 1921,23-24,31-36,47,49-51,57,58,
81,84, 2001
Fewest:
21 **NL:** Bos./Mil./Atl. 1907-09,11,20,23,25,28,
35-40,42,47,56,61,68,72,87
14 **AL:** Phil./KC/Oak. 1918,23,33,39,41,47,
51-52,54-57,60,84

Seasons, Consecutive, Leading League
Most:
16 **NL:** Brk./LA 1948-63
9 **AL:** Phil. 1902-10
Fewest:
6 **NL:** Bos. 1935-40
4 **AL:** Phil./KC 1954-57
Wash. 1961-64
Mil. 1977-80

WILD PITCHES

Most Wild Pitches, Game
10 **NL:** Lou.July 22, 1876
Since 1900:
6 **NL:** Hou. (LA) Apr. 10, 1979
Atl. (Hou.) Aug. 4(2g), 1979
Mtl. (Phil.) Apr. 10, 1982
AL: Cal. (Minn.) Apr. 13, 1991

Most Wild Pitches, Inning
4 **AL:** Wash. (Chi.) Sept. 21, 1914 (4th)
NL: Atl. (Hou.) Aug. 4, 1979 (5th)

BALKS

Most Balks, Game
6 **NL:** Mil. (Chi.) May 4, 1963
5 **AL:** Mil. (NY) Apr. 10, 1988
Oak. (Sea.) Apr. 13, 1988

Most Balks, Both Clubs, Game
7 **NL:** Pitt. 4 Cin. 3 Apr. 13, 1963
Mil. 6 Chi. 1 May 4, 1963
6 **AL:** Mil. 5 NY 1 Apr. 10, 1988
Chi. 4 Cal. 2 Apr. 12, 1988

Fewest Balks, Both Clubs, Game (Most Innings)
0 **NL:** Bos. (Brk.) May 1, 1920 (26 inn)
AL: Chi. (Mil.) May 8, 1984 (25 inn)

Most Balks, Inning
3 **AL:** Clev. (Phil.) May 12, 1930 (3rd)
Det. (Oak.) May 3, 1988 (6th)
NL: Cin. (LA) Apr. 24, 1963 (2nd)
Mil. (Chi.) May 4, 1963 (3rd)
Pitt. (NY) Aug. 6, 1988 (8th)

CLUB GENERAL — SEASON

	AL:1901-1960 NL:1900-1961 8 clubs 154 games		AL:1961-1968 NL:1962-1968 10 clubs 162 games		AL:1969- NL:1969- 12-16 clubs 162 games
Most Games Played					
AL:	162	Det. 1904	164	By many	163	By many
NL:	160	Cin. 1915	165	LA & SF 1962	164	Pitt. & StL. 1989
Fewest Games Played					
AL:	147	Clev. 1945	159	Wash. 1966	158	Balt. 1971
NL:	149	Phil. 1907, 34	160	Cin. 1966	160	By many
Highest Percentage Games Won, League Champion					
AL:	.721	Clev. 1954 (111-43)	.673	NY 1961 (109-53)	.704	NY 1998 (114-48)
NL:	.763	Chi. 1906 (116-36)	.627	StL. 1967 (101-60)	.667	Cin. 1975 (108-54) NY 1986 (108-54)
Highest Percentage Games Won, Last Place					
AL:	.431	Chi. 1924 (66-87)	.440	NY 1966 (70-89)	.469	Tor. 1997 (76-86)
NL:	.454	NY 1915 (69-83)	.444	Hou. 1968 (72-90)	.469	SD 1997, 2000 (76-86)
Lowest Percentage Games Won, League Champion					
AL:	.575	Det. 1945 (88-65)	.568	Bos. 1967 (92-70)	.525	Minn. 1987 (85-77)
NL:	.564	LA 1959 (88-68)	.574	StL. 1964 (93-69)	.509	NY 1973 (82-79)
Lowest Percentage Games Won, Last Place					
AL:	.235	Phil. 1916 (36-117)	.346	Wash. 1963 (56-106)	.327	Tor. 1979 (53-109) Det. 1996 (53-109)
NL:	.248	Bos. 1935 (38-115)	.250	NY 1962 (40-120)	.321	Mtl. 1969 (52-110) SD 1969 (52-110)
Most Games Won					
AL:	111	Clev. 1954	109	NY 1961	116	Sea. 2001
NL:	116	Chi. 1906	103	SF 1962	108	Cin. 1975; NY 1986
Fewest Games Won					
AL:	36	Phil. 1916	56	Wash. 1963	53	Tor. 1979; Det. 1996
NL:	38	Bos. 1935	40	NY 1962	52	Mtl. 1969; SD 1969
Most Games Won, Home					
AL:	62	NY 1932	65	NY 1961	62	NY 1998
NL:	60	StL. 1942 Brk. 1953	61	SF 1962	64	Cin. 1975
Fewest Games Won, Home					
AL:	18	StL. 1939	26	KC 1964	25	Tor. 1977
NL:	20	Phil. 1923	22	NY 1962	24	Mtl. 1969
Most Games Won, Away					
AL:	54	NY 1939	51	Det. 1961 Minn. 1965	59	Sea. 2001
NL:	60	Chi. 1906	52	StL. 1967	53	Cin. 1972,76; NY 1986 Atl. 1993; SF 1993
Fewest Games Won, Away					
AL:	13	Phil. 1916	24	Cal. 1961	20	Balt. 1988
NL:	13	Bos. 1935	17	NY 1963	21	Atl. 1977
Most Games Lost					
AL:	117	Phil. 1916	106	Wash. 1963	109	Tor. 1979; Det. 1996
NL:	115	Bos. 1935	120	NY 1962	110	Mtl. 1969; SD 1969
Fewest Games Lost					
AL:	43	Clev. 1954	53	NY 1961	46	Sea. 2001
NL:	36	Chi. 1906	60	StL. 1967	54	Cin. 1975; NY 1986
Most Games Lost, Home					
AL:	59	StL. 1939	55	KC 1964	55	Tor. 1977
NL:	55	Phil. 1923, 45 Bos. 1923	58	NY 1962	57	Mtl. 1969
Fewest Games Lost, Home					
AL:	15	NY 1932	16	NY 1961	19	NY 1998
NL:	17	StL. 1942 Brk. 1953	21	SF 1962	17	Cin. 1975
Most Games Lost, Away					
AL:	64	Phil. 1916	57	Wash. 1963	61	Balt. 1988
NL:	65	Bos. 1935	64	NY 1963	60	Atl. 1977

	AL:1901-1960 NL:1900-1961 8 clubs 154 games		AL:1961-1968 NL:1962-1968 10 clubs 162 games		AL:1969- NL:1969- 12-16 clubs 162 games	
Fewest Games Lost, Away						
AL:	20	NY 1939	30	Det. 1961 Minn. 1965	22	Sea. 2001
NL:	15	Chi. 1906	28	StL. 1967	25	Cin. 1972
Most Games Tied						
AL:	10	Det. 1904	2	By many	3	Chi 1974
NL:	9	StL. 1911	2	By many	3	Chi. 1981
Most Night Games						
AL:	87	Balt. 1960	107	Cal. 1964, 68	134	Sea. 1982
NL:	105	LA 1961	118	Hou. 1964	134	Hou. 1984
Fewest Night Games (Since 1935)						
AL:	2	Det. 1939	66	Minn. 1961 Bos. & NY 1962	62	Clev. 1973
NL:	0	NY 1935-39	43	Chi. 1962-65	46	Chi. 1969
Most Night Games Won						
AL:	47	Balt. 1960	64	Det. 1968	79	Balt. 1980; Sea. 2001
NL:	61	LA 1961	70	StL. 1967	75	Ari. 1999
Fewest Night Games Won						
AL:	1	By many	25	Bos. 1966	29	Chi. 1970
NL:	1	By many	11	Chi. 1962	17	Chi. 1980
Most Night Games Lost						
AL:	48	KC 1956	68	Wash. 1963	83	Sea. 1980
NL:	67	Phil. 1961	68	Hou. 1964	82	Atl. 1977
Fewest Night Games Lost						
AL:	1	By many	26	Det. & NY 1962	32	Oak. 1971
NL:	0	By many	26	Chi. 1963, 65	21	Chi. 1969
Most Night Games Tied						
AL:	2	Chi. 1959	2	Minn. 1967	1	By many
NL:	2	Phil. 1943	1	By many	1	By many
Most Extra-Inning Games						
AL:	31	Bos. 1943	26	NY 1964	26	Cal. 1976; Tex. 1976
NL:	27	Bos. 1943	27	LA 1967	27	Hou. 1990
Fewest Extra-Inning Games						
AL:	6	Det. 1958	9	KC 1961-62 Minn. & NY 1966 Det. 1967	6	Tex. 1998
NL:	6	Chi. 1945	7	Atl. 1964	6	Atl. 1998
Most Extra-Inning Games Won						
AL:	18	Clev. 1949	16	Clev. 1967	16	Balt. 1970
NL:	19	Pitt. 1959	15	StL. 1968	18	Mtl. 1988
Fewest Extra-Inning Games Won						
AL:	1	Det. 1958	3	KC 1962, 65	1	Chi. 1978 Minn. 1982 Tex. 1985
NL:	1	Phil. 1959 Pitt. 1961	2	Pitt. 1964 NY 1968	0	Mtl. 1969
Most Extra-Inning Games Lost						
AL:	18	StL. 1943	16	Bos. 1966	15	Clev. 1977, 89; Chi. 1988
NL:	17	Cin. 1942	17	LA 1967	17	NY 1978; Pitt. 1984
Fewest Extra-Inning Games Lost						
AL:	1	Clev. 1949	2	NY 1961	1	Oak. 1975
NL:	2	By many	2	Cin.& Mil. 1964 Phil. 1968	1	Pitt. 1969; NY 1984 Mtl. 1987; SD 2001
Most Extra-Inning Games Tied						
AL:	4	Det. 1953	1	By many	1	By many
NL:	3	By many	1	By many	2	Chi. 1981
Most Doubleheaders						
AL:	44	Chi. 1943	34	Chi. 1961	21	Chi. 1969 NY 1972; Clev. 1973
NL:	43	Phil. 1943	28	NY 1962	22	NY 1969

		AL:1901-1960 NL:1900-1961 8 clubs 154 games		AL:1961-1968 NL:1962-1968 10 clubs 162 games		AL:1969- NL:1969- 12-16 clubs 162 games
Fewest Doubleheaders						
AL:	11	Bos. 1959	10	Bos. 1968	0	By many
NL:	6	LA 1961	7	LA 1966	0	By many
Most Doubleheaders Won						
AL:	14	NY & Clev. 1943 Wash. 1945 Bos. 1946	15	Chi. 1961	10	NY 1972
NL:	20	Chi. 1945	8	Cin.& Mil. 1964	11	NY 1969
Fewest Doubleheaders Won						
AL:	0	Det. 1952 Wash. 1957	1	Minn. 1964, 68 Cal., Wash. 1968	0	By many
NL:	1	By many	0	SF 1963	0	By many
Most Doubleheaders Lost						
AL:	18	Phil. 1943	12	Cal. 1961, 65	13	Chi. 1970
NL:	17	Chi. 1950	15	NY 1962	11	NY 1974
Fewest Doubleheaders Lost						
AL:	0	NY 1950	1	By many	0	By many
NL:	0	By many	0	LA & StL. 1966	0	By many
Most Doubleheaders Split						
AL:	19	Phil. 1952 Balt. 1955	17	KC 1965, 67 Bos. 1966	14	Oak. 1969
NL:	24	Bos. 1945	13	NY 1967	12	Chi. 1973 Mtl. 1975
Most Players						
AL:	56	Phil. 1915	52	KC 1961	55	Clev. 2000
NL:	53	Brk. 1944	54	NY 1967	56	SD 2000
Fewest Players						
AL:	18	Bos. 1904	30	NY 1963 Bos. 1965	30	Balt.. 1969
NL:	20	Chi. 1905	30	LA 1962	29	Cin. 1975-76
Most Pitchers						
AL:	27	Phil. 1915 KC 1955	24	KC 1965	32	Clev. 2000
NL:	24	Cin. 1912 Brk. 1944 Phil. 1946	27	NY 1967	29	SD 2000
Fewest Pitchers						
AL:	5	Bos. 1904	12	Bos.& Chi. 1965 Minn. 1967	11	Balt. 1972, 74 Oak. 1974 Bos. 1976
NL:	5	Bos. 1901	12	LA 1962, 65 SF 1962, 68 Cin. 1963	11	Phil. 1976
Most Starting Pitchers						
AL:	24	Phil. 1915	17	Wash. 1963 Cal. 1967	18	Clev. 1993
NL:	19	Brk. 1944 Phil. 1946	20	NY 1967	15	By many; Last: StL. 1998
Most Relief Pitchers (Appearances)						
AL:	263	NY 1960	378	KC 1965	483	Clev. 2001
NL:	293	Chi. 1958	321	Cin. 1968	491	Mtl. 2001
Fewest Relief Pitchers (Appearances)						
AL:	9	Bos. 1904	168	Balt. 1961	139	Bos. 1974
NL:	9	StL. 1904	167	SF 1968	169	LA 1975
Most Pinch Hitters						
AL:	309	Wash. 1960	277	Wash. 1962	326	Mil. 1970
NL:	300	Cin. 1958	363	NY 1965	353	LA 1992
Most Managers						
AL:	3	Bos. 1907 StL. 1918, 33 NY 1946	3	Det. 1966	3	Tex. 1977 NY 1982
NL:	3	Cin. 1902 NY 1902; StL. 1905, 40 Pitt. 1917; Phil. 1948	3	Chi. 1961-62 Chi. 1925	2	By many

GAMES

Same Clubs, Consecutive
12 **NL:**Bos. vs Phil. Sept. 2-8, 1903
11 **AL:**Det. vs StL. Sept. 8-14, 1904

One Day
3 **NL:**Brk. vs Pitt. Sept. 1, 1890
Balt. vs Lou. Sept. 7, 1896
Cin. vs Pitt. Oct. 2, 1920
2 **AL:**By many clubs

TIME

Shortest Game
0:51 **NL:**NY 6 Phil. 1 Sept. 28(1g), 1919
0:55 **AL:**StL. 6 NY 2 Sept. 26(2g), 1926

Shortest Doubleheader
2:07 **AL:**NY vs StL. Sept. 26, 1926
2:20 **NL:**Chi. vs Brk. Aug. 14, 1919

Longest Game
4:27 **NL:**LA 11 SF 10, Oct. 5, 2001
4:22 **AL:**Balt. 13 NY 9 Sept. 5, 1997
    Extra Innings:
8:06 **AL:**Chi. 7 Mil. 6 May 8, 1984 (25 inn)
7:23 **NL:**SF 8 NY 6 May 31(2g), 1964 (23 inn)

Longest Doubleheader
7:39 **AL:**Tex. vs Chi. May 24, 1995
6:46 **NL:**Brk. vs NY Aug. 7, 1952
    Extra Innings:
9:52 **NL:**SF vs NY May 31, 1964 (32 inn)
9:05 **AL:**KC vs Det. June 17, 1967 (28 inn)

ATTENDANCE

Highest Attendance, Home, Season
4,483,350 **NL:**Col. 1993
4,057,947 **AL:**Tor. 1993

Highest Attendance, Road, Season
3,016,074 **NL:**Cin. 2000
2,876,506 **AL:**NY 2000

Highest Attendance, Game
84,587   **AL:**Clev. (NY) Sept. 12, 1954(dh)
80,227   **NL:**Col. (Mtl.) Apr. 9, 1993

INNINGS

Most Innings, Game
26 **NL:**Brk. (1) Bos. (1) May 1, 1920
25 **AL:**Chi. (7) Mil. (6) May 8, 1984

Most Innings, 2 Consecutive Games
45 **NL:**Bos. May 1-3, 1920
37 **AL:**Mil. May 12-13, 1972
    Minn. May 12-13, 1972

Most Innings, 3 Consecutive Games
58 **NL:**Brk. May 1-3, 1920
46 **AL:**Mil. May 10-13, 12-14, 1972
    Minn. May 10-13, 12-14, 1972

Most Innings, 2 Consecutive Games, Same Clubs
40 **NL:**Bos. vs Chi. May 14-17, 1927
37 **AL:**Mil. vs Minn. May 12-13, 1972

Most Innings, Opening-Day Game
15 **AL:**Wash. (1) Phil. (0) Apr. 13, 1926
    Det. (4) Clev. (2) Apr. 19, 1960
14 **NL:**Phil. (5) Brk. (5) Apr. 17, 1923
    Pitt. (4) Mil. (3) Apr. 15, 1958
    Pitt. (6) StL. (2) Apr. 8, 1969
    Cin. (2) LA (1) Apr. 7, 1975
    NY (1) Phil. (0) Mar. 31, 1998

Most Innings, Shutout
24 **NL:**Hou. (1) NY (0) Apr. 15, 1968
20 **AL:**Oak. (1) Cal. (0) July 9, 1971

Most Innings, 0-0 Game
19 **NL:**Brk. vs Cin. Sept. 11, 1946
18 **AL:**Det. vs Wash. July 16, 1909

Most Innings, 1-0 Game
24 **NL:**Hou. vs NY Apr. 15, 1968
20 **AL:**Oak. vs Cal. July 9, 1971

Most Innings, Tie Game
26 **NL:**Brk. vs Bos. May 1, 1920 (1-1)
24 **AL:**Det. vs Phil. July 21, 1945 (1-1)

FIRST PLACE

Most Seasons
39 **AL:**NY 1921-23,26-28,32,36-39,41-43,
    47,49-53,55-58, 60-64,76-78,80-81,
    94,96,98-2001
23 **NL:**NY/SF 1888-89, 1904-05,11-13,17,21-24,
    33,36-37,51,54,62,71,87,89,97, 2000

Most Seasons, Consecutive
7 **NL:**Atl. 1995-2001
5 **AL:**NY 1949-53, 60-64
    Oak. 1971-75
    Clev. 1995-99

Fewest Games Played to Clinch
136 **AL:**NY 1941 (Sept. 4)
137 **NL:**NY 1904 (Sept. 22)

Earliest Date To Clinch
Sept. 3 **AL:**Sea. 2001 (138 g)
Sept. 7 **NL:**Cin. 1975 (142 g)

Days In First Place
    Most:
183 **AL:**Sea. 2001 162g (entire season)
    (not including Sept. 11-16, 2001)
181 **NL:**Phil. 1993 162g
    Fewest (by team finishing in 1st place):
3 **NL:**NY 1951 154g (before playoff)
20 **AL:**Bos. 1967 162g

Largest Gain, Standings, From Previous Season
9 **NL:**Brk. 1899 (10th to 1st)
    Since 1900:
8 **AL:**Bos. 1967 (9th to 1st)
    NL:NY 1969 (9th to 1st)

LAST PLACE

Most Seasons
29 **AL:**Phil./KC/Oak. 1915-21,35-36 38,40-43,
    45-46,50,54,56,60-61,64-65,67,77,79,
    93,97-98
27 **NL:**Phil. 1883, 1904,19-21,23,26-28,30,36
    38-42,44-45,47,58-61,72,96-97, 2000

Most Seasons, Consecutive
7 **AL:**Phil. 1915-21
5 **NL:**Phil. 1938-42

GAMES AHEAD

Most, End of Season
30.0 **AL:**Clev. 1995
27.5 **NL:**Pitt. 1902

Most, 1st-Place Finisher, Through July 4
14.5 **NL:**NY 1912
13.0 **AL:**Clev. 1999

GAMES BEHIND

Most, End Of Season
80.0 **NL:**Clev. 1899
      Since 1900:
66.5 **NL:**Bos. 1906
64.5 **AL:**StL. 1939

Fewest, End Of Season, Last Place Club
10.0 **AL:**Cal. 1987
      AL: Tex. 1987
11.0 **NL:**SF 1995

Most, 1st-Place Finisher, Through July 4
15.0 **NL:**Bos, 1914 (8th place)
9.0 **AL:**NY 1978 (2nd place)

PERCENTAGE

One Month
  Highest:
.947 **UA:**StL. May 1884 (18-1)
.944 **NL:**Prov. Aug. 1884 (17-1)
    Since 1900:
.900 **AL:**Det. Apr. 1984 (18-2)
.897 **NL:**Chi. Aug. 1906 (26-3)
  Lowest:
.036 **NL:**Pitt. Aug. 1890 (1-27)
    Clev. Sept. 1899 (1-27)
    Since 1900:
.043 **AL:**Balt. Apr. 1988 (1-22)
.120 **NL:**Phil. May 1928 (3-22)

PLAYOFF WINNERS

One-Game Playoff:
  AL: Clev. (Bos.) 1948
    NY (Bos.) 1978
    Sea. (Cal.) 1995
  NL: Hou. (LA) 1980
    Chi. (SF) 1998 (wild card)
    NY (Cin.) 1999 (wild card)

Best-Of-Three Series:
  NL: StL. (Brk.) 1946 (2-0)
    NY (Brk.) 1951 (2-1)
    LA (Mil.) 1959 (2-0)
    SF (LA) 1962 (2-1)
  AL:none

GAMES WON

Opening Games Won, Consecutive Seasons
10 **NL:**Bos. 1887-96
    Since 1900:
9 **AL:**StL. 1937-45
  NL:NY 1975-83
    Cin. 1983-91

Most Seasons, 100 or more Games Won
15 **AL:**NY 1927-28,32,36-37,39,41-42,
    54 61,63,77-78,80,98
6 **NL:**Brk./LA 1899, 1941-42,53,62,74
    StL. 1931,42-44,67,85
    NY/SF 1904-05,12-13,62,93

Seasons, Consecutive, 100 or more Games Won
3 **AL:**Phil. 1929-31
    Balt. 1969-71
  NL: StL. 1942-44
    Atl. 1997-99

Most Games Won, 2 Consecutive Seasons
223 **NL:**Chi. 1906-07
217 **AL:**Balt. 1969-70

Most games Won, 3 Consecutive Seasons
322 **NL:**Chi. 1906-08
318 **AL:**Balt. 1969-71

Most Games Won, Consecutive, Season
26 **NL:**NY Sept. 7-30, 1916 (+1 tie)
19 **AL:**Chi. Aug. 2-23, 1906 (+1 tie)
    NY June 29-July 17, 1947

Most Games Won, Consecutive, Season (no ties)
21 **NL:**Chi. June 2-July 8, 1880
    Chi. Sept. 4-27, 1935
19 **AL:**NY June 29-July 17, 1947

Most Games Won, Consecutive, Start of Season
20 **UA:**StL. Apr. 20-May 22, 1884
13 **NL:**Atl. Apr. 6-21, 1982
    AL: Mil. Apr. 6-20, 1987

Most Games Won, vs. One Opponent, Season
21 **NL:**Chi. (Bos.) 1909 (lost 1)
    Pitt. (Cin.) 1937 (lost 1)
    Chi. (Cin.) 1945 (lost 1)
    AL:NY (StL.) 1927 (lost 1)

Most Games Won, Consecutive, vs.
One Opponent
23 **NL:**Cin. (StL) June 15, 1896-Sept. 26, 1897
    AL: Balt. (KC) May 10, 1969-Aug. 2, 1970
    NL Since 1900:
20 NL: StL. (Phil.) July 15, 1927-July 20, 1928
    Pitt. (Cin.) May 31, 1937-Apr. 24, 1938

Won, Consecutive Seasons, vs. One Opponent
40 **NL:**Pitt. (StL.) 1907-08
37 **AL:**Phil. (StL.) 1910-11
    Chi. (Phil.) 1915-16
    NY (Phil.) 1919-20
    NY (StL.) 1926-27

Won vs. Pennant Winner, Season
16 **NL:**StL. (Chi.) 1945 (lost 6)
14 **AL:**Phil. (Det.) 1909 (lost 8)
    Minn. (Oak) 1973 (lost 4)

Won Home, vs. One Club, Season
16 **NL:**Brk. (Pitt.) 1890 (lost 2)
    Phil. (Pitt.) 1890 (lost 1)
    Since 1900:
13 **NL:**NY (Phil.) 1904 (lost 2)
12 **AL:**Chi. (StL.) 1915 (lost 0)

Won Home, Consecutive, vs. One Club
32 **NL:**Balt. (Lou.) June 7, 1894-July 11, 1899
    Since 1900:
27 **AL:**Clev. (StL./Balt.) Aug. 13, 1952-
    Aug. 15, 1954
25 **NL:**StL. (Cin.) Apr. 27, 1929-May 31, 1931

Away, Consecutive, vs. One Club
19 **NL:**Brk. (Cin.) June 22, 1947-May 22, 1949
18 **AL:**Bos. (NY) Oct. 3, 1911-June 2, 1913

Away, vs. One Club, Season, No losses:
11 **NL:**Pitt. (StL.) 1908
    Chi. (Bos.) 1909
    Brk. (Phil.) 1945
    AL: Chi. (Phil.) 1915
    NY (StL.) 1927, 39
    Clev. (Bos.) 1954

Home, Consecutive, Season
- 26 **NL:** NY Sept. 7-30, 1916 (includes tie)
  - *(None away during streak)*
- 24 **AL:** Bos. June 25-Aug. 13, 1988
  - *(Lost away during streak)*
- 14 **AL:** Det. Aug. 19-Sept. 2, 1909
  - *(None away during streak)*

Away, Consecutive, Season
- 17 **NL:** NY May 9-29, 1916
  - **AL:** Det. Apr. 3-May 24, 1984

One Month
- 29 **NL:** NY Sept. 1916 (lost 5)
- 28 **AL:** NY Aug. 1938 (lost 4)

One Day
- 3 **NL:** Brk. (Pitt.) Sept. 1, 1890
  - Balt. (Lou.) Sept. 7, 1896
- 2 **AL:** By many clubs

Consecutive Days
- 5 **NL:** Balt. Sept. 7-8, 1896
- 4 **AL:** By many clubs

Days, 2 Wins, vs. One Club, Season
- 7 **AL:** Chi. (Phil.) 1943
  - **NL:** Chi. (Cin.) 1945

GAMES LOST

Opening Games Lost, Consecutive Seasons
- 9 **NL:** NY 1893-1901
  - Atl. 1972-80
- 8 **AL:** Wash. 1963-70

Seasons, 100 or more Games Lost
- 14 **NL:** Phil. 1904,21,23,27-28,30,36,
  - 38-42,45,61
- 16 **AL:** Phil./KC/Oak. 1915-16,19-21,36,40,43,
  - 46 50,54,56,61,64-65,79

Seasons, Consecutive, 100 or more Games Lost
- 5 **NL:** Phil. 1938-42
- 4 **AL:** Wash. 1961-64

Seasons, 2 Consecutive
- 231 **NL:** NY 1962-63 (162 g)
- 226 **AL:** Phil. 1915-16
- 220 **NL:** Phil. 1941-42(154 g)

Seasons, 3 Consecutive
- 340 **NL:** NY 1962-64 (162 g)
- 324 **AL:** Phil. 1915-17
- 323 **NL:** Phil. 1940-42 (154 g)

Consecutive, Season
- 26 **AA:** Lou. May 22-June 22, 1889
- 24 **NL:** Clev. Aug. 26-Sept. 16, 1899
  - **Since 1900:**
- 23 **NL:** Phil. July 29-Aug. 20, 1961
- 21 **AL:** Balt. Apr. 4-28, 1988

Consecutive, Start of Season
- 21 **AL:** Balt. Apr. 4-28, 1988
- 14 **NL:** Chi. Apr. 1-20, 1997

Home, Consecutive, Season
- 20 **AL:** StL. June 3-July 7, 1953
  - *(Won away during streak)*
- 19 **AL:** Bos. May 2-24, 1906
  - *(None away during streak)*
- 14 **NL:** Bos. May 9-24, 1911
  - *(None away during streak)*

Away, Consecutive, Season
- 22 **NL:** Pitt. Aug. 13-Sept. 2, 1890
  - *(None home during streak)*
  - NY June 16-July 28, 1963
  - *(Won home during streak)*
  - **AL:** Phil. July 11(2g)-Aug. 24(1g), 1943
  - *(Won home during streak)*

One Month
- 29 **AL:** Wash. July 1909 (won 5)
- 27 **NL:** Pitt. Aug. 1890 (won 1)
  - Clev. Sept. 1899 (won 1)
  - StL. Sept. 1908 (won 7)
  - Brk. Sept. 1908 (won 6)
  - Phil. Sept. 1939 (won 6)

One Day
- 3 **NL:** Pitt. (Brk.) Sept. 1, 1890
  - Lou. (Balt.) Sept. 7, 1896
- 2 **AL:** By many clubs

Consecutive Days
- 5 **NL:** Pitt. Aug. 30-Sept. 1, 1890
  - Lou. Sept. 7-8, 1896
- 4 **AL:** By many clubs

LOW HIT GAMES

No-Hit Games, vs. One Club, Season
- 2 **AL:** StL. (Chi.) 1917
  - **NL:** Mil. (Phil.) 1960

EXTRA-INNING GAMES

Consecutive, Season
- 5 **AL:** Det. Sept. 9-13, 1908
- 4 **NL:** Pitt. Aug. 18-22, 1917
  - Brk. Sept. 20-23, 1924
  - Cin. Aug. 21-23, 1926
  - Pitt. May 8-15, 1938
  - Cin. Sept. 5-7, 1939
  - SF July 7-10, 1987
  - Mil. Sept. 15-19, 1999

Consecutive, Same Clubs, Season
- 4 **AL:** Chi. vs Det. Sept. 9-12, 1908
  - Clev. vs StL. May 1-5, 1910
  - Bos. vs StL. May 31-June 2, 1943
- 3 **NL:** Brk. vs Pitt. Aug. 20-22, 1917
  - Cin. vs Bos. June 4-7, 1925
  - Bos. vs Cin. Aug. 21-22, 1926
  - Bos. vs Phil. July 2-3, 1928
  - NY vs Chi. Sept. 13-15, 1932
  - Pitt. vs Cin. Sept. 6-7, 1939
  - Chi. vs Pitt. Aug. 18-20, 1961
  - Mtl. vs NY June 17-19, 1975
  - Cin. vs NY May 5-7, 1980
  - Atl. vs LA Aug. 5-7, 1982
  - Mil. vs Chi. Sept. 17-19, 1999
  - NY vs Hou. July 31-Aug. 2, 2001

DOUBLEHEADERS

Consecutive, Season
- 9 **NL:** Bos. Sept. 4-15, 1928
- 8 **AL:** Wash. July 27-Aug. 5, 1909

Won, Consecutive, Season
- 5 **AL:** NY Aug. 30-Sept. 4, 1906
- 4 **NL:** Brk. Sept. 1-4, 1924
  - NY Sept. 10-14, 1928

Lost, Consecutive, Season
- 5 **NL:** Bos. Sept. 8-14, 1928
- 4 **AL:** Bos. June 29-July 5, 1921

Consecutive, Same Clubs, Season
5 **AL:** Phil. vs Wash. Aug. 5-10, 1901
4 **NL:** NY vs Bos. Sept. 10-14, 1928

PERSONNEL

Most Players, Game
27 **AL:** KC (Cal.) Sept. 10, 1969
26 **NL:** LA (Cin.) Oct. 6, 1985
   Extra-Inning Game:
30 **AL:** Oak. (Chi.) Sept. 19, 1972 (15 inn)
28 **NL:** LA (SD) Sept. 13, 1982 (16 inn)
   Doubleheader:
43 **NL:** LA (SD) Sept. 21, 1988
42 **AL:** Tex. (Balt.) Sept. 7, 1989
   Doubleheader, Extra Innings:
44 **AL:** Chi. (Minn.) Oct. 3, 1991 (22 inn)

Most Players, Both Clubs, Game
45 **NL:** Chi. (24) Mtl. (21) Sept. 5, 1978
43 **AL:** Sea. (24) Tex. (19) Sept. 27, 1987
   Extra-Inning Game:
54 **AL:** Sea. (29) Tex. (25) Sept. 25 1992(16 inn)
53 **NL:** Chi. (27) Hou. (26) Sept. 2, 1986 (18 inn)
   Doubleheader:
74 **NL:** SD (41) SF (33) May 30, 1977
71 **AL:** Tex. (42) Balt. (29) Sept. 7, 1989
   Doubleheader, Extra Innings:
83 **AL:** Minn. (42) Chi. (41) Oct. 3, 1991 (22 inn)
78 **NL:** Hou. (39) NY (39) Sept. 15, 1998 (21 inn)

Most Pitchers, Game
9 **AL:** StL. (Chi.) Oct. 2, 1949
   Chi. (Clev.) Sept. 14, 1997
   NL: Mtl. (Chi.) Sept. 10, 1996
   StL. (LA) Sept. 8, 2001
   Extra-Inning Game:
11 **AL:** Sea. (Tex.) Sept. 25, 1992 (16 inn)
10 **NL:** Chi. (Pitt.) Apr. 20, 1986 (17 inn)
   Hou. (Chi.) Sept. 28, 1995 (11 inn)
   Col. (Atl.) Aug. 22, 2000 (12 inn)
   Doubleheader:
13 **NL:** Mil. (Phil.) May 12, 1963 (23 inn)
   Col. (SD) June 28 1994 (20 inn)
   SD (SF) May 30, 1977
12 **AL:** Clev. (Det.) Sept. 7, 1959
   Cal. (Det.) Sept. 30, 1967
   Doubleheader, Extra Innings:
13 **AL:** Balt. (Tex.) Aug. 13, 1991 (21 inn)

Most Pitchers, Both Clubs, Game
15 **NL:** StL. (8) Cin. (7) Sept. 7(1g), 1993
   Mtl. (8) Atl. (7) Sept. 27, 1996
   Ari. (8) Mil. (7) Sept. 7, 1999
   AL: Det (8) Minn. (7) Oct. 1, 2000
   Extra-Inning Game:
   Sea. (9) Oak. (9) Sept. 20, 1997 (15 inn)
   Det. (10) Chi. (8) Sept. 14, 1998 (12 inn)
   NL: Hou. (10) Chi. (8) Sept. 28, 1995 (11 inn)
   Doubleheader:
22 **NL:** Mil. (11) NY (11) July 26, 1964
   StL. (11) Phil. (11) June 20, 1989
   Chi. (11) Pitt. (11) Sept. 27, 1996 (19 inn)
   AL: Wash. (12) Clev. (10) Sept. 14, 1971 (29 inn)
   Chi. (12) Minn(10) Oct. 3, 1991 (22 inn)
   Det. (12) NY (10) July 20, 1998 (22 inn)

Most Pitchers, Combination Shutout Win
6 By many clubs; last time:
   NL: Mtl. (NY) Sept. 23, 1998
   AL: Bos. (Tor.) Sept. 23, 1995 (1g)
   Extra-Inning Game:
8 **AL:** Bos. (Balt.) Oct. 3, 1999 (10 inn)
7 **NL:** Atl. (StL.) May 16, 1997 (13 inn)
   Ari. (SF) May 29, 2001 (18 inn)

Most Pitchers, Inning
6 **AL:** Oak. (Clev.) Sept. 3, 1983 (9th)
5 **NL:** By Many Clubs; Last:
   Ari. (SD) Sept. 1, 2001 (8th)

Most Pitchers, Both Clubs, Inning
8 **NL:** LA (5) NY (3) Aug. 26, 1987 (8th)
   LA (4) StL (4) May 14, 1995 (8th)
   AL: NY (4) Mil. (4) May 25, 1992 (8th)
   Minn. (4) NY (4) Aug. 8, 1993 (8th)
   Clev. (5) Minn, (3) May 10, 2000 (7th)

LEAGUE RECORDS – SEASON

BATTING

	AL:1901-1960 NL:1900-1961 8 clubs 154 games		AL:1961-1968 NL:1962-1968 10 clubs 162 games		AL:1969- NL:1969- 12-16 clubs 162 games	
Highest Batting Average						
AL	.292	1921	.256	1961	.277	1996
NL	.303	1930	.261	1962	.268	1999
Lowest Batting Average						
AL	.239	1908	.230	1968	.239	1972
NL	.239	1908	.243	1968	.246	1989
Highest Slugging Percentage						
AL	.421	1936	.395	1961	.445	1996
NL	.449	1930	.393	1962	.432	2000
Lowest Slugging Percentage						
AL	.314	1910	.339	1968	.343	1972
NL	.306	1908	.341	1968	.361	1976
Most Tie Games						
AL	19	1910	4	1961, 64	3	1974
NL	15	1911, 13	4	1965	4	1981
Fewest Tie Games						
AL	0	1930	0	1963, 65	0	Many
NL	0	1925, 54, 58	1	1963, 66-67	0	Many
Most Extra-Inning Games Won						
AL	91	1943	91	1965	117	1991
NL	86	1916	93	1967	135	1998
Most At-Bats						
AL	43,747	1936	55,239	1962	79,090	1996
NL	43,891	1936	55,449	1962	89,011	1999
Fewest At-Bats						
AL	40,424	1906	53,709	1968	64,641	1971
NL	39,337	1907	54,803	1963	65,156	1978
Most Runs						
AL	7,009	1936	7,342	1961	12,208	1996
NL	7,025	1930	7,278	1962	12,976	2000
Fewest Runs						
AL	4,272	1909	5,532	1968	7,472	1971
NL	4,136	1908	5,577	1968	7,522	1988
Most Hits						
AL	12,657	1936	14,068	1962	21,992	1996
NL	13,260	1930	14,453	1962	23,880	1999
Fewest Hits						
AL	9,719	1908	12,359	1968	15,957	1971
NL	9,566	1907	13,351	1968	16,215	1989
Most Total Bases						
AL	18,427	1936	21,762	1962	35,192	1996
NL	19,572	1930	21,781	1962	38,305	2000
Fewest Total Bases						
AL	12,307	1908	18,221	1968	23,537	1971
NL	12,143	1907	18,737	1968	23,767	1976
Most Extra-Base Hits						
AL	3,706	1936	4,190	1962	7,377	2000
NL	3,903	1930	3,977	1962	8,169	2000
Fewest Extra-Base Hits						
AL	1,877	1907	3,316	1968	4,177	1976
NL	1,791	1907	3,245	1968	4,264	1976
Most Singles						
AL	9,214	1921	9,878	1962	15,072	1980
NL	9,476	1922	10,476	1962	15,856	1999
Fewest Singles						
AL	7,573	1959	9,043	1968	11,696	1971
NL	7,466	1956	9,796	1963	11,536	1989

	AL:1901-1960 NL:1900-1961 8 clubs 154 games		AL:1961-1968 NL:1962-1968 10 clubs 162 games		AL:1969- NL:1969- 12-16 clubs 162 games	
Most Doubles						
AL	2,400	1936	2,238	1962	4,269	2000
NL	2,386	1930	2,161	1964	4,632	2000
Fewest Doubles						
AL	1,348	1910	1,874	1968	2,385	1969
NL	1,148	1907	1,984	1963	2,455	1969
Most Triples						
AL	694	1921	408	1966	644	1977
NL	685	1912	453	1962	554	1970
Fewest Triples						
AL	267	1959	333	1964	351	1971
NL	323	1942	359	1968	386	1973
Most Home Runs						
AL	1,091	1959	1,552	1962	2,742	1996
NL	1,263	1955	1,449	1962	3,005	2000
ML	2,294	1956	3,001	1962	5,693	2000
Fewest Home Runs						
AL	101	1907	1,104	1968	1,122	1976
NL	126	1906	891	1968	1,113	1976
ML	242	1907	1,995	1968	2,235	1976
Most Clubs, 100 or more Home Runs						
AL	8	1958, 60	10	1964	14	See Club Table
NL	8	1956, 58-59, 61	10	1962	16	1998-2001
ML	16	1958	19	1962	30	1998-2001
Fewest Clubs, 100 or more Home Runs						
AL	0	Many. Last: 1945	6	1968	5	1976
NL	0	Many. Last: 1943	4	1968	5	1976
ML	0	Many. Last: 1924	10	1968	10	1976
Most Grand Slam Home Runs						
AL	37	1938	48	1961	89	2000
NL	35	1950	37	1962	87	2000
ML	68	1950	77	1961	176	2000
Fewest Grand Slam Home Runs						
AL	0	1918	20	1967	23	1976
NL	1	1920	16	1968	21	1988
ML	3	1907	38	1968	51	1976
Most Home Runs, Pinch-hitters						
AL	29	1953	50	1961	53	1980
NL	42	1958	45	1962	95	2001
ML	70	1958	84	1962	131	2001
Most Grand Slam Home Runs, Pinch-hitters						
AL	5	1953	7	1961	5	1988, 98
NL	4	1959	3	1963, 67	9	1978, 95
ML	8	1953	7	1961	13	1978
Most Runs Batted In						
AL	6,520	1936	6,842	1961	11,583	1996
NL	6,582	1930	6,760	1962	12,321	1999
Most Sacrifice Hits						
AL	1,731	1917	779	1965	1,016	1978
NL	1,655	1908	794	1968	1,167	1998
Fewest Sacrifice Hits						
AL	531	1958	673	1964	507	1999
NL	510	1957	656	1962	809	1984
Most Sacrifice Flies (since 1954)						
AL	370	1954	448	1961	765	1979
NL	425	1954	410	1962	809	2000
Fewest Sacrifice Flies (since 1954)						
AL	312	1959	348	1967	484	1969
NL	304	1959	363	1966	430	1969

	AL:1901-1960 NL:1900-1961 8 clubs 154 games		AL:1961-1968 NL:1962-1968 10 clubs 162 games		AL:1969- NL:1969- 12-16 clubs 162 games	
Most Walks						
AL	5,627	1949	5,902	1961	8,592	1996
NL	4,537	1950	5,265	1962	9,735	2000
Fewest Walks						
AL	3,797	1922	4,881	1968	6,128	1976
NL	2,906	1921	4,275	1968	5,793	1988
Most Intentional Walks (since 1955)						
AL	353	1957	534	1965	734	1993
NL	504	1956	804	1967	865	2001
Fewest Intentional Walks (since 1955)						
AL	257	1959	290	1961	420	1998
NL	387	1957	452	1962	626	1991, 97
Most Hit by Pitch						
AL	435	1909	426	1968	921	2001
NL	415	1903	404	1965	969	2001
Fewest Hit by Pitch						
AL	132	1947	316	1965	372	1982
NL	157	1943	327	1964	249	1984
Most Strikeouts						
AL	6,081	1959	9,956	1964	14,617	1997
NL	6,824	1960	9,649	1965	17,908	2001
Fewest Strikeouts						
AL	3,245	1924	8,330	1961	9,143	1976
NL	3,359	1926	9,032	1962	9,602	1976
Most Stolen Bases						
AL	1,810	1912	811	1968	1,734	1987
NL	1,691	1911	788	1962	1,959	1999
Fewest Stolen Bases						
AL	278	1950	540	1964	863	1970
NL	337	1954	636	1964	817	1969
Most Grounded into Double Plays						
AL	1,181	1950	1,256	1961	1,968	1980
NL	1,047	1958	1,251	1962	1,978	2000
Fewest Grounded into Double Plays						
AL	890	1945	1,060	1967	1,305	1988
NL	820	1945	1,117	1963	1,198	1991
Most Left on Base						
AL	9,628	1936	11,680	1961	16,711	1996
NL	9,424	1945	11,416	1962	18,939	2000
Fewest Left on Base						
AL	8,619	1958	10,668	1966	13,494	1976
NL	8,254	1920	10,994	1966	13,295	1988

FIELDING

	AL:1901-1960 NL:1900-1961 8 clubs 154 games		AL:1961-1968 NL:1962-1968 10 clubs 162 games		AL:1969- NL:1969- 12-16 clubs 162 games	
Highest Fielding Average						
AL	.979	1958	.980	1964	.982	2001
NL	.977	1956	.978	1968	.982	2001
Lowest Fielding Average						
AL	.937	1901	.976	1961	.975	1975
NL	.949	1903	.975	1962	.976	1974
Most Total Chances						
AL	53,194	1910	62,296	1968	88,541	1980
NL	52,196	1917	63,636	1968	99,083	1998
Fewest Total Chances						
AL	47,293	1958	62,042	1966	74,387	1971
NL	47,539	1955	62,857	1962	74,562	1991
Most Chances Accepted						
AL	50,870	1910	60,997	1964	86,621	1980
NL	50,419	1920	62,247	1968	97,233	1998
Fewest Chances Accepted						
AL	46,086	1938	60,550	1961	72,875	1971
NL	46,404	1955	61,302	1962	72,495	1990
Most Putouts						
AL	33,830	1916	43,847	1964	61,146	1991
NL	33,724	1917	44,042	1968	69,720	1998
Fewest Putouts						
AL	32,235	1938	43,281	1961	51,821	1975
NL	32,296	1906	43,470	1962	52,000	1978
Most Assists						
AL	17,167	1910	17,269	1961	25,626	1980
NL	16,759	1920	18,205	1968	27,513	1998
Fewest Assists						
AL	13,219	1958	17,048	1963	21,001	1971
NL	13,345	1956	17,681	1963	20,351	1990
Most Errors						
AL	2,889	1901	1,506	1961	1,989	1977
NL	2,590	1904	1,586	1964	1,915	1999
Fewest Errors						
AL	1,002	1958	1,261	1964	1,512	1971
NL	1,082	1956	1,389	1968	1,401	1992
Most Passed Balls						
AL	178	1914	211	1965	267	1987
NL	202	1905	216	1962	217	1969
Fewest Passed Balls						
AL	53	1949	147	1963,66	127	1976
NL	65	1936	148	1968	122	1980
Most Double Plays						
AL	1,487	1949	1,585	1961	2,368	1980
NL	1,337	1951	1,596	1962	2,431	2000
Fewest Double Plays						
AL	818	1912	1,388	1967-68	1,821	1976
NL	1,007	1920	1,431	1963	1,527	1991
Most Triple Plays						
AL	7	1922,36	5	1968	10	1979
NL	7	1905,10,29	5	1964-65	5	1991
Fewest Triple Plays						
AL	0	1904, 33, 42, 56	0	1961-62	0	1974, 75, 87, 93, 98
NL	0	1928, 38, 41, 43 45-46, 59, 61	1	1963	0	1974, 84, 2001

PITCHING

	AL:1901-1960 NL:1900-1961 8 clubs 154 games		AL:1961-1968 NL:1962-1968 10 clubs 162 games		AL:1969- NL:1969- 12-16 clubs 162 games	
Lowest Earned Run Average						
AL	2.73	1914	2.98	1968	3.06	1972
NL	2.62	1916	2.99	1968	3.45	1988
Highest Earned Run Average						
AL	5.04	1936	4.02	1961	4.99	1996
NL	4.97	1930	3.94	1962	4.63	2000
Most Complete Games						
AL	1,100	1904	426	1968	650	1974
NL	1,089	1904	471	1968	546	1971
Fewest Complete Games						
AL	312	1960	323	1965	103	2001
NL	328	1961	402	1966	96	2001
Most Saves (since 1969)						
AL	–	–	–	–	637	1990
NL	–	–	–	–	675	1998
Fewest Saves (since 1969)						
AL	–	–	–	–	260	1974
NL	–	–	–	–	257	1974
Most Shutouts						
AL	146	1909	154	1968	193	1972
NL	164	1908	185	1968	166	1969
Fewest Shutouts						
AL	41	1930	100	1961	79	1996
NL	49	1925	95	1962	93	1999
Most No-Hit Games (9 or more innings)						
AL	5	1917	4	1962	5	1990
NL	3	1960	3	1963-64, 68	5	1969
ML	6	1917	5	1962, 68	7	1990
Fewest No-Hit Games (9 or more innings)						
AL	0	29 seasons Last: 1960	0	1961, 63-64	0	12 seasons Last: 2000
NL	0	29 seasons Last: 1959	0	1966	0	8 seasons Last: 2000
ML	0	14 seasons Last: 1959	1	1961, 66	0	1982, 85, 89, 2000
Most One-Hit Games						
AL	12	1910, 15	11	1968	13	1979, 88
NL	12	1906, 11	15	1965	12	1971
Fewest One-Hit Games						
AL	0	1922, 26-27, 30	2	1962	2	1998
NL	0	1924, 29, 32, 52	3	1962	2	1976, 96
Most 1-0 Games Won						
AL	41	1908	38	1968	42	1971
NL	43	1907	44	1968	45	2001
Fewest 1-0 Games Won						
AL	4	1930, 36	16	1961	10	1998
NL	5	1932, 56	13	1962	12	1997
Most Games Won By One Run						
AL	217	1943	281	1967-68	368	1978
NL	223	1946	294	1968	417	1998
Fewest Games Won By One Run						
AL	157	1938	242	1963	213	1993
NL	170	1949	245	1968	286	1990
Most Earned Runs						
AL	6,120	1936	6,451	1961	11,241	1996
NL	6,046	1930	6,345	1962	11,884	2000
Fewest Earned Runs						
AL	3,414	1914	4,817	1968	6,650	1971
NL	3,258	1916	4,870	1968	6,695	1988

	AL:1901-1960 NL:1900-1961 8 clubs 154 games		AL:1961-1968 NL:1962-1968 10 clubs 162 games		AL:1969- NL:1969- 12-16 clubs 162 games	
Most Wild Pitches						
AL	325	1936	513	1966	785	1997
NL	356	1961	550	1965	884	1999
Fewest Wild Pitches						
AL	166	1931	404	1962	491	1976
NL	174	1943	478	1967	443	1980
Most Balks						
AL	46	1950	51	1966	558	1988
NL	76	1950	147	1963	366	1988
Fewest Balks						
AL	18	1933, 41	29	1964	43	1973
NL	13	1936, 46, 56	25	1965	52	1971, 73
Most Pitchers 40 or more Games Won						
AL	1	1904, 08	0	1961-68	0	1969-to date
NL	0	1900-61	0	1962-68	0	1969-to date
Most Pitchers 30 or more Games Won						
AL	2	1912	1	1968	0	1969-to date
NL	2	1903-04	0	1962-68	0	1969-to date
Most Pitchers 20 or more Games Won						
AL	10	1907, 20	5	1963	12	1973
NL	9	1901, 03, 04	7	1965	9	1969
Fewest Pitchers 20 or more Games Won						
AL	0	1955, 60	2	1961, 64-66	0	1982, 95
NL	0	1931	2	1967	0	1983, 87, 95
Most Pitchers 20 or more Games Lost						
AL	7	1904	1	1962, 64, 67	2	1973-74
NL	8	1905	4	1962	3	1974
Fewest Pitchers 20 or more Games Lost						
AL	0	17 seasons Last: 1960	0	1962, 64-65, 67-68	0	Many seasons Last: 2001
NL	0	22 seasons Last: 1961	0	1967-68	0	Many seasons Last: 2001

GENERAL

	AL:1901-1960 NL:1900-1961 8 clubs 154 games		AL:1961-1968 NL:1962-1968 10 clubs 162 games		AL:1969- NL:1969- 12-16 clubs 162 games	
Most Players						
AL	323	1955	369	1962	610	2000
NL	333	1946	373	1967	699	2000
Fewest Players						
AL	166	1904	351	1968	416	1976
NL	188	1905	336	1968	420	1979
Most Pitchers						
AL	133	1946	170	1962	303	2000
NL	149	1946	167	1967	341	2000
Most Pinch-Hitters						
AL	1,950	1960	2,403	1967	2,993	1970
NL	1,911	1960	2,448	1965	4,260	2001
ML	3,861	1960	4,723	1967	5,804	1970
Most Batters, .300 Batting Average (Minimum: 300 at-bats)						
AL	35	1921	11	1962	31	1999
NL	44	1930	17	1962	38	2000
Fewest Batters, .300 Batting Average (Minimum: 300 at-bats)						
AL	3	1905	1	1968	6	1971-72
NL	4	1907	5	1968	9	1982
Most Players 150 or more Games						
AL	19	1921, 36	30	1962	46	1998
NL	23	1953	34	1965	42	1998
Most Players 600 or more At-Bats						
AL	15	1936	17	1962	22	1998
NL	13	1929	19	1962	16	1979, 96
Most Players 100 or more Runs						
AL	24	1936	6	1961	29	1999
NL	19	1929	10	1962	31	1999
Most Players 200 or more Hits						
AL	9	1936-37	1	1962, 64	6	1986
NL	12	1929-30	5	1963-64	6	1970
Most Players 300 or more Total Bases						
AL	12	1930, 37	7	1961	22	2000
NL	14	1930	9	1963, 65	20	1999, 2001
Most Players 40 or more Doubles						
AL	12	1937	3	1962, 65	15	2000
NL	12	1920	3	1968	11	1998-2000
Most Players 20 or more Triples						
AL	4	1912	0	1961	1	1979, 85, 2000-01
NL	3	1911-12	0	1962-68	1	1996
Most Players 50 or more Home Runs						
AL	2	1938	2	1961	2	1996
NL	2	1947	1	1965	3	1998, 2001
Most Players 40 or more Home Runs						
AL	3	1936	6	1961	8	1996, 98
NL	6	1954-55	2	1961-63, 66	9	2000
Most Players 30 or more Home Runs						
AL	6	1937-38, 40, 58-59	9	1964	23	2000
NL	9	1953, 56	10	1965	25	2001
Most Players 20 or more Home Runs						
AL	18	1959	25	1964	51	1987
NL	23	1956	25	1962	54	1999
Most Players 100 or more Runs Batted In						
AL	18	1936	8	1962	31	1999-2000
NL	17	1930	10	1962	27	1999
Most Players 100 or more Walks						
AL	8	1949	5	1961-62	10	2000
NL	4	1949, 51	1	1962-63	7	2000

	AL:1901-1960 NL:1900-1961 8 clubs 154 games		AL:1961-1968 NL:1962-1968 10 clubs 162 games		AL:1969- NL:1969- 12-16 clubs 162 games	
Most Players 100 or more Strikeouts						
AL	3	1958-60	15	1967	38	1997
NL	4	1960	17	1965	42	2001
Most Managers						
AL	12	1933, 46	15	1966	20	1986
NL	12	1902, 48	12	1965-68	18	2001
ML	21	1902, 33	27	1966	35	2001
Attendance						
AL	11,150,099	1948	11,336,923	1967	33,332,603	1993
NL	10,684,963	1960	15,015,471	1966	39,851,427	2000
ML	20,920,842	1948	25,182,209	1966	72,748,970	2000

MISCELLANEOUS SERVICE

Oldest Player
AL: Satchel Paige, KC, Sept. 25, 1965 (59 years, 78 days)
NL: Jim O'Rourke, NY, Sept. 22, 1904 (52 years, 29 days)

Youngest Player
AL: Carl Scheib, Phil., Sept. 6, 1943 (16 years, 248 days)
NL: Joe Nuxhall, Cin., June 10, 1944 (15 years, 316 days)
AA: Fred Chapman, Phil., July 22, 1887 (14 years, 140 days)

Oldest Manager
AL: Connie Mack, Phil., Oct. 1, 1950, (87 years, 282 days)
NL: Casey Stengel, NY, July 24, 1965 (74 years, 359 days)

Youngest Manager
AL: Roger Peckinpaugh, NY, Sept. 16, 1914 (23 years, 223 days)
NL: George Davis, NY, Apr. 18, 1895 (24 years, 238 days)

Umpire, Most Seasons
AL: 31 Tom Connolly, 1901-31
NL: 37 Bill Klem, 1905-41

Oldest Batting Leader
AL: Ted Williams, Bos., 40 years, 28 days (1958)
NL: Honus Wagner, Pitt., 37 years, 231 days (1911)

Youngest Batting Leader
AL: Al Kaline, Det., 20 years, 280 days (1955)
NL: Pete Reiser, Brk., 22 years, 195 days (1941)

Oldest Home Run Leader
AL: Darrell Evans, Det., 38 years, 133 days (1985)
NL: Cy Williams, Phil., 39 years, 286 days (1927)

Youngest Home Run Leader
AL: Tony Conigliaro, Bos., 20 years, 270 days (1965)
NL: Sam Crawford, Cin., 21 years, 171 days (1901)

CLUB SEASON RECORDS PRIOR TO 1900
(The following exceed or equal records listed in preceding sections)

BATTING

Highest Batting Average
.343 **NL:**Phil. 1894

Lowest Batting Average
.208 **NL:**Wash. 1888

Most Runs Scored
1,220 **NL:**Bos. 1894

Most Singles
1,338 **NL:**Phil. 1894

Most Triples
153 **NL:**Balt. 1894

Most Hit by Pitch
121 **NL:**:Balt. 1896

Most Stolen Bases
638 **AA:**Phil. 1887
426 **NL:**NY 1893

FIELDING

Most Errors
867 **NL:**Wash. 1886

Most Triple Plays
3 **AA:**Cin. 1882
Roch. 1890
NL:NY 1885

Most Passed Balls
167 **NL:**Bos. 1883

PITCHING

Fewest Shutouts Won
0 **NL:**Brk. StL. Wash 1898
Clev. 1899

Most No-Hit Games
2 **AA:**Lou. 1882
Colu. 1884
Phil. 1888

Most No-Hit Games Against
2 **AA:**Pitt. 1884
NL: Prov. 1885
Bos. 1898

GENERAL

Highest Pct. Games Won, First Place
.850 **UA:**StL. 1884 (91-16)
.798 **NL:**Chi. 1880 (67-17)

Lowest Pct. Games Won, Last Place
.130 **NL:**:Clev. 1899 (20-134)

Fewest Games Won
20 **NL:**Clev. 1899

Most Games Lost
134 **NL:**:Clev. 1899

Most Games Lost, Away
102 **NL:**Clev. 1899

MANAGERS

Most, Season
7 **AA:**Lou. 1889
4 **NL:**Wash. 1892, 98
StL. 1895, 96, 97

MANAGERS

Most Seasons, Lifetime
53 Connie Mack, NL:Pitt. (3) 1894-96; AL:Phil. (50) 1901-50

Most Seasons, League
50 Connie Mack, AL:Phil. 1901-50
32 John McGraw, NL:Balt. 1899; NY 1902-32

Most Seasons, One Club
50 Connie Mack, AL:Phil. 1901-50
31 John McGraw, NL:NY 1902-32

Most Clubs, Lifetime
7 Frank Bancroft, NL:Wor. 1880; Det. 81-82; Clev. 83; Prov. 84-85; Ind. 89; Cin. 1902; AA:Phil. 1887
Since 1900:
6 Jimmy Dykes, AL:Chi. 1934-46; Phil. 51-53; Balt. 54; Det. 59-60; Clev. 60-61; NL:Cin. 1958
Dick Williams, AL:Bos. 1967-69; Oak. 71-73; Cal. 74-76; Sea. 86-88; NL:Mtl. 1977-81; SD 82-85
John McNamara, AL:Oak 1969-70; Cal. 83-84; Bos. 85-88; Clev. 90-91; NL:SD 1974-77; Cin. 79-82

Most Clubs, League
6 Frank Bancroft, NL:Wor. 1880; Det. 81-82; Clev. 83; Prov. 84-85; Ind. 89; Cin. 1902
5 Jimmy Dykes, AL:Chi 1934-46; Phil. 51-53; Balt. 54; Det. 59-60; Clev. 60-61
Billy Martin, AL:Minn. 1969; Det. 71-73; Tex. 73-75; NY 75-78,79,83,85; Oak. 80-82
4 Bill McKechnie, NL:Pitt. 1922-26; StL. 28-29; Bos. 30-37; Cin. 38-46
Rogers Hornsby, NL:StL. 1925-26; Bos. 28; Chi. 30-32; Cin. 52-53
Leo Durocher, NL:Brk. 1939-46,48; NY 48-55; Chi. 66-72; Hou. 72-73

Most Clubs, Season
2 Joe Battin, AA:Pitt.-UA:Pitt. 1884
Bill Watkins, NL:Det.-AA: Colu. 1888
Gus Schmelz, NL:Clev.-AA: Colu. 1890
John McGraw, AL:Balt.-NL:NY 1902
Rogers Hornsby, AL:StL.-NL:Cin. 1952
Bill Virdon, AL:NY-NL:Hou. 1975
Pat Corrales, NL:Phil.-AL:Clev. 1983
Buck Rodgers, NL:Mtl.-AL:Cal. 1991
Also following item

Most Clubs, League, Season
2 Ted Sullivan UA:StL.-KC 1884
Billy Barnie, AA:Balt.-Phil. 1891
Leo Durocher. NL:Brk.-NY 1948; Chi.-Hou. 1972
Jimmy Dykes, AL:Det.-Clev. 1960
Joe Gordon, AL:Clev.-Det. 1960
(Dykes & Gordon switched teams Aug. 3, 1960)
Billy Martin, AL:Det.-Tex. 1973; Tex.-NY 1975
Bob Lemon, AL:Chi.-NY 1978
Tony LaRussa, AL:Chi.-Oak. 1986

Most Different Terms, Same Club
5 Billy Martin, AL:NY 1975-78; 1979; 1983; 1985; 1988
4 Danny Murtaugh, NL:Pitt. 1957-64; 1967; 1970-71; 1973-76

Most Seasons Manager, World Series Champions
10 John McGraw, NL:NY 1904-05,11-13,17,21-24
Casey Stengel, AL:NY 1949-53,55-58,60

Most Seasons, Consecutive, Manager, World Series Champions
5 Casey Stengel, AL:NY 1949-53
John McGraw, NL:NY 1921-24

AMERICAN LEAGUE

TEAM	No	Series W	L	All Games G	W	L	Home Games G	W	L	Road Games G	W	L
New York Yankees	38	26	12	213	128	84	103	64	38	110	64	46
Philadelphia/Oakland	14	9	5	75	41	34	37	22	15	38	19	19
Boston Red Sox	9	5	4	60	33	26	31	18	12	29	15	14
Detroit Tigers	9	4	5	56	26	29	28	12	16	28	14	13
St. Louis/Baltimore	7	3	4	39	21	18	20	11	9	19	10	9
Washington/Minnesota	6	3	3	40	19	21	22	17	5	18	2	16
Cleveland Indians	5	2	3	30	14	16	15	9	6	15	5	10
Chicago White Sox	4	2	2	26	13	13	13	6	7	13	7	6
Kansas City Royals	2	1	1	13	6	7	7	4	3	6	2	4
Toronto Blue Jays	2	2	0	12	8	4	6	4	2	6	4	2
Milwaukee Brewers	1	0	1	7	3	4	3	2	1	4	1	3
TOTALS	97	57	40	571	312	256	285	169	114	286	143	142

NATIONAL LEAGUE

TEAM	No	Series W	L	All Games G	W	L	Home Games G	W	L	Road Games G	W	L
Brooklyn/Los Angeles	18	6	12	105	45	60	51	30	21	54	15	39
New York/San Francisco	16	5	11	93	42	49	47	23	24	46	19	25
St. Louis Cardinals	15	9	6	96	48	48	47	24	23	49	24	25
Chicago Cubs	10	2	8	53	19	33	27	7	19	26	12	14
Boston/Milwaukee/Atlanta	9	3	6	53	24	29	26	14	12	27	10	17
Cincinnati Reds	9	5	4	51	26	25	26	12	14	25	14	11
Pittsburgh Pirates	7	5	2	47	23	24	23	12	11	24	11	13
Philadelphia Phillies	5	1	4	26	8	18	14	5	9	12	3	9
New York Mets	4	2	2	24	12	12	13	8	5	11	4	7
San Diego Padres	2	0	2	9	1	8	4	1	3	5	0	5
Arizona Diamondbacks	1	1	0	7	4	3	4	4	0	3	0	3
Florida Marlins	1	1	0	7	4	3	4	2	2	3	2	1
TOTALS	97	40	57	571	256	312	286	142	143	285	114	169

TIED GAMES

1907 Oct. 8	Detroit AL at Chicago NL	3-3	12 inn
1912 Oct. 9	New York NL at Boston AL	6-6	11 inn
1922 Oct. 5	New York NL at New York AL	3-3	10 inn

WORLD SERIES RECORDS

NOTE: Individual and Club records are listed under appropriate headings according to the duration of each annual Series, immediately preceding records for lifetime, game and inning. Players' complete names are found in the annual rosters.

8-Game Series records that tied or exceeded those shown are included under 7-Game Series

BATTING — INDIVIDUAL

4 Games	5 Games	6 Games	7 Games
Highest Batting Average			
.750 Hatcher, NL:Cin 1990	.500 Gordon, AL:NY 1941	.500 Robertson, NL:NY 1917	.500 Martin:NL:StL 1931
	Clendenon, NL:NY 1969	Martin, AL:NY 1953	Lindell, AL:NY 1947
		Molitor, AL:Tor 1993	Garner, NL:Pitt 1979
Highest Slugging Percentage			
1.727 Gehrig, AL:NY 1928	.929 Gordon, AL:NY 1941	1.250 Jackson, AL:NY 1977	.913 Tenace, AL:Oak 1972
Most At-Bats			
19 Koenig, AL:NY 1928	23 Janvrin, AL:Bos 1916	29 Duncan, NL:Phil 1993	36 Collins, AL:Bos 1903 (8g)
R.Henderson, AL:Oak 1989	Moore, NL:NY 1937		33 Harris, AL:Wash 1924
O'Neill, AL:NY 1998	Richardson, AL:NY 1961		Rice, AL:Wash 1925
			Moreno, NL:Pitt 1979
			White, NL:Fla. 1997
Most Runs			
9 Ruth, AL:NY 1928	6 Baker, AL:Phil 1910	10 Jackson, AL:NY 1977	8 By many players
Gehrig, AL:NY 1932	Murphy, AL Phil 1910	Molitor, AL:Tor 1993	
	Hooper, AL:Bos 1916		
	Simmons, AL:Phil 1929		
	May, NL:Cin 1970		
	Powell, AL:Balt 1970		
	Whitaker, AL:Det 1984		
	Jeter, AL:NY 2000		
Most Hits			
10 Ruth, AL:NY 1928	9 Baker, AL:Phil 1910,13	12 Martin, AL:NY 1953	13 Richardson, AL:NY 1964
	Collins, AL:Phil 1910	Alomar, AL:Tor 1993	Brock, NL:StL. 1968
	Groh, NL:NY 1922	Molitor, AL:Tor 1993	Barrett, AL:Bos 1986
	Moore, NL:NY 1937	Grissom, NL:Atl 1996	
	Richardson, AL:NY 1961		
	Blair, AL:Balt 1970		
	B.Robinson, AL:Balt 1970		
	Trammell, AL:Det 1984		
	Jeter, AL:NY 2000		
	O'Neill, AL:NY 2000		
Most Extra-Base Hits			
6 Ruth, AL:NY 1928	5 Dempsey, AL:Balt 1983	6 Jackson, AL:NY 1977	7 Stargell, NL:Pitt 1979
	Jeter, AL:NY 2000	Molitor & White AL:Tor 1993	
Most Total Bases			
22 Ruth, AL:NY 1928	19 Jeter, AL:NY 2000	25 Jackson, AL:NY 1977	25 Stargell, NL:Pitt 1979
Most Singles			
9 Munson, AL:NY 1976	8 Chance, NL:Chi 1908	10 Rolfe, AL:NY 1936	12 Rice, AL:Wash 1925
	Baker, AL:Phil 1913	Irvin, NL:NY 1951	
	Groh, NL:NY 1922		
	Moore, NL:NY 1937		
	Richardson, AL:NY 1961		
	Blair, AL:Balt 1970		
	Garvey, NL:LA 1974		
Most Doubles			
4 Hatcher, NL:Cin 1990	4 Collins, AL:Phil 1910	5 Hafey, NL:StL. 1930	6 Fox, AL:Det 1934
Boone, NL:Atl. 1999	Dempsey, AL:Balt 1983		
Most Triples			
2 Gehrig, AL:NY 1927	2 Collins, AL:Phil 1913	2 Rohe, AL:Chi 1906	4 Leach, NL:Pitt 1903 (8g)
Davis, NL:LA 1963	Brown, AL:NY 1949	R. Meusel, AL:NY 1923	3 Johnson, AL:NY 1947
R.Henderson, AL:Oak 1989	O'Neill, AL:NY 2000	Martin, AL:NY 1953	Lemke, NL:Atl 1991
		Molitor, AL:Tor 1993	
		White, AL:Tor 1993	

WORLD SERIES - INDIVIDUAL BATTING

4 Games	5 Games	6 Games	7 Games
Most Home Runs			
4 Gehrig, AL:NY 1928	3 Clendenon, NL:NY 1969	5 Jackson, AL:NY 1977	4 Ruth, AL:NY 1926
			Snider, NL:Brk 1952, 55
			Bauer, AL:NY 1958
			Tenace, AL:Oak 1972
Most Runs Batted In			
9 Gehrig, AL:NY 1928	8 Murphy, AL:Phil 1910	10 Kluszewski, AL:Chi 1959	12 Richardson, AL:NY 1960
	May, NL:Cin 1970		
Most Sacrifice Hits			
3 Westrum, NL:NY 1954	4 Lewis, AL:Bos 1916	3 Sheckard, NL:Chi 1906	5 Clarke. NL:Pitt 1909
		Steinfeldt, NL:Chi 1906	Daubert, NL:Cin 1919 (8g)
		Tinker, NL:Chi 1906	
		Barry, AL:Phil 1911	
		Lee, NL:Chi 1935	
Most Sacrifice Flies (since 1954)			
2 Westrum, NL:NY 1954	2 Nettles, NL:SD 1984	3 Carter, AL:Tor 1993	2 Campanella, NL:Brk 1956
	Brosius, AL:NY 2000		B.Robinson, AL:Balt 1971
			Stargell, NL:Pitt 1979
			Ramirez, AL:Clev 1997
			Williams, NL:Ari 2001
Most Walks			
7 Thompson, NL:NY 1954	7 Sheckard, NL:Chi 1910	9 Randolph, AL:NY 1981	11 Ruth, AL:NY 1926
	Cochrane, AL:Phil 1929		Tenace, AL:Oak 1973
	Gordon, AL:NY 1941		
Most Intentional Walks (Since 1955)			
3 Williams, AL:NY 1999	3 Posada, AL:NY 2000	3 Milbourne, AL:NY 1981	4 Puckett, AL:Minn 1991
Most Strikeouts			
7 R. Meusel, AL:NY 1927	9 Martinez, NL:SD 1984	12 Wilson, AL:KC 1980	11 Mathews, NL:Mil 1958
Caminiti, NL:SD 1998			Garrett, NL:NY 1973
			Gonzalez, NL:Ari 2001
			Miller, NL:Ari 2001
Most Stolen Bases			
3 R.Henderson, AL:Oak 1989-90	6 Slagle, NL:Chi 1907	6 Lofton,AL:Clev 1995	7 Brock, NL:StL. 1967,68
Jeter, AL:NY 1999			
Most Caught Stealing			
2 Aparicio, AL:Balt 1966	5 Schulte, NL:Chi 1910	3 Devore, NL:NY 1911	4 Neale, NL:Cin 1919 (8g)
Foster, NL:Cin 1976			3 Brock, NL:StL. 1968

SERVICE

Most Series, Lifetime
14 Yogi Berra, AL:NY 1947,49-53,55-58,60-63

Most Series, Consecutive
5 By many. See rosters AL:NY 1949-53; 60-64

CLUBS

Most Series, One Club, Lifetime
14 Yogi Berra, AL:NY 1947,49-53,55-58,60-63

Most Series, Winning Club
10 Yogi Berra, AL:NY 1947,49-53,56,58,61-62

Most Series, Losing Club
6 Pee Wee Reese, NL:Brk. 1941,47,49,52-53,56
   Elston Howard, AL:NY 1955,57,60,63-64; Bos. 67

Most Positions Played, Lifetime
4 Fred Snodgrass, NL:NY 1911-13 (CF, LF, RF, 1B)
   Babe Ruth, AL:Bos. 1915-16,18 (P, LF); NY 21-23,26-28,32 (LF, RF, 1B)
   Jackie Robinson, NL:Brk. 1947,49,52-53,55-56 (1B, 2B, LF, 3B)
   Tony Kubek, AL:NY 1957-58,60-63 (LF, 3B, CF, SS)
   Elston Howard, AL:NY 1955-58, 60-64 (LF, RF, 1B, C); Bos. 67 (C)
   Pete Rose, NL:Cin. 1970,72,75-76 (RF, LF, 3B); Phil. 80,83 (1B)

BATTING AVERAGE

Highest Batting Average (Minimum: 75 at-bats)
.391 Lou Brock, NL:StL. 1964,67-68 (Yrs-3,G-21,AB-87,H-34)

Most Series, .300 or Higher Batting Average
6 Babe Ruth, AL:NY 1921,23,26-28,32

Most Series Leading Club (Playing all games)
3 Frank Baker, AL:Phil. 1911,13-14
   Pee Wee Reese, NL:Brk. 1947,49,52
   Duke Snider, NL:Brk. 1952,55-56
   Gil Hodges, NL:Brk. 1953,56; LA 59
   Steve Garvey, NL:LA 1974,77,81

Highest Slugging Percentage (Minimum: 75 at-bats)
.755 Reggie Jackson, AL:Oak. 1973-74; NY 77-78,81 (Yrs-5,G-27,AB-98,TB-74)

GAMES

Most Games, Lifetime
75 Yogi Berra, AL:NY 1947,49-53,55-58,60-63

Most Games, One Club
75 Yogi Berra, AL:NY 1947,49-53,55-58,60-63

Most Games, Consecutive
30 Bobby Richardson, AL:NY 1960-64

AT-BATS

Most At-Bats, Lifetime
259 Yogi Berra, AL:NY 1947,49-53,55-58,60-63

Most At-Bats, Game
6 Pat Dougherty, AL:Bos. Oct. 7, 1903
Jimmy Collins, AL:Bos. Oct. 7, 1903
Jimmy Sheckard, NL:Chi. Oct. 10, 1908
Heinie Groh, NL:Cin. Oct. 9, 1919
George Burns, NL:NY Oct. 7, 1921
Mark Koenig, AL:NY Oct. 6, 1926
Frankie Crosetti, AL:NY Oct. 2, 1932
Bill Dickey, AL:NY Oct. 2, 1932
Joe Sewell, AL:NY Oct. 2, 1932
Red Rolfe, AL:NY Oct. 6, 1936
Joe DiMaggio, AL:NY Oct. 6, 1936
Jimmy Brown, NL:StL. Oct. 4, 1942
Red Schoendienst, NL:StL. Oct. 10, 1946
Enos Slaughter, NL:StL. Oct. 10, 1946
Pee Wee Reese, NL:Brk. Oct. 5, 1956
Tony Kubek, AL:NY Oct. 6, 1960
Moose Skowron, AL:NY Oct. 6, 1960
Clete Boyer, AL:NY Oct. 12, 1960
Bobby Richardson, AL:NY Oct. 9, 1961
Tony Kubek, AL:NY Oct. 9, 1961
Paul Molitor, AL:Mil. Oct. 12, 1982
Robin Yount, AL:Mil. Oct. 12. 1982
Jim Rice, AL:Bos. Oct. 19, 1986
Rickey Henderson, AL:Oak. Oct. 28, 1989
Roberto Alomar, AL:Tor. Oct. 20, 1993
Joe Carter, AL:Tor. Oct. 20, 1993
Tony Fernandez, AL:Tor. Oct. 20, 1993
Mariano Duncan, NL:Phil. Oct. 20, 1993
Tony Womack, NL:Ari. Nov. 3, 2001
Extra-Inning Game:
7 Don Hahn, NL:NY Oct. 14, 1973 (12 inn)

Most Appearances, No At-Bats, Game
5 Fred Clarke, NL:Pitt. Oct. 16, 1909

Most At-Bats, Inning
2 By many players

RUNS

Most Runs Lifetime
42 Mickey Mantle, AL:NY 1951-53,55-58,60-64

Most Runs, Game
4 Babe Ruth, AL:NY Oct. 6, 1926
Earle Combs, AL:NY Oct. 2, 1932
Frankie Crosetti, AL:NY Oct. 2, 1936
Enos Slaughter, NL:StL. Oct. 10, 1946
Reggie Jackson, AL:NY Oct. 18, 1977
Kirby Puckett, AL:Minn. Oct. 24, 1987
Carney Lansford, AL:Oak. Oct. 27, 1989
Lenny Dykstra, NL:Phil. Oct. 20, 1993

Most Runs, Inning
2 Frankie Frisch, NL:NY Oct. 7, 1921 (7th)
Al Simmons, AL:Phil. Oct. 12, 1929 (7th)
Jimmie Foxx, AL:Phil. Oct. 12, 1929 (7th)
Dick McAuliffe, AL:Det. Oct. 9, 1968 (3rd)
Mickey Stanley, AL:Det. Oct. 9, 1968 (3rd)
Al Kaline, AL:Det. Oct. 9, 1968 (3rd)
Greg Colbrunn, NL:Ari. Nov. 3, 2001 (3rd)

Most Games, Consecutive, Runs
9 Babe Ruth, AL:NY 1927-28,32
Frank Baker, AL:Phil. 1910-11

HITS

Most Hits, Lifetime
71 Yogi Berra, AL:NY 1947,49-53,55-58,60-63

Most Hits, Game
5 Paul Molitor, AL:Mil. Oct. 12, 1982

Most Games, 4 or more Hits
2 Robin Yount, AL:Mil. Oct. 12 & 17, 1982

Most Games, 4 or more Hits, One Series
2 Robin Yount, AL:Mil. Oct. 12 & 17, 1982

Most Hits, 2 Consecutive Games
7 Frank Isbell, AL:Chi. Oct. 13-14, 1906
   Freddie Lindstrom, NL:NY Oct. 7-8. 1924
   Monte Irvin, NL:NY Oct. 4-5, 1951
   Thurman Munson, AL:NY Oct. 19-21, 1976
   Paul Molitor, AL:Mil. Oct. 12-13, 1982
   Billy Hatcher, NL:Cin. Oct. 16-17, 1990

Most Hits, Inning
2 Ross Youngs, NL:NY Oct. 7, 1921 (7th)
   Al Simmons, AL:Phil. Oct. 12, 1929 (7th)
   Jimmie Foxx, AL:Phil. Oct. 12, 1929 (7th)
   Jimmy Dykes, AL:Phil. Oct. 12, 1929 (7th)
   Joe Moore, NL:NY Oct. 4, 1933 (6th)
   Dizzy Dean, NL:StL. Oct. 9, 1934 (3rd)
   Joe DiMaggio, AL:NY Oct. 6, 1936 (9th)
   Hank Leiber, NL:NY Oct. 9, 1937 (2nd)
   Stan Musial, NL:StL. Oct. 4, 1942 (4th)
   Elston Howard, AL:NY Oct. 6, 1960 (6th)
   Bobby Richardson, AL:NY Oct. 6, 1960 (6th)
   Bob Cerv, AL:NY Oct. 8, 1960 (1st)
   Frank Quilici, AL:Minn. Oct. 6, 1965 (3rd)
   Al Kaline, AL:Det. Oct. 9, 1968 (3rd)
   Norm Cash, AL:Det. Oct. 9, 1968 (3rd)
   Merv Rettenmund, AL:Balt. Oct. 11, 1971 (5th)
   Gary Gaetti, AL:Minn. Oct. 17, 1987 (4th)
   Matt Williams, NL:Ari. Nov. 3, 2001 (3rd)

Most Hits, Consecutive At-Bats
7 Thurman Munson, AL:NY 1976-77
   Billy Hatcher, NL:Cin. 1990

Most Hits, Consecutive At-Bats, One Series
7 Billy Hatcher, NL:Cin. 1990

Most Games, Consecutive, Hits
17 Hank Bauer, AL:NY 1956-58

Hitless At-Bats
  Most At-Bats, No Hits, Lifetime
  22 George Earnshaw, AL:Phil. 1929-31
  Consecutive At-Bats, No Hits
  31 Marv Owen, AL:Det. 1934-35
  One Series, Most At-Bats, No Hits:
  22 Dal Maxvill, NL:StL. 1968
  Game, Most At-Bats, No Hits:
  6 Travis Jackson, NL:NY Oct. 10, 1924 (12 inn)
     Hughie Critz, NL:NY Oct. 6, 1933 (11 inn)
     Felix Millan, NL:NY Oct. 14, 1973 (12 inn)
     Mickey Rivers, AL:NY Oct. 11, 1977 (12 inn)
     Ron Gant, NL:Atl. Oct. 22, 1991 (12 inn)
     Devon White, NL:Fla. Oct. 26, 1997 (11 inn)
     Craig Counsell, NL:Ari. Nov. 1, 2001 (12 inn)

EXTRA-BASE HITS

Most Extra-Base Hits, Lifetime
26 Mickey Mantle, AL:NY 1951-53,55-58,60-64

Most Extra-Base Hits, Game
4 Frank Isbell, AL:Chi. Oct. 13, 1906 (4-2b)

Most Extra-Base Hits, Inning
2 Ross Youngs, NL:NY Oct. 7, 1921 (7th: 2b,3b)
Matt Williams, NL:Ari. Nov. 3, 2001 (3rd; 2-2b)

TOTAL BASES

Most Total Bases, Lifetime
123 Mickey Mantle, AL:NY 1951-53,55-58,60-64

Most Total Bases, Game
12 Babe Ruth, AL:NY Oct. 6, 1926
Babe Ruth, AL:NY Oct. 9, 1928
Reggie Jackson, AL:NY Oct. 18, 1977

Most Total Bases, Inning
5 Ross Youngs, NL:NY Oct. 7, 1921 (7th)
Al Simmons, AL:Phil. Oct. 12, 1929 (7th)

SINGLES

Most Singles, Lifetime
49 Yogi Berra, AL:NY 1947,49-53,55-58,60-63

Most Singles. Game
5 Paul Molitor, AL:Mil. Oct. 12, 1982

Most Singles, Inning
2 Jimmie Foxx, AL:Phil. Oct. 12, 1929 (7th)
Joe Moore, NL:NY Oct. 4, 1933 (6th)
Joe DiMaggio, AL:NY Oct. 6, 1936 (9th)
Hank Leiber, NL:NY Oct. 9, 1937 (2nd)
Bob Cerv, AL:NY Oct. 8, 1960 (1st)
Al Kaline, AL:Det. Oct. 9, 1968 (3rd)
Norm Cash, AL:Det. Oct. 9, 1968 (3rd)
Merv Rettenmund, AL:Balt. Oct. 11, 1971 (5th)

DOUBLES

Most Doubles, Lifetime
10 Frankie Frisch, NL:NY 1921-24; StL. 28,30-31,34
Yogi Berra, AL:NY 1947,49-59,55-58,60-63

Most Doubles, Game
4 Frank Isbell, AL:Chi. Oct. 13, 1906

Most Doubles, Inning
2 Matt Williams, NL:Ari. Nov. 3, 2001 (3rd)

TRIPLES

Most Triples, Lifetime
4 Tommy Leach, NL:Pitt. 1903,09
Tris Speaker, AL:Bos. 1912,15; Clev. 20
Billy Johnson, AL:NY 1943,47,49-50

Most Triples, Game
2 Tommy Leach, NL:Pitt. Oct. 1, 1903
Patsy Dougherty, AL:Bos. Oct. 7, 1903
Dutch Ruether, NL:Cin. Oct. 1, 1919
Bobby Richardson, AL:NY Oct. 12, 1960
Tommy Davis, NL:LA Oct. 3, 1963
Mark Lemke, NL:Atl. Oct. 24, 1991

Most Triples, Inning
1 By many players

HOME RUNS

Most Home Runs, Lifetime
18 Mickey Mantle, AL:NY 1951-53,55-58,60-64

Most Home Runs, Game
3 Babe Ruth, AL:NY Oct. 6, 1926
3 Babe Ruth, AL:NY Oct. 9, 1928
Reggie Jackson, AL:NY Oct. 18, 1977

Most Home Runs, Game, Rookie
2 Charlie Keller, AL:NY Oct. 7, 1939
Tony Kubek, AL:NY Oct. 5, 1957
Willie McGee, NL:StL. Oct. 15, 1982
Andruw Jones, NL:Atl. Oct. 20, 1996

Most Games, Consecutive, Home Runs
4 Lou Gehrig, AL:NY Oct. 5,7 (2),9, 1928; Sept. 28, 1932
Reggie Jackson, AL:NY Oct. 15,16,18 (3), 1977; Oct. 10, 1978

Most Home Runs, First Game
2 Ted Kluszewski, AL:Chi. Oct. 1, 1959
Gene Tenace, AL:Oak. Oct. 14, 1972
Willie Aikens, AL:KC Oct. 14, 1980
Andruw Jones, NL:Atl. Oct. 20, 1996
Greg Vaughn, NL:SD Oct. 17, 1998

Most Games, 2 or more Home Runs
4 Babe Ruth, AL:NY Oct. 11, 1923; Oct. 6, 1926; Oct. 9, 1928; Oct. 1, 1932

Most Games, One Series, 2 or more Home Runs
2 Willie Aikens, AL:KC Oct. 14,18, 1980

Most Home Runs, Consecutive At-Bats
4 Reggie Jackson, AL:NY Oct. 16-18, 1977

Most Home Runs, Inning
1 By many players

Most Home Runs, Consecutive Innings
2 Babe Ruth, AL:NY Oct. 11, 1923 (4th-5th);
Babe Ruth, AL:NY Oct. 9, 1928 (7th-8th)
Ted Kluszewski, AL:Chi. Oct. 1, 1959 (3th-4th)
Reggie Jackson, AL:NY Oct. 18, 1977 (4th-5th)
Willie Aikens. AL:KC Oct. 18. 1980 (1st-2nd)
Dave Henderson, AL:Oak. Oct. 27, 1989 (4th-5th)
Chris Sabo, NL:Cin. Oct. 19, 1990 (2nd-3rd)
Andruw Jones, NL:Atl. Oct. 20, 1996 (2nd-3rd)
Scott Brosius, AL:NY, Oct. 21, 1998 (7th-8th)

Home Run, First Career At-Bat

Chick Fewster, AL:NY Oct. 11, 1921	Gene Tenace, AL:Oak. Oct. 14, 1972
Joe Harris, AL:Wash. Oct. 7, 1925	Jim Mason, AL:NY Oct. 19, 1976
George Watkins, NL:StL. Oct. 2, 1930	Doug DeCinces, AL:Balt. Oct. 10, 1979
Mel Ott, NL:NY Oct. 3, 1933	Amos Otis, AL:KC Oct. 14, 1980
George Selkirk, AL:NY Sept. 30, 1936	Bob Watson, AL:NY Oct. 20, 1981
Dusty Rhodes, NL:NY Sept. 29, 1954	Jim Dwyer, AL:Balt. Oct. 11, 1983
Elston Howard, AL:NY Sept. 28, 1955	Jose Canseco, AL:Oak. Oct. 15, 1988
Roger Maris, AL:NY Oct. 5, 1960	Mickey Hatcher, NL:LA Oct. 15, 1988
Don Mincher, AL:Minn. Oct. 6, 1965	Bill Bathe, NL:SF Oct. 27, 1989
Brooks Robinson, AL:Balt. Oct. 5, 1966	Eric Davis, NL:Cin. Oct. 16, 1990
Jose Santiago, AL:Bos. Oct. 4, 1967	Ed Sprague, AL:Tor. Oct. 18, 1992
Mickey Lolich, AL:Det. Oct. 3, 1968	Fred McGriff, NL:Atl. Oct. 21, 1995
Don Buford, AL:Balt. Oct. 11, 1969	Andruw Jones, NL:Atl. Oct. 20, 1996

Home Run, Each of First Two Career At-Bats
2 Gene Tenace, AL:Oak. Oct. 14, 1972
Andruw Jones, NL:Atl. Oct. 20, 1996

Home Run, Leading Off First Inning

Patsy Dougherty, AL:Bos. Oct. 2, 1903	Don Buford, AL:Balt. Oct. 11, 1969
Davy Jones, AL:Det. Oct. 13, 1909	Tommie Agee, NL:NY Oct. 14, 1969
Phil Rizzuto, AL:NY Oct. 5, 1942	Pete Rose, NL:Cin. Oct. 20, 1972
Dale Mitchell, AL:Clev. Oct. 10, 1948	Wayne Garrett, NL:NY Oct. 16, 1973
Gene Woodling, AL:NY Oct. 4, 1953	Davey Lopes, NL:LA Oct. 17, 1978
Al Smith, AL:Clev. Sept. 30, 1954	Lennie Dykstra, NL:NY Oct. 21, 1986
Bill Bruton, NL:Mil. Oct. 2, 1958	Rickey Henderson, AL:Oak. Oct. 28, 1989
Lou Brock, NL:StL. Oct. 6, 1968	Derek Jeter, AL:NY Oct. 25, 2000

Grand Slam Home Runs
    Elmer Smith (RF) AL:Clev. (Brk.) Oct. 10, 1920 (1st: Burleigh Grimes)
    Tony Lazzeri (2B) AL:NY (NY) Oct. 2, 1936 (3rd: Dick Coffman)
    Gil McDougald (2B) AL:NY (NY) Oct. 9, 1951 (3rd: Larry Jansen)
    Mickey Mantle (CF) AL:NY (Brk.) Oct. 4, 1953 (3rd: Russ Meyer)
    Yogi Berra (C) AL:NY (Brk.) Oct. 5, 1956 (2nd: Don Newcombe)
    Moose Skowron (1B) AL:NY (Brk.) Oct. 10, 1956 (7th: Roger Craig)
    Bobby Richardson (2B) AL:NY (Pitt.) Oct. 8, 1960 (1st: Clem Labine)
    Chuck Hiller (2B) NL:SF (NY) Oct. 8, 1962 (7th: Marshall Bridges)
    Ken Boyer (3B) NL:StL. (NY) Oct. 11, 1964 (6th: Al Downing)
    Joe Pepitone (1B) AL:NY (StL.) Oct. 14, 1964 (8th: Gordie Richardson)
    Jim Northrup (CF) AL:Det. (StL.) Oct. 9, 1968 (3rd: Larry Jaster)
    Dave McNally (P) AL:Balt. (Cin.) Oct. 13, 1970 (6th: Wayne Granger)
    Dan Gladden (LF) AL:Minn. (StL.) Oct. 17, 1987 (4th: Bob Forsch)
    Kent Hrbek (1B) AL:Minn. (StL.) Oct. 24, 1987 (6th: Ken Dayley)
    Jose Canseco (RF) AL:Oak. (LA) Oct. 15, 1988 (2nd: Tim Belcher)
    Lonnie Smith (DH) NL:Atl. (Tor.) Oct. 22, 1992 (5th: Jack Morris)
    Tino Martinez (1B) AL:NY (SD) Oct. 17, 1998 (7th: Mark Langston)

RUNS BATTED IN

Most Runs Batted In, Lifetime
    40 Mickey Mantle, AL:NY 1951-53,55-58,60-64

Most Runs Batted In, Game
    6 Bobby Richardson, AL:NY Oct. 8, 1960

Most Runs Batted In, Inning
    4 By many players

SACRIFICE HITS

Most Sacrifice Hits, Lifetime
    8 Eddie Collins, AL:Phil. 1910-11,13-14; Chi. 17,19

Most Sacrifice Hits, Game
    3 Joe Tinker, NL:Chi. Oct. 12, 1906
       Craig Counsell, NL:Ari. Oct. 31, 2001 (10 inn)

Most Sacrifice Hits, Inning
    1 By many players

SACRIFICE FLIES (Since 1954)

Most Sacrifice Flies, Lifetime
    4 Joe Carter, AL:Tor. 1992-93

Most Sacrifice Flies, Game
    2 Wes Westrum, NL:NY Oct. 2, 1954
       Manny Ramirez, AL:Clev. Oct. 25, 1997

Most Sacrifice Flies, Inning
    1 By many players

Most Runs Batted In, Sacrifice Fly
    2 Tommy Herr, NL:StL. Oct. 16, 1982 (2nd)

WALKS

Most Walks, Lifetime
    43 Mickey Mantle, AL:NY 1951-53,55-58,60-64

Most Walks, Consecutive
    5 Lou Gehrig, AL:NY Oct. 7-9, 1928

Most Walks, Game
    4 Fred Clarke, NL:Pitt. Oct. 16, 1909
       Dick Hoblitzel, AL:Bos. Oct. 9, 1916 (14 inn)
       Ross Youngs, NL:NY Oct. 10, 1924 (12 inn)
       Babe Ruth, AL:NY Oct. 10, 1926
       Jackie Robinson, NL:Brk. Oct. 5, 1952 (11 inn)
       Doug DeCinces, AL:Balt. Oct. 13, 1979

Most Walks, Inning
    2 Lefty Gomez, AL:NY Oct. 6, 1937 (6th)
       Dick McAuliffe, AL:Det. Oct. 9, 1968 (3rd)

Most Intentional Walks
    7 Bernie Williams, AL:NY 1996, 98-2000

HIT BY PITCH

Most Hit By Pitch, Lifetime
3 Honus Wagner, NL:Pitt. 1903,09
   Frank Chance, NL:Chi. 1906-07
   Fred Snodgrass, NL:NY 1911-12
   Max Carey, NL:Pitt. 1925
   Yogi Berra, AL:NY 1953,55
   Elston Howard, AL:NY 1960,62,64
   Frank Robinson, NL:Cin. 1961; AL:Balt. 71
   Bert Campaneris, AL:Oak. 1973-74
   Reggie Jackson, AL:NY 1977-78

Most Hit By Pitch, Game
2 Max Carey, NL:Pitt. Oct. 7, 1925
   Yogi Berra, AL:NY Oct. 2, 1953
   Frank Robinson, NL:Cin. Oct. 8, 1961
   Todd Pratt, NL:NY Oct. 21, 2000 (12 inn)

Most Hit By Pitch, Inning
1 By many players

STRIKEOUTS

Most Strikeouts, Lifetime
54 Mickey Mantle, AL:NY 1951-53,55-58,60-64

Most Strikeouts, Consecutive Plate Appearances
8 Vida Blue, AL:Oak. Oct. 14, 1973-Oct. 17, 1974
   David Justice, AL:NY Oct. 27-31, 2001

Most Strikeouts, Game
5 George Pipgras, AL:NY Oct. 1, 1932

Most Strikeouts, Inning
2 Edgar Renteria, NL:Fla. Oct. 23, 1997 (6th)

GROUNDED INTO DOUBLE PLAYS

Most Grounded Into Double Plays, Lifetime
8 George Kelly, NL:NY 1921-24

Most Grounded Into Double Plays, Game
3 Willie Mays, NL:NY Oct. 8, 1951

STOLEN BASES

Most Stolen Bases, Lifetime
14 Eddie Collins, AL:Phil. 1910-11,13-14; Chi. 17,19
    Lou Brock, NL:StL. 1964,67-68

Most Stolen Bases, Game
3 Honus Wagner, NL:Pitt. Oct. 11, 1909
   Willie Davis, NL:LA Oct. 11, 1965
   Lou Brock, NL:StL. Oct. 12, 1967
   Lou Brock, NL:StL. Oct. 5, 1968

Most Stolen Bases, Inning
2 George Browne, NL:NY Oct. 12, 1905 (9th)
   Jimmy Slagle, NL:Chi. Oct. 8, 1907 (10th)
   Ty Cobb, AL:Det. Oct. 12, 1908 (9th)
   Honus Wagner, NL:Pitt. Oct. 13, 1909 (7th)
   Eddie Collins, AL:Chi. Oct. 7, 1917 (6th)
   Babe Ruth, AL:NY Oct. 6, 1921 (5th)
   Lou Brock, NL:StL. Oct. 12, 1967 (5th)
   Davey Lopes, NL:LA Oct. 15, 1974 (1st)
   Roberto Alomar, AL:Tor. Oct. 19, 1993 (6th)
   Kenny Lofton, AL:Clev. Oct. 21, 1995 (1st)
   Omar Vizquel, AL:Clev. Oct. 20, 1997 (5th)

Most Steals of Home, Lifetime
2 Bob Meusel, AL:NY 1921,28

Most Steals of Home, Game
1 Bill Dahlen, NL:NY Oct. 12, 1905 (5th)
   George Davis, AL:Chi. Oct. 13, 1906 (3rd)
   Jimmy Slagle, NL:Chi. Oct. 11, 1907 (7th)
   Ty Cobb, AL:Det. Oct. 9, 1909 (3rd)
   Buck Herzog, NL:NY Oct. 14, 1912 (1st)
   Butch Schmidt, NL:Bos. Oct. 9, 1914 (8th)
   Mike McNally, AL:NY Oct. 5, 1921 (5th)
   Bob Meusel, AL:NY Oct. 6, 1921 (8th)
   Bob Meusel, AL:NY Oct. 7, 1928 (6th)
   Hank Greenberg, AL:Det. Oct. 6, 1934 (8th)
   Monte Irvin, NL:NY Oct. 4, 1951 (1st)
   Jackie Robinson, NL:Brk. Sept. 28, 1955 (8th)
   Tim McCarver, NL:StL. Oct. 15, 1964 (4th)

CAUGHT STEALING

Most Caught Stealing, Game
2 Frank Schulte, NL:Chi. Oct. 17,23, 1910
   Fred Luderus, NL:Phil. Oct. 8, 1915
   Jimmy Johnston, NL:Brk. Oct. 9, 1916
   Mickey Livingston, NL:Chi. Oct. 3, 1945
   Billy Martin, AL:NY Sept. 28, 1955

Most Caught Stealing, Inning
1 By many players

PINCH-HITTING

Most Games, Lifetime
12 Luis Polonia, AL:Oak. 1988, NY 2000; NL:Atl. 1995-96

Most Games, One Series
6 Luis Polonia, NL:Atl. 1996

Most At-Bats, Lifetime
11 Luis Polonia, AL:Oak. 1988, NY 2000; NL:Atl. 1995-96

Most Hits, Lifetime
3 Ken O'Dea, NL:Chi. 1935; StL. 42,44
   Bobby Brown, AL:NY 1947
   Johnny Mize, AL:NY 1949,52
   Dusty Rhodes, NL:NY 1954
   Carl Furillo, NL:Brk. 1947; LA 59
   Bob Cerv, AL:NY 1955-56,60
   Johnny Blanchard, AL:NY 1960-61,64
   Carl Warwick, NL:StL. 1964
   Gonzalo Marquez, AL:Oak. 1972
   Ken Boswell, NL:NY 1973

Most Hits, One Series
3 Bobby Brown, AL:NY 1947
   Dusty Rhodes, NL:NY 1954
   Carl Warwick. NL:StL. 1964
   Gonzalo Marquez, AL:Oak. 1972
   Ken Boswell, NL:NY 1973

Most Total Bases, One Series
8 Chuck Essegian, NL:LA 1959
   Bernie Carbo, AL:Bos. 1975

Most Home Runs, Lifetime
2   Chuck Essegian, NL:LA Oct. 2 (7th), 8 (9th), 1959
    Bernie Carbo, AL:Bos. Oct. 14 (7th), 21 (8th), 1975
1   Yogi Berra, AL:NY Oct. 2, 1947 (7th)
    Johnny Mize, AL:NY Oct. 3, 1952 (9th)
    George Shuba, NL:Brk. Sept. 30, 1953 (6th)
    Dusty Rhodes, NL:NY Sept. 29, 1954 (10th)
    Hank Majeski AL:Clev. Oct. 2, 1954 (5th)
    Bob Cerv, AL:NY Oct. 2, 1955 (7th)
    Elston Howard, AL:NY Oct. 5, 1960 (9th)
    Johnny Blanchard, AL:NY Oct. 7, 1961 (8th)
    Jay Johnstone, NL:LA Oct. 24, 1981 (6th)
    Kirk Gibson, NL:LA Oct. 15, 1988 (9th)
    Bill Bathe, NL:SF Oct. 27, 1989 (9th)
    Chili Davis, AL:Minn. Oct. 22, 1991 (8th)
    Ed Sprague, AL:Tor. Oct. 18, 1992 (9th)
    Jim Leyritz, AL:NY Oct. 27, 1999 (8th)

Most Runs Batted In, One Series
6   Dusty Rhodes, NL:NY 1954

Most Runs Batted In, Game
3   Dusty Rhodes, NL:NY Sept. 29, 1954
    Hank Majeski, AL:Clev. Oct. 2, 1954
    Bernie Carbo, AL:Bos. Oct. 21, 1975
    Bill Bathe, NL:SF Oct. 27. 1989

Most Walks, One Series
3   Bennie Tate, AL:Wash. 1924

Most Strikeouts, One Series
3   Gabby Hartnett, NL:Chi. 1929
    Rollie Hemsley, NL:Chi. 1932
    Otto Velez, AL:NY 1976
    Luis Polonia, NL:Atl. 1996

PINCH-RUNNING

Most Games, Lifetime
9   Allan Lewis, AL:Oak. 1972-73

Most Games, One Series
6   Allan Lewis, AL:Oak. 1972

BASE ON INTERFERENCE

Awarded First Base on Interference
1   Roger Peckinpaugh, AL:Wash. Oct. 15, 1925 (1st)
    Bud Metheny, AL:NY Oct. 6, 1943 (6th)
    Ken Boyer, NL:StL. Oct. 12, 1964 (1st)
    Pete Rose, NL:Cin. Oct. 10, 1970 (5th)
    George Hendrick, NL:StL. Oct. 15, 1982 (9th)

WORLD SERIES INDIVIDUAL FIELDING FIRST BASEMEN

4 Games	5 Games	6 Games	7 Games
Highest Average 1.000 (Most Chances)			
55 Schmidt, NL:Bos 1914	73 Hoblitzel, AL:Bos 1916	72 McInnis, AL:Bos 1918	93 Pipp, AL:NY 1921 (8g)
			Kelly, NL:NY 1921 (8g)
			80 Bottomley, NL:StL 1926
Chances Accepted			
55 Schmidt, NL:Bos 1914	73 Hoblitzel, AL:Bos 1916	87 Donahue, AL:Chi 1906	93 Pipp, AL:NY 1921 (8g)
			Kelly, NL:NY 1921 (8g)
			81 C.Cooper, AL:Mil 1982
Putouts			
52 Schmidt, NL:Bos 1914	69 Hoblitzel, AL:Bos 1916	79 Donahue, AL:Chi 1906	92 Pipp, AL:NY 1921 (8g)
			79 Bottomley,NL:StL 1926
Assists			
6 Wertz, AL:Clev 1954	5 Rossman, AL:Det 1908	9 Merkle, NL:Chi 1918	10 C.Cooper, AL:Mil 1982
Pepitone, AL:NY 1963	Camilli, NL:Brk 1941		
	Sanders, NL:StL 1943		
	Skowron, AL:NY 1961		
Errors			
2 McGwire, AL:Oak 1990	3 Chance, NL:Chi 1908	3 Greenberg, AL:Det 1935	5 Abstein, NL:Pitt 1909
Hunter, NL:Atl. 1999	Davis, AL:Phil 1910		
Double Plays			
7 Pepitone, AL:NY 196	7 Pipp, AL:NY 1922	8 E.Robinson, AL:Clev 1948	11 Hodges, NL:Brk 1955
		Rose, NL:Phil 1980	
Double Plays Started			
2 Hunter, NL:Atl. 1999	2 May, NL:Cin 1970	2 Garvey, NL:LA 1977	3 Hodges, NL:Brk 1955
	Garvey, NL:SD 1984	McGriff, NL:Atl. 1996	

FIELDING – FIRST BASEMEN

Most Series
8   Moose Skowron, AL:NY 1955-58,60-62; NL:LA 63

Games
38   Gil Hodges, NL:Brk. 1949,52-53,55-56; LA 59

Chances Accepted
   Lifetime:
351   Gil Hodges, NL:Brk. 1949,52-53,55-56; LA 59
   Game:
20   Fred McGriff, NL:Atl. Oct. 21, 1995
   Extra-Inning Game:
23   Dick Hoblitzell, AL:Bos. Oct. 16, 1916 (14 inn)
   Inning:
4   Bill Abstein, NL:Pitt. Oct. 12, 1909 (7th)
   Wally Pipp, AL:NY Oct. 7, 1922 (5th)
   George Kelly, NL:NY Oct. 11, 1923 (7th)
   Steve Garvey, NL:LA Oct. 12, 1977 (4th)

Putouts
   Lifetime:
326   Gil Hodges, NL:Brk. 1949,52-53,55-56; LA 59
   Game (9 inn):
19   George Kelly, NL:NY Oct. 15, 1923
   Fred McGriff, NL:Atl. Oct. 21, 1995
   Inning:
3   By many players

Assists:
   Lifetime
29   Moose Skowron, AL:NY 1955-58,60-62
   NL:LA 63
   Game:
4   Marv Owen, AL:Det. Oct. 6, 1935
   Don Mincher, AL:Minn. Oct. 7, 1965
   Inning:
2   By many players

Errors
   Lifetime:
8   Fred Merkle, NL:NY 1911-13; Brk. 16; Chi. 18
   Game:
2   By many players
   Inning:
2   Claude Rossman, AL:Det. Oct. 12, 1908 (4th)
   Hank Greenberg, AL:Det. Oct. 3, 1935 (5th)
   Johnny McCarthy, NL:NY Oct. 8, 1937 (5th)
   Frank Torre, NL:Mil. Oct. 9, 1958 (2nd)
   Brian Hunter, NL:Atl. Oct. 23, 1999 (8th)

Double Plays
   Lifetime:
31   Gil Hodges, NL:Brk. 1949,52-53,55-56; LA59
   Game:
4   Stuffy McInnis, AL:Phil. Oct. 9, 1914
   Joe Collins, AL:NY Oct. 8, 1951
   Gene Tenace, AL:Oak. Oct. 17, 1973
   Pete Rose, NL:Phil. Oct. 15, 1980
   Game, started:
2   Brian Hunter, NL:Atl. Oct. 26, 1999
   Game, unassisted:
1   George Grantham, NL:Pitt. Oct. 7, 1925
   Joe Judge, AL:Wash. Oct. 13, 1925
   Jimmie Foxx, AL:Phil. Oct. 8, 1930
   Jim Bottomley, NL:StL. Oct. 1, 1931
   Lou Gehrig, AL:NY Oct. 10, 1937
   Ripper Collins, NL:Chi. Oct. 5, 1938
   Joe Collins, AL:NY Oct. 7, 1956
   Gordy Coleman, NL:Cin. Oct. 8, 1961
   Tony Perez, NL:Cin. Oct. 11, 1975
   Steve Garvey, NL:SD Oct. 9, 1984
   Fred McGriff, NL:Atl. Oct. 24, 1996
   Jim Thome, AL:Clev. Oct. 22, 1997
   Tino Martinez, AL:NY Oct. 17, 1998
   Brian Hunter, NL:Atl. Oct. 26, 1999

FIELDING – SECOND BASEMEN

4 Games	5 Games	6 Games	7 Games
Highest Average 1.000 (Most Chances)			
26 Randolph, AL:Oak 1990	43 Gordon, AL:NY 1943	39 Gehringer, AL:Det 1935	49 Doerr, AL:Bos 1946
Chances Accepted			
28 Lazzeri, AL:NY 1927	43 Gordon, AL:NY 1943	40 Lopes, NL:LA 1981	54 Harris, AL:Wash 1924
Putouts			
14 Randolph, AL:Oak 1990	20 Gordon, AL:NY 1943	26 Lopes, NL:LA 1981	26 Harris, AL:Wash 1924
Assists			
18 Lazzeri, AL:NY 1927	23 Gordon, AL:NY 1943	27 Ward, AL:NY 1923	34 Ward AL:NY 1921 (8g)
			33 Gantner, AL:Mil 1982
Errors			
2 Lazzeri, AL:NY 1928	4 Murphy, AL:Phil 1905	6 Lopes, NL:LA 1981	5 Gantner, AL:Mil 1982
Gordon, AL:NY 1938			
Herman, NL:Chi 1938			
Morgan, NL:Cin 1976			
Double Plays			
6 Herman, NL:Chi 1932	6 Green, AL:Oak 1974	7 Frisch, NL:NY 1923	9 Garner, NL:Pitt 1979
		Gordon, AL:Clev 1948	
		Neal, NL:LA 1959	
		Baerga, AL:Clev 1995	
Double Plays Started			
5 Herman, NL:Chi 1932	4 Gordon, AL:NY 1941	3 Baerga, AL:Clev 1995	5 Herr, NL:StL 1985
	Green, AL:Oak 1974		

FIELDING – SECOND BASEMEN

Most Series
7 Frankie Frisch, NL:NY 1922-24; StL. 28,
   30-31,34

Games
42 Frankie Frisch,NL:NY 1922-24; StL. 28,
   30-31,34

Chances Accepted
Lifetime:
241 Frankie Frisch,NL:NY 1922-24; StL. 28,
   30-31,34
Game:
13 Claude Richey, NL:Pitt. Oct. 10, 1903
   Bucky Harris, AL:Wash. Oct. 11, 1925
   Davey Lopes, NL:LA Oct. 16, 1974
Extra-inning game:
14 Hughie Critz, NL:NY Oct. 6, 1933 (11 inn)
Inning:
4 Phil Garner, NL:Pitt. Oct. 11, 1979 (8th)

Putouts
Lifetime:
105 Frankie Frisch,NL:NY 1922-24; StL. 28,
   30-31,34
Game:
8 Bucky Harris, AL:Wash. Oct. 8, 1924
   Davey Lopes, NL:LA Oct. 16, 1974
Extra-Inning Game:
9 Hughie Critz, NL:NY Oct. 6, 1933 (11 inn)
Inning:
3 Larry Doyle, NL:NY Oct. 9, 1913 (7th)
   Bill Wambsganss, AL:Clev. Oct. 10, 1920 (5th)
   Johnny Rawlings, NL:NY Oct. 11. 1921 (9th)
   Frankie Frisch, NL:StL. Oct. 7, 1931 (7th)
   Davey Lopes, NL:LA Oct. 16, 1974 (6th)
   Davey Lopes, NL:LA Oct. 21, 1981 (4th)
   Lou Whitaker, AL:Det. Oct. 14, 1984 (8th)

Assists
Lifetime:
136 Frankie Frisch,NL:NY 1922-24; StL. 28
   30-31,34
Game:
8 Claude Richey, NL:Pitt. Oct. 10, 1903
   Germany Schaefer, AL:Det. Oct. 12, 1907
   Hal Janvrin, AL:Bos. Oct. 7, 1916
   Eddie Collins, AL:Chi. Oct. 15, 1917
   Bucky Harris, AL:Wash. Oct. 7, 1924
   Joe Gordon, AL:NY Oct. 5, 1943
   Bobby Doerr, AL:Bos. Oct. 9, 1946
   Mark Lemke, NL:Atl. Oct. 21, 1995
Inning:
3 Eddie Collins, AL:Phil. Oct. 12, 1914 (4th)
   Pete Kilduff, NL:Brk. Oct. 10, 1920 (3rd)
   Aaron Ward, AL:NY Oct. 12, 1921 (6th)
   Joe Gordon, AL:NY Oct. 11, 1943 (8th)
   Jackie Robinson, NL:Brk. Oct. 8, 1949 (7th)
   Gil McDougald, AL:NY Oct. 2, 1958 (2nd)
   Phil Garner, NL:Pitt. Oct. 13, 1979 (9th)
   Frank White, AL:KC Oct. 19, 1980 (8th)
   Marty Barrett, AL:Bos. Oct. 23, 1986 (1st)

Errors
Lifetime:
8 Larry Doyle, NL:NY 1911-13
   Eddie Collins, AL:Phil. 1910-11,13-14; Chi. 17,19
Game:
3 Danny Murphy, AL:Phil. Oct. 12, 1905
   Buddy Myer, AL:Wash. Oct. 3, 1933
   Davey Lopes, NL:LA Oct. 25, 1981
Inning:
2 Danny Murphy, AL:Phil. Oct. 12, 1905 (5th)
   Mike Andrews, AL:Oak. Oct. 14, 1973 (12th)
   Davey Lopes, NL:LA Oct. 25, 1981 (4th)

Double Plays
Lifetime:
24 Frankie Frisch,NL:NY 1922-24; StL. 28,
   30-31,34
Game
3 By many players
Game, started:
3 Dick Green, AL:Oak. Oct. 15, 1974
Game, Unassisted
1 Hobe Ferris, AL:Bos. Oct. 2, 1903
   Larry Doyle, NL:NY Oct. 9, 1913
   Buck Herzog, NL:NY Oct. 7, 1917
   Frank White, AL:KC Oct. 17, 1980
   Mark Lemke, NL:Atl. Oct. 27, 1991

Triple Plays
1 Bill Wambsganss, AL:Clev. Oct. 10, 1920
   (Unassisted, 5th)

FIELDING – THIRD BASEMEN

4 Games	5 Games	6 Games	7 Games
Highest Average 1.000 (Most Chances)			
25 Baker, AL:Phil 1914	20 Groh, NL:NY 1922	26 Nettles, AL:NY 1978	29 Menke, NL:Cin 1972
Chances Accepted			
25 Baker, AL:Phil 1914	25 Gardner, AL:Bos 1916	27 Thomson, NL:NY 1951	37 Frisch, NL:NY 1921 (8g)
			34 Higgins, AL:Det 1940
Putouts			
10 Baker, AL:Phil 1914	10 Steinfeldt, NL:Chi 1907	14 Rolfe, AL:NY 1936	13 Kurowski, NL:StL 1946
Assists			
15 Baker, AL:Phil 1914	18 Gardner, AL:Bos 1916	20 Nettles, AL:NY 1977	30 Higgins, AL:Det 1940
Errors			
2 Rolfe, AL:NY 1938	4 Steinfeldt, NL:Chi 1910	3 Rohe, AL:Chi 1906	4 Leach, NL:Pitt 1903 (8g)
Caminiti, NL:SD 1998		Herzog, NL:NY 1911	Gardner, AL:Bos 1912 (8g)
		T. Jackson, NL:NY 1936	Martin, NL:StL 1934
		Elliott, NL:Bos 1948	McDougald, AL:NY 1952
Double Plays			
3 Nettles, AL:NY 1976	2 Jackson, NL:NY 1933	4 Nettles, AL:NY 1978	4 Davenport, NL:SF 1962
	B.Robinson, AL:Balt 1970		Madlock, NL:Pitt 1979
Double Plays Started			
2 Rolfe, AL:NY 1939	2 Jackson, NL:NY 1933	3 Nettles, AL:NY 1978	4 Davenport, NL:SF 1962
Nettles, AL:NY 1976	B. Robinson, AL:Balt 1970	Madlock, NL:Pitt 1979	
Brosius, AL:NY 1999			

FIELDING — THIRD BASEMEN

Most Series
6 Red Rolfe, AL:NY 1936-39,41-42

Games
31 Gil McDougald, AL:NY 1951-53,55,60

Chances Accepted
Lifetime:
96 Graig Nettles, AL:NY 1976-78,81; NL:SD 84
Game:
10 Pinky Higgins, AL:Det. Oct. 5, 1940
Chris Sabo, NL:Cin. Oct. 19, 1990
Inning:
4 Eddie Mathews, NL:Mil. Oct. 5, 1957 (3rd)

Putouts
Lifetime:
37 Frank Baker, AL:Phil. 1910-11,13-14; NY 21
Game:
4 Art Devlin, NL:NY Oct. 13, 1905
Bill Coughlin, AL:Det. Oct. 10, 1907
Bobby Byrne, NL:Pitt. Oct. 9, 1909
Tommy Leach, NL:Pitt. Oct. 16, 1909
Buck Herzog, NL:NY Oct. 17, 1911
Frank Baker, AL:Phil. Oct. 24, 1911
Frank Baker; AL:Phil. Oct. 12, 1914
Heinie Zimmerman, NL:NY Oct. 7, 1917
Jimmy Dykes, AL:Phil. Oct. 2, 1930
Bob Elliott, NL:Bos. Oct. 11, 1948
Willie Jones, NL:Phil. Oct. 4, 1950
Inning:
3 Freddie Lindstrom, NL:NY Oct. 6, 1924 (9th)

Assists:
Lifetime:
68 Graig Nettles, AL:NY 1976-78,81; NL:SD 84
Game:
9 Pinky Higgins, AL:Det. Oct. 5, 1940
Inning:
3 Ossie Bluege, AL:Wash. Oct. 13, 1925 (3rd)
Jose Pagan, NL:Pitt. Oct. 14, 1971 (9th)
Sal Bando, AL:Oak. Oct. 16, 1974 (6th)
Wade Boggs, AL:Bos. Oct. 19, 1986 (3rd)
Terry Pendleton, NL:Atl. Oct. 27, 1991 (7th)

Errors
Lifetime:
8 Larry Gardner, AL:Bos. 1912,15-16; Clev. 20
Game:
3 Pepper Martin, NL:StL. Oct. 6, 1934
Buck Herzog, NL:NY Oct. 17, 1911 (11 inn)
Inning:
2 Harry Steinfeldt, NL:Chi. Oct. 18, 1910 (3rd)
Larry Gardner, AL:Bos. Oct. 16, 1912 (2nd)
Doug DeCinces, AL:Balt. Oct. 10, 1979 (6th)

Double Plays
Lifetime:
8 Graig Nettles, AL:NY 1976-78,81; NL:SD 84
Game:
2 By many players
Game, started:
2 Fred McMullin, AL:Chi. Oct. 13, 1917
Ossie Bluege, AL:Wash. Oct. 5, 1924
Whitey Kurowski, NL:StL. Oct. 13, 1946
Clete Boyer, AL:NY Oct. 12, 1960
Dalton Jones, AL:Bos. Oct. 4, 1967
Graig Nettles, AL:NY Oct. 19, 1976
Bobby Bonilla, NL:Fla. Oct. 19, 1997`
Game, unassisted:
None

Triple Plays
None

FIELDING – SHORTSTOPS

4 Games	5 Games	6 Games	7 Games
Highest Average 1.000 (Most Chances)			
27 Wills, NL:LA 1966	29 Dahlen, NL:NY 1905	36 Scott, AL:Bos 1918	42 Gelbert, NL:StL 1931
	Scott, AL:NY 1922		
	Marion, NL:StL 1942		
	Harrelson, NL:NY 1969		
Chances Accepted			
27 Wills, NL:LA 1966	38 Tinker, NL:Chi 1907	37 Rizzuto, AL:NY 1951	51 Risberg, AL:Chi 1919 (8g)
			42 Gelbert, NL:StL 1931
Putouts			
16 Crosetti, AL:NY 1938	15 Tinker, NL:Chi 1907	16 Jurges, NL:Chi 1935	24 Wagner, AL:Bos 1912 (8g)
	Rizzuto, AL:NY 1942		22 O.Smith, NL:StL 1982
Assists			
21 Barry, AL:Phil 1914	25 Scott, AL:Bos 1916	26 Russell, NL:LA 1981	32 Foli, NL:Pitt 1979
Errors			
4 Crosetti, AL:NY 1932	4 Olson, NL:Brk 1916	4 Fletcher, NL:NY 1911	8 Peckinpaugh, AL:Wash 1925
	English, NL:Chi 1929	Weaver, AL:Chi 1917	
Double Plays			
5 Jurges, NL:Chi 1932	6 Scott, AL:NY 1922	8 Rizzuto, AL:NY 1951	7 Reese, NL:Brk 1955-56
Kubek, AL:NY 1963	Rizzuto, AL:NY 1941		Foli, NL:Pitt 1979
			Renteria, NL:Fla. 1997
Double Plays Started			
3 Koenig, AL:NY 1928	4 Tinker, NL:Chi 1907	7 Bowa, NL:Phil 1980	4 Reese, NL:Brk 1947
			McDougald, AL:NY 1957
			Linz, AL:NY 1964
			Wills, NL:LA 1965
			Foli, NL:Pitt 1979

FIELDING – SHORTSTOPS

Most Series
9 Phil Rizzuto, AL:NY 1941-42,47,49-53,55

Games
52 Phil Rizzuto, AL:NY 1941-42,47,49-53,55

Chances Accepted
Lifetime:
250 Phil Rizzuto, AL:NY 1941-42, 47, 49-53, 55
Game:
13 Buck Weaver, AL:Chi. Oct. 7, 1917
Inning:
4 Charley Gelbert, NL:StL. Oct. 6, 1931 (3rd)
Alvin Dark, NL:NY Oct. 6, 1951 (3rd)

Putouts
Lifetime:
107 Phil Rizzuto, AL:NY 1941-42, 47, 49-53, 55
Game:
7 Buck Weaver, AL:Chi. Oct. 7, 1917
Phil Rizzuto, AL:NY Oct. 5, 1942
Inning:
3 Freddy Parent, AL:Bos. Oct. 1, 1903 (4th)
Art Fletcher, NL:NY Oct. 25, 1911 (9th)
Phil Rizzuto, AL:NY Oct. 5, 1947 (4th)
Mickey Stanley, AL:Det. Oct. 10, 1968 (6th)

Assists:
Lifetime:
143 Phil Rizzuto, AL:NY 1941-42, 47, 49-53, 55
Game:
9 Roger Peckinpaugh, AL:NY Oct. 5, 1921
Extra-Inning Game:
10 Johnny Logan, NL:Mil. Oct. 6, 1957 (10 inn)
Inning:
3 Everett Scott, AL:Bos. Sept. 6, 1918 (6th)
Everett Scott, AL:Bos. Sept. 10, 1918 (3rd)
Joe Sewell, AL:Clev. Oct. 9, 1920 (6th)
Dave Bancroft, NL:NY Oct. 8, 1922 (3rd)
Ossie Bluege, AL:Wash. Oct. 7, 1924 (6th)
Blondy Ryan, NL:NY Oct. 7. 1933 (3rd)
Glenn Wright, NL:Pitt. Oct. 8, 1927 (2nd)
Phil Rizzuto, AL:NY Oct. 3, 1942 (2nd)
Ernie Bowman, NL:SF Oct. 8, 1962 (9th)
Bud Harrelson, NL:NY Oct. 14, 1969 (5th)
Mark Belanger, AL:Balt. Oct. 16, 1971 (7th)
Bud Harrelson, NL:NY Oct. 13, 1973 (7th)
Tim Foli, NL:Pitt. Oct. 12, 1979 (2nd)
Omar Vizquel, AL:Clev. Oct. 18, 1997 (5th)

Errors
Lifetime:
12 Art Fletcher, NL:NY 1911-13,17
Game:
3 Jack Barry, AL:Phil. Oct. 26, 1911
Art Fletcher, NL:NY Oct. 9, 1912 (12 inn)
Buck Weaver, AL:Chi. Oct. 13, 1917
Inning:
2 Honus Wagner, NL:Pitt. Oct. 7, 1903 (6th)
Ivy Olson, NL:Brk. Oct. 12, 1916
Roger Peckinpaugh, AL:Wash. Oct. 8, 1925
(8th)
Woody English, NL:Chi. Oct. 8, 1929 (9th)
Dick Bartell, NL:NY Oct. 9, 1937 (3rd)
Pee Wee Reese, NL:Brk. Oct. 2, 1941 (8th)

Double Plays
Lifetime:
32 Phil Rizzuto, AL:NY 1941-42,47,49-53,55
Game:
4 Phil Rizzuto, AL:NY, Oct. 8, 1951
Game, started:
3 Phil Rizzuto, AL:NY Oct. 10, 1951
Maury Wills, NL:LA Oct. 11, 1965
Larry Bowa, NL:Phil. Oct. 15, 1980
Game, unassisted:
1 Joe Tinker, NL:Chi. Oct. 10, 1907
Joe Tinker, NL:Chi. Oct. 11, 1907
Charlie Gelbert, NL:StL. Oct. 2, 1930
Eddie Kasko, NL:Cin. Oct. 7, 1961
Greg Gagne, AL:Minn. Oct. 26, 1991

Triple Plays
None

FIELDING – OUTFIELDERS

	4 Games		5 Games		6 Games		7 Games
Highest Average 1.000 (Most Chances)							
16	Combs, AL:NY 1927	20	DiMaggio, AL:NY 1942	25	Rivers, AL:NY 1977	24	Murray, NL:NY 1912 (8g)
							Evans, AL:Bos 1975
							Geronimo, NL:Cin 1975
							Lynn, AL:Bos 1975
							McGee, NL:StL 1982
Chances Accepted							
16	Combs, AL:NY 1927	20	DiMaggio, AL:NY 1942	25	Rivers, AL:NY 1977	33	Roush, NL:Cin 1919 (8g)
						26	Pafko, NL:Chi 1945
							Gladden, AL:Minn 1991
Putouts							
16	Combs, AL:NY 1927	20	DiMaggio, AL:NY 1942	24	Rivers, AL:NY 1977	30	Roush, NL:Cin 1919 (8g)
						25	Gladden, AL:Minn 1991
Assists							
2	By many players	2	By many players	2	By many players	4	Rice, AL:Wash 1924
Errors							
3	W. Davis, NL:LA 1966	2	By many players	3	Murray, NL:NY 1911	2	Wheat, NL:Brk 1920
					J.Collins, AL:Chi 1917		Orsatti, NL:StL 1934
							Goslin, AL:Det 1934
							Mantle, AL:NY 1964
							Northrup, AL:Det 1968
Double Plays							
none		2	Murphy, AL:Phil 1910	1	By many players	2	Speaker, AL:Bos 1912 (8g)
							Roush, NL:Cin 1919 (8g)
							Howard, AL:NY 1958
Double Plays Started							
none		2	Murphy, AL:Phil 1910	1	By many players	2	See preceding record

FIELDING – OUTFIELDERS

Most Series
12 Mickey Mantle, AL:NY 1951-53,55-58,60-64

Games
63 Mickey Mantle, AL:NY 1951-53,55-58,60-64

Chances Accepted
Lifetime:
150 Joe DiMaggio, AL:NY 1936-39,41-42,47,49-51
Game, Left-fielder:
8 George Foster, NL:Cin. Oct. 21, 1976
Game, Center-fielder:
8 Edd Roush, NL:Cin. Oct. 1, 1919
Hank Leiber, NL:NY Oct. 2, 1936
Extra-Inning Game:
9 Edd Roush, NL:Cin. Oct. 7, 1919 (10 inn)
Mickey Rivers, AL:NY Oct. 11, 1977 (12 inn)
Amos Otis, AL:KC Oct. 17, 1980 (10 inn)
Game, Right-fielder:
7 Red Murray, NL:NY Oct. 14, 1912
Bing Miller, AL:Phil, Oct. 5, 1930
Ray Blades, NL:StL. Oct. 5, 1930
Tony Oliva, AL:Minn. Oct. 6, 1965
Al Kaline, AL:Det. Oct. 9, 1968
Frank Robinson, AL:Balt. Oct. 14, 1969
Inning:
3 By many players

Putouts
Lifetime:
150 Joe DiMaggio, AL:NY 1936-39,41-42,47,49-51
Game, Left-fielder:
8 George Foster, NL:Cin. Oct. 21, 1976
Game, Center-fielder:
8 Edd Roush, NL:Cin. Oct. 1, 1919
Extra-Inning Game:
9 Amos Otis, AL:KC Oct. 17, 1980 (10 inn)
Game, Right-fielder:
7 By many players; Last:
Frank Robinson, AL:Balt. Oct. 14, 1969
Inning, Left-fielder:
3 By many players; Last:
Deion Sanders, NL:Atl. Oct. 22, 1992 (5th)
Inning, Center-fielder:
3 By many players; Last:
Andruw Jones, NL:Atl. Oct. 24, 1999 (7th)
Inning, Right-fielder:
3 By many players; Last:
David Justice, NL:Atl. Oct. 22, 1995 (5th)

Assists
Lifetime:
5 Harry Hooper, AL:Bos. 1912,15-16,18
Ross Youngs, NL:NY 1921-24
Game:
2 By many players
Inning:
1 By many players

Errors
Lifetime:
4 Ross Youngs, NL:NY 1921-24
Game:
3 Willie Davis, NL:LA Oct. 6, 1966
Inning:
3 Willie Davis, NL:LA Oct. 6, 1966 (5th)

Double Plays
Lifetime:
2 By many players
Game:
2 Edd Roush, NL:Cin. Oct. 7, 1919 (10 inn)
Game, started:
2 Edd Roush, NL:Cin. Oct. 7, 1919 (10 inn)
Game, unassisted:
1 Tris Speaker, AL:Bos. Oct. 15, 1912

Triple Plays
None

FIELDING – CATCHERS

4 Games	5 Games	6 Games	7 Games
Highest Average 1.000 (Most Chances)			
43 Roseboro, NL:LA 1963	61 Cochrane, AL:Phil 1929	56 Campanella, NL:Brk 1953	71 Grote, NL:NY 1973
Chances Accepted			
43 Roseboro, NL:LA 1963	61 Cochrane, AL:Phil 1929	56 Campanella, NL:Brk 1953	73 Posada, AL:NY 2001
Putouts			
43 Roseboro, NL:LA 1963	59 Cochrane, AL:Phil 1929	55 W.Cooper, NL:StL 1944	69 Posada, AL:NY 2001
Assists			
7 Munson, AL:NY 1976	9 Kling, NL:Chi 1907 Schmidt, AL:Det 1907 Burns, NL:Phil 1915	12 Meyers, NL:NY 1911	15 Schalk, AL:Chi 1919 (8g) 11 Schmidt, AL:Det 1909
Errors			
3 Oliver, NL:Cin 1990	2 Schmidt, AL:Det 1907 W.Cooper, NL:StL 1943 Ferguson, NL:LA 1974	2 Schalk, AL:Chi 1917	5 Schmidt, AL:Det 1909
Double Plays			
2 Hartnett, NL:Chi 1932	2 Burns, NL:Phil 1915 Mancuso, NL:NY 1933	3 Kling, NL:Chi 1906	3 Schmidt, AL:Det 1909 Schang, AL:NY 1921 (8g) Bench, NL:Cin 1975
Double Plays Started			
1 By many players	1 By many players	1 By many players	3 Schang, AL:NY 1921 (8g) 2 Schmidt, AL:Det 1909 Crandall, NL:Mil 1957-58 Battey, AL:Minn 1965
Passed Balls			
2 Schang. AL:Phil 1914	2 Meyers, NL:Brk 1916	2 Kling, NL:Chi 1906 Killefer, AL:Chi 1918	3 Burgess, NL:Pitt 1960 Howard, AL:NY 1964

FIELDING — CATCHERS

Most Series
12 Yogi Berra, AL:NY 1947,49-53,55-58,60,62

Games
63 Yogi Berra, AL:NY 1947,49-53,55-58,60,62

Chances Accepted
Lifetime:
457 Yogi Berra, AL:NY 1947,49-53,55-58,60,62
Game:
18 Johnny Roseboro, NL:LA Oct. 2, 1963
Tim McCarver, NL:StL. Oct. 2, 1968
Inning:
4 Boss Schmidt, AL:Det. Oct. 14, 1908 (8th)
Ira Thomas, AL:Phil. Oct. 14, 1911 (6th)
Steve O'Neill, AL:Clev. Oct. 6, 1920 (3rd)
Jimmie Wilson, NL:StL. Oct. 1, 1931 (3rd)
Roy Campanella, NL:Brk. Sept. 29, 1955 (2nd)
Tim McCarver, NL:StL. Oct. 9, 1967 (9th)

Putouts
Lifetime:
421 Yogi Berra, AL:NY 1947,49-53,55-58,60,62
Game:
18 Johnny Roseboro, NL:LA Oct. 2, 1963
Inning:
3 By many players

Assists
Lifetime:
36 Yogi Berra, AL:NY 1947,49-53,55-58,60,62
Game:
4 Roger Bresnahan, NL:NY Oct. 12, 1905
Johnny Kling, NL:Chi. Oct. 9, 1907
Boss Schmidt, AL:Det. Oct. 11, 1907; Oct. 14, 1908
Bill Rariden, NL:NY Oct. 10, 1917
Sam Agnew, AL:Bos. Sept. 6, 1918
Bill DeLancey, NL:StL. Oct. 8, 1934
Extra-Inning Game:
6 Jack Lapp, AL:Phil. Oct. 17, 1911 (11 inn)
Inning:
2 By many players

Errors
Lifetime:
7 Boss Schmidt, AL:Det. 1907-09
Game:
2 Lou Criger, AL:Bos. Oct. 1, 1903
Billy Sullivan, Sr. AL:Chi. Oct. 10, 1906
Boss Schmidt, AL:Det. Oct. 8, 1907 (13 inn)
Jimmie Wilson, NL:StL. Oct. 7, 1928
Joe Ferguson, NL:LA Oct. 15, 1974
Carlton Fisk, AL:Bos. Oct. 14, 1975 (10 inn)
Inning:
2 Lou Criger, AL:Bos. Oct. 1, 1903 (1st)
Jimmie Wilson, NL:StL. Oct. 7, 1928 (6th)

Passed Balls
Lifetime:
4 Wally Schang, AL:Phil.1913-14; Bos.18; NY 21-23
Elston Howard, AL:NY 1955-58,60-64; Bos. 67
Game:
2 Johnny Kling, NL:Chi. Oct. 9, 1906
Bill Killefer, NL:Chi. Sept. 9, 1918
Paul Richards, AL:Det. Oct. 3, 1945
Bruce Edwards, NL:Brk. Oct. 4, 1947
Smoky Burgess, NL:Pitt. Oct. 6, 1960
Elston Howard, AL:NY Oct. 7, 1964
Inning:
1 By many players

Double Plays
Lifetime:
6 Yogi Berra, AL:NY 1947,49-53,55-58,60,62
Johnny Bench, NL:Cin. 1970,72,75
Game:
2 By many players
Game, started:
2 Boss Schmidt, AL:Det. Oct. 14, 1909
Wally Schang, AL:NY Oct. 11, 1921
Game, unassisted:
None

Triple Plays
None

FIELDING – PITCHERS

4 Games	5 Games	6 Games	7 Games
Highest Average 1.000 (Most Chances)			
6 Tyler, NL:Bos 1914 Ruffing, AL:NY 1938	8 Marquard, NL:NY 1913 Shore, AL:Bos 1916 Smith, NL:Brk 1916	17 Altrock, AL:Chi 1906 Vaughn, NL:Chi 1918	12 Mullin, AL:Det 1909
Chances Accepted			
6 Tyler, NL:Bos 1914 Ruffing, AL:NY 1938	10 Mathewson, NL:NY 1905 Brown, NL:Chi 1910	17 Altrock, AL:Chi 1906 Vaughn, NL:Chi 1918	12 Mullin, AL:Det 1909
Putouts			
3 Ford, AL:NY 1963 Stewart, AL:Oak 1989	5 Morris, AL:Det 1984	6 Altrock, AL:Chi 1906 Vaughn, NL:Chi 1918	5 Kaat, AL:Minn 1965
Assists			
5 Bush, AL:Phil 1914 Tyler, NL:Bos 1914 James, NL:Bos 1914 Moore, AL:NY 1927 Pearson, AL:NY 1939	10 Brown, NL:Chi 1910	12 Brown, NL:Chi 1906	12 Mullin, AL:Det 1909 Mathewson,NL:NY 1912 (8g)
Errors			
1 By many players	2 Coombs, AL:Phil 1910 Lanier, NL:StL 1942	2 Potter, AL:StL 1944	2 Phillippe, NL:Pitt 1909 Cicotte, AL:Cin 1919 (8g) Reynolds, AL:NY 1952
Double Plays			
2 Bender, AL:Phil 1914	2 Bush, AL:NY 1922	2 Faber, AL:Chi 1917 Reynolds, AL:NY 1951 Gura, AL:KC 1980	2 Johnson, AL:Wash 1924 Stafford, AL:NY 1960
Double Plays Started			
2 Bender, AL:Phil 1914	2 Bush, AL:NY 1922	2 Faber, AL:Chi 1917 Reynolds, AL:NY 1951	2 Stafford, AL:NY 1960

FIELDING – PITCHERS

Most Series
11 Whitey Ford, AL:NY 1950,53,55-58,60-64

Games:
22 Whitey Ford, AL:NY 1950,53,55-58,60-64

Chances Accepted
Lifetime:
40 Christy Mathewson, NL:NY 1905,11-13
Game:
11 Nick Altrock, AL:Chi. Oct. 12, 1906
Inning:
3 By many players

Putouts
Lifetime:
11 Whitey Ford, AL:NY 1950,53,55-58,60-64
Game:
5 Jim Kaat, AL:Minn. Oct. 7, 1965
Inning:
2 Johnny Beazley, NL:StL. Oct. 5, 1942 (8th)
Bob Turley, AL:NY Oct. 9, 1957 (7th)
Whitey Ford, AL:NY Oct. 8, 1960 (9th)
Bob Purkey, NL:Cin. Oct. 7, 1961 (9th)
John Denny, NL:Phil. Oct. 15, 1983 (5th)
Dave Stewart, AL:Oak. Oct. 16, 1990 (3rd)
Jeff Nelson, AL:NY Oct. 23, 1996 (7th)

Assists
Lifetime:
35 Christy Mathewson, NL:NY 1905,11-13
Game:
8 Nick Altrock, AL:Chi. Oct. 12, 1906
Lon Warneke, NL:Chi. Oct. 2, 1935
Inning:
3 Eddie Plank, AL:Phil. Oct. 13, 1905 (8th)
Ed Reulbach, NL:Chi. Oct. 10, 1908 (6th)
Rube Marquard, NL:NY Oct. 7, 1913 (4th)
Lon Warneke, NL:Chi. Oct. 2, 1935 (3rd)
Johnny Murphy, AL:NY Oct. 8, 1939 (8th)
Bob Rush, NL:Mil. Oct. 4, 1958 (3rd)
Ray Washburn, NL:Cin. Oct. 15, 1970 (7th)

Errors
Lifetime:
3 Deacon Phillippe, NL:Pitt. 1903,09
Eddie Cicotte, AL:Chi. 1917,19
Max Lanier, NL:StL. 1942-44
Dave Stewart, NL:LA 1981; AL:Oak. 1989-90
Game:
2 Deacon Phillippe, NL:Pitt. Oct. 12, 1909
Jack Coombs, AL:Phil. Oct. 18, 1910
Eddie Cicotte, AL:Chi. Oct. 4, 1919
Max Lanier, NL:StL. Sept. 30, 1942
Nels Potter, AL:StL. Oct. 5, 1944 (11 inn)
Inning:
2 Jack Coombs, AL:Phil. Oct. 18, 1910 (5th)
Eddie Cicotte, AL:Chi. Oct. 4, 1919 (5th)
Max Lanier, NL:StL. Sept. 30, 1942 (9th)
Nels Potter, AL:StL. Oct. 5, 1944 (3rd)

Double Plays
Lifetime:
3 Chief Bender, AL:Phil. 1905,10-11,13-14
Joe Bush, AL:Phil.1913-14; Bos.18; NY 22-23
Allie Reynolds, AL:NY 1947,49-53
Game:
2 Chief Bender, AL:Phil. Oct. 9, 1914
Joe Bush, AL:NY Oct. 8, 1922
Allie Reynolds, AL:NY Oct. 8, 1951
Larry Gura, AL:KC Oct. 19, 1980
Game, started:
2 Chief Bender, AL:Phil. Oct. 9, 1914
Joe Bush, AL:NY Oct. 8, 1922
Allie Reynolds, AL:NY Oct. 8, 1951
Game, unassisted:
None

Triple Plays
None

INDIVIDUAL PITCHING

4 Games	5 Games	6 Games	7 Games
Earned Run Average 0.00 (Most Innings)			
11.0 James, NL:Bos 1914	27.0 Mathewson, NL:NY 1905	14.0 Benton, NL:NY 1917	27.0 Hoyt, AL:NY 1921 (8g)
			18.0 Ford, AL:NY 1960
Games			
4 Nelson, AL:NY 1999	5 Marshall, NL:LA 1974	6 Quisenberry, AL:KC 1980	7 Knowles, AL:Oak 1973
Games Started			
2 By many players; Last:	3 Mathewson, NL:NY 1905	3 By many players; Last:	5 Phillippe, NL:Pitt 1903 (8g)
Brown, NL:SD 1998	Coombs, AL:Phil 1910	Wynn, AL:Chi 1959	3 By many players; Last:
			Schilling, NL:Ari 2001
Complete Games			
2 Rudolph, NL:Bos 1914	3 Mathewson, NL:NY 1905	3 Bender, AL:Phil 1911	5 Phillippe, NL:Pitt 1903 (8g)
Hoyt, AL:NY 1928	Coombs, AL:Phil 1910	Vaughn, NL:Chi 1918	3 Adams, NL:Pitt 1909
Ruffing, AL:NY 1938			Mullin, AL:Det 1909
Koufax, NL:LA 1963			Coveleski, AL:Clev 1920
			Johnson, AL:Wash 1925
			Newsom, AL:Det 1940
			Burdette, NL:Mil 1957
			Gibson, NL:StL 1967-68
			Lolich, AL:Det 1968
Games Finished			
3 Reniff, AL:NY 1963	5 Marshall, NL:LA 1974	6 Quisenberry, AL:KC 1980	6 Casey, NL:Brk 1947
Myers, NL:Cin 1990			
Rivera, AL:NY 1998-99			
Saves (Since 1969)			
3 Rivera, AL:NY 1998	2 Fingers, AL:Oak 1974	4 Wetteland, AL:NY 1996	3 Tekulve, NL:Pitt 1979
	T. Martinez, AL:Balt 1983		
	Hernandez, AL:Det. 1984		
	Rivera, AL:NY 2000		
Shutouts			
1 By many pitchers	3 Mathewson, NL:NY 1905	1 By many pitchers	2 Dineen, AL:Bos 1903 (8g)
			Burdette, NL:Mil 1957
			Ford, AL:NY 1960
			Koufax, NL:LA 1965
Most Games, Relief Pitcher			
4 Nelson, AL:NY 1999	5 Marshall, NL:LA 1974	6 Quisenberry, AL:KC 1980	7 Knowles, AL:Oak 1973
Won			
2 Rudolph, NL:Bos 1914	3 Mathewson, NL:NY 1905	3 Faber, AL:Chi 1917	3 Phillippe, NL:Pitt 1903 (8g)
James, NL:Bos 1914	Coombs, AL:Phil 1910		Dinneen, AL:Bos 1903 (8g)
Hoyt, AL:NY 1928			Adams, NL:Pitt 1909
Ruffing, AL:NY 1938			Wood, AL:Bos 1912 (8g)
Koufax,NL:LA 1963			Coveleski, AL:Clev 1920
Stewart, AL:Oak 1989			Brecheen, NL:StL 1946
Moore, AL:Oak 1989			Burdette, NL:Mil 1957
Rijo, NL:Cin 1990			Gibson, NL:StL 1967
			Lolich, AL:Det 1968
			Johnson, NL:Ari 2001
Lost			
2 Sherdel, NL:StL 1928	2 By many players; Last:	3 Frazier, AL:NY 1981	3 Williams, AL:Chi 1919 (8g)
Lee, NL:Chi 1938	Hudson, NL:Phil 1983		2 By many players; Last:
Walters, NL:Cin 1939	Davis, AL:Oak 1988		Hershiser, AL:Clev 1997
Lemon, AL:Clev 1954			Brown, NL:Fla 1997
Ford, AL:NY 1963			Pettitte, AL:NY 2001
Drysdale, NL:LA 1966			
Garrelts, NL:SF 1989			
Stewart, AL:Oak 1990			

4 Games	5 Games	6 Games	7 Games
Innings			
18.0 Rudolph, NL:Bos 1914	27.0 Mathewson, NL:NY 1905	27.0 Mathewson. NL:NY 1911	44.0 Phillippe, NL:Pitt 1903 (8g)
Hoyt, AL:NY 1928	Coombs, AL:Phil 1910	Faber, AL:Chi 1917	32.0 Mullin, AL:Det 1909
Ruffing, AL:NY 1938		Vaughn, NL:Chi 1918	
Koufax, NL:LA 1963			
Runs			
11 Alexander, NL:StL 1928	16 Brown, NL:Chi 1910	10 Sallee, NL:NY 1917	19 Phillippe, NL:Pitt 1903 (8g)
Lemon, AL:Clev 1954		Ruffing, AL:NY 1936	17 Burdette, NL:Mil 1958
		Gullett, AL:NY 1977	
		Sutton, NL:LA 1978	
		Morris, AL:Tor 1992	
Hits			
17 Ruffing, AL:NY 1938	23 Coombs, AL:Phil 1910	25 Mathewson, NL:NY 1911	38 Phillippe, NL:Pitt 1903 (8g)
	Brown, NL:Chi 1910		30 Johnson, AL:Wash 1924
Home Runs			
4 Sherdel, NL:StL 1928	4 Nolan, NL:Cin 1970	4 Reynolds, AL:NY 1953	5 Burdette, NL:Mil 1958
Root, NL:Chi 1932	Hudson, NL:Phil 1983		Hughes, NL:StL 1967
Thompson, NL:Cin 1939			
Garrelts, NL:SF 1989			
Walks			
8 Lemon, AL:Clev 1954	14 Coombs, AL:Phil 1910	11 Tyler, NL:Chi 1918	13 Nehf, NL:NY 1921 (8g)
		Gomez, AL:NY 1936	11 Johnson, AL:Wash 1924
		Reynolds, AL:NY 1951	Bevens, AL:NY 1947
Most Intentional Walks (since 1955)			
2 Brown, NL:SD 1998	3 Brosnan, NL:Cin 1961	2 By many players	3 Burdette, NL:Mil. 1958
			Pena, NL:Atl 1991
			Mussina, AL:NY 2001
Strikeouts			
23 Koufax, NL:LA 1963	18 Mathewson, NL:NY 1905	20 Bender, AL:Phil 1911	35 Gibson, NL:StL 1968

SERVICE

Most Series
11 Whitey Ford, AL:NY 1950,53,55-58,60-64

Most Series, Relief Pitcher
6 Johnny Murphy, AL:NY 1936-39,41,43

GAMES

Most Games
22 Whitey Ford, AL:NY 1950,53,55-58,60-64

Most Games, Relief Pitcher
20 Mike Stanton, NL:Atl. 1991-92; AL:NY 98-2001

Most Games, Consecutive
7 Darold Knowles, AL:Oak. 1973

GAMES STARTED

Most Games Started
22 Whitey Ford, AL:NY 1950,53,55-58,60-64

Most Games Started, Consecutive
22 Whitey Ford, AL:NY 1950,53,55-58,60-64

Most Opening Games Started
8 Whitey Ford, AL:NY 1955-58,61-64

COMPLETE GAMES

Most Complete Games
10 Christy Mathewson, NL:NY 1905,11-13

Most Complete Games, Consecutive
9 Chief Bender, AL:Phil. 1905,10-11,13

GAMES FINISHED

Most Games Finished
13 Mariano Rivera, AL:NY 1996, 98-2001

Most Games Finished, Consecutive
8 Johnny Murphy, AL:NY 1936-39,41,43
   Rich Gossage, AL:NY 1978,81; NL:SD 1984

SAVES (since 1969)

Most Saves
8 Mariano Rivera, AL:NY 1996, 98-2001

SHUTOUTS

Most Shutouts
4 Christy Mathewson, NL:NY 1905,13

Most Shutouts, Consecutive
3 Christy Mathewson, NL:NY 1905
   Whitey Ford, AL:NY 1960-61

Most Consecutive Scoreless Innings
   Complete game:
10 Christy Mathewson, NL:NY Oct. 8, 1913
   Clem Labine, NL:Brk. Oct. 9, 1956
   Jack Morris, AL:Minn. Oct. 27, 1991
   Game, consecutive:
13 Babe Ruth, AL:Bos. Oct. 9, 1916
   Consecutive:
33 Whitey Ford, AL:NY 1960-62

GAMES WON

Most Won
10 Whitey Ford, AL:NY 1950,53,55-58,60-64

Most Won, Consecutive
7 Bob Gibson, NL:StL. 1964,67-68

GAMES LOST

Most Lost
8 Whitey Ford, AL:NY 1950,53,55-58,60-64

Most Lost Consecutive
5 Joe Bush, AL:Phil. 1914; Bos. 18; NY 22-23

INNINGS PITCHED

Most Innings
146 Whitey Ford, AL:NY 1950,53,55-58,60-64

Most Innings, Game
14 Babe Ruth, AL:Bos. Oct. 9, 1916

RUNS

Most Runs
51 Whitey Ford, AL:NY 1950,53,55-58,60-64

Most Runs, Game
10 Brickyard Kennedy, NL:Pitt. Oct. 7, 1903

Most Runs, Inning
7 Hooks Wiltse, NL:NY Oct. 26, 1911 (7th)
   Carl Hubbell, NL:NY Oct. 6, 1937 (6th)

EARNED RUNS

Most Earned Runs
44 Whitey Ford, AL:NY 1950,53,59-58,60-64

Earned Runs, Game
8 Grover Alexander, NL:StL. Oct. 5, 1928
   Guy Bush, NL:Chi. Sept. 28, 1932
   Jay Witasick, AL:NY Nov. 3, 2001

Earned Runs, Inning
6 Bill Donovan, AL:Det. Oct. 11, 1908 (8th)
   Hooks Wiltse, NL:NY Oct. 26, 1911 (7th)
   Charlie Root, NL:Chi. Oct. 12, 1929 (7th)
   General Crowder, AL:Wash. Oct. 4, 1933 (6th)
   Harry Gumbert, NL:NY Oct. 2, 1936 (9th)
   Hank Borowy, AL:NY Oct. 4, 1942 (4th)
   Danny Cox, NL:StL. Oct. 18, 1987 (4th)
   Jay Witasick, AL:NY Nov. 3, 2001 (3rd)

HITS

Most Hits
132 Whitey Ford, AL:NY 1950,53,55-58,60-64

Most Hits, Game
15 Walter Johnson, AL:Wash. Oct. 15, 1925

Most Hits, Inning
8 Jay Witasick, AL:NY Nov. 3, 2001 (3rd)

Most Hits, Consecutive, Inning
6 Ed Summers, AL:Det. Oct. 10, 1908 (9th)

Most Hitless Innings, Consecutive
11.1 Don Larsen, AL:NY 1956-57

HOME RUNS

Most Home Runs
9 Catfish Hunter, AL:Oak. 1972-74; NY 76-78

Most Home Runs, Game
4 Charlie Root, NL:Chi. Oct. 1, 1932
Junior Thompson, NL:Cin. Oct. 7, 1939
Dick Hughes, NL:StL. Oct. 11, 1967

Most Home Runs, Inning
3 Dick Hughes, NL:StL. Oct. 11, 1967 (4th)

Most Home Runs, Consecutive, Inning
2 By many pitchers, Last:
David Wells, AL:NY Oct. 17, 1998 (5th)

Most Grand Slam Home Runs
1 By many pitchers. See Batter's record.

WALKS

Most Walks
34 Whitey Ford, AL:NY 1950,53,55-58,60-64

Most Walks, Game
10 Bill Bevens, AL:NY Oct. 3, 1947

Most Walks, Inning
4 Wild Bill Donovan, AL:Det. Oct. 16, 1909 (2nd)
Art Reinhart, NL:StL. Oct. 6, 1926 (5th)
Paul Derringer, NL:StL. Oct. 9, 1931 (5th)
Guy Bush, NL:Chi. Sept. 28, 1932 (6th)
Don Gullett, NL:Cin. Oct. 22, 1975 (3rd)
Bobby Castillo, NL:LA Oct. 20, 1981 (4th)
Tom Glavine, NL:Atl. Oct. 25, 1991 (6th)
Todd Stottlemyre, AL:Tor. Oct. 20, 1993 (1st)
Al Leiter, NL:Fla. Oct. 21, 1997 (4th)
Consecutive:
3 By many players; Last:
Charles Nagy, AL:Clev. Oct. 21, 1997 (3rd)

Most Intentional Walks (since 1955)
4 By many pitchers

HIT BATTERS

Most Hit Batters
4 Wild Bill Donovan, AL:Det. 1907,09
Eddie Plank, AL:Phil. 1905,11,13-14

Most Hit Batters, Game
3 Bruce Kison, NL:Pitt. Oct. 13, 1971

Most Hit Batters, Inning
2 Ed Willett, AL:Det. Oct. 11, 1909 (2nd)
Wayne Granger, NL:StL. Oct. 9, 1968 (8th)

STRIKEOUTS

Most Strikeouts
94 Whitey Ford, AL:NY 1950,53,55-58,60-64

Most Strikeouts, Game
17 Bob Gibson, NL:StL. Oct. 2, 1968
Relief pitcher:
11 Moe Drabowsky, AL:Balt. Oct. 5, 1966 (6.2 inn)

Most Strikeouts, Inning
4 Orval Overall, NL:Chi. Oct. 14, 1908 (1st)

Most Strikeouts, Consecutive Batters Faced
6 Hod Eller, NL:Cin. Oct. 6, 1919
Moe Drabowsky, AL:Balt. Oct. 5, 1966
Todd Worrell, NL:StL. Oct. 24, 1985

Most Strikeouts, Consecutive, Start of Game:
5 Mort Cooper, NL:StL. Oct. 11, 1943
Sandy Koufax, NL:LA, Oct. 2, 1963

WILD PITCHES

Most Wild Pitches
5 Hal Schumacher, NL:NY 1933,36-37
Jack Morris, AL:Det. 1984; Minn. 91; Tor. 92

Most Wild Pitches, Game
2 Jeff Tesreau, NL:NY Oct. 15, 1912
Jeff Pfeffer, NL:Brk. Oct. 12, 1916
Bob Shawkey, AL:NY Oct. 5, 1922
Vic Aldridge, NL:Pitt. Oct. 15, 1925
Johnny Miljus, NL:Pitt. Oct. 8, 1927
Tex Carleton, NL:Chi. Oct. 9, 1938
Glendon Rusch, NL:NY Oct. 21, 2000
Jim Bouton, AL:NY Oct. 5, 1963
John Stuper, NL:StL. Oct. 13, 1982
Doc Medich, AL:Mil. Oct. 19, 1982
Jack Morris, AL:Det. Oct. 13, 1984
Ron Darling, NL:NY Oct. 18, 1986
Mike Moore, AL:Oak. Oct. 15, 1989
Jack Morris, AL:Minn. Oct. 23, 1991
John Smoltz, NL:Atl. Oct. 18, 1992

Most Wild Pitches, Inning
2 Bob Shawkey, AL:NY Oct. 5, 1922 (5th)
Vic Aldridge, NL:Pitt. Oct. 15, 1925 (1st)
Johnny Miljus, NL:Pitt. Oct. 8, 1927 (9th)
Tex Carleton, NL:Chi. Oct. 9, 1938 (8th)
Doc Medich, AL:Mil. Oct. 19, 1982 (6th)

BALKS

1912	Oct	14	AL:Bos	O'Brien, Buck
1919	Oct.	2	NL:Cin.	Sallee, Slim
1925	Oct.	8	NL:Pitt.	Aldridge, Vic
1926	Oct.	6	NL:StL.	Bell, Hi
1935	Oct.	5	NL:Chi.	Carleton, Tex
1947	Sept.	30	AL:NY	Shea, Spec
1948	Oct.	10	AL:Clev.	Paige, Satchel
1948	Oct.	11	AL:Clev.	Lemon, Bob
1952	Oct.	6	NL:Brk.	Loes, Billy
1953	Oct.	2	AL:NY	Raschi, Vic
1965	Oct.	7	NL:LA	Perranoski, Ron
1967	Oct.	4	AL:Bos.	Wyatt, Whitlow
1975	Oct.	11	AL:Bos.	Tiant, Luis
1979	Oct.	12	AL:Balt.	McGregor, Scott
1982	Oct.	19	AL:Mil.	Sutton, Don
1983	Oct.	15	AL:Balt.	Stewart, Sammy
1984	Oct.	10	AL:Det.	Petry, Dan
1985	Oct.	22	NL:StL.	Horton, Ricky
1987	Oct.	20	AL:Minn.	Straker, Les
1987	Oct.	22	AL:Minn.	Atherton, Keith
1988	Oct.	15	AL:Oak.	Stewart, Dave
1988	Oct.	18	NL:LA	Leary, Tim
1989	Oct.	27	NL:SF	Brantley, Jeff
1991	Oct.	20	NL:Atl.	Glavine, Tom
1993	Oct.	17	AL:Tor.	Stewart, Dave
1995	Oct.	25	NL:Atl.	Avery, Steve
1996	Oct.	23	AL:NY	Weathers, David

CLUB BATTING – SERIES

BATTING AVERAGE

4 Games	5 Games	6 Games	7 Games
Highest Batting Average, Winning Club			
.317 NL:Cin (Oak) 1990	.316 AL:Phil (Chi) 1910	.311 AL:Tor (Phil) 1993	.323 NL:Pitt (Balt) 1979
Highest Batting Average, Losing Club			
.253 NL:Chi (NY) 1932	.265 NL:SD (Det) 1984	.300 NL:Brk (NY) 1953	.338 AL:NY (Pitt) 1960
Highest Batting Average, Both Clubs			
.283 AL:NY (Chi) 1932	.272 AL:Phil (Chi) 1910	.292 AL:Tor (Phil) 1993	.300 AL:NY (Pitt) 1960
Lowest Batting Average, Winning Club			
.200 AL:Balt (LA) 1966	.209 NL:NY (Phil) 1905	.186 AL:Bos (Chi) 1918	.199 AL:NY (SF) 1962
Lowest Batting Average, Losing Club			
.142 NL:LA (Balt) 1966	.146 AL:Balt (NY) 1969	.175 NL:NY (Phil) 1911	.183 AL:NY (Ari) 2001
Lowest Batting Average, Both Clubs			
.171 NL:LA (Balt) 1966	.184 AL:Balt (NY) 1969	.197 AL:Chi (Chi) 1906	.209 AL:Oak (Cin) 1972

SLUGGING PERCENTAGE

4 Games	5 Games	6 Games	7 Games
Highest Slugging Percentage, Winning Club			
.582 AL:Oak (SF) 1989	.509 AL:Balt (Cin) 1970	.510 AL:Tor (Phil) 1993	.438 NL:Pitt (Bal) 1979
Highest Slugging Percentage, Losing Club			
.397 NL:Chi (NY) 1932	.361 NL:SD (Det) 1984	.484 NL:Brk (NY) 1953	.528 AL:NY (Pitt) 1960
Highest Slugging Percentage, Both Clubs			
.468 AL:Oak (SF) 1989	.433 AL:Balt (Cin) 1970	.483 NL:Brk (NY) 1953	.447 AL:NY (Pitt) 1960
Lowest Slugging Percentage, Winning Club			
.304 AL:NY (Phil) 1950	.255 NL:NY (Phil) 1905	.233 AL:Bos (Chi) 1918	.276 AL:NY (SF) 1962
Lowest Slugging Percentage, Losing Club			
.192 NL:LA (Balt) 1966	.194 AL:Phil (NY) 1905	.243 NL:NY (Phil) 1911	.237 NL:Brk (Clev) 1920
Lowest Slugging Percentage, Both Clubs			
.267 AL:Balt (LA) 1966	.224 NL:NY (Phil) 1905	.241 NL:Chi (Bos) 1918	.285 AL:Clev (Brk) 1920

AT-BATS

4 Games	5 Games	6 Games	7 Games
Most At-Bats			
146 NL:Chi (NY) 1932	179 AL:NY 2000	222 AL:NY (LA) 1978	282 AL:Bos (Pitt) 1903 (8g)
AL:Oak (SF) 1989			269 AL:NY (Pitt) 1960
Most At-Bats, Both Clubs			
290 NL:Chi (NY) 1932	354 AL:NY (NY) 2000	421 AL:NY (LA) 1978	552 AL:Bos (Pitt) 1903 (8g)
			512 NL:StL. (Det.) 1934
Fewest At-Bats			
117 NL:LA (NY) 1963	142 AL:Oak (LA) 1974	172 AL:Bos (Chi) 1918	215 NL:Brk (Clev) 1920
			NL:Brk (NY) 1956
			AL:Minn (LA) 1965
Fewest At-Bats, Both Clubs			
240 AL:Balt (LA) 1966	300 AL:Oak (LA) 1974	348 NL:Chi (Bos) 1918	432 AL:Clev (Brk) 1920

RUNS

4 Games	5 Games	6 Games	7 Games
Most Runs			
37 AL:NY (Chi) 1932	35 AL:Phil (Chi) 1910	45 AL:Tor (Phil) 1993	55 AL:NY (Pitt) 1960
Most Runs, Losing Club			
19 NL:Chi (NY) 1932	20 NL:Cin (Balt) 1970	36 NL:Phil (Tor) 1993	55 AL:NY (Pitt) 1960
Most Runs, Both Clubs			
56 AL:NY (Chi) 1932	53 AL:Balt (Cin) 1970	81 AL:Tor (Phil) 1993	82 AL:NY (Pitt) 1960
Fewest Runs			
2 NL:LA (Balt) 1966	3 AL:Phil (NY) 1905	9 AL:Bos (Chi) 1918	8 NL:Brk (Clev) 1920
Fewest Runs, Both Clubs			
15 AL:Balt (LA) 1966	18 NL:NY (Phil) 1905	19 NL:Chi (Bos) 1918	29 AL:Clev (Brk) 1920

HITS

4 Games	5 Games	6 Games	7 Games
Most Hits			
45 AL:NY (Chi) 1932 NL:Cin (Oak) 1990	56 AL:Phil (Chi) 1910	68 AL:NY (LA) 1978	91 AL:NY (Pitt) 1960
Most Hits, Both Clubs			
82 AL:NY (Chi) 1932	91 AL:Phil (Chi) 1910 AL:Phil (Chi) 1929	122 AL:Tor (Phil) 1993	151 AL:NY (Pitt) 1960
Fewest Hits			
17 NL:LA (Balt) 1966	23 AL:Balt (NY) 1969	32 AL:Bos (Chi) 1918	40 NL:StL (KC) 1985
Fewest Hits, Both Clubs			
41 AL:Balt (LA) 1966	57 NL:NY (Phil) 1905	69 NL:Chi (Bos) 1918	92 AL:Oak (Cin) 1972

EXTRA-BASE HITS

Most Extra-Base Hits			
20 AL:Oak (SF) 1989	21 AL:Phil (Chi) 1910	24 AL:Tor (Phil) 1993	27 AL:NY (Pitt) 1960
Most Extra-Base Hits, Both Clubs			
29 AL:Oak (SF) 1989	33 AL:Phil (Chi) 1910	41 NL:Brk (NY) 1953	42 AL:NY (Pitt) 1960 NL:StL (Mil) 1982 NL:Atl (Minn) 1991
Fewest Extra-Base Hits			
4 NL:Cin (NY) 1939 NL:LA (Balt) 1966	3 AL:Det (Chi) 1907	5 AL:Bos (Chi) 1918	6 NL:Brk (Clev) 1920
Fewest Extra-Base Hits, Both Club			
12 AL:Balt (LA) 1966	10 NL:Chi (Det) 1907	11 NL:Chi (Bos) 1918	19 AL:Clev (Brk) 1920

TOTAL BASES

Most Total Bases			
85 AL:Oak (SF) 1989	87 AL:Balt (Cin) 1970	105 AL:Tor (Phil) 1993	142 AL:NY (Pitt) 1960
Most Total Bases, Both Clubs			
133 AL:NY (Chi) 1932	145 AL:Balt (Cin) 1970	200 NL:Brk (NY) 1953	225 AL:NY (Pitt) 1960
Fewest Total Bases			
23 NL:LA (Balt) 1966	30 AL:Phil (NY) 1905	40 AL:Bos (Chi) 1918	51 NL:Brk (Clev) 1920
Fewest Total Bases, Both Clubs			
64 AL:Balt (LA) 1966	69 NL:NY (Phil) 1905	84 NL:Chi (Bos) 1918	123 AL:Clev (Brk) 1920

SINGLES

Most Singles			
32 AL:NY (SD) 1998	46 NL:NY (NY) 1922	57 AL:NY (LA) 1978	64 AL:NY (Pitt) 1960
Most Singles, Both Clubs			
55 AL:NY (Chi) 1932	71 NL:Chi (Phil) 1929	95 AL:NY (LA) 1978	109 AL:NY (Pitt) 1960
Fewest Singles			
13 AL:Phil (Bos) 1914 NL:LA (Balt) 1966	19 NL:Brk (NY) 1941 AL:Balt (NY) 1969	17 AL:Phil (StL) 1930	27 AL:Minn (LA) 1965 NL:StL (KC) 1985
Fewest Singles, Both Clubs			
29 AL:Balt (LA) 1966	40 NL:NY (Balt) 1969	42 NL:StL (Phil) 1930	66 NL:StL (Bos) 1967

DOUBLES

	4 Games	5 Games	6 Games	7 Games
Most Doubles	10 NL:Cin (NY) 1976	19 AL:Phil (Chi) 1910	15 AL:Phil (NY) 1911	19 NL:StL (Bos) 1946
Most Doubles, Both Clubs	15 AL:Phil (Bos) 1914	30 AL:Phil (Chi) 1910	26 AL:Phil (NY) 1911	29 AL:Det (Pitt) 1909
Fewest Doubles	3 By many clubs	1 AL:Det (Chi) 1907 AL:Balt (NY) 1969	2 AL:Bos (Chi) 1918 NL:NY (NY) 1923	3 AL:Balt (Pitt) 1971
Fewest Doubles, Both Clubs	6 NL:LA (NY) 1963 AL:Balt (LA) 1966	6 NL:Phil (Bos) 1915	7 NL:Chi (Bos) 1918	11 AL:Bos (Pitt) 1903 (8g) NL:StL (Det) 1968

TRIPLES

	4 Games	5 Games	6 Games	7 Games
Most Triples	3 NL:Cin (NY) 1976 AL:Oak (SF) 1989	6 AL:Bos (Brk) 1916	5 AL:Tor (Phil) 1993	16 AL:Bos (Pitt) 1903 (8g) 5 NL:StL (Det) 1934 AL:NY (Brk) 1947
Most Triples, Both Clubs	4 NL:Cin (NY) 1976 AL:Oak (SF) 1989	11 AL:Bos (Brk) 1916	7 AL:NY (NY) 1923 AL:Tor (Phil) 1993	25 AL:Bos (Pitt) 1903 (8g) 8 AL:Minn (Atl) 1991
Fewest Triples	0 By many	0 By many	0 By many	0 By many
Fewest Triples, Both Clubs	1 NL:StL (NY) 1928 AL:Clev (NY) 1954 AL:Balt (LA) 1966 AL:NY (SD) 1998 AL:NY (Atl.) 1999	0 NL:NY (Phil) 1905 NL:NY (Wash) 1933 NL:NY (Balt) 1969 NL:SD (Det) 1984	0 AL:Clev (Bos) 1948 AL:NY (LA) 1978 AL:Tor (Atl) 1992	0 NL:StL (Phil) 1931 AL:NY (Ari) 2001

HOME RUNS

	4 Games	5 Games	6 Games	7 Games
Most Home Runs	9 AL:NY (StL) 1928 AL:Oak (SF) 1989	10 AL:Balt (Cin) 1970	9 AL:NY (Brk) 1953 NL:LA (NY) 1977	12 AL:NY (Brk) 1956
Most Home Runs, Both Clubs	13 AL:Oak (SF) 1989	15 AL:Balt (Cin) 1970	17 AL:NY (Brk) 1953 NL:LA (NY) 1977	17 NL:Brk (NY) 1955
Fewest Home Runs	0 By many	0 By many	0 By many	0 NL:Cin (Chi) 1919 (8g) NL:Brk (Clev) 1920
Fewest Home Runs, Both Clubs	1 NL:Bos (Phil) 1914	0 NL:NY (Phil) 1905 NL:Chi (Det) 1907	0 AL:Chi (Chi) 1906 AL:Bos (Chi) 1918	1 AL:Chi (Cin) 1919 (8g)

RUNS BATTED IN

	4 Games	5 Games	6 Games	7 Games
Most Runs Batted In	36 AL:NY (Chi) 1932	32 AL:Balt (Cin) 1970	45 AL:Tor (Phil) 1993	54 AL:NY (Pitt) 1960
Most Runs Batted In, Both Clubs	52 AL:NY (Chi) 1932	52 AL:Balt (Cin) 1970	80 AL:Tor (Phil) 1993	80 AL:NY (Pitt) 1960
Fewest Runs Batted In	2 NL:LA (Balt) 1966	2 AL:Phil (NY) 1905	6 AL:Bos (Chi) 1918	8 NL:Brk (Clev) 1920
Fewest Runs Batted In, Both Clubs	12 NL:LA (Balt) 1966	15 AL: Phil (NY) 1905	16 AL:Bos (Chi) 1918	25 NL:Brk (Clev) 1920

SACRIFICE HITS

4 Games	5 Games	6 Games	7 Games
Most Sacrifice Hits			
6 By many	12 AL:Bos (Brk) 1916	13 NL:Chi (Chi) 1906	13 NL:Cin (Chi) 1919 (8g)
			12 NL:Pitt (Det) 1909
			NL:StL (NY) 1926
Most Sacrifice Hits, Both Clubs			
12 AL:NY (Pitt) 1927	18 AL:Bos (Brk) 1916	19 NL:Chi (Chi) 1906	22 NL:StL (NY) 1926
Fewest Sacrifice Hits			
0 By many	0 By many	0 NL:NY (NY) 1923	0 NL:StL (Bos) 1967
		AL:NY (NY) 1951	
		NL:LA (NY) 1977	
		AL:Tor (Phil) 1993	
		AL:Clev (Atl) 1995	
Fewest Sacrifice Hits, Both Clubs			
0 NL:Cin (NY) 1976	0 AL:NY (Brk) 1941	1 AL:Tor (Phil) 1993	2 NL:StL (Mil) 1982
AL:Oak (SF) 1989	AL:Balt (Phil) 1983		

SACRIFICE FLIES (Since 1954)

Most Sacrifice Flies			
2 NL:NY (Clev) 1954	3 AL:Balt (Phil) 1983	7 AL:Tor (Phil) 1993	5 NL:Pitt (Balt) 1979
NL:Cin (NY) 1976	NL:SD (Det) 1984		
NL:SD (NY) 1998	AL:NY (NY) 2000		
Most Sacrifice Flies, Both Clubs			
3 NL:Cin (NY) 1976	5 NL:SD (Det) 1984	8 AL:Tor (Phil) 1993	5 NL:Brk (NY) 1956
AL:NY (SD) 1998			NL:Mil (NY) 1958
			AL:Bos (Cin) 1975
			AL:Balt. (Pitt) 1979
			NL:Atl (Minn) 1991
			NL:Fla. (Clev.) 1997
Fewest Sacrifice Flies			
0 By many	0 By many	0 By many	0 By many
Fewest Sacrifice Flies, Both Clubs			
0 AL:Balt (LA) 1966	1 NL:Cin (NY) 1961	0 AL:NY (LA) 1978	0 AL:Minn (LA) 1965
AL:NY (Atl.) 1999	AL:Balt (Cin) 1970		AL:KC (StL) 1985
	NL:LA (Oak) 1988		

WALKS

Most Walks			
23 AL:NY (Chi) 1932	25 AL:NY (NY) 2000	34 NL:Phil (Tor) 1993	40 AL:Clev. (Fla) 1997
Most Walks, Both Clubs			
34 AL:NY (Chi) 1932	37 AL:NY (Brk) 1941	59 NL:Phil (Tor) 1993	76 AL:Clev. (Fla) 1997
Fewest Walks			
4 NL:Pitt (NY) 1927	5 AL:Phil (NY) 1905	4 AL:Phil (NY)1911	9 NL:StL (Phil) 1931
Fewest Walks, Both Clubs			
15 AL:NY (Cin) 1939	15 NL:NY (Phil) 1913	17 AL:Chi (NY) 1917	27 AL:Bos (Pitt) 1903 (8g)
Most Intentional Walks			
4 NL:NY (Clev) 1954	7 AL:NY (NY) 2000	7 AL:NY (LA) 1981	8 NL:Cin (Oak) 1972

HIT BY PITCH

4 Games	5 Games	6 Games	7 Games
Most Hit By Pitch			
4 AL:NY (Chi) 1932	4 NL:Chi (Det) 1907	4 AL:NY (Brk) 1953	6 NL:Pitt (Det) 1909
			NL:Ari (NY) 2001
Most Hit By Pitch, Both Clubs			
4 AL:NY (Chi) 1932	6 AL:NY (NY) 2000	6 AL:NY (Brk) 1953	10 NL:Pitt (Det) 1909
Fewest Hit By Pitch			
0 By many	0 By many	0 By many	0 By many
Fewest Hit By Pitch, Both Clubs			
0 NL:LA (Balt) 1966	0 AL:Wash (NY) 1933	0 AL:StL (StL) 1944	0 AL:Clev (Brk) 1920
AL:NY (Atl.) 1999	AL:NY (StL) 1942-43		AL:Det (Cin) 1940
	AL:Balt (Cin) 1970		AL:NY (Brk) 1956
			AL:NY (Mil) 1958

STRIKEOUTS

4 Games	5 Games	6 Games	7 Games
Most Strikeouts			
37 AL:NY (LA) 1963	50 NL:Chi (Phil) 1929	50 NL:Phil (Tor) 1993	70 NL:Ari (NY) 2001
Most Strikeouts, Both Clubs			
62 AL:NY (LA) 1963	88 AL:NY (NY) 2000	92 AL:StL (StL) 1944	133 AL:NY (Ari) 2001
Fewest Strikeouts			
7 NL:Pitt (NY) 1927	15 NL:NY (NY) 1922	14 NL:Chi (Bos) 1918	20 NL:Brk (Clev) 1920
Fewest Strikeouts, Both Clubs			
32 AL:NY (Pitt) 1927	35 NL:NY(Phil) 1913	35 AL:Bos (Chi) 1918	41 AL:Clev (Brk) 1920
NL:Cin (NY) 1976	AL:NY (NY) 1922		

STOLEN BASES

4 Games	5 Games	6 Games	7 Games
Most Stolen Bases			
9 NL:Bos (Phil) 1914	18 NL:Chi (Det) 1907	15 NL:Atl (Tor) 1992	18 NL:Pitt (Det) 1909
Most Stolen Bases, Both Clubs			
11 NL:Bos (Phil) 1914	26 NL:Chi (Det) 1907	20 NL:Atl (Tor) 1992	24 NL:Pitt (Det) 1909
Fewest Stolen Bases			
0 By many	0 By many	0 By many	0 By many
Fewest Stolen Bases, Both Clubs			
1 NL:Cin (NY) 1939	1 NL:Chi (Phil) 1929	0 NL:StL (StL) 1944	1 NL:Cin (Det) 1940
NL:NY (Clev) 1954	AL:Wash (NY) 1933		
NL:LA (Balt) 1966	NL:NY (NY) 1937		
	AL:NY (Cin) 1961		
	NL:Cin (Balt) 1970		
	AL:NY (NY) 2000		

CAUGHT STEALING

4 Games	5 Games	6 Games	7 Games
Most Caught Stealing			
5 NL:Cin (NY) 1976	8 NL:Chi (Phil) 1910	10 NL:NY (Phil) 1911	10 NL:Cin (Chi) 1919 (8g)
			8 NL:StL. (Det) 1968
Most Caught Stealing, Both Clubs			
7 NL:Cin (NY) 1976	15 NL:Chi (Phil) 1910	16 NL:NY (Phil) 1911	15 AL:Chi (Cin) 1919 (8g)
			AL:NY (NY) 1921 (8g)
			10 NL:Pitt (Det) 1909
			AL:Det (StL) 1968
Fewest Caught Stealing (Most Attempts)			
0 AL:Oak (Cin) 1990 (7)	0 AL:NY (StL) 1942 (3)	0 AL:Tor (Atl) 1992 (5)	0 AL:Minn (StL) 1987 (6)
	AL:Oak (LA) 1988 (3)		
Fewest Caught Stealing, Both Clubs (Most Attempts)			
0 AL:NY (Pitt) 1927 (2)	0 AL:NY (Brk) 1949 (3)	0 NL:Bos (Clev) 1948 (3)	0 AL:NY (StL) 1964 (5)

LEFT ON BASE

4 Games	5 Games	6 Games	7 Games

Most Left on Base

37 AL:Clev (NY) 1954	52 AL:NY (NY) 2000	55 AL:NY (LA) 1981	72 NL:NY (Oak) 1973

Most Left on Base, Both Clubs

65 AL:Clev (NY) 1954	88 AL:NY (NY) 2000	101 AL:NY (LA) 1981	130 NL:NY (Oak) 1973

Fewest Left on Base

16 NY (Cin) 1939	23 NL:Phil (Bos) 1915 NL:Phil (Balt) 1983	29 AL:Phil (NY) 1911	36 AL:Minn (LA 1965

Most Left on Base, Both Clubs

65 AL:Clev (NY) 1954	88 AL:NY (NY) 2000	101 AL:NY (LA) 1981	130 NL:NY (Oak) 1973

Fewest Left on Base, Both Clubs

39 NL:Cin (NY) 1939	51 NL:Phil (Balt) 1983	61 NL:NY (Phil) 1911	82 AL:Clev (Brk) 1920 NL:Brk (NY) 1956 AL:NY (SF) 1962

PINCH-HITTING

Most Pinch-Hitters

16 AL:Clev (NY) 1954	15 NL:Cin (NY) 1961	14 NL:LA (NY) 1981	23 AL:Balt (Pitt) 1979

Most Pinch-Hitters, Both Clubs

19 AL:Clev (NY) 1954	23 AL:Balt (Phil) 1983	24 NL:LA (NY) 1981	37 AL:Minn (Atl) 1991

Fewest Pinch-Hitters

0 AL:NY (Cin) 1939 AL:Balt (LA) 1966 NL:Cin (NY) 1976	0 AL:Phil (Chi) 1910 AL:Phil (NY) 1913	0 AL:Phil (NY) 1911	1 NL:Pitt (Bos) 1903 (8g)

Fewest Pinch-Hitters, Both Clubs

3 NL:Cin (NY) 1939	2 NL:NY (Phil) 1905	6 NL:NY (Phil) 1911 AL:Chi (Chi) 1906	5 AL:Bos (Pitt) 1903 (8g) AL:NY (NY) 1921 (8g)

PINCH-RUNNING

Most Pinch-Runners

4 NL:Phil (NY) 1950	5 NL:NY (Phil) 1913	5 AL:NY (LA) 1981	8 AL:Oak (Cin) 1972

Most Pinch-Runners, Both Clubs

6 NL:Phil (NY) 1950	6 AL:Oak (LA) 1974 AL:Balt (Phil) 1983	7 AL:NY (LA) 1981	10 AL:Oak (Cin) 1972

Fewest Pinch-Runners

0 By many	0 By many	0 By many	0 By many

Fewest Pinch-Runners, Both Clubs

0 AL:NY (Chi) 1938 NL:LA (NY) 1963 NL:Cin (NY) 1976 AL:Oak (SF) 1989	0 NL:NY (Phil) 1905 AL:Phil (Chi) 1929 AL:NY (NY) 1937 AL:Balt (Cin) 1970	0 AL:Chi (NY) 1917 AL:Phil (StL) 1930 AL:Det (Chi) 1935 AL:NY (Brk) 1953	0 AL:Bos (Pitt) 1903 (8g) AL:NY (Brk) 1956 NL:Cin (Bos) 1975

AT-BATS

Most At-Bats, Game
46 NL:Ari. (NY) Nov. 3, 2001
   Extra-Inning Game:
54 NL:NY (Oak.) Oct. 14, 1973 (12)
   Fewest, 9-Inning Game:
23 NL:Cin. (Chi.) Oct. 2, 1919

Most At-Bats, Both Clubs, Game
   Most, 9 innings:
85 AL:Tor. (Phil.) Oct. 20, 1993
   Extra-Inning Game:
101 NL:NY (Oak.) Oct. 14, 1973 (12)
   Fewest, 9-Inning Game:
53 NL:Brk. (Clev.) Oct. 7, 1920
   AL:NY (NY) Oct. 6, 1921
   AL:NY (Brk.) Oct. 8, 1956
   NL:LA (NY) Oct. 5, 1963

Most At-Bats, Inning
13 AL:Phil. (Chi.) Oct. 12, 1929 (7th)

Most At-Bats, Both Clubs, Inning
17 AL:Phil. (Chi.) Oct. 12, 1929 (7th)

RUNS

Most Runs, Game
18 AL:NY (NY) Oct. 2, 1936

Most Earned Runs, Game
17 AL:NY (NY) Oct. 2, 1936

Most Runs, Both Clubs, Game
29 AL:Tor. (Phil.) Oct. 20, 1993

Most Runs, Inning
10 AL:Phil. (Chi.) Oct. 12, 1929 (7th)
   AL:Det. (StL.) Oct. 9, 1968 (3rd)

Most Runs, Both Clubs, Inning
11 AL:Phil. (Chi.) Oct. 12, 1929 (7th)
   NL:Brk. (NY) Oct. 5, 1956 (2nd)
   NL:Fla. (Clev.) Oct. 21, 1997 (9th)

Most innings Scoring a Run, Game
6 AL:NY (StL.) Oct. 6, 1926
   AL:NY (Brk.) Oct. 1, 1947
   AL:NY (Pitt.) Oct. 6, 1960
   NL:Phil. (Tor.) Oct. 20, 1993
   NL:Fla. (Clev.) Oct. 21, 1997

Most innings Scoring a Run, Both Clubs, Game
10 NL:Phil. (Tor.) Oct. 20, 1993
   NL:Fla. (Clev.) Oct. 21, 1997

Most Earned Runs, Both Clubs, Game
29 AL:Tor. (Phil.) Oct. 20, 1993

Most Runs, Each Inning, Club
7 1st: NL:Mil. (NY) Oct. 2, 1958
6 2nd: AL:NY (NY) Oct. 13, 1923
          NL:NY (NY) Oct. 9, 1937
          NL:Brk. (NY) Oct. 2, 1947
          NL:Brk. (NY) Oct. 5, 1956
10 3rd: AL:Det. (StL.) Oct. 9, 1968
7 4th: AL:Minn. (StL.) Oct. 17, 1987
6 5th: AL:Balt. (Pitt.) Oct. 11, 1971
          AL:KC (StL.) Oct. 27, 1985
7 6th: AL:NY (NY) Oct. 6, 1937
          AL:NY (Pitt.) Oct. 6, 1960
10 7th: AL:Phil. (Chi.) Oct. 12, 1929
6 8th: NL:Chi. (Det.) Oct. 11, 1908
          AL:Balt. (Pitt.) Oct. 13, 1979
          AL:Tor. (Phil.) Oct. 20, 1993
7 9th: AL:NY (NY) Oct. 6, 1936
          NL:Fla. (Clev.) Oct. 21, 1997
3 10th: NL:NY (Phil.) Oct. 8, 1913
          AL:NY (Cin.) Oct. 8, 1939
          NL:NY (Clev.) Sept. 29, 1954
          NL:Mil. (NY) Oct. 6, 1957
          NL:StL. (NY) Oct. 12, 1964
          NL:NY (Bos.) Oct. 25, 1986
2 11th: AL:Phil. (NY) Oct. 17, 1911
          AL:Tor. (Atl.) Oct. 24, 1992
4 12th: NL:NY (Oak.) Oct. 14, 1973
0 13th: No runs scored
1 14th: AL:Bos. (Brk.) Oct. 9, 1916

HITS

Most Hits, Game
22 NL:Ari. (NY) Nov. 3, 2001

Most Hits, Both Clubs, Game
32 AL:NY (Pitt.) Oct. 6, 1960
   AL:Tor. (Phil.) Oct. 20, 1993

Most Hits, Inning
10 AL:Phil. (Chi.) Oct. 12, 1929 (7th)

Most Hits, Both Clubs, Inning
12 AL:Phil. (Chi.) Oct. 12, 1929 (7th)

Most Hits, Consecutive, Inning
6 NL:Chi. (Det.) Oct. 10, 1908 (9th)

Most Hitless Innings, Consecutive
11 NL:Cin. (NY) Oct. 4-5, 1939
   Complete game:
9 NL:Brk. (NY) Oct. 8, 1956

EXTRA-BASE HITS

Most Extra-Base Hits, Game
9 NL:Pitt. (Wash.) Oct. 15, 1925

Most Extra-Base Hits, Both Clubs, Game
13 NL:Phil. (Tor.) Oct. 20, 1993

Most Extra-Base Hits, Inning
4 AL:Chi. (LA) Oct. 1, 1959 (3rd)
   AL:NY (Cin.) Oct. 9, 1961 (1st)
   AL:KC (Phil.) Oct. 18, 1980 (1st)

TOTAL BASES

Most Total Bases, Game
34 NL:Atl. (Minn.) Oct. 24, 1991

Most Total Bases, Both Clubs, Game
53 NL:Phil. (Tor.) Oct. 20, 1993

Most Total Bases, Inning
17 AL:Phil. (Chi.) Oct. 12, 1929 (7th)

Most Total Bases, Both Clubs, Inning
21 AL:Phil. (Chi.) Oct. 12, 1929 (7th)

SINGLES

Most Singles, Game
16 AL:NY (LA) Oct. 15, 1978
NL:Ari. (NY) Nov. 3, 2001

Most Singles, Both Clubs, Game
24 AL:NY (LA) Oct. 15, 1978

Most Singles, Inning
7 AL:Phil. (Chi.) Oct. 12, 1929 (7th)
NL:NY (Wash.) Oct. 4, 1933 (6th)
NL:NY (NY) Oct. 9, 1937 (2nd)
NL:Brk. (NY) Oct. 8, 1949 (6th)

Most Singles, Both Clubs, Inning
8 AL:Phil. (Chi.) Oct. 12, 1929 (7th)
NL:NY (Wash.) Oct. 4, 1933 (6th)
NL:NY (NY) Oct. 9, 1937 (2nd)
NL:Brk. (NY) Oct. 8, 1949 (6th)

DOUBLES

Most Doubles, Game
8 AL:Chi. (Chi.) Oct. 13, 1906
NL:Pitt. (Wash.) Oct. 15, 1925

Most Doubles, Both Clubs, Game
11 AL:Chi. (Chi.) Oct. 13, 1906

Most Doubles, Inning
3 AL:Chi. (Chi.) Oct. 13, 1906 (4th)
AL:Phil. (Chi.) Oct. 18, 1910 (7th)
AL:Phil. (NY) Oct. 24, 1911 (4th)
NL:Pitt. (Wash.) Oct. 15, 1925 (8th)
NL:StL. (Det.) Oct. 9, 1934 (3rd)
NL:Brk. (NY) Oct. 2, 1947 (2nd)
NL:Brk. (NY) Oct. 5, 1947 (3rd)
AL:NY (Brk.) Oct. 8, 1949 (4th)
AL:Chi. (LA) Oct. 1, 1959 (3rd)
NL:Cin. (Balt.) Oct. 15, 1970 (1st)
NL:StL. (KC) Oct. 20, 1985 (9th)
NL:Ari. (NY) Nov. 3, 2001 (3rd)

TRIPLES

Most Triples, Game
5 AL:Bos. (Pitt.) Oct. 7, 10, 1903

Most Triples, Both Clubs, Game
7 AL:Bos. (Pitt.) Oct. 10, 1903

Most Triples, Inning
2 AL:Bos. (Pitt.) Oct. 1, 1903 (7th)
AL:Bos. (Pitt.) Oct. 7, 1903 (6th)
AL:Bos. (Pitt.) Oct. 10, 1903 (1st, 4th)
AL:Bos. (NY) Oct. 12, 1912 (3rd)
AL:Phil. (NY) Oct. 7, 1913 (4th)
AL:Bos. (Chi.) Sept. 6, 1918 (9th)
AL:NY (Brk.) Oct. 1, 1947 (3rd)
AL:NY (Brk.) Sept 30, 1953 (1st)
AL:Det. (StL.) Oct. 7, 1968 (4th)

HOME RUNS

Most Home Runs, Game
5 AL:NY (StL.) Oct. 9, 1928
AL:Oak. (SF) Oct. 27, 1989

Most Home Runs, Both Clubs, Game
7 AL:Oak. (SF) Oct. 27, 1989

Most Home Runs, Inning
3 AL:Bos. (StL.) Oct. 11, 1967 (4th)

Most Home Runs, Both Clubs, Inning
3 NL:NY (NY) Oct. 11, 1921 (2nd)
AL:Bos. (StL.) Oct. 11, 1967 (4th)

Most Home Runs, Consecutive, Inning
2 AL:Wash. (Pitt.) Oct. 11, 1925 (3rd)
AL:NY (StL.) Oct. 9, 1928 (7th)
AL:NY (Chi.) Oct. 1, 1932 (5th)
AL:NY (StL.) Oct. 14, 1964 (6th)
AL:Balt. (LA) Oct. 5, 1966 (1st)
AL:Bos. (StL.) Oct. 11, 1967 (4th)
NL:Cin. (Bos.) Oct. 14, 1975 (5th)
AL:NY (LA) Oct. 16, 1977 (8th)
NL:LA (NY) Oct. 25, 1981 (7th)
AL:Bos. (NY) Oct. 27, 1986 (2nd)
NL:Fla. (Clev.) Oct. 18, 1997 (4th)
NL:SD (NY) Oct. 17, 1998 (5th)

Most Consecutive Games with a Home Run
9 AL:NY 1932-37
AL:NY 1952-53
Games, One Series
7 AL:Wash. (Pitt.) 1925
AL:NY (Brk.) 1952

RUNS BATTED IN

Most Runs Batted In, Game
18 AL:NY (NY) Oct. 2, 1936

Most Runs Batted In, Both Clubs, Game
29 AL:Tor. (Phil.) Oct. 20, 1993

Most Runs Batted In, Inning
10 AL:Phil. (Chi.) Oct. 12, 1929 (7th)
AL:Det. (StL.) Oct. 9, 1968 (3rd)

Most Runs Batted In, Both Clubs, Inning
11 AL:Phil. (Chi.) Oct. 12, 1929 (7th)
NL:Brk. (NY) Oct. 5, 1956 (2nd)

SACRIFICE HITS

Most Sacrifice Hits, Game
5 NL:Chi. (Chi.) Oct. 12, 1906
NL:Chi. (Det.) Oct. 10, 1908
NL:Pitt. (Det.) Oct. 16, 1909

Most Sacrifice Hits, Both Clubs, Game
7 NL:Chi. (Det.) Oct. 10, 1908

Most Sacrifice Hits, Inning
2 By many clubs

Most Sacrifice Hits, Consecutive, Inning
2 By many clubs

SACRIFICE FLIES (Since 1954)

Most Sacrifice Flies, Game
3 AL:Tor. (Phil.) Oct. 19, 1993

Most Sacrifice Flies, Both Clubs, Game
3 AL:Tor. (Phil.) Oct. 19, 1993
   AL:Tor. (Phil.) Oct. 23, 1993
   AL:Clev. (Fla.) Oct. 25, 1997

Most Sacrifice Flies, Inning
2 AL:Balt. (Pitt.) Oct. 13, 1971 (1st)

Most Sacrifice Flies, Both Clubs, Inning
2 AL:Balt. (Pitt.) Oct. 13, 1971 (1st)
   AL:Det. (SD) Oct. 10, 1984 (1st)
   AL:Clev. (Fla.) Oct. 25, 1997 (5th)

Most Sacrifice Flies, Consecutive, Inning
2 AL:Balt. (Pitt.) Oct. 13, 1971 (1st)

WALKS

Most Walks, Game
11 NL:Brk. (NY) Oct. 5, 1956
    AL:NY (Mil.) Oct. 5, 1957
    AL:Det. (SD) Oct. 12, 1984

Most Walks, Both Clubs, Game
19 AL:NY (Mil.) Oct. 5, 1957

Most Walks, Inning
5 AL:NY (StL.) Oct. 6, 1926 (5th)

Most Walks, Both Clubs, Inning
6 AL:NY (NY) Oct. 7, 1921 (3rd)
   AL:NY (StL.) Oct. 6, 1926 (5th)
   NL:LA (NY) Oct. 28, 1981 (6th)
   NL:Phil. (Tor.) Oct. 20, 1993 (1st)

Fewest Walks, Both Clubs, Game
0 AL:Phil. (NY) Oct. 16, 1911
   NL:NY (Chi.) Oct. 10, 1917
   NL:NY (NY) Oct. 9, 1921
   AL:Bos. (StL.) Oct. 7, 1967
   NL:Phil. (Balt.) Oct. 11, 1983

HIT BY PITCH

Most Hit By Pitch, Game
3 AL:Det. (StL.) Oct. 9, 1968
   AL:Balt. (Pitt.) Oct. 13, 1971

Most Hit By Pitch, Both Clubs, Game
3 NL:Phil. (Bos.) Oct. 13, 1915
   NL:Cin. (Chi.) Oct. 9, 1919
   NL:Pitt. (Wash.) Oct. 7, 1925
   AL:Det. (StL.) Oct. 9, 1968
   AL:Balt. (Pitt.) Oct. 13, 1971
   NL:NY (Oak.) Oct. 14, 1973 (12 inn)
   AL:Minn. (StL.) Oct. 21, 1987

Most Hit By Pitch, Inning
2 NL:Pitt. (Det.) Oct. 11, 1909 (2nd)
   AL:Det. (StL.) Oct. 9, 1968 (8th)
   NL:Pitt. (Balt.) Oct. 17, 1979 (9th)

STRIKEOUTS

Most Strikeouts, Game
17 AL:Det. (StL.) Oct. 2, 1968

Most Strikeouts, Both Clubs, Game
25 AL:NY (LA) Oct. 2, 1963
    AL:Oak. (NY) Oct. 14, 1973 (12 inn)
    AL:NY (NY) Oct. 24, 2000

Most Strikeouts, Inning
4 AL:Det. (Chi.) Oct. 14, 1908 (1st)

Most Strikeouts, Both Clubs, Inning
6 NL:Cin. (Oak.) Oct. 18, 1972 (5th)
   AL:KC (StL.) Oct. 24, 1985 (7th)
   AL:NY (NY) Oct. 24, 2000 (2nd)

Most Strikeouts, Consecutive, Game
6 AL:Chi. (Cin.) Oct. 6, 1919
   AL:KC (StL.) Oct. 24, 1985
   NL:LA (Balt.) Oct. 5, 1966

Fewest Strikeouts, Both Clubs, Game
0 NL:Pitt. (NY) Oct. 13, 1960

BASE ON ERROR

Most Base on Error Game
5 NL:Chi. (Chi.) Oct. 13, 1906

Most Base on Error, Both Clubs, Game
6 NL:Pitt. (Bos.) Oct. 10, 1903
   NL:Chi. (Phil.) Oct. 18, 1910
   NL:NY (Phil.) Oct. 26, 1911

STOLEN BASES

Most Stolen Bases, Game
6 NL:Chi. (Chi.) Oct. 10, 1906
   Extra-Inning Game:
7 NL:Chi. (Det.) Oct. 8, 1907 (13 inn)

Most Stolen Bases, Both Clubs, Game
7 NL:Chi. (Det.) Oct. 12, 1907
   Extra-Inning Game:
11 NL:Chi. (Det.) Oct. 8, 1907 (13 inn)

Most Stolen Bases, Inning
3 NL:Pitt. (Bos.) Oct. 1, 1903 (1st)
   NL:NY (Phil.) Oct. 12, 1905 (9th)
   NL:Chi. (Det.) Oct. 8, 1907 (10th)
   NL:Chi. (Det.) Oct. 11, 1908 (8th)
   AL:Det. (Chi.) Oct. 12, 1908 (9th)
   NL:NY (Bos.) Oct. 14, 1912 (1st)

CAUGHT STEALING

Most Caught Stealing, Game
3 By many clubs; Last:
   NL:LA (Oak.) Oct. 19, 1988
   Extra-Inning Game:
5 NL:NY (Phil.) Oct. 17, 1911 (11)

Most Caught Stealing, Both Clubs, Game
5 AL:Phil. (Chi.) Oct. 17, 1910
   Extra-Inning Game
6 NL:NY (Phil.) Oct. 17, 1911 (11 inn)

Most Caught Stealing Inning
2 NL:NY (Phil.) Oct. 12, 1905 (7th)
   NL:NY (Phil.) Oct. 17, 1911 (10th)
   NL:NY (Bos.) Oct. 9, 1912 (11th)
   AL:Bos. (Phil.) Oct. 9, 1915 (1st)
   AL:Bos. (Brk.) Oct. 12, 1916 (3rd)
   AL:Chi. (Cin.) Oct. 3, 1919 (6th)
   NL:Brk. (NY) Oct. 6, 1947 (1st)
   AL:NY (Brk.) Oct. 2, 1952 (1st)
   NL:StL. (Det.) Oct. 10, 1968 (6th)

LEFT ON BASE

Most Left on Base, Game
14 NL:Chi. (Phil.) Oct. 18, 1910
    NL:Mil. (NY) Oct. 5, 1957
    NL:Pitt. (Balt.) Oct. 11, 1971
    AL:Det. (SD) Oct. 12, 1984
    Extra-Inning Game:
15 NL:NY (Oak.) Oct. 14, 1973 (12 inn)
    NL:Phil. (KC) Oct. 17, 1980 (10 inn)
    AL:NY (NY) Oct. 21, 2000 (12 inn)

Most Left on Base, Both Clubs, Game
24 AL:Det. (SD) Oct. 12, 1984
    Extra-Inning Game:
27 NL:NY (Oak.) Oct. 14, 1973 (12 inn)

Fewest Left on Base, Game
0 NL:Brk. (NY) Oct. 8, 1956
   NL:LA (NY) Oct. 6, 1963

Fewest Left on Base, Both Clubs, Game
3 NL:Brk. (NY) Oct. 8, 1956

PINCH-HITTING

Most Pinch-Hitters, Game
6 NL:LA (Chi.) Oct. 6, 1959
   Extra-Inning Game:
8 AL:Minn. (Atl.) Oct. 22, 1991 (12 inn)

Most Pinch-Hitters, Both Clubs, Game
8 AL:Balt. (Phil.) Oct. 15, 1983
   AL:Oak. (NY) Oct. 14, 1973
   Extra-Inning Game:
12 AL:Minn. (Atl.) Oct. 22, 1991 (12 inn)

Most Pinch-Hitters, Inning
4 NL:NY (Oak.) Oct. 13, 1973 (9th)
   AL:Balt. (Phil.) Oct. 15, 1983 (6th)
   AL:KC (StL.) Oct. 26, 1985 (9th)
   AL:Minn. (StL.) Oct. 22, 1987 (9th)
   NL:SD (NY) Oct. 18, 1998 (8th)
   NL:Atl. (NY) Oct. 23, 1999 (8th)
   NL:NY (NY) Oct. 25, 2000 (7th)

Most Pinch-Hits, Series
6 AL:NY (Brk.) 1947 (7g)
   AL:NY (Pitt.) 1960 (7g)
   AL:Oak. (Cin.) 1972 (7g)
   AL:Balt. (Pitt.) 1979 (7g)

Most Pinch-Hits, Both Clubs, Series
11 AL:NY (Brk.) 1947 (7g)

Most Pinch-Hits, Game
3 AL:Oak. (Cin.) Oct. 19, 1972
   AL:Balt. (Pitt.) Oct. 13, 1979
   NL:SD (NY) Oct. 18, 1998

Most Pinch-Hits, Both Clubs, Game
3 by many

Most Pinch-Hits, Inning
3 AL:Oak. (Cin.) Oct. 19, 1972 (9th)
   NL:SD (NY) Oct. 18, 1998 (8th)

Most Pinch-Hit Home Runs
6 AL:NY 1947, 52, 55, 60-61, 99

Most Pinch-Hit Home Runs, One Series
2 NL:LA (Chi.) 1959 (6 g)
   AL:Bos. (Cin.) 1975 (7 g)

Most Pinch-Hit HRs, Both Clubs, One Series
2 AL:Clev. (NY) 1954
   NL:LA (Chi.) 1959
   AL:Bos. (Cin.) 1975

Most Pinch-Hit Walks, Inning
2 AL:NY (NY) Oct. 15, 1923 (8th)
   AL:Balt. (Pitt.) Oct. 11, 1979 (7th)
   AL:Balt. (Phil.) Oct. 15, 1983 (6th)
   AL:NY (Atl.) Oct. 23, 1999 (8th)

Most Pinch-Hit Strikeouts, Game
4 AL:StL. (StL.) Oct. 8, 1944
   AL:StL. (StL.) Oct. 9, 1944

Most Pinch-Hit Strikeouts, Inning
3 AL:StL. (StL.) Oct. 8, 1944 (9th)

PINCH-RUNNERS

Most Pinch-Runners, Game
2 By many

Most Pinch-Runners, Both Clubs, Game
4 NL:StL. (KC) Oct. 26, 1985

Most Pinch-Runners, Inning
2 NL:NY (NY) Oct. 10, 1923 (3rd)
   AL:NY (NY) Oct. 15, 1923 (8th)
   NL:Brk. (NY) Oct. 3, 1947 (9th)
   NL:Bos. (Clev.) Oct. 6, 1948 (8th)
   NL:Phil: (NY) Oct. 7, 1950 (9th)
   NL:LA (Chi.) Oct. 6, 1959 (7th)
   AL:Oak. (Cin.) Oct. 19, 1972 (9th)
   NL:StL. (KC) Oct. 26, 1985 (8th)
   AL:KC (StL.) Oct. 26, 1985 (9th)
   NL:Ari. (NY) Nov. 4, 2001 (9th)

Most Pinch-Runners, Both Clubs, Inning
2 By many; Last:
   NL:Ari. (NY) Nov. 4, 2001 (9th)

CLUB FIELDING

AVERAGE

	4 Games		5 Games		6 Games		7 Games
Highest Average (Most Chances)							
1.000	AL:Balt. (LA) 1966 (141 tc)	1.000	AL:NY (NY) 1937 (179 tc)	.996	AL:Bos. (Chi.) 1918	.993	NL:Cin. (Bos.) 1975
Highest Average, Both Clubs							
.986	AL:NY (LA) 1963	.986	AL:NY (Brk.) 1941	.992	NL:LA 1977	.990	NL:StL. (KC) 1985
Lowest Average							
.949	AL:NY (Chi.) 1932	.942	NL:Brk. (Bos.) 1916	.938	NL:NY (Phil.) 1911	.934	AL:Det. (Pitt.) 1909
Lowest Average, Both Clubs							
954	AL:NY (Chi.) 1932	.946	NL:Chi. (Phil.) 1910	.947	NL:NY (Phil.) 1911	.941	AL:Det. (Pitt.) 1909

CHANCES ACCEPTED

	4 Games		5 Games		6 Games		7 Games
Most Chances Accepted							
179	NL:Bos. (Phil.) 1914	237	AL:Bos. (Brk.) 1916	271	AL:Chi. (Chi.) 1906	329	NL:NY (Bos.) 1912 (8g) AL:Chi. (Cin.) 1919 (8g)
						300	AL:Wash. (NY) 1924
Most Chances Accepted, Both Clubs							
356	NL:Bos. (Phil.) 1914	449	AL:Bos. (Brk.) 1916	514	AL:Chi. (Chi.) 1906	652	NL:NY (Bos.) 1912 (8g)
						594	AL:Wash. (NY) 1924
Fewest Chances Accepted							
136	AL:NY (StL.) 1928 NL:Atl. (NY) 1999	166	NL:SD (Det.) 1984	197	AL:Phil. (StL.) 1930	234	NL:StL. (Det.) 1968
Fewest Chances Accepted, Both Clubs							
274	AL:NY (StL.) 1928	348	NL:LA (Oak.) 1988	404	AL:Phil. (StL.) 1930	490	AL:Minn. (LA) 1965

PUTOUTS

	4 Games		5 Games		6 Games		7 Games
Most Putouts							
117	AL:Bos. (Phil.) 1914	147	NL:Bos. (Brk.) 1916	168	AL:NY (LA) 1977	222	AL:Bos. (NY) 1912 (8g)
						202	AL:Minn. (Atl.) 1991
Most Putouts, Both Clubs							
228	NL:Bos. (Phil.) 1914	289	AL:Bos. (Brk.) 1916	333	AL:NY (LA) 1977	443	AL:Bos. (NY) 1912 (8g)
						401	NL:NY (Wash.) 1924
Fewest Putouts							
102	NL:StL. (NY) 1928 AL:Chi. (NY) 1932 NL:Chi. (NY) 1938 AL:NY (LA) 1963 AL:LA (Balt.) 1966 NL:SF (Oak.) 1989 NL:SD (NY) 1998	126	NL:LA (Oak.) 1974 NL:SD (Det.) 1984	153	NL:NY (Chi.) 1917 AL:StL. (Phil.) 1930 AL:NY (LA) 1981	177	AL:Brk. (Clev.) 1920 NL:StL. (Minn.) 1987
Fewest Putouts, Both Clubs							
210	NL:StL. (NY) 1928 NL:Chi. (NY) 1932,38 AL:NY (LA) 1963 NL:LA (Balt.) 1966 NL:SF (Oak.) 1989 AL:NY (SD) 1998	258	NL:LA (Oak.) 1974 NL:SD (Det.) 1984	309	NL:NY (Chi.) 1917 NL:StL. (Phil.) 1930 AL:NY (LA) 1981	357	NL:StL. (Minn.) 1987

ASSISTS

	4 Games		5 Games		6 Games		7 Games
Most Assists							
67	NL:Phil. (Bos.) 1914	90	NL:Bos. (Brk.) 1916	99	AL:Chi. (Chi.) 1906	116	AL:Chi. (Cin.) 1919 (8g)
							AL:Wash. (NY) 1924
Most Assists, Both Clubs							
129	AL:Phil. (Bos.) 1914	160	AL:Bos. (Brk.) 1916	183	AL:Chi. (Chi.) 1906	212	AL:Chi. (Cin.) 1919 (8g)
							193 AL:Wash. (NY) 1924
Fewest Assists							
28	AL:NY (StL.) 1928	36	NL:LA (Oak.) 1988	41	AL:Phil. (StL.) 1930	48	NL:StL. (Det.) 1968
Fewest Assists, Both Clubs							
64	AL:NY (StL.) 1928	79	NL:LA (Oak.) 1988	96	AL:Phil. (StL.) 1930	120	NL:StL. (Det.) 1968

ERRORS

	4 Games		5 Games		6 Games		7 Games
Most Errors							
8	AL:NY (Chi.) 1932	13	NL:Brk. (Bos.) 1916	16	NL:NY (Phil.) 1911	19	AL:Det. (Pitt.) 1909
Most Errors, Both Clubs							
14	AL:NY (Chi.) 1932	23	NL:Chi. (Phil.) 1910	27	NL:NY (Phil.) 1911	34	AL:Det. (Pitt.) 1909
Fewest Errors							
0	AL:Balt. (LA) 1966	0	AL:NY (NY) 1937	1	By many clubs	2	By many clubs
Fewest Errors, Both Clubs							
4	AL:NY (LA) 1963	5	AL:Oak. (LA) 1988	4	NL:LA (NY) 1977	5	NL:StL. (KC) 1985
Most Errorless Games							
4	AL:Balt. (LA) 1966	5	AL:NY (NY) 1937	5	AL:Bos. (Chi.) 1918	5	NL:NY (NY) 1921 (8g)
							NL:StL. (StL.) 1944	AL:Phil. (StL.) 1931
							AL:NY (Brk.) 1953	AL:NY (Brk.) 1955
							NL:LA (NY) 1977	NL:Brk. (NY) 1956
								NL:StL. (Det.) 1968
								NL:Cin. (Bos.) 1975
								AL:KC (StL.) 1985
								NL:StL. (KC) 1985
								AL:Bos. (NY) 1986
								AL:Clev. (Fla.) 1997
Most Errorless Games, Both Clubs							
3	AL:Balt (LA) 1966	2	AL:NY (NY) 1937	3	AL:NY (LA) 1977	4	AL:KC (StL) 1985
	NL:Cin (NY) 1976		NL:LA (Oak) 1988		AL:Tor. (Atl) 1992		
			AL:NY (NY) 2000				

DOUBLE PLAYS

	4 Games		5 Games		6 Games		7 Games
Most Double Plays							
7	NL:Chi (NY) 1932	7	AL:NY (NY) 1922	10	AL:NY (NY) 1951	12	NL:Brk (NY) 1955
	AL:NY (LA) 1963		AL:NY (Brk) 1941				
			NL:Cin (NY) 1961				
Most Double Plays, Both Clubs							
10	NL:Cin (NY) 1976	12	AL:NY (Brk) 1941	16	NL:Phil (KC) 1980	19	NL:Brk (NY) 1955
Fewest Double Plays							
1	AL:NY (Chi) 1932	0	NL:NY (Balt) 1969	2	AL:Chi (Chi) 1906	2	NL:StL (Det) 1934
	NL:Cin (NY) 1939				NL:NY (Phil) 1911		AL:Balt (Pitt) 1971
	NL:Phil (NY) 1950				AL:Phil (NY) 1911		NL:StL (Minn) 1987
	NL:LA (NY) 1963				AL:Phil (StL) 1930		
	AL:Oak (SF) 1989				AL:NY (NY) 1936		
					AL:Chi (LA) 1959		
					AL:NY (LA) 1977, 81		
					NL:Atl (Clev) 1995		
Fewest Double Plays, Both Clubs							
4	NL:NY (Clev) 1954	4	NL:NY (Balt) 1969	4	AL:Phil (NY) 1911	6	NL:StL (Minn) 1987
	AL:Oak (SF) 1989		AL:NY (NY) 2000				

TRIPLE PLAYS

4 Games	5 Games	6 Games	7 Games

Most Triple Plays

4 Games	5 Games	6 Games	7 Games
none	none	none	1 AL:Clev (Brk) 1920

PASSED BALLS

Most Passed Balls

4 Games	5 Games	6 Games	7 Games
2 AL:Phil (Bos) 1914	2 NL:Brk (Bos) 1916	2 NL:Chi (Chi) 1906 NL:Chi (Bos) 1918 NL:LA (NY) 1978	3 NL:Pitt (NY) 1960 AL:NY (StL) 1964

Most Passed Balls, Both Clubs

4 Games	5 Games	6 Games	7 Games
2 AL:Phil (Bos) 1914	3 NL:Brk (Bos) 1916	3 NL:Chi (Chi) 1906 NL:Chi (Bos) 1918	4 NL:Brk (NY) 1947

CHANCES ACCEPTED

Chances Accepted, Game
48 AL:Chi. (Chi.) Oct. 12, 1906
     AL:Chi. (NY) Oct. 7, 1917
     AL:Bos. (Chi.) Sept. 9, 1918
     Extra-Inning Game:
74 AL:Bos. (Brk.) Oct. 9, 1916 (14 inn)

Chances Accepted, Both Clubs, Game
91 AL:Chi. (Chi.) Oct. 12, 1906
     Extra-Inning Game:
137 AL:Bos. (Brk.) Oct. 9, 1916 (14 inn)

PUTOUTS

Putouts, Game
42 AL:Bos. (Brk.) Oct. 9, 1916 (14 inn)

Putouts, Both Clubs, Game
82 AL:Bos. (Brk.) Oct. 9, 1916 (14 inn)

ASSISTS

Assists, Game
21 AL:Chi. (Chi.) Oct. 12, 1906
     AL:Chi. (NY) Oct. 7, 1917
     AL:Bos. (Chi.) Sept. 9, 1918
     Extra-Inning Game:
32 AL:Bos. (Brk.) Oct. 9, 1916 (14 inn)

Assists, Both Clubs, Game
37 AL:Chi. (Chi.) Oct. 12, 1906
     Extra-Inning Game:
55 NL:Brk. (Bos.) Oct. 9, 1916 (14 inn)

ERRORS

Errors, Game
6 AL:Chi. (Chi.) Oct. 13, 1906
    NL:Pitt. (Det.) Oct. 12, 1909
    AL:Chi. (NY) Oct. 13, 1917
    NL:LA (Balt.) Oct. 6, 1966

Errors, Both Clubs, Game
9 AL:Chi. (NY) Oct. 13, 1917

Errors,Inning
3 By many clubs; Last:
    AL:Clev. (Fla.) Oct. 21, 1997 (9th)

DOUBLE PLAYS

Double Plays, Game
5 AL:Phil (Bos.) Oct. 9, 1914

Double Plays, Both Clubs, Game
6 AL:Phil. (Bos.) Oct. 9, 1914
    AL:NY (Brk.) Sept. 29, 1955
    NL:Phil. (KC) Oct. 15, 1980

TRIPLE PLAYS

Triple Plays
1 AL:Clev. (Brk.) Oct. 10, 1920 (5th)

PASSED BALLS

Passed Balls, Game
2 NL:Chi. (Chi.) Oct. 9, 1906
    NL:Chi. (Bos.) Sept. 9, 1918
    AL:Det. (Chi.) Oct. 3, 1945
    NL:Brk. (NY) Oct. 4, 1947
    NL:Pitt. (NY) Oct. 6, 1960
    AL:NY (StL.) Oct. 7, 1964
    NL:LA (NY) Oct. 5, 1978

Passed Balls, Inning
1 By many clubs

CLUB PITCHING

	4 Games	5 Games	6 Games	7 Games
Most Complete Games				
	4 AL:NY (StL) 1928	5 AL:Phil (NY) 1905,13 AL:Phil (Chi) 1910 AL:Bos (Phil) 1915	5 AL:Phil (NY) 1911 AL:Bos (Chi) 1918 AL:Det (Chi) 1935	7 AL:Bos (Pitt) 1903 (8g) 5 AL:Clev (Brk) 1920 AL:NY (Brk) 1956
Most Complete Games, Both Clubs				
	5 NL:Bos (Phil) 1914	9 AL:Phil (NY) 1905 AL:Bos (Phil) 1915	9 AL:Bos (Chi) 1918	13 AL:Bos (Pitt) 1903 (8g) 8 1909,20,25,34,40,56
Fewest Complete Games				
	0 By Many	0 By many clubs	0 By many clubs	0 By many clubs
Fewest Complete Games, Both Clubs				
	0 AL:NY (SD) 1998 AL:NY (Atl.) 1999	0 AL:Oak (LA) 1974 AL:NY (NY) 2000	0 AL:Chi (LA) 1959 AL:KC (Phil) 1980 AL:NY (Atl) 1996	0 AL:Oak (Cin) 1972 AL:Oak (NY) 1973 AL:Minn (StL) 1987 AL:Clev. (Fla.) 1997
Most Saves (Since 1969)				
	3 AL:NY (SD) 1998	3 AL:Oak (LA) 1974	4 AL:NY (Atl) 1996	4 AL:Oak (NY) 1973
Most Saves, Both Clubs (since 1969)				
	3 AL:NY (SD) 1998	4 AL:Oak (LA) 1974	4 NL:Phil (KC) 1980 AL:Tor (Atl) 1992 NL:Atl (Clev) 1995 AL:NY (Atl) 1996	7 AL:Oak (NY) 1973
Fewest Saves (since 1969)				
	0 AL:NY (Cin) 1976 NL:SF (Oak) 1989 AL:Oak (Cin) 1990 NL:SD (NY) 1998 NL:Atl. (NY) 1999	0 AL:Balt (NY) 1969 NL:Cin (Balt) 1970 AL:Oak (LA) 1988	0 NL:LA(NY) 1977 AL:NY (LA) 1977-78 NL:Atl. (NY) 1996	0 AL:Bos (Cin) 1975 AL:Balt (Pitt) 1979 AL:KC (StL) 1985 NL:Atl (Minn) 1991 NL:Ari (NY) 2001
Fewest Saves, Both Clubs (since 1969)				
	1 NL:SF (Oak) 1989 AL:Oak (Cin) 1990	1 AL:Oak (LA) 1988	0 AL:NY (LA) 1977	1 NL:Ari (NY) 2001
Most Shutouts				
	3 AL:Balt (LA) 1966	4 NL:NY (Phil) 1905	2 NL:NY (Chi) 1917 AL:Chi (LA) 1959	3 NL:LA (Minn) 1965
Most Shutouts, Both Clubs				
	3 AL:Balt. (LA) 1966	5 NL:NY (Phil) 1905	2 By many clubs	3 AL:Clev (Brk) 1920 AL:NY (Brk) 1956 AL:NY (Mil) 1958 AL:Minn (LA) 1965
Most Shutouts, Consecutive				
	3 AL:Balt (LA) 1966	3 NL:NY (Phil) 1905	2 NL:NY (Chi) 1917	2 AL:Cin (Chi) 1919 (8g) AL:Clev (Brk) 1920 NL:NY (NY) 1921 (8g)
Most Shutouts, Consecutive, Both Clubs				
	3 AL:Balt. (LA) 1966	5 NL:NY (Phil) 1905	2 NL:Chi. (Chi) 1906 NL:NY (Chi) 1917	3 NL:Cin (Chi) 1919 (8g) AL:NY (Brk) 1956 AL:NY (Mil) 1958
Fewest Shutouts				
	0 By many clubs	0 By many clubs	0 By many clubs	0 By many clubs
Fewest Shutouts, Both Clubs				
	0 1927,28,32,38,54,76,99	0 1910,15,16,29,37,41,70, 74,84, 2000	0 By many clubs	0 1912,24,47,64,87,97
Most Shutout Innings, Consecutive				
	33 AL:Balt (LA) 1966	28 NL:NY (Phil) 1905	24 NL:NY (Chi) 1917	26 NL:Cin (Chi) 1919 (8g) 22 NL:Pitt (Balt) 1971

4 Games	5 Games	6 Games	7 Games

Most Wild Pitches

4 Games	5 Games	6 Games	7 Games
3 NL:Pitt (NY) 1927	3 NL:LA (Oak) 1974	4 NL:Chi (Chi) 1906	5 NL:Pitt (NY) 1960
AL:Clev (NY) 1954			AL:Minn (Atl) 1991

Most Wild Pitches, Both Clubs

4 Games	5 Games	6 Games	7 Games
4 AL:Clev (NY) 1954	4 AL:Bos (Brk) 1916	6 AL:Chi (Chi) 1906	8 AL:NY (Brk) 1947
	AL:Wash (NY) 1933		
	NL:LA (Oak) 1974		
	AL:Balt (Phil) 1983		
	AL:Det (SD) 1984		

CLUB GENERAL

	4 Games	5 Games	6 Games	7 Games
Most Players, Club	25 AL:Oak (Cin) 1990 NL:Atl. (NY) 1999	25 NL:Brk (NY) 1949 NL:NY (NY) 2000	25 NL:LA (NY) 1977 AL:NY (Atl) 1996	26 AL:Det (Chi) 1945 AL:Bos (StL) 1946
Most Players, Both Clubs	48 AL:NY (Atl.) 1999	47 AL:NY (NY) 2000	49 AL:NY (Atl.) 1996	51 AL:Det (Chi) 1945
Fewest Players	13 NL:LA (NY) 1963 AL:Balt (LA) 1966	12 NL:NY (Phil) 1905 AL:Phil (Chi) 1910 AL:Phil (NY) 1913	14 NL:Chi (Chi) 1906 AL:Phil (NY) 1911	13 AL:Bos (Pitt) 1903 (8g) NL:NY (NY) 1921 (8g)
Fewest Players, Both Clubs	31 AL:Phil (Bos) 1914	25 AL:Phil (NY) 1905	29 NL:NY (Phil) 1911	27 AL:Bos (Pitt) 1903 (8g)
Most Pitchers	10 AL:Oak (Cin) 1990 NL:SD (NY) 1998	10 NL:SD (Det) 1984 AL:Oak (LA) 1988 NL:NY (NY) 2000	10 By many teams	11 AL:Bos (StL) 1946 AL:Clev. (Fla.) 1997
Most Pitchers, Both Clubs	19 AL:NY (SD) 1998	18 AL:Balt (Cin) 1970 AL:NY (NY) 2000	20 AL:Tor (Phil) 1993 AL:NY (Atl) 1996	21 NL:Fla. (Clev.) 1997
Fewest Pitchers	3 NL:Bos (Phil) 1914 AL:NY (StL) 1928	2 AL:Phil (Chi) 1910	3 AL:Phil (NY) 1911	3 AL:Bos (Pitt) 1903 (8g)
Fewest Pitchers, Both Clubs	9 NL:Bos (Phil) 1914 AL:NY (StL) 1928	6 AL:Phil (NY) 1905	8 AL:Chi (Chi) 1906 AL:Phil (NY) 1911 AL:Bos (Chi) 1918	8 AL:Bos (Pitt) 1903 (8g)
Largest Attendance	251,507 NL:NY (Clev) 1954	304,139 AL:Balt (Phil) 1983	420,784 NL:LA (Chi) 1959	403,617 NL:Fla (Clev) 1997
Smallest Attendance	111,009 NL:Bos (Phil) 1914	62,232 AL:Det (Chi) 1908	99,846 AL:Chi (Chi) 1906	100,429 AL:Bos (Pitt) 1903 (8g)
Most Extra-Inning Games	1 NL:Bos (Phil) 1914 AL:NY (Cin) 1939 AL:NY (Phil) 1950 NL:NY (Clev) 1954 AL:Oak (Cin) 1990 AL:NY (Atl.) 1999	2 NL:NY (Wash) 1933	2 AL:Phil (NY) 1911	3 AL:Minn (Atl) 1991
Most 1-Run Decisions	3 AL:NY (Phil) 1950	4 AL:Bos (Phil) 1915 AL:Oak (LA) 1974	5 NL:Atl (Clev) 1995	6 AL:Oak (Cin) 1972
Most 1-Run Decisions, Consecutive	3 AL:NY (Phil) 1950	4 AL:Bos (Phil) 1915	3 NL:LA (NY) 1981 AL:Tor (Atl) 1992 AL:Clev (Atl) 1995	5 AL:Oak (Cin) 1972
Most 1-Run Decisions Won	3 AL:NY (Phil) 1950	4 AL:Bos (Phil) 1915	4 AL:Bos (Chi) 1918 AL:Tor (Atl) 1992	4 AL:Oak (Cin) 1972
Most 1-Run Decisions Won, Consecutive	3 AL:NY (Phil) 1950	4 AL:Bos (Phil) 1915	3 NL:LA (NY) 1981 AL:Tor (Atl) 1992	3 AL:NY (Ari) 2001
Most 1-0 Games Won (See Table)	2 AL:Balt (LA) 1966	1 By many clubs	1 By many clubs	1 By many clubs

PERSONNEL

Most Players, Game
21   AL:NY (Brk.) Oct. 5, 1947
     NL:Cin. (NY) Oct. 9, 1961
     Extra-Inning Game:
23   AL:Minn. (Atl.) Oct. 22, 1991 (12 inn)

Most Players, Both Clubs, Game
38   AL:NY (Brk.) Oct. 5, 1947
     Extra-Inning Game:
42   AL:Minn. (Atl.) Oct. 22, 1991 (12 inn)

Most Pitchers, Game
     Winning Club:
6   NL:Cin. (Oak.) Oct. 20, 1972
     Extra-Inning Game:
7   AL:Tor. (Atl.) Oct. 24, 1992 (11 inn)
     AL:NY(Atl) Oct. 23, 1996 (10 inn)
     Losing Club:
8   NL:Cin. (NY) Oct. 9, 1961
     NL:StL. (Bos.) Oct. 11, 1967
     NL:Cin. (Bos.) Oct. 21, 1975 (12 inn)

Most Pitchers, Both Clubs, Game
11   NL:StL. (Bos.) Oct. 11, 1967
     NL:SF (Oak.) Oct. 28, 1989
     NL:Phil. (Tor.) Oct. 20, 1993
     AL:Clev. (Fla.) Oct. 21, 1997
     Extra-Inning Game:
13   AL:Minn. (Atl.) Oct. 22, 1991 (12 inn)
     AL:NY (Atl) Oct. 23, 1996 (10 inn)

Most Pitchers, Inning
5   AL:Balt. (Pitt.) Oct. 17, 1979 (9th)
     NL:StL. (KC) Oct. 27, 1985 (5th)

DATES

Earliest Date, First Game
     Sept. 5, 1918 Bos. at Chi.

Earliest Date, Last Game
     Sept. 11, 1918 AL:Bos. at Chi.

Latest Date, First Game
     Oct. 27, 2001 AL:NY at Ari.

Latest Date, Final Game
     Nov. 4, 2001 AL:NY at Ari.

ATTENDANCE

Game, Largest
     92,706 AL:Chi. at LA Oct. 6, 1959

Game, Smallest
     6,210 NL:Chi. at Det. Oct. 14, 1908

TIME

Longest Game
     Day 9 innings:
     3:48 AL:Balt. at Pitt. Oct. 13, 1979
     Night 9 innings
     4:14 AL:Tor. at Phil. Oct. 20, 1993
     Day Extra Innings:
     4:13 NL:NY at Oak. Oct. 14, 1973 (12 inn)
     Night Extra Innings:
     4:51 NL:NY at NY Oct. 21, 2000 (12 inn)

Shortest Game
     1:25 NL:Chi. at Det. Oct. 14, 1908

SCORELESS INNINGS

Most, Consecutive, By Pitchers
Total Series:
39 AL:Balt. (LA) 1966 (33); (NY) 1969 (6)

LOW-HIT GAMES (Pitching)

No Hits
1956	Oct. 8	AL:NY Don Larsen

1 Hit
1906	Oct. 10	NL:Chi. Ed Reulbach
1945	Oct. 5	NL:Chi. Claude Passeau
1947	Oct. 3	AL:NY Bill Bevens (Lost)
1967	Oct. 5	AL:Bos. Jim Lonborg
1995	Oct. 28	NL:Atl. Tom Glavine & Mark Wohlers

2 Hits
1906	Oct. 11	AL:Chi. Ed Walsh
1906	Oct. 12	NL:Chi. Three Finger Brown
1913	Oct. 11	AL:Phil. Eddie Plank
1914	Oct. 10	NL:Bos. Bill James
1921	Oct. 6	AL:NY Waite Hoyt
1931	Oct. 5	NL:StL . Burleigh Grimes
1931	Oct. 6	AL:Phil. George Earnshaw
1939	Oct. 5	AL:NY Monte Pearson
1944	Oct. 4	NL:StL. Mort Cooper & Blix Donnelly (Lost)
1948	Oct. 6	AL:Clev. Bob Feller (Lost)
1949	Oct. 5	AL:NY Allie Reynolds
1950	Oct. 4	AL:NY Vic Raschi
1958	Oct. 5	NL:Mil. Warren Spahn
1961	Oct. 4	AL:NY Whitey Ford
1963	Oct. 6	AL:NY Whitey Ford & Hal Reniff (Lost)
1969	Oct. 12	NL:NY Jerry Koosman & Ron Taylor
1971	Oct. 14	NL:Pitt. Nelson Briles
1990	Oct. 20	NL:Cin. Jose Rijo & Randy Myers
1995	Oct. 21	NL:Atl. Greg Maddux
1999	Oct. 23	AL:NY Orlando Hernandez, Jeff Nelson, Mike Stanton & Mariano Rivera

HIGH-HIT GAMES (Batting)

22 Hits
2001	Nov. 3	NL:Ari. vs. NY

20 Hits
1921	Oct. 7	NL:NY vs NY
1946	Oct. 10	NL:StL. vs Bos.

19 Hits
1932	Oct. 2	AL:NY vs Chi.
1960	Oct. 6	AL:NY vs Pitt.

18 Hits
1978	Oct. 15	AL:NY vs LA
1986	Oct. 19	AL:Bos. vs NY
1993	Oct. 20	AL:Tor. vs Phil.

17 Hits
1934	Oct. 9	NL:StL. vs Det.
1936	Oct. 2	AL:NY vs NY
1936	Oct. 6	AL:NY vs NY
1960	Oct. 12	AL:NY vs Pitt.
1979	Oct. 13	NL:Pitt. vs Balt.
1982	Oct. 12	AL:Mil. vs StL.
1991	Oct. 24	NL:Atl. vs Minn.

16 Hits
1912	Oct. 15	NL:NY vs Bos.
1919	Oct. 9	NL:Cin. vs Chi.
1960	Oct. 8	AL:NY vs Pitt.
1997	Oct. 21	NL:Fla. vs Clev.
1998	Oct. 18	AL:NY vs SD

EXTRA-INNING GAMES

14 AL:Bos. 2 Brk. 1 Oct. 9, 1916
12 NL:Chi. 3 Det. 3 Oct. 8, 1907
   NL:Bos. 5 Phil. 4, Oct. 12, 1914
   NL:NY 4 Wash. 3, Oct. 4, 1924
   AL:Wash. 4 NY 3, Oct. 10, 1924
   AL:Det. 3 StL. 2 Oct. 4 1934
   NL:Chi. 8 Det. 7, Oct. 8, 1945
   NL:NY 10 Oak. 7, Oct. 14, 1973
   AL:Bos. 7 Cin. 6 Oct. 21, 1975
   AL:NY 4 LA 3 Oct. 11, 1977
   NL:Atl. 5 Minn. 4, Oct. 22, 1991
   AL:NY 4 NY 3, Oct. 21, 2000
   AL:NY 3 Ari. 2, Nov. 1, 2001
11 AL:Phil. 3 NY 2, Oct. 17, 1911
   NL:NY 6 Bos. 6, Oct. 9, 1912
   NL:NY 2 Wash. 1, Oct. 6, 1933
   AL:Det. 6 Chi. 5, Oct. 4, 1935
   NL:StL. 3 StL. 2, Oct. 5, 1944
   NL:Brk. 6 NY 5, Oct. 5, 1952
   AL:Oak. 3 NY 2, Oct. 16, 1973
   AL:Minn. 4 Atl. 3, Oct. 26, 1991
   AL:Tor. 4 Atl. 3, Oct. 24, 1992
   AL:Clev. 7 Atl. 6, Oct. 24, 1995
   NL:Fla. 3 Clev. 2 Oct. 26, 1997
10 NL:Chi. 4 Phil. 3, Oct. 22, 1910
   NL:NY 4 Phil. 3, Oct. 25, 1911
   AL:Bos. 3 NY 2, Oct. 16, 1912
   NL:NY 3 Phil. 0, Oct. 8, 1913
   AL:Chi. 5 Cin. 4, Oct. 7, 1919
   NL:NY 3 NY 3, Oct. 5, 1922
   AL:NY 3 StL. 2 Oct. 7, 1926
   NL:NY 4 Wash. 3, Oct. 7, 1933
   NL:NY 5 NY 4 Oct. 5, 1936
   AL:NY 7 Cin. 4, Oct. 8, 1939
   AL:Bos. 3 StL. 2, Oct. 6, 1946
   AL:NY 2 Phil. 1, Oct. 5, 1950
   NL:NY 5 Clev. 2, Sept. 29, 1954
   NL:Brk. 1 NY 0, Oct. 9, 1956
   NL:Mil. 7 NY 5, Oct. 6, 1957
   NL:Mil. 4 NY 3, Oct. 1, 1958
   AL:NY 4 Mil. 3, Oct. 8, 1958
   NL:StL. 5 NY 2, Oct. 12, 1964
   NL:NY 2 Balt 1, Oct. 15, 1969
   AL:Balt. 3 Pitt. 2, Oct. 16, 1971
   NL:Cin. 6 Bos. 5, Oct. 14, 1975
   AL:NY 4 LA 3, Oct. 14, 1978
   AL:KC 4 Phil. 3, Oct. 17, 1980
   NL:NY 6 Bos. 5, Oct. 25, 1986
   NL:Cin. 5 Oak. 4, Oct. 17, 1990
   AL:Minn. 1 Atl. 0, Oct. 27, 1991
   AL:NY 8 Atl. 6, Oct. 23, 1996
   AL:NY 6 Atl. 5 Oct. 26, 1999
   AL:NY 4 Ari. 3 Oct. 31, 2001

WORLD SERIES – CLUB BATTING

AMERICAN LEAGUE	BA	SLG	G	AB	R	ER	H	TB	1B	2B	3B	HR	RBI	SH	SF	BB	HB	SO	SB	LOB
New York Yankees	.249	.385	213	7138	936	835	1780	2748	1272	254	51	204	884	106	18	747	45	1192	72	1472
Philadelphia/Oakland	.228	.338	75	2457	267	211	559	830	393	107	13	46	244	65	4	223	13	461	41	490
Boston Red Sox	.239	.355	60	1992	204	160	477	708	347	60	39	31	183	56	7	174	13	306	19	425
Detroit Tigers	.232	.323	56	1878	210	181	436	606	328	72	10	26	195	31	3	205	18	278	35	413
Washington/Minnesota	.238	.366	40	1340	145	128	319	491	228	46	9	36	140	24	2	128	6	229	23	279
St.Louis/Baltimore	.212	.329	39	1261	135	127	267	415	189	41	4	33	122	8	7	125	6	240	5	238
Cleveland Indians	.227	.341	30	987	110	94	224	337	158	40	5	21	101	14	3	114	2	158	17	212
Chicago White Sox	.239	.317	26	846	86	68	202	268	154	36	6	6	73	19	1	64	8	126	19	165
Kansas City Royals	.289	.422	13	443	51	49	128	187	93	21	4	10	48	5	3	54	1	105	13	110
Toronto Blue Jays	.271	.438	12	402	62	60	109	176	71	21	5	12	62	2	8	43	4	63	12	77
Milwaukee Brewers	.269	.399	7	238	33	26	64	95	45	12	2	5	29	1	1	19	1	28	1	44

NATIONAL LEAGUE	BA	SLG	G	AB	R	ER	H	TB	1B	2B	3B	HR	RBI	SH	SF	BB	HB	SO	SB	LOB
Brooklyn/Los Angeles	.232	.350	105	3420	347	310	794	1197	572	120	23	79	327	54	11	321	17	584	57	689
St. Louis Cardinals	.243	.346	96	3216	344	286	782	1113	564	149	25	44	324	64	6	226	7	503	62	632
New York/San Francisco	.243	.330	93	3091	307	248	752	1021	581	110	24	37	280	66	3	241	19	453	55	611
Boston/Milwaukee/Atlanta	.235	.353	53	1760	188	174	414	622	296	68	10	40	182	35	12	189	9	316	41	367
Chicago Cubs	.242	.325	53	1753	178	134	425	569	322	75	15	13	154	63	0	139	9	301	53	345
Cincinnati Reds	.243	.358	51	1690	192	166	411	605	289	77	18	27	187	29	9	148	13	225	40	332
Pittsburgh Pirates	.254	.359	47	1576	175	135	400	565	289	76	16	19	162	39	5	109	19	226	42	337
Philadelphia Phillies	.237	.342	26	848	87	78	201	290	147	34	5	15	82	14	6	73	6	145	14	167
New York Mets	.247	.362	24	835	87	74	206	302	154	29	2	21	73	15	4	73	8	162	8	192
San Diego Padres	.253	.367	9	300	28	26	76	110	55	14	1	6	25	1	5	23	0	55	3	61
Arizona Diamondbacks	.264	.394	7	246	37	30	65	97	45	14	0	6	36	5	2	17	6	70	2	49
Florida Marlins	.272	.424	7	250	37	33	68	106	47	12	1	8	34	1	2	36	1	48	4	62

WORLD SERIES – CLUB FIELDING

AMERICAN LEAGUE

	PCT	G	TC	CA	PO	A	E	DP	TP	PB
New York Yankees	.981	213	8104	7946	5698	2248	158	187	0	14
Philadelphia/Oakland	.972	75	2870	2791	2016	775	79	56	0	5
Boston Red Sox	.974	60	2413	2350	1623	727	63	43	0	5
Detroit Tigers	.963	56	2238	2155	1507	648	83	38	0	5
Washington/Minnesota	.976	40	1563	1526	1081	445	37	35	0	2
St.Louis/Baltimore	.972	39	1472	1431	1039	392	41	27	0	0
Cleveland Indians	.975	30	1164	1135	797	338	29	35	1	1
Chicago White Sox	.960	26	1088	1045	687	358	43	20	0	4
Kansas City Royals	.980	13	504	494	342	152	10	11	0	1
Toronto Blue Jays	.974	12	427	416	324	92	11	10	0	0
Milwaukee Brewers	.960	7	272	261	180	81	11	3	0	0

NATIONAL LEAGUE

	PCT	G	TC	CA	PO	A	E	DP	TP	PB
Brooklyn/Los Angeles	.975	105	3975	3875	2759	1116	100	89	0	9
St. Louis Cardinals	.976	96	3569	3485	2543	942	84	76	0	5
New York/San Francisco	.966	93	3752	3623	2496	1127	129	69	0	7
Boston/Milwaukee/Atlanta	.980	53	2092	2050	1436	614	42	50	0	1
Chicago Cubs	.969	53	2133	2066	1420	646	67	48	0	6
Cincinnati Reds	.976	51	1946	1899	1367	532	47	47	0	2
Pittsburgh Pirates	.966	47	1834	1772	1235	537	62	39	0	5
Philadelphia Phillies	.985	26	955	941	688	253	14	20	0	1
New York Mets	.976	24	905	883	659	224	22	10	0	0
San Diego Padres	.978	9	316	309	228	81	7	10	0	1
Arizona Diamondbacks	.988	7	259	256	195	61	3	6	0	0
Florida Marlins	.972	7	282	274	192	82	8	9	0	0

WORLD SERIES – CLUB PITCHING

AMERICAN LEAGUE

	ERA	OBA	G	CG	SV	SHO	AB	IP	H	TB	2B	3B	HR	RBI	R	ER	BB	HP	SO	WP	BK
New York Yankees	3.08	.240	213	79	14	16	7072	1899.1	1699	2477	283	45	135	711	752	650	606	38	1197	25	3
Philadelphia/Oakland	2.56	.228	75	34	11	3	2473	672.1	563	790	105	16	30	210	235	191	208	16	448	17	1
Boston Red Sox	2.76	.238	60	30	2	6	1983	541.0	471	674	77	27	24	187	202	166	160	15	275	8	3
Detroit Tigers	3.17	.257	56	34	2	2	1902	502.2	489	679	87	17	23	200	222	177	133	13	289	8	1
Washington/Minnesota	3.07	.263	39	12	3	3	1374	360.1	361	511	54	9	26	138	147	123	105	11	207	10	2
St.Louis/Baltimore	2.52	.235	39	15	5	4	1295	346.1	304	454	57	6	27	112	117	97	111	5	240	8	2
Cleveland Indians	3.18	.241	30	10	3	3	975	266.0	235	341	36	2	22	101	106	94	104	3	145	7	2
Chicago White Sox	2.87	.244	26	13	0	2	837	229.0	204	282	27	12	9	80	91	73	61	9	104	5	0
Kansas City Royals	2.92	.237	13	3	1	1	417	114.0	99	139	23	1	5	39	40	37	33	2	59	2	0
Toronto Blue Jays	4.25	.248	12	0	5	0	412	108.0	102	149	13	2	10	54	56	51	54	2	98	5	1
Milwaukee Brewers	4.80	.273	7	1	2	1	245	60.0	67	101	16	3	4	34	39	32	20	0	26	3	1

NATIONAL LEAGUE

	ERA	OBA	G	CG	SV	SHO	AB	IP	H	TB	2B	3B	HR	RBI	R	ER	BB	HP	SO	WP	BK
Brooklyn/Los Angeles	3.52	.239	105	32	4	9	3416	919.2	818	1263	119	28	90	379	407	360	365	21	610	22	3
St. Louis Cardinals	3.33	.240	96	36	7	10	3183	847.2	763	1149	126	19	74	339	368	314	331	19	575	20	2
New York/San Francisco	3.20	.239	93	40	0	11	3116	832.1	745	1081	118	28	54	324	360	296	271	13	444	23	1
Boston/Milwaukee/Atlanta	2.90	.218	53	16	4	7	1750	478.2	382	601	62	8	47	169	176	154	171	14	322	10	2
Chicago Cubs	3.59	.243	53	23	0	8	1764	473.1	428	594	75	11	23	207	225	189	177	19	246	12	1
Cincinnati Reds	3.34	.236	51	13	8	3	1687	455.2	398	608	56	11	44	179	190	169	173	6	259	8	1
Pittsburgh Pirates	4.08	.259	47	17	4	2	1597	412.1	413	620	60	24	33	202	221	187	127	17	224	14	1
Philadelphia Phillies	4.04	.265	26	6	5	1	871	229.1	231	361	35	10	25	105	109	103	85	6	153	6	0
New York Mets	2.70	.230	24	2	8	0	825	219.2	190	280	32	8	14	73	76	66	96	8	183	6	0
San Diego Padres	5.21	.279	9	0	1	0	297	76.0	83	131	9	0	13	48	49	44	44	3	56	3	0
Arizona Diamondbacks	1.94	.183	7	1	0	1	229	65.0	42	66	6	0	6	14	14	14	16	0	63	4	1
Florida Marlins	5.48	.291	7	0	2	0	247	64.0	72	107	12	1	7	42	44	39	40	0	51	1	0

	AB	R	H	TB	1B	2B	3B	HR	RBI	SH	SF	BB	HP	SO	SB	LOB	BA	SLG
1903 (8)																		
AL:Bos	282	39	71	113	49	4	16	2	35	6	-	13	2	27	5	55	.252	.401
NL:Pitt	270	24	64	92	47	7	9	1	23	3	-	14	1	45	7	51	.237	.341
1905 (5)																		
NL:NY	153	15	32	39	25	7	0	0	13	5	-	15	2	26	11	31	.209	.255
AL:Phil	155	3	25	30	20	5	0	0	2	3	-	5	1	25	2	26	.161	.194
1906 (6)																		
AL:Chi	187	22	37	53	24	10	3	0	19	6	-	18	3	35	6	33	.198	.283
NL:Chi	184	18	36	45	27	9	0	0	11	13	-	18	2	27	8	37	.196	.245
1907 (5)																		
NL:Chi	167	19	43	51	36	6	1	0	16	9	-	12	4	25	18	35	.257	.305
AL:Det	173	6	36	41	33	1	2	0	6	3	-	9	1	21	7	34	.208	.237
1908 (5)																		
NL:Chi	164	24	48	59	41	4	2	1	21	9	-	13	0	26	13	30	.293	.360
AL:Det	158	15	32	37	27	5	0	0	14	5	-	12	2	26	5	27	.203	.234
1909 (7)																		
NL:Pitt	223	34	49	70	34	12	1	2	26	12	-	20	6	34	18	44	.220	.320
AL:Det	234	28	55	77	37	16	0	2	25	4	-	20	4	22	6	50	.235	.329
1910 (5)																		
AL:Phil	177	35	56	80	35	19	1	1	29	7	-	17	2	24	7	36	.316	.452
NL:Chi	158	15	35	48	23	11	1	0	13	7	-	18	0	31	3	31	.222	.304
1911 (6)																		
AL:Phil	205	27	50	74	32	15	0	3	21	9	-	4	0	31	4	29	.244	.361
NL:NY	189	13	33	46	21	11	1	0	10	6	-	14	3	44	4	31	.175	.243
1912 (8)																		
AL:Bos	273	25	60	89	39	14	6	1	21	8	-	19	1	36	6	55	.220	.326
NL:NY	274	31	74	99	55	14	4	1	25	7	-	22	3	39	12	53	.270	.361
1913 (5)																		
AL:Phil	174	23	46	64	36	4	4	2	21	7	-	7	0	16	5	30	.264	.368
NL:NY	164	15	33	41	28	3	1	1	15	2	-	8	3	19	5	24	.201	.250
1914 (4)																		
NL:Bos	135	16	33	46	24	6	2	1	14	3	-	15	1	18	9	27	.244	.341
AL:Phil	128	6	22	31	13	9	0	0	5	3	-	13	0	28	2	21	.172	.242
1915 (5)																		
AL:Bos	159	12	42	57	35	2	2	3	11	7	-	11	1	25	1	35	.264	.358
NL:Phil	148	10	27	36	21	4	1	1	9	5	-	10	2	25	2	23	.182	.243
1916 (5)																		
AL:Bos	164	21	39	64	24	7	6	2	18	12	-	18	0	25	1	31	.238	.390
NL:Brk	170	13	34	49	26	2	5	1	11	6	-	14	2	19	1	32	.200	.288
1917 (6)																		
AL:Chi	197	21	54	63	47	6	0	1	18	3	-	11	0	28	6	37	.274	.320
NL:NY	199	17	51	70	40	5	4	2	16	3	-	6	2	27	4	37	.256	.352
1918 (6)																		
AL:Bos	172	9	32	40	27	2	3	0	6	8	-	16	1	21	3	32	.186	.233
NL:Chi	176	10	37	44	31	5	1	0	10	4	-	18	2	14	3	31	.210	.250
1919 (8)																		
NL:Cin	251	35	64	88	47	10	7	0	34	13	-	25	5	22	7	46	.255	.351
AL:Chi	263	20	59	78	45	10	3	1	17	7	-	15	3	30	5	52	.224	.297
1920 (7)																		
AL:Clev	217	21	53	72	40	9	2	2	18	3	-	21	0	21	2	43	.244	.332
NL:Brk	215	8	44	51	38	5	1	0	8	5	-	10	0	20	1	39	.205	.237
1921 (8)																		
NL:NY	264	29	71	98	52	13	4	2	28	6	-	22	1	38	7	54	.269	.371
AL:NY	241	22	50	65	40	7	1	2	20	9	-	27	1	44	6	43	.207	.270
1922 (5)																		
NL:NY	162	18	50	57	46	2	1	1	18	5	-	12	0	15	1	32	.309	.352
AL:NY	158	11	32	46	23	6	1	2	11	6	-	8	2	20	2	25	.203	.291
1923 (6)																		
AL:NY	205	30	60	91	43	8	4	5	29	6	-	20	1	22	1	43	.293	.444
NL:NY	201	17	47	70	37	2	3	5	17	0	-	12	1	18	1	35	.234	.348
1924 (7)																		
AL:Wash	248	26	61	85	47	9	0	5	23	6	-	29	0	34	5	57	.246	.343
NL:NY	253	27	66	91	51	9	2	4	22	7	-	25	2	40	3	59	.261	.360

	AB	R	H	TB	1B	2B	3B	HR	RBI	SH	SF	BB	HP	SO	SB	LOB	BA	SLG
1925 (7)																		
NL:Pitt	230	25	61	89	43	12	2	4	25	8	-	17	4	32	7	54	.265	.387
AL:Wash	225	26	59	91	43	8	0	8	25	10	-	17	2	31	2	46	.262	.404
1926 (7)																		
NL:StL	239	31	65	91	48	12	1	4	30	12	-	11	1	30	2	43	.272	.381
AL:NY	223	21	54	78	39	10	1	4	19	10	-	31	1	31	1	55	.242	.350
1927 (4)																		
AL:NY	136	23	38	54	28	6	2	2	20	6	-	13	1	25	2	29	.279	.397
NL:Pitt	130	10	29	37	22	6	1	0	10	6	-	4	1	7	0	23	.223	.285
1928 (4)																		
AL:NY	134	27	37	71	21	7	0	9	25	5	-	13	1	12	4	24	.276	.530
NL:StL	131	10	27	37	20	5	1	1	9	2	-	11	1	29	3	27	.206	.282
1929 (5)																		
AL:Phil	171	26	48	71	37	5	0	6	26	7	-	13	1	27	0	35	.281	.415
NL:Chi	173	17	43	56	34	6	2	1	15	2	-	13	0	50	1	36	.249	.324
1930 (6)																		
AL:Phil	178	21	35	67	17	10	2	6	21	7	-	24	1	32	0	36	.197	.376
NL:StL	190	12	38	56	25	10	1	2	11	4	-	11	0	33	1	37	.200	.295
1931 (7)																		
NL:StL	229	19	54	71	41	11	0	2	17	4	-	9	0	41	8	40	.236	.310
AL:Phil	227	22	50	64	42	5	0	3	20	4	-	28	1	46	0	52	.220	.282
1932 (4)																		
AL:NY	144	37	45	75	31	6	0	8	36	1	-	23	4	26	0	33	.313	.521
NL:Chi	146	19	37	58	24	8	2	3	16	1	-	11	0	24	2	31	.253	.397
1933 (5)																		
NL:NY	176	16	47	61	39	5	0	3	16	6	-	11	0	21	0	39	.267	.347
AL:Wash	173	11	37	47	31	4	0	2	11	3	-	13	0	24	1	37	.214	.272
1934 (7)																		
NL:StL	262	34	73	103	52	14	5	2	32	4	-	11	1	31	2	49	.279	.393
AL:Det	250	23	56	76	41	12	1	2	20	6	-	25	2	43	4	64	.224	.304
1935 (6)																		
AL:Det	206	21	51	67	38	11	1	1	18	3	-	25	2	27	1	51	.248	.325
NL:Chi	202	18	48	73	35	6	2	5	17	7	-	11	1	29	1	33	.238	.361
1936 (6)																		
AL:NY	215	43	65	96	49	8	1	7	41	3	-	26	1	35	1	43	.302	.447
NL:NY	203	23	50	71	37	9	0	4	20	7	-	21	0	33	0	46	.246	.350
1937 (5)																		
AL:NY	169	28	42	68	28	6	4	4	25	2	-	21	1	21	0	36	.249	.402
NL:NY	169	12	40	49	33	6	0	1	12	0	-	11	0	21	1	36	.237	.290
1938 (4)																		
AL:NY	135	22	37	60	25	6	1	5	21	1	-	11	1	16	3	24	.274	.444
NL:Chi	136	9	33	45	26	4	1	2	8	1	-	6	0	26	0	26	.243	.331
1939 (4)																		
AL:NY	131	20	27	54	15	4	1	7	18	2	-	9	0	20	0	16	.206	.412
NL:Cin	133	8	27	32	23	3	1	0	8	2	-	6	1	22	1	23	.203	.316
1940 (7)																		
NL:Cin	232	22	58	78	42	14	0	2	21	4	-	15	0	30	1	49	.250	.336
AL:Det	228	28	56	83	40	9	3	4	24	3	-	30	0	30	0	50	.246	.364
1941 (5)																		
AL:NY	166	17	41	54	33	5	1	2	16	0	-	23	2	18	2	42	.247	.325
NL:Brk	150	11	29	43	19	7	2	1	11	0	-	14	0	21	0	27	.182	.270
1942 (5)																		
NL:StL	163	23	39	53	31	4	2	2	23	7	-	17	0	19	0	32	.239	.325
AL:NY	178	18	44	59	35	6	0	3	14	1	-	8	0	22	3	34	.247	.331
1943 (5)																		
AL:NY	159	17	35	50	26	5	2	2	14	4	-	12	0	30	2	29	.220	.314
NL:StL	165	9	37	48	30	5	0	2	8	5	-	11	0	26	1	37	.224	.291
1944 (6)																		
NL:StL	204	16	49	69	36	9	1	3	15	7	-	19	0	43	0	51	.240	.338
AL:StL	197	12	36	50	25	9	1	1	9	1	-	23	0	49	0	44	.183	.254
1945 (7)																		
AL:Det	242	32	54	70	42	10	0	2	32	3	-	33	2	22	3	53	.223	.289
NL:Chi	247	29	65	90	45	16	3	1	27	10	-	19	0	48	2	50	.263	.364

	AB	R	H	TB	1B	2B	3B	HR	RBI	SH	SF	BB	HP	SO	SB	LOB	BA	SLG
1946 (7)																		
NL:StL	232	28	60	86	38	19	2	1	27	8	-	19	2	30	3	50	.259	.371
AL:Bos	233	20	56	77	44	7	1	4	18	3	-	22	1	28	2	53	.240	.330
1947 (7)																		
AL:NY	238	38	67	100	47	11	5	4	36	3	-	38	2	37	2	63	.282	.420
NL:Brk	226	29	52	70	37	13	1	1	26	3	-	30	1	32	7	46	.230	.310
1948 (6)																		
AL:Clev	191	17	38	57	27	7	0	4	16	3	-	12	1	26	2	34	.199	.298
NL:Bos	187	17	43	61	33	6	0	4	16	7	-	16	0	19	1	34	.230	.326
1949 (5)																		
AL:NY	164	21	37	57	23	10	2	2	20	3	-	18	0	27	2	32	.226	.348
NL:Brk	162	14	34	55	22	7	1	4	14	2	-	15	1	38	1	31	.210	.340
1950 (4)																		
AL:NY	135	11	30	41	24	3	1	2	10	2	-	13	1	12	1	33	.222	.304
NL:Phil	128	5	26	34	19	6	1	0	3	6	-	7	1	24	1	26	.203	.266
1951 (6)																		
AL:NY	199	29	49	75	35	7	2	5	25	0	-	26	1	23	0	41	.246	.377
NL:NY	194	18	46	61	36	7	1	2	15	2	-	25	1	22	2	45	.237	.314
1952 (7)																		
AL:NY	232	26	50	89	33	5	2	10	24	2	-	31	1	32	1	48	.216	.384
NL:Brk	233	20	50	75	37	7	0	6	18	6	-	24	1	49	5	52	.215	.322
1953 (6)																		
AL:NY	201	33	56	97	37	6	4	9	32	4	-	25	4	43	2	47	.279	.483
NL:Brk	213	27	64	103	42	13	1	8	26	2	-	15	2	30	2	49	.300	.484
1954 (4)																		
NL:NY	130	21	33	42	28	3	0	2	20	6	2	17	0	24	1	28	.254	.323
AL:Clev	137	9	26	42	17	5	1	3	9	3	0	16	1	23	0	37	.190	.307
1955 (7)																		
NL:Brk	223	31	58	95	40	8	1	9	30	6	2	33	2	38	2	55	.260	.426
AL:NY	222	26	55	87	41	4	2	8	25	1	0	22	1	39	3	41	.248	.392
1956 (7)																		
AL:NY	229	33	58	100	40	6	0	12	33	4	2	21	0	43	2	40	.253	.437
NL:Brk	215	25	42	61	30	8	1	3	24	2	3	32	0	47	1	42	.199	.284
1957 (7)																		
NL:Mil	225	23	47	79	32	6	1	8	22	6	0	22	3	40	1	46	.209	.351
AL:NY	230	25	57	87	42	7	1	7	25	3	1	22	0	34	1	45	.248	.378
1958 (7)																		
AL:NY	233	29	49	86	33	5	1	10	29	2	2	21	0	42	1	40	.210	.369
NL:Mil	240	25	60	81	46	10	1	3	24	4	3	27	0	56	1	58	.250	.338
1959 (6)																		
NL:LA	203	21	53	79	42	3	1	7	19	4	0	12	0	27	5	42	.261	.389
AL:Chi	199	23	52	74	38	10	0	4	19	3	1	20	2	33	2	43	.261	.372
1960 (7)																		
NL:Pitt	234	27	60	83	45	11	0	4	26	3	0	12	3	26	2	42	.256	.355
AL:NY	269	55	91	142	64	13	4	10	54	2	1	18	2	40	0	51	.338	.528
1961 (5)																		
AL:NY	165	27	42	73	26	8	1	7	26	3	1	24	0	25	1	34	.255	.442
NL:Cin	170	13	35	52	24	8	0	3	11	0	0	8	3	27	0	33	.206	.306
1962 (7)																		
AL:NY	221	20	44	61	34	6	1	3	17	1	1	21	2	39	4	43	.199	.276
NL:SF	226	21	51	80	34	10	2	5	19	4	0	12	1	39	1	39	.226	.354
1963 (4)																		
NL:LA	117	12	25	41	17	3	2	3	12	2	1	12	0	25	2	17	.214	.373
AL:NY	129	4	22	31	17	3	0	2	4	1	0	5	1	37	0	24	.171	.240
1964 (7)																		
NL:StL	240	32	61	90	45	8	3	5	29	4	2	18	0	30	3	47	.254	.375
AL:NY	239	33	60	101	39	21	0	10	33	1	2	25	2	54	2	47	.251	.423
1965 (7)																		
NL:LA	234	24	64	91	48	10	1	5	21	0	0	13	3	31	9	52	.274	.389
AL:Minn	215	20	42	71	27	7	2	6	19	2	0	19	0	54	2	36	.195	.330
1966 (4)																		
AL:Balt	120	13	24	41	16	3	1	4	10	2	0	11	0	17	0	18	.200	.342
NL:LA	120	2	17	23	13	3	0	1	2	1	0	13	0	28	1	24	.142	.192

	AB	R	H	TB	1B	2B	3B	HR	RBI	SH	SF	BB	HP	SO	SB	LOB	BA	SLG
1967 (7)																		
NL:StL	229	25	51	81	33	11	2	5	24	0	2	17	0	30	7	40	.223	.354
AL:Bos	222	21	48	80	33	6	1	8	19	4	2	17	2	49	1	43	.216	.360
1968 (7)																		
AL:Det	231	34	56	90	41	4	3	8	33	2	1	27	3	59	0	44	.242	.390
NL:StL	239	27	61	95	44	7	3	7	27	1	0	21	1	40	11	49	.255	.397
1969 (5)																		
NL:NY	159	15	35	61	21	8	0	6	13	2	1	15	1	35	1	34	.220	.384
AL:Balt	157	9	23	33	19	1	0	3	9	0	1	15	0	28	1	29	.146	.210
1970 (5)																		
AL:Balt	171	33	50	87	33	7	0	10	32	2	0	20	0	33	0	31	.292	.509
NL:Cin	164	20	35	58	23	6	1	5	20	2	1	15	0	23	1	28	.213	.354
1971 (7)																		
NL:Pitt	238	23	56	84	40	9	2	5	21	4	0	26	1	47	5	63	.235	.353
AL:Balt	219	24	45	65	36	3	1	5	22	2	3	20	4	35	1	39	.205	.297
1972 (7)																		
AL:Oak	220	16	46	65	37	4	0	5	16	6	0	21	1	37	1	45	.209	.295
NL:Cin	220	21	46	65	34	8	1	3	21	5	3	27	1	46	12	49	.209	.295
1973 (7)																		
AL:Oak	241	21	51	75	34	12	3	2	20	2	1	28	2	62	3	58	.212	.311
NL:NY	261	24	66	89	53	7	2	4	16	4	0	26	3	36	0	72	.253	.341
1974 (5)																		
AL:Oak	142	16	30	46	22	4	0	4	14	7	1	16	2	42	3	26	.211	.324
NL:LA	158	11	36	54	27	4	1	4	10	3	1	16	1	32	3	36	.228	.342
1975 (7)																		
NL:Cin	244	29	59	95	40	9	3	7	29	2	2	25	2	30	9	50	.242	.389
AL:Bos	239	30	60	89	45	7	2	6	30	4	3	30	1	40	0	52	.251	.372
1976 (4)																		
NL:Cin	134	22	42	70	25	10	3	4	21	0	2	12	0	16	7	22	.313	.522
AL:NY	135	8	30	38	25	3	1	1	8	0	1	12	1	16	1	33	.222	.281
1977 (6)																		
AL:NY	205	26	50	84	32	10	0	8	25	4	1	11	2	37	1	32	.244	.410
NL:LA	208	28	48	86	31	5	3	9	28	0	2	16	1	36	2	31	.231	.413
1978 (6)																		
AL:NY	222	36	68	85	57	8	0	3	34	1	0	16	2	40	5	47	.306	.383
NL:LA	199	23	52	78	38	8	0	6	22	1	0	20	0	31	5	38	.261	.392
1979 (7)																		
NL:Pitt	251	32	81	110	59	18	1	3	32	3	5	16	3	35	0	60	.323	.438
AL:Balt	233	26	54	78	39	10	1	4	23	1	0	26	1	41	2	49	.232	.335
1980 (6)																		
NL:Phil	201	27	59	81	43	13	0	3	26	2	4	15	2	17	3	41	.294	.403
AL:KC	207	23	60	97	41	9	2	8	22	2	3	26	0	49	6	54	.290	.469
1981 (6)																		
NL:LA	198	27	51	77	38	6	1	6	26	4	2	20	2	44	6	46	.258	.389
AL:NY	193	22	46	74	31	8	1	6	22	5	2	33	0	24	4	55	.238	.383
1982 (7)																		
NL:StL	245	39	67	101	44	16	3	4	34	1	1	20	0	26	7	49	.273	.412
AL:Mil	238	33	64	95	45	12	2	5	29	1	1	19	1	28	1	44	.269	.399
1983 (5)																		
AL:Balt	164	18	35	61	21	8	0	6	17	0	3	10	1	37	1	28	.213	.372
NL:Phil	159	9	31	49	22	4	1	4	9	0	1	7	0	29	1	23	.195	.308
1984 (5)																		
AL:Det	158	23	40	65	29	4	0	7	22	2	2	24	2	27	7	39	.253	.411
NL:SD	166	15	44	60	34	7	0	3	14	1	3	11	0	26	2	34	.265	.361
1985 (7)																		
AL:KC	236	28	68	90	52	12	2	2	26	3	0	28	1	56	7	56	.288	.381
NL:StL	216	13	40	58	27	10	1	2	13	3	0	18	0	42	2	38	.185	.269
1986 (7)																		
NL:NY	240	32	65	92	52	6	0	7	29	6	2	21	1	43	7	50	.271	.383
AL:Bos	248	27	69	99	51	11	2	5	26	4	2	28	3	53	0	69	.278	.398
1987 (7)																		
AL:Minn	238	38	64	101	44	10	3	7	38	1	0	29	3	36	6	56	.269	.424
NL:StL	232	26	60	74	50	8	0	2	25	2	1	13	1	44	12	43	.259	.319

	AB	R	H	TB	1B	2B	3B	HR	RBI	SH	SF	BB	HP	SO	SB	LOB	BA	SLG
1988 (5)																		
NL:LA	167	21	41	66	27	8	1	5	19	1	0	13	1	36	4	30	.246	.395
AL:Oak	158	11	28	37	23	3	0	2	11	1	1	17	1	41	3	34	.177	.234
1989 (4)																		
AL:Oak	146	32	44	85	24	8	3	9	30	0	0	18	1	22	4	31	.301	.582
NL:SF	134	14	28	46	19	4	1	4	14	0	1	8	0	27	2	21	.209	.343
1990 (4)																		
NL:Cin	142	22	45	67	31	9	2	3	22	1	1	15	1	9	2	32	.317	.472
AL:Oak	135	8	28	41	21	4	0	3	8	2	1	12	0	28	7	31	.207	.304
1991 (7)																		
AL:Minn	241	24	56	96	36	8	4	8	24	2	2	21	1	48	7	47	.232	.398
NL:Atl	249	29	63	105	41	10	4	8	29	4	3	26	1	39	5	52	.253	.422
1992 (6)																		
AL:Tor	196	17	45	71	31	8	0	6	17	2	1	18	1	33	5	38	.230	.362
NL:Atl	200	20	44	59	35	6	0	3	19	2	2	20	1	48	15	40	.220	.295
1993 (6)																		
AL:Tor	206	45	64	105	40	13	5	6	45	0	7	25	3	30	7	39	.311	.510
NL:Phil	212	36	58	90	42	7	2	7	35	1	1	34	1	50	7	54	.274	.425
1995 (6)																		
NL:Atl	193	23	47	81	29	10	0	8	23	5	1	25	2	34	5	44	.244	.420
AL:Clev	195	19	35	59	22	7	1	5	17	0	0	25	0	37	8	39	.179	303
1996 (6)																		
AL:NY	199	18	43	57	48	6	1	2	16	2	0	26	1	43	4	68	.216	.286
NL:Atl	201	26	51	74	37	9	1	4	26	4	3	23	1	36	3	41	.254	.368
1997 (7)																		
NL:Fla	250	37	68	106	47	12	1	8	34	1	2	36	1	48	4	62	.272	.424
AL:Clev	247	44	72	107	52	12	1	7	42	5	3	40	0	51	5	59	.291	.433
1998 (4)																		
AL:NY	139	26	43	66	32	5	0	6	25	1	1	20	1	29	1	34	.309	.475
NL:SD	134	13	32	50	21	7	1	3	11	0	2	12	0	29	1	27	.239	.373
1999 (4)																		
AL:NY	137	21	37	57	27	5	0	5	20	3	0	13	0	31	5	27	.270	.416
NL:Atl.	130	9	26	36	19	5	1	1	9	0	0	15	0	26	1	25	.200	.277
2000 (5)																		
AL:NY	179	19	47	73	32	8	3	4	18	1	3	25	3	40	1	52	.263	.408
NL:NY	175	16	40	60	28	8	0	4	15	3	1	11	3	48	0	36	.229	.343
2001 (7)																		
NL:Ari	246	37	65	97	45	14	0	6	36	5	2	17	6	70	2	49	.264	.394
AL:NY	229	14	42	66	30	6	0	6	14	1	0	16	1	63	1	38	.183	.288

WORLD SERIES CLUB PITCHING & FIELDING

[PL=Players Used   PI=Pitchers Used]

		Fielding:										Pitching:					
	PL	TC	CA	PO	A	E	DP	TP	PB	AVG		PI	IP	ER	ERA	CG	SHO
1903 (8)																	
AL:Bos	13	329	315	213	102	14	6	0	2	.957		3	71.0	16	2.03	7	2
NL:Pitt	14	324	306	210	96	18	5	0	0	.944		5	70.0	29	3.73	6	0
1905 (5)																	
NL:NY	12	219	213	135	78	6	3	0	0	.973		3	45.0	0	0.00	4	3
AL:Phil	13	194	185	129	56	9	3	0	0	.954		3	43.0	4	0.83	5	1
1906 (6)																	
AL:Chi	16	275	261	162	99	14	2	0	1	.949		4	54.0	10	1.67	4	1
NL:Chi	14	250	243	159	84	7	4	0	3	.972		4	53.0	19	3.22	4	1
1907 (5)																	
NL:Chi	15	219	209	144	65	10	6	0	1	.954		4	48.0	4	0.75	4	1
AL:Det	14	217	208	138	70	9	2	0	0	.959		4	46.0	11	2.15	4	0
1908 (5)																	
NL:Chi	13	214	209	135	74	5	4	0	1	.977		4	45.0	13	2.60	3	2
AL:Det	16	204	194	131	63	10	5	0	1	.951		5	44.0	18	3.68	3	0
1909 (7)																	
NL:Pitt	17	285	270	182	88	15	3	0	0	.947		6	61.0	18	2.65	4	1
AL:Det	16	289	270	183	87	19	4	0	1	.934		5	61.0	20	2.95	4	1
1910 (5)																	
AL:Phil	12	206	195	136	59	11	6	0	0	.947		2	45.2	14	2.75	5	0
NL:Chi	18	221	209	132	77	12	3	0	0	.946		7	44.0	23	4.70	1	0
1911 (6)																	
AL:Phil	14	250	239	167	72	11	2	0	0	.956		3	55.2	8	1.29	5	0
NL:NY	15	257	241	162	79	16	2	0	1	.938		5	54.0	17	2.83	2	0
1912 (8)																	
AL:Bos	17	337	323	222	101	14	5	0	0	.958		5	74.0	22	2.67	3	0
NL:NY	17	346	329	221	108	17	4	0	0	.951		5	73.2	15	1.83	6	0
1913 (5)																	
AL:Phil	12	197	192	138	54	5	6	0	0	.975		3	46.0	11	2.15	5	0
NL:NY	20	209	202	135	67	7	1	0	1	.967		5	45.0	19	3.80	3	1
1914 (4)																	
NL:Bos	15	183	179	117	62	4	4	0	0	.978		3	39.0	5	1.15	3	1
AL:Phil	16	180	177	111	66	3	4	0	1	.983		6	37.0	15	3.55	2	0
1915 (5)																	
AL:Bos	17	194	190	132	58	4	2	0	0	.979		3	44.0	9	1.84	5	0
NL:Phil	16	188	185	131	54	3	3	0	0	.984		4	43.2	10	2.06	4	0
1916 (5)																	
AL:Bos	20	243	237	147	90	6	5	0	1	.975		5	49.0	8	1.46	3	0
NL:Brk	20	225	212	142	70	13	2	0	2	.942		7	47.1	16	3.04	1	0
1917 (6)																	
AL:Chi	16	250	238	156	82	12	7	0	1	.952		5	52.0	16	2.38	4	0
NL:NY	17	236	225	153	72	11	3	0	1	.953		6	51.0	17	3.00	3	2
1918 (6)																	
AL:Bos	15	247	246	159	88	1	4	0	1	.996		4	53.0	10	1.70	5	1
NL:Chi	17	237	232	156	76	5	7	0	2	.979		4	52.0	6	1.04	4	1
1919 (8)																	
NL:Cin	17	324	312	216	96	12	7	0	0	.963		6	72.0	13	1.62	5	2
AL:Chi	19	341	329	213	116	12	9	0	1	.965		7	71.0	28	3.54	5	1
1920 (7)																	
AL:Clev	20	283	271	182	89	12	8	1	0	.958		5	61.0	6	0.88	5	2
NL:Brk	21	274	268	177	91	6	5	0	2	.978		7	59.0	16	2.44	3	1
1921 (8)																	
NL:NY	13	319	314	212	102	5	5	0	2	.984		4	71.0	20	2.53	5	1
AL:NY	19	322	316	210	106	6	8	0	0	.981		8	70.0	24	3.08	6	2
1922 (5)																	
NL:NY	16	214	208	138	70	6	4	0	0	.972		5	46.0	8	1.56	4	1
AL:NY	17	193	192	129	62	1	7	0	1	.995		5	43.0	16	3.35	2	0
1923 (6)																	
AL:NY	17	242	239	162	77	3	6	0	0	.988		5	54.0	17	2.83	2	0
NL:NY	22	245	239	159	80	6	8	0	0	.976		8	53.0	25	4.24	1	1

	Fielding:										Pitching:					
	PL	TC	CA	PO	A	E	DP	TP	PB	AVG	PI	IP	ER	ERA	CG	SHO
1924 (7)																
AL:Wash	21	312	300	201	99	12	10	0	1	.962	8	66.2	16	2.16	3	0
NL:NY	21	300	294	200	94	6	4	0	0	.980	9	67.1	23	3.07	2	0
1925 (7)																
NL:Pitt	18	278	271	182	89	7	4	0	0	.975	7	61.0	25	3.69	4	0
AL:Wash	21	264	255	180	75	9	8	0	1	.966	6	60.0	19	2.85	4	1
1926 (7)																
NL:StL	19	292	287	189	98	5	6	0	0	.983	8	63.0	19	2.71	4	1
AL:NY	19	278	271	189	82	7	3	0	1	.975	7	63.0	22	3.14	3	0
1927 (4)																
AL:NY	15	155	152	108	44	3	4	0	0	.981	4	36.0	8	2.00	3	0
NL:Pitt	21	156	150	104	46	6	2	0	0	.962	7	34.2	20	5.19	0	0
1928 (4)																
AL:NY	16	142	136	108	28	6	3	0	0	.958	3	36.0	9	2.25	4	0
NL:StL	20	143	138	102	36	5	3	0	0	.965	6	34.0	23	6.08	0	0
1929 (5)																
AL:Phil	17	179	175	135	40	4	2	0	0	.978	6	45.0	13	2.60	2	0
NL:Chi	19	182	175	131	44	7	4	0	0	.962	6	43.2	21	4.33	2	0
1930 (6)																
AL:Phil	15	200	197	156	41	3	2	0	0	.985	5	52.0	10	1.73	4	1
NL:StL	21	212	207	153	54	5	4	0	1	.976	7	51.0	21	5.40	4	1
1931 (7)																
NL:StL	21	263	259	186	73	4	7	0	0	.985	6	62.0	16	2.32	3	1
AL:Phil	20	254	252	183	69	2	4	0	0	.992	6	61.0	18	2.66	4	1
1932 (4)																
AL:NY	16	157	149	108	41	8	1	0	0	.949	6	36.0	13	3.25	2	0
NL:Chi	22	148	142	102	40	6	7	0	0	.959	8	34.0	35	9.26	1	0
1933 (5)																
NL:NY	15	212	208	141	67	4	5	0	0	.981	5	47.0	8	1.53	3	0
AL:Wash	19	202	201	138	65	4	4	0	0	.981	7	46.0	14	2.73	1	1
1934 (7)																
NL:StL	20	284	269	196	73	15	2	0	0	.947	8	65.1	17	2.34	4	1
AL:Det	17	277	265	195	70	12	6	0	0	.957	6	65.0	27	3.74	4	0
1935 (6)																
AL:Det	15	146	137	165	72	9	7	0	1	.963	5	55.0	14	2.29	5	0
NL:Chi	18	244	238	164	74	6	5	0	0	.975	7	54.2	18	2.96	2	1
1936 (6)																
AL:NY	16	225	219	162	57	6	2	0	0	.973	6	54.0	20	3.33	3	0
NL:NY	22	228	221	159	62	7	7	0	0	.969	8	53.0	40	6.79	3	0
1937 (5)																
AL:NY	17	179	179	132	47	0	2	0	0	1.000	7	44.0	12	2.45	3	0
NL:NY	20	184	175	129	46	9	5	0	0	.951	7	43.0	23	4.81	1	0
1938 (4)																
AL:NY	14	153	147	108	39	6	4	0	0	.961	4	36.0	7	1.75	3	0
NL:Chi	20	140	137	102	35	3	3	0	0	.979	8	34.0	19	5.03	0	0
1939 (4)																
AL:NY	15	163	161	111	50	2	5	0	0	.988	7	37.0	5	1.21	2	1
NL:Cin	18	144	140	106	34	4	1	0	0	.972	5	35.1	17	4.34	2	0
1940 (7)																
NL:Cin	23	257	249	183	66	8	9	0	1	.969	9	61.0	25	3.68	4	1
AL:Det	20	264	260	180	80	4	4	0	0	.985	8	60.0	20	3.00	4	1
1941 (5)																
AL:NY	18	192	190	135	55	2	7	0	0	.990	7	45.0	9	1.80	3	0
NL:Brk	20	196	192	132	60	4	5	0	0	.980	7	44.0	13	2.65	2	0
1942 (5)																
NL:StL	18	190	180	135	45	10	3	0	0	.947	6	45.0	13	2.60	3	1
AL:NY	20	182	177	132	45	5	2	0	0	.973	7	44.0	22	4.50	2	0
1943 (5)																
AL:NY	16	203	198	135	63	5	3	0	0	.975	5	45.0	7	1.40	3	0
NL:StL	20	192	182	129	53	10	4	0	0	.948	6	43.0	12	2.51	2	0
1944 (6)																
NL:StL	20	225	224	165	59	1	3	0	1	.996	8	55.0	12	1.96	2	1
AL:StL	22	233	223	163	60	10	4	0	0	.957	7	54.1	9	1.49	3	0

	Fielding:										Pitching:					
	PL	TC	CA	PO	A	E	DP	TP	PB	AVG	PI	IP	ER	ERA	CG	SHO
1945 (7)																
AL:Det	26	287	282	197	85	5	4	0	2	.983	9	65.2	28	3.83	4	0
NL:Chi	25	279	273	195	78	6	5	0	1	.978	8	65.0	30	4.15	2	2
1946 (7)																
NL:StL	19	258	254	186	68	4	7	0	1	.984	7	62.0	16	2.32	4	1
AL:Bos	26	269	259	183	76	10	5	0	0	.963	11	61.0	20	2.95	2	1
1947 (7)																
AL:NY	24	259	255	185	70	4	4	0	2	.985	9	61.2	28	4.09	3	0
NL:Brk	24	259	251	180	71	8	8	0	2	.969	8	60.0	37	5.55	0	0
1948 (6)																
AL:Clev	23	234	231	159	72	3	9	0	0	.987	8	53.0	16	2.72	4	1
NL:Bos	20	216	210	156	54	6	3	0	0	.972	6	52.0	15	2.60	2	1
1949 (5)																
AL:NY	20	182	179	135	44	3	5	0	0	.984	5	45.0	14	2.80	2	1
NL:Brk	25	177	172	132	40	5	1	0	0	.972	9	44.0	21	4.29	2	1
1950 (4)																
AL:NY	18	154	152	111	41	2	4	0	0	.987	5	37.0	3	0.73	2	1
NL:Phil	20	146	142	107	35	4	1	0	0	.973	5	35.2	9	2.27	1	0
1951 (6)																
AL:NY	21	230	226	159	67	4	10	0	1	.982	8	53.0	11	1.87	3	0
NL:NY	24	231	221	156	65	10	4	0	0	.957	9	52.0	27	4.67	1	0
1952 (7)																
AL:NY	19	268	258	192	66	10	7	0	1	.963	8	64.0	20	2.81	2	1
NL:Brk	19	267	263	192	71	4	4	0	0	.985	6	64.0	25	3.52	3	0
1953 (6)																
AL:NY	20	217	216	156	60	1	5	0	0	.995	9	52.0	26	4.50	2	0
NL:Brk	23	223	216	154	62	7	3	0	0	.969	10	51.1	28	4.94	2	0
1954 (4)																
NL:NY	15	157	150	111	39	7	2	0	0	.955	6	37.0	6	1.46	1	0
AL:Clev	24	150	146	106	40	4	2	0	0	.973	7	35.1	19	4.84	1	0
1955 (7)																
NL:Brk	22	270	264	180	84	6	12	0	0	.978	10	60.0	25	3.75	2	1
AL:NY	24	254	252	180	72	2	7	0	0	.992	9	60.0	28	4.20	2	0
1956 (7)																
AL:NY	22	257	251	185	66	6	7	0	0	.977	8	61.2	17	2.48	5	2
NL:Brk	21	254	252	183	69	2	8	0	0	.992	8	61.0	32	4.72	3	1
1957 (7)																
NL:Mil	23	282	279	186	93	3	10	0	1	.989	8	62.0	24	3.48	4	2
AL:NY	23	265	259	187	72	6	5	0	0	.977	9	62.1	20	2.89	2	0
1958 (7)																
AL:NY	22	259	256	191	65	3	5	0	1	.988	9	63.2	24	3.39	1	2
NL:Mil	19	274	267	189	78	7	5	0	0	.974	6	63.0	26	3.71	3	1
1959 (6)																
NL:LA	24	232	228	159	69	4	7	0	0	.983	9	53.0	19	3.23	0	0
AL:Chi	21	222	218	156	62	4	2	0	1	.982	7	52.0	20	3.46	0	2
1960 (7)																
NL:Pitt	25	257	253	186	67	4	7	0	3	.984	10	62.0	49	7.11	0	0
AL:NY	25	284	276	183	93	8	9	0	0	.972	10	61.0	24	3.54	2	2
1961 (5)																
AL:NY	18	190	185	135	50	5	1	0	1	.974	6	45.0	8	1.60	1	2
NL:Cin	24	178	174	132	42	4	7	0	1	.978	9	44.0	24	4.91	2	0
1962 (7)																
AL:NY	18	255	250	183	67	5	5	0	0	.980	6	61.0	20	2.95	4	1
NL:SF	21	258	250	183	67	8	9	0	1	.969	7	61.0	18	2.66	2	1
1963 (4)																
NL:LA	13	142	139	108	31	3	1	0	0	.979	4	36.0	4	1.00	3	1
AL:NY	20	153	152	102	50	1	7	0	0	.993	7	34.0	11	2.91	0	0
1964 (7)																
NL:StL	21	257	253	189	64	4	6	0	0	.984	8	63.0	30	4.29	2	0
AL:NY	21	277	268	186	82	9	6	0	3	.986	9	62.0	26	3.77	2	0
1965 (7)																
NL:LA	20	258	252	180	72	6	7	0	0	.977	7	60.0	14	2.10	4	3
AL:Minn	21	243	238	180	58	5	3	0	0	.979	9	60.0	21	3.15	3	0

	Fielding:										Pitching:					
	PL	TC	CA	PO	A	E	DP	TP	PB	AVG	PI	IP	ER	ERA	CG	SHO
1966 (4)																
AL:Balt	13	141	141	108	33	0	4	0	0	1.000	4	36.0	2	0.50	3	3
NL:LA	23	152	146	102	44	6	4	0	0	.961	8	34.0	10	2.65	1	0
1967 (7)																
NL:StL	23	253	249	183	66	4	3	0	0	.984	10	61.0	18	2.66	4	1
AL:Bos	25	253	249	183	66	4	4	0	1	.984	10	61.0	23	3.39	2	1
1968 (7)																
AL:Det	24	269	258	186	72	11	4	0	0	.959	9	62.0	24	3.48	4	0
NL:StL	25	236	234	186	48	2	7	0	0	.992	10	62.0	32	4.65	3	1
1969 (5)																
NL:NY	21	179	177	135	42	2	0	0	0	.989	6	45.0	9	1.80	2	1
AL:Balt	21	184	180	129	51	4	4	0	0	.978	7	43.0	13	2.72	2	0
1970 (5)																
AL:Balt	21	183	178	135	43	5	3	0	0	.973	9	45.0	17	3.40	2	0
NL:Cin	24	182	179	129	50	3	4	0	0	.984	9	43.0	32	6.70	0	0
1971 (7)																
NL:Pitt	25	258	255	185	70	3	7	0	1	.988	10	61.2	24	3.50	3	1
AL:Balt	21	261	252	183	69	9	2	0	0	.966	10	61.0	18	2.66	1	0
1972 (7)																
AL:Oak	23	260	251	186	65	9	4	0	0	.965	8	62.	21	3.05	0	0
NL:Cin	22	280	275	187	88	5	4	0	0	.982	8	62.1	15	2.17	0	1
1973 (7)																
AL:Oak	24	286	277	198	79	9	8	0	1	.969	8	66.0	17	2.32	0	0
NL:NY	22	275	265	195	70	10	3	0	1	.964	7	65.0	16	2.22	0	1
1974 (5)																
AL:Oak	20	188	183	132	51	5	6	0	0	.973	5	44.0	10	2.05	0	0
NL:LA	19	182	176	126	50	6	5	0	0	.967	6	42.0	13	2.79	0	0
1975 (7)																
NL:Cin	22	273	271	195	76	2	8	0	0	.993	9	65.0	28	3.88	0	0
AL:Bos	23	274	268	196	72	6	6	0	0	.978	10	65.1	28	3.86	2	1
1976 (4)																
NL:Cin	16	147	142	108	34	5	4	0	0	.966	7	36.0	8	2.00	0	0
AL:NY	21	146	144	104	40	2	6	0	0	.986	7	34.2	21	5.45	1	0
1977 (6)																
AL:NY	20	239	236	168	68	3	2	0	1	.987	7	56.0	25	4.02	3	0
NL:LA	25	235	234	165	69	1	4	0	0	.996	9	55.0	25	4.09	2	0
1978 (6)																
AL:NY	24	214	212	159	54	2	9	0	0	.991	8	53.0	22	3.74	2	0
NL:LA	23	229	222	158	64	7	2	0	2	.969	8	52.2	32	5.47	0	0
1979 (7)																
NL:Pitt	24	274	265	186	79	9	11	0	0	.967	9	62.0	22	3.19	0	1
AL:Balt	25	280	271	186	85	9	5	0	0	.968	8	62.0	30	4.35	2	0
1980 (6)																
NL:Phil	22	231	229	161	68	2	8	0	0	.991	10	53.2	22	3.69	0	0
AL:KC	21	235	228	156	72	7	8	0	0	.970	7	52.0	24	4.15	0	0
1981 (6)																
NL:LA	24	230	221	156	65	9	6	0	0	.961	10	52.0	19	3.29	2	0
AL:NY	24	212	208	153	55	4	2	0	1	.981	9	51.0	24	4.24	0	1
1982 (7)																
NL:StL	22	264	257	183	74	7	9	0	0	.973	8	61.0	23	3.39	1	0
AL:Mil	21	272	261	180	81	11	3	0	0	.960	9	60.0	32	4.80	1	1
1983 (5)																
AL:Balt	23	189	185	135	50	4	5	0	0	.979	7	45.0	8	1.60	2	1
NL:Phil	23	177	174	132	42	3	3	0	0	.983	8	44.0	17	3.48	0	0
1984 (5)																
AL:Det	22	188	184	132	52	4	2	0	0	.979	7	44.0	15	3.07	2	0
NL:SD	24	170	166	126	40	4	5	0	0	.976	10	42.0	22	4.71	0	0
1985 (7)																
AL:KC	22	269	266	186	80	3	3	0	1	.989	6	62.0	13	1.89	3	1
NL:StL	24	246	244	184	60	2	9	0	1	.992	9	61.1	27	3.96	1	1
1986 (7)																
NL:NY	22	257	252	189	63	5	4	0	0	.980	8	63.0	23	3.29	0	0
AL:Bos	21	271	267	188	79	4	7	0	1	.985	8	62.2	30	4.31	1	1

	Fielding:										Pitching:					
	PL	TC	CA	PO	A	E	DP	TP	PB	AVG	PI	IP	ER	ERA	CG	SHO
1987 (7)																
AL:Minn	24	256	253	180	73	3	4	0	0	.998	9	60.0	25	3.75	0	0
NL:StL	24	252	246	177	69	6	2	0	1	.976	9	59.0	37	5.64	0	0
1988 (5)																
NL:LA	22	172	169	133	36	3	3	0	1	.983	7	44.1	10	2.03	2	1
AL:Oak	24	176	174	131	43	2	2	0	1	.989	10	43.2	19	3.92	0	0
1989 (4)																
AL:Oak	19	144	143	108	35	1	1	0	1	.993	6	36.0	14	3.50	1	1
NL:SF	24	146	142	102	40	4	3	0	0	.973	9	34.0	31	8.21	0	0
1990 (4)																
NL:Cin	21	157	153	111	42	4	2	0	0	.975	8	37.0	7	1.70	0	1
AL:Oak	25	157	152	106	46	5	5	0	0	.968	10	35.1	15	3.82	1	0
1991 (7)																
AL:Minn	25	280	276	202	74	4	6	0	1	.986	9	67.1	28	3.74	1	1
NL:Atl	25	288	282	196	86	6	9	0	0	.979	10	65.1	21	2.89	1	0
1992 (6)																
AL:Tor	23	216	212	165	47	4	5	0	0	.981	10	55.0	17	2.78	0	0
NL:Atl	22	233	231	163	68	2	7	0	0	.991	8	54.1	16	2.65	2	0
1993 (6)																
AL:Tor	23	211	204	159	45	7	5	0	0	.967	10	53.0	34	5.77	0	0
NL:Phil	23	213	211	157	54	2	5	0	1	.991	10	52.1	44	7.57	1	1
1995 (6)																
NL:Atl	23	238	232	159	73	6	2	0	0	.975	10	54.0	16	2.67	1	1
AL:Clev	23	237	231	162	69	6	8	0	1	.975	9	53.0	21	3.57	0	0
1996 (6)																
AL:NY	25	233	228	165	63	5	7	0	0	.979	10	55.0	24	3.93	0	1
NL:Atl	24	239	235	162	73	4	6	0	0	.983	10	54.0	14	2.33	0	1
1997 (7)																
NL:Fla	25	282	274	192	82	8	9	0	0	.972	10	64.0	39	5.48	0	0
AL:Clev	23	260	255	191	64	5	8	0	0	.981	11	63.2	32	4.52	0	0
1998 (4)																
AL:NY	19	146	144	108	36	2	4	0	0	.986	9	36.0	11	2.75	0	1
NL:SD	23	146	143	102	41	3	5	0	1	.979	10	34.0	22	5.82	0	0
1999 (4)																
AL:NY	20	160	159	111	48	1	5	0	0	.994	9	37.0	9	2.19	0	0
NL:Atl	23	140	136	105	31	4	4	0	0	.971	9	35.0	17	4.37	0	0
2000 (5)																
AL:NY	22	189	187	141	46	2	1	0	1	.989	8	47.0	14	2.68	0	0
NL:NY	25	192	187	140	47	5	3	0	0	.974	10	46.2	18	3.47	0	0
2001 (7)																
NL:Ari.	25	259	256	195	61	3	6	0	0	.988	10	65.0	14	1.94	1	0
NL:NY	25	273	265	190	75	8	7	0	0	.971	10	63.1	30	4.26	0	0

BATTING AVERAGE LEADERS

(Playing all games)

Year	Player	AB	H	AVG
1903				
AL	Chick Stahl, Bos.	33	10	.303
NL	Jimmy Sebring, Pitt.	30	11	.367
1905				
AL	Topsy Hartsel, Phil.	17	5	.294
NL	Mike Donlin NY	19	6	.316
1906				
AL	George Rohe, Chi.	21	7	.333
AL	Jiggs Donahue, Chi.	18	6	.333
NL	Solly Hofman,Chi.	23	7	.304
1907				
AL	Claude Rossman, Det.	20	8	.400
NL	Harry Steinfeldt, Chi.	17	8	.471
1908				
AL	Ty Cobb, Det.	19	7	.368
NL	Frank Chance, Chi.	19	8	.421
1909				
AL	Jim Delahanty, Det.	26	9	.346
NL	Honus Wagner, Pitt.	24	8	.333
1910				
AL	Eddie Collins, Phil.	21	9	.429
NL	Frank Chance, Chi.	17	6	.353
NL	Wildfire Schulte, Chi.	17	6	.353
1911				
AL	Frank Baker, Phil.	24	9	.375
NL	Larry Doyle, NY	23	7	.304
1912				
AL	Tris Speaker, Bos.	30	9	.300
NL	Buck Herzog, NY	30	12	.400
1913				
AL	Frank Baker, Phil.	20	9	.450
NL	Larry McLean, NY	12	6	.500
1914				
AL	Frank Baker, Phil.	16	4	.250
NL	Hank Gowdy, Bos.	11	6	.545
1915				
AL	Duffy Lewis, Bos.	18	8	.444
NL	Fred Luderus,Phil.	16	7	.438
1916				
AL	Duffy Lewis, Bos.	17	6	.353
NL	Ivy Olson, Brk.	16	4	.250
1917				
AL	Eddie Collins, Chi.	22	9	.409
NL	Dave Robertson, NY	22	11	.500
1918				
AL	Stuffy McInnis, Bos.	20	5	.250
AL	George Whiteman, Bos.	20	5	.250
NL	Charlie Pick, Chi.	18	7	.389
1919				
AL	Joe Jackson,Chi.	32	12	.375
NL	Greasy Neale, Cin.	28	10	.357
1920				
AL	Steve O'Neill, Clev.	21	7	.333
NL	Zack Wheat, Brk.	27	9	.333
1921				
AL	Wally Schang,NY	21	6	.286
NL	Irish Meusel, NY	29	10	.345
1922				
AL	Bob Meusel, NY	20	6	.300
NL	Heinie Groh, NY	19	9	.474

Year	Player	AB	H	AVG
1923				
AL	Aaron Ward, NY	24	10	.417
NL	Casey Stengel, NY	12	5	.417
1924				
AL	Joe Judge, Wash.	26	10	.385
NL	Frankie Frisch, NY	30	10	.333
NL	Freddie Lindstrom. NY	30	10	.333
1925				
AL	Bucky Harris, Wash.	25	11	.440
NL	Max Carey, Pitt.	24	11	.458
1926				
AL	Earle Combs, NY	28	10	.357
NL	Tommy Thevenow, StL.	24	10	.417
1927				
AL	Mark Koenig, NY	18	9	.500
NL	Lloyd Waner, Pitt.	15	6	.400
1928				
AL	Babe Ruth, NY	16	10	.625
NL	Rabbit Maranville, StL.	13	4	.308
1929				
AL	Jimmy Dykes, Phil.	19	8	.421
NL	Hack Wilson, Chi.	17	8	.471
1930				
AL	Al Simmons, Phil.	22	8	.364
NL	Charlie Gelbert, StL.	17	6	.353
1931				
AL	Jimmie Foxx, Phil.	23	8	.348
NL	Pepper Martin, StL.	24	12	.500
1932				
AL	Lou Gehrig,NY	17	9	.529
NL	Riggs Stephenson, Chi.	18	8	.444
1933				
AL	Fred Schulte, Wash.	21	7	.333
NL	Mel Ott, NY	18	7	.389
1934				
AL	Charlie Gehringer, Det.	29	11	.379
NL	Joe Medwick, StL.	29	11	.379
1935				
AL	Pete Fox, Det.	26	10	.385
NL	Hank Gowdy, Bos.	11	6	.545
1936				
AL	Jake Powell, NY	22	10	.455
NL	Dick Bartell, NY	21	8	.381
1937				
AL	Tony Lazzeri, NY	15	6	.400
NL	Joe Moore, NY	23	9	.391
1938				
AL	Bill Dickey, NY	15	6	.400
AL	Joe Gordon, NY	15	6	.400
NL	Stan Hack, Chi.	17	8	.471
1939				
AL	Charlie Keller, NY	16	7	.438
NL	Frank McCormick, Cin.	15	6	.400
1940				
AL	Bruce Campbell, Det.	25	9	.360
NL	Bill Werber, Cin.	27	10	.370
1941				
AL	Joe Gordon, NY	14	7	.500
NL	Joe Medwick, Brk.	17	4	.235
1942				
AL	Phil Rizzuto, NY	21	8	.381
NL	Jimmy Brown, StL.	20	6	.300
1943				
AL	Billy Johnson, NY	20	6	.300
NL	Marty Marion, StL.	14	5	.357

YEAR	PLAYER	AB	H	AVG
1944				
AL	George McQuinn, StL.	16	7	.438
NL	Emil Verban, StL.	17	7	.412
1945				
AL	Doc Cramer, Det.	29	11	.379
NL	Phil Cavarretta, Chi.	26	11	.423
1946				
AL	Rudy York, Bos.	23	6	.261
NL	Harry Walker, StL.	17	7	.412
1947				
AL	Tommy Henrich, NY	31	10	.323
NL	Pee Wee Reese, Brk.	23	7	.304
1948				
AL	Larry Doby, Clev.	22	7	.318
NL	Bob Elliott, Bos.	21	7	.333
1949				
AL	Tommy Henrich, NY	19	5	.263
NL	Pee Wee Reese, Brk.	19	6	.316
1950				
AL	Gene Woodling, NY	14	6	.429
NL	Granny Hamner, Phil.	14	6	.429
1951				
AL	Phil Rizzuto, NY	25	8	.320
NL	Monte Irvin, NY	24	11	.458
1952				
AL	Gene Woodling, NY	23	8	.348
NL	Pee Wee Reese, Brk.	29	10	.345
AL	Duke Snider,Brk.	29	10	.345
1953				
AL	Billy Martin, NY	24	12	.500
NL	Gil Hodges, Brk.	22	8	.364
1954				
AL	Vic Wertz, Clev.	16	8	.500
NL	Alvin Dark, NY	7	7	.412
1955				
AL	Yogi Berra, NY	24	10	.417
NL	Duke Snider, Brk.	25	8	.320
1956				
AL	Yogi Berra, NY	25	9	.360
NL	Gil Hodges, Brk.	23	7	.304
NL	Duke Snider, Brk.	23	7	.304
1957				
AL	Jerry Coleman, NY	22	8	.364
NL	Hank Aaron, Mil.	28	11	.393
1958				
AL	Hank Bauer, NY	31	10	.323
NL	Bill Bruton, Mil.	17	7	.412
1959				
AL	Ted Kluszewski, Chi.	23	9	.391
NL	Gil Hodges, LA	23	9	.391
1960				
AL	Mickey Mantle, NY	25	10	.400
NL	Bill Mazeroski, Pitt.	25	8	.320
1961				
AL	Bobby Richardson, NY	23	9	.319
NL	Wally Post, Cin.	18	6	.333
1962				
AL	Tom Tresh, NY	28	9	.321
NL	Jose Pagan, SF	19	7	.368
1963				
AL	Elston Howard, NY	15	5	.333
NL	Tommy Davis, LA	15	6	.400
1964				
AL	Bobby Richardson, NY	32	13	.406
NL	Tim McCarver, StL.	23	11	.478

YEAR	PLAYER	AB	H	AVG
1965				
AL	Zoilo Versalles, Minn.	28	8	.286
AL	Harmon Killebrew, Minn.	21	6	.286
NL	Ron Fairly, LA	29	11	.379
1966				
AL	Boog Powell, Balt.	14	5	.357
NL	Lou Johnson, LA	15	4	.267
1967				
AL	Carl Yastrzemski, Bos.	25	10	.400
NL	Lou Brock, StL.	29	12	.414
1968				
AL	Norm Cash, Det.	26	10	.385
NL	Lou Brock, StL.	28	13	.464
1969				
AL	Boog Powell, Balt.	19	5	.263
NL	Al Weis, NY	11	5	.455
1970				
AL	Paul Blair, Balt.	19	9	.474
NL	Lee May, Cin.	18	7	.389
1971				
AL	Brooks Robinson, Balt.	22	7	.318
NL	Roberto Clemente, Pitt.	29	12	.414
1972				
AL	Gene Tenace, Oak	23	8	.348
NL	Tony Perez, Cin.	23	10	.435
1973				
AL	Joe Rudi, Oak.	27	9	.333
NL	Rusty Staub, NY	26	11	.423
1974				
AL	Bert Campaneris, Oak.	17	6	.353
NL	Steve Garvey, LA	21	8	.381
1975				
AL	Carl Yastrzemski, Bos.	29	9	.310
NL	Pete Rose, Cin.	27	10	.370
1976				
AL	Thurman Munson, NY	17	9	.529
NL	Johnny Bench, Cin.	15	8	.533
1977				
AL	Reggie Jackson, NY	20	9	.450
NL	Steve Garvey, LA	24	9	.375
1978				
AL	Brian Doyle, NY	16	7	.438
NL	Bill Russell, LA	26	11	.423
1979				
AL	Kiko Garcia, Balt.	20	8	.400
NL	Phil Garner, Pitt.	24	12	.500
1980				
AL	Amos Otis, KC	23	11	.478
NL	Bob Boone, Phil.	17	7	.412
1981				
AL	Lou Piniella, NY	16	7	.438
NL	Steve Garvey, LA	24	10	.417
1982				
AL	Robin Yount, Mil.	29	12	.414
NL	George Hendrick, StL.	28	9	.321
NL	Lonnie Smith, StL.	28	9	.321
1983				
AL	John Shelby, Balt	9	4	.444
NL	Bo Diaz, Phil.	15	5	.333
1984				
AL	Alan Trammell, Det.	20	9	.450
NL	Kurt Bevacqua, SD	17	7	.412
1985				
AL	George Brett, KC	27	10	.370
NL	Tito Landrum, StL.	25	9	.360

YEAR	PLAYER	AB	H	AVG
1986				
AL	Marty Barrett, Bos.	30	13	.433
NL	Ray Knight, NY	23	9	.391
1987				
AL	Kirby Puckett, Minn.	28	10	.357
NL	Tony Pena, StL.	22	9	.409
1988				
AL	Dave Henderson, Oak.	20	6	.300
NL	Mickey Hatcher, LA	19	7	.368
1989				
AL	Rickey Henderson, Oak.	19	9	.474
NL	Kevin Mitchell, SF	17	5	.294
1990				
NL	Billy Hatcher, Cin.	12	9	.750
AL	Rickey Henderson, Oak.	15	5	.333
1991				
AL	Brian Harper, Minn.	21	8	.381
NL	Rafael Belliard, Atl.	16	6	.375
1992				
AL	Pat Borders, Tor.	20	9	.450
NL	Otis Nixon, Atl.	27	8	.296
1993				
AL	Paul Molitor, Tor.	24	12	.500
NL	Lenny Dykstra, Phil.	23	8	.348
NL	John Kruk, Phil.	23	8	.348
1995				
AL	Albert Belle, Clev.	17	4	.235
NL	Marquis Grissom, Atl.	25	9	.360
1996				
NL	Marquis Grissom, Atl.	27	12	.444
AL	Cecil Fielder, NY	23	9	.391
1997				
AL	Matt Williams,Clev.	26	10	.385
NL	Darren Daulton, Fla.	18	7	.389
1998				
AL	Ricky Ledee, NY	10	6	.600
NL	Tony Gwynn, SD	16	8	.500
1999				
AL	Scott Brosius, NY	16	6	.375
NL	Bret Boone, Atl.	13	7	.538
2000				
AL	Paul O'Neill, NY	19	9	.474
NL	Todd Zeile, NY	20	8	.400
2001				
AL	Alfonso Soriano, NY	25	6	.240
NL	Steve Finley, Ari.	19	7	.368

HITTING SAFELY, EACH GAME, SERIES

YEAR	PLAYER	AB	H	AVG
1907 - (5 games)				
NL	Wildfire Schulte, Chi.	20	5	.250
1908 - (5 games)				
NL	Wildfire Schulte, Chi.	18	7	.389
1910 - (5 games)				
AL	Eddie Collins, Phil.	21	9	.429
AL	Danny Murphy, Phil.	20	7	.350
1914 - (4 games)				
NL	Johnny Evers, Bos.	16	7	.438
NL	Butch Schmidt, Bos.	17	5	.294
1915 - (5 games)				
AL	Duffy Lewis, Bos	18	8	.444
AL	Harry Hooper, Bos.	20	7	.350
1916 - (5 games)				
AL	Harry Hooper, Bos.	21	7	.333
1917 - (6 games)				
NL	Dave Robertson, NY	22	11	.500
1922 - (5 games)				
AL	Bob Meusel, N. Y.	20	6	.300
AL	Wally Pipp, NY	21	6	.286
NL	Heinie Groh, NY	19	9	.474
NL	Irish Meusel, NY	20	5	.250
1923 - (6 games)				
AL	Aaron Ward, NY	24	10	.417
AL	Babe Ruth, NY	19	7	.368
AL	Wally Schang, NY	22	7	.318
1924 - (7 games)				
AL	Bucky Harris, Wash.	33	11	.333
NL	George Kelly, NY	31	9	.290
1925 - (7 games)				
AL	Joe Harris, Wash.	25	11	.440
1926 - (7 games)				
AL	Earle Combs, NY	28	10	.357
NL	Jim Bottomley, StL.	29	10	.345
1927 - (4 games)				
AL	Mark Koenig, NY	18	9	.500
NL	Lloyd Waner, Pitt.	15	6	.400
NL	Clyde Barnhart, Pitt.	16	5	.313
1928 - (4 games)				
AL	Babe Ruth, NY	16	10	.625
AL	Lou Gehrig, NY	11	6	.545
1929 - (5 games)				
AL	Bing Miller, Phil.	19	7	.368
NL	Riggs Stephenson, Chi.	19	6	.316
1930 - (6 games)				
AL	Jimmie Foxx, Phil.	21	7	.333
1932 - (4 games)				
AL	Lou Gehrig, NY	17	9	.529
AL	Bill Dickey, NY	16	7	.438
AL	Babe Ruth, NY	15	5	.333
NL	Riggs Stephenson, Chi.	18	8	.444
NL	Gabby Hartnett, Chi.	16	5	.313
1933 - (5 games)				
NL	Kiddo Davis, NY	19	7	.368
1934 - (7 games)				
AL	Charlie Gehringer, Det.	29	11	.379
NL	Pepper Martin, StL.	31	11	.355
1935 - (6 games)				
AL	Pete Fox, Det.	26	10	.385
1936 - (6 games)				
AL	George Selkirk, NY	24	8	.333
NL	Dick Bartell, NY	21	8	.381
1937 - (5 games)				
AL	Tony Lazzeri, NY	15	6	.400
NL	Joe Moore, NY	23	9	.391
1938 - (4 games)				
AL	Joe Gordon, NY	15	6	.400
AL	Lou Gehrig, NY	14	4	.286
NL	Stan Hack, Chi.	17	8	.471
NL	Phil Cavarretta, Chi.	13	6	.462
1939 - (4 games)				
AL	Charlie Keller, NY	16	7	.438
AL	Joe DiMaggio, NY	16	5	.313
AL	Bill Dickey, NY	15	4	.267
1941 - (5 games)				
AL	Joe Gordon, NY	14	7	.500
AL	Johnny Sturm, NY	21	6	.286
1943 - (5 games)				
NL	Walker Cooper, StL.	17	5	.294
1944 - (6 games)				
NL	Ray Sanders, StL.	21	6	.286
1947 - (7 games)				
AL	Tommy Henrich, NY	31	10	.323
1950 - (4 games)				
AL	Gene Woodling, NY	14	6	.429
1951 - (6 games)				
AL	Phil Rizzuto, NY	25	8	.320
NL	Alvin Dark, NY	24	10	.417
1953 - (6 games)				
AL	Billy Martin, NY	24	12	.500
1954 - (4 games)				
AL	Vic Wertz, Clev.	16	8	.500
NL	Alvin Dark, NY	17	7	.412
NL	Hank Thompson, NY	11	4	.364
1955 - (7 games)				
AL	Yogi Berra, NY	24	10	.417
1956 - (7 games)				
AL	Billy Martin, NY	27	8	.296
AL	Hank Bauer, NY	32	9	.281
1957 - (7 games)				
AL	Hank Bauer, NY	31	8	.258
NL	Hank Aaron, Mil.	28	11	.393
1960 - (7 games)				
NL	Roberto Clemente, Pitt.	29	9	.310
1961 - (5 games)				
AL	Bobby Richardson, NY	23	9	.391
1964 - (7 games)				
AL	Bobby Richardson, NY	32	13	.406
NL	Tim McCarver, StL.	23	11	.478
1965 - (7 games)				
NL	Ron Fairly, LA	29	11	.379
1966 - (4 games)				
AL	Boog Powell, Balt.	14	5	.357
1968 - (7 games)				
NL	Lou Brock, StL.	28	13	.464
1970 - (5 games)				
AL	Brooks Robinson, Balt.	21	9	.429
NL	Lee May, Cin.	18	7	.389
1971 - (7 games)				
NL	Roberto Clemente, Pitt.	29	12	.414
1972 - (7 games)				
NL	Tony Perez, Cin.	23	10	.435
1974 - (5 games)				
NL	Steve Garvey, LA	21	8	.381
1975 - (7 games)				
AL	Denny Doyle, Bos.	30	8	.267

YEAR	PLAYER	AB	H	AVG
1976 - (4 games)				
AL	Thurman Munson, NY	17	9	.529
AL	Chris Chambliss, NY	16	5	.313
NL	Johnny Bench, Cin.	15	8	.533
NL	George Foster, Cin.	14	6	.429
NL	Dave Concepcion, Cin.	14	5	.357
NL	Joe Morgan, Cin.	15	5	.333
1977 - (6 games)				
AL	Thurman Munson, NY	25	8	.320
1978 - (6 games)				
AL	Bucky Dent, NY	24	10	.417
AL	Reggie Jackson, NY	23	9	.391
AL	Roy White, NY	24	8	.333
AL	Lou Piniella, NY	25	7	.350
NL	Bill Russell, LA	26	11	.423
1979 - (7 games)				
NL	Phil Garner, Pitt.	24	12	.500
1980 - (6 games)				
AL	George Brett, KC	24	9	.375
NL	Mike Schmidt, Phil.	21	8	.381
NL	Larry Bowa, Phil.	24	9	.375
1981 - (6 games)				
NL	Steve Garvey, LA	24	10	.417
1984 - (5 games)				
NL	Kurt Bevacqua, SD	17	7	.412
1985 - (7 games)				
AL	Willie Wilson, KC	30	11	.367
NL	Tito Landrum, StL.	25	9	.360
1986 - (7 games)				
AL	Marty Barrett, Bos.	30	13	.433
1987 - (7 games)				
AL	Dan Gladden, Minn.	31	9	.290
1988 - (5 games)				
NL	Mickey Hatcher, LA	19	6	.368
NL	Steve Sax, LA	20	6	.300
1989 - (4 games)				
AL	Rickey Henderson, Oak.	19	9	.474
AL	Carney Lansford, Oak.	16	7	.438
AL	Terry Steinbach, Oak.	16	4	.250
NL	Kevin Mitchell, SF	17	5	.294
1990 - (4 games)				
NL	Chris Sabo, Cin.	16	9	.563
NL	Joe Oliver, Cin.	18	6	.333
1992 - (6 games)				
AL	Pat Borders, Tor.	20	9	.450
1993 - (6 games)				
AL	Paul Molitor, Tor.	24	12	.500
AL	Roberto Alomar, Tor.	25	12	.480
1995 - (6 games)				
NL	Marquis Grissom, Atl.	25	9	.350
1996 - (6 games)				
NL	Marquis Grissom, Atl.	27	12	.444
1998 - (4 games)				
NL	Tony Gwynn, SD	16	8	.500
AL	Scott Brosius, NY	17	8	.471
AL	Chuck Knoblauch, NY	16	6	.375
AL	Derek Jeter, NY	17	6	.353
1999 - (4 games)				
NL	Bret Boone, Atl.	13	7	.538
AL	Derek Jeter, NY	17	6	.353
2000 - (5 games)				
AL	Derek Jeter, NY	22	9	.409
NL	Jay Payton, NY	21	7	.333
NL	Mike Piazza, NY	22	6	.273

1903 [3]
AL: BOSTON - 2
    Patsy Dougherty - lf (2)
NL: PITTSBURGH - 1
    Jimmy Sebring - rf

1904 No Series

1905 [0]
AL: PHILADELPHIA - 0
NL: NEW YORK - 0

1906 [0]
AL: CHICAGO - 0
NL: CHICAGO - 0

1907 [0]
AL: DETROIT - 0
NL: CHICAGO - 0

1908 [1]
AL: DETROIT - 0
NL: CHICAGO - 1
    Joe Tinker - ss

1909 [4]
AL: DETROIT - 2
    Sam Crawford - cf
    Davy Jones - lf
NL: PITTSBURGH - 2
    Fred Clarke - lf (2)

1910 [1]
AL: PHILADELPHIA - 1
    Danny Murphy - rf
NL: CHICAGO - 0

1911 [3]
AL: PHILADELPHIA - 3
    Frank Baker - 3b (2)
    Rube Oldring - cf
NL: NEW YORK - 0

1912 [2]
AL: BOSTON - 1
    Larry Gardner - 3b
NL: NEW YORK - 1
    Larry Doyle - 2b

1913 [3]
AL: PHILADELPHIA - 2
    Frank Baker - 3b
    Wally Schang - c
NL: NEW YORK - 1
    Fred Merkle - 1b

1914 [1]
AL: PHILADELPHIA - 0
NL: BOSTON - 1
    Hank Gowdy - c

1915 [4]
AL: BOSTON - 3
    Harry Hooper - rf (2)
    Duffy Lewis - lf
NL: PHILADELPHIA - 1
    Fred Luderus - 1b

1916 [3]
AL: BOSTON - 2
    Larry Gardner - 3b (2)
NL: BROOKLYN - 1
    Hy Myers - cf

1917 [3]
AL: CHICAGO - 1
    Happy Felsch - cf
NL: NEW YORK - 2
    Benny Kauff - cf (2)

1918 [0]
AL: BOSTON - 0
NL: CHICAGO - 0

1919 [1]
AL: CHICAGO - 1
    Joe Jackson - lf
NL: CINCINNATI - 0

1920 [2]
AL: CLEVELAND - 2
    Jim Bagby - p
    Elmer Smith - rf
NL: BROOKLYN - 0

1921 [4]
AL: NEW YORK - 2
    Chick Fewster - lf
    Babe Ruth - lf
NL: NEW YORK - 2
    Irish Meusel - lf
    Frank Snyder - c

1922 [3]
AL: NEW YORK - 2
    Aaron Ward - 2b (2)
NL: NEW YORK - 1
    Irish Meusel - lf

1923 [10]
AL: NEW YORK - 5
    Babe Ruth - rf (3)
    Joe Dugan - 3b
    Aaron Ward - 2b
NL: NEW YORK - 5
    Casey Stengel - cf (2)
    Irish Meusel - lf
    Frank Snyder - c
    Ross Youngs - rf

1924 [9]
AL: WASHINGTON - 5
    Goose Goslin - lf (3)
    Bucky Harris - 2b (2)
NL: NEW YORK - 4
    Jack Bentley - p
    George Kelly - cf
    Rosy Ryan - p
    Bill Terry - 1b

1925 [12]
AL: WASHINGTON - 8
    Goose Goslin - lf (3)
    Joe Harris - rf (3)
    Joe Judge - 1b
    Roger Peckinpaugh - ss
NL: PITTSBURGH - 4
    Kiki Cuyler - rf
    Eddie Moore - 2b
    Pie Traynor - 3b
    Glenn Wright - ss

1926 [8]
AL: NEW YORK - 4
    Babe Ruth - lf (3), rf (1)
NL: ST. LOUIS - 4
    Les Bell - 3b
    Jesse Haines - p
    Billy Southworth - rf
    Tommy Thevenow - ss

1927 [2]
AL: NEW YORK - 2
    Babe Ruth - lf (2)
NL: PITTSBURGH - 0

1928 [10]
AL: NEW YORK - 9
    Lou Gehrig - 1b (4)
    Babe Ruth - lf (3)
    Cedric Durst - cf
    Bob Meusel - lf
NL: ST. LOUIS - 1
    Jim Bottomley - 1b

1929 [7]
AL: PHILADELPHIA - 6
    Jimmie Foxx - 1b (2)
    Mule Haas - cf (2)
    Al Simmons - lf (2)
NL: CHICAGO - 1
    Charlie Grimm - 1b

1930 [8]
AL: PHILADELPHIA - 6
    Mickey Cochrane - c (2)
    Al Simmons - lf (1), cf (1)
    Jimmy Dykes - 3b
    Jimmie Foxx - 1b
NL: ST. LOUIS - 2
    Taylor Douthit - cf
    George Watkins - rf

1931 [5]
AL: PHILADELPHIA - 3
    Al Simmons - lf (2)
    Jimmie Foxx - 1b
NL: ST. LOUIS - 2
    Pepper Martin - cf
    George Watkins - rf

1932 [11]
AL: NEW YORK - 8
    Lou Gehrig - 1b (3)
    Tony Lazzeri - 2b (2)
    Babe Ruth - lf (2)
    Earle Combs - cf
NL: CHICAGO - 3
    Kiki Cuyler - rf
    Frank Demaree - cf
    Gabby Hartnett - c

1933 [5]
AL: WASHINGTON - 2
    Goose Goslin - rf
    Fred Schulte - cf
NL: NEW YORK - 3
    Mel Ott - rf (2)
    Bill Terry - 1b

1934 [4]
- AL: DETROIT - 2
  - Charlie Gehringer - 2b
  - Hank Greenberg - 1b
- NL: ST. LOUIS - 2
  - Bill DeLancey - c
  - Joe Medwick - lf

1935 [6]
- AL: DETROIT - 1
  - Hank Greenberg - 1b
- NL: CHICAGO - 5
  - Frank Demaree - rf (2)
  - Gabby Hartnett - c
  - Billy Herman - 2b
  - Chuck Klein - cf

1936 [11]
- AL: NEW YORK - 7
  - Lou Gehrig - 1b (2)
  - George Selkirk - rf (2)
  - Bill Dickey - c
  - Tony Lazzeri - 2b
  - Jake Powell - lf
- NL: NEW YORK - 4
  - Dick Bartell - ss
  - Joe Moore - lf
  - Mel Ott - rf
  - Jimmy Ripple - cf

1937 [5]
- AL: NEW YORK - 4
  - Joe DiMaggio - cf
  - Lou Gehrig - 1b
  - Myril Hoag - lf
  - Tony Lazzeri - 2b
- NL: NEW YORK - 1
  - Mel Ott - 3b

1938 [7]
- AL: NEW YORK - 5
  - Frankie Crosetti - ss
  - Bill Dickey - c
  - Joe DiMaggio - cf
  - Joe Gordon - 2b
  - Tommy Henrich - rf
- NL: CHICAGO - 2
  - Joe Marty - cf
  - Ken O'Dea - c

1939 [7]
- AL: NEW YORK - 7
  - Charlie Keller - rf (3)
  - Bill Dickey - c (2)
  - Babe Dahlgren - 1b
  - Joe DiMaggio - cf
- NL: CINCINNATI - 0

1940 [6]
- AL: DETROIT - 4
  - Bruce Campbell - rf
  - Hank Greenberg - lf
  - Pinky Higgins - 3b
  - Rudy York - 1b
- NL: CINCINNATI - 2
  - Jimmy Ripple - lf
  - Bucky Walters - p

1941 [3]
- AL: NEW YORK - 2
  - Joe Gordon - 2b
  - Tommy Henrich - rf
- NL: BROOKLYN - 1
  - Pete Reiser - cf

1942 [5]
- AL: NEW YORK - 3
  - Charlie Keller - lf (2)
  - Phil Rizzuto - ss
- NL: ST. LOUIS - 2
  - Whitey Kurowski - 3b
  - Enos Slaughter - rf

1943 [4]
- AL: NEW YORK - 2
  - Bill Dickey - c
  - Joe Gordon - 2b
- NL: ST. LOUIS - 2
  - Marty Marion - ss
  - Ray Sanders - 1b

1944 [4]
- AL: ST. LOUIS - 1
  - George McQuinn - 1b
- NL: ST. LOUIS - 3
  - Danny Litwhiler - lf
  - Stan Musial - rf
  - Ray Sanders - 1b

1945 [3]
- AL: DETROIT - 2
  - Hank Greenberg - lf (2)
- NL: CHICAGO - 1
  - Phil Cavarretta - 1b

1946 [5]
- AL: BOSTON - 4
  - Rudy York - 1b (2)
  - Leon Culberson - rf
  - Bobby Doerr - 2b
- NL: ST. LOUIS - 1
  - Enos Slaughter - rf

1947 [5]
- AL: NEW YORK - 4
  - Joe DiMaggio - cf (2)
  - Yogi Berra - ph
  - Tommy Henrich - rf
- NL: BROOKLYN - 1
  - Dixie Walker - rf

1948 [8]
- AL: CLEVELAND - 4
  - Larry Doby - cf
  - Joe Gordon - 2b
  - Jim Hegan - c
  - Dale Mitchell - lf
- NL: BOSTON - 4
  - Bob Elliott - 3b (2)
  - Marv Rickert - lf
  - Bill Salkeld - c

1949 [6]
- AL: NEW YORK - 2
  - Joe DiMaggio - cf
  - Tommy Henrich - 1b
- NL: BROOKLYN - 4
  - Roy Campanella - c
  - Gil Hodges - 1b
  - Luis Olmo - lf
  - Pee Wee Reese - ss

1950 [2]
- AL: NEW YORK - 2
  - Yogi Berra - c
  - Joe DiMaggio - cf
- NL: PHILADELPHIA - 0

1951 [7]
- AL: NEW YORK - 5
  - Joe Collins - 1b
  - Joe DiMaggio - cf
  - Gil McDougald - 2b
  - Phil Rizzuto - ss
  - Gene Woodling - lf
- NL: NEW YORK - 2
  - ALvin Dark - ss
  - Whitey Lockman - 1b

1952 [16]
- AL: NEW YORK - 10
  - Johnny Mize - 1b (2), ph (1)
  - Yogi Berra - c (2)
  - Mickey Mantle - cf (2)
  - Billy Martin - 2b
  - Gil McDougald - 3b
  - Gene Woodling - lf
- NL: BROOKLYN - 6
  - Duke Snider - cf (4)
  - Pee Wee Reese - ss
  - Jackie Robinson - 2b

1953 [17]
- AL: NEW YORK - 9
  - Mickey Mantle - cf (2)
  - Billy Martin - 2b (2)
  - Gil McDougald - 3b (2)
  - Yogi Berra - c
  - Joe Collins - 1b
  - Gene Woodling - lf
- NL: BROOKLYN - 8
  - Jim Gilliam - 2b (2)
  - Roy Campanella - c
  - Billy Cox - 3b
  - Carl Furillo - rf
  - Gil Hodges - 1b
  - George Shuba - ph
  - Duke Snider - cf

1954 [5]
- AL: CLEVELAND - 3
  - Hank Majeski - ph
  - AL Smith - lf
  - Vic Wertz - 1b
- NL: NEW YORK - 2
  - Dusty Rhodes - ph (1), lf (1)

1955 [17]
AL: NEW YORK - 8
   Joe Collins - 1b (2)
   Yogi Berra - c
   Bob Cerv - ph
   Elston Howard - lf
   Mickey Mantle - cf
   Gil McDougald - 3b
   Bill Skowron - 1b
NL: BROOKLYN - 9
   Duke Snider - cf (4)
   Roy Campanella - c (2)
   Sandy Amoros - lf
   Carl Furillo - rf
   Gil Hodges - 1b

1956 [15]
AL: NEW YORK - 12
   Yogi Berra - c (3)
   Mickey Mantle - cf (3)
   Billy Martin - 2b (2)
   Hank Bauer - rf
   Elston Howard - lf
   Bill Skowron - 1b
   Enos Slaughter - lf
NL: BROOKLYN - 3
   Gil Hodges - 1b
   Jackie Robinson - 3b
   Duke Snider - cf

1957 [15]
AL: NEW YORK - 7
   Hank Bauer - rf (2)
   Tony Kubek - lf (2)
   Yogi Berra - c
   Elston Howard - 1b
   Mickey Mantle - cf
NL: MILWAUKEE - 8
   Hank Aaron - cf (3)
   Frank Torre - 1b (2)
   Del Crandall - c
   Johnny Logan - ss
   Eddie Mathews - 3b

1958 [13]
AL: NEW YORK - 10
   Hank Bauer - rf (4)
   Mickey Mantle - cf (2)
   Gil McDougald - 2b (2)
   Bill Skowron - 1b (2)
NL: MILWAUKEE - 3
   Bill Bruton - cf
   Lew Burdette - p
   Del Crandall - c

1959 [11]
AL: CHICAGO - 4
   Ted Kluszewski - 1b (3)
   Sherm Lollar - c
NL: LOS ANGELES - 7
   Chuck Essegian - ph (2)
   Charlie Neal - 2b (2)
   Gil Hodges - 1b
   Wally Moon - lf
   Duke Snider - cf

1960 [14]
AL: NEW YORK - 10
   Mickey Mantle - cf (3)
   Roger Maris - rf (2)
   Bill Skowron - 1b (2)
   Yogi Berra - lf
   Elston Howard - ph
   Bobby Richardson - 2b
NL: PITTSBURGH - 4
   Bill Mazeroski - 2b (2)
   Rocky Nelson - 1b
   Hal W. Smith - c

1961 [10]
AL: NEW YORK - 7
   Johnny Blanchard -ph (1),rf (1)
   Yogi Berra - lf
   Elston Howard - c
   Hector Lopez - lf
   Roger Maris - rf
   Bill Skowron - 1b
NL: CINCINNATI - 3
   Gordy Coleman - 1b
   Wally Post - lf
   Frank Robinson - rf

1962 [8]
AL: NEW YORK - 3
   Clete Boyer - 3b
   Roger Maris - rf
   Tom Tresh - lf
NL: SAN FRANCISCO - 5
   Ed Bailey - c
   Tom Haller - c
   Chuck Hiller - 2b
   Willie McCovey - 1b
   Jose Pagan - ss

1963 [5]
AL: NEW YORK - 2
   Mickey Mantle - cf
   Tom Tresh - lf
NL: LOS ANGELES - 3
   Frank Howard - rf
   Johnny Roseboro - c
   Bill Skowron - 1b

1964 [15]
AL: NEW YORK - 10
   Mickey Mantle - rf (3)
   Phil Linz - ss (2)
   Tom Tresh - lf (2)
   Clete Boyer - 3b
   Roger Maris - cf
   Joe Pepitone - 1b
NL: ST. LOUIS - 5
   Ken Boyer - 3b (2)
   Lou Brock - lf
   Tim McCarver - c
   Mike Shannon - rf

1965 [11]
AL: MINNESOTA - 6
   Bob Allison - lf
   Mudcat Grant - p
   Harmon Killebrew - 3b
   Don Mincher - 1b
   Tony Oliva - rf
   Zoilo Versalles - ss
NL: LOS ANGELES - 5
   Ron Fairly - rf (2)
   Lou Johnson - lf (2)
   Wes Parker - 1b

1966 [5]
AL: BALTIMORE - 4
   Frank Robinson - rf (2)
   Paul Blair - cf
   Brooks Robinson - 3b
NL: LOS ANGELES - 1
   Jim Lefebvre - 2b

1967 [13]
AL: BOSTON - 8
   Carl Yastrzemski - lf (3)
   Rico Petrocelli - ss (2)
   Reggie Smith - cf (2)
   Jose Santiago - p
NL: ST. LOUIS - 5
   Lou Brock - lf
   Bob Gibson - p
   Julian Javier - 2b
   Roger Maris - rf
   Mike Shannon - 3b

1968 [15]
AL: DETROIT - 8
   AL Kaline - rf (2)
   Jim Northrup - cf (2)
   Norm Cash - 1b
   Willie Horton - lf
   Mickey Lolich - p
   Dick McAuliffe - 2b
NL: ST. LOUIS - 7
   Lou Brock - lf (2)
   Orlando Cepeda - 1b (2)
   Bob Gibson - p
   Tim McCarver - c
   Mike Shannon - 3b

1969 [9]
AL: BALTIMORE - 3
   Don Buford - lf
   Dave McNally - p
   Frank Robinson - rf
NL: NEW YORK - 6
   Donn Clendenon - 1b (3)
   Tommie Agee - cf
   Ed Kranepool - 1b
   AL Weis - 2b

1970 [15]
AL: BALTIMORE - 10
   Boog Powell - 1b (2)
   Brooks Robinson - 3b (2)
   Frank Robinson - rf (2)
   Don Buford - lf
   Ellie Hendricks - c
   Dave McNally - p
   Merv Rettenmund - lf
NL: CINCINNATI - 5
   Lee May - 1b (2)
   Johnny Bench - c
   Pete Rose - rf
   Bobby Tolan - cf

1971 [10]
AL: BALTIMORE - 5
   Don Buford - lf (2)
   Frank Robinson - rf (2)
   Merv Rettenmund - cf
NL: PITTSBURGH - 5
   Roberto Clemente - rf (2)
   Bob Robertson - 1b (2)
   Richie Hebner - 3b

1972 [8]
AL: OAKLAND - 5
   Gene Tenace - c (4)
   Joe Rudi - lf
NL: CINCINNATI - 3
   Johnny Bench - c
   Denis Menke - 3b
   Pete Rose - lf

1973 [6]
AL: OAKLAND - 2
   Bert Campaneris - ss
   Reggie Jackson - cf
NL: NEW YORK - 4
   Wayne Garrett - 3b (2)
   Cleon Jones - lf
   Rusty Staub - rf

1974 [8]
AL: OAKLAND - 4
   Ray Fosse - c
   Ken Holtzman - p
   Reggie Jackson - rf
   Joe Rudi - 1b
NL: LOS ANGELES - 4
   Bill Buckner - lf
   Willie Crawford - rf
   Joe Ferguson - rf
   Jimmy Wynn - cf

1975 [13]
AL: BOSTON - 6
   Bernie Carbo - ph (2)
   Carlton Fisk - c (2)
   Dwight Evans - rf
   Fred Lynn - cf
NL: CINCINNATI - 7
   Tony Perez - 1b (3)
   Cesar Geronimo - cf (2)
   Johnny Bench - c
   Dave Concepcion - ss

1976 [5]
AL: NEW YORK - 1
   Jim Mason - ss
NL: CINCINNATI - 4
   Johnny Bench - c (2)
   Dan Driessen - dh
   Joe Morgan - 2b

1977 [17]
AL: NEW YORK - 8
   Reggie Jackson - rf (5)
   Chris Chambliss - 1b
   Thurman Munson - c
   Willie Randolph - 2b
NL: LOS ANGELES - 9
   Reggie Smith - rf (3)
   Steve Yeager - c (2)
   Dusty Baker - lf
   Ron Cey - 3b
   Steve Garvey - 1b
   Davey Lopes - 2b

1978 [9]
AL: NEW YORK - 3
   Reggie Jackson - dh (2)
   Roy White - lf
NL: LOS ANGELES - 6
   Davey Lopes - 2b (3)
   Dusty Baker - lf
   Ron Cey - 3b
   Reggie Smith - rf

1979 [7]
AL: BALTIMORE - 4
   Benny Ayala - lf
   Rich Dauer - 2b
   Doug DeCinces - 3b
   Eddie Murray - 1b
NL: PITTSBURGH - 3
   Willie Stargell - 1b (3)

1980 [11]
AL: KANSAS CITY - 8
   Willie Aikens - 1b (4)
   Amos Otis - cf (3)
   George Brett - 3b
NL: PHILADELPHIA - 3
   Mike Schmidt - 3b (2)
   Bake McBride - rf

1981 [12]
AL: NEW YORK - 6
   Willie Randolph - 2b (2)
   Bob Watson - 1b (2)
   Rick Cerone - c
   Reggie Jackson - rf
NL: LOS ANGELES - 6
   Pedro Guerrero - rf (2)
   Steve Yeager - c (2)
   Ron Cey - 3b
   Jay Johnstone - ph

1982 [9]
AL: MILWAUKEE - 5
   Ted Simmons - c (2)
   Cecil Cooper - 1b
   Ben Oglivie - lf
   Robin Yount - ss
NL: ST. LOUIS - 4
   Willie McGee - cf (2)
   Keith Hernandez - 1b
   Darrell Porter - c

1983 [10]
AL: BALTIMORE - 6
   Eddie Murray - 1b (2)
   Rick Dempsey - c
   Jim Dwyer - rf
   Dan Ford - rf
   John Lowenstein - lf
NL: PHILADELPHIA - 4
   Joe Morgan - 2b (2)
   Garry Maddox - cf
   Gary Matthews - lf

1984 [10]
AL: DETROIT - 7
   Kirk Gibson - rf (2)
   Alan Trammell - ss (2)
   Marty Castillo - 3b
   Larry Herndon - lf
   Lance Parrish - c
NL: SAN DIEGO - 3
   Kurt Bevacqua - dh (2)
   Terry Kennedy - c

1985 [4]
AL: KANSAS CITY - 2
   Darryl Motley - rf
   Frank White - 2b
NL: ST. LOUIS - 2
   Tito Landrum - lf
   Willie McGee - cf

1986 [12]
AL: BOSTON - 5
   Dwight Evans - rf (2)
   Dave Henderson - cf (2)
   Rich Gedman - c
NL: NEW YORK - 7
   Gary Carter - c (2)
   Len Dykstra - cf (2)
   Ray Knight - 3b
   Darryl Strawberry - rf
   Tim Teufel - 2b

1987 [9]
AL: MINNESOTA - 7
   Don Baylor - dh
   Gary Gaetti - 3b
   Greg Gagne - ss
   Dan Gladden - lf
   Kent Hrbek - 1b
   Tim Laudner - c
   Steve Lombardozzi - 2b
NL: ST. LOUIS - 2
   Tommy Herr - 2b
   Tom Lawless - 3b

1988 [7]
AL: OAKLAND - 2
    Jose Canseco - rf
    Mark McGwire - 1b
NL: LOS ANGELES - 5
    Mickey Hatcher - lf (2)
    Mike Davis - dh
    Kirk Gibson - ph
    Mike Marshall - rf

1989 [13]
AL: OAKLAND - 9
    Dave Henderson - cf (2)
    Jose Canseco - rf
    Rickey Henderson - lf
    Carney Lansford - 3b
    Dave Parker - dh
    Tony Phillips - 2b
    Terry Steinbach - c
    Walt Weiss - ss
NL: SAN FRANCISCO - 4
    Bill Bathe - ph
    Greg Litton - 2b
    Kevin Mitchell - lf
    Matt Williams - ss

1990 [6]
AL: OAKLAND - 3
    Harold Baines - dh
    Jose Canseco - rf
    Rickey Henderson - lf
NL: CINCINNATI - 3
    Chris Sabo - 3b (2)
    Eric Davis - lf

1991 [16]
AL: MINNESOTA - 8
    Chili Davis - dh (1), ph (1)
    Kirby Puckett - cf (2)
    Greg Gagne - ss
    Kent Hrbek - 1b
    Scott Leius - 3b
    Mike Pagliarulo - 3b
NL: ATLANTA - 8
    Lonnie Smith - 1f (3)
    David Justice - rf (2)
    Terry Pendleton - 3b (2)
    Brian Hunter - 1b

1992 [9]
AL: TORONTO - 6
    Joe Carter - 1b (1), rf (1)
    Pat Borders - c
    Kelly Gruber - 3b
    Candy Maldonado - lf
    Ed Sprague - ph
NL: ATLANTA - 3
    Damon Berryhill - c
    David Justice - rf
    Lonnie Smith - dh

1993 [13]
AL: TORONTO - 6
    Joe Carter - rf (2)
    Paul Molitor - 1b (1) , dh (1)
    John Olerud - 1b
    Devon White - cf
NL: PHILADELPHIA - 7
    Len Dykstra - cf (4)
    Darren Daulton - c
    Jim Eisenreich - rf
    Milt Thompson - lf

1995 [13]
AL: CLEVELAND - 5
    ALbert Belle - 1f (2)
    Eddie Murray - 1b
    Manny Ramirez - rf
    Jim Thome - 3b
NL: ATLANTA - 8
    Ryan Klesko - dh (3)
    Fred McGriff - 1b (2)
    David Justice - rf
    Javier Lopez - c
    Luis Polonia - lf

1996 [6]
AL: NEW YORK - 2
    Jim Leyritz - c
    Bernie Williams - cf
NL: ATLANTA - 4
    Andruw Jones - lf (2)
    Fred McGriff - 1b (2)

1997 [15]
AL: CLEVELAND - 7
    Sandy Alomar, Jr. - c (2)
    Manny Ramirez - rf (2)
    Jim Thome - 1b (2)
    Matt Williams - 3b
NL: FLORIDA - 8
    Moises Alou - lf (3)
    Bobby Bonilla - 3b
    Darren Daulton - 1b
    Jim Eisenreich - dh
    Charles Johnson - c
    Gary Sheffield - rf

1998 [9]
AL: NEW YORK - 6
    Scott Brosius - 3b (2)
    Chuck Knoblauch - 2b
    Tino Martinez - 1b
    Jorge Posada - c
    Bernie Williams - cf
NL: SAN DIEGO - 3
    Greg Vaughn - lf (2)
    Tony Gwynn - rf

1999 [6]
AL: NEW YORK - 5
    Chad Curtis - lf (2)
    Chuck Knoblauch - 2b
    Jim Leyritz - ph/dh
    Tino Martinez - 1b
NL: ATLANTA - 1
    Chipper Jones - 3b

2000 [8]
AL: NEW YORK - 4
    Derek Jeter - ss (2)
    Scott Brosius - 3b
    Bernie Williams - cf
NL: NEW YORK - 4
    Mike Piazza - c (2)
    Jay Payton - cf
    Robin Ventura - 3b

2001 [12]
AL: NEW YORK - 6
    Scott Brosius - 3b
    Derek Jeter - ss
    Tino Martinez - 1b
    Jorge Posada - c
    Alfonso Soriano - 2b
    Shane Spencer - lf
NL: ARIZONA - 6
    Rod Barajas - c
    Craig Counsell - 2b
    Steve Finley - cf
    Luis Gonzalez - lf
    Mark Grace - 1b
    Matt Williams - 3b

1-0

Year	Date	Lg	Teams
1905	Oct. 13:	NL:	NY vs Phil. (Joe McGinnity)
1906	Oct. 12:	NL:	Chi. vs Chi. (Three Finger Brown)
1914	Oct. 10:	NL:	Bos. vs Phil. (Bill James)
1918	Sept. 5:	AL:	Bos. vs Chi. (Babe Ruth)
1920	Oct. 11:	AL:	Clev. vs Brk. (Duster Mails)
1921	Oct. 13:	NL:	NY vs NY (Art Nehf)
1923	Oct. 12:	NL:	NY vs NY (Art Nehf)
1948	Oct. 6:	NL:	Bos. vs Clev. (Johnny Sain)
1949	Oct. 5:	AL:	NY vs Brk. (Allie Reynolds)
1949	Oct. 6:	NL:	Brk. vs NY (Preacher Roe)
1950	Oct. 4:	AL:	NY vs Phil. (Vic Raschi)
1956	Oct. 9:	NL:	Brk. vs NY (Clem Labine, 10 inn)
1957	Oct. 7:	NL:	Mil. vs NY (Lew Burdette)
1959	Oct. 6:	AL:	Chi. vs LA (Bob Shaw, Billy Pierce & Dick Donovan)
1962	Oct. 16:	AL:	NY vs SF (Ralph Terry)
1963	Oct. 5:	NL:	LA vs NY (Don Drysdale)
1966	Oct. 8:	AL:	Balt. vs LA (Wally Bunker)
1966	Oct. 9:	AL:	Balt. vs LA (Dave McNally)
1972	Oct. 18:	NL:	Cin. vs Oak. (Jack Billingham & Clay Carroll)
1986	Oct. 18:	AL:	Bos. vs NY (Bruce Hurst & Calvin Schiraldi)
1991	Oct. 27:	AL:	Minn. vs Atl. (Jack Morris)
1995	Oct. 28:	NL:	Atl. vs Clev. (Tom Glavine & Mark Wohlers)
1996	Oct. 24	AL:	NY vs Atl. (Andy Pettitte & John Wetteland)

2-0

Year	Date	Lg	Teams
1905	Oct. 14:	NL:	NY vs Phil. (Christy Mathewson)
1907	Oct. 12:	NL:	Chi. vs Det. (Three Finger Brown)
1908	Oct. 14:	NL:	Chi. vs Det. (Orval Overall)
1917	Oct. 10:	NL:	NY vs Chi. (Rube Benton)
1919	Oct. 4:	NL:	Cin. vs Chi. (Jimmy Ring)
1930	Oct. 6:	AL:	Phil. vs StL. (George Earnshaw & Lefty Grove)
1931	Oct. 2:	NL:	StL. vs Phil. (Bill Hallahan)
1942	Oct. 3:	NL:	StL. vs NY (Ernie White)
1943	Oct. 11:	AL:	NY vs StL. (Spud Chandler)

Year	Date	Lg	Teams
1944	Oct. 8:	NL:	StL. vs StL. (Mort Cooper)
1948	Oct. 8:	AL:	Clev. vs Bos. (Gene Bearden)
1952	Oct. 4:	AL:	NY vs Brk. (Allie Reynolds)
1955	Oct. 4:	NL:	Brk. vs NY (Johnny Podres)
1956	Oct. 8:	AL:	NY vs Brk. (Don Larsen)
1961	Oct. 4:	AL:	NY vs Cin. (Whitey Ford)
1962	Oct. 5:	NL:	SF vs NY (Jack Sanford)
1965	Oct. 14:	NL:	LA vs Minn. (Sandy Koufax)
1973	Oct. 18:	NL:	NY vs Oak. (Jerry Koosman & Tug McGraw)
1993	Oct. 21:	NL:	Phil. vs Tor. (Curt Schilling)

3-0

Year	Date	Lg	Teams
1903	Oct. 2:	AL:	Bos. vs Pitt. (Bill Dinneen)
1903	Oct. 13:	AL:	Bos. vs Pitt. (Bill Dinneen)
1905	Oct. 9:	NL:	NY vs Phil. (Christy Mathewson)
1905	Oct. 10:	AL:	Phil. vs NY (Chief Bender)
1906	Oct. 11:	AL:	Chi. vs Chi. (Ed Walsh)
1908	Oct. 13:	NL:	Chi. vs Det. (Three Finger Brown)
1913	Oct. 8:	NL:	NY vs Phil. (Christy Mathewson, 10 inn)
1918	Sept. 10:	NL:	Chi. vs Bos. (Hippo Vaughn)
1919	Oct. 3:	AL:	Chi. vs Cin. (Dickie Kerr)
1920	Oct. 6:	NL:	Brk. vs Clev. (Burleigh Grimes)
1920	Oct. 12:	AL:	Clev. vs Brk. (Stan Coveleski)
1921	Oct. 5:	AL:	NY vs NY (Carl Mays)
1921	Oct. 6:	AL:	NY vs NY (Waite Hoyt)
1922	Oct. 6:	NL:	NY vs NY (Jack Scott)
1931	Oct. 6:	AL:	Phil. vs StL. (George Earnshaw)
1935	Oct. 2:	NL:	Chi. vs Det. (Lon Warneke)
1945	Oct. 5:	NL:	Chi. vs Det. (Claude Passeau)
1946	Oct. 7:	NL:	StL. vs Bos. (Harry Brecheen)
1958	Oct. 5:	NL:	Mil. vs NY (Warren Spahn)
1981	Oct. 21:	AL:	NY vs LA (Tommy John & Goose Gossage)
1985	Oct. 23:	NL:	StL. vs KC (John Tudor)
1998	Oct. 21	AL	NY vs SD (Andy Pettitte, Jeff Nelson & Mariano Rivera)

4-0

1925	Oct. 11:	AL:	Wash. vs Pitt. (Walter Johnson)
1926	Oct. 5:	NL:	StL. vs NY (Jesse Haines)
1933	Oct. 5:	AL:	Wash. vs NY (Earl Whitehill)
1939	Oct. 5:	AL:	NY vs Cin. (Monte Pearson)
1940	Oct. 7:	NL:	Cin. vs Det. (Bucky Walters)
1946	Oct. 9:	AL:	Bos. vs StL. (Boo Ferriss)
1958	Oct. 4:	AL:	NY vs Mil. (Don Larsen & Ryne Duren)
1965	Oct. 9:	NL:	LA vs Minn. (Claude Osteen)
1968	Oct. 2:	NL:	StL. vs Det. (Bob Gibson)
1971	Oct. 14:	NL:	Pitt. vs Balt. (Nellie Briles)
1979	Oct. 16:	NL:	Pitt. vs Balt. (John Candelaria & Kent Tekulve)
1996	Oct. 21:	NL:	Atl. vs NY (Greg Maddux)
2001	Oct. 28	NL:	Ari. vs NY (Randy Johnson)

5-0

1909	Oct. 12:	AL:	Det. vs Pitt. (George Mullin)
1917	Oct. 11:	NL:	NY vs Chi. (Ferdie Schupp)
1919	Oct. 6:	NL:	Cin. vs Chi. (Hod Eller)
1930	Oct. 4:	NL:	StL. vs Phil. (Bill Hallahan)
1957	Oct. 10:	NL:	Mil. vs NY (Lew Burdette)
1967	Oct. 5:	AL:	Bos. vs StL. (Jim Lonborg)
1969	Oct. 14:	NL:	NY vs Balt. (Gary Gentry & Nolan Ryan)
1983	Oct. 16:	AL:	Balt. vs Phil. (Scott McGregor)
1989	Oct. 14:	AL:	Oak. vs SF (Dave Stewart)

6-0

1966	Oct. 6:	AL:	Balt. vs LA (Jim Palmer)
1967	Oct. 8:	NL:	StL. vs Bos. (Bob Gibson)
1975	Oct. 11:	AL:	Bos. vs Cin. (Luis Tiant)
1988	Oct. 16:	NL:	LA vs Oak. (Orel Hershiser)

7-0

1958	Oct. 6:	AL:	NY vs Mil. (Bob Turley)
1961	Oct. 8:	AL:	NY vs Cin. (Whitey Ford & Jim Coates)
1965	Oct. 11:	NL:	LA vs Minn. (Sandy Koufax)
1990	Oct. 16:	NL:	Cin. vs Oak. (Jose Rijo, Rob Dibble & Randy Myers)

8-0

1909	Oct. 16:	NL:	Pitt. vs Det. (Babe Adams)
1940	Oct. 6:	AL:	Det. vs Cin. (Bobo Newsom)

9-0

1905	Oct. 12:	NL:	NY vs Phil. (Christy Mathewson)
1945	Oct. 3:	NL:	Chi. vs Det. (Hank Borowy)
1956	Oct. 10:	AL:	NY vs Brk. (Johnny Kucks)

10-0

1960	Oct. 8:	AL:	NY vs Pitt. (Whitey Ford)
1982	Oct. 12:	AL:	Mil. vs StL. (Mike Caldwell)

11-0

1934	Oct. 9:	NL:	StL. vs Det. (Dizzy Dean)
1959	Oct. 1:	AL:	Chi. vs LA (Early Wynn & Gerry Staley)
1985	Oct. 27:	AL:	KC vs StL. (Bret Saberhagen)

12-0

1960	Oct. 12:	AL:	NY vs Pitt. (Whitey Ford)

PITCHER, CLUB, YEAR		W	L
Adams, Babe NL:Pitt 1909		3	0
Aguilera, Rick	NL:NY 1986 (1-0)		
	AL:Minn 1991 (1-1)	2	1
Aldridge, Vic NL:Pitt 1925, 27		2	1
Alexander, Doyle AL:NY 1976		0	1
Alexander, Grover	NL:Phil 1915 (1-1)		
	NL:StL 1926, 28 (2-1)	3	2
Altrock, Nick AL:Chi 1906		1	1
Ames, Red NL:NY 1911		0	1
Anderson, Brian NL:Ari 2001		0	1
Anderson, Fred NL:NY 1917		0	1
Andujar, Joaquin NL:StL 1982, 85		2	1
Antonelli, Johnny NL:NY 1954		1	0
Arroyo, Luis AL:NY 1961		1	0
Ashby, Andy NL:SD 1998		0	1
Auker, Elden AL:Det 1934		1	1
Avery, Steve NL:Atl 1992, 95-96		1	2
Bagby, Jim AL:Clev 1920		1	1
Bair, Doug NL:StL 1982		0	1
Barnes, Jesse NL:NY 1921		2	0
Barnes, Virgil NL:NY 1924		0	1
Barney, Rex NL:Brk 1947, 49		0	2
Bearden, Gene AL:Clev 1948		1	0
Beattie, Jim AL:NY 1978		1	0
Beazley, Johnny NL:StL 1942		2	0
Bedient, Hugh AL:Bos 1912		1	0
Belcher, Tim NL:LA 1988		1	0
Bell, Gary AL:Bos 1967		0	1
Bender, Chief AL:Phil 1905,10-11,13-14		6	4
Bentley, Jack NL:NY 1923-24		1	3
Benton, Rube NL:NY 1917		1	1
Berenguer, Juan AL:Minn 1987		0	1
Bessent, Don NL:Brk 1956		1	0
Bevens, Bill AL:NY 1947		0	1
Bickford, Vern NL:Bos 1948		0	1
Billingham, Jack NL:Cin 1972, 76		2	0
Black, Bud AL:KC 1985		0	1
Black, Joe NL:Brk 1952		1	2
Blake, Sheriff AL:Chi 1929		0	1
Blass, Steve NL:Pitt 1971		2	0
Blue, Vida AL:Oak 1972-74		0	3
Blyleven, Bert	NL:Pitt 1979 (1-0)		
	AL:Minn 1987 (1-1)	2	1
Boddicker, Mike AL:Balt 1983		1	0
Bonham, Ernie AL:NY 1941-43		1	2
Borbon, Pedro, Sr. NL:Cin 1972		0	1
Borowy, Hank	AL:NY 1943 (1-0)		
	NL:Chi 1945 (2-2)	3	2
Bouton, Jim AL:NY 1963-64		2	1
Boyd, Oil Can AL:Bos 1986		0	1
Branca, Ralph NL:Brk 1947, 49		1	2
Brazle, Al NL:StL 1943, 46		0	2
Brecheen, Harry NL:StL 1943-44, 46		4	1
Bridges, Tommy AL:Det 1934-35, 40		4	1
Briles, Nellie	NL:StL 1967-68 (1-1)		
	NL:Pitt 1971 (1-0)	2	1
Kevin Brown	NL:Fla 1997 (0-2)		
	NL:SD 1998 (0-1)	0	3
Brown, Three Finger NL:Chi 1906-08, 10		5	4
Browning, Tom NL:Cin 1990		1	0
Bryant, Clay NL:Chi 1935		0	1
Buhl, Bob NL:Mil 1957		0	1
Bunker, Wally AL:Balt 1966		1	0
Burdette, Lew NL:Mil 1957-58		4	2
Burton, Jim AL:Bos 1975		0	1
Bush, Guy NL:Chi 1929, 32		1	1
Bush, Joe	AL:Phil 1913-14 (0-2)		
	AL:Bos 1918 (0-1)		
	AL:NY 1922-23 (2-2)	2	5

PITCHER, CLUB, YEAR		W	L
Byrne, Tommy AL:NY 1955		1	1
Cadore, Leon NL:Brk 1920		0	1
Caldwell, Mike AL:Mil 1982		2	0
Caldwell, Ray AL:Clev 1920		0	1
Camnitz, Howie, NL:Pitt 1909		0	1
Candelaria, John, NL:Pitt 1979		1	1
Carlton, Tex, NL:Chi 1935		0	1
Carlton, Steve	NL:StL 1965 (0-1)		
	NL:Phil 1980,83 (2-1)	2	2
Carroll, Clay, NL:Cin 1970, 72, 75		2	1
Casey, Hugh NL:Brk 1941, 47		2	2
Castillo, Tony AL:Tor 1993		1	0
Chalmers, George NL:Phil 1915		0	1
Chandler, Spud AL:NY 1941-43		2	2
Christenson, Larry NL:Phil 1980		0	1
Cicotte, Eddie AL:Chi 1917, 19		2	3
Clancy, Jim NL:Atl 1991		1	0
Clemens, Roger AL:NY 1999-2001		3	0
Cleveland, Reggie AL:Bos 1975		0	1
Cloninger, Tony NL:Cin 1970		0	1
Coakley, Andy AL:Phil 1905		0	1
Coates, Jim AL:NY 1962		0	1
Cone, David AL:NY 1996, 99		2	0
Cook, Dennis NL:Fla. 1997		1	0
Coombs, Jack	AL:Phil 1910-11 (4-0)		
	NL:Brk 1916 (1-0)	5	0
Cooper, Mort NL:StL 1942-44		2	3
Coveleski, Stan	AL:Clev 1920 (3-0)		
	AL:Wash 1925 (0-2)	3	2
Cox, Danny NL:StL 1987		1	2
Craig, Roger	NL:Brk 1955-56 (1-1)		
	NL:LA 1959 (0-1)		
	NL:StL 1964 (1-0)	2	2
Crandall, Doc NL:NY 1911		1	0
Crawford, Steve AL:Bos 1986		1	0
Crowder, General	AL:Wash 1933 (0-1)		
	AL:Det 1934-35 (1-1)	1	2
Cuellar, Mike AL:Balt 1969-71		2	2
Daley, Bud AL:NY 1961		1	0
Darcy, Pat NL:Cin 1975		0	1
Darling, Ron NL:NY 1986		1	1
Davis, Curt NL:Brk 1941		0	1
Davis, Storm	AL:Balt 1983 (1-0)		
	AL:Oak 1988 (0-2)	1	2
Dayley, Ken NL:StL 1985		1	0
Dean, Dizzy	NL:StL 1934 (2-1)		
	NL:Chi 1938 (0-1)	2	2
Dean, Paul NL:StL 1934		2	0
Demaree, Al NL:NY 1913		0	1
Denny, John NL:Phil 1983		1	1
Derringer, Paul	NL:StL 1931 (0-2)		
	NL:Cin 1939-40 (2-2)	2	4
Dibble, Rob NL:Cin 1990		1	0
Dickson, Murry NL:StL 1946		0	1
Dinneen, Bill AL:Bos 1903		3	1
Ditmar, Art AL:NY 1960		0	2
Dobson, Joe AL:Bos 1946		1	0
Donald, Atley AL:NY 1942		0	1
Donnelly, Blix NL:StL 1944		1	0
Donovan, Dick AL:Chi 1959		0	1
Donovan, Wild Bill AL:Det. 1907-09		1	4
Douglas, Phil	NL:Chi. 1918 (0-1)		
	NL:NY 1921 (2-1)	2	2
Downing, Al	AL:NY 1963-64 (0-2)		
	NL:LA 1974 (0-1)	0	3
Drabowsky, Moe AL:Balt 1966		1	0
Drago, Dick AL:Bos 1975		0	1
Drysdale, Don NL:LA 1959, 63, 65-66		3	3
Duren, Ryne AL:NY 1958		1	1

PITCHER, CLUB, YEAR		W	L
Earnshaw, George AL:Phil 1929-31		4	3
Eastwick, Rawly NL:Cin 1975		2	0
Eckersley, Dennis AL:Oak 1988, 90		0	2
Ehmke, Howard AL:Phil 1929		1	0
Eller, Hod NL:Cin 1919		2	0
Ellis, Dock	NL:Pitt 1971 (0-1)		
	AL:NY 1976 (0-1)	0	2
Erskine, Carl NL:Brk 1952-53, 56		2	2
Faber, Red AL:Chi 1917		3	1
Feller, Bob AL:Clev 1948		0	2
Ferguson, Alex AL:Wash 1925		1	1
Ferrick, Tom AL:NY 1950		1	0
Ferriss, Boo AL:Bos 1946		1	0
OJames, Bill NL:Bos 1914		2	0
Jansen, Larry NL:NY 1951		0	2
Figueroa, Ed AL:NY 1976, 78		0	2
Fingers, Rollie AL:Oak 1972-74		2	2
Fisher Ray, NL:Cin 1919		0	1
Fitzsimmons, Freddie NL:NY 1933, 36		0	3
Flanagan, Mike AL:Balt 1979		1	1
Ford, Whitey AL:NY 1950,53,55-58, 60-64		10	8
Forsch, Bob, NL:StL 1982, 85, 87		1	3
Foster, Rube AL:Bos 1915		2	0
Franco, John NL:NY 2000		1	0
Frazier, George AL:NY 1981		0	3
French, Larry NL:Chi 1935		0	2
Friend, Bob NL:Pitt 1960		0	2
Gale, Rich AL:KC 1980		0	1
Galehouse, Denny AL:StL 1944		1	1
Garcia, Mike AL:Clev 1954		0	1
Garrelts, Scott NL:SF 1989		0	2
Gentry, Gary NL:NY 1969		1	0
Gibson, Bob NL:StL 1964, 67-68		7	2
Glavine, Tom NL:Atl 1991-92, 95-96		4	3
Gomez, Lefty AL:NY 1932, 36-38		6	0
Gomez, Ruben NL:NY 1954		1	0
Gooden, Dwight NL:NY 1986		0	2
Gossage, Goose AL:NY 1978		1	0
Grant, Mudcat AL:Minn 1965		2	1
Gregg, Hal NL:Brk 1947		0	1
Grim, Bob AL:NY 1955, 57		0	2
Grimes, Burleigh	NL:Brk 1920 (1-2)		
	NL:StL 1930-31 (2-2)	3	4
Grimsley, Ross NL:Cin 1972		2	1
Grissom, Marv NL:NY 1954		1	0
Gromek, Steve AL:Clev 1948		1	0
Grove, Lefty AL:Phil 1930-31		4	2
Guidry, Ron AL:NY 1977-78, 81		3	1
Gullett, Don	NL:Cin 1975-76 (2-1)		
	AL:NY 1977 (0-1)	2	2
Guthrie, Mark AL:Minn 1991		0	1
Guzman, Juan AL:Tor 1993		0	1
Haddix, Harvey NL:Pitt 1960		2	0
Hadley, Bump AL:NY 1936-37, 39		2	1
Haines, Jesse NL:StL 1926, 28, 30		3	1
Hall, Dick AL:Balt 1969		0	1
Hallahan, Bill NL:StL 1930-31		3	1
Hampton, Mike NL:NY 2000		0	1
Harris, Mickey AL:Bos 1946		0	2
Hawkins, Andy NL:SD 1984		1	1
Hearn, Jim NL:NY 1951		1	0
Hentgen, Pat AL:Tor 1993		1	0
Hernandez, Livan NL:Fla. 1997		2	0
Hernandez, Orlando AL:NY 1998-2000		2	1
Hershiser, Orel	NL:LA 1988 (2-0)		
	AL:Clev 1995,97 (1-3)	3	3
Hill, Ken AL:Clev 1995		0	1
Hitchcock, Sterling AL:NY 2001		1	0
Hoerner, Joe NL:StL 1968		0	1

PITCHER, CLUB, YEAR		W	L
Hoffman, Trevor NL:SD 1998		0	1
Holtzman, Ken AL:Oak 1972-74		4	1
Honeycutt, Rick AL:Oak 1988		1	0
Hooton, Burt NL:LA 1977-78		3	3
Howe, Steve NL:LA 1981		1	0
Howell, Jay NL:LA 1988		0	1
Hoyt, Waite	AL:NY 1921-22,26-28 (6-3)		
	AL:Phil 1931 (0-1)	6	4
Hubbell, Carl NL:NY 1933, 36-37		4	2
Hudson, Charles NL:Phil 1983		0	2
Hughes, Dick NL:StL 1967		0	1
Hughes, Long Tom AL:Bos 1903		0	1
Hughson, Tex AL: Bos 1946		0	1
Hunter, Catfish	AL:Oak 1972-74 (4-0)		
	AL:NY 1976-78 (1-3)	5	3
Hurst, Bruce AL:Bos 1986		2	0
Jackson, Danny	AL:KC 1985 (1-1)		
	NL:Phil 1993 (0-1)	1	2
Jackson, Grant NL:Pitt 1979		1	0
Jakucki, Sig AL: StL 1944		0	1
Jay, Joey NL:Cin 1961		1	1
John, Tommy	NL:LA 1977-78 (1-1)		
	AL:NY 1981 (1-0)	2	1
Johnson, Bob NL:Pitt 1971		0	1
Johnson, Earl AL:Bos 1946		1	0
Johnson, Ernie NL:Mil 1957		0	1
Johnson, Randy NL:Ari. 2001		3	0
Johnson, Syl NL:StL 1931		0	1
Johnson, Walter AL:Wash 1924-25		3	3
Jones, Bobby J. NL:NY 2000		0	1
Jones, Sam	AL:Bos 1918 (0-1)		
	NY 1923 (0-1)	0	2
Kaat, Jim AL:Minn 1965		1	2
Kennedy, Brickyard NL:Pitt 1903		0	1
Kerr, Dickie AL:Chi 1919		2	0
Key, Jimmy	AL:Tor 1992 (2-0)		
	NY 1996 (1-1)	3	1
Kim, Byung-Hyun NL:Ari. 2001		0	1
Kison, Bruce NL:Pitt 1971, 79		1	1
Klinger, Bob AL:Bos 1946		0	1
Konstanty, Jim NL:Phil 1950		0	1
Koosman, Jerry NL:NY 1969, 73		3	0
Koslo, Dave NL:NY 1951		1	1
Koufax, Sandy NL:LA 1959, 63, 65-66		4	3
Kramer, Jack AL:StL 1944		1	0
Kremer, Ray NL:Pitt 1925, 27		2	2
Kucks, Johnny AL:NY 1956		1	0
Labine, Clem NL:Brk 1953, 55-56		2	2
Lamabe, Jack NL:StL 1967		0	1
Lanier, Max NL:StL 1942-44		2	1
Larsen, Don	AL:NY 1955-58 (3-2)		
	NL:SF 1962 (1-0)	4	2
Law, Vern NL:Pitt 1960		2	0
Lee, Bill NL:Chi 1938		0	2
Leever, Sam NL:Pitt 1903		0	2
Leibrandt, Charlie	AL:KC 1985 (0-1)		
	NL:Atl 1991-92 (0-3)	0	4
Leifield, Lefty NL:Pitt 1909		0	1
Leiter, Al	AL:Tor. 1998 (1-0)		
	NL:NY 2000 (0-1)	1	1
Lemon, Bob AL:Clev 1948, 54		2	2
Leonard, Dennis AL:KC 1980		1	1
Leonard, Dutch AL:Bos 1915-16		2	0
Liddle, Don NL:NY 1954		1	0
Lindblad, Paul AL:Oak 1973		1	0
Lloyd, Graeme AL:NY 1996		1	0
Loes, Billy NL:Brk 1952-53, 55		1	2
Lolich, Mickey AL:Det 1968		3	0
Lollar, Tim NL:SD 1984		0	1

PITCHER, CLUB, YEAR	W	L
Lombardi, Vic NL:Brk 1947	0	1
Lonborg, Jim AL:Bos 1967	2	1
Lopat, Ed AL:NY 1949, 51-53	4	1
Lopez, Albie NL:Ari. 2001	0	1
Lopez, Aurelio AL:Det 1984	1	0
Luque, Dolf NL:NY 1933	1	0
Lyle, Sparky AL:NY 1977	1	0
Maddox, Nick NL:Pitt 1909	1	0
Maddux, Greg NL:Atl 1995-96, 99	2	3
Maglie, Sal NL:NY 1951 (0-1)		
NL:Brk 1956 (1-1)	1	2
Magrane, Joe NL:StL 1987	0	1
Mails, Duster AL:Clev 1920	1	0
Malone, Pat NL:Chi 1929 (0-2)		
AL:NY 1936 (0-1)	0	3
Marberry, Firpo AL:Wash 1924	0	1
Marquard, Rube NL:NY 1911-13 (2-2)		
NL:Brk 1916, 20 (0-3)	2	5
Marshall, Mike NL:LA 1974	0	1
Martinez, Dennis AL:Clev 1995	0	1
Mathewson, Christy NL:NY 1905, 11-13	5	5
Matlack, Jon NL:NY 1973	1	2
May, Jakie NL:Chi 1932	0	1
Mayer, Erskine NL:Phil 1915	0	1
Mays, Carl AL:Bos 1916, 18 (2-1)		
AL:NY 1921-22 (1-3)	3	4
McClure, Bob AL:Mil 1982	0	2
McDonald, Jim AL:NY 1953	1	0
McDowell, Roger NL:NY 1986	1	0
McGinnity, Joe NL:NY 1905	1	1
McGraw, Tug NL:NY 1973 (1-0)		
NL:Phil 1980 (1-1)	2	1
McGregor, Scott AL:Balt 1979, 83	2	2
McIntire, Harry NL:Chi 1910	0	1
McLain, Denny AL, Det 1968	1	2
McNally, Dave AL:Balt 1966, 69-71	4	2
McQuillan, Hugh NL:NY 1922-24	2	1
Meadow, Lee NL:Pitt 1925, 27	0	2
Melton, Cliff NL:NY 1937	0	2
Mendoza, Ramiro AL:NY 1998	1	0
Merritt, Jim NL:Cin 1970	0	1
Mesa, Jose AL:Clev 1995	1	0
Messersmith, Andy NL:LA 1974	0	2
Meyer, Russ NL:Phil 1950	0	1
Mikkelsen, Pete AL:NY 1964	0	1
Miljus, Johnny NL:Pitt 1927	0	1
Miller, Bob J. NL:Phil 1950	0	1
Miller, Bob L. NL:Pitt 1971	0	1
Millwood, Kevin NL:Atl. 1999	0	1
Mizell, Vinegar Bend NL:Pitt 1960	0	1
Mogridge, George AL:Wash 1924	1	0
Moore, Mike AL:Oak 1989-90	2	1
Moore, Wilcy AL:NY 1927, 32	2	0
Morgan, Tom AL:NY 1956	0	1
Morris, Jack AL:Det 1984 (2-0)		
AL:Minn 1991 (2-0)		
AL:Tor 1992 (0-2)	4	2
Mulholland, Terry NL:Phil 1993	1	0
Mullin, George AL:Det 1907-09	3	3
Muncrief, Bob AL:StL 1944	0	1
Munger, George NL:StL 1946	1	0
Murphy, Johnny AL:NY 1939, 41	2	0
Nagy, Charles NL:Clev. 1997	0	1
Nehf, Art NL:NY 1921-24	4	4
Nelson, Jeff AL:NY 2000	1	0
Newcombe, Don NL:Brk 1949, 55-56	0	4
Newhouser, Hal AL:Det 1945	2	1
Newsom, Bobo AL:Det 1940 (2-1)		
AL:NY 1947 (0-1)	2	2

PITCHER, CLUB, YEAR	W	L
Nipper, Al AL:Bos 1986	0	1
Nolan, Gary NL:Cin 1970, 72, 76	1	2
Norman, Fred NL:Cin 1975	0	1
O'Brien, Buck AL:Bos 1912	0	2
O'Dell, Billy NL:SF 1962	0	1
Odom, Blue Moon AL:Oak 1972, 74	1	1
Ogea, Chad AL:Clev. 1997	2	0
Ojeda, Bob NL:NY 1986	1	0
Osteen, Claude NL:LA 1965-66	1	2
O'Toole, Jim NL:Cin 1961	0	2
Overall, Orval NL:Chi 1907-08,10	3	1
Overmire, Stubby AL:Det 1945	0	1
Page, Joe AL:NY 1947, 49	2	1
Palmer, Jim AL:Balt 1969-71, 79, 83	4	2
Parker, Harry NL:NY 1973	0	1
Pascual, Camilo AL:Minn 1965	0	1
Passeau, Claude NL:Chi 1945	1	0
Pearson, Monte AL:NY 1936-39	4	0
Pena, Alejandro NL:LA 1988 (1-0)		
NL:Atl 1991, 95 (0-2)	1	2
Pennock, Herb AL:NY 1923, 26-27	5	0
Petry, Dan AL:Det 1984	0	1
Pettitte, Andy AL:NY 1996,98, 2001	2	3
Pfeffer, Jeff NL:Brk 1916	0	1
Pfiester, Jack NL:Chi 1906-08	1	3
Phillippe, Deacon NL:Pitt 1903	3	2
Phoebus, Tom AL:Balt 1970	1	0
Pierce, Billy NL:SF 1962	1	1
Pipgras, George AL:NY 1927-28, 32	3	0
Plank, Eddie AL:Phil 1905, 11, 13-14	2	5
Plunk, Eric AL:Clev. 1997	0	1
Podres, Johnny NL:Brk 1953, 55 (2-1)		
NL:LA 1959, 63 (2-0)	4	1
Pollet, Howie NL:StL 1946	0	1
Poole, Jim AL:Clev 1995	0	1
Potter, Nels AL:StL 1944	1	1
Powell, Jay NL:Fla. 1997	1	0
Prim, Ray NL:Chi 1945	0	1
Purkey, Bob NL: Cin 1961	0	1
Quinn, Jack AL:NY 1921	0	1
Quisenberry, Dan AL:KC 1980, 85	2	2
Raschi, Vic AL:NY 1949-53	5	3
Rau, Doug NL:LA 1977	0	1
Reardon, Jeff NL:Atl 1992	0	1
Reinhart, Art NL:StL 1926	0	1
Remlinger, Mike NL:Atl. 1999	0	1
Reulbach, Ed NL:Chi 1906-07	2	0
Reuschel, Rick NL:SF 1989	0	1
Reuss, Jerry NL:LA 1981	1	1
Reynolds, Allie AL:NY 1947, 49-53	7	2
Rhem, Flint NL:StL 1930	0	1
Rhoden, Rick NL:LA 1977	0	1
Rijo, Jose NL:Cin 1990	2	0
Ring, Jimmy NL:Cin 1919	1	1
Rivera, Mariano, AL:NY 1999, 2001	2	1
Rixey, Eppa NL:Phil. 1915	0	1
Roberts, Robin, NL:Phil. 1950	0	1
Robinson, Don, NL:Pitt. 1979 (1-0)		
NL:SF 1989 (0-1)	1	1
Roe, Preacher NL:Brk 1949, 52-53	2	1
Rommel, Eddie AL:Phil 1929	1	0
Root, Charlie NL:Chi 1929, 32, 35	0	3
Rowe, Schoolboy AL:Det 1934-35, 40	2	5
Rudolph, Dick NL:Bos 1914	2	0
Ruether, Dutch NL:Cin 1919 (1-0)		
AL:NY 1926 (0-1)	1	1
Ruffing, Red AL:NY 1932, 36-39, 41-42	7	2
Rush, Bob NL:Mil 1958	0	1
Russell, Jack AL:Wash 1933	0	1

PITCHER, CLUB, YEAR		W	L
Russo, Marius AL:NY 1941, 43		2	0
Ruth, Babe AL:Bos 1916, 18		3	0
Ryan, Rosy NL:NY 1922-23		2	0
Saberhagen, Bret AL:KC 1985		2	0
Sadecki, Ray NL:StL 1964		1	0
Sain, Johnny	NL:Bos 1948 (1-1)		
	AL:NY 1952-53 (1-1)	2	2
Sallee, Slim	NL:NY 1917 (0-2)		
	NL:Cin 1919 (1-1)	1	3
Sanford, Jack NL:SF 1962		1	2
Santiago, Jose AL:Bos 1967		0	2
Saunders, Tony NL:Fla. 1997		0	1
Schatzeder, Dan AL:Minn 1987		1	0
Schilling, Curt	NL:Phil 1993 (1-1)		
	NL:Ari 2001 (1-0)	2	1
Schiraldi, Calvin AL:Bos 1986		0	2
Schultz, Barney NL:StL 1964		0	1
Schumacher, Hal NL:NY 1933, 36-37		2	2
Schupp, Ferdie NL:NY 1917		1	0
Scott, Jack NL:NY 1922-23		1	1
Seaver, Tom NL:NY 1969, 73		1	2
Shantz, Bobby AL:NY 1957		0	1
Shaw, Bob AL:Chi 1959		1	1
Shawkey, Bob	AL:Phil 1914 (0-1)		
	AL:NY 1921,23,26 (1-2)	1	3
Shea, Spec AL:NY 1947		2	0
Sherdel, Bill NL:StL 1926, 28		0	4
Sherry, Larry NL:LA 1959		2	0
Shocker, Urban AL:NY 1926		0	1
Shore, Ernie AL:Bos 1915-16		3	1
Show, Eric NL:SD 1984		0	1
Siever, Ed AL:Det 1907		0	1
Simmons, Curt NL:StL 1964		0	1
Slaton, Jim AL:Mil 1982		1	0
Smith, Sherry NL:Brk 1916, 20		1	2
Smoltz, John NL:Atl 1992, 96, 99		2	2
Spahn, Warren	NL:Bos 1948 (1-1)		
	NL:Mil 1957-58 (3-2)	4	3
Spooner, Karl NL:Brk 1955		0	1
Stafford, Bill AL:NY 1962		1	0
Staley, Gerry AL:Chi 1959		0	1
Stanhouse, Don AL:Balt 1979		0	1
Stanton, Mike	NL Atl. 1991 (1-0)		
	AL:NY 2000 (2-0)	3	0
Stewart, Dave	AL:Oak 1988-90 (2-3)		
	AL:Tor 1993 (0-1)	2	4
Stewart, Lefty AL: Wash 1933		0	1
Stoddard, Tim AL:Balt 1979		1	0
Stottlemyre, Mel AL:NY 1964		1	1
Stuper, John NL:StL 1982		1	0
Sturdivant, Tom AL:NY 1956		1	0
Summers, Ed AL:Det 1908-09		0	4
Sutter, Bruce NL:StL 1982		1	0
Sutton, Don	NL:LA 1974,77-78 (2-2)		
	AL:Mil 1982 (0-1)	2	3
Tapani, Kevin AL:Minn 1991		1	1
Tekulve, Kent NL:Pitt 1979		0	1
Terry, Ralph AL:NY 1960-62		2	4
Tesreau, Jeff NL:NY 1912-13		1	3
Thompson, Junior NL:Cin 1939-40		0	2
Thurmond, Mark NL:SD 1984		0	1
Tiant, Luis AL:Bos 1975		2	0
Torrez, Mike AL:NY 1977		2	0
Trout, Dizzy AL:Det 1940, 45		1	2
Trucks, Virgil AL:Det 1945		1	0
Tudor, John NL:StL 1985, 87		3	2
Turley, Bob AL:NY 1955, 58, 60		4	3
Turner, Jim NL:Cin 1940		0	1
Tyler, Lefty NL:Chi 1918		1	1

PITCHER, CLUB, YEAR		W	L
Valenzuela, Fernando NL:LA 1981		1	0
Vaughn, Hippo NL:Chi 1918		1	2
Viola, Frank AL:Minn 1987		2	1
Voiselle, Bill NL:Bos 1948		0	1
Vuckovich, Pete AL:Mil 1982		0	1
Walberg, Rube AL:Phil 1929-30		1	1
Walk, Bob NL:Phil 1980		1	0
Walker, Bill NL:StL 1934		0	2
Wall, Donne NL:SD 1998		0	1
Walsh, Ed AL:Chi 1906		2	0
Walters, Bucky NL:Cin 1939-40		2	2
Ward, Duane AL:Tor 1992-93		3	0
Warneke, Lon NL:Chi 1932, 35		2	1
Washburn, Ray NL:StL 1968		1	1
Watt, Eddie AL:Balt 1969-71		0	3
Weaver, Monte AL:Wash 1933		0	1
Welch, Bob NL:LA 1978		0	1
Wells, David AL:NY 1998		1	0
Wendell, Turk NL:NY 2000		0	1
White, Doc AL:Chi 1906		1	1
White, Ernie NL:StL 1942		1	0
Whitehill, Earl AL: Wash 1933		1	0
Wilcox, Milt	NL:Cin 1970 (0-1)		
	AL:Det 1984 (1-0)	1	1
Wilks, Ted NL:StL 1944		0	1
Williams, Lefty AL:Chi 1919		0	3
Williams, Mitch NL:Phil 1993		0	2
Willis, Vic NL:Pitt 1909		0	1
Willoughby, Jim AL:Bos 1975		0	1
Wilson, Earl AL:Det 1968		0	1
Wise, Rick AL:Bos 1975		1	0
Wood, Smoky Joe AL:Bos 1912		3	1
Worrell, Todd NL:StL 1985		0	1
Wright, Jaret NL:Clev. 1997		1	0
Wyatt, John AL:Bos 1967		1	0
Wyatt, Whitlow NL:Brk 1941		1	1
Wynn, Early	AL:Clev 1954 (0-1)		
	AL:Chi 1959 (1-1)	1	2
Wyse, Hank NL:Chi 1945		0	1
Yde, Emil NL: Pitt 1925		0	1
Young, Cy AL:Bos 1903		2	1
Zachary, Tom	AL:Wash 1924 (2-0)		
	AL:NY 928 (1-0)	3	0
Zachry, Pat NL:Cin 1976		1	0

AMERICAN LEAGUE WORLD SERIES MANAGERS

	SERIES			GAMES		YEARS	
	No.	Won	Lost	Won	Lost	Won	Lost
Altobelli, Joe Balt.	1	1	0	4	1	1983	
*Anderson, Sparky Det.	1	1	0	4	1	1984	
Baker, Del Det.	1	0	1	3	4		1940
Barrow, Ed Bos.	1	1	0	4	2	1918	
Bauer, Hank Balt.	1	1	0	4	0	1966	
*Berra, Yogi NY	1	0	1	3	4		1964
Boudreau, Lou Clev.	1	1	0	4	2	1948	
Carrigan, Bill Bos.	2	2	0	8	2	1915-16	
Cochrane, Mickey Det.	2	1	1	7	6	1935	1934
Collins, Jimmy Bos.	1	1	0	5	3	1903	
Cronin, Joe Wash.	1	0	1	1	4		1933
Bos.	1	0	1	3	4		1946
Totals	(2)	(0)	(2)	(4)	(8)		
*Dark, Alvin Oak.	1	1	0	4	1	1974	
Frey, Jim KC	1	0	1	2	4		1980
Gaston, Cito Tor.	2	2	0	8	4	1992-93	
Gleason, Kid Chi.	1	0	1	3	5		1919
Hargrove, Mike Clev.	2	0	2	5	8		1995, 97
Harris, Bucky Wash.	2	1	1	7	7	1924	1925
NY	1	1	0	4	3	1947	
Totals	(3)	(2)	(1)	(11)	(10)		
Houk, Ralph NY	3	2	1	8	8	1961-62	1963
Howser, Dick KC	1	1	0	4	3	1985	
Huggins, Miller NY	6	3	3	18	15	1923, 27-28	1921-22, 26
Jennings, Hughie Det.	3	0	3	4	12		1907-09
Johnson, Darrell Bos.	1	0	1	3	4		1975
Jones, Fielder Chi.	1	1	0	4	2	1906	
Kelly, Tom Minn.	2	2	0	8	6	1987, 91	
Kuenn, Harvey Mil.	1	0	1	3	4		1982
LaRussa, Tony Oak.	3	1	2	5	8	1989	1988, 90
Lemon, Bob NY	2	1	1	6	6	1978	1981
Lopez, Al Clev.	1	0	1	0	4		1954
Chi.	1	0	1	2	4		1959
Totals	(2)	(0)	(2)	(2)	(8)		
Mack, Connie Phil.	8	5	3	24	19	1910-11, 13, 29-30	1905, 14, 31
Martin, Billy NY	2	1	1	4	6	1977	1976
*McCarthy, Joe NY	8	7	1	29	9	1932, 36-39, 41, 43	1942
McNamara, John Bos.	1	0	1	3	4		1986
Mele, Sam Minn.	1	0	1	3	4		1965
O'Neill, Steve Det.	1	1	0	4	3	1945	
Rowland, Pants Chi.	1	1	0	4	3	1917	
Sewell, Luke StL.	1	0	1	2	4		1944
Smith, Mayo, Det.	1	1	0	4	3	1968	
Speaker, Tris Clev.	1	1	0	5	2	1920	
Stahl, Jake Bos.	1	1	0	4	3	1912	
Stengel, Casey NY	10	7	3	37	26	1949-53, 56, 58	1955, 57, 60
Torre, Joe NY	5	4	1	19	7	1996, 98-2000	2001
Weaver, Earl Balt.	4	1	3	11	13	1970	1969, 71, 79
*Williams, Dick Bos.	1	0	1	3	4		1967
Oak.	2	2	0	8	6	1972-73	
A.L. Totals	(3)	(2)	(1)	(11)	(10)		

* Also managed in the World Series for the National League (see next page)

NATIONAL LEAGUE WORLD SERIES MANAGERS

	SERIES			GAMES		YEARS	
	No.	Won	Lost	Won	Lost	Won	Lost
Alston, Walter Brk.	2	1	1	7	7	1955	1956
LA	5	3	2	13	13	1959, 63, 65	1966, 74
Totals	(7)	(4)	(3)	(20)	(20)		
*Anderson, Sparky Cin.	4	2	2	12	11	1975-76	1970, 72
*Berra, Yogi NY	1	0	1	3	4		1973
Bochy, Bruce SD	1	0	1	0	4		1998
Brenly, Bob Ari.	1	1	0	4	3	2001	
Bush, Donie Pitt.	1	0	1	0	4		1927
Chance, Frank Chi.	4	2	2	11	9	1907-08	1906, 10
Clarke, Fred Pitt.	2	1	1	7	8	1909	1903
Cox, Bobby Atl.	5	1	4	11	18	1995	1991-92, 96, 99
Craig, Roger SF	1	0	1	0	4		1989
*Dark, Alvin SF	1	0	1	3	4		1962
Dressen, Chuck Brk.	2	0	2	5	8		1952-53
Durocher, Leo Brk.	1	0	1	1	4		1941
NY	2	1	1	6	4	1954	1951
Totals	(3)	(1)	(2)	(7)	(8)		
Dyer, Eddie StL.	1	1	0	4	3	1946	
Fregosi, Jim Phil.	1	0	1	2	4		1993
Frisch, Frankie StL.	1	1	0	4	3	1934	
Green, Dallas Phil.	1	1	0	4	2	1980	
Grimm, Charlie Chi.	3	0	3	5	12		1932, 35, 45
Haney, Fred Mil.	2	1	1	7	7	1957	1958
Hartnett, Gabby Chi.	1	0	1	0	4		1938
Herzog, Whitey StL.	3	1	2	10	11	1982	1985, 87
Hodges, Gil NY	1	1	0	4	1	1969	
Hornsby, Rogers StL.	1	1	0	4	3	1926	
Hutchinson, Fred Cin.	1	0	1	1	4		1961
Johnson, Davey NY	1	1	0	4	3	1986	
Keane, Johnny StL.	1	1	0	4	3	1964	
Lasorda, Tommy LA	4	2	2	12	11	1981, 88	1977-78
Leyland, Jim Fla.	1	1	0	4	3	1997	
*McCarthy, Joe Chi.	1	0	1	1	4		1929
McGraw, John NY	9	3	6	26	28	1905, 21-22	1911-13, 17, 23-24
McKechnie, Bill Pitt.	1	1	0	4	3	1925	
Cin.	2	1	1	4	7	1940	1939
StL.	1	0	1	0	4		1928
Totals	(4)	(2)	(2)	(8)	(14)		
Mitchell, Fred Chi.	1	0	1	2	4		1918
Moran, Pat Phil.	1	0	1	1	4		1915
Cin.	1	1	0	5	3	1919	
Totals	(2)	(1)	(1)	(6)	(7)		
Murtaugh, Danny Pitt.	2	2	0	8	6	1960, 71	
Owens, Paul Phil.	1	0	1	1	4		1983
Piniella, Lou Cin.	1	1	0	4	0	1990	
Robinson, Wilbert Brk.	2	0	2	3	9		1916, 20
Sawyer, Eddie Phil.	1	0	1	0	4		1950
Schoendienst, Red StL.	2	1	1	7	7	1967	1968
Shotton, Burt Brk.	2	0	2	4	8		1947, 49
Southworth, Billy StL.	3	2	1	9	7	1942, 44	1943
Bos.	1	0	1	2	4		1948
Totals	(4)	(2)	(2)	(11)	(11)		
Stallings, George Bos.	1	1	0	4	0	1914	
Street, Gabby StL.	2	1	1	6	7	1931	1930
Tanner, Chuck Pitt.	1	1	0	4	3	1979	
Terry, Bill NY	3	1	2	7	9	1933	1936-37
Valentine, Bobby NY	1	0	1	1	4		2000
*Williams, Dick SD	1	0	1	1	4		1984

* Also managed in the World Series for the American League (see previous page)

World Series Umpires

Ashford, Emmett L. 1970
Ballanfant, E. Lee 1940, 46, 51, 55
Barlick, Albert J. 1946, 50, 51, 54, 58, 62, 67
Barnett, Lawrence R. 1975, 81, 84, 90
Barr, George 1937, 42, 48-49
Basil, Stephen J. 1937, 40
Berry, Charles F. 1946, 50, 54, 58, 62
Boggess, Lynton R. 1940, 52, 56, 60
Boyer, James M. 1947
Bremigan, Nicholas G. 1980
Brennan, William T. 1911
Brinkman, Joseph 1978, 86, 95
Burkhart, William K. 1962, 64, 70
Byron, William J. 1914
Chill, Ollie P. 1921
Chylak, Nestor 1957, 60, 66, 71, 77
Clark, Alan M. 1983, 89
Coble, Drew 1991
Colosi, Nicholas, 1975, 81
Conlan, John B. 1945, 50, 54, 57, 61
Connolly, Thomas H. 1903, 08, 10-11, 13, 16, 20, 24
Cooney, Terrance J. 1981
Cousins, Derryl 1988, 99
Crawford, Gerald J. 1988, 92, 98, 2000
Crawford, Henry C. 1961, 63, 69
Dale, Jerry P. 1977
Dascoli, Frank 1953, 55, 59
Davidson, David L. 1975, 82
Davidson, Robert 1992
Davis, Gerald 1996, 99
Deegan, William E. 1976
DeMuth, Dana A. 1993, 98, 2001
Denkinger, Donald A. 1974, 80, 85, 91
DiMuro, Louis J. 1969, 76
Dinneen, William H. 1911, 14, 16, 20, 26, 29, 32
Dixon, Hal H. 1959
Donatelli, August J. 1955, 57, 61, 67, 73
Drummond, Calvin T. 1966
Dunn, Thomas P. 1944
Egan, John J. 1913
Engel, Robert A. 1972, 79, 85
Evans, James B. 1977, 82, 86, 96
Evans, William G. 1909, 12, 15, 17, 19, 23
Flaherty, John F. 1955, 58, 65, 70
Ford, Robert D. 1986, 97
Frantz, Arthur F. 1975
Froemming, Bruce N. 1976, 84, 88, 95
Garcia, Richard R. 1981, 84, 89, 98
Geisel, Harry C. 1930, 34, 36
Goetz, Lawrence J. 1941, 47, 52
Goetz, Russell 1973, 79
Gore, Arthur J. 1951, 53
Gorman, Thomas D. 1956, 58, 63, 68, 74
Gregg, Eric E. 1989
Grieve, William T. 1941, 48, 53
Haller, William E. 1968, 72, 78, 82
Hart, Eugene F. 1923
Harvey, H. Douglas 1968,74, 81, 84, 88
Hendry, Gene 1990
Hildebrand, George A. 1914, 18, 22, 26
Hirschbeck, John F. 1995
Hirschbeck, Mark 1998, 2001
Honochick, G. James 1952, 55, 60, 62, 68, 72
Hubbard, Calvin 1938, 42, 46, 49
Hurley, Edwin 1949, 53, 59, 65
Jackowski, William 1958, 60, 66
Johnson, Mark S. 1993
Johnstone, James E. 1906, 09
Jorda, Louis D. 1945, 49
Joyce, James A. 1999, 2001
Kaiser, Kenneth S. 1987, 97
Kellogg, Jeffrey 2000
Kibler, John W. 1971, 78, 82, 86
Kinnamon, William E. 1968
Klem, William J. 1908-09,11-15,17-18,20,22,24,26,29,31-32,34,40
Kolls, Louis C. 1938
Kosc, Gregory J. 1987, 97
Kunkel, William G. 1974, 80
Landes, Stanley 1960, 62, 68
Luciano, Ronald M. 1974
Magerkurth, George L. 1932, 36, 42, 47
Maloney, George P. 1975
Marsh, Randy 1990, 97, 99
McClelland, Timothy R. 1993, 2000
McCormick, William J. 1922, 25
McCoy, Larry S. 1977, 88
McGowan, William A. 1928, 31, 35, 39, 41, 44, 47, 50

McKean, James 1979, 85, 95
McKinley, William F. 1950, 52, 57, 64
McSherry, John P. 1977, 87
Merrill, E. Durwood 1988
Montague, Edward M. 1986, 91, 97, 2000
Moran, Charles B. 1927, 29, 33, 38
Moriarty, George 1921, 25, 30, 33, 35
Morrison, Daniel 1992
Nallin, Richard F. 1919, 23, 27, 31
Napp, Larry A. 1954, 56, 63, 69
Neudecker, Jerome A. 1973, 79
O'Day, Henry 1903, 05, 07-08, 10, 16, 18, 20, 23, 26
Odom, James C. 1971
O'Loughlin, Francis H. 1906, 09, 12, 15, 17
Olsen, Andrew H. 1974
Ormsby, Emmett T. 1927, 33, 37, 40
Owens, Clarence B. 1918, 22, 25, 28, 34
Palermo, Stephen M. 1983
Paparella, Joseph 1948, 51, 57, 63
Passarella, Arthur 1945, 49, 52
Pelekoudas, Chris G. 1966, 72
Pfirman, Charles H. 1928, 33, 36
Phillips, David R. 1976, 82, 87, 93
Pinelli, Ralph A. 1939, 41, 47-48, 52, 56
Pipgras, George W. 1944
Pryor, J. Paul 1967, 73, 80
Pulli, Frank V. 1978, 83, 90, 95
Quick, James E. 1985, 90
Quigley, Ernest C. 1916, 19, 21, 24, 27, 35
Rapuano, Ed 2001
Reardon, John E. 1930, 34, 39, 43, 49
Reed, Rick 1991
Reilly, Michael 1984, 92
Reliford, Charles H. 2000
Rennert, Laurence H. 1980, 83, 89
Rice, John L. 1959, 63, 66, 71
Rigler, Charles 1910, 12-13, 15, 17, 19, 21, 25, 28,30
Rippley, T. Steve 1996, 99, 2001
Roe, John 1990, 99
Rommel, Edwin A. 1943, 47
Rue, Joseph 1943
Runge, Edward P. 1956, 61, 67
Runge, Paul E. 1979, 84, 89, 93
Scott, Dale 1998, 2001
Sears, John W. 1938, 44
Secory, Frank E. 1957, 59, 64, 69
Sheridan, John F. 1905, 07-08, 10
Shulock, John R. 1985, 92
Smith, Vincent A. 1964
Smith, W. Alaric 1964
Soar, A. Henry 1953, 56, 62, 64, 69
Springstead, Martin J. 1973, 78, 83
Stark, Albert D. 1931, 35
Steiner, Melvin J. 1966, 72
Stello, Richard J. 1975, 81
Stevens, John W. 1951, 54, 60, 67
Stewart, Robert W. 1961, 65, 70
Stewart, William J. 1937, 43, 48, 53
Sudol, Edward L. 1965, 71, 77
Summers, William R. 1936, 39, 42, 45, 48, 51, 55, 59
Tata, Terry A. 1979, 87, 91, 96
Tschida, Timothy 1998
Umont, Frank 1958, 61, 67, 72
Van Graflan, Roy 1929, 32
Vargo, Edward P. 1965, 71, 78, 83
Venzon, Anthony 1963, 65, 70
Voltaggio, Vito H. 1989
Warneke, Lon 1954
Welke, Timothy J. 1996, 2000
Wendelstedt, Harry H. 1973, 80, 86, 91, 95
West, Joseph 1992, 97
Weyer, Lee H. 1969, 76, 82, 87
Williams, Charles H. 1993
Williams, William G. 1970, 76, 85
Young, Larry E. 1996

1903 - BOSTON RED SOX A.L. (5) vs. PITTSBURGH PIRATES N.L. (3)
(Huntington Grounds)/(Exposition Park)

Oct. 1	@ Bos.	Pittsburgh (Phillippe)	7	Boston (Young)	3
Oct. 2	@ Bos.	Boston (Dinneen)	3	Pittsburgh (Leever)	0
Oct. 3	@ Bos.	Pittsburgh (Phillippe)	4	Boston (Hughes)	2
Oct. 6	@ Pitt.	Pittsburgh (Phillippe)	5	Boston (Dinneen)	4
Oct. 7	@ Pitt.	Boston (Young)	11	Pittsburgh (Kennedy)	2
Oct. 8	@ Pitt.	Boston (Dinneen)	6	Pittsburgh (Leever)	3
Oct. 10	@ Pitt.	Boston (Young)	7	Pittsburgh (Phillippe)	3
Oct. 13	@ Bos.	Boston (Dinneen)	3	Pittsburgh (Phillippe)	0

POSTPONED: (Rain) Oct. 5,12(Cold) Oct. 9

MANAGERS: Jimmy Collins, Red Sox; Fred Clarke, Pirates

Red Sox – Lou Criger, Duke Farrell, catchers; Bill Dinneen, Long Tom Hughes, Cy Young,pitchers; Jimmy Collins, Hobe Ferris, Candy LaChance, Freddy Parent, infielders; Patsy Dougherty, Buck Freeman, Jack O'Brien, Chick Stahl, outfielders.

Pirates – Ed Phelps, Harry Smith, catchers; Brickyard Kennedy, Sam Leever, Deacon Phillippe, Gus Thompson, Bucky Veil, pitchers; Kitty Bransfield, Tommy Leach, Claude Ritchey, Honus Wagner, infielders; Ginger Beaumont, Fred Clarke, Jimmy Sebring, outfielders.

1904 - NO WORLD SERIES PLAYED

1905 - NEW YORK GIANTS N.L. (4) vs. PHILADELPHIA ATHLETICS A.L. (1)
(Polo Grounds)/(Columbia Park)

Oct. 9	@ Phil.	New York (Mathewson)	3	Philadelphia (Plank)	0
Oct. 10	@ N.Y.	Philadelphia (Bender)	3	New York (McGinnity)	0
Oct. 12	@ Phil.	New York (Mathewson)	9	Philadelphia (Coakley)	0
Oct. 13	@ N.Y.	New York (McGinnity)	1	Philadelphia (Plank)	0
Oct. 14	@ N.Y.	New York (Mathewson)	2	Philadelphia (Bender)	0

MANAGERS: John McGraw, Giants; Connie Mack, Athletics

Giants – Frank Bowerman, Roger Bresnahan, Boileryard Clarke, catchers; Leon Ames, Claude Elliott, Christy Mathewson, Joe McGinnity, Dummy Taylor, Hooks Wiltse, pitchers; Bill Dahlen, Art Devlin, Billy Gilbert, Dan McGann, Sammy Strang, infielders; George Browne, Mike Donlin, Sam Mertes, outfielders.

Athletics – Mike Powers, Ossee Schreckengost, catchers; Chief Bender, Andy Coakley, Jimmy Dygert, Weldon Henley, Eddie Plank, Rube Waddell, pitchers; Lave Cross, Monte Cross, Harry Davis, John Knight, Danny Murphy, infielders; Harry Barton, Topsy Hartsel, Danny Hoffman, Bris Lord, Socks Seybold, outfielders.

1906 - CHICAGO WHITE SOX A.L. (4) vs. CHICAGO CUBS N.L. (2)
(South Side Park)/(West Side Park)

Oct. 9	@ N.L.	White Sox (Altrock)	2	Cubs (Brown)	1
Oct. 10	@ A.L.	Cubs (Reulbach)	7	White Sox (White)	1
Oct. 11	@ N.L.	White Sox (Walsh)	3	Cubs (Pfiester)	0
Oct. 12	@ A.L.	Cubs (Brown)	1	White Sox (Altrock)	0
Oct. 13	@ N.L.	White Sox (Walsh)	8	Cubs (Pfiester)	6
Oct. 14	@ A.L.	White Sox (White)	8	Cubs (Brown)	3

MANAGERS: Fielder Jones, White Sox; Frank Chance, Cubs

White Sox – Hub Hart, Ed McFarland, Billy Sullivan, Sr., Babe Towne, catchers; Nick Altrock, Lou Fiene, Frank Owen, Roy Patterson, Frank Smith, Ed Walsh, Doc White, pitchers; George Davis, Jiggs Donahue, Gus Dundon, Frank Isbell, Bill O'Neill, George Rohe, Lee Tannehill, infielders; Patsy Dougherty, Ed Hahn, Fielder Jones, outfielders.

Cubs – Johnny Kling, Pat Moran, Tom Walsh, catchers; Three Finger Brown, Jack Harper, Carl Lundgren, Orval Overall, Jack Pfiester, Ed Reulbach, Jack Taylor, pitchers; Frank Chance, Johnny Evers, Barry McCormick, Harry Steinfeldt, Joe Tinker, infielders; Doc Gessler, Solly Hofman, Wildfire Schulte, Jimmy Sheckard, Jimmy Slagle, outfielders.

1907 – CHICAGO CUBS N.L. (4) vs. DETROIT TIGERS A.L. (0) 1 tie
(West Side Park)/(Bennett Park)

Oct. 8	@ Chi.	Chicago (tie)	3	Detroit (tie)	3	(12 Innings, tie)
Oct. 9	@ Chi.	Chicago (Pfiester)	3	Detroit (Mullin)	1	
Oct. 10	@ Chi.	Chicago (Reulbach)	5	Detroit (Siever)	1	
Oct. 11	@ Det.	Chicago (Overall)	6	Detroit (Donovan)	1	
Oct. 12	@ Det.	Chicago (Brown)	2	Detroit (Mullin)	0	

MANAGERS: Frank Chance, Cubs; Hughie Jennings, Tigers

Cubs – Johnny Kling, Pat Moran, Tom Walsh, catchers; Three Finger Brown, Chick Fraser, Carl Lundgren, Orval Overall, Jack Pfiester, Ed Reulbach, pitchers; Frank Chance, Johnny Evers, Del Howard, Harry Steinfeldt, Joe Tinker, Heinie Zimmerman, infielders; Kid Durbin, Solly Hofman, Wildfire Schulte, Jimmy Sheckard, Jimmy Slagle, outfielders.

Tigers – Jimmy Archer, Fred Payne, Boss Schmidt, catchers; Wild Bill Donovan, Ed Killian, George Mullin, Ed Siever, Ed Willett, pitchers; Bill Coughlin, Red Downs, Bobby Lowe, Charley O'Leary, Claude Rossman, Germany Schaefer, infielders; Ty Cobb, Sam Crawford, Davy Jones, Matty McIntyre, outfielders.

1908 – CHICAGO CUBS N.L. (4) vs. DETROIT TIGERS A.L. (1)
(West Side Park)/(Bennett Park)

Oct. 10	@ Det.	Chicago (Brown)	10	Detroit (Summers)	6
Oct. 11	@ Chi.	Chicago (Overall)	6	Detroit (Donovan)	1
Oct. 12	@ Chi.	Detroit (Mullin)	8	Chicago (Pfiester)	3
Oct. 13	@ Det.	Chicago (Brown)	3	Detroit (Summers)	0
Oct. 14	@ Det.	Chicago (Overall)	2	Detroit (Donovan)	0

MANAGERS: Frank Chance, Cubs; Hughie Jennings, Tigers

Cubs – Johnny Kling, Doc Marshall, Pat Moran, catchers; Three Finger Brown, Chick Fraser, Rube Kroh, Carl Lundgren, Orval Overall, Jack Pfiester, Ed Reulbach, pitchers; Frank Chance, Johnny Evers, Del Howard, Harry Steinfeldt, Joe Tinker, Heinie Zimmerman, infielders; Kid Durbin, Solly Hofman, Wildfire Schulte. Jimmy Sheckard, Jimmy Slagle, outfielders.

Tigers – Boss Schmidt, Ira Thomas, catchers; Wild Bill Donovan, Ed Killian, George Mullin, George Suggs, Ed Summers, Ed Willett, George Winter, pitchers; Bill Coughlin, Red Downs, Red Killefer, Charley O'Leary, Claude Rossman, Germany Schaefer, infielders; Ty Cobb, Sam Crawford, Davy Jones, Matty McIntyre, outfielders.

1909 – PITTSBURGH PIRATES N.L. (4) vs. DETROIT TIGERS A.L. (3)
(Forbes Field)/(Bennett Park)

Oct. 8	@ Pitt.	Pittsburgh (Adams)	4	Detroit (Mullin)	1
Oct. 9	@ Pitt.	Detroit (Donovan)	7	Pittsburgh (Camnitz)	2
Oct. 11	@ Det.	Pittsburgh (Maddox)	8	Detroit (Summers)	6
Oct. 12	@ Det.	Detroit (Mullin)	5	Pittsburgh (Leifield)	0
Oct. 13	@ Pitt.	Pittsburgh (Adams)	8	Detroit (Summers)	4
Oct. 14	@ Det.	Detroit (Mullin)	5	Pittsburgh (Willis)	4
Oct. 16	@ Det.	Pittsburgh (Adams)	8	Detroit (Donovan)	0

MANAGERS: Fred Clarke, Pirates; Hughie Jennings, Tigers

Pirates – George Gibson, Paddy O'Connor, Mike Simon, catchers; Babe Adams, Chick Brandom, Howie Camnitz, Sam Frock, Sam Leever, Lefty Leifield, Nick Maddox, Gene Moore, Deacon Phillippe, Bill Powell, Vic Willis, pitchers; Ed Abbaticchio, Bill Abstein, Bobby Byrne, Dots Miller, Honus Wagner, infielders; Fred Clarke, Ham Hyatt, Tommy Leach, Owen Wilson, outfielders.

Tigers – Heinie Beckendorf, Boss Schmidt, Oscar Stanage, catchers; Wild Bill Donovan, Ed Killian, George Mullin, George Speer, Ed Summers, Ed Willett, Ralph Works, pitchers; Donie Bush, Jim Delahanty, Tom Jones, George Moriarty, Charley O'Leary, infielders; Ty Cobb, Sam Crawford, Davy Jones, Matty McIntyre, outfielders.

1910 – PHILADELPHIA ATHLETICS A.L. (4) vs. CHICAGO CUBS N.L. (1)
(Shibe Park)/(West Side Park)

Oct. 17	@ Phil.	Philadelphia (Bender)	4	Chicago (Overall)	1	
Oct. 18	@ Phil.	Philadelphia (Coombs)	9	Chicago (Brown)	3	
Oct. 20	@ Chi.	Philadelphia (Coombs)	12	Chicago (McIntyre)	5	
Oct. 22	@ Chi.	Chicago (Brown)	4	Philadelphia (Bender)	3	(10 Innings)
Oct. 23	@ Chi.	Philadelphia (Coombs)	7	Chicago (Brown)	2	

MANAGERS: Connie Mack, Athletics; Frank Chance, Cubs

Athletics – Pat Donahue, Jack Lapp, Paddy Livingston, Ira Thomas, catchers; Tommy Atkins, Chief Bender, Jack Coombs, Jimmy Dygert, Harry Krause, Cy Morgan, Eddie Plank, pitchers; Frank Baker, Jack Barry, Eddie Collins, Harry Davis, Claud Derrick, Ben Houser, Stuffy McInnis, infielders; Topsy Hartsel, Bristol Lord, Danny Murphy, Rube Oldring, Amos Strunk, outfielders.

Cubs – Jimmy Archer, Johnny Kling, Tom Needham, catchers; Three Finger Brown, King Cole, Bill Foxen, Harry McIntyre, Orval Overall, Big Jeff Pfeffer, Jack Pfiester, Ed Reulbach, Lew Richie, Orlie Weaver, pitchers; Frank Chance, Johnny Evers, Harry Steinfeldt, Joe Tinker, Heinie Zimmerman, infielders; Ginger Beaumont, Solly Hofman, John Kane, Wildfire Schulte, Jimmy Scheckard, outfielders.

1911 – PHILADELPHIA ATHLETICS A.L. (4) vs. NEW YORK GIANTS N.L. (2)
(Shibe Park)/(Polo Grounds)

Oct. 14	@ N.Y.	New York (Mathewson)	2	Philadelphia (Bender)	1	
Oct. 16	@ Phil.	Philadelphia (Plank)	3	New York (Marquard)	1	
Oct. 17	@ N.Y.	Philadelphia (Coombs)	3	New York (Mathewson)	2	(11 Innings)
Oct. 24	@ Phil.	Philadelphia (Bender)	4	New York (Mathewson)	2	
Oct. 25	@ N.Y.	New York (Crandall)	4	Philadelphia (Plank)	3	(10 Innings)
Oct. 26	@ Phil.	Philadelphia (Bender)	13	New York (Ames)	2	

POSTPONED: (Rain) Oct. 18,19,20,21,23

MANAGERS: Connie Mack, Athletics; John McGraw, Giants

Athletics – Jack Lapp, Paddy Livingston, Ira Thomas, catchers; Chief Bender, Jack Coombs, Dave Danforth, Harry Krause, Doc Martin, Cy Morgan, Eddie Plank, pitchers; Frank Baker, Jack Barry, Eddie Collins, Harry Davis, Claud Derrick, Stuffy McInnis, infielders; Topsy Hartsel, Bristol Lord, Danny Murphy, Rube Oldring, Amos Strunk, outfielders.

Giants – Grover Hartley, Chief Meyers, Art Wilson, catchers; Leon Ames, Doc Crandall, Louis Drucke, Rube Marquard, Christy Mathewson, Hooks Wiltse, pitchers; Art Devlin, Larry Doyle, Art Fletcher, Buck Herzog, Fred Merkle, Gene Paulette, infielders; Beals Becker, Josh Devore, Red Murray, Fred Snodgrass, outfielders.

1912 – BOSTON RED SOX A.L. (4) vs. NEW YORK GIANTS N.L. (3) 1 tie
(Fenway Park)/(Polo Grounds)

Oct. 8	@ N.Y.	Boston (Wood)	4	New York (Tesreau)	3	
Oct. 9	@ Bos.	Boston (tie)	6	New York (tie)	6	(11 innings, tie)
Oct. 10	@ Bos.	New York (Marquard)	2	Boston (O'Brien)	1	
Oct. 11	@ N.Y.	Boston (Wood)	3	New York (Tesreau)	1	
Oct. 12	@ Bos.	Boston (Bedient)	2	New York (Mathewson)	1	
Oct. 14	@ N.Y.	New York (Marquard)	5	Boston (O'Brien)	2	
Oct. 15	@ Bos.	New York (Tesreau)	11	Boston (Wood)	4	
Oct. 16	@ Bos.	Boston (Wood)	3	New York (Mathewson)	2	(10 Innings)

MANAGERS: Garland Stahl, Red Sox; John McGraw, Giants

Red Sox – Hick Cady, Bill Carrigan, Les Nunamaker, Pinch Thomas, catchers; Hugh Bedient, Ray Collins, Charley Hall, Buck O'Brien, Larry Pape, Smoky Joe Wood, pitchers; Neal Ball, Hugh Bradley, Clyde Engle, Larry Gardner, Marty Krug, Garland Stahl, Heinie Wagner, Steve Yerkes, infielders; Olaf Henriksen, Harry Hooper, Duffy Lewis, Tris Speaker, outfielders.

Giants – Grover Hartley, Chief Meyers, Art Wilson, catchers; Red Ames, Doc Crandall, Rube Marquard, Christy Mathewson, Jeff Tesreau, Hooks Wiltse, pitchers; Larry Doyle, Art Fletcher, Heinie Groh, Buck Herzog, Fred Merkle, Tillie Shafer, infielders; Beals Becker, George Burns, Josh Devore, Red Murray, Moose McCormick, Fred Snodgrass, outfielders.

1913 – PHILADELPHIA ATHLETICS A.L. (4) vs. NEW YORK GIANTS N.L. (1)
(Shibe Park)/(Polo Grounds)

Oct. 7	@ N.Y.	Philadelphia (Bender)	6	New York (Marquard)	4		
Oct. 8	@ Phil.	New York (Mathewson)	3	Philadelphia (Plank)	0	(10 Innings)	
Oct. 9	@ N.Y.	Philadelphia (Bush)	8	New York (Tesreau)	2		
Oct. 10	@ Phil.	Philadelphia (Bender)	6	New York (Demaree)	5		
Oct. 11	@ N.Y.	Philadelphia (Plank)	3	New York (Mathewson)	1		

MANAGERS: Connie Mack, Athletics; John McGraw, Giants

Athletics – Jack Lapp, Wally Schang, Ira Thomas, catchers; Chief Bender, Boardwalk Brown, Joe Bush, Jack Coombs, Byron Houck, Herb Pennock, Eddie Plank, Bob Shawkey, John Wyckoff, pitchers; Frank Baker, Jack Barry, Eddie Collins, Harry Davis, Doc Lavan, Stuffy McInnis, Bill Orr, infielders; Tom Daley, Danny Murphy, Eddie Murphy, Rube Oldring, Amos Strunk, James Walsh, outfielders.

Giants – Grover Hartley, Chief Meyers, Larry McLean, Art Wilson, catchers; Doc Crandall, Al Demaree, Art Fromme, Rube Marquard, Christy Mathewson, Jeff Tesreau, Hooks Wiltse, pitchers; Larry Doyle, Art Fletcher, Eddie Grant, Buck Herzog, Fred Merkle, Tillie Shafer, infielders; George Burns, Claude Cooper, Moose McCormick, Red Murray, Fred Snodgrass, Jim Thorpe, outfielders.

1914 – BOSTON BRAVES N.L. (4) vs. PHILADELPHIA ATHLETICS A.L. (0)
(Fenway Park)/(Shibe Park)

Oct. 9	@ Phil.	Boston (Rudolph)	7	Philadelphia (Bender)	1		
Oct. 10	@ Phil.	Boston (James)	1	Philadelphia (Plank)	0		
Oct. 12	@ Bos.	Boston (James)	5	Philadelphia (Bush)	4	(12 Innings)	
Oct. 13	@ Bos.	Boston (Rudolph)	3	Philadelphia (Shawkey)	1		

MANAGERS: George Stallings, Braves; Connie Mack, Athletics

Braves – Hank Gowdy, Bert Whaling, catchers; Gene Cocreham, Ensign Cottrell, Dick Crutcher, George Davis, Otto Hess, Bill H. James, Dick Rudolph, Paul Strand, Lefty Tyler, pitchers; Charlie Deal, Oscar Dugey, Johnny Evers, Rabbit Maranville, Bill Martin, Butch Schmidt, Red Smith, infielders; Ted Cather, Joe Connolly, Josh Devore, Larry Gilbert, Les Mann, Herbie Moran, Possum Whitted, outfielders.

Athletics – Jack Lapp, Wickey McAvoy, Wally Schang, Ira Thomas, catchers; Chief Bender, Rube Bressler, Joe Bush, Jack Coombs, Chick Davies, Herb Pennock, Eddie Plank, Bob Shawkey, John Wyckoff, pitchers; Frank Baker, Jack Barry, Eddie Collins, Harry Davis, Larry Kopf, Stuffy McInnis, infielders; Eddie Murphy, Rube Oldring, Amos Strunk, Shag Thompson, Jimmy Walsh, outfielders.

1915 – BOSTON RED SOX A.L. (4) vs. PHILADELPHIA PHILLIES N.L. (1)
(Braves Field)/(Baker Bowl)

Oct. 8	@ Phil.	Philadelphia (Alexander)	3	Boston (Shore)	1
Oct. 9	@ Phil.	Boston (Foster)	2	Philadelphia (Mayer)	1
Oct. 11	@ Bos.	Boston (Leonard)	2	Philadelphia (Alexander)	1
Oct. 12	@ Bos.	Boston (Shore)	2	Philadelphia (Chalmers)	1
Oct. 13	@ Phil.	Boston (Foster)	5	Philadelphia (Rixey)	4

MANAGERS: Bill Carrigan, Red Sox; Pat Moran, Phillies

Red Sox – Hick Cady, Bill Carrigan, Pinch Thomas, catchers; Ray Collins, Rube Foster, Vean Gregg, Dutch Leonard, Carl Mays, Babe Ruth, Ernie Shore, Smoky Joe Wood, pitchers; Jack Barry, Del Gainor, Larry Gardner, Dick Hoblitzel, Hal Janvrin, Mike McNally, Everett Scott, Heinie Wagner, infielders; Olaf Henriksen, Harry Hooper, Duffy Lewis, Tris Speaker, outfielders.

Phillies – Bert Adams, Ed Burns, Bill Killefer, catchers; Grover Alexander, Stan Baumgartner, George Chalmers, Al Demaree, Erskine Mayer, George McQuillan, Eppa Rixey, Ben Tincup, pitchers; Dave Bancroft, Bobby Byrne, Oscar Dugey, Fred Luderus, Bert Niehoff, Milt Stock, infielders; Beats Becker, Gavvy Cravath, Dode Paskert, Bud Weiser, Possum Whitted, outfielders.

1916 – BOSTON RED SOX A.L. (4) vs. BROOKLYN DODGERS N.L. (1)
(Braves Field)/(Ebbets Field)

Oct. 7	@ Bos.	Boston (Shore)	6	Brooklyn (Marquard)	5	
Oct. 9	@ Bos.	Boston (Ruth)	2	Brooklyn (Smith)	1	(14 Innings)
Oct. 10	@ Brk.	Brooklyn (Coombs)	4	Boston (Mays)	3	
Oct. 11	@ Brk.	Boston (Leonard)	6	Brooklyn (Marquard)	2	
Oct. 12	@ Bos.	Boston (Shore)	4	Brooklyn (Pfeffer)	1	

MANAGERS: Bill Carrigan, Red Sox; Wilbert Robinson, Dodgers

Red Sox – Sam Agnew, Hick Cady, Bill Carrigan, Pinch Thomas, catchers; Rube Foster, Vean Gregg, Sam Jones, Dutch Leonard, Carl Mays, Babe Ruth, Ernie Shore, John Wyckoff, pitchers; Jack Barry, Del Gainor, Larry Gardner, Dick Hoblitzel, Hal Janvrin, Mike McNally, Everett Scott, Heinie Wagner, infielders; Olaf Henriksen, Harry Hooper, Duffy Lewis, Chick Shorten, Tilly Walker, Jimmy Walsh, outfielders.

Dodgers – Chief Meyers, Otto Miller, catchers; Ed Appleton, Larry Cheney, Jack Coombs, Wheezer Dell, Duster Mails, Rube Marquard, Jeff Pfeffer, Nap Rucker, Sherry Smith, pitchers; George Cutshaw, Jake Daubert, Gus Getz, Fred Merkle, Mike Mowrey, Ivy Olson, Ollie O'Mara, infielders; Jimmy Johnston, Hy Myers, Casey Stengel, Zack Wheat, outfielders.

1917 – CHICAGO WHITE SOX A.L. (4) vs. NEW YORK GIANTS N.L. (2)
(Comiskey Park)/(Polo Grounds)

Oct. 6	@ Chi.	Chicago (Cicotte)	2	New York (Sallee)	1
Oct. 7	@ Chi.	Chicago (Faber)	7	New York (Anderson)	2
Oct. 10	@ N.Y.	New York (Benton)	2	Chicago (Cicotte)	0
Oct. 11	@ N.Y.	New York (Schupp)	5	Chicago (Faber)	0
Oct. 13	@ Chi.	Chicago (Faber)	8	New York (Sallee)	5
Oct. 15	@ N.Y.	Chicago (Faber)	4	New York (Benton)	2

MANAGERS: Pants Rowland, White Sox; John McGraw, Giants

White Sox – Joe Jenkins, Byrd Lynn, Ray Schalk, catchers; Joe Benz, Eddie Cicotte, Dave Danforth, Red Faber, Reb Russell, Jim Scott, Lefty Williams, Red Wolfgang, pitchers; Bobby Byrne, Eddie Collins, Chick Gandil, Ziggy Hasbrook, Ted Jourdan, Fred McMullin, Swede Risberg, Buck Weaver,infielders; Shano Collins, Happy Felsch, Joe Jackson, Nemo Leibold, Eddie Murphy, outfielders.

Giants – George Gibson, Lew McCarty, Jack Onslow, Bill Rariden, catchers; Fred Anderson, Rube Benton, Al Demaree, Pol Perritt, Slim Sallee, Ferdie Schupp, Jeff Tesreau, pitchers; Al Baird, Art Fletcher, Buck Herzog, Walter Holke, Hans Lobert, Jimmy Smith, Heinie Zimmerman, infielders; George Burns, Benny Kauff, Red Murray, Dave Robertson, Jim Thorpe, Joe Wilhoit, outfielders.

1918 – BOSTON RED SOX A.L. (4) vs. CHICAGO CUBS N.L. (2)
(Fenway Park)/(Comiskey Park)

Sept. 5	@ Chi.	Boston (Ruth)	1	Chicago (Vaughn)	0
Sept. 6	@ Chi.	Chicago (Tyler)	3	Boston (Bush)	1
Sept. 7	@ Chi.	Boston (Mays)	2	Chicago (Vaughn)	1
Sept. 9	@ Bos.	Boston (Ruth)	3	Chicago (Douglas)	2
Sept. 10	@ Bos.	Chicago (Vaughn)	3	Boston (Jones)	0
Sept. 11	@ Bos.	Boston (Mays)	2	Chicago (Tyler)	1

POSTPONED: (Rain) Sept. 4

MANAGERS: Ed Barrow, Red Sox; Fred Mitchell, Cubs

Red Sox – Sam Agnew, Wally Mayer, Wally Schang, catchers; Joe Bush, Jean Dubuc, Sam Jones, Walt Kinney, Carl Mays, Bill Pertica, Babe Ruth, pitchers; George Cochran, Jack Coffey, Stuffy McInnis, Everett Scott, Dave Shean, Fred Thomas, Heinie Wagner, infielders; Harry Hooper, Hack Miller, Amos Strunk, George Whiteman, outfielders.

Cubs – Tommy Clarke, Bill Killefer, Bob O'Farrell, catchers; Paul Carter, Phil Douglas, Claude Hendrix, Speed Martin, Lefty Tyler, Hippo Vaughn, Roy Walker, pitchers; Charlie Deal, Charlie Hollocher, Otto Knabe, Bill McCabe, Fred Merkle, Charlie Pick, Chuck Wortman, Rollie Zeider, infielders; Turner Barber, Max Flack, Les Mann, Dode Paskert, outfielders.

1919 - CINCINNATI REDS N.L. (5) vs. CHICAGO WHITE SOX A.L. (3)
(Redland Field)/(Comiskey Park)

Oct. 1	@ Cin.	Cincinnati (Ruether)	9	Chicago (Cicotte)	1	
Oct. 2	@ Cin.	Cincinnati (Sallee)	4	Chicago (Williams)	2	
Oct. 3	@ Chi.	Chicago (Kerr)	3	Cincinnati (Fisher)	0	
Oct. 4	@ Chi.	Cincinnati (Ring)	2	Chicago (Cicotte)	0	
Oct. 6	@ Chi.	Cincinnati (Eller)	5	Chicago (Williams)	0	
Oct. 7	@ Cin.	Chicago (Kerr)	5	Cincinnati (Ring)	4	(10-Innings)
Oct. 8	@ Cin.	Chicago (Cicotte)	4	Cincinnati (Sallee)	1	
Oct. 9	@ Chi.	Cincinnati (Eller)	10	Chicago (Williams)	5	

MANAGERS: Pat Moran, Reds; Kid Gleason, White Sox

Reds — Nick Allen, Bill Rariden, Ivy Wingo, catchers; Hod Eller, Ray Fisher, Ed Gerner, Dolf Luque, Roy Mitchell, Jimmy Ring, Dutch Ruether, Slim Sallee, pitchers; Jake Daubert, Heinie Groh, Larry Kopf, Morrie Rath, Hank Schreiber, Jimmy Smith, infielders; Rube Bressler, Pat Duncan, Sherry Magee, Greasy Neale, Edd Roush, Charlie See, outfielders.

White Sox — Joe Jenkins, Byrd Lynn, Ray Schalk, catchers; Eddie Cicotte, Red Faber, Bill James, Dickie Kerr, Grover Lowdermilk, Erskine Mayer, John Sullivan, Roy Wilkinson, Lefty Williams, pitchers; Eddie Collins, Chick Gandil, Hervey McClellan, Fred McMullin, Swede Risberg, Buck Weaver, infielders; Shano Collins, Happy Felsch, Joe Jackson, Nemo Leibold, Eddie Murphy, outfielders.

1920 - CLEVELAND INDIANS A.L. (5) vs. BROOKLYN DODGERS N.L. (2)
(League Park)/(Ebbets Field)

Oct. 5	@ Brk.	Cleveland (Coveleski)	3	Brooklyn (Marquard)	1
Oct. 6	@ Brk.	Brooklyn (Grimes)	3	Cleveland (Bagby)	0
Oct. 7	@ Brk.	Brooklyn (Smith)	2	Cleveland (Caldwell)	1
Oct. 9	@ Clev.	Cleveland (Coveleski)	5	Brooklyn (Cadore)	1
Oct. 10	@ Clev.	Cleveland (Bagby)	8	Brooklyn (Grimes)	1
Oct. 11	@ Clev.	Cleveland (Mails)	1	Brooklyn (Smith)	0
Oct. 12	@ Clev.	Cleveland (Coveleski)	3	Brooklyn (Grimes)	0

MANAGERS: Tris Speaker, Indians; Wilbert Robinson, Dodgers

Indians — Les Nunamaker, Steve O'Neill, Pinch Thomas, catchers; Jim Bagby, Ray Caldwell, Bob Clark, Stan Coveleski, George Ellison, Duster Mails, Guy Morton, George Uhle, pitchers; Tioga George Burns, Larry Gardner, Doc Johnston, Harry Lunte, Joe Sewell, Bill Wambsganss, infielders; Joe Evans, Jack Graney, Charlie Jamieson, Elmer Smith, Tris Speaker, Smoky Joe Wood, outfielders.

Dodgers — Rowdy Elliott, Ernie Krueger, Otto Miller, Zack Taylor, catchers; Leon Cadore, Burleigh Grimes, Al Mamaux, Rube Marquard, Johnny Miljus, Clarence Mitchell, George Mohart, Jeff Pfeffer, Sherry Smith, pitchers; Jimmy Johnston, Pete Kilduff, Ed Konetchy, Bill McCabe, Ivy Olson, Ray Schmandt, Jack Sheehan, Chuck Ward, infielders; Tommy Griffith, Bill Lamar, Hy Myers, Bernie Neis, Zack Wheat, outfielders.

1921 - NEW YORK GIANTS N.L. (5) vs. NEW YORK YANKEES A.L. (3)
(Polo Grounds)/(Polo Grounds)

Oct. 5	@ N.Y.G.	Yankees (Mays)	3	Giants (Douglas)	0
Oct. 6	@ N.Y.Y.	Yankees (Hoyt)	3	Giants (Nehf)	0
Oct. 7	@ N.Y.G.	Giants (Barnes)	13	Yankees (Quinn)	5
Oct. 9	@ N.Y.Y.	Giants (Douglas)	4	Yankees (Mays)	2
Oct. 10	@ N.Y.G.	Yankees (Hoyt)	3	Giants (Nehf)	1
Oct. 11	@ N.Y.Y.	Giants (Barnes)	8	Yankees (Shawkey)	5
Oct. 12	@ N.Y.G.	Giants (Douglas)	2	Yankees (Mays)	1
Oct. 13	@ N.Y.Y.	Giants (Nehf)	1	Yankees (Hoyt)	0

MANAGERS: John McGraw, Giants; Miller Huggins, Yankees

Giants — Alex Gaston, Earl Smith, Frank Snyder, catchers; Jesse Barnes, Red Causey, Phil Douglas, Art Nehf, Rosy Ryan, Slim Sallee, Red Shea, Fred Toney, pitchers; Dave Bancroft, Frankie Frisch, Mike Gonzalez, George Kelly, Wally Kopf, Johnny Rawlings, infielders; Eddie Brown, George Burns, Bill Cunningham, Irish Meusel, Casey Stengel, Ross Youngs, outfielders.

Yankees — Al DeVormer, Wally Schang, catchers; Rip Collins, Alex Ferguson, Harry Harper, Waite Hoyt, Carl Mays, Bill Piercy, Jack Quinn, Tom Rogers, Bob Shawkey, pitchers; Frank Baker, Mike McNally, Johnny Mitchell, Roger Peckinpaugh, Wally Pipp, Aaron Ward, infielders; Chick Fewster, Chicken Hawks, Bob Meusel, Elmer Miller, Braggo Roth, Babe Ruth, outfielders.

1922 - NEW YORK GIANTS N.L. (4) vs. NEW YORK YANKEES A.L. (0) 1 tie
(Polo Grounds)/(Polo Grounds)

Oct. 4	@ N.Y.G.	Giants (Ryan)	3	Yankees (Bush)	2	
Oct. 5	@ N.Y.Y.	Giants (tie)	3	Yankees (tie)	3	(10 Innings, tie)
Oct. 6	@ N.Y.G.	Giants (Scott)	3	Yankees (Hoyt)	0	
Oct. 7	@ N.Y.Y.	Giants (McQuillan)	4	Yankees (Mays)	3	
Oct. 8	@ N.Y.G.	Giants (Nehf)	5	Yankees (Bush)	3	

MANAGERS: John McGraw, Giants; Miller Huggins, Yankees

Giants – Alex Gaston, Earl Smith, Frank Snyder, catchers; Jesse Barnes, Virgil Barnes, Clint Blume, Carmen Hill, Claude Jonnard, Hugh McQuillan, Art Nehf, Rosy Ryan, Jack Scott, pitchers; Dave Bancroft, Frankie Frisch, Heinie Groh, George Kelly, Johnny Rawlings, infielders; Bill Cunningham, Lee King, Irish Meusel, Dave Robertson, Casey Stengel, Ross Youngs, outfielders.

Yankees – Al DeVoraner, Fred Hofmann, Wally Schang, catchers; Joe Bush, Waite Hoyt, Sam Jones, Carl Mays, George Murray, Lefty O'Doul, Bob Shawkey, pitchers; Frank Baker, Joe Dugan, Mike McNally, Wally Pipp, Everett Scott, Aaron Ward, infielders; Norm McMillan, Bob Meusel, Babe Ruth,Camp Skinner, Elmer Smith, Whitey Witt, outfielders.

1923 - NEW YORK YANKEES A.L. (4) vs. NEW YORK GIANTS N.L. (2)
(Yankee Stadium)/(Polo Grounds)

Oct. 10	@ N.Y.Y.	Giants (Ryan)	5	Yankees (Bush)	4
Oct. 11	@ N.Y.G.	Yankees (Pennock)	4	Giants (McQuillan)	2
Oct. 12	@ N.Y.Y.	Giants (Nehf)	1	Yankees (Jones)	0
Oct. 13	@ N.Y.G.	Yankees (Shawkey)	8	Giants (Scott)	4
Oct. 14	@ N.Y.Y.	Yankees (Bush)	8	Giants (Bentley)	1
Oct. 15	@ N.Y.G.	Yankees (Pennock)	6	Giants (Nehf)	4

MANAGERS: Miller Huggins, Yankees; John McGraw, Giants

Yankees – Benny Bengough, Fred Hofmann, Wally Schang, catchers; Joe Bush, Waite Hoyt, Sam Jones, Carl Mays, Herb Pennock, George Pipgras, Oscar Roettger, Bob Shawkey, pitchers; Joe Dugan,Mike Gazella, Ernie Johnson, Mike McNally, Wally Pipp, Everett Scott, Aaron Ward, infielders; Hinkey Haines, Harvey Hendrick, Bob Meusel, Babe Ruth, Elmer Smith, Whitey Witt, outfielders.

Giants – Alex Gaston, Hank Gowdy, Frank Snyder, catchers; Virgil Barnes, Jack Bentley, Dinty Gearin, Claude Jonnard, Hugh McQuillan, Art Nehf, Rosy Ryan, Jack Scott, Mule Watson, pitchers; Dave Bancroft, Frankie Frisch, Heinie Groh, Travis Jackson, George Kelly, Freddie Maguire, infielders; Bill Cunningham, Irish Meusel, Jimmy O'Connell, Ralph Shinners, Casey Stengel, Ross Youngs, outfielders.

1924 - WASHINGTON SENATORS A.L. (4) vs. NEW YORK GIANTS N.L. (3)
(Griffith Stadium)/(Polo Grounds)

Oct. 4	@ Wash.	New York (Nehf)	4	Washington (Johnson)	3	(12 Innings)
Oct. 5	@ Wash.	Washington (Zachary)	4	New York (Bentley)	3	
Oct. 6	@ N.Y.	New York (McQuillan)	6	Washington (Marberry)	4	
Oct. 7	@ N.Y.	Washington (Mogridge)	7	New York (Barnes)	4	
Oct. 8	@ N.Y.	New York (Bentley)	6	Washington (Johnson)	2	
Oct. 9	@ Wash.	Washington (Zachary)	2	New York (Nehf)	1	
Oct. 10	@ Wash.	Washington (Johnson)	4	New York (Bentley)	3	(12 Innings)

MANAGERS: Bucky Harris, Senators; John McGraw, Giants

Senators – Pinky Hargrave, Muddy Ruel, Bennie Tate, catchers; Walter Johnson, Firpo Marberry, Joe Martina, George Mogridge, Curly Ogden, Allan Russell, Byron Speece, Tom Zachary, Paul Zahniser, pitchers; Ossie Bluege, Bucky Harris, Joe Judge, Ralph Miller, Roger Peckinpaugh, Mule Shirley, Tommy Taylor, infielders; Showboat Fisher, Goose Goslin, Nemo Leibold, Earl McNeely, Sam Rice, outfielders.

Giants – Hank Gowdy, Frank Snyder, catchers; Harry Baldwin, Virgil Barnes, Jack Bentley, Wayland Dean, Walter Huntzinger, Claude Jonnard, Ernie Maun, Hugh McQuillan, Art Nehf, Rosy Ryan, Mule Watson, pitchers; Frankie Frisch, Heinie Groh, Travis Jackson, George Kelly, Fred Lindstrom, Bill Terry, infielders; Irish Meusel, Jimmy O'Connell, Billy Southworth, Hack Wilson, Ross Youngs, outfielders.

1925 – PITTSBURGH PIRATES N.L. (4) vs. WASHINGTON SENATORS A.L. (3)
(Forbes Field)/(Griffith Stadium)

Oct. 7	@ Pitt.	Washington (Johnson)	4	Pittsburgh (Meadows)	1	
Oct. 8	@ Pitt.	Pittsburgh (Aldridge)	3	Washington (Coveleski)	2	
Oct. 10	@Wash.	Washington (Ferguson)	4	Pittsburgh (Kremer)	3	
Oct. 11	@Wash.	Washington (Johnson)	4	Pittsburgh (Yde)	0	
Oct. 12	@ Wash.	Pittsburgh (Aldridge)	6	Washington (Coveleski)	3	
Oct. 13	@ Pitt.	Pittsburgh (Kremer)	3	Washington (Ferguson)	2	
Oct. 15	@ Pitt.	Pittsburgh (Kremer)	9	Washington (Johnson)	7	

POSTPONED: *(Rain) Oct. 14*

MANAGERS: Bill McKechnie, Pirates; Bucky Harris, Senators

Pirates – Johnny Gooch, Earl Smith, Roy Spencer, catchers; Babe Adams, Vic Aldridge, Bud Culloton, Remy Kremer, Lee Meadows, Johnny Morrison, Red Oldham, Tom Sheehan, Emil Yde, pitchers; Jewel Ens, George Grantham, Stuffy McInnis, Eddie Moore, Johnny Rawlings, Fresco Thompson, Pie Traynor, Glenn Wright, infielders; Clyde Barnhart, Carson Bigbee, Max Carey, Kiki Cuyler, Mule Haas, outfielders.

Senators – Muddy Ruel, Hank Severeid, Bennie Tate, catchers; Win Ballou, Stan Coveleski, Alex Ferguson, Walter Johnson, Firpo Marberry, Dutch Ruether, Allan Russell, Tom Zachary, pitchers; Spencer Adams, Ossie Bluege, Bucky Harris, Joe Judge, Buddy Myer, Roger Peckinpaugh, Everett Scott, infielders; Goose Goslin, Joe Harris, Tex Jeanes, Nemo Leibold, Earl McNeely, Sam Rice, Bobby Veach, outfielders.

1926 – ST. LOUIS CARDINALS N.L. (4) vs. NEW YORK YANKEES A.L. (3)
(Sportsmans Park)/(Yankee Stadium)

Oct. 2	@ N.Y.	New York (Pennock)	2	St. Louis (Sherdel)	1	
Oct. 3	@ N.Y.	St. Louis (Alexander)	6	New York (Shocker)	2	
Oct. 5	@ St.L.	St. Louis (Haines)	4	New York (Ruether)	0	
Oct. 6	@ St.L.	New York (Hoyt)	10	St. Louis (Reinhart	5	
Oct. 7	@ St.L.	New York (Pennock)	3	St. Louis (Sherdel)	2	(10 Innings)
Oct. 9	@ N.Y.	St. Louis (Alexander)	10	New York (Shawkey)	2	
Oct. 10	@ N.Y.	St. Louis (Haines)	3	New York (Hoyt)	2	

MANAGERS: Rogers Hornsby, Cardinals; Miller Huggins, Yankees

Cardinals – Bob O'Farrell, Ernie Vick, catchers; Grover Alexander, Herman Bell, Ed Clough, Jesse Haines, Bill Hallahan, Syl Johnson, Vic Keen, Art Reinhart, Flint Rhem, Bill Sherdel, Allen Sothoron, pitchers; Les Bell, Jim Bottomley, Jake Flowers, Rogers Hornsby, Tommy Thevenow, Specs Toporcer, infielders; Ray Blades, Taylor Douthit, Chick Hafey, Roscoe Holm, Billy Southworth, outfielders.

Yankees – Benny Bengough, Pat Collins, Hank Severeid, catchers; Walter Beall, Garland Braxton, Waite Hoyt, Sam Jones, Herb McQuaid, Herb Pennock, Dutch Ruether, Bob Shawkey, Urban Shocker, Myles Thomas, pitchers; Spencer Adams, Joe Dugan, Michael Gazella, Lou Gehrig, Mark Koenig, Tony Lazzeri, Aaron Ward, infielders; Roy Carlyle, Earle Combs, Bob Meusel, Ben Paschal, Babe Ruth, outfielders.

1927 – NEW YORK YANKEES A.L. (4) vs. PITTSBURGH PIRATES N.L. (0)
(Yankee Stadium)/(Forbes Field)

Oct. 5	@ Pitt.	New York (Hoyt)	5	Pittsburgh (Kremer)	4
Oct. 6	@ Pitt.	New York (Pipgras)	6	Pittsburgh (Aldridge)	2
Oct. 7	@ N.Y.	New York (Pennock)	8	Pittsburgh (Meadows)	1
Oct. 8	@ N.Y.	New York (Moore)	4	Pittsburgh (Miljus)	3

MANAGERS: Miller Huggins, Yankees; Donie Bush, Pirates

Yankees – Benny Bengough, Pat Collins, Johnny Grabowski, catchers; Joe Giard, Waite Hoyt, Wilcy Moore, Herb Pennock, George Pipgras, Dutch Ruether, Bob Shawkey, Urban Shocker, Myles Thomas, pitchers; Joe Dugan, Mike Gazella, Lou Gehrig, Mark Koenig, Tony Lazzeri, Ray Morehart, Julie Wera, infielders; Earle Combs, Cedric Durst, Bob Meusel, Ben Paschal, Babe Ruth, outfielders.

Pirates – Johnny Gooch, Earl Smith, Roy Spencer, catchers; Vic Aldridge, Mike Cvengros, Joe Dawson, Carmen Hill, Remy Kremer, Lee Meadows, Johnny Miljus, Emil Yde, pitchers; Joe Cronin, George Grantham, Heinie Groh, Joe Harris, Hal Rhyne, Pie Traynor, Glenn Wright, infielders; Clyde Barnhart, Fred Brickell, Kiki Cuyler, Lloyd Waner, Paul Waner, outfielders.

1928 – NEW YORK YANKEES A.L. (4) vs. ST. LOUIS CARDINALS N.L. (0)
(Yankee Stadium)/(Sportsmans Park)

Oct. 4	@ N.Y.	New York (Hoyt)	4	St. Louis (Sherdel)	1
Oct. 5	@ N.Y.	New York (Pipgras)	9	St. Louis (Alexander)	3
Oct. 7	@ St.L.	New York (Zachary)	7	St. Louis (Haines)	3
Oct. 9	@ St.L.	New York (Hoyt)	7	St. Louis (Sherdel)	3

MANAGERS: Miller Huggins, Yankees; Bill McKechnie, Cardinals

Yankees – Benny Bengough, Pat Collins, Bill Dickey, Johnny Grabowski, catchers; Fred Heimach, Waite Hoyt, Herb Pennock, George Pipgras, Rosy Ryan, Myles Thomas, Tom Zachary, pitchers; Joe Dugan, Leo Durocher, Mike Gazella, Lou Gehrig, Mark Koenig, Tony Lazzeri, Gene Robertson, infielders; Earle Combs, Cedric Durst, Bob Meusel, Ben Paschal, Babe Ruth, outfielders.

Cardinals – Earl Smith, Jimmie Wilson, catchers; Grover Alexander, Fred Frankhouse, Hal Haid, Jesse Haines, Syl Johnson, Clarence Mitchell, Art Reinhart, Flint Rhem, Bill Sherdel, pitchers; Jim Bottomley, Frankie Frisch, Andy High, Wattie Holm, Rabbit Maranville, Tommy Thevenow, infielders; Ray Blades, Taylor Douthit, Chick Hafey, George Harper, Pepper Martin, Ernie Orsatti, Wally Roettger, Howie Williamson, outfielders.

1929 – PHILADELPHIA ATHLETICS A.L. (4) vs. CHICAGO CUBS N.L. (1)
(Shibe Park)/(Wrigley Field)

Oct. 8	@ Chi.	Philadelphia (Ehmke)	3	Chicago (Root)	1
Oct. 9	@ Chi.	Philadelphia (Earnshaw)	9	Chicago (Malone)	3
Oct. 11	@ Phil.	Chicago (Bush)	3	Philadelphia (Earnshaw)	1
Oct. 12	@ Phil.	Philadelphia (Rommel)	10	Chicago (Blake)	8
Oct. 14	@ Phil.	Philadelphia (Walberg)	3	Chicago (Malone)	2

MANAGERS: Connie Mack, Athletics; Joe McCarthy, Cubs

Athletics – Mickey Cochrane, Cy Perkins, catchers; Bill Breckinridge, George Earnshaw, Howard Ehmke, Lefty Grove, Jack Quinn, Ed Rommel, Bill Shores, Rube Walberg, Carroll Yerkes, pitchers; Max Bishop, Joe Boley, Tioga George Burns, Eddie Collins, Jim Cronin, Jimmy Dykes, Jimmie Foxx, Sammy Hale, infielders; Walter French, Mule Haas, Bevo LeBourveau, Bing Miller, Al Simmons, Homer Summa, outfielders.

Cubs – Mike Gonzalez, Gabby Hartnett, Johnny Schulte, Zack Taylor, catchers; Sheriff Blake, Guy Bush, Hal Carlson, Mike Cvengros, Henry Grampp, Pat Malone, Art Nehf, Ken Penner, Charlie Root, pitchers; Clyde Beck, Footsie Blair, Woody English, Charlie Grimm, Rogers Hornsby, Norm McMillan, Chick Tolson, infielders; Kiki Cuyler, Cliff Heathcote, Johnny Moore, Riggs Stephenson, Hack Wilson, outfielders.

1930 – PHILADELPHIA ATHLETICS A.L. (4) vs. ST. LOUIS CARDINALS N.L. (2)
(Shibe Park)/(Sportsmans Park)

Oct. 1	@ Phil.	Philadelphia (Grove)	5	St. Louis (Grimes)	2
Oct. 2	@ Phil.	Philadelphia (Earnshaw)	6	St. Louis (Rhem)	1
Oct. 4	@ St.L.	St. Louis (Hallahan)	5	Philadelphia (Walberg)	0
Oct. 5	@ St.L.	St. Louis (Haines)	3	Philadelphia (Grove)	1
Oct. 6	@ St.L.	Philadelphia (Grove)	2	St. Louis (Grimes)	0
Oct. 8	@ Phil.	Philadelphia (Earnshaw)	7	St. Louis (Hallahan)	1

MANAGERS: Connie Mack, Athletics; Gabby Street, Cardinals

Athletics – Mickey Cochrane, Cy Perkins, Wally Schang, catchers; George Earnshaw, Lefty Grove, Lee Roy Mahaffey, Jack Quinn, Ed Rommel, Bill Shores, Rube Walberg, pitchers; Max Bishop, Joe Boley, Eddie Collins, Jimmy Dykes, Jimmie Foxx, Pinky Higgins, Eric McNair, Dib Williams, infielders; Mule Haas, Bing Miller, Jimmy Moore, Al Simmons, Homer Summa, outfielders.

Cardinals – Gus Mancuso, Jimmie Wilson, catchers; Hi Bell, Al Grabowski, Burleigh Grimes, Jesse Haines, Bill Hallahan, Syl Johnson, Jim Lindsey, Flint Rhem, pitchers; Sparky Adams, Jim Bottomley, Frankie Frisch, Charley Gelbert, Andy High, infielders; Ray Blades, Taylor Douthit, Showboat Fisher, Chick Hafey, Ernie Orsatti, George Puccinelli, George Watkins, outfielders.

1931- ST. LOUIS CARDINALS N.L. (4) vs. PHILADELPHIA ATHLETICS A.L. (3)

(Sportsmans Park)/(Shibe Park)

Oct. 1	@ St.L.	Philadelphia (Grove)	6	St. Louis (Derringer)	2	
Oct. 2	@ St.L.	St. Louis (Hallahan)	2	Philadelphia (Earnshaw)	0	
Oct. 5	@ Phil.	St. Louis (Grimes)	5	Philadelphia (Grove)	2	
Oct. 6	@ Phil.	Philadelphia (Earnshaw)	3	St. Louis (Johnson)	0	
Oct. 7	@ Phil.	St. Louis (Hallahan)	5	Philadelphia (Hoyt)	1	
Oct. 9	@ St.L.	Philadelphia (Grove)	8	St. Louis (Derringer)	1	
Oct. 10	@ St.L.	St. Louis (Grimes)	4	Philadelphia (Earnshaw)	2	

POSTPONED: (Rain) Oct. 4

MANAGERS: Gabby Street, Cardinals; Connie Mack, Athletics

Cardinals — Mike Gonzalez, Gus Mancuso, Jimmie Wilson, catchers; Paul Derringer, Burleigh Grimes, Jesse Haines, Bill Hallahan, Syl Johnson, Tony Kaufman, Jim Lindsey, Flint Rhem, Allyn Stout, pitchers; Sparky Adams, Jim Bottomley, Ripper Collins, Jake Flowers, Frankie Frisch, Charley Gelbert, Andy High, infielders; Ray Blades, Chick Hafey, Pepper Martin, Ernie Orsatti, Wally Roettger, George Watkins, outfielders.

Athletics — Mickey Cochrane, Johnnie Heving, Joe Palmisano, catchers; George Earnshaw, Lefty Grove, Waite Hoyt, Lew Krausse, Lee Roy Mahaffey, Hank McDonald, Jim Peterson, Ed Rommel, Rube Walberg, pitchers; Max Bishop, Joe Boley, Jimmy Dykes, Jimmie Foxx, Eric McNair, Philip Todt, Dib Williams, infielders; Doc Cramer, Mule Haas, Bing Miller, Jimmy Moore, Al Simmons, outfielders.

1932 - NEW YORK YANKEES A.L. (4) vs. CHICAGO CUBS N.L. (0)

(Yankee Stadium)/(Wrigley Field)

Sept. 28	@ N.Y.	New York (Ruffing)	12	Chicago (Bush)	6
Sept. 29	@ N.Y.	New York (Gomez)	5	Chicago (Warneke)	2
Oct. 1	@ Chi.	New York (Pipgras)	7	Chicago (Root)	5
Oct. 2	@ Chi.	New York (Moore)	13	Chicago (May)	6

MANAGERS: Joe McCarthy, Yankees; Charlie Grimm, Cubs

Yankees — Bill Dickey, Arndt Jorgens, catchers; Johnny Allen, Jumbo Brown, Charlie Devens, Lefty Gomez, Danny MacFayden, Wilcy Moore, Herb Pennock, George Pipgras, Red Ruffing, Ed Wells, pitchers; Frankie Crosetti, Doc Farrell, Lou Gehrig, Lyn Lary, Tony Lazzeri, Joe Sewell, infielders; Sammy Byrd, Ben Chapman, Earle Combs, Myril Hoag, Babe Ruth, outfielders.

Cubs — Gabby Hartnett, Rollie Hemsley, Zack Taylor, catchers; Guy Bush, Burleigh Grimes, LeRoy Herrmann, Pat Malone, Frank May, Charlie Root, Bob Smith, Bud Tinning, Lon Warneke, pitchers; Woody English, Charlie Grimm, Stan Hack, Billy Herman, Billy Jurges, Mark Koenig, infielders; Kiki Cuyler, Frank Demaree, Marv Gudat, Johnny Moore, Riggs Stephenson, outfielders.

1933 - NEW YORK GIANTS N.L. (4) vs. WASHINGTON SENATORS A.L. (1)

(Polo Grounds)/(Griffith Stadium)

Oct. 3	@ N.Y.	New York (Hubbell)	4	Washington (Stewart)	2	
Oct. 4	@ N.Y.	New York (Schumacher)	6	Washington (Crowder)	1	
Oct. 5	@ Wash.	Washington (Whitehill)	4	New York (Fitzsimmons)	0	
Oct. 6	@ Wash.	New York (Hubbell)	2	Washington (Weaver)	1	(11 Innings)
Oct. 7	@ Wash.	New York (Luque)	4	Washington (Russell)	3	(10 Innings)

MANAGERS: Bill Terry, Giants; Joe Cronin, Senators

Giants — Harry Danning, Gus Mancuso, Paul Richards, catchers; Hi Bell, Watty Clark, Freddie Fitzsimmons, Carl Hubbell, Dolf Luque, Roy Parmelee, Jack Salveson, Hal Schumacher, Glenn Spencer, pitchers; Hughie Critz, Chuck Dressen, Travis Jackson, Bernie James, Blondy Ryan, Bill Terry, Johnny Vergez, infielders; Kiddo Davis, Joe Moore, Lefty O'Doul, Mel Ott, Homer Peel, outfielders.

Senators — Moe Berg, Cliff Bolton, Luke Sewell, catchers; Bobby Burke, Ed Chapman, General Crowder, Alex McColl, Jack Russell, Lefty Stewart, Tommy Thomas, Monte Weaver, Earl Whitehill, pitchers; Ossie Bluege, Bob Boken, Joe Cronin, John Kerr, Joe Kuhel, Buddy Myer, infielders. Goose Goslin, Dave Harris, Heinie Manush, Sam Rice, Fred Schulte, outfielders.

1934 - ST. LOUIS CARDINALS N.L. (4) vs. DETROIT TIGERS A.L. (3)
(Sportsmans Park)/(Navin Field)

Oct. 3	@ Det.	St. Louis (Dizzy Dean)	8	Detroit (Crowder)	3	
Oct. 4	@ Det.	Detroit (Rowe)	3	St. Louis (Walker)	2	(12 Innings)
Oct. 5	@ St.L.	St. Louis (Daffy Dean)	4	Detroit (Bridges)	1	
Oct. 6	@ St.L.	Detroit (Auker)	10	St. Louis (Walker)	4	
Oct. 7	@ St.L.	Detroit (Bridges)	3	St. Louis (Dizzy Dean)	1	
Oct. 8	@ Det.	St. Louis (Daffy Dean)	4	Detroit (Rowe)	3	
Oct. 9	@ Det.	St. Louis (Dizzy Dean)	11	Detroit (Auker)	0	

MANAGERS: Frankie Frisch, Cardinals; Mickey Cochrane, Tigers

Cardinals — Spud Davis, Bill DeLancey, Francis Healy, catchers; Tex Carleton, Dizzy Dean, Daffy Dean, Jesse Haines, Bill Hallahan, Jim Mooney, Dazzy Vance, Bill Walker, pitchers; Ripper Collins, Pat Crawford, Leo Durocher, Frankie Frisch, Pepper Martin, Burgess Whitehead, infielders; Chick Fullis, Joe Medwick, Ernie Orsatti, Jack Rothrock, outfielders.

Tigers — Mickey Cochrane, Ray Hayworth, catchers; Elden Auker, Tommy Bridges, General Crowder, Carl Fischer, Luke Hamlin, Chief Hogsett, Firpo Marberry, Schoolboy Rowe, Vic Sorrell, pitchers; Flea Clifton, Charlie Gehringer, Hank Greenberg, Marv Owen, Billy Rogell, Heinie Schuble, infielders; Frank Doljack, Pete Fox, Goose Goslin, Gee Walker, JoJo White, outfielders.

1935 - DETROIT TIGERS A.L. (4) vs. CHICAGO CUBS N.L. (2)
(Navin Field)/(Wrigley Field)

Oct. 2	@ Det.	Chicago (Warneke)	3	Detroit (Rowe)	0	
Oct. 3	@ Det.	Detroit (Bridges)	8	Chicago (Root)	3	
Oct. 4	@ Chi.	Detroit (Rowe)	6	Chicago (French)	5	(11 Innings)
Oct. 5	@ Chi.	Detroit (Crowder)	2	Chicago (Carleton)	1	
Oct. 6	@ Chi.	Chicago (Warneke)	3	Detroit (Rowe)	1	
Oct. 7	@ Det.	Detroit (Bridges)	4	Chicago (French)	3	

MANAGERS: Mickey Cochrane, Tigers; Charlie Grimm, Cubs

Tigers — Mickey Cochrane, Ray Hayworth, Frank Reiber, catchers; Elden Auker, Tommy Bridges, General Crowder, Chief Hogsett, Roxie Lawson, Schoolboy Rowe, Vic Sorrell, Joe Sullivan, pitchers; Flea Clifton, Charlie Gehringer, Hank Greenberg, Marv Owen, Billy Rogell, Heinie Schuble, infielders; Pete Fox, Goose Goslin, Hugh Shelley, Gee Walker, JoJo White, outfielders.

Cubs — Gabby Hartnett, Ken O'Dea, Walter Stephenson, catchers; Tex Carleton, Hugh Casey, Larry French, Roy Henshaw, Fabian Kowalik, Bill Lee, Charlie Root, Clyde Shoun, Lon Warneke, pitchers; Phil Cavarretta, Woody English, Charlie Grimm, Stan Hack, Billy Herman, Bill Jurges, infielders; Frank Demaree, Augie Galan, Chuck Klein, Freddie Lindstrom, Tuck Stainback, outfielders.

1936 - NEW YORK YANKEES A.L. (4) vs. NEW YORK GIANTS N.L. (2)
(Yankee Stadium)/(Polo Grounds)

Sept. 30	@ N.Y.G.	Giants (Hubbell)	6	Yankees (Ruffing)	1	
Oct. 2	@ N.Y.G.	Yankees (Gomez)	18	Giants (Schumacher)	4	
Oct. 3	@ N.Y.Y.	Yankees (Hadley)	2	Giants (Fitzsimmons)	1	
Oct. 4	@ N.Y.Y.	Yankees (Pearson)	5	Giants (Hubbell)	2	
Oct. 5	@ N.Y.Y.	Giants (Schumacher)	5	Yankees (Malone)	4	(10 Innings)
Oct. 6	@ N.Y.G.	Yankees (Gomez)	13	Giants (Fitzsimmons)	5	
POSTPONED: (Rain) Oct. 1						

MANAGERS: Joe McCarthy, Yankees; Bill Terry, Giants

Yankees — Bill Dickey, Joe Glenn, Arndt Jorgens, catchers; Johnny Broaca, Jumbo Brown, Lefty Gomez, Bump Hadley, Pat Malone, Johnny Murphy, Monte Pearson, Red Ruffing, Kemp Wicker, pitchers; Frankie Crosetti, Lou Gehrig, Don Heffner, Tony Lazzeri, Red Rolfe, Jack Saltzgaver, infielders; Joe DiMaggio, Roy Johnson, Jake Powell, Bob Seeds, George Selkirk, outfielders.

Giants — Harry Danning, Gus Mancuso, Roy Spencer, catchers; Slick Castleman, Dick Coffman, Freddie Fitzsimmons, Frank Gabler, Harry Gumbert, Carl Hubbell, Hal Schumacher, Al Smith, pitchers; Dick Bartell, Travis Jackson, Mark Koenig, Sam Leslie, Eddie Mayo, Bill Terry, Burgess Whitehead, infielders; Kiddo Davis, Hank Leiber, Joe Moore, Mel Ott, Jimmy Ripple, outfielders.

1937 - NEW YORK YANKEES A.L. (4) vs. NEW YORK GIANTS N.L. (1)
(Yankee Stadium)/(Polo Grounds)

Oct. 6	@ N.Y.Y.	Yankees (Gomez)	8	Giants (Hubbell)	1
Oct. 7	@ N.Y.Y.	Yankees (Ruffing)	8	Giants (Melton)	1
Oct. 8	@ N.Y.G.	Yankees (Pearson)	5	Giants (Schumacher)	1
Oct. 9	@ N.Y.G.	Giants (Hubbell)	7	Yankees (Hadley)	3
Oct. 10	@ N.Y.G.	Yankees (Gomez)	4	Giants (Melton)	2

MANAGERS: Joe McCarthy, Yankees; Bill Terry, Giants

Yankees – Bill Dickey, Joe Glenn, Arndt Jorgens, catchers; Ivy Andrews, Spud Chandler, Lefty Gomez, Bump Hadley, Frank Makosky, Pat Malone, Johnny Murphy, Monte Pearson, Red Ruffing, Kemp Wicker, pitchers; Frankie Crosetti, Lou Gehrig, Don Heffner, Tony Lazzeri, Red Rolfe, Jack Saltzgaver, infielders; Joe DiMaggio, Tommy Henrich, Myril Hoag, Jake Powell, George Selkirk, outfielders.

Giants – Harry Danning, Ed Madjeski, Gus Mancuso, catchers; Tom Baker, Don Brennan, Slick Castleman, Dick Coffman, Harry Gumbert, Carl Hubbell, Cliff Melton, Hal Schumacher, Al Smith, pitchers; Dick Bartell, Lou Chiozza, Mickey Haslin, Sam Leslie, Johnny McCarthy, Mel Ott, Blondy Ryan, Burgess Whitehead, infielders; Wally Berger, Hank Leiber, Joe Moore, Jimmy Ripple, outfielders.

1938 - NEW YORK YANKEES A.L. (4) vs. CHICAGO CUBS N.L. (0)
(Yankee Stadium)/(Wrigley Field)

Oct. 5	@ Chi.	New York (Ruffing)	3	Chicago (Lee)	1
Oct. 6	@ Chi.	New York (Gomez)	6	Chicago (Dean)	3
Oct. 8	@ N.Y.	New York (Pearson)	5	Chicago (Bryant)	2
Oct. 9	@ N.Y.	New York (Ruffing)	8	Chicago (Lee)	3

MANAGERS: Joe McCarthy, Yankees; Gabby Hartnett, Cubs

Yankees – Bill Dickey, Joe Glenn, Arndt Jorgens, catchers; Ivy Andrews, Spud Chandler, Wes Ferrell, Lefty Gomez, Bump Hadley, Johnny Murphy, Monte Pearson, Red Ruffing, Steve Sundra, pitchers; Frankie Crosetti, Babe Dahlgren, Lou Gehrig, Joe Gordon, Billy Knickerbocker, Red Rolfe, infielders; Joe DiMaggio, Tommy Henrich, Myril Hoag, Jake Powell, George Selkirk, outfielders.

Cubs – Bob Garbark, Gabby Hartnett, Ken O'Dea, catchers; Clay Bryant, Tex Carleton, Dizzy Dean, Larry French, Bill Lee, Vance Page, Charlie Root, Jack Russell, pitchers; Phil Cavarretta, Ripper Collins, Stan Hack, Billy Herman, Billy Jurges, Tony Lazzeri, infielders; Jim Asbell, Frank Demaree, Augie Galan, Joe Marty, Carl Reynolds, outfielders.

1939 - NEW YORK YANKEES A.L. (4) vs. CINCINNATI REDS N.L. (0)
(Yankee Stadium)/(Crosley Field)

Oct. 4	@ N.Y.	New York (Ruffing)	2	Cincinnati (Derringer)	1	
Oct. 5	@ N.Y.	New York (Pearson)	4	Cincinnati (Walters)	0	
Oct. 7	@ Cin.	New York (Hadley)	7	Cincinnati (Thompson)	3	
Oct. 8	@ Cin.	New York (Murphy)	7	Cincinnati (Walters)	4	(10 Innings)

MANAGERS: Joe McCarthy, Yankees; Bill McKechnie, Reds

Yankees – Bill Dickey, Arndt Jorgens, Buddy Rosar, catchers; Spud Chandler, Atley Donald, Lefty Gomez, Bump Hadley, Oral Hildebrand, Johnny Murphy, Monte Pearson, Red Ruffing, Marius Russo, Steve Sundra, pitchers; Frankie Crosetti, Babe Dahlgren, Lou Gehrig, Joe Gordon, Billy Knickerbocker, Red Rolfe, infielders; Joe DiMaggio, Tommy Henrich, Charlie Keller, Jake Powell, George Selkirk, outfielders.

Reds – Willard Hershberger, Ernie Lombardi, catchers; Paul Derringer, Lee Grissom, Hank Johnson, Whitey Moore, Johnny Niggeling, Milt Shoffner, Junior Thompson, Johnny Vander Meer, Bucky Walters, pitchers; Lonny Frey, Eddie Joost, Frank McCormick, Billy Myers, Lew Riggs, Les Scarsella, Bill Werber, infielders; Wally Berger, Tony Bongiovanni, Frenchy Bordagaray, Harry Craft, Lee Gamble, Ival Goodman, Al Simmons, outfielders.

1940 – CINCINNATI REDS N.L. (4) vs. DETROIT TIGERS A.L. (3)
(Crosley Field)/(Briggs Stadium)

Oct. 2	@ Cin.	Detroit (Newsom)	7	Cincinnati (Derringer)	2
Oct. 3	@ Cin.	Cincinnati (Walters)	5	Detroit (Rowe)	3
Oct. 4	@ Det.	Detroit (Bridges)	7	Cincinnati (Turner)	4
Oct. 5	@ Det.	Cincinnati (Derringer)	5	Detroit (Trout)	2
Oct. 6	@ Det.	Detroit (Newsom)	8	Cincinnati (Thompson)	0
Oct. 7	@ Cin.	Cincinnati (Walters)	4	Detroit (Rowe)	0
Oct. 8	@ Cin.	Cincinnati (Derringer)	2	Detroit (Newsom)	1

MANAGERS: Bill McKechnie, Reds; Del Baker, Tigers

Reds – Bill Baker, Ernie Lombardi, Jimmie Wilson, catchers; Joe Beggs, Paul Derringer, Witt Guise, Johnny Hutchings, Whitey Moore, Elmer Riddle, Milt Shoffner, Junior Thompson, Jim Turner, Johnny Vander Meer, Bucky Walters, pitchers; Lonny Frey, Eddie Joost, Frank McCormick, Billy Myers, Lew Riggs, Bill Werber, infielders; Morris Arnovich, Harry Craft, Ival Goodman, Myron McCormick, Jimmy Ripple, outfielders.

Tigers – Billy Sullivan, Jr., Birdie Tebbetts, catchers; Al Benton, Tommy Bridges, Johnny Gorsica, Fred Hutchinson, Archie McKain, Hal Newhouser, Bobo Newsom, Schoolboy Rowe, Tom Seats, Clay Smith, Dizzy Trout, pitchers; Dick Bartell, Frank Croucher, Charlie Gehringer, Pinky Higgins, Dutch Meyer, Rudy York, infielders; Earl Averill, Bruce Campbell, Pete Fox, Hank Greenberg, Barney McCosky, Tuck Stainback, outfielders.

1941 – NEW YORK YANKEES A.L. (4) vs. BROOKLYN DODGERS N.L. (1)
(Yankee Stadium)/(Ebbets Field)

Oct. 1	@ N.Y.	New York (Ruffing)	3	Brooklyn (Davis)	2
Oct. 2	@ N.Y.	Brooklyn (Wyatt)	3	New York (Chandler)	2
Oct. 4	@ Brk.	New York (Russo)	2	Brooklyn (Casey)	1
Oct. 5	@ Brk.	New York (Murphy)	7	Brooklyn (Casey)	4
Oct. 6	@ Brk.	New York (Bonham)	3	Brooklyn (Wyatt)	1

POSTPONED: (Rain) Oct. 3

MANAGERS: Joe McCarthy, Yankees; Leo Durocher, Dodgers

Yankees – Bill Dickey, Buddy Rosar, Ken Silvestri, catchers; Ernie Bonham, Norm Branch, Marv Breuer, Spud Chandler, Atley Donald, Lefty Gomez, Johnny Murphy, Steve Peek, Red Ruffing, Marius Russo, Charley Stanceu, pitchers; Frankie Crosetti, Joe Gordon, Jerry Priddy, Phil Rizzuto, Red Rolfe, Johnny Sturm, infielders; Frenchy Bordagaray, Joe DiMaggio, Tommy Henrich, Charlie Keller, George Selkirk, outfielders.

Dodgers – Herman Franks, Mickey Owen, catchers; Ed Albosta, Johnny Allen, Hugh Casey, Curt Davis, Tom Drake, Freddie Fitzsimmons, Larry French, Luke Hamlin, Kirby Higbe, Newt Kimball, Whit Wyatt, pitchers; Dolph Camilli, Pete Coscarart, Leo Durocher, Billy Herman, Cookie Lavagetto, Pee Wee Reese, Lew Riggs, infielders; Augie Galan, Joe Medwick, Pete Reiser, Dixie Walker, Jimmy Wasdell, outfielders.

1942 – ST. LOUIS CARDINALS N.L. (4) vs. NEW YORK YANKEES A.L. (1)
(Sportsmans Park)/(Yankee Stadium)

Sept. 30	@ St.L.	New York (Ruffing)	7	St. Louis (M.Cooper)	4
Oct. 1	@ St.L.	St. Louis (Beazley)	4	New York (Bonham)	3
Oct. 3	@ N.Y.	St. Louis (White)	2	New York (Chandler)	0
Oct. 4	@ N.Y.	St. Louis (Lanier)	9	New York (Donald)	6
Oct. 5	@ N.Y.	St. Louis (Beazley)	4	New York (Ruffing)	2

MANAGERS: Billy Southworth, Cardinals; Joe McCarthy, Yankees

Cardinals – Walker Cooper, Sam Narron, Ken O'Dea, catchers; Johnny Beazley, Mort Cooper, Murry Dickson, Harry Gumbert, Howie Krist, Max Lanier, Whitey Moore, Howie Pollet, Ernie White, pitchers; Jimmy Brown, Creepy Crespi, Johnny Hopp, Whitey Kurowski, Marty Marion, Ray Sanders, infielders; Terry Moore, Stan Musial, Enos Slaughter, Coaker Triplett, Harry Walker, outfielders.

Yankees – Bill Dickey, Rollie Hemsley, Buddy Rosar, catchers; Ernie Bonham, Hank Borowy, Marv Breuer, Spud Chandler, Atley Donald, Lefty Gomez, Johnny Lindell, Johnny Murphy, Red Ruffing, Marius Russo, Jim Turner, pitchers; Frankie Crosetti, Joe Gordon, Buddy Hassett, Gerry Priddy, Phil Rizzuto, Red Rolfe, infielders; Roy Cullenbine, Joe DiMaggio, Charlie Keller, George Selkirk, Tuck Stainback, outfielders.

1943 - NEW YORK YANKEES A.L. (4) vs. ST. LOUIS CARDINALS N.L. (1)

(Yankee Stadium)/(Sportsmans Park)

Oct. 5	@ N.Y.	New York (Chandler)	4	St. Louis (Lanier)	2
Oct. 6	@ N.Y.	St. Louis (M.Cooper)	4	New York (Bonham)	3
Oct. 7	@ N.Y.	New York (Borowy)	6	St. Louis (Brazle)	2
Oct. 10	@ St.L.	New York (Russo)	2	St. Louis (Brecheen)	1
Oct. 11	@ St.L.	New York (Chandler)	2	St. Louis (M.Cooper)	0

MANAGERS: Joe McCarthy, Yankees; Billy Southworth, Cardinals

Yankees – Bill Dickey, Rollie Hemsley, Ken Sears, catchers; Ernie Bonham, Hank Borowy, Marv Breuer, Tommy Byrne, Spud Chandler, Atley Donald, Johnny Murphy, Marius Russo, Jim Turner, Butch Wensloff, Bill Zuber, pitchers; Frankie Crosetti, Nick Etten, Joe Gordon, Oscar Grimes, Billy Johnson, Snuffy Stirnweiss, infielders; Charlie Keller, Johnny Lindell, Bud Metheny, Tuck Stainback, Roy Weatherly, outfielders.

Cardinals – Walker Cooper, Sam Narron, Ken O'Dea, catchers; Al Brazle, Harry Brecheen, Mort Cooper, Murry Dickson, Harry Gumbert, Howie Krist, Max Lanier, George Munger, Ernie White, pitchers; George Fallon, Debs Garms, Lou Klein, Whitey Kurowski, Marty Marion, Ray Sanders, infielders; Frank Demaree, Johnny Hopp, Danny Litwhiler, Stan Musial, Harry Walker, outfielders.

1944 - ST. LOUIS CARDINALS N.L. (4) vs. ST. LOUIS BROWNS A.L. (2)

(Sportsmans Park)/(Sportsmans Park)

Oct. 4	@ Cards	Browns (Galehouse)	2	Cardinals (M.Cooper)	1	
Oct. 5	@ Cards	Cardinals (Donnelly)	3	Browns (Muncrief)	2	(11 Innings)
Oct. 6	@ Browns	Browns (Kramer)	6	Cardinals (Wilks)	2	
Oct. 7	@ Browns	Cardinals (Brecheen)	5	Browns (Jakucki)	1	
Oct. 8	@ Browns	Cardinals (M.Cooper)	2	Browns (Galehouse)	0	
Oct. 9	@ Cards	Cardinals (Lanier)	3	Browns (Potter)	1	

MANAGERS: Billy Southworth, Cardinals; Luke Sewell, Browns

Cardinals – Walker Cooper, Bob Keely, Ken O'Dea, catchers; Harry Brecheen, Bud Byerly, Mort Cooper, Blix Donnelly, Al Jurisich, Max Lanier, Freddy Schmidt, Ted Wilks, pitchers; George Fallon, Whitey Kurowski, Marty Marion, Ray Sanders, Emil Verban, infielders; Augie Bergamo, Debs Garms, Johnny Hopp, Danny Litwhiler, Pepper Martin, Stan Musial, outfielders.

Browns – Red Hayworth, Frank Mancuso, Tom Turner, catchers; George Caster, Denny Galehouse, Al Hollingsworth, Willis Hudlin, Sig Jakucki, Jack Kramer, Bob Muncrief, Nels Potter, Tex Shirley, Sam Zoldak, pitchers; Floyd Baker, Mark Christman, Ellis Clary, Don Gutteridge, George McQuinn, Vern Stephens, infielders; Milt Byrnes, Mike Chartak, Mike Kreevich, Chet Laabs, Gene Moore, Al Zarilla, outfielders.

1945 - DETROIT TIGERS A.L. (4) vs. CHICAGO CUBS N.L. (3)

(Briggs Stadium)/(Wrigley Field)

Oct. 3	@ Det.	Chicago (Borowy)	9	Detroit (Newhouser)	0	
Oct. 4	@ Det.	Detroit (Trucks)	4	Chicago (Wyse)	1	
Oct. 5	@ Det.	Chicago (Pasaeau)	3	Detroit (Overmire)	0	
Oct. 6	@ Chi.	Detroit (Trout)	4	Chicago (Prim)	1	
Oct. 7	@ Chi.	Detroit (Newhouser)	8	Chicago (Borowy)	4	
Oct. 8	@ Chi.	Chicago (Borowy)	8	Detroit (Trout)	7	(12 Innings)
Oct. 10	@ Chi.	Detroit (Newhouser)	9	Chicago (Borowy)	3	

MANAGERS: Steve O'Neill, Tigers; Charlie Grimm, Cubs

Tigers – Hack Miller, Paul Richards, Bob Swift, catchers; Al Benton, Tommy Bridges, George Caster, Zeb Eaton, Art Houtteman, Les Mueller, Hal Newhouser, Stubby Overmire, Billy Pierce, Jim Tobin, Dizzy Trout, Virgil Trucks, Walter Wilson, pitchers; Red Borom, Joe Hoover, Bob Meier, Eddie Mayo, John McHale, Jimmy Outlaw, Skeeter Webb, Rudy York, infielders; Doc Cramer, Roy Cullenbine, Hank Greenberg, Chuck Hostetler, Ed Mierkowicz, Hub Walker, outfielders.

Cubs – Paul Gillespie, Mickey Livingston, Clyde McCullough, Len Rice, Dewey Williams, catchers; Hi Bithorn, Hank Borowy, Bob Chipman, Paul Derringer, Paul Erickson, Ed Hanyzewski, Claude Passeau, Ray Prim, Walter Signer, Ray Starr, Hy Vandenberg, Lon Warneke, Hank Wyse, pitchers; Heinz Becker, Sy Block, Phil Cavarretta, Stan Hack, Roy Hughes, Don Johnson, Lennie Merullo, Bill Schuster, infielders; Peanuts Lowrey, Bill Nicholson, Andy Pafko, Ed Sauer, Frank Secory, outfielders.

1946 - ST. LOUIS CARDINALS N.L. (4) vs. BOSTON RED SOX A.L. (3)
(Sportsmans Park)/(Fenway Park)

Oct. 6	@ St.L.	Boston (Johnson)	3	St. Louis (Pollet)	2	(10 Innings)
Oct. 7	@ St.L.	St. Louis (Brecheen)	3	Boston (Harris)	0	
Oct. 9	@ Bos.	Boston (Ferriss)	4	St. Louis (Dickson)	0	
Oct. 10	@ Bos.	St. Louis (Munger)	12	Boston (Hughson)	3	
Oct. 11	@ Bos.	Boston (Dobson)	6	St. Louis (Brazle)	3	
Oct. 13	@ St.L.	St. Louis (Brecheen)	4	Boston (Harris)	1	
Oct. 15	@ St.L.	St. Louis (Brecheen)	4	Boston (Klinger)	3	

MANAGERS: Eddie Dyer, Cardinals; Joe Cronin, Red Sox

Cardinals – Joe Garagiola, Clyde Kluttz, Del Rice, catchers; Red Barrett, Johnny Beazley, Al Brazle, Harry Brecheen, Ken Burkhart, Murry Dickson, Johnny Grodzicki, Howie Krist, George Munger, Howie Pollet, Freddy Schmidt, Ted Wilks, pitchers; Jeff Cross, Nippy Jones, Whitey Kurowski, Marty Marion, Stan Musial, Red Schoendienst, infielders; Buster Adams, Erv Dusak, Bill Endicott, Terry Moore, Walter Sessi, Dick Sisler, Enos Slaughter, Harry Walker, outfielders.

Red Sox – Ed McGah, Roy Partee, Hal Wagner, catchers; Jim Bagby, Mace Brown, Joe Dobson, Clem Dreisewerd, Boo Ferriss, Mickey Harris, Tex Hughson, Earl Johnson, Bob Klinger, Mike Ryba, Charlie Wagner, Bill Zuber, pitchers; Paul Campbell, Bobby Doerr, Don Gutteridge, Pinky Higgins, Eddie Pellagrini, Johnny Pesky, Rip Russell, Rudy York, infielders; Leon Culberson, Dom DiMaggio, Johnny Lazor, Tom McBride, George Metkovich, Wally Moses, Ted Williams, outfielders.

1947 - NEW YORK YANKEES A.L. (4) vs. BROOKLYN DODGERS N.L. (3)
(Yankee Stadium)/(Ebbets Field)

Sept. 30	@ N.Y.	New York (Shea)	5	Brooklyn (Branca)	3
Oct. 1	@ N.Y.	New York (Reynolds)	10	Brooklyn (Lombardi)	3
Oct. 2	@ Brk.	Brooklyn (Casey)	9	New York (Newsom)	8
Oct. 3	@ Brk.	Brooklyn (Casey)	3	New York (Bevens)	2
Oct. 4	@ Brk	New York (Shea)	2	Brooklyn (Barney)	1
Oct. 5	@ N.Y.	Brooklyn (Branca)	8	New York (Page)	6
Oct. 6	@ N.Y.	New York (Page)	5	Brooklyn (Gregg)	2

MANAGERS: Bucky Harris, Yankees; Burt Shotton, Dodgers

Yankees – Yogi Berra, Ralph Houk, Sherm Lollar, Aaron Robinson, catchers; Bill Bevens, Spud Chandler, Karl Drews, Randy Gumpert, Don Johnson, Bobo Newsom, Joe Page, Vic Raschi, Allie Reynolds, Spec Shea, Butch Wensloff, pitchers; Bobby Brown, Lonny Frey, Billy Johnson, George McQuinn, Jack Phillips, Phil Rizzuto, Snuffy Stirnweiss, infielders; Allie Clark, Joe DiMaggio, Tommy Henrich, Charlie Keller, Johnny Lindell, outfielders.

Dodgers – Bobby Bragan, Bruce Edwards, Gil Hodges, catchers; Dan Bankhead, Rex Barney, Hank Behrman, Ralph Branca, Hugh Casey, Hal Gregg, Joe Hatten, Clyde King, Vic Lombardi, Harry Taylor, pitchers; Tommy Brown, Spider Jorgensen, Cookie Lavagetto, Eddie Miksis, Pee Wee Reese, Jackie Robinson, Stan Rojek, Eddie Stanky, Arky Vaughan, infielders; Carl Furillo, Al Gionfriddo, Gene Hermanski, Pete Reiser, Dixie Walker, outfielders.

1948 - CLEVELAND INDIANS A.L. (4) vs. BOSTON BRAVES N.L. (2)
(Cleveland Stadium)/(Braves Field)

Oct. 6	@ Bos.	Boston (Sain)	1	Cleveland (Feller)	0
Oct. 7	@ Bos.	Cleveland (Lemon)	4	Boston (Spahn)	1
Oct. 8	@ Clev.	Cleveland (Beardon)	2	Boston (Bickford)	0
Oct. 9	@ Clev.	Cleveland (Gromek)	2	Boston (Sain)	1
Oct. 10	@ Clev.	Boston (Spahn)	11	Cleveland (Feller)	5
Oct. 11	@ Bos.	Cleveland (Lemon)	4	Boston (Voiselle)	3

MANAGERS: Lou Boudreau, Indians; Billy Southworth, Braves

Indians – Jim Hegan, Joe Tipton, catchers; Gene Bearden, Russ Christopher, Bob Feller, Steve Gromek, Eddie Klieman, Bob Lemon, Bob Muncrief, Satchel Paige, Sam Zoldak, pitchers; Johnny Berardino, Ray Boone, Lou Boudreau, Joe Gordon, Ken Keltner, Eddie Robinson, Al Rosen, infielders; Allie Clark, Larry Doby, Walt Judnich, Bob Kennedy, Dale Mitchell, Hal Peck, Thurman Tucker, outfielders.

Braves – Phil Masi, Bill Salkeld, catchers; Red Barrett, Vern Bickford, Bobby Hogue, Al Lyons, Nels Potter, Johnny Sain, Clyde Shoun, Warren Spahn, Bill Voiselle, Ernie White, pitchers; Alvin Dark, Bob Elliott, Frank McCormick, Connie Ryan, Ray Sanders, Sibby Sisti, Eddie Stanky, Bobby Sturgeon, Earl Torgeson, infielders; Clint Conatser, Tommy Holmes, Mike McCormick, Marv Rickert, outfielders.

1949 - NEW YORK YANKEES A.L. (4) vs. BROOKLYN DODGERS N.L. (1)

(Yankee Stadium)/(Ebbets Field)

Oct. 5	@ N.Y.	New York (Reynolds)	1	Brooklyn (Newcombe)	0	
Oct. 6	@ N.Y.	Brooklyn (Roe)	1	New York (Raschi)	0	
Oct. 7	@ Brk.	New York (Page)	4	Brooklyn (Branca)	3	
Oct. 8	@ Brk.	New York (Lopat)	6	Brooklyn (Newcombe)	4	
Oct. 9	@ Brk.	New York (Raschi)	10	Brooklyn (Barney)	6	

MANAGERS: Casey Stengel, Yankees; Burt Shotton, Dodgers

Yankees – Yogi Berra, Gus Niarhos, Charlie Silvera, catchers; Ralph Buxton, Tommy Byrne, Ed Lopat, Cuddles Marshall, Joe Page, Duane Pillette, Vic Raschi, Allie Reynolds, Fred Sanford, pitchers; Bobby Brown, Jerry Coleman, Tommy Henrich, Billy Johnson, Johnny Mize, Phil Rizzuto, Snuffy Stirnweiss, infielders; Hank Bauer, Joe DiMaggio, Charlie Keller, Johnny Lindell, Cliff Mapes, Gene Woodling, outfielders.

Dodgers – Roy Campanella, Bruce Edwards, catchers; Jack Banta, Rex Barney, Ralph Branca, Carl Erskine, Joe Hatten, Paul Minner, Don Newcombe, Erv Palica, Preacher Roe, pitchers; Billy Cox, Gil Hodges, Spider Jorgensen, Eddie Miksis, Pee Wee Reese, Jackie Robinson, infielders; Tommy Brown, Carl Furillo, Gene Hermanski, Mike McCormick, Luis Olmo, Marv Rackley, Duke Snider, Dick Whitman, outfielders.

1950 - NEW YORK YANKEES A.L. (4) vs. PHILADELPHIA PHILLIES N.L. (0)

(Yankee Stadium)/(Shibe Park)

Oct. 4	@ Phil.	New York (Raschi)	1	Philadelphia (Konstanty)	0	
Oct. 5	@ Phil.	New York (Reynolds)	2	Philadelphia (Roberts)	1	(10 Innings)
Oct. 6	@ N.Y.	New York (Ferrick)	3	Philadelphia (Meyer)	2	
Oct. 7	@ N.Y.	New York (Ford)	5	Philadelphia (Miller)	2	

MANAGERS: Casey Stengel, Yankees; Eddie Sawyer, Phillies

Yankees – Yogi Berra, Ralph Houk, Charlie Silvera, catchers; Tommy Byrne, Tom Ferrick, Whitey Ford, Ed Lopat, Joe Ostrowski, Joe Page, Vic Raschi, Allie Reynolds, Fred Sanford, pitchers; Bobby Brown, Jerry Coleman, Joe Collins, Johnny Hopp, Billy Johnson, Billy Martin, Johnny Mize, Phil Rizzuto, infielders; Hank Bauer, Joe DiMaggio, Jackie Jensen, Cliff Mapes, Gene Woodling, outfielders.

Phillies – Stan Lopata, Andy Seminick, Ken Silvestri, catchers; Milo Candini, Bubba Church, Blix Donnelly, Ken Heintzelman, Ken Johnson, Jim Konstanty, Russ Meyer, Bob Miller, Robin Roberts, Jocko Thompson, pitchers; Jimmy Bloodworth, Ralph Caballero, Mike Goliat, Granny Hamner, Willie Jones, Eddie Waitkus, infielders; Richie Ashburn, Del Ennis, Stan Hollmig, Jackie Mayo, Dick Sisler, Dick Whitman, outfielders.

1951 - NEW YORK YANKEES A.L. (4) vs. NEW YORK GIANTS N.L. (2)

(Yankee Stadium)/(Polo Grounds)

Oct. 4	@ N.Y.Y.	Giants (Koslo)	5	Yankees (Reynolds)	1
Oct. 5	@ N.Y.Y.	Yankees (Lopat)	3	Giants (Jansen)	1
Oct. 6	@ N.Y.G.	Giants (Hearn)	6	Yankees (Raschi)	2
Oct. 8	@ N.Y.G.	Yankees (Reynolds)	6	Giants (Maglie)	2
Oct. 9	@ N.Y.G.	Yankees (Lopat)	13	Giants (Jansen)	1
Oct. 10	@ N.Y.Y.	Yankees (Raschi)	4	Giants (Koslo)	3

POSTPONED: (Rain) Oct. 7

MANAGERS: Casey Stengel, Yankees; Leo Durocher, Giants

Yankees – Yogi Berra, Ralph Houk, Charlie Silvera, catchers; Bobby Hogue, Bob Kuzava, Ed Lopat, Tom Morgan, Joe Ostrowskl, Stubby Overmire, Vic Raschi, Allie Reynolds, Johnny Sain, Art Schallock, Spec Shea, pitchers; Bobby Brown, Jerry Coleman, Joe Collins, Johnny Hopp, Billy Martin, Gil McDougald, Johnny Mize, Phil Rizzuto, infielders; Hank Bauer, Joe DiMaggio, Mickey Mantle, Gene Woodling, outfielders.

Giants – Ray Noble, Wes Westrum, Sal Yvars, catchers; Al Corwin, Jim Hearn, Larry Jansen, Sheldon Jones, Monte Kennedy, Alex Konikowski, Dave Koslo, Sal Maglie, George Spencer, pitchers; Alvin Dark, Whitey Lockman, Jack Lohrke, Bill Rigney, Hank Schenz, Eddie Stanky, Hank Thompson, Bobby Thomson, Davey Williams, infielders; Clint Hartung, Monte Irvin, Willie Mays, Don Mueller, outfielders.

1952 – NEW YORK YANKEES A.L. (4) vs. BROOKLYN DODGERS N.L. (3)

(Yankee Stadium)/(Ebbets Field)

Oct. 1	@ Brk.	Brooklyn (Black)	4	New York (Reynolds)	2	
Oct. 2	@ Brk.	New York (Raschi)	7	Brooklyn (Erskine)	1	
Oct. 3	@ N.Y.	Brooklyn (Roe)	5	New York (Lopat)	3	
Oct. 4	@ N.Y.	New York (Reynolds)	2	Brooklyn (Black)	0	
Oct. 5	@ N.Y.	Brooklyn (Erskine)	6	New York (Sain)	5	(11 Innings)
Oct. 6	@ Brk.	New York (Raschi)	3	Brooklyn (Loes)	2	
Oct. 7	@ Brk.	New York (Reynolds)	4	Brooklyn (Black)	2	

MANAGERS: Casey Stengel, Yankees; Chuck Dressen, Dodgers

Yankees – Yogi Berra, Ralph Houk, Charlie Silvera, catchers; Ewell Blackwell, Tom Gorman, Bob Kuzava, Ed Lopat, Jim McDonald, Bill Miller, Joe Ostrowski, Vic Raschi, Allle Reynolds, Johnny Sain, Ray Scarborough, pitchers; Loren Babe, Jim Brideweser, Joe Collins, Billy Martin, Gil McDougald, Johnny Mize, Phil Rizzuto, infielders; Hank Bauer, Mickey Mantle, Irv Noren, Gene Woodling, outfielders.

Dodgers – Roy Campanella, Rube Walker, catchers; Joe Black, Ralph Branca, Carl Erskine, Clyde King, Clem Labine, Joe Landrum, Ken Lehman, Billy Loes, Ray Moore, Preacher Roe, Johnny Rutherford, Ben Wade, pitchers; Rocky Bridges, Billy Cox, Gil Hodges, Bobby Morgan, Rocky Nelson, Pee Wee Reese, Jackie Robinson, infielders; Sandy Amoros, Carl Furillo, Tommy Holmes, Andy Pafko, George Shuba, Duke Snider, outfielders.

1953 – NEW YORK YANKEES A.L. (4) vs. BROOKLYN DODGERS N.L. (2)

(Yankee Stadium)/(Ebbets Field)

Sept. 30	@ N.Y.	New York (Sain)	9	Brooklyn (Labine)	5
Oct. 1	@ N.Y.	New York (Lopat)	4	Brooklyn (Roe)	2
Oct. 2	@ Brk.	Brooklyn (Erskine)	3	New York (Raschi)	2
Oct. 3	@ Brk.	Brooklyn (Loes)	7	New York (Ford)	3
Oct. 4	@ Brk.	New York (McDonald)	11	Brooklyn (Podres)	7
Oct. 5	@ N.Y.	New York (Reynolds)	4	Brooklyn (Labine)	3

MANAGERS: Casey Stengel, Yankees; Chuck Dressen, Dodgers

Yankees – Yogi Berra, Charlie Silvera, Gus Triandos, catchers; Whitey Ford, Tom Gorman, Steve Kraly, Bob Kuzava, Ed Lopat, Jim McDonald, Bill Miller, Vic Raschi, Allie Reynolds, Johnny Saln, Art Schallock, pitchers; Don Bollweg, Andy Carey, Jerry Coleman, Joe Collins, Billy Martin, Gil McDougald, Willie Miranda, Johnny Mize, Phil Rizzuto, infielders; Hank Bauer, Mickey Mantle, Irv Noren, Bill Renna, Gene Woodling, outfielders.

Dodgers – Roy Campanella, Rube Walker, catchers; Joe Black, Carl Erskine, Jim Hughes, Clem Labine, Billy Loes, Russ Meyer, Bob Milliken, Erv Palica, Johnny Podres, Preacher Roe, Ben Wade, pitchers; Wayne Belardi, Billy Cox, Jim Gilliam, Gil Hodges, Bobby Morgan, Pee Wee Reese, infielders; Bill Antonello, Carl Furillo, Jackie Robinson, George Shuba, Duke Snider, Don Thompson, Dick Williams, outfielders.

1954 – NEW YORK GIANTS N.L. (4) vs. CLEVELAND INDIANS A.L. (0)

(Polo Grounds)/(Cleveland Stadium)

Sept. 29	@ N.Y.	New York (Grissom)	5	Cleveland (Lemon)	2	(10 Innings)
Sept. 30	@ N.Y.	New York (Antonelli)	3	Cleveland (Wynn)	1	
Oct. 1	@ Clev.	New York (Gomez)	6	Cleveland (Garcia)	2	
Oct. 2	@ Clev.	New York (Liddle)	7	Cleveland (Lemon)	4	

MANAGERS: Leo Durocher, Giants; Al Lopez, Indians

Giants – Ray Katt, Wes Westrnm, catchers; Johnny Antonelli, Al Corwin, Paul Giel, Ruben Gomez, Marv Grissom, Jim Hearn, Alex Konikowskl, Don Liddle, Sal Maglie, Windy McCall, Hoyt Wilhelm, Al Worthington, pitchers; Joey Amalfitano, Foster Castleman, Alvin Dark, Billy Gardner, Bobby Hofman, Whitey Lockman, Hank Thompson, Davey Williams, infielders; Monte Irvin, Willie Mays, Don Mueller, Dusty Rhodes, Bill Taylor, outfielders.

Indians – Mickey Grasso, Jim Hegan, Hal Naragon, catchers; Bob Feller, Mike Garcia, Bob Hooper, Art Houtteman, Bob Lemon, Don Mossi, Ray Narleski, Hal Newhouser, Early Wynn, pitchers; Bobby Avila, Sam Dente, Bill Glynn, Hank Majeski, Rudy Regalado, Al Rosen, George Strickland, Vic Wertz, infielders; Larry Doby, Dale Mitchell, Dave Phllley, David Pope, Al Smith, Wally Westlake, outfielders.

1955 - BROOKLYN DODGERS N.L. (4) vs. NEW YORK YANKEES A.L. (3)

(Ebbets Field)/(Yankee Stadium)

Sept. 28	@ N.Y.	New York (Ford)	6	Brooklyn (Newcombe)	5
Sept. 29	@ N.Y.	New York (Byrne)	4	Brooklyn (Loes)	2
Sept. 30	@ Brk.	Brooklyn (Podres)	8	New York (Turley)	3
Oct. 1	@ Brk.	Brooklyn (Labine)	8	New York (Larsen)	5
Oct. 2	@ Brk.	Brooklyn (Craig)	5	New York (Grim)	3
Oct. 3	@ N.Y.	New York (Ford)	5	Brooklyn (Spooner)	1
Oct. 4	@ N.Y.	Brooklyn (Podres)	2	New York (Byrne)	0

MANAGERS: Walter Alston, Dodgers; Casey Stengel, Yankees

Dodgers — Roy Campanella, Dixie Howell, Rube Walker, catchers; Don Bessent, Roger Craig, Carl Erskine, Sandy Koufax, Clem Labine, Billy Loes, Russ Meyer, Don Newcombe, Johnny Podres, Ed Roebuck, Karl Spooner, pitchers; Jim Gilliam, Don Hoak, Gil Hodges, Frank Kellert, Jackie Robinson, Pee Wee Reese, Don Zimmer, infielders; Sandy Amoros, Carl Furillo, George Shuba, Duke Snider, outfielders.

Yankees — Yogi Berra, Charlie Silvera, catchers; Tommy Byrne, Rip Coleman, Whitey Ford, Bob Grim, Johnny Kucks, Don Larsen, Tom Morgan, Tom Sturdivant, Bob Turley, Bob Wiesler, pitchers; Andy Carey, Tommy Carroll, Jerry Coleman, Joe Collins, Frank Leja, Gil McDougald, Billy Martin, Phil Rizzuto, Eddie Robinson, Bill Skowron, infielders; Hank Bauer, Bob Cerv, Elston Howard, Mickey Mantle, Irv Noren, outfielders.

1956 - NEW YORK YANKEES A.L. (4) vs. BROOKLYN DODGERS N.L. (3)

(Yankee Stadium)/(Ebbets Field)

Oct. 3	@ Brk.	Brooklyn (Maglie)	6	New York (Ford)	3	
Oct. 5	@ Brk.	Brooklyn (Bessent)	13	New York (Morgan)	8	
Oct. 6	@ N.Y.	New York (Ford)	5	Brooklyn (Craig)	3	
Oct. 7	@ N.Y.	New York (Sturdivant)	6	Brooklyn (Erskine)	2	
Oct. 8	@ N.Y.	New York (Larsen)	2	Brooklyn (Maglie)	0	
Oct. 9	@ Brk.	Brooklyn (Labine)	1	New York (Turley)	0	(10 Innings)
Oct. 10	@ Brk.	New York (Kucks)	9	Brooklyn (Newcombe)	0	

POSTPONED: (Rain) Oct. 4

MANAGERS: Casey Stengel, Yankees; Walter Alston, Dodgers

Yankees — Yogi Berra, Charlie Silvera, catchers; Tommy Byrne, Rip Coleman, Whitey Ford, Bob Grim, Johnny Kucks, Don Larsen, Mickey McDermott, Tom Morgan, Tom Sturdivant, Bob Turley, pitchers; Andy Carey, Tommy Carroll, Jerry Coleman, Joe Collins, Billy Hunter, Billy Martin, Gil McDougald, Bill Skowron, infielders; Hank Bauer, Bob Cerv, Elston Howard, Mickey Mantle, Norm Siebern, Enos Slaughter, Ted Wilson, outfielders.

Dodgers — Roy Campanella, Dixie Howell, Rube Walker, catchers; Don Bessent, Roger Craig, Don Drysdale, Carl Erskine, Sandy Koufax, Clem Labine, Ken Lehman, Sal Maglie, Don Newcombe, Ed Roebuck, pitchers; Chico Fernandez, Jim Gilliam, Gil Hodges, Randy Jackson, Charlie Neal, Pee Wee Reese, Jackie Robinson, infielders; Sandy Amoros, Gino Cimoli, Carl Furillo, Dale Mitchell, Duke Snider, outfielders.

1957 - MILWAUKEE BRAVES N.L. (4) vs. NEW YORK YANKEES A.L. (3)

(County Stadium)/(Yankee Stadium)

Oct. 2	@ N.Y.	New York (Ford)	3	Milwaukee (Spahn)	1	
Oct. 3	@ N.Y.	Milwaukee (Burdette)	4	New York (Shantz)	2	
Oct. 5	@ Mil.	New York (Larsen)	12	Milwaukee (Buhl)	3	
Oct. 6	@ Mil.	Milwaukee (Spahn)	7	New York (Grim)	5	(10 Innings)
Oct. 7	@ Mil.	Milwaukee (Burdette)	1	New York (Ford)	0	
Oct. 9	@ N.Y.	New York (Turley)	3	Milwaukee (Johnson)	2	
Oct. 10	@ N.Y.	Milwaukee (Burdette)	5	New York (Larsen)	0	

MANAGERS: Fred Haney, Braves; Casey Stengel, Yankees

Braves — Del Crandall, Del Rice, Carl Sawatski, catchers; Bob Buhl, Lew Burdette, Gene Conley, Ernie Johnson, Dave Jolly, Don McMahon, Taylor Phillips, Juan Pizarro, Warren Spahn, Bob Trowbridge, pitchers; Joe Adcock, Nippy Jones, Johnny Logan, Felix Mantilla, Eddie Mathews, Mel Roach, Red Schoendienst, Frank Torre, infielders; Hank Aaron, Wes Covington, John DeMerit, Bob Hazle, Andy Pafko, outfielders.

Yankees — Yogi Berra, Darrell Johnson, catchers; Tommy Byrne, Al Cicotte, Art Ditmar, Whitey Ford, Bob Grim, Johnny Kucks, Don Larsen, Bobby Shantz, Tom Sturdivant, Bob Turley, pitchers; Andy Carey, Jerry Coleman, Joe Collins, Tony Kubek, Jerry Lumpe, Gil McDougald, Bobby Richardson, Bill Skowron, infielders; Hank Bauer, Elston Howard, Mickey Mantle, Harry Simpson, Enos Slaughter, outfielders.

1958 - NEW YORK YANKEES A.L. (4) vs. MILWAUKEE BRAVES N.L. (3)

(Yankee Stadium)/(County Stadium)

Oct. 1	@ Mil.	Milwaukee (Spahn)	4	New York (Duren)	3	(10 Innings)
Oct. 2	@ Mil.	Milwaukee (Burdette)	13	New York (Turley)	5	
Oct. 4	@ N.Y.	New York (Larsen)	4	Milwaukee (Rush)	0	
Oct. 5	@ N.Y.	Milwaukee (Spahn)	3	New York (Ford)	0	
Oct. 6	@ N.Y.	New York (Turley)	7	Milwaukee (Burdette)	0	
Oct. 8	@ Mil.	New York (Duren)	4	Milwaukee (Spahn)	3	(10 Innings)
Oct. 9	@ Mil.	New York (Turley)	6	Milwaukee (Burdette)	2	

MANAGERS: Casey Stengel, Yankees; Fred Haney, Braves

Yankees – Yogi Berra, Elston Howard, Darrell Johnson, catchers; Murry Dickson, Art Ditmar, Ryne Duren, Whitey Ford, Johnny Kucks, Don Larsen, Duke Maas, Zack Monroe, Bobby Shantz, Tom Sturdivant, Bob Turley, pitchers; Andy Carey, Tony Kubek, Jerry Lumpe, Gil Gil McDougald, Bobby Richardson, Bill Skowron, Marv Throneberry, infielders; Hank Bauer, Mickey Mantle, Norm Siebern, Enos Slaughter, outfielders.

Braves – Del Crandall, Del Rice, catchers; Bob Buhl, Lew Burdette, Gene Conley, Ernie Johnson, Don McMahon, Juan Pizarro, Humberto Robinson, Bob Rush, Warren Spahn, Bob Trowbridge, Carl Willey, pitchers; Joe Adcock, Harry Hanebrink, Johnny Logan, Felix Mantilla, Eddie Mathews, Red Schoendienst, Frank Torre, Casey Wise, infielders; Hank Aaron, Bill Bruton, Wes Covington, Andy Pafko, outfielders.

1959 - LOS ANGELES DODGERS N.L. (4) vs. CHICAGO WHITE SOX A.L. (2)

(Memorial Coliseum)/(Comiskey Park)

Oct. 1	@ Chi.	Chicago (Wynn)	11	Los Angeles (Craig)	0
Oct. 2	@ Chi.	Los Angeles (Podres)	4	Chicago (Shaw)	3
Oct. 4	@ LA.	Los Angeles (Drysdale)	3	Chicago (Donovan)	1
Oct. 5	@ LA.	Los Angeles (Sherry)	5	Chicago (Staley)	4
Oct. 6	@ LA.	Chicago (Shaw)	1	Los Angeles (Koufax)	0
Oct. 8	@ Chi.	Los Angeles (Sherry)	9	Chicago (Wynn)	3

MANAGERS: Walter Alston, Dodgers; Al Lopez, White Sox

Dodgers – Joe Pignatano, Johnny Roseboro, catchers; Chuck Churn, Roger Craig, Don Drysdale, Johnny Klippstein, Sandy Koufax, Clem Labine, Danny McDevitt, Johnny Podres, Larry Sherry, Stan Williams, pitchers; Jim Gilliam, Gil Hodges, Charlie Neal, Maury Wills, Don Zimmer, infielders; Don Demeter, Chuck Essegian, Ron Fairly, Carl Furillo, Norm Larker, Wally Moon, Rip Repulski, Duke Snider, outfielders.

White Sox – Earl Battey, Sherm Lollar, Johnny Romano, catchers; Rudy Arias, Dick Donovan, Barry Latman, Turk Lown, Ken McBride, Ray Moore, Billy Pierce, Bob Shaw, Gerry Staley, Early Wynn, pitchers; Luis Aparicio, Norm Cash, Sammy Esposito, Nellie Fox, Billy Goodman, Ted Kluszewskl, Bubba Phillips, Earl Torgeson, infielders; Jim Landis, Jim McAnany, Jim Rivera, Al Smith, outfielders.

1960 - PITTSBURGH PIRATES N.L. (4) vs. NEW YORK YANKEES A.L. (3)

(Forbes Field)/(Yankee Stadium)

Oct. 5	@ Pitt.	Pittsburgh (Law)	6	New York (Ditmar)	4
Oct. 6	@ Pitt.	New York (Turley)	16	Pittsburgh (Friend)	3
Oct. 8	@ N.Y.	New York (Ford)	10	Pittsburgh (Mizell)	0
Oct. 9	@ N.Y.	Pittsburgh (Law)	3	New York (Terry)	2
Oct. 10	@ N.Y.	Pittsburgh (Haddix)	5	New York (Ditmar)	2
Oct. 12	@ Pitt.	New York (Ford)	12	Pittsburgh (Friend)	0
Oct. 13	@ Pitt.	Pittsburgh (Haddix)	10	New York (Terry)	9

MANAGERS: Danny Murtaugh, Pirates; Casey Stengel, Yankees

Pirates – Smoky Burgess, Bob Oldis, Hal W. Smith, catchers; Tom Cheney, ElRoy Face, Bob Friend, Joe Gibbon, Fred Green, Harvey Haddix, Clem Labine, Vern Law, Vinegar Bend Mizell, George Witt, pitchers; Gene Baker, Dick Groat, Don Hoak, Bill Mazeroski, Rocky Nelson, Dick Schofield, Dick Stuart, infielders; Joe Christopher, Gino Cimoli, Roberto Clemente, Bob Skinner, Bill Virdon, outfielders.

Yankees – Yogi Berra, Johnny Blanchard, Elston Howard, catchers; Luis Arroyo, Jim Coates, Art Ditmar, Ryne Duren, Whitey Ford, Eli Grba, Duke Maas, Bobby Shantz, Bill Stafford, Ralph Terry, Bob Turley, pitchers; Clete Boyer, Joe DeMaestri, Tony Kubek, Dale Long, Gil McDougald, Bobby Richardson, Bill Skowron, infielders; Bob Cerv, Hector Lopez, Mickey Mantle, Roger Maris, outfielders.

1961 - NEW YORK YANKEES A.L. (4) vs. CINCINNATI REDS N.L. (1)
(Yankee Stadium)/(Crosley Field)

Oct. 4	@ N.Y.	New York (Ford)	2	Cincinnati (O'Toole)	0
Oct. 5	@ N.Y.	Cincinnati (Jay)	6	New York (Terry)	2
Oct. 7	@ Cin.	New York (Arroyo)	3	Cincinnati (Purkey)	2
Oct. 8	@ Cin.	New York (Ford)	7	Cincinnati (O'Toole)	0
Oct. 9	@ Cin.	New York (Daley)	13	Cincinnati (Jay)	5

MANAGERS: Ralph Houk, Yankees; Fred Hutchinson, Reds

Yankees — Johnny Blanchard, Elston Howard, catchers; Luis Arroyo, Tex Clevenger, Jim Coates, Bud Daley, Al Downing, Whitey Ford, Hal Reniff, Rollie Sheldon, Bill Stafford, Ralph Terry, Bob Turley, pitchers; Clete Boyer, Joe DeMaestri, Billy Gardner, Bob Hale, Tony Kubek, Bobby Richardson, Bill Skowron, infielders; Yogi Berra, Hector Lopez, Mickey Mantle, Roger Maris, Jack Reed, outfielders.

Reds — Johnny Edwards, Darrell Johnson, Jerry Zimmerman, catchers; Jim Brosnan, Bill Henry, Jay Hook, Ken Hunt, Joey Jay, Ken Johnson, Jim Maloney, Jim O'Toole, Bob Purkey, pitchers; Don Blasingame, Leo Cardenas, Elio Chacon, Gordy Coleman, Gene Freese, Dick Gernert, Eddie Kasko, infielders; Gus Bell, Jerry Lynch, Vada Pinson, Wally Post, Frank Robinson, outfielders.

1962 - NEW YORK YANKEES A.L. (4) vs. SAN FRANCISCO GIANTS N.L. (3)
(Yankee Stadium)/(Candlestick Park)

Oct. 4	@ S.F.	New York (Ford)	6	San Francisco (O'Dell)	2
Oct. 5	@ S.F.	San Francisco (Sanford)	2	New York (Terry)	0
Oct. 7	@ N.Y.	New York (Stafford)	3	San Francisco (Pierce)	2
Oct. 8	@ N.Y.	San Francisco (Larsen)	7	New York (Coates)	3
Oct. 10	@ N.Y.	New York (Terry)	5	San Francisco (Sanford)	3
Oct. 15	@ S.F.	San Francisco (Pierce)	5	New York (Ford)	2
Oct. 16	@ S.F.	New York (Terry)	1	San Francisco (Sanford)	0

POSTPONED: *(Rain) Oct. 9,12,13,14*

MANAGERS: Ralph Houk, Yankees; Alvin Dark, Giants

Yankees — Johnny Blanchard, Elston Howard, catchers; Luis Arroyo, Jim Bouton, Marshall Bridges, Tex Clevenger, Jim Coates, Bud Daley, Whitey Ford, Rollie Sheldon, Bill Stafford, Ralph Terry, Bob Turley, pitchers; Clete Boyer, Tony Kubek, Phil Linz, Dale Long, Bobby Richardson, Bill Skowron, infielders; Yogi Berra, Hector Lopez, Mickey Mantle, Roger Maris, Jack Reed, Tom Tresh, outfielders.

Giants — Ed Bailey, Tom Haller, John Orsino, catchers; Bobby Bolin, Jim Duffalo, Bob Garibaldi, Don Larsen, Juan Marichal, Mike McCormick, Stu Miller, Billy O'Dell, Billy Pierce, Jack Sanford, pitchers; Ernie Bowman, Orlando Cepeda, Jim Davenport, Chuck Hiller, Willie McCovey, Jose Pagan, infielders; Felipe Alou, Matty Alou, Carl Boles, Harvey Kuenn, Willie Mays, Bob Nieman, outfielders.

1963 - LOS ANGELES DODGERS N.L. (4) vs. NEW YORK YANKEES A.L. (0)
(Dodger Stadium)/(Yankee Stadium)

Oct. 2	@ N.Y.	Los Angeles (Koufax)	5	New York (Ford)	2
Oct. 3	@ N.Y.	Los Angeles (Podres)	4	New York (Downing)	1
Oct. 5	@ L.A.	Los Angeles (Drysdale)	1	New York (Bouton)	0
Oct. 6	@ L.A.	Los Angeles (Koufax)	2	New York (Ford)	1

MANAGERS: Walter Alston, Dodgers; Ralph Houk, Yankees

Dodgers — Doug Camilli, Johnny Roseboro, catchers; Dick Calmus, Don Drysdale, Sandy Koufax, Bob Miller, Ron Perranoski, Johnny Podres, Pete Richert, Ken Rowe, Larry Sherry, pitchers; Marv Breeding, Ron Fairly, Jim Gilliam, Ken McMullen, Bill Skowron, Dick Tracewski, Maury Wills, infielders; Tommy Davis, Willie Davis, Al Ferrara, Frank Howard, Wally Moon, Lee Walls, outfielders.

Yankees — Yogi Berra, Elston Howard, catchers; Jim Bouton, Marshall Bridges, Al Downing, Whitey Ford, Steve Hamilton, Bill Kunkel, Tom Metcalf, Hal Reniff, Bill Stafford, Ralph Terry, Stan Williams, pitchers; Clete Boyer, Harry Bright, Tony Kubek, Phil Linz, Joe Pepitone, Bobby Richardson, infielders; Johnny Blanchard, Hector Lopez, Mickey Mantle, Roger Maris, Jack Reed, Tom Tresh, outfielders.

1964 - ST. LOUIS CARDINALS N.L. (4) vs. NEW YORK YANKEES A.L. (3)

(Busch Stadium)/(Yankee Stadium)

Oct. 7	@ St.L.	St. Louis (Sadecki)	9	New York (Ford)	5	
Oct. 8	@ St.L.	New York (Stottlemyre)	8	St. Louis (Gibson)	3	
Oct. 10	@ N.Y.	New York (Bouton)	2	St. Louis (Schultz)	1	
Oct. 11	@ N.Y.	St. Louis (Craig)	4	New York (Downing)	3	
Oct. 12	@ N.Y.	St. Louis (Gibson)	5	New York (Mikkelsen)	2	(10 Innings)
Oct. 14	@ St.L.	New York (Bouton)	8	St. Louis (Simmons)	3	
Oct. 15	@ St.L.	St. Louis (Gibson)	7	New York (Stottlemyre)	5	

MANAGERS: Johnny Keane, Cardinals; Yogi Berra, Yankees

Cardinals — Tim McCarver. Bob Uecker, catchers; Roger Craig, Mike Cuellar, Bob Gibson, Bob Humphreys, Gordie Richardson, Ray Sadecki, Barney Schultz, Curt Simmons, Ron Taylor, Ray Washburn, pitchers; Ken Boyer. Jerry Buchek, Dick Groat, Julian Javier, Dal Maxvill, Ed Spiezio, Bill White, infielders; Lou Brock, Curt Flood, Charlie James, Mike Shannon, Bob Skinner, Carl Warwick, outfielders.

Yankees — Johnny Blanchard, Elston Howard, catchers: Jim Bouton, Al Downing, Whitey Ford, Steve Hamilton, Pete Mikkelsen, Hal Reniff, Rollie Sheldon, Bill Stafford, Mel Stottlemyre, Ralph Terry, Stan Williams, pitchers. Clete Boyer, Pedro Gonzalez, Mike Hegan, Phil Linz, Joe Pepitone, Bobby Richardson, Chet Trail, infielders: Hector Lopez, Mickey Mantle, Roger Maris, Archie Moore, Tom Tresh, outfielders.

1965 - LOS ANGELES DODGERS N.L. (4) vs. MINNESOTA TWINS A.L. (3)

(Dodger Stadium)/(Metropolitan Stadium)

Oct. 6	@ Minn.	Minnesota (Grant)	8	Los Angeles (Drysdale)	2
Oct. 7	@ Minn.	Minnesota (Kaat)	5	Los Angeles (Koufax)	1
Oct. 9	@ L.A.	Los Angeles (Osteen)	4	Minnesota (Pascual)	0
Oct. 10	@ L.A.	Los Angeles (Drysdale)	7	Minnesota (Grant)	2
Oct. 11	@ L.A.	Los Angeles (Koufax)	7	Minnesota (Kaat)	0
Oct. 13	@ Minn.	Minnesota (Grant)	5	Los Angeles (Osteen)	1
Oct. 14	@ Minn.	Los Angeles (Koufax)	2	Minnesota (Kaat)	0

MANAGERS: Walter Alston, Dodgers; Sam Mele, Twins

Dodgers — Johnny Roseboro, Jeff Torborg, catchers: Jim Brewer, Don Drysdale, Mike Kekich, Sandy Koufax, Bob Miller, Claude Osteen, Ron Perranoski, Johnny Podres, John Purdin, Howie Reed, Nick Willhite, pitchers; Ron Fairly, Jim Gilliam, John Kennedy, Jim Lefebvre, Don LeJohn, Wes Parker, Dick Tracewski, Maury Wills, infielders; Willie Crawford, Willie Davis, Lou Johnson, Wally Moon, outfielders.

Twins — Earl Battey, John Sevcik, Jerry Zimmerman, catchers: Dave Boswell, Mudcat Grant, Jim Kaat, Johnny Klippstein, Jim Merritt, Mel Nelson, Camilo Pascual, Jim Perry, Bill Pleis, Dick Stigman, Al Worthington, pitchers; Harmon Killebrew, Jerry Kindall, Don Mincher, Frank Quilici, Rich Rollins, Zoilo Versalles, infielders: Bob Allison, Jimmie Hall, Joe Nossek, Tony Oliva, Sandy Valdespino, outfielders.

1966 - BALTIMORE ORIOLES A.L. (4) vs. LOS ANGELES DODGERS N.L. (0)

(Memorial Stadium)/(Dodger Stadium)

Oct. 5	@ L.A.	Baltimore (Drabowsky)	5	Los Angeles (Drysdale)	2
Oct. 6	@ L.A.	Baltimore (Palmer)	6	Los Angeles (Koufax)	0
Oct. 8	@ Balt.	Baltimore (Bunker)	1	Los Angeles (Osteen)	0
Oct. 9	@ Balt.	Baltimore (McNally)	1	Los Angeles (Drysdale)	0

MANAGERS: Hank Bauer, Orioles; Walter Alston, Dodgers

Orioles — Andy Etchebarren, Larry Haney, Vic Roznovsky, catchers; Frank Bertaina, Gene Brabender, Wally Bunker, Moe Drabowsky, Eddie Fisher, Dick Hall, Dave McNally, John Miller, Stu Miller, Jim Palmer, Eddie Watt, pitchers; Luis Aparicio, Woody Held, Dave Johnson, Bob Johnson, Boog Powell, Brooks Robinson, Infielders; Paul Blair, Curt Blefary, Sam Bowens, Frank Robinson, Russ Snyder, outfielders.

Dodgers — Johnny Roseboro, Jeff Torborg, catchers; Jim Brewer, Don Drysdale, Sandy Koufax, Bob Miller, Joe Moeller, Claude Osteen, Ron Perranoski, Phil Regan, Don Sutton, pitchers; Jim Gilliam, John Kennedy, Jim Lefebvre, Nate Oliver, Wes Parker, Dick Stuart, Maury Wills, infielders; Jim Barbieri, Wes Covington, Tommy Davis, Willie Davis, Ron Fairly, Al Ferrara, Lou Johnson, outfielders.

1967 - ST. LOUIS CARDINALS N.L. (4) vs. BOSTON RED SOX A.L. (3)
(Busch Memorial Stadium)/(Fenway Park)

Oct. 4	@ Bos.	St. Louis (Gibson)	2	Boston (Santiago)	1
Oct. 5	@ Bos.	Boston (Lonborg)	5	St. Louis (Hughes)	0
Oct. 7	@ St.L.	St. Louis (Briles)	5	Boston (Bell)	2
Oct. 8	@ St.L.	St. Louis (Gibson)	6	Boston (Santiago)	0
Oct. 9	@ St.L.	Boston (Lonborg)	3	St. Louis (Carlton)	1
Oct. 11	@ Bos.	Boston (Wyatt)	8	St. Louis (Lamabe)	4
Oct. 12	@ Bos.	St. Louis (Gibson)	7	Boston (Lonborg)	2

MANAGERS: Red Schoendienst, Cardinals; Dick Williams, Red Sox

Cardinals — Tim McCarver, Dave Ricketts, catchers; Nellie Briles, Steve Carlton, Bob Gibson, Joe Hoerner, Dick Hughes, Al Jackson, Larry Jaster, Jack Lamabe, Ray Washburn, Ron Willis, Hal Woodeshick, pitchers; Eddie Bressoud, Orlando Cepeda, Phil Gagliano, Julian Javier, Dal Maxvill, Mike Shannon, Ed Spiezio, infielders; Lou Brock, Curt Flood, Alex Johnson, Roger Maris, Bobby Tolan, outfielders.
Red Sox — Russ Gibson, Elston Howard, Mike Ryan, catchers; Gary Bell, Ken Brett, Jim Lonborg, Dave Morehead, Dan Osinski, Jose Santiago, Lee Stange, Jerry Stephenson, Gary Waslewski, John Wyatt, pitchers; Jerry Adair, Mike Andrews, Joe Foy, Dalton Jones, Rico Petrocelli, George Scott, infielders; Ken Harrelson, Norm Siebern, Reggie Smith, Jose Tartabull, George Thomas, Carl Yastrzemski, outfielders.

1968 - DETROIT TIGERS A.L. (4) vs. ST. LOUIS CARDINALS N.L. (3)
(Tiger Stadium)/(Busch Memorial Stadium)

Oct. 2	@ St.L.	St. Louis (Gibson)	4	Detroit (McLain)	0
Oct. 3	@ St.L.	Detroit (Lolich)	8	St. Louis (Briles)	1
Oct. 5	@ Det.	St. Louis (Washburn)	7	Detroit (Wilson)	3
Oct. 6	@ Det.	St. Louis (Gibson)	10	Detroit (McLain)	1
Oct. 7	@ Det.	Detroit (Lolich)	5	St. Louis (Hoerner)	3
Oct. 9	@ St.L.	Detroit (McLain)	13	St. Louis (Washburn)	1
Oct. 10	@ St.L.	Detroit (Lolich)	4	St. Louis (Gibson)	1

MANAGERS: Mayo Smith, Tigers; Red Schoendienst, Cardinals

Tigers — Bill Freehan, Jim Price, catchers; Pat Dobson, John Hiller, Fred Lasher, Mickey Lolich, Dennis McLain, Don McMahon, Daryl Patterson, Joe Sparma, Jon Warden, Earl Wilson, pitchers; Norm Cash, Tommy Matchick, Eddie Mathews, Dick McAuliffe, Ray Oyler, Mickey Stanley, Dick Tracewski, Don Wert, infielders; Gates Brown, Wayne Comer, Willie Horton, Al Kaline, Jim Northrup, outfielders.
Cardinals — Johnny Edwards, Tim McCarver, Dave Ricketts, catchers; Nellie Briles, Steve Carlton, Bob Gibson, Wayne Granger, Joe Hoerner, Dick Hughes, Larry Jaster, Mel Nelson, Ray Washburn, Ron Willis, pitchers; Orlando Cepeda, Phil Gagliano, Julian Javier, Dall Maxvill, Dick Schofield, Mike Shannon, Ed Spiezio, infielders; Lou Brock, Ron Davis, Curt Flood, Roger Maris, Bobby Tolan, outfielders.

1969 - NEW YORK METS N.L. (4) vs. BALTIMORE ORIOLES A.L. (1)
(Shea Stadium)/(Memorial Stadium)

Oct. 11	@ Balt.	Baltimore (Cuellar)	4	New York (Seaver)	1	
Oct. 12	@ Balt.	New York (Koosman)	2	Baltimore (McNally)	1	
Oct. 14	@ N.Y.	New York (Gentry)	5	Baltimore (Palmer)	0	
Oct. 15	@ N.Y.	New York (Seaver)	2	Baltimore (Hall)	1	(10 Innings)
Oct. 16	@ N.Y.	New York (Koosman)	5	Baltimore (Watt)	3	

MANAGERS: Gil Hodges, Mets; Earl Weaver, Orioles

Mets — Duffy Dyer, Jerry Grote, J.C. Martin, catchers; Don Cardwell, Jack DiLauro, Gary Gentry, Cal Koonce, Jerry Koosman, Jim McAndrew, Tug McGraw, Nolan Ryan, Tom Seaver, Ron Taylor, pitchers; Ken Boswell, Ed Charles, Donn Clendenon, Wayne Garrett, Buddy Harrelson, Ed Kranepool, Al Weis, infielders; Tommie Agee, Rod Gaspar, Cleon Jones, Art Shamsky, Ron Swoboda, outfielders.
Orioles — Clay Dalrymple, Andy Etchebarren, Elrod Hendricks, catchers; Mike Cuellar, Dick Hall, Jim Hardin, Dave Leonhard, Marcelino Lopez, Dave McNally, Jim Palmer, Tom Phoebus, Pete Richert, Eddie Watt, pitchers; Mark Belanger, Bobby Floyd, Dave Johnson, Boog Powell, Brooks Robinson, Chico Salmon, infielders; Paul Blair, Don Buford, Dave May, Curt Motton, Merv Rettenmund, Frank Robinson, outfielders.

1970 - BALTIMORE ORIOLES A.L. (4) vs. CINCINNATI REDS N.L. (1)
(Memorial Stadium)/(Riverfront Stadium)

Oct. 10	@ Cin.	Baltimore (Palmer)	4	Cincinnati (Nolan)	3
Oct. 11	@ Cin.	Baltimore (Phoebus)	6	Cincinnati (Wilcox)	5
Oct. 13	@ Balt.	Baltimore (McNally)	9	Cincinnati (Cloninger)	3
Oct. 14	@ Balt.	Cincinnati (Carroll)	6	Baltimore (Watt)	5
Oct. 15	@ Balt.	Baltimore (Cuellar)	9	Cincinnati (Merritt)	3

MANAGERS: Earl Weaver, Orioles; Sparky Anderson, Reds

Orioles — Andy Etchebarren, Elrod Hendricks, catchers; Mike Cuellar, Moe Drabowsky, Dick Hall, Jim Hardin, Dave Leonhard, Marcelino Lopez, Dave McNally, Jim Palmer, Tom Phoebus, Pete Richert, Eddie Watt, pitchers; Mark Belanger, Bobby Grich, Dave Johnson, Boog Powell, Brooks Robinson, Chico Salmon, infielders; Paul Blair, Don Buford, Terry Crowley, Curt Motton, Merv Rettenmund, Frank Robinson, outfielders.

Reds — Johnny Bench, Pat Corrales, catchers; Mel Behney, Clay Carroll, Tony Cloninger, Wayne Granger, Don Gullett, Jim McGlothlin, Jim Merritt, Gary Nolan, Ray Washburn, Milt Wilcox, pitchers; Darrell Chaney, Dave Concepcion, Tommy Helms, Lee May, Tony Perez, Jim Stewart, Woody Woodward, infielders; Angel Bravo, Bernie Carbo, Ty Cline, Hal McRae, Pete Rose, Bobby Tolan, outfielders.

1971 - PITTSBURGH PIRATES N.L. (4) vs. BALTIMORE ORIOLES A.L. (3)
(Three Rivers Stadium)/(Memorial Stadium)

Oct. 9	@ Balt.	Baltimore (McNally)	5	Pittsburgh (Ellis)	3	
Oct. 11	@ Balt.	Baltimore (Palmer)	11	Pittsburgh (Johnson)	3	
Oct. 12	@ Pitt.	Pittsburgh (Blass)	5	Baltimore (Cuellar)	1	
Oct. 13n	@ Pitt.	Pittsburgh (Kison)	4	Baltimore (Watt)	3	
Oct. 14	@ Pitt.	Pittsburgh (Briles)	4	Baltimore (McNally)	0	
Oct. 16	@ Balt.	Baltimore (McNally)	3	Pittsburgh (Miller)	2	(10 Innings)
Oct. 17	@ Balt.	Pittsburgh (Blass)	2	Baltimore (Cuellar)	1	

POSTPONED: (Rain) Oct. 10

MANAGERS: Danny Murtaugh, Pirates; Earl Weaver, Orioles

Pirates — Milt May, Charlie Sands, Manny Sanguillen, catchers; Steve Blass, Nellie Briles, Dock Ellis, Dave Giusti, Bob Johnson, Bruce Kison, Bob Miller, Bob Moose, Bob Veale, Luke Walker, pitchers; Gene Alley, Dave Cash, Richie Hebner, Jackie Hernandez, Bill Mazeroski, Jose Pagan, Bob Robertson, infielders; Roberto Clemente, Gene Clines, Vic Davalillo, Al Oliver, Willie Stargell, outfielders.

Orioles — Clay Dalrymple, Andy Etchebarren, Elrod Hendricks, catchers; Mike Cuellar, Pat Dobson, Tom Dukes, Dick Hall, Grant Jackson, Dave Leonhard, Dave McNally, Jim Palmer, Pete Richert, Eddie Watt, pitchers; Mark Belanger, Jerry DaVanon, Dave Johnson, Boog Powell, Brooks Robinson, Chico Salmon, infielders; Paul Blair, Don Buford, Curt Motton, Merv Rettenmund, Frank Robinson, Tom Shopay, outfielders.

1972 - OAKLAND ATHLETICS A.L. (4) vs. CINCINNATI REDS N.L. (3)
(Oakland Coliseum)/(Riverfront Stadium)

Oct. 14	@ Cin.	Oakland (Holtzman)	3	Cincinnati (Nolan)	2
Oct. 15	@ Cin.	Oakland (Hunter)	2	Cincinnati (Grimsley)	1
Oct. 18n	@ Oak.	Cincinnati (Billingham)	1	Oakland (Odom)	0
Oct. 19n	@ Oak.	Oakland (Fingers)	3	Cincinnati (Carroll)	2
Oct. 20	@ Oak.	Cincinnati (Grimsley)	5	Oakland (Fingers)	4
Oct. 21	@ Cin.	Cincinnati (Grimsley)	8	Oakland (Blue)	1
Oct. 22	@ Cin.	Oakland (Hunter)	3	Cincinnati (Borbon, Sr.)	2

POSTPONED: (Rain) Oct. 17

MANAGERS: Dick Williams, Athletics; Sparky Anderson, Reds

Athletics — Dave Duncan, Gene Tenace, catchers; Vida Blue, Rollie Fingers, Dave Hamilton, Ken Holtzman, Joel Horlen, Catfish Hunter, Bob Locker, Blue Moon Odom, pitchers; Sal Bando, Bert Campaneris, Tim Cullen, Mike Epstein, Dick Green, Mike Hegan, Ted Kubiak, Gonzalo Marquez, Dal Maxvill, Don Mincher, infielders: Matty Alou, George Hendrick, Allan Lewis, Angel Mangual, Joe Rudi, outfielders.

Reds — Johnny Bench, Bill Plummer, catchers; Jack Billingham, Pedro Borbon, Sr., Clay Carroll, Ross Grimsley, Don Gullett, Tom Hall, Jim McGlothlin, Gary Nolan, Wayne Simpson, Ed Sprague, pitchers; Darrell Chaney, Dave Concepcion, Julian Javier, Denis Menke, Joe Morgan, Tony Perez, infielders; George Foster, Cesar Geronimo, Joe Hague, Hal McRae, Pete Rose, Bobby Tolan, Ted Uhlaender, outfielders.

1973 - OAKLAND ATHLETICS A.L. (4) vs. NEW YORK METS N.L. (3)

(Oakland Coliseum)/(Shea Stadium)

Oct. 13	@ Oak.	Oakland (Holtzman)	2	New York (Matlack)	1	
Oct. 14	@ Oak.	New York (McGraw)	10	Oakland (Fingers)	7	(12 Innings)
Oct. 16n	@ N.Y.	Oakland (Lindblad)	3	New York (Parker)	2	(11 Innings)
Oct. 17n	@ N.Y.	New York (Matlack)	6	Oakland (Holtzman)	1	
Oct. 18n	@ N.Y.	New York (Koosman)	2	Oakland (Blue)	0	
Oct. 20	@ Oak.	Oakland (Hunter)	3	New York (Seaver)	1	
Oct. 21	@ Oak.	Oakland (Holtzman)	5	New York (Matlack)	2	

MANAGERS: Dick Williams, Athletics; Yogi Berra, Mets

Athletics — Ray Fosse, catcher; Vida Blue, Rollie Fingers, Ken Holtzman, Catfish Hunter, Darold Knowles, Paul
Lindblad, Blue Moon Odom, Horacio Pina, pitchers; Mike Andrews, Sal Bando, Pat Bourque, Bert Campaneris,
Vic Davalillo, Dick Green, Deron Johnson, Ted Kubiak, Gene Tenace infielders; Jesus Alou, Billy Conigliaro,
Reggie Jackson, Allan Lewis, Angel Mangual, Joe Rudi, outfielders.

Mets — Duffy Dyer, Jerry Grote, Ron Hodges, catchers; Buzz Capra, Jerry Koosman, Jon Matlack, Jim McAndrew, Tug
McGraw, Harry Parker, Ray Sadecki, Tom Seaver, George Stone, pitchers; Jim Beauchamp, Ken Boswell, Wayne
Garrett, Bud Harrelson, Ed Kranepool, Teddy Martinez, Felix Millan, infielders; Don Hahn, Cleon Jones, Willie
Mays, John Milner, Rusty Staub, George Theodore, outfielders.

1974 - OAKLAND ATHLETICS A.L. (4) vs. LOS ANGELES DODGERSN.L. (1)

(Oakland Coliseum)/(Dodger Stadium)

Oct. 12	@ L.A.	Oakland (Fingers)	3	Los Angeles (Messersmith)	2
Oct. 13	@ L.A.	Los Angeles (Sutton)	3	Oakland (Blue)	2
Oct. 15n	@ Oak.	Oakland (Hunter)	3	Los Angeles (Downing)	2
Oct. 16n	@ Oak.	Oakland (Holtzman)	5	Los Angeles (Messersmith)	2
Oct. 17n	@ Oak.	Oakland (Odom)	3	Los Angeles (Marshall)	2

MANAGERS: Alvin Dark, Athletics; Walter Alston, Dodgers

Athletics — Ray Fosse, Larry Haney, catchers; Glenn Abbott, Vida Blue, Rollie Fingers, Dave Hamilton, Ken
Holtzman, Catfish Hunter, Darold Knowles, Paul Lindblad, Blue Moon Odom, pitchers; Sal Bando, Bert
Campaneris, Dick Green, Jim Holt, Ted Kubiak, Dal Maxvill, Gene Tenace, infielders; Jesus Alou, Reggie
Jackson, Angel Mangual, Billy North, Joe Rudi, Claudell Washington, Herb Washington, outfielders.

Dodgers — Steve Yeager, catcher; Jim Brewer, Al Downing, Charlie Hough, Mike Marshall, Andy Messersmith, Doug
Rau, Eddie Solomon, Don Sutton, Geoff Zahn, pitchers; Rick Auerbach, Ron Cey, Steve
Garvey, Gail Hopkins, Lee Lacy, Davey Lopes, Ken McMullen, Bill Russell, infielders; Bill Buckner, Willie
Crawford, Joe Ferguson, Von Joshua, Manny Mota, Tom Paciorek, Jimmy Wynn, outfielders.

1975 - CINCINNATI REDS N.L. (4) vs. BOSTON RED SOX A.L. (3)

(Riverfront Stadium)/(Fenway Park)

Oct. 11	@ Bos.	Boston (Tiant)	6	Cincinnati (Gullett)	0	
Oct. 12	@ Bos.	Cincinnati (Eastwick)	3	Boston (Drago)	2	
Oct. 14n	@ Cin.	Cincinnati (Eastwick)	6	Boston (Willoughby)	5	(10 Innings)
Oct. 15n	@ Cin.	Boston (Tiant)	5	Cincinnati (Norman)	4	
Oct. 16n	@ Cin.	Cincinnati (Gullett)	6	Boston (Cleveland)	2	
Oct. 21n	@ Bos.	Boston (Wise)	7	Cincinnati (Darcy)	6	(12 Innings)
Oct. 22n	@ Bos.	Cincinnati (Carroll)	4	Boston (Burton)	3	

POSTPONED: (Rain) Oct. 18,19,20

MANAGERS: Sparky Anderson, Reds; Darrell Johnson, Red Sox

Reds — Johnny Bench, Bill Plummer, catchers; Jack Billingham, Pedro Borbon, Sr., Clay Carroll, Pat Darcy, Rawley
Eastwick, Don Gullett, Clay Kirby, Will McEnaney, Gary Nolan, Fredie Norman, pitchers; Darrell Chaney, Dave
Concepcion, Dan Driessen, Doug Flynn, Joe Morgan, Tony Perez, Pete Rose, infielders; Ed Armbrister, Terry
Crowley, George Foster, Cesar Geronimo, Ken Griffey, Sr., Merv Rettenmund, outfielders.

Red Sox — Tim Blackwell, Carlton Fisk, Bob Montgomery, catchers; Jim Burton, Reggie Cleveland, Dick Drago, Bill
Lee, Roger Moret, Dick Pole, Diego Segui, Luis Tiant, Jim Willoughby, Rick Wise, pitchers: Rick Burleson, Cecil
Cooper, Denny Doyle, Doug Griffin, Bob Heise, Rico Petrocelli, Carl Yastrzemski, infielders; Juan Beniquez,
Bernie Carbo, Dwight Evans, Fred Lynn, Rick Miller, outfielders

1976 - CINCINNATI REDS N.L. (4) vs. NEW YORK YANKEES A.L. (0)
(Riverfront Stadium)/(Yankee Stadium)

Oct. 16	@ Cin.	Cincinnati (Gullett)	5	New York (Alexander)	1	
Oct. 17n	@ Cin.	Cincinnati (Billingham)	4	New York (Hunter)	3	
Oct. 19n	@ N.Y.	Cincinnati (Zachry)	6	New York (Ellis)	2	
Oct. 21n	@ N.Y.	Cincinnati (Nolan)	7	New York (Figueroa)	2	

POSTPONED: (Rain) Oct. 20

MANAGERS: Sparky Anderson, Reds; Billy Martin, Yankees

Reds — Johnny Bench, Bill Plummer, catchers; Santo Alcala, Jack Billingham, Pedro Borbon, Sr., Rawley Eastwick, Don Gullett, Will McEnaney, Gary Nolan, Fredie Norman, Manny Sarmiento, Pat Zachry, pitchers; Bob Bailey, Dave Concepcion, Dan Driessen, Doug Flynn, Joe Morgan, Tony Perez, Pete Rose, infielders; Ed Armbrister, George Foster, Cesar Geronimo, Ken Griffey, Sr., Mike Lum, Joel Youngblood, outfielders.

Yankees — Fran Healy, Elrod Hendricks, Thurman Munson, catchers; Doyle Alexander, Dock Ellis, Ed Figueroa, Ron Guidry, Ken Holtzman, Catfish Hunter, Grant Jackson, Sparky Lyle, Dick Tidrow, pitchers; Sandy Alomar, Sr., Chris Chambliss, Jim Mason, Graig Nettles, Willie Randolph, Fred Stanley, infielders; Oscar Gamble, Elliott Maddox, Carlos May, Lou Piniella, Mickey Rivers, Otto Velez, Roy White, outfielders.

1977 - NEW YORK YANKEES A.L. (4) vs. LOS ANGELES DODGERS N.L. (2)
(Yankee Stadium)/(Dodger Stadium)

Oct. 11n	@ N.Y.	New York (Lyle)	4	Los Angeles (Rhoden)	3	(12 Innings)
Oct. 12n	@ N.Y.	Los Angeles (Hooton)	6	New York (Hunter)	1	
Oct. 14n	@ L.A.	New York (Torrez)	5	Los Angeles (John)	3	
Oct. 15	@ L.A.	New York (Guidry)	4	Los Angeles (Rau)	2	
Oct. 16	@ L.A.	Los Angeles (Sutton)	10	New York (Gullett)	4	
Oct. 18n	@ N.Y.	New York (Torrez)	8	Los Angeles (Hooton)	4	

MANAGERS: Billy Martin, Yankees; Tommy Lasorda, Dodgers

Yankees — Fran Healy, Cliff Johnson, Thurman Munson, catchers; Ken Clay, Ed Figueroa, Ron Guidry, Don Gullett, Ken Holtzman, Catfish Hunter, Sparky Lyle, Dick Tidrow, Mike Torrez, pitchers;Chris Chambliss, Bucky Dent, Mickey Klutts, Graig Nettles, Willie Randolph, Fred Stanley, George Zeber, infielders; Paul Blair, Reggie Jackson, Johnny Oates, Lou Piniella, Mickey Rivers, Roy White, outfielders,

Dodgers — Jerry Grote, Johnny Oates, Steve Yeager, catchers; Mike Garman, Burt Hooton, Charlie Hough, Tommy John, Doug Rau, Lance Rautzhan, Rick Rhoden, Elias Sosa, Don Sutton, pitchers; Ron Cey, Steve Garvey, Ed Goodson, Rafael Landestoy, Davey Lopes, Bill Russell, infielders; Dusty Baker, Glenn Burke, Vic Davalillo, Lee Lacy, Rick Monday, Manny Mota, Reggie Smith, outfielders.

1978 - NEW YORK YANKEES A.L. (4) vs LOS ANGELES DODGERS N.L. (2)
(Yankee Stadium)/(Dodger Stadium)

Oct. 10n	@ L.A.	Los Angeles (John)	11	New York Figueroa)	5	
Oct. 11n	@ L.A.	Los Angeles (Hooton)	4	New York (Hunter)	3	
Oct. 13n	@ N.Y.	New York (Guidry)	5	Los Angeles (Sutton)	1	
Oct. 14	@ N.Y.	New York (Gossage)	4	Los Angeles (Welch)	3	(10 Innings)
Oct. 15	@ N.Y.	New York (Beattie)	12	Los Angeles (Hooton)	2	
Oct. 17n	@ L.A.	New York (Hunter)	7	Los Angeles (Sutton)	2	

MANAGERS: Bob Lemon, Yankees; Tommy Lasorda, Dodgers

Yankees — Mike Heath, Cliff Johnson, Thurman Munson, catchers: Jim Beattie, Ken Clay Ed Figueroa, Goose Gossage Ron Guidry, Catfish Hunter Paul Lindblad, Sparky Lyle, Dick Tidrow pitchers; Chris Chambliss, Bucky Dent, Brian Doyle, Graig Nettles, Jim Spencer, Fred Stanley, infielders; Paul Blair, Reggie Jackson, Jay Johnstone, Lou Piniella, Mickey Rivers, Gary Thomasson, Roy White, outfielders.

Dodgers — Joe Ferguson, Jerry Grote, Johnny Oates, Steve Yeager. catchers; Terry Forster, Burt Hooton, Charlie Hough, Tommy John, Doug Rau, Lance Rautzhan, Rick Rhoden, Don Sutton, Bob Welch, pitchers; Ron Cey, Steve Garvey, Davey Lopes, Teddy Martinez, Bill Russell, infielders; Dusty Baker, Vic Davalillo, Lee Lacy, Rick Monday, Manny Mota, Billy North, Reggie Smith, outfielders.

1979 – PITTSBURGH PIRATES N.L. (4) vs. BALTIMORE ORIOLES A.L. (3)

(Three Rivers Stadium)/(Memorial Stadium)

Oct. 10n	@ Balt.	Baltimore (Flanagan)	5	Pittsburgh (Kison)	4
Oct. 11n	@ Balt.	Pittsburgh (D.Robinson)	3	Baltimore (Stanhouse)	2
Oct. 12n	@ Pitt.	Baltimore (McGregor)	8	Pittsburgh (Candelaria)	4
Oct. 13	@ Pitt.	Baltimore (Stoddard)	9	Pittsburgh (Tekulve)	6
Oct. 14	@ Pitt.	Pittsburgh (Blyleven)	7	Baltimore (Flanagan)	1
Oct. 16n	@ Balt.	Pittsburgh (Candelaria)	4	Baltimore (Palmer)	0
Oct. 17n	@ Balt.	Pittsburgh (Jackson)	4	Baltimore (McGregor)	1

POSTPONED: (Rain) Oct. 9

MANAGERS: Chuck Tanner, Pirates; Earl Weaver, Orioles

Pirates – Steve Nicosia, Ed Ott, Manny Sanguillen, catchers; Jim Bibby, Bert Blyleven,John Candelaria, Grant Jackson, Bruce Kison, Dave Roberts, Don Robinson, Enrique Romo, Jim Rooker, Kent Tekulve, pitchers; Tim Foli, Phil Garner, Bill Madlock, Willie Stargell, Rennie Stennett, infielders; Matt Alexander, Mike Easler, Lee Lacy, John Milner, Omar Moreno, Dave Parker, Bill Robinson, outfielders.

Orioles – Rick Dempsey, Dave Skaggs, catchers; Mike Flanagan, Dennis Martinez, Tippy Martinez, Scott McGregor, Jim Palmer, Don Stanhouse, Sammy Stewart, Tim Stoddard, Steve Stone, pitchers; Mark Belanger, Terry Crowley, Rich Dauer, Doug DeCinces, Kiko Garcia, Lee May, Eddie Murray, Billy Smith, infielders; Benny Ayala, Al Bumbry, Pat Kelly, John Lowenstein, Gary Roenicke, Ken Singleton, outfielders.

1980 – PHILADELPHIA PHILLIES N.L. (4) vs. KANSAS CITY ROYALS A.L. (2)

(Veterans Stadium)/(Royals Stadium)

Oct. 14n	@ Phil.	Philadelphia (Walk)	7	Kansas City (Leonard)	6	
Oct. 15n	@ Phil.	Philadelphia (Carlton)	6	Kansas City (Quisenberry)	4	
Oct. 17n	@ K.C.	Kansas City (Quisenberry)	4	Philadelphia (McGraw)	3	(10 innings)
Oct. 18	@ K.C.	Kansas City (Leonard)	5	Philadelphia (Christenson)	3	
Oct. 19	@ K.C.	Philadelphia (McGraw)	4	Kansas City (Quisenberry)	3	
Oct. 21n	@ Phil.	Philadelphia (Carlton)	4	Kansas City (Gale)	1	

MANAGERS: Dallas Green, Phillies; Jim Frey, Royals

Phillies – Bob Boone, Keith Moreland, catchers; Warren Brusstar, Marty Bystrom, Steve Carlton, Larry Christenson, Tug McGraw, Dickie Noles, Ron Reed, Dick Ruthven, Kevin Saucier, Bob Walk, pitchers; Ramon Aviles, Larry Bowa, Pete Rose, Mike Schmidt, Manny Trillo, John Vukovich, infielders; Greg Gross, Greg Luzinski, Garry Maddox, Bake McBride, Lonnie Smith, Del Unser, George Vukovich, outfielders.

Royals – Darrel Porter, Jamie Quirk, John Wathan, catchers; Ken Brett, Rich Gale, Larry Gura, Dennis Leonard, Renie Martin, Marty Pattin, Dan Quisenberry, Paul Splittorff, Jeff Twitty, pitchers; Willie Aikens, George Brett, Dave Chalk, Onix Concepcion, Pete LaCock, Rance Mulliniks, U.L. Washington, Frank White, infielders; Jose Cardenal, Clint Hurdle, Hal McRae, Amos Otis, Willie Wilson, outfielders.

1981 – LOS ANGELES DODGERS N.L. (4) vs. NEW YORK YANKEES A.L. (2)

(Dodger Stadium)/(Yankee Stadium)

Oct. 20n	@ N.Y.	New York (Guidry)	5	Los Angeles (Reuss)	3
Oct. 21n	@ N.Y.	New York (John)	3	Los Angeles (Hooton)	0
Oct. 23n	@ L.A.	Los Angeles (Valenzuela)	5	New York (Frazier)	4
Oct. 24	@ L.A.	Los Angeles (Howe)	8	New York (Frazier)	7
Oct. 25	@ L.A.	Los Angeles (Reuss)	2	New York (Guidry)	1
Oct. 28n	@ N.Y.	Los Angeles (Hooton)	9	New York (Frazier)	2

POSTPONED: (Rain) Oct. 27

MANAGERS: Tommy Lasorda, Dodgers; Bob Lemon, Yankees

Dodgers – Mike Scioscia, Steve Yeager, catchers; Bobby Castillo, Terry Forster, Dave Goltz, Burt Hooton, Steve Howe, Tom Niedenfuer, Alejandro Pena, Jerry Reuss, Dave Stewart, Fernando Valenzuela, Bob Welch, pitchers; Ron Cey, Steve Garvey, Davey Lopes, Bill Russell, Steve Sax, Derrel Thomas, infielders; Dusty Baker, Pedro Guerrero, Jay Johnstone, Ken Landreaux, Rick Monday, Reggie Smith, outfielders.

Yankees – Rick Cerone, Barry Foote, catchers; Ron Davis, George Frazier, Goose Gossage, Ron Guidry, Tommy John, Dave LaRoche, Rudy May, Rick Reuschel, Dave Righetti, pitchers; Larry Milbourne, Graig Nettles, Willie Randolph, Dave Revering, Andre Robertson, Aurelio Rodriguez, Bob Watson, infielders; Bobby Brown, Oscar Gamble, Reggie Jackson, Jerry Mumphrey, Bobby Murcer, Lou Piniella, Dave Winfield, outfielders.

1982 - ST. LOUIS CARDINALS N.L. (4) vs. MILWAUKEE BREWERS A.L. (3)
(Busch Stadium)/(County Stadium)

Oct. 12n	@ St.L.	Milwaukee (Caldwell)	10	St. Louis (Forsch)	0
Oct. 13n	@ St.L.	St. Louis (Sutter)	5	Milwaukee (McClure)	4
Oct. 15n	@ Mil.	St. Louis (Andujar)	6	Milwaukee (Vuckovich)	2
Oct. 16	@ Mil.	Milwaukee (Slaton)	7	St. Louis (Bair)	5
Oct. 17	@ Mil.	Milwaukee (Caldwell)	6	St. Louis (Forsch)	4
Oct. 19n	@ St.L.	St. Louis (Stuper)	13	Milwaukee (Sutton)	1
Oct. 20n	@ St.L.	St. Louis (Andujar)	6	Milwaukee (McClure)	3

MANAGERS: Whitey Herzog, Cardinals; Harvey Kuenn, Brewers

Cardinals – Glenn Brummer, Darrell Porter, Gene Tenace, catchers; Joaquin Andujar, Doug Bair, Bob Forsch, Jim Kaat, Jeff Lahti, Dave LaPoint, John Martin, Steve Mura, John Stuper, Bruce Sutter, pitchers; Julio Gonzalez, Keith Hernandez, Tommy Herr, Ken Oberkfell, Mike Ramsey, Ozzie Smith, infielders; Steve Braun, David Green, George Hendrick, Dane Iorg, Willie McGee, Lonnie Smith, outfielders.

Brewers – Ted Simmons, Ned Yost, catchers; Dwight Bernard, Pete Ladd, Bob McClure, Doc Medich, Mike Caldwell, Rollie Fingers, Moose Haas, Jim Slaton, Don Sutton, Pete Vuckovich, pitchers; Roy Howell, Paul Molitor, Cecil Cooper, Jim Gantner, Don Money, Rob Picciolo, Ed Romero, Robin Yount, infielders; Mark Brouhard, Marshall Edwards, Charlie Moore, Ben Oglivie, Gorman Thomas, outfielders.

1983 - BALTIMORE ORIOLES A.L. (4) vs. PHILADELPHIA PHILLIES N.L. (1)
(Memorial Stadium)/(Veterans Stadium)

Oct. 11n	@ Balt.	Philadelphia (Denny)	2	Baltimore (McGregor)	1
Oct. 12n	@ Balt.	Baltimore (Boddicker)	4	Philadelphia (Hudson)	1
Oct. 14n	@ Phil.	Baltimore (Palmer)	3	Philadelphia (Carlton)	2
Oct. 15	@ Phil.	Baltimore (Davis)	5	Philadelphia (Denny)	4
Oct. 16	@ Phil.	Baltimore (McGregor)	5	Philadelphia (Hudson)	0

MANAGERS: Joe Altobelli, Orioles; Paul Owens, Phillies

Orioles – Rick Dempsey, Joe Nolan, catchers; Mike Boddicker, Storm Davis, Mike Flanagan, Dennis Martinez, Tippy Martinez, Scott McGregor, Jim Palmer, Sammy Stewart, Tim Stoddard, pitchers; Todd Cruz, Rich Dauer, Eddie Murray, Cal Ripken, Lenn Sakata, infielders; Benny Ayala, Al Bumbry, Jim Dwyer, Darnell Ford, Terry Landrum, John Lowenstein, Gary Roenicke, John Shelby, Ken Singleton, outfielders.

Phillies – Bo Diaz, Ozzie Virgil, catchers; Larry Andersen, Marty Bystrom, Steve Carlton, John Denny, Kevin Gross, Willie Hernandez, Al Holland, Charles Hudson, Tug McGraw, Ron Reed, pitchers; Ivan DeJesus, Kiko Garcia, Joe Morgan, Tony Perez, Pete Rose, Juan Samuel, Mike Schmidt, infielders; Bob Dernier, Greg Gross, Von Hayes, Joe Lefebvre, Sixto Lezcano, Garry Maddox, Gary Matthews, outfielders.

1984 - DETROIT TIGERS A.L. (4) vs. SAN DIEGO PADRES N.L. (1)
(Tiger Stadium)/(Jack Murphy Stadium)

Oct. 9n	@ S.D.	Detroit (Morris)	3	San Diego (Thurmond)	2
Oct. 10n	@ S.D.	San Diego (Hawkins)	5	Detroit (Petry)	3
Oct. 12n	@ Det.	Detroit (Wilcox)	5	San Diego (Lollar)	2
Oct. 13	@ Det.	Detroit (Morris)	4	San Diego (Show)	2
Oct. 14	@ Det.	Detroit (Lopez)	8	San Diego (Hawkins)	4

MANAGERS: Sparky Anderson, Tigers; Dick Williams, Padres

Tigers – Lance Parrish, catcher; Doug Bair, Juan Berenguer, Willie Hernandez, Aurelio Lopez, Jack Morris, Dan Petry, Dave Rozema, Bill Scherrer, Milt Wilcox, pitchers; Doug Baker, Dave Bergman, Tom Brookens, Marty Castillo, Darrell Evans, Howard Johnson, Alan Trammell, Lou Whitaker, infielders; Barbaro Garbey, Kirk Gibson, Johnny Grubb, Larry Herndon, Ruppert Jones, Rusty Kuntz, Chet Lemon, outfielders.

Padres – Bruce Bochy, Terry Kennedy, catchers; Greg Booker, Dave Dravecky, Goose Gossage, Greg Harris, Andy Hawkins, Craig Lefferts, Tim Lollar, Eric Show, Mark Thurmond, Ed Whitson, pitchers; Kurt Bevacqua, Tim Flannery, Steve Garvey, Graig Nettles, Mario Ramirez, Luis Salazar, Garry Templeton, Alan Wiggins, infielders; Bobby Brown, Tony Gwynn, Carmelo Martinez, Ron Roenicke, Champ Summers, outfielders.

1985 - KANSAS CITY ROYALS A.L. (4) vs. ST. LOUIS CARDINALS N.L. (3)
(Royals Stadium)/(Busch Stadium)

Oct. 19n	@ K.C.	St. Louis (Tudor)	3	Kansas City (Jackson)	1
Oct. 20n	@ K.C.	St. Louis (Daley)	4	Kansas City (Leibrandt)	2
Oct. 22n	@ St.L.	Kansas City (Saberhagen)	6	St. Louis (Andujar)	1
Oct. 23n	@ St.L.	St. Louis (Tudor)	3	Kansas City (Black)	0
Oct. 24n	@ St.L.	Kansas City (Jackson)	6	St. Louis (Forsch)	1
Oct. 26n	@ K.C.	Kansas City (Quisenberry)	2	St. Louis (Worrell)	1
Oct. 27n	@ K.C.	Kansas City (Saberhagen)	11	St. Louis (Tudor)	0

MANAGERS: Dick Howser, Royals; Whitey Herzog, Cardinals

Royals — Jamie Quirk, Jim Sundberg, John Wathan, catchers; Joe Beckwith, Bud Black, Steve Farr, Mark Gubicza, Danny Jackson, Charlie Leibrandt, Dan Quisenberry, Bret Saberhagen, pitchers; Steve Balboni, Buddy Biancalana, George Brett, Onix Concepcion, Greg Pryor, Frank White, infielders; Dane Iorg, Lynn Jones, Hal McRae, Darryl Motley, Jorge Orta, Pat Sheridan, Lonnie Smith, Willie Wilson, outfielders.

Cardinals — Tom Nieto, Darrell Porter, catchers; Joaquin Andujar, Bill Campbell, Danny Cox, Ken Dayley, Bob Forsch, Rick Horton, Jeff Lahti, John Tudor, Todd Worrell, pitchers; Jack Clark, Ivan DeJesus, Tommy Herr, Mike Jorgensen, Tom Lawless, Terry Pendleton, Ozzie Smith, infielders; Steve Braun, Cesar Cedeno, Vince Coleman, Brian Harper, Terry Landrum, Willie McGee, Andy Van Slyke, outfielders.

1986 - NEW YORK METS N.L. (4) vs. BOSTON RED SOX A.L. (3)
(Shea Stadium)/(Fenway Park)

Oct. 18n	@ N.Y.	Boston (Hurst)	1	New York (Darling)	0	
Oct. 19n	@ N.Y.	Boston (Crawford)	9	New York (Gooden)	3	
Oct. 21n	@ Bos.	New York (Ojeda)	7	Boston (Boyd)	1	
Oct. 22n	@ Bos.	New York (Darling)	6	Boston (Nipper)	2	
Oct. 23n	@ Bos.	Boston (Hurst)	4	New York (Gooden)	2	
Oct. 25n	@ N.Y.	New York (Aguilera)	6	Boston (Schiraldi)	5	(10 innings)
Oct. 27n	@ N.Y.	New York (McDowell)	8	Boston (Schiraldi)	5	

POSTPONED: (Rain) Oct. 26

MANAGERS: Davey Johnson, Mets; John McNamara, Red Sox

Mets — Gary Carter, Ed Hearn, catchers; Rick Aguilera, Ron Darling, Sid Fernandez, Dwight Gooden, Roger McDowell, Randy Niemann, Bob Ojeda, Jesse Orosco, Doug Sisk, pitchers; Wally Backman, Kevin Elster, Keith Hernandez, Howard Johnson, Ray Knight, Lee Mazzilli, Kevin Mitchell, Rafael Santana, Tim Teufel, infielders; Len Dykstra, Danny Heep, Darryl Strawberry, Mookie Wilson, outfielders.

Red Sox — Rich Gedman, Marc Sullivan, catchers; Oil Can Boyd, Roger Clemens, Steve Crawford, Bruce Hurst, Tim Lollar, Al Nipper, Joe Sambito, Calvin Schiraldi, Bob Stanley, Sammy Stewart, pitchers; Marty Barrett, Wade Boggs, Bill Buckner, Spike Owen, Ed Romero, Dave Stapleton, infielders; Tony Armas, Don Baylor, Dwight Evans, Mike Greenwell, Dave Henderson, Jim Rice, outfielders.

1987 - MINNESOTA TWINS A.L. (4) vs. ST. LOUIS CARDINALS N.L. (3)
(Metrodome)/(Busch Stadium)

Oct. 17n	@ Minn.	Minnesota (Viola)	10	St. Louis (Magrane)	1
Oct. 18n	@ Minn.	Minnesota (Blyleven)	8	St. Louis (Cox)	4
Oct. 20n	@ St.L.	St. Louis (Tudor)	3	Minnesota (Berenguer)	1
Oct. 21n	@ St.L.	St. Louis (Forsch)	7	Minnesota (Viola)	2
Oct. 22n	@ St.L.	St. Louis (Cox)	4	Minnesota (Blyleven)	2
Oct. 24	@ Minn.	Minnesota (Schatzeder)	11	St. Louis (Tudor)	5
Oct. 25n	@ Minn.	Minnesota (Viola)	4	St. Louis (Cox)	2

MANAGERS: Tom Kelly, Twins Whitey Herzog, Cardinals

Twins — Sal Butera, Tim Laudner, catchers; Keith Atherton, Juan Berenguer, Bert Blyleven, George Frazier, Joe Niekro, Jeff Reardon, Dan Schatzeder, Les Straker, Frank Viola, pitchers; Don Baylor, Gary Gaetti, Greg Gagne, Kent Hrbek, Gene Larkin, Steve Lombardozzi, Al Newman, Roy Smalley, infielders; Tom Brunansky, Randy Bush, Mark Davidson, Dan Gladden, Kirby Puckett, outfielders.

Cardinals — Steve Lake, Tom Pagnozzi, Tony Pena, catchers; Danny Cox, Bill Dawley, Ken Dayley, Bob Forsch, Ricky Horton, Joe Magrane, Greg Mathews, John Tudor, Lee Tunnell, Todd Worrell, pitchers; Dan Driessen, Tommy Herr, Tom Lawless, Jim Lindeman, Jose Oquendo, Terry Pendleton, Ozzie Smith, infielders; Vince Coleman, Curt Ford, Lance Johnson, Willie McGee, John Morris, outfielders.

1988 – LOS ANGELES DODGERS N.L. (4) vs. OAKLAND ATHLETICS A.L. (1)
(Dodger Stadium)/(Oakland Coliseum)

Oct. 15n	@ L.A.	Los Angeles (Pena)	5	Oakland (Eckersley)	4	
Oct. 16n	@ L.A.	Los Angeles (Hershiser)	6	Oakland (Davis)	0	
Oct. 18n	@ Oak.	Oakland (Honeycutt)	2	Los Angeles (J.Howell)	1	
Oct. 19n	@ Oak.	Los Angeles (Belcher)	4	Oakland (Stewart)	3	
Oct. 20n	@ Oak.	Los Angeles (Hershiser)	5	Oakland (Davis)	2	

MANAGERS: Tommy Lasorda, Dodgers; Tony LaRussa, Athletics.

Dodgers – Rick Dempsey, Mike Scioscia, catchers; Tim Belcher, Orel Hershiser, Brian Holton, Ricky Horton, Jay Howell, Tim Leary, Jesse Orosco, Alejandro Pena, John Tudor, pitchers; Dave Anderson, Alfredo Griffin, Jeff Hamilton, Danny Heep, Steve Sax, Mike Sharperson, Franklin Stubbs, Tracy Woodson, infielders; Mike Davis, Kirk Gibson, Jose Gonzalez, Mickey Hatcher, Mike Marshall, John Shelby, outfielders.

Athletics – Ron Hassey, Terry Steinbach, catchers; Todd Burns, Greg Cadaret, Storm Davis, Dennis Eckersley, Rick Honeycutt, Gene Nelson, Eric Plunk, Dave Stewart, Bob Welch, Curt Young, pitchers; Mike Gallego, Glenn Hubbard, Carney Lansford, Mark McGwire, Tony Phillips, Walt Weiss, infielders. Don Baylor, Jose Canseco, Dave Henderson, Stan Javier, Doug Jennings, Dave Parker, Luis Polonia, outfielders.

1989 – OAKLAND ATHLETICS A.L. (4) vs. SAN FRANCISCO GIANTS N.L. (0)
(Oakland Coliseum)/(Candlestick Park)

Oct. 14n	@ Oak.	Oakland (Stewart)	5	San Francisco (Garrelts)	0
Oct. 15n	@ Oak.	Oakland (Moore)	5	San Francisco (Reuschel)	1
Oct. 27n	@ S.F.	Oakland (Stewart)	13	San Francisco (Garrelts)	7
Oct. 28n	@ S.F.	Oakland (Moore)	9	San Francisco (Robinson)	6

POSTPONED: (Earthquake) Oct. 17 through Oct. 26

MANAGERS: Tony LaRussa, Athletics; Roger Craig, Giants

Athletics – Ron Hassey, Terry Steinbach, catchers; Todd Burns, Storm Davis, Dennis Eckersley, Rick Honeycutt, Mike Moore, Gene Nelson, Dave Stewart, Bob Welch, Curt Young, Matt Young, pitchers; Lance Blankenship, Mike Gallego, Carney Lansford, Mark McGwire, Ken Phelps, Tony Phillips, Walt Weiss, infielders; Jose Canseco, Dave Henderson, Rickey Henderson, Stan Javier, Dave Parker, outfielders.

Giants – Bill Bathe, Terry Kennedy, Kirt Manwaring, catchers; Steve Bedrosian, Jeff Brantley, Kelly Downs, Scott Garrelts, Atlee Hammaker, Mike LaCoss, Craig Lefferts, Rick Reuschel, Don Robinson, pitchers; Will Clark, Greg Litton, Ken Oberkfell, Ernest Riles, Rob Thompson, Jose Uribe, Matt Williams, infielders; Brett Butler, Candy Maldonado, Kevin Mitchell, Donnel Nixon, Pat Sheridan, outfielders.

1990 – CINCINNATI REDS N.L. (4) vs. OAKLAND ATHLETICS A.L. (0)
(Riverfront Stadium)/(Oakland Coliseum)

Oct. 16n	@ Cin.	Cincinnati (Rijo)	7	Oakland (Stewart)	0	
Oct. 17n	@ Cin.	Cincinnati (Dibble)	5	Oakland (Eckersley)	4	(10 innings)
Oct. 19n	@ Oak.	Cincinnati (Browning)	8	Oakland (Moore)	3	
Oct. 20n	@ Oak.	Cincinnati (Rijo)	2	Oakland (Stewart)	1	

MANAGERS: Lou Piniella, Reds; Tony LaRussa, Athletics

Reds – Joe Oliver, Jeff Reed, catchers; Jack Armstrong, Tom Browning, Norm Charlton, Rob Dibble, Danny Jackson, Rick Mahler, Randy Myers, Jose Rijo, Scott Scudder, pitchers; Billy Bates, Todd Benzinger, Mariano Duncan, Barry Larkin, Terry Lee, Hal Morris, Ron Oester, Luis Quinones, Chris Sabo, infielders; Glenn Braggs, Eric Davis, Billy Hatcher, Paul O'Neill, Herm Winningham, outfielders.

Athletics – Ron Hassey, Jamie Quirk, Terry Steinbach, catchers; Todd Burns, Dennis Eckersley, Rick Honeycutt, Joe Klink, Mike Moore, Gene Nelson, Scott Sanderson, Dave Stewart, Bob Welch, Curt Young, pitchers; Lance Blankenship, Mike Bordick, Mike Gallego, Carney Lansford, Mark McGwire, Willie Randolph, infielders; Harold Baines, Jose Canseco, Dave Henderson, Rickey Henderson, Doug Jennings, Willie McGee, outfielders.

1991 - MINNESOTA TWINS A.L. (4) vs. ATLANTA BRAVES N.L. (3)
(Metrodrome)/(Atlanta-Fulton County Stadium)

Oct. 19n	@ Minn.	Minnesota (Morris)	5	Atlanta (Leibrandt)	2	
Oct. 20n	@ Minn.	Minnesota (Tapani)	3	Atlanta (Glavine)	2	
Oct. 22n	@ Atl.	Atlanta (Clancy)	5	Minnesota (Aguilera)	4	(12 innings)
Oct. 23n	@ Atl.	Atlanta (Stanton)	3	Minnesota (Guthrie)	2	
Oct. 24n	@ Atl.	Atlanta (Glavine)	14	Minnesota (Tapani)	5	
Oct. 26n	@ Minn.	Minnesota (Aguilera)	4	Atlanta (Leibrandt)	3	(11 innings)
Oct. 27n	@ Minn.	Minnesota (Morris)	1	Atlanta (Pena)	0	(10 innings)

MANAGERS: Tom Kelly, Twins; Bobby Cox, Braves

Twins – Brian Harper, Junior Oritz, catchers; Rick Aguilera, Steve Bedrosian, Scott Erickson, Mark Guthrie, Terry Leach, Jack Morris, Kevin Tapani, David West, Carl Willis, pitchers; Greg Gagne, Kent Hrbek, Chuck Knoblauch, Scott Leius, Al Newman, Mike Pagliarulo, Paul Sorrento, infielders; Jarvis Brown, Randy Bush, Chili Davis, Dan Gladden, Gene Larkin, Shane Mack, Kirby Puckett, outfielders.

Braves – Francisco Cabrera, Greg Olson, Jerry Willard, catchers; Steve Avery, Jim Clancy, Tom Glavine, Charlie Leibrandt, Kent Mercker, Alejandro Pena, John Smoltz, Mike Stanton, Randy St. Claire, Mark Wohlers, pitchers; Rafael Belliard, Jeff Blauser, Sid Bream, Brian Hunter, Mark Lemke, Terry Pendleton, Jeff Treadway, infielders. Ron Gant, Tommy Gregg, David Justice, Keith Mitchell, Lonnie Smith, outfielders.

1992 - TORONTO BLUE JAYS A.L. (4) vs. ATLANTA BRAVES N.L. (2)
(Skydome)/(Atlanta-Fulton County Stadium)

Oct. 17n	@ Atl.	Atlanta (Glavine)	3	Toronto (Morris)	1	
Oct. 18n	@ Atl.	Toronto (D. Ward)	5	Atlanta (Reardon)	4	
Oct. 20n	@ Tor.	Toronto (D. Ward)	3	Atlanta (Avery)	2	
Oct. 21n	@ Tor.	Toronto (Key)	2	Atlanta (Glavine)	1	
Oct. 22n	@ Tor.	Atlanta (Smoltz)	7	Toronto (Morris)	2	
Oct. 24n	@ Atl.	Toronto (Key)	4	Atlanta (Leibrandt)	3	(11 innings)

MANAGERS: Cito Gaston, Blue Jays; Bobby Cox, Braves

Blue Jays – Pat Borders, Randy Knorr, Ed Sprague, catchers; David Cone, Mark Eichhorn, Juan Guzman, Tom Henke, Jimmy Key, Jack Morris, Todd Stottlemyre, Mike Timlin, Duane Ward, David Wells, pitchers; Roberto Alomar, Alfredo Griffin, Kelly Gruber, Manuel Lee, Rance Mulliniks, John Olerud, Pat Tabler, infielders; Derek Bell, Joe Carter, Candy Maldonado, Devon White, Dave Winfield, outfielders.

Braves – Damon Berryhill, Francisco Cabrera, Javier Lopez, catchers; Steve Avery, Tom Glavine, Charlie Leibrandt, Kent Mercker, David Nied, Jeff Reardon, Pete Smith, John Smoltz, Mike Stanton, Mark Wohlers, pitchers; Rafael Belliard, Jeff Blauser, Sid Bream, Brian Hunter, Mark Lemke, Terry Pendleton, Jeff Treadway, infielders; Ron Gant, David Justice, Otis Nixon, Deion Sanders, Lonnie Smith, outfielders.

1993 - TORONTO BLUE JAYS A.L. (4) vs. PHILADELPHIA PHILLIES N.L. (2)
(Skydome)/(Veterans Stadium)

Oct. 16n	@ Tor.	Toronto (Leiter)	8	Philadelphia (Schilling)	5
Oct. 17n	@ Tor.	Philadelphia (Mulholland)	6	Toronto (Stewart)	4
Oct. 19n	@ Phil.	Toronto (Hentgen)	10	Philadelphia (Jackson)	3
Oct. 20n	@ Phil.	Toronto (Castillo)	15	Philadelphia (Williams)	14
Oct. 21n	@ Phil.	Philadelphia (Schilling)	2	Toronto (Guzman)	0
Oct. 23n	@ Tor.	Toronto (D. Ward)	8	Philadelphia (Williams)	6

MANAGERS: Cito Gaston, Blue Jays; Jim Fregosi, Phillies

Blue Jays — Pat Borders, Randy Knorr, catchers; Tony Castillo, Danny Cox, Mark Eichhorn, Juan Guzman, Pat Hentgen, Al Leiter, Dave Stewart, Todd Stottlemyre, Mike Timlin, Duane Ward, pitchers; Roberto Alomar, Tony Fernandez, Alfredo Griffin, Paul Molitor, John Olerud, Dick Schofield, Ed Sprague, infielders; Rob Butler, William Canate, Joe Carter, Darnell Coles, Rickey Henderson, Devon White, outfielders.

Phillies — Darren Daulton, Todd Pratt, catchers; Larry Andersen, Tommy Greene, Danny Jackson, Roger Mason, Terry Mulholland, Ben Rivera, Curt Schilling, Bobby Thigpen, David West, Mitch Williams, pitchers; Kim Batiste, Mariano Duncan, Dave Hollins, Ricky Jordan, John Kruk, Mickey Morandini, Kevin Stocker, infielders; Wes Chamberlain, Lenny Dykstra, Jim Eisenreich, Pete Incaviglia, Tony Longmire, Milt Thompson, outfielders.

1994 - NO WORLD SERIES PLAYED

1995 - ATLANTA BRAVES N.L. (4) vs CLEVELAND INDIANS A.L. (2)
(Atlanta-Fulton County Stadium)/(Jacobs Field)

Oct. 21n	@ Atl.	Atlanta (Maddux)	3	Cleveland (Hershiser)	2	
Oct. 22n	@ Atl.	Atlanta (Glavine)	4	Cleveland (Martinez)	3	
Oct. 24n	@ Clev.	Cleveland (Mesa)	7	Atlanta (Pena)	6	(11 innings)
Oct. 25n	@ Clev.	Atlanta (Avery)	5	Cleveland (Hill)	2	
Oct. 26n	@ Clev.	Cleveland (Hershiser)	5	Atlanta (Maddux)	4	
Oct. 28n	@ Atl.	Atlanta (Glavine)	1	Cleveland (Poole)	0	

MANAGERS: Bobby Cox, Braves; Mike Hargrove, Indians

Braves — Javier Lopez, Charlie O'Brien, Eduardo Perez, catchers; Steve Avery, Pedro Borbon, Jr., Brad Clontz, Tom Glavine, Greg Maddux, Greg McMichael, Kent Mercker, Alejandro Pena, John Smoltz, Mark Wohlers, pitchers; Rafael Belliard, Jeff Blauser, Chipper Jones, Mark Lemke, Fred McGriff, Mike Mordecai, infielders; Mike Devereaux, Marquis Grissom, David Justice, Ryan Klesko, Luis Polonia, Dwight Smith, outfielders.

Indians — Sandy Alomar, Jr., Tony Pena, catchers; Paul Assenmacher, Alan Embree, Orel Hershiser, Ken Hill, Dennis Martinez, Jose Mesa, Charles Nagy, Chad Ogea, Eric Plunk, Jim Poole, Julian Tavarez, pitchers; Carlos Baerga, Alvaro Espinoza, Eddie Murray, Herbert Perry, Paul Sorrento, Jim Thome, Omar Vizquel, infielders; Ruben Amaro, Jr., Albert Belle, Wayne Kirby, Kenny Lofton, Manny Ramirez, outfielders

1996 - NEW YORK YANKEES A.L. (4) vs ATLANTA BRAVES N.L. (2)

(Yankee Stadium)/(Atlanta-Fulton County Stadium)

Oct. 20n	@ N.Y.	Atlanta (Smoltz)	12	New York (Pettitte)	1	
Oct. 21n	@ N.Y.	Atlanta (Maddux)	4	New York (Key)	0	
Oct. 22n	@ Atl.	New York (Cone)	5	Atlanta (Glavine)	2	
Oct. 23n	@ Atl.	New York (Lloyd)	8	Atlanta (Avery)	6	(10 innings)
Oct. 24n	@ Atl.	New York (Pettitte)	1	Atlanta (Smoltz)	0	
Oct. 26n	@ N.Y.	New York (Key)	3	Atlanta (Maddux)	2	

POSTPONED: (Rain) Oct. 19

MANAGERS: Joe Torre, Yankees; Bobby Cox, Braves

Yankees — Joe Girardi, Jim Leyritz, catchers; Brian Boehringer, David Cone, Jimmy Key, Graeme Lloyd, Jeff Nelson, Andy Pettitte, Mariano Rivera, Kenny Rogers, David Weathers, John Wetteland, pitchers; Wade Boggs, Mariano Duncan, Cecil Fielder, Andy Fox, Charlie Hayes, Derek Jeter, Tino Martinez, Luis Sojo, infielders; Mike Aldrete, Paul O'Neill, Tim Raines, Darryl Strawberry, Bernie Williams, outfielders.

Braves — Joe Ayrault, Javier Lopez, Eduardo Perez, catchers; Steve Avery, Mike Bielecki, Brad Clontz, Tom Glavine, Greg Maddux, Greg McMichael, Denny Neagle, John Smoltz, Terrell Wade, Mark Wohlers, pitchers; Rafael Belliard, Jeff Blauser, Chipper Jones, Mark Lemke, Fred McGriff, Mike Mordecai, Terry Pendleton, infielders; Jermaine Dye, Marquis Grissom, Andruw Jones, Ryan Klesko, Luis Polonia, outfielders.

1997 - FLORIDA MARLINS N.L. (4) vs CLEVELAND INDIANS A.L. (3)

(Pro Player Stadium)/(Jacobs Field)

Oct. 18n	@ Fla.	Florida (Hernandez)	7	Cleveland (Hershiser)	4	
Oct. 19n	@ Fla.	Cleveland (Ogea)	6	Florida (Brown)	1	
Oct. 21n	@ Clev.	Florida (Cook)	14	Cleveland (Plunk)	11	
Oct. 22n	@ Clev.	Cleveland (Wright)	10	Florida (Saunders)	3	
Oct. 23n	@ Clev.	Florida (Hernandez)	8	Cleveland (Hershiser)	7	
Oct. 25n	@ Fla.	Cleveland (Ogea)	4	Florida (Brown)	1	
Oct. 26n	@ Fla.	Florida (Powell)	3	Cleveland (Nagy)	2	(11 innings)

MANAGERS: Jim Leyland, Marlins; Mike Hargrove, Indians

Marlins — Charles Johnson, Gregg Zaun, catchers; Antonio Alfonseca, Kevin Brown, Dennis Cook, Felix Heredia, Livan Hernandez, Al Leiter, Robb Nen, Jay Powell, Tony Saunders, Ed Vosberg, pitchers; Kurt Abbott, Alex Arias, Bobby Bonilla, Jeff Conine, Darren Daulton, Cliff Floyd, Edgar Renteria, infielders; Moises Alou, John Cangelosi, Craig Counsell, Jim Eisenreich, Gary Sheffield, Devon White, outfielders.

Indians — Sandy Alomar, Jr., Pat Borders, catchers; Brian Anderson, Paul Assenmacher, Orel Hershiser, Mike Jackson, Jeff Juden, Jose Mesa, Alvin Morman, Charles Nagy, Chad Ogea, Eric Plunk, Jaret Wright, pitchers; Jeff Branson, Tony Fernandez, Jeff Manto, Bip Roberts, Kevin Seitzer, Jim Thome, Omar Vizquel, Matt Williams, infielders; Brian Giles, Marquis Grissom, David Justice, Manny Ramirez, outfielders.

1998 – NEW YORK YANKEES A.L. (4) vs SAN DIEGO PADRES N.L. (0)
(Yankee Stadium)/(Qualcomm Stadium)

Oct. 17n	@ N.Y.	New York (Wells)	9	San Diego (Wall)	6
Oct. 18n	@ N.Y.	New York (Hernandez)	9	San Diego (Ashby)	3
Oct. 20n	@ S.D.	New York (Mendoza)	5	San Diego (Hoffman)	4
Oct. 21n	@ S.D.	New York (Pettitte)	3	San Diego (Brown)	0

MANAGERS: Joe Torre, Yankees; Bruce Bochy, Padres

Yankees – Joe Girardi, Jorge Posada, catchers; David Cone, Orlando Hernandez, Hideki Irabu. Graeme Lloyd, Ramiro Mendoza, Jeff Nelson, Andy Pettitte, Mariano Rivera, Mike Stanton, David Wells, pitchers; Scott Brosius, Homer Bush, Derek Jeter, Chuck Knoblauch, Tino Martinez, Luis Sojo, infielders; Chad Curtis, Chili Davis, Ricky Ledee, Paul O'Neill, Tim Raines, Shane Spencer, Bernie Williams, outfielders.

Padres – Carlos Hernandez, Jim Leyritz, Greg Myers, catchers; Andy Ashby, Brian Boehringer, Kevin Brown, Joey Hamilton, Sterling Hitchcock, Trevor Hoffman, Mark Langston, Dan Miceli, Randy Myers, Donne Wall, pitchers; George Arias, Ken Caminiti, Chris Gomez, Wally Joyner, Andy Sheets, Quilvio Veras, infielders; Steve Finley, Tony Gwynn, Ruben Rivera, Mark Sweeney, John Vander Wal, Greg Vaughn, outfielders.

1999 – NEW YORK YANKEES A.L. (4) vs ATLANTA BRAVES N.L. (0)
(Yankee Stadium)/(Turner Field)

Oct. 23n	@ Atl.	New York (Hernandez)	4	Atlanta (Maddux)	1	
Oct. 24n	@ Atl.	New York (Cone)	7	Atlanta (Millwood)	2	
Oct. 26n	@ N.Y.	New York (Rivera)	6	Atlanta (Remlinger)	5	(10 innings)
Oct. 27n	@ N.Y.	New York (Clemens)	4	Atlanta (Smoltz)	1	

MANAGERS: Joe Torre, Yankees; Bobby Cox, Braves

Yankees – Joe Girardi, Jorge Posada, catchers; Roger Clemens, David Cone, Jason Grimsley, Orlando Hernandez, Ramiro Mendoza, Jeff Nelson, Andy Pettitte, Mariano Rivera, Mike Stanton, Allen Watson, pitchers; Clay Bellinger, Scott Brosius, Derek Jeter, Chuck Knoblauch, Jim Leyritz, Tino Martinez, Luis Sojo, infielders; Chad Curtis, Chili Davis, Ricky Ledee, Paul O'Neill, Darryl Strawberry, Bernie Williams, outfielders.

Braves – Jorge Fabregas, Greg Myers, Eddie Perez, catchers; Tom Glavine, Greg Maddux, Kevin McGlinchy, Kevin Millwood, Terry Mulholland, Mike Remlinger, John Rocker, John Smoltz, Russ Springer, pitchers; Howard Battle, Bret Boone, Ozzie Guillen, Jose Hernandez, Brian Hunter, Chipper Jones, Ryan Klesko, Keith Lockhart, Walt Weiss, infielders; Andruw Jones, Brian Jordan, Otis Nixon, Gerald Williams, outfielders.

2000 - NEW YORK YANKEES A.L. (4) vs NEW YORK METS N.L. (1)
(Yankee Stadium) / (Shea Stadium)

Oct. 21n	@ N.Y.Y.	Yankees (Stanton)	4	Mets (Wendell)	3	(12 innings)
Oct. 22n	@ N.Y.Y.	Yankees (Clemens)	6	Mets (Hampton)	5	
Oct. 24n	@ N.Y.M.	Mets (J. Franco)	4	Yankees (Hernandez)	2	
Oct. 25n	@ N.Y.M.	Yankees (Nelson)	3	Mets (Jones)	2	
Oct. 26n	@ N.Y.M.	Yankees (Stanton)	4	Mets (Leiter)	2	

MANAGERS: Joe Torre, Yankees; Bobby Valentine, Mets

Yankees – Jorge Posada, Chris Turner, catchers; Roger Clemens, David Cone, Dwight Gooden, Jason Grimsley, Orlando Hernandez, Denny Neagle, Jeff Nelson, Andy Pettitte, Mariano Rivera, Mike Stanton, pitchers; Clay Bellinger, Scott Brosius, Derek Jeter, Chuck Knoblauch, Tino Martinez, Luis Sojo, Jose Vizcaino, infielders; Jose Canseco, Glenallen Hill, David Justice, Paul O'Neill, Luis Polonia, Bernie Williams, outfielders.

Mets – Mike Piazza, Todd Pratt, catchers; Armando Benitez, Dennis Cook, John Franco, Mike Hampton, Bobby J. Jones, Al Leiter, Rick Reed, Glendon Rusch, Turk Wendell, Rick White, pitchers; Kurt Abbott, Edgardo Alfonzo, Mike Bordick, Matt Franco, Lenny Harris, Robin Ventura, Todd Zeile, infielders; Benny Agbayani, Darryl Hamilton, Joe McEwing, Jay Payton, Timo Perez, Bubba Trammell, outfielders.

2001 - ARIZONA DIAMONDBACKS N.L. (4) vs NEW YORK YANKEES A.L. (3)
(Bank One Ballpark / Yankee Stadium)

Oct. 27n	@ Ari.	Arizona (Schilling)	9	New York (Mussina)	1	
Oct. 28n	@ Ari.	Arizona (Johnson)	4	New York (Pettitte)	0	
Oct. 30n	@ N.Y.	New York (Clemens)	2	Arizona (Anderson)	1	
Oct. 31n	@ N.Y.	New York (Rivera)	4	Arizona (Kim)	3	(10 innings)
Nov. 1n	@ N.Y.	New York (Hitchcock)	3	Arizona (Lopez)	2	(12 innings)
Nov. 3n	@ Ari.	Arizona (Johnson)	15	New York (Pettitte)	2	
Nov. 4n	@ Ari.	Arizona (Johnson)	3	New York (Rivera)	2	

MANAGERS: Bob Brenly, Diamondbacks; Joe Torre, Yankees

Diamondbacks – Rod Barajas, Damian Miller, catchers; Brian Anderson, Miguel Batista, Troy Brohawn, Randy Johnson, Byung-Hyun Kim, Albie Lopez, Mike Morgan, Curt Schilling, Greg Swindell, Bobby Witt, pitchers; Jay Bell, Greg Colbrunn, Craig Counsell, Erubiel Durazo, Mark Grace, Matt Williams, Tony Womack, infielders; Danny Bautista, Midre Cummings, David Dellucci, Steve Finley, Luis Gonzalez, Reggie Sanders, outfielders.

Yankees – Todd Greene, Jorge Posada, catchers; Randy Choate, Roger Clemens, Orlando Hernandez, Sterling Hitchcock, Ramiro Mendoza, Mike Mussina, Andy Pettitte, Mariano Rivera, Mike Stanton, Jay Witasick, pitchers; Scott Brosius, Derek Jeter, Tino Martinez, Luis Sojo, Alfonso Soriano, Randy Velarde, Enrique Wilson infielders; Clay Bellinger, David Justice, Chuck Knoblauch, Paul O'Neill, Shane Spencer, Bernie Williams, outfielders.

AMERICAN LEAGUE CHAMPIONSHIP SERIES

	SERIES			GAMES			YEARS	
	No.	W	L	No.	W	L	WON	LOST
Baltimore	9	5	4	37	21	16	1969-71,79,83	1973-74,96,97
Boston	5	2	3	23	8	15	1975,86	1988,90,99
California	3	0	3	16	6	10		1979,82,86
Chicago	2	0	2	10	3	7		1983,93
Cleveland	3	2	1	18	10	8	1995,97	1998
Detroit	3	1	2	13	6	7	1984	1972,87
Kansas City	6	2	4	27	12	15	1980,85	1976-78,84
Milwaukee	1	1	0	5	3	2	1982	
Minnesota	4	2	2	16	8	8	1987, 91	1969-70
New York	10	9	1	47	32	15	1976-78,81,96,98-01	1980
Oakland	10	6	4	42	23	19	1972-74,88-90	1971,75,81,92
Seattle	3	0	3	17	5	12		1995, 2000-01
Toronto	5	2	3	29	13	16	1992-93	1985,89, 91

*(Note: 1994 Championship Series Not Played; Winner capitalized; *Home club)*

1969	Oct. 4	Oct. 5	Oct. 6
BALT	*4 10 1	*1 8 0	11 18 0
Minn	3 4 2	0 3 1	*2 10 2
	39,324	41,704	32,735
	3:29	3:17	2:48
	12 inn	11 inn	

1970	Oct. 3	Oct. 4	Oct. 5
BALT	10 13 0	11 13 0	*6 10 0
Minn	*6 11 2	*3 6 2	1 7 2
	26,847	27,490	27,608
	2:36	2:59	2:20

1971	Oct. 3	Oct. 4	Oct. 5
BALT	*5 7 1	*5 7 0	5 12 0
Oak	3 9 0	1 6 0	*3 7 0
	42,621	35,003	33,176
	2:23	2:04	2:49

1972	Oct. 7	Oct. 8	Oct. 10	Oct. 11	Oct. 12
OAK	*3 10 1	*5 8 0	0 7 0	3 9 2	2 4 0
Det	2 6 2	0 3 1	*3 8 1	*4 10 1	*1 5 2
	29,536	31,088	41,156	37,615	50,276
	3:09	2:37	2:27	3:04	2:48
	11 inn			10 inn	

1973	Oct. 6	Oct. 7	Oct. 9	Oct. 10	Oct. 11
OAK	0 5 1	6 9 0	*2 4 3	*4 7 0	*3 7 0
Balt	*6 12 0	*3 8 0	1 3 0	5 8 0	0 5 2
	41,279	48,425	34,367	27,497	24,265
	2:51	2:42	2:23	2:31	2:11
			11 inn		

1974	Oct. 5	Oct. 6	Oct. 8	Oct. 9
OAK	*3 9 0	*5 8 0	1 4 2	2 1 0
Balt	6 10 0	0 5 2	*0 2 1	*1 5 1
	41,609	42,810	32,060	28,136
	2:29	2:23	1:57	2:46

1975	Oct. 4	Oct. 5	Oct. 7n
BOS	*7 8 3	*6 12 0	5 11 1
Oak	1 3 4	3 10 0	*3 6 2
	35,578	35,578	49,358
	2:40	2:27	2:30

1976	Oct. 9	Oct. 10n	Oct. 12n	Oct. 13	Oct. 14n
NY	4 12 0	3 12 5	*5 9 0	*4 11 0	*7 11 1
KC	*1 5 2	*7 9 0	3 6 0	7 9 1	6 11 1
	41,077	41,091	56,808	56,355	56,821
	2:06	2:45	3:00	2:50	3:13

1977	Oct. 5	Oct. 6n	Oct. 7n	Oct. 8	Oct. 9n
NY	*2 9 0	*6 10 1	2 4 1	6 13 0	5 10 0
KC	7 9 0	2 3 1	*6 12 1	*4 8 2	*3 10 1
	54,930	56,230	41,285	41,135	41,133
	2:40	2:58	2:19	3:08	3:04

1978	Oct. 3n	Oct. 4	Oct. 6	Oct. 7n
NY	7 16 0	4 12 1	*6 10 0	*2 4 0
KC	*1 2 2	*10 16 1	5 10 1	1 7 0
	41,143	41,158	55,535	56,356
	2:57	2:42	2:13	2:20

1979	Oct. 3n	Oct. 4	Oct. 5	Oct. 6
BALT	*6 6 0	*9 11 1	3 8 3	8 12 1
Cal	3 7 1	8 10 1	*4 9 0	*0 6 0
	52,787	52,108	43,199	43,199
	3:10	2:51	2:59	2:56
	10 inn			

1980	Oct. 8	Oct. 9n	Oct. 10n
KC	*7 10 0	*3 6 0	4 12 1
NY	2 10 1	2 8 0	*2 8 0
	42,598	42,633	56,588
	3:00	2:51	2:59

1981	Oct. 13n	Oct. 14	Oct. 15n
NY	*3 7 1	*13 19 0	4 10 0
Oak	1 6 1	3 11 1	*0 5 2
	55,740	48,497	47,302
	2:52	3:08	3:19

1982	Oct. 5n	Oct. 6n	Oct. 8	Oct. 9	Oct. 10
MIL	3 7 2	2 5 0	*5 6 0	*9 9 2	*4 6 4
Cal	*8 10 0	*4 6 0	3 8 0	5 5 3	3 11 1
	64,406	64,179	50,135	51,003	54,968
	2:31	2:06	2:41	3:10	3:01

1983	Oct. 5	Oct. 6n	Oct. 7n	Oct. 8
BALT	*1 5 1	*4 6 0	11 8 1	3 9 0
Chi	2 7 0	0 5 2	*1 6 1	*0 10 0
	51,289	52,347	46,635	45,477
	2:38	2:51	2:58	3:41
				10 inn

1984	Oct. 2n	Oct. 3n	Oct. 5n
DET	8 14 0	5 8 1	*1 3 0
KC	*1 5 1	*3 10 3	0 3 3
	41,973	42,019	52,168
	2:42	3:37	2:39
		11 inn	

1985	Oct. 8n	Oct. 9	Oct. 11n	Oct. 12n	Oct. 13	Oct. 15n	Oct. 16n
KC	1 5 1	5 10 3	*6 10 1	*1 2 0	*2 8 0	5 8 1	6 8 0
Tor	*6 11 0	*6 10 0	5 13 1	3 7 0	0 8 0	*3 8 2	*2 8 1
	39,114	34,029	40,224	41,112	40,046	37,557	32,084
	2:24	3:39	2:51	3:02	2:21	3:12	2:49
		10 inn					

1986	Oct. 7n	Oct. 8	Oct. 10n	Oct. 11n	Oct. 12	Oct. 14n	Oct. 15n
BOS	*1 5 1	*9 13 2	3 9 1	3 6 1	7 12 0	*10 16 1	*8 8 1
Cal	8 11 0	2 11 3	*5 8 0	*4 11 2	*6 13 0	4 11 1	1 6 2
	32,993	32,786	64,206	64,223	64,223	32,998	33,001
	2:52	2:47	2:48	3:50	3:54	3:23	2:39
					11 inn		

1987	Oct. 7n	Oct. 8n	Oct. 10	Oct. 11n	Oct. 12
MINN	*8 10 0	*6 6 0	6 8 1	5 7 1	9 15 1
Det	5 10 0	3 7 1	*7 7 0	*3 7 3	*5 9 1
	53,269	55,245	49,730	51,939	47,448
	2:46	2:54	3:29	3:24	3:14

1988

	Oct. 5	Oct. 6	Oct. 8n	Oct. 9
OAK	2 6 0	4 10 1	*10 15 1	*4 10 1
Bos	*1 6 0	*3 4 1	6 12 0	1 4 0
	34,104	34,605	49,261	49,406
	2:44	3:14	3:14	2:55

1989

	Oct. 3n	Oct. 4	Oct. 6n	Oct. 7	Oct. 8
OAK	*7 11 0	*6 9 1	3 8 1	6 11 1	4 4 0
Tor	3 5 1	3 5 1	*7 8 0	*5 13 0	*3 9 1
	44,435	49,444	50,268	50,076	50,024
	2:52	3:20	2:54	3:29	2:52

1990

	Oct. 6n	Oct. 7n	Oct. 9	Oct. 10
OAK	9 13 0	4 13 1	*4 6 0	*3 6 0
Bos	*1 5 1	*1 6 0	1 8 3	1 4 1
	35,192	35,070	49,026	49,052
	3:26	3:42	2:47	3:02

1991

	Oct. 8n	Oct. 9	Oct. 11n	Oct. 12n	Oct. 13
MIN	*5 11 0	*2 5 1	3 7 0	9 13 1	8 14 2
Tor	4 9 3	5 9 0	*2 5 1	*3 11 2	*5 9 1
	54,776	54,816	51,454	51,526	51,425
	3:17	3:02	3:36	3:15	3:29

1992

	Oct. 7n	Oct. 8n	Oct. 10	Oct. 11	Oct. 12	Oct. 14
TOR	*3 9 0	*3 4 0	7 9 1	7 17 4	2 7 3	*9 13 0
Oak	4 6 1	1 6 0	*5 13 3	*6 12 2	*6 8 0	2 7 1
	51,039	51,114	46,911	47,732	44,955	51,355
	2:47	2:58	3:40	4:25	2:51	3:15
				11 inn		

1993

	Oct. 5n	Oct. 6	Oct. 8n	Oct. 9n	Oct. 10	Oct. 12n
TOR	7 17 1	3 8 0	*1 7 1	*4 9 0	*5 14 0	6 10 0
Chi	*1 6 1	*1 7 2	6 12 0	7 11 0	3 5 1	*3 ⌐ 3
	46,246	46,101	51,783	51,889	51,375	45,527
	3:38	3:00	2:56	3:30	3:09	3:31

1995

	Oct. 10n	Oct. 11n	Oct. 13n	Oct. 14n	Oct. 15n	Oct. 17n
CLEV	2 10 1	5 12 0	*2 4 2	*7 9 0	*3 10 4	4 8 0
Sea	*3 7 0	*2 6 1	5 9 1	0 6 1	2 5 2	*0 4 1
	57,065	58,144	43,643	43,686	43,607	58,489
	3:07	3:14	3:18	3:30	3:37	2:54
		11 inn				

1996

	Oct. 9	Oct. 10	Oct. 11n	Oct. 12n	Oct. 13
NY	*5 11 0	*3 11 1	5 8 0	8 9 0	6 11 0
Balt	4 11 1	5 10 0	*2 3 2	*4 11 0	*4 4 1
	56,495	56,432	48,635	48,974	48,718
	4:23	4:13	2:50	3:45	2:57
	11 inn				

1997

	Oct. 8n	Oct. 9n	Oct. 11	Oct. 12n	Oct. 13n	Oct. 15
CLEV	0 4 1	5 6 1	*2 6 1	*8 13 2	*2 8 0	1 3 0
Balt	*3 6 1	*4 8 3	1 8 0	7 12 0	4 10 1	*0 10 0
	49,029	49,131	45,047	45,081	45,068	49,075
	2:33	3:53	4:51	3:32	3:08	3:52
			12 inn			11 inn

1998

	Oct. 6n	Oct. 7	Oct. 9n	Oct. 10n	Oct. 11	Oct. 13n
NY	*7 11 0	*1 7 1	1 4 0	4 4 0	5 6 0	*9 11 1
Clev	2 5 0	4 7 1	*6 12 0	*0 4 3	*3 8 0	5 8 3
	57,138	57,128	44,904	44,981	44,966	57,142
	3:31	4:28	2:53	3:31	3:33	3:31
		12 inn				

1999

	Oct. 13n	Oct. 14n	Oct. 16	Oct. 17n	Oct. 18n
NY	*4 10 1	*3 7 0	1 3 3	9 11 0	6 11 1
Bos	3 8 3	2 10 0	*13 21 1	*2 10 4	*1 5 2
	57,181	57,180	33,190	33,586	33,589
	3:39	3:46	3:14	3:39	4:09
	10 inn				

2000	Oct. 10n	Oct. 11	Oct. 13n	Oct. 14	Oct. 15	Oct. 17n
NY	*0 6 1	*7 14 0	8 13 0	5 5 0	2 8 0	*9 11 0
Sea	2 5 0	1 7 2	*2 10 1	*0 1 0	*6 8 0	7 10 0
	54,481	55,317	47,827	47,803	47,802	56,598
	3:45	3:36	3:35	2:59	4:14	4:03

2001	Oct. 17	Oct. 18n	Oct. 20	Oct. 21n	Oct. 22n
NY	4 9 0	3 9 1	*3 7 2	*3 4 0	*12 13 1
Sea	*2 4 0	*2 6 0	14 15 0	1 2 0	3 9 1
	47,644	47,791	56,517	56,375	56,370
	3:06	3:25	3:49	3:24	3:18

NATIONAL LEAGUE CHAMPIONSHIP SERIES

	SERIES			GAMES			YEARS	
	No.	W	L	No.	W	L	WON	LOST
Arizona	1	1	0	5	4	1	2001	
Atlanta	11	5	6	60	27	33	1991-92,95-96,99	1969,82,93,97-98, 2001
Chicago	2	0	2	10	3	7		1984,89
Cincinnati	8	5	3	32	18	14	1970,72,75-76,90	1973,79,95
Florida	1	1	0	6	4	2	1997	
Houston	2	0	2	11	4	7		1980,86
Los Angeles	7	5	2	34	19	15	1974,77-78,81,88	1983,85
Montreal	1	0	1	5	2	3		1981
New York	6	4	2	32	19	13	1969,73,86, 2000	1988,99
Philadelphia	6	3	3	26	12	14	1980,83,93	1976-78
Pittsburgh	9	2	7	42	17	25	1971,79	1970,72,74-75,90-92
St. Louis	5	3	2	28	15	13	1982,85,87	1996, 2000
San Diego	2	2	0	11	7	4	1984,98	
San Francisco	3	1	2	16	8	8	1989	1971,87

*(Note: 1994 Championship Series Not Played; Winner capitalized; *Home club)*

1969	Oct. 4	Oct. 5	Oct. 6		
NY	9 10 1	11 13 1	*7 14 0		
Atl	*5 10 2	*6 9 3	4 8 1		
	50,122	50,270	53,195		
	2:37	3:10	2:24		

1970	Oct. 3	Oct. 4	Oct. 5		
CIN	3 9 0	3 8 1	*3 5 0		
Pitt	*0 8 0	*1 5 2	2 10 0		
	33,088	39,317	40,538		
	2:23	2:10	2:38		
	10 inn				

1971	Oct. 2	Oct. 3	Oct. 5	Oct. 6	
PITT	4 9 0	9 15 0	*2 4 1	*9 11 2	
SF	*5 7 2	*4 9 0	1 5 2	5 10 0	
	40,977	42,562	38,322	35,487	
	2:44	3:23	2:26	3:00	

1972	Oct. 7	Oct. 8	Oct. 9	Oct. 10	Oct. 11
CIN	1 8 0	5 8 1	*2 8 1	*7 11 1	*4 7 1
Pitt	*5 6 0	*3 7 1	3 7 0	1 2 3	3 8 0
	50,476	50,584	52,420	39,447	41,887
	1:57	2:43	2:33	1:58	2:19

1973	Oct. 6	Oct. 7	Oct. 8	Oct. 9	Oct. 10
NY	1 3 0	5 7 0	*9 11 1	*1 3 2	*7 13 1
Cin	*2 6 0	*0 2 0	2 8 1	2 8 0	2 7 1
	53,431	54,041	53,967	50,786	50,323
	2:00	2:19	2:48	3:07	2:40
			12 inn		

1974	Oct. 5	Oct. 6	Oct. 8	Oct. 9	
LA	3 9 2	5 12 0	*0 4 5	*12 12 0	
Pitt	*0 4 0	*2 8 3	7 10 0	1 3 1	
	40,638	49,247	55,953	54,424	
	2:25	2:44	2:41	2:36	

1975	Oct. 4	Oct. 5	Oct. 7		
CIN	*8 11 0	*6 12 1	5 6 0		
Pitt	3 8 0	1 5 0	*3 7 2		
	54,633	54,752	46,355		
	3:00	2:51	2:47		
		10 inn			

1976	Oct. 9n	Oct. 10	Oct. 12		
CIN	6 10 0	6 6 0	*7 9 2		
Phil	*3 6 1	*2 10 1	6 11 0		
	62,640	62,651	55,047		
	2:39	2:24	2:43		

1977	Oct. 4n	Oct. 5n	Oct. 7	Oct. 8n		
LA	*5 9 2	*7 9 1	6 12 2	4 5 0		
Phil	7 9 0	1 9 1	*5 6 2	*1 7 0		
	55,968	55,973	63,719	64,924		
	2:35	2:14	2:51	2:39		

1978	Oct. 4n	Oct. 5	Oct. 6	Oct. 7		
LA	9 13 1	4 8 0	*4 8 2	*4 13 0		
Phil	*5 12 1	*0 4 0	9 11 1	3 8 2		
	63,460	60,642	55,043	55,124		
	2:37	2:06	2:18	2:53		
				10 inn		

1979	Oct. 2n	Oct. 3	Oct. 5			
PITT	5 10 0	3 11 0	*7 7 0			
Cin	*2 7 0	*2 8 0	1 8 1			
	55,006	55,000	42,240			
	3:14	3:24	2:45			
	11 inn	10 inn				

1980	Oct. 7n	Oct. 8n	Oct. 10	Oct. 11	Oct. 12n	
PHIL	*3 8 1	*4 14 2	0 7 1	5 13 0	8 13 2	
Hou	1 7 0	7 8 1	*1 6 1	*3 5 1	*7 14 0	
	65,277	65,476	44,443	44,952	44,802	
	2:35	3:34	3:22	3:55	3:38	
		10 inn	11 inn	10 inn	10 inn	

1981	Oct. 13	Oct. 14n	Oct. 16n	Oct. 17	Oct. 19	
LA	*5 8 0	*0 5 1	1 7 0	7 12 1	2 6 0	
Mtl	1 9 0	3 10 1	*4 7 1	*1 5 1	*1 3 1	
	51,273	53,463	54,372	54,499	36,491	
	2:47	2:48	2:27	3:14	2:41	

1982	Oct. 7n	Oct. 9n	Oct. 10n			
STL	*7 13 1	*4 9 1	6 12 0			
Atl	0 3 0	3 6 0	*2 6 1			
	53,008	53,408	52,173			
	2:45	2:46	2:51			

1983	Oct. 4n	Oct. 5n	Oct. 7	Oct. 8n		
PHIL	1 5 1	1 7 1	*7 9 1	*7 13 1		
LA	*0 7 0	*4 6 1	2 4 0	2 10 0		
	55,254	55,967	53,490	64,494		
	2:17	2:44	2:51	2:50		

1984	Oct. 2	Oct. 3	Oct. 4n	Oct. 6n	Oct. 7	
SD	0 6 1	2 5 0	*7 11 0	*7 11 0	*6 8 0	
Chi	*13 16 0	*4 8 1	1 5 0	8 1	3 5 1	
	36,282	36,282	58,346	58,354	58,359	
	2:49	2:18	2:19	3:13	2:41	

1985	Oct. 9n	Oct. 10n	Oct. 12	Oct. 13n	Oct. 14	Oct. 16
STL	1 8 1	2 8 1	*4 8 0	*12 15 0	*3 5 1	7 12 1
LA	*4 8 0	*8 13 1	2 7 2	2 5 2	2 5 1	*5 8 0
	55,270	55,222	53,708	53,708	53,708	55,208
	2:42	3:04	3:21	2:47	2:56	3:32

1986	Oct. 8n	Oct. 9n	Oct. 11	Oct. 12n	Oct. 14	Oct. 15
NY	0 5 0	5 10 0	*6 10 1	*1 3 0	*2 4 0	7 11 0
Hou	*1 7 1	*1 10 2	5 8 1	3 4 1	1 9 1	*6 11 1
	44,131	44,391	55,052	55,038	54,986	45,718
	2:56	2:40	2:55	2:23	3:45	4:42
					12 inn	16 inn

1987	Oct. 6n	Oct. 7	Oct. 9n	Oct. 10n	Oct. 11	Oct. 13n	Oct. 14n
STL	*5 10 1	*0 2 1	6 11 1	2 9 0	3 7 0	*1 5 0	*6 12 0
SF	3 7 1	5 10 0	*5 7 1	*4 9 2	*6 7 1	0 6 0	0 8 1
	55,331	55,331	57,913	57,997	59,363	55,331	55,331
	2:34	2:33	3:27	2:23	2:48	3:09	2:59

1988

	Oct. 4n	Oct. 5n	Oct. 8	Oct. 9n	Oct. 10	Oct. 11n	Oct. 12n
LA	*2 4 0	*6 7 0	4 7 1	5 7 1	7 12 0	*1 5 2	*6 10 0
NY	3 8 1	3 6 0	*8 9 2	*4 10 2	*4 9 1	5 11 0	0 5 2
	55,582	55,780	44,672	54,014	52,069	55,885	55,693
	2:45	3:10	3:44	4:29	3:07	3:16	2:51
				12 inn			

1989

	Oct. 4n	Oct. 5n	Oct. 7n	Oct. 8n	Oct. 9
SF	11 13 0	5 10 0	*5 8 3	*6 9 1	*3 4 1
Chi	*3 10 1	*9 11 0	4 10 0	4 2 1	2 10 1
	39,195	39,195	62,065	62,078	62,084
	2:51	3:08	2:58	3:13	2:47

1990

	Oct. 4n	Oct. 5	Oct. 8	Oct. 9n	Oct. 10n	Oct. 12n
CIN	*3 5 0	*2 5 0	6 13 1	5 10 1	2 7 0	*2 9 0
Pitt	4 7 1	1 6 0	*3 8 0	*3 8 0	*3 6 1	1 1 3
	55,700	54,456	45,611	50,461	48,221	56,079
	2:51	2:38	2:51	3:00	2:38	2:57

1991

	Oct. 9n	Oct. 10n	Oct. 12	Oct. 13n	Oct. 14	Oct. 16n	Oct. 17n
ATL	1 5 1	1 8 0	*10 11 0	*2 7 1	*0 9 1	1 7 0	4 6 1
Pitt	*5 8 1	*0 6 0	3 10 2	3 11 1	1 6 2	*0 4 0	*0 6 0
	57,347	57,523	50,905	51, 109	51, 109	54,504	46,932
	2:52	2:46	3:21	3:43	2:51	3:09	3:04
			10 inn				

1992

	Oct. 6n	Oct. 7	Oct. 9n	Oct. 10n	Oct. 11n	Oct. 13n	Oct. 14n
ATL	*5 8 0	*13 14 0	2 5 0	6 11 1	1 3 0	*4 9 1	*3 7 0
Pitt	1 5 1	5 7 0	*3 8 1	*4 6 1	*7 13 0	13 13 1	2 7 1
	51,971	51,975	56,610	57,164	52,929	51,975	51,975
	3:00	3:20	2:37	3:10	2:52	2:50	3:22

1993

	Oct. 6n	Oct. 7n	Oct. 9	Oct. 10n	Oct. 11	Oct. 13n
PHIL	*4 9 1	*3 7 2	4 10 1	2 8 1	4 6 1	*6 7 1
Atl	3 9 0	14 16 0	*9 12 0	*1 10 1	*3 7 1	3 5 3
	62,012	62,436	52,032	52,032	52,032	62,502
	3:33	3:14	2:44	3:33	3:21	3:04
	10 inn				10 inn	

1995

	Oct. 10n	Oct. 11n	Oct. 13n	Oct. 14n
ATL	2 7 0	6 11 1	*5 12 1	*6 12 1
Cin	*1 8 0	*2 9 1	2 8 0	0 3 1
	40,382	44,624	51,424	52,067
	3:18	3:26	2:42	2:54
	11 inn	10 inn		

1996

	Oct. 9n	Oct. 10n	Oct. 12	Oct. 13n	Oct. 14n	Oct. 16n	Oct. 17n
ATL	*4 9 0	*3 5 2	2 8 1	3 9 1	14 22 0	*3 5 2	*15 17 0
StL	2 5 1	8 11 2	*3 7 0	*4 5 0	*0 7 0	1 6 1	0 4 2
	48,686	52,067	56,769	56,764	56,782	52,067	52,067
	2:35	2:53	2:46	3:17	2:57	2:41	2:25

1997

	Oct. 7n	Oct. 8	Oct. 10n	Oct. 11n	Oct. 12	Oct. 14n
FLA	5 6 2	1 3 0	*5 8 1	*0 4 0	*2 5 0	7 10 1
Atl	*3 5 0	*7 13 1	2 6 1	4 11 0	1 3 0	*4 11 1
	49,244	48,933	53,857	54,890	51,982	50,446
	3:04	2:57	2:59	2:48	2:27	3:10

1998

	Oct. 7n	Oct. 8n	Oct. 10	Oct. 11	Oct. 12n	Oct. 14
SD	3 7 0	3 11 0	*4 7 0	*3 8 0	*6 10 1	5 10 0
Atl	*2 8 3	*0 3 1	1 8 2	8 12 0	7 14 1	*0 2 1
	42,117	43,083	62,779	65,042	58,988	50,988
	3:27	2:54	3:00	2:58	3:17	3:10
	10 inn					

1999

	Oct. 12n	Oct. 13	Oct. 15n	Oct. 16n	Oct. 17	Oct. 19n
ATL	*4 8 2	*4 9 1	1 3 1	2 3 0	3 13 2	*10 10 1
NY	2 6 2	3 5 1	*0 7 2	*3 5 0	*4 11 1	9 15 2
	44,172	44,624	55,911	55,872	55,723	52,335
	3:09	2:42	3:04	2:20	5:46	4:25
					15 inn	11 inn

2000	Oct. 11n	Oct. 12n	Oct. 14	Oct. 15n	Oct. 16n
NY	6 8 3	6 9 0	*2 7 1	*10 9 0	*7 10 0
StL	*2 9 0	*5 10 3	8 14 0	6 11 2	0 3 2
	52,255	52,250	55,693	55,665	55,695
	3:08	3:59	3:23	3:14	3:17

2001	Oct. 16	Oct. 17n	Oct. 19n	Oct. 20n	Oct. 21n
ARI	*2 8 0	*1 5 1	5 9 1	11 12 0	3 6 1
Atl	0 3 1	8 8 0	*1 4 1	*4 13 4	*2 7 1
	37,729	49,334	41,624	42,291	35,652
	2:44	2:54	2:59	3:47	3:13

AMERICAN LEAGUE CLUB CHAMPIONSHIP SERIES RECORDS

(Winning club first. IB = innings batted)

YEAR	G	IB	AB	R	ER	H	TB	1B	2B	3B	HR	RBI	SH	SF	BB	HP	SO	SB	CS	GDP	BA	SLG	LOB	PO	A	E	DP	ERA	CG	SHO
1969	3																													
Balt		31.1	123	16	14	36	58	23	8	1	4	15	2	0	13	0	14	0	4	2	.293	.472	28	96	31	1	2	1.13	2	1
Minn		32.	110	5	4	17	25	12	3	1	1	5	0	1	12	0	27	2	0	2	.155	.227	22	94	34	5	3	4.06	0	0
1970	3																													
Balt		26	109	27	22	36	61	23	7	0	6	24	1	2	12	1	19	1	0	4	.330	.560	20	81	29	0	3	3.33	2	0
Minn		27	101	10	10	24	39	16	4	1	3	10	1	0	9	0	22	0	0	3	.238	.386	20	78	28	6	5	7.62	0	0
1971	3																													
Balt		25	95	15	15	26	47	14	7	1	4	14	0	1	13	0	22	0	0	2	.274	.495	19	81	31	1	3	2.33	2	0
Oak		27	96	7	7	22	41	10	8	1	3	7	2	0	5	0	16	0	2	3	.229	.427	15	75	15	0	4	5.40	1	0
1972	5																													
Oak		46.1	170	13	11	38	49	29	8	0	1	10	4	1	12	3	35	7	2	2	.224	.288	38	138	59	3	5	1.76	1	1
Det		46	162	10	9	32	52	21	6	1	4	10	3	0	13	0	25	0	2	5	.198	.321	30	139	48	7	4	2.14	1	1
1973	5																													
Oak		45	160	15	14	32	54	21	5	1	5	15	4	1	17	2	39	3	1	2	.200	.338	34	138	47	4	4	2.74	2	1
Balt		46	171	15	14	36	52	26	7	0	3	15	0	0	16	2	25	1	4	2	.211	.304	36	135	51	2	2	2.80	2	1
1974	4																													
Oak		35	120	11	7	22	37	14	4	1	3	11	2	1	22	1	16	3	3	3	.183	.308	30	108	43	2	4	1.75	2	2
Balt		36	124	7	7	22	32	18	1	0	3	7	2	0	5	0	20	0	3	3	.177	.258	16	105	50	4	4	1.80	1	0
1975	3																													
Bos		25	98	18	12	31	45	21	8	0	2	14	5	1	3	0	12	3	0	3	.316	.459	14	81	33	4	3	1.67	1	0
Oak		27	98	7	5	19	28	12	6	0	1	7	0	0	9	0	14	0	0	2	.194	.286	19	75	40	6	4	4.32	0	0
1976	5																													
NY		43	174	23	21	55	84	36	13	2	4	21	2	2	16	0	15	4	3	4	.316	.483	41	132	60	6	3	4.70	1	0
KC		44	162	24	23	40	60	28	6	4	2	24	0	4	11	1	18	5	5	3	.247	.370	22	129	51	4	5	4.40	0	0
1977	5																													
NY		44	175	21	16	46	64	32	12	0	2	17	1	2	9	0	16	2	0	1	.263	.366	34	132	51	2	2	4.50	1	0
KC		44	163	22	22	42	66	27	9	3	3	21	2	2	15	0	22	5	4	2	.258	.405	28	132	54	5	2	3.27	1	0
1978	4																													
NY		34	140	19	18	42	62	33	3	1	5	18	0	1	7	0	18	0	1	3	.300	.443	27	105	35	1	2	3.86	0	0
KC		35	133	17	15	35	59	22	6	3	4	16	1	2	14	0	21	6	3	0	.263	.444	28	102	36	4	4	4.76	1	0
1979	4																													
Balt		35.2	133	26	23	37	53	28	5	1	3	25	1	3	18	1	24	5	1	4	.278	.398	23	109	52	5	5	2.97	1	1
Cal		36.1	137	15	12	32	48	22	7	0	3	14	0	2	7	0	13	2	1	4	.234	.350	22	107	37	2	7	5.80	0	0
1980	3																													
KC		25	97	14	12	28	45	18	6	1	3	14	0	0	9	1	15	3	5	2	.289	.464	18	81	29	1	3	1.67	1	0
NY		27.	102	6	5	26	44	15	7	1	3	5	1	0	6	0	16	0	0	2	.255	.431	22	75	41	1	2	4.32	1	0

AMERICAN LEAGUE CLUB CHAMPIONSHIP SERIES RECORDS

YEAR	G	IP	AB	R	ER	H	TB	2B	3B	HR	RBI	SH	SF	BB	HP	SO	SB	CS	GDP	BA	SLG	LOB	PO	A	E	DP	ERA	CG	SHO
1981	3																												
NY		25	107	20	17	36	49	4	0	3	20	2	1	13	2	10	2	2	1	.336	.458	30	81	29	1	6	1.33	0	1
Oak		27.	99	4	4	22	28	4	1	0	4	4	0	6	0	23	2	0	6	.222	.283	20	75	31	4	1	6.12	0	0
1982	5																												
Mil		42	151	23	20	33	52	4	0	5	20	2	3	15	1	28	2	2	3	.219	.344	24	129	45	8	6	4.19	1	0
Cal		43	157	23	20	40	62	8	1	4	23	5	2	16	1	34	1	2	4	.255	.395	29	126	47	4	3	4.29	2	0
1983	4																												
Balt		36	129	19	16	28	46	9	0	3	17	2	3	16	2	24	2	0	5	.217	.357	24	111	49	2	4	0.49	1	2
Chi		37	133	3	2	28	32	4	0	0	2	5	0	12	3	26	4	1	2	.211	.241	35	108	50	3	5	4.00	1	0
1984	3																												
Det		28.	107	14	11	25	43	4	1	4	14	4	1	8	0	17	4	0	2	.234	.402	20	87	27	1	0	1.24	0	1
KC		29.	106	4	4	18	21	1	1	0	4	0	0	6	0	21	0	1	0	.170	.198	21	84	26	7	2	3.54	1	0
1985	7																												
KC		62.	227	26	26	51	83	9	1	7	26	4	2	22	1	51	2	4	4	.225	.366	44	188	87	6	7	3.16	1	1
Tor		62.2	242	25	22	65	90	19	0	2	23	0	2	16	3	37	2	2	4	.269	.372	50	186	60	4	4	3.77	0	0
1986	7																												
Bos		64.	254	41	28	69	102	11	2	6	35	3	2	19	3	31	1	0	7	.272	.402	48	196	73	7	5	3.58	1	0
Cal		65.1	256	30	26	71	103	11	0	7	29	4	2	20	4	44	1	4	5	.277	.402	60	192	78	8	7	3.94	0	0
1987	7																												
Minn		43.	171	34	32	46	85	13	1	8	33	3	2	20	5	25	4	1	1	.269	.497	37	132	41	3	3	4.50	0	0
Det		44.	167	23	22	40	65	4	0	7	21	2	2	18	3	35	5	0	3	.240	.389	37	129	56	5	1	6.70	1	0
1988	4																												
Oak		34	137	20	20	41	70	8	0	7	20	1	1	10	0	35	1	3	1	.299	.511	26	108	30	3	5	2.00	0	0
Bos		36	126	11	8	26	36	4	0	2	10	0	2	18	1	23	0	0	4	.206	.286	30	102	34	1	2	5.29	1	0
1989	5																												
Oak		43	158	26	24	43	75	9	1	7	23	4	3	20	1	32	13	2	2	.272	.475	29	132	40	3	4	3.89	0	0
Tor		44	165	21	19	40	54	5	0	3	19	1	3	15	0	24	11	0	3	.242	.327	30	129	45	2	5	5.02	0	0
1990	4																												
Oak		34	127	20	17	38	42	4	0	0	18	4	2	19	4	21	9	3	4	.299	.331	35	108	43	1	3	1.00	0	0
Bos		36	126	4	4	23	31	5	0	1	4	1	1	6	0	16	1	0	3	.183	.246	23	102	47	5	6	4.50	1	0
1991	5																												
Minn		45	181	27	23	50	70	9	1	3	25	2	2	15	1	37	8	4	4	.276	.387	38	138	51	4	3	3.33	0	0
Tor		46	173	19	17	43	52	6	0	1	18	3	1	15	0	30	7	1	3	.249	.301	35	135	49	7	5	4.60	1	0
1992	6																												
Tor		54	210	31	23	59	99	8	3	10	30	1	4	23	0	29	7	5	4	.281	.471	45	165	60	8	7	3.44	1	0
Oak		55	207	24	21	52	71	5	1	4	23	3	2	24	1	33	16	2	5	.251	.343	48	162	65	7	5	4.50	1	0
1993	6																												
Tor		53	216	26	21	65	85	8	2	2	24	1	1	21	2	36	7	2	5	.301	.394	56	162	57	2	7	3.67	0	0
Chi		54	194	23	22	46	68	5	1	5	22	5	1	32	3	43	3	2	4	.237	.351	50	159	56	7	5	3.57	1	0

AMERICAN LEAGUE CLUB CHAMPIONSHIP SERIES RECORDS

YEAR	G	IB	AB	R	ER	H	TB	1B	2B	3B	HR	RBI	SH	SF	BB	HP	SO	SB	CS	GDP	BA	SLG	LOB	PO	A	E	DP	ERA	CG	SHO
1995	**6**																													
Clev		54	206	23	20	53	86	37	6	3	7	21	1	2	25	1	37	9	1	6	.257	.417	50	165	66	7	4	1.64	0	2
Sea		55	201	12	10	37	60	24	8	0	5	10	1	0	15	3	46	9	2	2	.184	.299	43	162	59	6	7	3.33	0	0
1996	**5**																													
NY		46	183	27	21	50	91	30	9	1	10	24	0	0	20	2	37	3	0	6	.273	.497	40	141	44	1	2	3.64	0	0
Balt		47	176	19	19	39	70	26	4	0	9	19	0	3	15	0	33	0	0	1	.222	.398	34	138	33	1	0	4.11	0	0
1997	**6**																													
Clev		58	207	18	17	40	63	27	8	0	5	15	2	0	23	4	62	5	0	3	.193	.304	44	174	61	5	11	2.95	0	1
Balt		58	218	19	19	54	86	36	11	0	7	19	1	0	23	1	47	3	1	10	.248	.394	50	174	60	5	4	2.64	0	1
1998	**6**																													
NY		55	197	27	22	43	65	30	8	1	4	25	3	3	35	2	42	9	2	7	.218	.330	48	168	54	2	5	3.21	0	1
Clev		56	205	20	20	45	77	32	3	1	9	19	0	1	16	5	51	6	2	5	.220	.376	39	165	77	7	7	3.60	1	0
1999	**5**																													
NY		45	176	23	18	42	72	29	4	1	8	21	2	0	18	1	44	3	1	0	.239	.409	42	135	38	5	7	3.80	0	0
Bos		45	184	21	19	54	86	34	13	2	5	19	1	0	15	1	38	4	1	6	.293	.467	45	132	40	10	0	3.68	0	0
2000	**6**																													
NY		52	204	31	31	57	85	41	10	0	6	31	3	3	25	3	41	4	2	4	.279	.417	49	159	54	1	5	3.06	1	0
Sea		53	191	18	18	41	68	24	12	0	5	18	2	1	21	0	48	3	2	2	.215	.356	38	156	58	3	4	5.37	0	1
2001	**5**																													
NY		43.1	159	25	21	42	70	28	7	0	7	24	4	1	23	2	31	3	3	4	.264	.440	34	135	47	4	4	3.80	0	0
Sea		45	171	22	19	36	59	25	4	2	5	20	1	0	18	1	35	3	0	3	.211	.345	34	130	45	1	5	4.36	0	0

NATIONAL LEAGUE CLUB CHAMPIONSHIP SERIES RECORDS

(Winning club first. IB = innings batted)

YEAR	G	IB	AB	R	ER	H	TB	1B	2B	3B	HR	RBI	SH	SF	BB	HP	SO	SB	CS	GDP	BA	SLG	LOB	PO	A	E	DP	ERA	CG	SHO
1969	3																													
NY		26	113	27	20	37	65	22	8	1	6	24	1	0	10	0	25	5	1	2	.327	.575	19	81	23	2	2	5.00	0	0
Atl		27.	106	15	15	27	51	13	9	0	5	15	0	1	11	1	20	1	0	2	.255	.481	23	78	37	6	4	6.92	0	0
1970	3																													
Cin		27.	100	9	8	22	36	15	3	1	3	8	0	0	8	0	12	1	1	2	.220	.360	18	84	39	1	1	0.96	0	1
Pitt		28.	102	3	3	23	29	17	6	0	0	3	2	0	12	0	19	0	2	1	.225	.284	29	81	37	2	3	2.67	0	0
1971	4																													
Pitt		34.	144	24	23	39	67	27	4	0	8	23	1	0	5	2	33	2	1	0	.271	.465	26	105	32	3	3	3.34	0	0
SF		35.	132	15	13	31	51	21	5	0	5	14	4	0	16	1	28	2	0	3	.235	.386	33	102	37	4	1	6.09	2	0
1972	5																													
Cin		43.2	166	19	16	42	67	27	9	2	4	16	3	1	10	0	28	4	1	1	.253	.404	30	132	53	4	3	3.07	1	0
Pitt		44.	158	15	15	30	47	20	6	1	3	14	2	0	9	2	27	0	1	2	.190	.297	24	131	38	4	3	3.30	0	0
1973	5																													
NY		46	168	23	23	37	51	29	5	0	3	22	3	1	19	0	28	0	0	3	.220	.304	30	142	44	4	3	1.33	3	1
Cin		47.1	167	8	7	31	52	20	6	0	5	8	3	1	13	1	42	0	1	3	.186	.311	35	138	59	2	3	4.50	0	0
1974	4																													
LA		35	138	20	20	37	56	25	8	1	3	19	1	0	30	0	16	5	0	2	.268	.406	44	108	46	7	8	2.00	1	1
Pitt		36	129	10	8	25	35	21	1	0	3	10	2	0	8	2	17	1	0	5	.194	.271	24	105	37	4	2	5.14	0	0
1975	3																													
Cin		26	102	19	19	29	45	21	4	0	4	18	0	3	9	0	28	11	0	2	.284	.441	17	84	31	1	2	2.25	1	0
Pitt		28	101	7	7	20	26	16	3	0	1	7	0	0	10	1	18	0	0	2	.198	.257	21	78	20	2	3	6.58	0	0
1976	3																													
Cin		26.1	99	19	15	25	45	14	5	3	3	17	1	3	15	0	16	5	1	1	.253	.455	20	81	32	2	3	3.33	0	0
Phil		27	100	11	10	27	40	17	8	1	1	11	3	2	12	0	9	0	1	2	.270	.400	25	79	34	2	3	5.13	0	0
1977	4																													
LA		35	133	22	21	35	52	25	6	1	3	20	2	0	14	0	22	3	1	2	.263	.391	22	108	44	5	3	2.25	2	0
Phil		36	138	14	9	31	40	26	3	0	2	12	2	0	11	3	21	1	0	3	.225	.290	32	105	49	3	3	5.40	0	0
1978	4																													
LA		36.2	147	21	19	42	80	23	8	3	8	21	2	0	9	1	22	2	1	4	.286	.544	28	111	50	3	4	3.41	1	1
Phil		37	140	17	14	35	57	25	3	2	5	16	2	1	9	0	21	0	1	4	.250	.407	24	110	46	4	4	4.66	1	0
1979	3																													
Pitt		29	105	15	14	28	47	19	3	2	4	14	5	3	13	0	13	4	0	2	.267	.448	24	90	34	0	2	1.50	1	0
Cinn		30.	107	5	5	23	35	16	4	1	2	5	1	1	11	0	26	4	2	2	.215	.327	25	87	39	1	2	4.34	0	0
1980	5																													
Phil		49	190	20	19	55	68	45	8	1	1	19	5	1	13	1	37	7	3	3	.289	.358	43	148	71	6	7	3.31	0	0
Hou		49.1	172	19	18	40	57	28	7	5	0	18	7	2	31	0	19	4	3	2	.223	.331	45	147	52	3	4	3.49	0	1
1981	5																													
LA		44	163	15	14	38	55	30	3	1	4	15	4	0	12	1	23	5	0	7	.233	.337	33	132	55	2	5	1.84	0	1
Mtl		44	158	10	9	34	44	26	7	0	1	8	3	0	12	0	25	2	1	4	.215	.278	31	132	53	4	8	2.86	2	0
1982	3																													
StL		25.1	103	17	17	34	45	27	4	2	1	16	5	3	12	1	16	1	0	2	.327	.575	19	81	23	2	2	5.00	0	0
Atl		27	89	5	4	15	16	14	1	0	0	3	2	1	6	0	15	1	2	2	.255	.481	23	78	37	6	4	6.92	0	0

NATIONAL LEAGUE CLUB CHAMPIONSHIP SERIES RECORDS

(Winning club first. IB = innings batted)

YEAR	G	IB	AB	R	ER	H	TB	1B	2B	3B	HR	RBI	SH	SF	BB	HP	SO	SB	CS	GDP	BA	SLG	LOB	PO	A	E	DP	ERA	CG	SHO
1983	4																													
Phil		34	130	16	15	34	53	25	4	0	5	15	3	1	15	0	22	2	1	2	.220	.360	18	84	39	1	1	0.96	0	1
LA		35	129	8	4	27	40	19	5	1	2	7	2	0	11	2	31	3	3	2	.225	.284	29	81	37	2	3	2.67	0	0
1984	5																													
SD		42.1	155	22	20	41	54	33	5	1	2	20	2	4	14	1	22	2	2	0	.271	.465	26	105	32	3	3	3.34	0	0
Chi		43	162	26	25	42	80	22	11	0	9	25	1	2	20	2	28	6	2	3	.235	.386	33	102	37	4	1	6.09	2	0
1985	6																													
StL		51.1	201	29	20	56	77	42	10	1	3	26	2	1	30	0	34	6	6	1	.253	.404	30	132	53	4	3	3.07	1	0
LA		52	197	23	20	46	75	28	12	1	5	23	1	1	19	0	31	4	1	2	.190	.297	24	131	38	4	3	3.30	0	0
1986	6																													
NY		62.2	227	21	20	43	60	34	4	2	3	19	1	3	14	0	57	4	0	3	.220	.304	30	142	44	4	3	1.33	3	1
Hou		63	225	17	16	49	70	38	6	0	5	17	2	0	17	1	40	8	4	3	.186	.311	35	138	59	2	3	4.50	0	0
1987	7																													
StL		60	215	23	22	56	74	46	4	4	2	22	5	4	16	0	42	4	4	2	.268	.406	44	108	46	7	8	2.00	1	1
SF		61	226	23	20	54	90	37	7	1	9	20	3	1	17	2	51	5	4	5	.194	.271	24	105	37	4	2	5.14	0	0
1988	7																													
LA		64	243	31	28	52	70	41	7	1	3	30	1	2	25	2	54	9	1	2	.284	.441	17	84	31	1	2	2.25	1	0
NY		65	240	27	24	58	87	40	12	1	5	27	3	1	28	4	42	6	2	2	.198	.257	21	78	20	2	3	6.58	0	0
1989	5																													
SF		42	165	30	26	44	78	38	6	2	8	29	2	2	17	1	29	2	1	1	.253	.455	20	81	32	2	3	3.33	0	0
Chi		44	175	22	20	53	77	38	9	3	3	21	3	2	16	1	27	3	0	2	.270	.400	25	79	34	2	3	5.13	0	0
1990	6																													
Cin		52	192	20	19	49	70	36	9	0	4	20	3	3	10	1	37	6	3	2	.263	.391	22	108	44	5	3	2.25	2	0
Pitt		53	186	15	14	36	58	22	9	2	3	14	0	1	27	1	49	6	2	3	.225	.290	32	105	49	3	3	5.40	0	0
1991	7																													
Atl		63	229	19	18	53	80	37	9	0	5	19	5	1	22	2	42	10	4	4	.286	.544	28	111	50	3	4	3.41	1	1
Pitt		63	228	12	11	51	70	38	10	0	3	11	4	1	22	0	57	6	2	4	.250	.407	24	110	46	4	4	4.66	1	0
1992	7																													
Atl		60.2	234	34	30	57	90	38	11	2	6	32	3	2	29	0	28	5	0	2	.267	.448	24	90	34	0	2	1.50	1	0
Pitt		61	231	35	32	59	100	31	20	3	5	32	5	3	29	2	42	1	2	2	.215	.327	25	87	39	1	2	4.34	0	0
1993	6																													
Phil		54.1	207	23	19	47	87	25	11	4	7	22	3	2	26	0	51	2	0	2	.289	.358	43	148	71	6	7	3.31	0	0
Atl		55	215	33	29	59	88	40	14	0	5	32	5	2	22	1	54	0	3	4	.223	.331	45	147	52	3	4	3.49	1	1
1995	4																													
Atl		37	149	19	19	42	62	31	6	1	4	17	1	0	16	0	22	2	1	3	.282	.416	36	117	54	3	8	1.15	0	0
Cin		39	134	5	5	28	35	22	5	0	0	4	1	1	12	2	31	4	3	8	.209	.261	28	111	43	2	4	4.62	0	1
1996	7																													
Atl		60	249	44	44	77	118	55	11	3	8	43	2	3	25	3	51	4	1	3	.309	.474	58	183	55	4	6	1.92	0	2
StL		61	221	18	13	45	65	35	4	2	4	15	1	1	11	1	53	1	1	5	.204	.294	34	180	43	0	1	6.60	0	0

NATIONAL LEAGUE CLUB CHAMPIONSHIP SERIES RECORDS

(Winning club first. 1B = innings batted)

YEAR	G	IB	AB	R	ER	H	TB	1B	2B	3B	HR	RBI	SH	SF	BB	HP	SO	SB	CS	GDP	BA	SLG	LOB	PO	A	E	DP	ERA	CG	SHO
1997	6																													
Fla		52	181	20	15	36	47	27	8	0	1	20	5	0	23	3	52	2	1	4	.199	.260	36	159	57	3	4	3.57	2	0
Atl		53	194	21	21	49	76	36	5	2	6	21	5	3	16	2	49	1	1	3	.253	.392	40	156	57	4	7	2.60	1	1
1998	6																													
SD		54	208	24	21	53	75	41	7	0	5	20	2	0	27	1	48	2	1	6	.255	.361	52	165	60	1	6	2.78	1	2
Atl		55	200	18	17	47	65	38	4	1	4	17	2	1	26	0	54	3	1	4	.235	.325	46	162	74	8	6	3.50	0	0
1999	6																													
ATL		60	206	24	23	46	72	31	9	1	5	22	7	1	31	4	47	14	3	5	.223	.350	47	181	55	7	4	2.69	0	0
NY		61	225	21	18	49	70	36	9	0	4	21	3	2	14	0	49	7	3	3	.218	.311	42	178	82	8	9	3.49	0	0
2000	5																													
NY		43	164	31	28	43	69	52	12	1	4	27	3	3	27	3	24	2	3	3	.262	.421	40	135	39	4	1	3.60	1	1
StL		45	177	21	18	47	64	51	11	0	2	18	4	2	11	1	39	3	0	0	.266	.362	39	129	49	7	3	5.86	0	0
2001	5																													
ARI		44	172	22	13	40	52	32	6	0	2	19	2	0	18	1	32	3	1	5	.233	.302	39	135	43	3	3	3.00	2	1
Atl		45	169	15	15	35	56	24	6	0	5	14	0	0	11	0	39	0	1	3	.207	.331	30	132	53	7	5	2.66	0	0

CHAMPIONSHIP SERIES – INDIVIDUAL BATTING

	3 Games	4 Games	5 Games	6 Games	7 Games
Batting Average (Minimum: 3 at-bats per game)					
AL:	.583 B. Robinson Balt 1970	.462 Jackson NY 1978	.611 Lynn Cal 1982	.458 Lofton Clev 1995	.455 Boone Cal 1986
NL:	.778 Johnstone Phil 1976	.467 Baker LA 1978 / Schmidt Phil 1983	.650 Clark SF 1989	.500 Perez Atl 1999	.542 Lopez Atl 1996
Slugging Percentage (Minimum: 3 at-bats per game)					
AL:	.917 By many players	1.056 Brett KC 1978	1.000 Brunansky Minn 1987	.826 Thome Clev 1998	.826 Brett KC 1985
NL:	1.182 Stargell Pitt 1979	1.250 Robertson Pitt 1971	1.000 Clark SF 1989	.900 Perez Atl 1999	1.000 Lopez Atl 1996
Plate Appearances					
AL:	17 Blair & Buford Balt 1969	20 Bumbry Balt 1979	25 Offerman Bos 1999 / Valentin Bos 1999	30 Knoblauch NY 1998	35 Boggs Bos 1986
NL:	16 Agee NY 1969	20 Lopes LA 1974	25 Rose & Schmidt Phil 1980 / Sandberg Chi 1989	31 Williams Atl 1999	35 Grissom Atl 1996
At-Bats					
AL:	15 Belanger Balt 1969 / Blair Balt 1969 / Law Chi 1983	18 Brett KC 1978 / Munson NY 1978	24 Puckett Minn 1987 / Jeter NY 1996 / Offerman Bos 1999	27 Carter & White Tor 1993 / Raines Chi 1993 / Lofton Clev 1998	32 DeCinces Cal 1986
NL:	15 Oberkfell StL 1982	19 Cash Pitt 1971 / Maddox Phil 1978 / Grissom Atl 1995	24 Schmidt Phil 1980	28 Williams Atl 1999	35 Grissom Atl 1996
Runs					
AL:	5 Belanger Balt 1970	7 Brett KC 1978	8 R.Henderson Oak 1989	7 Winfield Tor 1992 / Molitor Tor 1993	8 Rice Bos 1986
NL:	4 By many players	6 Garvey LA 1978	8 Clark SF 1989 / Perez NY 2000	6 McGee StL 1985 / McGriff Atl 1993 / Sheffield Fla 1997	8 Lopez Atl 1996
Hits					
AL:	7 B. Robinson Balt 1969-70	7 Brett KC 1978; Carew Cal 1979 / R. Law Chi 1983 / Boggs Bos; Lansford Oak 1990	11 Chambliss NY 1976 / Lynn Cal 1982 / Offerman Bos 1999	12 Raines Chi & White Tor 1993	11 Barrett Bos 1986
NL:	7 Shamsky NY 1969 / Johnstone Phil 1976	8 Cash Pitt 1971	13 Clark SF 1989	10 O. Smith StL 1985 / McGriff Atl 1993 / Perez Atl 1999	13 Lopez Atl 1996
Extra-Base Hits					
AL:	4 Watson NY 1980	5 Brett KC 1978	6 Brunansky Minn 1987	5 Buhner Sea 1995	5 Brett KC 1985
NL:	5 Aaron Atl 1969	6 Garvey LA 1978	6 Clark SF 1989	5 Herr StL 1985	7 Lopez Atl 1996

CHAMPIONSHIP SERIES – INDIVIDUAL BATTING

		3 Games	4 Games	5 Games	6 Games	7 Games
Total Bases	AL:	11 By many players	19 Brett KC 1978	20 Chambliss NY 1976	19 Thome Clev 1998	19 Brett KC 1985
	NL:	16 H. Aaron Atl 1969	22 Garvey LA 1978	24 Clark SF 1989	18 Madlock LA 1985 / Perez Atl 1999	24 Lopez Atl 1996
Singles	AL:	6 B. Robinson Balt 1969	6 Chambliss NY 1978 / R. Law Chi 1983 / Lansford Oak 1990	10 Offerman Bos 1999	10 Raines Chi 1993 / Vizquel Clev 1998	9 Barrett Bos 1986 / Boone Cal 1986
	NL:	7 Shamsky NY 1969	7 Russell LA 1974	8 Puhl Hou 1980 / Rose Phil 1980 / Walton Chi 1989	7 Clark StL 1985 / O. Smith StL 1985 / McGriff & Pendleton Atl 1983	9 Bell Pitt 1991 / C. Jones Atl 1996 / Lemke Atl 1996
Doubles	AL:	3 Watson NY 1980	3 Carew Cal 1979	4 M. Alou Oak 1972 / Brunansky Minn 1987	3 Giles Clev 1997 / Olerud & McLemore Sea 2000	4 Garcia Tor 1985
	NL:	3 Morgan Cin 1975 / Porter StL 1982	4 McGriff Atl 1995	4 Rose Cin 1972	4 Herr StL 1985 / Alfonzo NY 1999	5 Lopez Atl 1996
Triples	AL:	1 By many players	1 By many players	2 Brett KC 1977	2 Lofton Clev 1995	1 By many players
	NL:	2 McGee StL 1982	1 By many players	1 By many players	2 Duncan Phil 1993	1 By many players
Home Runs	AL:	2 By many players	3 Brett KC 1978 / Canseco Oak 1988	3 Strawberry NY 1996 / Williams NY 2001	4 Thome Clev 1998	3 Brett KC 1985
	NL:	3 H. Aaron Atl 1969	4 Robertson Pitt 1971 / Garvey LA 1978	3 Staub NY 1973	3 Madlock LA 1985	4 Leonard SF 1987
Runs Batted In	AL:	9 Nettles NY 1981	6 Jackson NY 1978	10 Baylor Cal 1982	8 Thome Clev 1998 / Justice NY 2000	7 Downing Cal 1986
	NL:	7 H. Aaron Atl 1969	8 Baker LA 1977 / Matthews Phil 1983	9 Williams SF 1989	7 Madlock LA 1985	7 McGriff Atl 1996
Walks	AL:	6 Killebrew Minn 1969	5 Jackson Oak 1974 / Murray Balt 1979 / Roenicke Balt 1983 / Canseco Oak 1990	7 Whitaker Det 1987 / R.Henderson Oak 1989	10 Thomas Chi 1993	7 Brett KC 1985
	NL:	6 Morgan Cin 1976	9 Wynn LA 1974	8 Cruz Hou 1980	9 C. Jones Atl 1999	6 By many players

CHAMPIONSHIP SERIES – INDIVIDUAL BATTING

	3 Games	4 Games	5 Games	6 Games	7 Games
Intentional Walks					
AL:	1 By many players	2 Rudi Oak 1974 / Murray Balt 1979 / Baines Oak 1990	2 By many players	2 By many players	3 Brett KC 1985
NL:	2 Morgan Cin 1976 / Hernandez StL 1982	3 McCovey SF 1971 / Cey LA 1974	4 Cruz Hou 1980	5 Guerrero LA 1985	2 Gibson 1988 / Bonilla Pitt & Belliard Atl 1991 / Bonds & Slaught Pitt 1992 / Justice Atl 1992 / Blauser Atl 1996
Hit by Pitch					
AL:	1 By many players	1 By many players	1 Gladden Minn 1987 / Sheridan Det 1987	2 Cora Sea 1995 / Grich Cal 1986	2 Baylor Bos 1986
NL:	1 By many players	1 By many players	1 By many players	1 By many players	2 Dykstra NY 1986 / Blauser Atl 1996
Strikeouts					
AL:	7 Cardenas Minn 1969	7 D.Henderson Oak 1988	8 Gibson Det 1987 / Davis Minn 1991	10 Palmeiro Balt 1997 / Vizquel Clev 1997	8 By many players
NL:	7 Geronimo Cin 1975	10 R. Sanders Cin 1995	9 Edmonds StL 2000	12 Strawberry NY 1986	12 Shelby LA 1988
Stolen Bases					
AL:	2 By many players	4 Otis KC 1978	8 R.Henderson Oak 1989	7 Wilson Oak 1992	1 By many players
NL:	4 Morgan Cin 1975	3 Lopes LA 1974	5 Lopes LA 1981	3 Hatcher Hou 1986 / Larkin Cin 1990 / C. Jones & Williams Atl 1999	7 Gant Atl 1991
Caught Stealing					
AL:	3 McRae KC 1980	2 By many players	3 Patek KC 1976	4 White Tor 1992	2 Pettis Cal 1986
NL:	1 By many players	2 Marshall LA 1983	2 Rose Phil 1980	3 McGee StL 1985 / Bass Hou 1986	2 Coleman StL 1987 / Thompson SF 1987 / L. Smith Atl 1991
Grounded into Double Plays					
AL:	2 Thompson Minn 1970	2 Anderson Cal 1979 / Singleton Balt 1983 / Benzinger Bos 1988 / Pena Bos 1990	3 Taylor Det 1972	3 Sorrento Clev 1995	3 DeCinces Cal 1986
NL:	2 Jones NY 1969 / Royster Atl 1982	2 Bowa Phil 1977 / Boone Cin 1995 / Devereaux Atl 1995	4 Guerrero LA 1981	3 Gomez SD 1998	3 Herr StL 1987

Most Series
11 Reggie Jackson, AL:Oak 1971-75, NY 77-78,80-81,Cal 82,86
8 Richie Hebner, NL:Pitt 1970-72,74-75, Phil 77-78, Chi 84

Most Games
46 David Justice, NL:Atl; AL:Clev-NY
45 Reggie Jackson, AL:Oak-NY-Cal
38 Terry Pendleton, NL:StL-Atl

Highest Batting Average (25 or more at-bats)
.517 Fred Lynn, AL:Bos-Cal (29ab-15h)
.515 Mark Grace, NL:Chi-Ari (33ab-17h)

Highest Slugging Percentage (25 or more ABs)
.840 Tony Oliva, AL:Minn (25ab-21tb)
.828 Gary Matthews, NL:Phi-Chi (29ab-24tb)

Most Plate Appearances
195 David Justice, NL:Atl; AL:Clev-NY
181 Reggie Jackson, AL:Oak-NY-Cal
154 Chipper Jones, NL:Atl

Most Plate Appearances, Game
6 By many players
Extra-Inning Game:
8 Mookie Wilson NL:NY Oct. 15, 1986 (16 inn)
Chipper Jones, NL:Atl Oct. 17 1999 (15 inn)
Brian Jordan, NL:Atl Oct. 17, 1999 (15 inn)
Gerald Williams, NL:Atl Oct. 17, 1999 (15inn)

Most Plate Appearances, Inning
2 By many players

Most At-Bats
166 David Justice, NL:Atl; AL:Clev-NY
163 Reggie Jackson, AL:Oak-NY-Cal
135 Terry Pendleton, NL:StL-Atl

Most At-Bats, Game
6 Paul Blair, AL:Balt Oct. 6, 1969
Dan Gladden, AL:Minn Oct. 12 1987
Kirby Puckett, AL:Minn Oct. 12, 1987
Rickey Henderson, AL:Tor Oct. 5, 1993
Jose Offerman, AL:Bos Oct. 16, 1999
John Valentin, AL:Bos Oct. 16, 1999
Marquis Grissom, NL:Atl Oct. 14,17 1996
Fred McGriff, NL:Atl Oct. 14, 1996
Jermaine Dye, NL:Atl Oct. 14, 1996
Tony Womack, NL:Ari Oct. 20, 2001
Craig Counsell, NL:Ari Oct. 20, 2001
Extra-Inning Game:
7 Mookie Wilson NL:NY Oct. 15, 1986 (16 inn)
Keith Hernandez NL:NY Oct. 15, 1986 (16 inn)
Bill Doran NL:Hou Oct. 15, 1986 (16 inn)
Billy Hatcher NL:Hou Oct. 15, 1986 (16 inn)
Glenn Davis NL:Hou Oct. 15, 1986 (16 inn)
Brian Jordan NL:Atl Oct. 17, 1999 (15 inn)
Robin Ventura NL:NY Oct. 17, 1999 (15 inn)
Gerald Williams NL:Atl Oct.17, 1999 (15 inn)

Most At-Bats, Inning
2 By many players

Most Runs
24 David Justice, NL:Atl; AL:Clev-NY
22 George Brett, AL:KC
Bernie Williams, AL:NY
20 Chipper Jones, NL:Atl

Most Runs, Game
4 Bob Robertson, NL:Pitt Oct. 3, 1971
Steve Garvey, NL:LA Oct. 9, 1974
Will Clark, NL:SF Oct. 4, 1989
Javier Lopez, NL:Atl Oct. 14, 1996
Fred McGriff, NL:Atl Oct. 17, 1996
Mark Brouhard, AL:Mil Oct. 9, 1982
Eddie Murray, AL:Balt Oct. 7, 1983
George Brett, AL:KC Oct. 11, 1985

Most Runs, Inning
2 Jack Clark, NL:StL Oct. 13, 1985 (2nd)
Cesar Cedeno, NL:StL Oct. 13, 1985 (2nd)
1 By many AL players

Most Hits
45 Pete Rose, NL:Cin-Phil
37 Reggie Jackson AL:Oak-NY-Cal

Most Hits, Game
5 Paul Blair, AL:Balt Oct. 6, 1969
4 Bob Robertson, NL:Pitt Oct. 3, 1971
Ron Cey, NL:LA Oct. 6, 1974
Steve Garvey, NL:LA Oct. 9, 1974
Dusty Baker, NL:LA Oct. 7, 1978 (10 inn)
Terry Puhl, NL:Hou Oct. 12, 1980 (10 inn)
Steve Garvey, NL:SD Oct. 6, 1984
Tito Landrum, NL:StL Oct. 13, 1985
Kevin McReynolds, NL:NY Oct. 11, 1988
Will Clark, NL:SF Oct. 4, 1989
Otis Nixon, NL:Atl Oct. 10, 1992
Chipper Jones, NL:Atl Oct. 9, 1996
Mark Lemke, NL:Atl Oct. 14, 1996
Javier Lopez, NL:Atl Oct. 14, 1996
Keith Lockhart, NL:Atl Oct. 14, 1997

Most Hits, Inning
2 Graig Nettles, AL:NY Oct. 14, 1981 (4th)
Rickey Henderson, AL:Oak Oct. 6, 1990 (9th)
Jack Clark, NL:StL Oct. 13, 1985 (2nd)
Tito Landrum, NL:StL Oct. 13, 1985 (2nd)
Jerome Walton, NL:Chi Oct. 5, 1989 (1st)
Barry Bonds, NL:Pitt Oct. 13, 1992 (2nd)
Lloyd McClendon, NL:Pitt Oct. 13, 1992 (2nd)

Most Extra-Base Hits
18 George Brett, AL:KC
12 Steve Garvey, NL:LA-SD
Will Clark, NL:SF-StL
Javy Lopez, NL:Atl

Most Extra-Base Hits, Game
4 Bob Robertson, NL:Pitt Oct. 3, 1971
3 Paul Blair, AL:Balt Oct. 6, 1969
George Brett, AL:KC Oct. 6, 1978
George Brett, AL:KC Oct. 11, 1985
Alex Rodriguez, AL:Sea Oct. 17, 2000

Most Extra-Base Hits, Inning
1 By many players

Most Total Bases
75 George Brett, AL:KC
63 Pete Rose, NL:Cin-Phil

Most Total Bases Game
14 Bob Robertson, NL:Pitt Oct. 3, 1971
12 George Brett, AL:KC Oct. 6, 1978

Most Total Bases Inning
5 Barry Bonds, NL:Pitt Oct. 13, 1992 (2nd)
4 By many players

Most Singles
34 Pete Rose, NL:Cin-Phil
29 Roberto Alomar, AL:Tor-Balt

Most Singles, Game
4 Brooks Robinson, AL:Balt Oct. 4, 1969 (12 inn)
Chris Chambliss, AL:NY Oct. 4, 1978
Kelly Gruber, AL:Tor Oct. 7, 1989
Jerry Browne, AL:Oak Oct. 12, 1992
Terry Puhl, NL:Hou Oct. 12, 1980 (10 inn)
Tito Landrum, NL:StL Oct. 13, 1985
Chipper Jones, NL:Atl Oct. 9, 1996
Keith Lockhart, NL:Atl Oct. 14, 1997

Most Singles, Inning

2 Graig Nettles, AL:NY Oct. 14, 1981 (4th)
  Rickey Henderson, AL:Oak Oct. 6, 1990 (9th)
  Jack Clark, NL:StL Oct. 13, 1985 (2nd)
  Tito Landrum, NL:StL Oct. 13, 1985 (2nd)
  Jerome Walton, NL:Chi Oct. 5, 1989 (1st)
  Lloyd McClendon, NL:Pitt Oct. 13, 1992 (2nd)

Most Doubles

7 David Justice, NL:Atl; AL:Clev-NY
  Rickey Henderson, AL:Oak-Tor-Sea; NL:NY
  Pete Rose, NL:Cin-Phil
  Richie Hebner, NL:Pitt-Phil
  Mike Schmidt, NL:Phil
  Ron Cey, NL:LA-Chi
  Javier Lopez, NL:Atl
  Fred McGriff, NL:Atl
  Will Clark, NL:SF-StL
  Chipper Jones, NL:Atl
  Reggie Jackson AL:Oak-NY-Cal
  Hal McRae AL:KC
  Chuck Knoblauch, AL:Minn-NY

Most Doubles, Game

2 By many players
  Extra-Inning Game:
3 Fred McGriff, NL:Atl Oct. 11, 1995 (10 inn)

Most Doubles, Inning

1 By many players

Most Triples

4 George Brett, AL:KC
3 Willie McGee, NL:StL
  Mariano Duncan, NL:LA-Phil
  Keith Lockhart, NL:Atl

Most Triples, Game

2 Mariano Duncan, NL:Phil Oct. 9, 1993
1 By many AL players

Most Triples, Inning

1 By many players

Most Home Runs

9 George Brett, AL:KC
8 Steve Garvey, NL:LA-SD

Most Home Runs, Game

3 Bob Robertson, NL:Pitt Oct. 3, 1971
  George Brett, AL:KC Oct. 6, 1978

Most Games, Consecutive, Home Runs

4 Jeffrey Leonard, NL:SF Oct. 6-7-9-10, 1987
3 Bernie Williams, AL:NY Oct. 20-21-22, 2001

Grand Slam Home Runs

1 Mike Cuellar, AL:Balt Oct. 3, 1970
  Don Baylor, AL:Cal Oct. 9, 1982
  Jim Thome, AL:Clev Oct. 13, 1998
  Ricky Ledee, AL:NY Oct. 17, 1999
  Ron Cey, NL:LA Oct. 4, 1977
  Dusty Baker, NL:LA Oct. 5, 1977
  Will Clark, NL:SF Oct. 4, 1989
  Ron Gant, NL:Atl Oct. 7, 1992
  Gary Gaetti, NL:StL Oct. 10, 1996
  Andres Galarraga, NL:Atl Oct. 11, 1998

Most Runs Batted In

27 David Justice, NL:Atl; AL:Clev-NY
21 Steve Garvey, NL:LA-SD
   Bernie Williams, AL:NY

Most Runs Batted In, Game

6 Will Clark, NL:SF Oct. 4, 1989
5 Paul Blair, AL:Balt Oct. 6, 1969
  Don Baylor, AL:Cal Oct. 5, 1982
  John Valentin, AL:Bos Oct. 16, 1999
  Bret Boone, AL:Sea Oct. 20, 2001

Most Runs Batted In, Inning

4 Mike Cuellar, AL:Balt Oct. 3, 1970 (4th)
  Don Baylor, AL:Cal Oct. 5, 1982 (8th)
  Jim Thome, AL:Clev Oct. 13, 1998 (5th)
  Ricky Ledee, AL:NY Oct. 17, 1999 (9th)
  Ron Cey, NL:LA Oct. 4, 1977 (7th)
  Dusty Baker, NL:LA Oct. 5, 1977 (4th)
  Will Clark, NL:SF Oct. 4, 1989 (4th)
  Ron Gant, NL:Atl Oct. 7, 1992 (5th)
  Gary Gaetti, NL:StL Oct. 10, 1996 (7th)
  Andres Galarraga, NL:Atl Oct. 11, 1998 (7th)

Most Sacrifice Hits

6 Greg Maddux, NL:Chi-Atl
4 Scott Brosius, AL:NY

Most Sacrifice Hits, Game

2 Dock Ellis, NL:Pitt Oct. 3, 1970 (10 inn)
  Gaylord Perry, NL:SF Oct. 2, 1971
  Jim Bibby, NL:Pitt Oct. 3, 1979 (10 inn)
  Manny Trillo, NL:Phil Oct. 8, 1980 (10 inn)
  Joaquin Andujar, NL:StL Oct. 10, 1982
  Greg Mathews, NL:StL Oct. 6, 1987
  Tim Wakefield, NL:Pitt Oct. 13, 1992
  Otis Nixon, NL:Atl Oct. 10, 1993
  Greg Maddux, NL:Atl Oct. 13, 1993
  Tommy Greene, NL:Phil Oct. 13, 1993
  Freddie Patek, AL:KC Oct. 7, 1977
  Mike Gallego, AL:Oak Oct. 8, 1989
  Joey Cora, AL:Chi Oct. 8, 1993

Most Sacrifice Flies

3 Robin Ventura, AL:Chi; NL:NY
2 By many AL & NL players

Most Sacrifice Flies, Game

1 By many players

Most Walks

24 David Justice, NL:Atl; AL:Clev-NY
   Chipper Jones, NL:Atl
21 Bernie Williams, AL:NY

Most Walks, Game

4 Ruppert Jones AL:Cal Oct. 11, 1986 (11 inn)
  Frank Thomas, AL:Chi Oct. 5, 1993
  Darren Daulton, NL:Phil Oct. 10, 1993
  Ken Caminiti, NL:SD Oct. 8, 1998

Most Walks, Inning

1 By many players

Most Intentional Walks

6 Keith Hernandez, NL:StL-NY
4 Eddie Murray, AL:Balt-Clev

Most Intentional Walks, Game

2 By many players
  Extra-Inning Game:
3 Jose Cruz, NL:Hou Oct. 10, 1980 (11 inn)

Most Intentional Walks, Inning

1 By many players

Most Hit By Pitch

4 Richie Hebner, NL:Pitt-Phil-Chi
3 Hal McRae, AL:KC
  Bobby Grich, AL:Balt-Cal
  Don Baylor, AL:Bos-Minn
  Joey Cora, AL:Sea
  Tino Martinez, AL:Sea-NY
  David Justice, AL:Clev-NY

Most Hit by Pitch, Game

2 Dan Gladden, AL:Minn Oct. 11, 1987
  Pat Sheridan, AL:Det Oct. 12, 1987
1 By many NL players

Most Strikeouts
41 Reggie Jackson, AL:Oak-NY-Cal
26 Ron Gant, NL:Atl-Cin-StL

Most Strikeouts, Game
4 Dave Boswell, AL:Minn Oct. 5, 1969 (11 inn)
  Marquis Grissom, AL:Clev Oct. 11, 1997 (12 inn)
  Rafael Palmeiro, AL:Balt Oct. 11, 1997 (12 inn)
  Marquis Grissom, AL:Clev Oct. 15, 1997 (11 inn)
  John Kruk, NL:Phil Oct. 10, 1993
  Reggie Sanders, NL:Cin Oct. 11, 1995 (11 inn)
  Bobby Bonilla, AL:Balt Oct. 10, 1996
  Gerald Williams, NL:Atl Oct. 10, 1998

Most Strikeouts, Inning
2 Ron Karkovice, AL:Chi Oct. 8, 1993 (3rd)

Most Stolen Bases
17 Rickey Henderson, AL:Oak-Tor; NL:NY
16 Rickey Henderson, AL:Oak-Tor
9 Davey Lopes, NL:LA-Chi-Hou

Most Stolen Bases, Game
4 Rickey Henderson, AL:Oak Oct. 4, 1989
3 Joe Morgan, NL:Cin Oct. 4, 1975
  Ken Griffey, Sr. NL:Cin Oct. 5, 1975
  Steve Sax, NL:LA Oct. 9, 1988 (12 inn)
  Ron Gant, NL:Atl Oct. 10, 1991
  Edgar Renteria, NL:StL Oct. 12, 2000

Most Stolen Bases, Inning
2 Bert Campaneris, AL:Oak Oct. 8, 1972 (1st)
  Reggie Jackson, AL:Oak Oct. 12, 1972 (2nd)
  Juan Beniquez, AL:Bos Oct. 4, 1975 (7th)
  Randy Bush, AL:Minn Oct. 8, 1987 (4th)
  Rickey Henderson, AL:Oak Oct. 4, 1989 (4th)
  Rickey Henderson, AL:Oak Oct. 4, 1989 (7th)
  Willie Wilson, AL:Oak Oct. 8, 1992 (5th)
  Joe Morgan, NL:Cin Oct. 4, 1975 (3rd)
  Ken Griffey, Sr. NL:Cin Oct. 5, 1975 (6th)
  Steve Sax, NL:LA Oct. 9, 1988 (3rd)
  Barry Bonds, NL:Pitt Oct. 10, 1991 (2nd)
  Ron Gant, NL:Atl Oct. 10, 1991 (3rd)
  Roger Cedeno, NL:NY Oct. 16, 1999 (8th)

Most Times Stealing Home
1 Reggie Jackson, AL:Oak Oct. 12, 1972
  Marquis Grissom, AL:Clev Oct. 11, 1997
  Jeff Branson, NL:Cin Oct. 11, 1995

Most Caught Stealing
6 Hal McRae, AL:KC
  Devon White, AL:Cal-Tor
4 Vince Coleman, NL:StL
  Willie McGee, NL:StL

Most Caught Stealing, Game
1 By many players
  Extra-Inning Game:
2 Brooks Robinson, AL:Balt Oct. 4, 1969 (12 inn)
  Kevin Bass NL:Hou Oct. 15, 1986 (16 inn)

Most Caught Stealing, Inning
1 By many players

Most Grounded into Double Plays
5 David Justice, NL:Atl; AL:Clev-NY
  Pedro Guerrero, NL:LA
  Willie Randolph, AL:NY-Oak
  Roberto Alomar, AL:Tor-Balt

Most Grounded into Double Plays, Game
3 Tony Taylor, AL:Det Oct. 10, 1972
2 Cleon Jones, NL:NY Oct. 4, 1969
  Garry Maddox, NL:Phil Oct. 12, 1980 (10 inn)
  Pedro Guerrero, NL:LA Oct. 16, 1981
  Jerry Royster, NL:Atl Oct. 10, 1982
  Bret Boone, NL:Cin Oct. 10, 1995 (11 inn)
  Chris Gomez, NL:SD Oct. 7, 1998 (10 inn)
  Gerald Williams, NL:Atl Oct. 13, 1999
  Damian Miller, NL:Ari. Oct. 20, 2001

Most Bases on Interference
1 Richie Hebner, NL:Pitt Oct. 8, 1974
  Mike Scioscia, NL:LA Oct. 14, 1985

CHAMPIONSHIP SERIES FIELDING RECORDS
FIRST BASEMEN – FIELDING

	3 Games	4 Games	5 Games	6 Games	7 Games
Highest Percentage 1.000 (Most Chances)					
AL:	34 Powell Balt 1969	40 McGwire Oak 1990	57 Epstein Oak 1972	57 Palmeiro Balt 1997	54 Buckner Bos 1986
NL:	36 Hernandez StL 1982	49 Garvey LA 1978	60 Rose Phil 1980	79 Hernandez NY 1986	57 Bream Atl 1992
Games					
AL:	3 By many players	4 By many players	5 By many players	6 By many players	7 By many players
NL:	3 By many players	4 By many players	5 By many players	6 By many players	7 By many players
Total Chances					
AL:	34 Powell Balt 1969 / Watson NY 1980	49 Murray Balt 1979	57 Epstein Oak 1972	58 Olerud Tor 1993	81 Balboni KC 1985
NL:	36 Hernandez StL 1982	49 Garvey LA 1978	60 Rose Phil 1980	79 Hernandez NY 1986	71 W. Clark SF 1987
Chances Accepted					
AL:	34 Powell Balt 1969	47 Murray Balt 1979	57 Epstein Oak 1972	57 Olerud Tor 1993 / Palmeiro Balt 1997	79 Balboni KC 1985
NL:	36 Hernandez StL 1982	49 Garvey LA 1978	60 Rose Phil 1980	79 Hernandez NY 1986	70 W. Clark SF 1987
Putouts					
AL:	34 Powell Balt 1969	44 Murray Balt 1979	55 Epstein Oak 1972	55 Palmeiro Balt 1997	72 Balboni KC 1985
NL:	35 Hernandez StL 1982	44 Garvey LA 1978	53 Rose Phil 1980	67 Hernandez NY 1986	63 W. Clark SF 1987
Assists					
AL:	5 Reese Minn 1969	3 Murray Balt 1979, 83 / Paciorek Chi 1983	8 Hrbek Minn 1991	9 Olerud Tor 1993	7 Balboni KC 1985 / Upshaw Tor 1985
NL:	5 Perez Cin 1975 / Chambliss Atl 1982	5 Garvey LA 1978	7 Rose Phil 1980 / Franco Atl 2001	12 Hernandez NY 1986	7 W. Clark SF 1987
Errors					
AL:	1 By many players	2 Murray Balt 1979	2 Mayberry KC 1977 / Cooper Mil 1982	2 Sorrento Clev 1995	2 Balboni KC 1985
NL:	2 Cepeda Atl 1969	1 By many players	2 Clark StL 2000	4 Galarraga Atl 1998	2 Hatcher LA 1988 / Redus Pitt 1991
Double Plays					
AL:	5 Watson NY 1981	6 Carew Cal 1979	6 Palmeiro Balt 1996 / Martinez NY 1999	8 Thome Clev 1997	5 Balboni KC 1985 / Grich Cal 1986
NL:	3 Hernandez StL 1982	8 McGriff Atl 1995	7 Cromartie Mtl 1981	6 Galarraga Atl 1998	10 W. Clark SF 1987

FIRST BASEMEN

Most Series
6 John Olerud AL:Tor 1991-93; Sea 2000-01;
    NL:NY 1999
    Tino Martinez, AL:Sea 1995; NY 96,98-2001
5 Bob Robertson, NL:Pitt 1970-72,74-75
    Tony Perez, NL:Cin 1970,72-73,75-76
    Steve Garvey, NL:LA 1974,77-78,81 SD 84

Most Games
34 John Olerud, AL:Tor-Sea; NL:NY
33 Tino Martinez AL:Sea-NY
23 Fred McGriff, NL:Atl

Highest Percentage (Most Chances)
1.000 Boog Powell, AL:Balt (118 tc)
        Sid Bream, NL:Pitt-Atl (110 tc)

Most Total Chances
318 John Olerud, AL:Tor-Sea; NL:NY
285 Tino Martinez AL:Sea-NY
222 Steve Garvey, NL:LA-SD

Most Total Chances, Game
18 Steve Garvey, NL:LA Oct. 6, 1978
16 Steve Balboni, AL:KC Oct. 12, 1985
    George Hendrick, AL:Cal Oct. 11, 1986 (11 inn)
    John Olerud, AL:Tor Oct. 11, 1991 (10 inn)
    Herbert Perry, AL:Clev Oct 13, 1995 (11 inn)
    Extra-Inning Game:
27 Keith Hernandez, NL:NY Oct. 15, 1986 (16 inn)

Most Total Chances, Inning
4 Dick Allen, NL:Phil Oct. 10, 1976 (6th)
    Enos Cabell, NL:LA Oct. 9, 1985 (4th)
    Mark McGwire, AL:Oak Oct. 4, 1989 (3rd)
    Will Clark, NL:StL Oct. 12, 2000 (9th)

Most Chances Accepted
315 John Olerud, AL:Tor-Sea; NL:NY
283 Tino Martinez AL:Sea-NY
221 Steve Garvey, NL:LA-SD

Most Chances Accepted, Game
18 Steve Garvey, NL:LA Oct. 6, 1978
16 Steve Balboni, AL:KC Oct. 12, 1985
    George Hendrick, AL:Cal Oct. 11, 1986 (11 inn)
    John Olerud, AL:Tor Oct. 11, 1991 (10 inn)
    Herbert Perry, AL:Clev Oct. 13, 1995 (11 inn)
    Extra-Inning Game:
27 Keith Hernandez, NL:NY Oct. 15, 1986 (16 inn)

Most Chances Accepted, Inning
4 Enos Cabell, NL:LA Oct. 9, 1985 (4th)

Most Putouts
288 John Olerud, AL:Tor-Sea; NL:NY
256 Tino Martinez, AL:Sea-NY
208 Steve Garvey, NL:LA-SD

Most Putouts, Game
17 Andres Galarraga, NL:Atl Oct. 14, 1998
15 Chris Chambliss, AL:NY Oct. 14, 1976
    Mark McGwire, AL:Oak Oct. 4, 1989
    Extra-Inning Game:
21 Glenn Davis, NL:Hou Oct. 15, 1986 (16 inn)
16 John Olerud, AL:Tor Oct. 11, 1991 (10 inn)
    Herbert Perry, AL:Clev Oct. 13, 1995 (11 inn)

Most Assists
27 John Olerud, AL:Tor-Sea; NL:NY
    Tino Martinez, AL:Sea-NY
17 Keith Hernandez, NL:StL-NY
    Will Clark, NL:SF-StL

Most Assists, Game
4 Steve Balboni, AL:KC Oct. 12, 1985
    Andres Galarraga, NL:Atl Oct. 10, 1998
    Extra-Inning Game:
7 Keith Hernandez, NL:NY Oct. 15, 1986 (16 inn)

Most Assists, Inning
2 By many players

Most Errors
4 Andres Galarraga, NL:Atl
3 Cecil Cooper, AL:Bos-Mil
    Eddie Murray, AL:Balt
    Steve Balboni, AL:KC
    John Olerud, AL:Tor-Sea

Most Errors, Game
2 Paul Sorrento, AL:Clev Oct. 15, 1995
    Andres Galarraga, NL:Atl Oct. 7, 1998
    (10 inn)
    Ryan Klesko NL:Atl Oct. 17, 1999 (15 inn)

Most Errors, Inning
2 Paul Sorrento, AL:Clev Oct. 15, 1995 (7th)
    Andres Galarraga, NL:Atl Oct. 7, 1998 (10th)

Most Double Plays
28 John Olerud, AL:Tor-Sea; NL:NY
27 Tino Martinez AL:Sea-NY
21 Steve Garvey, NL:LA-SD

Most Double Plays, Game
4 Will Clark, NL:SF Oct. 10, 1987
3 Rich Reese, AL:Minn Oct. 3, 1970
    Mike Epstein, AL:Oak Oct. 10, 1972
    Gene Tenace, AL:Oak Oct. 5, 1975
    Eddie Murray, AL:Balt Oct. 6, 1979
    Bobby Grich, AL:Cal Oct. 14, 1986
    Jim Thome, AL:Clev Oct. 9, 1998
    Tino Martinez, AL:NY Oct. 17, 1999
    Extra-Inning Game:
5 Fred McGriff, NL:Atl Oct. 10, 1995 (11 inn)

Double Plays, Unassisted
1 Tino Martinez, AL:NY Oct. 11 1996 (5th)
    Tino Martinez, AL:NY Oct. 22, 2001 (4th)
    John Mabry, NL:StL Oct. 14, 1996 (2nd)
    Will Clark, NL:StL Oct. 14, 2000 (4th)

SECOND BASEMEN – FIELDING

		3 Games	4 Games	5 Games	6 Games	7 Games
Highest Percentage 1.000 (Most Chances)						
	AL:	25 Randolph NY 1981	23 J. Cruz Chi 1983	29 White KC 1977	34 Baerga Clev 1995	40 Barrett Bos 1986
	NL:	23 Helms Cin 1970 Morgan Cin 1979	29 Lemke Atl 1995	39 Morgan Cin 1973	38 Lind Pitt 1990	34 Sax LA 1988
Games						
	AL:	3 By many players	4 By many players	5 By many players	6 By many players	7 By many players
	NL:	3 By many players	4 By many players	5 By many players		7 By many players
Total Chances						
	AL:	25 Randolph NY 1981	26 Grich Balt 1974	42 Alomar Balt 1996	41 Cora Chi 1993	40 Barrett Bos 1986
	NL:	23 Helms Cin 1970	29 Lemke Atl 1995	44 Trillo Phil 1980	38 Lind Pitt 1990	41 Lind Pitt 1992
Chances Accepted						
	AL:	25 Randolph NY 1981	25 Grich Balt 1974	40 Alomar Balt 1996	38 Cora Chi 1993	40 Barrett Bos 1986
	NL:	23 Helms Cin 1970	29 Lemke Atl 1995	43 Trillo Phil 1980	38 Lind Pitt 1990	39 Lind Pitt 1992
Putouts						
	AL:	12 Randolph NY 1981	13 Grich Balt 1974	16 Grich Balt 1973	18 Cora Chi 1993	19 Barrett Bos 1986
	NL:	12 Morgan Cin 1979	13 Lemke Atl 1995	18 Trillo Phil 1980	19 Lind Pitt 1990	16 Lind Pitt 1992
Assists						
	AL:	13 Randolph NY 1981	14 J. Cruz Chi 1983	25 Alomar Balt 1996	22 Baerga Clev 1995	28 White KC 1985
	NL:	12 Helms Cin 1970	18 Lopes LA 1974	27 Morgan Cin 1973	21 Sax LA 1985	24 Lind Pitt 1991
Errors						
	AL:	1 By many players	2 Green Oak 1974	2 Green Oak 1973 Offerman Bos 1999	3 Cora Chi 1993	2 Grich Cal 1986
	NL:	1 By many players	2 Sizemore Phil 1977 Lopes LA 1978	2 Giles Atl 2001	1 Duncan Cin 1990 & Phil 1993 Counsell Fla 1997 Alfonzo NY 1999	2 Backman NY 1988 Lind Pitt 1992
Double Plays						
	AL:	4 Randolph NY 1981	4 Grich Cal 1979 5 Reed Bos 1990	7 Alomar Balt 1996	5 Alomar Tor 1993 Roberts Clev 1997 Knoblauch NY 1998	6 Wilfong Cal 1986
	NL:	3 Cash Pitt 1970	5 Lemke Atl 1995 Herr StL 1982	7 Scott Mtl 1981	6 Alfonzo NY 1999	6 Thompson SF 1987 Sax LA 1988

SECOND BASEMEN

Most Series
- 7 Joe Morgan, NL:Cin 1972-73,75-76,79;
Hou 80; Phil 83
- 6 Frank White, AL:KC 1976-78,80,84-85

Most Games
- 31 Mark Lemke, NL:Atl
- 28 Roberto Alomar, AL:Tor-Balt

Highest Percentage (Most Chances)
- 1.000 Joe Morgan, NL:Cin-Hou-Phil (148 tc)
Willie Randolph, AL:NY-Oak (93 tc)

Most Total Chances
- 158 Roberto Alomar, AL:Tor-Balt
- 148 Joe Morgan, NL:Cin-Hou-Phil

Most Total Chances, Game
- 13 Bobby Grich, AL:Balt Oct. 6, 1974
Manny Trillo, NL:Phil Oct. 7, 1980
Roberto Alomar, AL:Tor Oct. 11, 1992 (11 inn)

Most Total Chances, Inning
- 4 Dick Green, AL:Oak Oct. 9, 1973 (7th)
Rodney Scott, NL:Mtl Oct. 16, 1981 (2nd)

Most Chances Accepted
- 154 Roberto Alomar, AL:Tor-Balt
- 148 Joe Morgan, NL:Cin-Hou-Phil

Most Chances Accepted, Game
- 13 Manny Trillo, NL:Phil Oct. 7, 1980
- 12 Bobby Grich, AL:Balt Oct. 6, 1974
Willie Randolph, AL:NY Oct. 13, 1981
  Extra-Inning Game:
- 13 Roberto Alomar, AL:Tor Oct. 11, 1992 (11 inn)

Most Chances Accepted, Inning
- 3 By many players

Most Putouts
- 69 Roberto Alomar, AL:Tor-Balt
- 62 Joe Morgan, NL:Cin-Hou-Phil

Most Putouts, Game
- 7 Bobby Grich, AL:Balt Oct. 6 1974
- 6 Dave Cash, NL:Phil Oct. 12, 1976
Davey Lopes, NL:LA Oct. 13, 1981
Jose Lind, NL:Pitt Oct. 12, 1990
  Extra-Inning Game:
- 8 Roberto Alomar, AL:Tor Oct. 11, 1992
- 7 Steve Sax, NL:LA Oct. 9, 1988 (12 inn)

Most Putouts, Inning
- 3 Dick Green, AL:Oak Oct. 8, 1974 (7th)
Joe Morgan, NL:Cin Oct. 10, 1976 (8th)
Ryne Sandberg, NL:Chi Oct. 4, 1984 (5th)

Most Assists
- 86 Joe Morgan, NL:Cin-Hou-Phil
- 85 Roberto Alomar, AL:Tor-Balt

Most Assists, Game
- 9 Joey Cora, AL:Chi Oct. 6, 1993
- 8 Manny Trillo, NL:Phil Oct. 7, 1980
  Extra-Inning Game:
- 9 Wally Backman, NL:NY Oct. 14, 1986 (12 inn)

Most Assists, Inning
- 3 Tony Phillips, AL:Oak Oct. 4, 1989 (5th)
Joey Cora, AL:Chi Oct. 6, 1993 (6th)
Mark Lemke, NL:Atl. Oct. 13, 1993 (1st)
Edgardo Alfonzo, NL:NY Oct. 11, 2000 (1st)

Most Errors
- 4 Dick Green, AL:Oak
Bobby Grich, AL:Balt-Cal
Joey Cora, AL:Chi-Sea
Roberto Alomar, AL:Tor-Balt
Davey Lopes, NL:LA

Most Errors, Game
- 2 Dick Green, AL:Oak Oct. 9, 1973 (11 inn)
Dick Green, AL:Oak Oct. 8, 1974
Lance Blankenship, AL:Oak Oct. 10, 1992
- 1 By many NL players

Most Errors, Inning
- 1 By many players

Most Double Plays
- 20 Roberto Alomar, AL:Tor-Balt
- 14 Joe Morgan, NL:Cin-Hou-Phil
Mark Lemke, NL:Atl

Most Double Plays, Game
- 4 Davey Lopes, NL:LA Oct. 13, 1981
- 3 Rob Wilfong, AL:Cal Oct. 14, 1986
Bip Roberts, AL:Clev Oct. 11, 1997 (12 inn)

Double Plays, Unassisted
- 1 Joe Morgan, NL:Cin Oct. 10, 1976 (8th)

THIRD BASEMEN — FIELDING

		3 Games	4 Games	5 Games	6 Games	7 Games
Highest Percentage 1.000 (Most Chances)						
	AL:	16 B Robinson Balt 1969	19 T. Cruz Balt 1983	22 Bando Oak 1972	15 Ripken Balt 1997	15 Iorg Tor 1985
	NL:	8 Madlock Pitt 1979	19 Schmidt Phil 1977	17 Williams SF 1989	21 Ventura NY 1999	22 Buechele Pitt 1991 / Pendleton Atl 1992
Games						
	AL:	3 By many players	4 By many players	5 By many players	6 By many players	7 By many players
	NL:	3 By many players	4 By many players	5 By many players	6 By many players	7 By many players
Total Chances						
	AL:	16 B. Robinson Balt 1969	19 T. Cruz Balt 1983	24 DeCinces Cal 1982	26 Williams Clev 1997	26 DeCinces Cal 1986
	NL:	14 Schmidt Phil 1976	23 Schmidt Phil 1978	22 Cey LA 1981	25 Pendleton StL 1985 / Knight NY 1986	31 King Pitt 1992
Chances Accepted						
	AL:	16 B. Robinson Balt 1969	19 T. Cruz Balt 1983	22 Bando Oak 1972	24 Williams Clev 1997	24 DeCinces Cal 1986
	NL:	13 Schmidt Phil 1976	21 Cey LA 1977 / Schmidt Phil 1978	21 Cey LA 1981	24 Pendleton StL 1985 / Knight NY 1986	30 King Pitt 1992
Putouts						
	AL:	6 By many players	7 Lansford Oak 1988	9 Decinces Cal 1982	6 Ventura Chi 1993 / Williams Clev 1997	7 Brett KC 1985 / Boggs Bos 1986
	NL:	5 Perez Cin 1970	7 Cey LA 1977	5 By many players	7 Sabo Cin 1990 / Pendleton Atl 1993	11 King Pitt 1992
Assists						
	AL:	10 B. Robinson Balt 1969 / Bando Oak 1975	13 B. Robinson Balt 1974 / T. Cruz Balt 1983	16 Bando Oak 1972	18 Williams Clev 1997	18 DeCinces Cal 1986
	NL:	9 Schmidt Phil 1976	18 Schmidt Phil 1978	17 Schmidt Phil 1980	19 Knight NY 1986	19 King Pitt 1992
Errors						
	AL:	1 By many players	1 By many players	3 Brett KC 1976 / DeCinces Cal 1982 / Gruber Tor 1991	2 Williams Clev 1997	2 By many players
	NL:	1 By many players	2 By many players	3 Williams Ari. 2001	2 C. Jones Atl 1999	2 Hamilton LA 1988
Double Plays						
	AL:	2 Bando Oak 1971 / Nettles NY 1981	3 Lansford Cal 1979	3 DeCinces Cal 1982	3 Ripken Balt 1997 / Williams Clev 1997	3 DeCines Cal 1986
	NL:	2 Schmidt Phil 1976	2 Jones Atl 1995	3 Parrish Mtl 1981	4 Ventura NY 1999	5 King Pitt 1992

THIRD BASEMEN

Most Series
6 Graig Nettles, AL:NY 1976-78, 80-81; NL:SD 84
   George Brett, AL:KC 1976-78, 80, 84-85
   Terry Pendleton, NL:StL 1985,87; Atl 91-93,96
   Chipper Jones, NL:Atl 1995-99, 2001

Most Games
34 Terry Pendleton, NL:StL-Atl
    Chipper Jones, NL:Atl
27 George Brett, AL:KC

Highest Percentage (Minimum: 40 chances)
.989 Terry Pendleton, NL:Stl-Atl (90 tc)
.986 Sal Bando, AL:Oak (73 tc)

Most Total Chances
91 Mike Schmidt, NL:Phil
79 George Brett, AL:KC

Most Total Chances, Game
10 Ron Cey, NL:LA Oct. 16, 1981
9 Todd Cruz, AL:Balt Oct. 5, 1983
   Wade Boggs, AL:Bos Oct. 10, 1990

Most Total Chances, Inning
3 Denis Menke, NL:Cin Oct. 11, 1972 (9th)
   Ron Cey, NL:LA Oct. 4, 1977 (4th)
   Ron Cey, NL:LA Oct. 7, 1977 (8th)
   Ron Cey, NL:LA Oct. 16, 1981 (8th)
   Larry Parrish, NL:Mtl Oct. 17, 1981 (3rd)
   Jeff Hamilton, NL:LA Oct. 8, 1988 (6th)
   Jeff King, NL:Pitt Oct. 6, 1992 (1st)
   Gary Gaetti, NL:StL Oct. 17, 1996 (1st)
   George Brett, AL:KC Oct. 9, 1976 (1st)
   Todd Cruz, AL:Balt Oct. 5, 1983 (5th)
   Kelly Gruber, AL:Tor Oct. 12, 1992 (5th)

Most Chances Accepted
89 Terry Pendelton, NL:StL-Atl
72 Sal Bando, AL:Oak

Most Chances Accepted, Game
10 Ron Cey, NL:LA Oct. 16, 1981
9 Todd Cruz, AL:Balt Oct. 5, 1983
   Wade Boggs, AL:Bos Oct. 10, 1990

Most Chances Accepted, Inning
3 Denis Menke, NL:Cin Oct. 11, 1972 (9th)
   Ron Cey, NL:LA Oct. 4, 1977 (4th)
   Ron Cey, NL:LA Oct. 16, 1981 (8th)
   Jeff King, NL:Pitt Oct. 6, 1992 (1st)
   Gary Gaetti, NL:StL Oct. 17, 1996 (1st)
   Todd Cruz, AL:Balt Oct. 5, 1983 (5th)

Most Putouts
25 Sal Bando, AL:Oak
    Terry Pendleton, NL:StL-Atl

Most Putouts, Game
4 Carney Lansford, AL:Cal Oct. 6, 1979
   Wade Boggs, AL:Bos Oct. 10, 1990
3 By many NL players

Most Putouts, Inning
2 By many players

Most Assists
66 Mike Schmidt, NL:Phil
49 Brooks Robinson, AL:Balt
    George Brett, AL:KC

Most Assists, Game
8 Ron Cey, NL:LA Oct. 16, 1981
6 Sal Bando, AL:Oak Oct. 8, 1972
   Todd Cruz, AL:Balt Oct. 5, 1983
   Tom Brookens, AL:Det Oct. 11, 1987
   Wade Boggs, AL:NY Oct. 13, 1996
   Cal Ripken, AL:Balt Oct. 8, 1997
   Extra-Inning Game:
7 Aurelio Rodriguez, AL:Det Oct. 11, 1972 (11)

Most Assists, Inning
3 Ron Cey, NL:LA Oct. 4, 1977 (4th)
   Ron Cey, NL:LA Oct. 16, 1981 (8th)
   Todd Cruz, AL:Balt Oct. 5, 1983 (5th)

Most Errors
8 George Brett, AL:KC
5 Mike Schmidt, NL:Phil

Most Errors, Game
2 Ron Cey, NL:LA Oct. 5, 1974
   Fernando Tatis, NL:StL Oct. 15, 2000
   George Brett, AL:KC Oct. 9, 1976
   Doug DeCinces, AL:Cal Oct. 9, 1982
   Darrell Evans, AL:Det Oct. 11, 1987
   Kelly Gruber, AL:Tor Oct. 8, 1991

Most Errors, Inning
2 George Brett, AL:KC Oct. 9, 1976 (1st)
1 By many NL players

Most Double Plays
8 Terry Pendleton, NL:StL-Atl
7 Doug DeCinces, AL:Balt-Cal
   Carney Lansford, AL:Cal-Oak

Most Double Plays, Game
2 Mike Schmidt, NL:Phil Oct. 9, 1976
   Mike Schmidt, NL:Phil Oct. 11, 1980 (10 inn)
   Larry Parrish, NL:Mtl Oct. 16, 1981
   Jeff King, NL:Pitt Oct. 9-10, 1992
   Robin Ventura NL:NY Oct. 17, 1999 (15 inn)
   Doug DeCinces, AL:Cal Oct. 14, 1986

Double Plays, Unassisted
1 Mike Schmidt, NL:Phil Oct. 9, 1976 (5th)
   Jeff King, NL:Pitt Oct. 14, 1992 (6th)

SHORTSTOP – FIELDING

	3 Games	4 Games	5 Games	6 Games	7 Games
Highest Percentage 1.000 (Most Chances)					
AL:	21 Dent NY 1980	20 Campaneris Oak 1974	31 Patek KC 1976	31 Vizquel Clev 1997	29 Biancalana KC 1985
NL:	17 Concepcion Cin 1979	29 Russell LA 1974	31 Santana NY 1986	31 Santana NY 1986 / Ordonez NY 1999	30 Griffin LA 1988
Games					
AL:	3 By many players	4 By many players	5 By many players	6 By many players	7 By many players
NL:	3 By many players	4 By many players	5 By many players	6 By many players	7 By many players
Total Chances					
AL:	26 Cardenas Minn 1969	24 Garcia Balt 1979	31 Patek KC 1976	38 Vizquel Clev 1998	38 Owen Bos 1986
NL:	18 Ramirez, Atl 1982	29 Russell LA 1974	33 Speier Mtl 1981	37 Larkin Cin 1990	33 Uribe SF 1987 / Bell Pitt 1991
Chances Accepted					
AL:	25 Cardenas Minn 1969	22 Garcia Balt 1979	31 Patek KC 1976	37 Vizquel Clev 1998	36 Schofield Cal 1986
NL:	17 Concepcion Cin 1979	29 Russell LA 1974	31 Speier Mtl 1981	36 Larkin Cin 1990	32 Uribe SF 1987 / Bell Pitt 1991
Putouts					
AL:	13 Cardenas Minn 1969	9 Patek KC 1978	13 Patek KC 1976	16 Vizquel Clev 1997	13 Schofield Cal 1986
NL:	16 By many players	13 Russell LA 1974	19 Templeton SD 1984	21 Larkin Cin 1990	17 Griffin LA 1988
Assists					
AL:	14 Belanger Balt 1970	17 Campaneris Oak 1974	18 Patek KC 1976, 77	26 Vizquel Clev 1998	23 Schofield Cal 1986
NL:	14 Concepcion Cin 1979	17 Bowa Phil 1977	16 Chaney Cin 1972	24 Ordonez NY 1999	21 Uribe SF 1987
Errors					
AL:	2 Cardenas Minn 1970	2 Patek KC 1978 / Garcia Balt 1979	4 Garciaparra Bos 1999	3 Lee Tor 1992	5 Owen Bos 1986
NL:	1 By many players	2 Russell LA 1977 / DeJesus Phil 1983	3 Chaney Cin 1972	2 Reynolds Hou 1986	2 Elster NY 1988 / Blauser Atl 1992
Double Plays					
AL:	3 By many players	3 Ripkin Balt 1983 / Weiss Oak 1988 / Rivera Bos 1990	5 Ripken Balt 1996 / Jeter NY 1999	8 Vizquel Clev 1997	4 Biancalana KC 1985 / Schofield Cal 1986
NL:	3 Garrido Atl 1969 / Alley Pitt 1970	6 Russel LA 1974	6 Bowa Chi 1984	6 Speier Mtl 1981	7 Uribe SF 1987 / Griffin LA 1988

SHORTSTOPS

Most Series
6 Walt Weiss,AL:Oak 1988-90,92;NL:Atl 98-99
Mark Belanger, AL:Balt 1969-71,73-74,79
Bert Campaneris, AL:Oak 1971-75; Cal 79
Jeff Blauser, NL:Atl 1991-93, 95-97

Most Games
29 Jeff Blauser, NL:Atl
27 Derek Jeter, AL:NY

Highest Percentage (Minimum: 40 chances)
1.000 Mike Bordick, AL:Balt; NL:NY (60 tc)
Edgar Renteria, NL:Fla-StL (46 tc)
.990 Mark Belenger, AL:Balt

Most Total Chances
109 Bill Russell, NL:LA
103 Derek Jeter, AL:NY

Most Total Chances, Game
13 Bill Russell, NL:LA Oct. 8, 1974
11 Kiko Garcia, AL:Balt Oct. 4, 1979
Omar Vizquel, AL:Clev Oct. 9, 1998
Extra-Inning Game:
12 Leo Cardenas, AL:Minn Oct. 5, 1969 (11 inn)

Most Total Chances, Inning
3 By many players

Most Chances Accepted
106 Bill Russell, NL:LA
101 Derek Jeter, AL:NY

Most Chances Accepted, Game
13 Bill Russell, NL:LA Oct. 8, 1974
11 Leo Cardenas, AL:Minn Oct. 5, 1969 (11 inn)
Kiko Garcia, AL:Balt Oct. 4, 1979
Omar Vizquel, AL:Clev Oct. 9, 1998

Most Chances Accepted, Inning
3 By many players

Most Putouts
41 Bill Russell, NL:LA
40 Derek Jeter, AL:NY

Most Putouts, Game
7 Garry Templeton, NL:SD Oct. 4, 1984
6 By many AL players

Most Putouts, Inning
3 Mark Belanger, AL:Balt Oct. 5, 1974 (3rd)
Freddie Patek, AL:KC Oct. 5, 1977 (2nd)
Omar Vizquel, AL:Clev Oct. 15, 1995 (8th)
Chris Speier, NL:Mtl Oct. 14, 1981 (5th)

Most Assists
70 Larry Bowa, NL:Phil-Chi
67 Mark Belanger, AL:Balt

Most Assists, Game
9 Bill Russell, NL:LA Oct. 5, 1978
Kiko Garcia, AL:Balt Oct. 4, 1979

Most Assists, Inning
3 Mark Belanger, AL:Balt Oct. 7, 1973 (7th)
Walt Weiss, AL:Oak Oct. 8, 1989 (1st)
Manuel Lee, AL:Tor Oct. 13, 1991 (5th)
Omar Vizquel, AL:Clev Oct. 10, 1995 (2nd)
Dave Concepcion, NL:Cin Oct. 3, 1979 (4th)
Barry Larkin, NL:Cin Oct. 10, 1990 (6th)
Jeff Blauser, NL:Atl Oct. 13, 1993 (7th)

Most Errors
5 Spike Owen, AL:Bos
Jeff Blauser, NL:Atl

Most Errors, Game
2 Leo Cardenas, AL:Minn Oct. 4, 1970
Manuel Lee, AL:Tor Oct. 11, 1992 (11 inn)
Nomar Garciaparra, AL:Bos Oct. 13, 1999 (10 inn)
Gene Alley, NL:Pitt Oct. 10, 1972
Bill Russell, NL:LA Oct. 4, 1977
Kevin Elster, NL:NY Oct. 9, 1988 (12 inn)
Rey Sanchez, NL:Atl Oct. 20, 2001

Most Errors, Inning
2 Gene Alley, NL:Pitt Oct. 10, 1972 (4th)
Kevin Elster, NL:NY Oct. 9, 1988 (5th)
1 By many AL players

Most Double Plays
18 Bill Russell, NL:LA
Omar Vizquel, AL:Clev

Most Double Plays, Game
3 Bill Russell, NL:LA Oct. 8, 1974
Bill Russell, NL:LA Oct. 5, 1983
Jose Uribe, NL:SF Oct. 10, 1987
Ozzie Smith, NL:StL Oct. 14, 1987
Jeff Blauser, NL:Atl Oct. 10, 1995 (11 inn)
Bert Campaneris, AL:Oak Oct. 5, 1975
Omar Vizquel, AL:Clev Oct. 11, 1997 (12 inn)
Omar Vizquel, AL:Clev Oct. 13, 1997
Omar Vizquel, AL:Clev Oct. 9, 1998

Double Plays, Unassisted
1 Bill Russell, NL:LA Oct. 8, 1974 (6th)
Alfredo Griffin, NL:LA Oct. 5, 1988 (1st)
Walt Weiss NL:Atl Oct. 19, 1999 (6th)
Robin Yount, AL:Mil Oct. 5, 1982 (4th)
Buddy Biancalana, AL:KC Oct. 12, 1985 (6th)
Tony Fernandez, AL:Tor Oct. 4, 1989 (1st)
Omar Vizquel, AL:Clev Oct. 15, 1995 (8th)

OUTFIELDERS – FIELDING

		3 Games	4 Games	5 Games	6 Games	7 Games
Highest Percentage 1.000 (Most Chances)						
	AL:	12 Oliva Minn 1970	16 Miller Cal 1979	22 D.Henderson Oak 1989	16 Wilson Oak 1992 / Cameron Sea 2000 / A. Jones & Jordan Atl 1999	18 Downing Cal 1986
	NL:	14 Parker Pitt 1975	13 Stargell Pitt 1974	23 Maddox Phil 1980 / Wilson NY 1986	17 McGee StL 1985	22 Justice Atl 1992
Games						
	AL:	3 By many players	4 By many players	5 By many players	6 By many players	7 By many players
	NL:	3 By many players	4 By many players	5 By many players	6 By many players	7 By many players
Total Chances						
	AL:	14 Lynn Bos 1975	16 Miller Cal 1979	22 D.Henderson Oak 1989	18 R. Henderson Oak 1992	29 Pettis Cal 1986
	NL:	14 Parker Pitt 1975	17 Maddox Phil 1978	23 Maddox Phil 1980	17 By many players	22 Justice Atl 1992
Chances Accepted						
	AL:	13 Lynn Bos 1975	16 Miller Cal 1979	22 D.Henderson Oak 1989	16 Wilson Tor & White Tor. 1992 / Cameron Sea 2000	28 Pettis Cal 1986
	NL:	14 Parker Pitt 1975	16 Maddox Phil 1978	23 Maddox Phil 1980	18 McGee StL 1985	22 Justice Atl 1992
Putouts						
	AL:	12 Lynn Bos 1975	14 North Oak 1974 / Miller Cal 1979 / Canseco Oak 1990	22 D.Henderson Oak 1989	16 Wilson Oak & White Tor 1992 / Cameron Sea 2000	28 Pettis Cal 1986
	NL:	13 Parker Pitt 1975 / Geronimo Cin 1975	16 Maddox Phil 1978	23 Maddox Phil 1980	18 McGee StL 1985	20 Van Slyke Pitt 1992
Assists						
	AL:	2 By many players	2 Miller Cal 1979	1 By many players	2 Raines Chi 1993	3 L. Smith KC 1985
	NL:	2 Foster Cin 1979	2 McBride Phil 1977	3 McBride Phil 1980	3 Mora NY 1999	3 Justice Atl 1992
Errors						
	AL:	2 Oliva Minn 1969 / Washington Oak 1975	2 D. Henderson Oak 1988	2 Gamble NY 1976 / Oglivie Mil 1982	3 R. Henderson Oak 1992	2 Barfield Tor 1985 / L. Smith KC 1985
	NL:	1 By many players	1 By many players	2 By many players	2 Lofton Atl 1997	1 C. Davis SF 1987 / Justice Atl 1991 / Bonds Pitt 1991 / Grissom ATL 1996 / McGee StL 1996
Double Plays						
	AL:	1 By many players	2 Miller Cal 1979	1 O'Neill NY 1996	1 Carter & Maldonado Tor 1992	0
	NL:	1 Parker Pitt 1975	1 McBride Phil 1977	2 McBride Phil 1980	1 By many players	1 By many players

OUTFIELDERS

Most Series
10 Reggie Jackson, AL:Oak 1971-75;
   NY 77-78, 80-81; Cal 82
5 Cesar Geronimo, NL:Cin 1972-73, 75-76, 79
   Garry Maddox, NL:Phil 1976-78, 80, 83
   Ron Gant, NL:Atl 1991-93; Cin 95; StL 96
   Andruw Jones, NL:Atl 1996-99, 2001

Most Games
33 Rickey Henderson, AL:Oak-Tor-Sea; NL:NY
32 Reggie Jackson, AL:Oak-NY-Cal
31 Ron Gant, NL:Atl-Cin-Stl

Highest Percentage (Minimum: 30 chances)
1.000 Paul O'Neil, NL:Cin; AL:NY (64 tc)
   Andruw Jones, NL:Atl (63 tc)
   Paul O'Neil, AL:NY (53 tc)

Most Total Chances
74 Reggie Jackson, AL:Oak-NY-Cal
66 Ron Gant, NL:Atl-Cin-Stl

Most Total Chances, Game
9 Jesse Barfield, AL:Tor Oct. 11, 1985
   Gary Pettis, AL:Cal Oct. 10, 1986
8 Al Oliver, NL:Pitt Oct. 7, 1972
   Don Hahn, NL:NY Oct. 8, 1973
   Brian Jordan, NL:Atl Oct. 21, 2001

Most Total Chances, Inning
3 By many players

Most Chances Accepted
73 Reggie Jackson, AL:Oak-NY-Cal
65 Ron Gant, NL:Atl-Cin-Stl

Most Chances Accepted, Game
9 Jesse Barfield, AL:Tor Oct. 11, 1985
   Gary Pettis, AL:Cal Oct. 10, 1986
8 Al Oliver, NL:Pitt Oct. 7, 1972
   Don Hahn, NL:NY Oct. 8, 1973
   Brian Jordan, NL:Atl Oct. 21, 2001

Most Chances Accepted, Inning
3 By many players

Most Putouts
70 Bernie Williams, AL:NY
63 Garry Maddox, NL:Phil

Most Putouts, Game
9 Jesse Barfield, AL:Tor Oct. 11, 1985
   Gary Pettis, AL:Cal Oct. 10, 1986
8 Al Oliver, NL:Pitt Oct. 7, 1972
   Don Hahn, NL:NY Oct. 8, 1973
   Brian Jordan, NL:Atl Oct. 21, 2001

Most Putouts, Inning
3 Andre Dawson, NL:Mtl Oct. 19, 1981 (7th)
   Andruw Jones, NL:Atl Oct. 10, 1997 (7th)
   Brian Jordan, NL:Atl Oct. 21, 2001 (7th)
   By many AL players

Most Assists
6 Lonnie Smith, NL:Phil-StL-Atl; AL:KC
5 Bake McBride, NL:Phil
4 Reggie Jackson, AL:Oak-NY-Cal

Most Assists, Game
2 Tony Oliva, AL:Minn Oct. 4, 1970
   Rickey Henderson, NL:NY Oct. 15, 1999
   George Foster, NL:Cin Oct. 3, 1979 (10 inn)
   Bake McBride, NL:Phil Oct. 11, 1980 (10 inn)
   Wes Chamberlain, NL:Phil Oct. 11, 1993
   (10 inn)

Most Assists, Inning
1 By many players

Most Errors
7 Rickey Henderson, AL:Oak-Tor-Sea; NL:NY
6 Rickey Henderson, AL:Oak-Tor-Sea
2 Marquis Grissom, NL:Atl
   David Justice, NL:Atl
   Kenny Lofton, NL:Atl
   Garry Maddox, NL:Phil
   Willie McGee, NL:StL
   Reggie Smith, NL:LA

Most Errors, Game
2 Tony Oliva, AL:Minn Oct. 6, 1969
   Ben Oglivie, AL:Mil Oct. 10, 1982
   Albert Belle, AL:Chi Oct. 15, 1995
1 By many NL players

Most Errors, Inning
2 Albert Belle, AL:Clev Oct. 15, 1995 (5th)
1 By many NL players

Most Double Plays
3 Bake McBride, NL:Phil
2 Rick Miller, AL:Cal

Most Double Plays, Game
1 By many players
   Extra-Inning Game:
2 Bake McBride, NL:Phil Oct. 11, 1980 (10 inn)

Double Plays, Unassisted
0 Not Accomplished

CATCHERS – FIELDING

	3 Games	4 Games	5 Games	6 Games	7 Games
Highest Percentage 1.000 (Most Chances)					
AL:	25 Cerone NY 1981	39 Gedman Bos 1988	39 Simmons Mil 1982	54 Posada NY 2000	53 Whitt Tor 1985
NL:	28 Ott Pitt 1979	36 Dietz SF 1971	41 Piazza NY 2000	60 Ashby Hou 1986	63 Olson Atl 1991
Games					
AL:	3 By many players	4 By many players	5 By many players	6 By many players	7 By many players
NL:	3 By many players	4 By many players	5 By many players	6 By many players	7 By many players
Total Chances					
AL:	25 Cerone NY 1981	39 Gedman Bos 1988	46 Varitek Bos 1999	54 Posada NY 2000	53 Whitt Tor 1985
NL:	31 Sanguillen Pitt 1975	36 Dietz SF 1971	44 Grote NY 1973	60 Ashby Hou 1986	63 Olson Atl 1991
Chances Accepted					
AL:	25 Cerone NY 1981	39 Gedman Bos 1988	45 Varitek Bos 1999	54 Posada NY 2000	53 Whitt Tor 1985
NL:	30 Sanguillen Pitt 1975	36 Dietz SF 1971	43 Grote NY 1973	60 Ashby Hou 1986	63 Olson Atl 1991
Putouts					
AL:	23 Cerone NY 1981	34 Gedman Bos 1988	44 Varitek Bos 1999	51 Posada NY 2000	50 Whitt Tor 1985
NL:	29 Sanguillen Pitt 1975	34 Dietz SF 1971	42 Grote NY 1973	59 Ashby Hou 1986	62 Olson Atl 1991
Assists					
AL:	4 Mitterwald Minn 1969, Cerone NY 1980	5 Gedman Bos 1988, Dempsey Balt 1983	6 Munson NY 1976	7 Steinbach Oak 1992	4 Gedman Bos 1986
NL:	4 Bench Cin 1975-76	2 By many players	4 Kennedy SD 1984	5 Carter NY 1986	5 Pena StL 1987, Slaught Pitt 1991, Berryhill Atl 1992
Errors					
AL:	3 Slaught KC 1984	1 Dempsey Balt 1983, Pena Bos 1990	2 Munson NY 1976, Borders Tor 1991	2 Webster Balt 1997, Alomar Clev 1998	1 Sundberg KC 1985
NL:	1 Sanguillen Pitt 1970, 75	2 Sanguillen Pitt 1974	1 By many players	3 Piazza NY 1999	0
Passed Balls					
AL:	1 Cerone NY 1981	1 By many players	2 Borders Tor 1991	3 Borders Tor 1992	2 Boone Cal 1986
NL:	2 Sanguillen Pitt 197+5	1 By many players	1 By many players	2 Ashby Hou 1986, Daulton Phil 1993	2 Slaught Pitt 1992
Double Plays					
AL:	2 Mitterwald Minn 1970	1 By many players	2 Fosse Oak 1973	1 Borders Tor 1992-93, Alomar Clev 1997, Posada NY 2000	1 By many players
NL:	1 By many players	1 By many players	2 Kennedy SF 1989	2 Lopez Atl 1997, Piazza NY 1999	2 Olson Atl 1991

CATCHERS

Most Series
6 Bob Boone, NL:Phil 1976-78,80; AL:Cal 82,86
Johnny Bench, NL:Cin 1970,72-73,75-76,79
Steve Yeager, NL:LA 1974,77-78,81,83,85
Javy Lopez, NL:Atl 1992,95-98, 2001
5 Andy Etchebarren, AL:Balt 1969-71,73-74

Most Games
27 Bob Boone, NL:Phil; AL:Cal
Javy Lopez, NL:Atl
19 Jorge Posada, AL:NY

Highest Percentage (Most Chances)
1.000 Gary Carter, NL:Mtl-NY (136 tc)
Rich Gedman AL:Bos (88 tc)

Most Total Chances
195 Javy Lopez, NL:Atl
149 Jorge Posada, AL:NY

Most Total Chances, Game
16 Rick Dempsey, AL:Balt Oct. 6, 1983
Chris Hoiles, AL:Balt Oct. 11, 1997 (12 inn)
Charles Johnson, NL:Fla Oct. 12, 1997
Extra-Inning Game:
18 Mike Piazza, NL:NY Oct. 17, 1999 (15 inn)

Most Total Chances, Inning
4 Pat Borders, AL:Tor Oct. 8, 1991 (3rd)
Jorge Posada, AL:NY Oct. 16, 1999 (5th)
3 By many NL players

Most Chances Accepted
193 Javy Lopez, NL:Atl
148 Jorge Posada, AL:NY

Most Chances Accepted, Game
16 Rick Dempsey, AL:Balt Oct. 6, 1983
Chris Hoiles, AL:Balt Oct. 11, 1997 (12 inn)
Charles Johnson, NL:Fla Oct. 12, 1997
Extra-Inning Game:
18 Mike Piazza, NL:NY Oct. 17, 1999 (15 inn)

Most Chances Accepted, Inning
4 Pat Borders, AL:Tor Oct. 8, 1991 (3rd)
3 By many NL players

Most Putouts
183 Javy Lopez, NL:Atl
140 Jorge Posada, AL:NY

Most Putouts, Game
15 Rick Dempsey, AL:Balt Oct. 6, 1983
Chris Hoiles, AL:Balt Oct. 11, 1997 (12 inn)
Jorge Posada, AL:NY Oct. 14, 2000
Charles Johnson, NL:Fla Oct. 12, 1997
Extra-Inning Game:
16 Mike Piazza NL:NY Oct. 17, 1999 (15 inn)

Most Putouts, Inning
3 By many players

Most Assists
18 Johnny Bench, NL:Cin
14 Thurman Munson, AL:NY

Most Assists, Game
3 Johnny Bench, NL:Cin Oct. 3, 1970 (10 inn)
Johnny Bench, NL:Cin Oct. 5, 1975
Gary Carter, NL:NY Oct. 15, 1986 (16 inn)
Rich Gedman, AL:Bos Oct. 8, 1988
Terry Steinbach, AL:Oak Oct. 10, 1992
Pat Borders, AL:Tor Oct. 8, 1993
Dan Wilson, AL:Sea Oct. 11, 2000

Most Assists, Inning
2 Johnny Bench, NL:Cin Oct. 7, 1973 (8th)
Mike Scioscia, NL:LA Oct. 10, 1985 (1st)
Gary Carter, NL:NY Oct. 15, 1986 (12th)
Rich Gedman, AL:Bos Oct. 8, 1988 (1st)
Tom Lampkin, AL:Sea Oct. 21, 2001 (2nd)

Most Errors
5 Manny Sanguillen, NL:Pitt
3 Don Slaught, AL:KC
Pat Borders, AL:Tor
Sandy Alomar, Jr. AL:Clev

Most Errors, Game
2 Manny Sanguillen, NL:Pitt Oct. 6, 1974
Mike Piazza, NL:NY Oct. 19, 1999 (11 inn)
Thurman Munson, AL:NY Oct. 10, 1976
Don Slaught, AL:KC Oct. 5, 1984
Sandy Alomar, Jr. AL:Clev Oct. 10, 1998

Most Errors, Inning
1 By many players

Most Passed Balls
5 Pat Borders, AL:Tor
4 Manny Sanguillen, NL:Pitt

Most Passed Balls, Game
2 Manny Sanguillen, NL:Pitt Oct. 4, 1975
Alan Ashby, NL:Hou Oct. 11, 1986
Don Slaught, NL:Pitt Oct. 13, 1992
Pat Borders, AL:Tor Oct. 13, 1991
Pat Borders, AL:Tor Oct. 14, 1992

Most Passed Balls, Inning
2 Pat Borders, AL:Tor Oct. 13, 1991 (2nd)
1 By many NL players

Most Double Plays
4 Ray Fosse, AL:Oak
3 Manny Sanguillen, NL:Pitt
Terry Kennedy, NL:SD-SF

Most Double Plays, Game
1 By many players

Double Plays, Unassisted
0 Not accomplished

PITCHERS – FIELDING

	3 Games	4 Games	5 Games	6 Games	7 Games
Highest Percentage 1.000 (Most Chances)					
AL:	5 By many players	5 By many players	5 John Cal 1982 / Flanagan Tor 1989 / Rivera NY 2001	5 Erickson Balt 1997	10 Leibrandt KC 1985
NL:	5 Gullet Cin 1975	6 Marichal SF 1971 / Carlton Phil 1983	5 Blass Pitt 1972 / Ryan Hou 1980 / Kile StL 2000 / Glavine Atl 2001	8 Ashby SD 1998	9 Cox StL 1987
Games					
AL:	3 By many players	4 Eckersley Oak 1988	5 Acker Tor 1989	5 Assenmacher Clev 1997 / Jackson Clev 1997 / Shuey Clev 1998	4 By many players
NL:	3 By many players	4 Guisti Pitt 1971 / Wohlers Atl 1995	5 McGraw Phil 1980	6 Rocker Atl 1998-99	6 Petkovsek StL 1996
Total Chances					
AL:	5 By many players	5 By many players	5 John Cal 1982 / Flannagan Tor 1989 / Morris Minn 1991 / Rivera NY 2001	5 Erickson Balt 1997	10 Leibrandt KC 1985
NL:	5 Gullett Cin 1975	6 Marichal SF 1971 / Carlton Phil 1983	6 Maddux Atl 2001	10 Maddux Atl 1993	9 Cox StL 1987
Chances Accepted					
AL:	5 By many players	5 By many players	5 John Cal 1982 / Flanagan Tor 1989 / Morris Minn 1991 / Rivera NY 2001	5 Erickson Balt 1997	10 Leibrandt KC 1985
NL:	5 Gullett Cin 1975	6 Marichal SF 1971 / Carlton Phil 1983	5 Blass Pitt 1972 / Ryan Hou 1980 / Kile StL 2000 / Glavine Atl 2001 / Maddux Atl 2001	9 Maddux Atl 1993	9 Cox StL 1987
Putouts					
AL:	2 By many players	3 Hunter Oak 1974	4 Rivera NY 2001	4 Tomko Sea 2000	3 Leibrandt KC 1985
NL:	4 Gullett Cin 1975	2 By many players	2 By many players	4 Maddux Atl 1993 / Ashby SD 1998	4 Cox StL 1987

PITCHERS – FIELDING

	3 Games	4 Games	5 Games	6 Games	7 Games
Most Assists					
AL:	4 By many players	5 Cuellar Balt 1974	3 By many players	5 Erickson Balt 1997	7 Leibrandt KC 1985
NL:	3 By many players	5 Carlton Phil 1983	4 Kile StL 2000	7 Maddux Atl 1997	5 Cox StL 1987
Errors					
AL:	1 Saberhagen KC 1984	1 Clemens Bos 1988 / Gray & Boddicker Bos 1990	1 By many players	1 By many players	0
NL:	1 Walker Pitt 1970	1 By many players	1 By many players	2 Andujar StL 1985	1 Reuschel SF 1987
Double Plays					
AL:	1 By many players	0	2 Flanagan Tor 1989	2 Nelson Sea 1995	1 By many players
NL:	1 Jarvis & Upshaw Atl 1969	1 By many players	2 Maddux Atl 2001	2 Mahomes NY 1999	2 Cox StL 1987

PITCHERS

Most Series
9 Tom Glavine NL:Atl 1991-93; 95-99, 2001
  John Smoltz, NL:Atl 1991-93, 95-99, 2001
6 Catfish Hunter, AL:Oak 1971-74; NY 76,78
  Jim Palmer, AL:Balt 1969-71, 73-74,79
  Jimmy Key, AL:Tor 1985,89,91-92; NY 96;
    Balt 97
  Roger Clemens, AL:Bos. 1986,88,90;
    NY 99-2001
  Jeff Nelson, AL:Sea. 1995, 2001;
    NY:1996,98-2000

Most Games
20 Rick Honeycutt, NL:LA-StL; AL:Oak
18 Mark Wohlers, NL:Atl
16 Mariano Rivera, AL:NY

Highest Percentage (Most Chances)
1.000 Tom Glavine, NL:Atl (27 tc)
      Mariano Rivera, AL:NY (15 tc)

Most Total Chances
39 Greg Maddux, NL:Chi-Atl
15 Mariano Rivera, AL:NY

Most Total Chances, Game
8 Charlie Leibrandt, AL:KC Oct. 12, 1985
6 Juan Marichal, NL:SF Oct. 5, 1971

Most Total Chances, Inning
3 Pat Zachry, NL:Cin Oct. 10, 1976 (4th)
  John Smoltz, NL:Atl Oct. 7, 1998 (1st)
  Bud Black, AL:KC Oct. 9, 1985 (7th)
  Mariano Rivera, AL:NY Oct. 17, 2001 (9th)

Most Chances Accepted
36 Greg Maddux, NL:Chi-Atl
15 Mariano Rivera, AL:NY

Most Chances Accepted, Game
8 Charlie Leibrandt, AL:KC Oct. 12, 1985
6 Juan Marichal, NL:SF Oct. 5, 1971

Most Chances Accepted, Inning
3 Pat Zachry, NL:Cin Oct. 10, 1976 (4th)
  Bud Black, AL:KC Oct. 9, 1985 (7th)
  Mariano Rivera, AL:NY Oct. 17, 2001 (9th)

Most Putouts
11 Greg Maddux, NL:Chi-Atl
9 Mariano Rivera, AL:NY

Most Putouts, Game
4 Don Gullett, NL:Cin Oct. 4, 1975
3 Tommy John, AL:Cal Oct. 5, 1982
  Charlie Leibrandt, AL:KC Oct. 12, 1985
  Charles Nagy, AL:Clev Oct. 7, 1998 (12 inn)

Most Putouts, Inning
2 Don Gullett, NL:Cin Oct. 4, 1975 (3rd)
  Roger McDowell, NL:NY Oct. 15, 1986 (10th)
  Mike Torrez, AL:NY Oct. 7, 1977 (2nd)
  Charlie Leibrandt, AL:KC Oct. 12, 1985 (5th)
  Bret Saberhagen, AL:KC Oct. 16, 1985 (3rd)
  Mike Witt, AL:Cal Oct. 12, 1986 (1st)
  Mariano Rivera, AL:NY Oct. 17, 2001 (9th)

Most Assists
25 Greg Maddux, NL:Chi-Atl
12 Mike Cuellar, AL:Balt

Most Assists, Game
5 Charlie Leibrandt, AL:KC Oct. 12, 1985
4 Juan Marichal, NL:SF Oct. 5, 1971
  Greg Maddux, NL:Atl Oct. 7, 1997
  Tom Glavine NL:Atl Oct. 14, 1997
  Andy Ashby, NL:SD Oct. 7, 1998 (10 inn)
  Greg Maddux, NL:Atl Oct. 12, 1999
  Kenny Rogers, NL:NY Oct. 13, 1999

Most Assists, Inning
3 Pat Zachry, NL:Cin Oct. 10, 1976 (4th)
2 By many AL players

Most Errors
3 Greg Maddux, NL:Chi-Atl
2 Bret Saberhagen, AL:KC-Bos

Most Errors, Game
1 By many players

Most Errors, Inning
1 By many players

Most Double Plays
3 Greg Maddux, NL:Chi-Atl
  Mike Flanagan, AL:Tor
  Jeff Nelson, AL:Sea

Most Double Plays, Game
2 Danny Cox, NL:StL Oct. 14, 1987
  Greg Maddux, NL:Atl Oct. 16, 2001
  Mike Flanagan, AL:Tor Oct. 7, 1989
  Jeff Nelson, AL:Sea Oct. 14, 1995

Double Plays, Unassisted
0 Not accomplished

CHAMPIONSHIP SERIES PITCHING RECORDS

	3 Games	4 Games	5 Games	6 Games	7 Games
Games					
AL:	3 Perranoski Minn 1969 / Todd Oak 1975 / Hernandez Det 1984	4 Eckersley Oak 1988	5 Acker Tor 1989	5 Assenmacher Clev 1997 / Jackson Clev 1997 / Shuey Clev 1998 / Paniagua Sea 2000	4 By many players
NL:	3 By many players	4 Guisti Pitt 1971 / Wohlers Atl 1995	5 McGraw Phil 1980	6 Rocker Atl 1998-99	6 Petkovsek StL 1996
Games Started					
AL:	2 Holtzman Oak 1975	2 By many players	2 By many players	2 By many players	3 Stieb Tor 1985 / Clemens Bos 1986
NL:	1 By many players	2 By many players	2 By many players	2 By many players	3 Hershiser LA 1988 / Drabek Pitt; Smoltz Atl 1992
Complete Games					
AL:	1 By many players	1 By many players	1 By many players	1 By many players	1 By many players
NL:	1 By many players	1 By many players	1 By many players	2 Scott Hou 1986	2 Cox StL 1987 / Wakefield Pitt 1992
Games Finished					
AL:	3 Perranoski Minn 1969	4 Eckersley Oak 1988	4 Lyle NY 1977 / Reardon Minn 1987 / Eckersley Oak 1989 / Rivera NY 2001	4 Henke Tor 1992 / Hernandez Chi 1993 / Ward Tor 1993	4 Quisenberry KC 1985 / Schiraldi Bos 1986
NL:	2 By many players	4 Giusti Pitt 1971	4 Borbon Cin 1973 / Bedrosian SF 1989	4 Orosco NY 1986 / Wohlers Atl 1993	4 Pena Atl 1991
Saves					
AL:	2 Drago Bos 1975	4 Eckersley Oak 1988	3 Eckersley Oak 1989 / Aguilera Minn 1991	3 Henke Tor 1992	1 By many players
NL:	2 Gullett Cin 1970	3 Giusti Pitt 1971	3 Bedrosian SF 1989	3 Myers Cin 1990	3 Pena Atl 1991
Most Decisions					
AL:	2 Holtzman Oak 1975	2 By many players	2 By many players	2 By many players	3 Leibrandt KC 1985
NL:	1 By many players	2 By many players	2 By many players	3 Orosco NY 1986	3 Drabek Pitt 1992
Most Won					
AL:	1 By many players	2 Nelson Oak 1988 / Stewart Oak 1990	2 By many players	2 By many players	2 Henke Tor 1985
NL:	1 By many players	2 Sutton LA 1974 / Carlton Phil 1983	2 Lefferts SD 1984 / Hampton NY 2000 / Johnson Ari 2001	3 Orosco NY 1986	2 Myers NY 1988 / Belcher LA 1988 / Avery Atl 1991 / Smoltz NL Atl 1991-92, 96 / Wakefield Pitt 1992

CHAMPIONSHIP SERIES PITCHING RECORDS

		3 Games	4 Games	5 Games	6 Games	7 Games
Most Lost	AL:	2 Holtzman Oak 1975	2 Leonard KC 1978 / Hurst Bos 1988	2 Fryman Det 1972 / Alexander Det 1987 / Stieb Tor 1989 / Sele Sea 2001	2 Moore Oak 1992 / Fernandez & McDowell Chi 1993 / Benitez Balt 1997 / Ogea Clev 1997 / Neagle NY 2000	2 Leibrandt KC 1985 / McCaskill Cal 1986
	NL:	1 By many players	2 Reuss Pitt 1974; LA 83	2 Gullickson Mtl 1981 / Kile StL 2000 / Maddux Atl 2001	2 Niedenfuer LA 1985 / Z. Smith Pitt 1990 / Maddux Atl 1997 / Glavine Atl 1998 / Rogers NY 1999	3 Drabek Pitt 1992
Innings	AL:	11.0 McNally Balt 1969 / Holtzman Oak 1975	16.0 Stewart Oak 1990	19.0 Lolich Det 1972	16.2 Stewart Oak 1992	22.2 Clemens Bos 1986
	NL:	9.2 Ellis Pitt 1970	17.0 Sutton LA 1974	17.0 Burris Mtl 1981	18.0 Scott Hou 1986	24.2 Hershiser LA 1988
Runs	AL:	9 Perry Minn 1970	10 Frost Cal 1979	10 Alexander Det 1987	10 McDowell Chi 1993	13 McCaskill Cal 1986
	NL:	9 Niekro Atl 1969	11 Perry SF 1971	12 Maddux Chi 1989	10 Andujar StL 1985 / Greene Phil 1993	11 Drabek Pitt 1992 / Glavine Atl 1992 / Stottlemyre StL 1996
Earned Runs	AL:	8 Perry Minn 1970	9 Frost Cal 1979	10 Alexander Det 1987	10 McDowell Chi 1993	11 Clemens Bos 1986
	NL:	6 Jarvis Atl 1969 / Koosman NY 1969	10 Perry SF 1971	11 Maddux Chi 1989	10 Greene Phil 1993	11 Stottlemyre StL 1996
Hits	AL:	12 Holtzman Oak 1975	13 Leonard KC 1978	18 Gura KC 1976	18 McDowell Chi 1993	22 Clemens Bos 1986
	NL:	10 Jarvis Atl 1969	19 Perry SF 1971 / Perez Atl 1982	16 Ryan Hou 1980 / Garrelts SF 1989	17 Hershiser LA 1985	19 Andy Benes StL 1996
Home Runs	AL:	4 Hunter Oak 1971	3 Hunter Oak 1974 & NY 1978 / Boddicker Bos 1988	4 McNally 1973 / Pettitte NY 1996	4 Pettitte NY 1998	4 Alexander Tor 1985
	NL:	3 Jarvis Atl 1969	4 Blass Pitt 1971	5 Show SD 1984	3 Greene Phil 1993	4 Wakefield Pitt 1992
Walks	AL:	7 Boswell Minn 1969	13 Cuellar Balt 1974	8 Palmer Balt 1973 / Abbott Sea 2001	9 Morris Tor 1992 / Guzman Tor 1993	10 Stieb Tor 1985
	NL:	5 Norman Cin 1974 / Carlton Phil 1978	8 Reuss Pitt 1974 / Carlton Phil 1977	8 Carlton Phil 1980 / Sutcliffe Chi 1984	11 Glavine Atl 1997	10 Smoltz Atl 1992

CHAMPIONSHIP SERIES PITCHING RECORDS

		3 Games	4 Games	5 Games	6 Games	7 Games
Intentional Walks						
AL:		2 Segui Oak 1971	2 Gardner Bos 1988	3 Henneman Det 1987	3 Fernandez Chi 1993	2 Stieb Tor 1985 / Schiraldi Bos 1986
NL:		2 By many players	4 Giusti Pitt 1974	3 McGraw Phil 1980 / Christenson Phil 1980	3 Welch LA 1985 / Lopez Hou 1986 / Avery Atl 1993 / Glavine Atl 1997	2 Tudor StL 1987 / Gooden NY 1988 / Glavine Atl 1991 / Smoltz Atl 1992
Hit Batters						
AL:		1 By many players	2 Boddicker Balt 1983 / Boddicker Bos 1990	3 Tanana Det 1987	3 Key Balt 1997	2 Clemens Bos 1986
NL:		1 By many players	2 John LA 1977	1 By many players	2 Leiter NY 1999	2 Hershiser LA 1988 / Glavine Atl 1992
Strikeouts						
AL:		12 Palmer Balt 1970	14 Boddicker Balt 1983	15 Palmer Balt 1973	25 Mussina Balt 1997	18 Stieb Tor 1985
NL:		14 Candelaria Pitt 1975	13 Sutton LA 1974 / Carlton Phil 1983 / Schourek Cin 1995	19 Johnson Ari 2001	19 Scott Hou 1986	20 Gooden NY 1988
Wild Pitches						
AL:		1 By many players	1 By many players	3 John Cal 1982	3 Guzman Tor 1993	2 Black KC 1985
NL:		2 McGraw Phil 1976 / Eastwick Cin 1976 / Andujar StL 1982	2 Marichal SF 1971 / Carlton Phil 1983 / Pena LA 1983	4 Ankiel StL 2000	2 Worrell StL 1985 / Calhoun Hou 1986 / Avery Atl 1993 / Hitchcock SD 1998	2 Gooden NY 1988 / Hershiser LA 1988 / Pena Atl 1991 / Smoltz Atl 1996
Balks						
AL:		See Game Record	See Game Record	See Game Record	See Game Record	1 See Game Record
NL:		See Game Record	See Game Record	See Game Record	See Game Record	See Game Record

INDIVIDUAL PITCHING

Most Series
9 Tom Glavine, NL:Atl 1991-93; 95-99, 2001
John Smoltz, NL:Atl 1991-93, 95-99, 2001
6 Catfish Hunter, AL:Oak 1971-74; NY 76,78
Jim Palmer, AL:Balt 1969-71, 73-74,79
Jimmy Key, AL:Tor 1985,89,91-92; NY 96;
    Balt 97
Roger Clemens, AL:Bos 1986,88,90;
    NY 99-2001
Jeff Nelson, AL:Sea 1995, 2001;
    NY 96,98-2000

Lowest Earned Run Average (Minimum: 20 IP)
0.397 Tommy John, NL:LA (22.2 inn)
0.403 Blue Moon Odom, AL:Oak (22.1 inn)

Most Games
20 Rick Honeycutt, NL:LA-StL-AL:Oak
18 Mark Wohlers NL:Atl
16 Mariano Rivera, AL:NY

Most Games Started
15 Tom Glavine, NL:Atl
10 Catfish Hunter, AL:Oak-NY
Dave Stewart, AL:Oak-Tor

Most Complete Games
5 Jim Palmer, AL:Balt
2 Kevin Brown, NL:Fla-SD
Danny Cox, NL:StL
Doug Drabek, NL:Pitt
Orel Hershiser, NL:LA
Tommy John, NL:LA
Mike Scott, NL:Hou
Don Sutton, NL:LA
Tim Wakefield, NL:Pitt

Most Games Finished
16 Dennis Eckersley, AL:Oak; NL:StL
14 Mark Wohlers, NL:Atl
Mariano Rivera, AL:NY

Most Saves
11 Dennis Eckersley, AL:Oak-NL:StL
10 Dennis Eckersley, AL:Oak
5 Tug McGraw, NL:NY-Phil

Shutouts
1 By many players

Most Games Won
8 Dave Stewart, AL:Oak-Tor
6 John Smoltz, NL:Atl

Most Games Lost
9 Tom Glavine, NL:Atl
4 Doyle Alexander, AL:Bal-Tor-Det

Most Innings
95.1 John Smoltz, NL:Atl
75.1 Dave Stewart, AL:Oak-Tor

Most Innings, Game
11.0 Dave McNally, AL:Balt Oct. 5, 1969
Ken Holtzman, AL:Oak Oct. 9, 1973
10.0 Joe Niekro, NL:Hou Oct. 10, 1980
Dwight Gooden, NL:NY Oct. 14, 1986

Most Runs
50 Greg Maddux, NL:Chi-Atl
25 Catfish Hunter, AL:Oak-NY

Most Runs, Game
9 Phil Niekro, NL:Atl Oct. 4, 1969
8 Jim Perry, AL:Minn Oct. 3, 1970
Roger Clemens, AL:Bos Oct. 7, 1986
Hideki Irabu, AL:NY Oct. 16, 1999

Most Runs, Inning
8 Tom Glavine, NL:Atl Oct. 13, 1992 (2nd)
6 Jim Perry, AL:Minn Oct. 3, 1970 (4th)
Scott Erickson, AL:Balt Oct. 13, 1996 (3rd)

Most Earned Runs
36 Greg Maddux, AL:Chi-Atl
25 Catfish Hunter, AL:Oak-NY

Most Earned Runs, Game
8 Greg Maddux, NL:Chi Oct. 4, 1989
7 Jim Perry, AL:Minn Oct. 3, 1970
Roger Clemens, AL:Bos Oct. 7, 1986
Jack McDowell, Al:Chi Oct. 5, 1993
Hideki Irabu AL:NY Oct. 16, 1999

Most Earned Runs, Inning
7 Tom Glavine, NL:Atl Oct. 13, 1992 (2nd)
6 Jim Perry, AL:Minn Oct. 3, 1970 (4th)

Most Hits
91 Tom Glavine, NL:Atl
57 Catfish Hunter, AL:Oak-NY

Most Hits, Game
13 Jack McDowell, AL:Chi Oct. 5, 1993
Hideki Irabu AL:NY Oct. 16, 1999
11 Kevin Brown, NL:Fla Oct. 14, 1997

Fewest Hits, Complete Game
1 Roger Clemens, AL:NY Oct. 14, 2000
2 Ross Grimsley, NL:Cin Oct. 10, 1972
Jon Matlack, NL:NY Oct. 7, 1973
Dave Dravecky, NL:SF Oct. 7, 1987

Most Hits, Inning
6 Jim Perry, AL:Minn Oct. 3, 1970 (4th)
Kirk McCaskill, AL:Cal Oct. 14, 1986 (3rd)
Greg Harris, NL:SD Oct. 2, 1984 (5th)
Tom Glavine, NL:Atl Oct. 13, 1992 (2nd)
Todd Stottlemyre, NL:StL Oct. 14, 1996 (1st)

Most Home Runs
12 Catfish Hunter, AL:Oak-NY
8 John Smoltz, NL:Atl
Tom Glavine, NL:Atl

Most Home Runs, Game
4 Catfish Hunter, AL:Oak Oct. 4, 1971
Dave McNally, AL:Balt Oct. 7, 1973
Andy Pettitte, AL:NY Oct. 9, 1998
3 Pat Jarvis, NL:Atl Oct. 6, 1969
Eric Show, NL:SD Oct. 2, 1984
Danny Cox, NL:StL Oct. 10, 1987

Most Home Runs, Inning
3 Scott Erickson, AL:Balt Oct. 13 1996 (3rd)
Jaret Wright, AL:Clev Oct. 12, 1997 (3rd)
Andy Pettitte, AL:NY Oct. 9, 1998 (5th)
2 By many NL players

Most Grand Slam Home Runs
2 Greg Maddux, NL:Atl
1 Jim Perry, AL:Minn
Moose Haas, AL:Mil
David Cone, AL:NY
Rod Beck, AL:Bos

Most Walks
37 Tom Glavine, NL:Atl
25 Dave Stewart, AL:Oak-Tor

Most Walks, Game
9 Mike Cuellar, AL:Balt Oct. 9, 1974
8 Fernando Valenzuela, NL:LA Oct. 14, 1985

Most Walks, Inning
4 Mike Cuellar, AL:Balt Oct. 9, 1974 (5th)
Burt Hooton, NL:LA Oct. 7, 1977 (2nd)
Bob Welch, NL:LA Oct. 12, 1985 (1st)

Most Walks, Consecutive
4   Mike Cuellar, AL:Balt Oct. 9, 1974
     Burt Hooton, NL:LA Oct. 7, 1977

Most Intentional Walks
7   Tom Glavine, NL:Atl
     Greg Maddux, NL:Chi-Atl
3   Mike Henneman, AL:Det
     Alex Fernandez, AL:Chi

Most Intentional Walks, Game
3   Dave Giusti, NL:Pitt Oct. 5, 1974
     Tug McGraw, NL:Phil Oct. 10, 1980
     Bob Welch, NL:LA Oct. 12, 1985
     Steve Avery, NL:Atl Oct. 6, 1993
     Tom Glavine, NL:Atl Oct. 14, 1997
2   Diego Segui, AL:Oak Oct. 5, 1971
     Mark Littell, AL:KC Oct. 5, 1977
     Dave Stieb, AL:Tor Oct. 12, 1985
     Calvin Schiraldi, AL:Bos Oct. 11, 1986 (11 inn)
     Mike Henneman, AL:Det Oct. 10, 1987
     Wes Gardner, AL:Bos Oct. 8, 1988
     Alex Fernandez, AL:Chi Oct. 6, 1993
     Danny Cox, AL:Tor Oct. 8, 1993

Most Intentional Walks, Inning
2   Tom Seaver, NL:NY Oct. 4, 1969 (3rd)
     Dave Giusti, NL:Pitt Oct. 5, 1974 (9th)
     Lance Rautzhan, NL:LA Oct. 6, 1978 (7th)
     Tug McGraw, NL:Phil Oct. 10, 1980 (11th)
     Joe Beckwith, NL:LA Oct. 8, 1983 (5th)
     Bob Welch, NL:LA Oct. 12, 1985 (1st)
     Dwight Gooden, NL:NY Oct. 12, 1988 (2nd)
     Rick Sutcliffe, NL:Chi Oct. 7, 1989 (1st)
     Steve Avery, NL:Atl Oct. 6, 1993 (6th)
     Mike Jackson, NL:Cin Oct. 14, 1995 (7th)
     John Smoltz, NL:Atl Oct. 10, 1997 (6th)
     Kenny Rogers, NL:NY Oct. 19, 1999 (11th)
1   By many AL players

Most Hit Batters
5   Tom Glavine, NL:Atl
     Greg Maddux, NL:Chi-Atl
4   Frank Tanana, AL:Cal-Det
     Mike Boddicker, AL:Bal-Bos

Most Hit Batters, Game
3   Frank Tanana, AL:Det Oct. 11, 1987
     Jimmy Key AL:Balt Oct. 9, 1997
2   Orel Hershiser, NL:LA Oct. 12, 1988
     Al Leiter, NL:NY Oct. 19, 1999

Most Hit Batters, Inning
3   Jimmy Key AL:Balt Oct. 9, 1997 (1st)
2   Al Leiter, NL:NY Oct. 19, 1999 (1st)

Most Strikeouts
89   John Smoltz, NL:Atl
53   Roger Clemens, AL:Bos-NY

Most Strikeouts, Game
15   Livan Hernandez, NL:Fla Oct. 12, 1997
     Mike Mussina, AL:Balt Oct. 11, 1997 (12 inn)
     Roger Clemens, AL:NY Oct. 14, 2000

Most Strikeouts, Inning
3   By many players

Most Strikeouts, Consecutive
5   Curt Schilling, NL:Phil Oct. 6, 1993
     Mark Wohlers, NL:Atl Oct. 7-10, 1993
     Mike Mussina, AL:Balt Oct. 11, 1997

Most Strikeouts, 2 Consecutive Innings
6   Jim Palmer, AL:Balt Oct. 6, 1973
5   By many NL players

Most Wild Pitches
4   Orel Hershiser, NL:LA; AL:Clev
     Rick Ankiel, NL:StL
     Alejandro Pena, NL:LA-Atl
     Juan Guzman, AL:Tor
     Tommy John, AL:NY-Cal

Most Wild Pitches, Game
3   Tommy John, AL:Cal Oct. 9, 1982
     Juan Guzman, AL:Tor Oct. 5, 1993
2   By many NL players

Most Wild Pitches, Inning
2   Chris Zachary, AL:Det Oct. 8, 1972 (5th)
     Tommy John, AL:Cal Oct. 9, 1982 (4th)
     David West, AL:Minn Oct. 11, 1991 (5th)
     Juan Guzman, AL:Tor Oct. 5, 1993 (1st)
     Mariano Rivera, AL:NY Oct. 17, 2001 (9th)
     Jeff Calhoun, NL:Hou Oct. 15, 1986 (16th)
     Sterling Hitchcock, NL:SD Oct. 14, 1998 (2nd)
     Rick Ankiel, NL:StL Oct. 12, 2000 (1st)
     Rick Ankiel, NL:StL Oct. 16, 2000 (7th)

Most Balks
1   By many

Most Balks, Game
1   By many

Shutouts

American League: *(* = Winning Pitcher)*

1-0	1969 Oct. 4	Dave McNally, Balt (vs Minn)
3-0	1972 Oct. 8	Blue Moon Odom, Oak (vs Det)
3-0	1972 Oct. 10	Joe Coleman, Det (vs Oak)
6-0	1973 Oct. 6	Jim Palmer, Balt (vs Oak)
3-0	1973 Oct. 11	Catfish Hunter, Oak (vs Balt)
5-0	1974 Oct. 6	Ken Holtzman, Oak (vs Balt)
1-0	1974 Oct. 8	Vida Blue, Oak (at Balt)
8-0	1979 Oct. 6	Scott McGregor, Balt (at Cal)
4-0	1981 Oct. 15	Dave Righetti*, Ron Davis, Goose Gossage, NY (at Oak)
4-0	1983 Oct. 6	Mike Boddicker, Balt (vs Chi)
3-0	1983 Oct. 8	Storm Davis, Tippy Martinez*, Balt (at Chi)
1-0	1984 Oct. 5	Milt Wilcox*, Willie Hernandez, Det (vs KC)
2-0	1985 Oct. 13	Danny Jackson, KC (vs Tor)
7-0	1995 Oct. 14	Ken Hill*, Jim Poole, Chad Ogea Alan Embree, Clev (vs Sea)
4-0	1995 Oct. 17	Dennis Martinez*, Julian Tavarez, Jose Mesa, Clev (at Sea)
3-0	1997 Oct. 8	Scott Erickson*, Randy Myers, Balt (vs Clev)
4-0	1998 Oct. 10	Orlando Hernandez*, Mike Stanton, Mariano Rivera, NY (at Clev)
2-0	2000 Oct. 10	Freddy Garcia*, Jose Paniagua, Arthur Rhodes, Kazuhiro Sasaki, Sea. (at NY)
5-0	2000 Oct. 14	Roger Clemens, NY (at Sea)

National League: *(* = Winning Pitcher)*

3-0	1970 Oct. 3	Gary Nolan*, Clay Carroll, Cin (at Pitt)
5-0	1973 Oct. 7	Jon Matlack, NY (at Cin)
3-0	1974 Oct. 5	Don Sutton, LA (at Pitt)
7-0	1974 Oct. 8	Bruce Kison*, Ramon Hernandez, Pitt (at LA)
4-0	1978 Oct. 5	Tommy John, LA (at Phil)
1-0	1980 Oct. 10	Joe Niekro, Dave Smith*, Hou (vs Phil)
3-0	1981 Oct. 14	Ray Burris, Mtl (at LA)
7-0	1982 Oct. 7	Bob Forsch, StL (vs Atl)
1-0	1983 Oct. 4	Steve Carlton*, Al Holland, Phil (at LA)
13-0	1984 Oct. 2	Rick Sutcliffe*, Warren Brusstar, Chi (vs SD)
1-0	1986 Oct. 8	Mike Scott, Hou (vs NY)
5-0	1987 Oct. 7	Dave Dravecky, SF (at StL)
1-0	1987 Oct. 13	John Tudor*, Todd Worrell, Ken Dayley, StL (vs SF)
6-0	1987 Oct. 14	Danny Cox, StL (vs SF)
6-0	1988 Oct. 12	Orel Hershiser, LA (vs NY)
1-0	1991 Oct. 10	Steve Avery*, Alejandro Pena, Atl (at Pitt)
1-0	1991 Oct. 14	Zane Smith*, Roger Mason, Pitt (at Atl)
1-0	1991 Oct. 16	Steve Avery*, Alejandro Pena, Atl (at Pitt)
4-0	1991 Oct. 17	John Smoltz, Atl (at Pitt)
6-0	1995 Oct. 14	Steve Avery*, Greg McMichael, Alejandro Pena, Mark Wohlers, Atl (vs Cin)
14-0	1996 Oct. 14	Greg Maddux*, Mark Wohlers, Atl (at StL)
15-0	1996 Oct. 17	Tom Glavine*, Mike Bielecki, Steve Avery, Atl (vs StL)
4-0	1997 Oct. 11	Denny Neagle, Atl (at Fla)
3-0	1998 Oct. 8	Kevin Brown, SD (at Atl)
5-0	1998 Oct. 14	Sterling Hitchcock*, Brian Boehringer, Mark Langston, Joey Hamilton, Trevor Hoffman, SD (at Atl)
1-0	1999 Oct. 15	Tom Glavine*, Mike Remlinger, John Rocker, Atl (at NY)
7-0	2000 Oct. 16	Mike Hampton, NY (vs StL)
2-1	2001 Oct. 16	Randy Johnson, Ari (vs. Atl)

CHAMPIONSHIP SERIES – CLUB BATTING

	3 Games	4 Games	5 Games	6 Games	7 Games
Batting Average					
AL:	.336 New York 1981	.300 New York 1978	.316 New York 1976	.301 Toronto 1993	.277 California 1986
NL:	.330 St Louis 1982	.286 Los Angeles 1978	.303 Chicago 1989	.279 St Louis 1985.	.309 Atlanta 1996
Batting Average Both Clubs					
AL:	.286 Balt .330 Minn .238 1970	.282 NY .300 KC .263 1978	.283 NY .316 KC .247 1976	.271 Tor .301 Chi .237 1993	.275 Cal .277 Bos .272 1986
NL:	.292 NY .327 Atl .255 1969	.268 LA .286 Phil .250 1978	.285 Chi .303 SF .267 1989	.256 StL .279 LA .234 1985	.260 Atl .309 StL .204
Slugging Percentage					
AL:	.560 Baltimore 1970	.511 Oakland 1988	.497 Minn 1987 & NY 1996	.471 Toronto 1992	.402 Bos & Cal 1986
NL:	.575 New York 1969	.544 Los Angeles 1978	.494 Chicago 1984	.420 Philadelphia 1993	.474 Atlanta 1996
Slugging Percentage Both Clubs					
AL:	.476 Balt .560 & Minn .386 1970	.443 KC .444 NY .443 1978	.448 NY .497 Balt .398 1996	.408 Tor .471 Oak .343 1992	.402 Cal .402 Bos .402 1986
NL:	.530 NY .575 Atl .481 1969	.477 LA .544 Phil .407 1978	.456 SF .473 Chi .440 1989	.415 Phil .420 Atl .409 1993	.409 Pitt .433 Atl .385 1992
At-Bats					
AL:	123 Baltimore 1969	140 New York 1978	184 Boston 1999	218 Baltimore 1997	256 California 1986
NL:	113 New York 1969	149 Atlanta 1995	190 Philadelphia 1980	227 New York 1986	249 Atlanta 1996
At-Bats, Both Clubs					
AL:	233 Balt 123 Minn 110 1969	273 NY 140 KC 133 1978	360 NY 176 Bos 184 1999	425 Balt 218 Clev 207 1997	510 Cal 256 Bos 254 1966
NL:	219 NY 113 Atl 106 1969	287 LA 147 Phil 140 1978	362 Phil 190 Hou 172 1980	452 NY 227 Hou 225 1986	483 LA 243 NY 240 1988
Runs					
AL:	27 Baltimore 1970	26 Baltimore 1979	34 Minnesota 1987	31 Tor 1992 & NY 2000	41 Boston 1986
NL:	27 New York 1969	24 Pittsburgh 1971	31 New York 2000	33 Atlanta 1993	44 Atlanta 1996
Runs, Both Clubs					
AL:	37 Balt 27 Minn 10 1970	41 Balt 26 Cal 15 1979	57 Minn 34 Det 23 1987	55 Tor 31 Oak 24 1992	71 Bos 41 Cal 30 1986
NL:	42 NY 27 Atl 15 1969	39 Pitt 24 SF 15 1971	52 SF 30 Chi 22 1989 / NY 31 StL 21 2000	56 Atl 33 Phil 23 1993	69 Pitt 35 Atl 34 1992
Hits					
AL:	36 Balt 1969-70; NY 1981	42 New York 1978	55 New York 1976	65 Toronto 1993	71 California 1986
NL:	37 New York 1969	42 Los Angeles 1978	55 Philadelphia 1980	59 Atlanta 1993	77 Atlanta 1996
Hits, Both Clubs					
AL:	60 Balt 36 Minn 24 1970	77 NY 42 KC 35 1978	96 NY 42 Bos 54 1999	111 Tor 59 Oak 52 1992 / Tor 65 Chi 46 1993	140 Cal 71 Bos 69 1986
NL:	64 NY 37 Atl 27 1969	77 LA 42 Phil 35 1978	97 Chi 53 SF 44 1989	106 Atl 59 Phil 47 1993	122 Atl 77 StL 45
Extra-Base Hits					
AL:	13 Baltimore 1969-70	15 Oakland 1988	22 Minnesota 1987	19 Toronto 1992	21 Toronto 1985
NL:	15 New York 1969	19 Los Angeles 1978	20 Chicago 1984	22 Philadelphia 1993	28 Pittsburgh 1992

CHAMPIONSHIP SERIES – CLUB BATTING

	3 Games	4 Games	5 Games	6 Games	7 Games
Extra-Base Hits, Both Clubs					
AL:	24 Balt 12 Oak 12 1971	22 KC 13 NY 9 1978	33 Minn 22 Det 11 1987 NY 20 Balt 13 1996 Bos 20 NY 13 1999	33 Sea 17 NY 16 2000	38 Tor 21 KC 17 1985
NL:	29 NY 15 Atl 14 1969	29 LA 19 Phil 10 1978	30 NY 17 StL 13 2000	41 Phil 22 Atl 19 1993	47 Pitt 28 Atl 19 1992
Total Bases					
AL:	61 Baltimore 1970	70 Oakland 1988	91 New York 1996	99 Toronto 1992	103 California 1986
NL:	65 New York 1969	80 Los Angeles 1978	80 Chicago 1984	88 Atlanta 1993	118 Atlanta 1996
Total Bases, Both Clubs					
AL:	100 Balt 61 Minn 39 1970	121 NY 62 KC 59 1978	161 NY 91 Balt 70 1996	170 Tor 99 Oak 71 1992	205 Cal 103 Bos 102 1986
NL:	116 NY 65 Atl 51 1969	137 LA 80 Phil 57 1978	155 SF 78 Chi 77 1989	175 Atl 88 Phil 87 1993	190 Pitt 100 Atl 90 1992
Singles					
AL:	29 New York 1981	34 Oakland 1990	37 Minnesota 1991	52 Toronto 1993	53 California 1986
NL:	27 St Louis 1982	31 Atlanta 1995	45 Philadelphia 1980	42 St Louis 1985	55 Atlanta 1996
Singles, Both Clubs					
AL:	46 NY 29 Oak 17 1981	55 NY 33 KC 22 1978	73 Minn 37 Tor 36 1991	87 Tor 52 Chi 35 1993	103 Cal 53 Bos 50 1986
NL:	41 StL 27 Atl 14 1962	53 Atl 31 Cin 22 1995	73 Phil 45 Hou 28 1980	79 SD (41) Atl (38) 1998	90 Atl 55 StL 35 1996
Doubles					
AL:	8 By many clubs	9 Baltimore 1983	13 NY 1976 Minn 1987 Boston 1999	12 Seattle 2000	19 Toronto 1985
NL:	9 Atlanta 1969	8 Los Angeles 1974 78	12 New York 2000	14 Atlanta 1993	20 Pittsburgh 1992
Doubles, Both Clubs					
AL:	15 Oak 8 Balt 7 1971	13 Balt 9 Chi 4 1983	21 NY 12 KC 9 1977	22 Sea 12 NY 10 2000	28 Tor 19 KC 9 1985
NL:	17 Atl 9 NY 8 1969	11 LA 8 Phil 3 1978 Atl 6 Cin 5 1995	23 NY 12 StL 11 2000	25 Atl 14 Phil 11 1993	31 Pitt 20 Atl 11 1992
Triples					
AL:	1 By many clubs	3 Kansas City 1978	4 Kansas City 1976	3 Toronto 1993 Cleveland 1995	2 Boston 1986
NL:	3 Cincinnati 1976	3 Los Angeles 1978	5 Houston 1980	4 Philadelphia 1993	4 St Louis 1987
Triples, Both Clubs					
AL:	2 Balt 1 Minn 1 1969 Balt 1 Oak 1 1971 KC 1 NY 1 1980	4 KC 3 NY 1 1978	6 KC 4 NY 2 1976	4 Tor 3 Chi 1 1993	2 Bos 2 Cal 0 1986
NL:	4 Cin 3 Phil 1 1976	5 LA 3 Phil 2 1978	6 Hou 5 Phil 1 1980	4 Phil 4 Atl 0 1993	5 StL 4 SF 1 1987 Pitt 3 Atl 2 1992 Atl 3 StL 2 1996

CHAMPIONSHIP SERIES – CLUB BATTING

		3 Games	4 Games	5 Games	6 Games	7 Games
Home Runs						
	AL:	6 Baltimore 1970	7 Oakland 1988	10 New York 1996	10 Toronto 1992	7 KC 1985 Cal 1986
	NL:	6 New York 1969	8 By many clubs	9 Chicago 1984	7 Philadelphia 1993	9 San Francisco 1987
Home Runs, Both Clubs						
	AL:	9 Balt 6 Minn 3 1970	9 NY 5 KC 4 1978 / Oak 7 Bos 2 1988	19 NY 10 Balt 9 1996	14 Tor 10 Oak 4 1992	13 Cal 7 Bos 6 1986
	NL:	11 NY 6 Atl 5 1969	13 Pitt 8 SF 5 1971 / LA 8 Phil 5 1978	11 Chi 9 SD 2 1984 / SF 9 StL 2 1987	12 Phil 7 Atl 5 1993	12 Atl 8 StL 4 1996
Runs Batted In						
	AL:	24 Baltimore 1970	25 Baltimore 1979	33 Minnesota 1987	31 New York 2000	35 Boston 1986
	NL:	24 New York 1969	23 Pittsburgh 1971	29 San Francisco 1989	32 Atlanta 1993	43 Atlanta 1996
Runs Batted In, Both Clubs						
	AL:	34 Balt 24 Minn 10 1970	39 Balt 25 Cal 14 1979	54 Minn 33 Det 21 1987	53 Tor 30 Oak 23 1992	64 Bos 35 Cal 29 1986
	NL:	39 NY 24 Atl 15 1969	37 Pitt 23 SF 14 1971 / LA 21 Phil 16 1978	50 SF 29 Chi 21 1989	54 Atl 32 Phil 22 1993	64 Atl 32 Pitt 32 1992
Sacrifice Hits						
	AL:	5 Boston 1975	4 Oakland 1990	5 California 1982	5 Chicago 1993	4 KC 1985 Cal 1986
	NL:	5 Pitt 1979; StL 1982	4 San Francisco 1971	7 Houston 1980	5 Atlanta 1993 / Atlanta 1997 / Florida 1997	5 St Louis 1987 / Atlanta 1991
Sacrifice Hits, Both Clubs						
	AL:	5 Bos 5 Oak 0 1975	5 Oak 4 Bos 1 1990	7 Oak 4 Det 3 1972 / Cal 5 Mil 2 1982	6 Chi 5 Tor 1 1993	7 Cal 4 Bos 3 1986
	NL:	7 StL 5 Atl 2 1982	5 SF 4 Pitt 1 1971 / Phil 3 LA 2 1983	12 Hou 7 Phil 5 1980	10 Atl 5 Fla 5 1997	9 Atl 5 Pitt 4 1991
Sacrifice Flies						
	AL:	2 Baltimore 1970	3 Baltimore 1979 / Oakland 1990	4 Kansas City 1976	4 Toronto 1992	2 KC & Tor / Bos &Cal 1986
	NL:	3 By many clubs	1 Philadelphia 1978 83 / Cincinnati 1995	4 San Diego 1984	3 New York 1986 / Cincinnati 1990; Atlanta 1997	4 St Louis 1987
Sacrifice Flies, Both Clubs						
	AL:	2 Balt 2 Minn 0 1970	5 Balt 3 Cal 2 1979 / Oak 3 Bos 2 1990	5 KC 4 NY 1 1976 / Mil 3 Cal 2 1982 / Tor 3 Oak 2 1989	6 Tor 4 Oak 2 1982	4 KC 2 Tor 2 1985
	NL:	5 Cin 3 Phil 2 1976	1 Phil 1 LA 0 1978, 83 / Cin 1 Atl 0 1995	6 SD 4 Chi 2 1984	4 Cin 3 Pitt 1 1990 / Atl 2 Phil 2 1993	5 StL 4 SF 1 1987 / Pitt 3 Atl 2 1992

CHAMPIONSHIP SERIES – CLUB BATTING

	3 Games	4 Games	5 Games	6 Games	7 Games
Walks					
AL:	13 Balt 1969 71; NY 81	22 Oakland 1974	23 New York 2001	35 New York 1998	22 Kansas City 1985
NL:	15 Cincinnati 1976	30 Los Angeles 1974	31 Houston 1980	31 Atlanta 1999	29 Atl & Pitt 1992
Walks, Both Clubs					
AL:	25 Balt 13 Minn 12 1969	28 Balt 16 Chi 12 1983 / Bos 18 Oak 10 1988	41 NY 23 Sea 18 2001	53 Chi 32 Tor 21 1993	39 Cal 20 Bos 19 1986
NL:	27 Cin 15 Phil 12 1976	38 LA 30 Pitt 8 1974	44 Hou 31 Phil 13 1980	53 SD 27 Atl 26 1998	58 Atl 29Pitt 29 1992
Intentional Walks					
AL:	2 By many clubs	3 By many clubs	3 Oak 1973 Minn 1987 / New York 1999	4 Chi & Tor 1993	4 KC 1985 Cal 1986
NL:	4 By many clubs	8 Los Angeles 1984	9 Houston 1980	10 Atlanta 1999	4 LA 1988 Pitt 1992 / Atlanta 1996
Hit by Pitch					
AL:	2 New York 1981	4 Oakland 1990	5 Minnesota 1987	5 Cleveland 1998	4 California 1986
NL:	1 By many clubs	3 Philadelphia 1977	3 New York 2000	4 Atlanta 1999	4 New York 1988
Hit by Pitch, Both Clubs					
AL:	2 NY 2 Oak 0 1981	5 Oak 3 Balt 2 1983	8 Minn 5 Det 3 1987	7 NY 2 Clev 5 1998	7 Cal 4 Bos 3 1986
NL:	1 Atl 1 NY 0 1969 / Pitt 1 Cin 0 1975	3 Pitt 2 SF 1 1971 / Phil 3 LA 0 1977	4 NY 3 StL 1 2000	5 Fla 3 Atl 2 1997	6 NY 4 LA 2 1988
Strikeouts					
AL:	27 Minnesota 1969	35 Oakland 1988	44 New York 1999	62 Cleveland 1997	51 Kansas City 1985
NL:	28 Cincinnati 1975	33 Pittsburgh 1971	42 Cincinnati 1973	57 New York 1986	57 Pittsburgh 1991
Strikeouts, Both Clubs					
AL:	41 Minn 27 Balt 14 1969 / Minn 22 Balt 19 1970	58 Oak 35 Bos 23 1988	82 NY 44 Bos 38 1999	109 Clev 62 Balt 47 1997	88 KC 51 Tor 37 1985
NL:	46 Cin 28 Pitt 18 1975	61 Pitt 33 SF 28 1971	71 Atl 39 Ari 32 2001	105 Atl 54 Phil 51 1993	104 StL 53 Atl 51 1996
Stolen Bases					
AL:	4 Detroit 1984	9 Oakland 1990	13 Oakland 1989	16 Oakland 1992	2 KC & Tor 1985
NL:	11 Cincinnati 1975	5 Los Angeles 1974	7 Philadelphia 1980	14 Atlanta 1999	10 Atlanta 1991
Stolen Bases, Both Clubs					
AL:	4 NY 2 Oak 2 1981 / Det 4 KC 0 1984	10 Oak 9 Bos 1 1990	24 Oak 13 Tor 11 1989	23 Oak 16 Tor 7 1992	4 Tor 2 KC 2 1985
NL:	11 Cin 11 Pitt 0 1975	6 LA 5 Pitt 1 1974 / Cin 4 Atl 2 1995	11 Phil 7 Hou 4 1980	21 Atl 14 NY 7 1999	16 Atl 10 Pitt 6 1991

CHAMPIONSHIP SERIES – CLUB BATTING

	3 Games	4 Games	5 Games	6 Games	7 Games
Caught Stealing					
AL:	5 Kansas City 1980	3 By many clubs	5 Kansas City 1976	5 Toronto 1992	4 KC 1985 Cal 1986 4 StL & SF 1987 Atlanta 1991
NL:	2 By many clubs	3 Los Angeles 1983 Cincinnati 1995	3 Philadelphia 1980 Chicago 1984	6 St Louis 1985	
Caught Stealing, Both Clubs					
AL:	5 KC 5 NY 0 1980	6 Oak 3 Balt 3 1974	8 KC 5 NY 3 1976	7 Tor 5 Oak 2 1992	6 KC 4 Tor 2 1985
NL:	3 Pitt 2 Cin 1 1970	4 Cin 3 Atl 1 1995	5 Chi 3 SD 2 1984	7 StL 6 LA 1 1985	8 SF 4 StL 4 1987
Grounded into Double Plays					
AL:	6 Oakland 1981	5 Baltimore 1983	6 New York 1996 Boston 1999	10 Baltimore 1997	7 Boston 1986
NL:	3 Atlanta 1982	8 Cincinnati 1995	7 Los Angeles 1981	6 San Diego 1998	8 St Louis 1987
Grounded into Double Plays, Both Clubs					
AL:	7 Balt 4 Minn 3 1970 Oak 6 NY 1 1981	8 Balt 4 Cal 4 1979	7 Det 5 Oak 2 1972 NY 4 KC 3 1976 Cal 4 Mil 3 1982 Minn 4 Tor 3 1991 NY 6 Balt 1 1996 NY 4 Sea 3 2001	13 Balt 10 Clev 3 1997	12 Bos 7 Cal 5 1986
NL:	4 NY 2 Atl 2 1969 Cin 2 Pitt 2 1975 Pitt 2 Cin 2 1979	11 Cin 8 Atl 3 1995	11 LA 7 Mtl 4 1981	10 SD 6 Atl 4 1998	13 StL 8 SF 5 1987
Left on Base					
AL:	30 New York 1981	35 Chicago 1983 Oakland 1990	45 Boston 1999	56 Toronto 1993	60 California 1986
NL:	31 St Louis 1982	44 Los Angeles 1974	45 Houston 1980	52 Philadelphia 1993 San Diego 1998	58 Atlanta 1996
Left on Base, Both Clubs					
AL:	50 Balt 28 Minn 22 1969 NY 30 Oak 20 1981	59 Chi 35 Balt 24 1983	87 Bos 45 NY 42 1999	106 Tor 56 Chi 50 1993	108 Cal 60 Bos 48 1986
NL:	49 Cin 25 Pitt 24 1979	68 LA 44 Pitt 24 1974	88 Hou 45 Phil 43 1980	99 Phil 52 Atl 47 1993	105 Pitt 54 Atl 51 1991

BATTING

Highest Batting Average, Game
.468 Atlanta NL Oct. 14, 1996
.467 Boston AL Oct. 16, 1999

Highest Slugging Percentage, Game
.895 Chicago NL Oct. 2, 1984
.844 Boston AL Oct. 16, 1999

Most Plate Appearances, Game
52 Atlanta NL Oct. 14, 1996
Seattle AL Oct. 20, 2001
Extra-Inning Game:
67 Atlanta NL Oct. 17, 1999 (15 inn)
54 Toronto AL Oct. 11, 1992 (11 inn)

Most Plate Appearances, Both Clubs, Game
89 Minn (48) Det (41) AL Oct. 12, 1987
Tor (46) Chi (43) AL Oct. 5, 1993
90 Ari (50) Atl (40) NL Oct. 20, 2001
Extra-Inning Game:
126 NY (59) Atl (67) NL Oct. 17, 1999 (15 inn)
104 Tor (54) Oak (50) AL Oct. 11, 1992 (11 inn)

Most Plate Appearances, Inning
14 St Louis NL Oct. 13, 1985 (2nd)
12 New York AL Oct. 14, 1981 (4th)
New York AL Oct. 17, 2000 (7th)

Most At-Bats, Game
47 Atlanta NL Oct. 14, 1996
45 Boston AL Oct. 16, 1999
Seattle AL Oct. 20, 2001
Extra-Inning Game:
56 Houston NL Oct. 15, 1986 (16 inn)
49 Toronto AL Oct. 11, 1992 (11 inn)

Most At-Bats, Both Clubs, Game
80 Balt (44) Minn (36) AL Oct. 6, 1969
Atl (47) StL (33) NL Oct. 14, 1996
Ari (42) Atl (38) NL Oct. 20, 2001
Extra-Inning Game
110 Hou (56) NY (54) NL Oct. 15, 1986 (16 inn)
91 Tor (49) Oak (42) AL Oct. 11, 1992 (11 inn)

Most At-Bats, Inning
12 St Louis NL Oct. 13, 1985 (2nd)
10 New York AL Oct. 14, 1981 (4th)
Toronto AL Oct. 11, 1985 (5th)

Most Runs, Game
15 Atlanta NL Oct. 17, 1996
14 Seattle AL Oct. 20, 2001

Most Runs, Both Clubs, Game
18 Atl (13) Pitt (5) NL Oct. 7, 1992
17 Balt (9) Cal (8) AL Oct. 4, 1979
Sea (14) NY (3) AL Oct. 20, 2001
Extra-Inning Game
19 Atl (10) NY (9) NL Oct. 19, 1999 (11 inn)

Most Runs, Inning
9 St Louis NL Oct. 13, 1985 (2nd)
7 Baltimore AL Oct. 3, 1970 (4th)
Baltimore AL Oct. 4, 1970 (9th)
New York AL Oct. 14, 1981 (4th)
Oakland AL Oct. 6, 1990 (9th)
New York AL Oct. 11, 2000 (8th)
Seattle AL Oct. 20, 2001 (6th)

Most Earned Runs, Game
15 Atlanta NL Oct. 17, 1996
13 New York AL Oct. 14, 1981

Most Earned Runs, Both Clubs, Game
17 Atl (13) Pitt (4) NL Oct. 7, 1992
16 NY (13) Oak (3) AL Oct. 14, 1981
NY (9) Sea (7) AL Oct. 17, 2000
Extra-Inning Game
18 Atl (10) NY (8) NL Oct. 19, 1999 (11 inn)

Most Earned Runs, Inning
7 Baltimore AL Oct. 3, 1970 (4th)
New York AL Oct. 14, 1981 (4th)
New York AL Oct. 11, 2000 (8th)
Pittsburgh NL Oct. 13, 1992 (2nd)

Most Innings Scoring, Game
6 New York NL Oct. 5, 1969
Los Angeles NL Oct. 9, 1974
Atlanta NL Oct. 14, 1996
Detroit AL Oct. 2, 1984
Toronto AL Oct. 10, 1992
Boston AL Oct. 16, 1999

Most Innings Scoring, Consecutive, Game
5 New York NL Oct. 5, 1969
Seattle AL Oct. 20, 2001

Most Innings Scoreless, Consecutive
30 Baltimore AL Oct. 5-9, 1974
26 Atlanta NL Oct. 13-16, 1991

Most Hits, Game
22 Atlanta NL Oct. 14, 1996
21 Boston AL Oct. 16, 1999

Most Hits, Both Clubs, Game
30 NY (19) Oak (11) AL Oct. 14, 1981
29 Atl (22) StL (7) Oct. 14, 1996

Fewest Hits, Game
1 Oakland AL Oct. 9, 1974
Seattle AL Oct. 14, 2000
Pittsburgh NL Oct. 12, 1990

Most Hits, Inning
8 St Louis NL Oct. 13, 1985 (2nd)
Pittsburgh NL Oct. 13, 1992 (2nd)
New York AL Oct. 11, 2000 (8th)

Most Total Bases, Game
38 Boston AL Oct. 16, 1999
34 Chicago NL Oct. 2, 1984
Atlanta NL Oct. 14, 1996

Most Total Bases, Both Clubs, Game
47 LA (30) Phil (17) NL Oct. 4, 1978
Oak (30) Bos (17) AL Oct. 8, 1988

Fewest Total Bases, Game
2 Cincinnati NL Oct. 7, 1973
St Louis NL Oct. 7, 1987
Pittsburgh NL Oct. 12, 1990
Atlanta NL Oct. 14, 1998
Baltimore AL Oct. 8, 1974
Oakland AL Oct. 9, 1974
Kansas City AL Oct. 12, 1985
Seattle AL Oct. 14, 2000

Most Total Bases, Inning
16 Baltimore AL Oct. 3, 1970 (4th)
Pittsburgh NL Oct. 13, 1992 (2nd)

Most Extra-Base Hits, Game
10 Boston AL Oct. 16, 1999
8 Cincinnati NL Oct. 9, 1976
Chicago NL Oct. 2, 1984

Most Extra-Base Hits, Both Clubs, Game
12 Oak (6) Bos (6) AL Oct. 5, 1975
Phil (7) Atl (5) NL Oct. 9, 1993

Most Extra-Base Hits, Inning
5 New York NL Oct. 15, 2000 (1st)
4 Baltimore AL Oct. 12, 1997 (3rd)
Seattle AL Oct. 20, 2001 (6th)

Most Singles, Game
15 New York AL Oct. 14, 1981
Atlanta NL Oct. 14, 1996

Most Singles, Both Clubs, Game
25 KC (13) NY (12) AL Oct. 4, 1978
22 Atl (15) StL (7) NL Oct. 14, 1996

Most Singles, Inning
8 St Louis NL Oct. 13, 1985 (2nd)
6 New York AL Oct. 6, 1998 (1st)

Most Doubles, Game
6 Baltimore AL Oct. 6, 1969
   Boston AL Oct. 16, 1999
   Seattle AL Oct. 17, 2000
   Philadelphia NL Oct. 12, 1976
   Atlanta NL Oct. 17, 1999 (15 inn)
   New York NL Oct. 15, 2000

Most Doubles, Both Clubs, Game
9 Oak (5) Balt (4) AL Oct. 3, 1971
   Oak (5) Bos (4) AL Oct. 5, 1975
8 LA (5) StL (3) NL Oct. 12, 1985
   Phil (5) Atl (3) NL Oct. 6, 1993 (10 inn)
   Atl (5) Phil (3) NL Oct. 9, 1993
   NY (6) StL (2) NL Oct. 15, 2000

Most Doubles, Inning
5 New York NL Oct. 15, 2000 (1st)
3 Oakland AL Oct. 10, 1973 (2nd)
   Boston AL Oct. 4, 1975 (7th)
   Minnesota AL Oct. 8, 1987 (2nd)

Most Triples, Game
3 Philadelphia NL Oct. 9, 1993
2 Kansas City AL Oct. 13, 1976
   Kansas City AL Oct. 8, 1977
   Seattle AL Oct. 20, 2001

Most Triples, Both Clubs, Game
3 LA (2) Phil (1) NL Oct. 4, 1978
   Phil (3) Atl (0) NL Oct. 9, 1993
2 Balt (1) Minn (1) AL Oct. 6, 1969
   KC (1) NY (1) AL Oct. 9, 1976
   KC (2) NY (0) AL Oct. 13, 1976
   KC (2) NY (0) AL Oct. 8, 1977
   Det (1) KC (1) AL Oct. 2, 1984
   Chi (1) Tor (1) AL Oct. 9, 1993
   Sea (2) NY (0) AL Oct. 20, 2001

Most Triples, Inning
2 Kansas City AL Oct. 8, 1977 (3rd)
   Philadelphia NL Oct. 9, 1993 (4th)

Most Home Runs, Game
5 Chicago NL Oct. 2, 1984
4 Baltimore AL Oct. 4, 1971
   Oakland AL Oct. 7, 1973
   Oakland AL Oct. 9, 1988
   New York AL Oct. 12, 1996
   Cleveland AL Oct. 9, 1998

Most Home Runs, Both Clubs, Game
6 Atl (4) Phil (2) NL Oct. 7, 1993
   Balt (3) NY (3) AL Oct. 13, 1996

Most Home Runs, Inning
3 Baltimore AL Oct. 3, 1970 (4th)
   New York AL Oct. 13, 1996 (3rd)
   Baltimore AL:Oct. 12, 1997 (3rd)
   Cleveland AL Oct. 9, 1998 (5th)
2 By many NL clubs

Most Grand Slam Home Runs, Game
1 Baltimore AL Oct. 3, 1970 (4th)
   California AL Oct. 9, 1982 (8th)
   Cleveland AL Oct. 13, 1998 (5th)
   New York AL Oct. 17, 1999 (9th)
   Los Angeles NL Oct. 4, 1977 (7th)
   Los Angeles NL Oct. 5, 1977 (4th)
   San Francisco NL Oct. 4, 1989 (4th)
   Atlanta NL Oct. 7, 1992 (5th)
   St Louis NLOct. 10, 1996 (7th)
   Atlanta NL Oct. 11, 1998 (7th)

Most Runs Batted In, Game
14 Atlanta NL Oct. 7, 1993
    Atlanta NL Oct. 14, 1996
    Atlanta NL Oct. 17, 1996
13 New York AL Oct. 14, 1981
    Seattle AL Oct. 20, 2001

Most Runs Batted In, Both Clubs, Game
17 NY (11) Atl (6) NL Oct. 5, 1969
    Atl (13) Pitt (4) NL Oct. 7, 1992
    Atl (14) Phil (3) NL Oct. 7, 1993
16 Balt (8) Cal (8) AL Oct. 4, 1979
    NY (13) Oak (3) AL Oct. 14, 1981
    Oak (10) Bos (6) AL Oct. 8, 1988
    NY (9) Sea (7) AL Oct. 17, 2000
    Sea (13) NY (3) AL Oct. 20, 2001
Extra-Inning Game
18 Atl (9) NY (9) NL Oct. 19, 1999 (11 inn)

Most Runs Batted In, Inning
8 St Louis NL Oct. 13, 1985 (2nd)
7 Baltimore AL Oct. 3, 1970 (4th)
   New York AL Oct. 14, 1981 (4th)
   New York AL Oct. 11, 2000 (8th)

Most Sacrifice Hits, Game
3 Pittsburgh NL Oct. 3, 1979 (10 inn)
   Philadelphia NL Oct. 8, 1980 (10 inn)
   Los Angeles NL Oct. 17, 1981
   Atlanta NL Oct. 19, 1999 (11 inn)
   St Louis NL Oct. 10, 1982
   California AL Oct. 10, 1982
   California AL Oct. 12, 1986 (11 inn)

Most Sacrifice Hits, Both Clubs, Game
4 LA (3) Mtl (1) NL Oct. 17, 1981
   StL (2) Atl (2) NL Oct. 9, 1982
   Atl (2) Phil (2) NL Oct. 13, 1993
3 Cal (3) Mil (0) AL Oct. 10, 1982
   Bos (2) Cal (1) AL Oct. 11, 1986 (11 inn)
   Cal (3) Bos (0) AL Oct. 12, 1986 (11 inn)
   Oak (2) Bos (1) AL Oct. 6, 1990
Extra-Inning Game:
5 Phil (3) Hou (2) NL Oct. 8, 1980 (10 inn)

Most Sacrifice Hits, Inning
2 Philadelphia NL Oct. 10, 1976 (4th)
1 By many AL clubs

Most Sacrifice Flies, Game
3 St Louis NL Oct. 7, 1982
2 By many AL clubs

Most Sacrifice Flies, Both Clubs, Game
3 StL (3) Atl (0) NL Oct. 7, 1982
   StL (2) SF (1) NL Oct. 11, 1987
   NY (2) Atl (1) NL Oct. 19, 1999 (11 inn)
2 By many AL clubs

Most Sacrifice Flies, Inning
2 Milwaukee AL Oct. 8, 1982 (4th)
   Baltimore AL Oct. 7, 1983 (9th)
   Detroit AL Oct. 7, 1987 (8th)
   San Diego NL Oct. 7, 1984 (6th)

Most Walks, Game
11 Oakland AL Oct. 9, 1974
    New York AL Oct. 11, 1998
    Los Angeles NL Oct. 9, 1974

Most Walks, Both Clubs, Game
15 NY (10) Sea (5) AL Oct. 21, 2001
13 LA (5) StL (8) NL Oct. 12, 1985
    LA (6) NY (7) NL Oct. 8, 1988
    Pitt (8) Atl (5) NL Oct. 7, 1992
Extra-Inning Game
15 Atl (10) NY (5) NL Oct. 17, 1999 (15 inn)

Most Walks, Inning
4 Oakland AL Oct. 9, 1974 (5th)
  Philadelphia NL Oct. 7, 1977 (2nd)
  St Louis NL Oct. 12, 1985 (1st)
  San Francisco NL Oct. 9, 1989 (8th)

Most Walks, Consecutive, Inning
4 Oakland AL Oct. 9, 1974 (5th)
  Philadelphia NL Oct. 7, 1977 (2nd)

Most Intentional Walks, Game
5 Houston NL Oct. 10, 1980 (11 inn)
  St Louis NL Oct. 12, 1985
  Atlanta NL Oct. 17, 1999 (15 inn)
3 New York AL Oct. 17, 1999

Most Intentional Walks, Both Clubs, Game
6 StL (5) LA (1) NL Oct. 12, 1985
3 NY (3) Bos (0) AL Oct. 17, 1999
  NY (2) Sea (1) AL Oct. 17, 2000
  Extra-Inning Game:
7 Hou (5) Phil (2) NL Oct. 10, 1980 (11 inn)

Most Intentional Walks, Inning
2 By many clubs

Most Hit by Pitch, Game
3 Minnesota AL Oct. 11, 1987
  Cleveland AL Oct. 9, 1997
2 New York NL Oct. 12, 1988
  Atlanta NL Oct. 16, 1996
  Atlanta NL Oct. 7, 1997
  Extra-Inning Game:
3 Atlanta NL Oct. 19, 1999 (11 inn)

Most Hit by Pitch, Both Clubs, Game
4 Det (2) Minn (2) AL Oct. 12, 1987
  NY (2) Clev (2) AL Oct. 11, 1998
3 Atl (2) Fla (1) NL Oct. 7, 1997
  Atl (3) NY (0) NL Oct. 19, 1999 (11 inn)

Most Hit by Pitch, Inning
3 Cleveland AL Oct. 9, 1997 (1st)
2 Atlanta NL Oct. 19, 1999 (1st)

Most Strikeouts, Game
15 Philadelphia NL Oct. 10, 1993
   Atlanta NL Oct. 12, 1997
   Seattle AL Oct. 14, 2000
   Extra-Inning Game:
21 Cleveland AL Oct. 11, 1997 (12 inn)
19 Atlanta NL Oct. 17, 1999 (15 inn)

Most Strikeouts, Both Clubs, Game
25 Atl (15) Fla (10) NL Oct. 12, 1997
22 NY (13) Sea (9) Oct. 10, 2000
   Extra-Inning Game:
33 Clev (21) Balt (12) AL Oct. 11, 1997 (12 inn)
32 Atl (19) NY (13) NL Oct. 17, 1999 (15 inn)

Fewest Strikeouts, Game
0 Pittsburgh NL Oct. 6, 1974
1 Baltimore AL Oct. 11, 1973
  New York AL Oct. 13, 1976
  Kansas City AL Oct. 4, 1978
  Toronto AL Oct. 12, 1985
  Boston AL Oct. 10, 1990

Most Strikeouts, Inning
3 By many clubs

Most Strikeouts, Consecutive, Game
5 Atlanta NL Oct. 6, 1993
  Arizona NL Oct. 20, 2001
  Cleveland AL Oct. 11, 1997

Most Stolen Bases, Game
7 Cincinnati NL Oct. 5, 1975
6 Oakland AL Oct. 4, 1989 & Oct. 8, 1992

Most Stolen Bases, Both Clubs, Game
8 Oak (6) Tor (2) AL Oct. 4, 1989
  Oak (6) Tor (2) AL Oct. 8, 1992
7 Cin (7) Pitt (0) NL Oct. 5, 1975
  Extra-Inning Game:
8 Atl (6) NY (2) NL Oct. 19, 1999 (11 inn)

Most Stolen Bases, Inning
3 Oakland AL Oct. 12, 1972 (2nd)
  Oakland AL Oct. 4, 1989 (7th)
  Oakland AL Oct. 8, 1992 (5th)
  New York NL Oct. 16, 1999 (8th)

Most Caught Stealing, Game
2 By many clubs

Most Caught Stealing, Both Clubs, Game
3 Balt (2) Oak (1) AL Oct. 10, 1973
  KC (2) NY (1) AL Oct. 12, 1976
  Mil (2) Cal (1) AL Oct. 9, 1982
  Chi (2) SD (1) NL Oct. 7, 1984
  StL (2) LA (1) NL Oct. 12, 1985
  SF (2) StL (1) NL Oct. 7, 1987

Most Caught Stealing, Inning
2 St Louis NL Oct. 10, 1985 (1st)
  St Louis NL Oct. 12, 1985 (2nd)
1 By many AL clubs

Most Grounded into Double Plays, Game
3 By many AL & NL clubs
  Extra Innings:
5 Cincinnati NL Oct. 10, 1995 (11 inn)

**Most Grounded into Double Plays,
Both Clubs, Game**
4 By many AL & NL clubs
  Extra Innings:
5 Cin (5) Atl (0) NL Oct. 10, 1995 (11 inn)

Most Left on Base, Game
15 Philadelphia NL Oct. 10, 1993
   New York AL Oct. 15, 2000
   Extra-Inning Game:
19 Atlanta NL Oct. 17, 1999 (15 inn)

Most Left on Base, Both Clubs, Game
26 Phil (15) Atl (11) NL Oct. 10, 1993
25 Chi (13) Tor (12) AL Oct. 5, 1993
   Tor (14) Oak (11) AL Oct. 11, 1992 (11 inn)
   Extra-Inning Game:
31 Atl. (19) NY (12) Oct. 17, 1999 (15 inn)

Fewest Left on Base, Game
0 Atlanta NL Oct. 16, 1999
1 Baltimore AL Oct. 11, 1996

Most Wild Pitches, Game
3 California AL Oct. 9, 1982
  Oakland AL Oct. 10, 1992
  Toronto AL Oct. 5, 1993
2 By many NL clubs

Most Wild Pitches, Both Clubs, Game
3 Cal (3) Mil (0) AL Oct. 9, 1982
  KC (2) Tor (1) AL Oct. 15, 1985
  Det (2) Min (1) AL Oct. 11, 1987
  Oak (3) Tor (0) AL Oct. 10, 1992
  Tor (3) Chi (0) AL Oct. 5, 1993
  StL (2) NY (1) NL Oct. 12, 2000

Most Wild Pitches, Inning
2 Detroit AL Oct. 8, 1972 (5th)
  California AL Oct. 9, 1982 (4th)
  Toronto AL Oct. 5, 1993 (1st)
  New York AL Oct. 17, 2001 (9th)
  San Diego NL Oct. 14, 1998 (2nd)
  St. Louis NL Oct. 12, 2000 (1st)

CLUB FIELDING

	3 Games	4 Games	5 Games	6 Games	7 Games
Highest Percentage (1.000 Most Chances)					
AL:	1.000 (110) Baltimore 1970	.9934 Oakland 1990	.9946 New York 1996	.9953 New York 2000	.9840 Toronto 1985
NL:	1.000 (124) Pittsburgh 1979	.9929 Los Angeles 1983	.9942 San Diego 1984	.9964 New York 1986	.9922 Atlanta 1992
Highest Percentage, Both Clubs					
AL:	.995 Oak 1.000 Balt. .991 1971	.986 Bos .993 Oak .979 1988	.987 NY .995 Balt .980 1996	.990 NY .995 Sea .986 2000	.981 Tor .984 KC .979 1985
NL:	.996 Pitt 1.000 Cin .992 1979	.996 LA .993 Phil .966 1983	.989 SD .994 Chi .983 1984	.985 NY .996 Hou .973 1986	.983 Stl .988 SF .977 1987
Total Chances					
AL:	133 Minnesota 1969	166 Baltimore 1979	200 Oakland 1972 / Baltimore 1996	249 Cleveland 1998	281 Kansas City 1985
NL:	127 Cincinnati 1979	174 Atlanta 1995	225 Philadelphia 1980	284 New York 1986	269 Pittsburgh 1991
Total Chances, Both Clubs					
AL:	261 Minn 133 Balt 128 1969	323 Balt 162 Chi 161 1983	395 Oak 200 Det 195 1972	479 Clev 240 Balt 239 1997	554 Cal 278 Bos 276 1986
NL:	244 Cinn 124 Pitt 120 1970	330 Atl 174 Cin 156 1995	427 Phil 225 Hou 202 1980	545 NY 284 Hou 261 1986	522 NY 262 LA 260 1988
Chances Accepted					
AL:	128 Minnesota 1969	161 Baltimore 1979	197 Oakland 1972	242 Cleveland 1998	275 Kansas City 1985
NL:	126 Cincinnati 1979	171 Atlanta 1995	219 Philadelphia 1980	283 New York 1986	263 Pittsburgh 1991
Chances Accepted, Both Clubs					
AL:	255 Minn 128 Balt 127 1969	318 Balt 160 Chi 158 1983	384 Oak 197 Det 187 1972	469 Clev 235 Balt 234 1997	539 Cal 270 Bos 269 1980
NL:	241 Cinn 123 Pitt 118 1970	325 Atl 171 Cin 154 1995	418 Phil 219 Hou 199 1980	537 NY 283 Hou 254 1986	510 LA 256. NY 254 1988
Putouts					
AL:	96 Baltimore 1969	111 Baltimore 1983	141 New York 1996	174 Baltimore 1997 / Cleveland 1997	196 Boston 1986
NL:	90 Pittsburgh 1979 / 90 Atlanta 1982	117 Atlanta 1995	148 Philadelphia 1980	189 New York 1986	195 Los Angeles 1988
Putouts, Both Clubs					
AL:	190 Balt 96 Minn 94 1969	219 Balt 111 Chi 108 1983	279 NY 141 Balt 138 1996	348 Balt 174 Clev 174 1997	388 Bos 196 Cal 192 1986
NL:	177 Pitt 90 Cin 87 1979	228 Atl 117 Cin 111 1995	295 Phil 148 Hou 147 1980	377 NY 189 Hou 188 1986	387 LA 195 NY 192 1988
Assists					
AL:	41 New York 1980	52 Baltimore 1979	60 New York 1976	77 Cleveland 1998	87 Kansas City 1985
NL:	39 Cincinnati 1979 / Atlanta 1982	54 Atlanta 1995	71 Philadelphia 1980	94 New York 1986	77 San Francisco 1987
Assists, Both Clubs					
AL:	73 Oak 40 Bos 33 1975	100 Chi 51 Balt 49 1983	111 NY 60 KC 51 1976	131 Clev 77 NY 54 1998	151 Cal 78 Bos 73 1986
NL:	76 Cin 39 Pitt 37 1970	97 Atl 54 Cin 43 1995	123 Phil 71 Hou 52 1980	160 NY 94 Hou 66 1986	144 SF 77 StL 67 1987

CHAMPIONSHIP SERIES – CLUB FIELDING

		3 Games	4 Games	5 Games	6 Games	7 Games
Errors						
	AL:	7 Kansas City 1984	5 Baltimore 1979 / Boston 1990	10 Boston 1999	8 Toronto 1992	8 California 1986
	NL:	6 Atlanta 1969	7 Los Angeles 1974	7 St. Louis 2000 / Atlanta 2001	8 Atlanta 1998 / New York 1999	8 New York 1988
Errors, Both Clubs						
	AL:	10 Oak 6 Bos 4 1975	7 Balt 5 Cal 2 1979	15 Bos 10 NY 5 1999	15 Tor 8 Oak 7 1992	15 Cal 8 Bos 7 1986
	NL:	8 Atl 6 NY 2 1969	11 LA 7 Pitt 4 1974	11 StL 7 NY 4 2000	15 NY 8 Atl 7 1999	13 NY 8 LA 5 1988
Passed Balls						
	AL:	1 New York 1981	1 By many clubs	2 Toronto 1991	3 Toronto 1992	2 California 1986
	NL:	2 Pittsburgh 1975	1 By many clubs	2 Chicago 1989	2 Houston 1986 / Philadelphia 1993	2 Pittsburgh 1992
Passed Balls, Both Clubs						
	AL:	1 By many clubs	2 NY 1 KC 1 1978 / Bos 1 Oak 1 1988	2 Tor 1 Oak 1 1989	3 Tor 3 Oak 0 1992	2 Cal 2 Bos 0 1986
	NL:	2 NY 1 Atl 1 1969 / Pitt 2 Atl 1 1992	2 Pitt 1 SF 1 1971	3 Chi 2 SF 1 1989 / Pitt 2 Cin 0 1975	2 Hou 2 NY 0 1986 / Phil 2 Atl 0 1993	3 Pitt 2 Atl 1 1992
Double Plays						
	AL:	6 New York 1981	7 California 1979	7 Baltimore 1996 / New York 1999	11 Cleveland 1997	7 Kansas City 1985 / California 1986
	NL:	4 Atlanta 1969	8 Los Angeles 1974 / Atlanta 1995	8 Montreal 1981	9 New York 1999	10 San Francisco 1987
Double Plays, Both Clubs						
	AL:	8 Minn 5 Balt 3 1970	12 Cal 7 Balt 5 1979	9 Oak 5 Det 4 1972 / Tor 5 Oak 4 1989 / Balt 7 NY 2 1996 / Sea 5 NY 4 2001	15 Clev 11 Balt 4 1997	12 Cal 7 Bos 5 1986
	NL:	6 Atl 4 NY 2 1969 / Cin 3 Phil 3 1976	12 Atl 8 Cin 4 1995	13 Pitt 8 LA 5 1981	13 NY 9 Atl 4 1999	15 SF 10 StL 5 1987

FIELDING

Most Total Chances Game
48 Atlanta NL Oct. 4, 1969
   Los Angeles NL Oct. 5, 1978
46 Boston AL Oct. 7, 1975
   Extra-Inning Game:
79 New York NL Oct. 15, 1986 (16 inn)
55 Toronto AL Oct. 11, 1992 (11 inn)

Most Total Chances, Inning
10 New York AL Oct. 10, 1976 (7th)
 9 Atlanta NL Oct. 13, 1992 (2nd)
   Atlanta NL Oct. 20, 2001 (3rd)

Most Chances Accepted, Game
48 Los Angeles NL Oct. 5, 1978
45 Boston AL Oct. 7, 1975
   Extra-Inning Game:
79 New York NL Oct. 15, 1986 (16 inn)
51 Toronto AL Oct. 11, 1992 (11 inn)

Most Chances Accepted, Inning
 8 New York AL Oct. 10, 1976 (7th)
   Los Angeles NL Oct. 7, 1978 (5th)
   Los Angeles NL Oct. 9, 1985 (4th)
   San Francisco NL Oct. 14, 1987 (1st)
   Atlanta NL Oct. 13, 1992 (2nd)
   New York NL Oct. 13, 1999 (2nd)

Most Assists, Game
21 Los Angeles NL Oct. 5, 1978
   Atlanta NL Oct. 3, 1995
18 Boston AL Oct. 7, 1975
   Extra-Inning Game:
31 New York NL Oct. 15, 1986 (16 inn)

Most Assists, Both Clubs, Game
33 Bos (18) Oak (15) AL Oct. 7, 1975
30 LA (21) Phil (9) NL Oct. 5, 1978
   Extra-Inning Game:
56 NY (31) Hou (25) NL Oct. 15, 1986 (16 inn)

Most Assists, Inning
 5 New York AL Oct. 10, 1976 (7th)
   Los Angeles NL Oct. 7, 1978 (5th)
   Los Angeles NL Oct. 9, 1985 (4th)
   San Francisco NL Oct. 14, 1987 (1st)
   Atlanta NL Oct. 13, 1992 (2nd)
   New York NL Oct. 13, 1999 (2nd)

Most Errors, Game
 5 Los Angeles NL Oct. 8, 1974
   New York AL Oct. 10, 1976

Most Errors, Both Clubs, Game
 7 Oak (4) Bos (3) AL Oct. 4, 1975
 5 LA (5) Pitt (0) NL Oct. 8, 1974

Most Errors, Inning
 3 Oakland AL Oct. 4, 1975 (1st)
   California AL Oct. 8, 1986 (7th)
   Arizona NL Oct. 20, 2001 (3rd)

Most Double Plays, Game
 4 Oakland AL Oct. 5, 1975
   Los Angeles NL Oct. 13, 1981
   San Francisco NL Oct. 10, 1987
   Extra Innings:
 5 Atlanta NL Oct. 13, 1995 (11 inn)

Most Double Plays, Both Clubs, Game
 6 Oak (4) Bos (2) AL Oct. 5, 1975
 5 Pitt (3) Cin (2) NL Oct. 5, 1975
   Extra-Inning Game:
 6 Atl (5) Cin (1) Oct. 10, 1995 (11 inn)

Most Passed Balls, Game
 2 Pittsburgh NL Oct. 4, 1975
   Houston NL Oct. 11, 1986
   Pittsburgh NL Oct. 13, 1992
   Toronto AL Oct. 13, 1991
   Toronto AL Oct. 14, 1992

Most Passed Balls, Both Clubs, Game
 2 NY (1) Atl (1) NL Oct. 4, 1969
   Pitt (1) LA (1) NL Oct. 8, 1974
   Pitt (2) Cin (0) NL Oct. 4, 1975
   Hou (2) NY (0) NL Oct. 11, 1986
   Pitt (2) Atl (0) NL Oct. 13, 1992
   Tor (2) Minn (0) AL Oct. 13, 1991
   Tor (2) Oak (0) AL Oct. 14, 1992

Most Passed Balls, Inning
 2 Toronto AL Oct. 13, 1991 (2nd)
 1 By many NL clubs

CLUB PITCHING

	3 Games	4 Games	5 Games	6 Games	7 Games
Earned Run Average, Lowest					
AL:	1.13 Baltimore 1969	0.49 Baltimore 1983	1.76 Oakland 1972	1.64 Cleveland 1995	3.16 Kansas City 1985
NL:	0.96 Cincinnati 1970	1.03 Philadelphia 1983	1.33 New York 1973	2.29 New York 1986	1.57 Atlanta 1991
Earned Run Average, Lowest, Both Clubs					
AL:	2.37 Det 1.24 KC 3.54 1984	1.77 Oak 1.75 Balt 1.80 1974	1.94 Oak 1.76 Det 2.14 1972	2.47 Clev 1.64 Sea 3.33 1995	3.47 Bos 3.58 Cal 3.49 1986
NL:	1.80 Cin 0.96 Pitt 2.67 1970	2.47 Phil 1.03 LA 3.97 1983	2.35 LA 1.84 Mtl 2.86 1981	2.58 NY 2.29 Hou 2.87 1986	2.07 Atl 1.57 Pitt 2.57 1991
Earned Run Average, Highest					
AL:	7.62 Minnesota 1970	5.80 California 1979	6.70 Detroit 1987	5.37 Seattle 2000	3.94 California 1986
NL:	6.92 Atlanta 1969	6.09 San Francisco 1971	5.86 St. Louis 2000	4.75 Philadelphia 1993	6.60 St Louis 1996
Earned Run Average, Highest, Both Clubs					
AL:	5.43 Minn 7.62 Balt 3.33 1970	4.38 Cal 5.80 Balt 2.97 1979	5.59 Det 6.70 Minn 4.50 1987	4.20 NY 3.06 Sea 5.37 2000	3.37 Cal 3.94 Bos 3.58 1986
NL:	5.94 Atl 6.92 NY 5.00 1969	4.70 SF 6.09 Pitt 3.34 1971	4.81 Chi 5.57 SF 4.09 1989	3.95 Phil 4.75 Atl 3.15 1993	4.59 Atl 4.72 Pitt 4.45 1992
Complete Games					
AL:	2 Baltimore 1969-70-71	2 Oakland 1974	2 By many clubs	1 By many clubs	1 Kansas City 1985 / Bos & Cal 1986
NL:	1 By many clubs	2 By many clubs / Florida 1997	3 New York 1973	2 Houston 1986 / Florida 1997	3 Pittsburgh 1992
Complete Games, Both Clubs					
AL:	3 Balt 2 Oak 1 1971	3 Oak 2 Balt 1 1974	4 Balt 2 Oak 2 1973	2 Tor 1 Oak 1 1992	2 Cal 1 Bos 1 1986
NL:	1 Cin 1 Pitt 0 1975 / Pitt 1 Cin 0 1979 / StL 1 Atl 0 1982	2 SF 2 Pitt 0 1971 / LA 2 Phil 0 1977 / LA 1 Phil 1 1978	3 NY 3 Cin 0 1973	3 Hou 2 NY 1 1986 / Fla 2 Atl 1 1997	4 SF 2 StL 2 1987
Saves					
AL:	2 Boston 1975	4 Oakland 1988	3 Mil 1982; Minn 1987 & 1991 / Oakland 1989; New York 1999	3 Toronto 1992	1 Kansas City 1985 / Bos & Cal 1986
NL:	3 Cincinnati 1970	3 Pittsburgh 1971	3 San Francisco 1989	4 Cincinnati 1990	3 St Louis 1987 / Los Angeles 1988 / Atlanta 1991
Saves, Both Clubs					
AL:	2 Bos 2 Oak 0 1975	4 Oak 4 Bos 0 1988	4 Minn 3 Tor 1 1991	4 Tor 3 Oak 1 1992	2 Cal 1 Bos 1 1986
NL:	3 Cin 3 Pitt 0 1970	3 Pitt 3 SF 0 1971	5 Hou 3 Phil 2 1980	6 Cin 4 Pitt 2 1990	5 Atl 3 Pitt 2 1991
Shutouts					
AL:	1 Balt 1969; NY 1981; Det 1984	2 Oak 1974; Balt 1983	1 By many clubs	2 Cleveland 1995	2 Kansas City 1985
NL:	1 Cin 1970; StL 1982	1 LA 1974 78; Phil 1983	1 By many clubs	2 San Diego 1998	3 Atlanta 1991 / Atlanta 1997

CLUB PITCHING

		3 Games	4 Games	5 Games	6 Games	7 Games
Shutouts, Both Clubs	AL	1 Balt 1 Minn 0 1969 / Oak 0 1981 / Det 1 KC 0 1984	2 Oak 2 Balt 0 1974 / Balt 2 Chi 0 1983	2 Oak 1 Det 1 1972 / Oak 1 Balt 1 1973	2 Clev 2 Sea 0 1995 / Balt 1 Clev 1 1997 / NY 1 Sea 1 2000	1 KC 1 Tor 0 1985
	NL	1 Cin 1 Pitt 0 1970 / StL 1 Atl 0 1982	2 LA 1 Pitt 1 1974 / Hou 1 Phil 0 1980	1 By many clubs	2 SD 2 Atl 0 1998	4 Atl 3 Pitt 1 1991
Total Batters Faced	AL	138 Minnesota 1969	157 Boston 1990	205 Baltimore 1996	243 Cleveland 1997	286 Boston 1986
	NL	126 Cincinnati 1979	169 Pitt 1974 Phil 1993	212 Philadelphia 1980	249 New York 1999	282 St Louis 1996
Total Batters Faced, Both Clubs	AL	261 Minn 138 Balt 123 1969	302 Cal 156 Balt 146 1979	399 Balt 205 NY 194 1996	479 Clev 243 Balt 236 1997	567 Bos 286 Cal 281 1986
	NL	246 Cin 126 Pitt 120 1979	316 Cin 166 Atl 150 1995	422 Phil 212 Hou 210 1980	493 NY 249 Atl 244 1999	549 LA 276 NY 273 1988
Innings	AL	32.0 Baltimore 1969	37.0 Baltimore 1983	47.0 New York 1996	58.0 Baltimore 1997 / Cleveland 1997	65.1 Boston 1986
	NL	30.0 Pittsburgh 1979	39.0 Atlanta 1995	49.1 Philadelphia 1980	63.0 New York 1986	65.0 Los Angeles 1988
Innings, Both Clubs	AL	63.1 Balt 32.0 Minn 31.1 1969	73.0 Balt 37.0 Chi 36.0 1983	93.0 NY 47.0 Balt 46.0 1996	116.0 Balt 58 Clev 58 1997	129.1 Bos 65.1 Cal 64.0 1986
	NL	59.0 Pitt 30.0 Cinn 29.0 1979	76.0 Atl 39.0 Cin 37.0 1995	98.1 Phil 49.1 Hou 49.0 1980	125.2 NY 63.0 Hou 62.2 1986	129.0 LA 65.0 NY 64.0 1988
Earned Runs, Most	AL	22 Minnesota 1970	23 California 1979	32 Detroit 1987	31 Seattle 2000	28 California 1986
	NL	20 Atlanta 1969	23 San Francisco 1971	28 St. Louis 2000	29 Philadelphia 1993	44 St Louis 1996
Earned Runs, Most, Both Clubs	AL	32 Minn 22 Balt 10 1970	35 Cal 23 Balt 12 1979	44 NY 23 KC 21 1976	49 Sea 31 NY 18 2000	54 Cal 28 Bos 26 1986 / Det 32 Minn 22 1987
	NL	35 Atl 20 NY 15 1969	36 SF 23 Pitt 13 1971	46 Chi 26 SF 20 1989 / StL 28 NY 18 2000	48 Phil 29 Atl 19 1993	62 Atl 32 Pitt 30 1992
Earned Runs, Fewest	AL	4 Balt 1969; NY 1981; Det 1984	2 Baltimore 1983	9 Oakland 1972	10 Cleveland 1995	22 Kansas City 1985
	NL	3 Cincinnati 1970	4 Philadelphia 1983	7 New York 1973	14 Cincinnati 1990	11 Atlanta 1991
Earned Runs, Fewest, Both Clubs	AL	15 Det 4 KC 11 1984	14 Oak 7 Balt 7 1974	20 Oak 9 Det 11 1972	30 Clev 10 Sea 20 1995	48 KC 22 Tor 26 1985
	NL	11 Cin 3 Pitt 8 1970	19 Phil 4 LA 15 1983	23 LA 9 Mtl 14 1981	33 Cin 14 Pitt 19 1990	29 Atl 11 Pitt 18 1991

CLUB MISCELLANEOUS

	3 Games	4 Games	5 Games	6 Games	7 Games
Wild Pitches					
AL:	2 By many clubs	3 California 1979	4 Minnesota 1991	5 Toronto 1993	3 Kansas City 1985
NL:	2 By many clubs	4 Los Angeles 1983	5 St. Louis 2000	4 San Diego 1998	4 Atlanta 1996
Wild Pitches, Both Clubs					
AL:	3 Balt 2 Minn 1 1969	3 Cal 3 Balt 0 1979	6 Minn 4 Tor 2 1991	7 Tor 5 Chi 2 1993	4 KC 3 Tor 1 1985
NL:	4 Cin 2 Phil 2 1976 Atl 2 StL 2 1982	6 LA 4 Phil 2 1983	7 StL 5 NY 2 2000	4 LA 2 StL 2 1985 SD 4 Atl 0 1998	6 Atl 4 StL 2 1996
Balks					
AL:	1 Kansas City 1980	2 Baltimore 1983	1 See individuals	1 Toronto 1993	1 California 1986
NL:	2 Pittsburgh 1975	1 See individuals	1 See individuals	1 Atlanta 1998	2 New York 1988
Balks, Both Clubs					
AL:	1 KC 1 NY 0 1980	2 Balt 2 Chi 0 1983 Bos 1 Oak 1 1988	1 Det 1 Oak 0 1972 KC 1 NY 0 1977 NY 1 Balt 0 1996	1 Tor 1 Chi 0 1993	1 Cal 1 Bos 0 1986
NL:	2 Pitt 2 Cin 0 1975	2 LA 1 Phil 1 1977	1 Chi 1 SF 0 1989	1 Atl 1 SD 0 1998	2 NY 2 LA 0 1988
Players					
AL:	24 Minnesota 1970 Oakland 1981	23 California 1979 Chicago 1983 Boston 1990	25 Oakland 1972 Seattle 2001	25 Oakland 1992 Cleveland 1995, 98 Seattle 1995, 2000	24 Toronto 1985 California 1986
NL:	24 Pittsburgh 1975	24 Cincinnati 1995	25 St. Louis 2000	25 Los Angeles 1985 Atlanta 1993 New York & Atlanta 1999	25 Pittsburgh 1991-92 Atl 1992 & StL 1996
Players, Both Clubs					
AL:	46 Oak 24 NY 22 1981	45 Chi 23 Balt 22 1983	49 Oak 25 Det 24 1972	50 Clev 25 Sea 25 1995	46 Tor 24 KC 22 1985
NL:	42 Pitt 24 Cin 18 1975	46 Cin 24 Atl 22 1995	49 StL 25 NY 24 2000	50 Atl (25) NY (25) 1999	50 Pitt 25 Atl 25 1992
Pitchers					
AL:	9 Minnesota 1969,70	10 Boston 1990	11 Seattle 2001	11 Oakland 1992 Cleveland 1997-98	9 California 1986
NL:	10 Pittsburgh 1975	9 San Francisco 1971 Los Angeles 1977,78 Cincinnati 1995	11 Atlanta 2001	11 New York 1999	11 Pittsburgh 1991

CLUB MISCELLANEOUS

	3 Games	4 Games	5 Games	6 Games	7 Games
Pitchers, Both Clubs					
AL:	16 Minn 9 Balt 7 1969	16 Oak 9 Bos 7 1988 Bos 10 Oak 6 1990	20 NY 10 Bos 10 1999 Sea 11 NY 9 2001	20 Oak 11 Tor 9 1992 Clev 10 Sea 10 1995 Clev 11 Balt 9 1997 Clev 11 NY 9 1998 NY 10 Sea 10 2000	16 Cal 9 Bos 7 1986
NL:	17 Pitt 10 Cin 7 1975 Cin 9 Pitt 8 1979	17 LA 9 Phil 8 1978 Cin 9 Atl 8 1995	20 NY 10 StL 10 2000 Atl 11 Ari 9 2001	20 NY 11 Atl 9 1999	20 Pitt 11 Atl 9 1991 Atl 10 StL 10 1996
Pinch-Hitters					
AL:	10 Minnesota 1970	8 Baltimore 1983	14 Oakland 1972	10 Seattle 1995	13 Toronto 1985
NL:	9 Pittsburgh 1975	13 Cincinnati 1995	18 St. Louis 2000	20 New York 1999	15 Los Angeles 1988 Atlanta 1992
Pinch-Hitters, Both Clubs					
AL:	13 Oak 8 NY 5 1981	13 Balt 8 Chi 5 1983	22 Oak 14 Det 8 1972	14 Balt 8 Clev 6 1997	21 Tor 13 KC 8 1985
NL:	12 Pitt 9 Cin 3 1975	21 Cin 13 Atl 8 1995	28 StL 18 NY 10 2000	32 NY 20 Atl 12 1999	26 LA 15 NY 11 1988 StL 14 Atl 12 1996
Pinch-Runners					
AL:	4 Kansas City 1984	5 Oakland 1974 1990	3 Oakland 1972 Toronto 1991 New York & Boston 1999	4 Oakland 1992 Cleveland 1995 New York 2000	3 Kansas City 1985 Toronto 1985
NL:	3 New York 1969	1 By many clubs	4 Houston 1980 New York 2000	5 Atlanta 1998	2 SF 1987; NY 1988 LA 1988; Atl 1996
Pinch-Runners, Both Clubs					
AL:	5 KC 4 Det 1 1984	8 Oak 5 Balt 3 1974	6 NY 3 Bos 3 1999	7 Oak 4 Tor 3 1992	6 KC 3 Tor 3 1985
NL:	3 NY 3 Atl 0 1969 Pitt 2 Cin 1 1970	2 LA 1 Pitt 1 1974 Atl 1 Cin 1 1995	7 Hou 4 Phil 3 1980 NY 4 StL 3 2000	5 Atl 5 SD 0 1998	4 LA 2 NY 2 1988
Extra-Inning Games					
AL:	2 Balt & Minn 1969	1 Balt & Chi 1983	2 Det & Oak 1972	2 Balt & Clev 1997	2 Bos & Cal 1986
NL:	2 Cin & Pitt 1979	2 Atl & Cin 1995	4 Hou & Phil 1980	2 NY & Hou 1986 Atl & Phil 1993 Atl & NY 1999	1 LA & NY 1988 Atl & Pitt 1991

PERSONNEL

Most Players, Game
21 St. Louis NL Oct. 16, 2000
20 Oakland AL Oct. 10, 1972
   Oakland AL Oct. 11, 1972 (10 inn)
   Extra-Inning Game:
23 New York NL Oct. 17, 1999 (15 inn)

Most Players, Both Clubs, Game
39 SD (20) Atl (19) NL Oct. 12, 1998
36 NY (19) Sea (17) AL Oct. 20, 2001
   Extra-Inning Game:
45 NY (23) Atl (22) NL Oct. 17, 1999 (15 inn)
37 Balt (19) Clev (18) AL Oct. 11, 1997 (12 inn)

Most Pitchers, Game
7 Minnesota AL Oct. 6, 1969
   Cleveland AL Oct. 11, 1997 (12 inn)
   Cleveland AL Oct. 7 1998 (12 inn)
   San Francisco NL Oct. 14, 1987
   Pittsburgh NL Oct. 7, 1992
   Atlanta NL Oct. 19, 2001
   Extra-Inning Game:
9 New York NL Oct. 17, 1999 (15 inn)

Most Pitchers, Both Clubs, Game
12 Pitt (7) Atl (5) NL Oct. 7, 1992
   Ari (6) Atl (6) NL Oct. 20, 2001
11 Balt (6) NY(5) AL Oct. 12, 1996
   Clev (6) Balt (5) AL Oct. 12, 1997
   Extra-Inning Game:
15 NY (9) Atl (6) NL Oct. 17, 1999 (15 inn)
12 Clev (7) NY (5) AL Oct. 7, 1998 (12 inn)

Most Pitchers, Inning
5 Kansas City AL Oct. 12, 1976 (6th)
   New York AL Oct. 18, 1999 (8th)
4 Los Angeles NL Oct. 8, 1988 (8th)
   St. Louis NL Oct. 13, 1996 (6th)

Most Pinch-Hitters, Game
6 Oakland AL Oct. 10, 1972
5 Los Angeles NL Oct. 8, 1974
   Philadelphia NL Oct. 5, 1983
   Los Angeles NL Oct. 12, 1985
   Pittsburgh NL Oct. 12, 1991
   Atlanta, NL Oct. 14, 1992
   San Diego NL Oct. 12, 1998
   St. Louis NL Oct. 16, 2000
   Extra-Inning Game:
6 Los Angeles NL Oct. 9, 1988 (12 inn)
   Atlanta NL Oct. 19, 1999 (11 inn)

Most Pinch-Hitters, Both Clubs, Game
7 Oak (6) Det (1) AL Oct. 10, 1972
   Chi (4) SF (3) NL Oct. 4, 1989
   Extra-Inning Game:
11 Atl (6) NY (5) NL Oct. 19, 1999 (11 inn)

Most Pinch-Hitters, Inning
4 Philadelphia NL Oct. 5, 1983 (9th)
   Atlanta NL Oct. 7, 1998 (8th)
   Baltimore AL Oct. 7, 1983 (9th)

Most Pinch-Runners, Game
2 By many clubs
   Extra-Inning Game:
3 Kansas City AL Oct. 3, 1984 (11 inn)

Most Pinch-Runners, Both Clubs, Game
3 Phil (2) Hou (1) NL Oct. 12, 1980 (10 inn)
   Atl (2) NY (1) NL Oct. 17, 1999 (15 inn)
   NY (2) StL (1) NL Oct. 11, 2000
   By many AL clubs
   Extra-Inning Game:
4 Bos (2) Cal (2) AL Oct. 12, 1986 (11 inn)

Most Pinch-Runners, Inning
2 Oakland AL Oct. 7, 1972 (11th)
   Baltimore AL Oct. 9, 1974 (9th)
   Boston AL Oct. 14, 1999 (8th)
   New York AL Oct. 13, 2000 (9th)
1 By many NL clubs

ATTENDANCE

Largest Attendance
NL: 65,476 Hou at Phil Oct. 8, 1980
AL: 64,406 Mil at Cal Oct. 5, 1982

Smallest Attendance
AL: 24,265 Balt at Oak Oct. 11 1973
NL: 33,088 Cin at Pitt Oct. 3, 1970

INNINGS – TIME

Most Innings, Game
NL: 16 NY 7 at Hou 6 Oct. 15, 1986
AL: 12 Minn 3 at Balt 4 Oct. 4, 1969
        Balt 1 at Clev 2 Oct. 11, 1997
        Clev 4 at NY 1 Oct. 7, 1998

Longest Game, Time
AL: 4:14 Sea at NY Oct. 15, 2000
NL: 3:59 NY at StL Oct. 12, 2000
        Extra-Inning Game:
NL: 5:46 Atl at NY Oct. 17, 1999 (15 inn)
AL: 4:51 Balt at Clev Oct. 11, 1997 (12 inn)

Shortest Game, Time
AL: 1:57 Oak at Balt Oct. 8, 1974
NL: 1:57 Cin at Pitt Oct. 7, 1972

ALL-STAR GAME

No. 1 AL: Chicago July 6, 1933
```
NL   000  002  000    2   8   0
AL   012  001  00x    4   9   1
```
HALLAHAN, Warneke(3), Hubbell(7)
GOMEZ, Crowder(4), Grove(7)
A-47,595   T-2:05

No. 2 NL: New York July 10, 1934
```
AL   000  261  000    9  14   1
NL   103  030  000    7   8   1
```
Gomez, Ruffing(4), HARDER(5)
Hubbell, Warneke(4), MUNGO(5)
Dean(6), Frankhouse(9)
A-48,363   T-2:44

No. 3 AL: Cleveland July 8, 1935
```
NL   000  100  000    1   4   1
AL   210  010  00x    4   8   0
```
WALKER, Schumacher(3), Derringer(7), Dean(8)
GOMEZ, Harder(7)
A-69,831   T-2:06

No. 4 NL: Boston July 7, 1936
```
AL   000  000  300    3   7   1
NL   020  020  00x    4   9   0
```
GROVE, Rowe(4), Harder(7)
DEAN, Hubbell(4), Davis(7), Warneke(7)
A-25,556   T-2:00

No. 5 AL: Washington July 7, 1937
```
NL   000  111  000    3  13   0
AL   002  312  00x    8  13   2
```
DEAN, Hubbell(4), Blanton(4), Grissom(5), Mungo(6),
   Walters(8)
GOMEZ, Bridges(4), Harder(7)
A-31,391   T-2:30

No. 6 NL: Cincinnati July 6, 1938
```
AL   000  000  001    1   7   4
NL   100  100  20x    4   8   0
```
GOMEZ, Allen(4), Grove(7)
VANDER MEER, Lee(4), Brown(7)
A-27,067   T-1:58

No. 7 AL: New York July 11, 1939
```
NL   001  000  000    1   7   1
AL   000  210  00x    3   6   1
```
Derringer, LEE(4), Fette(7)
Ruffing, BRIDGES(4), Feller(6)
A-62,892   T-1:55

No. 8 NL: St. Louis July 9, 1940
```
AL   000  000  000    0   3   1
NL   300  000  01x    4   7   0
```
RUFFING, Newsom(4), Feller(7)
DERRINGER, Walters(3), Wyatt(5),
   French(7), Hubbell(9)
A-32,373   T-1:53

No. 9 AL: Detroit July 8, 1941
```
NL   000  001  220    5  10   2
AL   000  101  014    7  11   3
```
Wyatt, Derringer(3), Walters(5), PASSEAU(7)
Feller, Lee(4), Hudson(7), SMITH(8)
A-54,674   T-2:23

No. 10 NL: New York July 6n, 1942
```
AL   300  000  000    3   7   0
NL   000  000  010    1   6   1
```
CHANDLER, Benton(5)
COOPER, Vander Meer(4), Passeau(7), Walters(9)
A-33,694   T-2:07

No. 11 AL: Philadelphia July 13n, 1943
```
NL   100  000  101    3  10   3
AL   031  010  00x    5   8   1
```
COOPER, Vander Meer(3), Sewell(6), Javery(7)
LEONARD, Newhouser(4), Hughson(7)
A-31,938   T-2:07

No. 12 NL: Pittsburgh July 11n, 1944
```
AL   010  000  000    1   6   3
NL   000  040  21x    7  12   1
```
Borowy, HUGHSON(4), Muncrief(5), Newhouser(7),
   Newsom(8)
Walters, RAFFENSBERGER(4), Sewell(6), Tobin(9)
A-29,589   T-2:11

1945 No Game (World War II)

No. 13 AL: Boston July 9, 1946
```
NL   000  000  000    0   3   0
AL   200  130  24x   12  14   1
```
PASSEAU, Higbe(4), Blackwell (5), Sewell(8)
FELLER, Newhouser(4), Kramer(7)
A-34,906   T-2:19

No. 14 NL: Chicago July 8, 1947
```
AL   000  001  100    2   8   0
NL   000  100  000    1   5   1
```
Newhouser, SHEA(4), Masterson(7), Page(8)
Blackwell, Brecheen(4), SAIN(7), Spahn(8)
A-41,123   T-2:19

No. 15 AL: St. Louis July 13, 1948
```
NL   200  000  000    2   8   0
AL   011  300  00x    5   6   0
```
Branca, SCHMITZ(4), Sain(4), Blackwell(6)
Masterson, RASCHI(4), Coleman(7)
A-34,009   T-2:27

No. 16 NL: Brooklyn July 12, 1949
```
AL   400  202  300   11  13   1
NL   212  002  000    7  12   5
```
Parnell, TRUCKS(2), Brissie(4), Raschi(7)
Spahn, NEWCOMBE(2), Munger(5), Bickford(6),
   Pollet(7), Blackwell(8), Roe(9)
A-32,577   T-3:04

No. 17 AL: Chicago July 11, 1950
```
NL   020  000  001  000  01    4  10   0
AL   001  020  000  000  00    3   8   1
```
Roberts, Newcombe(4), Konstanty(6), Jansen(7),
   BLACKWELL(12)
Raschi, Lemon(4), Houtteman(7), Reynolds(10),
   GRAY(13), Feller(14)
A-46,127   T-3:19

No. 18 AL: Detroit July 10, 1951
```
NL   100  302  110    8  12   1
AL   010  110  000    3  10   2
```
Roberts, MAGLIE(3), Newcombe(6), Blackwell(9)
Garver, LOPAT(4), Hutchinson(5), Parnell(8), Lemon(9)
A-52,075   T-2:41

No. 19 NL: Philadelphia July 8, 1952 (rain)
```
AL   000  20        2   5   0
NL   100  20        3   3   0
```
Raschi, LEMON(3), Shantz(5)
Simmons, RUSH(4)
A-32,785   T-1:29

No. 20 NL: Cincinnati July 14, 1953
```
AL   000  000  001    1   5   0
NL   000  020  12x    5  10   0
```
Pierce, REYNOLDS(4), Garcia(6), Paige(8)
Roberts, SPAHN(4), Simmons(6), Dickson(8)
A-30,846   T-2:19

No. 21 AL: Cleveland July 13, 1954

NL	000	520	020	9	14	0
AL	004	121	03x	11	17	1

Roberts, Antonelli(4), Spahn(6), Grissom(6),
CONLEY(8), Erskine(8)
Ford, Consuegra(4), Lemon(4), Porterfield(5),
Keegan(8), STONE(8), Trucks(9)
A-68,751   T-3:10

No. 22 NL: Milwaukee July 12, 1955

AL	400	001	000	000	5	10	2
NL	000	000	230	001	6	13	1

Pierce, Wynn(4), Ford(7), SULLIVAN(8)
Roberts, Haddix(4), Newcombe(7), Jones(8),
Nuxhall(8), CONLEY(12)
A-45,314   T-3:17

No. 23 AL: Washington July 10, 1956

NL	001	211	200	7	11	0
AL	000	003	000	3	11	0

FRIEND, Spahn(4), Antonelli(6), PIERCE, Ford(4),
Wilson(5), Brewer(6), Score(8), Wynn(9)
A-28,843   T-2:45

No. 24 NL: St. Louis July 9, 1957

AL	020	001	003	6	10	0
NL	000	000	203	5	9	1

BUNNING, Loes(4), Wynn(7), Pierce(7), Mossi(9),
Grim(9)
SIMMONS, Burdette(2), Sanford(6), Jackson(7),
Labine(9)
A-30,693   T-2:43

No. 25 AL: Baltimore July 8, 1958

NL	210	000	000	3	4	2
AL	110	011	00x	4	9	2

Spahn, FRIEND(4), Jackson(6), Farrell(7)
Turley, Narleski(2), WYNN(6), O'Dell(7)
A-48,829   T-2:13

No. 26 NL: Pittsburgh July 7, 1959

AL	000	100	030	4	8	0
NL	100	000	22x	5	9	1

Wynn, Duren(4), Bunning(7), FORD(8), Daley(8)
Drysdale, Burdette(4), Face(7), ANTONELLI(8),
Elston(9)
A-35,277   T-2:33

No. 27 NL: Los Angeles August 3, 1959

AL	012	000	110	5	6	0
NL	100	010	100	3	6	3

WALKER, Wynn(4), Wilhelm(6), O'Dell(7), McLish(8)
DRYSDALE, Conley(4), Jones(6), Face(8)
A-55,105   T-2:42

No. 28 AL: Kansas City July 11, 1960

NL	311	000	000	5	12	4
AL	000	001	020	3	6	1

FRIEND, McCormick(4), Face(6), Buhl(8), Law (9)
MONBOUQUETTE, Estrada(3), Coates(4), Bell(6),
Lary(8), Daley(9)
A-30,619   T-2:39

No. 29 AL: New York July 13, 1960

NL	021	000	102	6	10	0
AL	000	000	000	0	8	0

LAW, Podres(3), Williams(5), Jackson(7), Henry (8),
McDaniel (9)
FORD, Wynn(4), Staley(6), Lary(8), Bell(9)
A-38,362   T-2:42

No. 30 NL: San Francisco July 11, 1961

AL	000	001	002	1	4	4	2
NL	010	100	010	2	5	11	5

Ford, Lary(4), Donovan(4), Bunning(6), Fornieles(8),
WILHELM(8)
Spahn, Purkey(4), McCormick(6), Face(9), Koufax(9),
MILLER(9)
A-44,115   T-2:53

No. 31 AL: Boston July 31, 1961 (rain)

NL	000	001	000	1	5	1
AL	100	000	000	1	4	0

Purkey, Mahaffey(3), Koufax(5), Miller(7)
Bunning, Schwall(4), Pascual(7)
A-31,851   T-2:27

No. 32 AL: Washington July 10, 1962

NL	000	002	010	3	8	0
AL	000	001	000	1	4	0

Drysdale, MARICHAL(4), Purkey(6), Shaw(8)
Bunning, PASCUAL(4), Donovan(7), Pappas(9)
A-45,480   T-2:33

No. 33 NL: Chicago July 30, 1962

AL	001	201	302	9	10	0
NL	010	000	111	4	10	4

Stenhouse, HERBERT(3), Aguirre(6), Pappas(9)
Podres, MAHAFFEY(3), Gibson(5), Farrell(7),
Marichal(8)
A-38,359   T-2:28

No. 34 AL: Cleveland July 9, 1963

NL	012	010	010	5	6	0
AL	012	000	000	3	11	1

O'Toole, JACKSON(3), Culp(5), Woodeshick(6),
Drysdale(8)
McBride, BUNNING(4), Bouton(6), Pizarro(7),
Radatz(8)
A-44,160   T-2:20

No. 35 NL: New York July 7, 1964

AL	100	002	100	4	9	1
NL	000	210	004	7	8	0

Chance, Wyatt(4), Pascual(5), RADATZ(7)
Drysdale, Bunning(4), Short(6), Farrell(7),
MARICHAL(9)
A-50,844   T-2:27

No. 36 AL: Minnesota July 13, 1965

NL	320	000	000	6	11	0
AL	000	140	000	5	8	0

Marichal, Maloney(4), Dryrdale(5), KOUFAX(6),
Farrell(7), Gibson(8)
Pappas, Grant(2), Richert(4), McDOWELL(6), Fisher(8)
A-46,706   T-2:45

No. 37 NL: St. Louis July 12, 1966

AL	010	000	000	0	1	6	0
NL	000	100	000	1	2	6	0

McLaln, Kaat(4), Stottlemyre(6), Siebert(8),
RICHERT(10)
Koufax, Bunning(4), Marichal(6), PERRY(9)
A-49,936   T-2:19

No. 38 AL: California July 11, 1967

NL	010	000	000	000	001	2	9	0
AL	000	001	000	000	000	1	8	0

Marichal, Jenkins(4), Gibson(7), Short(9), Cuellar(11),
DRYSDALE(13), Seaver(15), Chance, McGlothlin(4),
Peters(6), Downing(9), HUNTER(11)
A-46,309   T-3:41

No. 39 NL: Houston July 9n, 1968

```
AL    000  000  000    0    3    1
NL    100  000  00x    1    5    0
```
TIANT, Odom(3), McLain(5), McDowell(7),
Stottlemyre(8), John(8)
DRYSDALE, Marichal(4), Carlton(6), Seaver(7), Reed
(9), Koosman(9)
A-48,321   T-2:10

No. 40 AL: Washington July 23, 1969

```
NL    125  100  000    9   11    0
AL    011  100  000    3    6    2
```
CARLTON, Gibson(4), Singer(5), Koosman(7),
Dierker(8), Niekro(9)
STOTTLEMYRE, Odom(3), Knowles(3), McLain(4),
McNally(5), McDowell(7), Culp(9)
A-45,259   T-2:38

No. 41 NL: Cincinnati July 14n, 1970

```
AL    000  001  120  000    4   12    0
NL    000  000  103  001    5   10    0
```
Palmer, McDowell(4), J.Perry(7), Hunter(9),
Peterson(9), Stottlemyre(9), WRIGHT(11)
Seaver, Merritt(4), G.Perry(6), Gibson(8), OSTEEN(10)
A-51,838   T-3:19

No. 42 AL: Detroit July 13n, 1971

```
NL    021  000  010    4    5    0
AL    004  002  00x    6    7    0
```
ELLIS, Marichal(4), Jenkins(6), Wilson(7)
BLUE, Palmer(4), Cuellar(6), Lolich(8)
A-53,559   T-2:05

No. 43 NL: Atlanta July 25n, 1972

```
AL    001  000  020    0    3    6    0
NL    000  002  001    1    4    8    0
```
Palmer, Lolich(4), G. Perry(6), Wood(8), McNALLY(10)
Gibson, Blass(3), Sutton(4), Carlton(6), Stoneman(7),
McGRAW(9)
A-53,107   T-2:26

No. 44 AL: Kansas City July 24n, 1973

```
NL    002  122  000    7   10    0
AL    010  000  000    1    5    0
```
WISE, Osteen(3), Sutton(5), Twitchell(6), Giusti(7),
Seaver(8), Brewer(9)
Hunter, Holtzman(2), BLYLEVEN(3), Singer(4), Ryan(6),
Lyle(8), Fingers(9)
A-40,849   T-2:45

No. 45 NL: Pittsburgh July 23n, 1974

```
AL    002  000  000    2    4    1
NL    010  210  12x    7   10    1
```
G.Perry, TIANT(4), Hunter(6), Fingers(8)
Messersmith, BRETT(4), Matlack(6), McGlothen(7),
Marshall(8)
A-50,706   T-2:37

No. 46 AL: Milwaukee July 15n, 1975

```
NL    021  000  003    6   13    1
AL    000  003  000    3   10    1
```
Reuss, Sutton(4), Seaver(6), MATLACK(7), R.Jones(9)
Blue, Busby(3), Kaat(5), HUNTER(7), Gossage(9)
A-51,480   T-2:35

No. 47 NL: Philadelphia July 13n, 1976

```
AL    000  100  000    1    5    0
NL    202  000  03x    7   10    0
```
FIDRYCH, Hunter(3), Tiant(5), Tanana(7)
R.JONES, Seaver(4), Montefusco(6), Rhoden(8),
K.Forsch(9)
A-63,974   T-2:12

No. 48 AL: New York July 19n, 1977

```
NL    401  000  020    7    9    1
AL    000  002  102    5    8    0
```
SUTTON, Lavelle(4),Seaver (6), Reuschel(8),Gossage (9)
PALMER, Kern(3), Eckersley(4), LaRoche(6)
A-56,683   T-2:34

No. 49 NL: San Diego July 11n, 1978

```
AL    201  000  000    3    8    1
NL    003  000  04x    7   10    0
```
Palmer, Keough(3), Sorensen(4), Kern(7), Guidry(7),
GOSSAGE(8)
Blue, Rogers(4), Fingers(6), SUTTER(8), P.Niekro(9)
A-51,549   T-2:37

No.50 AL: Seattle July 17n, 1979

```
NL    211  001  011    7   10    1
AL    302  001  000    6   10    1
```
Carlton, Andujar(2), Rogers(4), Perry(6) Sambito(6),
LaCoss(6), SUTTER(7)
Ryan, Stanley(3), Clear(5), KERN(7) Guidry(9)
A-58,905   T-3:11

No. 51 NL: Los Angeles July 8n, 1980

```
AL    000  020  000    2    7    2
NL    000  012  10x    4    7    0
```
Stone, JOHN(4), Farmer(6), Stieb(7), Gossage(8)
Richard, Welch(3), REUSS(6), Bibby(7), Sutter(8)
A-58,088   T-2:33

No.52 AL: Cleveland August 9n, 1981

```
NL    000  011  120    5    9    1
AL    010  003  000    4   11    1
```
Valenzuela, Seaver(2), Knepper(3), Hooton(5),
Ruthven(6), BLUE(7), Ryan(8), Sutter(9)
Morris, Barker(3), K.Forsch(5), Norris(6), Davis(7),
FINGERS(8), Stieb(8)
A-72,086   T-2:59

No. 53 NL: Montreal July 13n, 1982

```
AL    100  000  000    1    8    2
NL    021  001  00x    4    8    1
```
ECKERSLEY, Clancy(4), Bannister(5), Quisenberry(6),
Fingers(8)
ROGERS, Carlton(4), Soto(6),
Valenzuela(8), Minton(8),
Howe(9), Hume(9)
A-59,057   T-2:53

No. 54 AL: Chicago July 6n, 1983

```
NL    100  110  000    3    8    3
AL    117  000  22x   13   15    2
```
SOTO, Hammaker(3), Dawley(3), Dravecky(5), Perez(7),
Orosco(7), L.Smith(8)
STIEB, Honeycutt(4), Stanley(6), Young(8),
Quisenberry(9)
A-43,801   T-3:05

No. 55 NL: San Francisco July 10n, 1984

```
AL    010  000  000    1    7    2
NL    110  000  01x    3    8    0
```
STIEB, Morris(3), Dotson(5), Caudill(7), Hernandez(8)
LEA, Valenzuela(3), Gooden(5), Soto(7), Gossage(9)
A-57,756   T-2:29

No. 56 AL: Minnesota July 16n, 1985

```
NL    011  020  002    6    9    1
AL    100  000  000    1    5    0
```
HOYT, Ryan(4), Valenzuela(7), Reardon(8), Gossage(9)
MORRIS, Key(3), Blyleven(4), Stieb(6), Moore(7),
Petry(9), Hernandez(9)
A-54,960   T-2:54

No. 57 NL: Houston July 15n, 1986

AL	020	000	100	3	5	0
NL	000	000	020	2	5	1

CLEMENS, Higuera(4), Hough(7), Righetti(8), Aase(9)
GOODEN, Valenzuela(4), Scott(7), Fernandez(8),
   Krukow(9)
A-45,774   T-2:28

No. 58 AL: Oakland July 14n, 1987

NL	000 000	000	000	2	2	8	2
AL	000 000	000	000	0	0	6	1

Scott, Sutcliffe(3), Hershiser(5), Reuschel(7), Franco(8),
   Bedrosian(9), L.SMITH (10),Fernandez(13)
Saberhagen, Morris(4), Langston(6), Plesac(8),
   Righetti(9), Henke(9), HOWELL(12)
A-44,671   T-3:39

No. 59 NL: Cincinnati July 12n, 1988

AL	001	100	000	2	6	2
NL	000	100	000	1	5	0

VIOLA, Clemens(3), Gubicza(4), Stieb(6)
Russell(7), D.Jones(8), Plesac(8), Eckersley(9)
GOODEN, Knepper(4), Cone(5), Gross(6), Davis(7),
   Walk(7), Hershiser(8), Worrell(9)
A-55,837   T-2:26

No. 60 AL: California July 11n, 1989

NL	200	000	010	3	9	1
AL	212	000	00x	5	12	0

Reuschel, SMOLTZ(2), Sutcliffe(3),Burke(4), M.Davis(6),
   Howell(7), M.Williams(8)
Stewart, RYAN(2), Gubicza(4), Moore(5), Swindell(6),
   Russell(7), Plesac(8), D.Jones(8)
A-64,036   T-2:48

No. 61 NL: Chicago July 10n, 1990

AL	000	000	200	2	7	0
NL	000	000	000	0	2	1

Welch, Stieb(3), SABERHAGEN(5), Thigpen(7),
   Finley(8), Eckersley(9)
Armstrong, R.Martinez(3), D.Martinez(4), Viola(5),
   D.Smith(6), BRANTLEY(6), Dibble(7), Myers(8),
   Franco(9)
A-39,071   T-2:53

No. 62 NL: Toronto July 9n, 1991

NL	100	100	000	2	10	1
AL	003	000	10x	4	8	0

Glavine, D. MARTINEZ(3), Viola(5), Harnish(6),
   Smiley(7), Dibble(7), Morgan(8)
Morris, KEY(3), Clemens(4), McDowell(5), Reardon(7),
   Aguilera(7), Eckersley(9)
A-52,313   T-3:04

No. 63 NL: San Diego July 14n, 1992

AL	411	004	030	13	19	1
NL	000	001	032	6	12	1

BROWN, McDowell(2), Guzman(3), Clemens(4),
   Mussina(5), Langston(6), Nagy(7), Montgomery(8),
   Aguilera(8), Eckersley(9)
GLAVINE, Maddux(2), Cone(4), Tewksbury(5),
   Smoltz(6), D.Martinez(7), Jones(8), Charlton(9)
A-59,372   T-2:55

No. 64 AL: Baltimore July 13n, 1993

NL	200	001	000	3	7	2
AL	011	033	10x	9	11	0

Mulholland, Benes(3), BURKETT(5), Avery(6),
   Smoltz(6), Beck(7), Harvey(8)
Langston, R. Johnson(3), McDOWELL(5), Key(6),
   Montgomery(7), Aguilera(8), Ward(9)
A-48,147   T-2:49

No. 65 NL: Pittsburgh July 12n, 1994

AL	100	003	300	0	7	15	0
NL	103	001	002	1	8	12	1

Key, Cone(3), Mussina(5), Johnson(6), Hentgen(7),
   Alvarez(8), L. Smith(9) BERE(10)
Maddux, Hill(4), Drabek(6), Hudek(6), Jackson(7),
   Beck(7), Myers(9), JONES(10)
A-59, 568   T-3:14

No. 66 AL: Texas July 11n, 1995

NL	000	001	110	3	3	0
AL	000	200	000	2	8	0

Nomo, Smiley(3), Green(5), Neagle(6), Perez(7),
   SLOCUMB(7), Henke(8), Myers(9)
Johnson, Appier(3), D.Martinez(5), Rogers(7),
   ONTIVEROS(8), Wells(8), Mesa(9)
A-50,920   T-2:40

No. 67 NL: Philadelphia July 9n, 1996

AL	000	000	000	0	7	0
NL	121	002	00x	6	12	1

NAGY, Finley(3), Pavlik(5), Percival(7), R.Hernandez(8)
SMOLTZ, Brown(3), Glavine(4), Bottalico(5),
   P.Martinez(6), Trachsel(7), Worrell(8), Wohlers(9),
   Leiter(9)
A-62,670   T-2:35

No. 68 AL: Cleveland July 8n, 1997

NL	000	000	100	1	3	0
AL	010	000	20x	3	7	0

Maddux, Schilling (3), Brown (5),P.Martinez (6), ESTES
   (7), B.Jones (8)
Johnson, Clemens (3), Cone (4), Thompson (5),
   Hentgen (6), ROSADO (7), Myers (8),
   Rivera (9)
A-44,916   T-2:36

No. 69 NL: Colorado July 7n, 1998

AL	000	413	113	13	19	2
NL	002	130	020	8	12	1

Wells, Clemens (3), Radke (4), COLON (5), Arrojo (6),
   Wetteland (7), Gordon (8), Percival (9)
Maddux, Glavine (3), Brown (4), Ashby (5), URBINA
   (6), Hoffman (7), Shaw (8), Nen (9)
A-51,267   T-3:38

No. 70 AL: Boston July 13n, 1999

NL	001	000	000	1	7	1
AL	200	000	00x	4	6	2

SCHILLING, Johnson (3), Bottenfield (4), Lima (5)
   Millwood (6), Ashby (7), Hampton (7), Hoffman (8),
   Wagner (8)
MARTINEZ, Cone (3), Mussina (5), Rosado (6),
   Zimmerman (7), Hernandez (8) Wetteland (9)
A-34,187   T-2:53

No. 71 NL: Atlanta July 11n, 2000

AL	001	200	003	6	10	2
NL	001	010	001	3	9	2

Wells, BALDWIN (3), Sele (4), Isringhausen (5), Lowe
   (6), Jones (7), Hudson (8), Rivera (9)
Johnson, Graves (3), Brown (3), LEITER (4), Glavine (5),
   Kile (6), Wickman (8), Hoffman (9)
A-51,323   T-2:56

No. 72 AL: Seattle July 10n, 2001

NL	000	001	000	1	3	1
AL	001	012	00x	4	8	0

Johnson, PARK (3), Burkett (4), Hampton (5), Lieber
   (6), Morris (7), Shaw (8), Wagner (8), Sheets (9)
Clemens, GARCIA (3), Pettitte (4), Mays (5), Quantrill
   (6), Stanton (6), Nelson (7), Percival (8), Sasaki (9)
A-47,364   T-2:48

ALL-STAR GAME CLUB BATTING

YEAR	AB	R	ER	H	TB	1B	2B	3B	HR	RBI	SH	SF	BB	HP	SO	SB	CS	BAT	SLG
1933																			
NL	34	2	2	8	14	5	1	1	1	2	0	0	0	0	4	0	0	.235	.412
AL	31	4	4	9	12	8	0	0	1	4	1	0	6	0	4	1	0	.290	.387
1934																			
AL	39	9	9	14	23	7	5	2	0	9	0	0	9	0	12	2	0	.359	.590
NL	36	7	7	8	15	5	1	0	2	6	0	0	3	0	5	2	0	.222	.417
1935																			
NL	31	1	1	4	6	2	2	0	0	1	0	0	2	0	5	1	0	.129	.194
AL	32	4	4	8	15	4	2	1	1	4	0	0	3	0	9	0	0	.250	.469
1936																			
AL	32	3	3	7	11	5	1	0	1	3	0	0	7	0	7	0	1	.219	.344
NL	31	4	3	9	14	7	0	1	1	4	0	0	3	0	6	0	0	.290	.452
1937																			
NL	41	3	3	13	16	10	3	0	0	3	0	0	0	0	0	0	0	.317	.390
AL	35	8	8	13	21	8	3	1	1	8	0	0	4	0	7	0	0	.371	.600
1938																			
AL	34	1	1	7	9	5	2	0	0	1	0	0	2	0	5	1	0	.206	.265
NL	33	4	1	8	10	7	0	1	0	2	0	0	0	1	7	1	0	.242	.303
1939																			
NL	34	1	1	7	8	6	1	0	0	1	0	0	3	0	9	0	0	.206	.235
AL	31	3	2	6	9	5	0	0	1	2	0	0	4	0	6	0	0	.194	.290
1940																			
AL	29	0	0	3	4	2	1	0	0	0	0	0	2	0	7	0	0	.103	.138
NL	29	4	4	7	10	6	0	0	1	4	2	0	3	1	6	0	0	.241	.345
1941																			
NL	35	5	5	10	19	5	3	0	2	5	2	0	1	0	7	0	1	.286	.543
AL	36	7	7	11	17	7	3	0	1	7	0	0	4	0	6	0	0	.306	.472
1942																			
AL	35	3	3	7	14	4	1	0	2	3	0	0	0	0	8	0	0	.200	.400
NL	31	1	1	6	9	5	0	0	1	1	0	0	2	1	3	0	0	.194	.290
1943																			
NL	37	3	3	10	16	7	1	1	1	3	0	0	1	0	3	0	0	.270	.432
AL	29	5	4	8	13	5	2	0	1	4	2	0	3	1	10	0	0	.276	.448
1944																			
AL	32	1	1	6	6	6	0	0	0	1	0	0	1	0	5	0	0	.188	.188
NL	33	7	5	12	16	9	2	1	0	7	3	0	4	0	4	1	0	.364	.485
1945																			
No Game (World War II)																			
1946																			
NL	31	0	0	3	3	3	0	0	0	0	0	0	1	0	10	0	0	.097	.097
AL	36	12	12	14	25	9	2	0	3	12	0	0	4	0	3	0	0	.389	.694
1947																			
AL	34	2	2	8	10	6	2	0	0	1	0	0	1	0	8	1	0	.235	.294
NL	32	1	1	5	8	4	0	0	1	1	0	0	4	0	6	0	0	.156	.250
1948																			
NL	35	2	2	8	11	7	0	0	1	2	0	0	4	0	7	1	0	.229	.314
AL	29	5	5	6	9	5	0	0	1	5	1	0	7	0	7	3	0	.207	.310
1949																			
AL	41	11	7	13	18	8	5	0	0	10	0	0	5	0	5	1	0	.317	.439
NL	37	7	7	12	20	8	2	0	2	6	0	0	8	1	3	0	0	.324	.541
1950 (14 innings)																			
NL	52	4	4	10	19	6	1	1	2	4	0	0	3	0	7	0	0	.192	.365
AL	49	3	3	8	12	5	2	1	0	3	0	0	2	0	12	0	0	.163	.245
1951																			
NL	39	8	7	12	25	7	1	0	4	7	0	0	4	0	3	0	1	.308	.641
AL	35	3	3	10	21	5	1	2	2	3	1	0	3	0	7	0	1	.286	.600
1952 (five innings, rain)																			
AL	18	2	2	5	7	3	2	0	0	2	0	0	2	0	4	0	1	.278	.389
NL	18	3	3	3	10	0	1	0	2	3	0	0	2	1	6	0	0	.167	.556

ALL-STAR GAME CLUB BATTING

YEAR	AB	R	ER	H	TB	1B	2B	3B	HR	RBI	SH	SF	BB	HP	SO	SB	CS	BAT	SLG
1953																			
AL	31	1	1	5	5	5	0	0	0	1	0	0	3	0	5	0	1	.161	.161
NL	32	5	5	10	11	9	1	0	0	5	0	0	3	1	3	1	0	.313	.344
1954																			
NL	40	9	9	14	23	9	3	0	2	9	0	0	2	0	2	0	1	.350	.575
AL	39	11	11	17	29	13	0	0	4	11	0	1	4	0	10	0	0	.436	.744
1955 (12 innings)																			
AL	44	5	5	10	14	8	1	0	1	4	2	0	6	1	12	0	0	.227	.318
NL	45	6	4	13	17	11	1	0	1	4	0	0	2	0	8	0	0	.289	.378
1956																			
NL	36	7	7	11	19	7	2	0	2	6	1	0	4	0	12	1	1	.306	.528
AL	37	3	3	11	17	9	0	0	2	3	0	0	0	0	5	0	0	.297	.459
1957																			
AL	37	6	4	10	12	8	2	0	0	6	1	0	4	0	1	0	0	.270	.324
NL	34	5	5	9	13	6	2	1	0	4	0	0	2	0	6	0	0	.265	.382
1958																			
NL	30	3	3	4	4	4	0	0	0	2	0	1	3	1	2	1	0	.133	.133
AL	31	4	2	9	9	9	0	0	0	3	1	0	3	0	4	0	0	.290	.290
1959 #1																			
AL	36	4	4	8	12	6	1	0	1	4	0	0	3	0	9	0	0	.222	.333
NL	30	5	5	9	16	5	2	1	1	5	1	0	2	0	9	0	0	.300	.533
1959 #2																			
AL	33	5	4	6	15	3	0	0	3	5	0	0	6	0	12	1	1	.182	.455
NL	31	3	3	6	13	3	1	0	2	3	0	1	5	0	4	0	0	.194	.419
1960 #1																			
NL	38	5	5	12	23	6	3	1	2	5	0	0	1	1	6	1	0	.316	.605
AL	34	3	1	6	9	5	0	0	1	3	0	0	5	0	7	0	0	.176	.265
1960 #2																			
NL	34	6	6	10	22	6	0	0	4	6	1	0	3	0	3	1	1	.294	.647
AL	33	0	0	8	9	7	1	0	0	0	0	0	6	0	4	0	0	.242	.273
1961 #1 (10 innings)																			
AL	38	4	2	4	8	2	1	0	1	3	0	0	2	0	12	0	0	.105	.211
NL	37	5	4	11	18	7	2	1	1	5	0	2	1	1	6	1	0	.297	.486
1961 #2 (nine innings, rain)																			
NL	32	1	1	5	6	4	1	0	0	1	0	0	2	1	7	0	0	.156	.188
AL	30	1	1	4	7	3	0	0	1	1	0	0	3	0	8	1	0	.133	.233
1962 #1																			
NL	33	3	3	8	9	7	1	0	0	3	0	1	1	0	3	2	1	.242	.273
AL	29	1	1	4	6	3	0	1	0	1	0	1	3	2	5	0	0	.138	.207
1962 #2																			
AL	37	9	8	10	21	5	2	0	3	9	0	1	4	0	8	0	0	.270	.568
NL	35	4	4	10	17	6	2	1	1	4	0	0	2	1	3	0	0	.286	.486
1963																			
NL	34	5	4	6	6	6	0	0	0	5	0	0	3	0	6	3	0	.176	.176
AL	34	3	3	11	12	10	1	0	0	3	1	0	1	1	9	0	0	.324	.353
1964																			
AL	35	4	3	9	12	7	1	1	0	4	0	1	1	1	10	0	0	.257	.343
NL	34	7	7	8	18	4	1	0	3	6	0	0	2	0	8	1	0	.235	.529
1965																			
NL	36	6	6	11	20	8	0	0	3	6	1	0	3	0	7	0	0	.306	.556
AL	34	5	5	8	15	5	1	0	2	5	0	0	6	0	5	0	0	.235	.441
1966 (10 innings)																			
AL	35	1	1	6	8	5	0	1	0	0	0	0	1	0	6	0	0	.171	.229
NL	33	2	2	6	7	5	1	0	0	2	1	0	1	0	5	0	0	.182	.212
1967 (15 innings)																			
NL	51	2	2	9	16	6	1	0	2	2	1	0	0	0	13	1	0	.176	.314
AL	49	1	1	8	12	6	1	0	1	1	2	0	2	0	17	0	2	.163	.245
1968																			
AL	30	0	0	3	6	0	3	0	0	0	0	0	0	0	11	0	0	.100	.200
NL	27	1	0	5	6	4	1	0	0	0	0	0	6	0	9	1	0	.185	.231

ALL-STAR GAME CLUB BATTING

YEAR	AB	R	ER	H	TB	1B	2B	3B	HR	RBI	SH	SF	BB	HP	SO	SB	CS	BAT	SLG
1969																			
NL	40	9	7	11	22	6	2	0	3	8	0	0	3	0	10	0	0	.275	.550
AL	33	3	3	6	13	3	1	0	2	3	0	0	2	0	7	0	0	.182	.394
1970 (12 innings)																			
AL	44	4	4	12	16	9	2	1	0	4	1	1	3	0	7	0	1	.273	.364
NL	43	5	5	10	13	9	0	0	1	4	0	1	5	1	11	0	0	.233	.302
1971																			
NL	31	4	4	5	14	2	0	0	3	4	0	0	1	1	8	0	0	.161	.452
AL	29	6	6	7	16	4	0	0	3	6	0	0	3	0	5	0	0	.241	.552
1972 (10 innings)																			
AL	33	3	3	6	11	3	2	0	1	3	1	0	2	0	8	0	0	.182	.333
NL	33	4	4	8	11	7	0	0	1	4	1	0	3	0	5	1	0	.242	.333
1973																			
NL	34	7	7	10	21	5	2	0	3	7	1	0	5	0	6	0	0	.294	.618
AL	32	1	1	5	9	2	2	1	0	1	0	0	3	0	5	1	0	.156	.281
1974																			
AL	30	2	2	4	5	3	1	0	0	1	1	0	6	0	7	1	0	.133	.167
NL	33	7	6	10	18	5	3	1	1	6	0	1	3	0	7	1	0	.303	.545
1975																			
NL	37	6	6	13	20	10	1	0	2	6	0	1	0	1	3	1	1	.351	.541
AL	36	3	3	10	13	9	0	0	1	3	0	0	1	1	10	3	1	.278	.361
1976																			
AL	29	1	1	5	8	4	0	0	1	1	0	0	3	0	5	1	0	.172	.276
NL	33	7	7	10	20	6	0	2	2	7	0	0	1	0	5	0	0	.303	.606
1977																			
NL	33	7	7	9	21	3	3	0	3	7	1	0	3	1	9	0	1	.273	.636
AL	35	5	4	8	12	6	1	0	1	5	0	0	3	1	10	0	0	.229	.343
1978																			
AL	31	3	3	8	13	5	1	2	0	3	0	2	1	0	7	1	2	.258	.419
NL	32	7	7	10	13	8	1	1	0	6	0	0	6	0	6	1	1	.313	.406
1979																			
NL	35	7	7	10	18	5	3	1	1	7	0	1	6	0	5	0	0	.286	.514
AL	35	6	5	10	16	6	3	0	1	5	1	0	5	1	5	0	0	.286	.457
1980																			
AL	32	2	2	7	11	5	1	0	1	2	0	0	4	0	11	1	0	.219	.344
NL	31	4	3	7	10	6	0	0	1	2	0	0	2	0	4	2	0	.226	.323
1981																			
NL	35	5	5	9	23	3	2	0	4	5	0	0	4	0	6	2	0	.257	.657
AL	37	4	4	11	15	9	1	0	1	4	0	1	2	0	8	0	1	.297	.405
1982																			
AL	33	1	1	8	9	7	1	0	0	1	0	1	5	0	10	1	0	.242	.273
NL	29	4	4	8	14	5	1	1	1	4	0	1	2	0	2	2	3	.276	.483
1983																			
NL	35	3	2	8	9	7	1	0	0	2	0	0	1	0	6	2	0	.229	.257
AL	38	13	10	15	28	8	3	2	2	13	1	3	4	0	8	0	0	.395	.737
1984																			
AL	32	1	1	7	13	3	3	0	1	1	0	0	0	0	11	0	0	.219	.406
NL	32	3	2	8	15	5	1	0	2	2	0	0	2	0	10	4	0	.250	.469
1985																			
NL	35	6	6	9	13	5	4	0	0	6	0	0	7	1	8	2	0	.257	.371
AL	30	1	0	5	5	5	0	0	0	1	0	1	4	0	6	3	0	.167	.167
1986																			
AL	33	3	3	5	12	2	1	0	2	3	0	0	2	0	12	2	0	.152	.364
NL	32	2	1	5	6	4	1	0	0	1	0	0	1	0	7	1	0	.156	.188
1987 (13 innings)																			
NL	46	2	2	8	11	6	1	1	0	2	0	0	1	0	10	1	1	.174	.239
AL	42	0	0	6	7	5	1	0	0	0	3	0	5	0	7	0	0	.143	.167
1988																			
AL	31	2	2	6	11	3	2	0	1	2	0	1	2	0	3	0	0	.194	.355
NL	33	1	1	5	5	5	0	0	0	0	0	0	1	0	7	2	0	.152	.152

ALL-STAR GAME CLUB BATTING

YEAR	AB	R	ER	H	TB	1B	2B	3B	HR	RBI	SH	SF	BB	HP	SO	SB	CS	BAT	SLG
1989																			
NL	33	3	3	9	9	9	0	0	0	3	0	0	3	0	8	3	1	.273	.273
AL	35	5	5	12	20	8	2	0	2	5	0	0	1	0	5	1	0	.343	.571
1990																			
AL	32	2	2	7	8	6	1	0	0	2	0	0	7	0	5	4	0	.219	.250
NL	29	0	0	2	2	2	0	0	0	0	0	0	2	0	6	1	0	.069	.069
1991																			
NL	35	2	2	10	14	8	1	0	1	2	0	0	2	0	6	1	0	.286	.400
AL	30	4	3	8	11	7	0	0	1	4	1	1	3	0	6	0	0	.267	.367
1992																			
AL	44	13	13	19	29	13	4	0	2	13	0	0	1	0	7	2	0	.432	.659
NL	39	6	4	12	17	9	2	0	1	6	0	0	2	0	7	0	0	.308	.436
1993																			
NL	33	3	3	7	13	3	3	0	1	3	0	1	1	0	9	0	0	.212	.394
AL	35	9	6	11	21	5	4	0	2	7	0	0	4	1	7	1	0	.314	.600
1994 (10 innings)																			
AL	44	7	5	15	18	12	3	0	0	6	0	0	2	0	8	3	0	.341	.409
NL	36	8	8	12	21	7	3	0	2	8	0	1	1	1	5	0	0	.333	.583
1995																			
NL	29	3	3	3	12	0	0	0	1	3	0	0	3	0	1	0	1	.103	.414
AL	34	2	2	8	12	6	1	0	1	2	0	0	2	0	2	1	1	.235	.353
1996																			
AL	34	0	0	7	8	6	1	0	0	0	0	0	0	0	8	2	0	.206	.235
NL	35	6	6	12	23	6	3	1	2	6	0	0	0	0	8	1	2	.343	.657
1997																			
NL	29	1	1	3	6	0	0	0	1	1	0	0	4	0	7	1	0	.103	.207
AL	30	3	3	7	14	0	1	0	2	3	0	0	1	0	8	0	1	.233	.467
1998																			
AL	43	13	11	19	26	16	1	0	2	11	0	2	6	0	5	5	0	.442	.605
NL	36	8	7	12	17	10	0	1	1	8	1	0	5	1	8	0	0	.333	.472
1999																			
NL	32	1	1	7	9	5	2	0	0	1	0	0	4	0	12	0	2	.219	.281
AL	31	4	4	6	6	6	0	0	0	4	0	0	2	1	10	1	0	.194	.194
2000																			
AL	38	6	5	10	13	7	3	0	0	6	0	1	4	0	7	1	0	.263	.342
NL	36	3	2	9	12	8	0	0	1	3	0	0	1	0	4	0	0	.250	.333
2001																			
NL	29	1	1	3	4	2	1	0	0	1	0	1	2	0	5	1	0	.103	.138
AL	33	4	3	8	19	3	2	0	3	4	0	0	0	0	7	1	0	.242	.576

ALL-STAR GAME – INDIVIDUAL RECORDS

BATTING – GAME

Most At-Bats
5 By many players
Extra-Inning Game:
7 Willie Jones, NL:Phil. 1950 (14 inn)

Most Runs
4 Ted Williams, AL:Bos. 1946
3 Frankie Frisch. NL:StL. 1934
Jackie Robinson, NL:Brk. 1949

Most Hits
4 Joe Medwick, NL:StL. 1937
Ted Williams, AL:Bos.1946
Carl Yastrzemski, AL:Bos. 1970 (12 inn)

Most Total Bases
10 Ted Williams, AL:Bos. 1946
9 Arky Vaughan, NL:Pitt. 1941

Most Singles
3 By many players; Last:
Ken Boyer, NL:StL. 1956
Ivan Rodrigiez, AL:Tex. 1998

Most Doubles
2 Joe Medwick, NL:StL. 1937
Ted Kluszewski, NL:Cin. 1956
Ernie Banks, NL:Chi. 1959
Barry Bonds, NL:SF 1993
Al Simmons, AL:Chi. 1934

Most Triples
2 Rod Carew, AL:Minn. 1978

Most Home Runs
2 Arky Vaughan, NL:Pitt. 1941 (cons)
Willie McCovey, NL:SF 1969 (cons)
Gary Carter, NL:Mtl. 1981 (cons)
Ted Williams, AL:Bos. 1946
Al Rosen, AL:Clev. 1954 (cons)

Most Runs Batted In
5 Ted Williams, AL:Bos. 1946
Al Rosen, AL:Clev. 1954
4 Arky Vaughan, NL:Pitt. 1941

Most Walks
3 Charlie Gehringer, AL:Det. 1934
Phil Cavarretta, NL:Chi. 1944

Most Strikeouts
3 Lou Gehrig, AL:NY 1934
Bob Johnson, AL:Phil. 1935
Joe Gordon, AL:NY 1942
Ken Keltner, AL:Clev. 1943
Jim Hegan, AL:Clev. 1950 (14 inn)
Mickey Mantle, AL:NY 1956
Tony Oliva, AL:Minn. 1967 (15 inn)
Kirby Puckett. AL:Minn. 1987 (12 inn)
Stan Hack, NL:Chi. 1939
John Roseboro, NL:LA 1961 (2g)
Willie McCovey, NL:SF 1968
Johnny Bench, NL:Cin 1970
Craig Biggio, NL:Hou 1998
Extra-Inning Game:
4 Roberto Clemente, NL:Pitt. 1967 (15 inn)

Most Stolen Bases
2 Willie Mays, NL:SF 1963
Kelly Gruber, AL:Tor. 1990
Roberto Alomar, AL:Tor. 1992
Kenny Lofton, AL:Clev. 1996

Most Stolen Bases, Inning
2 Roberto Alomar, AL:Tor. 1992 (2nd)
1 By many NL players

Most Caught Stealing
2 Stan Musial, NL:StL. 1951
Tony Oliva, AL:Minn. 1967

Most Hit By Pitch
1 By many players

Most Grounded Into Double Plays
2 Bobby Richardson, AL:NY 1963
1 By many NL players

PITCHING – GAME

Most Innings
6 Lefty Gomez, AL:NY 1935
5 Larry Jansen, NL:NY 1950

Most Runs
7 Atlee Hammaker, NL:SF 1983
5 Sandy Consuegra, AL:Chi. 1954
Whitey Ford, AL:NY 1955
Blue Moon Odom, AL:Oak. 1969
Jim Palmer, AL:Balt. 1977

Most Earned Runs
7 Atlee Hammaker, NL:S,F. 1983
5 Sandy Consuegra, AL:Chi. 1954
Jim Palmer, AL:Balt. 1977

Most Hits
9 Tom Glavine, NL:Atl 1992
7 Tommy Bridges, AL:Det, 1937

Most Hits, Inning
7 Tom Glavine, NL:Atl 1992 (1st)
5 Tex Hughson, AL:Bos. 1944 (5th)
Sandy Consuegra, AL:Chi. 1954 (4th)
Blue Moon Odom, AL:Oak. 1969 (3rd)

Most Walks
5 Bill Hallahan, NL:StL. 1933
4 Jim Palmer. AL:Balt. 1978

Most Walks, Inning
3 Early Wynn, AL:Chi. 1959 (5th)
Jim Palmer, AL:Balt. 1978 (3rd)
Jim Kern, AL:Tex. 1979 (9th)
Dan Petry, AL:Det. 1985 (9th)
Kevin Brown, NL:LA 2000 (3rd)

Most Strikeouts
6 Carl Hubbell, NL:NY 1934
Johnny Vander Meer, NL:.Cin. 1943
Larry Jansen, NL:NY 1950
Ferguson Jenkins, NL:Chi. 1967
5 Billy Pierce, AL:Chi. 1956
Dick Radatz, AL:Bos. 1963,64
Pedro Martinez, AL:Bos. 1999

Most Strikeouts, Consecutive
5 Carl Hubbell, NL:NY 1934
Fernando Valenzuela, NL:LA 1986
4 Pedro Martinez, AL:Bos. 1999

Most Strikeouts, Consecutive Innings
6 Carl Hubbell, NL:NY 1934
5 Dick Radatz, AL:Bos. 1963
Pedro Martinez, AL:Bos. 1999

ALL-STAR GAME – INDIVIDUAL RECORDS

Most Strikeouts, Inning (only batters faced)
3 Johnny Sain, NL:Bos. 1948 (5th)
   Gene Conley, NL:Mil. 1955 (12th)
   Jerry Reuss, NL:LA 1980 (6th)
   Fernando Valenzuela, NL:LA 1984 (4th)
   Fernando Valenzuela, NL:LA 1986 (4th)
   Dwight Gooden, NL:NY 1984 (5th)
   Bobby Shantz, AL:Phil. 1952 (5th)
   Bill Caudill, AL:Oak. 1984 (7th)
   Pedro Martinez, AL:Bos. 1999 (1st)

Most Home Runs Allowed
3 Jim Palmer, AL:Balt. 1977
2 By many NL players; Last:
   Jon Lieber, NL:Chi 2001

Most Home Runs Allowed, Inning
2 By many players; Last:
   Jim Palmer, AL:Balt. 1977 (1st)
   Jon Lieber, NL:Chi 2001 (6th)

Most Hit Batters
1 By many players

Most Wild Pitches
2 Tom Brewer, AL:Bos. 1956
   Dave Stieb, AL:Tor. 1980
   Juan Marichal, NL:SF 1962
   John Smoltz, NL:Atl 1993

Most Balks
1 Bob Friend, NL:Pitt. 1960
   Stu Miller, NL:SF 1961
   Dwight Gooden, NL:NY 1986,88
   Steve Busby, AL:KC 1975
   Jim Kern, AL:Tex. 1979
   Charlie Hough, AL:Tex. 1986

BATTING – LIFETIME

Most Games
24 Hank Aaron, NL:Mil./Atl; AL: Mil.
    Stan Musial, NL:StL.
    Willie Mays, NL:NY/SF-NY
18 Ted Williams, AL:Bos.
    Brooks Robinson, AL:Balt.
    Cal Ripken, AL:Balt.

Most Games, Consecutive
24 Stan Musial, NL:StL.
    Willie Mays, NL:NY/SF-NY
18 Brooks Robinson, AL:Balt.

Most Winning Teams
17 Willie Mays, NL:NY/SF-NY
    Hank Aaron, NL:Mil./Atl
12 Cal Ripken, AL:Balt.

Most Losing Teams
15 Brooks Robinson, AL:Balt
10 Stan Musial, NL:StL.

Highest Batting Avg. (Minimum: 20 at-bats)
.500 Charlie Gehringer, AL:Det. (20-10)
.433 Billy Herman, NL:Chi.-Brk. (30-13)

Highest Slugging Pct. (Minimum: 20 at-bats)
.900 Fred Lynn, AL:Bos.-Cal. (20-18)
.821 Steve Garvey, NL:LA-SD (28-23)

Most At-Bats
75 Willie Mays, NL:NY/SF-NY
49 Cal Ripken, AL:Balt.

Most Runs
20 Willie Mays, NL:NY/SF
10 Ted Williams, AL:Bos.

Most Hits
23 Willie Mays, NL:NY/SF
14 Ted Williams, AL:Bos.
    Nellie Fox, AL:Chi.

Most Extra Base Hits
8 Stan Musial, NL:StL.
   Willie Mays, NL:NY/SF
7 Ted Williams, AL:Bos.

Most Total Bases
40 Stan Musial, NL:StL.
    Willie Mays, NL:NY/SF
30 Ted Williams, AL:Bos.

Most Singles
15 Willie Mays, NL:NY/SF
14 Nellie Fox, AL:Chi.

Most Doubles
7 Dave Winfield, NL-SD AL:NY
5 Dave Winfield, AL:NY
3 Ted Kluszewski, NL:Cin.
   Ernie Banks, NL:Chi.
   Al Oliver, NL:Pitt.-Mtl.
   Barry Bonds, NL:Pitt.-SF

Most Triples
3 Willie Mays, NL:NY/SF
   Brooks Robinson, AL:Balt.

Most Home Runs
6 Stan Musial, NL:StL.
4 Ted Williams, AL:Bos
   Fred Lynn, AL:Bos.-Cal.

Most Runs Batted In
12 Ted Williams, AL:Bos.
10 Stan Musial, NL:StL.

Most Walks
11 Ted Williams, AL:Bos.
7 Stan Musial, NL:StL.
   Willie Mays, NL:NY/SF

Most Strikeouts
17 Mickey Mantle, AL:NY
14 Willie Mays, NL:NY/SF-NY

Most Stolen Bases
6 Willie Mays, NL:NY/SF
5 Roberto Alomar, AL:Tor.-Balt.
   Kenny Lofton, AL:Clev.

Most Hit By Pitch
1 By many players

PITCHING – LIFETIME

Most Games
8 Jim Bunning, AL:Det. NL:Phil.
   Don Drysdale, NL:LA
   Juan Marichal, NL:SF
   Tom Seaver, NL:NY-Cin.
7 Early Wynn, AL:Clev.-Chi.
   Dave Stieb, AL:Tor.
   Roger Clemens, AL:Bos.-Tor.-NY

Most Games, Consecutive
6 Ewell Blackwell, NL:Cin.
   Early Wynn, AL:Clev.-Chi.

Most Games Started
5 Lefty Gomez, AL:NY
   Robin Roberts, NL:Phil.
   Don Drysdale, NL:LA

ALL-STAR GAME – INDIVIDUAL RECORDS

Most Games Finished
6 Goose Gossage, NL:Pitt.-SD AL:Chi.-NY
4 Mel Harder, AL:Clev.
  Dennis Eckersley, AL:Bos.-Oak.
3 Ewell Blackwell, NL:Cin.
  Bruce Sutter, NL:Chi.-StL
  Goose Gossage, NL:Pitt.-SD

Most Saves (since 1969)
3 Dennis Eckersley, AL:Clev.-Bos.-Oak.
2 Bruce Sutter, NL:Chi.-StL.

Most Games Won
3 Lefty Gomez, AL:NY
2 Bob Friend, NL:Pitt.
  Juan Marichal, NL:SF
  Don Drysdale, NL:LA
  Bruce Sutter, NL:Chi.

Most Games Lost
2 Mort Cooper, NL:StL.
  Claude Passeau, NL:Chi.
  Dwight Gooden, NL:NY
  Whitey Ford, AL:NY
  Luis Tiant, AL:Clev.-Bos.
  Catfish Hunter, AL:Oak.-NY

Lowest Earned Run Average (Minimum: 12 IP)
0.00 Mel Harder, AL:Clev. (13 inn)
0.50 Juan Marichal, NL:SF (18 inn)

Most Innings
19.1 Don Drysdale, NL:LA
18.0 Lefty Gomez, AL:NY

Most Runs
13 Whitey Ford, AL:NY
10 Robin Roberts, NL:Phil.
  Warren Spahn, NL:Bos/Mil.

Most Earned Runs
11 Whitey Ford, AL:NY
10 Robin Roberts, NL:Phil.

Most Hits
19 Whitey Ford, AL:NY
17 Robin Roberts, NL:Phil.
  Warren Spahn, NL:Bos.-Mil.

Most Home Runs
4 Vida Blue, AL:Oak
  Catfish Hunter, AL:KC-Oak.-NY
3 Robin Roberts, NL:Phil.
  Mort Cooper, NL:StL.
  Tom Seaver, NL:NY-Cin.
  Steve Carlton, NL:StL.-Phil.

Most Walks
7 Jim Palmer, AL:Balt.
6 Lon Warneke, NL:Chi.
  Carl Hubbell, NL:NY
  Robin Roberts, NL:Phil.

Most Strikeouts
19 Don Drysdale, NL:LA
14 Jim Palmer, AL:Balt.

Most Hit Batters
1 By many.players; See batters' record

Most Wild Pitches
2 Ewell Blackwell, NL:Cin.
  Robin Roberts, NL:Phil.
  Juan Marichal, NL:SF
  Steve Rogers, NL:Mtl.
  John Smoltz, NL:Atl
  Tom Brewer, AL:Bos.
  Dave Stieb, AL:Tor.

Most Balks
2 Dwight Gooden, NL:NY
1 Steve Busby, AL:KC
  Jim Kern, AL:Tex.
  Charlie Hough, AL:Tex.

ALL-STAR GAME – MOST VALUABLE PLAYER

1962 (1g)	Maury Wills, NL:LA	1981	Gary Carter, NL:Mtl.
1962 (2g)	Leon Wagner, AL:LA	1982	Dave Concepcion, NL:Cin.
1963	Willie Mays, NL:SF	1983	Fred Lynn, AL:Cal.
1964	Johnny Callison, NL:Phil.	1984	Gary Carter, NL:Mtl.
1965	Juan Marichal, NL:SF	1985	LaMarr Hoyt, NL:SD
1966	Brooks Robinson, AL:Balt.	1986	Roger Clemens, AL:Bos.
1967	Tony Perez, NL:Cin.	1987	Tim Raines, NL:Mtl.
1968	Willie Mays, NL:SF	1988	Terry Steinbach, AL:Oak.
1969	Willie McCovey, NL:SF	1989	Bo Jackson, AL:KC
1970	Carl Yastrzemski, AL:Bos.	1990	Julio Franco, AL:Tex.
1971	Frank Robinson, AL:Balt.	1991	Cal Ripken, AL:Balt.
1972	Joe Morgan, NL:Cin.	1992	Ken Griffey, Jr AL:Sea.
1973	Bobby Bonds, NL:SF	1993	Kirby Puckett, AL:Minn.
1974	Steve Garvey NL:LA	1994	Fred McGriff, NL:Atl
1975	Bill Madlock, NL:Chi. &	1995	Jeff Conine, NL:Fla.
	Jon Matlack, NL:NY	1996	Mike Piazza, NL:LA
1976	George Foster, NL:Cin.	1997	Sandy Alomar, Jr., AL:Clev.
1977	Don Sutton, NL:LA	1998	Roberto Alomar, AL:Balt.
1978	Steve Garvey, NL:LA	1999	Pedro Martinez, NL:Bos.
1979	Dave Parker, NL:Pitt.	2000	Derek Jeter, AL:NY
1980	Ken Griffey, Sr., NL:Cin.	2001	Cal Ripken, AL:Balt.

AMERICAN LEAGUE CLUB STANDINGS - 1901-1968

	BALT	BOS	CAL	CHI	CLEV	DET	KC	MIL	MINN	NY	OAK	PHIL	STL	WASH	WASH
1901	5	2	-	1	7	3	-	8	-	-	-	4	-	6	-
1902	8	3	-	4	5	7	-	-	-	-	-	1	2	6	-
1903	-	1	-	7	3	5	-	-	-	4	-	2	6	8	-
1904	-	1	-	3	4	7	-	-	-	2	-	5	6	8	-
1905	-	4	-	2	5	3	-	-	-	6	-	1	8	7	-
1906	-	8	-	1	3	6	-	-	-	2	-	4	5	7	-
1907	-	7	-	3	4	1	-	-	-	5	-	2	6	8	-
1908	-	5	-	3	2	1	-	-	-	8	-	6	4	7	-
1909	-	3	-	4	6	1	-	-	-	5	-	2	7	8	-
1910	-	4	-	6	5	3	-	-	-	2	-	1	8	7	-
1911	-	5	-	4	3	2	-	-	-	6	-	1	8	7	-
1912	-	1	-	4	5	6	-	-	-	8	-	3	7	2	-
1913	-	4	-	5	3	6	-	-	-	7	-	1	8	2	-
1914	-	2	-	6	8	4	-	-	-	6	-	1	5	3	-
1915	-	1	-	3	7	2	-	-	-	5	-	8	6	4	-
1916	-	1	-	2	6	3	-	-	-	4	-	8	5	7	-
1917	-	2	-	1	3	4	-	-	-	6	-	8	7	5	-
1918	-	1	-	6	2	7	-	-	-	4	-	8	5	3	-
1919	-	6	-	1	2	4	-	-	-	3	-	8	5	7	-
1920	-	5	-	2	1	7	-	-	-	3	-	8	4	6	-
1921	-	5	-	7	2	6	-	-	-	1	-	8	3	4	-
1922	-	8	-	5	4	3	-	-	-	1	-	7	2	6	-
1923	-	8	-	7	3	2	-	-	-	1	-	6	5	4	-
1924	-	7	-	8	6	3	-	-	-	2	-	5	4	1	-
1925	-	8	-	5	6	4	-	-	-	7	-	2	3	1	-
1926	-	8	-	5	2	6	-	-	-	1	-	3	7	4	-
1927	-	8	-	5	6	4	-	-	-	1	-	2	7	3	-
1928	-	8	-	5	7	6	-	-	-	1	-	2	3	4	-
1929	-	8	-	7	3	6	-	-	-	2	-	1	4	5	-
1930	-	8	-	7	4	5	-	-	-	3	-	1	6	2	-
1931	-	6	-	8	4	7	-	-	-	2	-	1	5	3	-
1932	-	8	-	7	4	5	-	-	-	1	-	2	6	3	-
1933	-	7	-	6	4	5	-	-	-	2	-	3	8	1	-
1934	-	4	-	8	3	1	-	-	-	2	-	5	6	7	-
1935	-	4	-	5	3	1	-	-	-	2	-	8	7	6	-
1936	-	6	-	3	5	2	-	-	-	1	-	8	7	4	-
1937	-	5	-	3	4	2	-	-	-	1	-	7	8	6	-
1938	-	2	-	6	3	4	-	-	-	1	-	8	7	5	-
1939	-	2	-	4	3	5	-	-	-	1	-	7	8	6	-
1940	-	4	-	4	2	1	-	-	-	3	-	8	6	7	-
1941	-	2	-	3	4	4	-	-	-	1	-	8	6	6	-
1942	-	2	-	6	4	5	-	-	-	1	-	8	3	7	-
1943	-	7	-	4	3	5	-	-	-	1	-	8	6	2	-
1944	-	4	-	7	5	2	-	-	-	3	-	5	1	8	-
1945	-	7	-	6	5	1	-	-	-	4	-	8	3	2	-
1946	-	1	-	5	6	2	-	-	-	3	-	8	7	4	-
1947	-	3	-	6	4	2	-	-	-	1	-	5	8	7	-
1948	-	2	-	8	1	5	-	-	-	3	-	4	6	7	-
1949	-	2	-	6	3	4	-	-	-	1	-	5	7	8	-
1950	-	3	-	6	4	2	-	-	-	1	-	8	7	5	-
1951	-	3	-	4	2	5	-	-	-	1	-	6	8	7	-
1952	-	6	-	3	2	8	-	-	-	1	-	4	7	5	-
1953	-	4	-	3	2	6	-	-	-	1	-	7	8	5	-
1954	7	4	-	3	1	5	-	-	-	2	-	8	-	6	-
1955	7	4	-	3	2	5	6	-	-	1	-	-	-	8	-
1956	6	4	-	3	2	5	8	-	-	1	-	-	-	7	-
1957	5	3	-	2	6	4	7	-	-	1	-	-	-	8	-
1958	6	3	-	2	4	5	7	-	-	1	-	-	-	8	-
1959	6	5	-	1	2	4	7	-	-	3	-	-	-	8	-
1960	2	7	-	3	4	6	8	-	-	1	-	-	-	5	-
1961	3	6	8	4	5	2	9	-	7	1	-	-	-	-	9
1962	7	8	3	5	6	4	9	-	2	1	-	-	-	-	10
1963	4	7	9	2	5	5	8	-	3	1	-	-	-	-	10
1964	3	8	5	2	6	4	10	-	6	1	-	-	-	-	9
1965	3	9	7	2	5	4	10	-	1	6	-	-	-	-	8
1966	1	9	6	4	5	3	7	-	2	10	-	-	-	-	8
1967	6	1	5	4	8	2	10	-	2	9	-	-	-	-	6
1968	2	4	8	8	3	1	-	-	7	5	6	-	-	-	10

AMERICAN LEAGUE CLUB STANDINGS 1969 –

	EAST						WEST					
---	BALT	BOS	CLEV	DET	NY	WASH	CAL	CHI	KC	SEA MIL	MINN	OAK
1969	1	3	6	2	5	4	3	5	4	6	1	2
1970	1	3	5	4	2	6	3	6	4	4	1	2
1971	1	3	6	2	4	5	4	3	2	6	5	1

	BALT	BOS	CLEV	DET	MIL	NY	CAL	CHI	KC	MINN	OAK	TEX
1972	3	2	5	1	6	4	5	2	4	3	1	6
1973	1	2	6	3	5	4	4	5	2	3	1	6
1974	1	3	4	6	5	2	6	4	5	3	1	2
1975	2	1	4	6	5	3	6	5	2	4	1	3
1976	2	3	4	5	6	1	4	6	1	3	2	4

	BALT	BOS	CLEV	DET	MIL	NY	TOR	CAL	CHI	KC	MINN	OAK	TEX	SEA
1977	2	2	5	4	6	1	7	5	3	1	4	7	2	6
1978	4	2	6	5	3	1	7	2	5	1	4	6	2	7
1979	1	3	6	5	2	4	7	1	5	2	4	7	3	6
1980	2	4	6	5	3	1	7	6	5	1	3	2	4	7
1981 *Split Season*														
1st Half	2	5	6	4	3	1	7	4	3	5	7	1	2	6
2nd Half	4	2	5	2	1	6	7	7	6	1	4	2	3	5
1982	2	3	6	4	1	5	6	1	3	2	7	5	6	4
1983	1	6	7	2	5	3	4	5	1	2	5	4	3	7
1984	5	4	6	1	7	3	2	2	5	1	2	4	7	5
1985	4	5	7	3	6	2	1	2	3	1	4	4	7	6
1986	7	1	5	3	6	2	4	1	5	3	6	3	2	7
1987	6	5	7	1	3	4	2	6	5	2	1	3	6	4
1988	7	1	6	2	3	5	3	4	5	3	2	1	6	7
1989	2	3	6	7	4	5	1	3	7	2	5	1	4	6
1990	5	1	4	3	6	7	2	4	2	6	7	1	3	5
1991	6	2	7	2	4	5	1	7	2	6	1	4	3	5
1992	3	7	4	6	2	4	1	5	3	5	2	1	4	7
1993	3	5	6	3	7	2	1	5	1	3	5	7	2	4

	EAST					CENTRAL					WEST			
---	BALT	BOS	DET	NY	TOR	CHI	CLEV	KC	MIL	MIN	ANA	OAK	SEA	TEX
1994	2	4	5	1	3	1	2	3	5	4	4	2	3	1
1995	3	1	4	2	5	3	1	2	4	5	2	4	1	3
1996	2	3	5	1	4	2	1	5	3	4	4	3	2	1
1997	1	4	3	2	5	2	1	5	3	4	2	4	1	3
	BALT	BOS	NY	TB	TOR	CHI	CLEV	DET	KC	MIN	ANA	OAK	SEA	TEX
1998	4	2	1	5	3	2	1	5	3	4	2	4	3	1
1999	4	2	1	5	3	2	1	3	4	5	4	2	3	1
2000	4	2	1	5	3	1	2	3	4	5	3	1	2	4
2001	4	2	1	5	3	3	1	4	5	2	3	2	1	4

NATIONAL LEAGUE CLUB STANDINGS 1876-1899

	BALT	BOS	BRK	BUFF	CHI	CIN	CLEV	DET	HART	IND	KC	LOU	MIL	NY	PHIL	PITT	PROV	STL	SYR	TROY	WASH	WOR
1876	·	4	·	·	1	8	·	·	2	·	·	5	·	6	7	·	·	3	·	·	·	·
1877	·	1	·	·	5	6	·	·	3	·	·	2	·	·	·	·	·	4	·	·	·	·
1878	·	1	·	·	4	2	·	·	·	5	·	·	6	·	·	·	3	·	·	·	·	·
1879	·	2	·	3	4	5	6	·	·	·	·	·	·	·	·	·	1	·	7	8	·	·
1880	·	6	·	7	1	8	3	·	·	·	·	·	·	·	·	·	2	·	·	4	·	5
1881	·	6	·	3	1	·	7	4	·	·	·	·	·	·	·	·	2	·	·	5	·	8
1882	·	3	·	4	1	·	5	6	·	·	·	·	·	·	·	·	2	·	·	7	·	8
1883	·	1	·	5	2	·	4	7	·	·	·	·	·	6	8	·	3	·	·	·	·	·
1884	·	2	·	3	4	·	7	8	·	·	·	·	·	5	6	·	1	·	·	·	·	·
1885	·	5	·	7	1	·	·	6	·	·	·	·	·	2	3	·	4	8	·	·	·	·
1886	·	5	·	·	1	·	·	2	·	·	7	·	·	3	4	·	·	6	·	·	8	·
1887	·	5	·	·	3	·	·	1	·	8	·	·	·	4	2	6	·	·	·	·	7	·
1888	·	4	·	·	2	·	·	5	·	7	·	·	·	1	3	6	·	·	·	·	8	·
1889	·	2	·	·	3	·	6	·	·	7	·	·	·	1	4	5	·	·	·	·	8	·
1890	·	5	1	·	2	4	7	·	·	·	·	·	·	6	3	8	·	·	·	·	·	·
1891	·	1	6	·	2	7	5	·	·	·	·	·	·	3	4	8	·	·	·	·	·	·
1892-1st	12	1	2	·	8	4	5	·	·	·	·	11	·	7	3	6	·	9	·	·	10	·
1892-2nd	10	3	2	·	7	6	1	·	·	·	·	9	·	8	5	4	·	11	·	·	12	·
1893	8	1	7	·	9	6	3	·	·	·	·	11	·	5	4	2	·	10	·	·	12	·
1894	1	3	5	·	8	10	6	·	·	·	·	12	·	2	4	7	·	9	·	·	11	·
1895	1	5	6	·	4	8	2	·	·	·	·	12	·	9	3	7	·	11	·	·	10	·
1896	1	4	9	·	5	3	2	·	·	·	·	12	·	7	8	6	·	11	·	·	9	·
1897	2	1	7	·	9	4	5	·	·	·	·	11	·	3	10	8	·	12	·	·	6	·
1898	2	1	10	·	4	3	5	·	·	·	·	9	·	7	6	8	·	12	·	·	11	·
1899	4	2	1	·	8	6	12	·	·	·	·	9	·	10	3	7	·	5	·	·	11	·

NOTE: 1892 Split season. Boston defeated Cleveland, 5 games to 0 (1 tie) in best-of-nine playoff.

NATIONAL LEAGUE CHAMPIONS 1876-1899

	Club & Manager	W	L	PCT	GA
1876	Chicago (Al Spalding)	52	14	.788	6
1877	Boston (Harry Wright)	31	17	.646	7
1878	Boston (Harry Wright)	41	19	.683	4
1879	Providence (George Wright)	55	23	.705	5
1980	Chicago (Cap Anson)	67	17	.798	15
1881	Chicago (Cap Anson)	56	28	.667	9
1882	Chicago (Cap Anson)	55	29	.655	3
1883	Boston (John Morill)	63	35	.643	4
1884	Providence (Frank Bancroft)	84	28	.750	10.5
1885	Chicago (Cap Anson)	87	25	.777	2
1886	Chicago (Cap Anson)	90	34	.726	21
1887	Detroit (Bill Watkins)	79	45	.637	31
1888	New York (Jim Mutrie)	84	47	.641	9
1889	New York (Jim Mutrie)	83	43	.659	1
1890	Brooklyn (Bill McGunnigle)	86	43	.667	6
1891	Boston (Frank Selee)	87	51	.630	3.5
1892	Boston (Frank Selee)	102	48	.680	8.5
1893	Boston (Frank Selee)	86	44	.662	5
1894	Baltimore (Ned Hanlon)	89	39	.695	3
1895	Baltimore (Ned Hanlon)	87	43	.669	3
1896	Baltimore (Ned Hanlon)	90	39	.698	9.5
1897	Boston (Frank Selee)	93	39	.705	2
1898	Boston (Frank Selee)	102	47	.685	6
1899	Brooklyn (Ned Hanlon)	89	41	.685	5

NATIONAL LEAGUE CLUB STANDINGS 1900-1968

	ATL	BOS	BRK	CHI	CINN	HOU	LA	MIL	NYG	NYM	PHIL	PITT	STL	SF
1900	-	4	1	5	7	-	-	-	8	-	3	2	5	-
1901	-	5	3	6	8	-	-	-	7	-	2	1	4	-
1902	-	3	2	5	4	-	-	-	8	-	7	1	6	-
1903	-	6	5	3	4	-	-	-	2	-	7	1	8	-
1904	-	7	6	2	3	-	-	-	1	-	8	4	5	-
1905	-	7	8	3	5	-	-	-	1	-	4	2	6	-
1906	-	8	5	1	6	-	-	-	2	-	4	3	7	-
1907	-	7	5	1	6	-	-	-	4	-	3	2	8	-
1908	-	6	7	1	5	-	-	-	2	-	4	2	8	-
1909	-	8	6	2	4	-	-	-	3	-	5	1	7	-
1910	-	8	6	1	5	-	-	-	2	-	4	3	7	-
1911	-	8	7	2	6	-	-	-	1	-	4	3	5	-
1912	-	8	7	3	4	-	-	-	1	-	5	2	6	-
1913	-	5	6	3	7	-	-	-	1	-	2	4	8	-
1914	-	1	5	4	8	-	-	-	2	-	6	7	3	-
1915	-	2	3	4	7	-	-	-	8	-	1	5	6	-
1916	-	3	1	5	7	-	-	-	4	-	2	6	7	-
1917	-	6	7	5	4	-	-	-	1	-	2	8	3	-
1918	-	7	5	1	3	-	-	-	2	-	6	4	8	-
1919	-	6	5	3	1	-	-	-	2	-	8	4	7	-
1920	-	7	1	5	3	-	-	-	2	-	8	4	5	-
1921	-	4	5	7	6	-	-	-	1	-	8	2	3	-
1922	-	8	6	5	2	-	-	-	1	-	7	3	3	-
1923	-	7	6	4	2	-	-	-	1	-	8	3	5	-
1924	-	8	2	5	4	-	-	-	1	-	7	3	6	-
1925	-	5	6	8	3	-	-	-	2	-	6	1	4	-
1926	-	7	6	4	2	-	-	-	5	-	8	3	1	-
1927	-	7	6	4	5	-	-	-	3	-	8	4	1	-
1928	-	7	6	3	5	-	-	-	2	-	8	4	1	-
1929	-	8	6	1	7	-	-	-	3	-	5	2	4	-
1930	-	6	4	2	7	-	-	-	3	-	8	5	1	-
1931	-	7	4	3	8	-	-	-	2	-	6	5	1	-
1932	-	5	3	1	8	-	-	-	6	-	4	2	6	-
1933	-	4	6	3	8	-	-	-	1	-	7	2	5	-
1934	-	4	6	3	8	-	-	-	2	-	7	5	1	-
1935	-	8	5	1	6	-	-	-	3	-	7	4	2	-
1936	-	6	7	2	5	-	-	-	1	-	8	4	2	-
1937	-	5	6	2	8	-	-	-	1	-	7	3	4	-
1938	-	5	7	1	4	-	-	-	3	-	8	2	6	-
1939	-	7	3	4	1	-	-	-	5	-	8	6	2	-
1940	-	7	2	5	1	-	-	-	6	-	8	4	3	-
1941	-	7	1	6	3	-	-	-	5	-	8	4	2	-
1942	-	7	2	6	4	-	-	-	3	-	8	5	1	-
1943	-	6	3	5	2	-	-	-	8	-	7	4	1	-
1944	-	6	7	4	3	-	-	-	5	-	8	2	1	-
1945	-	6	3	1	7	-	-	-	5	-	8	4	2	-
1946	-	4	2	3	6	-	-	-	8	-	5	7	1	-
1947	-	3	1	6	5	-	-	-	4	-	7	7	2	-
1948	-	1	3	8	7	-	-	-	5	-	6	4	2	-
1949	-	4	1	8	7	-	-	-	5	-	3	6	2	-
1950	-	4	2	7	6	-	-	-	3	-	1	8	5	-
1951	-	4	2	8	6	-	-	-	1	-	5	7	3	-
1952	-	7	1	5	6	-	-	-	2	-	4	8	3	-
1953	-	-	1	7	6	-	-	2	5	-	3	8	3	-
1954	-	-	2	7	5	-	-	3	1	-	4	8	6	-
1955	-	-	1	6	5	-	-	2	3	-	4	8	7	-
1956	-	-	1	8	3	-	-	2	6	-	5	7	4	-
1957	-	-	3	7	4	-	-	1	6	-	5	7	2	-
1958	-	-	-	5	4	-	7	1	-	-	8	2	5	3
1959	-	-	-	5	5	-	1	2	-	-	8	4	7	3
1960	-	-	-	7	6	-	4	2	-	-	8	1	3	5
1961	-	-	-	7	1	-	2	4	-	-	8	6	5	3
1962	-	-	-	9	3	8	2	5	-	10	7	4	6	1
1963	-	-	-	7	5	9	1	6	-	10	4	8	2	3
1964	-	-	-	8	2	9	6	5	-	10	6	3	1	4
1965	-	-	-	8	4	9	1	5	-	10	6	3	7	2
1966	5	-	-	10	7	8	1	-	-	9	4	3	6	2
1967	7	-	-	3	4	9	8	-	-	10	5	6	1	2
1968	5	-	-	3	4	10	7	-	-	9	7	6	1	2

NATIONAL LEAGUE CLUB STANDINGS 1969 –

| | EAST | | | | | | | WEST | | | | |
	CHI	MTL	NY	PHIL	PITT	STL		ATL	CIN	HOU	LA	SD	SF
1969	2	6	1	5	3	4		1	3	5	4	6	2
1970	2	6	3	5	1	4		5	1	4	2	6	3
1971	3	5	3	6	1	2		3	4	4	2	6	1
1972	2	5	3	6	1	4		4	1	2	3	6	5
1973	5	4	1	6	3	2		5	1	4	2	6	3
1974	6	4	5	3	1	2		3	2	4	1	6	5
1975	5	5	3	2	1	3		5	1	6	2	4	3
1976	4	6	3	1	2	5		6	1	3	2	5	4
1977	4	5	6	1	2	3		6	2	3	1	5	4
1978	3	4	6	1	2	5		6	2	5	1	4	3
1979	5	2	6	4	1	3		6	1	2	3	5	4
1980	6	2	5	1	3	4		4	3	1	2	6	5
1981 *Split Season*													
1st Half	6	3	5	1	4	2		4	2	3	1	6	5
2nd Half	5	1	4	3	6	2		5	2	1	4	6	3
1982	5	3	6	2	4	1		1	6	5	2	4	3
1983	5	3	6	1	2	4		2	6	3	1	4	5
1984	1	5	2	4	6	3		2	5	2	4	1	6
1985	4	3	2	5	6	1		5	2	3	1	3	6
1986	5	4	1	2	6	3		6	2	1	5	4	3
1987	6	3	2	4	4	1		5	2	3	4	6	1
1988	4	3	1	6	2	5		6	2	5	1	3	4
1989	1	4	2	6	5	3		6	5	3	4	2	1
1990	4	3	2	4	1	6		6	1	4	2	4	3
1991	4	6	5	3	1	2		1	5	6	2	3	4
1992	4	2	5	6	1	3		1	2	4	6	3	5

	CHI	FLA	MTL	NY	PHI	PITT	STL		ATL	CIN	COL	HOU	LA	SD	SF
1993	4	6	2	7	1	5	3		1	5	6	3	4	7	2

| | EAST | | | | | | CENTRAL | | | | | | WEST | | | |
	ATL	FLA	MTL	NY	PHI		CHI	CIN	HOU	PITT	STL		COL	LA	SD	SF
1994	2	5	1	3	4		5	1	2	3	3		3	1	4	2
1995	1	4	5	2	2		3	1	2	5	4		2	1	3	4
1996	1	3	2	4	5		4	3	2	5	1		3	2	1	4
1997	1	2	4	3	5		5	3	1	2	4		3	2	4	1

	ATL	FLA	MTL	NY	PHI		CHI	CIN	HOU	MIL	PITT	STL		ARI	COL	LA	SD	SF
1998	1	5	4	2	3		2	4	1	5	6	3		5	4	3	1	2
1999	1	5	4	2	3		6	2	1	5	3	4		1	5	3	4	2
2000	1	3	4	2	5		6	2	4	3	5	1		3	4	2	5	1
2001	1	4	5	3	2		3	5	1	4	6	2		1	5	3	4	2

AMERICAN LEAGUE CHAMPIONS (1901 to 1968)

YEAR	CLUB (MANAGER)	WON	LOST	PCT.	GA
1901	Chicago (Clark Griffith)	83	53	.610	4
1902	Philadelphia (Connie Mack)	83	53	.610	5
1903	Boston (Jimmy Collins)	91	47	.659	14.5
1904	Boston (Jimmy Collins)	95	59	.617	1.5
1905	Philadelphia (Connie Mack)	92	56	.622	2
1906	Chicago (Fielder Jones)	93	58	.616	3
1907	Detroit (Hughie Jennings)	92	58	.613	1.5
1908	Detroit (Hughie Jennings)	90	63	.588	0.5
1909	Detroit (Hughie Jennings)	98	54	.645	3.5
1910	Philadelphia (Connie Mack)	102	48	.680	14.5
1911	Philadelphia (Connie Mack)	101	50	.669	13.5
1912	Boston (Jake Stahl)	105	47	.691	14
1913	Philadelphia (Connie Mack)	96	57	.627	6.5
1914	Philadelphia (Connie Mack)	99	53	.651	8.5
1915	Boston (Bill Carrigan)	101	50	.669	2.5
1916	Boston (Bill Carrigan)	91	63	.591	2
1917	Chicago (Pants Rowland)	100	54	.649	9
1918	Boston (Ed Barrow)	75	51	.595	3.5
1919	Chicago (Kid Gleason)	88	52	.629	3.5
1920	Cleveland (Tris Speaker)	98	56	.636	2
1921	New York (Miller Huggins)	98	55	.641	4.5
1922	New York (Miller Huggins)	94	60	.610	1
1923	New York (Miller Huggins)	98	54	.645	16
1924	Washington (Bucky Harris)	92	62	.597	2
1925	Washington (Bucky Harris)	96	55	.636	8.5
1926	New York (Miller Huggins)	91	63	.591	3
1927	New York (Miller Huggins)	110	44	.714	19
1928	New York (Miller Huggins)	101	53	.656	2.5
1929	Philadelphia (Connie Mack)	104	46	.693	18
1930	Philadelphia (Connie Mack)	102	52	.662	8
1931	Philadelphia (Connie Mack)	107	45	.704	13.5
1932	New York (Joe McCarthy)	107	47	.695	13
1933	Washington (Joe Cronin)	99	53	.651	7
1934	Detroit (Mickey Cochrane)	101	53	.656	7
1935	Detroit (Mickey Cochrane)	93	58	.616	3
1936	New York (Joe McCarthy)	102	51	.667	19.5
1937	New York (Joe McCarthy)	102	52	.662	13
1938	New York (Joe McCarthy)	99	53	.651	9.5
1939	New York (Joe McCarthy)	106	45	.702	17
1940	Detroit (Del Baker)	90	64	.584	1
1941	New York (Joe McCarthy)	101	53	.656	17
1942	New York (Joe McCarthy)	103	51	.669	9
1943	New York (Joe McCarthy)	98	56	.636	13.5
1944	St. Louis (Luke Sewell)	89	65	.578	1
1945	Detroit (Steve O'Neill)	88	65	.575	1.5
1946	Boston (Joe Cronin)	104	50	.675	12
1947	New York (Bucky Harris)	97	57	.630	12
1948	Cleveland (Lou Boudreau)	97	58	.626	1
1949	New York (Casey Stengel)	97	57	.630	1
1950	New York (Casey Stengel)	98	56	.636	3
1951	New York (Casey Stengel)	98	56	.636	5
1952	New York (Casey Stengel)	95	59	.617	2
1953	New York (Casey Stengel)	99	52	.656	8.5
1954	Cleveland (Al Lopez)	111	43	.721	8
1955	New York (Casey Stengel)	96	58	.623	3
1956	New York (Casey Stengel)	97	57	.630	9
1957	New York (Casey Stengel)	98	56	.636	8
1958	New York (Casey Stengel)	92	62	.597	10
1959	Chicago (Al Lopez)	94	60	.610	5
1960	New York (Casey Stengel)	97	57	.630	8
1961	New York (Ralph Houk)	109	53	.673	8
1962	New York (Ralph Houk)	96	66	.593	5
1963	New York (Ralph Houk)	104	57	.646	10.5
1964	New York (Yogi Berra)	99	63	.611	1
1965	Minnesota (Sam Mele)	102	60	.630	7
1966	Baltimore (Hank Bauer)	97	63	.606	9
1967	Boston (Dick Williams)	92	70	.568	1
1968	Detroit (Mayo Smith)	103	59	.636	12

AMERICAN LEAGUE DIVISION CHAMPIONS (1969 to 1993)
(Championship Series Winner Capitalized)
(E = East; W = West)
(= mid-season replacement)*

YEAR	CLUB (MANAGER)	WON	LOST	PCT.	GA
1969	(E) BALTIMORE (Earl Weaver)	109	53	.673	19
	(W) Minnesota (Billy Martin)	97	65	.599	9
1970	(E) BALTIMORE (Earl Weaver)	108	54	.667	15
	(W) Minnesota (Bill Rigney)	98	64	.605	9
1971	(E) BALTIMORE (Earl Weaver)	101	57	.639	12
	(W) Oakland (Dick Williams)	101	60	.627	16
1972	(W) OAKLAND (Dick Williams)	93	62	.600	5.5
	(E) Detroit (Billy Martin)	86	70	.551	0.5
1973	(W) OAKLAND (Dick Williams)	94	68	.580	6
	(E) Baltimore (Earl Weaver)	97	65	.599	8
1974	(W) OAKLAND (Alvin Dark)	90	72	.556	5
	(E) Baltimore (Earl Weaver)	91	71	.562	2
1975	(E) BOSTON (Darrell Johnson)	95	65	.594	4.5
	(W) Oakland (Alvin Dark)	98	64	.605	7
1976	(E) NEW YORK (Billy Martin)	97	62	.610	10.5
	(W) Kansas City (Whitey Herzog)	90	72	.556	2.5
1977	(E) NEW YORK (Billy Martin)	100	62	.617	2.5
	(W) Kansas City (Whitey Herzog)	102	60	.630	8
1978	(E) NEW YORK (Bob Lemon*)	100	63	.613	1
	(W) Kansas City (Whitey Herzog)	92	70	.568	5
1979	(E) BALTIMORE (Earl Weaver)	102	57	.642	8
	(W) California (Jim Fregosi)	88	74	.543	3
1980	(W) KANSAS CITY (Jim Frey)	97	65	.599	14
	(E) New York (Dick Howser)	103	59	.636	3
1981	(E) NEW YORK (Bob Lemon*)	59	48	.551	--
	(W) Oakland (Billy Martin)	64	45	.587	--

Due to players' strike, 1981 season was divided into two halves. Leaders of each half met in a best-of-five series to determine the ALCS participants. East: New York 3, Milwaukee 2; West: Oakland 3, Kansas City 0.

YEAR	CLUB (MANAGER)	WON	LOST	PCT.	GA
1982	(E) MILWAUKEE (Harvey Kuenn*)	95	67	.586	1
	(W) California (Gene Mauch)	93	69	.574	3
1983	(E) BALTIMORE (Joe Altobelli)	98	64	.605	6
	(W) Chicago (Tony LaRussa)	99	63	.611	20
1984	(E) DETROIT (Sparky Anderson)	104	58	.642	15
	(W) Kansas City (Dick Howser)	84	78	.519	3
1985	(W) KANSAS CITY (Dick Howser)	91	71	.562	1
	(E) Toronto (Bobby Cox)	99	62	.615	2
1986	(E) BOSTON John (McNamara)	95	66	.590	5.5
	(W) California (Gene Mauch)	92	70	.568	5
1987	(W) MINNESOTA (Tom Kelly)	85	77	.525	2
	(E) Detroit (Sparky Anderson)	98	64	.605	2
1988	(W) OAKLAND (Tony LaRussa)	104	58	.642	13
	(E) Boston (Joe Morgan*)	89	73	.549	1
1989	(W) OAKLAND (Tony LaRussa)	99	63	.611	7
	(E) Toronto (Cito Gaston*)	89	73	.549	2.
1990	(W) OAKLAND (Tony LaRussa)	103	59	.636	9
	(E) Boston (Joe Morgan)	88	74	.543	2
1991	(W) MINNESOTA (Tom Kelly)	95	67	.586	8
	(E) Toronto (Cito Gaston)	91	71	.562	7
1992	(E) TORONTO (Cito Gaston)	96	66	.593	4
	(W) Oakland (Tony LaRussa)	96	66	.593	6
1993	(E) TORONTO (Cito Gaston)	95	67	.586	7
	(W) Chicago (Gene Lamont)	94	68	.580	8

AMERICAN LEAGUE POSTSEASON PARTICIPANTS (since 1995)

(Championship Series Winner Capitalized)
(E = East; C = Central; W = West; WC = Wild Card)

YEAR	CLUB (MANAGER)	WON	LOST	PCT.	GA
1995	(C) CLEVELAND (Mike Hargrove)	100	44	.694	30
	(W) Seattle (Lou Piniella)	79	66	.545	1
	(E) Boston (Kevin Kennedy)	86	58	.597	7
	(WC) New York (Buck Showalter)	79	65	.549	--
1996	(E) NEW YORK (Joe Torre)	92	70	.568	4
	(WC) Baltimore (Davey Johnson)	88	74	.543	--
	(C) Cleveland (Mike Hargrove)	99	62	.615	14.5
	(W) Texas (Johnny Oates)	90	72	.556	4.5
1997	(C) CLEVELAND (Mike Hargrove)	86	75	.534	6
	(E) Baltimore (Davey Johnson)	98	64	.605	2
	(W) Seattle (Lou Piniella)	90	72	.556	6
	(WC) New York (Joe Torre)	96	66	.593	--
1998	(E) NEW YORK (Joe Torre)	114	48	.704	22
	(C) Cleveland (Mike Hargrove)	89	73	.549	9
	(W) Texas (Johnny Oates)	88	74	.543	3
	(WC) Boston (Jimy Williams)	92	70	.568	--
1999	(E) NEW YORK (Joe Torre)	98	64	.605	4
	(WC) Boston (Jimy Williams)	94	68	.580	--
	(C) Cleveland (Mike Hargrove)	97	65	.599	21.5
	(W) Texas (Johnny Oates)	95	67	.586	8
2000	(E) NEW YORK (Joe Torre)	87	74	.540	2.5
	(WC) Seattle (Lou Piniella)	91	71	.562	--
	(W) Oakland (Art Howe)	91	70	.565	0.5
	(C) Chicago (Jerry Manuel)	95	67	.586	5
2001	(E) NEW YORK (Joe Torre)	95	65	.594	13.5
	(W) Seattle (Lou Piniella)	116	46	.716	14
	(C) Cleveland (Charlie Manuel)	91	71	.562	6
	(WC) Oakland (Art Howe)	102	60	.630	--

NATIONAL LEAGUE CHAMPIONS (1901 to 1968)

(* = mid-season replacement)

YEAR	CLUB (MANAGER)	WON	LOST	PCT.	GA
1900	Brooklyn (Ned Hanlon)	82	54	.603	4.5
1901	Pittsburgh (Fred Clarke)	90	49	.647	7.5
1902	Pittsburgh (Fred Clarke)	103	36	.741	27.5
1903	Pittsburgh (Fred Clarke)	91	49	.650	6.5
1904	New York (John McGraw)	106	47	.693	13
1905	New York (John McGraw)	105	48	.686	9
1906	Chicago (Frank Chance)	116	36	.763	20
1907	Chicago (Frank Chance)	107	45	.704	17
1908	Chicago (Frank Chance)	99	55	.643	1
1909	Pittsburgh (Fred Clarke)	110	42	.724	6.5
1910	Chicago (Frank Chance)	104	50	.675	13
1911	New York (John McGraw)	99	54	.647	7.5
1912	New York (John McGraw)	103	48	.682	10
1913	New York (John McGraw)	101	51	.664	12.5
1914	Boston (George Stallings)	94	59	.614	10.5
1915	Philadelphia (Pat Moran)	90	62	.592	7
1916	Brooklyn (Wilbert Robinson)	94	60	.610	2.5
1917	New York (John McGraw)	98	56	.636	10
1918	Chicago (Fred Mitchell)	84	45	.651	10.5
1919	Cincinnati (Pat Moran)	96	44	.686	9
1920	Brooklyn (Wilbert Robinson)	93	61	.604	7
1921	New York (John McGraw)	94	59	.614	4
1922	New York (John McGraw)	93	61	.604	7
1923	New York (John McGraw)	95	58	.621	4.5
1924	New York (John McGraw)	93	60	.608	1.5
1925	Pittsburgh (Bill McKechnie)	95	58	.621	8.5
1926	St. Louis (Rogers Hornsby)	89	65	.578	2
1927	Pittsburgh (Donie Bush)	94	60	.610	1.5
1928	St. Louis (Bill McKechnie)	95	59	.617	2
1929	Chicago (Joe McCarthy)	98	54	.645	10.5
1930	St. Louis (Gabby Street)	92	62	.597	2
1931	St. Louis (Gabby Street)	101	53	.656	13
1932	Chicago (Charlie Grimm*)	90	64	.584	4
1933	New York (Bill Terry)	91	61	.599	5
1934	St. Louis (Frankie Frisch)	95	58	.621	2
1935	Chicago (Charlie Grimm)	100	54	.649	4
1936	New York (Bill Terry)	92	62	.597	5
1937	New York (Bill Terry)	95	57	.625	3
1938	Chicago (Gabby Hartnett*)	89	63	.586	2
1939	Cincinnati (Bill McKechnie)	97	57	.630	4.5
1940	Cincinnati (Bill McKechnie)	100	53	.654	12
1941	Brooklyn (Leo Durocher)	100	54	.649	2.5
1942	St. Louis (Billy Southworth)	106	48	.688	2
1943	St. Louis (Billy Southworth)	105	49	.682	18
1944	St. Louis (Billy Southworth)	105	49	.682	14.5
1945	Chicago (Charlie Grimm)	98	56	.636	3
1946	St. Louis (Eddie Dyer)	98	58	.628	2
1947	Brooklyn (Burt Shotton*)	94	60	.610	5
1948	Boston (Billy Southworth)	91	62	.595	6.5
1949	Brooklyn (Burt Shotton)	97	57	.630	1
1950	Philadelphia (Eddie Sawyer)	91	63	.591	2
1951	New York (Leo Durocher)	98	59	.624	1
1952	Brooklyn (Chuck Dressen)	96	57	.627	4.5
1953	Brooklyn (Chuck Dressen)	105	49	.682	13
1954	New York (Leo Durocher)	97	57	.630	5
1955	Brooklyn (Walter Alston)	98	55	.641	13.5
1956	Brooklyn (Walter Alston)	93	61	.604	1
1957	Milwaukee (Fred Haney)	95	59	.617	8
1958	Milwaukee (Fred Haney)	92	62	.597	8
1959	Los Angeles (Walter Alston)	88	68	.564	2
1960	Pittsburgh (Danny Murtaugh)	95	59	.617	7
1961	Cincinnati (Fred Hutchinson)	93	61	.604	4
1962	San Francisco (Alvin Dark)	103	62	.624	1
1963	Los Angeles (Walter Alston)	99	63	.611	6
1964	St. Louis (Johnny Keane)	93	69	.574	1
1965	Los Angeles (Walter Alston)	97	65	.599	2
1966	Los Angeles (Walter Alston)	95	67	.586	1.5
1967	St. Louis (Red Schoendienst)	101	60	.627	10.5
1968	St. Louis (Red Schoendienst)	97	65	.599	9

NATIONAL LEAGUE DIVISION CHAMPIONS (1969 to 1993)

(Championship Series Winner Capitalized)
(E = East; W = West)
(* = mid-season replacement)

YEAR	CLUB (MANAGER)	WON	LOST	PCT.	GA
1969	(E) NEW YORK (Gil Hodges)	100	62	.617	8
	(W) Atlanta (Lum Harris)	93	69	.574	3
1970	(W) CINCINNATI (Sparky Anderson)	102	60	.630	14.5
	(E) Pittsburgh (Danny Murtaugh)	89	73	.549	5
1971	(E) PITTSBURGH (Danny Murtaugh)	97	65	.599	7
	(W) San Francisco (Charlie Fox)	90	72	.556	1
1972	(W) CINCINNATI (Sparky Anderson)	95	59	.617	10.5
	(E) Pittsburgh (Bill Virdon)	96	59	.619	11
1973	(E) NEW YORK (Yogi Berra)	82	79	.509	1.5
	(W) Cincinnati (Sparky Anderson)	99	63	.611	3.5
1974	(W) LOS ANGELES (Walter Alston)	102	60	.630	4
	(E) Pittsburgh (Danny Murtaugh)	88	74	.543	1.5
1975	(W) CINCINNATI (Sparky Anderson)	108	54	.667	20
	(E) Pittsburgh (Danny Murtaugh)	92	69	.571	6.5
1976	(W) CINCINNATI (Sparky Anderson)	102	60	.630	10
	(E) Philadelphia (Danny Ozark)	101	61	.623	9
1977	(W) LOS ANGELES (Tommy Lasorda)	98	64	.605	10
	(E) Philadelphia (Danny Ozark)	101	61	.623	5
1978	(W) LOS ANGELES (Tommy Lasorda)	95	67	.586	2.5
	(E) Philadelphia (Danny Ozark)	90	72	.556	1.5
1979	(E) PITTSBURGH (Chuck Tanner)	98	64	.605	2
	(W) Cincinnati (John McNamara)	90	71	.559	1.5
1980	(E) PHILADELPHIA (Dallas Green)	91	71	.562	1
	(W) Houston (Bill Virdon)	93	70	.571	1
1981	(W) LOS ANGELES (Tommy Lasorda)	63	47	.573	--
	(E) Montreal (Jim Fanning*)	60	48	.556	--

Due to players' strike, 1981 season was divided into two halves. Leaders of each half met in a best-of-five series to determine the NLCS participants. West: Los Angeles 3, Houston 2; East: Montreal 3, Philadelphia 2.

YEAR	CLUB (MANAGER)	WON	LOST	PCT.	GA
1982	(E) ST. LOUIS (Whitey Herzog)	92	70	.568	3
	(W) Atlanta (Joe Torre)	89	73	.549	1
1983	(E) PHILADELPHIA (Paul Owens*)	90	72	.556	6
	(W) Los Angeles (Tommy Lasorda)	91	71	.562	3
1984	(W) SAN DIEGO (Dick Williams)	92	70	.568	12
	(E) Chicago (Jimmy Frey)	96	65	.596	6.5
1985	(E) ST. LOUIS (Whitey Herzog)	101	61	.623	3
	(W) Los Angeles (Tommy Lasorda)	95	67	.586	5.5
1986	(E) NEW YORK (Davey Johnson)	108	54	.667	21.5
	(W) Houston (Hal Lanier)	96	66	.593	10
1987	(E) ST. LOUIS (Whitey Herzog)	95	67	.586	3
	(W) San Francisco (Roger Craig)	90	72	.556	6
1988	(W) LOS ANGELES (Tommy Lasorda)	94	67	.584	7
	(E) New York (Davey Johnson)	100	60	.625	15
1989	(W) SAN FRANCISCO (Roger Craig)	92	70	.568	3
	(E) Chicago (Don Zimmer)	93	69	.574	6
1990	(W) CINCINNATI (Lou Piniella)	91	71	.562	5
	(E) Pittsburgh (Jim Leyland)	95	67	.586	4
1991	(W) ATLANTA (Bobby Cox)	94	68	.580	1
	(E) Pittsburgh (Jim Leyland)	98	64	.605	14
1992	(E) ATLANTA (Bobby Cox)	98	64	.605	8
	(W) Pittsburgh (Jim Leyland)	96	66	.593	9
1993	(E) PHILADELPHIA (Jim Fregosi)	97	65	.599	3
	(W) Atlanta (Bobby Cox)	104	58	.642	1

NATIONAL LEAGUE POSTSEASON PARTICIPANTS (since 1995)

(Championship Series Winner Capitalized)
(E = East; C = Central; W = West; WC = Wild Card)
(* = mid-season replacement)

YEAR	CLUB (MANAGER)	WON	LOST	PCT.	GA
1995	(E) ATLANTA (Bobby Cox)	90	54	.625	21
	(C) Cincinnati (Davey Johnson)	85	59	.590	9
	(W) Los Angeles (Tommy Lasorda)	78	66	.542	1
	(WC) Colorado (Don Baylor)	77	67	.535	--
1996	(E) ATLANTA (Bobby Cox)	96	66	.593	8
	(C) St. Louis (Tony LaRussa)	88	74	.543	6
	(W) San Diego (Bruce Bochy)	91	71	.562	1
	(WC) Los Angeles (Bill Russell*)	90	72	.556	--
1997	(WC) FLORIDA (Jim Leyland)	92	70	.568	--
	(E) Atlanta (Bobby Cox)	101	61	.623	9
	(C) Houston (Larry Dierker)	84	78	.519	5
	(W) San Francisco (Dusty Baker)	90	72	.556	2
1998	(W) SAN DIEGO (Bruce Bochy)	98	64	.605	9.5
	(E) Atlanta (Bobby Cox)	106	56	.654	18
	(C) Houston (Larry Dierker)	102	60	.630	12.5
	(WC) Chicago (Jim Riggleman)	90	73	.552	--
1999	(E) ATLANTA (Bobby Cox)	103	59	.636	6.5
	(WC) New York (Bobby Valentine)	97	66	.595	--
	(C) Houston (Larry Dierker)	97	65	.599	1.5
	(W) Arizona (Buck Showalter)	100	62	.617	14
2000	(WC) NEW YORK (Bobby Valentine)	94	68	.580	--
	(C) St. Louis (Tony LaRussa)	95	67	.586	10
	(E) Atlanta (Bobby Cox)	95	67	.586	1
	(W) San Francisco (Dusty Baker)	97	65	.599	11
2001	(W) ARIZONA (Bob Brenly)	92	70	.568	2
	(E) Atlanta (Bobby Cox)	88	74	.543	2
	(C) Houston (Larry Dierker)	93	69	.574	--
	(WC) St. Louis (Tony LaRussa)	93	69	.574	--

CONSECUTIVE VICTORIES
NATIONAL LEAGUE

No.	Club	H	A	Year
26	New York	26	0	1916
21	Chicago	11	10	1880
	Chicago	18	3	1935
20	Providence	16	4	1884
18	Chicago	14	4	1885
	Boston	16	2	1891
	Baltimore	13	5	1894
	New York	13	5	1904
17	Boston	16	1	1897
	New York	14	3	1907
	New York	0	17	1916
16	Philadelphia	5	11	1887
	Philadelphia	14	2	1890
	Philadelphia	11	5	1892
	Pittsburgh	12	4	1909
	New York	11	5	1912
	New York	13	3	1951
15	Detroit	12	3	1886
	Pittsburgh	11	4	1903
	Brooklyn	3	12	1924
	Chicago	11	4	1936
	New York	8	7	1936
	Atlanta	9	6	2000

AMERICAN LEAGUE

No.	Club	H	A	Year
19	Chicago	11	8	1906
	New York	6	13	1947
18	New York	3	15	1953
17	Washington	1	16	1912
	Philadelphia	5	12	1931
16	New York	12	4	1926
	Kansas City	9	7	1977
15	New York	12	3	1906
	Philadelphia	13	2	1913
	Boston	11	4	1946
	New York	9	6	1960
	Minnesota	8	7	1991
	Seattle	5	10	2001

AMERICAN ASSOCIATION

No.	Club	H	A	Year
15	St. Louis	15	0	1887

UNION ASSOCIATION

No.	Club	H	A	Year
20	St. Louis	16	4	1884

CONSECUTIVE LOSSES
NATIONAL LEAGUE

No.	Club	H	A	Year
24	Cleveland	5	19	1899
23	Pittsburgh	1	22	1890
	Philadelphia	6	17	1961
20	Louisville	0	20	1894
	Montreal	12	8	1969
19	Boston	3	16	1906
	Cincinnati	6	13	1914
18	Cincinnati	9	9	1876
	Louisville	0	18	1894
17	Washington	7	10	1894
	New York	7	10	1962
	Atlanta	8	9	1977
16	Troy	5	11	1882
	Detroit	5	11	1884
	Cleveland	0	16	1899
	Boston	5	11	1907
	Boston	8	8	1911
	Brooklyn	0	16	1944
15	St. Louis	11	4	1909
	Boston	0	15	1909
	Boston	0	15	1927
	Boston	0	15	1935
	New York	8	7	1963
	New York	6	9	1982

AMERICAN LEAGUE

No.	Club	H	A	Year
21	Baltimore	8	13	1988
20	Boston	19	1	1906
	Philadelphia	1	19	1916
	Philadelphia	3	17	1943
19	Detroit	9	10	1975
18	Philadelphia	0	18	1920
	Washington	8	10	1948
	Washington	3	15	1959
17	Boston	14	3	1926
16	Boston	9	7	1907
15	Boston	10	5	1927
	Philadelphia	10	5	1937
	Philadelphia	10	5	1937
	Texas	5	10	1972

AMERICAN ASSOCIATION

No.	Club	H	A	Year
26	Louisville	5	21	1889

LONGEST GAMES, 18 OR MORE INNINGS

AMERICAN LEAGUE

25	Chi. 7 Mil. 6, May 8, 1984
24	Phil. 4 Bos. 1, Sept 1, 1906
	Det. 1 Phil. 1, July 21, 1945
22	NY 9 Det. 7, June 24, 1962
	Wash. 6 Chi. 5, June 12, 1967
	Mil. 4 Minn. 3, May 12, 1972
	Minn. 5 Clev. 4, Aug. 31, 1993
21	Det. 6 Chi. 5, May 24, 1929
	Oak. 5 Wash. 3, June 4, 1971
	Chi. 6 Clev. 3, May 26, 1973
20	Phil. 4 Bos. 2, July 4, 1905
	Wash. 9 Minn. 7, Aug. 9, 1967
	NY 4 Bos. 3, Aug. 29(2g), 1967
	Bos. 5 Sea. 3, July 27, 1969
	Oak. 1 Cal. 0, July 9, 1971
	Wash. 8 Clev. 6, Sept. 14(2g), 1971
	Sea. 8 Bos. 7, Sept 3, 1981
	Cal. 4 Sea. 3, Apr. 13, 1982
19	Wash. 5 Phil. 4, Sept. 27, 1912
	Chi 5 Clev. 4, June 24, 1915
	Clev. 3 NY 2, May 24, 1918
	StL. 8 Wash. 6, Aug. 9, 1921
	Chi. 5 Bos. 4, July 13, 1951
	Clev. 4 StL. 3, July 1, 1952
	Clev. 3 Wash. 2, June 14(2g), 1963
	Balt. 7 Wash. 5, June 4, 1967
	KC 6 Det. 5, June 17(2g), 1967
	NY 3 Det. 3, Aug. 23(2g), 1968
	Oak. 5 Chi. 3, Aug. 10, 1972
	NY 5 Minn. 4, Aug. 25, 1976
	Clev. 8 Det. 4, Apr. 27, 1984
	Mil. 10 Chi. 9, May 1, 1991
	Bos. 7 Clev. 5 Apr. 11, 1992
	Sea. 5 Bos. 4 Aug. 1, 2000
18	Chi. 6 NY 6, June 25, 1903
	Det. 0 Wash. 0, July 16, 1909
	Wash. 1 Chi. 0, May 15, 1918
	Det. 7 Wash. 6, Aug. 4(2g), 1918
	Bos. 12 NY 11, Sept 5(1g), 1927
	Phil. 18 Clev. 17, July 10, 1932
	NY 3 Chi. 3, Aug. 21, 1933
	Wash. 1 Chi. 0, June 8(1g), 1947
	Wash. 5 StL. 5, June 20, 1952
	Chi. 1 Balt. 1, Aug. 6, 1959
	NY 7 Bos. 6, Apr. 16, 1967
	Minn. 3 NY 2, July 26(2g), 1967
	Balt. 3 Bos. 2, Aug. 25, 1968
	Minn. 11 Sea. 7, July 19, 1969
	Oak 9 Balt. 8, Aug. 24(2g), 1969
	Minn. 8 Oak. 6, Sept. 6, 1969
	Wash. 2 NY 1, Apr. 22, 1970
	Tex. 4 KC 3, May 17, 1972
	Det. 4 Clev. 3, June 9(2g), 1982
	NY 5 Det. 4, Sept. 11, 1988
	KC 4 Tex 3, June 6, 1991
	Bos. 4 Det. 3, June 5, 2001
	Tex. 8 Bos. 7, Aug. 25, 2001

NATIONAL LEAGUE

26	Brk. 1 Bos. 1, May 1, 1920
25	StL. 4 NY 3, Sept. 11 1974
24	Hou. 1 NY 0, Apr. 15, 1968
23	Brk. 2 Bos. 2, June 27, 1939
	SF 8 NY 6, May 31(2g), 1964
22	Brk. 6 Pitt. 5, Aug. 22, 1917
	Chi. 4 Bos. 3, May 17 1927
	Hou. 5 LA 4, June 3, 1989
	LA 1 Mtl. 0, Aug. 23, 1989

21	NY 3 Pitt. 1, July 17, 1914
	Chi. 2 Phil. 1, July 17, 1918
	Pitt. 2 Bos. 0, Aug. 1, 1918
	SF 1 Cin. 0, Sept. 1, 1967
	Hou. 2 SD 1, Sept. 24(1g), 1971
	SD 11 Mtl. 8, May 21, 1977
	LA 2 Chi. 1, Aug. 17, 1982
20	Chi. 7 Cinn. 7, June 30, 1892
	Chi. 2 Phil 1, Aug. 24, 1905
	Brk. 9 Phil. 9, Apr. 30, 1919
	StL. 8 Chi. 7, Aug. 28, 1930
	Brk. 6 Bos. 2, July 5, 1940
	Phil. 5 Atl. 4, May 4, 1973
	Pitt. 5 Chi. 4, July 6, 1980
	Hou. 3 SD 1, Aug. 15, 1980
	Phil. 7 LA 6, July 7, 1993
19	Chi. 3 Pitt. 2, June 22, 1902
	Pitt. 7 Bos. 6, July 31, 1912
	Chi. 4 Brk. 3, June 17, 1915
	StL. 8 Phil. 8, June 13, 1918
	Bos. 2 Brk. 1, May 3, 1920
	Chi. 3 Bos. 2, Aug. 17, 1932
	Brk. 9 Chi. 9, May 17, 1939
	Cin. 0 Brk. 0, Sept. 11, 1946
	Phil. 8 Cin. 7, Sept. 15(2g), 1950
	Pitt. 4 Mil. 3, July 19, 1955
	Cin. 2 LA 1, Aug. 8, 1972
	NY 7 LA 3, May 24, 1973
	Pitt. 4 SD 3, Aug. 25, 1979
	NY 16 Atl. 13, July 4, 1985
	Mtl. 6 Hou. 3, July 7, 1985
	Atl. 7 StL. 5, May 14, 1988
18	Prov. 1 Det. 0, Aug. 17, 1882
	Brk. 7 StL.7, Aug. 17, 1902
	Chi. 2 StL. 1, June 24, 1905
	Pitt. 3 Chi. 2, June 28(2g), 1916
	Phil. 10 Brk. 9, June 1, 1919
	NY 9 Pitt 8, July 7, 1922
	Chi. 7 Bos. 2, May 14, 1927
	NY 1 StL. 0, July 2(1g), 1933
	StL. 8 Cin. 6, July 1(1g), 1934
	Chi. 10 Cin. 8, Aug. 9(1g), 1942
	Phil. 4 Pitt. 3, June 9, 1949
	Cin. 7 Chi. 6, Sept. 7, 1951
	NY 0 Phil 0, Oct. 2(2g), 1965
	Cin. 3 Chi. 2, July 19, 1966
	Phil. 2 Cin. 1, May 21, 1967
	Pitt. 1 SD 0, June 7(2g), 1972
	NY 3 Phil 2, Aug. 1(1g), 1972
	Mtl. 5 Chi. 4, June 27(2g), 1973
	Chi. 8 Mtl. 7, June 28(1g), 1974
	NY 4 Mtl. 3, Sept. 16, 1975
	Pitt. 2 Chi. 1, Aug. 10, 1977
	Chi. 9 Cin. 8, May 10, 1979
	Hou. 3 NY 2, June 18, 1979
	SD 8 NY 6, Aug. 26, 1980
	StL. 3 Hou. 1, May 27, 1983
	Pitt. 4 SF 3, July 13(2g), 1984
	Atl. 3 LA 2, Sept. 6, 1984
	NY 5 Pitt. 4, Apr. 28, 1985
	SF 5 Atl. 4, June 11, 1985
	Hou. 8 Chi. 7, Sept. 2, 1986
	Pitt. 5 Chi. 4, Aug. 6, 1989
	Atl. 5 LA 3, Aug. 3, 1996
	Ari. 1 SF 0, May 29, 2001

AMERICAN LEAGUE CLUB HOME RUNS

(* = Leader)

(1901 Milwaukee total under StL.)

	Balt	Bos	Chi	Clev	Det	KC	NY	Phil	StL	Wash	Total
1901	24	*37	32	12	29	-	-	35	26	33	*228
1902	33	42	14	33	22	-	-	38	29	*47	*258
1903	-	*48	14	31	12	-	18	32	12	17	184
1904	-	26	14	27	11	-	27	*31	10	10	156
1905	-	*29	11	18	13	-	23	24	16	22	156
1906	-	13	7	12	10	-	17	*32	20	26	137
1907	-	18	5	11	11	-	15	*22	10	12	104
1908	-	14	3	18	19	-	13	*21	20	8	116
1909	-	20	4	10	19	-	16	*21	10	9	109
1910	-	*43	7	9	28	-	20	19	12	9	147
1911	-	*35	20	20	30	-	25	*35	17	16	198
1912	-	*29	17	12	19	-	18	22	19	20	156
1913	-	17	24	16	24	-	8	*33	18	19	159
1914	-	18	19	10	25	-	12	*29	17	18	148
1915	-	14	25	20	23	-	*31	16	19	12	160
1916	-	14	17	16	17	-	*35	19	14	12	144
1917	-	14	18	13	25	-	*27	17	15	4	133
1918	-	15	8	9	13	-	20	*22	5	4	96
1919	-	33	25	24	23	-	*45	35	31	24	240
1920	-	22	37	35	30	-	*115	44	50	36	*369
1921	-	17	35	42	58	-	*134	82	67	42	*477
1922	-	45	45	32	54	-	95	*111	98	45	*525
1923	-	34	42	59	41	-	*105	53	82	26	442
1924	-	30	41	41	35	-	*98	63	67	22	397
1925	-	41	38	52	50	-	*110	76	*110	56	*533
1926	-	32	32	27	36	-	*121	61	72	43	424
1927	-	28	36	26	51	-	*158	56	55	29	439
1928	-	38	24	34	62	-	*133	89	63	40	483
1929	-	28	37	62	110	-	*142	122	46	48	*595
1930	-	47	63	72	82	-	*152	125	75	57	*673
1931	-	37	27	71	43	-	*155	118	76	49	576
1932	-	53	36	78	80	-	160	*172	67	61	*707
1933	-	50	43	50	57	-	*144	139	64	60	607
1934	-	51	71	100	74	-	135	*144	62	51	688
1935	-	69	74	93	106	-	104	*112	73	32	663
1936	-	86	60	123	94	-	*182	72	79	62	*758
1937	-	100	67	103	150	-	*174	94	71	47	*806
1938	-	98	67	113	137	-	*174	98	92	85	*864
1939	-	124	64	85	124	-	*166	98	91	44	796
1940	-	145	73	101	134	-	*155	105	118	52	*883
1941	-	124	47	103	81	-	*151	85	91	52	734
1942	-	103	25	50	76	-	*108	33	98	40	533
1943	-	57	33	55	77	-	*100	26	78	47	473
1944	-	69	23	70	60	-	*96	36	72	33	459
1945	-	50	22	65	77	-	*93	33	63	27	430
1946	-	109	37	79	108	-	*136	40	84	60	653
1947	-	103	53	112	103	-	*115	61	90	42	679
1948	-	121	55	*155	78	-	139	68	63	31	710
1949	-	*131	43	112	88	-	115	82	117	81	769
1950	-	161	93	*164	114	-	159	100	106	76	*973
1951	-	127	86	*140	104	-	*140	102	86	54	839
1952	-	113	80	*148	103	-	129	89	82	50	794
1953	-	101	74	*160	108	-	139	116	112	69	879
1954	52	123	94	*156	90	-	133	94	-	81	823
1955	54	137	116	148	130	121	*175	-	-	80	961
1956	91	139	128	153	150	112	*190	-	-	112	*1075
1957	87	153	106	140	116	*166	145	-	-	111	1024
1958	108	155	101	161	109	138	*164	-	-	121	1057
1959	109	125	97	*167	160	117	153	-	-	163	*1091
1960	123	124	112	127	150	110	*193	-	-	147	1086

AMERICAN LEAGUE CLUB HOME RUNS

(* = Leader)

	ANA	BALT	BOS	CHI	CLEV	DET	KC	MIL	MINN	NY	OAK	SEA	TEX	TOR	WASH	TOTAL
1961	189	149	112	138	150	130	90	-	167	*240	-	-	-	-	119	*1534
1962	137	156	146	92	180	*209	116	-	185	199	-	-	-	-	132	*1552
1963	95	146	171	114	169	148	95	-	*225	188	-	-	-	-	138	1489
1964	102	162	186	106	164	157	166	-	*221	162	-	-	-	-	125	1551
1965	92	125	*165	125	156	162	110	-	150	149	-	-	-	-	136	1370
1966	122	175	145	87	155	*179	110	-	144	162	-	-	-	-	126	1365
1967	114	138	*158	89	131	152	69	-	131	100	-	-	-	-	115	1197
1968	83	133	125	71	75	*185	-	-	105	109	94	-	-	-	124	1104
1969	88	175	*197	112	119	182	98	-	163	94	148	125	-	-	148	*1649
1970	114	179	*203	123	183	148	97	126	153	111	171	-	-	-	138	*1746
1971	96	158	161	138	109	*179	80	124	116	97	160	-	-	-	86	1484
1972	78	100	124	108	91	122	78	88	93	103	*134	-	56	-	-	1175
1973	93	119	147	111	*158	157	114	145	120	131	147	-	110	-	-	1552
1974	95	116	109	*135	131	131	89	120	111	101	132	-	99	-	-	1369
1975	55	124	134	94	*153	125	118	146	124	110	151	-	134	-	-	1465
1976	63	119	*134	73	85	101	65	88	81	120	113	-	80	-	-	1122
1977	131	148	*213	192	100	166	146	125	123	184	117	133	135	100	-	*2013
1978	108	154	172	106	106	129	98	*173	125	100	97	132		98	-	1680
1979	164	181	*194	127	138	164	116	185	112	150	108	132	140	95	-	2006
1980	106	156	162	91	89	143	115	*203	99	189	137	104	124	126	-	1844
1981	97	88	90	76	39	65	61	96	47	100	*104	89	49	61	-	1062
1982	186	179	136	136	109	177	132	*216	148	161	149	130	115	106	-	*2080
1983	154	*168	142	157	86	156	109	132	141	153	121	111	106	167	-	1903
1984	150	160	181	172	123	*187	117	96	114	130	158	129	120	143	-	1980
1985	153	*214	162	146	116	202	154	101	141	176	155	171	129	158	-	*2178
1986	167	169	144	121	157	*198	137	127	196	188	163	158	184	181	-	*2290
1987	172	211	174	173	187	*225	168	163	196	196	199	161	194	215	-	*2634
1988	124	137	124	132	134	143	121	113	151	148	156	148	112	*158	-	1901
1989	*145	129	108	94	127	116	101	126	117	130	127	134	122	142	-	1718
1990	147	132	106	106	110	*172	100	128	100	147	164	107	110	167	-	1796
1991	115	170	126	139	79	*209	117	116	140	147	159	126	177	133	-	1953
1992	88	148	84	110	127	*182	75	82	104	163	142	149	159	163	-	1776
1993	114	157	114	162	141	178	125	125	121	178	158	161	*181	159	-	2074
1994	120	139	120	121	*167	161	100	99	103	139	113	153	124	115	-	1774
1995	186	173	175	146	*207	159	119	128	120	122	169	182	138	140	-	2164
1996	192	*257	209	195	218	204	123	178	118	162	243	245	221	177	-	*2742
1997	161	196	185	158	220	176	158	135	132	161	197	*264	187	147	-	2477

	ANA	BALT	BOS	CHI	CLEV	DET	KC	-	MINN	NY	OAK	SEA	TEX	TOR	TB	TOTAL
1998	147	214	205	198	198	165	134		115	207	149	*234	201	221	111	2499
1999	158	203	176	162	209	212	151		105	193	235	*244	230	212	145	2635
2000	236	184	167	216	221	177	150		116	205	239	198	173	*244	162	2688
2001	158	136	198	214	212	139	152		164	203	199	169	*246	195	121	2506

NATIONAL LEAGUE CLUB HOME RUNS

(= Leader)*

	BOS	BRK	CHI	CIN	LA	MIL	NY	PHIL	PITT	STL	SF	TOTAL
1900	*48	26	33	33	-	-	23	29	26	36	-	*254
1901	28	32	18	38	-	-	19	24	28	*39	-	226
1902	14	*19	6	18	-	-	6	5	18	10	-	96
1903	25	15	9	28	-	-	20	12	*34	8	-	151
1904	24	15	22	21	-	-	*31	23	15	24	-	175
1905	17	29	12	27	-	-	*39	16	22	20	-	182
1906	16	*25	20	16	-	-	15	12	12	10	-	126
1907	22	18	13	15	-	-	*23	12	19	18	-	140
1908	17	*28	19	14	-	-	20	11	25	17	-	151
1909	14	16	20	22	-	-	*26	12	25	15	-	150
1910	31	25	*34	23	-	-	31	22	33	15	-	214
1911	37	28	54	21	-	-	41	*60	49	26	-	*316
1912	35	32	42	21	-	-	*47	43	39	27	-	286
1913	32	39	59	27	-	-	31	*73	35	15	-	311
1914	35	31	42	16	-	-	30	*62	18	33	-	267
1915	17	14	53	15	-	-	24	*58	24	20	-	225
1916	22	28	*46	14	-	-	42	42	20	25	-	239
1917	22	25	17	26	-	-	*39	38	9	26	-	202
1918	13	10	21	15	-	-	13	25	15	*27	-	139
1919	24	25	21	20	-	-	40	*42	17	18	-	207
1920	23	28	34	18	-	-	46	*64	16	32	-	261
1921	61	59	37	20	-	-	75	*88	37	83	-	*460
1922	32	56	42	45	-	-	80	*116	52	107	-	*530
1923	32	62	90	45	-	-	85	*112	49	63	-	*538
1924	25	72	66	36	-	-	*95	94	44	67	-	499
1925	41	64	86	44	-	-	*114	100	78	109	-	*636
1926	16	40	66	35	-	-	73	75	44	*90	-	439
1927	37	39	74	29	-	-	*109	57	54	84	-	483
1928	52	66	92	32	-	-	*118	85	52	113	-	610
1929	33	99	139	34	-	-	136	*153	60	100	-	*754
1930	66	122	*171	74	-	-	143	126	86	104	-	*892
1931	34	71	84	21	-	-	*101	81	41	60	-	493
1932	63	110	69	47	-	-	116	*122	48	76	-	651
1933	54	62	72	34	-	-	*82	60	39	57	-	460
1934	83	79	101	55	-	-	*126	56	52	104	-	656
1935	75	59	88	73	-	-	*123	92	66	86	-	662
1936	67	33	76	82	-	-	97	*103	60	88	-	606
1937	63	37	96	73	-	-	*111	103	47	94	-	624
1938	54	61	65	110	-	-	*125	40	65	91	-	611
1939	56	78	91	98	-	-	*116	49	63	98	-	649
1940	59	93	86	89	-	-	91	75	76	*119	-	688
1941	48	*101	99	64	-	-	95	64	56	70	-	597
1942	68	62	75	66	-	-	*109	44	54	60	-	538
1943	39	39	52	43	-	-	*81	66	42	70	-	432
1944	79	56	71	51	-	-	93	55	70	*100	-	575
1945	101	57	57	56	-	-	*114	56	72	64	-	577
1946	44	55	56	65	-	-	*121	80	60	81	-	562
1947	85	83	71	95	-	-	*221	60	156	115	-	886
1948	95	91	87	104	-	-	*164	91	108	105	-	845
1949	103	*152	97	86	-	-	147	122	126	102	-	*935
1950	148	*194	161	99	-	-	133	125	138	102	-	*1100
1951	130	*184	103	88	-	-	179	108	137	95	-	1024
1952	110	*153	107	104	-	-	151	93	92	97	-	907
1953	-	*208	137	166	-	156	176	115	99	140	-	*1197
1954	-	*186	159	147	-	139	*186	102	76	119	-	1114
1955	-	*201	164	181	-	182	169	132	91	143	-	*1263
1956	-	179	142	*221	-	177	145	121	110	124	-	1219
1957	-	147	147	187	-	*199	157	117	92	132	-	1178
1958	-	-	*182	123	172	167	-	124	134	111	170	1183
1959	-	-	163	161	148	*177	-	113	112	118	167	1159
1960	-	-	119	140	126	*170	-	99	120	138	130	1042
1961	-	-	176	158	157	*188	-	103	128	103	183	1196

NATIONAL LEAGUE CLUB HOME RUNS

(* = Leader)

	ATL	CHI	CIN	HOU	LA	MIL	MTL	NY	PHIL	PITT	STL	SD	SF	TOTAL
1962	-	126	167	105	140	181	-	139	142	108	137	-	*204	*1449
1963	-	127	122	62	110	139	-	96	126	108	128	-	*197	1215
1964	-	145	130	70	79	159	-	103	130	121	109	-	*165	1211
1965	-	134	183	97	78	*196	-	107	144	111	109	-	159	1318
1966	*207	140	149	112	108	-	-	98	117	158	108	-	181	1378
1967	*158	128	109	93	82	-	-	83	103	91	115	-	140	1102
1968	80	*130	106	66	67	-	-	81	100	80	73	-	108	891
1969	141	142	*171	104	97	-	125	109	137	119	90	99	136	*1470
1970	160	179	*191	129	87	-	136	120	101	130	113	172	165	*1683
1971	153	128	138	71	95	-	88	98	123	*154	95	96	104	1379
1972	144	133	124	134	98	-	91	105	98	110	70	102	*150	1359
1973	*206	117	137	134	110	-	125	85	134	154	75	112	161	1550
1974	120	110	135	110	*139	-	86	96	95	114	83	99	93	1280
1975	107	95	124	84	118	-	98	101	125	*138	81	78	84	1233
1976	82	105	*141	66	91	-	94	102	110	110	63	64	85	1113
1977	139	111	181	114	*191	-	138	88	186	133	96	120	134	1631
1978	123	72	136	70	*149	-	121	86	133	115	79	75	117	1276
1979	126	135	132	49	*183	-	143	74	119	148	100	93	125	1427
1980	144	107	113	75	*148	-	114	61	117	116	101	67	80	1243
1981	64	57	64	45	*82	-	81	57	69	55	50	32	63	719
1982	*146	102	82	74	138	-	133	97	112	134	67	81	133	1299
1983	130	140	107	97	*146	-	102	112	125	121	83	93	142	1398
1984	111	136	106	79	102	-	96	107	*147	98	75	109	112	1278
1985	126	*150	114	121	129	-	118	134	141	80	87	109	115	1424
1986	138	*155	144	125	130	-	110	148	154	111	58	136	114	1523
1987	152	*209	192	122	125	-	120	192	169	131	94	113	205	*1824
1988	96	113	122	96	99	-	107	*152	106	110	71	94	113	1279
1989	128	124	128	97	89	-	100	*147	123	95	73	120	141	1365
1990	162	136	125	94	129	-	114	*172	103	138	73	123	152	1521
1991	141	159	*164	79	108	-	95	117	111	126	68	121	141	1430
1992	*138	104	99	96	72	-	102	93	118	106	94	135	105	1262

	ATL	CHI	CIN	COL	FLA	HOU	LA	MTL	NY	PHIL	PITT	STL	SD	SF	TOTAL
1993	*169	161	137	142	94	138	130	122	158	156	110	118	153	168	*1956
1994	*137	109	124	125	94	120	115	108	117	80	80	108	92	123	1532
1995	168	158	161	*200	144	109	140	118	125	94	125	107	116	152	1917
1996	197	175	191	*221	150	129	150	148	147	132	138	142	147	153	*2220
1997	174	127	142	*239	136	133	174	172	153	116	129	144	152	172	2163

	ARI	ATL	CHI	CIN	COL	FLA	HOU	LA	MIL	MTL	NY	PHIL	PITT	STL	SD	SF	TOTAL
1998	159	215	212	138	183	114	166	159	152	147	136	126	107	*223	167	161	*2565
1999	216	197	189	209	*223	128	168	187	165	163	181	161	171	194	153	188	*2893
2000	179	179	183	200	161	160	*249	211	177	178	198	144	168	235	157	226	*3005
2001	208	174	194	176	213	166	208	206	209	131	147	164	161	199	161	*235	2952

MANAGERS –
AMERICAN LEAGUE

Adcock, Joe Clev. 1967
Altobelli, Joe Balt. 1983-85
Anderson, Sparky Det. 1979-95
Appling, Luke KC 1967
Armour, Bill Clev. 1902-04
  Det. 1905-06
Aspromonte, Ken Clev. 1972-74
Austin, Jimmy StL. 1923
Baker, Del Det. 1933, 38-42
Bamberger, George Mil. 1978-80; 85-86
Barrow, Ed Det. 1903-04
  Bos. 1918-20
Barry, Jack Bos. 1917
Bauer, Hank KC 1961-62
  Balt. 1964-68
  Oak. 1969
Bell, Buddy Det. 1996-98
Berra, Yogi NY 1964;84-85
Bevington, Terry Chi. 1995-97
Birmingham, Joe Clev. 1912-15
Blackburne, Lena Chi. 1928-29
Bluege, Ossie Wash. 1943-47
Boone, Bob KC 1995-97
Boros, Steve Oak. 1983-84
Bottomley, Jim StL. 1937
Boudreau, Lou Clev. 1942-50
  Bos. 1952-54
  KC 1955-57
Bragan, Bobby Clev. 1958
Bristol, Dave Mil. 1970-72
Burke, Jimmy StL. 1918-20
Bush, Donie Wash. 1923
  Chi. 1930-31
Callahan, Nixey Chi. 1903-04;12-14
Cantillon, Joe Wash. 1907-09
Carrigan, Bill Bos. 1913-16;27-29
Chance, Frank NY 1913-14
  Bos. 1923
Chase, Hal NY 1910-11
Cobb, Ty Det. 1921-26
Cochrane, Mickey Det. 1934-38
Collins, Eddie Chi. 1925-26
Collins, Jimmy Bos. 1901-06
Collins, Shano Bos. 1931-32
Collins, Terry Ana. 1997-99
Corrales, Pat Tex. 1978-80
  Clev. 1983-87
Corriden, Red Chi. 1950
Cottier, Chuck Sea. 1984-86
Cox, Bobby Tor. 1982-85
Craft, Harry KC 1957-59
Crandall, Del Mil. 1972-75
  Sea. 1983-84
Cronin, Joe Wash. 1933-34
  Bos. 1935-47
Dark, Alvin KC /Oak. 1966-67; 74-75
  Clev. 1968-71
Davis, Harry Clev. 1912
Dent, Bucky NY 1989-90
Dickey, Bill NY 1946
Doby, Larry Chi. 1978
Donovan, Patsy Wash. 1904
  Bos. 1910-11
Donovan, Wild Bill NY 1915-17
Dressen, Chuck Wash. 1955-57
  Det. 1963-66
Duffy, Hugh Mil. 1901
  Chi. 1910-11
  Bos. 1921-22
Dwyer, Frank Det. 1902

Dykes, Jimmy Chi. 1934-46
  Phil. 1951-53
  Balt. 1954
  Det. 1959-60
  Clev. 1960-61
Edwards, Doc Clev. 1987-89
Elberfeld, Kid NY 1908
Elliot, Bob KC 1960
Ermer, Cal Minn. 1967-68
Evers, Johnny Chi. 1924
Farrell, Kerby Clev. 1957
Ferraro, Mike Clev. 1983
  KC 1986
Fohl, Lee Clev. 1915-19
  StL. 1921-23
  Bos. 1924-26
Fonseca, Lew Chi. 1932-34
Fregosi, Jim Cal. 1978-81
  Chi. 1986-88
  Tor. 1999-2000
Frey, Jim KC 1980-81
Garcia, Dave Cal. 1977-78
  Clev. 1979-82
Gardner, Billy Minn. 1981-85
  KC 1987
Garner, Phil Mil. 1992-97
  Det. 2000-
Gaston, Cito Tor. 1989-97
Gleason, Kid Chi. 1919-23
Gordon, Joe Clev. 1958-60
  Det. 1960
  KC 1961;69
Goryl, John Minn. 1980-81
Grammas, Alex Mil. 1976-77
Green, Dallas NY 1989
Griffith, Clark Chi. 1901-02
  NY 1903-08
  Wash. 1912-20
Gutteridge, Don Chi. 1969-70
Haney, Fred StL. 1939-41
Hargrove, Mike Clev. 1991-99
  Balt. 2000-
Harrah, Toby Tex. 1992
Harris, Lum Balt. 1961
Harris, Bucky Wash. 1924-28;35-42;50-54
  Det. 1929-33;1955-56
  Bos. 1934
  NY 1947-48
Hart, John Clev. 1989
Hartsfield, Roy Tor. 1977-79
Herman, Billy Bos. 1965-66
Herzog, Whitey Tex. 1973
  KC 1975-79
Higgins, Pinky Bos. 1955-62
Hitchcock, Billy Balt. 1962-63
Hobson, Butch Bos. 1992-1994
Hodges, Gil Wash. 1963-67
Hornsby, Rogers StL. 1933-37;52
Houk, Ralph NY 1961-63;66-73
  Det. 1974-78
  Bos. 1981-84
Howe, Art Oak. 1996-
Howley, Dan StL. 1927-29
Howser, Dick NY 1980
  KC 1981-86
Huff, George Bos. 1907
Huggins, Miller NY 1918-29
Hunter, Billy Tex. 1977-78
Hutchinson, Fred Det. 1952-54
Jennings, Hughie Det. 1907-20
Johnson, Darrell Bos. 1974-76
  Sea. 1977-80
  Tex. 1982
Johnson, Davey Balt. 1996-97
Johnson, Tim Tor. 1998

Johnson, Walter Wash. 1929-32
  Clev. 1933-35
Jones, Fielder Chi. 1904-08
  StL. 1916-18
Joost, Eddie Phil. 1954
Jurges, Billy Bos. 1959-60
Kasko, Eddie Bos. 1970-73
Keane, Johnny NY 1965-66
Kelly, Tom Minn. 1986-2001
Kennedy, Bob Oak. 1968
Kennedy, Kevin Tex. 1993-1994
  Bos. 1995-96
Kerrigan, Joe Bos. 2001-
Kessinger, Don Chi. 1979
Killefer, Bill StL. 1930-33
King, Clyde NY 1982
Kittridge, Malachi Wash. 1904
Kuenn, Harvey Mil. 1982-83
Kuhel, Joe Wash. 1948-49
Lachemann, Marcel Cal. 1994-96
Lachemann, Rene Sea. 1981-83
  Mil. 1984
Lajoie, Nap Clev. 1905-09
Lake, Fred Bos. 1908-09
Lamont, Gene Chi. 1992-95
LaRussa, Tony Chi. 1979-86
  Oak. 1986-95
Lavagetto, Cookie Wash./Minn. 1957-61
Lefebvre, Jim Sea. 1989-91
Lemon, Jim Wash. 1968
Lemon, Bob KC 1970-72
  Chi. 1977-78
  NY 1978-79;81-82
Lipon, Johnny Clev. 1971
Loftus, Tom Wash. 1902-03
Lopat, Ed KC 1963-64
Lopez, Al Clev. 1951-56
  Chi. 1957-65;68-69
Lowe, Bobby Det. 1904
Lucchesi, Frank Tex. 1975-77
Lyons, Ted Chi. 1946-48
Mack, Connie Phil. 1901-50
Maddon, Joe Ana. 1999
Manning, Jimmy Wash. 1901
Manuel, Charlie, Clev. 2000-
Manuel, Jerry Chi. 1998-
Marion, Marty StL. 1952-53
  Chi. 1954-56
Marshall Jim Oak. 1979
Martin, Billy Minn. 1969
  Det. 1971-73
  Tex. 1973-75
  NY 1975-78;79;83;85;88
  Oak. 1980-82
Martinez, Buck Tor. 2001-
Mattick, Bobby Tor. 1980-81
Mauch, Gene Minn. 1976-80
  Cal. 1981-82;85-87
McAleer, Jimmy Clev. 1901
  StL. 1902-09
  Wash. 1910-11
McBride, George Wash. 1921
McCallister, Jack Clev. 1927
McCarthy, Joe NY 1931-46
  Bos. 1948-50
McGaha, Mel Clev. 1962
  KC 1964-65
McGraw, John Balt. 1901-02
McGuire, Deacon Bos. 1907-08
  Clev. 1909-11
McKeon, Jack KC 1973-75
  Oak. 1977;78
McManus, Marty Bos. 1932-33

McNamara, John Oak. 1969-70
Cal. 1983-84;96
Bos. 1985-88
Clev. 1990-91
McRae, Hal KC 1991-1994
TB 2001-
Mele, Sam Minn. 1961-67
Merrill, Stump NY 1990-91
Metro, Charlie KC 1970
Michael, Gene NY 1981;82
Milan, Clyde Wash. 1922
Miller, Ray Minn. 1985-86
Balt. 1998-99
Moore, Jackie, Oak. 1984-86
Morgan, Joe M. Bos. 1988-91
Moriarty, George Det. 1927-28
Moss, Les Det. 1979
Muser, Tony KC 1998-
Narron, Jerry Tex. 2001-
Neun, Johnny NY 1946
Norman, Bill Det. 1958-59
Oates, Johnny Balt. 1991-1994
Tex. 1995-2001
O'Connor, Jack StL. 1910
O'Neill, Steve Clev. 1935-37
Det. 1943-48
Bos. 1950-51
Onslow, Jack Chi. 1949-50
Parrish, Larry Det. 1998-99
Peckinpaugh, Roger NY 1914
Clev. 1928-33;41
Pesky, Johnny Bos. 1963-64
Philips, Lefty Cal. 1969-71
Piniella, Lou NY 1986-87;88
Sea. 1993-
Plummer, Bill Sea. 1992
Queen, Mel Tor. 1997
Quilici, Frank Minn. 1972-75
Rader, Doug Tex. 1983-85
Cal. 1989-91
Regan, Phil Balt. 1995
Rice, Del Cal. 1972
Richards, Paul Chi. 1951-54;76
Balt. 1955-61
Rickey, Branch, StL. 1913-15
Rigney, Bill Cal. 1961-69
Minn. 1970-72
Ripken, Cal, Sr. Balt. 1987-88
Robinson, Frank Clev. 1975-77
Balt. 1988-91
Robinson, Wilbert Balt. 1902
Rodgers, Buck Mil. 1980-82
Cal. 1991-1994
Rojas, Cookie Cal. 1988
Rolfe, Red Det. 1949-52
Rothschild, Larry TB 1998-2001
Rowland, Pants Chi. 1915-18
Ruel, Muddy StL. 1947
Ryan, Connie Tex. 1977
Schalk, Ray Chi. 1927-28
Scheffing, Bob Det. 1961-63
Schultz, Joe Sea. 1969
Scioscia, Mike Ana. 2000-
Sewell, Luke StL. 1941-46
Shawkey, Bob NY 1930
Sherry, Norm Cal. 1976-77
Showalter, Buck NY 1992-95
Sisler, George StL. 1924-26
Skaff, Frank Det. 1966
Smith, Mayo Det. 1967-70
Snyder, Jimmy Sea. 1988
Speaker, Tris Clev. 1919-26
Stahl, Jake Wash. 1905-06
Bos. 1912-13
Stahl, Chick Bos. 1906

Stallings, George Det. 1901
NY 1909-10
Stanky, Eddie Chi. 1966-68
Tex. 1977
Stengel, Casey NY 1949-60
Stovall, George Clev. 1911
StL. 1912-13
Street, Gabby StL. 1938
Strickland, George Clev. 1966
Stubing, Moose Cal. 1988
Sullivan, Haywood, KC 1965
Sullivan, Billy, Sr. Chi. 1909
Swift, Bob Det. 1965-66
Tanner, Chuck Chi. 1970-75
Oak. 1976
Taylor, Zack StL. 1948-51
Tebbetts, Birdie Clev. 1963-66
Tighe, Jack Det. 1957-58
Torborg, Jeff Clev. 1977-79
Chi. 1989-1991
Torre, Joe NY 1996-
Trebelhorn, Tom Mil. 1986-91
Unglaub, Bob Bos. 1907
Valentine, Bobby Tex. 1985-92
Vernon, Mickey Wash. 1961-63
Virdon, Bill NY 1974-75
Vitt, Ossie Clev. 1938-40
Wagner, Heinie Bos. 1930
Wallace, Bobby StL. 1911-12
Wathan, John KC 1987-1991
Weaver, Earl Balt. 1968-82;85-86
Williams, Jimy Tor. 1986-89
Bos. 1997-2001
Williams, Dick Bos. 1967-69
Oak. 1971-73
Cal. 1974-76
Sea. 1986-88
Williams, Ted Wash./Tex. 1969-72
Wills, Maury Sea 1980-81
Winkles, Bobby Cal. 1973-74
Oak. 1977-78
Wolverton, Harry NY 1912
Zimmer, Don Bos. 1976-80
Tex. 1981-82

MANAGERS — NATIONAL LEAGUE

(Since 1901)
Alou, Felipe Mtl. 1992-2001
Alston, Walter Brk/LA 1954-76
Altobelli, Joe SF 1977-79
Amalfitano, Joey Chi. 1980-81
Anderson, Sparky Cin. 1970-78
Baker, Dusty SF 1993-
Bamberger, George NY 1982-83
Bancroft, Dave Bos. 1924-27
Bancroft, Frank Cin. 1902
Baylor, Don Col. 1993-98
Chi. 2000-
Bell, Buddy Col. 2000-
Berra, Yogi NY 1972-75
Bezdek, Hugo Pitt. 1917-19
Bissonette, Del Bos. 1945
Blades, Ray StL. 1939-40
Bochy, Bruce SD 1995-
Boles, John Fla. 1996,99-2001
Boros, Steve SD 1986
Boudreau, Lou Chi. 1960
Bowa, Larry SD, 1987-88
Phil. 2001-
Bowerman, Frank Bos. 1909
Boyer, Ken StL. 1978-80
Bragan, Bobby Pitt. 1956-57
Mil./Atl 1963-66

Bob Brenly Ari. 2001-
Bresnahan, Roger StL. 1909-12
Chi. 1915
Bristol, Dave Cin. 1966-69
Atl. 1976-77
SF 1979-80
Buckenberger, Al Bos. 1902-04
Burke, Jimmy StL. 1905
Bush, Donie Pitt. 1927-29
Cin. 1933
Callahan, Nixey Pitt. 1916-17
Carey, Max Brk. 1932-33
Cavarretta, Phil Chi. 1951-53
Chance, Frank Chi. 1905-12
Chapman, Ben Phil. 1945-48
Clarke, Fred Pitt. 1901-15
Coleman, Bob Bos. 1944-45
Coleman, Jerry SD 1980
Collins, Terry Hou. 1994-96
Coombs, Jack Phil. 1919
Corrales, Pat Phil. 1982-83
Cox, Bobby Atl. 1978-81;90-
Craft, Harry Chi. 1961
Hou. 1962-64
Craig, Roger SD 1978-79
SF 1985-92
Cravath, Gavvy Phil. 1919-20
Dahlen, Bill Brk. 1910-13
Dark, Alvin SF 1961-64
SD 1977
Davenport, Jim SF 1985
Davis, George NY 1901
Dierker, Larry Hou. 1997-2001
Donovan, Patsy StL. 1901-03
Brk. 1906-08
Donovan, Wild Bill Phil. 1921
Dooin, Red Phil. 1910-14
Dressen, Chuck Cin. 1934-37
Brk. 1951-53
Mil. 1960-61
Duffy, Hugh Phil. 1904-06
Durocher, Leo Brk. 1939-46;48
NY 1948-55
Chi. 1966-72
Hou. 1972-73
Dyer, Eddie StL. 1946-50
Dykes, Jimmy Cin. 1958
Elia, Lee Chi. 1982-83
Phil. 1987-88
Ens, Jewell Pitt. 1929-31
Essian, Jim Chi. 1991
Evers, Johnny Chi. 1913;21
Fanning, Jim Mtl. 1981-82;84
Felske, John Phil. 1985-87
Fitzsimmons, Freddie Phil. 1943-45
Fletcher, Art Phil. 1923-26
Fogel, Horace NY 1902
Fox, Charlie SF 1970-74
Mtl. 1976
Chi. 1983
Francona, Terry Phil. 1997-2000
Franks, Herman L. SF 1965-68
Chi. 1977-79
Frazier, Joe NY 1976-77
Fregosi, Jim Phil. 1991-96
Frey, Jim Chi. 1984-86
Frisch, Frankie StL. 1933-38
Pitt. 1940-46
Chi. 1949-51
Fuchs, Judge Bos. 1929
Ganzel, John Cin. 1908
Garner, Phil Mil 1998-99
Gibson, George Pitt. 1920-22;32-34
Chi. 1925

Gomez, Preston SD 1969-72
  Hou. 1974-75
  Chi. 1980
Gonzales, Mike StL. 1938;40
Green, Dallas Phil. 1979-81
  NY 1993-96
Griffith, Clark Cin. 1909-11
Grimes, Burleigh Brk. 1937-38
Grimm, Charlie Chi. 1932-38;44-49;60
  Bos./Mil. 1952-56
Haas, Eddie Atl. 1985
Hack, Stan Chi. 1954-56
  StL. 1958
Haney, Fred Pitt. 1953-55
  Mil. 1956-59
Hanlon, Ned Brk. 1901-05
  Cin. 1906-07
Harrelson, Bud NY 1990-91
Harris, Lum Hou. 1964-65
  Atl. 1968-72
Harris, Bucky Phil. 1943
Hartnett, Gabby Chi. 1938-40
Hatton, Grady Hou. 1966-68
Heffner, Don Cin. 1966
Helms, Tommy Cin. 1989
Hemus, Solly StL. 1959-61
Hendricks, Jack StL. 1918
  Cin. 1924-29
Herman, Billy Pitt. 1947
Herzog, Buck Cin. 1914-16
Herzog, Whitey StL. 1980-90
Himsl, Vedie Chi. 1961
Hitchcock, Billy Atl. 1966-67
Hodges, Gil NY 1968-71
Hoffman, Glenn LA 1998
Holmes, Tommy Bos. 1951-52
Hornsby, Rogers StL. 1925-26
  Bos. 1928
  Chi. 1930-32
  Cin. 1952-53
Howard, Frank SD 1981
  NY 1983
Howe, Art Hou. 1989-93
Howley, Dan Cin. 1930-32
Huggins, Miller StL. 1913-17
Hutchinson, Fred Phil. 1956-58
  Cin. 1959-64
Johnson, Davey NY 1984-90
  Cin. 1993-95
  LA 1999-2000
Jorgensen, Mike StL. 1995
Keane, Johnny StL. 1961-64
Kelley, Joe Cin. 1902-05
  Bos. 1908
Kennedy, Bob Chi. 1963-65
Killefer, Bill Chi. 1921-25
King, Clyde SF 1969-70
  Atl. 1974-75
Klein, Lou Chi. 1961;62;65
Kling, Johnny Bos. 1912
Knight, Ray Cin. 1996-97
Kuehl, Karl Mtl. 1976
Lachemann, Rene Fla. 1993-96
Lake, Fred Bos. 1910
Lamont, Gene Pitt. 1997-2000
Lanier, Hal Hou. 1986-88
LaRussa, Tony StL. 1996-
Lasorda, Tommy LA 1977-96
Lefebvre, Jim Chi. 1992-93
  Mil. 1999
Leyland, Jim Pitt. 1986-96
  Fla. 1997-98
  Col. 1999
Leyva, Nick Phil. 1989-91
Lillis, Bob Hou. 1982-85
Lobert, Hans Phil. 1938;42

Lockman, Whitey Chi. 1972-74
Loftus, Tom Chi. 1901
Lopes, Davey Mil. 2000-
Lucchesi, Frank Phil. 1970-72
  Chi. 1987
Lumley, Harry Brk. 1909
Maranville, Rabbit Chi. 1925
Marion, Marty StL. 1951
Marshall, Jim Chi. 1974-76
Mathews, Eddie Atl. 1972-74
Mathewson, Christy Cin. 1916-18
Mauch, Gene Phil. 1960-68
  Mtl. 1969-75
McCarthy, Joe Chi. 1926-30
McClendon, Lloyd Pitt. 2001-
McCloskey, John StL. 1906-08
McGraw, John NY 1902-32
McInnis, Stuffy Phil. 1927
McKechnie, Bill Pitt. 1922-26
  StL. 1928-29
  Bos. 1930-37
  Cin. 1938-46
McKeon, Jack SD 1988-90
  Cin. 1997-2000
McMillan, Roy NY 1975
McNamara, John SD 1974-77
  Cin. 1979-82
McPhee, Bid Cin. 1901-02
Metro, Charlie Chi. 1962
Meyer, Billy Pitt. 1948-52
Michael, Gene Chi. 1986-87
Mitchell, Fred Chi. 1917-20
  Bos. 1921-23
Moore, Terry Phil. 1954
Moran, Pat Phil. 1915-18
  Cin. 1919-23
Murray, Billy Phil. 1907-09
Murtaugh, Danny Pitt.1957-64;67,
  70-71;73-76
Myatt, George Phil. 1969
Neun, Johnny Cin. 1947-48
Nichols, Kid StL. 1904-05
Nixon, Russ Cin. 1982-83
  Atl. 1988-90
O'Day, Hank Cin. 1912
  Chi. 1914
O'Farrell, Bob StL. 1927
  Cin. 1934
O'Neill, Steve Phil. 1952-54
Ott, Mel NY 1942-48
Owens, Paul Phil. 1972;83-84
Ozark, Danny Phil. 1973-79
  SF 1984
Perez, Tony Cin. 1993
  Fla. 2001
Piniella, Lou Cin. 1990-92
Prothro, Doc Phil. 1939-41
Rapp, Vern StL. 1977-78
  Cin. 1984
Rickey, Branch StL. 1919-25
Riddoch, Greg SD 1990-92
Riggleman, Jim SD 1992-1994
  Chi. 1995-99
Rigney, Bill NY/SF 1956-60;76
Robinson, Frank SF 1981-84
Robinson, Wilbert Brk. 1914-31
Rodgers, Buck Mtl. 1985-91
Rojas, Cookie Fla. 1996
Rose, Pete Cin. 1984-89
Runnells, Tom Mtl. 1991-92
Russell, Bill LA 1996-98
Ryan, Connie Atl. 1975
Sawyer, Eddie Phil. 1948-52;58-60
Scheffing, Bob Chi. 1957-59
Schoendienst, Red StL. 1965-76;80;90

Selee, Frank Bos. 1901
  Chi. 1902-05
Sewell, Luke Cin. 1950-52
Sheehan, Tom SF 1960
Shepard, Larry Pitt. 1968-69
Shettsline, Bill Pitt. 1901-02
Shotton, Burt Phil. 1928-33
  Brk. 1947-50
Showalter, Buck Ari. 1998-2000
Sisler, Dick Cin. 1964-65
Skinner, Bob Phil. 1968-69
Slattery, Jack Bos. 1928
Smith, Heinie NY 1902
Smith, Harry Bos. 1909
Smith, Mayo StL. 1955-58
  Cin. 1959
Southworth, Billy StL. 1929;40-45
  Bos. 1946-51
Stallings, George Bos. 1913-20
Stanky, Eddie StL. 1952-55
Stengel, Casey Brk. 1934-36
  Bos. 1938-43
  NY 1962-65
Street, Gabby StL. 1930-33
Tanner, Chuck Pitt. 1977-85
  Atl. 1986-88
Tappe, El Chi. 1961;62
Tebbetts, Birdie Cin. 1954-58
  Mil. 1961-62
Tenney, Fred Bos. 1905-07;11
Terry, Bill NY 1932-41
Tinker, Joe Cin. 1913
  Chi. 1916
Torborg, Jeff NY 1992-93
  Mtl. 2001
Torre, Joe NY 1977-81
  Atl. 1982-84
  StL. 1990-95
Tracy, Jim LA 2001-
Traynor, Pie Pitt. 1934-39
Trebelhorn, Tom Chi. 1994
Valentine, Bobby NY 1996-
Virdon, Bill Pitt. 1972-73
  Hou. 1975-82
  Mtl. 1983-84
Wagner, Honus Pitt. 1917
Walker, Harry StL. 1955
  Pitt. 1965-67
  Hou. 1968-72
Wallace, Bobby Cin. 1937
Walters, Bucky Cin. 1948-49
Westrum, Wes NY 1965-67
  SF 1974-75
Wilhelm, Kaiser Phil. 1921-22
Williams, Dick Mtl. 1977-81
  SD 1982-85
Wilson, Jimmie Phil.1934-38
  Chi. 1941-44
Wine, Bobby Atl. 1985
Zimmer, Chief Phil. 1903
Zimmer, Don SD 1972-73
  Chi. 1988-91

HOME RUN
FIRST MAJOR LEAGUE AT-BAT

= Pinch-hitter
* = NOT first plate appearance

Alyea, Brant AL:Wash. Sept. 12, 1965#
Anderson, Marlon NL:Phil. Sept. 8, 1998#
Averill, Earl AL:Clev. Apr. 16, 1929
Ayala, Benny NL:NY Aug. 27, 1974
Bankhead, Dan NL:Brk. Aug. 26, 1947
Barragan, Cuno NL:Chi. Sept. 1, 1961
Bates, Johnny NL:Bos. Apr. 12, 1906
Bell, Jay AL:Clev. Sept. 29, 1986
Brown, Gates AL:Det. June 19, 1963#
Bullinger, Jim NL:Chi. June 8, 1992
Cabrera, Alex NL:Ari. June 26, 2000
Campaneris, Bert AL:KC July 23, 1964
Clark, Will NL:SF Apr. 8, 1986
David, Andre AL:Minn. June 29, 1984
Dudley, Clise NL:Brk. Apr. 27, 1929
Duggleby, Bill NL:Phil. Apr. 21, 1898
Dye, Jermaine NL:Atl. May 17, 1996
Eiland, Dave NL:SD Apr. 10, 1992
Ernaga, Frank NL:Chi May 24, 1957
Felix, Junior AL:Tor. May 4, 1989
Fitzgerald, Mike NL:NY Sept. 13, 1983
Fullmer, Brad NL:Mtl. Sept. 2, 1997#
Gaetti, Gary AL:Minn. Sept. 20, 1981
Gainer, Jay NL:Col. May 14, 1993
Gillespie, Paul NL:Chi. Sept. 11, 1942
Gumbert, Billy NL:Pitt. June 19, 1890
Harrington, Joe NL:Bos. Sept. 10, 1895
Hasson, Gene AL:Phil. Sept. 9, 1937
Hermanson, Dustin NL:Mtl. Apr. 16, 1997
Ingram, Garey NL:LA May 19, 1994#
Jordan, Ricky NL:Phil. July 17, 1988*
Kennedy, John AL:Wash. Sept. 5, 1962#
Keough, Joe AL:Oak. Aug. 7 1968#
Kerr, Buddy NL:NY Sept. 8, 1943
Koy, Ernie NL:Brk. Apr. 19, 1938
Lamont, Gene AL:Det. Sept. 2, 1970
Layton, Les NL:NY May 21, 1948#
Lee, Carlos AL:Chi. May 7, 1999
LeFebvre, Bill AL:Bos. June 10, 1938
LeMaster, Johnnie NL:SF Sept. 2, 1975#
Leppert, Don NL:Pitt. June 18, 1961
Lockman, Whitey NL:NY July 5, 1945
Lyden, Mitch NL:Fla. June 16, 1993
Machemer, Dave AL:Cal. June 21, 1978
Martinez, Carmelo NL:Chi. Aug. 22, 1983*
McDonald, Keith NL:StL July 4, 2000
McKay, Dave AL:Minn. July 22 1975#
Miller, John AL:NY Sept. 11, 1966
Miller, Hack AL:Det. Apr. 23, 1944
Montefusco, John NL:SF Sept. 3, 1974*
Moon, Wally NL:StL. Apr. 13, 1954
Morgan, Eddie NL:StL. Apr. 14, 1936#
Mota, Guillermo NL:Mtl. June 9, 1999
Mueller, Walter NL:Pitt. May 7, 1922
Mueller, Emmett NL:Phil Apr. 19, 1938
Narum, Buster AL:Balt. May 3, 1963
Nieman, Bob AL:StL. Sept. 14, 1951
Nunnally, Jon AL:KC Apr. 29, 1995
Offerman, Jose NL:LA Aug. 19, 1990
Parker, Ace AL:Phil. Apr. 30, 1937#
Pellagrini, Eddie AL:Bos. Apr. 22, 1946

Renick, Rick AL:Minn. July 11, 1968
Richard, Chris NL:StL July 17, 2000
Roman, Bill AL:Det. Sept. 30, 1964#
Rose, Don AL:Cal. May 24, 1972
Sanders, Reggie AL:Det. Sept 1, 1974
Sanicki, Ed NL:Phil. Sept. 14, 1949
Slade, Gordon NL:Brk. May 24, 1930
Sosa, Jose NL:Hou. July 30, 1975#
Steinbach, Terry AL:Oak. Sept. 12, 1986
Stechschulte, Gene NL:StL. Apr. 17, 2001#
Stuart, Luke AL:StL. Aug. 8, 1921
Tanner, Chuck NL:Mil. Apr. 12, 1955#
Tappe, Ted NL:Cin. Sept 14, 1950#
Tillman, Bob AL:Bos. May 19, 1962*
Vico, George AL:Det. Apr. 20, 1948
Vollmer, Clyde NL:Cin. May 31, 1942
Wallach, Tim NL:Mtl. Sept. 6, 1980*
White, Bill NL:NY May 7, 1956
Wilhelm, Hoyt NL:NY Apr. 23, 1952
Woods, Al AL:Tor. Apr. 7, 1977#
Yan, Esteban, AL:TB June 4, 2000

TRIPLE CROWN WINNERS

Rogers Hornsby NL:StL. 1922
Rogers Hornsby NL:StL. 1925
Jimmie Foxx AL:Phil. 1933
Chuck Klein NL:Phil. 1933
Lou Gehrig AL:NY 1934
Joe Medwick NL:StL. 1937
Ted Williams AL:Bos. 1942
Ted Williams AL:Bos. 1947
Mickey Mantle AL:NY 1956
Frank Robinson AL:Balt. 1966
Carl Yastrzemski AL:Bos. 1967

50 OR MORE HOME RUNS, SEASON

73	Barry Bonds NL:SF 2001
70	Mark McGwire NL:StL. 1998
66	Sammy Sosa NL:Chi. 1998
65	Mark McGwire NL:StL. 1999
64	Sammy Sosa NL:Chi. 2001
63	Sammy Sosa NL:Chi. 1999
61	Roger Maris AL:NY 1961
60	Babe Ruth AL:NY 1927
59	Babe Ruth AL:NY 1921
58	Jimmie Foxx AL:Phil. 1932
58	Hank Greenberg AL:Det. 1938
58	Mark McGwire AL:Oak.-NL:StL. 1997
57	Luis Gonzalez NL:Ari. 2001
56	Hack Wilson NL:Chi. 1930
56	Ken Griffey, Jr. AL:Sea. 1997
56	Ken Griffey, Jr. AL:Sea. 1998
54	Babe Ruth AL:NY 1920
54	Babe Ruth AL:NY 1928
54	Ralph Kiner NL:Pitt. 1949
54	Mickey Mantle AL:NY 1961
52	Mickey Mantle AL:NY 1956
52	Willie Mays NL:SF 1965
52	Mark McGwire AL:Oak. 1996
52	George Foster NL:Cin. 1977
52	Alex Rodriguez AL:Tex. 2001
51	Ralph Kiner NL:Pitt. 1947
51	Johnny Mize NL:NY 1947
51	Willie Mays NL:NY 1955
51	Cecil Fielder AL:Det. 1990
50	Jimmie Foxx AL:Bos. 1938
50	Albert Belle AL:Clev. 1995
50	Brady Anderson AL:Balt. 1996
50	Greg Vaughn NL:SD 1998
50	Sosa, Sammy NL:Chi. 2000

MOST HRs, LIFETIME, BY POSITION

National League:

1B:	439	Willie McCovey (2045 g)
2B:	277	Ryne Sandberg (1985 g)
3B:	509	Mike Schmidt (2212 g)
SS:	277	Ernie Banks (1125 g)
OF:	661	Hank Aaron (2756 g)
C:	327	Johnny Bench (1744 g)
P:	35	Warren Spahn (750 g)
DH:	6	Greg Vaughn (13 g)

American League:

1B:	493	Lou Gehrig (2150 g)
2B:	246	Joe Gordon (1519 g)
3B:	319	Graig Nettles (1997 g)
SS:	345	Cal Ripken (2302 g)
OF:	692	Babe Ruth (2212 g)
C:	351	Carlton Fisk (2226 g)
P:	36	Wes Ferrell (369 g)
DH:	235	Harold Baines (1644 g)

Major Leagues (higher than league records):

OF:	698	Babe Ruth AL: 692; NL: 6 (2238 g)
1B:	566	Mark McGwire AL: 349; NL: 217 (1763 g)

MOST HRs, SEASON, BY POSITION

National League:

1B:	69	Mark McGwire, StL. 1998 (155 g)
2B:	42	Rogers Hornsby, StL. 1922 (154 g)
		Davey Johnson, Atl. 1973 (157 g)
3B:	48	Mike Schmidt, Phil. 1980 (162 g)
SS:	47	Ernie Banks, Chi. 1958 (154 g)
OF:	71	Barry Bonds, SF 2001 (143 g)
C:	41	Todd Hundley, NY 1996 (150 g)
P:	7	Don Newcombe, Brk. 1955 (34 g)
		Don Drysdale, LA 1958 (44 g)
		Don Drysdale, LA 1965 (44 g)
		Mike Hampton, Col. 2001 (32 g)
DH:	2	By many players

American League:

1B:	58	Hank Greenberg, Det. 1938 (154 g)
2B:	36	Bret Boone, Sea. 2001 (156 g)
3B:	46	Troy Glaus, Ana. 2000 (156 g)
SS:	52	Alex Rodriguez, Tex. 2001 (161 g)
OF:	61	Roger Maris, NY 1961 (161 g)
C:	35	Ivan Rodriguez, Tex. 1999 (141 g)
P:	9	Wes Ferrell, Clev. 1931 (40 g)
DH:	37	Rafael Palmeiro, Tex. 1999 (128 g)
		Edgar Martinez, Sea. 2000 (146 g)

CLUB HOME RUN LEADERS, SEASON

National League:

ARIZONA	57	Luis Gonzalez 2001
ATLANTA	47	Eddie Mathews (Mil.) 1953
		Hank Aaron 1971
CHICAGO	66	Sammy Sosa 1998
CINCINNATI	52	George Foster 1977
COLORADO	49	Larry Walker 1997
		Todd Helton 2001
FLORIDA	42	Gary Sheffield 1996
HOUSTON	47	Jeff Bagwell 2000
LOS ANGELES	49	Shawn Green 2001
MILWAUKEE	45	Gorman Thomas (AL) 1979
		Richie Sexson 2001
MONTREAL	44	Vladimir Guerrero 2000
NEW YORK	41	Todd Hundley 1996
PHILADELPHIA	48	Mike Schmidt 1980
PITTSBURGH	54	Ralph Kiner 1949
ST. LOUIS	70	Mark McGwire 1998
SAN DIEGO	50	Greg Vaughn 1998
SAN FRANCISCO	73	Barry Bonds 2001

American League:

ANAHEIM	47	Troy Glaus 2000
BALTIMORE	50	Brady Anderson 1996
BOSTON	50	Jimmie Foxx 1938
CHICAGO	49	Albert Belle 1998
CLEVELAND	50	Albert Belle 1995
DETROIT	58	Hank Greenberg 1938
KANSAS CITY	36	Steve Balboni 1985
MINNESOTA	49	Harmon Killebrew 1964
		Harmon Killebrew 1969
NEW YORK	61	Roger Maris 1961
OAKLAND	58	Jimmie Foxx (Phil.) 1932
SEATTLE	56	Ken Griffey, Jr. 1997
		Ken Griffey, Jr. 1998
TAMPA BAY	34	Jose Canseco 1999
TEXAS	52	Alex Rodriguez 2001
TORONTO	47	George Bell 1987

200 OR MORE HOMERS

(At-Bats per Home Run in parentheses; Active Players in Boldface)

755 Aaron, Hank (16.38)
714 Ruth, Babe (11.76)
660 Mays, Willie (16.49)
586 Robinson, Frank (17.08)
583 McGwire, Mark (10.61)
573 Killebrew, Harmon (14.22)
567 Bonds, Barry (13.99)
563 Jackson, Reggie (17.52)
548 Schmidt, Mike (15.24)
536 Mantle, Mickey (15.12)
534 Foxx, Jimmie (15.23)
521 McCovey, Willie (15.73)
521 Williams, Ted (14.79)
512 Banks, Ernie (18.40)
512 Mathews, Eddie (16.67)
511 Ott, Mel (18.50)
504 Murray, Eddie (22.49)
493 Gehrig, Lou (16.23)
475 Musial, Stan (23.10)
475 Stargell, Willie (16.69)
465 Winfield, Dave (23.66)
462 Canseco, Jose (15.27)
460 Griffey, Ken, Jr. (14.60)
452 Yastrzemski, Carl (26.52)
450 Sosa, Sammy (14.38)
448 McGriff, Fred (17.56)
447 Palmeiro, Rafael (18.89)
442 Kingman, Dave (15.11)
438 Dawson, Andre (22.66)
431 Ripken, Cal (26.80)
426 Williams, Billy (21.95)
414 Evans, Darrell (21.67)
407 Snider, Duke (17.59)
399 Kaline, Al (25.35)
398 Murphy, Dale (20.00)
397 Gonzalez, Juan (14.67)
396 Carter, Joe (21.27)
390 Nettles, Graig (23.04)
389 Bench, Johnny (19.69)
385 Evans, Dwight (23.37)
384 Baines, Harold (25.80)
382 Howard, Frank (16.98)
382 Rice, Jim (21.53)
381 Belle, Albert (15.36)
379 Cepeda, Orlando (20.92)
379 Perez,Tony (25.80)
377 Cash, Norm (17.79)
377 Galarraga, Andres (19.95)
376 Fisk, Carlton (23.29)
374 Colavito, Rocky (17.39)
370 Hodges, Gil (19.00)
369 Kiner, Ralph (14.11)
362 Williams, Matt (18.37)
361 DiMaggio, Joe (18.89)
360 Gaetti, Gary (24.86)
359 Mize, Johnny (17.95)
358 Berra, Yogi (21.10)
354 May, Lee (21.49)
351 Allen, Dick (18.04)
350 Davis, Chili (24.78)
349 Bagwell, Jeff (17.05)
348 Foster, George (20.18)
348 Thomas, Frank (15.93)
344 Vaughn, Greg (16.90)
342 Santo, Ron (23.81)
340 Clark, Jack (20.14)
339 Parker, Dave (27.60)
339 Powell, Boog (19.71)
338 Baylor, Don (24.25)
336 Adcock, Joe (19.66)
335 Strawberry, Darryl (16.17)
332 Bonds, Bobby (21.21)
331 Greenberg, Hank (15.69)
325 Horton, Willie (22.46)
324 Carter, Gary (24.60)
324 Parrish, Lance (21.28)
319 Fielder, Cecil (16.17)
318 Sievers, Roy (20.08)
317 Brett, George (32.65)

316 Cey, Ron (22.66)
315 Sheffield, Gary (17.97)
314 Piazza, Mike (14.77)
314 Smith, Reggie (22.40)
313 Burks, Ellis (20.71)
310 Buhner, Jay (16.17)
309 Walker, Larry (17.49)
307 Luzinski, Greg (21.19)
307 Simmons, Al (28.54)
306 Lynn, Fred (22.63)
302 Gant, Ron (20.20)
301 Hornsby, Rogers (27.15)
300 Klein, Chuck (21.62)
299 Vaughn, Mo (16.61)
294 Justice, David (17.78)
293 Hrbek, Kent (21.13)
292 Staub, Rusty (33.29)
291 Wynn, Jimmy (22.86)
290 Henderson, Rickey (36.93)
288 Ennis, Del (25.19)
288 Johnson, Bob (24.03)
288 Sauer, Hank (16.65)
287 Bonilla, Bobby (25.13)
286 Thomas, Frank J. (21.98)
284 Clark, Will (25.26)
282 Boyer, Ken (26.44)
282 Davis, Eric (18.87)
282 Sandberg, Ryne (29.73)
282 Thome, Jim (14.75)
281 O'Neill, Paul (26.04)
279 Kluszewski, Ted (21.25)
277 Ramirez, Manny (14.44)
277 York, Rudy (21.27)
275 Downing, Brian (28.56)
275 Maris, Roger (18.55)
275 Palmer, Dean (17.47)
274 Bichette, Dante (23.29)
272 Garvey, Steve (32.48)
271 Brunansky, Tom (23.21)
271 Scott, George (27.43)
268 Morgan, Joe (34.62)
268 Robinson, Brooks (39.75)
268 Thomas, Gorman (17.45)
267 Hendrick, George (26.70)
266 Wertz, Vic (22.93)
265 Bell, George (23.11)
264 Thomson, Bobby (23.88)
263 Martinez, Tino (20.39)
263 Sierra, Ruben (25.90)
262 Tartabull, Danny (19.13)
260 Wallach, Tim (31.15)
258 Martinez, Edgar (22.88)
257 Karros, Eric (21.32)
256 Allison, Bob (19.66)
256 Parrish, Larry (26.53)
256 Pinson, Vada (37.68)
255 Gibson, Kirk (22.74)
255 Mayberry, John (21.36)
253 Doby, Larry (21.14)
253 Gordon, Joe (22.56)
253 Thornton, Andre (20.91)
252 Murcer, Bobby (26.71)
252 Torre, Joe (31.25)
251 Armas, Tony (20.57)
251 Williams, Cy (27.01)
251 Yount, Robin (43.86)
248 Ventura, Robin (24.42)
248 Goslin, Goose (34.90)
247 Salmon, Tim (18.32)
247 Stephens, Vern (26.30)
246 Singleton, Ken (29.22)
245 Johnson, Deron (24.25)
245 Tettleton, Mickey (19.18)
244 Whitaker, Lou (35.12)
244 Wilson, Hack (19.51)
242 Baker, Dusty (29.41)
242 Bando, Sal (29.17)
242 Berger, Wally (21.33)
242 Campanella, Roy (17.38)
241 Barfield, Jesse (19.75)
241 Cooper, Cecil (30.49)
241 Monday, Rick (25.46)
241 Rodriguez, Alex (15.59)

240 Burroughs, Jeff (23.07)
240 Clemente, Roberto (39.39)
239 Camilli, Dolph (22.40)
239 Caminiti, Ken (26.31)
238 Averill, Earl (26.69)
237 DeCinces, Doug (24.51)
237 Zernial, Gus (17.43)
236 Hartnett, Gabby (27.25)
235 Nicholson, Bill (23.60)
235 Oglivie, Ben (25.16)
234 Castilla, Vinny (18.74)
234 Matthews, Gary (30.54)
234 Mitchell,Kevin (17.67)
234 Molitor, Paul (46.30)
230 Deer, Rob (16.87)
229 Delgado, Carlos (15.17)
228 Johnson, Howard (21.67)
228 Stuart, Dick (17.53)
228 Trosky, Hal (22.64)
227 Jones, Chipper (17.80)
226 Callison, Johnny (29.43)
226 Lankford, Ray (23.64)
224 Grich, Bobby (30.76)
223 Doerr, Bobby (31.81)
222 Mattingly, Don (31.55)
221 Gonzalez, Luis (25.81)
220 Oliva, Tony (28.64)
219 Bottomley, Jim (34.11)
219 Oliver, Al (41.32)
219 Pepitone, Joe (23.27)
218 Horner, Bob (17.33)
216 Kent, Jeff (22.85)
215 Fairly, Ron (33.41)
215 Guerrero, Pedro (25.08)
215 Lemon, Chet (31.94)
215 Zeile, Todd (29.86)
214 Mondesi, Raul (20.78)
213 Pafko, Andy (29.54)
212 Fryman, Travis (28.70)
211 McReynolds, Kevin (25.70)
211 Skowron, Bill (26.29)
211 Wagner, Leon (20.98)
210 Petrocelli, Rico (25.67)
210 Post, Wally (19.08)
209 Anderson, Brady (30.71)
208 Thompson, Jason (23.09)
208 White, Devon (35.31)
207 Olerud, John (28.51)
207 Puckett, Kirby (35.00)
207 Williams, Bernie (25.83)
207 Zisk, Richie (24.85)
206 Alou, Felipe (35.63)
206 Bell, Gus (31.45)
206 Incaviglia, Pete (20.55)
205 Medwick, Joe (37.24)
204 Carty, Rico (27.48)
204 Joyner, Wally (34.94)
203 Hebner, Richie (30.27)
202 Alou, Moises (20.98)
202 Dickey, Bill (31.19)
202 Finley, Steve (33.77)
202 Gordon, Sid (24.71)
202 White, Bill (29.56)
201 Bell, Buddy (44.75)
201 Tenace, Gene (21.84)
200 Freehan, Bill (30.37)
200 Gamble, Oscar (22.51)
200 Mincher, Don (20.13)

3+ HOME RUNS, GAME
*Consecutive; ( ) extra innings
(Four-HR Games in Boldface)

AMERICAN ASSOCIATION

Hecker, Guy Lou.	*Aug. 15, 1886

AMERICAN LEAGUE

Allison, Bob Minn	May 17, 1963
Alomar, Roberto Balt.	*Apr. 26, 1997
Averill, Earl Clev.	*Sept. 17, 1930
Avila, Bobby Clev.	June 20, 1951
Baerga, Carlos Clev.	June 17, 1993
Baines, Harold Chi.	July 7, 1982
Baines, Harold Chi. #2	Sept. 17, 1984
Baines, Harold Oak. #3	May 7, 1991
Baylor, Don Balt.	*July 2, 1975
Bell, George Tor	Apr. 4, 1988
Belle, Albert Clev. (12)	Sept. 6, 1992
Belle, Albert Clev. #2	*Sept. 19, 1995
Belle, Albert Balt. #3 (11)	July 25, 1999
Beniquez, Juan Balt.	*June 12, 1986
Berroa, Geronimo Oak.	May 22, 1996
Berroa, Geronimo Oak #2	Aug. 12, 1996
Blair, Paul Balt.	Apr. 29, 1970
Blefary, Curt Balt	June 6, 1967
Boros, Steve Det	Aug. 6, 1962
Brantley, Mickey Sea.	Sept. 14, 1987
Brett, George KC	July 22, 1979
Brett, George KC #2	Apr. 20, 1983
Brunansky, Tom Bos.	*Sept. 29, 1990
Burks, Ellis Clev. (12)	June 19, 2001
Burroughs, Jeff Sea.	Aug. 14, 1981
Canseco, Jose Oak(16)	July 3, 1988
Canseco, Jose Tex.#2	June 13, 1994
Carter, Joe Clev.	Aug. 29, 1986
Carter, Joe Clev. #2	May 28, 1987
Carter, Joe Clev. #3	*June 24, 1989
Carter, Joe Clev. #4	July 19, 1989
Carter, Joe Tor. #5	Aug. 23, 1993
Cerv, Bob KC	Aug. 20, 1959
Chapman, Sam Phil.	Aug. 15, 1946
Chapman, Ben NY	July 9, 1932
Clark, Jack Bos. (14)	July 31, 1991
Cobb, Ty Det.	May 5, 1925
Cochrane, Mickey Phil.	May 21, 1925
Colavito, Rocky Clev.	*June 10, 1959
Colavito, Rocky Det. #2	Aug. 27, 1961
Colavito, Rocky Det. #3	*July 5, 1962
Coleman, Ed Phil.	*Aug. 17, 1934
Coles, Darnell Tor.NL:1	July 5, 1994
Connors, Merv Chi.	*Sept. 17, 1938
Cooper, Cecil Mil.	July 27, 1979
DeCinces, Doug Cal.	*Aug. 3, 1982
DeCinces, Doug Cal. #2	Aug. 8, 1982
Delgado, Carlos Tor.	*Aug. 4, 1998
Delgado, Carlos Tor. #2	Aug. 6, 1999
Delgado, Carlos Tor. #3	*Apr. 4, 2001
Delgado, Carlos Tor. #4	Apr. 20, 2001
Dickey, Bill NY	July 26, 1939
DiMaggio, Joe NY (11)	June 13, 1937
DiMaggio, Joe NY #2	*May 23, 1948
DiMaggio, Joe NY #3	Sept. 10, 1950
Doby, Larry Clev.	*Aug. 2, 1950
Doerr, Bobby Bos.	*June 8, 1950
Epstein, Mike Wash.	May 16, 1969
Fielder, Cecil Det.	*May 6, 1990
Fielder, Cecil Det. #2	*June 6, 1990
Fielder, Cecil Det. #3	Apr. 16, 1996
Fletcher, Darrin Tor.	Aug. 27, 2000
Ford, Dan Balt.	July 20, 1983
Foxx, Jimmie Phil. (18)	July 10, 1932
Foxx, Jimmie Phil. #2	June 8, 1933
Freehan, Bill Det.	Aug. 9, 1971
Garciaparra, Nomar Bos.	May 10, 1999
Gehrig, Lou NY	June 23, 1927
Gehrig, Lou NY #2	May 4, 1929

Gehrig, Lou NY #3	May 22, 1930
Gehrig, Lou NY #4	***June 3, 1932**
Glynn, Bill Clev.	*July 5, 1954
Gonzalez, Juan Tex.	June 7, 1992
Gonzalez, Juan Tex.#2	Aug. 28, 1993
Gonzalez, Juan Tex. #3	Sept. 24, 1999
Goslin, Goose Wash. (12)	June 19, 1925
Goslin, Goose StL. #2	*Aug. 19, 1930
Goslin, Goose StL. #3	June 23, 1932
Grich, Bobby Balt.	*June 18, 1974
Griffey, Ken Jr. Sea.	May 24, 1996
Griffey, Ken Jr. Sea. #2	Apr. 25, 1997
Harrelson, Ken Bos.	June 14, 1968
Hauser, Joe Phil.	Aug. 2, 1924
Henderson, Dave Oak.	*Aug. 3, 1991
Hendrick, George Clev.	*June 19, 1973
Herndon, Larry Det.	*May 18, 1982
Higgins, Pinky Phil.	June 27, 1935
Higgins, Pinky Det. #2	*May 20, 1940
Higginson, Bobby Det.	June 30, 1997
Higginson, Bobby Det. #2	June 24, 2000
Horton, Tony Clev. (11)	May 24, 1970
Horton, Willie Det.	June 9, 1970
Horton, Willie Tex. #2	May 15, 1977
Jackson, Bo KC	*July 17, 1990
Jackson, Reggie Oak.	July 2, 1969
Jackson, Reggie Cal.#2	Sept. 18, 1986
Jacoby, Brook Clev.	*July 3, 1987
Jimenez, Manny KC	*July 4, 1964
Johnson, Cliff NY	June 30, 1977
Joyner, Wally Cal.	Oct. 3, 1987
Kaline, Al Det.	Apr. 17, 1955
Keller, Charlie NY	July 28, 1940
Keltner, Ken Clev.	*May 25, 1939
Killebrew, Harmon Minn.	Sept. 21, 1963
King, Jim Wash.	June 8, 1964
Kingman, Dave Oak NL:4	*Apr. 16, 1984
Kirkland, Willie Clev.	*July 9, 1961
Lacy, Lee Balt.	June 8, 1986
Lahoud, Joe Bos.	*June 11, 1969
Lansford, Carney Cal.	*Sept. 1, 1979
Lazzeri, Tony NY (11)	June 8, 1927
Lazzeri, Tony NY #2	May 24, 1936
Lemon, Jim Wash.	Aug. 31, 1956
Leppert, Don Wash.	Apr. 11, 1963
Lopez, Hector KC (12)	June 26, 1958
Lynn, Fred Bos.	June 18, 1975
Madlock, Bill Det. (11)	June 28, 1987
Mantle, Mickey NY	May 13, 1955
Martinez, Edgar Sea.	July 6, 1996
Martinez, Edgar Sea. #2	*May 18, 1999
Martinez, Tino NY	*Apr. 2, 1997
Maxwell, Charlie Det.	*May 3, 1959
Mayberry, John KC	*July 1, 1975
Mayberry, John KC #2	*June 1, 1977
McCraw, Tommy Chi.	May 24, 1967
McGwire, Mark Oak.	June 27, 1987
McGwire, Mark Oak #2 NL:3	June 11, 1995
Melton, Bill Chi.	*June 24, 1969
Milligan, Randy Balt.	*June 9, 1990
Mize, Johnny NY NL:5	*Sept. 15, 1950
Molitor, Paul Mil.	May 12, 1982
Mullin, Pat Det.	June 26, 1949
Murcer, Bobby NY	June 24, 1970
Murcer, Bobby NY #2	July 13, 1973
Murray, Eddie Balt.	Aug. 29, 1979
Murray, Eddie Balt. #2 (13)	Sept. 14, 1980
Murray, Eddie Balt. #3	Aug. 26, 1985
Nixon, Trot Bos.	July 24, 1999
Oglivie, Ben Mil.	July 8, 1979
Oglivie, Ben Mil. #2	*June 20, 1982
Oglivie, Ben Mil. #3 (10)	May 14, 1983
Oliva, Tony Minn.	July 3, 1973
Oliver, Al Tex.	May 23, 1979
Oliver, Al Tex. #2	*Aug. 17, 1980
O'Neill, Paul, NY	*Aug. 31, 1995

Parrish, Larry Tex. NL:3	*Apr. 29, 1985
Patek, Freddie Cal.	June 20, 1980
Powell, Boog Balt.	*Aug. 10, 1963
Powell, Boog Balt. #2	June 27, 1964
Powell, Boog Balt. #3 (11)	Aug. 15, 1966
Presley, Jim Sea.	Sept. 1, 1986
Raines, Tim Chi.	Apr. 18, 1994
Ramirez, Manny, Clev.	*Sept. 15, 1998
Ramirez, Manny, Clev. #2	Aug. 25, 1999
Reynolds, Carl Chi.	July 2, 1930
Rice, Jim Bos.	Aug. 29, 1977
Rice, Jim Bos. #2	Aug. 29, 1983
Ripken, Cal Balt.	May 28, 1996
Rodriguez, Alex Sea.	Apr. 16, 2000
Rodriguez, Ivan Tex.	*Sept. 11, 1997
Rosen, Al Clev.	Apr. 29, 1952
Ruth, Babe NY NL:1	May 21, 1930
Seerey, Pat Clev.	July 13, 1945
Seerey, Pat Chi. #2 (11)	**July 18, 1948**
Simmons, Al Phil. (11)	July 15, 1932
Snyder, Cory Clev.NL:1	May 21, 1987
Solaita, Tony KC (11)	*Sept 7, 1975
Solters, Moose StL.	*July 7, 1935
Stanley, Mike NY (1g)	Aug. 10, 1995
Stanton, LeRoy Cal. (10)	July 10, 1973
Stevens, Lee, Tex.	Apr. 13, 1998
Strawberry,Darryl NY NL:1	*Aug. 6, 1996
Sveum, Dale Mil.	July 17, 1987
Tabor, Jim Bos.	July 4, 1939
Tartabull, Danny KC	July 6, 1991
Tejada, Miguel Oak.	June 11, 1999
Tejada, Miguel Oak. #2	June 30, 2001
Thomas, Frank Chi.	*Sept 15, 1996
Thomas, Gorman, Sea.	*Apr. 11, 1985
Thomas, Lee LA	Sept. 5, 1961
Thome, Jim Clev.	*July 22, 1994
Thome, Jim Clev. #2	July 6, 2001
Tresh, Tom NY	*June 6, 1965
Trosky, Hal Clev.	May 30, 1934
Trosky, Hal Clev. #2	July 5, 1937
Valentin, John Bos. (10)	June 2, 1995
Varitek, Jason Bos.	May 20, 2001
Vaughn, Mo Bos.	*Sept 24, 1996
Vaughn, Mo Bos. #2	*May 30, 1997
Velez, Otto Tor. (10)	May 4, 1980
Vollmer, Clyde Bos.	July 26, 1951
Ward, Preston KC	Sept. 9, 1958
Washington,Claudell Chi. NL:1	July 14, 1979
Whitt, Ernie Tor.	Sept. 14, 1987
Williams, Ken StL.	Apr. 22, 1922
Williams, Matt Clev.	Apr. 25, 1997
Williams, Ted Bos.	July 14, 1946
Williams, Ted Bos #2	May 8, 1957
Williams, Ted Bos #3	June 13, 1957
Wilson,Dan Sea.	Apr 11, 1996
Winfield, Dave Cal.	*Apr 13, 1991
Yastrzemski, Carl Bos.	May 19, 1976
York, Rudy Det.	Sept. 1, 1941
Young, Ernie Oak.	May 10, 1996
Zauchin, Norm Bos.	May 27, 1955
Zernial, Gus Chi.	Oct. 1, 1950

3+ HOME RUNS, GAME
Consecutive; ( ) extra innings
(Four-HR Games in Boldface)

NATIONAL LEAGUE

Aaron, Hank Mil.	June 21, 1959
Adcock, Joe Mil.	**July 31, 1954**
Alfonzo, Edgardo NY	Aug. 30, 1999
Allen, Dick Phil.	Sept. 29, 1968
Anson, Cap Chi.	*Aug. 6, 1884
Bagwell, Jeff Hou.	*June 24, 1994
Bagwell, Jeff Hou. #2	Apr. 21, 1999
Bagwell, Jeff Hou. #3	*June 9, 1999
Bailey, Ed Cin.	June 24, 1956
Banks, Ernie Chi.	Aug. 4, 1955
Banks, Ernie Chi. #2	*Sept. 14, 1957
Banks, Ernie Chi.#3	*May 2, 1962
Banks, Ernie Chi.#4	June 9, 1963
Beckley, Jake Cin.	Sept. 26, 1897
Bell, Gus Cin.	*July 21, 1955
Bell, Gus Cin #2	*May 29, 1956
Bell, Les Bos.	June 2, 1928
Bench, Johnny Cin.	*July 26, 1970
Bench, Johnny Cin. #2	May 9, 1973
Bench, Johnny Cin. #3	May 29, 1980
Blauser, Jeff Atl. (10)	July 12, 1992
Bonds, Barry SF	Aug. 2, 1994
Bonds, Barry SF #2	May 19, 2001
Bonds, Barry SF #3	Sept. 9, 2001
Boone, Bret Cin.	*Sept. 20, 1998
Boone, Bret S.D. #2	*June 23, 2000
Brouthers, Dennis Det.	Sept. 10, 1886
Brown, Brant Chi.	June 18, 1998
Brown, Tommy Brk.	*Sept. 18, 1950
Burgess, Smoky Cin.	July 29, 1955
Burnitz, Jeromy Mil.	May 10, 2000
Burnitz, Jeromy Mil. #2	*Sept. 25, 2001
Callison, Johnny Phil.	Sept. 27, 1964
Callison, Johnny Phil. #2	June 6, 1965
Caminiti, Ken, SD	July 12, 1998
Campanella, Roy Brk.	*Aug. 26, 1950
Carter, Gary Mtl.	*Apr. 20, 1977
Carter, Gary NY #2	*Sept. 3, 1985
Carty, Rico Atl.	May 31, 1970
Castilla, Vinny Col.	June 5, 1999
Castilla, Vinny Hou. #2 (13)	July 28, 2001
Cepeda, Orlando Atl.	July 26, 1970
Cirillo, Jeff Col.	June 28, 2000
Clemente, Roberto Pitt.	May 15, 1967
Clemente, Roberto Pitt. #2	*Aug. 13, 1969
Colbert, Nate SD	Aug. 1, 1972
Coles, Darnell, Pitt. AL:1	Sept. 30, 1987
Connor, Roger NY	May 9, 1888
Cooper, Walker Cin.	July 6, 1949
Davis, Eric Cin	Sept. 10, 1986
Davis, Eric Cin. #2	*May 3, 1987
Davis, Glenn Hou.	*Sept. 10, 1987
Davis, Glenn Hou. #2 (11)	*June 1, 1990
Dawson, Andre Mtl.	Sept. 24, 1985
Dawson, Andre Chi. #2	*Aug. 1, 1987
Delahanty, Ed Phil.	**July 13, 1896**
Demeter, Don LA (11)	Apr. 21, 1959
Demeter, Don Phil. #2	Sept. 12, 1961
Elliott, Bob Bos.	Sept. 24, 1949
Elster, Kevin LA	Apr. 11, 2000
Ennis, Del Phil.	July 23, 1955
Estalella, Bobby Phil.	Sept. 4, 1997
Evans, Darrell SF	June 15, 1983
Finley, Steve SD	May 19, 1997
Finley, Steve SD #2	June 23, 1997
Finley, Steve Ari. #3	*Sept. 8, 1999
Foster, George Cin.	*July 14, 1977
Fournier, Jack Brk.	*July 13, 1926
Galarraga, Andres Col.	*June 25, 1995
Gonzalez, Luis Ari.	June 8, 2001
Green, Shawn LA	Aug. 15, 2001
Greene, Willie Cin.	Sept. 24, 1996
Griffey, Ken, Sr. Atl. (11)	Jully 22, 1986
Hammonds, Jeffery Cin.	May 19, 1999
Harper, George StL.	Sept. 20, 1928
Hayes, Von Phil.	Aug. 29, 1989
Helton, Todd Col.	May 1, 2000
Henline, Butch Phil.	Sept. 15, 1922
Herman, Babe Chi.	July 20, 1933
Hermanski, Gene Brk.	*Aug. 5, 1948
Hickman, Jim NY	*Sept. 3, 1965
Hodges, Gil Brk.	**Aug. 31, 1950**
Hollandsworth, Todd Col.	*Apr. 15, 2001
Horner, Bob Atl.	**July 6, 1986**
Hornsby, Rogers Chi.	*Apr. 24, 1931
Houston, Tyler Mil.	*July 9, 2000
Jenkins, Geoff Mil.	*Apr. 28, 2001
Johnson, Deron Phil.	*July 11, 1971
Joyce, Bill Wash.	*Aug. 20, 1894
Kampouris, Alex Cin.	May 9, 1937
Kelly, George NY	*Sept. 17, 1923
Kelly, George NY #2	June 14, 1924
Kiner, Ralph Pitt.	Aug. 16, 1947
Kiner, Ralph Pitt. #2	Sept. 11, 1947
Kiner, Ralph Pitt. #3	July 5, 1948
Kiner, Ralph Pitt. #4	July 18, 1951
Kingman, Dave NY	*June 4, 1976
Kingman, Dave Chi #2 (15)	May 14, 1978
Kingman, Dave Chi #3 (10)	May 4, 1979
Kingman, Dave Chi. #4 AL:1	*July 28, 1979
Klein, Chuck Phil. (10)	**July 10, 1936**
Kluszewski, Ted Cin. (10)	July 1, 1956
Lansing, Mike, Col.	Sept. 22, 1998
Larkin, Barry Cin.	*June 28, 1991
Lee, Hal Bos.	July 6, 1934
Leiber, Hank Chi.	*July 4, 1939
Lopes, Davey LA	Aug. 20, 1974
Lowe, Bobby Bos.	***May 30, 1894**
Lum, Mike Atl.	July 3, 1970
Manning, Jack Phil.	Oct. 9, 1884
Marshall, Willard NY	*July 18, 1947
Mathews, Eddie Bos.	*Sept. 27, 1952
Matthews, Gary SF	Sept. 25, 1976
May, Lee Hou.	June 21, 1973
Mays, Willie SF	**Apr. 30, 1961**
Mays, Willie SF #2 (10)	June 29, 1961
Mays, Willie SF #3	June 2, 1963
McCovey, Willie SF	*Sept. 22, 1963
McCovey, Willie SF #2	*Apr. 22, 1964
McCovey, Willie SF #3 (10)	Sept. 17, 1966
McCreery, Tom Lou.	*July 12, 1897
McCullough, Clyde Chi.	*July 26, 1942
McGwire, Mark, StL.	Apr. 14, 1998
McGwire, Mark StL. #2	May 19, 1998
McGwire, M. StL #3 AL:2	May 18, 2000
Mejias, Roman Pitt.	May 4, 1958
Mitchell, Kevin SF	*May 25, 1990
Mitterwald, George Chi.	Apr. 17, 1974
Mize, Johnny StL.	*July 13, 1938
Mize, Johnny StL. #2	July 20, 1938
Mize, Johnny StL. #3 (14)	May 13, 1940
Mize, Johnny StL. #4	*Sept. 8, 1940
Mize, Johnny NY #5 AL:1	*Apr. 24, 1947
Monday, Rick Chi.	*May 16, 1972
Moore, Johnny Phil.	*July 22, 1936
Moryn, Walt Chi.	May 30, 1958
Mueller, Don NY	Sept. 1, 1951
Murphy, Dale Atl.	May 18, 1979
Musial, Stan StL.	May 2, 1954
Musial, Stan StL. #2	*July 8, 1962
Nevin, Phil SD	Oct. 6, 2001
Nicholson, Bill Chi.	*July 23, 1944
Oliver, Gene Atl. (2g)	July 30, 1966
Ortiz, Jose Col.	*Aug. 17, 2001
Ott, Mel NY	Aug. 31, 1930
Pafko, Andy Chi.	Aug. 2, 1950
Parrish, Larry Mtl.	*May 29, 1977
Parrish, Larry Mtl. #2	*July 30, 1978
Parrish, Larry Mtl. #3 (11) AL:1	Apr. 25, 1980
Pendleton, Jim Mil.	*Aug. 30, 1953
Phillips, Adolfo Chi.	*June 11, 1967
Piazza, Mike LA	June 29, 1996
Ramirez, Aramis Pitt.	*Apr. 8, 2001
Rhodes, Dusty NY	Apr. 26, 1953
Rhodes, Dusty NY #2	*July 28, 1954
Rhodes, Karl Chi.	*Apr. 4, 1994
Robinson, Bill Pitt. (15)	June 5, 1976
Robinson, Frank Cin.	Aug. 22, 1959
Rose, Pete Cin.	Apr. 29, 1978
Ruth, Babe Bos. AL:1	May 25, 1935
Sanders, Reggie Cin.	*Aug. 15, 1995
Santiago, Benito Phil.	Sept. 15, 1996
Sauer, Hank Chi.	Aug. 28, 1950
Sauer, Hank Chi. #2	June 11, 1952
Schmidt, Mike Phil. (10)	***Apr. 17, 1976**
Schmidt, Mike Phil.#2	*July 7, 1979
Schmidt, Mike Phil #3	*June 14, 1987
Seminick, Andy Phil.	*June 2, 1949
Sexson, Richie, Mil.	Sept. 25, 2001
Shamsky, Art Cin. (13)	*Aug. 12, 1966
Shugart, Frank StL.	*May 10, 1894
Smith, Reggie StL.	*May 22, 1976
Snider, Duke Brk.	*May 30, 1950
Snider, Duke Brk. #2	June 1, 1955
Snyder, Cory LA AL:1	Apr. 17, 1994
Sosa, Sammy Chi.	*June 5, 1996
Sosa, Sammy Chi. #2	June 15, 1998
Sosa, Sammy Chi. #3	*Aug. 9, 2001
Sosa, Sammy Chi. #4	Aug. 22, 2001
Sosa, Sammy Chi. #5	*Sept. 23, 2001
Stargell, Wilie Pitt.	June 24, 1965
Stargell, Willie Pitt. #2	May 22, 1968
Stargell, Willie Pitt. #3 (12)	Apr. 10, 1971
Stargell, Willie Pitt. #4	*Apr. 21, 1971
Strawberry, Darryl NY AL:1	Aug. 5, 1985
Stuart, Dick Pitt.	*June 30, 1960
Terry, Bill NY	*Aug. 13, 1932
Thomas, Frank Pitt.	Aug. 16, 1958
Thompson, Hank NY	*June 3, 1954
Thurman, Bob Cin.	*Aug. 18, 1956
Tillman, Bob Atl.	*July 30, 1969
Tobin, Jim Bos.	*May 13, 1942
Treadway, Jeff Atl.	May 26, 1990
Valentin, Jose, Mil.	Apr. 3, 1998
Vaughn, Greg Cin.	Sept. 7, 1999
Walker, Larry Col.	*Apr. 5, 1997
Walker, Larry Col. #2	Apr. 28, 1999
Wallach, Tim Mtl.	May 4, 1987
Walls, Lee Chi.	Apr. 24, 1958
Washington, Claudell NY AL:1	June 22, 1980
Watkins, George StL.	June 24, 1931
Westrum, Wes NY	June 24, 1950
White, Bill StL.	*July 5, 1961
Whiten, Mark StL.	**Sept. 7, 1993**
Wilber, Del Phil.	*Aug. 27, 1951
Williams, Billy Chi.	Sept. 10, 1968
Williams, Fred Phil.	May 11, 1923
Williamson, Ned Chi.	May 30, 188
Wilson, Hack Chi.	July 26, 1930
Wynn, Jimmy Hou.	*June 15, 1967
Wynn, Jimmy LA #2	May 11, 1974

GRAND SLAM HOME RUNS

Career Leaders
(Active Players in Boldface)

23	Lou Gehrig
19	Eddie Murray
18	Willie McCovey
17	Jimmie Foxx
17	Ted Williams
16	Hank Aaron
16	Dave Kingman
16	Babe Ruth
15	**Robin Ventura**
14	**Ken Griffey, Jr.**
14	Gil Hodges
14	Mark McGwire
14	**Manny Ramirez**
13	**Harold Baines**
13	Albert Belle
13	Joe DiMaggio
13	George Foster
13	Ralph Kiner
12	Ernie Banks
12	Don Baylor
12	Rogers Hornsby
12	**Mike Piazza**
12	Joe Rudi
12	Rudy York
11	Johnny Bench
11	Gary Carter
11	Eric Davis
11	Cecil Fielder
11	Gary Gaetti
11	Hank Greenberg
11	Reggie Jackson
11	Harmon Killebrew
11	Lee May
11	Willie Stargell
11	Danny Tartabull
11	**Devon White**
11	Dave Winfield

3000 OR MORE HITS

(Active Players in Boldface)

4256	Pete Rose
4191	Ty Cobb
3771	Hank Aaron
3630	Stan Musial
3515	Tris Speaker
3430	Honus Wagner
3419	Carl Yastrzemski
3319	Paul Molitor
3314	Eddie Collins
3283	Willie Mays
3255	Eddie Murray
3252	Nap Lajoie
3184	Cal Ripken
3154	George Brett
3152	Paul Waner
3142	Robin Yount
3141	Tony Gwynn
3110	Dave Winfield
3081	Cap Anson
3053	Rod Carew
3023	Lou Brock
3010	Wade Boggs
3007	Al Kaline
3000	Roberto Clemente
3000	**Rickey Henderson**

BATTERS' HITTING STREAKS, 30 OR MORE GAMES, SEASON

AMERICAN LEAGUE:

G	Year	Player & Club
56	1941	Joe DiMaggio, NY
41	1922	George Sisler, StL.
40	1911	Ty Cobb, Det.
39	1987	Paul Molitor, Mil.
35	1917	Ty Cobb, Det.
34	1925	George Sisler, StL.
34	1938	George McQuinn, StL.
34	1949	Dom DiMaggio, Bos.
33	1907	Hal Chase, NY
33	1933	Heinie Manush, Wash.
31	1906	Nap Lajoie, Clev.
31	1924	Sam Rice, Wash.
31	1980	Ken Landreaux, Minn.
30	1912	Tris Speaker, Bos.
30	1929	Bing Miller, Phil.
30	1934	Goose Goslin, Det.
30	1976	Ron LeFlore, Det.
30	1980	George Brett, KC
30	1997	Sandy Alomar, Jr., Clev.
30	1997	Nomar Garciaparra, Bos.
30	1998	Eric Davis, Balt.

NATIONAL LEAGUE:

G	Year	Player & Club
44	1897	Willie Keeler, Balt.
44	1978	Pete Rose, Cin.
42	1894	Bill Dahlen, Chi.
37	1945	Tommy Holmes, Bos.
36	1894	Billy Hamilton, Phil.
35	1895	Fred Clarke, Lou.
34	1987	Benito Santiago, SD
33	1893	George Davis, NY
33	1922	Rogers Hornsby, StL.
31	1899	Ed Delahanty, Phil.
31	1969	Willie Davis, LA
31	1970	Rico Carty, Atl.
31	1999	Vladimir Guerrero, Mtl.
30	1898	Elmer Smith, Cin.
30	1950	Stan Musial, StL.
30	1989	Jerome Walton, Chi
30	1999	Luis Gonzalez, Ari.

PITCHERS: GAMES WON, CONSECUTIVE, SEASON

19   Tim Keefe, NL:NY 1888
     Rube Marquard, NL:NY 1912
18   Hoss Radbourn, NL:Prov. 1884
17   Mickey Welch, NL:NY 1883
     John Luby, NL:Chi. 1890
     Roy Face, NL:Pitt. 1959
16   Jim McCormick, NL:Chi. 1886
     Smoky Joe Wood, AL:Bos. 1912
     Walter Johnson, AL: Wash. 1912
     Lefty Grove, AL:Phil. 1931
     Schoolboy Rowe, AL:Det. 1934
     Carl Hubbell, NL:NY 1936
     Ewell Blackwell, NL:Cin. 1947
     Jack Sanford, NL:SF 1962
     Roger Clemens, AL:NY 2001
15   Scott Stratton, AA:Lou. 1890
     Dazzy Vance, NL:Brk. 1924
     General Crowder, AL:Wash. 1932
     Johnny Allen, AL:Clev. 1937
     Bob Gibson, NL:StL. 1968
     Dave McNally, AL:Balt. 1969
     Steve Carlton, NL:Phil. 1972
     Gaylord Perry, AL:Clev. 1974
     Roger Clemens, AL:Tor. 1998
14   Jocko Flynn, NL:Chi. 1886
     Joe McGinnity, NL:NY 1904
     Jim McCormick, UA:Cin. 1884
     Jack Chesbro, AL:NY 1904
     Ed Reulbach, NL:Chi. 1909
     Walter Johnson, AL:Wash. 1913
     Chief Bender, AL:Phil. 1914
     Lefty Grove, AL:Phil. 1928
     Whitey Ford, AL:NY. 1961
     Steve Stone, AL:Balt. 1980
     Rick Sutcliffe, NL:Chi. 1984
     Dwight Gooden, NL:NY 1985
     Roger Clemens, AL:Bos. 1986
     John Smoltz, NL:Atl. 1996
13   Larry Corcoran, NL:Chi. 1880
     Charlie Buffinton, NL:Bos. 1884
     Cy Young, NL:Clev. 1892
     Frank Killen, NL:Pitt. 1893
     Frank Dwyer, NL:Cin. 1896
     Fred Klobedanz, NL:Bos. 1897
     Ed Lewis, NL:Bos. 1898
     Christy Mathewson, NL:NY 1909
     Deacon Phillippe, NL:Pitt. 1910
     Walter Johnson, AL:Wash. 1924
     Stan Coveleski, AL:Wash. 1925
     Burleigh Grimes, NL:NY 1927
     Wes Ferrell, AL:Clev. 1930
     Bobo Newsom, AL:Det. 1940
     Ellis Kinder, AL:Bos. 1949
     Brooks Lawrence, NL:Cin, 1956
     Phil Regan, NL:LA 1966
     Dock Ellis, NL:Pitt. 1971
     Dave McNally, AL:Balt. 1971
     Catfish Hunter, AL:Oak. 1973
     Ron Guidry, AL:NY 1978
     Lamarr Hoyt, AL:Chi. 1983
     Tom Glavine, NL:Atl. 1992

PITCHERS: GAMES LOST, CONSECUTIVE, SEASON

19   Jack Nabors, AL:Phil. 1916
18   Cliff Curtis, NL:Bos. 1910
     Roger Craig, NL:NY 1963
16   Dory Dean, NL:Cin. 1876
     Jim Hughey, NL:Clev. 1899
     Craig Anderson, NL:NY 1962
     Mike Parrott, AL:Sea. 1980
15   Bob Groom, AL:Wash. 1909
14   Frank Gilmore, NL:Wash. 1887
     Frank Bates, NL:Clev. 1899
     Joe Harris, AL:Bos. 1906
     Jim Pastorius, NL:Brk. 1908
     Buster Brown, NL:Bos. 1911
     Howie Judson, AL:Chi. 1949
     Paul Calvert, AL:Wash. 1949
     Matt Keough, AL:Oak. 1979
     Anthony Young, NL:NY 1992
13   Sam Moffet, NL:Clev. 1884
     Guy Morton, AL:Clev. 1914
     Burleigh Grimes, NL:Pitt. 1917
     Roy Moore, AL:Phil. 1920
     Joe Oeschger, NL:Bos. 1922
     Dutch Henry, AL:Chi. 1930
     Ben Cantwell, NL:Bos. 1935
     Lum Harris, AL:Phil. 1943
     Dutch McCall, NL:Chi. 1948
     Terry Felton, AL:Minn. 1982
     Rick Honeycutt, NL:LA (11)-AL:Oak. (2) 1987
     Anthony Young, NL:NY 1993
     Jose Lima, NL:Hou. 2000

WINNING TWO COMPLETE GAMES, ONE DAY

Joe McGinnity, (3) NL:NY Aug. 1, 8, 31, 1903
Grover Alexander, (2) NL:Phil. Sept. 23, 1916; Sept. 3, 1917
Mark Baldwin, (2) NL:Pitt. Sept. 12, 1891; May 30, 1892
Pud Galvin, (2) NL:Buff. July 12, 1879; July 4, 1882
Hi Bell, NL:StL. July 19, 1924
John Clarkson, NL:Bos. Sept. 12, 1889
Ray Collins, AL:Bos. Sept. 22, 1914
Cannonball Crane, PL:NY Sept. 27, 1890
Candy Cummings, NL:Hart. Sept. 9, 1876
Bert Cunningham, PL:Buff. Aug. 20, 1890
Dave Davenport, AL:StL. July 29, 1916
Al Demaree, NL:Phil. Sept. 20, 1916
Bill Doak, NL:StL. Sept. 18, 1917
Charlie Ferguson, NL:Phil. Oct. 9, 1886
Henry Gruber, PL:Clev. July 26, 1890
Guy Hecker, AA:Lou. July 4, 1884
Bill Hutchinson, NL:Chi. May 30, 1890
Tim Keefe, AA:NY July 4, 1883
Dutch Levsen, AL:Clev. Aug. 28, 1926
Carl Mays, AL:Bos. Aug. 30, 1918
Tony Mullane, AA:Cin. Sept. 20, 1888
George Mullin, AL:Det.Sept. 22, 1906
Frank Owen, AL:Chi. July 1, 1905
Pol Perritt, NL:NY Sept. 9, 1916
Hoss Radbourn, NL:Prov. May 30, 1884
Ed Reulbach, NL:Chi. Sept. 26, 1908
Amos Rusie, NL:NY Sept. 26, 1891
Doc Scanlon, NL:Brk. Oct. 3, 1905
Cy Seymour, NL:NY June 3, 1897
Urban Shocker, AL:StL. Sept. 6, 1924
Johnny Stuart, NL:StL. July 10, 1923
Ed Summers, AL:Det. Sept. 25, 1908
Fred Toney, NL:Cin. July 1, 1917
Ed Walsh, AL:Chi. Sept. 29, 1908
Monte Ward, NL:Prov. Aug. 8, 1878
Mule Watson, NL:Bos. Aug. 13, 1921
Mickey Welch, NL:Troy July 4, 1881
Jim Whitney, NL:Wash. Aug. 20, 1887
Cy Young, NL:Clev. Oct. 4, 1890

TWO OR MORE NO-HIT GAMES, LIFETIME

7	Nolan Ryan, AL:Cal. 1973(2)-75; NL:Hou.1981; AL:Tex. 90-91
4	Sandy Koufax, NL:LA 1962-65
3	Larry Corcoran, NL:Chi. 1880, 82, 84
	Bob Feller, AL:Clev. 1940, 46, 51
	Cy Young, NL:Clev. 1897; AL:Bos. 1904, 08
2	Al Atkinson, AA:Phil. 1884, 86
	Ted Breitenstein, AA:StL. 1891; NL:Cin. 1898
	Jim Bunning, AL:Det. 1958; NL:Phil. 1964
	Steve Busby, AL:KC 1973-74
	Carl Erskine, NL:Brk. 1952, 56
	Bob Forsch, NL:StL. 1978, 83
	Pud Galvin, NL:Buff. 1880, 84
	Ken Holtzman, NL:Chi. 1969, 71
	Addie Joss, AL:Clev. 1908, 10
	Dutch Leonard, AL:Bos. 1916, 18
	Jim Maloney, NL:Cin. 1965, 69
	Christy Mathewson, NL:NY 1901, 05
	Hideo Nomo, NL:LA 1996; AL:Bos. 2001
	Allie Reynolds, AL:NY 1951(2)
	Frank Smith AL:Chi 1905, 08
	Warren Spahn, NL:Mil. 1960-61
	Bill Stoneman, NL:Mtl. 1969, 72
	Adonis Terry, AA:Brk 1886, 88
	Virgil Trucks, AL:Det. 1952 (2)
	Johnny Vander Meer, NL:Cin. 1938 (2)
	Don Wilson, NL:Hou. 1967, 69

NO-HIT GAMES – INACTIVE LEAGUES

9 OR MORE INNINGS

UNION ASSOCIATION (2)

1884

Burns, Dick, Cin. Aug. 26 (at KC) 3-1
Cushman, Ed, Mil. Sept. 28, (Wash.) 5-0

AMERICAN ASSOCIATION (15)

1882

Mullane, Tony, Lou. Sept. 11 (at Cin.) 2-0
Hecker, Guy, Lou. Sept. 19 (at Pitt.) 3-1

1884

Atkinson, Al, Phil. May 24 (Pitt.) 10-1
Morris, Ed, Colu. May 29 (at Pitt.) 5-0
Mountain, Frank, Colu. June 5 (at Wash.) 12-0
Kimber, Sam, Brk. Oct. 4 (Tol.) 0-0 (10 inn)

1886

Atkinson, Al, Phil. May 1 (NY) 3-2
Terry, Adonis, Brk. July 24 (StL.) 1-0
Kilroy, Matt, Balt. Oct. 6 (at Pitt.) 6-0

1888

Terry, Adonis, Brk. May 27 (Lou.) 4-0
Porter, Henry, KC June 6 (at Balt.) 4-0
Seward, Ed, Phil. July 26 (Cin.) 12-2
Weyhing, Gus, Phil. July 31 (KC) 4-0

1890

Titcomb, Cannonball, Roch. Sept. 15 (Syr.) 7-0

1891

Breitenstein, Ted, StL. Oct. 4(1g) (Lou.) 8-0
(First major-league start)

NO-HIT GAMES — AMERICAN LEAGUE

*9 OR MORE INNINGS   * Denotes Perfect Game*

1902
Callahan, Nixey, Chi. Sept. 20(1g) (Det.) 3-0

1904
*Young, Cy, Bos. May 5 (Phil.) 3-0
Tannehill, Jess, Bos. Aug. 17 (Chi.) 6-0

1905
Henley, Weldon, Phil. July 22(1g) (StL.) 6-0
Dinneen, Bill, Bos. Sept. 27(1g) (Chi.) 2-0
Smith, Frank, Chi. Sept. 6(2g) (Det.) 15-0

1908
Young, Cy, Bos. June 30 (NY) 8-0
Rhoades, Bob, Clev. Sept. 18 (Bos.) 2-1
Smith, Frank, Chi. Sept. 20 (Phil.) 1-0
*Joss, Addie, Clev. Oct. 2 (Chi.) 1-0

1910
Joss, Addie, Clev. Apr. 20 (at Chi.) 1-0
Bender, Chief, Phil. May 12 (Clev.) 4-0

1911
Wood, Joe, Bos. July 29(1g) (StL.) 5-0
Walsh, Ed, Chi. Aug. 27 (Bos.) 5-0

1912
Mullin, George, Det. July 4(2g) (StL.) 7-0
Hamilton, Earl, StL. Aug. 30 (at Det.) 5-1

1914
Benz, Joe, Chi. May 31 (Clev.) 6-1

1916
Foster, Rube, Bos. June 21 (NY) 2-0
Bush, Joe, Phil. Aug. 26 (Clev.) 5-0
Leonard, Dutch, Bos. Aug. 30 (StL.) 4-0

1917
Cicotte, Eddie, Chi. Apr. 14 (StL.) 11-0
Mogridge, George, NY Apr. 24 (at Bos.) 2-1
Koob, Ernie, StL. May 5 (Chi.) 1-0
Groom, Bob, StL. May 6(2g) (Chi.) 3-0
Ruth, Babe (0 inn) & Shore, Ernie (9 inn) Bos.
June 23(1g) (Wash.) 4-0

1918
Leonard, Dutch, Bos. June 3 (at Det.) 5-0

1919
Caldwell, Ray, Clev. Sept. 10(1g) (at NY) 3-0

1920
Johnson, Walter, Wash. July 1 (at Bos.) 1-0

1922
*Robertson, Charlie, Chi. Apr. 30 (at Det.) 2-0

1923
Jones, Sam, NY Sept. 4 (at Phil.) 2-0
Ehmke, Howard, Bos. Sept. 7 (at Phil.) 4-0

1926
Lyons, Ted, Chi. Aug. 21 (Bos.) 6-0

1931
Ferrell, Wes, Clev. Apr. 29 (StL.) 9-0
Burke, Bobby, Wash. Aug. 8 (Bos.) 5-0

1935
Kennedy, Vern, Chi. Aug. 31 (Clev.) 5-0

1937
Dietrich, Bill, Chi. June 1 (StL.) 8-0

1938
Pearson, Monte, NY Aug. 27(2g) (Clev.) 13-0

1940
Feller, Bob, Clev. Apr. 16 (at Chi.) 1-0
(Opening Day)

1945
Fowler, Dick, Phil. Sept. 9(2g) (StL.) 1-0

1946
Feller, Bob, Clev. Apr. 30 (at NY) 1-0

1947
Black, Don, Clev. July 10(1g) (Phil.) 3-0
McCahan, Bill, Phil. Sept. 3 (Wash.) 3-0

1948
Lemon, Bob, Clev. June 30 (at Det.) 2-0

1951
Feller, Bob, Clev. July 1(1g) (Det.) 2-1
Reynolds, Allie, NY July 12 (at Clev.) 1-0
Reynolds, Allie, NY Sept. 28(1g) (Bos.) 8-0

1952
Trucks, Virgil, Det. May 15 (Wash.) 1-0
Trucks, Virgil, Det. Aug. 25 (at NY) 1-0

1953
Holloman, Bobo, StL. May 6 (Phil.) 6-0
(First major-league start)

1956
Parnell, Mel, Bos. July 14 (Chi.) 4-0

1957
Keegan, Bob, Chi. Aug. 20(2g) (Wash.) 6-0

1958
Bunning, Jim, Det. July. 20(1g) (Bos.) 3-0
Wilhelm, Hoyt, Balt. Sept. 20 (NY) 1-0

1962
Belinsky, Bo, LA May 5 (Balt.) 2-0
Wilson, Earl, Bos. June 26 (LA) 2-0
Monbouquette, Bill, Bos. Aug. 1(1g) (at Chi.) 1-0
Kralick, Jack, Minn. Aug. 26 (KC) 1-0

1965
Morehead, Dave, Bos. Sept. 16 (Clev.) 2-0

1966
Siebert, Sonny, Clev. June 10 (Wash.) 2-0

1967
Barber, Steve (8.2 inn.)& Miller, Stu (1 inn.) Balt.
Apr. 30 (1g) (Det.) 1-2 lost
Chance, Dean, Minn. Aug. 25(2g) (at Clev.) 2-1
Horlen, Joe, Chi. Sept. 10(1g) (Det.) 6-0

1968
Phoebus, Tom, Balt. Apr. 27 (Bos.) 6-0
*Hunter, Catfish, Oak. May 8 (Minn.) 4-0

1969
Palmer, Jim, Balt. Aug. 13 (Oak.) 8-0

1970
Wright, Clyde, Cal. July 3 (Oak.) 4-0
Blue, Vida, Oak. Sept. 21 (Minn.) 6-0

1973
Busby, Steve, KC Apr. 27 (at Det.) 3-0
Ryan, Nolan, Cal. May 15 (at KC) 3-0
Ryan, Nolan, Cal. July 15 (at Det.) 6-0
Bibby, Jim, Tex. July 30 (at Oak.) 6-0

1974
Busby, Steve, KC June 19 (at Mil.) 2-0
Bosman, Dick, Clev. July 19 (Oak.) 4-0
Ryan, Nolan, Cal. Sept. 28 (Minn.) 4-0

1975
Ryan, Nolan, Cal. June 1 (Balt.) 1-0
Blue, Vida (5 inn), Abbott, Glenn (1 inn), Lindblad, Paul
(1 inn) & Fingers, Rollie (2 inn), Oak. Sept. 28
(Cal.) 5-0

NO-HIT GAMES — AMERICAN LEAGUE

*9 OR MORE INNINGS * Denotes Perfect Game*
(continued)

1976
Odom, Blue Moon (5 inn) & Barrios, Francisco (4 inn),
Chi. July 28 (at Oak.) 2-1

1977
Colborn, Jim, KC May 14 (Tex.) 6-0
Eckersley, Dennis, Clev. May 30 (Cal.) 1-0
Blyleven, Bert, Tex. Sept. 22 (at Cal.) 6-0

1981
*Barker, Len, Clev. May 15 (Tor.) 3-0

1983
Righetti, Dave, NY July 4 (Bos.) 4-0
Warren, Mike, Oak. Sept. 29 (Chi.)3-0

1984
Morris, Jack, Det. Apr. 7 (at Chi.) 4-0
*Witt, Mike, Cal. Sept. 30 (at Tex.) 1-0

1986
Cowley, Joe, Chi. Sept. 19 (at Cal.) 7-1

1987
Nieves, Juan, Mil. Apr. 15 (at Balt.) 7-0

1990
Langston, Mark (7 inn) & Witt, Mike (2 inn) Cal.,
Apr. 11 (Sea.) 1-0
Johnson, Randy, Sea. June 2 (Det.) 2-0
Ryan, Nolan, Tex. June 11 (at Oak.) 5-0
Stewart, Dave, Oak. June 29 (at Tor.) 5-0
Stieb, Dave, Tor. Sept. 2 (at Clev.) 3-0

1991
Ryan, Nolan, Tex. May 1 (Tor.) 3-0
Milacki, Bob (6 inn), Flanagan, Mike (1 inn),
Williamson, Mark (1 inn) & Olson, Greg (1 inn) Balt.
July 13 (at Oak.) 2-0
Alvarez, Wilson, Chi. Aug. 11 (at Balt.) 7-0
Saberhagen, Bret, KC Aug. 26 (Chi.) 7-0

1993
Bosio,Chris, Sea. Apr. 22 (Bos.) 7-0
Abbott, Jim, NY Sept. 4 (Clev.) 4-0

1994
Erickson, Scott, Minn. Apr. 27 (Mil.) 6-0
*Rogers, Kenny, Tex. July 28 (Cal.) 4-0

1996
Gooden, Dwight, NY May 14 (Sea.) 2-0

1998
*Wells, David, NY May 17 (Minn.) 4-0

1999
*Cone, David, NY July 18 (Mtl.) 6-0
Milton, Eric, Minn. Sept. 11 (Ana.) 7-0

2001
Nomo, Hideo, Bos. Apr. 4 (at Balt.) 3-0

NO-HIT GAMES — NATIONAL LEAGUE

9 OR MORE INNINGS *Denotes Perfect Game*

1876
Bradley, George, StL. July 15 (Hart.) 2-0

1880
*Richmond, Lee, Wor. June 12 (Clev.) 1-0
*Ward, Monte, Prov. June 17 (Buff.) 5-0
Corcoran, Larry, Chi. Aug. 19 (Bos.) 6-0
Galvin, Pud, Buff. Aug. 20 (at Wor.) 1-0

1882
Corcoran, Larry, Chi. Sept. 20 (Wor.) 5-0

1883
Radbourn, Hoss, Prov. July 25 (at Clev.) 8-0
Dailey, Hugh, Clev. Sept. 13 (at Phil.) 1-0

1884
Corcoran, Larry, Chi. June 27 (Prov.) 6-0
Galvin, Pud, Buff. Aug. 4 (at Det.) 18-0

1885
Clarkson, John, Chi. July 27 (at Prov.) 4-0
Ferguson, Charlie, Phil. Aug. 29 (Prov.) 1-0

1891
Lovett, Tom, Brk. June 22 (NY) 4-0
Rusie, Amos, NY July 31 (Brk.) 6-0

1892
Stivetts, Jack, Bos. Aug. 6 (Brk.) 11-0
Sanders, Ben, Lou. Aug. 22 (Balt.) 6-2
Jones, Bumpus, Cin. Oct. 15 (Pitt.) 7-1
(First major league game)

1893
Hawke, Bill, Balt. Aug. 16 (Wash.) 5-0

1897
Young, Cy, Clev. Sept. 18 (Cin.) 6-0

1898
Breitenstein, Ted, Cin. Apr. 22 (Pitt.) 11-0
Hughes, Jim, Balt. Apr. 22 (Bos.) 8-0
Donahue, Red, Phil. July 8 (Bos.) 5-0
Thornton, Walter, Chi. Aug. 21(2g) (Brk.) 2-0

1899
Phillippe, Deacon, Lou. May 25 (NY) 7-0
Willis, Vic, Bos. Aug. 7 (Wash.) 7-1

1900
Hahn, Noodles, Cin. July 12 (Phil.) 4-0

1901
Mathewson, Christy, NY July 15 (at StL.) 5-0

1903
Fraser, Chick, Phil. Sept. 18(2g) (at Chi.) 10-0

1905
Mathewson, Christy, NY June 13 (at Chi.) 1-0

1906
Lush, Johnny, Phil. May 1 (at Brk.) 1-0
Eason, Mal, Brk. July 20 (at StL.) 2-0

1907
Pfeffer, Jeff, Bos. May 8 (Cin.) 6-0
Maddox, Nick, Pitt. Sept. 20 (Brk.) 2-1

1908
Wiltse, Hooks, NY July 4(1g) 10 inn. (Phil.) 1-0
Rucker, Nap, Brk. Sept. 5(2g) (Bos.) 6-0

1912
Tesreau, Jeff, NY Sept. 6(1g) (at Phil.) 3-0

1914
Davis, George, Bos. Sept. 9(2g) (Phil.) 7-0

1915
Marquard, Rube, NY Apr. 15 (Brk.) 2-0
Lavender, Jimmy, Chi. Aug. 31(1g) (at NY) 2-0

1916
Hughes, Tom, Bos. June 16 (Pitt.) 2-0

1917
Toney, Fred, Cin. May 2 10 inn. (at Chi.) 1-0

1919
Eller, Hod, Cin. May 11 (StL.) 6-0

1922
Barnes, Jesse, NY May 7 (Phil.) 6-0

1924
Haines, Jesse, StL. July 17 (Bos.) 5-0

1925
Vance, Dazzy, Brk. Sept. 13(1g) (Phil.) 10-1

1929
Hubbell, Carl, NY May 8 (Pitt.) 11-0

1934
Dean, Paul, StL. Sept. 21(2g) (at Brk.) 3-0

1938
Vander Meer, Johnny, Cin. June 11 (Bos.) 3-0
Vander Meer, Johnny, Cin. June 15 (at Brk.) 6-0
(consecutive appearances)

1940
Carleton, Tex, Brk. Apr. 30 (at Cin.) 3-0

1941
Warneke, Lon, StL. Aug. 30 (at Cin.) 2-0

1944
Tobin, Jim, Bos. Apr. 27 (Brk.) 2-0
Shoun, Clyde, Cin. May 15 (Bos.) 1-0

1946
Head, Ed, Brk. Apr. 23 (Bos.) 5-0

1947
Blackwell, Ewell, Cin. June 18 (Bos.) 6-0

1948
Barney, Rex, Brk. Sept. 9 (at NY) 2-0

1950
Bickford, Vern, Bos. Aug. 11 (Brk.) 7-0

1951
Chambers, Cliff, Pitt. May 6(2g) (at Bos.) 3-0

1952
Erskine, Carl, Brk. June 19 (Chi.) 5-0

1954
Wilson, Jim, Mil. June 12 (Phil.) 2-0

1955
Jones, Sam, Chi. May 12 (Pitt.) 4-0

1956
Erskine, Carl, Brk. May 12 (NY) 3-0
Maglie, Sal, Brk. Sept. 25 (Phil.) 5-0

1960
Cardwell, Don, Chi. May 15(2g) (StL.) 4-0
Burdette, Lew, Mil. Aug. 18 (Phil.) 1-0
Spahn, Warren, Mil. Sept. 16 (Phil.) 4-0

1961
Spahn, Warren, Mil. Apr. 28 (SF) 1-0

1962
Koufax, Sandy, LA June 30 (NY) 5-1

1963
Koufax, Sandy, LA May 11 (SF) 8-0
Nottebart, Don, Hou. May 17 (Phil.) 4-1
Marichal, Juan, SF June 15 (Hou.) 1-0

NO-HIT GAMES — NATIONAL LEAGUE

(continued)
*9 OR MORE INNINGS * Denotes Perfect Game*

1964
Johnson, Ken, Hou. Apr. 23 (Cin.) 0-1 lost
Koufax, Sandy, LA June 4 (at Phil.) 3-0
*Bunning, Jim, Phil. June 21(1g) (at NY) 6-0

1965
Maloney, Jim, Cin. Aug. 19(1g) (10 inn.) (at Chi.) 1-0
*Koufax, Sandy, LA Sept. 9 (Chi.) 1-0

1967
Wilson, Don, Hou. June 18 (Atl.) 2-0

1968
Culver, George, Cin. July 29n(2g) (Phil.) 6-1
Perry, Gaylord, SF Sept. 17 (StL.) 1-0
Washburn, Ray, StL. Sept. 18 (at SF) 2-0

1969
Stoneman, Bill, Mtl. Apr. 17 (at Phil.) 7-0
Maloney, Jim, Cin. Apr. 30 (Hou.) 10-0
Wilson, Don, Hou. May 1 (at Cin.) 4-0
Holtzman, Ken, Chi. Aug. 19 (Atl.) 3-0
Moose, Bob, Pitt. Sept. 20 (at NY) 4-0

1970
Ellis, Dock, Pitt. June 12n(1g) (at SD) 2-0
Singer, Bill, LA July 20 (Phil.) 5-0

1971
Holtzman, Ken, Chi. June 3 (at Cin.) 1-0
Wise, Rick, Phil. June 23 (at Cin.) 4-0
Gibson, Bob, StL. Aug. 14 (at Pitt.) 11-0

1972
Hooton, Burt, Chi. Apr. 16 (Phil.) 4-0
Pappas, Milt, Chi. Sept. 2 (SD) 8-0
Stoneman, Bill, Mtl. Oct. 2(1g) (NY) 7-0

1973
Niekro, Phil, Atl. Aug. 5 (SD) 9-0

1975
Halicki, Ed, SF Aug. 24(2g) (NY) 6-0

1976
Dierker, Larry, Hou. July 9 (Mtl.) 6-0
Candelaria, John, Pitt. Aug. 9 (LA) 2-0
Montefusco, John, SF Sept. 29 (at Atl.) 9-0

1978
Forsch, Bob, StL. Apr. 16 (Phil.) 5-0
Seaver, Tom, Cin. June 16 (StL.) 4-0

1979
Forsch, Ken, Hou. Apr. 7 (Atl.) 6-0

1980
Reuss, Jerry, LA June 27 (at SF) 8-0

1981
Lea, Charlie, Mtl. May 10(2g) (SF) 4-0
Ryan, Nolan, Hou. Sept. 26 (LA) 5-0

1983
Forsch, Bob, StL. Sept. 26 (Mtl.) 3-0

1986
Scott, Mike, Hou. Sept. 25 (SF) 2-0

1988
*Browning, Tom, Cin. Sept. 16 (LA) 1-0

1990
Valenzuela, Fernando, LA June 29 (StL.) 6-0
Mulholland, Terry, Phil. Aug. 15 (SF) 6-0

1991
Greene, Tommy, Phil. May 23 (at Mtl.) 2-0
*Martinez, Dennis, Mtl. July 28 (at LA) 2-0
Mercker, Kent (6 inn) & Wohlers, Mark (2 inn) & Pena,
Alejandro (1 inn) Atl. Sept. 11 (SD) 1-0

1992
Gross, Kevin, LA Aug. 17 (SF) 2-0

1993
Kile, Darryl, Hou. Sept. 8 (NY) 7-1

1994
Mercker, Kent, Atl. Apr. 8 (at LA) 6-0

1995
Martinez, Ramon, LA July 14 (Fla.) 7-0

1996
Leiter, Al, Fla. May 11 (Col.) 11-0
Nomo, Hideo, LA Sept. 17 (at Col.) 9-0

1997
Brown, Kevin, Fla. June 10 (at SF) 9-0
Cordova, Francisco (9 inn)& Rincon, Ricardo (1 inn), Pitt.
July 12 (10 inn) (Hou.) 3-0

1999
Jimenez, Jose, StL. June 25 (at Ari.) 1-0

2001
Burnett, A.J., Fla. May 12 (at SD) 3-0
Smith, Bud, StL. Sept. 3 (at SD) 4-0

NO-HIT GAMES

FEWER THAN NINE INNINGS

EIGHT INNINGS

Gagus, Charlie UA:Wash. Aug. 21, 1884 (Wil) 2-1
King, Charles PL:Chi. June 21, 1890 (Brk.) lost 0-1
Gastright, Henry AA: Colu. Oct. 12, 1890 (Tol.) 6-0
Frankhouse, Fred NL:Brk. Aug. 27, 1937 (Cin.) 5-0
  (7.2 inn, rain)
Hawkins, Andy AL:NY July 1, 1990 (@Chi.) lost 0-4
Young, Matt AL:Bos. Apr. 12(1g), 1992 (@Clev) lost 1-2

SEVEN INNINGS

Crane, Ed NL:NY Sept. 27, 1888 (Wash) 3-0
Kilroy, Matt AA:Balt. July 29(2g), 1889 (StL.) 0-0
Nicol, George AA:StL. Sept 23, 1890 (Phil.) 21-2
Chamberlain, Elton NL:Cin. Sept. 23(2g), 1893 (Bos.) 6-0
Weimer, John NL:Cin. Aug. 24(2g), 1906 (Brk.) 1-0
McGlynn, Grant NL:StL. Sept. 24(2g), 1906 (Brk.) 1-1
Karger, Ed NL:StL. Aug. 11(2g), 1907 (Bos.) perfect 4-0
Cole, Len NL:Chi. July 31(2g), 1910 (@StL.) 4-0
Johnson, Walter AL:Wash. Aug. 25, 1924 (StL.) 2-0
Jones, Sam NL:SF Sept. 26, 1959 (@StL.) 4-0

SIX INNINGS

McKeon, Larry AA:Ind. May 6, 1884 (@Cin.) 0-0
Getzein, Charlie NL:Det. Oct. 1, 1884 (Phil.) 1-0
Van Haltren, George NL:Chi. June 21, 1888 (Pitt.) 1-0
Stein, Ed NL:Brk. June 2, 1894 (Chi.) 1-0
Leifield, Al NL:Pitt. Sept. 26(2g), 1906 (Phil.) 8-0
Lush, John NL:StL. Aug. 6, 1908 (@Brk.) 2-0
Cashion, Carl AL:Wash. Aug. 20(2g), 1912 (Clev.) 2-0
Whitehead, Johnny AL:StL. Aug. 5(2g), 1940 (Det.) 4-0
Perez, Melido AL:Chi. July 12n 1990 (@NY) 8-0

FIVE INNINGS

Sweeney, Charlie (2 inn) & Henry Boyle (3 inn) UA:StL. Oct. 5, 1884 (St.P.) lost 0-1
Shaw, Fred NL:Prov. Oct. 7(1g), 1885 (@Buff.) 4-0
Stivetts, John NL:Bos. Oct. 15(2g), 1892 (@Wash.) 4-0
Ames, Leon NL:NY Sept. 14(2g), 1903 (@StL.) 5-0
  (First major league game)
Waddell, Rube AL:Phil. Aug. 15, 1905 (StL.) 2-0
Dygert, Jim (3 inn) & Rube Waddell (2 inn)
AL:Phil. Aug. 29, 1906 (Chi.) 4-3
Walsh, Ed AL:Chi. May 26, 1907 (NY) 8-1
Camnitz, Howie NL:Pitt. Aug. 23(2g), 1907 (@NY) 1-0
Vickers, Harry AL:Phil. Oct. 5(2g), 1907 (@Wash.) perfect 4-0
Tobin, Jim NL:Bos. June 22(2g), 1944 (Phil.) 7-0
McCormick, Mike NL:SF June 12, 1959 (@Phil.) 3-0
  (allowed hit in 6th inning before game was rained out and reverted to last full inning)
Chance, Dean AL:Minn. Aug. 6, 1967 (Bos.) perfect 2-0
Palmer, David NL:Mtl. Apr. 21(2g), 1984 (@StL.) perfect 4-0
Perez, Pascual NL:Mtl. Sept 24, 1988 (@Phil.) 1-0

NO HITS THROUGH NINE INNINGS, ALLOWED HIT IN EXTRA-INNING

Earl Moore, AL:Clev. (Chi.) May 9, 1901
  (allowed hit in 10th, lost)
Bob Wicker, NL:Chi. (NY) June 11, 1904
  (allowed hit in 10th, won in 12th)
Harry McIntyre, NL:Brk. (Pitt.) Aug. 1, 1906
  (allowed hit in 11th, lost in 13th)
Red Ames, NL:NY (Brk.) Apr. 15, 1909
  (allowed hit in 10th, lost in 13th)
Tom Hughes, AL:NY (Clev.) Aug. 30, 1910
  (allowed hit in 10th, lost in 11th)
Jim Scott, AL:Chi. (Wash.) May 14, 1914
  (allowed hit in 10th, lost)
Hippo Vaughn, NL:Chi. (Cin.) May 2, 1917
  (allowed hit in 10th, lost)
Bobo Newsom, AL:StL. (Bos.) Sept. 18, 1934
  (allowed hit in 10th, lost)
Johnny Klippstein (7 inn), Hershell Freeman (1 inn),
Joe Black (2.1 inn), NL:Cin. (Mil.) May 26, 1956
  (allowed hit in 10th, 2 hits in 11th, lost)
Harvey Haddix, NL:Pitt. (Mil.) May 26, 1959
  (12 innings perfect; allowed hit in 13th, lost)
Jim Maloney, NL:Cin. (NY) June 14, 1965
  (allowed 2 hits in 11th, lost)
Mark Gardner, NL:Mtl. (LA) July 26, 1991
  (allowed 2 hits in 10th, lost)
Pedro Martinez, NL:Mtl. (SD) June 3, 1995
  (9 innings perfect, allowed hit in 10th, won)

BATTING AVERAGE

Year	AVG	Player
1900:	.381	Wagner, Honus NL:Pitt.
1901:	.422	Lajoie, Nap AL:Phil.
	.382	Burkett, Jess NL:StL.
1902:	.376	Delahanty, Ed AL:Wash.
	.357	Beaumont, Ginger NL:Pitt.
1903:	.355	Wagner, Honus NL:Pitt. [2]
	.355	Lajoie, Nap AL:Clev. [2]
1904:	.381	Lajoie, Nap AL:Clev. [3]
	.349	Wagner, Honus NL:Pitt. [3]
1905	.377	Seymour, Cy NL:Cin.
	.306	Flick, Elmer AL:Clev.
1906	.358	Stone, George AL:StL.
	.339	Wagner, Honus NL:Pitt. [4]
1907:	.350	Cobb, Ty AL:Det.
	.350	Wagner, Honus NL:Pitt. [5]
1908:	.354	Wagner, Honus NL:Pitt. [6]
	.324	Cobb, Ty AL:Det. [2]
1909:	.377	Cobb, Ty AL:Det. [3]
	.339	Wagner, Honus NL:Pitt. [7]
1910:	.385	Cobb, Ty AL:Det. [4]
	.331	Magee, Sherry NL:Phil.
1911:	.420	Cobb, Ty AL:Det. [5]
	.334	Wagner, Honus NL:Pitt. [8]
1912:	.410	Cobb, Ty AL:Det. [6]
	.372	Zimmerman, Heinie NL:Cin.
1913:	.390	Cobb, Ty AL:Det. [7]
	.350	Daubert, Jake NL:Brk.
1914:	.368	Cobb, Ty AL:Det. [8]
	.329	Daubert, Jake NL:Brk. [2]
1915:	.369	Cobb, Ty AL:Det. [9]
	.320	Doyle, Larry NL:NY
1916:	.386	Speaker, Tris AL:Clev.
	.339	Chase, Hal NL:Cin.
1917:	.383	Cobb, Ty AL:Det. [10]
	.341	Roush, Edd NL:Cin.
1918:	.382	Cobb, Ty AL:Det. [11]
	.335	Wheat, Zack NL:Brk.
1919:	.384	Cobb, Ty AL:Det. [12]
	.321	Roush, Edd NL:Cin. [2]
1920:	.407	Sisler, George AL:StL.
	.370	Hornsby, Rogers NL:StL.
1921:	.397	Hornsby, Rogers NL:StL. [2]
	.394	Heilmann, Harry AL:Det.
1922:	.420	Sisler, George AL:StL. [2]
	.401	Hornsby, Rogers NL:StL. [3]
1923:	.403	Heilmann, Harry AL:Det. [2]
	.384	Hornsby, Rogers NL:StL. [4]
1924:	.424	Hornsby, Rogers NL:StL. [5]
	.378	Ruth, Babe AL:NY
1925:	.403	Hornsby, Rogers NL:StL. [6]
	.393	Heilmann, Harry AL:Det. [3]
1926:	.378	Manush, Heinie AL:Det.
	.353	Hargrave, Bubbles NL:Cin.
1927:	.398	Heilmann, Harry AL:Det. [4]
	.380	Waner, Paul NL:Pitt.
1928:	.387	Hornsby, Rogers NL:Bos. [7]
	.379	Goslin, Goose AL:Wash.
1929:	.398	O'Doul, Lefty NL:Phil.
	.369	Fonseca, Lew AL:Clev.
1930:	.401	Terry, Bill NL:NY
	.381	Simmons, Al AL:Phil.
1931:	.390	Simmons, Al AL:Phil. [2]
	.349	Hafey, Chick NL:StL.
1932:	.368	O'Doul, Lefty NL:Brk. [2]
	.367	Alexander, Dale AL:Det.-Bos.
1933:	.368	Klein, Chuck NL:Phil.
	.356	Foxx, Jimmie AL:Phil.
1934:	.363	Gehrig, Lou AL:NY
	.362	Waner, Paul NL:Pitt. [2]
1935:	.385	Vaughan, Arky NL:Pitt.
	.349	Myer, Buddy AL:Wash.
1936:	.388	Appling, Luke AL:Chi.
	.373	Waner, Paul NL:Pitt. [3]
1937:	.374	Medwick, Joe NL:StL.
	.371	Gehringer, Charlie AL:Det.
1938:	.349	Foxx, Jimmie AL:Bos. [2]
	.342	Lombardi, Ernie NL:Cin.
1939:	.381	DiMaggio, Joe AL:NY
	.349	Mize, Johnny NL:StL.
1940:	.355	Garms, Deb NL:Pitt.
	.352	DiMaggio, Joe AL:NY [2]
1941:	.406	Williams, Ted AL:Bos.
	.343	Reiser, Pete NL:Brk.
1942:	.356	Williams, Ted AL:Bos. [2]
	.330	Lombardi, Ernie NL:Bos. [2]
1943:	.357	Musial, Stan NL:StL.
	.328	Appling, Luke AL:Chi. [2]
1944:	.357	Walker, Dixie NL:Brk.
	.327	Boudreau, Lou AL:Clev.
1945:	.355	Cavarretta, Phil NL:Chi.
	.309	Stirnweiss, Snuffy AL:NY
1946:	.365	Musial, Stan NL:StL. [2]
	.353	Vernon, Mickey AL:Wash.
1947:	.363	Walker, Harry NL:StL.-Phil.
	.343	Williams, Ted AL:Bos. [3]
1948:	.376	Musial, Stan NL:StL. [3]
	.369	Williams, Ted AL:Bos. [4]
1949:	.343	Kell, George AL:Det.
	.342	Robinson, Jackie NL:Brk.
1950:	.354	Goodman, Billy AL:Bos.
	.346	Musial, Stan NL:StL. [4]
1951:	.355	Musial, Stan NL:StL. [5]
	.344	Fain, Ferris AL:Phil.
1952:	.336	Musial, Stan NL:StL. [6]
	.327	Fain, Ferris AL:Phil. [2]
1953	.344	Furillo, Carl NL:Brk.
	.337	Vernon, Mickey AL:Wash. [2]
1954:	.345	Mays, Willie NL:NY
	.341	Avila, Bobby AL:Clev.
1955:	.340	Kaline, Al AL:Det.
	.338	Ashburn, Richie NL:Phil.
1956:	.353	Mantle, Mickey AL:NY
	.328	Aaron, Hank NL:Mil.
1957:	.388	Williams, Ted AL:Bos. [5]
	.351	Musial, Stan NL:StL. [7]
1958:	.350	Ashburn, Richie NL:Phil. [2]
	.328	Williams, Ted AL:Bos. [6]
1959:	.355	Aaron, Hank NL:Mil. [2]
	.353	Kuenn, Harvey AL:Det.
1960:	.325	Groat, Dick NL:Pitt.
	.320	Runnels, Pete AL:Bos.
1961:	.361	Cash, Norm AL:Det.
	.351	Clemente, Roberto NL:Pitt.
1962:	.346	Davis, Tommy NL:LA
	.326	Runnels, Pete AL:Bos. [2]
1963:	.326	Davis, Tommy NL:LA [2]
	.321	Yastrzemski, Carl AL:Bos.
1964:	.339	Clemente, Roberto NL:Pitt. [2]
	.323	Oliva, Tony AL:Minn.

BATTING AVERAGE (CONTINUED)

1965:	.329	Clemente, Roberto NL:Pitt. [3]
	.321	Oliva, Tony AL:Minn. [2]
1966:	.342	Alou, Matty NL:Pitt.
	.316	Robinson, Frank AL:Balt.
1967:	.357	Clemente, Roberto NL:Pitt. [4]
	.326	Yastrzemski, Carl AL:Bos. [2]
1968:	.335	Rose, Pete NL:Cin.
	.301	Yastrzemski, Carl AL:Bos. [3]
1969:	.348	Rose, Pete NL:Cin. [2]
	.332	Carew, Rod AL:Minn.
1970:	.366	Carty, Rico NL:Atl.
	.329	Johnson, Alex AL:Cal.
1971:	.363	Torre, Joe NL:StL.
	.337	Oliva, Tony AL:Minn. [3]
1972:	.333	Williams, Billy NL:Chi.
	.318	Carew, Rod AL:Minn. [2]
1973:	.350	Carew, Rod AL:Minn. [3]
	.338	Rose, Pete NL:Cin. [3]
1974:	.364	Carew, Rod AL:Minn. [4]
	.353	Garr, Ralph NL:Atl.
1975:	.359	Carew, Rod AL:Minn. [5]
	.354	Madlock, Bill NL:Chi.
1976:	.339	Madlock, Bill NL:Chi. [2]
	.333	Brett, George AL:KC
1977:	.388	Carew, Rod AL:Minn. [6]
	.338	Parker, Dave NL:Pitt
1978:	.334	Parker, Dave NL:Pitt. [2]
	.333	Carew, Rod AL:Minn. [7]
1979:	.344	Hernandez, Keith NL:StL.
	.333	Lynn, Fred AL:Bos.
1980:	.390	Brett, George AL:KC [2]
	.324	Buckner, Bill NL:Chi.
1981:	.341	Madlock, Bill NL:Pitt. [3]
	.336	Lansford, Carney AL:Bos.
1982:	.332	Wilson, Willie AL:KC
	.331	Oliver, Al NL:Mtl.
1983:	.361	Boggs, Wade AL:Bos.
	.323	Madlock, Bill NL:Pitt. [4]
1984:	.351	Gwynn, Tony NL:SD
	.343	Mattingly, Don AL:NY
1985:	.368	Boggs, Wade AL:Bos. [2]
	.353	McGee, Willie NL:StL.
1986:	.357	Boggs, Wade AL:Bos. [3]
	.334	Raines, Tim NL:Mtl.
1987:	.370	Gwynn, Tony NL:SD [2]
	.363	Boggs, Wade AL:Bos. [4]
1988:	.366	Boggs, Wade AL:Bos. [5]
	.313	Gwynn, Tony NL:SD [3]
1989:	.339	Puckett, Kirby AL:Minn.
	.336	Gwynn, Tony NL:SD [4]
1990:	.335	McGee, Willie NL:StL. [2]
	.329	Brett, George AL:KC [3]
1991:	.341	Franco, Julio AL:Tex.
	.319	Pendleton, Terry NL:Atl.
1992:	.343	Martinez, Edgar AL:Sea.
	.330	Sheffield, Gary NL:SD
1993:	.370	Galarraga, Andres NL:Col.
	.363	Olerud, John AL:Tor.
1994:	.394	Gwynn, Tony NL:SD [5]
	.359	O'Neill, Paul AL:NY
1995:	.368	Gwynn, Tony NL:SD [6]
	.356	Martinez, Edgar AL:Sea. [2]
1996:	.358	Rodriguez, Alex AL:Sea.
	.353	Gwynn, Tony NL:SD [7]

1997	.372	Gwynn, Tony NL:SD [8]
	.347	Thomas, Frank AL:Chi.
1998	.363	Walker, Larry NL:Col.
	.339	Williams, Bernie AL:NY
1999	.379	Walker, Larry NL:Col. [2]
	.357	Garciaparra, Nomar AL:Bos.
2000	.372	Helton, Todd NL:Col.
	.372	Garciaparra, Nomar AL:Bos [2]
2001	.350	Walker, Larry NL:Col. [3]
	.350	Suzuki, Ichiro AL:Sea.

TOTAL BASES

1900:	305	Flick, Elmer NL:Phil.
1901:	345	Lajoie, Nap AL:Phil.
	314	Burkett, Jesse NL:StL.
1902:	289	Piano Legs Hickman AL:Bos.-Clev.
	256	Crawford, Sam NL:Cin.
1903:	281	Freeman, Buck AL:Bos.
	272	Beaumont, Ginger NL:Pitt.
1904:	304	Lajoie, Nap AL:Clev. [2]
	255	Wagner, Honus NL:Pitt.
1905:	325	Seymour, Cy NL:Cin.
	259	Stone, George AL:StL.
1906:	291	Stone, George AL:StL. [2]
	237	Wagner, Honus NL:Pitt. [2]
1907:	286	Cobb, Ty AL:Det.
	264	Wagner, Honus NL:Pitt. [3]
1908:	308	Wagner, Honus NL:Pitt. [4]
	276	Cobb, Ty AL:Det. [2]
1909:	296	Cobb, Ty AL:Det. [3]
	242	Wagner, Honus NL:Pitt. [5]
1910:	304	Lajoie, Nap AL:Clev. [3]
	263	Magee, Sherry NL:Phil.
1911:	367	Cobb, Ty AL:Det. [4]
	308	Schulte, Wildfire NL:Chi.
1912:	331	Jackson, Joe AL:Clev.
	318	Zimmerman, Heinie NL:Chi.
1913:	298	Cravath, Gavvy NL:Phil.
	298	Crawford, Sam AL:Det.
1914:	287	Speaker, Tris AL:Bos.
	277	Magee, Sherry NL:Phil. [2]
1915:	274	Cobb, Ty AL:Det. [5]
	266	Cravath, Gavvy NL:Phil. [2]
1916:	293	Jackson, Joe AL:Chi. [2]
	262	Wheat, Zack NL:Brk.
1917:	336	Cobb, Ty AL:Det. [6]
	253	Hornsby, Rogers NL:StL.
1918:	236	Burns, George AL:Phil.
	202	Hollocher, Charlie NL:Chi.
1919:	284	Ruth, Babe AL:Bos.
	223	Myers, Hy NL:Brk.
1920:	399	Sisler, George AL:StL.
	329	Hornsby, Rogers NL:StL. [2]
1921:	457	Ruth, Babe AL:NY [2]
	378	Hornsby, Rogers NL:StL. [3]
1922:	450	Hornsby, Rogers NL:StL. [4]
	367	Williams, Ken AL:StL.
1923:	399	Ruth, Babe AL:NY [3]
	311	Frisch, Frankie NL:NY
1924:	391	Ruth, Babe AL:NY [4]
	373	Hornsby, Rogers NL:StL. [5]
1925:	392	Simmons, Al AL:Phil.
	381	Hornsby, Rogers NL:StL. [6]
1926:	365	Ruth, Babe AL:NY [5]
	305	Bottomley, Jim NL:StL.
1927:	447	Gehrig, Lou AL:NY
	342	Waner, Paul NL:Pitt.
1928:	380	Ruth, Babe AL:NY [6]
	362	Bottomley, Jim NL:StL. [2]
1929:	409	Hornsby, Rogers NL:Chi. [7]
	373	Simmons, Al AL:Phil. [2]
1930:	445	Klein, Chuck NL:Phil.
	419	Gehrig, Lou AL:NY [2]
1931:	410	Gehrig, Lou AL:NY [3]
	347	Klein, Chuck NL:Phil. [2]
1932:	438	Foxx, Jimmie AL:Phil.
	420	Klein, Chuck NL:Phil. [3]
1933:	403	Foxx, Jimmie AL:Phil. [2]
	365	Klein, Chuck NL:Phil. [4]
1934:	409	Gehrig, Lou AL:NY [4]
	369	Collins, Ripper NL:StL.
1935:	389	Greenberg, Hank AL:Det.
	365	Medwick, Joe NL:StL.
1936:	405	Trosky, Hal AL:Clev.
	367	Medwick, Joe NL:StL. [2]
1937:	418	DiMaggio, Joe AL:NY
	406	Medwick, Joe NL:StL. [3]
1938:	398	Foxx, Jimmie AL:Bos. [3]
	326	Mize, Johnny NL:StL.
1939:	353	Mize, Johnny NL:StL. [2]
	344	Williams, Ted AL:Bos.
1940:	384	Greenberg, Hank AL:Det. [2]
	368	Mize, Johnny NL:StL. [3]
1941:	348	DiMaggio, Joe AL:NY [2]
	299	Reiser, Pete NL:Brk.
1942:	338	Williams, Ted AL:Bos. [2]
	292	Slaughter, Enos NL:StL.
1943:	347	Musial, Stan NL:StL.
	301	York, Rudy AL:Det.
1944:	317	Nicholson, Bill NL:Chi.
	297	Lindell, Johnny AL:NY
1945:	367	Holmes, Tommy NL:Bos.
	301	Stirnweiss, Snuffy AL:NY
1946:	366	Musial, Stan NL:StL. [2]
	343	Williams, Ted AL:Bos. [3]
1947:	361	Kiner, Ralph NL:Pitt.
	335	Williams, Ted AL:Bos. [4]
1948:	429	Musial, Stan NL:StL. [3]
	355	DiMaggio, Joe AL:NY [3]
1949:	382	Musial, Stan NL:StL. [4]
	368	Williams, Ted AL:Bos. [5]
1950:	343	Snider, Duke NL:Brk.
	326	Dropo, Walt AL:Bos.
1951:	355	Musial, Stan NL:StL. [5]
	295	Williams, Ted AL:Bos. [6]
1952:	311	Musial, Stan NL:StL. [6]
	297	Rosen, Al AL:Clev.
1953:	370	Snider, Duke NL:Brk. [2]
	367	Rosen, Al AL:Clev. [2]
1954:	378	Snider, Duke NL:Brk. [3]
	304	Minoso, Minnie AL:Chi.
1955:	382	Mays, Willie NL:NY
	321	Kaline, Al AL:Det.
1956:	376	Mantle, Mickey AL:NY
	340	Aaron, Hank NL:Mil.
1957:	369	Aaron, Hank NL:Mil. [2]
	331	Sievers,Roy AL:Wash.
1958:	379	Banks, Ernie NL:Chi.
	307	Mantle, Mickey AL:NY [2]
1959:	400	Aaron, Hank NL:Mil. [3]
	301	Colavito, Rocky AL:Clev.
1960:	334	Aaron, Hank NL:Mil. [4]
	294	Mantle, Mickey AL:NY [3]
1961:	366	Maris, Roger AL:NY
	358	Aaron, Hank NL:Mil. [5]
1962:	382	Mays, Willie NL:SF [2]
	309	Colavito, Rocky AL:Det. [2]
1963:	370	Aaron, Hank NL:Mil. [6]
	319	Stuart, Dick AL:Bos.
1964:	374	Oliva, Tony AL:Minn.
	352	Allen, Dick NL:Phil.
1965:	360	Mays, Willie NL:SF [3]
	308	Versalles, Zoilo AL:Minn.

TOTAL BASES (CONTINUED)

1966:	367	Robinson, Frank AL:Balt.
	355	Alou, Felipe NL:Atl.
1967:	360	Yastrzemski, Carl AL:Bos.
	344	Aaron, Hank NL:Atl. [7]
1968:	330	Howard, Frank AL:Wash.
	321	Williams, Billy NL:Chi.
1969:	340	Howard, Frank AL:Wash. [2]
	332	Aaron, Hank NL:Atl. [8]
1970:	373	Williams, Billy NL:Chi. [2]
	335	Yastrzemski, Carl AL:Bos. [2]
1971:	352	Torre, Joe NL:StL.
	302	Smith, Reggie AL:Bos.
1972:	348	Williams, Billy NL:Chi. [3]
	314	Murcer, Bobby AL:NY
1973:	341	Bonds, Bobby NL:SF
	295	Bando, Sal AL:Oak.
	295	May, Dave AL:Mil.
	295	Scott, George AL:Mil.
1974:	315	Bench, Johnny NL:Cin.
	287	Rudi, Joe AL:Oak.
1975:	322	Luzinski, Greg NL:Phil.
	318	Scott, George AL:Mil. [2]
1976:	306	Schmidt, Mike NL:Phil.
	298	Brett, George AL:KC
1977:	388	Foster, George NL:Cin.
	382	Rice, Jim AL:Bos.
1978:	406	Rice, Jim AL:Bos. [2]
	340	Parker, Dave NL:Pitt.
1979:	369	Rice, Jim AL:Bos. [3]
	333	Winfield, Dave NL:SD
1980:	342	Schmidt, Mike NL:Phil. [2]
	335	Cooper, Cecil AL:Mil.
1981:	228	Schmidt, Mike NL:Phil. [3]
	215	Evans, Dwight AL:Bos.
1982:	367	Yount, Robin AL:Mil.
	317	Oliver, Al NL:Mtl.
1983:	344	Rice, Jim AL:Bos. [4]
	341	Dawson, Andre NL:Mtl.
1984:	339	Armas, Tony AL:Bos.
	332	Murphy, Dale NL:Atl.
1985:	370	Mattingly, Don AL:NY
	350	Parker, Dave NL:Cin. [2]
1986:	388	Mattingly, Don AL:NY [2]
	304	Parker, Dave NL:Cin. [3]
1987:	369	Bell, George AL:Tor.
	353	Dawson, Andre NL:Chi. [2]
1988:	358	Puckett, Kirby AL:Minn.
	329	Galarraga, Andres NL:Mtl.
1989:	345	Mitchell, Kevin NL:SF
	344	Sierra, Ruben AL:Tex.
1990:	344	Sandberg, Ryne NL:Chi.
	339	Fielder, Cecil AL:Det.
1991:	368	Ripken, Cal AL:Balt.
	303	Clark, Will NL:SF
	303	Pendleton, Terry NL:Atl.
1992:	323	Sheffield, Gary NL:SD
	313	Puckett, Kirby AL:Minn. [2]
1993:	365	Bonds, Barry NL:SF
	359	Griffey, Ken, Jr. AL:Sea.
1994:	300	Bagwell, Jeff NL:Hou.
	294	Belle, Albert AL:Clev.
1995:	377	Belle, Albert AL:Clev [2]
	359	Bichette, Dante NL:Col.

1996:	392	Burks, Ellis NL:Col.
	379	Rodriguez, Alex AL:Sea.
1997:	409	Walker, Larry NL:Col.
	393	Griffey, Ken, Jr. AL:Sea. [2]
1998	416	Sosa, Sammy NL:Chi.
	399	Belle, Albert AL:Chi. [3]
1999	397	Sosa, Sammy NL:Chi. [2]
	361	Green, Shawn AL:Tor.
2000	405	Helton, Todd NL:Col.
	378	Delgado, Carlos AL:Tor.
2001	425	Sosa, Sammy NL:Chi. [3]
	393	Rodriguez, Alex AL:Tex. [2]

RUNS BATTED IN

1920:	137	Ruth, Babe AL:NY
	94	Hornsby, Rogers NL:StL.
	94	Kelly, George NL:NY
1921:	171	Ruth, Babe AL:NY [2]
	126	Hornsby, Rogers NL:StL. [2]
1922:	155	Williams, Ken AL:StL.
	152	Hornsby, Rogers NL:StL. [3]
1923:	131	Ruth, Babe AL:NY [3]
	125	Meusel, Irish NL:NY
1924:	136	Kelly, George NL:NY [2]
	129	Goslin, Goose AL:Wash.
1925:	143	Hornsby, Rogers NL:StL. [4]
	138	Meusel, Bob AL:NY
1926:	145	Ruth, Babe AL:NY [4]
	120	Bottomley, Jim NL:StL.
1927:	175	Gehrig, Lou AL:NY
	131	Waner, Paul NL:Pitt.
1928:	142	Gehrig, Lou AL:NY [2]
	142	Ruth, Babe AL:NY [5]
	136	Bottomley, Jim NL:StL. [2]
1929:	159	Wilson, Hack NL:Chi.
	157	Simmons, Al AL:Phil.
1930:	191	Wilson, Hack NL:Chi. [2]
	174	Gehrig, Lou AL:NY [3]
1931:	184	Gehrig, Lou AL:NY [4]
	121	Klein, Chuck NL:Phil.
1932:	169	Foxx, Jimmie AL:Phil.
	143	Hurst, Don NL:Phil.
1933:	163	Foxx, Jimmie AL:Phil. [2]
	120	Klein, Chuck NL:Phil. [2]
1934:	165	Gehrig, Lou AL:NY [5]
	135	Ott, Mel NL:NY
1935:	170	Greenberg, Hank AL:Det.
	130	Berger, Wally NL:Bos.
1936:	162	Trosky, Hal AL:Clev.
	138	Medwick, Joe NL:StL.
1937:	183	Greenberg, Hank AL:Det. [2]
	154	Medwick, Joe NL:StL. [2]
1938:	175	Foxx, Jimmie AL:Bos. [3]
	122	Medwick, Joe NL:StL. [3]
1939:	145	Williams, Ted AL:Bos.
	128	McCormick, Frank NL:Cin.
1940:	150	Greenberg, Hank AL:Det. [3]
	137	Mize, Johnny NL:StL.
1941:	125	DiMaggio, Joe AL:NY
	120	Camilli, Dolph NL:Brk.
1942:	137	Williams, Ted AL:Bos. [2]
	110	Mize, Johnny NL:NY [2]
1943:	128	Nicholson, Bill NL:Chi.
	118	York, Rudy AL:Det.
1944:	122	Nicholson, Bill NL:Chi. [2]
	109	Stephens, Vern AL:StL.
1945:	124	Walker, Dixie NL:Brk.
	111	Etten, Nick AL:NY
1946:	130	Slaughter, Enos NL:StL.
	127	Greenberg, Hank AL:Det. [4]
1947:	138	Mize, Johnny NL:NY [3]
	114	Williams, Ted AL:Bos. [3]
1948:	155	DiMaggio, Joe AL:NY [2]
	131	Musial, Stan NL:StL
1949:	159	Williams, Ted AL:Bos. [4]
	159	Stephens, Vern AL:Bos. [2]
	127	Kiner, Ralph NL:Pitt.

1950:	144	Dropo, Walt AL:Bos.
	144	Stephens, Vern AL:Bos. [3]
	126	Ennis, Del NL:Phil.
1951:	129	Zernial, Gus AL:Chi.-Phil.
	121	Irvin, Monte NL:NY
1952:	121	Sauer, Hank NL:Chi.
	105	Rosen, Al AL:Clev.
1953:	145	Rosen, Al AL:Clev. [2]
	142	Campanella, Roy NL:Brk.
1954:	141	Kluszewski, Ted NL:Cin.
	126	Doby, Larry AL:Clev.
1955:	136	Snider, Duke NL:Brk.
	116	Boone, Ray AL:Det.
	116	Jensen, Jackie AL:Bos.
1956:	130	Mantle, Mickey AL:NY
	109	Musial, Stan NL:StL. [2]
1957:	132	Aaron, Hank NL:Mil.
	114	Sievers, Roy AL:Wash.
1958:	129	Banks, Ernie NL:Chi.
	122	Jensen, Jackie AL:Bos. [2]
1959:	143	Banks, Ernie NL:Chi. [2]
	112	Jensen, Jackie AL:Bos. [3]
1960:	126	Aaron, Hank NL:Mil. [2]
	112	Maris, Roger AL:NY
1961:	142	Cepeda, Orlando NL:SF
	142	Maris, Roger AL:NY [2]
1962:	153	Davis, Tommy NL:LA
	126	Killebrew, Harmon AL:Minn.
1963:	130	Aaron, Hank NL:Mil. [3]
	118	Stuart, Dick AL:Bos.
1964:	119	Boyer, Ken NL:StL.
	118	Robinson, Brooks AL:Balt.
1965:	130	Johnson, Deron NL:Cin.
	108	Colavito, Rocky AL:Clev.
1966:	127	Aaron, Hank NL:Atl. [4]
	122	Robinson, Frank AL:Balt.
1967:	121	Yastrzemski, Carl AL:Bos.
	111	Cepeda, Orlando NL:StL. [2]
1968:	109	Harrelson, Ken AL:Bos.
	105	McCovey, Willie NL:SF
1969:	140	Killebrew, Harmon AL:Minn. [2]
	126	McCovey, Willie NL:SF [2]
1970:	148	Bench, Johnny NL:Cin.
	126	Howard, Frank AL:Wash.
1971:	137	Torre, Joe NL:StL.
	119	Killebrew, Harmon AL:Minn. [3]
1972:	125	Bench, Johnny NL:Cin. [2]
	113	Allen, Dick AL:Chi.
1973:	119	Stargell, Willie NL:Pitt.
	117	Jackson, Reggie AL:Oak
1974:	129	Bench, Johnny NL:Cin. [3]
	118	Burroughs, Jeff AL:Tex
1975:	120	Luzinski, Greg NL:Phil.
	109	Scott, George AL:Mil.
1976:	121	Foster, George NL:Cin.
	109	May, Lee AL:Balt.
1977:	149	Foster, George NL:Cin. [2]
	119	Hisle, Larry AL:Minn.
1978:	139	Rice, Jim AL:Bos.
	120	Foster, George NL:Cin. [3]
1979:	139	Baylor, Don AL:Cal.
	118	Winfield, Dave NL:SD
1980:	122	Cooper, Cecil AL:Mil.
	121	Schmidt, Mike NL:Phil.
1981:	91	Schmidt, Mike NL:Phil. [2]
	78	Murray, Eddie AL:Balt.

RUNS BATTED IN (CONTINUED)

1982:	133	McRae, Hal AL:KC
	109	Murphy, Dale NL:Atl.
	109	Oliver, Al NL:Mtl.
1983:	126	Cooper, Cecil AL:Mil. [2]
	126	Rice, Jim AL:Bos. [2]
	121	Murphy, Dale NL:Atl. [2]
1984:	123	Armas, Tony AL:Bos.
	106	Carter, Gary NL:Mtl.
	106	Schmidt, Mike NL:Phil. [3]
1985:	145	Mattingly, Don AL:NY
	125	Parker, Dave NL:Cin.
1986:	121	Carter, Joe AL:Clev.
	119	Schmidt, Mike NL:Phil. [4]
1987:	137	Dawson, Andre NL:Chi.
	134	Bell, George AL:Tor.
1988:	124	Canseco, Jose AL:Oak.
	109	Clark, Will NL:SF
1989:	125	Mitchell, Kevin NL:SF
	119	Sierra, Ruben AL:Tex.
1990:	132	Fielder, Cecil AL:Det.
	122	Williams, Matt NL:SF
1991:	133	Fielder, Cecil AL:Det. [2]
	117	Johnson, Howard NL:NY
1992:	124	Fielder, Cecil AL:Det. [3]
	109	Daulton, Darren NL:Phil.
1993:	129	Belle, Albert AL:Clev.
	123	Bonds, Barry NL:SF
1994:	116	Bagwell, Jeff NL:Hou.
	112	Puckett, Kirby AL:Minn.
1995:	128	Bichette, Dante NL:Col.
	126	Belle, Albert AL:Clev. [2]
	126	Vaughn, Mo AL:Bos.
1996	150	Galarraga, Andres NL:Col.
	148	Belle, Albert AL:Clev. [3]
1997	147	Griffey, Ken, Jr. AL:Sea.
	140	Galarraga, Andres NL:Col.
1998	158	Sosa, Sammy NL:Chi.
	157	Gonzalez, Juan AL:Tex.
1999	165	Ramirez, Manny AL:Clev.
	147	McGwire, Mark NL:StL.
2000	147	Helton, Todd NL:Col.
	145	Martinez, Edgar AL:Sea.
2001	160	Sosa, Sammy NL:Chi. [2]
	141	Boone, Bret AL:Sea.

RUNS SCORED

Year	Runs	Player
1900:	131	Thomas, Roy NL:Phil.
1901:	145	Lajoie, Nap AL:Phil.
	139	Burkett, Jesse NL:StL.
1902:	109	Fultz, Dave AL:Phil.
	109	Hartsel, Topsy AL:Phil.
	105	Wagner, Honus NL:Pitt.
1903:	137	Beaumont, Ginger NL:Pitt.
	108	Dougherty, Patsy AL:Bos.
1904:	113	Dougherty, Patsy AL:Bos.-NY [2]
	99	Browne, George NL:NY
1905:	124	Donlin, Mike NL:NY
	92	Davis, Harry AL:Phil.
1906:	103	Chance, Frank NL:Chi.
	103	Wagner, Honus NL:Pitt. [2]
	98	Flick, Elmer AL:Clev.
1907:	104	Shannon, Spike NL:NY
	102	Crawford, Sam AL:Det.
1908:	105	McIntyre, Matty AL:Det.
	101	Tenney, Fred NL:NY
1909:	126	Leach, Tommy NL:Pitt.
	116	Cobb, Ty AL:Det.
1910:	110	Magee, Sherry NL:Phil.
	106	Cobb, Ty AL:Det. [2]
1911:	147	Cobb, Ty AL:Det. [3]
	121	Sheckard,Jimmy NL:Chi.
1912:	137	Collins, Eddie AL:Phil.
	120	Bescher, Bob NL:Cin.
1913:	125	Collins, Eddie AL:Phil. [2]
	99	Carey, Max NL:Pitt.
	99	Leach, Tommy NL:Chi. [2]
1914:	122	Collins, Eddie AL:Phil. [3]
	100	Burns, George NL:NY
1915:	144	Cobb, Ty AL:Det. [4]
	89	Cravath, Gavvy NL:Phil.
1916:	113	Cobb, Ty AL:Det. [5]
	105	Burns, George NL:NY [2]
1917:	112	Bush, Donie AL:Det.
	103	Burns, George NL:NY [3]
1918:	88	Groh, Heinie NL:Cin.
	84	Chapman, Ray AL:Clev.
1919:	103	Ruth, Babe AL:Bos.
	86	Burns, George NL:NY [4]
1920:	158	Ruth, Babe AL:NY [2]
	115	Burns, George NL:NY [5]
1921:	177	Ruth, Babe AL:NY [3]
	131	Hornsby, Rogers NL:StL.
1922:	141	Hornsby, Rogers NL:StL. [2]
	134	Sisler, George AL:StL.
1923:	151	Ruth, Babe AL:NY [4]
	121	Youngs, Ross NL:NY
1924:	143	Ruth, Babe AL:NY [5]
	121	Frisch, Frankie NL:NY
	121	Hornsby, Rogers NL:StL. [3]
1925:	144	Cuyler, Kiki NL:Pitt.
	135	Mostil, Johnny AL:Chi.
1926:	139	Ruth, Babe AL:NY [6]
	113	Cuyler, Kiki NL:Pitt. [2]
1927:	158	Ruth, Babe AL:NY [7]
	133	Hornsby, Rogers NL:NY [4]
	133	Waner, Lloyd NL:Pitt.
1928:	163	Ruth, Babe AL:NY [8]
	142	Waner, Paul NL:Pitt.
1929:	156	Hornsby, Rogers NL:Chi. [5]
	131	Gehringer, Charlie AL:Det.
1930:	158	Klein, Chuck NL:Phil.
	152	Simmons, Al AL:Phil
1931:	163	Gehrig, Lou AL:NY
	121	Klein, Chuck NL:Phil. [2]
	121	Terry, Bill NL:NY
1932:	152	Klein, Chuck NL:Phil. [3]
	151	Foxx, Jimmie AL:Phil.
1933:	138	Gehrig, Lou AL:NY [2]
	122	Martin, Pepper NL:StL.
1934:	134	Gehringer, Charlie AL:Det. [2]
	122	Waner, Paul NL:Pitt. [2]
1935:	133	Galan, Augie NL:Chi.
	125	Gehrig, Lou AL:NY [3]
1936:	167	Gehrig, Lou AL:NY [4]
	122	Vaughan, Arky NL:Pitt.
1937:	151	DiMaggio, Joe AL:NY
	111	Medwick, Joe NL:StL.
1938:	144	Greenberg, Hank AL:Det.
	116	Ott, Mel NL:NY
1939:	139	Rolfe, Red AL:NY
	115	Werber, Bill NL:Cin.
1940:	134	Williams, Ted AL:Bos.
	113	Vaughan, Arky NL:Pitt. [2]
1941:	135	Williams, Ted AL:Bos. [2]
	117	Reiser, Pete NL:Brk.
1942:	141	Williams, Ted AL:Bos. [3]
	118	Ott, Mel NL:NY [2]
1943:	112	Vaughan, Arky NL:Brk. [3]
	102	Case, George AL:Wash.
1944:	125	Stirnweiss, Snuffy AL:NY
	116	Nicholson, Bill NL:Chi.
1945:	128	Stanky, Eddie NL:Brk.
	107	Stirnweiss, Snuffy AL:NY [2]
1946:	142	Williams, Ted AL:Bos. [4]
	124	Musial, Stan NL:StL.
1947:	137	Mize, Johnny NL:NY
	125	Williams, Ted AL:Bos. [5]
1948:	138	Henrich, Tommy AL:NY
	135	Musial, Stan NL:StL. [2]
1949:	150	Williams, Ted AL:Bos. [6]
	132	Reese, Pee Wee NL:Brk.
1950:	131	DiMaggio, Dom AL:Bos.
	120	Torgeson, Earl NL:Bos.
1951:	124	Kiner, Ralph NL:Pitt.
	124	Musial, Stan NL:StL. [3]
	113	DiMaggio, Dom AL:Bos. [2]
1952:	105	Hemus, Solly NL:StL.
	105	Musial, Stan NL:StL. [4]
	104	Doby, Larry AL:Clev.
1953:	132	Snider, Duke NL:Brk.
	115	Rosen, Al AL:Clev.
1954:	129	Mantle, Mickey AL:NY
	120	Musial, Stan NL:StL. [5]
	120	Snider, Duke NL:Brk. [2]
1955:	126	Snider, Duke NL:Brk. [3]
	123	Smith, Al AL:Clev.
1956:	132	Mantle, Mickey AL:NY [2]
	122	Robinson, Frank NL:Cin.
1957:	121	Mantle, Mickey AL:NY [3]
	118	Aaron, Hank NL:Mil.
1958:	127	Mantle, Mickey AL:NY [4]
	121	Mays, Willie NL:SF
1959:	131	Pinson, Vada NL:Cin.
	115	Yost, Eddie AL:Det.

RUNS SCORED (CONTINUED)

1960:	119	Mantle, Mickey AL:NY [5]
	112	Bruton, Bill NL:Mil.
1961:	132	Mantle, Mickey AL:NY [6]
	132	Maris, Roger AL:NY
	129	Mays, Willie NL:SF [2]
1962:	134	Robinson, Frank NL:Cin. [2]
	115	Pearson, Albie AL:LA
1963:	121	Aaron, Hank NL:Mil. [2]
	99	Allison, Bob AL:Minn.
1964:	125	Allen, Dick NL:Phil.
	109	Oliva, Tony AL:Minn.
1965:	126	Harper, Tommy NL:Cin.
	126	Versalles, Zoilo AL:Minn.
1966:	122	Alou, Felipe NL:Atl.
	122	Robinson, Frank AL:Balt.
1967:	113	Aaron, Hank NL:Atl. [3]
	113	Brock, Lou NL:StL.
	112	Yastrzemski, Carl AL:Bos.
1968	98	Beckert, Glenn NL:Chi.
	95	McAuliffe, Dick AL:Det.
1969:	123	Jackson, Reggie AL:Oak.
	120	Bonds, Bobby NL:SF
	120	Rose, Pete NL:Cin.
1970:	137	Williams, Billy NL:Chi.
	125	Yastrzemski, Carl AL:Bos. [2]
1971:	126	Brock, Lou NL:StL. [2]
	99	Buford, Don AL:Balt.
1972:	122	Morgan, Joe NL:Cin.
	102	Murcer, Bobby AL:NY
1973:	131	Bonds, Bobby NL:SF [2]
	99	Jackson, Reggie AL:Oak. [2]
1974:	110	Rose, Pete NL:Cin. [2]
	93	Yastrzemski, Carl AL:Bos. [3]
1975:	112	Rose, Pete NL:Cin. [3]
	103	Lynn, Fred AL:Bos.
1976:	130	Rose, Pete NL:Cin. [4]
	104	White, Roy AL:NY
1977:	128	Carew, Rod AL:Minn.
	124	Foster, George NL:Cin.
1978:	126	LeFlore, Ron AL:Det.
	104	DeJesus, Ivan NL:Chi.
1979:	120	Baylor, Don AL:Cal.
	116	Hernandez, Keith NL:StL.
1980:	133	Wilson, Willie AL:KC
	111	Hernandez, Keith NL:StL. [2]
1981:	89	Henderson, Rickey AL:Oak.
	78	Schmidt, Mike NL:Phil.
1982:	136	Molitor, Paul AL:Mil.
	120	Smith, Lonnie NL:StL.
1983:	133	Raines, Tim NL:Mtl.
	121	Ripken, Cal AL:Balt.
1984:	121	Evans, Dwight AL:Bos.
	114	Sandberg, Ryne NL:Chi.
1985:	146	Henderson, Rickey AL:NY [2]
	118	Murphy, Dale NL:Atl.
1986:	130	Henderson, Rickey AL:NY [3]
	107	Gwynn, Tony NL:SD
	107	Hayes, Von NL:Phil.
1987:	123	Raines, Tim NL:Mtl. [2]
	114	Molitor, Paul AL:Mil. [2]
1988:	128	Boggs, Wade AL:Bos.
	109	Butler, Brett NL:SF

1989:	113	Boggs, Wade AL:Bos. [2]
	113	Henderson, Rickey AL:NY-Oak. [4]
	104	Clark, Will NL:SF
	104	Johnson, Howard NL:NY
	104	Sandberg, Ryne NL:Chi. [2]
1990:	119	Henderson, Rickey AL:Oak. [5]
	116	Sandberg, Ryne NL:Chi. [3]
1991:	133	Molitor, Paul AL:Mil. [3]
	112	Butler, Brett NL:LA [2]
1992:	114	Phillips, Tony AL:Det.
	109	Bonds, Barry NL:Pitt.
1993:	143	Dykstra, Len NL:Phil.
	124	Palmeiro, Rafael AL:Tex.
1994:	106	Thomas, Frank AL:Chi.
	104	Bagwell, Jeff NL:Hou.
1995:	123	Biggio, Craig NL:Hou.
	121	Belle, Albert AL:Clev.
	121	Martinez, Edgar AL:Sea.
1996	142	Burks, Ellis NL:Col.
	141	Rodriguez, Alex AL:Sea
1997	146	Biggio, Craig NL:Hou. [2]
	125	Griffey, Ken, Jr. AL:Sea.
1998	134	Sosa, Sammy NL:Chi.
	127	Jeter, Derek AL:NY
1999	143	Bagwell, Jeff NL:Hou. [2]
	138	Alomar, Roberto AL:Clev.
2000	152	Bagwell, Jeff NL:Hou. [3]
	136	Damon, Johnny AL:KC
2001	146	Sosa, Sammy NL:Chi. [2]
	133	Rodriguez, Alex AL:Tex. [2]

HITS

1900:	208	Keeler, Willie NL:Brk.
1901:	229	Lajoie, Nap AL:Phil.
	228	Burkett, Jesse NL:StL.
1902:	194	Beaumont, Ginger NL:Pitt.
	194	Hickman, Piano Legs AL:Bos.-Clev.
1903:	209	Beaumont, Ginger NL:Pitt. [2]
	195	Dougherty, Patsy AL:Bos.
1904:	211	Lajoie, Nap AL:Clev. [2]
	185	Beaumont, Ginger NL:Pitt. [3]
1905:	219	Seymour, Cy NL:Cin.
	187	Stone, George AL:StL.
1906:	214	Lajoie, Nap AL:Clev. [3]
	176	Steinfeldt, Harry NL:Chi.
1907:	212	Cobb, Ty AL:Det.
	187	Beaumont, Ginger NL:Bos. [4]
1908:	201	Wagner, Honus NL:Pitt.
	188	Cobb, Ty AL:Det. [2]
1909:	216	Cobb, Ty AL:Det. [3]
	172	Doyle, Larry NL:NY
1910:	227	Lajoie, Nap AL:Clev. [4]
	178	Byrne, Bobby NL:Pitt.
	178	Wagner, Honus NL:Pitt. [2]
1911:	248	Cobb, Ty AL:Det. [4]
	192	Miller, Doc NL:Bos.
1912:	227	Cobb, Ty AL:Det. [5]
	207	Zimmerman, Heinie NL:Chi.
1913:	197	Jackson, Joe AL:Clev.
	179	Cravath, Gavvy NL:Phil.
1914:	193	Speaker, Tris AL:Bos.
	171	Magee, Sherry NL:Phil.
1915:	208	Cobb, Ty AL:Det. [6]
	189	Doyle, Larry NL:NY [2]
1916:	211	Speaker, Tris AL:Clev. [2]
	184	Chase, Hal NL:Cin.
1917:	225	Cobb, Ty AL:Det. [7]
	182	Groh, Heinie NL:Cin.
1918:	178	Burns, George AL:Phil.
	161	Hollocher, Charlie NL:Chi.
1919:	191	Cobb, Ty AL:Det. [8]
	191	Veach, Bob AL:Det.
	164	Olson, Ivy NL:Brk.
1920:	257	Sisler, George AL:StL.
	218	Hornsby, Rogers NL:StL.
1921:	237	Heilmann, Harry AL:Det.
	235	Hornsby, Rogers NL:StL. [2]
1922:	250	Hornsby, Rogers NL:StL. [3]
	246	Sisler, George AL:StL. [2]
1923:	223	Frisch, Frankie NL:NY
	222	Jamieson, Charlie AL:Clev.
1924:	227	Hornsby, Rogers NL:StL. [4]
	216	Rice, Sam AL:Wash.
1925:	253	Simmons, Al AL:Phil.
	227	Bottomley, Jim NL:StL.
1926:	216	Burns, George AL:Clev. [2]
	216	Rice, Sam AL:Wash. [2]
	201	Brown, Eddie NL:Bos.
1927:	237	Waner, Paul NL:Pitt.
	231	Combs, Earle AL:NY
1928:	241	Manush, Heinie AL:StL.
	231	Lindstrom, Freddie NL:NY
1929:	254	O'Doul, Lefty NL:Phil.
	215	Alexander, Dale AL:Det.
	215	Gehringer, Charlie AL:Det.
1930:	254	Terry, Bill NL:NY
	225	Hodapp, Johnny AL:Clev.
1931:	214	Waner, Lloyd NL:Pitt.
	211	Gehrig, Lou AL:NY
1932:	226	Klein, Chuck NL:Phil.
	216	Simmons, Al AL:Phil. [2]
1933:	223	Klein, Chuck NL:Phil. [2]
	221	Manush, Heinie AL:Wash. [2]
1934:	217	Waner, Paul NL:Pitt. [2]
	214	Gehringer, Charlie AL:Det. [2]
1935:	227	Herman, Billy NL:Chi.
	216	Vosmik, Joe AL:Clev.
1936:	232	Averill, Earl AL:Clev.
	223	Medwick, Joe NL:StL.
1937:	237	Medwick, Joe NL:StL. [2]
	218	Bell, Beau AL:StL.
1938:	209	McCormick, Frank NL:Cin.
	201	Vosmik, Joe AL:Bos. [2]
1939:	213	Rolfe, Red AL:NY
	209	McCormick, Frank NL:Cin. [2]
1940:	200	Cramer, Doc AL:Bos.
	200	McCosky, Barney AL:Det.
	200	Radcliff, Rip AL:StL.
	191	Hack, Stan NL:Chi.
	191	McCormick, Frank NL:Cin. [3]
1941:	218	Travis, Cecil AL:Wash.
	186	Hack,Stan NL:Chi. [2]
1942:	205	Pesky, Johnny AL:Bos.
	188	Slaughter, Enos NL:StL.
1943:	220	Musial, Stan NL:StL.
	200	Wakefield, Dick AL:Det.
1944:	205	Stirnweiss, Snuffy AL:NY
	197	Cavarretta, Phil NL:Chi.
	197	Musial, Stan NL:StL. [2]
1945:	224	Holmes, Tommy NL:Bos.
	195	Stirnweiss, Snuffy AL:NY [2]
1946:	228	Musial, Stan NL:StL. [3]
	208	Pesky, Johnny AL:Bos. [2]
1947:	207	Pesky, Johnny AL:Bos. [3]
	191	Holmes, Tommy NL:Bos. [2]
1948:	230	Musial, Stan NL:StL. [4]
	207	Dillinger, Bob AL:StL.
1949:	207	Musial, Stan NL:StL. [5]
	203	Mitchell, Dale AL:Clev.
1950:	218	Kell, George AL:Det.
	199	Snider, Duke NL:Brk.
1951:	221	Ashburn, Richie NL:Phil.
	191	Kell, George AL:Det. [2]
1952:	194	Musial, Stan NL:StL. [6]
	192	Fox, Nellie AL:Chi.
1953:	209	Kuenn, Harvey AL:Det.
	205	Ashburn, Richie NL:Phil. [2]
1954:	212	Mueller, Don NL:NY
	201	Fox, Nellie AL:Chi. [2]
	201	Kuenn, Harvey AL:Det. [2]
1955:	200	Kaline, Al AL:Det.
	192	Kluszewski,Ted NL:Cin.
1956:	200	Aaron, Hank NL:Mil.
	196	Kuenn, Harvey AL:Det. [3]
1957:	200	Schoendienst, Red NL:NY-Mil.
	196	Fox, Nellie AL:Chi. [3]
1958:	215	Ashburn, Richie NL:Phil. [3]
	187	Fox, Nellie AL:Chi. [4]
1959:	223	Aaron, Hank NL:Mil. [2]
	198	Kuenn, Harvey AL:Det. [4]
1960:	190	Mays, Willie NL:SF
	184	Minoso, Minnie AL:Chi.

HITS (CONTINUED)

1961:	208	Pinson, Vada NL:Cin.
	193	Cash, Norm AL:Det.
1962:	230	Davis, Tommy NL:LA
	209	Richardson, Bobby AL:NY
1963:	204	Pinson, Vada NL:Cin. [2]
	183	Yastrzemski, Carl AL:Bos.
1964:	217	Oliva, Tony AL:Minn.
	211	Clemente, Roberto NL:Pitt.
	211	Flood, Curt NL:StL.
1965:	209	Rose, Pete NL:Cin.
	185	Oliva, Tony AL:Minn. [2]
1966:	218	Alou, Felipe NL:Atl.
	191	Oliva, Tony AL:Minn. [3]
1967:	209	Clemente, Roberto NL:Pitt. [2]
	189	Yastrzemski, Carl AL:Bos. [2]
1968:	210	Alou, Felipe NL:Atl. [2]
	210	Rose, Pete NL:Cin. [2]
	177	Campaneris, Bert AL:Oak.
1969:	231	Alou, Matty NL:Pitt.
	197	Oliva, Tony AL:Minn. [4]
1970:	205	Rose Pete NL:Cin. [3]
	205	Williams, Billy NL:Chi.
	204	Oliva, Tony AL:Minn. [5]
1971:	230	Torre, Joe NL:StL.
	204	Tovar, Cesar AL:Minn.
1972:	198	Rose, Pete NL:Cin. [4]
	181	Rudi, Joe AL:Oak.
1973:	230	Rose, Pete NL:Cin. [5]
	203	Carew, Rod AL:Minn.
1974:	218	Carew, Rod AL:Minn. [2]
	214	Garr, Ralph NL:Atl.
1975:	213	Cash, Dave NL:Phil.
	195	Brett, George AL:KC
1976:	215	Rose, Pete NL:Cin. [6]
	215	Brett, George AL:KC [2]
1977:	239	Carew, Rod AL:Minn. [3]
	215	Parker, Dave NL:Pitt.
1978:	213	Rice, Jim AL:Bos.
	202	Garvey, Steve NL:LA
1979:	212	Brett, George AL:KC [3]
	211	Templeton, Garry NL:StL.
1980:	230	Wilson, Willie AL:KC
	200	Garvey, Steve NL:LA [2]
1981:	140	Rose, Pete NL:Phil. [7]
	135	Henderson, Rickey AL:Oak.
1982:	210	Yount, Robin AL:Mil.
	204	Oliver, Al NL:Mtl.
1983:	211	Ripken, Cal AL:Balt.
	189	Cruz, Jose NL:Hou.
	189	Dawson, Andre NL:Mtl.
1984:	213	Gwynn, Tony NL:SD
	207	Mattingly, Don AL:NY
1985:	240	Boggs, Wade AL:Bos.
	216	McGee, Willie NL:StL.
1986:	238	Mattingly Don AL:NY [2]
	211	Gwynn, Tony NL:SD [2]
1987:	218	Gwynn, Tony NL:SD [3]
	207	Puckett, Kirby AL:Minn.
	207	Seitzer, Kevin AL:KC
1988:	234	Puckett, Kirby AL:Minn. [2]
	184	Galarraga, Andres NL:Mtl.
1989:	215	Puckett, Kirby AL:Minn. [3]
	203	Gwynn, Tony NL:SD [4]

1990:	199	McGee, Willie NL:StL.-AL:Oak.
	192	Butler, Brett NL:SF
	192	Dykstra, Len NL:Phil.
	191	Palmeiro, Rafael AL:Tex.
1991:	216	Molitor, Paul AL:Mil.
	187	Pendleton, Terry NL:Atl.
1992:	210	Puckett, Kirby AL:Minn. [4]
	199	Pendleton, Terry NL:Atl. [2]
	199	Van Slyke, Andy NL:Pitt.
1993:	211	Molitor, Paul AL:Tor. [2]
	194	Dykstra, Len NL:Phil. [2]
1994:	165	Gwynn, Tony NL:SD [5]
	160	Lofton, Kenny AL:Clev.
1995:	197	Bichette, Dante NL:Col.
	197	Gwynn, Tony NL:SD [6]
	186	Johnson, Lance AL:Chi.
1996	227	Johnson, Lance NL:NY (AL=1)
	225	Molitor, Paul AL:Minn. [3]
1997	220	Gwynn, Tony NL:SD [7]
	209	Garciaparra, Nomar, Bos
1998	219	Bichette, Dante NL:Col.[2]
	213	Rodriguez, Alex AL:Sea.
1999	219	Jeter, Derek AL:NY
	206	Gonzalez, Luis NL:Ari.
2000	240	Erstad, Darin AL:Ana.
	216	Helton, Todd NL:Col.
2001	242	Suzuki, Ichiro AL:Sea.
	206	Aurilia, Rich, NL:SF

SINGLES

1900	179	Keeler, Willie Brk.
1901:	180	Burkett, Jesse NL:StL.
	155	Waldron, Irv AL:Mil.-Wash.
1902:	167	Beaumont, Ginger NL:Pitt.
	150	Jones, Fielder AL:Chi.
1903:	166	Beaumont, Ginger NL:Pitt. [2]
	160	Dougherty, Patsy AL:Bos.
1904:	162	Keeler, Willie AL:NY [2]
	158	Beaumont, Ginger NL:Pitt. [3]
1905:	162	Donlin, Mike NL:NY
	147	Keeler, Willie AL:NY [3]
1906:	167	Keeler, Willie AL:NY [4]
	141	Huggins, Miller NL:Cin.
	141	Shannon, Spike NL:StL.-NY
1907:	163	Cobb, Ty AL:Det.
	163	Stone, George AL:StL.
	150	Beaumont, Ginger NL:Bos. [4]
1908:	153	Donlin, Mike NL:NY [2]
	131	McIntyre, Matty AL:Det.
	131	Stone, George AL:StL. [2]
1909:	164	Cobb, Ty AL:Det. [2]
	147	Grant, Eddie NL:Phil.
1910:	165	Lajoie, Nap AL:Clev.
	134	Grant, Eddie NL:Phil. [2]
1911:	169	Cobb, Ty AL:Det. [3]
	146	Daubert, Jake NL:Brk.
	146	Miller, Doc NL:Bos.
1912:	167	Cobb, Ty AL:Det. [4]
	159	Sweeney, Bill NL:Bos.
1913:	152	Daubert, Jake NL:Brk. [2]
	145	Collins, Eddie AL:Phil.
1914:	160	McInnis, Stuffy AL:Phil.
	128	Becker, Beals NL:Phil.
1915:	161	Cobb, Ty AL:Det. [5]
	135	Doyle, Larry NL:NY
1916:	160	Speaker, Tris AL:Clev.
	142	Robertson, Dave NL:NY
1917:	151	Cobb, Ty AL:Det. [6]
	151	Milan, Clyde AL:Wash.
	141	Kauff, Benny NL:NY
	141	Roush, Edd NL:Cin.
1918:	141	Burns, George AL:Phil.
	130	Hollocher, Charlie NL:Chi.
1919:	144	Rice, Sam AL:Wash.
	140	Olson, Ivy NL:Brk.
1920:	171	Sisler, George AL:StL.
	170	Stock, Milt NL:StL.
1921:	179	Tobin, Jack AL:StL.
	161	Bigbee, Carson NL:Pitt.
1922:	178	Sisler, George AL:StL. [2]
	166	Bigbee, Carson NL:Pitt. [2]
1923:	172	Jamieson, Charlie AL:Clev.
	169	Frisch, Frankie NL:NY
1924:	168	Jamieson, Charlie AL:Clev. [2]
	149	Wheat, Zack NL:Brk.
1925:	182	Rice, Sam AL:Wash. [2]
	164	Stock, Milt NL:Brk. [2]
1926:	167	Rice, Sam AL:Wash. [3]
	160	Brown, Eddie NL:Bos.
1927:	198	Waner, Lloyd NL:Pitt.
	166	Combs, Earle AL:NY
1928:	180	Waner, Lloyd NL:Pitt. [2]
	161	Manush, Heinie AL:StL.

1929:	181	O'Doul, Lefty NL:Phil.
	181	Waner, Lloyd NL:Pitt. [3]
	151	Combs, Earle AL:NY [2]
1930:	177	Terry, Bill NL:NY
	158	Rice, Sam AL:Wash. [4]
1931:	172	Waner, Lloyd NL:Pitt. [4]
	142	Melillo, Oscar AL:StL.
	142	Stone, John AL:Det.
1932:	158	O'Doul, Lefty AL:Brk. [2]
	145	Manush, Heinie AL:Wash. [2]
1933:	167	Manush, Heinie AL:Wash. [3]
	162	Fullis, Chick NL:Phil.
1934:	169	Terry, Bill NL:NY [2]
	158	Cramer, Doc AL:Phil.
1935:	170	Cramer, Doc AL:Phil. [2]
	160	Jensen, Woody NL:Pitt.
1936:	161	Radcliff, Rip AL:Chi.
	160	Moore, Joe NL:NY
1937:	178	Waner, Paul NL:Pitt.
	162	Lewis, Buddy AL:Wash.
1938:	160	McCormick, Frank NL:Cin.
	158	Almada, Mel AL:Wash.-StL.
1939:	162	Hassett, Buddy NL:Bos.
	147	Cramer, Doc AL:Bos. [3]
1940:	160	Cramer, Doc AL:Bos. [4]
	141	Whitehead, Burgess NL:NY
1941:	153	Travis, Cecil AL:Wash.
	141	Hack, Stan NL:Chi.
1942:	165	Pesky, Johnny AL:Bos.
	127	Slaughter, Enos NL:StL.
1943:	172	Witek, Mickey NL:NY
	159	Cramer, Doc AL:Det. [5]
1944:	146	Stirnweiss, Snuffy AL:NY
	142	Cavarretta, Phil NL:Chi.
1945:	155	Hack, Stan NL:Chi. [2]
	139	Hall, Irv AL:Phil.
1946:	159	Pesky, Johnny AL:Bos. [2]
	142	Musial, Stan NL:StL.
1947:	172	Pesky, Johnny AL:Bos. [3]
	146	Holmes, Tommy NL:Bos.
1948:	162	Mitchell, Dale AL:Clev.
	150	Rojek, Stan NL:Pitt.
1949:	161	Mitchell, Dale AL:Clev. [2]
	160	Schoendienst, Red NL:StL.
1950:	150	Rizzuto, Phil AL:NY
	143	Waitkus, Eddie NL:Phil.
1951:	181	Ashburn, Richie NL:Phil.
	150	Kell, George AL:Det.
1952:	157	Fox, Nellie AL:Chi.
	145	Adams, Bobby NL:Cin.
1953:	169	Ashburn, Richie NL:Phil. [2]
	167	Kuenn, Harvey AL:Det.
1954:	167	Fox, Nellie AL:Chi. [2]
	165	Mueller, Don NL:NY
1955:	157	Fox, Nellie AL:Chi. [3]
	152	Mueller, Don NL:NY [2]
1956:	158	Fox, Nellie AL:Chi. [4]
	157	Temple, Johnny NL:Cin.
1957:	155	Fox, Nellie AL:Chi. [5]
	152	Ashburn, Richie NL:Phil. [3]
1958:	176	Ashburn, Richie NL:Phil. [4]
	160	Fox, Nellie AL:Chi. [6]
1959:	149	Fox, Nellie AL:Chi. [7]
	144	Blasingame, Don NL:StL.
1960:	154	Groat, Dick NL:Pitt.
	139	Fox, Nellie AL:Chi. [8]

SINGLES (CONTINUED)

1961:	150	Pinson, Vada NL:Cin.
	150	Wills, Maury NL:LA
	148	Richardson, Bobby AL:NY
1962:	179	Wills, Maury NL:LA [2]
	158	Richardson, Bobby AL:NY [2]
1963:	152	Flood, Curt NL:StL.
	139	Pearson, Albie AL:LA
1964:	178	Flood, Curt NL:StL. [2]
	148	Richardson, Bobby AL:NY [3]
1965:	165	Wills, Maury NL:LA [3]
	129	Buford, Don AL:Chi.
1966:	160	Jackson, Sonny NL:Hou.
	143	Aparicio, Luis AL:Balt.
1967:	162	Wills, Maury NL:Pitt. [4]
	140	Clarke, Horace AL:NY
1968:	160	Flood, Curt NL:StL. [3]
	139	Campaneris, Bert AL:Oak.
1969:	183	Alou, Matty NL:Pitt.
	146	Clarke, Horace AL:NY [2]
1970:	171	Alou, Matty NL:Pitt. [2]
	156	Johnson, Alex AL:Cal.
1971:	180	Garr, Ralph NL:Atl.
	171	Tovar, Cesar AL:Minn.
1972:	156	Brock, Lou NL:StL.
	143	Carew, Rod AL:Minn.
1973:	181	Rose, Pete NL:Cin.
	156	Carew, Rod AL:Minn. [2]
1974:	180	Carew, Rod AL:Minn. [3]
	167	Cash, Dave NL:Phil.
1975:	166	Cash, Dave NL:Phil. [2]
	151	Munson, Thurman AL:NY
1976:	164	Montanez, Willie NL:SF-Atl.
	160	Brett, George AL:KC
1977:	171	Carew, Rod AL:Minn. [4]
	155	Templeton, Garry NL:StL.
1978:	153	Bowa, Larry NL:Phil.
	153	LeFlore, Ron AL:Det.
1979:	159	Rose, Pete NL:Phil. [2]
	148	Wilson, Willie AL:KC
1980:	184	Wilson, Willie AL:KC [2]
	155	Richards, Gene NL:SD
1981:	117	Rose, Pete NL:Phil. [3]
	115	Wilson, Willie AL:KC [3]
1982:	157	Wilson, Willie AL:KC [4]
	147	Buckner, Bill NL:Chi.
1983:	160	Ramirez, Rafael NL:Atl.
	154	Boggs, Wade AL:Bos.
1984:	177	Gwynn, Tony NL:SD
	162	Boggs, Wade AL:Bos. [2]
1985:	187	Boggs, Wade AL:Bos. [3]
	162	McGee, Willie NL:StL.
1986:	161	Fernandez, Tony AL:Tor.
	157	Gwynn, Tony NL:SD [2]
	157	Sax, Steve NL:LA
1987:	162	Gwynn, Tony NL:SD [3]
	151	Seitzer, Kevin AL:KC
1988:	163	Puckett, Kirby AL:Minn.
	147	Sax, Steve NL:LA [2]
1989:	171	Sax, Steve NL:NY (NL=2)
	165	Gwynn, Tony NL:SD [4]
1990:	160	Butler, Brett NL:SF
	136	Palmeiro, Rafael AL:Tex.
1991:	162	Butler, Brett NL:LA [2]
	156	Franco, Julio AL:Tex.

1992:	152	Baerga, Carlos AL:Clev.
	143	Butler, Brett NL:LA [3]
1993:	149	Butler, Brett NL:LA [4]
	148	Lofton, Kenny AL:Clev.
1994:	117	Gwynn, Tony NL:SD [5]
	107	Lofton, Kenny AL:Clev. [2]
	107	Molitor, Paul AL:Tor.
1995:	154	Gwynn, Tony NL:SD [6]
	151	Nixon, Otis AL:Tex.
1996	167	Molitor, Paul AL:Minn. [2]
	166	Johnson, Lance NL:NY
1997	152	Gwynn, Tony NL:SD [7]
	142	Anderson, Garret AL:Ana.
	142	Jeter, Derek AL:NY
1998	151	Jeter, Derek AL:NY [2]
	149	Womack, Tony NL:Pitt.
1999	152	Velarde, Randy AL:Ana.-Oak.
	149	Glanville, Doug NL:Phil.
2000	170	Erstad, Darin AL:Ana.
	158	Castillo, Luis NL:Fla.
2001	192	Suzuki, Ichiro AL:Sea.
	163	Pierre, Juan NL:Col.

DOUBLES

1900:	45	Wagner, Honus NL:Pitt.
1901:	48	Lajoie, Nap AL:Phil.
	39	Beckley, Jake NL:Cin.
	39	Wagner, Honus NL:Pitt. [2]
1902:	43	Davis, Harry AL:Phil.
	43	Delahanty, Ed AL:Wash.
	33	Wagner, Honus NL:Pitt. [3]
1903:	45	Seybold, Socks AL:Phil.
	32	Clarke, Fred NL:Pitt.
	32	Mertes, Sam NL:NY
	32	Steinfeldt, Harry NL:Cin.
1904:	50	Lajoie, Nap AL:Clev. [2]
	44	Wagner, Honus NL:Pitt. [4]
1905:	47	Davis, Harry AL:Phil. [2]
	40	Seymour, Cy NL:Cin.
1906:	49	Lajoie, Nap AL:Clev. [3]
	38	Wagner, Honus NL:Pitt. [5]
1907:	38	Wagner, Honus NL:Pitt. [6]
	37	Davis, Harry AL:Phil. [3]
1908:	39	Wagner, Honus NL:Pitt. [7]
	36	Cobb, Ty AL:Det.
1909:	39	Wagner, Honus NL:Pitt. [8]
	35	Crawford, Sam AL:Det.
1910:	51	Lajoie, Nap AL:Clev. [4]
	43	Byrne, Bobby NL:Pitt.
1911:	47	Cobb, Ty AL:Det. [2]
	38	Konetchy, Ed NL:StL.
1912:	53	Speaker, Tris AL:Bos.
	41	Zimmerman, Heinie NL:Chi.
1913:	40	Smith, Red NL:Brk.
	39	Jackson, Joe AL:Clev.
1914:	46	Speaker, Tris AL:Bos. [2]
	39	Magee, Sherry NL:Phil.
1915:	40	Doyle, Larry NL:NY
	40	Veach, Bobby AL:Det.
1916:	42	Niehoff, Bert NL:Phil.
	41	Graney, Jack AL:Clev.
	41	Speaker, Tris AL:Clev. [3]
1917:	44	Cobb, Ty AL:Det. [3]
	39	Groh, Heinie NL:Cin.
1918:	33	Speaker, Tris AL:Clev. [4]
	28	Groh, Heinie NL:Cin. [2]
1919:	45	Veach, Bobby AL:Det. [2]
	31	Youngs, Ross NL:NY
1920:	50	Speaker, Tris AL:Clev. [5]
	44	Hornsby, Rogers NL:StL.
1921:	52	Speaker, Tris AL:Clev. [6]
	44	Hornsby, Rogers NL:StL. [2]
1922:	48	Speaker, Tris AL:Clev. [7]
	46	Hornsby, Rogers NL:StL. [3]
1923:	59	Speaker, Tris AL:Clev. [8]
	41	Roush, Edd NL:Cin.
1924:	45	Heilmann, Harry AL:Det.
	45	Sewell, Joe AL:Clev.
	43	Hornsby, Rogers NL:StL. [4]
1925:	44	Bottomley, Jim NL:StL.
	44	McManus, Marty AL:StL.
1926:	64	Burns, George AL:Clev.
	40	Bottomley, Jim NL:StL. [2]
1927:	52	Gehrig, Lou AL:NY
	46	Stephenson, Riggs NL:Chi.
1928:	50	Waner, Paul NL:Pitt.
	47	Gehrig, Lou AL:NY [2]
	47	Manush, Heinie AL:StL.
1929:	52	Frederick, Johnny NL:Brk.
	45	Gehringer, Charlie AL:Det.
	45	Johnson, Roy AL:Det.
	45	Manush, Heinie AL:StL. [2]
1930:	59	Klein, Chuck NL:Phil.
	51	Hodapp, Johnny AL:Clev.
1931:	67	Webb, Earl AL:Bos.
	46	Adams, Sparky NL:StL.
1932:	62	Waner, Paul NL:Pitt. [2]
	47	McNair, Eric AL:Phil.
1933:	45	Cronin, Joe AL:Wash.
	44	Klein, Chuck NL:Phil. [2]
1934:	63	Greenberg, Hank AL:Det.
	42	Allen, Ethan NL:Phil.
	42	Cuyler, Kiki NL:Chi.
1935:	57	Herman, Billy NL:Chi.
	47	Vosmik, Joe AL:Clev.
1936:	64	Medwick, Joe NL:StL.
	60	Gehringer, Charlie AL:Det. [2]
1937:	56	Medwick, Joe NL:StL. [2]
	51	Bell, Beau AL:StL.
1938:	51	Cronin, Joe AL:Bos. [2]
	47	Medwick, Joe NL:StL. [3]
1939:	52	Slaughter, Enos NL:StL.
	46	Rolfe, Red AL:NY
1940:	50	Greenberg, Hank AL:Det. [2]
	44	McCormick, Frank NL:Cin.
1941:	45	Boudreau, Lou AL:Clev.
	39	Mize, Johnny NL:StL.
	39	Reiser, Pete NL:Brk.
1942:	40	Kolloway, Don AL:Chi.
	38	Marion, Marty NL:StL.
1943:	48	Musial, Stan NL:StL.
	38	Wakefield, Dick AL:Det.
1944:	51	Musial, Stan NL:StL. [2]
	45	Boudreau, Lou AL:Clev. [2]
1945:	47	Holmes, Tommy NL:Bos.
	35	Moses, Wally AL:Chi.
1946:	51	Vernon, Mickey AL:Wash.
	50	Musial, Stan NL:StL. [3]
1947:	45	Boudreau, Lou AL:Clev. [3]
	38	Miller, Eddie NL:Cin.
1948:	46	Musial, Stan NL:StL. [4]
	44	Williams, Ted AL:Bos.
1949:	41	Musial, Stan NL:StL. [5]
	39	Williams, Ted AL:Bos. [2]
1950:	56	Kell, George AL:Det.
	43	Schoendienst, Red NL:StL.
1951:	41	Dark, Alvin NL:NY
	36	Kell, George AL:Det. [2]
	36	Mele, Sam AL:Wash.
	36	Yost, Eddie AL:Wash.
1952:	43	Fain, Ferris AL:Phil.
	42	Musial, Stan NL:StL. [6]
1953:	53	Musial, Stan NL:StL. [7]
	43	Vernon, Mickey AL:Wash. [2]
1954:	41	Musial, Stan NL:StL. [8]
	33	Vernon, Mickey AL:Wash. [3]
1955:	38	Kuenn, Harvey AL:Det.
	37	Aaron, Hank NL:Mil.
	37	Logan, Johnny NL:Mil.
1956:	40	Piersall, Jimmy AL:Bos.
	34	Aaron, Hank NL:Mil. [2]
1957:	39	Hoak, Don NL:Cin.
	36	Gardner, Billy AL:Balt.
	36	Minoso, Minnie AL:Chi.

DOUBLES (CONTINUED)

1958:	39	Kuenn, Harvey AL:Det. [2]
	38	Cepeda, Orlando NL:SF
1959:	47	Pinson, Vada NL:Cin.
	42	Kuenn, Harvey AL:Det. [3]
1960:	37	Pinson, Vada NL:Cin. [2]
	36	Francona, Tito AL:Clev.
1961:	41	Kaline, Al AL:Det.
	39	Aaron, Hank NL:Mil. [3]
1962:	51	Robinson, Frank NL:Cin.
	45	Robinson, Floyd AL:Chi.
1963:	43	Groat, Dick NL:StL.
	40	Yastrzemski, Carl AL:Bos.
1964:	44	Maye, Lee NL:Mil.
	43	Oliva, Tony AL:Minn.
1965:	45	Versalles Zoilo AL:Minn.
	45	Yastrzemski, Carl AL:Bos. [2]
	40	Aaron, Hank NL:Mil. [4]
1966:	40	Callison, Johnny NL:Phil.
	39	Yastrzemski, Carl AL:Bos. [3]
1967:	44	Staub, Rusty NL:Hou.
	34	Oliva, Tony AL:Minn. [2]
1968:	46	Brock, Lou NL:StL.
	37	Smith, Reggie AL:Bos.
1969:	41	Alou, Matty NL:Pitt.
	39	Oliva, Tony AL:Minn. [3]
1970:	47	Parker, Wes NL:LA
	36	Oliva, Tony AL:Minn. [4]
	36	Otis, Amos AL:KC
	36	Tovar, Cesar AL:Minn.
1971:	40	Cedeno, Cesar NL:Hou.
	33	Smith, Reggie AL:Bos. [2]
1972:	39	Cedeno, Cesar NL:Hou. [2]
	39	Montanez, Willie NL:Phil.
	33	Piniella, Lou AL:KC
1973:	43	Stargell, Willie NL:Pitt.
	32	Bando, Sal AL:Oak
	32	Garcia, Pedro AL:Mil.
1974:	45	Rose, Pete NL:Cin.
	39	Rudi, Joe AL:Oak.
1975:	47	Lynn, Fred AL:Bos.
	47	Rose, Pete NL:Cin. [2]
1976:	42	Rose, Pete NL:Cin. [3]
	40	Otis, Amos AL:KC [2]
1977:	54	McRae, Hal AL:KC
	44	Parker, Dave NL:Pitt.
1978:	51	Rose, Pete NL:Cin. [4]
	45	Brett, George AL:KC
1979:	48	Hernandez, Keith NL:StL.
	44	Cooper, Cecil AL:Mil.
	44	Lemon, Chet AL:Chi.
1980:	49	Yount, Robin AL:Mil.
	42	Rose, Pete NL:Phil. [5]
1981:	35	Buckner, Bill NL:Chi.
	35	Cooper, Cecil AL:Mil. [2]
1982:	46	McRae, Hal AL:KC [2]
	46	Yount, Robin AL:Mil. [2]
	43	Oliver, Al NL:Mtl.
1983:	47	Ripken, Cal AL:Balt.
	38	Buckner, Bill NL:Chi. [2]
	38	Oliver, Al NL:Mtl. [2]
	38	Ray, Johnny NL:Pitt.
1984:	44	Mattingly, Don AL:NY
	38	Raines, Tim NL:Mtl.
	38	Ray, Johnny NL:Pitt. [2]

1985:	48	Mattingly, Don AL:NY [2]
	42	Parker, Dave NL:Cin. [2]
1986:	53	Mattingly, Don AL:NY [3]
	46	Hayes, Von NL:Phil.
1987:	42	Wallach, Tim NL:Mtl.
	41	Molitor, Paul AL:Mil.
1988:	45	Boggs, Wade AL:Bos.
	42	Galarraga, Andres NL:Mtl.
1989:	51	Boggs, Wade AL:Bos. [2]
	42	Guerrero, Pedro NL:StL.
	42	Wallach, Tim NL:Mtl. [2]
1990:	45	Brett, George AL:KC [2]
	45	Reed, Jody AL:Bos.
	40	Jefferies, Gregg NL:NY
1991:	49	Palmeiro, Rafael AL:Tex.
	44	Bonilla, Bobby NL:Pitt.
1992:	46	Martinez, Edgar AL:Sea.
	46	Thomas, Frank AL:Chi.
	45	Van Slyke, Andy NL:Pitt.
1993:	54	Olerud, John AL:Tor.
	45	Hayes, Charlie NL:Col.
1994:	45	Knoblauch, Chuck AL:Minn.
	44	Biggio, Craig NL:Hou.
	44	Walker, Larry NL:Mtl.
1995:	52	Belle, Albert AL:Clev.
	52	Martinez, Edgar AL:Sea. [2]
	51	Grace, Mark NL:Chi.
1996	54	Rodriguez, Alex AL:Sea.
	48	Bagwell, Jeff NL:Hou.
1997	54	Grudzielanek, Mark NL:Mtl.
	47	Valentin, John AL:Bos
1998	51	Biggio, Craig NL:Hou [2]
	50	Gonzalez, Juan AL:Tex.
1999	56	Biggio, Craig NL:Hou. [3]
	45	Green, Shawn AL:Tor.
2000	59	Helton, Todd NL:Col.
	57	Delgado, Carlos AL:Tor.
2001	55	Berkman, Lance NL:Hou.
	47	Giambi, Jason AL:Oak.

TRIPLES

1900:	22	Wagner, Honus NL:Pitt.		1929:	20	Waner, Lloyd NL:Pitt.
1901:	21	Keister, Bill AL:Balt.			19	Gehringer, Charlie AL:Det.
	19	Sheckard, Jimmy NL:Brk.		1930:	23	Comorosky, Adam NL:Pitt.
1902:	23	Crawford, Sam NL:Cin.			22	Combs, Earle AL:NY [3]
	21	Williams, Jimmy AL:Balt.		1931:	20	Terry, Bill NL:NY
1903:	25	Crawford, Sam AL:Det.			19	Johnson, Roy AL:Det.
	19	Wagner, Honus NL:Pitt. [2]		1932:	19	Herman, Babe NL:Cin.
1904:	19	Cassidy, Joe AL:Wash.			18	Cronin, Joe AL:Wash.
	19	Freeman, Buck AL:Bos.		1933:	19	Vaughan, Arky NL:Pitt.
	19	Stahl, Chick AL:Bos.			17	Manush, Heinie AL:Wash.
	18	Lumley, Harry NL:Brk.		1934:	18	Medwick, Joe NL:StL.
1905:	21	Seymour, Cy NL:Cin.			13	Chapman, Ben AL:NY
	19	Flick, Elmer AL:Clev.		1935:	20	Vosmik, Joe AL:Clev.
1906:	22	Flick, Elmer AL:Clev. [2]			18	Goodman, Ival NL:Cin.
	13	Clarke, Fred NL:Pitt.		1936:	15	Averill, Earl AL:Clev.
	13	Schulte, Wildfire NL:Chi.			15	DiMaggio, Joe AL:NY
1907:	18	Flick, Elmer AL:Clev. [3]			15	Rolfe, Red AL:NY
	16	Alperman, Whitey NL:Brk.			14	Goodman, Ival NL:Cin. [2]
	16	Ganzel, John NL:Cin.		1937:	17	Vaughan, Arky NL:Pitt. [2]
1908:	20	Cobb, Ty AL:Det.			16	Kreevich, Mike AL:Chi.
	19	Wagner, Honus NL:Pitt. [3]			16	Walker, Dixie AL:Chi.
1909:	19	Baker, Frank AL:Phil.		1938:	18	Heath, Jeff AL:Clev.
	17	Mitchell, Mike NL:Cin.			16	Mize, Johnny NL:StL.
1910:	19	Crawford, Sam AL:Det. [2]		1939:	18	Herman, Billy NL:Chi.
	18	Mitchell, Mike NL:Cin. [2]			16	Lewis, Buddy AL:Wash.
1911:	25	Doyle, Larry NL:NY		1940:	19	McCosky, Barney AL:Det.
	24	Cobb, Ty AL:Det. [2]			15	Vaughan, Arky NL:Pitt. [3]
1912:	36	Wilson, Owen NL:Pitt.		1941:	20	Heath, Jeff AL:Clev. [2]
	26	Jackson, Joe AL:Clev.			17	Reiser, Pete NL:Brk.
1913:	23	Crawford, Sam AL:Det. [3]		1942:	17	Slaughter, Enos NL:StL.
	21	Saier, Vic NL:Chi.			15	Spence, Stan AL:Wash.
1914:	26	Crawford, Sam AL:Det. [4]		1943:	20	Musial, Stan NL:StL.
	17	Carey, Max NL:Pitt.			12	Lindell, Johnny AL:NY
1915:	25	Long, Tommy NL:StL.			12	Moses, Wally AL:Chi.
	19	Crawford, Sam AL:Det. [5]		1944:	19	Barrett, Johnny NL:Pitt.
1916:	21	Jackson, Joe AL:Chi. [2]			16	Lindell, Johnny AL:NY [2]
	16	Hinchman, Bill NL:Pitt.			16	Stirnweiss, Snuffy AL:NY
1917:	23	Cobb, Ty AL:Det. [3]		1945:	22	Stirnweiss, Snuffy AL:NY [2]
	17	Hornsby, Rogers NL:StL.			13	Olmo, Luis NL:Brk.
1918:	15	Daubert, Jake NL:Brk.		1946:	20	Musial, Stan NL:StL. [2]
	14	Cobb, Ty AL:Det. [4]			16	Edwards, Hank AL:Clev.
1919:	17	Veach, Bobby AL:Det.		1947:	16	Walker, Harry NL:StL.-Phil.
	14	Myers, Hy NL:Brk.			13	Henrich, Tommy AL:NY
	14	Southworth, Billy NL:Pitt.		1948:	18	Musial, Stan NL:StL. [3]
1920:	22	Myers, Hy NL:Brk. [2]			14	Henrich, Tommy AL:NY [2]
	20	Jackson, Joe AL:Chi. [3]		1949:	23	Mitchell, Dale AL:Clev.
1921:	19	Shanks, Howard AL:Wash.			13	Musial, Stan NL:StL. [4]
	18	Hornsby, Rogers NL:StL. [2]			13	Slaughter, Enos NL:StL. [2]
	18	Powell, Ray NL:Bos.		1950:	14	Ashburn, Richie NL:Phil.
1922:	22	Daubert, Jake NL:Cin. [2]			11	DiMaggio, Dom AL:Bos.
	18	Sisler, George AL:StL.			11	Doerr, Bobby AL:Bos.
1923:	19	Carey, Max NL:Pitt. [2]			11	Evers, Hoot AL:Det.
	19	Traynor, Pie NL:Pitt.		1951:	14	Minoso, Minnie AL:Clev.-Chi.
	18	Goslin, Goose AL:Wash.			12	Bell, Gus NL:Pitt.
	18	Rice, Sam AL:Wash.			12	Musial, Stan NL:StL. [5]
1924:	21	Roush, Edd NL:Cin.		1952:	14	Thomson, Bobby NL:NY
	19	Pipp, Wally AL:NY			11	Avila, Bobby AL:Clev.
1925:	26	Cuyler, Kiki NL:Pitt.		1953:	17	Gilliam, Jim NL:Brk.
	20	Goslin, Goose AL:Wash. [2]			16	Rivera, Jim AL:Chi.
1926:	22	Waner, Paul NL:Pitt.		1954:	18	Minoso, Minnie. AL:Chi. [2]
	20	Gehrig, Lou AL:NY			13	Mays, Willie NL:NY
1927:	23	Combs, Earle AL:NY		1955:	13	Long, Dale NL:Pitt.
	18	Waner, Paul NL:Pitt. [2]			13	Mays, Willie NL:NY [2]
1928:	21	Combs, Earle AL:NY [2]			11	Carey, Andy AL:NY
	20	Bottomley, Jim NL:StL.			11	Mantle, Mickey AL:NY

TRIPLES (CONTINUED)

1956:	15	Bruton, Bill NL:Mil.
	11	Jensen, Jackie AL:Bos.
	11	Lemon, Jim AL:Wash.
	11	Minoso, Minnie. AL:Chi. [3]
	11	Simpson, Harry AL:KC
1957:	20	Mays, Willie NL:NY [3]
	9	Bauer, Hank AL:NY
	9	McDougald, Gil AL:NY
	9	Simpson, Harry AL:KC-NY [2]
1958:	13	Ashburn, Richie NL:Phil. [2]
	10	Power, Vic AL:KC-Clev.
1959:	11	Moon, Wally NL:LA
	11	Neal, Charlie NL:LA
	9	Allison, Bob AL:Wash.
1960:	13	Bruton, Bill NL:Mil. [2]
	10	Fox, Nellie AL:Chi.
1961:	14	Wood, Jake AL:Det.
	12	Altman, George NL:Chi.
1962:	15	Cimoli, Gino AL:KC
	10	Callison, Johnny NL:Phil.
	10	Davis, Willie NL:LA
	10	Virdon, Bill NL:Pitt.
	10	Wills, Maury NL:LA
1963:	14	Pinson, Vada NL:Cin.
	13	Versalles, Zoilo AL:Minn.
1964:	13	Allen, Dick NL:Phil.
	13	Santo, Ron NL:Chi.
	10	Rollins, Rich AL:Minn.
	10	Versalles, Zoilo AL:Minn. [2]
1965:	16	Callison, Johnny NL:Phil. [2]
	12	Campaneris, Bert AL:KC
	12	Versalles, Zoilo AL:Minn. [3]
1966:	13	McCarver, Tim NL:StL.
	11	Knoop, Bobby AL:Cal.
1967:	13	Pinson, Vada NL:Cin. [2]
	12	Blair, Paul AL:Balt.
1968:	14	Brock, Lou NL:StL.
	13	Fregosi, Jim AL:Cal.
1969:	12	Clemente, Roberto NL:Pitt.
	8	Unser, Del AL:Wash.
1970:	16	Davis, Willie NL:LA [2]
	13	Tovar, Cesar AL:Minn.
1971:	11	Metzger, Roger NL:Hou.
	11	Morgan, Joe NL:Hou.
	11	Patek, Freddie AL:KC
1972:	13	Bowa, Larry NL:Phil.
	9	Fisk, Carlton AL:Bos.
	9	Rudi, Joe AL:Oak.
1973:	14	Metzger, Roger NL:Hou. [2]
	11	Bumbry, Al AL:Balt.
	11	Carew, Rod AL:Minn.
1974:	17	Garr, Ralph NL:Atl.
	11	Rivers, Mickey AL:Cal.
1975:	13	Brett, George AL:KC
	13	Rivers, Mickey AL:Cal. [2]
	11	Garr, Ralph NL:Atl. [2]
1976:	14	Brett, George AL:KC [2]
	12	Cash, Dave NL:Phil.
1977:	18	Templeton, Garry NL:StL.
	16	Carew, Rod AL:Minn. [2]
1978:	15	Rice, Jim AL:Bos.
	13	Templeton, Garry NL:StL. [2]
1979:	20	Brett, George AL:KC [3]
	19	Templeton, Garry NL:StL. [3]

1980:	15	Griffin, Alfredo AL:Tor.
	15	Wilson, Willie AL:KC
	13	Moreno, Omar NL:Pitt.
	13	Scott, Rodney NL:Mtl.
1981:	12	Reynolds, Craig NL:Hou.
	12	Richards, Gene NL:SD
	9	Castino, John AL:Minn.
1982:	15	Wilson, Willie AL:KC [2]
	10	Thon, Dickie NL:Hou.
1983:	13	Butler, Brett NL:Atl.
	10	Yount, Robin AL:Mil.
1984:	19	Samuel, Juan NL:Phil.
	19	Sandberg, Ryne NL:Chi.
	15	Collins, Dave AL:Tor.
	15	Moseby, Lloyd AL:Tor.
1985:	21	Wilson, Willie AL:KC [3]
	18	McGee, Willie NL:StL.
1986:	14	Butler, Brett AL:Clev. (NL=1)
	13	Webster, Mitch NL:Mtl.
1987:	15	Samuel, Juan NL:Phil. [2]
	15	Wilson, Willie AL:KC [4]
1988:	15	Van Slyke, Andy NL:Pitt.
	11	Reynolds, Harold AL:Sea.
	11	Wilson, Willie AL:KC [5]
	11	Yount, Robin AL:Mil. [2]
1989:	14	Sierra, Ruben AL:Tex
	11	Thompson, Robby NL:SF
1990:	17	Fernandez, Tony AL:Tor.
	11	Duncan, Mariano NL:Cin.
1991:	15	Lankford, Ray NL:StL.
	13	Johnson, Lance AL:Chi.
	13	Molitor, Paul AL:Mil.
1992:	14	Sanders, Deion NL:Atl.
	12	Johnson, Lance AL:Chi. [2]
1993:	14	Johnson, Lance AL:Chi. [3]
	13	Finley, Steve NL:Hou.
1994:	14	Johnson, Lance AL:Chi. [4]
	9	Butler, Brett NL:LA [2] (AL=1)
	9	Lewis, Darren NL:SF
1995:	13	Lofton, Kenny AL:Clev.
	9	Butler, Brett NL:NY-LA [3] (AL=1)
	9	Young, Eric NL:Col.
1996	21	Johnson, Lance NL:NY (AL=4)
	14	Knoblauch, Chuck AL:Minn.
1997	14	DeShields, Delino NL:StL.
	11	Garciaparra, Nomar AL:Bos.
1998	13	Offerman, Jose AL:KC
	12	Dellucci, David NL:Ari.
1999	11	Abreu, Bobby NL:Phil.
	11	Perez, Neifi NL:Col.
	11	Offerman, Jose AL:Bos. [2]
2000	20	Guzman, Cristian AL:Minn.
	14	Womack, Tony NL:Ari.
2001	14	Guzman, Cristian AL:Minn. [2]
	12	Rollins, Jimmy NL:Phil.

HOME RUNS

1900:	12	Long, Herman NL:Bos.
1901:	16	Crawford, Sam NL:Cin.
	14	Lajoie, Nap AL:Phil.
1902:	16	Seybold, Socks AL:Phil.
	6	Leach, Tommy NL:Pitt.
1903:	13	Freeman, Buck AL:Bos.
	9	Sheckard, Jimmy NL:Brk.
1904:	10	Davis, Harry AL:Phil.
	9	Lumley, Harry NL:Brk.
1905:	9	Odwell, Fred NL:Cin.
	8	Davis, Harry AL:Phil. [2]
1906:	12	Davis, Harry AL:Phil. [3]
	12	Jordan, Tim NL:Brk.
1907:	10	Brain, Dave NL:Bos.
	8	Davis, Harry AL:Phil. [4]
1908:	12	Jordan, Tim NL:Brk. [2]
	7	Crawford, Sam AL:Det.
1909:	9	Cobb, Ty AL:Det.
	7	Murray, Red NL:NY
1910:	10	Beck, Fred NL:Bos.
	10	Schulte, Wildfire NL:Chi.
	10	Stahl, Jake AL:Bos.
1911:	21	Schulte, Wildfire NL:Chi. [2]
	11	Baker, Frank AL:Phil.
1912:	14	Zimmerman, Heinie NL:Chi.
	10	Baker, Frank AL:Phil. [2]
	10	Speaker, Tris AL:Bos.
1913:	19	Cravath, Gavvy NL:Phil.
	12	Baker, Frank AL:Phil. [3]
1914:	19	Cravath, Gavvy NL:Phil. [2]
	9	Baker, Frank AL:Phil. [4]
1915:	24	Cravath, Gavvy NL:Phil. [3]
	7	Roth, Braggo AL:Chi.-Clev.
1916:	12	Pipp, Wally AL:NY
	12	Robertson, Dave NL:NY
	12	Williams, Cy NL:Chi.
1917:	12	Cravath, Gavvy NL:Phil. [4]
	12	Robertson, Dave NL:NY [2]
	9	Pipp, Wally AL:NY [2]
1918:	11	Ruth, Babe AL:Bos.
	11	Walker, Tilly AL:Phil.
	8	Cravath, Gavvy NL:Phil. [5]
1919:	29	Ruth, Babe AL:Bos. [2]
	12	Cravath, Gavvy NL:Phil. [6]
1920:	54	Ruth, Babe AL:NY [3]
	15	Williams, Cy NL:Phil. [2]
1921:	59	Ruth, Babe AL:NY [4]
	23	Kelly, George NL:NY
1922:	42	Hornsby, Rogers NL:StL.
	39	Williams, Ken AL:StL.
1923:	41	Ruth, Babe AL:NY [5]
	41	Williams, Cy NL:Phil. [3]
1924:	46	Ruth, Babe AL:NY [6]
	27	Fournier, Jack NL:Brk.
1925:	39	Hornsby, Rogers NL:StL. [2]
	33	Meusel, Bob AL:NY
1926:	47	Ruth, Babe AL:NY [7]
	21	Wilson, Hack NL:Chi.
1927:	60	Ruth, Babe AL:NY [8]
	30	Williams, Cy NL:Phil. [4]
	30	Wilson, Hack NL:Chi. [2]
1928:	54	Ruth, Babe AL:NY [9]
	31	Bottomley, Jim NL:StL.
	31	Wilson, Hack NL:Chi. [3]

1929:	46	Ruth, Babe AL:NY [10]
	43	Klein, Chuck NL:Phil.
1930:	56	Wilson, Hack NL:Chi. [4]
	49	Ruth, Babe AL:NY [11]
1931:	46	Gehrig, Lou AL:NY
	46	Ruth, Babe AL:NY [12]
	31	Klein, Chuck NL:Phil. [2]
1932:	58	Foxx, Jimmie AL:Phil.
	38	Klein, Chuck NL:Phil. [3]
	38	Ott, Mel NL:NY
1933:	48	Foxx, Jimmie AL:Phil. [2]
	28	Klein, Chuck NL:Phil. [4]
1934:	49	Gehrig, Lou AL:NY [2]
	35	Collins, Ripper NL:StL.
	35	Ott, Mel NL:NY [2]
1935:	36	Foxx, Jimmie AL:Phil. [3]
	36	Greenberg, Hank AL:Det.
	34	Berger, Wally NL:Bos.
1936:	49	Gehrig, Lou AL:NY [3]
	33	Ott, Mel NL:NY [3]
1937:	46	DiMaggio, Joe AL:NY
	31	Medwick, Joe NL:StL.
	31	Ott, Mel NL:NY [4]
1938:	58	Greenberg, Hank AL:Det. [2]
	36	Ott, Mel NL:NY [5]
1939:	35	Foxx, Jimmie AL:Bos. [4]
	28	Mize, Johnny NL:StL.
1940:	43	Mize, Johnny NL:StL. [2]
	41	Greenberg, Hank AL:Det. [3]
1941:	37	Williams, Ted AL:Bos.
	34	Camilli, Dolph NL:Brk.
1942:	36	Williams, Ted AL:Bos. [2]
	30	Ott, Mel NL:NY [6]
1943:	34	York, Rudy AL:Det.
	29	Nicholson, Bill NL:Chi.
1944:	33	Nicholson, Bill NL:Chi. [2]
	22	Etten, Nick AL:NY
1945:	28	Holmes, Tommy NL:Bos.
	24	Stephens, Vern AL:StL.
1946:	44	Greenberg, Hank AL:Det. [4]
	23	Kiner, Ralph NL:Pitt.
1947:	51	Kiner, Ralph NL:Pitt. [2]
	51	Mize, Johnny NL:NY [3]
	32	Williams, Ted AL:Bos. [3]
1948:	40	Kiner, Ralph NL:Pitt. [3]
	40	Mize, Johnny NL:NY [4]
	39	DiMaggio, Joe AL:NY [2]
1949:	54	Kiner, Ralph NL:Pitt. [4]
	43	Williams, Ted AL:Bos. [4]
1950:	47	Kiner, Ralph NL:Pitt. [5]
	37	Rosen, Al AL:Clev.
1951:	42	Kiner, Ralph NL:Pitt. [6]
	33	Zernial, Gus AL:Chi.-Phil.
1952:	37	Kiner, Ralph NL:Pitt. [7]
	37	Sauer, Hank NL:Chi.
	32	Doby, Larry AL:Clev.
1953:	47	Mathews, Eddie NL:Mil.
	43	Rosen, Al AL:Clev. [2]
1954:	49	Kluszewski, Ted NL:Cin.
	32	Doby, Larry AL:Clev. [2]
1955:	51	Mays, Willie NL:NY
	37	Mantle, Mickey AL:NY
1956:	52	Mantle, Mickey AL:NY [2]
	43	Snider, Duke NL:Brk.
1957:	44	Aaron, Hank NL:Mil.
	42	Sievers, Roy AL:Wash.

HOME RUNS (CONTINUED)

1958:	47	Banks, Ernie NL:Chi.
	42	Mantle, Mickey AL:NY [3]
1959:	46	Mathews, Eddie NL:Mil. [2]
	42	Colavito, Rocky AL:Clev.
	42	Killebrew, Harmon AL:Wash.
1960:	41	Banks, Ernie NL:Chi. [2]
	40	Mantle, Mickey AL:NY [4]
1961:	61	Maris, Roger AL:NY
	46	Cepeda, Orlando NL:SF
1962:	49	Mays, Willie NL:SF [2]
	48	Killebrew, Harmon AL:Minn. [2]
1963:	45	Klllebrew, Harmon AL:Minn. [3]
	44	Aaron, Hank NL:Mil. [2]
	44	McCovey, Willie NL:SF
1964:	49	Killebrew, Harmon AL:Minn. [4]
	47	Mays, Willie NL:SF [3]
1965:	52	Mays, Willie NL:SF [4]
	32	Conigliaro, Tony AL:Bos.
1966:	49	Robinson, Frank AL:Balt.
	44	Aaron, Hank NL:Atl. [3]
1967:	44	Killebrew, Harmon AL:Minn. [5]
	44	Yastrzemski, Carl AL:Bos.
	39	Aaron, Hank NL:Atl. [4]
1968:	44	Howard, Frank AL:Wash.
	36	McCovey, Willie NL:SF [2]
1969:	49	Killebrew, Harmon AL:Minn. [6]
	45	McCovey, Willie NL:SF [3]
1970:	45	Bench, Johnny NL:Cin.
	44	Howard, Frank AL:Wash. [2]
1971:	48	Stargell, Willie NL:Pitt.
	33	Melton, Bill AL:Chi.
1972:	40	Bench, Johnny NL:Cin. [2]
	37	Allen, Dick AL:Chi.
1973:	44	Stargell, Willie NL:Pitt. [2]
	32	Jackson, Reggie AL:Oak.
1974:	36	Schmidt, Mike NL:Phil.
	32	Allen, Dick AL:Chi. [2]
1975:	38	Schmidt, Mike NL:Phil. [2]
	36	Jackson, Reggie AL:Oak. [2]
	36	Scott, George AL:Mil.
1976:	38	Schmidt, Mike NL:Phil. [3]
	32	Nettles, Graig AL:NY
1977:	52	Foster, George NL:Cin.
	39	Rice, Jim AL:Bos.
1978:	46	Rice, Jim AL:Bos. [2]
	40	Foster, George NL:Cin. [2]
1979:	48	Kingman, Dave NL:Chi.
	45	Thomas, Gorman AL:Mil.
1980:	48	Schmidt, Mike NL:Phil. [4]
	41	Jackson, Reggie AL:NY [3]
	41	Oglivie, Ben AL:Mil.
1981:	31	Schmidt, Mike NL:Phil. [5]
	22	Armas, Tony AL:Oak.
	22	Evans, Dwight AL:Bos.
	22	Grich, Bobby AL:Cal.
	22	Murray, Eddie AL:Balt.
1982:	39	Jackson, Reggie AL:Cal. [4]
	39	Thomas, Gorman AL:Mil. [2]
	37	Kingman, Dave NL:NY [2]
1983:	40	Schmidt, Mike NL:Phil. [6]
	39	Rice, Jim AL:Bos. [3]
1984:	43	Armas, Tony AL:Bos. [2]
	36	Murphy, Dale NL:Atl.
	36	Schmidt, Mike NL:Phil. [7]

1985:	40	Evans, Darrell AL:Det.
	37	Murphy, Dale NL:Atl. [2]
1986:	40	Barfield, Jesse AL:Tor.
	37	Schmidt, Mike NL:Phil. [8]
1987:	49	Dawson, Andre NL:Chi.
	49	McGwire, Mark AL:Oak.
1988:	42	Canseco, Jose AL:Oak.
	39	Strawberry, Darryl NL:NY
1989:	47	Mitchell, Kevin NL:SF
	36	McGriff, Fred AL:Tor.
1990:	51	Fielder, Cecil AL:Det.
	40	Sandberg, Ryne NL:Chi.
1991:	44	Canseco, Jose AL:Oak. [2]
	44	Fielder, Cecil AL:Det. [2]
	38	Johnson, Howard NL:NY
1992:	43	Gonzalez, Juan AL:Tex.
	35	McGriff, Fred NL:SD (AL=1)
1993:	46	Bonds, Barry NL:SF
	46	Gonzalez, Juan AL:Tex. [2]
1994:	43	Williams, Matt NL:SF
	40	Griffey, Ken, Jr. AL:Sea.
1995:	50	Belle, Albert AL:Clev.
	40	Bichette, Dante NL:Col.
1996	52	McGwire, Mark AL:Oak. [2]
	47	Galarraga, Andres NL:Col.
1997	58	McGwire, Mark AL:Oak.-NL:StL. [ML=3]
	56	Griffey, Ken, Jr. AL:Sea. [2]
	49	Walker, Larry NL:Col.
1998	70	McGwire, Mark NL:StL. [ML=4]
	56	Griffey, Ken, Jr. AL:Sea. [3]
1999	65	McGwire, Mark NL:StL. [2, ML=5]
	48	Griffey, Ken, Jr. AL:Sea. [4]
2000	50	Sosa, Sammy NL:Chi.
	47	Glaus, Troy AL:Ana.
2001	73	Bonds, Barry NL:SF [2]
	52	Rodriguez, Alez, AL:Tex.

WALKS

1913:	99	Shotton, Burt AL:StL.
	94	Bescher, Bob NL:Cin.
1914:	112	Bush, Donie AL:Det.
	105	Huggins, Miller NL:StL.
1915:	119	Collins, Eddie AL:Chi.
	86	Cravath, Gavvy NL:Phil.
1916:	111	Shotton, Burt AL:StL. [2]
	84	Groh, Heinie NL:Cin.
1917:	94	Graney, Jack AL:Clev.
	75	Burns, George NL:NY
1918:	84	Chapman, Ray AL:Clev.
	62	Carey, Max NL:Pitt.
1919:	105	Graney, Jack AL:Clev. [2]
	82	Burns, George NL:NY [2]
1920:	150	Ruth, Babe AL:NY
	76	Burns, George NL:NY [3]
1921:	145	Ruth, Babe AL:NY [2]
	80	Burns, George NL:NY [4]
1922:	89	Witt, Whitey AL:NY
	80	Carey, Max NL:Pitt. [2]
1923:	170	Ruth, Babe AL:NY [3]
	101	Burns, George NL:NY [5]
1924:	142	Ruth, Babe AL:NY [4]
	89	Hornsby, Rogers NL:StL.
1925:	90	Kamm, Willie AL:Chi.
	90	Mostil, Johnny AL:Chi.
	86	Fournier, Jack NL:Brk.
1926:	144	Ruth, Babe AL:NY [5]
	69	Wilson, Hack NL:Chi.
1927:	137	Ruth, Babe AL:NY [6]
	86	Hornsby, Rogers NL:NY [2]
1928:	137	Ruth, Babe AL:NY [7]
	107	Hornsby, Rogers NL:Bos. [3]
1929:	128	Bishop, Max AL:Phil.
	113	Ott, Mel NL:NY
1930:	136	Ruth, Babe AL:NY [8]
	105	Wilson, Hack NL:Chi. [2]
1931:	128	Ruth, Babe AL:NY [9]
	80	Ott, Mel NL:NY [2]
1932:	130	Ruth, Babe AL:NY [10]
	100	Ott, Mel NL:NY [3]
1933:	114	Ruth, Babe AL:NY [11]
	75	Ott, Mel NL:NY [4]
1934:	111	Foxx, Jimmie AL:Phil.
	94	Vaughan, Arky NL:Pitt.
1935:	132	Gehrig, Lou AL:NY
	97	Vaughan, Arky NL:Pitt. [2]
1936:	130	Gehrig, Lou AL:NY [2]
	118	Vaughan, Arky NL:Pitt. [3]
1937:	127	Gehrig, Lou AL:NY [3]
	102	Ott, Mel NL:NY [5]
1938:	119	Camilli, Dolph NL:Brk.
	119	Foxx, Jimmie AL:Bos. [2]
	119	Greenberg, Hank AL:Det.
1939:	111	Clift, Harlond AL:StL.
	110	Camilli, Dolph NL:Brk. [2]
1940:	119	Fletcher, Elbie NL:Pitt.
	106	Keller, Charlie AL:NY
1941:	145	Williams, Ted AL:Bos.
	118	Fletcher, Elbie NL:Pitt. [2]
1942:	145	Williams, Ted AL:Bos. [2]
	109	Ott, Mel NL:NY [6]
1943:	106	Keller, Charlie AL:NY [2]
	103	Galan, Augie NL:Brk.
1944:	101	Galan, Augie NL:Brk. [2]
	97	Etten, Nick AL:NY
1945:	148	Stanky, Eddie NL:Brk.
	112	Cullenbine, Roy AL:Clev.-Det.
1946:	156	Williams, Ted AL:Bos. [3]
	137	Stanky, Eddie NL:Brk. [2]
1947:	162	Williams, Ted AL:Bos. [4]
	104	Greenberg, Hank NL:Pitt.
	104	Reese, Pee Wee NL:Brk.
1948:	131	Elliott, Bob NL:Bos.
	126	Williams, Ted AL:Bos. [5]
1949:	162	Williams, Ted AL:Bos. [6]
	117	Kiner, Ralph NL:Pitt.
1950:	144	Stanky, Eddie NL:NY [3]
	141	Yost, Eddie AL:Wash.
1951:	144	Williams, Ted AL:Bos. [7]
	137	Kiner, Ralph NL:Pitt. [2]
1952:	129	Yost, Eddie AL:Wash. [2]
	110	Kiner, Ralph NL:Pitt. [3]
1953:	123	Yost, Eddie AL:Wash. [3]
	105	Musial, Stan NL:StL
1954:	136	Williams, Ted AL:Bos. [8]
	125	Ashburn, Richie NL:Phil.
1955:	113	Mantle, Mickey AL:NY
	109	Mathews, Eddie NL:Mil.
1956:	151	Yost, Eddie AL:Wash. [4]
	99	Snider, Duke NL:Brk.
1957:	146	Mantle, Mickey AL:NY [2]
	94	Ashburn, Richie NL:Phil. [2]
	94	Temple, Johnny NL:Cin.
1958:	129	Mantle, Mickey AL:NY [3]
	97	Ashburn, Richie NL:Phil. [3]
1959:	135	Yost, Eddie AL:Det. [5]
	96	Gilliam, Jim NL:LA
1960:	125	Yost, Eddie AL:Det. [6]
	116	Ashburn, Richie NL:Phil. [4]
1961:	126	Mantle, Mickey AL:NY [4]
	93	Mathews, Eddie NL:Mil. [2]
1962:	122	Mantle, Mickey AL:NY [5]
	101	Mathews, Eddie NL:Mil. [3]
1963:	124	Mathews, Eddie NL:Mil. [4]
	95	Yastrzemski, Carl AL:Bos.
1964:	106	Siebern, Norm AL:Balt.
	86	Santo, Ron NL:Chi.
1965:	97	Morgan, Joe NL:Hou.
	93	Colavito, Rocky AL:Clev.
1966:	103	Killebrew, Harmon AL:Minn.
	95	Santo, Ron NL:Chi. [2]
1967:	131	Killebrew, Harmon AL:Minn. [2]
	96	Santo, Ron NL:Chi. [3]
1968:	119	Yastrzemski, Carl AL:Bos. [2]
	96	Santo, Ron NL:Chi. [4]
1969:	148	Wynn, Jimmy NL:Hou.
	145	Killebrew, Harmon AL:Minn. [3]
1970:	137	McCovey, Willie NL:SF
	132	Howard, Frank AL:Wash.
1971:	114	Killebrew, Harmon AL:Minn. [4]
	112	Mays, Willie NL:SF
1972:	115	Morgan, Joe NL:Cin. [2]
	99	Allen, Dick AL:Chi.
	99	White, Roy AL:NY
1973:	124	Evans, Darrell NL:Atl.
	122	Mayberry, John AL:KC
1974:	126	Evans, Darrell NL:Atl. [2]
	110	Tenace, Gene AL:Oak.

WALKS (CONTINUED)

Year	Walks	Player
1975:	132	Morgan, Joe NL:Cin. [3]
	119	Mayberry, John AL:KC [2]
1976:	127	Wynn, Jimmy NL:Atl. [2]
	97	Hargrove, Mike AL:Tex.
1977:	125	Tenace, Gene NL:SD
	109	Harrah, Toby AL:Tex.
1978:	117	Burroughs, Jeff NL:Atl.
	107	Hargrove, Mike AL:Tex. [2]
1979:	121	Porter, Darrell AL:KC
	120	Schmidt, Mike NL:Phil.
1980:	119	Randolph, Willie AL:NY
	93	Driessen, Dan NL:Cin.
	93	Morgan, Joe NL:Hou. [4]
1981:	85	Evans, Dwight AL:Bos.
	73	Schmidt, Mike NL:Phil. [2]
1982:	116	Henderson, Rickey AL:Oak.
	107	Schmidt, Mike NL:Phil. [3]
1983:	128	Schmidt, Mike NL:Phil. [4]
	103	Henderson, Rickey AL:Oak. [2]
1984:	107	Murray, Eddie AL:Balt.
	103	Matthews, Gary NL:Chi.
1985:	114	Evans, Dwight AL:Bos. [2]
	90	Murphy, Dale NL:Atl.
1986:	105	Boggs, Wade AL:Bos.
	94	Hernandez, Keith NL:NY
1987:	136	Clark, Jack NL:StL.
	106	Downing, Brian AL:Cal.
	106	Evans, Dwight AL:Bos. [3]
1988:	125	Boggs, Wade AL:Bos. [2]
	100	Clark, Will NL:SF
1989:	132	Clark, Jack NL:SD [2]
	126	Henderson, Rickey AL:NY-Oak. [3]
1990:	110	McGwire, Mark AL:Oak.
	104	Clark, Jack NL:SD [3]
1991:	138	Thomas, Frank AL:Chi.
	108	Butler, Brett NL:LA
1992:	127	Bonds, Barry NL:Pitt.
	122	Tettleton, Mickey AL:Det.
	122	Thomas, Frank AL:Chi. [2]
1993:	132	Phillips, Tony AL:Det.
	129	Dykstra, Len NL:Phil.
1994:	109	Thomas, Frank AL:Chi. [3]
	74	Bonds, Barry NL:SF [2]
1995:	136	Thomas, Frank AL:Chi. [4]
	120	Bonds, Barry NL:SF [3]
1996	151	Bonds, Barry NL:SF [4]
	125	Phillips, Tony AL:Chi. [2]
1997	145	Bonds, Barry NL:SF [5]
	120	Thome, Jim AL:Clev.
1998	162	McGwire, Mark NL:StL. [AL=1]
	118	Henderson, Rickey AL:Oak. [4]
1999	149	Bagwell, Jeff NL:Hou.
	127	Thome, Jim AL:Clev. [2]
2000	137	Giambi, Jason AL:Oak.
	117	Bonds, Barry NL:SF [6]
2001	177	Bonds, Barry NL:SF [7]
	129	Giambi, Jason AL:Oak. [2]

STRIKEOUTS

1910:	81	Hummell, John NL:Brk.
1911:	78	Bescher, Bob NL:Cin.
	78	Coulson, Bob NL:Brk.
1912:	91	McDonald, Ed NL:Bos.
1913:	103	Moeller, Danny AL:Wash.
	74	Burns, George NL:NY
1914:	120	Williams, Gus AL:StL.
	80	Merkle, Fred NL:NY
1915:	88	Baird, Doug NL:Pitt.
	83	Lavan, Doc AL:StL.
1916:	89	Cravath, Gavvy NL:Phil.
	82	Pipp, Wally AL:NY
1917:	78	Williams, Cy NL:Chi
	73	Roth, Braggo AL:Clev.
1918:	58	Ruth, Babe AL:Bos.
	49	Paskert, Dode NL:Chi.
	49	Youngs, Ross NL:NY
1919:	79	Powell, Ray NL:Bos.
	70	Shannon, Red AL:Phil.-Bos.
1920:	92	Kelly, George NL:NY
	84	Ward, Aaron AL:NY
1921:	88	Meusel, Bob AL:NY
	85	Powell, Ray NL:Bos. [2]
1922:	98	Dykes, Jimmy AL:Phil.
	93	Parkinson, Frank NL:Phil.
1923:	93	Ruth, Babe AL:NY [2]
	92	Grantham, George NL:Chi.
1924:	81	Ruth, Babe AL:NY [3]
	63	Grantham, George NL:Chi. [2]
1925:	77	Hartnett, Gabby NL:Chi.
	69	McManus, Marty AL:StL.
1926:	96	Lazzeri, Tony AL:NY
	77	Friberg, Barney NL:Phil.
1927:	89	Ruth, Babe AL:NY [4]
	70	Wilson, Hack NL:Chi.
1928:	94	Wilson, Hack NL:Chi. [2]
	87	Ruth, Babe AL:NY [5]
1929:	83	Wilson, Hack NL:Chi. [3]
	70	Foxx, Jimmie AL:Phil.
1930:	84	Wilson, Hack NL:Chi. [4]
	66	Foxx, Jimmie AL:Phil. [2]
	66	Morgan, Ed AL:Clev.
1931:	86	Cullop, Nick NL:Cin.
	84	Foxx, Jimmie AL:Phil. [3]
1932:	104	Campbell, Bruce AL:Chi.-StL.
	85	Wilson. Hack NL:Brk. [5]
1933:	93	Foxx, Jimmie AL:Phil. [4]
	77	Berger, Wally NL:Bos.
1934:	100	Clift, Harlond AL:StL.
	94	Camilli, Dolph NL:Chi.-Phil.
1935:	113	Camilll, Dolph NL:Phil. [2]
	99	Foxx, Jimmie AL:Phil. [5]
1936:	119	Foxx, Jimmie AL:Bos. [6]
	96	Brubaker, Bill NL:Pitt.
1937:	111	DiMaggio, Vince NL:Bos.
	105	Crosetti, Frankie AL:NY
1938:	134	DiMaggio, Vince NL:Bos. [2]
	99	Crosetti, Frankie AL:NY [2]
1939:	107	Camilli, Dolph NL:Brk. [3]
	95	Greenberg, Hank AL:Det.
1940:	127	Ross, Chet NL:Bos.
	96	Chapman, Sam AL:Phil.
1941:	115	Camilli, Dolph NL:Brk. [4]
	103	Foxx, Jimmie AL:Bos. [7]
1942:	95	Gordon, Joe AL:NY
	87	DiMaggio, Vince NL:Pitt. [3]
1943:	126	DiMaggio, Vince NL:Pitt. [4]
	105	Laabs, Chet AL:StL.
1944:	99	Seerey, Pat AL:Clev.
	83	DiMaggio, Vince NL:Pitt. [5]
1945:	97	Seerey, Pat AL:Clev. [2]
	91	DiMaggio, Vince NL:Phil. [6]
1946:	109	Kiner, Ralph NL:Pitt.
	101	Keller, Charlie AL:NY
	101	Seerey, Pat AL:Clev. [3]
1947:	110	Joost, Eddie AL:Phil.
	83	Nicholson, Bill NL:Chi.
1948:	102	Seerey, Pat AL:Clev.-Chi. [4]
	85	Sauer, Hank NL:Cin.
1949:	92	Snider, Duke NL:Brk.
	91	Kokos, Dick AL:StL.
1950:	114	Smalley, Roy NL:Chi.
	110	Zernial, Gus AL:Chi.
1951:	101	Zernial, Gus AL:Chi.-Phil. [2]
	99	Hodges, Gil NL:Brk.
1952:	115	Mathews, Eddie NL:Bos.
	111	Doby, Larry AL:Clev.
	111	Mantle, Mickey AL:NY
1953:	125	Bilko, Steve NL:StL.
	121	Doby, Larry AL:Clev. [2]
1954:	107	Mantle. Mickey AL:NY [2]
	96	Snider, Duke NL:Brk. [2]
1955:	105	Zauchin, Norm AL:Bos.
	102	Post, Wally NL:Cin.
1956:	138	Lemon, Jim AL:Wash.
	124	Post, Wally NL:Cin. [2]
1957:	104	Snider, Duke NL:Brk. [3]
	94	Lemon, Jim AL:Wash. [2]
1958:	120	Lemon. Jim AL:Wash. [3]
	120	Mantle, Mickey AL:NY [3]
	95	Anderson, Harry NL:Phil.
1959:	126	Mantle, Mickey AL:NY [4]
	101	Post, Wally NL:Phil. [3]
1960:	136	Herrera, Pancho NL:Phil.
	125	Mantle, Mickey AL:NY [5]
1961:	141	Wood, Jake AL:Det.
	121	Stuart, Dick NL:Pitt.
1962:	142	Killebrew, Harmon AL:Minn.
	129	Hubbs, Ken NL:Chi.
1963:	175	Nicholson, Dave AL:Chi.
	136	Clendenon, Donn NL:Pitt.
1964:	143	Mathews, Nelson AL:KC
	138	Allen, Dick NL:Phil.
1965:	150	Allen, Dick NL:Phil. [2]
	122	Versalles, Zoilo AL:Minn.
1966:	152	Scott, George AL:Bos.
	143	Browne, Byron NL:Chi.
1967:	155	Howard, Frank AL:Wash.
	137	Wynn, Jimmy NL:Hou.
1968:	171	Jackson, Reggie AL:Oak.
	163	Clendenon, Donn NL:Pitt. [2]
1969:	187	Bonds, Bobby NL:SF
	142	Jackson, Reggie AL:Oak. [2]
1970:	189	Bonds, Bobby NL:SF [2]
	135	Jackson, Reggie AL:Oak. [3]
1971:	161	Jackson, Reggie AL:Oak. [4]
	154	Stargell, Willie NL:Pitt.

STRIKEOUTS (CONTINUED)

1972:	145	Darwin, Bobby AL:Minn.
	145	May, Lee NL:Hou.
1973:	148	Bonds, Bobby NL:SF [3]
	137	Darwin, Bobby AL:Minn. [2]
1974:	138	Schmidt, Mike NL:Phil.
	127	Darwin, Bobby AL:Minn. [3]
1975:	180	Schmidt, Mike NL:Phil. [2]
	155	Burroughs, Jeff AL:Tex.
1976:	149	Schmidt, Mike NL:Phil. [3]
	123	Rice, Jim AL:Bos.
1977:	162	Hobson, Butch AL:Bos.
	140	Luzinski, Greg :NL:Phil.
1978:	166	Alexander, Gary AL:Oak.-Clev.
	145	Murphy, Dale NL:Atl.
1979:	175	Thomas, Gorman AL:Mil.
	131	Kingman, Dave NL:Chi.
1980:	170	Thomas, Gorman AL:Mil. [2]
	133	Murphy, Dale NL:Atl. [2]
1981:	115	Armas, Tony AL:Oak.
	105	Kingman, Dave NL:NY [2]
1982:	156	Jackson, Reggie AL:Cal. [5]
	156	Kingman, Dave NL:NY [3]
1983:	150	Kittle, Ron AL:Chi.
	148	Schmidt, Mike NL:Phil. [4]
1984:	168	Samuel, Juan NL:Phil.
	156	Armas, Tony AL:Bos. [2]
1985:	166	Balboni, Steve AL:KC
	141	Murphy, Dale NL:Atl. [3]
	141	Samuel, Juan NL:Phil. [2]
1986:	185	Incaviglia, Pete AL:Tex
	142	Samuel, Juan NL:Phil. [3]
1987:	186	Deer, Rob AL:Mil.
	162	Samuel, Juan NL:Phil. [4]
1988:	153	Galarraga, Andres NL:Mtl.
	153	Deer, Rob AL:Mil. [2]
	153	Incaviglia, Pete AL:Tex. [2]
1989:	172	Jackson, Bo AL:KC
	158	Galarraga, Andres NL:Mtl. [2]
1990:	182	Fielder, Cecil AL:Det.
	169	Galarraga, Andres NL:Mtl. [3]
1991:	175	Deer, Rob AL:Det. [3]
	151	DeShields, Delino NL:Mtl.
1992:	154	Palmer, Dean AL:Tex.
	147	Lankford, Ray NL:StL.
1993:	169	Deer, Rob AL:Det.-Bos. [4]
	147	Snyder, Cory NL:LA
1994:	128	Fryman, Travis AL:Det.
	114	Sanders, Reggie NL:Cin.
1995	150	Vaughn, Mo AL:Bos.
	146	Galarraga, Andres NL:Col. [4]
1996	160	Rodriguez, Henry NL:Mtl.
	159	Buhner, Jay AL:Sea.
1997:	175	Buhner, Jay AL:Sea.[2]
	174	Sosa, Sammy NL:Chi.
1998:	171	Sosa, Sammy NL:Chi. [2]
	159	Canseco, Jose AL:Tor.
1999:	171	Sosa, Sammy NL:Chi. [3]
	171	Thome, Jim AL:Clev.
2000:	187	Wilson, Preston NL:Fla.
	181	Vaughn, Mo AL:Ana. [2]
2001:	185	Hernandez, Jose NL:Mil.
	185	Thome, Jim AL:Clev. [2]

STOLEN BASES

1900:	45	Donovan, Patsy NL:StL.
	45	Van Haltren, George NL:NY
1901:	52	Wagner, Honus NL:Pitt.
	48	Isbell, Frank AL:Chi.
1902:	47	Hartsell, Topsy AL:Phil.
	42	Wagner, Honus NL:Pitt. [2]
1903:	67	Chance, Frank NL:Chi.
	67	Sheckard, Jimmy NL:Brk.
	45	Bay, Harry AL:Clev. [2]
1904:	53	Wagner, Honus NL:Pitt. [3]
	42	Flick, Elmer AL:Clev.
1905:	59	Devlin, Art NL:NY
	59	Maloney, Billy NL:Chi.
	46	Hoffman, Danny AL:Phil.
1906:	57	Chance, Frank NL:Chi. [2]
	39	Anderson, John AL:Wash.
	39	Flick, Elmer AL:Clev. [2]
1907:	61	Wagner, Honus NL:Pitt. [4]
	49	Cobb, Ty AL:Det.
1908:	53	Wagner, Honus NL:Pitt. [5]
	47	Dougherty, Patsy AL:Chi.
1909:	76	Cobb, Ty AL:Det. [2]
	54	Bescher, Bob NL:Cin.
1910:	81	Collins, Eddie AL:Phil.
	70	Bescher, Bob NL:Cin. [2]
1911:	83	Cobb, Ty AL:Det. [3]
	81	Bescher, Bob NL:Cin. [3]
1912:	88	Milan, Clyde AL:Wash.
	67	Bescher, Bob NL:Cin. [4]
1913:	75	Milan, Clyde AL:Wash. [2]
	61	Carey, Max NL:Pitt.
1914:	74	Maisel, Fritz AL:NY
	62	Burns, George NL:NY
1915:	96	Cobb, Ty AL:Det. [4]
	36	Carey, Max NL:Pitt. [2]
1916:	68	Cobb, Ty AL:Det. [5]
	63	Carey, Max NL:Pitt. [3]
1917:	55	Cobb, Ty AL:Det. [6]
	46	Carey, Max NL:Pitt. [4]
1918:	58	Carey, Max NL:Pitt. [5]
	45	Sisler, George AL:StL.
1919:	40	Burns, George NL:NY [2]
	33	Collins, Eddie AL:Chi. [2]
1920:	63	Rice, Sam AL:Wash. [6]
	52	Carey, Max NL:Pitt.
1921:	49	Frisch, Frankie NL:NY
	35	Sisler, George AL:StL. [2]
1922:	51	Carey, Max NL:Pitt. [7]
	51	Sisler, George AL:StL. [3]
1923:	51	Carey, Max NL:Pitt. [8]
	47	Collins, Eddie AL:Chi. [3]
1924:	49	Carey, Max NL:Pitt. [9]
	42	Collins, Eddie AL:Chi. [4]
1925:	46	Carey, Max NL:Pitt. [10]
	43	Mostil, Johnny AL:Chi.
1926:	35	Cuyler, Kiki NL:Pitt.
	35	Mostil, Johnny AL:Chi. [2]
1927:	48	Frisch, Frankie NL:StL. [2]
	27	Sisler, George AL:StL. [4]
1928:	37	Cuyler, Kiki NL:Chi. [2]
	30	Myer, Buddy AL:Bos.
1929:	43	Cuyler, Kiki NL:Chi. [3]
	27	Gehringer, Charlie AL:Det.
1930:	37	Cuyler, Kiki NL:Chi. [4]
	23	McManus, Marty AL:Det.
1931:	61	Chapman, Ben AL:NY
	28	Frisch, Frankie NL:StL. [3]
1932:	38	Chapman, Ben AL:NY [2]
	20	Klein, Chuck NL:Phil.
1933:	27	Chapman, Ben AL:NY [3]
	26	Martin, Pepper NL:StL.
1934:	40	Werber, Bill AL:Bos.
	23	Martin, Pepper NL:StL. [2]
1935:	29	Werber, Bill AL:Bos. [2]
	22	Galan,Augie NL:Chi.
1936:	37	Lary, Lyn AL:StL.
	23	Martin, Pepper NL:StL. [3]
1937:	35	Chapman, Ben AL:Wash.-Bos. [4]
	35	Werber, Bill AL:Phil. [3]
	23	Galan, Augie NL:Chi. [2]
1938:	27	Crosetti, Frankie AL:NY
	16	Hack, Stan NL:Chi.
1939:	51	Case, George AL:Wash.
	17	Hack, Stan NL:Chi. [2]
	17	Handley, Lee NL:Pitt.
1940:	35	Case, George AL:Wash. [2]
	22	Frey, Lonny NL:Cin.
1941:	33	Case, George AL:Wash. [3]
	18	Murtaugh, Danny NL:Phil.
1942:	44	Case, George AL:Wash. [4]
	20	Reiser, Pete NL:Brk.
1943:	61	Case, George AL:Wash. [5]
	20	Vaughan, Arky NL:Brk.
1944:	55	Stirnweiss, Snuffy AL:NY
	28	Barrett, Johnny NL:Pitt.
1945:	33	Stirnweiss, Snuffy AL:NY [2]
	26	Schoendienst, Red NL:StL.
1946:	34	Reiser, Pete NL:Brk. [2]
	28	Case, George AL:Clev. [6]
1947:	34	Dillinger, Bob AL:StL.
	29	Robinson, Jackie NL:Brk.
1948:	32	Ashburn, Richie NL:Phil.
	28	Dillinger, Bob AL:StL. [2]
1949:	37	Robinson, Jackie NL:Brk. [2]
	20	Dillinger, Bob AL:StL. [3]
1950:	35	Jethroe, Sam NL:Bos.
	15	DiMaggio, Dom AL:Bos.
1951:	35	Jethroe, Sam NL:Bos. [2]
	31	Minoso, Minnie AL:Clev.-Chi.
1952:	30	Reese, Pee Wee NL:Brk.
	22	Minoso, Minnie AL:Chi. [2]
1953:	26	Bruton, Bill NL:Mil.
	25	Minoso, Minnie AL:Chi. [3]
1954:	34	Bruton, Bill NL:Mil. [2]
	22	Jensen, Jackie AL:Bos.
1955:	25	Bruton, Bill NL:Mil. [3]
	25	Rivera, Jim AL:Chi.
1956:	40	Mays, Willie NL:NY
	21	Aparicio, Luis AL:Chi.
1957:	38	Mays, Willie NL:NY [2]
	28	Aparicio, Luis AL:Chi. [2]
1958:	31	Mays, Willie NL:SF [3]
	29	Aparicio, Luis AL:Chi. [3]
1959:	56	Aparicio, Luis AL:Chi. [4]
	27	Mays, Willie NL:SF [4]
1960:	51	Aparicio, Luis AL:Chi. [5]
	50	Wills, Maury NL:LA
1961:	53	Aparicio, Luis AL:Chi. [6]
	35	Wills, Maury NL:LA [2]
1962:	104	Wills, Maury NL:LA [3]
	31	Aparicio, Luis AL:Chi. [7]

STOLEN BASES (CONTINUED)

1963:	40	Aparicio, Luis AL:Balt. [8]
	40	Wills, Maury NL:LA [4]
1964:	57	Aparicio, Luis AL:Balt. [9]
	53	Wills, Maury NL:LA [5]
1965:	94	Wills, Maury NL:LA [6]
	51	Campaneris, Bert AL:KC
1966:	74	Brock, Lou NL:StL.
	52	Campaneris, Bert AL:KC [2]
1967:	55	Campaneris, Bert AL:KC [3]
	52	Brock, Lou NL:StL. [2]
1968:	62	Brock, Lou NL:StL. [3]
	62	Campaneris. Bert AL:Oak. [4]
1969:	73	Harper, Tommy AL:Sea.
	53	Brock, Lou NL:StL. [4]
1970:	57	Tolan, Bobby NL:Cin.
	42	Campaneris, Bert AL:Oak. [5]
1971:	64	Brock, Lou NL:StL. [5]
	52	Otis, Amos AL:KC
1972:	63	Brock, Lou NL:StL. [6]
	52	Campaneris, Bert AL:Oak. [6]
1973:	70	Brock, Lou NL:StL. [7]
	54	Harper, Tommy AL:Bos. [2]
1974:	118	Brock, Lou NL:StL. [8]
	54	North, Billy AL:Oak.
1975:	77	Lopes, Davey NL:LA
	70	Rivers, Mickey AL:Cal.
1976:	75	North, Billy AL:Oak. [2]
	63	Lopes, Davey NL:LA [2]
1977:	70	Taveras, Frank NL:Pitt.
	53	Patek, Freddie AL:KC
1978:	71	Moreno, Omar NL:Pitt.
	68	LeFlore, Ron AL:Det.
1979:	83	Wilson, Willie AL:KC
	77	Moreno, Omar NL:Pitt. [2]
1980:	100	Henderson, Rickey AL:Oak.
	97	LeFlore, Ron NL:Mtl.
1981:	71	Raines, Tim NL:Mtl.
	56	Henderson, Rickey AL:Oak. [2]
1982:	130	Henderson, Rickey AL:Oak. [3]
	78	Raines, Tim NL:Mtl. [2]
1983:	108	Henderson, Rickey AL:Oak. [4]
	90	Raines, Tim NL:Mtl. [3]
1984:	75	Raines, Tim NL:Mtl. [4]
	66	Henderson, Rickey AL:Oak. [5]
1985:	110	Coleman, Vince NL:StL.
	80	Henderson, Rickey AL:NY [6]
1986:	107	Coleman, Vince NL:StL. [2]
	87	Henderson, Rickey AL:NY [7]
1987:	109	Coleman, Vince NL:StL. [3]
	60	Reynolds, Harold AL:Sea.
1988:	93	Henderson, Rickey AL:NY [8]
	81	Coleman, Vince NL:StL. [4]
1989:	77	Henderson, Rickey AL:NY-Oak. [9]
	65	Coleman, Vince NL:StL. [5]
1990:	77	Coleman, Vince NL:StL. [6]
	65	Henderson, Rickey AL:Oak. [10]
1991:	76	Grissom, Marquis NL:Mtl.
	58	Henderson, Rickey AL:Oak. [11]
1992:	78	Grissom, Marquis NL:Mtl. [2]
	66	Lofton, Kenny AL:Clev.
1993:	70	Lofton, Kenny AL:Clev. [2]
	58	Carr, Chuck NL:Fla.
1994:	60	Lofton, Kenny AL:Clev. [3]
	39	Biggio, Craig NL:Hou
1995:	56	Veras, Quilvio NL:Fla.
	54	Lofton, Kenny AL:Clev. [4]
1996	75	Lofton, Kenny AL:Clev. [5]
	53	Young, Eric NL:Col.
1997	74	Hunter, Brian AL:Det.
	60	Womack, Tony NL:Pitt.
1998	66	Henderson, Rickey AL:Oak. [12]
	58	Womack, Tony NL:Pitt. [2]
1999	72	Womack, Tony NL:Ari. [3]
	44	Hunter, Brian AL:Det.-Sea. [2]
2000	62	Castillo, Luis NL:Fla.
	46	Damon, Johnny AL:KC
2001	56	Suzuki, Ichiro AL:Sea.
	46	Pierre, Juan NL:Col.
	46	Rollins, Jimmy NL:Phil.

EARNED RUN AVERAGE

1912:	1.96	Tesreau, Jeff NL:NY		1945:	1.81	Newhouser, Hal AL:Det.
1913:	1.14	Johnson, Walter AL:Wash.			2.14	Borowy, Hank NL:Chi.
	2.06	Mathewson, Christy NL:NY		1946:	1.94	Newhouser, Hal AL:Det. [2]
1914:	1.00	Leonard, Dutch AL:Bos.			2.10	Pollet, Howie NL:StL. [2]
	1.72	Doak Bill NL:StL.		1947:	2.33	Spahn, Warren NL:Bos.
1915:	1.22	Alexander, Grover NL:Phil.			2.46	Chandler, Spud AL:NY [2]
	1.49	Wood, Smoky Joe AL:Bos.		1948:	2.24	Brecheen, Harry NL:StL.
1916:	1.55	Alexander, Grover NL:Phil. [2]			2.43	Bearden, Gene AL:Clev.
	1.75	Ruth, Babe AL:Bos.		1949:	2.50	Koslo, Dave NL:NY
1917:	1.53	Cicotte, Eddie AL:Chi.			2.78	Parnell, Mel AL:Bos.
	1.85	Alexander, Grover NL:Phil. [3]		1950:	2.49	Hearn, Jim NL:StL.NY
1918:	1.28	Johnson, Walter AL:Wash. [2]			3.20	Wynn, Early AL:Clev.
	1.74	Vaughn, Hippo NL:Chi.		1951:	2.78	Rogovin, Saul AL:Det.-Chi.
1919:	1.49	Johnson, Walter AL:Wash. [3]			2.88	Nichols, Chet NL:Bos.
	1.72	Alexander, Grover NL:Chi. [4]		1952:	2.07	Reynolds, Allie AL:NY
1920:	1.91	Alexander, Grover NL:Chi. [5]			2.43	Wilhelm, Hoyt NL:NY
	2.46	Shawkey, Bob AL:NY		1953:	2.10	Spahn, Warren NL:Mil. [2]
1921:	2.48	Faber, Red AL:Chi.			2.43	Lopat, Ed AL:NY
	2.58	Doak, Bill NL:StL. [2]		1954:	2.29	Antonelli, Johnny NL:NY
1922:	2.81	Faber, Red AL:Chi. [2]			2.64	Garcia, Mike AL:Clev.
	3.00	Ryan, Rosy NL:NY		1955	1.97	Pierce, Billy AL:Chi.
1923:	1.93	Luque, Dolf NL:Cin.			2.84	Friend, Bob NL:Pitt.
	2.76	Coveleski, Stan AL:Clev.		1956:	2.47	Ford, Whitey AL:NY
1924:	2.16	Vance, Dazzy NL:Brk.			2.71	Burdette, Lew NL:Mil.
	2.72	Johnson, Walter AL:Wash. [4]		1957:	2.45	Shantz, Bobby AL:NY
1925:	2.63	Luque, Dolf NL:Cin. [2]			2.66	Podres, Johnny NL:Brk.
	2.84	Coveleski, Stan AL:Wash. [2]		1958:	2.01	Ford, Whitey AL:NY [2]
1926:	2.51	Grove, Lefty AL:Phil.			2.47	Miller, Stu NL:SF
	2.61	Kremer, Ray NL:Pitt.		1959:	2.19	Wilhelm, Hoyt AL:Balt. [NL=1]
1927:	2.28	Moore, Wilcy AL:NY			2.82	Jones, Sam NL:SF
	2.47	Kremer, Ray NL:Pitt. [2]		1960:	2.68	Baumann, Frank AL:Chi.
1928:	2.09	Vance, Dazzy NL:Brk. [2]			2.70	McCormick, Mike NL:SF
	2.52	Braxton, Garland AL:Wash.		1961:	2.40	Donovan, Dick AL:Wash.
1929:	2.82	Grove, Lefty AL:Phil. [2]			3.01	Spahn, Warren NL:Mil. [3]
	3.08	Walker, Bill NL:NY		1962:	2.21	Aguirre, Hank AL:Det.
1930:	2.54	Grove, Lefty AL:Phil. [3]			2.54	Koufax, Sandy NL:LA
	2.61	Vance, Dazzy NL:Brk. [3]		1963:	1.88	Koufax, Sandy NL:LA [2]
1931:	2.05	Grove, Lefty AL:Phil. [4]			2.33	Peters, Gary AL:Chi.
	2.26	Walker, Bill NL:NY [2]		1964:	1.65	Chance, Dean AL:LA
1932:	2.37	Warneke, Lon NL:Chi.			1.74	Koufax, Sandy NL:LA [3]
	2.84	Grove, Lefty AL:Phil. [5]		1965:	2.04	Koufax, Sandy NL:LA [4]
1933:	1.66	Hubbell, Carl NL:NY [2]			2.18	McDowell, Sam AL:Clev.
	2.33	Pearson, Monte AL:Clev.		1966:	1.73	Koufax, Sandy NL:LA [5]
1934:	2.30	Hubbell, Carl NL:NY [3]			1.98	Peters, Gary AL:Chi. [2]
	2.33	Gomez, Lefty AL:NY		1967:	1.87	Niekro, Phil NL:Atl.
1935:	2.59	Blanton, Cy NL:Pitt.			2.06	Horlen, Joel AL:Chi.
	2.70	Grove, Lefty AL:Bos. [6]		1968:	1.12	Gibson, Bob NL:StL.
1936:	2.31	Hubbell, Carl NL:NY [4]			1.60	Tiant, Luis AL:Clev.
	2.81	Grove, Lefty AL:Bos. [7]		1969:	2.10	Marichal, Juan NL:SF
1937:	2.33	Gomez, Lefty AL:NY [2]			2.19	Bosman, Dick AL:Wash.
	2.38	Turner, Jim NL:Bos.		1970:	2.56	Segui, Diego AL:Oak.
1938:	2.66	Lee, Bill NL:Chi.			2.81	Seaver, Tom NL:NY
	3.07	Grove, Lefty AL:Bos. [8]		1971:	1.76	Seaver, Tom NL:NY [2]
1939:	2.29	Walters, Bucky NL:Cin.			1.82	Blue, Vida AL:Oak.
	2.54	Grove, Lefty AL:Bos. [9]		1972:	1.91	Tiant, Luis AL:Bos. [2]
1940:	2.48	Walters, Bucky NL:Cin. [2]			1.98	Carlton, Steve NL:Phil.
	2.62	Feller, Bob AL:Clev.		1973:	2.08	Seaver, Tom NL:NY [3]
1941:	2.24	Riddle, Elmer NL:Cin.			2.40	Palmer, Jim AL:Balt.
	2.37	Lee, Thornton AL:Chi.		1974:	2.28	Capra, Buzz NL:Atl.
1942:	1.77	Cooper, Mort NL:StL.			2.49	Hunter, Catfish AL:Oak.
	2.10	Lyons, Ted AL:Chi.		1975:	2.09	Palmer, Jim AL:Balt. [2]
1943:	1.64	Chandler, Spud AL:NY			2.24	Jones, Randy NL:SD
	1.75	Pollet, Howie NL:StL.		1976:	2.34	Fidrych, Mark AL:Det.
1944:	2.12	Trout, Dizzy AL:Det.			2.52	Denny, John NL:StL.
	2.38	Heusser, Ed NL:Cin.		1977:	2.34	Candelaria, John NL:Pitt.
					2.54	Tanana, Frank AL:Cal.

EARNED RUN AVERAGE (CONTINUED)

1978:	1.74	Guidry, Ron AL:NY
	2.43	Swan, Craig NL:NY
1979:	2.71	Richard, J.R. NL:Hou.
	2.78	Guidry, Ron AL:NY [2]
1980:	2.21	Sutton, Don NL:LA
	2.47	May, Rudy AL:NY
1981:	1.69	Ryan, Nolan NL:Hou.
	2.32	McCatty, Steve AL:Oak.
1982:	2.40	Rogers, Steve NL:Mtl.
	2.96	Sutcliffe, Rick AL:Clev.
1983:	2.25	Hammaker, Atlee NL:SF
	2.42	Honeycutt, Rick AL:Tex.
1984:	2.48	Pena, Alejandro NL:LA
	2.79	Boddicker, Mike AL:Balt.
1985:	1.53	Gooden, Dwight NL:NY
	2.48	Stieb, Dave AL:Tor.
1986:	2.22	Scott, Mike NL:Hou.
	2.48	Clemens, Roger AL:Bos.
1987:	2.76	Key, Jimmy AL:Tor.
	2.76	Ryan, Nolan NL:Hou. [2]
1988:	2.18	Magrane, Joe NL:StL.
	2.45	Anderson, Allan AL:Minn.
1989:	2.16	Saberhagen, Bret AL:KC
	2.28	Garrelts, Scott NL:SF
1990:	1.93	Clemens, Roger AL:Bos. [2]
	2.21	Darwin, Danny NL:Hou.
1991:	2.39	Martinez, Dennis NL:Mtl.
	2.62	Clemens, Roger AL:Bos. [3]
1992:	2.08	Swift, Bill NL:SF
	2.41	Clemens, Roger AL:Bos. [4]
1993:	2.36	Maddux, Greg NL:Atl.
	2.56	Appier, Kevin AL:KC
1994:	1.56	Maddux, Greg NL:Atl. [2]
	2.65	Ontiveros, Steve AL:Oak.
1995	1.63	Maddux, Greg NL:Atl. [3]
	2.48	Johnson, Randy AL:Sea.
1996	1.89	Brown, Kevin NL:Fla.
	2.93	Guzman, Juan AL:Tor.
1997	1.90	Martinez, Pedro NL:Mtl.
	2.05	Clemens, Roger AL:Tor. [5]
1998	2.22	Maddux, Greg NL:Atl. [4]
	2.65	Clemens, Roger AL:Tor. [6]
1999	2.07	Martinez, Pedro AL:Bos. [NL=1]
	2.48	Johnson, Randy NL:Ari. [AL=1]
2000	1.74	Martinez, Pedro AL:Bos. [AL=2; NL=1]
	2.58	Brown, Kevin NL:LA[2]
2001	2.49	Johnson, Randy NL:Ari. [AL=1; NL=2]
	3.05	Garcia, Freddy AL:Sea.

WINNING PERCENTAGE

Minimum 15 Decisions

Year	Pct	W-L	Player
1900	.763	29- 9	McGinnity, Joe NL:Brk.
1901:	.774	24- 7	Griffith, Clark AL:Chi.
	.737	14- 5	Leever, Sam NL:Pitt.
1902:	.824	28- 6	Chesbro, Jack NL:Pitt.
	.783	18- 5	Bernhard, Bill AL:Clev.
1903:	.781	25- 7	Leever, Sam NL:Pitt. [2]
	.757	28- 9	Young, Cy AL:Bos.
1904:	.814	35- 8	McGinnity, Joe NL:NY [2]
	.774	41-12	Chesbro, Jack AL:NY
1905:	.800	20- 5	Leever, Sam NL:Pitt. [3]
	.730	27-10	Waddell, Rube AL:Phil.
1906:	.826	19- 4	Ruelbach, Ed NL:Chi.
	.760	19- 6	Plank, Eddie AL:Phil.
1907:	.862	25- 4	Donovan, Wild Bill AL:Det.
	.810	17- 4	Ruelbach,Ed NL:Chi. [2]
1908:	.774	24- 7	Ruelbach, Ed NL:Chi. [3]
	.727	40-15	Walsh, Ed AL:Chi.
1909:	.806	25- 6	Camnitz, Howie NL:Pitt.
	.806	25- 6	Mathewson, Christy NL:NY
	.784	29- 8	Mullin, George AL:Det.
1910:	.875	14- 2	Phillippe, Deacon NL:Pitt.
	.821	23- 5	Bender, Chief AL:Phil.
1911:	.774	24- 7	Marquard, Rube NL:NY
	.773	17- 5	Bender, Chief AL:Phil. [2]
1912:	.872	34- 5	Wood, Smoky Joe AL:Bos.
	.727	24- 9	Hendrix, Claude NL:Pitt.
1913:	.837	36- 7	Johnson, Walter AL:Wash.
	.800	16- 4	Humphries, Bert NL:Chi.
1914:	.850	17- 3	Bender, Chief AL:Phil. [3]
	.788	26- 7	James, Bill NL:Bos.
1915:	.756	31-10	Alexander, Grover NL:Phil.
	.750	15- 5	Wood, Smoky Joe AL:Bos. [2]
1916:	.842	16- 3	Hughes, Tom NL:Bos.
	.656	21-11	Coveleski, Harry AL:Det.
1917:	.765	13- 4	Klepfer, Ed AL:Clev.
	.750	21- 7	Schupp, Ferdie NL:NY
1918:	.762	16- 5	Jones, Sam AL:Bos.
	.741	24- 9	Hendrix, Claude NL:Pitt. [2]
1919:	.805	29- 7	Cicotte, Eddie AL:Chi.
	.760	19- 6	Ruether, Dutch NL:Cin.
1920:	.721	31-12	Bagby, Jim AL:Clev.
	.676	23-11	Grimes, Burleigh NL:Brk.
1921:	.750	27- 9	Mays, Carl AL:NY
	.737	14- 5	Adams, Babe NL:Pitt.
	.737	14- 5	Glazner, Whitey NL:Pitt.
1922:	.788	26- 7	Bush, Joe AL:NY
	.733	11- 4	Douglas, Phil NL:NY
1923:	.771	27- 8	Luque, Dolf NL:Cin.
	.760	19- 6	Pennock, Herb AL:NY
1924:	.842	16- 3	Yde, Emil NL:Pitt.
	.767	23- 7	Johnson, Walter AL:Wash. [2]
1925:	.800	20- 5	Coveleski, Stan AL:Wash.
	.714	15- 6	Sherdel, Bill NL:StL.
1926:	.769	20- 6	Kremer, Ray NL:Pitt.
	.711	27-11	Uhle, George AL:Clev.
1927:	.759	22- 7	Hoyt, Waite AL:NY
	.708	17- 7	Benton, Larry NL:NY
1928:	.808	21- 5	Crowder, General AL:StL.
	.735	25- 9	Benton, Larry NL:NY [2]
1929:	.769	20- 6	Grove, Lefty AL:Phil.
	.760	19- 6	Root, Charlie NL:Chi.
1930:	.848	28- 5	Grove, Lefty AL:Phil. [2]
	.731	19- 7	Fitzsimmons, Freddie NL:NY
1931:	.886	31- 4	Grove, Lefty AL:Phil. [3]
	.800	12- 3	Haines, Jesse NL:StL.
1932:	.810	17- 4	Allen, Johnny AL:NY
	.786	22- 6	Warneke, Lon NL:Chi.
1933:	.750	24- 8	Grove, Lefty AL:Phil. [4]
	.684	13- 6	Tinning, Bud NL:Chi.
1934:	.839	26- 5	Gomez, Lefty AL:NY
	.811	30- 7	Dean, Dizzy NL:StL.
1935:	.769	20- 6	Lee, Bill NL:Chi.
	.720	18- 7	Auker, Elden AL:Det.
1936:	.813	26- 6	Hubbell, Carl NL:NY
	.778	14- 4	Hadley, Bump AL:NY
1937:	.938	15- 1	Allen, Johnny AL:Clev. [2]
	.733	22- 8	Hubbell, Carl NL:NY [2]
1938:	.778	14- 4	Grove, Lefty AL:Bos. [5]
	.710	22- 9	Lee, Bill NL:Chi. [2]
1939:	.813	13- 3	Donald, Atley AL:NY
	.781	25- 7	Derringer, Paul NL:Cin.
1940:	.889	16- 2	Fitzsimmons, Freddie NL:Brk. [2]
	.842	16- 3	Rowe, Schoolboy AL:Det.
1941:	.826	19- 4	Riddle, Elmer NL:Cin.
	.750	15- 5	Gomez, Lefty AL:NY [2]
1942:	.813	13- 3	Krist, Howie NL:StL.
	.808	21- 5	Bonham, Ernie AL:NY
1943:	.833	20- 4	Chandler, Spud AL:NY
	.737	14- 5	Shoun, Clyde NL:Cin.
	.737	14- 5	Wyatt, Whit NL:Brk.
1944:	.810	17- 4	Wilks, Ted NL:StL.
	.783	18- 5	Hughson, Tex AL:Bos.
1945:	.789	15- 4	Brecheen, Harry NL:StL.
	.765	13- 4	Muncrief, Bob AL:StL.
1946:	.806	25- 6	Ferriss, Boo AL:Bos.
	.733	11- 4	Rowe, Schoolboy NL:Phil.
1947:	.808	21- 5	Jansen, Larry NL:NY
	.737	14- 5	Shea, Spec AL:NY
1948:	.813	13- 3	Sewell, Rip NL:Pitt.
	.783	18- 5	Kramer, Jack AL:Bos.
1949:	.793	23- 6	Kinder, Ellis AL:Bos.
	.722	13- 5	Branca, Ralph NL:Brk.
1950:	.818	18- 4	Maglie, Sal NL:NY
	.724	21- 8	Raschi, Vic AL:NY
1951:	.880	22- 3	Roe, Preacher NL:Brk.
	.733	22- 8	Feller, Bob AL:Clev.
	.733	11- 4	Martin, Morrie AL:Phil.
1952:	.833	15- 3	Wilhelm, Hoyt NL:NY
	.774	24- 7	Shantz, Bobby AL:Phil.
1953:	.800	16- 4	Lopat, Ed AL:NY
	.769	20- 6	Erskine, Carl NL:Brk.
1954:	.842	16- 3	Consuegra, Sandy AL:Chi.
	.750	21- 7	Antonelli, Johnny NL:NY
	.750	12- 4	Wilhelm, Hoyt NL:NY [2]
1955:	.800	20- 5	Newcombe, Don NL:Brk.
	.762	16- 5	Byrne, Tommy AL:NY
1956:	.794	27- 7	Newcombe, Don NL:Brk. [2]
	.760	19- 6	Ford, Whitey AL:NY
1957:	.727	16- 6	Donovan, Dick AL:Chi.
	.727	16- 6	Sturdivant, Tom AL:NY
	.720	18- 7	Buhl, Bob NL:Mil.
1958:	.750	21- 7	Turley, Bob AL:NY
	.667	22-11	Spahn, Warren NL:Mil.
	.667	20-10	Burdette, Lew NL:Mil.
1959:	.947	18- 1	Face, Roy NL:Pitt.
	.750	18- 6	Shaw, Bob AL:Chi.
1960:	.813	13- 3	Coates, Jim AL:NY
	.750	12- 4	McDaniel, Lindy NL:StL.

WINNING PERCENTAGE (CONTINUED)

1961:	.862 25- 4	Ford, Whitey AL:NY [2]
	.783 18- 5	Podres, Johnny NL:LA
1962	.821 23- 5	Purkey, Bob NL:Cin.
	.733 11- 4	Wickersham, Dave AL:KC
1963	.842 16- 3	Perranoski, Ron NL:LA
	.774 24- 7	Ford, Whitey AL:NY [3]
1964	.792 19- 5	Bunker, Wally AL:Balt.
	.792 19- 5	Koufax, Sandy NL:LA
1965:	.765 26- 8	Koufax, Sandy NL:LA [2]
	.750 21- 7	Grant, Mudcat AL:Minn.
1966:	.933 14- 1	Regan, Phil NL:LA
	.706 12- 5	Boswell, Dave AL:Minn.
1967:	.750 12- 4	Santiago, Jose AL:Bos.
	.737 14- 5	Briles Nellie NL:StL.
1968:	.838 31- 6	McLain, Denny AL:Det.
	.750 18- 6	Blass, Steve NL:Pitt.
1969:	.824 14- 3	Moose, Bob NL:Pitt.
	.800 16- 4	Palmer, Jim AL:Balt.
1970:	.824 14- 3	Simpson, Wayne NL:Cin.
	.750 24- 8	Cuellar, Mike AL:Balt.
1971:	.808 21- 5	McNally, Dave AL:Balt.
	.733 11- 4	McGraw, Tug NL:NY
1972:	.750 21- 5	Hunter, Catfish AL:Oak.
	.750 15- 5	Nolan, Gary NL:Cin.
1973:	.867 13- 2	Moret, Roger AL:Bos.
	.800 12- 3	Stone, George NL:NY
1974:	.813 13- 3	John, Tommy NL:LA
	.688 22-10	Cuellar, Mike AL:Balt. [2]
1975:	.824 14- 3	Moret, Roger AL:Bos. [2]
	.813 13- 3	Hrabosky, Al NL:StL.
1976:	.800 12- 3	Rhoden, Rick NL:LA
	.773 17- 5	Campbell, Bill AL:Minn.
1977:	.800 20- 5	Candelaria, John NL:Pitt.
	.778 14- 4	Gullett, Don AL:NY
1978:	.893 25- 3	Guidry, Ron AL:NY
	.778 21- 6	Perry, Gaylord NL:SD
1979:	.875 14- 2	Davis, Ron AL:NY
	.750 12- 4	Bibby, Jim NL:Pitt.
1980:	.781 25- 7	Stone, Steve AL:Balt.
	.760 19- 6	Bibby, Jim NL:Pitt. [2]
1981:	.875 14- 2	Seaver, Tom NL:Cin.
	.800 8- 2	Comer, Steve AL:Tex.
1982:	.810 17- 4	Niekro, Phil NL:Atl.
	.750 15- 5	Palmer, Jim AL:Balt. [2]
	.750 18- 6	Vuckovich, Pete AL:Mil. [2]
1983:	.813 13- 3	Haas, Moose AL:Mil.
	.760 19- 6	Denny, John NL:Phil.
1984:	.941 16- 1	Sutcliffe, Rick NL:Chi.
	.739 17- 6	Alexander, Doyle AL:Tor.
1985:	.864 19- 3	Hershiser, Orel NL:LA
	.786 22- 6	Guidry, Ron AL:NY [2]
1986:	.857 24- 4	Clemens, Roger AL:Bos.
	.783 18- 5	Ojeda, Bob NL:NY
1987:	.733 11- 4	Martinez, Dennis NL:Mtl.
	.733 11- 4	Cerutti, John AL:Tor.
	.733 11- 4	Guetterman, Lee AL:Sea.
1988:	.870 20- 3	Cone, David NL:NY
	.774 24- 7	Viola, Frank AL:Minn.
1989:	.793 23- 6	Saberhagen, Bret AL:KC
	.737 14- 5	Fernandez, Sid NL:NY
	.737 14- 5	Garrelts, Scott NL:SF
1990:	.818 27- 6	Welch, Bob AL:Oak.
	.786 22- 6	Drabek, Doug NL:Pitt.
1991:	.750 12- 4	Hesketh, Joe AL:Bos.
	.714 20- 8	Smiley, John NL:Pitt.
	.714 15- 6	Rijo, Jose NL:Cin.
1992:	.783 18- 5	Mussina, Mike AL:Balt.
	.762 16- 5	Tewksbury, Bob NL:StL.
1993:	.824 14- 3	Guzman, Juan AL:Tor.
	.818 18- 4	Portugal, Mark NL:Hou.
1994:	.857 12- 2	Bere, Jason AL:Chi.
	.833 10- 2	Freeman, Marvin NL:Col.
1995	.905 19- 2	Maddux, Greg NL:Atl.
	.900 18- 2	Johnson, Randy AL:Sea.
1996	.813 13- 3	Moyer, Jamie AL:Bos.-Sea.
	.750 24- 8	Smoltz, John NL:Atl.
1997	.833 20- 4	Johnson, Randy AL:Sea. [2]
	.824 19- 4	Maddux, Greg NL:Atl. [2]
1998	.850 17- 3	Smoltz, John NL:Atl. [2]
	.818 18- 4	Wells, David AL:NY
1999	.852 23-4	Martinez, Pedro AL:Bos.
	.846 22-4	Hampton, Mike NL:Hou.
2000	.769 20-6	Hudson, Tim AL:Oak.
	.731 19-7	Johnson, Randy NL:Ari. [AL=2]
2001	.870 20-3	Clemens, Roger AL:NY [2]
	.824 14-3	Oswalt, Roy NL:Hou.

STRIKEOUTS

1900:	130	Waddell, Rube NL:Pitt.
1901:	239	Hahn, Noodles NL:Cin.
	158	Young, Cy AL:Bos.
1902:	225	Willis, Vic NL:Bos.
	210	Waddell, Rube AL:Phil.
1903:	302	Waddell, Rube AL:Phil. [2]
	267	Mathewson, Christy NL:NY
1904:	349	Waddell, Rube AL:Phil. [3]
	212	Mathewson, Christy NL:NY [2]
1905:	287	Waddell, Rube AL:Phil. [4]
	206	Mathewson, Christy NL:NY [3]
1906:	196	Waddell, Rube AL:Phil. [5]
	171	Beebe, Fred NL:Chi.-StL.
1907:	232	Waddell, Rube AL:Phil. [6]
	178	Mathewson, Christy NL:NY [4]
1908:	269	Walsh, Ed AL:Chi.
	259	Mathewson, Christy NL:NY [5]
1909:	205	Overall, Orval NL:Chi.
	177	Smith, Frank AL:Chi.
1910:	313	Johnson, Walter AL:Wash.
	185	Moore, Earl NL:Phil.
1911:	255	Walsh, Ed AL:Chi. [2]
	237	Marquard, Rube NL:NY
1912:	303	Johnson, Walter AL:Wash. [2]
	195	Alexander, Grover NL:Phil.
1913:	243	Johnson, Walter AL:Wash. [3]
	168	Seaton, Tom NL:Phil.
1914:	225	Johnson, Walter AL:Wash. [4]
	214	Alexander, Grover NL:Phil. [2]
1915:	241	Alexander, Grover NL:Phil. [3]
	203	Johnson, Walter AL:Wash. [5]
1916:	228	Johnson, Walter AL:Wash. [6]
	167	Alexander, Grover NL:Phil. [4]
1917:	200	Alexander,Grover NL:Phil. [5]
	188	Johnson, Walter AL:Wash. [7]
1918:	162	Johnson, Walter AL:Wash. [8]
	148	Vaughn, Hippo NL:Chi.
1919:	147	Johnson, Walter AL:Wash. [9]
	141	Vaughn, Hippo NL:Chi. [2]
1920:	173	Alexander, Grover NL:Chi. [6]
	133	Coveleski, Stan AL:Clev.
1921:	143	Johnson, Walter AL:Wash. [10]
	136	Grimes, Burleigh NL:Brk.
1922:	149	Shocker, Urban AL:StL.
	134	Vance, Dazzy NL:Brk.
1923:	197	Vance, Dazzy NL:Brk. [2]
	130	Johnson, Walter AL:Wash. [11]
1924:	262	Vance, Dazzy NL:Brk. [3]
	158	Johnson, Walter AL:Wash. [12]
1925:	221	Vance, Dazzy NL:Brk. [4]
	116	Grove, Lefty AL:Phil.
1926:	194	Grove, Lefty AL:Phil. [2]
	140	Vance, Dazzy NL:Brk. [5]
1927:	184	Vance, Dazzy NL:Brk. [6]
	174	Grove, Lefty AL:Phil. [3]
1928:	200	Vance, Dazzy NL:Brk. [7]
	183	Grove, Lefty AL:Phil. [4]
1929:	170	Grove, Lefty AL:Phil. [5]
	166	Malone, Pat NL:Chi.
1930:	209	Grove, Lefty AL:Phil. [6]
	177	Hallahan, Bill NL:StL.
1931:	175	Grove, Lefty AL:Phil. [7]
	159	Hallahan, Bill NL:StL. [2]
1932:	191	Dean, Dizzy NL:StL.
	190	Ruffing, Red AL:NY
1933:	199	Dean, Dizzy NL:StL. [2]
	163	Gomez, Lefty AL:NY
1934:	195	Dean, Dizzy NL:StL. [3]
	158	Gomez, Lefty AL:NY [2]
1935:	190	Dean, Dizzy NL:StL. [4]
	163	Bridges, Tommy AL:Det.
1936:	238	Mungo, Van NL:Brk.
	175	Bridges, Tommy AL:Det. [2]
1937:	194	Gomez, Lefty AL:NY [3]
	159	Hubbell, Carl NL:NY
1938:	240	Feller, Bob AL:Clev.
	135	Bryant, Clay NL:Chi.
1939:	246	Feller, Bob AL:Clev. [2]
	137	Passeau, Claude NL:Phil.-Chi.
	137	Walters, Bucky NL:Cin.
1940:	261	Feller, Bob AL:Clev. [3]
	137	Higbe, Kirby NL:Phil.
1941:	260	Feller, Bob AL:Clev. [4]
	202	Vander Meer, Johnny NL:Cin.
1942:	186	Vander Meer, Johnny NL:Cin. [2]
	113	Hughson, Tex AL:Bos.
	113	Newsom, Bobo AL:Wash.
1943:	174	Vander Meer, Johnny NL:Cin. [3]
	151	Reynolds, Allie AL:Clev.
1944:	187	Newhouser, Hal AL:Det.
	161	Voiselle, Bill NL:NY
1945:	212	Newhouser, Hal AL:Det. [2]
	148	Roe, Preacher NL:Pitt.
1946:	348	Feller, Bob AL:Clev. [5]
	135	Schmitz, Johnny NL:Chi.
1947:	196	Feller, Bob AL:Clev. [6]
	193	Blackwell, Ewell NL:Cin.
1948:	164	Feller, Bob AL:Clev. [7]
	149	Brecheen, Harry NL:StL.
1949:	153	Trucks, Virgil AL:Det.
	151	Spahn, Warren NL:Bos.
1950:	191	Spahn, Warren NL:Bos. [2]
	170	Lemon, Bob AL:Clev.
1951:	164	Newcombe, Don NL:Brk.
	164	Spahn, Warren NL:Bos. [3]
	164	Raschi, Vic AL:NY
1952:	183	Spahn, Warren NL:Bos. [4]
	160	Reynolds Allie AL:NY [2]
1953:	198	Roberts, Robin NL:Phil.
	186	Pierce, Billy AL:Chi.
1954:	185	Roberts, Robin NL:Phil. [2]
	185	Turley, Bob AL:Balt.
1955:	245	Score, Herb AL:Clev.
	198	Jones, Sam NL:Chi.
1956:	263	Score, Herb AL:Clev. [2]
	176	Jones, Sam NL:Chi. [2]
1957:	188	Sanford, Jack NL:Phil.
	184	Wynn, Early AL:Clev.
1958:	225	Jones, Sam NL:StL. [3]
	179	Wynn, Early AL:Chi. [2]
1959:	242	Drysdale, Don NL:LA
	201	Bunning, Jim AL:Det.
1960:	246	Drysdale, Don NL:LA [2]
	201	Bunning, Jim AL:Det. [2]
1961:	269	Koufax, Sandy NL:LA
	221	Pascual, Camilo AL:Minn.
1962:	232	Drysdale, Don NL:LA [3]
	206	Pascual, Camilo AL:Minn. [2]

STRIKEOUTS (CONTINUED)

1963:	306	Koufax, Sandy NL:LA [2]
	202	Pascual, Camilo AL:Minn. [3]
1964:	250	Veale, Bob NL:Pitt.
	217	Downing, Al AL:NY
1965:	382	Koufax, Sandy NL:LA [3]
	325	McDowell, Sam AL:Clev.
1966:	317	Koufax, Sandy NL:LA [4]
	225	McDowell, Sam AL:Clev. [2]
1967:	253	Bunning, Jim NL:Phil.
	246	Lonborg, Jim AL:Bos.
1968:	283	McDowell, Sam AL:Clev. [3]
	268	Gibson, Bob NL:StL.
1969:	279	McDowell, Sam AL:Clev. [4]
	273	Jenkins, Ferguson NL:Chi.
1970:	304	McDowell, Sam AL:Clev. [5]
	283	Seaver, Tom NL:NY
1971:	308	Lolich, Mickey AL:Det.
	289	Seaver, Tom NL:NY [2]
1972:	329	Ryan, Nolan AL:Cal.
	310	Carlton, Steve NL:Phil.
1973:	383	Ryan, Nolan AL:Cal. [2]
	251	Seaver, Tom NL:NY [3]
1974:	367	Ryan, Nolan AL:Cal. [3]
	240	Carlton, Steve NL:Phil. [2]
1975:	269	Tanana, Frank AL:Cal.
	243	Seaver, Tom NL:NY [4]
1976:	327	Ryan, Nolan AL:Cal. [4]
	235	Seaver, Tom NL:NY [5]
1977:	341	Ryan, Nolan AL:Cal. [5]
	262	Niekro, Phil. NL:Atl.
1978:	303	Richard, J.R. NL:Hou.
	260	Ryan, Nolan AL:Cal. [6]
1979:	313	Richard, J.R. NL:Hou. [2]
	223	Ryan, Nolan AL:Cal. [7]
1980:	286	Carlton, Steve NL:Phil. [3]
	187	Barker, Len AL:Clev.
1981:	180	Valenzuela, Fernando NL:LA
	127	Barker, Len AL:Clev. [2]
1982:	286	Carlton, Steve NL:Phil. [4]
	209	Bannister, Floyd AL:Sea.
1983:	275	Carlton, Steve NL:Phil. [5]
	232	Morris, Jack AL:Det.
1984:	276	Gooden, Dwight NL:NY
	204	Langston, Mark AL:Sea.
1985:	268	Gooden, Dwight NL:NY [2]
	206	Blyleven, Bert AL:Clev.-Minn.
1986:	306	Scott, Mike NL:Hou.
	245	Langston, Mark AL:Sea. [2]
1987:	270	Ryan, Nolan NL:Hou.
	262	Langston, Mark AL:Sea. [3]
1988:	291	Clemens, Roger AL:Bos.
	228	Ryan, Nolan NL:Hou. [2]
1989:	301	Ryan, Nolan AL:Tex. [8]
	201	DeLeon, Jose NL:StL.
1990:	233	Cone, David NL:NY
	232	Ryan, Nolan AL:Tex. [9]
1991:	241	Clemens, Roger AL:Bos. [2]
	241	Cone, David NL:NY [2]
1992:	261	Cone, David NL:NY-AL:Tor (ML=3)
	241	Johnson, Randy AL:Sea.
	215	Smoltz, John NL:Atl.
1993:	308	Johnson, Randy AL:Sea. [2]
	227	Rijo, Jose NL:Cin.
1994:	204	Johnson, Randy AL:Sea. [3]
	189	Benes, Andy NL:SD

1995	294	Johnson, Randy AL:Sea. [4]
	236	Nomo, Hideo NL:LA
1996	276	Smoltz, John NL:Atl. [2]
	257	Clemens, Roger AL:Bos. [3]
1997	319	Schilling, Curt NL:Phil.
	292	Clemens, Roger AL:Tor. [4]
1998	329	Johnson, Randy AL:Sea.-NL:Hou. [ML=4]
	300	Schilling, Curt NL:Phil. [2]
	271	Clemens, Roger AL:Tor. [5]
1999	364	Johnson, Randy NL:Ari [ML=5]
	313	Martinez, Pedro AL:Bos.
2000	347	Johnson, Randy NL:Ari. [NL=2; ML=6]
	284	Martinez, Pedro AL:Bos. [2]
2001	372	Johnson, Randy NL:Ari. [NL=3;ML=7]
	220	Nomo, Hideo AL:Bos. [NL=1]

MOST VALUABLE PLAYER
Baseball Writers Association of America *(Unanimous Selections Capitalized)*

AMERICAN LEAGUE	YEAR	NATIONAL LEAGUE
Grove, Lefty Phil. (P)	1931	Frisch, Frankie St.L. (2B)
Foxx, Jimmie Phil. (1B)	1932	Klein, Chuck Phil. (OF)
Foxx, Jimmie Phil. (1B)	1933	HUBBELL, CARL NY (P)
Cochrane Mickey Det. (C)	1934	Dean, Dizzy St.L. (P)
GREENBERG, HANK Det. (1B)	1935	Hartnett, Gabby Chi. (C)
Gehrig, Lou NY (1B)	1936	Hubbell, Carl NY (P)
Gehringer, Charlie Det. (2B)	1937	Medwick, Joe St.L. (OF)
Foxx, Jimmie Bos. (1B)	1938	Lombardi, Ernie Cin. (C)
DiMaggio, Joe NY (OF)	1939	Walters, Bucky Cin. (P)
Greenberg, Hank Det. (OF)	1940	McCormick, Frank Cin. (1B)
DiMaggio, Joe NY (OF)	1941	Camilli, Dolph Brk. (1B)
Gordon, Joe NY (2B)	1942	Cooper, Mort St.L. (P)
Chandler, Spud NY (P)	1943	Musial, Stan St.L. (OF)
Newhouser, Hal Det. (P)	1944	Marion, Marty St.L. (SS)
Newhouser, Hal Det. (P)	1945	Cavarretta, Phil Chi. (1B)
Williams, Ted Bos. (OF)	1946	Musial, Stan St.L. (1B)
DiMaggio, Joe NY (OF)	1947	Elliott, Bob Bos. (3B)
Boudreau, Lou Clev. (SS)	1948	Musial, Stan St.L. (OF)
Williams, Ted Bos. (OF)	1949	Robinson, Jackie Brk. (2B)
Rizzuto, Phil NY (SS)	1950	Konstanty, Jim Phil. (P)
Berra, Yogi NY (C)	1951	Campanella, Roy Brk. (C)
Shantz, Bobby Phil. (P)	1952	Sauer, Hank Chi. (OF)
ROSEN, AL Clev. (3B)	1953	Campanella, Roy Brk. (C)
Berra, Yogi NY (C)	1954	Mays, Willie NY (OF)
Berra, Yogi NY (C)	1955	Campanella, Roy Brk. (C)
MANTLE, MICKEY NY (OF)	1956	Newcombe, Don Brk. (P)
Mantle, Mickey NY (OF)	1957	Aaron, Hank Mil. (OF)
Jensen, Jackie Bos. (OF)	1958	Banks, Ernie Chi. (SS)
Fox, Nellie Chi. (2B)	1959	Banks, Ernie Chi. (SS)
Maris, Roger NY (OF)	1960	Groat, Dick Pitt. (SS)
Maris, Roger NY (OF)	1961	Robinson, Frank Cin. (OF)
Mantle, Mickey NY (OF)	1962	Wills, Maury LA (SS)
Howard, Elston NY (C)	1963	Koufax, Sandy LA (P)
Robinson, Brooks Balt. (3B)	1964	Boyer, Ken St.L. (3B)
Versalles, Zoilo Minn. (SS)	1965	Mays, Willie SF (OF)
ROBINSON, FRANK, Balt. (OF)	1966	Clemente, Roberto Pitt. (OF)
Yastrzemski, Carl Bos. (OF)	1967	CEPEDA, ORLANDO St.L. (1B)
McLAIN, DENNY Det. (P)	1968	Gibson, Bob St.L. (P)
Killebrew, Harmon Minn. (3B)	1969	McCovey, Willie SF (1B)
Powell, Boog Balt. (1B)	1970	Bench, Johnny Cin. (C)
Blue, Vida Oak. (P)	1971	Torre, Joe St.L. (3B)
Allen, Dick Chi. (1B)	1972	Bench, Johnny Cin. (C)
JACKSON, REGGIE Oak. (OF)	1973	Rose, Pete Cin. (OF)
Burroughs, Jeff Tex. (OF)	1974	Garvey, Steve LA (1B)
Lynn, Fred Bos. (OF)	1975	Morgan, Joe Cin. (2B)
Munson, Thurman NY (C)	1976	Morgan, Joe Cin. (2B)
Carew, Rod Minn. (1B)	1977	Foster, George Cin. (OF)
Rice, Jim Bos. (OF)	1978	Parker, Dave Pitt. (OF)
Baylor, Don Cal. (OF)	1979	Hernandez, Keith StL (1B) &
	1979	Stargell, Willie Pitt. (1B) (tied)
Brett, George KC (3B)	1980	SCHMIDT, MIKE Phil. (3B)
Fingers, Rollie Mil. (P)	1981	Schmidt, Mike Phil. (3B)
Yount, Robin Mil. (SS)	1982	Murphy, Dale Atl. (OF)
Ripken, Cal Balt. (SS)	1983	Murphy, Dale Atl. (OF)
Hernandez, Willie Det. (P)	1984	Sandberg, Ryne Chi. (2B)
Mattingly, Don NY (1B)	1985	McGee, Willie StL. (OF)
Clemens, Roger Bos. (P)	1986	Schmidt, Mike Phil. (3B)
Bell, George Tor. (OF)	1987	Dawson, Andre Chi. (OF)
CANSECO, JOSE Oak. (OF)	1988	Gibson, Kirk LA (OF)
Yount, Robin Mil. (OF)	1989	Mitchell, Kevin SF (OF)
Henderson, Rickey Oak. (OF)	1990	Bonds, Barry Pitt. (OF)
Ripken, Cal Balt. (SS)	1991	Pendleton, Terry Atl. (3B)
Eckersley, Dennis Oak. (P)	1992	Bonds, Barry Pitt. (OF)
THOMAS, FRANK Chi. (1B)	1993	Bonds, Barry SF (OF)
Thomas, Frank Chi. (1B)	1994	BAGWELL, JEFF Hou. (1B)
Vaughn, Mo Bos. (1B)	1995	Larkin, Barry Cin. (SS)
Gonzalez, Juan Tex. (OF)	1996	CAMINITI, KEN SD (3B)
GRIFFEY, KEN, JR. Sea. (OF)	1997	Walker, Larry, Col. (OF)
Gonzalez, Juan Tex. (OF)	1998	Sosa, Sammy Chi. (OF)
Rodriguez, Ivan Tex. (C)	1999	Jones, Chipper Atl. (3B)
Giambi, Jason Oak. (1B)	2000	Kent, Jeff SF (2B)
Suzuki, Ichiro Sea. (OF)	2001	Bonds, Barry SF (OF)

CHALMERS AWARD

AMERICAN LEAGUE	YEAR	NATIONAL LEAGUE
COBB, TY Det. (OF)	1911	Schulte, Wildfire Chi. (OF)
Speaker, Tris Bos. (OF)	1912	Doyle, Larry NY (2B)
Johnson, Walter Wash. (P)	1913	Daubert, Jake Brk. (1B)
Collins, Eddie Phil. (2B)	1914	Evers, Johnny Bos. (2B)

LEAGUE AWARD

AMERICAN LEAGUE	YEAR	NATIONAL LEAGUE
Sisler, George StL. (1B)	1922	No selection
RUTH, BABE NY (OF)	1923	No selection
Johnson, Walter Wash. (P)	1924	Vance, Dazzy Brk. (P)
Peckinpaugh, Roger Wash. (SS)	1925	Hornsby, Rogers StL. (2B)
Burns, George Clev. (1B)	1926	O'Farrell, Bob StL. (C)
Gehrig, Lou NY (1B)	1927	Waner, Paul Pitt. (OF)
Cochrane, Mickey Phil. (C)	1928	Bottomley, Jim StL. (1B)
No selection	1929	Hornsby, Rogers Chi. (2B)

CY YOUNG AWARD

1956	Newcombe, Don NL:Brk.	1962	Drysdale, Don NL:LA
1957	Spahn, Warren NL:Mil.	1963	KOUFAX, SANDY NL:LA
1958	Turley, Bob AL:NY	1964	Chance, Dean AL:LA
1959	Wynn, Early AL:Chi.	1965	KOUFAX, SANDY NL:LA
1960	Law, Vern NL:Pitt.	1966	KOUFAX, SANDY NL:LA
1961	Ford, Whitey AL:NY		

AMERICAN LEAGUE	YEAR	NATIONAL LEAGUE
Lonborg, Jim Bos.	1967	McCormick, Mike SF
McLAIN, DENNY Det.	1968	GIBSON, BOB StL.
Cuellar, Mike Balt. (tied)	1969	Seaver, Tom NY
McLain, Denny Det.	1969	
Perry, Jim Minn.	1970	Gibson, Bob StL.
Blue, Vida Oak.	1971	Jenkins, Ferguson, Chi.
Perry, Gaylord Clev.	1972	CARLTON, STEVE Phil.
Palmer, Jim Balt.	1973	Seaver, Tom NY
Hunter, Catfish Oak.	1974	Marshall, Mike LA
Palmer, Jim Balt.	1975	Seaver. Tom NY
Palmer, Jim Balt.	1976	Jones, Randy SD
Lyle, Sparky NY	1977	Carlton, Steve Phil.
GUIDRY, RON NY	1978	Perry, Gaylord SD
Flanagan, Mike Balt.	1979	Sutter, Bruce Chi.
Stone, Steve Balt.	1980	Carlton, Steve Phil.
Fingers, Rollie Mil.	1981	Valenzuela, Fernando LA
Vuckovich, Pete Mil.	1982	Carlton, Steve Phil.
Hoyt, LaMarr Chi.	1983	Denny, John Phil.
Hernandez, Willie Det.	1984	SUTCLIFFE, RICK Chi.
Saberhagen, Bret KC	1985	GOODEN, DWIGHT NY
CLEMENS, ROGER Bos.	1986	Scott, Mike Hou.
Clemens, Roger Bos.	1987	Bedrosian, Steve Phil.
Viola, Frank Minn.	1988	HERSHISER, OREL LA
Saberhagen, Bret KC	1989	Davis, Mark SD
Welch, Bob Oak.	1990	Drabek, Doug Pitt.
Clemens, Roger Bos.	1991	Glavine, Tom Atl.
Eckersley, Dennis Oak.	1992	Maddux, Greg Chi.
McDowell, Jack Chi.	1993	Maddux, Greg Atl.
Cone, David KC	1994	MADDUX, GREG Atl.
Johnson, Randy Sea.	1995	MADDUX, GREG Atl.
Hentgen, Pat Tor.	1996	Smoltz, John Atl.
Clemens, Roger Tor.	1997	Martinez, Pedro, Mtl.
CLEMENS, ROGER TOR.	1998	Glavine, Tom Atl.
MARTINEZ, PEDRO BOS.	1999	Johnson, Randy Ari.
MARTINEZ, PEDRO BOS.	2000	Johnson, Randy Ari.
Clemens, Roger NY	2001	Johnson, Randy Ari.

ROOKIE OF THE YEAR AWARD

(Unanimous Selections Capitalized)

AMERICAN LEAGUE	YEAR	NATIONAL LEAGUE
One selection	1947	Robinson, Jackie Brk. (1B)
One selection	1948	Dark, Alvin Bos. (SS)
Sievers, Roy StL. (OF)	1949	Newcombe, Don Brk. (P)
Dropo, Walt Bos. (1B)	1950	Jethroe, Sam Bos. (OF)
McDougald, Gil NY (3B)	1951	Mays, Willie NY (OF)
Byrd, Harry Phil. (P)	1952	Black, Joe Brk. (P)
Kuenn, Harvey Det. (SS)	1953	Gilliam, Jim Brk. (2B)
Grim, Bob NY (P)	1954	Moon, Wally StL. (OF)
Score, Herb Clev. (P)	1955	Virdon, Bill StL. (OF)
Aparicio, Luis Chi. (SS)	1956	ROBINSON, FRANK, Cin. (OF)
Kubek, Tony NY (OF)	1957	Sanford, Jack Phil. (P)
Pearson, Albie Wash. (OF)	1958	CEPEDA, ORLANDO SF (1B)
Allison, Bob Wash. (OF)	1959	McCOVEY, WILLIE SF (1B)
Hansen, Ron Balt. (SS)	1960	Howard, Frank LA (OF)
Schwall, Don Bos. (P)	1961	Williams, Billy Chi. (OF)
Tresh, Tom NY (SS)	1962	Hubbs, Ken Chi. (2B)
Peters, Gary Chi. (P)	1963	Rose, Pete Cin. (2B)
Oliva, Tony Minn. (OF)	1964	Allen, Dick Phil. (3B)
Blefary, Curt Balt. (OF)	1965	Lefebvre, Jim LA (2B)
Agee, Tommie Chi. (OF)	1966	Helms, Tommy Cin. (3B)
Carew, Rod Minn. (2B)	1967	Seaver, Tom NY (P)
Bahnsen, Stan NY (P)	1968	Bench, Johnny Cin. (C)
Piniella, Lou KC (OF)	1969	Sizemore, Ted LA (2B)
Munson, Thurman NY (C)	1970	Morton, Carl Mtl. (P)
Chambliss, Chris Clev. (1B)	1971	Williams, Earl Atl. (C)
FISK, CARLTON Bos. (C)	1972	Matlack, Jon NY (P)
Bumbry, Al Balt. (OF)	1973	Matthews, Gary SF (OF)
Hargrove, Mike Tex. (1B)	1974	McBride, Bake StL. (OF)
Lynn, Fred Bos. (OF)	1975	Montefusco, John SF (P)
	1976	Metzger, Butch SD (P) (tied)
Fidrych, Mark Det. (P)	1976	Zachry, Pat Cin (P)
Murray, Eddie Balt. (DH)	1977	Dawson, Andre Mtl. (OF)
Whitaker, Lou Det. (2B)	1978	Horner, Bob Atl. (3B)
Castino, John Minn. (3B) (tied)	1979	Sutcliffe, Rick LA (P)
Griffin, Alfredo Tor. (SS)	1979	
Charboneau, Joe Clev. (OF)	1980	Howe, Steve LA (P)
Righetti, Dave NY (P)	1981	Valenzuela, Fernando LA (P)
Ripken, Cal Balt. (SS)	1982	Sax, Steve LA (2B)
Kittle, Ron Chi. (OF)	1983	Strawberry, Darryl NY (OF)
Davis, Alvin Sea. (1B)	1984	Gooden, Dwight NY (P)
Guillen, Ozzie Chi. (SS)	1985	COLEMAN, VINCE StL. (OF)
Canseco, Jose Oak. (OF)	1986	Worrell, Todd StL. (P)
McGWIRE, MARK Oak. (1B)	1987	SANTIAGO, BENITO SD (C)
Weiss, Walt Oak (SS)	1988	Sabo, Chris Cin (3B)
Olson, Gregg Balt. (P)	1989	Walton, Jerome Chi. (OF)
ALOMAR, SANDY, JR Clev. (C)	1990	Justice, Dave Atl. (OF)
Knoblauch, Chuck Minn. (2B)	1991	Bagwell, Jeff Hou. (1B)
Listach, Pat Mil. (SS)	1992	Karros, Eric LA (1B)
SALMON, TIM Cal. (OF)	1993	PIAZZA, MIKE LA (C)
Hamelin, Bob KC (DH)	1994	MONDESI, RAUL LA (OF)
Cordova, Marty Minn. (OF)	1995	Nomo, Hideo LA (P)
JETER, DEREK NY (SS)	1996	Hollandsworth, Todd LA (OF)
GARCIAPARRA, NOMAR Bos. (SS)	1997	ROLEN, SCOTT Phil. (3B)
Grieve, Ben Oak. (OF)	1998	Wood, Kerry Chi. (P)
Beltran, Carlos KC (OF)	1999	Williamson, Scott Cin (P)
Sasaki, Kazuhiro Sea. (P)	2000	Furcal, Rafael Atl. (SS)
Suzuki, Ichiro Sea (OF)	2001	PUJOLS, ALBERT StL. (OF)

JOE DiMAGGIO, NEW YORK AL – 1941
56 CONSECUTIVE GAME BATTING STREAK

Date		Opp	Club and Pitcher	AB	R	H	2B	3B	HR	RBI
May	15	Chi	Edgar Smith	4	0	1	0	0	0	1
	16	Chi	Thornton Lee	4	2	2	0	1	1	1
	17	Chi	Johnny Rigney	3	1	1	0	0	0	0
	18	StL	Bob Harris (2)							
			Johnny Niggeling (1)	3	3	3	1	0	0	1
	19	StL	Denny Galehouse	3	0	1	1	0	0	0
	20	StL	Elden Auker	5	1	1	0	0	0	1
	21	Det	Schoolboy Rowe (1)							
			Al Benton (1)	5	0	2	0	0	0	1
	22	Det	Archie McKain	4	0	1	0	0	0	1
	23	Bos	Dick Newsome	5	0	1	0	0	0	2
	24	Bos	Earl Johnson	4	2	1	0	0	0	2
	25	Bos	Lefty Grove	4	0	1	0	0	0	0
	27	Wash	Ken Chase (1)							
			Red Anderson (2)							
			Alex Carrasquel (1)	5	3	4	0	0	1	3
	28n	Wash	Sid Hudson	4	1	1	0	1	0	0
	29	Wash	Steve Sundra	3	1	1	0	0	0	0
	30	Bos	Earl Johnson	2	1	1	0	0	0	0
	30	Bos	Mickey Harris	3	0	1	1	0	0	0
June	1	Clev	Al Milnar	4	1	1	0	0	0	0
	1	Clev	Mel Harder	4	0	1	0	0	0	0
	2	Clev	Bob Feller	4	2	2	1	0	0	0
	3	Det	Dizzy Trout	4	1	1	0	0	1	1
	5	Det	Hal Newhouser	5	1	1	0	1	0	1
	7	StL	Bob Muncrief (1)							
			Johnny Allen (1)							
			George Caster(1)	5	2	3	0	0	0	1
	8	StL	Elden Auker	4	3	2	0	0	2	4
	8	StL	George Caster (1)							
			Jack Kramer (1)	4	1	2	1	0	1	3
	10	Chi	Johnny Rigney	5	1	1	0	0	0	0
	12n	Chi	Thornton Lee	4	1	2	0	1	1	1
	14	Clev	Bob Feller	2	0	1	1	0	0	1
	15	Clev	Jim Bagby	3	1	1	0	0	1	1
	16	Clev	Al Milnar	5	0	1	1	0	0	0
	17	Chi	Johnny Rigney	4	1	1	0	0	0	0
	18	Chi	Thornton Lee	3	1	1	0	0	0	0
	19	Chi	Edgar Smith (1)							
			Buck Ross (2)	3	2	3	0	0	1	2
	20	Det	Bobo Newsom (2)							
			Archie McKain (2)	5	3	4	1	0	0	1
	21	Det	Dizzy Trout	4	0	1	0	0	0	1
	22	Det	Hal Newhouser (1)							
			Bobo Newsom (1)	5	1	2	1	0	1	2
	24	StL	Bob Muncrief	4	1	1	0	0	0	0
	25	StL	Denny Galehouse	4	1	1	0	0	1	3
	26	StL	Elden Auker	4	0	1	1	0	0	1
	27	Phil	Chubby Dean	3	1	2	0	0	1	2
	28	Phil	Johnny Babich (1)							
			Lum Harris(1)	5	1	2	1	0	0	0
	29	Wash	Dutch Leonard	4	1	1	1	0	0	0
	29	Wash	Red Anderson	5	1	1	0	0	0	1
July	1	Bos	Mickey Harris (1)							
			Mike Ryba (1)	4	0	2	0	0	0	1
	1	Bos	Jack Wilson	3	1	1	0	0	0	1
	2	Bos	Dick Newsome	5	1	1	0	0	1	3
	5	Phil	Phil Marchildon	4	2	1	0	0	1	2
	6	Phil	Johnny Babich (1)							
			Bump Hadley (3)	5	2	4	1	0	0	2
	6	Phil	Jack Knott	4	0	2	0	1	0	2
	10n	StL	Johnny Niggeling	2	0	1	0	0	0	0
	11	StL	Bob Harris (3)							
			Jack Kramer (1)	5	1	4	0	0	1	2
	12	StL	Elden Auker (1)							
			Bob Muncrief (1)	5	1	2	1	0	0	1
	13	Chi	Ted Lyons (2)							
			Jack Hallett (1)	4	2	3	0	0	0	0
	13	Chi	Thornton Lee	4	0	1	0	0	0	0
	14	Chi	Johnny Rigney	3	0	1	0	0	0	0
	15	Chi	Edgar Smith	4	1	2	1	0	0	2
	16	Clev	Al Milnar (2)							
			Joe Krakauskas (1)	4	3	3	1	0	0	0
	17n	Clev	Stopped in Cleveland (Al Smith and Jim Bagby)							

	PCT	AB	R	H	2B	3B	HR	RBI
TOTALS	.408	223	56	91	16	4	15	55

ROGER MARIS, NEW YORK AL — 1961   61 HOME RUNS

HR	Team Game	Ind Game	Date	Inn	Opponent	Pitcher
1	11	11	Apr 26	5	@ Detroit	Paul Foytack
2	17	17	May 3	7	@ Minnesota	Pedro Ramos
3	20	20	May 6n	5	@ Los Angeles	Eli Grba
4	29	29	May 17	8	Washington	Pete Burnside (L)
5	30	30	May 19n	1	@ Cleveland	Jim Perry
6	31	31	May 20	3	@ Cleveland	Gary Bell
7	32	32	May 21	1	Baltimore	Chuck Estrada
8	35	35	May 24	4	Boston	Gene Conley
9	38	38	May 28	2	Chicago	Cal McLish
10	40	40	May 30	6	@ Boston	Gene Conley
11	40	40	May 30	8	@ Boston	Mike Fornieles
12	41	41	May 31n	3	@ Boston	Billy Muffett
13	43	43	June 2n	3	@ Chicago	Cal McLish
14	44	44	June 3	8	@ Chicago	Bob Shaw
15	45	45	June 4	3	@ Chicago	Russ Kemmerer
16	48	48	June 6n	6	Minnesota	Ed Palmquist
17	49	49	June 7	3	Minnesota	Pedro Ramos
18	52	52	June 9n	7	Kansas City	Ray Herbert
19	55	55	June 11	3	Los Angeles	Eli Grba
20	55	55	June 11	7	Los Angeles	Johnny James
21	57	57	June 13n	6	@ Cleveland	Jim Perry
22	58	58	June 14n	4	@ Cleveland	Gary Bell
23	61	61	June 17n	4	@ Detroit	Don Mossi (L)
24	62	62	June 18	8	@ Detroit	Jerry Casale
25	63	63	June 19n	9	@ Kansas City	Jim Archer (L)
26	64	64	June 20n	1	@ Kansas City	Joe Nuxhall (L)
27	66	66	June 22n	2	@ Kansas City	Norm Bass
28	74	74	July 1	9	Washington	Dave Sisler
29	75	75	July 2	3	Washington	Pete Burnside (L)
30	75	75	July 2	7	Washington	Johnny Klippstein
31	77	77	July 4	8	Detroit	Frank Lary
32	78	78	July 5	7	Cleveland	Frank Funk
33	82	82	July 9	7	Boston	Bill Monbouquette
34	84	84	July 13n	1	@ Chicago	Early Wynn
35	86	86	July 15	3	@ Chicago	Ray Herbert
36	92	92	July 21n	1	@ Boston	Bill Monbouquette
37	95	95	July 25n	4	Chicago	Frank Baumann (L)
38	95	95	July 25n	8	Chicago	Don Larsen
39	96	96	July 25n	4	Chicago	Russ Kemmerer
40	96	96	July 25n	6	Chicago	Warren Hacker
41	106	105	Aug. 4n	1	Minnesota	Camilo Pascual
42	114	113	Aug. 11n	5	@ Washington	Pete Burnside (L)
43	115	114	Aug. 12	4	@ Washington	Dick Donovan
44	116	115	Aug. 13	4	@ Washington	Bennie Daniels
45	117	116	Aug. 13	1	@ Washington	Marty Kutyna
46	118	117	Aug. 15n	4	Chicago	Juan Pizarro (L)
47	119	118	Aug. 16	1	Chicago	Billy Pierce (L)
48	119	118	Aug. 16	3	Chicago	Billy Pierce (L)
49	123	122	Aug. 20	3	@ Cleveland	Jim Perry
50	125	124	Aug. 22n	6	@ Los Angeles	Ken McBride
51	129	128	Aug. 26	6	@ Kansas City	Jerry Walker
52	135	134	Sept. 2	6	Detroit	Frank Lary
53	135	134	Sept. 2	8	Detroit	Hank Aguirre (L)
54	140	139	Sept. 6	4	Washington	Tom Cheney
55	141	140	Sept. 7n	3	Cleveland	Dick Stigman (L)
56	143	142	Sept. 9	7	Cleveland	Mudcat Grant
57	151	150	Sept. 16	3	@ Detroit	Frank Lary
58	152	151	Sept. 17	12	@ Detroit	Terry Fox
59	155	154	Sept. 20n	3	@ Baltimore	Milt Pappas
60	159	158	Sept. 26n	3	Baltimore	Jack Fisher
61	163	161	Oct. 1	4	Boston	Tracy Stallard

Home–30   Road–31   Off RHP–49   Off LHP–12   Day-36   Night-25

BARRY BONDS, SAN FRANCISCO NL – 2001   73 HOME RUNS

HR	Team Game	Ind Game	Date	Inn	Opponent	Pitcher
1	1	1	Apr. 2	5	San Diego	Woody Williams
2	9	8	Apr. 12	4	@ San Diego	Adam Eaton
3	10	9	Apr. 13n	1	@ Milwaukee	Jamey Wright
4	11	10	Apr. 14n	5	@ Milwaukee	Jimmy Haynes
5	12	11	Apr. 15	8	@ Milwaukee	David Weathers
6	13	12	Apr. 17n	8	Los Angeles	Terry Adams
7	14	13	Apr. 18n	7	Los Angeles	Chan Ho Park
8	16	15	Apr. 20n	4	Milwaukee	Jimmy Haynes
9	19	18	Apr. 24n	3	Cincinnati	Jim Brower
10	21	20	Apr. 26	8	Cincinnati	Scott Sullivan
11	24	22	Apr. 29	4	Chicago (NL)	Manny Aybar
12	26	24	May 2n	5	@ Pittsburgh	Todd Ritchie
13	27	25	May 3n	1	@ Pittsburgh	Jimmy Anderson (L)
14	28	26	May 4n	6	@ Philadelphia	Bruce Chen (L)
15	35	32	May 11n	4	New York (NL)	Steve Trachsel
16	40	37	May 17n	3	@ Florida	Chuck Smith
17	41	38	May 18n	8	@ Atlanta	Mike Remlinger (L)
18	42	39	May 19n	3	@ Atlanta	Odalis Perez (L)
19	42	39	May 19n	7	@ Atlanta	Jose Cabrera
20	42	39	May 19n	8	@ Atlanta	Jason Marquis
21	43	40	May 20	1	@ Atlanta	John Burkett
22	43	40	May 20	7	@ Atlanta	Mike Remlinger (L)
23	44	41	May 21n	4	@ Arizona	Curt Schilling
24	45	42	May 22n	9	@ Arizona	Russ Springer
25	47	44	May 24n	3	Colorado	John Thomson
26	50	46	May 27	1	Colorado	Denny Neagle (L)
27	53	49	May 30n	2	Arizona	Robert Ellis
28	53	49	May 30n	6	Arizona	Robert Ellis
29	54	50	June 1n	3	@ Colorado	Shawn Chacon
30	57	53	June 4n	4	San Diego	Bobby J. Jones
31	58	54	June 5n	3	San Diego	Wascar Serrano
32	60	55	June 7	7	San Diego	Brian Lawrence
33	64	59	June 12n	1	Anaheim	Pat Rapp
34	66	61	June 14	6	Anaheim	Lou Pote
35	67	62	June 15n	1	Oakland	Mark Mulder (L)
36	67	62	June 15n	6	Oakland	Mark Mulder (L)
37	70	65	June 19n	5	@ San Diego	Adam Eaton
38	71	66	June 20n	8	@ San Diego	Rodney Myers
39	74	68	June 23n	1	@ St. Louis	Darryl Kile
40	89	82	July 12n	1	@ Seattle	Paul Abbott
41	95	88	July 18n	4	Colorado	Mike Hampton (L)
42	95	88	July 18n	5	Colorado	Mike Hampton (L)
43	103	96	July 26n	4	@ Arizona	Curt Schilling
44	103	96	July 26n	5	@ Arizona	Curt Schilling
45	104	97	July 27n	4	@ Arizona	Brian Anderson (L)
46	108	101	Aug. 1n	1	Pittsburgh	Joe Beimel (L)
47	111	103	Aug. 4	6	Philadelphia	Nelson Figueroa
48	113	105	Aug. 7n	11	@ Cincinnati	Danny Graves
49	115	107	Aug. 9n	3	@ Cincinnati	Scott Winchester
50	117	108	Aug. 11	2	@ Chicago (NL)	Joe Borowski
51	119	110	Aug. 14n	6	Florida	Ricky Bones
52	121	112	Aug. 16	4	Florida	A.J. Burnett
53	121	112	Aug. 16	8	Florida	Vic Darensbourg (L)
54	123	114	Aug. 18	8	Atlanta	Jason Marquis
55	127	118	Aug. 23n	9	@ Montreal	Graeme Lloyd (L)
56	131	122	Aug. 27	5	@ New York (NL)	Kevin Appier
57	135	126	Aug. 31n	8	Colorado	John Thomson
58	138	129	Sept. 3	4	Colorado	Jason Jennings
59	139	130	Sept. 4n	7	Arizona	Miguel Batista
60	141	132	Sept. 6	2	Arizona	Albie Lopez
61	144	135	Sept. 9	1	@ Colorado	Scott Elarton
62	144	135	Sept. 9	5	@ Colorado	Scott Elarton
63	144	135	Sept. 9	11	@ Colorado	Todd Belitz (L)
64	147	138	Sept. 20	5	Houston	Wade Miller
65	150	141	Sept. 23	2	@ San Diego	Jason Middlebrook
66	150	141	Sept. 23	4	@ San Diego	Jason Middlebrook
67	151	142	Sept. 24n	7	@ Los Angeles	James Baldwin
68	154	145	Sept. 28n	2	San Diego	Jason Middlebrook
69	155	146	Sept. 29	6	San Diego	Chuck McElroy (L)
70	159	150	Oct. 4n	9	@ Houston	Wilfredo Rodriguez (L)
71	160	151	Oct. 5n	1	Los Angeles	Chan Ho Park
72	160	151	Oct. 5n	3	Los Angeles	Chan Ho Park
73	162	153	Oct. 7	1	Los Angeles	Dennis Springer

Home–37   Road–36   Off RHP–56   Off LHP–17   Day–26   Night–47

RICKEY HENDERSON, OAKLAND – 1982

130 STOLEN BASES *(* = 2nd Game)*

No.	Date	Game	Opp.
1	Apr. 8	3	Cal.
2	8	3	Cal.
3	9	4	Sea.
4	11	5	Sea.
5	11	5	Sea.
6	13	7	@Minn.
7	14	8	@Minn.
8	14	8	@Minn.
9	15	9	@Minn.
10	16	10	@Sea.
11	17	11	@Sea.
12	17	11	@Sea.
13	18	12	@Sea.
14	20	14	Minn.
15	21	15	Minn.
16	23	16	@Cal.
17	23	16	@Cal
18	28	19	@Balt.
19	28*	20	@Balt.
20	29	21	@Balt.
21	29	21	@Balt.
22	30	22	@Clev.
23	May 1	23	@Clev.
24	1	23	@Clev.
25	2	24	@Clev.
26	3	25	@NY
27	6	27	Clev.
28	6	27	Clev.
29	8	29	Clev.
30	8	29	Clev.
31	8	29	Clev.
32	9	30	Clev.
33	10	31	Balt.
34	11	32	Balt.
35	11	32	Balt.
36	15	36	NY
37	16	37	NY
38	16	37	NY
39	19	39	@Det.
40	22	42	@Bos.
41	22	42	@Bos.
42	23	43	@Bos.
43	26	45	@Mil.
44	26	45	@Mil.
45	26	45	@Mil.
46	30*	49	Det.
47	30*	49	Det.
48	30*	49	Det.
49	30*	49	Det.
50	June 1	51	Bos.
51	1	51	Bos.
52	4	53	Mil.
53	6	55	Mil.
54	6	55	Mil.
55	8	57	@ Chi.
56	8	57	@ Chi.
57	8	57	@ Chi.
58	9	58	@ Chi.
59	13	61	@ Tor.
60	13	61	@ Tor.
61	13	61	@ Tor.
62	13	61	@ Tor.
63	14	62	@ Tor.
64	15	63	Chi.
65	18	66	Tor.
66	18	66	Tor.
67	22	70	KC
68	22	70	KC
69	25	73	@ Tex.
70	25	73	@ Tex.

No.	Date	Game	Opp.
71	26	74	@ Tex.
72	29	77	@ KC
73	30	78	@ KC
74	July 2	79	Tex.
75	2	79	Tex.
76	3	80	Tex.
77	4	81	Tex.
78	6	83	Clev.
79	6	83	Clev.
80	8	85	NY
81	8	85	NY
82	9	86	Balt.
83	10	87	Balt.
84	11	88	Balt.
85	15	89	@ NY
86	16	90	@ NY
87	19	92	@ Clev.
88	20	93	@ Clev.
89	20	93	@ Clev.
90	24	96	@ Balt.
91	24	96	@ Balt.
92	25	97	@ Balt.
93	26	98	@ Cal.
94	26	98	@ Cal.
95	27	99	@ Cal.
96	29	101	Minn.
97	30	102	Minn.
98	30	102	Minn.
99	30	102	Minn.
100	Aug. 2	105	Sea.
101	4	107	Sea.
102	4*	108	Sea.
103	4*	108	Sea.
104	6	109	@Minn.
105	8	111	@Minn.
106	11	113	@Sea.
107	11	113	@Sea.
108	14	115	Cal.
109	15	116	Cal.
110	17	118	Mil.
111	19	120	Mil.
112	21	122	Bos.
113	21	122	Bos.
114	21	122	Bos.
115	23	124	Det.
116	24	125	Det.
117	24	125	Det.
118	26	126	@Mil.
119	27	127	@Mil
120	27	127	@Mil.
121	27	127	@Mil.
122	27	127	@Mil.
123	30	128	@Bos.
124	Sept. 3	131	@Det.
125	25	142	KC
126	28	145	@Tex.
127	Oct. 1	148	@KC
128	2	149	@KC
129	2	149	@KC
130	2	149	@KC

CAUGHT STEALING: 42

STOLENS BASES BY OPPONENT

Opponent	Home	Away
Baltimore	6	7
Boston	5	4
California	4	5
Chicago	1	4
Cleveland	8	7
Detroit	7	2

Opponent	Home	Away
Kansas City	3	6
Milwaukee	5	8
Minnesota	6	6
New York	5	3
Seattle	7	6
Texas	4	4
Toronto	2	5
	63	67

HALL OF FAME
EXECUTIVES, MANAGERS, UMPIRES, NEGRO LEAGUE PLAYERS

Walter Alston (1983)	Manager
Sparky Anderson (2000)	Manager
Al Barlick (1989)	Umpire
Ed Barrow (1953)	Manager-Executive
Cool Papa Bell (1974)	Negro League Player
Morgan Bulkeley (1937)	Executive
Alexander Cartwright (1938)	Executive
Henry Chadwick (1938)	Writer-Statistican
Happy Chandler (1982)	Commissioner
Oscar Charleston (1976)	Negro League Player
Nestor Chylak (1999)	Umpire
Charles Comiskey (1939)	Player-Executive
Jocko Conlan (1974)	Umpire
Tom Connolly (1953)	Umpire
Candy Cummings (1939)	Pitcher
Ray Dandridge (1987)	Negro League Player
Leon Day (1995)	Negro League Player
Martin Dihigo (1977)	Negro League Player
Leo Durocher (1994)	Player-Manager
Billy Evans (1973)	Umpire-Executive
Bill Foster (1996)	Negro League Player
Rube Foster (1981)	Negro League Player
Ford Frick (1970)	Commissioner-Executive
Josh Gibson (1972)	Negro League Player
Warren Giles (1979)	Executive
Clark Griffith (1946)	Player-Manager-Executive
Ned Hanlon (1996)	Manager
Will Harridge (1972)	Executive
Bucky Harris (1975)	Player-Manager
Cal Hubbard (1976)	Umpire
Miller Huggins (1964)	Manager
William Hulbert (1995)	Executive
Monte Irvin (1973)	Negro League Player
Ban Johnson (1937)	Executive
Judy Johnson (1975)	Negro League Player
Bill Klem (1953)	Umpire
Kenesaw M. Landis (1944)	Commissioner
Tommy Lasorda (1997)	Pitcher-Manager
Buck Leonard (1972)	Negro League Player
Pop Lloyd (1977)	Negro League Player
Al Lopez (1977)	Player-Manager
Connie Mack (1937)	Manager-Executive
Larry MacPhail (1978)	Executive
Lee MacPhail (1998)	Executive
Joe McCarthy (1957)	Manager
Bill McGowan (1992)	Umpire
John McGraw (1937)	Player-Manager
Bill McKechnie (1962)	Manager
Satchel Paige (1971)	Negro League Player
Branch Rickey (1967)	Manager-Executive
Wilbert Robinson (1945)	Player-Manager
Joe Rogan (1998)	Negro League Player
Frank Selee (1999)	Manager
Hilton Smith (2001)	Negro League Player
Al Spalding (1939)	Player-Executive
Turkey Stearns (2000)	Negro League Player
Casey Stengel (1966)	Player-Manager
Bill Veeck (1991)	Executive
Earl Weaver (1996)	Manager
George Weiss (1971)	Executive
Willie Wells (1997)	Negro League Player
Smokey Joe Williams (1999)	Negro League Player
George Wright (1937)	Player-Manager
Harry Wright (1953)	Manager
Tom Yawkey (1980)	Executive

HALL OF FAME PITCHERS

*Special Committee Selection
(Capitalized pitchers were elected in their first year of eligibility.)

	Selected	Years	G	IP	W	L	PCT.
Grover Alexander	1938	1911-1930	696	5189	373	208	.642
*Chief Bender	1953	1903-1925	459	3017	212	127	.625
*Three Finger Brown	1949	1903-1916	481	3171	239	130	.648
*Jim Bunning	1996	1955-1971	591	3759	224	184	.549
STEVE CARLTON	1994	1965-1988	741	5216	329	244	.574
*Jack Chesbro	1946	1899-1909	392	2898	198	132	.600
*John Clarkson	1963	1882-1894	531	4537	327	177	.649
*Stan Coveleski	1969	1912-1928	450	3091	215	142	.602
Dizzy Dean	1953	1930-1947	317	1967	150	83	.644
Don Drysdale	1984	1956-1969	518	3432	209	166	.557
*Red Faber	1964	1914-1933	669	4086	254	213	.544
BOB FELLER	1962	1936-1956	570	3828	266	162	.621
Rollie Fingers	1992	1968-1985	944	1701	114	118	.491
Whitey Ford	1974	1950-1967	498	3171	236	106	.690
*Pud Galvin	1965	1879-1892	697	5941	361	302	.544
BOB GIBSON	1981	1959-1975	528	3885	251	174	.591
*Lefty Gomez	1972	1930-1943	368	2503	189	102	.649
*Clark Griffith	1946	1891-1914	428	3370	237	140	.629
*Burleigh Grimes	1964	1916-1934	615	4180	270	212	.560
Lefty Grove	1947	1925-1941	616	3940	300	141	.680
*Jesse Haines	1970	1918-1937	555	3208	210	158	.571
*Waite Hoyt	1969	1918-1938	674	3762	237	182	.566
Carl Hubbell	1947	1928-1943	535	3590	253	154	.622
Catfish Hunter	1987	1965-1979	500	3449	224	166	.574
Ferguson Jenkins	1991	1965-1983	664	4499	284	226	.557
WALTER JOHNSON	1936	1907-1927	802	5917	417	279	.599
*Addie Joss	1978	1902-1910	286	2327	160	97	.623
*Tim Keefe	1964	1880-1893	601	5072	341	223	.605
SANDY KOUFAX	1972	1955-1966	397	2325	165	87	.655
Bob Lemon	1976	1946-1958	460	2849	207	128	.618
Ted Lyons	1955	1923-1946	594	4162	260	230	.531
Juan Marichal	1983	1960-1975	471	3506	243	142	.631
*Rube Marquard	1971	1908-1925	536	3309	201	177	.532
CHRISTY MATHEWSON	1936	1900-1916	635	4783	373	188	.665
*Joe McGinnity	1946	1899-1908	466	3459	246	141	.636
*Hal Newhouser	1992	1939-1955	488	2992	207	150	.580
*Kid Nichols	1949	1890-1906	621	5084	360	205	.637
Phil Niekro	1997	1964-1987	864	5404	318	274	.537
JIM PALMER	1990	1965-1984	558	3947	268	152	.638
Herb Pennock	1948	1912-1934	617	3572	241	162	.598
Gaylord Perry	1991	1962-1983	777	5352	314	265	.542
*Eddie Plank	1946	1901-1917	622	4502	326	194	.627
*Hoss Radbourn	1939	1881-1891	528	4535	310	196	.613
*Eppa Rixey	1963	1912-1933	692	4494	266	251	.515
Robin Roberts	1976	1948-1966	676	4689	286	245	.539
Red Ruffing	1967	1924-1947	624	4342	273	225	.548
*Amos Rusie	1977	1889-1901	463	3769	248	171	.592
BABE RUTH	1936	1914-1935	163	1221	94	46	.671
NOLAN RYAN	1999	1966-1993	807	5387	324	292	.526
TOM SEAVER	1992	1967-1986	656	4782	311	205	.603
WARREN SPAHN	1973	1942-1965	750	5246	363	245	.597
Don Sutton	1998	1966-1988	774	5282	324	256	.559
Dazzy Vance	1955	1915-1935	442	2967	197	140	.585
*Rube Waddell	1946	1897-1910	407	2962	193	143	.574
*Ed Walsh	1946	1904-1917	430	2962	195	126	.607
*Mickey Welch	1973	1880-1892	564	4801	309	212	.593
Hoyt Wilhelm	1985	1952-1972	1070	2253	143	122	.540
*Vic Willis	1995	1898-1910	513	3997	249	207	.546
Early Wynn	1972	1939-1963	691	4566	300	244	.551
Cy Young	1937	1890-1911	906	7356	511	315	.619

HALL OF FAME BATTERS

*Special Committee Selection
(Capitalized batters were elected in their first year of eligibility.)

	Selected	Years	G	AB	R	H	BA
HANK AARON	1982	1954-1976	3298	12364	2174	3771	.305
*Cap Anson	1939	1876-1897	2253	9084	1712	3081	.339
Luis Aparicio	1984	1956-1973	2599	10230	1335	2677	.262
Luke Appling	1964	1930-1950	2422	8856	1319	2749	.310
*Richie Ashburn	1995	1948-1962	2189	8365	1322	2574	.308
*Earl Averill	1975	1929-1941	1668	6353	1224	2019	.318
*Frank Baker	1955	1908-1922	1575	5985	887	1838	.307
*Dave Bancroft	1971	1915-1930	1913	7182	1048	2004	.279
ERNIE BANKS	1977	1953-1971	2528	9421	1305	2583	.274
*Jake Beckley	1971	1888-1907	2376	9476	1601	2930	.309
JOHNNY BENCH	1989	1967-1983	2158	7658	1091	2048	.267
Yogi Berra	1972	1946-1965	2120	7555	1175	2150	.285
*Jim Bottomley	1974	1922-1937	1991	7471	1177	2313	.310
Lou Boudreau	1970	1938-1952	1646	6029	861	1779	.295
*Roger Bresnahan	1945	1897-1915	1430	4480	684	1251	.279
GEORGE BRETT	1999	1973-1993	2707	10349	1583	3154	.305
LOU BROCK	1985	1961-1979	2616	10332	1610	3023	.293
*Dan Brouthers	1945	1879-1904	1658	6725	1507	2349	.349
*Jesse Burkett	1946	1890-1905	2062	8389	1708	2872	.342
Roy Campanella	1969	1948-1957	1215	4205	627	1161	.276
ROD CAREW	1991	1967-1985	2469	9315	1424	3053	.328
*Max Carey	1961	1910-1929	2476	9363	1545	2665	.285
*Orlando Cepeda	1999	1958-1974	2124	7927	1131	2351	.297
*Frank Chance	1946	1898-1914	1246	4279	796	1273	.297
*Fred Clarke	1945	1894-1915	2238	8584	1620	2703	.315
ROBERTO CLEMENTE	1973	1955-1972	2433	9454	1416	3000	.317
TY COBB	1936	1905-1928	3034	11429	2245	4191	.367
Mickey Cochrane	1947	1925-1937	1482	5169	1041	1652	.320
Eddie Collins	1939	1906-1930	2826	9951	1820	3314	.333
*Jimmy Collins	1945	1895-1908	1719	6791	1057	1998	.294
*Earle Combs	1970	1924-1935	1454	5746	1186	1866	.325
*Roger Connor	1976	1880-1897	1987	7807	1607	2535	.325
*Sam Crawford	1957	1899-1917	2505	9579	1392	2964	.309
Joe Cronin	1956	1926-1945	2124	7579	1233	2285	.301
*Kiki Cuyler	1968	1921-1938	1879	7161	1305	2299	.321
*George Davis	1998	1890-1909	2376	9027	1546	2683	.297
*Ed Delahanty	1945	1888-1903	1825	7493	1596	2593	.346
Bill Dickey	1954	1928-1946	1789	6300	930	1969	.313
Joe DiMaggio	1955	1936-1951	1736	6821	1390	2214	.325
*Larry Doby	1998	1947-1959	1533	5348	960	1515	.283
*Bobby Doerr	1986	1937-1951	1865	7093	1094	2042	.288
*Hugh Duffy	1945	1888-1906	1722	6999	1545	2307	.330
*Johnny Evers	1946	1902-1929	1773	6136	919	1569	.270
*Buck Ewing	1939	1880-1897	1281	5348	1118	1663	.311
*Rick Ferrell	1984	1929-1947	1884	6028	687	1692	.281
Carlton Fisk	2000	1969-1993	2499	8756	1276	2356	.269
*Elmer Flick	1963	1898-1910	1481	5601	951	1767	.315
*Nellie Fox	1997	1947-1965	2367	9232	1279	2663	.288
Jimmie Foxx	1951	1925-1945	2317	8134	1751	2646	.325
Frankie Frisch	1947	1919-1937	2311	9112	1532	2880	.316
LOU GEHRIG	1939	1923-1939	2164	8001	1888	2721	.340
Charlie Gehringer	1949	1924-1942	2323	8860	1774	2839	.320
*Goose Goslin	1968	1921-1938	2287	8656	1483	2735	.316
Hank Greenberg	1956	1930-1947	1394	5193	1051	1628	.313
*Chick Hafey	1971	1924-1937	1283	4625	777	1466	.317
*Billy Hamilton	1961	1888-1901	1578	6262	1691	2157	.344
Gabby Hartnett	1955	1922-1941	1990	6432	867	1912	.297
Harry Heilmann	1952	1914-1932	2146	7787	1291	2660	.342
*Billy Herman	1975	1931-1947	1922	7707	1163	2345	.304
*Harry Hooper	1971	1909-1925	2308	8785	1429	2466	.281
Rogers Hornsby	1942	1915-1937	2259	8173	1579	2930	.358
REGGIE JACKSON	1993	1967-1987	2820	9864	1551	2584	.262
*Travis Jackson	1982	1922-1936	1656	6086	833	1768	.291
*Hughie Jennings	1945	1891-1918	1264	4842	989	1520	.314
AL KALINE	1980	1953-1974	2834	10116	1622	3007	.297
Willie Keeler	1939	1892-1910	2124	8564	1720	2955	.345
*George Kell	1983	1943-1957	1795	6702	881	2054	.306
*Joe Kelley	1971	1891-1908	1835	6989	1425	2245	.321
*George Kelly	1973	1915-1932	1622	5993	819	1778	.297
*King Kelly	1945	1878-1893	1434	5992	1359	1853	.313
Harmon Killebrew	1984	1954-1975	2435	8147	1283	2086	.256

HALL OF FAME BATTERS (CONTINUED)

*Special Committee Selection
(Capitalized batters were elected in their first year of eligibility.)

	Selected	Years	G	AB	R	H	BA
Ralph Kiner	1975	1946-1955	1472	5205	971	1451	.279
*Chuck Klein	1980	1928-1944	1753	6486	1168	2076	.320
Nap Lajoie	1937	1896-1916	2475	9589	1506	3252	.339
*Tony Lazzeri	1991	1926-1939	1739	6297	986	1840	.292
*Freddie Lindstrom	1976	1924-1936	1438	5611	895	1747	.311
*Ernie Lombardi	1986	1931-1947	1853	5855	601	1792	.306
MICKEY MANTLE	1974	1951-1968	2401	8102	1677	2415	.298
*Heinie Manush	1964	1923-1939	2009	7653	1287	2524	.330
Rabbitt Maranville	1954	1912-1935	2670	10078	1255	2605	.258
Eddie Mathews	1978	1952-1968	2391	8537	1509	2315	.271
WILLIE MAYS	1979	1951-1973	2992	10881	2062	3283	.302
*Bill Mazeroski	2001	1956-1972	2163	7755	769	2016	.260
*Tommy McCarthy	1946	1884-1896	1258	5055	1050	1485	.294
WILLIE McCOVEY	1986	1959-1980	2588	8197	1229	2211	.270
*John McGraw	1937	1891-1906	1082	3919	1019	1307	.334
*Bid McPhee	2000	1882-1899	2127	8348	1674	2342	.281
Joe Medwick	1968	1932-1948	1984	7635	1198	2471	.324
*Johnny Mize	1981	1936-1953	1884	6443	1118	2011	.312
JOE MORGAN	1990	1963-1984	2649	9277	1650	2517	.271
STAN MUSIAL	1969	1941-1963	3026	10972	1949	3630	.331
*Jim O'Rourke	1945	1876-1904	1750	7365	1425	2314	.314
Mel Ott	1951	1926-1947	2730	9456	1859	2876	.304
Tony Perez	2000	1964-1986	2777	9778	1272	2732	.279
KIRBY PUCKETT	2001	1984-1995	1783	7244	1071	2304	.318
*Pee Wee Reese	1984	1940-1958	2166	8058	1338	2170	.269
*Sam Rice	1963	1915-1934	2404	9269	1515	2987	.322
*Phil Rizzuto	1994	1941-1956	1661	5816	878	1588	.273
BROOKS ROBINSON	1983	1955-1977	2896	10654	1232	2848	.267
FRANK ROBINSON	1982	1956-1976	2808	10006	1829	2943	.294
JACKIE ROBINSON	1962	1947-1956	1382	4877	947	1518	.311
*Wilbert Robinson	1945	1886-1902	1316	4942	632	1386	.280
*Edd Roush	1962	1913-1931	1967	7363	1099	2376	.323
BABE RUTH	1936	1914-1935	2503	8399	2174	2873	.342
*Ray Schalk	1955	1912-1929	1760	5306	579	1345	.253
MIKE SCHMIDT	1995	1972-1989	2404	8352	1506	2234	.267
*Red Schoendienst	1989	1945-1963	2216	8479	1223	2449	.289
*Joe Sewell	1977	1920-1933	1902	7132	1141	2226	.312
Al Simmons	1953	1924-1944	2215	8763	1507	2927	.334
George Sisler	1939	1915-1930	2055	8267	1284	2812	.340
*Enos Slaughter	1985	1938-1959	2380	7946	1247	2383	.300
OZZIE SMITH	2002	1978-1996	2573	9396	1257	2460	.262
Duke Snider	1980	1947-1964	2143	7161	1259	2116	.295
Tris Speaker	1937	1907-1928	2789	10195	1881	3515	.345
WILLIE STARGELL	1988	1962-1982	2360	7927	1195	2232	.282
Bill Terry	1954	1923-1936	1721	6428	1120	2193	.341
*Sam Thompson	1974	1885-1906	1405	6004	1259	2016	.336
*Joe Tinker	1946	1902-1916	1805	6441	773	1695	.263
Pie Traynor	1948	1920-1937	1941	7559	1183	2416	.320
*Arky Vaughan	1985	1932-1948	1817	6622	1173	2103	.318
HONUS WAGNER	1936	1897-1917	2787	10427	1740	3430	.329
*Bobby Wallace	1953	1894-1918	2385	8629	1056	2308	.267
*Lloyd Waner	1967	1927-1945	1993	7772	1201	2459	.316
Paul Waner	1952	1926-1945	2549	9459	1627	3152	.333
*Monte Ward	1964	1878-1894	1819	7597	1403	2151	.283
*Zack Wheat	1959	1909-1927	2410	9106	1289	2884	.317
Billy Williams	1987	1959-1976	2488	9350	1410	2711	.290
TED WILLIAMS	1966	1939-1960	2292	7706	1798	2654	.344
*Hack Wilson	1979	1923-1934	1348	4760	844	1461	.307
DAVE WINFIELD	2001	1973-1995	2973	11003	1669	3110	.283
CARL YASTRZEMSKI	1989	1961-1983	3308	11988	1816	3419	.285
*Ross Youngs	1972	1917-1926	1211	4627	812	1491	.322
ROBIN YOUNT	1999	1974-1993	2856	11008	1632	3142	.285

BATTERS – 1,000 OR MORE GAMES - ACTIVE

(OBA = On-Base Average)   XBH = Extra-Base Hits)

PLAYER	YR	BA	SLG	OBA	G	AB	R	H	TB	XBH	1B	2B	3B	HR	RBI	BB	HBP	SO	SB	CS	GDP
Alicea, Luis	12	.262	.374	.347	1247	3734	523	977	1398	278	699	181	51	46	399	468	47	590	79	47	69
Alomar, Roberto	14	.306	.455	.378	2034	7796	1341	2389	3549	708	1681	446	72	190	1018	902	45	949	446	106	173
Alomar, Sandy Jr.	14	.275	.415	.313	1063	3649	434	1002	1514	309	693	203	9	97	480	180	37	407	25	24	107
Alou, Moises	10	.306	.524	.372	1181	4238	696	1297	2221	491	806	260	29	202	834	446	33	578	81	33	112
Anderson, Brady	14	.257	.427	.363	1800	6419	1058	1648	2743	610	1038	334	67	209	756	942	152	1167	311	100	60
Anderson, Garret	8	.296	.461	.325	1048	4179	530	1237	1926	399	838	244	20	135	633	190	4	569	54	34	111
Ausmus, Brad	9	.259	.366	.332	1041	3430	442	889	1256	237	652	160	24	53	333	347	35	571	78	38	93
Baerga, Carlos	10	.291	.427	.330	1280	4807	659	1400	2052	387	1013	246	17	124	686	253	58	511	52	23	135
Bagwell, Jeff	11	.303	.554	.415	1637	5949	1199	1803	3296	769	1034	394	26	349	1223	1098	103	1157	178	67	166
Baines, Harold	22	.289	.465	.356	2830	9908	1299	2866	4604	921	1945	488	49	384	1628	1062	14	1441	34	34	298
Bell, Derek	11	.276	.421	.336	1210	4578	642	1262	1926	381	881	232	15	134	668	377	61	955	170	51	123
Bell, Jay	16	.267	.420	.344	1959	7233	1109	1934	3039	652	1282	392	67	193	846	826	54	1396	91	60	159
Belle, Albert	12	.295	.564	.369	1539	5853	974	1726	3300	791	935	389	21	381	1239	683	55	961	88	41	193
Bichette, Dante	14	.299	.499	.336	1704	6381	934	1906	3183	702	1204	401	27	274	1141	355	41	1078	152	73	176
Biggio, Craig	14	.291	.436	.381	1955	7383	1305	2149	3218	663	1486	437	46	180	811	913	197	1146	365	110	93
Bonds, Barry	16	.292	.585	.419	2296	7932	1713	2313	4639	1121	1192	483	71	567	1542	1724	65	1282	484	138	127
Bonilla, Bobby	16	.279	.472	.358	2113	7213	1084	2010	3401	756	1254	408	61	287	1173	912	28	1204	45	57	169
Boone, Bret	10	.265	.435	.321	1230	4534	621	1202	1974	431	771	252	17	162	677	347	49	868	52	38	110
Borders, Pat	13	.256	.381	.291	1006	3052	267	782	1162	234	548	155	12	67	327	149	10	507	6	13	88
Bordick, Mike	12	.261	.361	.323	1501	5060	600	1321	1825	323	998	220	25	78	536	432	58	677	86	53	128
Brosius, Scott	11	.257	.422	.323	1146	3889	544	1001	1640	349	652	200	8	141	531	348	47	699	57	30	84
Buhner, Jay	15	.254	.494	.359	1472	5013	798	1273	2474	562	711	233	19	310	965	792	56	1406	6	24	123
Burks, Ellis	15	.292	.512	.364	1796	6483	1128	1893	3319	738	1155	363	62	313	1086	719	50	1178	176	80	153
Caminiti, Ken	15	.272	.447	.347	1760	6288	894	1710	2809	604	1106	348	17	239	983	727	84	1163	88	39	152
Canseco, Jose	17	.266	.515	.353	1887	7057	1186	1877	3631	816	1061	340	14	462	1407	906	84	1942	200	88	178
Castilla, Vinny	11	.288	.504	.331	1187	4385	609	1262	2211	462	800	209	19	234	744	272	34	670	24	38	135
Cirillo, Jeff	8	.311	.459	.383	1084	3937	627	1224	1809	378	846	265	19	94	570	440	47	507	47	29	114
Clayton, Royce	11	.258	.372	.312	1347	4809	608	1242	1790	347	895	225	43	79	499	366	28	888	182	82	133
Conine, Jeff	11	.289	.453	.354	1245	4328	562	1252	1961	396	856	229	21	146	694	443	25	795	27	22	111
Curtis, Chad	10	.264	.396	.349	1204	4017	648	1061	1591	312	749	195	16	101	461	510	40	676	212	98	102
Davis, Eric	17	.269	.482	.359	1626	5321	938	1430	2567	547	883	239	26	282	934	740	33	1398	349	66	112
DeShields, Delino	12	.270	.379	.354	1548	5633	852	1520	2135	388	1132	238	73	77	551	733	20	1023	453	146	99
DiSarcina, Gary	12	.258	.341	.292	1086	3744	444	966	1276	234	732	186	20	28	355	154	36	306	47	44	105
Dunston, Shawon	17	.270	.419	.297	1742	5780	729	1563	2421	498	1065	287	62	149	659	200	40	967	211	82	98
Durham, Ray	7	.276	.427	.349	1050	4134	713	1143	1765	377	766	229	51	97	436	435	43	699	199	68	65
Easley, Damion	10	.257	.407	.334	1106	3885	554	998	1580	340	658	209	20	111	476	372	92	688	104	49	88
Edmonds, Jim	9	.293	.519	.374	1011	3669	688	1075	1904	430	645	224	13	193	626	470	25	861	41	32	62
Fernandez, Tony	17	.288	.399	.347	2158	7911	1057	2276	3156	600	1676	414	92	94	844	690	64	784	246	138	161

BATTERS – 1,000 OR MORE GAMES - ACTIVE

(OBA = On-Base Average)

XBH = Extra-Base Hits

PLAYER	YR	BA	SLG	OBA	G	AB	R	H	TB	XBH	1B	2B	3B	HR	RBI	BB	HBP	SO	SB	CS	GDP
Finley, Steve	13	.275	.439	.332	1830	6822	1071	1873	2996	625	1248	329	94	202	818	581	38	920	265	95	108
Fletcher, Darrin	13	.270	.426	.320	1200	3775	369	1020	1607	337	683	208	8	121	561	251	49	386	2	6	118
Franco, Julio	17	.301	.418	.366	1916	7334	1117	2204	3069	530	1674	339	47	144	992	763	34	1026	260	101	258
Fryman, Travis	12	.278	.449	.339	1580	6084	853	1690	2731	580	1110	331	37	212	967	562	39	1287	72	38	142
Galarraga, Andres	16	.289	.503	.347	2036	7522	1128	2172	3784	826	1346	417	32	377	1341	534	166	1858	125	76	161
Gant, Ron	14	.256	.468	.337	1713	6099	1018	1564	2856	639	925	288	49	302	945	732	30	1343	239	96	89
Gilkey, Bernard	12	.275	.434	.352	1239	4061	606	1115	1761	386	729	244	24	118	546	466	42	708	115	71	116
Girardi, Joe	13	.270	.355	.318	1171	3870	434	1044	1375	236	808	176	25	35	408	260	25	568	43	31	125
Gonzalez, Juan	13	.297	.568	.345	1503	5824	957	1727	3308	765	962	346	22	397	1282	417	56	1125	23	17	160
Gonzalez, Luis	12	.286	.484	.363	1599	5705	878	1632	2762	637	995	365	51	221	917	652	79	770	101	74	123
Goodwin, Tom	11	.269	.340	.335	1046	3416	576	919	1161	161	758	102	37	22	252	332	13	580	329	111	37
Grace, Mark	14	.307	.447	.386	2055	7632	1123	2343	3409	695	1648	487	45	163	1082	1013	33	597	68	48	181
Green, Shawn	9	.285	.515	.353	1039	3742	621	1066	1927	454	612	239	23	192	600	368	41	738	120	34	65
Griffey, Ken Jr.	13	.296	.566	.379	1791	6716	1220	1987	3799	857	1130	362	35	460	1335	885	60	1173	175	64	124
Grissom, Marquis	13	.270	.404	.318	1716	6646	962	1794	2688	515	1279	302	47	166	723	467	26	989	409	110	120
Gwynn, Tony	20	.338	.459	.388	2440	9288	1383	3141	4259	763	2378	543	85	135	1138	790	24	434	319	125	259
Hamilton, Darryl	13	.291	.385	.360	1328	4577	707	1333	1764	292	1041	204	37	51	454	493	17	494	163	73	82
Harris, Lenny	14	.271	.350	.319	1531	3417	411	925	1197	191	734	141	19	31	314	239	14	280	126	52	101
Hayes, Charlie	14	.262	.398	.316	1547	5262	580	1379	2094	411	968	251	16	144	740	420	21	918	47	31	155
Henderson, Rickey	23	.280	.420	.402	2979	10710	2248	3000	4503	858	2142	503	65	290	1094	2141	93	1631	1395	333	169
Hernandez, Jose	10	.250	.420	.306	1021	2977	421	743	1250	263	480	128	26	109	394	234	16	865	32	28	72
Hill, Glenallen	11	.271	.482	.321	1162	3715	528	1005	1792	394	611	187	21	186	586	270	20	845	96	38	89
Howard, Thomas	11	.264	.384	.311	1015	2483	297	655	954	189	466	123	22	44	264	165	11	432	66	41	39
Hundley, Todd	12	.237	.445	.321	1112	3470	461	821	1545	349	472	158	7	184	553	413	31	895	14	10	65
Javier, Stan	17	.269	.363	.345	1763	5047	781	1358	1834	322	1036	225	40	57	503	578	25	839	246	52	102
Jones, Chipper	8	.307	.545	.400	1094	4041	773	1240	2204	487	753	237	23	227	737	652	7	609	106	36	107
Jordan, Brian	10	.287	.469	.337	1077	3931	599	1128	1845	388	740	208	31	149	656	259	59	622	112	43	90
Joyner, Wally	16	.289	.440	.362	2033	7127	973	2060	3133	639	1421	409	26	204	1106	833	38	825	60	39	168
Justice, David	13	.280	.507	.378	1492	5227	875	1465	2651	577	888	262	21	294	968	833	17	933	49	45	89
Karros, Eric	11	.268	.462	.326	1459	5478	700	1466	2531	542	924	276	9	257	903	480	25	1031	53	27	154
Kelly, Roberto	14	.290	.430	.337	1337	4797	687	1390	2063	395	995	241	30	124	585	317	49	862	235	84	113
Kent, Jeff	10	.285	.495	.351	1350	4936	764	1409	2442	570	839	323	31	216	899	452	82	973	68	46	110
Klesko, Ryan	10	.282	.526	.369	1083	3463	567	978	1822	428	550	207	26	195	655	480	19	693	72	27	79
Knoblauch, Chuck	11	.293	.411	.382	1552	6066	1091	1776	2493	469	1307	313	64	92	593	776	135	698	388	114	111
Lankford, Ray	12	.274	.483	.366	1528	5342	912	1464	2581	613	851	335	52	226	826	769	32	1434	254	113	68
Lansing, Mike	9	.271	.401	.324	1110	4150	554	1124	1664	355	769	254	17	84	440	299	37	570	119	38	116
Larkin, Barry	16	.299	.454	.377	1854	6843	1163	2048	3104	624	1424	373	70	181	851	839	50	689	362	73	142
Lewis, Darren	12	.250	.322	.323	1296	4002	600	1002	1289	197	805	134	36	27	335	396	45	503	246	104	58

BATTERS – 1,000 OR MORE GAMES - ACTIVE

(OBA = On-Base Average)
XBH = Extra-Base Hits)

PLAYER	YR	BA	SLG	OBA	G	AB	R	H	TB	XBH	1B	2B	3B	HR	RBI	BB	HBP	SO	SB	CS	GDP
Lofton, Kenny	11	.302	.425	.377	1366	5439	1050	1642	2312	417	1225	256	69	92	551	663	22	731	479	122	75
Magadan, Dave	16	.288	.377	.390	1582	4059	516	1197	1567	273	924	218	13	42	495	718	12	546	11	11	98
Martin, Al	10	.278	.449	.341	1132	4004	645	1112	1799	383	729	208	46	129	459	373	22	828	171	63	55
Martinez, Tino	12	.274	.481	.343	1466	5363	773	1468	2577	566	902	286	17	263	1002	565	36	801	18	16	145
Martinez, Dave	16	.276	.389	.341	1919	5795	795	1599	2254	401	1198	238	72	91	580	567	28	893	183	94	84
Martinez, Edgar	15	.319	.530	.425	1672	5902	1060	1882	3129	716	1166	443	15	258	1041	1066	74	931	47	28	152
McGriff, Fred	16	.287	.514	.381	2201	7865	1243	2260	4045	867	1393	397	22	448	1400	1202	34	1698	71	36	205
McGwire, Mark	16	.263	.588	.394	1874	6187	1167	1626	3639	841	785	252	6	583	1414	1317	75	1596	12	8	147
McLemore, Mark	16	.260	.340	.349	1552	5296	826	1377	1798	294	1083	209	43	42	516	735	11	816	249	102	123
Merced, Orlando	11	.279	.428	.359	1145	3535	509	987	1514	316	671	199	23	94	529	446	11	578	50	27	77
Mondesi, Raul	9	.282	.499	.335	1161	4447	709	1253	2219	495	758	238	43	214	669	335	32	864	192	71	66
Offerman, Jose	12	.277	.375	.363	1387	5120	759	1417	1920	339	1078	223	68	48	471	695	16	828	162	93	83
O'Leary, Troy	9	.276	.457	.332	1008	3563	502	984	1630	370	614	213	38	119	526	286	24	583	13	20	94
Olerud, John	13	.300	.476	.404	1714	5902	927	1768	2812	618	1150	399	12	207	960	1016	69	802	11	13	176
Oliver, Joe	13	.247	.391	.299	1076	3367	320	831	1317	279	552	174	3	102	476	248	15	637	13	13	93
O'Neill, Paul	17	.288	.470	.363	2053	7318	1041	2105	3441	753	1352	451	21	281	1269	892	22	1166	141	73	221
Palmeiro, Rafael	16	.294	.519	.372	2258	8446	1357	2485	4386	971	1514	488	36	447	1470	1036	68	1073	89	79	191
Palmer, Dean	12	.253	.479	.326	1327	4804	731	1217	2301	519	698	229	15	275	843	492	52	1299	48	31	91
Piazza, Mike	10	.325	.579	.391	1258	4638	782	1507	2685	546	961	228	4	314	975	506	18	719	17	17	149
Raines, Tim Sr.	22	.295	.427	.386	2404	8783	1562	2588	3748	709	1879	427	113	169	973	1308	41	947	808	146	139
Ramirez, Manny	9	.312	.594	.406	1109	3999	758	1248	2375	560	688	270	13	277	929	622	45	927	28	25	107
Ripken, Cal	21	.276	.447	.340	3001	11551	1647	3184	5168	1078	2106	603	44	431	1695	1129	66	1305	36	39	350
Rodriguez, Ivan	10	.304	.485	.341	1371	5248	785	1595	2547	534	1061	312	26	196	769	279	37	692	75	36	174
Salmon, Tim	10	.285	.511	.391	1250	4526	779	1288	2315	516	772	252	17	247	806	779	45	1080	38	36	70
Sanchez, Rey	11	.274	.337	.311	1167	3821	440	1047	1289	194	853	158	24	12	300	182	32	407	51	27	109
Sanders, Reggie	11	.268	.484	.350	1167	4144	718	1112	2005	459	653	220	44	195	630	489	44	1089	229	90	76
Santiago, Benito	16	.261	.411	.305	1689	5874	630	1531	2416	484	1047	267	33	184	767	366	32	1093	86	64	162
Segui, David	12	.293	.447	.360	1345	4469	639	1308	1998	413	895	267	15	131	636	482	12	605	16	18	120
Sheffield, Gary	14	.295	.521	.399	1592	5661	982	1668	2948	629	1039	293	21	315	1016	952	80	688	170	81	131
Sierra, Ruben	15	.270	.455	.317	1776	6813	947	1837	3103	683	1154	363	57	263	1121	514	7	1023	135	51	160
Snow, J.T.	11	.264	.433	.351	1207	4132	596	1092	1791	370	722	200	11	159	669	548	34	867	14	21	105
Sosa, Sammy	13	.277	.542	.343	1725	6470	1093	1795	3505	769	1026	278	41	450	1239	635	44	1690	231	105	139
Spiers, Bill	13	.271	.370	.341	1252	3408	477	922	1261	230	692	158	35	37	388	355	18	496	97	43	73
Sprague, Ed Jr.	11	.247	.419	.318	1203	4095	506	1010	1715	389	621	225	12	152	558	358	91	833	6	12	106
Surhoff, B.J.	15	.281	.416	.331	2004	7218	946	2026	3006	601	1425	392	39	170	1019	561	30	727	136	79	149
Thomas, Frank	12	.319	.577	.438	1550	5542	1091	1770	3198	722	1048	364	10	348	1193	1198	46	847	29	21	165
Thome, Jim	11	.285	.555	.411	1230	4160	816	1186	2308	540	646	240	18	282	809	875	37	1238	17	12	81
Valentin, Jose	10	.247	.444	.328	1030	3415	559	845	1517	360	485	191	26	143	503	407	17	805	106	40	34

BATTERS – 1,000 OR MORE GAMES - ACTIVE

(OBA = On-Base Average)

XBH = Extra-Base Hits

PLAYER	YR	BA	SLG	OBA	G	AB	R	H	TB	XBH	1B	2B	3B	HR	RBI	BB	HBP	SO	SB	CS	GDP
Vander Wal, John	11	.265	.442	.357	1129	2154	292	570	953	217	353	126	16	75	361	312	7	516	36	17	41
Vaughn, Greg	13	.245	.477	.339	1640	5815	981	1427	2772	636	791	271	21	344	1038	816	34	1418	118	57	96
Vaughn, Mo	10	.298	.533	.387	1346	4966	784	1479	2646	559	920	250	10	299	977	652	96	1262	30	17	119
Velarde, Randy	15	.278	.410	.353	1217	4111	611	1141	1687	327	814	206	23	98	437	448	44	821	75	37	114
Ventura, Robin	13	.271	.447	.364	1698	6055	877	1638	2708	561	1077	300	13	248	1006	905	21	960	21	37	148
Vizcaino, Jose	13	.270	.339	.319	1288	4097	498	1106	1387	200	906	141	37	22	353	294	14	574	68	53	80
Vizquel, Omar	13	.274	.351	.340	1775	6420	919	1761	2254	363	1398	276	44	43	565	643	26	648	273	110	121
Walker, Larry	13	.315	.572	.396	1527	5403	1057	1702	3091	725	977	370	46	309	1029	660	103	950	209	66	119
White, Devon	17	.263	.419	.319	1941	7344	1125	1934	3078	657	1277	378	71	208	846	541	87	1526	346	98	98
Williams, Bernie	11	.305	.499	.389	1383	5346	964	1629	2666	573	1056	316	50	207	896	744	28	830	130	76	134
Williams, Gerald	10	.259	.415	.305	1012	2852	437	739	1183	268	471	172	16	80	348	167	31	488	97	56	57
Williams, Matt	15	.269	.491	.316	1762	6651	951	1789	3263	717	1072	322	33	362	1162	432	53	1296	50	34	173
Young, Eric	10	.289	.395	.365	1237	4524	762	1307	1788	332	975	238	39	55	427	489	68	323	377	128	89
Young, Kevin	10	.262	.445	.324	1007	3345	468	875	1490	347	528	205	16	126	548	274	58	756	78	43	91
Zeile, Todd	13	.267	.429	.349	1777	6420	855	1717	2752	584	1133	348	21	215	946	801	37	1050	51	50	177

PITCHERS – 100 OR MORE GAMES WON – ACTIVE

PLAYER	YR	ERA	W	L	PCT	G	GS	GF	SV	SHO	INN	H	AB	BFP	R	ER	HR	BB	HBP	SO	WP	BK
Appier, Kevin	13	3.63	147	115	.561	357	345	2	0	12	2291.1	2107	8625	9642	1002	923	188	823	64	1805	91	6
Astacio, Pedro	10	4.50	103	96	.518	308	265	9	0	10	1742.2	1798	6695	7480	937	872	218	572	89	1366	47	14
Benes, Andy	13	4.02	150	135	.526	385	370	6	1	9	2408.1	2297	9154	10228	1167	1076	279	858	50	1936	63	16
Brown, Kevin	15	3.18	180	118	.604	402	399	1	0	17	2776.1	2588	10495	11511	1132	982	169	768	119	2021	89	14
Burba, Dave	12	4.46	105	80	.568	408	211	51	1	1	1512.0	1510	5789	6584	811	749	173	660	43	1218	61	2
Burkett, John	13	4.23	141	119	.542	384	364	7	1	5	2293.2	2465	8946	9779	1173	1077	212	603	73	1535	28	7
Clemens, Roger	18	3.10	280	145	.659	545	544	7	0	45	3887.0	3306	14451	16007	1479	1338	279	1258	129	3717	106	19
Cone, David	16	3.44	193	123	.611	445	415	9	1	22	2880.2	2484	10711	12099	1209	1102	254	1124	106	2655	149	32
Erickson, Scott	11	4.43	135	116	.538	326	322	2	0	16	2106.1	2281	8171	9123	1126	1037	191	745	88	1152	60	3
Fassero, Jeff	11	3.87	104	95	.523	486	217	98	22	2	1669.0	1658	6434	7176	814	717	168	580	35	1405	73	6
Fernandez, Alex	10	3.74	107	87	.552	263	261	1	0	2	1760.1	1693	6674	7370	804	731	190	552	25	1252	38	2
Finley, Chuck	16	3.83	189	158	.545	492	435	24	0	14	3006.2	2886	11321	12829	1420	1278	291	1254	75	2436	127	22
Glavine, Tom	15	3.40	224	132	.629	469	469	4	0	21	3120.0	2964	11758	13094	1303	1178	226	1062	42	1927	57	7
Gordon, Tom	14	4.13	105	98	.517	491	203	198	98	4	1690.1	1548	6376	7329	853	776	137	823	29	1498	93	4
Harnisch, Pete	14	3.89	111	103	.519	321	318	2	0	11	1959.0	1822	7428	8332	926	846	223	716	49	1368	50	12
Hentgen, Pat	11	4.18	122	91	.573	294	264	11	0	1	1812.1	1840	6966	7773	915	842	222	665	40	1146	60	9
Hill, Ken	14	4.06	117	109	.518	332	315	4	0	0	1973.0	1938	7460	8520	977	891	162	852	47	1181	78	13
Johnson, Randy	14	3.13	200	101	.664	401	391	5	2	8	2748.1	2113	9951	11376	1076	956	241	1160	125	3412	88	24
Kile, Darryl	11	4.14	128	115	.527	345	317	8	0	9	2080.2	2053	7877	9065	1063	957	205	890	109	1618	97	19
Leiter, Al	16	3.69	117	90	.565	293	263	7	0	2	1690.0	1490	6249	7248	751	692	131	805	77	1449	54	17
Maddux, Greg	16	2.84	257	146	.638	505	501	3	0	34	3551.0	3206	13282	14396	1281	1121	196	760	97	2523	49	26
Martinez, Pedro	10	2.66	132	59	.691	296	229	23	3	15	1693.0	1262	6137	6750	553	501	129	467	75	1981	43	4
Morgan, Mike	21	4.22	140	185	.431	568	411	47	8	10	2737.2	2902	10519	11716	1409	1283	263	929	71	1390	102	5
Moyer, Jamie	15	4.22	151	117	.563	405	353	13	0	6	2292.0	2388	8882	9757	1170	1075	267	664	71	1381	41	10
Mulholland, Terry	15	4.30	113	125	.475	510	311	62	5	10	2212.1	2384	8640	9446	1171	1056	237	572	51	1166	57	2
Mussina, Mike	11	3.49	164	92	.641	322	322	0	0	18	2238.1	2097	8461	9110	923	869	230	509	26	1749	45	1
Nagy, Charles	12	4.40	128	99	.564	294	290	2	0	0	1893.2	2097	7452	8172	1003	926	207	570	49	1213	44	4
Neagle, Denny	11	4.07	114	77	.597	350	251	23	3	7	1690.2	1670	6463	7146	816	764	212	519	42	1283	42	5
Pettitte, Andy	7	3.99	115	65	.639	221	221	0	0	2	1449.2	1530	5603	6204	706	643	116	497	26	998	33	8
Reynolds, Shane	11	3.91	100	80	.556	261	235	5	0	2	1548.1	1658	6071	6543	742	672	158	332	32	1262	37	7
Rijo, Jose	13	3.15	111	87	.561	345	260	37	28	4	1803.0	1621	6733	7527	724	632	134	643	27	1568	29	28
Rogers, Kenny	13	4.23	132	98	.574	556	271	132	28	6	2049.1	2093	7896	8868	1076	964	204	778	59	1315	56	16
Saberhagen, Bret	16	3.34	167	117	.588	399	371	13	1	16	2562.2	2452	9733	10421	1036	952	218	471	33	1715	53	12
Schilling, Curt	14	3.37	132	101	.567	390	279	60	13	16	2158.2	1924	8077	8799	864	809	217	538	33	2032	57	7
Sele, Aaron	9	4.33	107	68	.611	242	241	0	0	0	1466.1	1580	5744	6458	783	706	137	548	79	1082	35	0
Smoltz, John	13	3.35	160	116	.580	392	361	20	10	14	2473.1	2145	9191	10185	1010	920	202	784	40	2155	119	14
Stottlemyre, Todd	13	4.25	138	119	.537	367	335	11	1	6	2171.1	2174	8317	9349	1113	1025	242	809	83	1575	64	10
Swindell, Greg	16	3.82	123	120	.506	630	269	88	7	12	2200.1	2275	8484	9158	1030	934	253	496	21	1519	30	12
Tapani, Kevin	13	4.35	143	125	.534	361	354	1	0	10	2265.0	2407	8844	9600	1168	1094	260	554	53	1482	44	6
Wells, David	15	4.08	166	114	.593	495	325	65	13	10	2407.1	2462	9310	10051	1183	1090	285	559	56	1555	87	15
Witt, Bobby	16	4.83	142	157	.475	430	397	13	0	11	2465.0	2493	9413	11003	1449	1324	252	1375	39	1955	128	26

WORLD SERIES (continued)

CHAMPIONSHIP SERIES

ALL-STAR GAME